Numerical Simulation and Computational Methods in Engineering and Sciences

Numerical Simulation and Computational Methods in Engineering and Sciences

Editors

Zhuojia Fu
Yiqian He
Hui Zheng

MDPI

Basel • Beijing • Wuhan • Barcelona • Belgrade • Novi Sad • Cluj • Manchester

Editors

Zhuojia Fu
College of Mechanics and Engineering Science,
Hohai University
Nanjing
China

Yiqian He
Dalian University of Technology
Dalian
China

Hui Zheng
Nanchang University
Nanchang
China

Editorial Office
MDPI
St. Alban-Anlage 66
4052 Basel, Switzerland

This is a reprint of articles from the Special Issue published online in the open access journal *Mathematics* (ISSN 2227-7390) (available at: https://www.mdpi.com/si/mathematics/Numeri_Simulation_Comput_Method_Engin_Sci).

For citation purposes, cite each article independently as indicated on the article page online and as indicated below:

Lastname, A.A.; Lastname, B.B. Article Title. *Journal Name* **Year**, *Volume Number*, Page Range.

ISBN 978-3-7258-0955-4 (Hbk)
ISBN 978-3-7258-0956-1 (PDF)
doi.org/10.3390/books978-3-7258-0956-1

Contents

About the Editors

Zhuojia Fu

Zhuojia Fu is a professor at the College of Mechanics and Engineering Science, Hohai University. His research interests include semi-analytical and numerical methods in computational mechanics, numerical modeling of wave propagation, and structural vibration.

Yiqian He

Yiqian He is a professor at the State Key Lab of Structural Analysis for Industrial Equipment, Department of Engineering Mechanics, International Research Centre for Computational Mechanics, Dalian University of Technology. His research interests include computational mechanics, biomechanics for soft tissues, and inverse problems.

Hui Zheng

Hui Zheng is a Professor at the Institute of Aerospace, School of Infrastructure Engineering, Nanchang University. His research interests include computational solid mechanics, biomechanics, and phononic crystals.

mathematics

MDPI

Article

Vibrational Resonance and Electrical Activity Behavior of a Fractional-Order FitzHugh–Nagumo Neuron System

Jia-Wei Mao and Dong-Liang Hu *

College of Mechanics and Materials, Hohai University, Nanjing 211100, China; 191308040019@hhu.edu.cn
* Correspondence: dlhu@hhu.edu.cn

Abstract: Making use of the numerical simulation method, the phenomenon of vibrational resonance and electrical activity behavior of a fractional-order FitzHugh–Nagumo neuron system excited by two-frequency periodic signals are investigated. Based on the definition and properties of the Caputo fractional derivative, the fractional L1 algorithm is applied to numerically simulate the phenomenon of vibrational resonance in the neuron system. Compared with the integer-order neuron model, the fractional-order neuron model can relax the requirement for the amplitude of the high-frequency signal and induce the phenomenon of vibrational resonance by selecting the appropriate fractional exponent. By introducing the time-delay feedback, it can be found that the vibrational resonance will occur with periods in the fractional-order neuron system, i.e., the amplitude of the low-frequency response periodically changes with the time-delay feedback. The weak low-frequency signal in the system can be significantly enhanced by selecting the appropriate time-delay parameter and the fractional exponent. In addition, the original integer-order model is extended to the fractional-order model, and the neuron system will exhibit rich dynamical behaviors, which provide a broader understanding of the neuron system.

Keywords: fractional-order system; time-delay feedback; vibrational resonance; FitzHugh–Nagumo neuron; numerical simulation

Citation: Mao, J.-W.; Hu, D.-L. Vibrational Resonance and Electrical Activity Behavior of a Fractional-Order FitzHugh–Nagumo Neuron System. *Mathematics* **2022**, *10*, 87. https://doi.org/10.3390/math10010087

Academic Editors: Yiqian He, Zhuojia Fu and Hui Zheng

Received: 13 December 2021
Accepted: 23 December 2021
Published: 27 December 2021

1. Introduction

Vibrational resonance (VR) has attracted considerable attention in the field of nonlinear sciences in the last twenty years. Based on the study of stochastic resonance (SR) [1], VR is firstly proposed by Landa and McClintock [2]. When replacing the noise in SR with an appropriate high-frequency signal, the weak low-frequency signal can be greatly amplified, which is similar to the typical "Inverted Bell" resonance phenomenon in SR, and is named as VR. Compared with the noise in SR, the high-frequency signal in VR is more controllable. Biharmonic signals are common in various fields, such as acoustics [3], optics [4], engineering [5], neuroscience [6], etc. Recently, the research hotspots of VR have changed from classic bistable systems [7–9] to fractional-order systems [10], delay systems [11], and network dynamical systems [12].

Due to the complex definition and lack of corresponding application background, the research on fractional calculus has been limited to the field of mathematics for a long time. However, compared with integer calculus, the power-law characteristic of complex social and physical phenomena can be accurately approximated through fractional calculus. Hence, this theory is gradually used in viscoelastic materials [13], electrification process [14], control theory [15], and neuron models [16], etc. To the best of our knowledge, the research on VR for fractional-order systems is quite few, and most of which are limited to bistable and multi-stable systems [17–19]. However, it is found that fractional calculus has its own unique advantages in describing certain neuronal characteristics. For example, fractional-order differentiation can be used to account for the firing rate of neocortical pyramidal neurons when stimulated by sinusoidal current [20]. Anastasio et al. [21] thought that the net output of the motor neurons in the visual system is consistent with fractional-order differentiation relative to eye position. Therefore, it is of great significance to study VR in the fractional-order neuron system.

In this study, we consider the FitzHugh–Nagumo (FHN) neuron model. As one of the simplest mathematical models for disclosing the dynamical behavior of neurons, the FHN model is widely used in integer-order systems for studying VR [22,23]. In brain activities [24], the neurons may exhibit two quite different time scales, and then, it is reasonable to reveal the mechanism of weak signal detection of neuron by VR. Since time delay is inherent in the neuron system, great progress has been made in the research on the effect of time delay on VR. Adding the time-delay feedback to the recovery variable of the FHN neuron model, the phenomenon of multiple VR can be induced in the neuron [25]. It is found that the bifurcation point and equilibrium point change periodically with the increase of time delay in a fractional order quantic oscillator system, and the output can be enhanced by selecting appropriate time delay [26].

Inspired by the above-mentioned ideas, the effects of fractional order and time delay on VR and dynamical behavior are studied in the fractional-order FHN neuron model. The VR can be induced in the fractional-order neuron model without strict requirement for the amplitude of high-frequency signal. It can be found that multiple VR occurs in the neuron with the increase of delay. Compared with integer-order model, the fractional-order FHN neuron exhibits rich electrical activities. The remainder of this paper is organized as follows: In Section 2, the fractional-order FHN neuron model excited by two periodic signals is briefly introduced. In Section 3, the VR in the fractional-order FHN model without and with time delay is studied. In Section 4, the effects of fractional exponent and time delay on the dynamical behavior in the fractional-order FHN model are discussed. Several conclusions are given in Section 5.

2. Fractional-Order FitzHugh–Nagumo Neuron Model

There are three common definitions of fractional calculus, namely Riemann–Liouville (R-L) definition, Grünwald–Letnikov (G-L) definition, and the Caputo definition. With the property of supersingularity, R-L definition is mainly used for the analysis of mathematical theory and is not convenient for engineering and physical modeling. G-L definition can be regarded as the extension of the limit form of integral calculus difference definition, which is widely applied to early numerical calculation. As its initial condition is the form of integer calculus, and it has clear physical meaning, the Caputo definition is used in this paper.

The fractional derivative of univariate function $f(t)$ is defined as

$$\frac{\mathrm{d}^{\alpha} f(t)}{\mathrm{d}t^{\alpha}} = {}_{t_0}D_t^{\alpha} f(t) = \frac{1}{\Gamma(n-\alpha)} \int_{t_0}^{t} \frac{f^{(n)}(\tau)\mathrm{d}\tau}{(t-\tau)^{\alpha-n+1}}, \ (n-1 < \alpha < n), \tag{1}$$

where $\Gamma(n-\alpha)$ is the gamma function, t_0 and t are the lower limit and upper limit of the definite integral, n is the minimum positive integer greater than α, and $f^{(n)}(\tau)$ is the nth derivative of the function $f(\tau)$. Under the joint excitation of harmonic signals, the fractional-order FHN neuron model with time delay (the model comes from the model involved in Ref. [27]) is given by the following form:

$$\begin{aligned} \varepsilon \frac{\mathrm{d}^{\alpha} x}{\mathrm{d}t^{\alpha}} &= x(t) - \frac{x(t)^3}{3} - y(t), \\ \frac{\mathrm{d}^{\alpha} y}{\mathrm{d}t^{\alpha}} &= x(t) + a + f\cos(\omega t) + F\cos(\Omega t) + K(y(t-\tau) - y(t)), \end{aligned} \tag{2}$$

where $x(t)$ and $y(t)$ represent the fast-varying membrane potential and the slow-varying recovery variable of neuronal cells, respectively; $\alpha(0 < \alpha \leq 1)$ is the fractional exponent; K is the strength of time-delay feedback. $\tau \geq 0$ is the delay parameter, and Equation (2) degenerates into the fractional-order FHN neuron model without delay when $\tau = 0$. $\varepsilon = 0.05$ is the time scale ratio, which is chosen to ensure that the membrane potential

$x(t)$ evolves faster than the recovery variable $y(t)$. $f\cos(\omega t)$ and $F\cos(\Omega t)$ represent the low-frequency signal and the high-frequency signal, respectively, which satisfy $f << 1$, $\omega << \Omega$. The value of a determines the behavior of the system under the conditions that $f = F = \tau = 0$ and $\alpha = 1$. If $|a| > 1.0$, the system is excitable and has only a stable fixed point; if $|a| < 1.0$, a limit cycle in the system arises. Here, the parameter $a = 1.05$ is chosen to make the system in the excitable state [28]. The variables in the model are dimensionless.

We consider the fractional derivative of $x(t)$ defined with the Caputo fractional derivative,

$$\frac{\mathrm{d}^{\alpha}x(t)}{\mathrm{d}t^{\alpha}} = f(x,t). \tag{3}$$

The discrete format of fractional-order L1 algorithm is [29]:

$$\frac{\mathrm{d}^{\alpha}x(t)}{\mathrm{d}t^{\alpha}} \approx \frac{(\mathrm{d}t)^{-\alpha}}{\Gamma(2-\alpha)}\left[\sum_{k=0}^{N-1}[x(t_{k+1}) - x(t_k)]\left[(N-k)^{1-\alpha} - (N-1-k)^{1-\alpha}\right]\right], \tag{4}$$

where $t_k = k\Delta t$. Combining the right sides of Equations (3) and (4) and solving for x at time t_N, it can be concluded that the discrete format of Equation (3) is

$$x(t_N) \approx (\mathrm{d}t)^{\alpha}\Gamma(2-\alpha)f(x,t) + x(t_{N-1}) - \left[\sum_{k=0}^{N-2}[x(t_{k+1}) - x(t_k)]\left[(N-k)^{1-\alpha} - (N-1-k)^{1-\alpha}\right]\right]. \tag{5}$$

where the Markov term weighted by the gamma function is given by

$$(\mathrm{d}t)^{\alpha}\Gamma(2-\alpha)f(x,t) + x(t_{N-1}) \tag{6}$$

and the memory trace is given by

$$\sum_{k=0}^{N-2}[x(t_{k+1}) - x(t_k)]\left[(N-k)^{1-\alpha} - (N-1-k)^{1-\alpha}\right] \tag{7}$$

The memory trace integrates information of all the previous activities and has a memory effect, which is the typical property of fractional-order system. When $\alpha = 1$, the memory trace has no effect, and Equation (5) degenerates into classical Euler algorithm.

According to Equation (5), the discrete format of Equation (2) can be obtained as follows:

$$\begin{aligned} x(t_N) \approx{}& \tfrac{1}{\varepsilon}(\mathrm{d}t)^{\alpha}\Gamma(2-\alpha)(x(t_{N-1}) - \tfrac{(x(t_{N-1}))^3}{3} - y(t_{N-1})) + x(t_{N-1}) \\ &- \left[\sum_{k=0}^{N-2}[x(t_{k+1}) - x(t_k)]\left[(N-k)^{1-\alpha} - (N-1-k)^{1-\alpha}\right]\right], \\ y(t_N) \approx{}& (\mathrm{d}t)^{\alpha}\Gamma(2-\alpha)(x(t_{N-1}) + a + f\cos(\omega t_{N-1}) + F\cos(\Omega t_{N-1}) + K(y(t_{N-m}) - y(t_{N-1}))) + y(t_{N-1}) \\ &- \left[\sum_{k=0}^{N-2}[y(t_{k+1}) - y(t_k)]\left[(N-k)^{1-\alpha} - (N-1-k)^{1-\alpha}\right]\right], \end{aligned} \tag{8}$$

where m is the number of discrete points caused by time delay.

3. Vibrational Resonance in the Fractional-Order FHN Neuron Model

3.1. VR in the Fractional-Order FHN Neuron Model without Time Delay

The response amplitude Q at the low-frequency signal is usually used as the index to measure the VR, which is defined by:

$$Q = \sqrt{Q_s^2 + Q_c^2}, \tag{9}$$

with

$$Q_s = \frac{2}{nT}\int_0^{nT} x(t)\sin(\omega t)dt, \quad Q_c = \frac{2}{nT}\int_0^{nT} x(t)\cos(\omega t)dt, \tag{10}$$

where $T = 2\pi/\omega$ and n is a positive integer. For the numerical simulation, the parameters are selected as $\varepsilon = 0.05,\ K = 0.2,\ f = 0.01,\ n = 50$.

Under fixed parameters $\omega = 0.5$, $\Omega = 5$, the curves of VR in the fractional-order FHN neuron without time delay are plotted in Figure 1a. It can be seen that different fractional exponents correspond to different phenomena of the VR. In Figure 1b, with the decrease of α, the region of the VR in the neuron changes, and the amplitude of low-frequency Q corresponding to the optimal F gradually decreases. Compared with the integer-order FHN neuron model, it is found that the low-frequency signal can also be amplified without strict requirement for the amplitude of high-frequency F in the fractional-order neuron. For example, in Figure 1b, the integer-order FHN neuron model fails to reach the state of the VR for $F = 0.15$, while for $\alpha = 0.96$, the VR occurs for the same value of F. Hence, it is shown that the VR in the FHN neuron can be induced by adjusting appropriate fractional exponent and the high-frequency force.

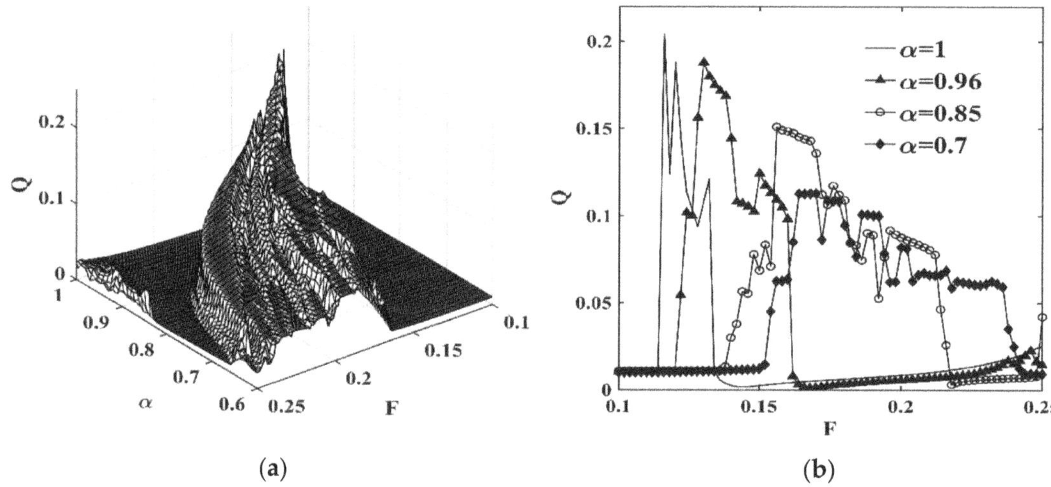

Figure 1. Response amplitude Q as a function of α and F. (**a**) The three-dimensional surface of response amplitude Q versus α and F; (**b**) response amplitude Q versus F for different values of α.

In order to further discuss the effect of α on the VR, the response amplitude $Q_{\max}$ versus α for $F \in [0.1, 0.25]$ is depicted in Figure 2a. For a certain range of F, although the response amplitude $Q_{\max}$ is not a strictly monotonic increasing function of α, in general, with the increase of α, the response amplitude Q can be optimized under the appropriate high-frequency force. However, when the value of F is fixed, the function of Q versus α shows different monotonic characteristics, as shown in Figure 2b. For $F = 0.11$, the curve of response amplitude is approximately a straight line, which indicates that VR does not occur with the change of α, while for $F = 0.15$ or $F = 0.2$, the response amplitude Q is a nonlinear function of α, and the low-frequency signal can be significantly enhanced by selecting an appropriate fractional-order α compared with the integer-order system.

3.2. Multiple VR in Fractional-Order FHN Neuron Model with Delay

For the fractional-order FitzHugh–Nagumo neuron with time delay, the numerical result of functional curves of the response amplitude Q versus τ can be obtained by combining Equation (8) with Equation (9). The response amplitude Q versus time delay τ in the fractional-order FHN neuron excited by two frequency signals is given in Figure 3. Figure 3e,f are partial, enlarged views of Figure 3a,d, respectively. From Figure 3a–d, it is seen that multiple resonance occurs in the neuron with the increase of the time-delay parameter. Therefore, the response amplitude Q can reach the maximum by selecting appropriate time-delay parameters, and the response amplitude Q can be greatly amplified compared with the neuron without time delay. Another notable phenomenon is that the response amplitude Q is periodic with the change of τ. From Figure 3a–d, it is clear that that the period of response amplitude Q is $2\pi/\omega$, while Figure 3e,f shows that the response amplitude Q varies with another period of $2\pi/\Omega$. Therefore, the response amplitude Q in the fractional-order FHN neuron with time-delay feedback presents two different periods, namely fast period $2\pi/\Omega$ and slow period $2\pi/\omega$, which exactly correspond to the period of high-frequency signal and low-frequency signal. Utilizing the periodicity of response amplitude Q and selecting appropriate time-delay parameters are helpful to realizing the effective control of the fractional-order FHN neuron. The only regret is that the parameters involved in the system are difficult to be optimized quickly to satisfy the requirement of resonance, which is consistent with the conclusion in Ref. [30].

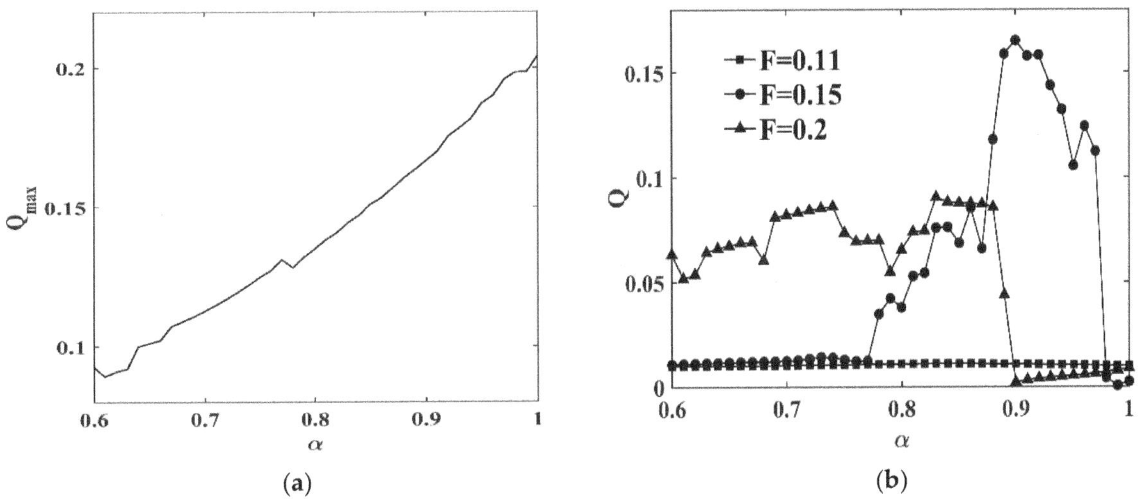

Figure 2. Relationship curve between response amplitude Q and fractional-order α. (**a**) Response amplitude Q_{max} versus α; (**b**) response amplitude Q versus α for three different values of F.

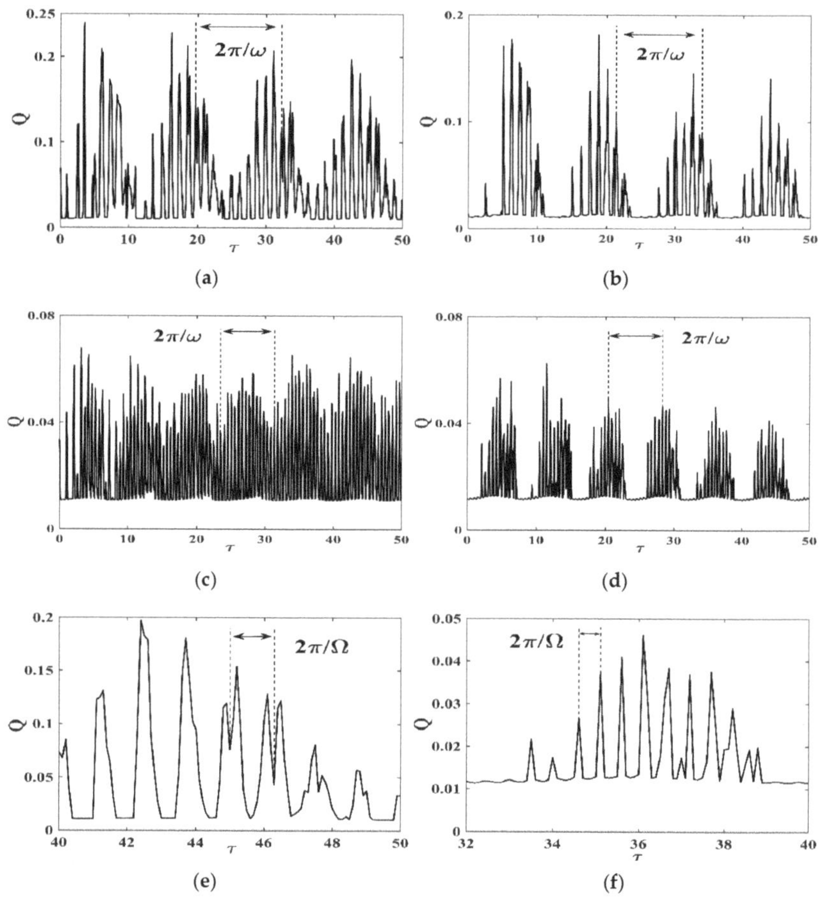

Figure 3. Relationship curve between response amplitude Q and τ: (**a**) $\omega = 0.5$, $\Omega = 5$, $\alpha = 0.96$, $F = 0.123$; (**b**) $\omega = 0.5$, $\Omega = 5$, $\alpha = 0.85$, $F = 0.138$; (**c**) $\omega = \pi/4$, $\Omega = 12$, $\alpha = 0.7$, $F = 0.395$; (**d**) $\omega = \pi/4$, $\Omega = 12$, $\alpha = 0.6$, $F = 0.298$; (**e**) $\omega = 0.5$, $\Omega = 5$, $\alpha = 0.96$, $F = 0.123$; (**f**) $\omega = \pi/4$, $\Omega = 12$, $\alpha = 0.6$, $F = 0.298$.

4. Dynamical Behavior of Fractional-Order FHN Neuron Model

4.1. Effect of the Fractional-Order

In this subsection, the dynamical behavior of the fractional-order FHN neuron without time-delay feedback is studied. Figure 4 shows the bifurcation diagram of interspike interval (ISI) of the neuron versus the fractional-order α, where $\alpha \in [0.6, 1]$. From Figure 4, when α is small, it can be seen that the fractional-order FHN neuron does not fire, and when the α is relatively large, various periodic and irregular firing patterns appear in the neuron. It can be found that the fractional-order FHN neuron displays complex dynamics by adjusting a single parameter α, which is also observed in other neurons [31,32].

In order to intuitively depict the effect of the fractional-order α on the dynamical behavior of the FHN neuron, the evolution of the membrane potential $x(t)$ is given in Figure 5. From Figure 5a, when $\alpha = 0.6$, the neuron is in the quiescent state. As can be seen from Figure 5b,c, when $\alpha = 0.792$ and $\alpha = 0.84$, the firing pattern of the neuron is period 1 bursting. Obviously, their interspike intervals are different, which are four times and two times $2\pi/\omega$, respectively. In Figure 5a, when $\alpha = 0.934$, the discharge rhythm of the FHN neuron alternates between period 1 and period 2. From Figure 5a–d, it is found that the fractional-order FHN neuron is more active with the increase of α, which is consistent with that revealed in Figure 4.

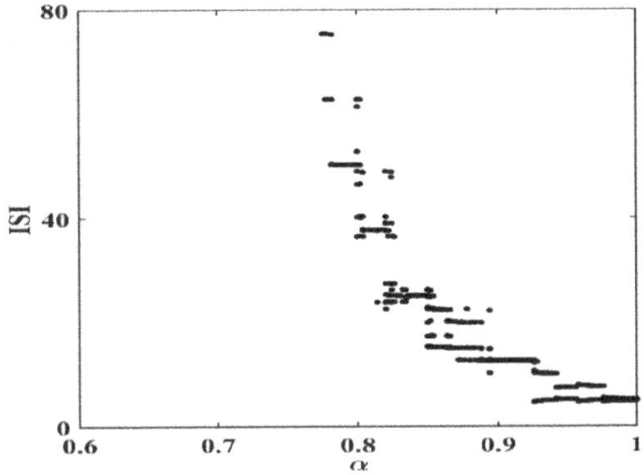

Figure 4. Bifurcation diagram of interspike interval (ISI) versus the fractional-order α; other parameters are $\omega = 0.5,\ \Omega = 5,\ F = 0.15$.

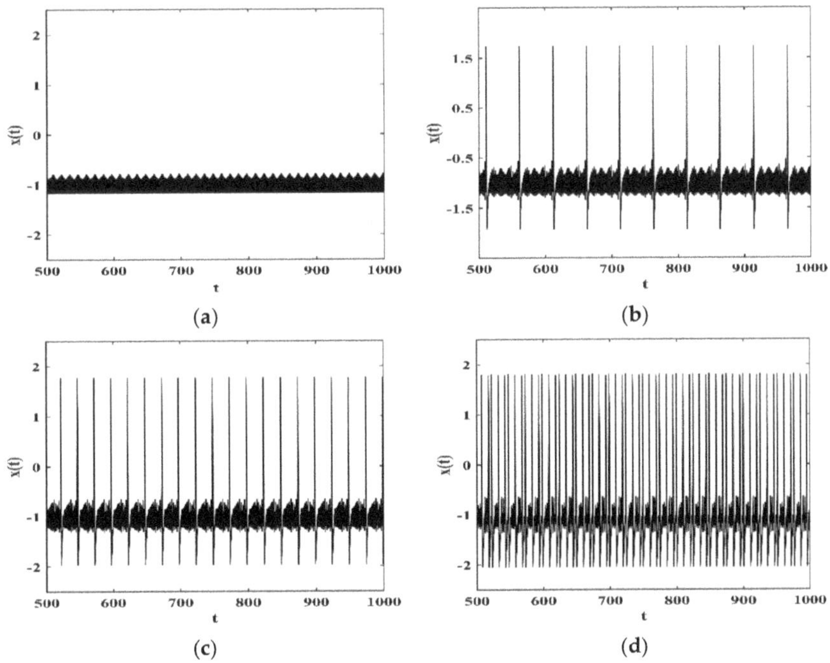

Figure 5. Time evolution of the membrane potential $x(t)$ for different values of α; other parameters are $\omega = 0.5,\ \Omega = 5,\ F = 0.15$; **(a)** $\alpha = 0.6$; **(b)** $\alpha = 0.792$; **(c)** $\alpha = 0.84$; **(d)** $\alpha = 0.934$.

4.2. Effect of the Time Delay

In order to study the effect of time-delay feedback on the dynamical behavior of the fractional-order FHN neuron, $\alpha = 0.84$ in Figure 5c is selected. Figure 6 depicts the bifurcation diagram of interspike interval (ISI) of the neuron versus the time-delay parameter τ, from which it can be seen that the fractional-order FHN neuron with time-delay feedback exhibits rich dynamical behaviors. The time series of the membrane potential $x(t)$ for different values of τ are given in Figure 7. When $\tau = 0$, the neuron fires with period

1, which corresponds to the case of the neuron without time delay in Figure 5c. When $\tau = 5.6$, it is seen that the firing pattern of the neuron is period 2 bursting. It can be seen from Figure 7c that a new firing pattern appears in the neuron, which regularly alters between period 2 and period 1. The multiple spiking of the firing pattern also appears in the neuron, as shown in Figure 7d. Thus, bursting patterns and interspike intervals of the fractional-order FHN neuron can be controlled by adjusting α or τ.

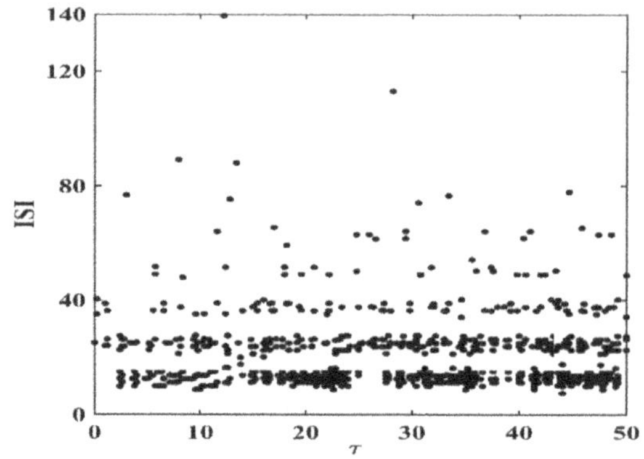

Figure 6. Bifurcation diagram of interspike interval (ISI) versus the time-delay τ; other parameters are $\alpha = 0.84,\ \omega = 0.5,\ \Omega = 5,\ F = 0.15$.

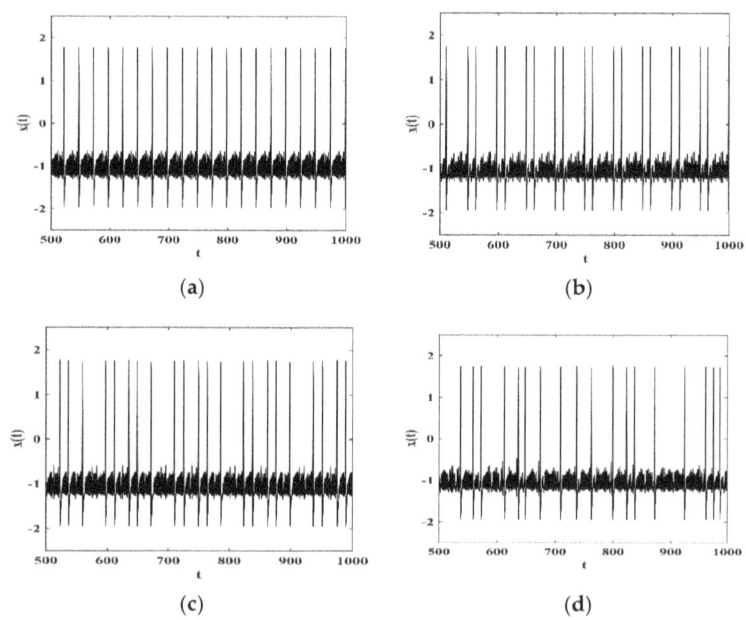

Figure 7. Time evolution of the membrane potential $x(t)$ for different values of τ; other parameters are $\alpha = 0.84,\ \omega = 0.5,\ \Omega = 5,\ F = 0.15$; (**a**) $\tau = 0$; (**b**) $\tau = 5.6$; (**c**) $\tau = 25$; (**d**) $\tau = 31.8$.

5. Conclusions

The vibrational resonance and electrical activity behaviors in the fractional-order FHN neuron are studied in this paper. When the original integer-order model is extended to the fractional-order model, the region of the VR will be wider, so the requirement for the amplitude of high-frequency signal can be relaxed, and then, the VR phenomenon can be induced by choosing the appropriate fractional-order α. Introducing time-delay feedback, it is found that the phenomenon of vibrational resonance appears with two different periods in the fractional FHN neuron, which are exactly equal to the periods of two frequency signals. The fractional-order FHN neuron exhibits rich electrical activities, and its bursting patterns and interspike interval can be controlled by adjusting α or τ.

Author Contributions: Conceptualization, J.-W.M. and D.-L.H.; methodology, J.-W.M. and D.-L.H.; validation, J.-W.M. and D.-L.H.; formal analysis, J.-W.M.; investigation, J.-W.M.; resources, D.-L.H.; data curation, J.-W.M.; writing—original draft preparation, J.-W.M.; writing—review and editing, D.-L.H.; visualization, D.-L.H.; supervision, D.-L.H.; project administration, D.-L.H.; funding acquisition, D.-L.H. All authors have read and agreed to the published version of the manuscript.

Funding: This work in the present paper was supported by the National Natural Science Foundation of China (Grant No. 11502067), and Natural Science Foundation of Jiangsu Province of China (Grant No. BK20191295).

Institutional Review Board Statement: Not applicable.

Informed Consent Statement: Not applicable.

Data Availability Statement: Not applicable.

Conflicts of Interest: The authors declare no conflict of interest. The funders had no role in the design of the study; in the collection, analyses, or interpretation of data; in the writing of the manuscript, or in the decision to publish the results.

References

1. Landa, P.S.; Mcclintock, P. Vibrational resonance. *J. Phys. A* **2000**, *33*, L433–L438. [CrossRef]
2. Mcnamara, B.; Wiesenfeld, K. Theory of stochastic resonance. *Phys. Rev. A* **1989**, *39*, 4854–4869. [CrossRef] [PubMed]
3. Maksimov, A.O. On the subharmonic emission of gas bubbles under two-frequency excitation. *Ultrasonics* **1997**, *35*, 79–86. [CrossRef]
4. Volkov, E.I.; Ullner, E.; Zaikin, A.A.; Kurths, J. Oscillatory amplification of stochastic resonance in excitable systems. *Phys. Rev. E* **2003**, *68*, 026214. [CrossRef] [PubMed]
5. Gherm, V.E.; Zernov, N.N.; Lundborg, B.; Västberg, A. The two-frequency coherence function for the fluctuating ionosphere: Narrowband pulse propagation. *J. Atmos. Sol.-Terr. Phys.* **1997**, *59*, 1831–1841. [CrossRef]
6. Victor, J.D.; Conte, M.M. Two-frequency analysis of interactions elicited by Vernier stimuli. *Vis. Neurosci.* **2000**, *17*, 959–973. [CrossRef]
7. Yao, C.; Liu, Y.; Zhan, M. Frequency-resonance-enhanced vibrational resonance in bistable systems. *Phys. Rev. E* **2011**, *83*, 061122. [CrossRef]
8. Abusoua, A.; Daqaq, M.F. Experimental evidence of vibrational resonance in a mechanical bistable twin-well oscillator. *J. Comput. Nonlinear Dyn.* **2018**, *3*, 061002. [CrossRef]
9. Chizhevsky, V.N. Vibrational higher-order resonances in an overdamped bistable system with biharmonic excitation. *Phys. Rev. E* **2014**, *90*, 042924. [CrossRef]
10. Yang, J.; Sanjuan, M.; Liu, H. Bifurcation and resonance in a fractional Mathieu-Duffing oscillator. *Eur. Phys. J. B* **2015**, *88*, 310. [CrossRef]
11. Yang, Z.; Ning, L. Vibrational resonance in a harmonically trapped potential system with time delay. *Pramana* **2019**, *92*, 1–12. [CrossRef]
12. Uzuntarla, M.; Yilmaz, E.; Wagemakers, A.; Ozer, M. Vibrational resonance in a heterogeneous scale free network of neurons. *Commun. Nonlinear Sci. Numer. Simul.* **2015**, *22*, 367–374. [CrossRef]
13. Meral, F.C.; Royston, T.J.; Magin, R. Fractional calculus in viscoelasticity: An experimental study. *Commun. Nonlinear Sci. Numer. Simul.* **2010**, *15*, 939–945. [CrossRef]
14. Matouk, A.E. Chaos, feedback control and synchronization of a fractional-order modified Autonomous Van der Pol–Duffing circuit. *Commun. Nonlinear Sci. Numer. Simul.* **2011**, *16*, 975–986. [CrossRef]
15. Chaudhary, N.I.; Raja, M.; Khan, A.R. Design of modified fractional adaptive strategies for Hammerstein nonlinear control autoregressive systems. *Nonlinear Dyn.* **2015**, *82*, 1811–1830. [CrossRef]
16. Khanday, F.A.; Kant, N.A.; Dar, M.R.; Zulkifli, T.Z.A.; Psychalinos, C. Low-Voltage low-power integrable CMOS circuit implementation of integer and fractional-order FitzHugh-Nagumo Neuron model. *IEEE Trans. Neural Netw. Learn. Syst.* **2019**, *30*, 2108–2122. [CrossRef]
17. Yang, J.H.; Zhu, H. Vibrational resonance in Duffing systems with fractional-order damping. *Chaos* **2012**, *22*, 013112. [CrossRef]
18. Mbong, T.L.M.D.; Siewe, M.S.; Tchawoua, C. The effect of the fractional derivative order on vibrational resonance in a special fractional quintic oscillator. *Mech. Res. Commun.* **2016**, *78*, 13–19. [CrossRef]

19. Qin, T.; Xie, T.; Luo, M.; Deng, K. Vibrational resonance in fractional-order overdamped multistable systems. *Chin. J. Phys.* **2017**, *55*, 546–555. [CrossRef]
20. Lundstrom, B.N.; Higgs, M.H.; Spain, W.J.; Fairhall, A.L. Fractional differentiation by neocortical pyramidal neurons. *Nat. Neurosci.* **2008**, *11*, 1335–1342. [CrossRef]
21. Anastasio, T.J. The fractional-order dynamics of brainstem vestibulo-oculomotor neurons. *Biol. Cybern.* **1994**, *72*, 69–79. [CrossRef]
22. Ullner, E.; Zaikin, A.; García-Ojalvo, J.; Bascones, R.; Kurths, J. Vibrational resonance and vibrational propagation in excitable systems. *Phys. Lett. A* **2003**, *312*, 348–354. [CrossRef]
23. Deng, B.; Wang, J.; Wei, X.; Tsang, K.M.; Chan, W.L. Vibrational resonance in neuron populations. *Chaos* **2010**, *20*, 013113. [CrossRef]
24. Izhikevich, E.M. Simple model of spiking neurons. *IEEE Trans. Neural Netw.* **2003**, *14*, 1569–1572. [CrossRef] [PubMed]
25. Hu, D.L.; Yang, J.H.; Liu, X.B. Delay-induced vibrational multiresonance in FitzHugh-Nagumo system. *Commun. Nonlinear Sci. Numer. Simul.* **2012**, *17*, 1031–1035. [CrossRef]
26. Guo, W.; Ning, L. Vibrational resonance in a fractional order quintic oscillator system with time delay feedback. *Int. J. Bifurc. Chaos* **2020**, *30*, 2050025. [CrossRef]
27. Abdelouahab, M.S.; Lozi, R.P.; Chen, G. Complex Canard Explosion in a Fractional-Order FitzHugh–Nagumo Model. *Int. J. Bifurc. Chaos* **2019**, *29*, 1950111. [CrossRef]
28. Wu, D.; Zhu, S. Stochastic resonance in FitzHugh–Nagumo system with time-delayed feedback. *Phys. Lett. A* **2008**, *372*, 5299–5304. [CrossRef]
29. Teka, W.; Marinov, T.M.; Santamaria, F. Neuronal spike timing adaptation described with a fractional leaky integrate-and-fire model. *PLoS Comput. Biol.* **2014**, *10*, e1003526. [CrossRef] [PubMed]
30. Wu, C.; Yang, J.; Huang, D.; Liu, H.; Hu, E. Weak signal enhancement by the fractional-order system resonance and its application in bearing fault diagnosis. *Meas. Sci. Technol.* **2019**, *30*, 035004. [CrossRef]
31. Teka, W.W.; Upadhyay, R.K.; Mondal, A. Spiking and bursting patterns of fractional-order Izhikevich model. *Commun. Nonlinear Sci. Numer. Simul.* **2018**, *56*, 161–176. [CrossRef]
32. Mondal, A.; Sharma, S.K.; Upadhyay, R.K.; Mondal, A. Firing activities of a fractional-order FitzHugh-Rinzel bursting neuron model and its coupled dynamics. *Sci. Rep.* **2019**, *9*, 15721. [CrossRef] [PubMed]

mathematics

MDPI

Article

A Hybrid Localized Meshless Method for the Solution of Transient Groundwater Flow in Two Dimensions

Qiang Wang [1,2], Pyeoungkee Kim [1,*] and Wenzhen Qu [3,*]

[1] Division of Computer Software Engineering, Silla University, Busan 612022, Korea; wangqiang@sdivc.edu.cn
[2] Shandong Vocational College of Industry, Zibo 256414, China
[3] School of Mathematics and Statistics, Qingdao University, Qingdao 266071, China
* Correspondence: pkkim@silla.ac.kr (P.K.); quwz@qdu.edu.cn (W.Q.)

Abstract: In this work, a hybrid localized meshless method is developed for solving transient groundwater flow in two dimensions by combining the Crank–Nicolson scheme and the generalized finite difference method (GFDM). As the first step, the temporal discretization of the transient groundwater flow equation is based on the Crank–Nicolson scheme. A boundary value problem in space with the Dirichlet or mixed boundary condition is then formed at each time node, which is simulated by introducing the GFDM. The proposed algorithm is truly meshless and easy to program. Four linear or nonlinear numerical examples, including ones with complicated geometry domains, are provided to verify the performance of the developed approach, and the results illustrate the good accuracy and convergency of the method.

Keywords: groundwater flow; generalized finite difference method; Crank–Nicolson; transient

Citation: Wang, Q.; Kim, P.; Qu, W. A Hybrid Localized Meshless Method for the Solution of Transient Groundwater Flow in Two Dimensions. *Mathematics* **2022**, *10*, 515. https://doi.org/10.3390/math10030515

Academic Editors: Zhuojia Fu, Yiqian He and Hui Zheng

Received: 14 January 2022
Accepted: 3 February 2022
Published: 5 February 2022

1. Introduction

As an important component of the hydrological cycle system, groundwater is a key source of domestic and industrial water supply. Therefore, the analysis of the groundwater flow has great significance for water supply security. Due to the complexity of the problem, an analytical solution is rarely available for most models of groundwater flow. With the development of computing techniques, more and more numerical approaches have been developed and applied to numerical simulations of science and engineering problems, such as the finite element method (FEM) [1–3], the boundary element method (BEM) [4,5], and the meshless method [6–10].

As a new approach in recent years, the meshless method is now widely applied in various fields [11–19], particularly in computational fluid dynamics (CFD). The developed meshless approaches can be classified into collocation-based and Galerkin-based methods. Compared with the latter, the meshless collocation methods have the advantages of no numerical quadrature and mesh generation, and some of these are the localized method of fundamental solutions (LMFS) [20–22], the generalized finite difference method (GFDM) [23–33], the localized Chebyshev collocation method [34], the singular boundary method (SBM) [35–43], and the localized knot method (LKM) [44].

The GFDM, as a popular localized meshless collocation method, employs the Taylor series expansions and moving least squares (MLS) approximations [45,46] to form the system of algebraic equations with a spare matrix [47,48]. Thanks to this spare system, this method is highly efficient and suitable for the numerical simulations of large-scale problems. Many physical applications have been addressed by the GFDM, such as the thin elastic plate bending analysis [49], the electroelastic analysis of 3D piezoelectric structures [50], the acoustic wave propagation [51], the inverse Cauchy problem in 2D elasticity [52], the heat conduction problems [53], and the stationary flow in a dam [54].

A hybrid localized meshless method is proposed in this paper for the solution of transient groundwater flow in a two-dimensional space by combining the Crank–Nicolson scheme and the GFDM. As the first step, the Crank–Nicolson scheme is applied to the temporal discretization of the transient groundwater flow equation. At each time node, a boundary value problem in space is then formed and subsequently solved with the GFDM. Through the above process, a hybrid localized meshless approach is finally established, which is truly meshless and easy to program. The rest of the work is organized as follows. The governing equation of transient groundwater flow with boundary and initial conditions is described in Section 2. The formulations of the hybrid localized meshless method are derived in Section 3. Several linear and nonlinear numerical examples are provided in Section 4 to verify the performance of the developed method. Some conclusions are presented in Section 5.

2. Problem Definition

The movement of transient groundwater flow of a constant density in a homogeneous and anisotropic two-dimensional (2D) medium with the domain Ω can be described by using the following equation:

$$T_x \frac{\partial^2 H(x,y,t)}{\partial x^2} + T_y \frac{\partial^2 H(x,y,t)}{\partial y^2} + W(x,y,t) = u_s \frac{\partial H(x,y,t)}{\partial t}, \ (x,y) \in \Omega, \ t > 0, \quad (1)$$

where H denotes hydraulic head, W is the volumetric flow rate of a source or sink per unit volume, u_s means the specific aquifer storativity, T_x and T_y are hydraulic conductivities along the x- and y-axis, and t is the time.

To obtain the solution of Equation (1), the boundary and initial conditions are imposed as the following:

$$H(x,y,t) = g_1(x,y,t), \ (x,y) \in \partial\Omega_D, \ t \geq 0, \quad (2)$$

$$\frac{\partial H(x,y,t)}{\partial \boldsymbol{n}(x,y)} = g_2(x,y,t), \ (x,y) \in \partial\Omega_N, \ t \geq 0, \quad (3)$$

$$H(x,y,0) = g_3(x,y), \ (x,y) \in \Omega, \quad (4)$$

where $g_i(i = 1,2,3)$ are given functions, $\partial\Omega_D \cup \partial\Omega_N = \partial\Omega$ $(\partial\Omega_D \cap \partial\Omega_N = \varnothing)$, and $\boldsymbol{n}$ is unit outward normal vector to $\partial\Omega_N$.

3. Hybrid Localized Meshless Method

To solve the transient groundwater flow of Equations (1)–(4), the temporal discretization of this system is first made by using the Crank–Nicolson scheme. The spatial equation is then formed at each time node. The GFDM is finally used for the solution of the spatial equation with corresponding boundary conditions.

3.1. Temporal Discretization by the Crank–Nicolson Scheme

We insert n nodes $\left\{t_1 = 0, t_2, \ldots, t_n = T_f\right\}$ in the time domain $[0, T_f]$ where T_f is the final time. By using the Crank–Nicolson scheme, the governing Equation (1) at each time node t_{i+1} is then recast as the following:

$$\begin{aligned} &\tfrac{1}{2}\left[T_x \tfrac{\partial^2 H(x,y,t_{i+1})}{\partial x^2} + T_y \tfrac{\partial^2 H(x,y,t_{i+1})}{\partial y^2} + W(x,y,t_{i+1}) + T_x \tfrac{\partial^2 H(x,y,t_i)}{\partial x^2} + T_y \tfrac{\partial^2 H(x,y,t_i)}{\partial y^2} + W(x,y,t_i)\right] \\ &= u_s \tfrac{H(x,y,t_{i+1}) - H(x,y,t_i)}{\Delta t_i}, \ i = 1,2,\ldots,n-1, \end{aligned} \quad (5)$$

where the time step size $\Delta t_i = t_{i+1} - t_i$. Then we can reformulate Equation (5) as the following:

$$\begin{aligned} &\tfrac{\Delta t_i}{2}\left[T_x \tfrac{\partial^2 H(x,y,t_{i+1})}{\partial x^2} + T_y \tfrac{\partial^2 H(x,y,t_{i+1})}{\partial y^2}\right] - u_s H(x,y,t_{i+1}) = \\ &= -u_s H(x,y,t_i) - \tfrac{\Delta t_i}{2}\left[T_x \tfrac{\partial^2 H(x,y,t_i)}{\partial x^2} + T_y \tfrac{\partial^2 H(x,y,t_i)}{\partial y^2} + W(x,y,t_i) + W(x,y,t_{i+1})\right], \ i = 1,2,\ldots,n-1, \end{aligned} \quad (6)$$

As a result, a system of spatial equations with the boundary conditions (2) and (3) at time node t_{i+1} is formed and will be solved by using the GFDM.

3.2. Spatial Discretization by the GFDM

For the GFDM, some collocation nodes are first distributed in the computational domain Ω and its boundary Γ. A supporting domain called a star for each node $\boldsymbol{x}_0 = (x_0, y_0)$ is defined by collecting $\boldsymbol{m}$ nearest nodes $\boldsymbol{x}_j = (x_j, y_j)(j = 1, 2, \ldots, m)$ as shown in Figure 1. In the star, x_0 and $\boldsymbol{x}_j(j = 1, 2, \ldots, m)$ are respectively named as the central node and the supporting nodes. This distance criterion is the simplest way of star selection. However, it should be noted that distorted (ill-conditioned) stars may be formed based on this distance criterion, particularly for cases with very irregular distributions of collocation nodes. To overcome the above drawback, the "cross" and the "Voronoi neighbours" criterions discussed in Refs. [55,56] can be used to form more reasonable stars.

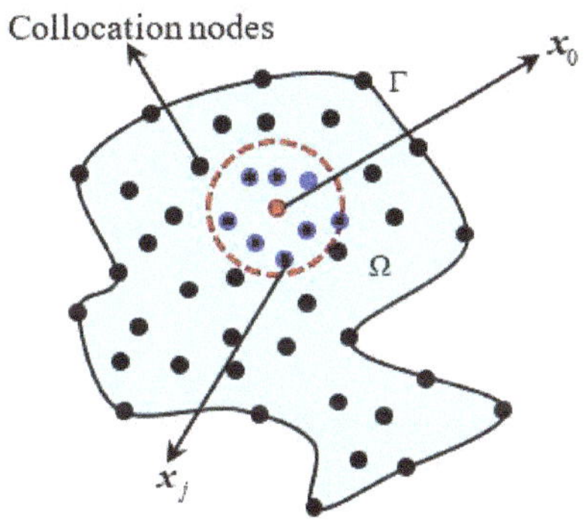

Figure 1. A star of collocation node x_0.

To conveniently derive the system of algebraic equations, the $H_j(j = 0, 1, \ldots, m)$ are employed to denote the values of hydraulic head at nodes $\boldsymbol{x}_j(j = 0, 1, \ldots, m)$ in the star of central node $\boldsymbol{x}_0$. Based on Taylor series expansions, H_j can be given as

$$H_j = H_0 + a_j \frac{\partial H_0}{\partial x} + b_j \frac{\partial H_0}{\partial y} + \frac{1}{2}\left(a_j^2 \frac{\partial^2 H_0}{\partial x^2} + b_j^2 \frac{\partial^2 H_0}{\partial y^2} \right) + a_j b_j \frac{\partial^2 H_0}{\partial x \partial y} + \ldots\ldots,\ j = 1, 2, \ldots, m, \tag{7}$$

with

$$a_j = x_j - x_0, \text{ and } b_j = y_j - y_0. \tag{8}$$

By truncating the expansion (7) after second-order derivatives of hydraulic head H, we can define a residual function $R(H)$ as the following:

$$R(H) = \sum_{j=1}^{m} \left[\left(H_0 - H_j + a_j \frac{\partial H_0}{\partial x} + b_j \frac{\partial H_0}{\partial y} + \frac{a_j^2}{2} \frac{\partial^2 H_0}{\partial x^2} + \frac{b_j^2}{2} \frac{\partial^2 H_0}{\partial y^2} + a_j b_j \frac{\partial^2 H_0}{\partial x \partial y} \right) \kappa_j \right]^2, \tag{9}$$

with the following weighting function κ_j [57,58]:

$$\kappa_j = \frac{\exp\left(-\lambda_j^2\right) - \exp\left(-\lambda_m^2\right)}{1 - \exp\left(-\lambda_m^2\right)},\quad j = 1, 2, \ldots, m, \tag{10}$$

in which $\lambda_j = |\boldsymbol{x}_j - \boldsymbol{x}_0|$, and $\lambda_m = \max\{\lambda_j, j = 1, 2, \ldots, m\}$. It should be noted that the weighting function in the GFDM should be a monotonic decreasing function of λ_j. Because the Taylor series approximation becomes more accurate when the distance λ_j is smaller, which should have a higher weight κ_j in residual function $R(H)$ of Equation (9). Some other weighting functions can be found in [53,59].

A vector $\boldsymbol{P}_H$ is defined by the following:

$$\boldsymbol{P}_H = \left[\frac{\partial H_0}{\partial x}, \frac{\partial H_0}{\partial y}, \frac{\partial^2 H_0}{\partial x^2}, \frac{\partial^2 H_0}{\partial y^2}, \frac{\partial^2 H_0}{\partial x \partial y} \right]^T \tag{11}$$

Minimizing the residual function $R(H)$ with respect to each element in the vector $\boldsymbol{P}_H$, i.e.,

$$\frac{\partial R(H)}{\partial\left\{\frac{\partial H_0}{\partial x}\right\}} = 0,\ \frac{\partial R(H)}{\partial\left\{\frac{\partial H_0}{\partial y}\right\}} = 0,\ \frac{\partial R(H)}{\partial\left\{\frac{\partial^2 H_0}{\partial x^2}\right\}} = 0,\ \frac{\partial R(H)}{\partial\left\{\frac{\partial^2 H_0}{\partial y^2}\right\}} = 0,\ \frac{\partial R(H)}{\partial\left\{\frac{\partial^2 H_0}{\partial x \partial y}\right\}} = 0, \tag{12}$$

we can have a system of linear equations as the following:

$$\boldsymbol{A}\boldsymbol{P}_H = \boldsymbol{b}, \tag{13}$$

with the following:

$$\boldsymbol{A} = \sum_{j=1}^{m} diag\left(\boldsymbol{E}_1^{(j)}\right) \coprod diag\left(\boldsymbol{E}_2^{(j)}\right), \tag{14}$$

$$\boldsymbol{b} = \boldsymbol{B}\boldsymbol{H} = \left(-\sum_{j=1}^{m} \kappa_j \boldsymbol{E}_2^{(j)},\ \kappa_1 \boldsymbol{E}_2^{(1)},\ \kappa_2 \boldsymbol{E}_2^{(2)},\ \cdots,\ \kappa_m \boldsymbol{E}_2^{(m)}\right)_{5\times(m+1)} \begin{pmatrix} H_0 \\ H_1 \\ H_2 \\ \vdots \\ H_m \end{pmatrix}_{(m+1)\times 1}, \tag{15}$$

where $\coprod$ is a 5×5 square matrix that all elements are one, $diag\left(\boldsymbol{E}_1^{(j)}\right)$ and $diag\left(\boldsymbol{E}_2^{(j)}\right)$ are both diagonal matrices with their diagonal elements as the following:

$$\boldsymbol{E}_1^{(j)} = \kappa_j \begin{bmatrix} a_j & b_j & a_j^2 & b_j^2 & a_j b_j \end{bmatrix}^T, \text{ and } \boldsymbol{E}_2^{(j)} = \frac{\kappa_j}{2} \begin{bmatrix} 2a_j & 2b_j & a_j^2 & b_j^2 & 2a_j b_j \end{bmatrix}^T, \tag{16}$$

and $\boldsymbol{H} = [H_0,\ H_1,\ H_2,\ \ldots, H_m]^T$.

With the help of Equation (13) and Equation (15), the vector $\boldsymbol{P}_H$ can be formulated as the following:

$$\boldsymbol{P}_H = \boldsymbol{A}^{-1}\boldsymbol{B}[H_0,\ H_1,\ H_2,\ \ldots, H_m]^T. \tag{17}$$

As a result, all the first- and second-order derivatives of hydraulic head H at central node $\boldsymbol{x}_0$ are expressed as the linear combinations of values H_j $(j = 0, 1, \ldots, m)$. By substituting the corresponding second-order derivatives of Equation (17) into Equation (6), we can easily recast Equation (6) as the following:

$$\sum_{j=0}^{m} \alpha_j H_j = Q, \tag{18}$$

where α_j $(j = 0, 1, \ldots, m)$ and Q are obviously known and can be determined by Equations (6) and (17). For each collocation node excepting that of satisfying boundary condition (2), one equation can be obtained by using the above similar derivation. It should be noted that $H_0 = g(x_0, y_0, t_{i+1})$ is directly used as one equation for collocation nodes of satisfying boundary condition (2). Finally, by using the GFDM, the spatial equation with the corresponding boundary conditions has been transformed into a system of linearly algebraic equations with a sparse matrix. The values of hydraulic head H at all collocation nodes can be calculated once this system is solved.

In addition, we consider a case with a nonlinear volumetric flow rate in the following numerical example 4 to further verify the proposed approach. Through a similar derivation process, a nonlinear system of algebraic equations is established and solved by using "fsolve" function of MATLAB.

4. Numerical Examples

In this section, four numerical examples with square and complicated domains are given to test the accuracy and stability of the proposed method. To preferably estimate the precision of numerical results, two different error definitions are provided as the following [60,61]:

$$\text{Global error} = \sqrt{\sum_{i=1}^{N} (\overline{H}_i - H_i)^2} / \sqrt{\sum_{i=1}^{N} H_i^2}, \tag{19}$$

$$\text{Max error} = \max_{1 \le i \le N} \left\{ \frac{|\overline{H}_i - H_i|}{|H_i|} \right\} \tag{20}$$

in which N denotes the number of collocation nodes, H_i and $\overline{H}_i$ represents the exact and numerical results of hydraulic head at the i-th node. Unless otherwise specified, the number of supporting nodes in a star is set to $m = 12$ in all numerical examples.

4.1. Example 1: Hydraulic Head Distribution in a Square Domain

As the first numerical example, we consider the distribution of hydraulic heads in a unit square domain with its central point $(0.5, 0.5)$. The specific aquifer storativity is $u_s = 1$, and the hydraulic conductivities are $T_x = 1$ and $T_y = 3$. The volumetric flow rate W is given as the following:

$$W(x,y,t) = \sin(0.5\pi x)\sin(0.5\pi y)\left(\pi^2 \sin t + \cos t\right). \tag{21}$$

The Dirichlet boundary condition $H(x,y,t) = 0$ is imposed on the boundaries $x = 0$, and $y = 0$. The Neumann boundary condition $\frac{\partial H(x,y,t)}{\partial n} = 0$ is applied to the boundaries $x = 1$, and $y = 1$. The initial condition is $H(x,y,0) = 0$. Based on these, the exact solution can be determined as the following:

$$H(x,y,t) = \sin(0.5\pi x)\sin(0.5\pi y)\sin t. \tag{22}$$

In the numerical simulation, the final time is set to $T_f = 2$, and the time step size is $\Delta t = 0.05$. For the spatial discretization, 396 collocation nodes are distributed in the domain and its boundary, which have the following two different patterns: regular distribution (case 1) and irregular distribution (case 2), as shown in Figure 2a. From $t = 0$ to $t = 2$, the variations of global and max errors of hydraulic head H calculated by the GFDM with the Crank–Nicolson scheme (CN-GFDM) are plotted in Figure 2b. As we can see from this figure, the developed method has good performance for two different collocation node distributions. We also find that errors obtained by employing the irregular distribution (case 2) are larger than those obtained by using the regular distribution (case 1).

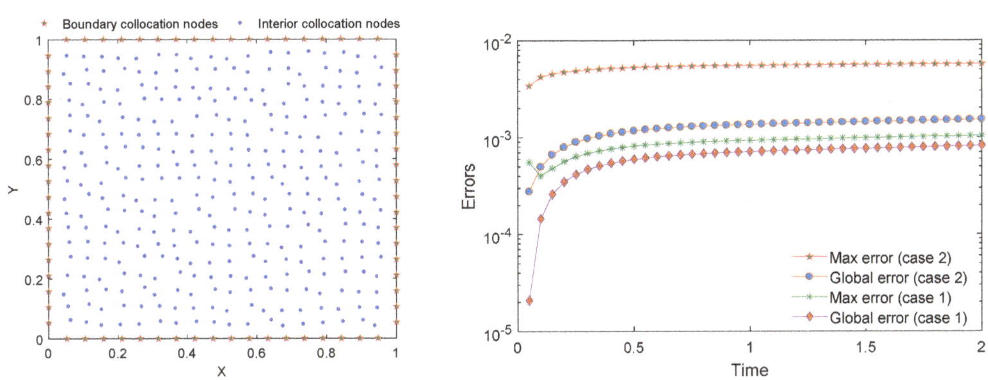

(a) **(b)**

Figure 2. (**a**) Irregular distribution of 396 collocation nodes, (**b**) Global and max errors of hydraulic head H from $t = 0$ to $t = 2$.

To investigate the convergence behavior of the CN-GFDM, the program is rerun by only changing the number of collocation nodes compared with the previous setting. Here, the distribution of nodes is regular. By using the developed method with a different number of collocation nodes (or a different mean distance of collocation nodes), Table 1 provides the max and global errors of the numerical results of the hydraulic head at time $t = 2$. It can be obviously observed that the errors decay with an increasing collocation node number, which indicates the CN-GFDM has a good convergence property for this case.

Table 1. Max and global errors of hydraulic head H with different number of collocation nodes.

Number of collocation nodes	21	96	192	285	396
Mean distance of collocation nodes	2.50×10^{-1}	1.11×10^{-1}	7.69×10^{-2}	6.25×10^{-2}	5.26×10^{-2}
Max error	1.01×10^{-2}	3.75×10^{-3}	2.05×10^{-3}	1.42×10^{-3}	1.04×10^{-3}
Global error	5.94×10^{-3}	2.74×10^{-3}	1.57×10^{-3}	1.11×10^{-3}	8.18×10^{-4}

4.2. Example 2: Hydraulic Head Distribution in a Heart-Shaped Domain

The second numerical example is a hydraulic head distribution in a heart-shaped domain, and the dimension of this domain is shown in Figure 3. The specific aquifer storativity and hydraulic conductivity are assumed to be as the following:

$$u_s = 3,\ T_x = 2T_y = 2. \tag{23}$$

The volumetric flow rate is $W = 0$. In this case, the Dirichlet boundary and initial conditions are imposed as the following:

$$H(x,y,t) = e^{-t}\cos x \cos y + c,\ \ (x,y) \in \Gamma, \tag{24}$$

$$H(x,y,0) = \cos x \cos y + c,\ \ (x,y) \in \Omega, \tag{25}$$

where $c = 0.2$. The exact solution for this example is determined as $H(x,y,t) = e^{-t}\cos x \cos y + c$.

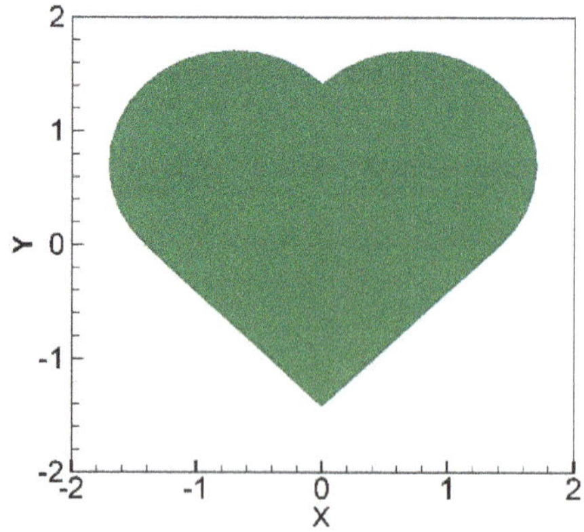

Figure 3. The dimension of a heart-shaped domain.

To simulate the solution from $t = 0$ to $t = 5$, the developed method employs 218, 464 (see Figure 4), and 1700 collocation nodes. The time step size is set to $\Delta t = 0.05$. Figure 5 provides the contours of relative errors (RE) of the hydraulic head at final time $t = 5$ by using these three distributions of collocation nodes. It can be found that the max relative error of numerical results in the computational domain is less than 3×10^{-4} even only using

218 collocation nodes. Moreover, all numerical errors overall decreased with an increasing number of collocation nodes.

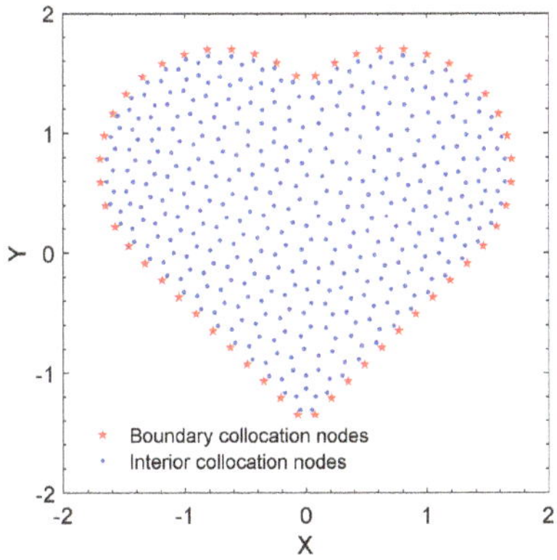

Figure 4. Distribution of 464 collocation nodes.

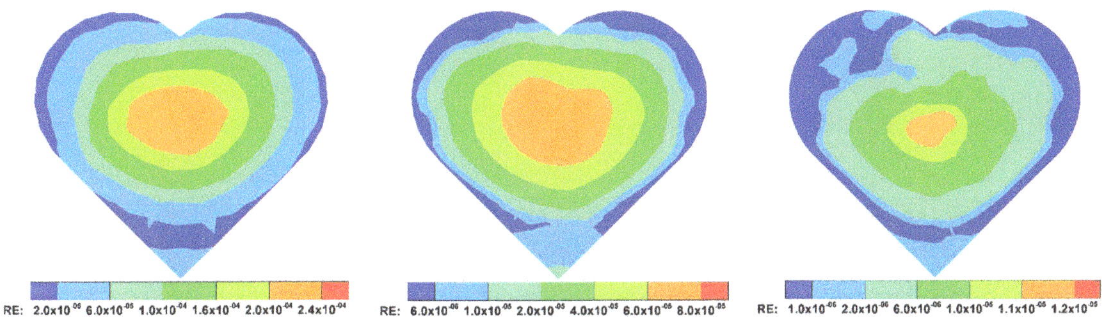

(**a**) 218 (**b**) 464 (**c**) 1700

Figure 5. The contours of relative errors of hydraulic head H with three distributions of collocation nodes.

Next, we keep the above-mentioned setting and distribute 1700 collocation nodes. The mean distance of these nodes is 0.101. Table 2 lists the max and global errors of hydraulic head H at final time $t = 5$, which are calculated by the CN-GFDM with different time step sizes. As we can observe, the errors decay rapidly when decreasing the time step size.

Table 2. Max and global errors of hydraulic head H with different time step size.

Time step size	0.625	0.50	0.25	0.125	0.05
Max error	2.51×10^{-3}	1.60×10^{-3}	4.05×10^{-4}	8.42×10^{-5}	1.17×10^{-5}
Global error	1.20×10^{-3}	7.80×10^{-4}	1.91×10^{-4}	3.89×10^{-5}	4.97×10^{-6}

Finally, we investigate the influence of supporting node number m on the precision and computational efficiency of the developed approach. The time step size is reset as $\Delta t = 0.25$. Table 3 provides the variations of two kinds of errors and CPU time with different numbers of supporting nodes. As we can observe, the accuracy of numerical results obtained by the present method is relatively insensitive to the number of supporting nodes. To have a higher computing efficiency of the CN-GFDM, we should choose a relatively small number of supporting nodes when the numerical results satisfy the accuracy requirement.

Table 3. Max and global errors of hydraulic head H and CPU time with different supporting node numbers.

m	12	16	20	24	28
Max error	4.05×10^{-4}	3.53×10^{-4}	3.45×10^{-4}	3.38×10^{-4}	3.23×10^{-4}
Global error	1.91×10^{-4}	1.71×10^{-4}	1.66×10^{-4}	1.61×10^{-4}	1.55×10^{-4}
CPU time (s)	0.27	0.34	0.38	0.44	0.49

4.3. Example 3: Hydraulic Head Distribution in a Complicated Domain

As the third numerical example, the distribution of hydraulic head in a complicated domain is considered. The dimension of this domain is 2.7×1.4, as shown in Figure 6. The specific aquifer storativity is set to $u_s = 0.3$, and hydraulic conductivities are assumed to be functions as the following:

$$T_x = e^{|x|}, \text{ and } T_y = e^{|y|}. \tag{26}$$

The volumetric flow rate is given as the following:

$$W(x, y, t) = e^{x+y}\left[u_s \cos t - (T_x + T_y)\sin t\right] \tag{27}$$

The Dirichlet boundary condition is imposed as the following:

$$H(x, y, t) = e^{x+y} \sin t, \ \ (x, y) \in \Gamma, \tag{28}$$

and initial condition is $H = 0$. The exact solution for this example is $H(x, y, t) = e^{x+y} \sin t$.

Figure 6. The dimension of a complicated domain.

We first consider the simulation from $t = 0$ to $t = 5$, and set the time step size as $\Delta t = 0.1$. By using the present approach with 3398 (see Figure 7) and 8918 collocation nodes, Figures 8 and 9 respectively plot the contours of relative errors of hydraulic head H and its flux $\frac{\partial H}{\partial x}$ at final time $t = 5$. The numerical results in these figures illustrate the availability and convergency of the developed CN-GFDM.

Finally, a long-time simulation of hydraulic head H from $t = 0$ to $t = 100$ is considered. The number of collocation nodes is 8918, and the time step size is $\Delta t = 0.1$. Figure 10 shows the max and global errors of hydraulic head H, which are changed as functions of time. As we can see from this figure, the two kinds of errors both remain stable in this simulation.

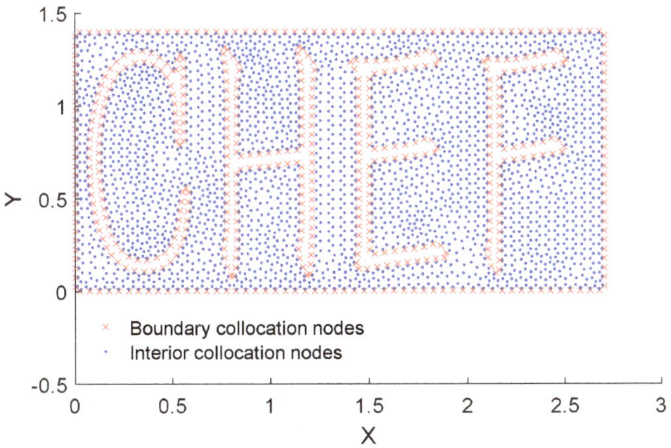

Figure 7. Distribution of 3398 collocation nodes.

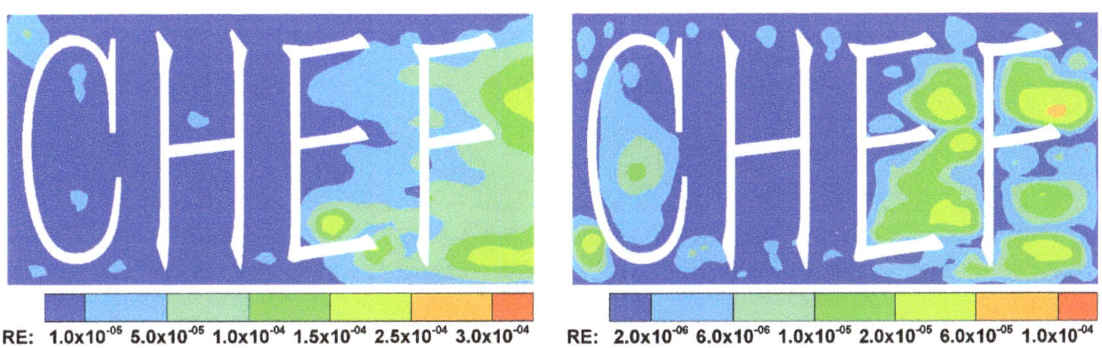

(**a**) 3398 (**b**) 8918

Figure 8. The contours of relative errors of hydraulic head H with two distributions of collocation nodes.

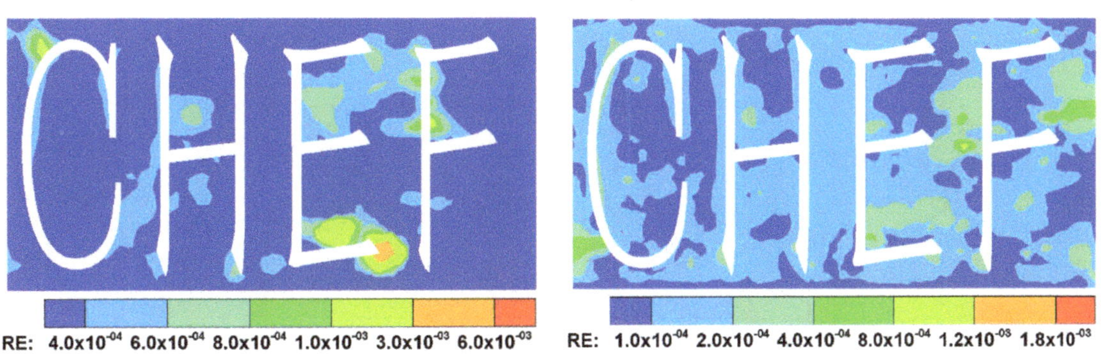

(**a**) 3398 (**b**) 8918

Figure 9. Relative error distributions of flux $\partial H/\partial x$ with different number of collocation nodes.

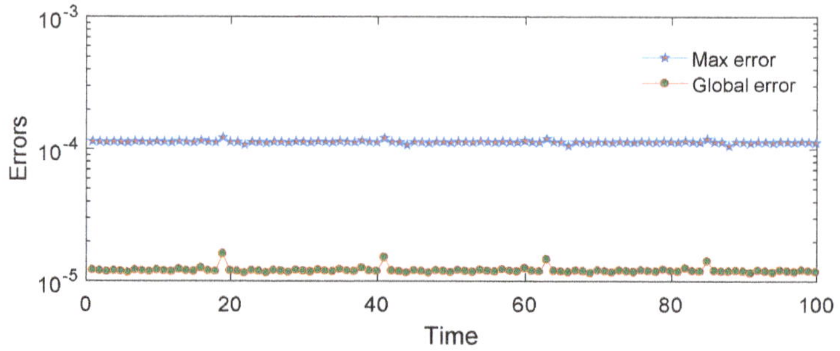

Figure 10. Two types of error curves of hydraulic head H from $t = 0$ to $t = 100$.

4.4. Example 4: Nonlinear Hydraulic Head Distribution in a Gear Domain

As the final numerical example, we consider the distribution of nonlinear hydraulic head in a gear domain. Figure 11 shows the dimension of the gear domain. The specific aquifer storativity is assumed to be $u_s = 1200$, and hydraulic conductivities are the following:

$$T_x = x^2, \text{ and } T_y = y^2. \tag{29}$$

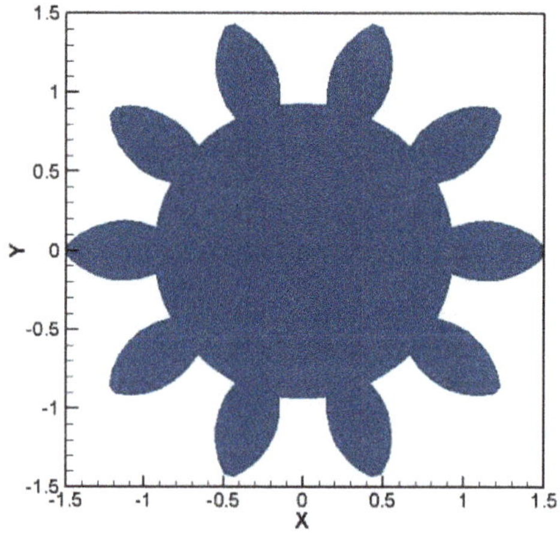

Figure 11. The dimension of a gear domain.

The volumetric flow rate is a nonlinear term given as the following:

$$W(x,y,t) = H^2(x,y,t) - \left[\left(x^4 + y^4\right)e^{\frac{t}{100}} + 0.1\right]^2 \tag{30}$$

The Dirichlet boundary condition is imposed as the following:

$$H(x,y,t) = \left(x^4 + y^4\right)e^{\frac{t}{100}} + 0.1, \ (x,y) \in \Gamma, \tag{31}$$

and initial condition is the following:

$$H(x,y,t) = x^4 + y^4 + 0.1, \ (x,y) \in \Omega. \tag{32}$$

The exact solution for this case is determined as the following:

$$H(x,y,t) = \left(x^4 + y^4\right)e^{\frac{t}{100}} + 0.1 \tag{33}$$

The numerical simulation for this case is run from $t = 0$ to $t = 10$. The time step size is set to $\Delta t = 0.05$, and 1186 collocation nodes are distributed in the gear domain and its boundary as shown in Figure 12. The contours of relative errors of the hydraulic head H at $t = 5$ and $t = 10$ are plotted in Figure 13. As we can see from this figure, the present approach obtains the satisfied numerical results for this nonlinear case, and max relative error is less than 4×10^{-3}. Figure 14 provides the max and global errors of hydraulic head H at each time node, which illustrates that the developed CN-GFDM yields accurate numerical results as an increasing time.

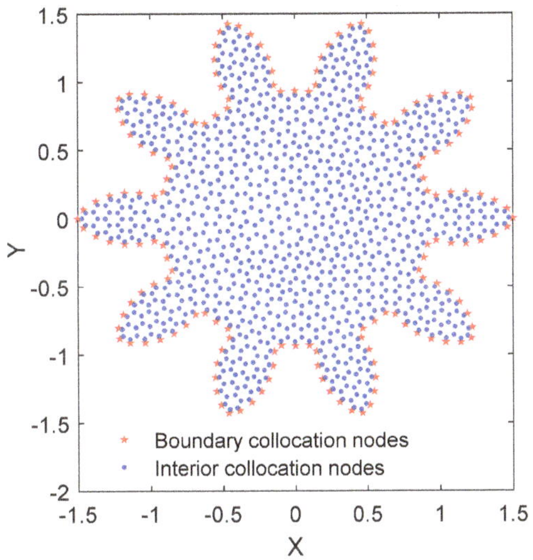

Figure 12. Distribution of 1186 collocation nodes.

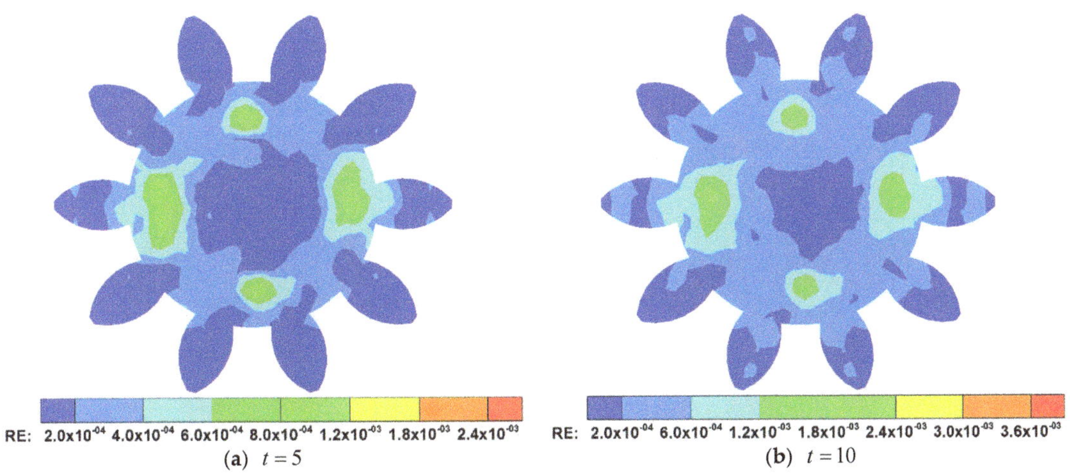

Figure 13. The contours of relative errors of hydraulic head H at $t = 5$ and $t = 10$.

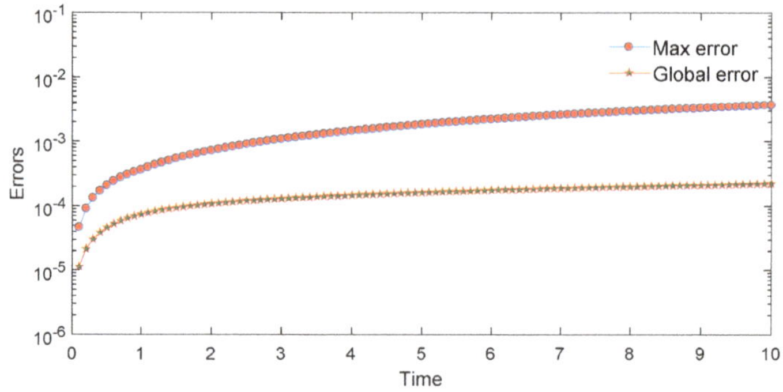

Figure 14. Two types of error curves of hydraulic head H from $t = 0$ to $t = 10$.

5. Concluding Remarks

To simulate the transient groundwater flow in homogeneous and anisotropic two-dimensional mediums, a hybrid localized meshless method is constructed based on the Crank–Nicolson scheme for temporal discretization and the GFDM for spatial discretization. The present approach is truly meshless and easy to program.

To fully investigate the performance of the developed method, the max and global errors of hydraulic head are both provided for numerical examples with different boundary conditions, complicated geometry domains, and several kinds of hydraulic conductivities. Numerical results indicate that the hybrid localized meshless method developed in this work obtains the satisfied accuracy and convergency in time and space.

Author Contributions: Conceptualization, Q.W. and W.Q.; methodology, W.Q.; software, Q.W. and P.K.; investigation, Q.W.; writing—original draft preparation, Q.W.; writing—review and editing, P.K. and W.Q.; visualization, Q.W.; supervision, P.K. and W.Q.; funding acquisition, Q.W. All authors have read and agreed to the published version of the manuscript.

Funding: The work described in this paper was supported by the Government of Shandong's Education System for studying abroad, and the key R & D plan of Zibo city: Intelligent Water IoT cloud service platform of "Zishui Online" (NO. 2019ZBXC246).

Institutional Review Board Statement: Not applicable.

Informed Consent Statement: Not applicable.

Data Availability Statement: Not applicable.

Conflicts of Interest: The authors declare no conflict of interest.

References

1. Hughes, T.J. *The Finite Element Method: Linear Static and Dynamic Finite Element Analysis*; Courier Corporation: Chelmsford, MA, USA, 2012.
2. Chai, Y.; Li, W.; Liu, Z. Analysis of transient wave propagation dynamics using the enriched finite element method with interpolation cover functions. *Appl. Math. Comput.* **2022**, *412*, 126564. [CrossRef]
3. Li, W.; Zhang, Q.; Gui, Q.; Chai, Y. A coupled FE-meshfree triangular element for acoustic radiation problems. *Int. J. Comput. Methods* **2021**, *18*, 2041002. [CrossRef]
4. Qu, W.; Zhang, Y.; Liu, C.-S. Boundary stress analysis using a new regularized boundary integral equation for three-dimensional elasticity problems. *Arch. Appl. Mech.* **2017**, *87*, 1213–1226. [CrossRef]
5. Gu, Y.; Zhang, C. Fracture analysis of ultra-thin coating/substrate structures with interface cracks. *Int. J. Solids Struct.* **2021**, *225*, 111074. [CrossRef]
6. Zhang, X.; Liu, X.H.; Song, K.Z.; Lu, M.W. Least-squares collocation meshless method. *Int. J. Numer. Methods Eng.* **2001**, *51*, 1089–1100. [CrossRef]
7. Atluri, S.N.; Shen, S. *The Meshless Method*; Tech Science Press: Encino, CA, USA, 2002.
8. Wang, C.; Wang, F.; Gong, Y. Analysis of 2D heat conduction in nonlinear functionally graded materials using a local semi-analytical meshless method. *AIMS Math.* **2021**, *6*, 12599–12618. [CrossRef]

9. Xing, Y.; Song, L.; Fan, C.-M. A generalized finite difference method for solving elasticity interface problems. *Eng. Anal. Bound. Elem.* **2021**, *128*, 105–117. [CrossRef]
10. Li, X.; Dong, H. An element-free Galerkin method for the obstacle problem. *Appl. Math. Lett.* **2021**, *112*, 106724. [CrossRef]
11. Xi, Q.; Fu, Z.; Wu, W.; Wang, H.; Wang, Y. A novel localized collocation solver based on Trefftz basis for potential-based inverse electromyography. *Appl. Math. Comput.* **2021**, *390*, 125604. [CrossRef]
12. Tang, Z.; Fu, Z.; Chen, M.; Ling, L. A localized extrinsic collocation method for Turing pattern formations on surfaces. *Appl. Math. Lett.* **2021**, *122*, 107534. [CrossRef]
13. Xi, Q.; Fu, Z.; Rabczuk, T.; Yin, D. A localized collocation scheme with fundamental solutions for long-time anomalous heat conduction analysis in functionally graded materials. *Int. J. Heat Mass Transf.* **2021**, *180*, 121778. [CrossRef]
14. Lin, J.; Zhang, Y.; Reutskiy, S.; Feng, W. A novel meshless space-time backward substitution method and its application to nonhomogeneous advection-diffusion problems. *Appl. Math. Comput.* **2021**, *398*, 125964. [CrossRef]
15. Qiu, L.; Hu, C.; Qin, Q.-H. A novel homogenization function method for inverse source problem of nonlinear time-fractional wave equation. *Appl. Math. Lett.* **2020**, *109*, 106554. [CrossRef]
16. Sun, L.; Zhang, C.; Yu, Y. A boundary knot method for 3D time harmonic elastic wave problems. *Appl. Math. Lett.* **2020**, *104*, 106210. [CrossRef]
17. Sun, L.; Chen, Z.; Zhang, S.; Chu, L. A wave based method for two-dimensional time-harmonic elastic wave propagation in anisotropic media. *Appl. Math. Lett.* **2021**, *120*, 107292. [CrossRef]
18. García, Á.; Negreanu, M.; Ureña, F.; Vargas, A.M. A Note on a Meshless Method for Fractional Laplacian at Arbitrary Irregular Meshes. *Mathematics* **2021**, *9*, 2843. [CrossRef]
19. Rao, X.; Zhan, W.; Zhao, H.; Xu, Y.; Liu, D.; Dai, W.; Gong, R.; Wang, F. Application of the least-square meshless method to gas-water flow simulation of complex-shape shale gas reservoirs. *Eng. Anal. Bound. Elem.* **2021**, *129*, 39–54. [CrossRef]
20. Qu, W.; Fan, C.-M.; Li, X. Analysis of an augmented moving least squares approximation and the associated localized method of fundamental solutions. *Comput. Math. Appl.* **2020**, *80*, 13–30. [CrossRef]
21. Gu, Y.; Fan, C.-M.; Fu, Z. Localized Method of Fundamental Solutions for Three-Dimensional Elasticity Problems: Theory. *Adv. Appl. Math. Mech.* **2021**, *13*, 1520–1534.
22. Li, W. Localized method of fundamental solutions for 2D harmonic elastic wave problems. *Appl. Math. Lett.* **2021**, *112*, 106759. [CrossRef]
23. Qu, W.; Gao, H.; Gu, Y. Integrating Krylov deferred correction and generalized finite difference methods for dynamic simulations of wave propagation phenomena in long-time intervals. *Adv. Appl. Math. Mech.* **2021**, *13*, 1398–1417.
24. Qu, W.; He, H. A spatial–temporal GFDM with an additional condition for transient heat conduction analysis of FGMs. *Appl. Math. Lett.* **2020**, *110*, 106579. [CrossRef]
25. Song, L.; Li, P.-W.; Gu, Y.; Fan, C.-M. Generalized finite difference method for solving stationary 2D and 3D Stokes equations with a mixed boundary condition. *Comput. Math. Appl.* **2020**, *80*, 1726–1743. [CrossRef]
26. Shao, M.; Song, L.; Li, P.-W. A generalized finite difference method for solving Stokes interface problems. *Eng. Anal. Bound. Elem.* **2021**, *132*, 50–64. [CrossRef]
27. Xing, Y.; Song, L.; Li, P.-W. A generalized finite difference method for solving biharmonic interface problems. *Eng. Anal. Bound. Elem.* **2022**, *135*, 132–144. [CrossRef]
28. Li, P.-W. Space–time generalized finite difference nonlinear model for solving unsteady Burgers' equations. *Appl. Math. Lett.* **2021**, *114*, 106896. [CrossRef]
29. Li, Y.-D.; Tang, Z.-C.; Fu, Z.-J. Generalized Finite Difference Method for Plate Bending Analysis of Functionally Graded Materials. *Mathematics* **2020**, *8*, 1940. [CrossRef]
30. Fan, C.-M.; Chu, C.-N.; Šarler, B.; Li, T.-H. Numerical solutions of waves-current interactions by generalized finite difference method. *Eng. Anal. Bound. Elem.* **2019**, *100*, 150–163. [CrossRef]
31. Ureña, F.; Gavete, L.; Garcia, A.; Benito, J.J.; Vargas, A.M. Solving second order non-linear parabolic PDEs using generalized finite difference method (GFDM). *J. Comput. Appl. Math.* **2019**, *354*, 221–241. [CrossRef]
32. Salete, E.; Vargas, A.M.; García, Á.; Negreanu, M.; Benito, J.J.; Ureña, F. Complex Ginzburg–Landau Equation with Generalized Finite Differences. *Mathematics* **2020**, *8*, 2248. [CrossRef]
33. Huang, J.; Lyu, H.; Fan, C.-M.; Chen, J.-H.; Chu, C.-N.; Gu, J. Wave-Structure Interaction for a Stationary Surface-Piercing Body Based on a Novel Meshless Scheme with the Generalized Finite Difference Method. *Mathematics* **2020**, *8*, 1147. [CrossRef]
34. Wang, F.; Zhao, Q.; Chen, Z.; Fan, C.-M. Localized Chebyshev collocation method for solving elliptic partial differential equations in arbitrary 2D domains. *Appl. Math. Comput.* **2021**, *397*, 125903. [CrossRef]
35. Li, J.; Gu, Y.; Qin, Q.-H.; Zhang, L. The rapid assessment for three-dimensional potential model of large-scale particle system by a modified multilevel fast multipole algorithm. *Comput. Math. Appl.* **2021**, *89*, 127–138. [CrossRef]
36. Li, J.; Fu, Z.; Gu, Y.; Qin, Q.-H. Recent Advances and Emerging Applications of the Singular Boundary Method for Large-Scale and High-Frequency Computational Acoustics. *Adv. Appl. Math. Mech.* **2021**, *14*, 315–343. [CrossRef]
37. Li, W.; Chen, W.; Pang, G. Singular boundary method for acoustic eigenanalysis. *Comput. Math. Appl.* **2016**, *72*, 663–674. [CrossRef]
38. Lin, J.; Qiu, L.; Wang, F. Localized singular boundary method for the simulation of large-scale problems of elliptic operators in complex geometries. *Comput. Math. Appl.* **2022**, *105*, 94–106. [CrossRef]

39. Qiu, L.; Wang, F.; Lin, J. A meshless singular boundary method for transient heat conduction problems in layered materials. *Comput. Math. Appl.* **2019**, *78*, 3544–3562. [CrossRef]
40. Wei, X.; Luo, W. 2.5D singular boundary method for acoustic wave propagation. *Appl. Math. Lett.* **2021**, *112*, 106760. [CrossRef]
41. Wei, X.; Huang, A.; Sun, L. Singular boundary method for 2D and 3D heat source reconstruction. *Appl. Math. Lett.* **2020**, *102*, 106103. [CrossRef]
42. Qu, W.; Chen, W. Solution of two-dimensional stokes flow problems using improved singular boundary method. *Adv. Appl. Math. Mech.* **2015**, *7*, 13–30. [CrossRef]
43. Li, W.; Wang, F. Precorrected-FFT Accelerated Singular Boundary Method for High-Frequency Acoustic Radiation and Scattering. *Mathematics* **2022**, *10*, 238. [CrossRef]
44. Wang, F.; Wang, C.; Chen, Z. Local knot method for 2D and 3D convection–diffusion–reaction equations in arbitrary domains. *Appl. Math. Lett.* **2020**, *105*, 106308. [CrossRef]
45. Li, X.; Zhao, Q.; Long, K.; Zhang, H. Multi-material topology optimization of transient heat conduction structure with functional gradient constraint. *Int. Commun. Heat Mass Transf.* **2022**, *131*, 105845. [CrossRef]
46. Li, X.; Li, S. On the stability of the moving least squares approximation and the element-free Galerkin method. *Comput. Math. Appl.* **2016**, *72*, 1515–1531. [CrossRef]
47. Liszka, T. An interpolation method for an irregular net of nodes. *Int. J. Numer. Methods Eng.* **1984**, *20*, 1599–1612. [CrossRef]
48. Liszka, T.; Orkisz, J. The finite difference method at arbitrary irregular grids and its application in applied mechanics. *Comput. Struct.* **1980**, *11*, 83–95. [CrossRef]
49. Qu, W.; He, H. A GFDM with supplementary nodes for thin elastic plate bending analysis under dynamic loading. *Appl. Math. Lett.* **2022**, *124*, 107664. [CrossRef]
50. Xia, H.; Gu, Y. Generalized finite difference method for electroelastic analysis of three-dimensional piezoelectric structures. *Appl. Math. Lett.* **2021**, *117*, 107084. [CrossRef]
51. Qu, W. A high accuracy method for long-time evolution of acoustic wave equation. *Appl. Math. Lett.* **2019**, *98*, 135–141. [CrossRef]
52. Li, P.-W.; Fu, Z.-J.; Gu, Y.; Song, L. The generalized finite difference method for the inverse Cauchy problem in two-dimensional isotropic linear elasticity. *Int. J. Solids Struct.* **2019**, *174*, 69–84. [CrossRef]
53. Qu, W.; Gu, Y.; Zhang, Y.; Fan, C.M.; Zhang, C. A combined scheme of generalized finite difference method and Krylov deferred correction technique for highly accurate solution of transient heat conduction problems. *Int. J. Numer. Methods Eng.* **2019**, *117*, 63–83. [CrossRef]
54. Chávez-Negrete, C.; Santana-Quinteros, D.; Domínguez-Mota, F. A Solution of Richards' Equation by Generalized Finite Differences for Stationary Flow in a Dam. *Mathematics* **2021**, *9*, 1604. [CrossRef]
55. Orkisz, J. Finite Difference Method; Part III. In *Handbook of Computational Solid Mechanics*; Kleiber, M., Ed.; Springer: Berlin/Heidelberg, Germany, 1998; pp. 336–432.
56. Milewski, S. Meshless finite difference method with higher order approximation—Applications in mechanics. *Arch. Comput. Methods Eng.* **2012**, *19*, 1–49. [CrossRef]
57. Belytschko, T.; Krongauz, Y.; Organ, D.; Fleming, M.; Krysl, P. Meshless methods: An overview and recent developments. *Comput. Methods Appl. Mech. Eng.* **1996**, *139*, 3–47. [CrossRef]
58. Zhou, Y.; Qu, W.; Gu, Y.; Gao, H. A hybrid meshless method for the solution of the second order hyperbolic telegraph equation in two space dimensions. *Eng. Anal. Bound. Elem.* **2020**, *115*, 21–27. [CrossRef]
59. Gavete, L.; Ureña, F.; Benito, J.J.; García, A.; Ureña, M.; Salete, E. Solving second order non-linear elliptic partial differential equations using generalized finite difference method. *J. Comput. Appl. Math.* **2017**, *318*, 378–387. [CrossRef]
60. Qu, W.; Chen, W.; Gu, Y. Fast multipole accelerated singular boundary method for the 3D Helmholtz equation in low frequency regime. *Comput. Math. Appl.* **2015**, *70*, 679–690. [CrossRef]
61. Qu, W.; Fan, C.-M.; Zhang, Y. Analysis of three-dimensional heat conduction in functionally graded materials by using a hybrid numerical method. *Int. J. Heat Mass Transf.* **2019**, *145*, 118771. [CrossRef]

mathematics

Article

A Novel Spatial–Temporal Radial Trefftz Collocation Method for 3D Transient Wave Propagation Analysis with Specified Sound Source Excitation

Lin Chen, Wenzhi Xu * and Zhuojia Fu *

College of Mechanics and Materials, Hohai University, Nanjing 211100, China; chenlin@hhu.edu.cn
* Correspondence: xwz@hhu.edu.cn (W.X.); paul212063@hhu.edu.cn (Z.F.)

Abstract: In this paper, a novel semi-analytical collocation solver, the spatial–temporal radial Trefftz collocation method (STRTCM) is proposed to solve 3D transient wave equations with specified sound source excitations. Unlike the traditional time discretization strategies, the proposed numerical scheme introduces the spatial–temporal radial Trefftz functions (STRTFs) as the basis functions for the spatial and temporal discretization of the transient wave equations. The STRTFs are constructed in the spatial–temporal domain, which is a combination of 3D Euclidean space and time into a 4D manifold. Moreover, since the initial and boundary conditions are imposed on the spatial–temporal domain boundaries, the original transient wave propagation problem can be converted to an inverse boundary value problem. To deal with the specified time-dependent sound source excitations, the composite multiple reciprocity technique is extended from the spatial domain to the spatial–temporal domain, which transforms the original problem with a source term into a high-order problem without a source term. By deriving the related STRTFs for the considered high-order problem, the proposed scheme only requires the node discretization on the spatial–temporal domain boundaries. The efficiency of the proposed method is numerically verified by four benchmark examples under 3D transient wave equations with specified time-dependent sound source excitation.

Keywords: meshless collocation method; semi-analytical; radial Trefftz basis functions; transient wave propagation analysis

MSC: 65M70; 35L05

Citation: Chen, L.; Xu, W.; Fu, Z. A Novel Spatial–Temporal Radial Trefftz Collocation Method for 3D Transient Wave Propagation Analysis with Specified Sound Source Excitation. *Mathematics* **2022**, *10*, 897. https://doi.org/10.3390/math10060897

Academic Editor: Efstratios Tzirtzilakis

Received: 25 January 2022
Accepted: 8 March 2022
Published: 11 March 2022

1. Introduction

As is well known, the phenomenon of wave propagation [1–7] widely exists in various areas of science and engineering, such as acoustics, elastodynamics, electromagnetics, and fluid dynamics. Numerical simulation plays an important role in understanding and mastering the fundamental laws of such wave propagation. Traditional numerical methods [8–10], such as the finite difference method and finite element method (FEM), have been widely used in wave propagation analysis. However, they usually have the problems of low computational efficiency and poor computational accuracy due to the use of universal polynomial functions. To overcome these drawbacks, several basis functions, including wave characteristics, have been introduced, and then a series of semi-analytical numerical methods have been constructed, such as the wave-based method [11], scaled boundary finite element method [12] and boundary element method [13–15], and so on. The aforementioned numerical methods belong to the mesh-based methods, which are sensitive to the mesh quality. To eliminate the effect of mesh generation, a group of meshless methods is developed. Similarly, by introducing the basis functions including the wave characteristics, several boundary-type meshless methods are proposed. They can be divided into two categories: weak-form boundary meshless methods and strong-form boundary meshless methods. The weak-form boundary meshless methods mainly include the local boundary integral equation method [16], boundary node method [17], hybrid boundary node method [18], boundary face method [19], null-field boundary integral equation method [20], and so on. The strong-form boundary meshless methods mainly include the wave superposition method [21,22], method of fundamental solutions (MFS) [23,24], regularized meshless method [25], boundary distributed source method [26], singular boundary method (SBM) [27–31], collocation Trefftz method (CTM) [32,33], and so on. Due to their simpler form, integral-free and easy-to-use merits, this study focused on the strong-form boundary meshless methods based on the semi-analytical basis functions.

A broader and more challenging problem in wave propagation analysis is the simulation of wave propagation in the time domain. The following three popular approaches have been widely used to treat transient wave propagation problems: (1) Time-stepping methods (TSM) [23,34] transform the transient wave propagation problem into a series of time-independent problems, and the accuracy and stability of this method highly depend on the time-step size. (2) Frequency domain techniques (FDT) [35,36] use the transformation technique to eliminate the time derivative leading to a time-independent equation in the frequency domain, and then employ a numerical inversion scheme to invert the frequency domain solutions back into the time-dependent solutions. The FDT does not require time stepping, and thus avoids the effect of the time step on numerical accuracy. However, for systems with no intrinsic damping and mismatched initial and ending responses, the numerical inversion transformation fails to produce accurate results. This is why in practical calculations often small artificial damping is added to the model. (3) Spatial–temporal semi-analytical basis function methods [37–39] employ the spatial–temporal semi-analytical basis function a priori to satisfy the transient wave equation and then solve it directly. Among these three time-discretization schemes, the first two have been widely used for transient wave propagation analysis; the last one has not been widely used because the time-dependent semi-analytical basis functions are not easy to construct, in particular, the transient wave equation, including the source excitations.

Fortunately, the composite multiple reciprocity method (CMRM) [40] has been proposed and applied to deal with some specified source terms in time-independent nonhomogeneous PDEs. In this study, the CMRM is extended from the spatial domain to the spatial–temporal domain, which transforms the original transient wave propagation problem with a source term into the high-order time-dependent problem without a source term. Then a group of spatial–temporal semi-analytical basis functions and spatial–temporal radial Trefftz functions are derived to satisfy the governing equation of such high-order time-dependent problem in advance. Correspondingly, the so-called spatial–temporal radial Trefftz collocation method (STRTCM) is constructed to solve 3D transient wave equations with specified sound source excitations, which only require the node discretization on the spatial–temporal domain boundaries.

In this paper, a novel spatial–temporal radial Trefftz collocation method is proposed without differential approximation for the temporal derivatives, which may cause the accumulated error to solve the 3D transient wave equations, and the composite multiple reciprocity method is extended from the space domain to the spatial–temporal domain to treat the time-dependent source term. Due to the use of the related spatial–temporal radial Trefftz functions, the proposed STRTCM requires fewer node discretizations to obtain more accurate results. A brief outline of this paper is as follows. In Section 2, the numerical procedure of the spatial–temporal radial Trefftz collocation method for solving 3D transient wave equations with specified sound source excitations is introduced. The efficiency of the proposed method is numerically verified by four benchmark examples in Section 3. In Section 4, several conclusions are drawn based on the present study.

2. Methodology

Considering a transient wave equation in 3D finite domain Ω bounded by Γ, the governing equation of 3D transient wave propagation problem with sound source excitations is stated as follows:

$$\left(\frac{\partial^2}{\partial t^2} - v^2\Delta\right)u(\boldsymbol{x},t) = f(\boldsymbol{x},t), \quad \boldsymbol{x} \in \Omega,\ 0 < t \leq T \tag{1}$$

subjected to the initial conditions

$$u(\boldsymbol{x},t)|_{t=0} = u_0, \boldsymbol{x} \in \Omega \tag{2}$$

$$\frac{\partial u(\boldsymbol{x},t)}{\partial t}|_{t=0} = u_1,\ \boldsymbol{x} \in \Omega \tag{3}$$

and the Dirichlet boundary condition

$$u(\boldsymbol{x},t)|_\Gamma = \overline{u}, \quad \boldsymbol{x} \in \Gamma,\ 0 < t \leq T. \tag{4}$$

where Δ is the Laplace operator, v denotes the wave speed, T represents the final time instant, u_0, u_1 and $\overline{u}$ are the known functions, and $f(\boldsymbol{x},t)$ is the known sound source function.

If the sound source function $f(\boldsymbol{x},t) = 0$, then the homogeneous type of Equation (1) is obtained as

$$\left(\frac{\partial^2}{\partial t^2} - v^2\Delta\right)u(\boldsymbol{x},t) = 0,\ \boldsymbol{x} \in \Omega,\ 0 < t \leq T. \tag{5}$$

By using the derived spatial–temporal radial Trefftz function [41],

$$G_0(\boldsymbol{x},t;\mathbf{s},\tau) = \left[\cos(v(t-\tau)) + \frac{\sin(v(t-\tau))}{v}\right]\frac{\sin(r(\boldsymbol{x},\mathbf{s}))}{r(\boldsymbol{x},\mathbf{s})} \tag{6}$$

the approximate solution of Equation (5) by using the spatial–temporal radial Trefftz collocation method can be represented as follows

$$u^0(\boldsymbol{x},t) = \sum_{j=1}^{N_S} \alpha_{0j} G_0(\boldsymbol{x},t;\mathbf{s}_j,\tau_j) \tag{7}$$

where $r(\boldsymbol{x},\mathbf{s}) = \|\boldsymbol{x}-\mathbf{s}\|_2$ denotes the Euclidean distance between collocation nodes $\boldsymbol{x}_i$ and source nodes $\mathbf{s}_j$, t and τ are the time variables corresponding to the collocation nodes $\boldsymbol{x}_i$ and source nodes $\mathbf{s}_j$, respectively. $\{\alpha_{0j}\}$ are the unknown coefficients and N_S represents the number of the source node pair $(\mathbf{s}_j,\tau_j) \in \partial(\Omega \times \langle 0,T\rangle)$, in which $\partial(\Omega \times \langle 0,T\rangle) = [\Gamma \times \langle 0,T\rangle] \cup [\Omega \times \{0,T\}]$ stands for the boundaries of the considered spatial–temporal domain $\Omega \times \langle 0,T\rangle$. Substituting expression (7) into the initial conditions (2) (3) and boundary conditions (4), one may have

$$\sum_{j=1}^{N_S} \alpha_{0j} G_0(\boldsymbol{x},0;\mathbf{s}_j,\tau_j) = u_0, \boldsymbol{x} \in \Omega, t = 0 \tag{8}$$

$$\sum_{j=1}^{N_S} \alpha_{0j} \frac{\partial G_0(\boldsymbol{x},0;\mathbf{s}_j,\tau_j)}{\partial t} = u_1, \boldsymbol{x} \in \Omega, t = 0 \tag{9}$$

$$\sum_{j=1}^{N_S} \alpha_{0j} G_0(\boldsymbol{x},t;\mathbf{s}_j,\tau_j) = \overline{u}, \quad \boldsymbol{x} \in \Gamma, \quad 0 < t \leq T \tag{10}$$

To determine the unknown coefficient $\{\alpha_{0j}\}$, N collocation node pairs $(x_i, t_i) \in [\Gamma \times \langle 0, T\rangle] \cup [\Omega \times \{0\}]$ are placed on the boundaries of the considered spatial-temporal domain, and then the discretized formulation can be represented as follows

$$\sum_{j=1}^{N_S} \alpha_{0j} G_0(x_i, t_i; \mathbf{s}_j, \tau_j) = u_0, x_i \in \Omega, t_i = 0 \tag{11}$$

$$\sum_{j=1}^{N_S} \alpha_{0j} \frac{\partial G_0(x_i, t_i; \mathbf{s}_j, \tau_j)}{\partial t} = u_1, x_i \in \Omega, t_i = 0 \tag{12}$$

$$\sum_{j=1}^{N_S} \alpha_{0j} G_0(x_i, t_i; \mathbf{s}_j, \tau_j) = \overline{u}, x_i \in \Gamma, 0 < t_i \leq T. \tag{13}$$

which can be also written as the following matrix form

$$\begin{bmatrix} [G_0(x_i, t_i; \mathbf{s}_j, \tau_j)]_{N_i \times N_S} \\ \left[\frac{\partial G_0(x_i, t_i; \mathbf{s}_j, \tau_j)}{\partial t}\right]_{N_i \times N_S} \\ [G_0(x_i, t_i; \mathbf{s}_j, \tau_j)]_{N_b N_t \times N_S} \end{bmatrix} [\alpha_{0j}]_{N_S \times 1} = \begin{bmatrix} [u_0]_{N_i \times 1} \\ [u_1]_{N_i \times 1} \\ [\overline{u}]_{N_b N_t \times 1} \end{bmatrix} \tag{14}$$

where $N = 2N_i + N_b N_t$, in which N_i and N_b represent the number of the collocation nodes inside the spatial domain Ω and on the boundary Γ of spatial domain Ω, respectively. The total node number in the spatial domain Ω is $N_{Total} = N_i + N_b$, and N_t represents the number of the collocation nodes along the time axis. If the same set of nodes to the collocation node discretization is used in the source node discretization inside the spatial domain Ω and on the boundary Γ of spatial domain Ω, the resultant matrix in Equation (14) is square due to $N_S = 2N_i + N_b N_t$.

Next, consider 3D transient wave propagation problems (1–4) with the non-zero sound source function $f(x, t)$. The approximate solution can be first divided into two parts, homogeneous solution $u_h(x, t)$ and particular solution $u_p(x, t)$, i.e.,

$$u(x, t) = u_h(x, t) + u_p(x, t) \tag{15}$$

where the particular solution $u_p(x, t)$ is constructed to satisfy the following equation

$$\left(\frac{\partial^2}{\partial t^2} - v^2 \Delta\right) u_p(x, t) = f(x, t) \tag{16}$$

and then the following updated homogeneous problem can be represented by substituting Equations (15) and (16) into the original transient wave propagation problems (1–4),

$$\begin{cases} \left(\frac{\partial^2}{\partial t^2} - v^2 \Delta\right) u_h(x, t) = 0, \; x \in \Omega, \; 0 < t \leq T \\ u_h(x, t) \mid_\Gamma = \overline{u} - u_p \\ u_h(x, t) \mid_{t=0} = u_0 - u_p \\ \frac{\partial u_h(x)}{\partial t} \mid_{t=0} = u_1 - \frac{\partial u_p}{\partial t} \end{cases}, \tag{17}$$

where the homogeneous solution $u_h(x, t)$ of Equation (17) can be obtained by using the spatial–temporal radial Trefftz collocation method with node discretization on the boundaries of the considered spatial–temporal domain.

To evaluate the particular solution $u_p(x, t)$, the composite multiple reciprocity method (CMRM) is extended from the spatial domain to the spatial–temporal domain. The key issue is to introduce the different spatial/spatial–temporal differential operators $L_1, L_2, \cdots L_M$ to eliminate the related non-zero sound source function $f(x,t)$ in Equation (16), namely,

$$L_M \cdots L_2 L_1 f(x,t) \cong 0 \tag{18}$$

It should be pointed out that the commonly used differential operators (Laplace, Helmholtz, modified Helmholtz, diffusion equation and wave equation operators) can be chosen as $L_1, L_2, \cdots L_M$ according to the form of $f(x,t)$, which could be the polynomial, exponential and trigonometric functions, or a combination of these functions. For complex functions, e.g., non-smooth functions, a set of discrete measured data or large-gradient functions in the source term $f(x,t)$, we can express the complex functions or a set of discrete measured data by a series representation of polynomial or trigonometric functions, and then Laplace and Helmholtz operators can be chosen as $L_1, L_2, \cdots L_M$ to satisfy Equation (18). In the numerical implementation, the order M is usually finite, or can be determined by a specified truncation error.

Then the particular solution $u_p(x,t)$ can be obtained by solving the following m-order homogeneous equation with $m-1$ constraint conditions

$$\begin{cases} L_m \cdots L_2 L_1 \Re u_p(x,t) = 0 & (x,t) \in (\Omega \times (0,T]) \\ \vdots & \\ L_2 L_1 \Re u_p(x,t) = L_2 L_1 f(x,t) & (x,t) \in \partial(\Omega \times (0,T]) \\ L_1 \Re u_p(x,t) = L_1 f(x,t) & (x,t) \in \partial(\Omega \times (0,T]) \\ \Re u_p(x,t) = f(x,t) & (x,t) \in \partial(\Omega \times (0,T]) \end{cases} \tag{19}$$

where $\Re = (\frac{\partial^2}{\partial t^2} - v^2\Delta)$ denotes the governing differential operator. Then the particular solution $u_p(x,t)$ can be represented by a linear combination of high-order spatial–temporal radial Trefftz functions $G_1(x,t;\mathbf{s},\tau), \cdots, G_m(x,t;\mathbf{s},\tau)$, namely,

$$u_p(x,t) = \sum_{k=1}^{m} \sum_{j=1}^{N_S} \alpha_{kj} G_k(x,t;\mathbf{s}_j,\tau_j) \tag{20}$$

where the high-order spatial–temporal radial Trefftz functions are derived by satisfying the following equations:

$$\begin{cases} L_1 \Re G_1(x,t;\mathbf{s}_j,\tau_j) = 0 \\ \vdots \\ L_m \cdots L_2 L_1 \Re G_m(x,t;\mathbf{s}_j,\tau_j) = 0 \end{cases} \tag{21}$$

Table 1 lists the related radial Trefftz functions for several commonly used spatial/spatial–temporal differential operators.

Table 1. Radial Trefftz functions of some commonly used spatial/spatial–temporal differential operators [41].

L_k	3D
$\Delta + k^2$	$\sin(kr)/(4\pi r)$
$\Delta - k^2$	$\sinh(kr)/(4\pi r)$
$\frac{\partial}{\partial t} - k\Delta$	$\frac{e^{-k(t-\tau)}\sin(r)}{r}$,
$\frac{\partial^2}{\partial t^2} - v_k^2\Delta$	$\left[\cos(v_k(t-\tau)) + \frac{\sin(v_k(t-\tau))}{v_k}\right]\frac{\sin(r)}{r}$

By combining Equations (7), (15) and (20), the approximate solution of 3D transient wave propagation problems (1–4) can be expressed as follows:

$$u(\boldsymbol{x},t)=\sum_{k=0}^{m}\sum_{j=1}^{N_S}\alpha_{kj}G_k(\boldsymbol{x},t;\mathbf{s}_j,\tau_j), \tag{22}$$

By employing Equation (22) to discretize Equations (17) and (19), the unknown coefficients $\left\{\alpha_{kj}\right\}_{k=0,1,\cdots,m}^{j=1,2,\cdots,N_S}$ can be obtained. After that, the numerical solution at any node pair $(\boldsymbol{x},t)\in[\Omega\times\langle 0,T\rangle]$ can be calculated by using Equation (22).

3. Numerical Results and Discussions

This section presents four benchmark examples of 3D transient wave propagation problems with specified sound source excitations to verify the efficiency of the proposed spatial–temporal radial Trefftz collocation method (STRTCM). To assess the performance of the proposed solver, the following L_2 relative error $Lerr$, relative error $Rerr$ and maximum relative error MRE are adopted as follows:

$$Lerr=\sqrt{\frac{1}{NN}\sum_{n=1}^{NN}\left(\frac{u_{num}(\boldsymbol{x}_n,t)-u_{ana}(\boldsymbol{x}_n,t)}{u_{ana}(\boldsymbol{x}_n,t)}\right)^2} \tag{23}$$

$$Rerr=\left|\frac{u_{num}(\boldsymbol{x}_n,t)-u_{ana}(\boldsymbol{x}_n,t)}{u_{ana}(\boldsymbol{x}_n,t)}\right| \tag{24}$$

$$MRE=\max_{1\le n\le NN}\left|\frac{u_{num}(\boldsymbol{x}_n,t)-u_{ana}(\boldsymbol{x}_n,t)}{u_{ana}(\boldsymbol{x}_n,t)}\right| \tag{25}$$

where $u_{ana}(\boldsymbol{x}_n,t)$ and $u_{num}(\boldsymbol{x}_n,t)$ stand for the analytical solution and the numerical solution on the test nodes $\boldsymbol{x}_n\in\Omega, n=1,\cdots,NN$ at time instant t, respectively. NN denotes the number of test nodes $\{\boldsymbol{x}_n\}$. Unless otherwise specified, the test nodes $\{\boldsymbol{x}_n\}$ are chosen as the same set of the collocation nodes inside 3D spatial domain $\{\boldsymbol{x}_i\}\in\Omega\backslash\Gamma$ and $NN=N_i$ in this study.

Example 1. *Transient wave equation with specified sound source excitation under a unit cube.*

In this example, the efficiency and accuracy of the proposed spatial–temporal radial Trefftz collocation method (STRTCM) in the solution of transient wave equations with the sound source $f(\boldsymbol{x},t)=-(\sin(x_1)+\cos(x_2)+\sin(x_3))\cos(\sqrt{2}t)$ under the unit cubic domain $\Omega_1=\{(x_1,x_2,x_3)|0\le x_1,x_2,x_3\le 1\}$ are investigated. The geometry and node distribution are depicted in Figure 1. The governing equation is represented as

$$\left(\frac{\partial^2}{\partial t^2}-v^2\Delta\right)u(\boldsymbol{x},t)=-(\sin(x_1)+\cos(x_2)+\sin(x_3))\cos(\sqrt{2}t),\ \boldsymbol{x}\in\Omega,\ 0<t\le T, \tag{26}$$

subjected to the initial conditions

$$u(\boldsymbol{x},t)|_{t=0}=(\sin(x_1)+\cos(x_2)+\sin(x_3)),\boldsymbol{x}\in\Omega, \tag{27}$$

$$\frac{\partial u(\boldsymbol{x},t)}{\partial t}|_{t=0}=0,\boldsymbol{x}\in\Omega, \tag{28}$$

and the Dirichlet boundary condition

$$u(\boldsymbol{x},t)\Big|_{\Gamma}=(\sin(x_1)+\cos(x_2)+\sin(x_3))\cos(\sqrt{2}t),\ \boldsymbol{x}\in\Gamma,\ 0<t\le T \tag{29}$$

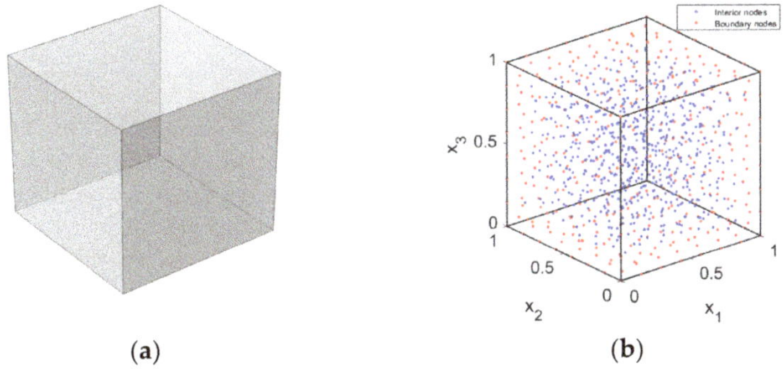

Figure 1. Schematic configurations of the unit cube model. (**a**) Geometry, (**b**) Node distribution.

Its analytical solution of Example 1 is

$$u(\mathbf{x},t) = (\sin(x_1) + \cos(x_2) + \sin(x_3))\cos(\sqrt{2}t) \tag{30}$$

Table 2 presents L_2 relative errors obtained by the proposed STRTCM and COMSOL at different time instants in Example 1. It can be found that under the same node discretization, the proposed STRTCM produces more accurate results with a slight longer computational time than the COMSOL (FEM). Figure 2 shows the numerical errors along with the time evolution by using the proposed STRTCM in Example 1. From Table 2 and Figure 2, it can be observed that the numerical errors may slightly increase with the time evolution. Table 3 presents L_2 relative errors obtained by the proposed STRTCM with different total node numbers, it can be found that with the increasing total node number, the L_2 relative error decreases rapidly and then remains at the same level.

Table 2. Relative errors obtained by the proposed STRTCM and COMSOL at different time instants in Example 1.

	T = 0.1 s	**t = 0.5 s**	**T = 1.0 s**	**CPU Time**
STRTCM	1.92×10^{-7}	6.21×10^{-7}	1.20×10^{-6}	1.76 s
COMSOL	2.14×10^{-3}	2.33×10^{-2}	5.98×10^{-2}	1.00 s

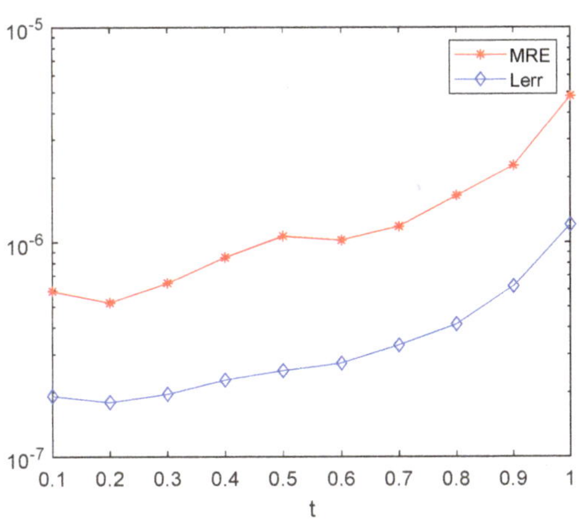

Figure 2. Numerical errors along with the time evolution by using the proposed STRTCM in Example 1.

Table 3. Relative errors obtained by the proposed STRTCM with different total node numbers in Example 1.

N_{Total}	32	81	432	896	1600	4725
Lerr	1.01×10^{-1}	4.04×10^{-6}	1.30×10^{-6}	1.31×10^{-6}	1.06×10^{-6}	1.34×10^{-6}

For ease of comparison, the same set of discretized nodes are used in both the proposed STRTCM and COMSOL, in which the number of collocation nodes is $N_{Total} = 1023$, the boundary nodes number is $N_b = 374$ and the interior nodes number is $N_i = 649$, and the number of total nodes distributed on the boundaries of spatial–temporal domain is $N = 5421$. It should be mentioned that, based on these collocation nodes, 4892 four-node tetrahedral elements are used in the COMSOL simulation. In addition, some other parameters are set as follows: the wave speed v = 1.0 m/s, the final time T = 1.0 s, the time interval dt = 0.1 s. The annihilation spatial–temporal differential operator $L_1 = \left(\frac{\partial^2}{\partial t^2} - 2\Delta\right)$ is employed to vanish the specified sound source excitation $f(x,t)$ in Equation (26) by using the extended CMRM.

Example 2. *Transient wave equation with specified sound source excitation under a circular tube.*

This example considers the transient wave equations with the sound source $f(x,t) = -\sin(\frac{x_1+x_2+x_3}{\sqrt{3}})\cos(340\sqrt{2}t)$ under the circular tube domain as shown in Figure 3a. The distribution of boundary nodes and interior nodes is depicted in Figure 3b. The governing equation is represented as

$$\left(\frac{\partial^2}{\partial t^2} - v^2\Delta\right)u(x,t) = -\sin(\frac{x_1+x_2+x_3}{\sqrt{3}})\cos(340\sqrt{2}t),\ x \in \Omega,\ 0 < t \le T, \tag{31}$$

subjected to the initial conditions

$$u(x,t)|_{t=0} = -\sin(\frac{x_1+x_2+x_3}{\sqrt{3}}), x \in \Omega \tag{32}$$

$$\frac{\partial u(x,t)}{\partial t}|_{t=0} = 0, x \in \Omega \tag{33}$$

and the Dirichlet boundary condition

$$u(x,t)|_{\Gamma} = \sin(\frac{x_1+x_2+x_3}{\sqrt{3}})\cos(340\sqrt{2}t),\ x \in \Gamma,\ 0 < t \le T \tag{34}$$

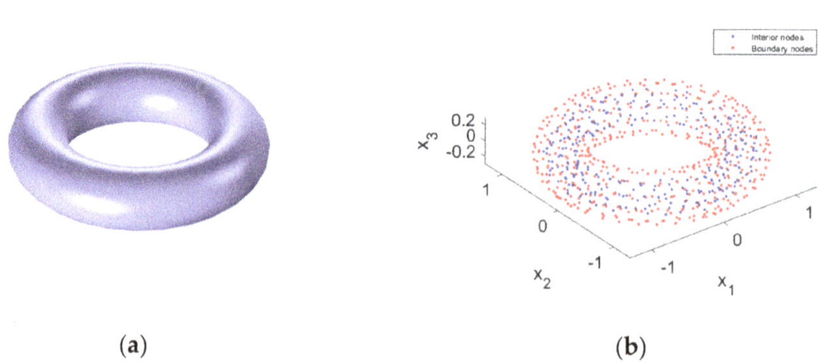

Figure 3. Schematic configurations of the circular tube model. (**a**) Geometry, (**b**) Node distribution.

Its analytical solution of Example 2 is

$$u(\boldsymbol{x}, t) = \sin\left(\frac{x_1 + x_2 + x_3}{\sqrt{3}}\right)\cos(340\sqrt{2}t) \tag{35}$$

In the proposed STRTCM implementation, the number of collocation nodes is $N_{Total} = 780$, the boundary nodes number is $N_b = 499$, the interior nodes number is $N_i = 281$, the wave speed is $v = 340$ m/s, the final time instant is $T = 10$ s, and the annihilation spatial–temporal differential operator $L_1 = \left(\frac{\partial^2}{\partial t^2} - 231200\Delta\right)$ is employed to vanish the specified sound source excitation $f(\boldsymbol{x}, t)$ in Equation (31) by using the extended CMRM.

Table 4 presents numerical errors at final time instant $T = 10$ s obtained by using the proposed STRTCM with different time intervals dt in Example 2. From Table 3, it can be found that the proposed STRTCM with different time intervals dt can provide equally accurate results, which reveals that the time interval dt has a slight influence on the numerical accuracy. Figure 4 plots the absolute and relative error distributions at two time instants (t = 5 s and 10 s) by using the proposed STRTCM with a large time interval dt = 5.0 s. Numerical results given in Figure 4 show that the proposed STRTCM performs very accurate results, even with large time interval dt = 5.0 s.

Table 4. Numerical errors at final time instant T = 10 s obtained by using the proposed STRTCM with different time intervals dt in Example 2.

dt	0.5 s	1.0 s	2.0 s	2.5 s	5 s	10 s
Lerr	1.55×10^{-5}	3.84×10^{-6}	3.76×10^{-6}	2.34×10^{-5}	2.54×10^{-6}	3.23×10^{-5}
MRE	3.14×10^{-5}	9.94×10^{-6}	9.96×10^{-6}	8.98×10^{-5}	9.77×10^{-6}	9.86×10^{-5}

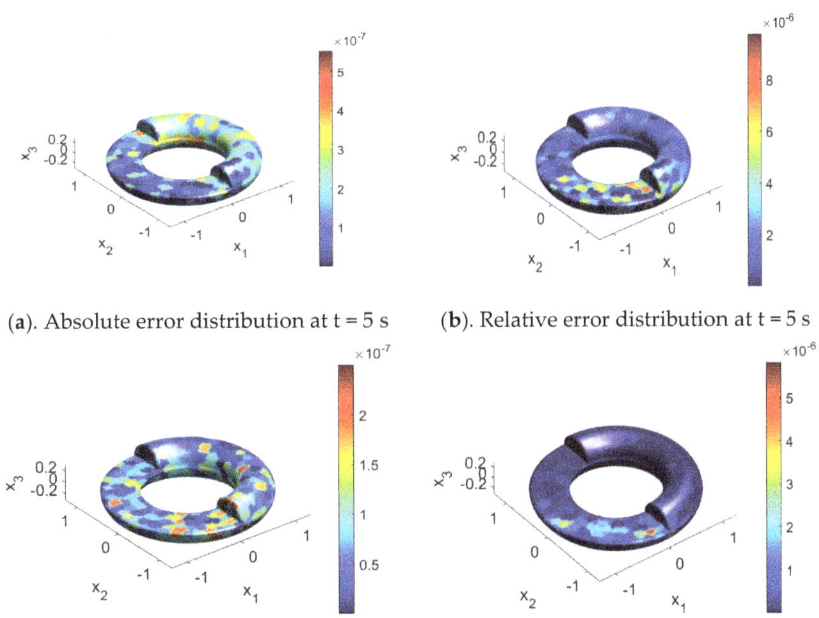

(**a**). Absolute error distribution at t = 5 s (**b**). Relative error distribution at t = 5 s

(**c**). Absolute error distribution at t = 10 s (**d**). Relative error distribution at t = 10 s

Figure 4. Error distributions at two time instants (t = 5 s and 10 s) by using the proposed STRTCM with large time interval dt = 5.0 s: (**a**) absolute error distribution and (**b**) relative error distribution at t = 5 s; (**c**) absolute error distribution and (**d**) relative error distribution at t = 10 s.

Example 3. *Transient wave equation with specified sound source excitation under a room model.*

This example considers the transient wave equations with the sound source $f(\boldsymbol{x},t) = -(\cos(x_1)+\sin(x_2)+\cos(x_3))\sin(\sqrt{2}t)$ under the room model [42] with principal dimensions being 5.0 m in length, 4.0 m in width and 3.0 m in height (see Figure 5a). The distributions of boundary nodes and interior nodes are depicted in Figure 5b. The governing equation is represented as

$$\left(\frac{\partial^2}{\partial t^2} - v^2\Delta\right)u(\boldsymbol{x},t) = -(\cos(x_1)+\sin(x_2)+\cos(x_3))\sin(\sqrt{2}t),\ \boldsymbol{x}\in\Omega,\ 0<t\le T \quad (36)$$

subjected to the initial conditions

$$u(\boldsymbol{x},t)|_{t=0} = 0, \boldsymbol{x}\in\Omega \quad (37)$$

$$\frac{\partial u(\boldsymbol{x},t)}{\partial t}|_{t=0} = \sqrt{2}(\cos(x_1)+\sin(x_2)+\cos(x_3))\cos(\sqrt{2}t),\ \boldsymbol{x}\in\Omega \quad (38)$$

and the Dirichlet boundary condition

$$u(\boldsymbol{x},t)\Big|_{\Gamma} = (\cos(x_1)+\sin(x_2)+\cos(x_3))\sin(\sqrt{2}t),\ \boldsymbol{x}\in\Gamma,\ 0<t\le T \quad (39)$$

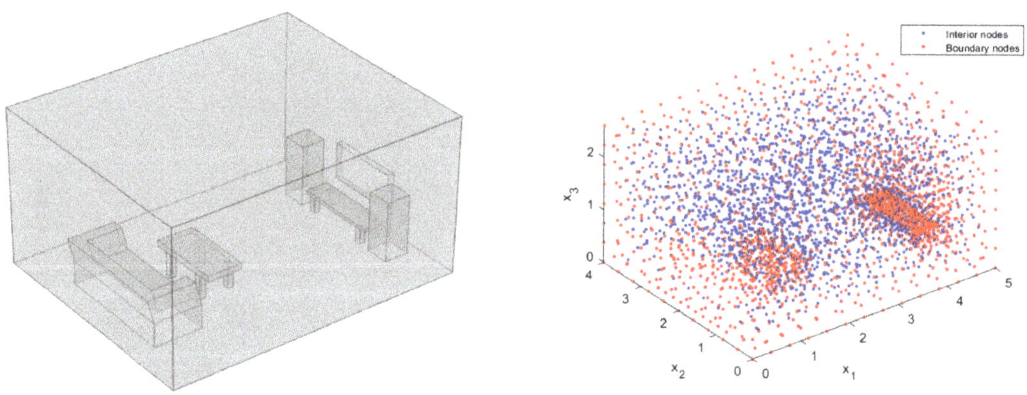

(a) **(b)**

Figure 5. Schematic configurations of the room model. (**a**) Geometry, (**b**) Node distribution.

Its analytical solution of Example 3 is

$$u(\boldsymbol{x},t) = (\cos(x_1)+\sin(x_2)+\cos(x_3))\sin(\sqrt{2}t) \quad (40)$$

In the proposed STRTCM implementation, the number of collocation nodes is $N_{Total} = 3588$, the boundary nodes number is $N_b = 1447$, the interior nodes number is $N_i = 2141$, the number of total nodes distributed on the boundaries of the spatial–temporal domain is N = 17,305, the wave speed is $v = 1.0$ m/s, the final time instant is $T = 1000$ s, the time interval is $dt = 125$ s, and the annihilation spatial–temporal differential operator $L_1 = \left(\frac{\partial^2}{\partial t^2} - 2\Delta\right)$ is employed to vanish the specified sound source excitation $f(\boldsymbol{x},t)$ in Equation (36) by using the extended CMRM.

Figure 6 shows the relative error distributions on the plane $x_3 = 1.5$ at different time instants (t = 250, 500, 750, 1000 s) by using the proposed STRTCM with time interval $dt = 125$ s in Example 3. It can be observed that the proposed STRTCM with a large time interval can still obtain very accurate results in the solution of the transient wave problem under a complicated geometry domain (room model). This is because the semi-analytical spatial–temporal radial Trefftz functions are employed as the basis functions in the proposed STRTCM, which allows the few temporal discretizations to simulate the long-term evolution of the wave propagation.

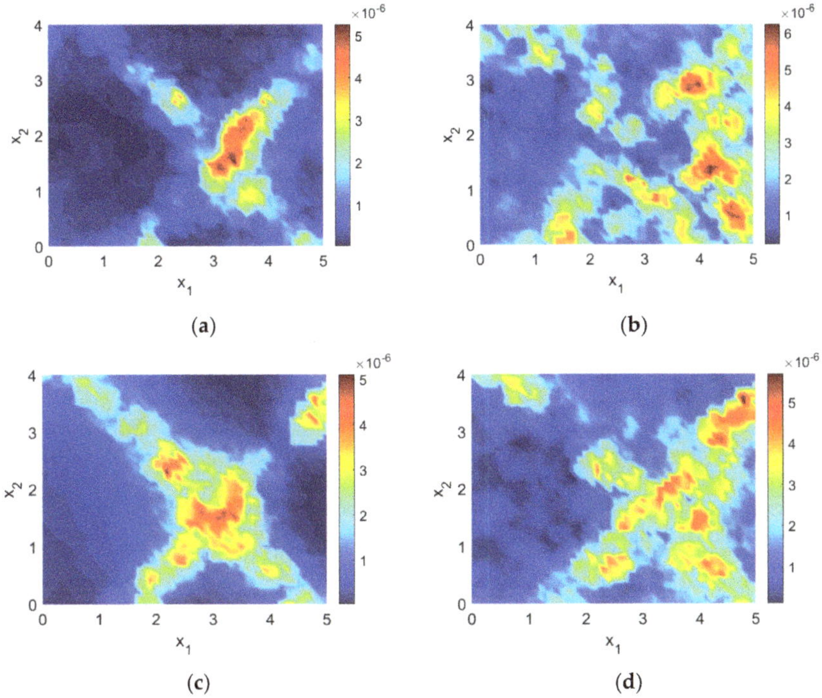

Figure 6. Relative error distributions on the plane x_3 = 1.5 at different time instants ((**a**) t = 250, (**b**) t = 500, (**c**) t = 750, (**d**) t = 1000 s) by using the proposed STRTCM with time interval $dt = 125$ s in Example 3.

Example 4. *Transient wave equation with specified sound source excitation under a submarine model.*

The final example considers the transient wave equations with the sound source $f(\boldsymbol{x}, t) = -(\cos(x_1) + \sin(x_2) + \cos(x_3))\sin(\sqrt{2}t)$ under the submarine model with the principal dimensions being 15.0 m in length, 4.0 m in width and 6.0 m in height (see Figure 7a). The distribution of boundary nodes and interior nodes are depicted in Figure 7b.

The governing equation is represented as

$$\left(\frac{\partial^2}{\partial t^2} - v^2\Delta\right)u(\boldsymbol{x}, t) = -(\cos(x_1) + \sin(x_2) + \cos(x_3))\sin(\sqrt{2}t),\ \boldsymbol{x} \in \Omega,\ 0 < t \leq T \quad (41)$$

subjected to the initial conditions

$$u(\boldsymbol{x}, t)|_{t=0} = 0, \boldsymbol{x} \in \Omega \quad (42)$$

$$\frac{\partial u(\boldsymbol{x}, t)}{\partial t}|_{t=0} = \sqrt{2}(\cos(x_1) + \sin(x_2) + \cos(x_3))\cos(\sqrt{2}t),\ \boldsymbol{x} \in \Omega \quad (43)$$

and the Dirichlet boundary condition

$$u(x,t)\Big|_{\Gamma} = (\cos(x_1) + \sin(x_2) + \cos(x_3))\sin(\sqrt{2}t),\ x \in \Gamma,\ 0 < t \le T \tag{44}$$

Its analytical solution of Example 4 is

$$u(x,t) = (\cos(x_1) + \sin(x_2) + \cos(x_3))\sin(\sqrt{2}t) \tag{45}$$

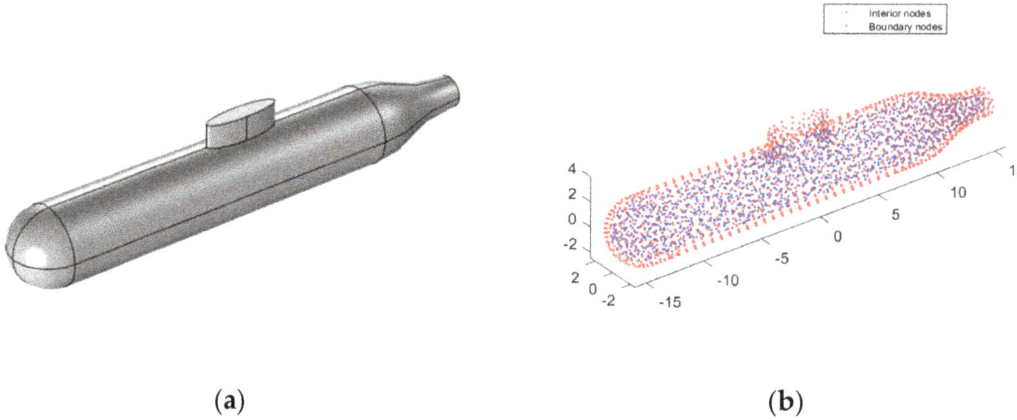

Figure 7. Schematic configurations of the submarine model. (**a**) Geometry, (**b**) Node distribution.

In the proposed STRTCM implementation, the number of collocation nodes is $N_{Total} = 2804$, the boundary nodes number is $N_b = 1312$, and the interior nodes number is $N_i = 1492$, the wave speed is $v = 1.0$ m/s, the time interval is $dt = 1$ s, the final time is $T = 10$ s, and the annihilation spatial–temporal differential operator $L_1 = \left(\frac{\partial^2}{\partial t^2} - 2\Delta\right)$ is employed to vanish the specified sound source excitation $f(x,t)$ in Equation (41) by using the extended CMRM.

By using the proposed STRTCM for Example 4, very accurate results with $Lerr = 4.40 \times 10^{-6}$ can be obtained in 1 min. However, it requires about 9 GB memory storage for getting the results in a large time instant $T = 10$ s. To enhance the ability of the proposed STRTCM for long-time evolution simulation, the entire time interval [0, 10] is divided into NP sub-time intervals $([0, 10/NP], \cdots, [10(NP-1)/NP, 10])$, and the STRTCM is used to solve the problems (41–44) in each sub-time interval in sequence. For each problem in the considered sub-time interval (np), the initial conditions are updated by using the final solution at the previous sub-time interval $(np-1)$, $np = 1, \cdots, NP$. Table 5 gives the numerical results of Example 4 by using the proposed STRTCM with different numbers of sub-time intervals. It can be found from Table 5 that with the increasing NP, the proposed STRTCM can perform enough accurate results with less computational cost (CPU time and memory storage).

Table 5. Numerical results of Example 4 by using the proposed STRTCM with different numbers of sub-time intervals.

NP	**1**	**2**	**5**	**10**
CPU time	53.0 s	20.0 s	15.9 s	15.7 s
Lerr	4.40×10^{-6}	6.92×10^{-6}	1.39×10^{-5}	5.17×10^{-5}
Memory requirement	9973 MB	5671 MB	4794 MB	4647 MB

4. Conclusions

In this paper, the spatial–temporal radial Trefftz collocation method (STRTCM) is proposed to solve transient wave propagation problems with specified sound source excitations.

To deal with the specified sound source excitations, the extended composite multiple reciprocity method (CMRM) is presented from the spatial domain to the spatial–temporal domain for constructing the high-order homogeneous equation with the related constraint conditions. Then, the particular solution can be obtained by using a linear combination of the related high-order spatial–temporal radial Trefftz functions. Therefore, the proposed STRTCM only requires the node discretization on the boundaries of the spatial–temporal domain in 3D transient wave propagation analysis.

Numerical investigation shows that the proposed STRTCM produces more accurate results with a slight longer computational time than the COMSOL (FEM) under the same node discretization. The time interval dt has a slight influence on the numerical accuracy of the proposed STRTCM. The iterative strategy is feasible to reduce the storage and CPU time. Due to the use of the spatial–temporal radial Trefftz functions, the proposed STRTCM only requires few temporal discretizations to accurately simulate the long-term evolution of the wave propagation.

Overall, it is concluded that the proposed STRTCM could be considered as a competitive alternative for the transient wave problems with specified sound source excitations under 3D complicated structures after further theoretical and numerical investigations. Moreover, it should be mentioned that as the first step, only 3D transient wave propagation with specified sound source excitations is considered in this paper, whose analytical solutions with regular form can be easily derived. The STRTCM for 3D transient wave problems with general sound source excitations is still under our intensive investigation. In addition, the present STRTCM scheme cannot handle the problems with heterogeneous materials because it is a nontrivial task to derive the corresponding semi-analytical basis solutions. For this, combining with the localized collocation scheme [43] and the extended multiple reciprocity method—generalized reciprocity method [44]—may be a good way. These topics are under study and will be reported in a subsequent paper.

Author Contributions: Conceptualization, L.C.; formal analysis, Z.F.; methodology, W.X.; writing—original draft, L.C. All authors contributed equally to writing this article. All authors have read and agreed to the published version of the manuscript.

Funding: This research was funded by the National Natural Science Foundation of China (Grant Nos. 12122205, 11772119), the Six Talent Peaks Project in Jiangsu Province of China (Grant No. 2019-KTHY-009).

Institutional Review Board Statement: Not applicable.

Informed Consent Statement: Not applicable.

Data Availability Statement: Not applicable.

Acknowledgments: The authors thank the anonymous reviewers of this article for their very helpful comments and suggestions to significantly improve the academic quality of this article. The work described in this paper was supported by the National Natural Science Foundation of China (Grant Nos. 12122205, 11772119) and the Six Talent Peaks Project in Jiangsu Province of China (Grant No. 2019-KTHY-009).

Conflicts of Interest: The authors declare no conflict of interest.

Nomenclature

$u(\boldsymbol{x}, t)$	acoustic pressure	$r(\boldsymbol{x}, \mathbf{s})$	distance between source node and colocation node
v	wave speed	$\{\alpha\}$	unknown coefficients
Δ	Laplace operator	N_i	number of interior nodes on spatial domain
$f(\boldsymbol{x}, t)$	spatial-temporal source function	N_b	number of boundary nodes on spatial domain
$\boldsymbol{x}$	collocation node	N_t	number of collocation nodes along with time axis
$\mathbf{s}$	source node	N_{Total}	number of total nodes on spatial domain
T	final time instant	$G_0(\boldsymbol{x}, t; \mathbf{s}, \tau)$	spatial–temporal radial Trefftz function
t	time variable corresponding to collocation node	$u_h(\boldsymbol{x}, t)$	homogeneous solution
τ	time variable corresponding to source node	$u_p(\boldsymbol{x}, t)$	particular solution
u_0, u_1	known functions on boundary	$L_M \cdots L_2 L_1$	differential operators
Ω	computational domain	MRE	maximum absolute error
Γ	boundary of computational domain	$Lerr\ L_2$	relative error
$\Re$	partial differential operator matrix	$Rerr$	relative error
N	number of collocation node pairs	NP	numbers of evolution steps
N_S	number of source node pairs		

References

1. Bellis, C.; Lombard, B. Simulating transient wave phenomena in acoustic metamaterials using auxiliary fields. *Wave Motion* **2019**, *86*, 175–194. [CrossRef]
2. Gao, J.; Ma, X.; Zang, J.; Dong, G.; Ma, X.; Zhu, Y.; Zhou, L. Numerical investigation of harbor oscillations induced by focused transient wave groups. *Coast. Eng.* **2020**, *158*, 103670. [CrossRef]
3. Chen, J.; Shou, Y.; Zhou, X. Implementation of the novel perfectly matched layer element for elastodynamic problems in time-domain finite element method. *Soil Dyn. Earthq. Eng.* **2022**, *152*, 107054. [CrossRef]
4. Ghafoor, A.; Haq, S.; Hussain, M.; Kumam, P.; Jan, M.A. Approximate Solutions of Time Fractional Diffusion Wave Models. *Mathematics* **2019**, *7*, 923. [CrossRef]
5. Weng, J.; Liu, X.; Zhou, Y.; Wang, J. A Space-Time Fully Decoupled Wavelet Integral Collocation Method with High-Order Accuracy for a Class of Nonlinear Wave Equations. *Mathematics* **2021**, *9*, 2957. [CrossRef]
6. Qing, H.L.; Gang, Z. Review of PSTD methods for transient electromagnetics. *Int. J. Numer. Model. Electron. Netw. Devices Fields* **2004**, *17*, 299–323. [CrossRef]
7. Fu, Z.J.; Xie, Z.Y.; Ji, S.Y.; Tsai, C.C.; Li, A.L. Meshless generalized finite difference method for water wave interactions with multiple-bottom-seated-cylinder-array structures. *Ocean. Eng.* **2020**, *195*, 106736. [CrossRef]
8. Cohen, G. *Higher-Order Numerical Methods for Transient Wave Equations*; Springer Science & Business Media: Berlin, Germany, 2001.
9. Astley, R.J.; Hamilton, J.A. The stability of infinite element schemes for transient wave problems. *Comput. Methods Appl. Mech. Eng.* **2006**, *195*, 3553–3571. [CrossRef]
10. Chai, Y.; Li, W.; Liu, Z. Analysis of transient wave propagation dynamics using the enriched finite element method with interpolation cover functions. *Appl. Math. Comput.* **2022**, *412*, 126564. [CrossRef]
11. Deckers, E.; Atak, O.; Coox, L.; D'Amico, R.; Devriendt, H.; Jonckheere, S.; Koo, K.; Pluymers, B.; Vandepitte, D.; Desmet, W. The wave based method: An overview of 15 years of research. *Wave Motion* **2014**, *51*, 550–565. [CrossRef]
12. Chen, D.; Birk, C.; Song, C.; Du, C. A high-order approach for modelling transient wave propagation problems using the scaled boundary finite element method. *Int. J. Numer. Methods Eng.* **2014**, *97*, 937–959. [CrossRef]
13. Demirel, V.; Wang, S. An efficient boundary element method for two-dimensional transient wave propagation problems. *Appl. Math. Model.* **1987**, *11*, 411–416. [CrossRef]
14. Jiang, F.; Chen, L.; Wang, J.; Miao, X.; Chen, H. Topology optimization of multimaterial distribution based on isogeometric boundary element and piecewise constant level set method. *Comput. Methods Appl. Mech. Eng.* **2022**, *390*, 114484. [CrossRef]
15. Jelich, C.; Zhao, W.; Chen, H.; Marburg, S. Fast multipole boundary element method for the acoustic analysis of finite periodic structures. *Comput. Methods Appl. Mech. Eng.* **2022**, *391*, 114528. [CrossRef]
16. Ilati, M.; Dehghan, M. Direct local boundary integral equation method for numerical solution of extended Fisher-Kolmogorov equation. *Eng. Comput.* **2018**, *34*, 203–213. [CrossRef]
17. Li, X.L.; Li, S.L. Meshless boundary node methods for Stokes problems. *Appl. Math. Model.* **2015**, *39*, 1769–1783. [CrossRef]
18. Yan, F.; Jiang, Q.; Bai, G.F.; Li, S.J.; Li, Y.; Qiao, Z.B. Dual reciprocity hybrid boundary node method for nonlinear problems. *Eng. Anal. Bound. Elem.* **2019**, *108*, 385–392. [CrossRef]
19. Zhang, J.M.; Ju, C.M.; Wen, P.H.; Shu, X.M.; Lin, W.C.; Chi, B.T. A dual interpolation boundary face method for 3D elasticity. *Eng. Anal. Bound. Elem.* **2021**, *122*, 102–116. [CrossRef]
20. Chen, J.T.; Kao, S.K.; Hsu, Y.H.; Fan, Y. Scattering problems of the SH Wave by Using the Null-Field Boundary Integral Equation Method. *J. Earthq. Eng.* **2018**, *22*, 1–35. [CrossRef]
21. Ergin, A.A.; Shanker, B.; Michielssen, E. The plane-wave time-domain algorithm for the fast analysis of transient wave phenomena. *IEEE Antennas Propag. Mag.* **1999**, *41*, 39–52. [CrossRef]

22. Geng, L.; Zhang, X.-Z.; Bi, C.-X. Reconstruction of transient vibration and sound radiation of an impacted plate using time domain plane wave superposition method. *J. Sound Vib.* **2015**, *344*, 114–125. [CrossRef]
23. Young, D.L.; Gu, M.H.; Fan, C.M. The time-marching method of fundamental solutions for wave equations. *Eng. Anal. Bound. Elem.* **2009**, *33*, 1411–1425. [CrossRef]
24. Fairweather, G.; Karageorghis, A.; Martin, P.A. The method of fundamental solutions for scattering and radiation problems. *Eng. Anal. Bound. Elem.* **2003**, *27*, 759–769. [CrossRef]
25. Liu, L. Single layer regularized meshless method for three dimensional exterior acoustic problem. *Eng. Anal. Bound. Elem.* **2017**, *77*, 138–144. [CrossRef]
26. Kim, S. An improved boundary distributed source method for two-dimensional Laplace equations. *Eng. Anal. Bound. Elem.* **2013**, *37*, 997–1003. [CrossRef]
27. Chen, W.; Li, J.; Fu, Z.J. Singular boundary method using time-dependent fundamental solution for scalar wave equations. *Comput. Mech.* **2016**, *58*, 717–730. [CrossRef]
28. Fu, Z.J.; Chen, W.; Wen, P.; Zhang, C. Singular boundary method for wave propagation analysis in periodic structures. *J. Sound Vib.* **2018**, *425*, 170–188. [CrossRef]
29. Fu, Z.J.; Xi, Q.; Li, Y.; Huang, H.; Rabczuk, T. Hybrid FEM–SBM solver for structural vibration induced underwater acoustic radiation in shallow marine environment. *Comput. Methods Appl. Mech. Eng.* **2020**, *369*, 113236. [CrossRef]
30. Qu, W.; Zheng, C.; Zhang, Y.; Gu, Y.; Wang, F. A wideband fast multipole accelerated singular boundary method for three-dimensional acoustic problems. *Comput. Struct.* **2018**, *206*, 82–89. [CrossRef]
31. Fu, Z.-J.; Yang, L.-W.; Xi, Q.; Liu, C.-S. A boundary collocation method for anomalous heat conduction analysis in functionally graded materials. *Comput. Math. Appl.* **2021**, *88*, 91–109. [CrossRef]
32. Li, Z.-C.; Lu, T.-T.; Huang, H.-T.; Cheng, A.H.D. Trefftz, collocation, and other boundary methods—A comparison. *Numer. Methods Partial Differ. Equ.* **2007**, *23*, 93–144. [CrossRef]
33. Liu, C.-S.; Kuo, C.-L. A multiple-direction Trefftz method for solving the multi-dimensional wave equation in an arbitrary spatial domain. *J. Comput. Phys.* **2016**, *321*, 39–54. [CrossRef]
34. Siraj, U.I.; Šarler, B.; Vertnik, R.; Kosec, G. Radial basis function collocation method for the numerical solution of the two-dimensional transient nonlinear coupled Burgers' equations. *Appl. Math. Model.* **2012**, *36*, 1148–1160. [CrossRef]
35. Sun, L.; Wei, X. A frequency domain formulation of the singular boundary method for dynamic analysis of thin elastic plate. *Eng. Anal. Bound. Elem.* **2019**, *98*, 77–87. [CrossRef]
36. Sun, L.; Chen, W.; Cheng, A.H.D. Singular boundary method for 2D dynamic poroelastic problems. *Wave Motion* **2016**, *61*, 40–62. [CrossRef]
37. Huang, Y.; Skandari, M.H.N.; Mohammadizadeh, F.; Tehrani, H.A.; Georgiev, S.G.; Tohidi, E.; Shateyi, S. Space–Time Spectral Collocation Method for Solving Burgers Equations with the Convergence Analysis. *Symmetry* **2019**, *11*, 1439. [CrossRef]
38. Ku, C.-Y.; Hong, L.-D.; Liu, C.-Y. Solving Transient Groundwater Inverse Problems Using Space–Time Collocation Trefftz Method. *Water* **2020**, *12*, 3580. [CrossRef]
39. Rezazadeh, A.; Mahmoudi, M.; Darehmiraki, M. Space–time spectral collocation method for one-dimensional PDE constrained optimisation. *Int. J. Control.* **2020**, *93*, 1231–1241. [CrossRef]
40. Xi, Q.; Fu, Z.-J.; Rabczuk, T. An efficient boundary collocation scheme for transient thermal analysis in large-size-ratio functionally graded materials under heat source load. *Comput. Mech.* **2019**, *64*, 1221–1235. [CrossRef]
41. Chen, W.; Fu, Z.-J.; Chen, C.-S. *Recent Advances in Radial Basis Function Collocation Methods*; Springer: Heidelberg, Germany, 2014.
42. COMSOL. Available online: https://www.comsol.com/model/full-wave-time-domain-room-acoustics-with-frequency-dependent-impedance-90551 (accessed on 3 March 2022).
43. Xi, Q.; Fu, Z.J.; Wu, W.; Wang, H.; Wang, Y. A novel localized collocation solver based on Trefftz basis for potential-based inverse electromyography. *Appl. Math. Comput.* **2021**, *390*, 125604. [CrossRef]
44. Xi, Q.; Fu, Z.J.; Zhang, C.; Yin, D. An efficient localized Trefftz-based collocation scheme for heat conduction analysis in two kinds of heterogeneous materials under temperature loading. *Comput. Struct.* **2021**, *255*, 106619. [CrossRef]

mathematics

Article

Localized Boundary Knot Method for Solving Two-Dimensional Inverse Cauchy Problems

Yang Wu [1], Junli Zhang [1], Shuang Ding [2,3] and Yan-Cheng Liu [1,*]

1 School of Civil Engineering and Architecture, Nanchang University, Nanchang 330031, China; wuy_96@outlook.com (Y.W.); zhangjunli_@outlook.com (J.Z.)
2 Shanghai Engineering Research Center of Underground Infrastructure Detection and Maintenance Equipment, Shanghai 200092, China; dingshuang525@hotmail.com
3 Shanghai Tongyan Civil Engineering Technology Co., Ltd., Shanghai 200092, China
* Correspondence: yanchengliu1113@gmail.com

Abstract: In this paper, a localized boundary knot method is adopted to solve two-dimensional inverse Cauchy problems, which are controlled by a second-order linear differential equation. The localized boundary knot method is a numerical method based on the local concept of the localization method of the fundamental solution. The approach is formed by combining the classical boundary knot method with the localization method. It has the potential to solve many complex engineering problems. Generally, in an inverse Cauchy problem, there are no boundary conditions in specific boundaries. Additionally, in order to be close to the actual engineering situation, a certain level of noise is added to the known boundary conditions to simulate the measurement error. The localized boundary knot method can be used to solve two-dimensional Cauchy problems more stably and is truly free from mesh and numerical quadrature. In this paper, the stability of the method is verified by using multi-connected domain and simply connected domain examples in Laplace equations.

Keywords: inverse Cauchy problem; Laplace equation; localized boundary knot method; noise; multiply domain

MSC: 65N21

Citation: Wu, Y.; Zhang, J.; Ding, S.; Liu, Y.-C. Localized Boundary Knot Method for Solving Two-Dimensional Inverse Cauchy Problems. *Mathematics* **2022**, *10*, 1324. https://doi.org/10.3390/math10081324

Academic Editors: Zhuojia Fu and Yiqian He

Received: 8 March 2022
Accepted: 14 April 2022
Published: 15 April 2022

1. Introduction

In the engineering field, due to the limitations of engineering measurement technology, some information that is required for engineering calculations can be difficult to obtain. Such problems are called inverse problems. The lack of information about inverse problems can be mainly classified into two modes: the detection of the boundary location and the determination of boundary conditions. Chang, Yeih and Shieh (2001) [1] showed that neither the traditional Tikhonov's regularization method, nor the singular value decomposition method can yield an acceptable numerical result for the inverse Cauchy problem of Laplace equations, when the influence matrix is highly ill-posed. In order to obtain sufficiently stable and accurate numerical results for inverse Cauchy problems, different numerical methods have been studied by scholars in previous works.

In order to obtain stable solutions, some mesh-based methods have been widely used to solve inverse problems, including the finite element method (FEM) [2], the finite difference method (FDM) [3] and the boundary element method (BEM) used by Lesnic et al. [4–6]. However, as a mesh-based method, it is still nontrivial of the BEM to generate a well-behaved mesh for complex-shaped surfaces. As a competitor to the mesh-based method, the meshless method has been proposed by researchers to solve inverse Cauchy problems. Similar to the FEM, the domain-type meshless method needs to employ arbitrarily distributed interior and boundary collocations to represent the domain and boundary of the problem. The domain-type meshless methods are the radial basis function method

(RBFCM) and the generalized finite-difference method (GFDM), which are commonly used recently. The RBFCM was proposed by Kansa in 1990 [7,8], after which the selection of its optimal parameters was studied [9–11], and then this method became popular [12]. The GFDM has been applied to inverse problems and is widely used for engineering problems [13–16]. Similar to the BEM, boundary-type methods have the advantages of reducing the calculation dimensions and can easily obtain highly accurate numerical results. Considering their merits, boundary-type methods, including the Trefftz method [17–19], the modified collocation Trefftz method (MCTM) [20,21], the singular boundary method (SBM) [22] and the boundary particle method (BPM) have been widely studied for use in inverse Cauchy problems [23].

It is worth emphasizing that among the boundary-type meshless methods, the method of fundamental solutions (MFS) proposed by Kupradze and Aleksidze in 1964 [24] is the most popular in the application of inverse problems [25,26] due to its high accuracy. Young [27] studied the condition number of MFS in a Cauchy problem, and Fan [28] further extended the scheme to solve a Cauchy problem involving Stokes equations. Despite the popularity of the method, determining the appropriate location of the source nodes is one of the difficulties that the MFS needs to overcome. Therefore, in 2002, Chen and Tanaka [29,30] proposed a boundary-type method with a nonsingular general solution instead of a singular fundamental solution as its basis function, named the boundary knot method (BKM). Since then, the BKM has also been applied to solve different problems [31,32], especially inverse problems [33,34].

In recent years, the concept of localization has been proposed to overcome the problems caused by the full matrix. The localized radial basis function collocation method (LRBFCM) [35–38], the first localized meshless method, was developed from the combination of the localization method and the RBFCM. Then, this method was applied to the study of an inverse Cauchy problem by Chan and Fan in 2013 [39]. After that, in 2019, in order to expand the application of the MFS in large-scale problems, Fan [40] proposed the localized method of fundamental solutions (LMFS) by combining a similar localization concept with MFS. This localized method was used to solve inverse Cauchy problems by Wang [41], who proved its accuracy. In addition, the localized Trefftz method (LTM) and the localized singular boundary method (LSBM) were studied by Liu et al. [42] and Wang et al. [43], respectively. In this paper, the traditional BKM is improved into a localized meshless method, which is called the localized boundary knot method (LBKM). Moreover, large-scale problems that were difficult to solve in the past using the traditional methods can be solved efficiently by the LBKM, and successful tests for solving direct problems can be found in recent works [44,45]. Considering the merits of the LBKM, we take the Laplace equation as the governing equation and discuss the application of the LBKM for the inverse Cauchy problem for the first time.

The structure of this paper can be studied as follows: In the first section, we introduce previous research on the use of numerical methods in inverse problems and discuss their merits and drawbacks. In the second section, we give the details and formulations of the inverse Cauchy problem. In the third section, we illustrate the LBKM calculation process with a specific description. Six numerical examples are shown in the fourth section. Then, the defined errors and numerical results are compared and analyzed. In the last section, the discussion and conclusions about the entire work can be found.

2. Inverse Cauchy Problem

In this paper, we use the localized boundary knot method to solve the two-dimensional Cauchy inverse problem. The core of the problem is that some of the boundary conditions are unknown, so we need to add the overdetermined boundary condition to the known boundary section. The governing equation and boundary conditions are:

$$\nabla^2 U(x,y) = 0, \quad (x,y) \in \Omega, \tag{1}$$

$$U(x,y) = p(x,y), \quad (x,y) \in \Gamma^D, \tag{2}$$

$$U_N = (\nabla U) \cdot \vec{n} = q(x,y), \quad (x,y) \in \Gamma^N, \tag{3}$$

$$U(x,y) = k(x,y), \quad (x,y) \in \Gamma^{os}, \tag{4}$$

$$U_N = (\nabla U) \cdot \vec{n} = d(x,y), \quad (x,y) \in \Gamma^{os}, \tag{5}$$

where $\nabla^2 = \frac{\partial^2}{\partial x^2} + \frac{\partial^2}{\partial y^2}$ is the two-dimensional Laplacian, $U(x,y)$ represents any unknown variable in the field Ω, $\partial\Omega = \Gamma^D \cup \Gamma^N \cup \Gamma^{os} \cup \eta$ is the boundary of the computational domain and we assume that the boundary $\partial\Omega$ consists of two components that are disjointed from each other $\Gamma^{os} \cap \eta = \varnothing$. Γ^D and Γ^N are the Dirichlet boundary condition and the Neumann boundary condition, respectively. Γ^{os} represents the boundary portions with overspecified boundary conditions. η represents the boundary portions without boundary conditions. $\vec{n} = (n_x, n_y)$ is the unit outward normal vector on the boundary. $p(x,y)$ and $q(x,y)$ are the given boundary conditions.

3. Numerical Method

In this study, we used a localized BKM to solve this two-dimensional Cauchy inverse problem, whose governing equation is the Laplace equation. However, the traditional boundary knot method is extended from the method of the fundamental solution, and this study improves the global-type meshless method by changing it into the local type. $N = n_i + n_{b1} + n_{b2}$ is assumed to represent the total number of points to be calculated, where n_i represents the number of internal points, while n_{b1} and n_{b2} represent the points of two kinds of boundary, i.e., Γ^D and Γ^N, respectively. A schematic diagram of the calculation nodes of the localized BKM method is shown in Figure 1a.

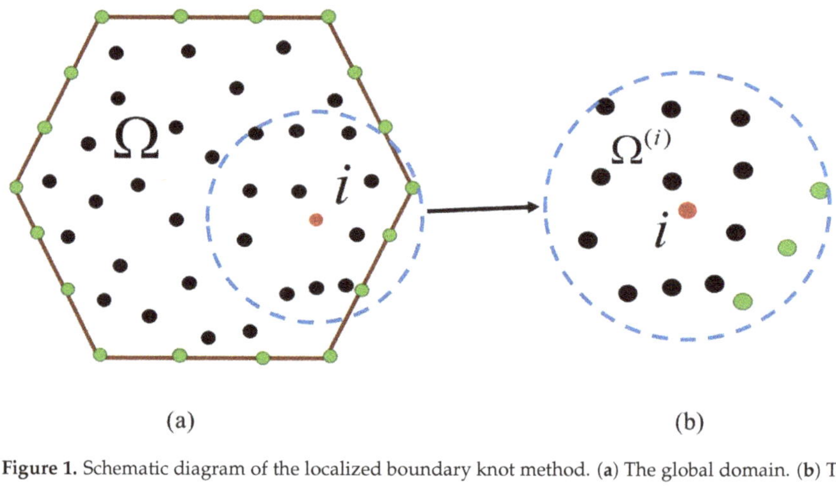

Figure 1. Schematic diagram of the localized boundary knot method. (**a**) The global domain. (**b**) The local domain of the ith node.

In the localized BKM method, a subdomain is formed in each node, as shown in Figure 1b. The numerical solution for each subdomain can be approximately expressed as follows:

$$U(x_i, y_i) = \sum_{k=1}^{n_k} \alpha_k G(r_k), \quad x, y \in \Omega, \tag{6}$$

in which α_j stands for the unknown coefficients, and N is the number of adjacent nodes. $G(r_k) = e^{(-c(x^2-y^2))}\cos(2cxy)$ is the BKM basis function, which satisfies the two-dimensional Laplace equation. n_k is the number of nodes in a subdomain. c is the shape parameter. $c = 0.1$ is adopted in the following case. $r = \sqrt{x^2+y^2}$ $(x = \|x - x_k\|,\ y = \|y - y_k\|)$ is the Euclidean distance, where x_k and y_k represent the x and y coordinates of the local node near the computing node, respectively. The source points are obtained from the nearest computing nodes in the subdomain.

By introducing the spatial coordinates of the nearest nodes into Equation (6), the following system is obtained:

$$U^{(i)} = C\alpha^{(i)}, \tag{7}$$

where $U^{(i)} = \left[u_1^{(i)}\ u_2^{(i)}\ u_3^{i}\ \ldots\ u_N^{(i)}\right]^T$ is the vector of unknown variables at n_k nodes, and $\alpha^{(i)} = \left[\alpha_1^{(i)}\ \alpha_2^{(i)}\ \alpha_3^{(i)}\ \ldots\ \alpha_m^{(i)}\right]^T$ is the vector of the unknown coefficients. C is the coefficient matrix. The unknown coefficients can be expressed by unknown variables:

$$\alpha^{(i)} = C^{-1}U^{(i)}. \tag{8}$$

The inverse matrix C^{-1} is calculated by using the MATLAB command ***pinv***, and we set the tolerance to be 10^{-3}–10^{-4} in this article.

The numerical solution for the ith node can be obtained from introducing the node coordinates of this point into Equation (7). The form is as follows:

$$U_{(i)} = \sum_{k=1}^{n_k} \alpha_k^{(i)} G(r_k) = c^{(i)T}\alpha^{(i)} = c^{(i)T}C^{(-1)}U^{(i)} = \sum_{k=1}^{n_k} \psi_k^i U_k^i, \tag{9}$$

where $c^{(i)} = \left[G(r_{i1})\ G(r_{i2})\ G(r_{i3})\ \ldots G(r_{in_k})\right]^T$ is the vector of the fundamental solution at the ith node. $\{\psi_k^{(i)}\}_{k=1}^{n_k}$ represents the weighting coefficients.

In addition, according to Equation (3), we have

$$\left.\frac{\partial U}{\partial x}\right|_i = \left.\sum_{k=1}^{n_k} \alpha_k^{(i)} \frac{\partial}{\partial x} G(r_k)\right|_i = h_x^{(i)T}\alpha^{(i)} = h_x^{(i)T}H^{-1}U^{(i)} = \sum_{k=1}^{n_k} \psi_k^{x(i)} U_k^i, \tag{10}$$

and

$$\left.\frac{\partial U}{\partial y}\right|_i = \left.\sum_{k=1}^{n_k} \alpha_k^{(i)} \frac{\partial}{\partial y} G(r_k)\right|_i = h_y^{(i)T}\alpha^{(i)} = h_y^{(i)T}H^{-1}U^{(i)} = \sum_{k=1}^{n_k} \psi_k^{y(i)} U_k^i, \tag{11}$$

where

$$h_x^{(i)} = \left[\left.\frac{\partial G(r_1)}{\partial x}\right|_i \left.\frac{\partial G(r_2)}{\partial x}\right|_i \left.\frac{\partial G(r_3)}{\partial x}\right|_i \cdots \left.\frac{\partial G(r_k)}{\partial x}\right|_i\right]^T, \tag{12}$$

$$h_y^{(i)} = \left[\left.\frac{\partial G(r_1)}{\partial y}\right|_i \left.\frac{\partial G(r_2)}{\partial y}\right|_i \left.\frac{\partial G(r_3)}{\partial y}\right|_i \cdots \left.\frac{\partial G(r_k)}{\partial y}\right|_i\right]^T \tag{13}$$

In order to obtain the expression for the Neumann boundary conditions, we can bring Equations (10) and (11) into Equation (3):

$$\frac{\partial U}{\partial n} = \frac{\partial U}{\partial x}n_x + \frac{\partial U}{\partial y}n_y = q(x,y),\ x,y \in \Gamma^N \tag{14}$$

The linear equations that satisfy the Laplace equation, Dirichlet boundary conditions and Neumann boundary conditions are combined to form sparse linear algebraic equations,

$$\mathbf{AU} = \mathbf{b}, \tag{15}$$

where $\mathbf{A}_{N\times N}$ is the sparse coefficient matrix that avoids the ill-conditioned matrix, $\mathbf{U} = \left[U_1\ U_2\ U_3\ \ldots U_N\right]^T$ is the unknown field quantity at every node and $\mathbf{b}$ represents the known conditions. Therefore, $\mathbf{U}$ can be calculated from Equation (15). The localized BKM, which combines BKM with the localization concept of localized MFS, is simple and clear, and the method of determining local points is also novel. In addition, due to the sparse matrix generated in the calculation of linear algebraic equations, it can also be applied to some complex fields.

4. Numerical Results and Comparisons

In this section, we present an analysis and comparison of the results of five cases. These five examples include a simply connected domain and a multi-connected domain. At the same time, different levels of noise are added to the boundary conditions to verify the stability of the localized BKM. For the last case, we carry out the process of forward calculation and then reverse calculation by guessing the analytical solution and relative error of the Laplace equation. In this paper, we compare the analytical solution u_a with the numerical solution U and take the maximum relative error as the index of error analysis.

$$error = max(|(U - u_a)/u_a|).$$

4.1. Case 1

In the first example, we use a square computing field, as shown in Figure 2. The field is denoted by $\partial\Omega = \Gamma_1 + \Gamma_2 + \Gamma_3 + \Gamma_4$. The boundary corner points are removed, and the internal points and boundary points are evenly distributed throughout the entire calculation domain. The analytical solution of the applied boundary condition is as follows:

$$u_a(x, y) = e^x \cos(y) + e^y \sin(x) + 5, \tag{16}$$

where the Γ_1 boundary is unknown, and the overdetermined boundary conditions (Dirichlet and Neumann) are added to the remaining edges, which are Γ_2, Γ_3 and Γ_4. Hence, the points on this edge are calculated as interior points. The following parameters are used in this example: $N = 4896$, $n_b = 272$, $n_k = 100$, $c = 0.1$, where N is the number of total nodes, while n_b is the number of boundary nodes.

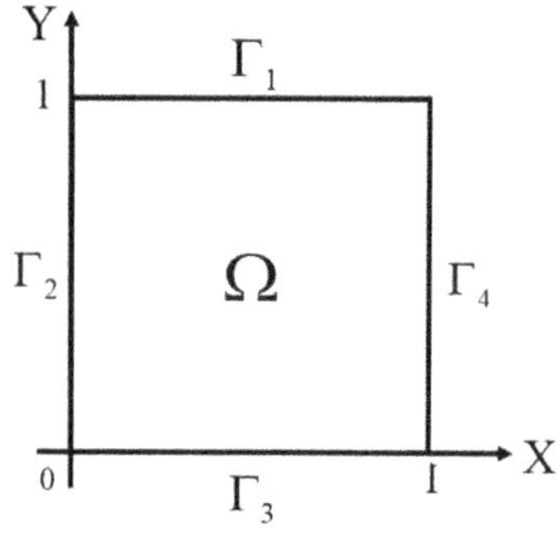

Figure 2. Schematic diagram for case 1.

In order to reflect the real boundary conditions, different levels of noise s are added to the boundary to consider possible errors in advance. Therefore, the boundary conditions take the following forms:

$$u_a = f(x, y)(1 + \frac{s}{100} \times rand), \quad (x, y) \in \Gamma_2 + \Gamma_3 + \Gamma_4, \tag{17}$$

$$\begin{aligned} u_{an} &= [(\nabla u) \cdot \vec{n}](1 + \tfrac{s}{100} \times rand) = g(x, y)(1 + \tfrac{s}{100} \times rand) \\ &= [\nabla(u_a(x, y)) \cdot \vec{n}](1 + \tfrac{s}{100} \times rand), \quad (x, y) \in \Gamma_2 + \Gamma_3 + \Gamma_4 \end{aligned} \tag{18}$$

where s is the percentage of added noise, *rand* is the random number and the range is $-1 \le rand \le 1$. The function ***rand*** in MATLAB software is used in this paper to generate the noise.

In order to show the calculation results more clearly, we draw the solution along the boundary Γ_1, as shown in Figure 3. In this figure, we can see that, although different degrees of noise interference are added, the numerical solution along the boundary Γ_1 is relatively stable, and the line-fitting degree with the analytical solution is relatively high.

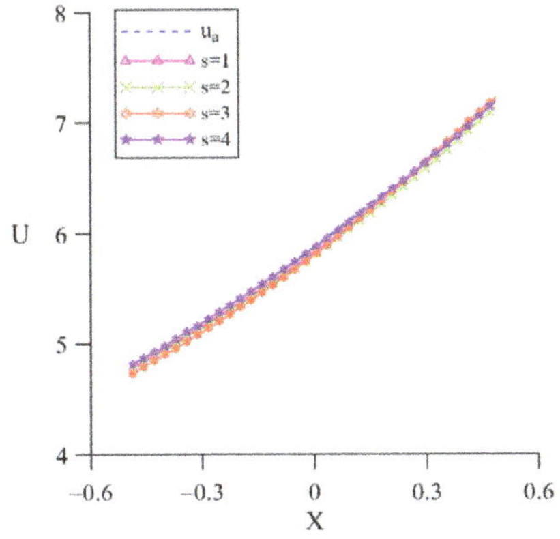

Figure 3. The profiles of numerical solutions along Γ_1 for case 1.

In Figure 4, we use a solid line to represent the internal numerical solution and a dotted line to represent the internal analytical solution. It can be seen from these four pictures that the errors increase with an increase in added noise, but they are all within the acceptable range, and those near the unknown boundary increase significantly. In Table 1, we describe the maximum relative error corresponding to different degrees of disturbance in detail.

Table 1. The maximum relative error obtained by adding different percentages of noise for case 1.

Percentage of Noise	$s = 1$	$s = 2$	$s = 3$	$s = 4$	$s = 5$	$s = 6$	$s = 7$
Maximum relative error	0.00943	0.0136	0.0147	0.0184	0.0189	0.0209	0.0286

4.2. Case 2

In this case, a circle is used as the calculation domain, as shown in Figure 5. The radius of the circle is 1, and half of the boundary is unknown. Γ_1 is an unknown boundary, while Γ_2 is a known boundary. The analytical solution for this example is:

$$u_a = x^2 - y^2 + xy + 5 \tag{19}$$

The following parameters are used in this example: $N = 2809,\ n_b = 200, n_k = 100, c = 0.1$. The boundary conditions take the following forms:

$$\begin{aligned} u &= f(x,y)(1 + \tfrac{s}{100} \times rand) \\ &= (x^2 - y^2 + xy + 5)(1 + \tfrac{s}{100} \times rand), \quad (x,y) \in \Gamma_2 \end{aligned} \tag{20}$$

$$\begin{aligned} u_{an} &= [(\nabla u) \cdot \vec{n}](1 + \tfrac{s}{100} \times rand) = g(x,y)(1 + \tfrac{s}{100} \times rand) \\ &= [\nabla(x^2 - y^2 + xy + 5) \cdot \vec{n}](1 + \tfrac{s}{100} \times rand), \quad (x,y) \in \Gamma_2 \end{aligned} \tag{21}$$

The marked solid lines in Figure 6 represent the numerical results for the unknown boundary Γ_1 under different noise disturbances, and the dotted line represents the analytical solution curve of Γ_1. Obviously, the numerical solutions are in good agreement with the analytical solution.

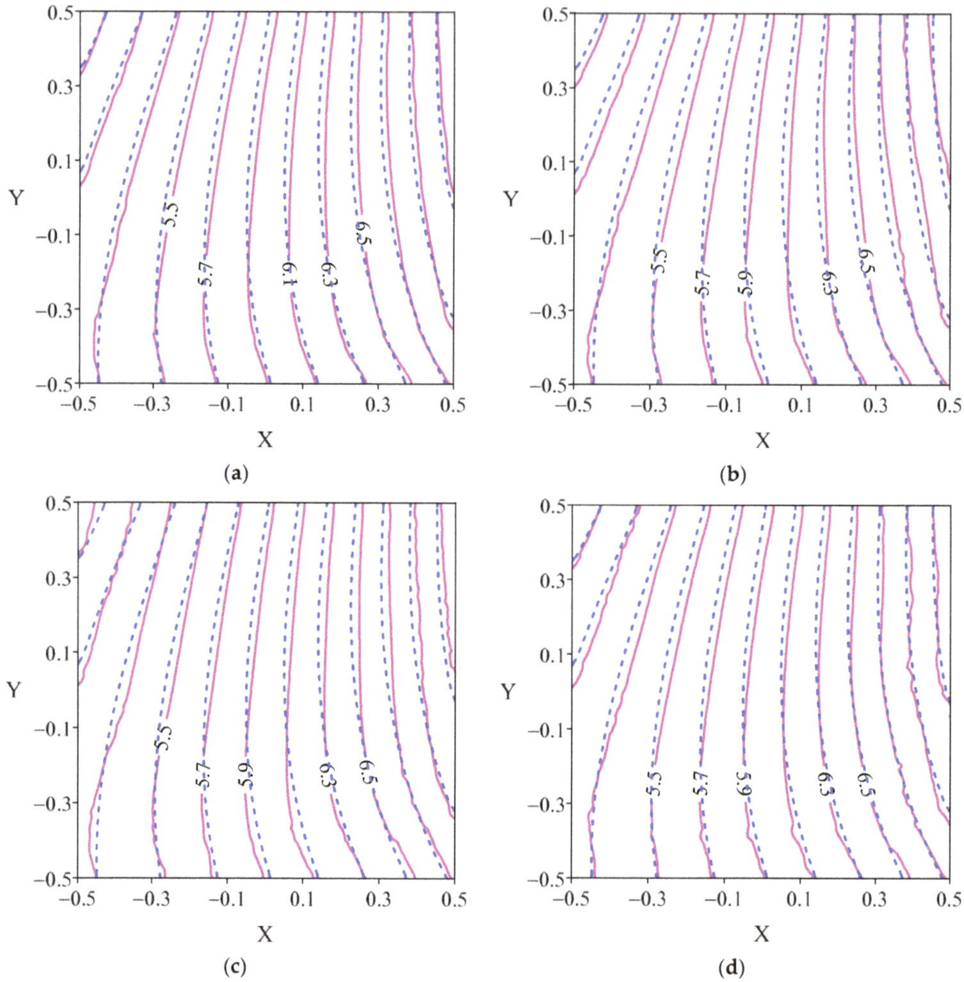

Figure 4. The distributions of numerical (solid lines) and analytical solutions (dashed lines) (**a**) s = 1 (**b**) s = 2 (**c**) s = 3 (**d**) s = 4.

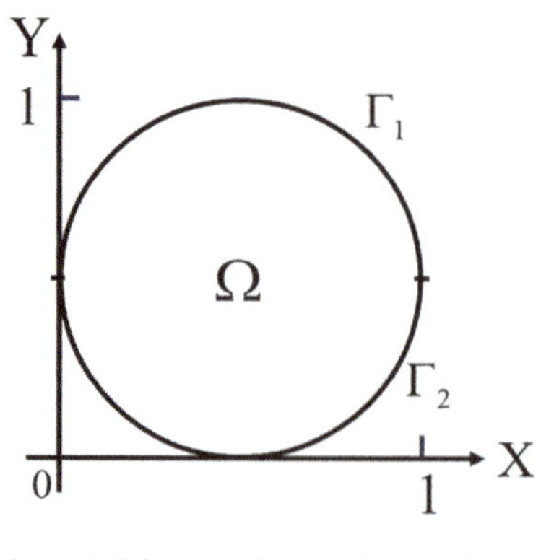

Figure 5. Schematic diagram for case 2.

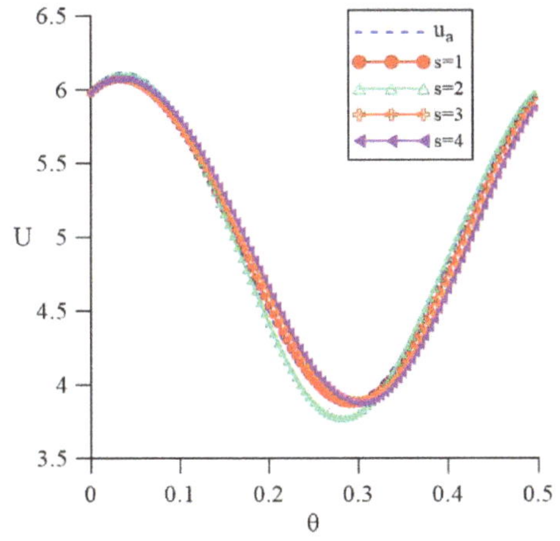

Figure 6. The profiles of numerical solutions along Γ_1 for case 2.

In Table 2, we list the maximum relative error obtained when adding different degrees of noise, and they are all very small. In Figure 7, we draw the internal distributions under different disturbances. The error near the unknown boundary is relatively large but is still within the acceptable range. The analytical solution line and the numerical solution line near the boundary with known boundary conditions fit well.

Table 2. The maximum relative error obtained by adding different percentages of noise for case 2.

Percentage of Noise	$s = 1$	$s = 2$	$s = 3$	$s = 4$	$s = 5$	$s = 6$	$s = 7$
Maximum relative error	0.0198	0.0272	0.0347	0.0428	0.0504	0.0596	0.0779

4.3. Case 3

For the third inverse problem, we use a doubly connected domain. The computational domain is concentric annular, as shown in Figure 8. The radius of the outer circle is 2, and the radius of the inner circle is 1. The analytical solution for this example is:

$$u_a = \sinh(y)\sin(x) + \cosh(x)\cos(y) + 5. \tag{22}$$

The outer boundary has two kinds of boundary conditions, while the inner boundary has no boundary conditions. The given boundary conditions are obtained by the analytical solution, and the nodes are uniformly distributed in the computational domain and on the boundary. The parameters used in this example are as follows:

$N = 1476$, $n_{b1} = 380$, $n_{b2} = 180$, $n_k = 60$, $c = 0.1$, where n_{b1} and n_{b2} represent the numbers of nodes on the outer and inner boundaries, respectively.

In Table 3, we list the maximum relative errors obtained when adding different degrees of noise, and the errors are also stable. A comparison of the analytical and numerical solutions drawn along the unknown boundary is shown in Figure 9. An internal contour map of different degrees of disturbance is shown in Figure 10. It can be seen from the figures that the numerical solution and the analytical solution are very similar.

Table 3. The maximum relative error obtained by adding different percentages of noise for case 3.

Percentage of Noise	$s = 0$	$s = 1$	$s = 2$	$s = 3$	$s = 4$	$s = 5$	$s = 6$	$s = 7$
Maximum relative error	9.45×10^{-5}	0.0056	0.0146	0.0214	0.0274	0.0375	0.0465	0.0654

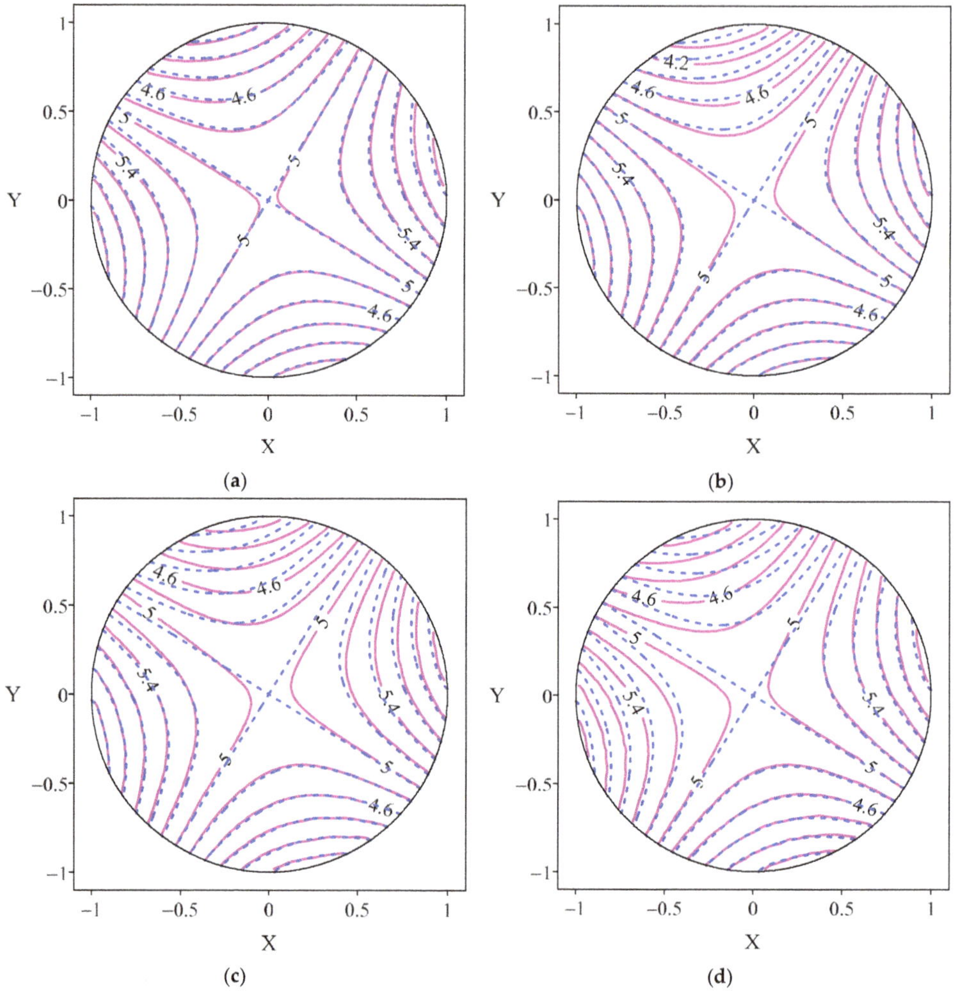

Figure 7. The distributions of numerical (solid lines) and analytical solutions (dashed lines). (**a**) s = 1 (**b**) s = 2 (**c**) s = 3 (**d**) s = 4.

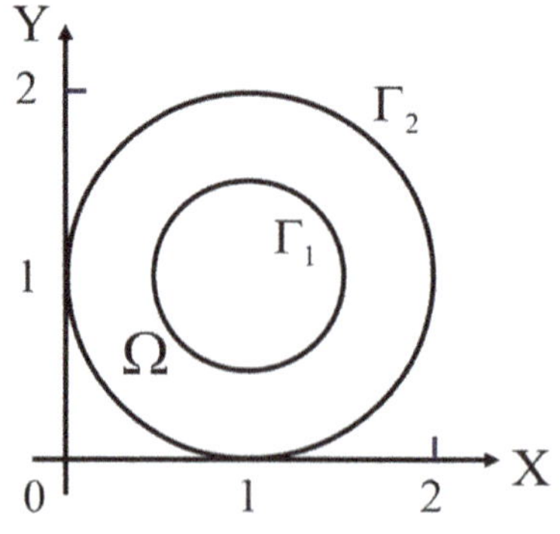

Figure 8. Schematic diagram for case 3.

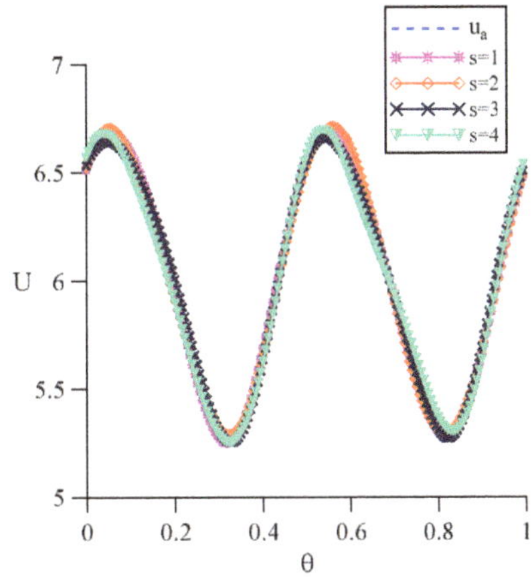

Figure 9. The profiles of numerical solutions along Γ_1 for case 3.

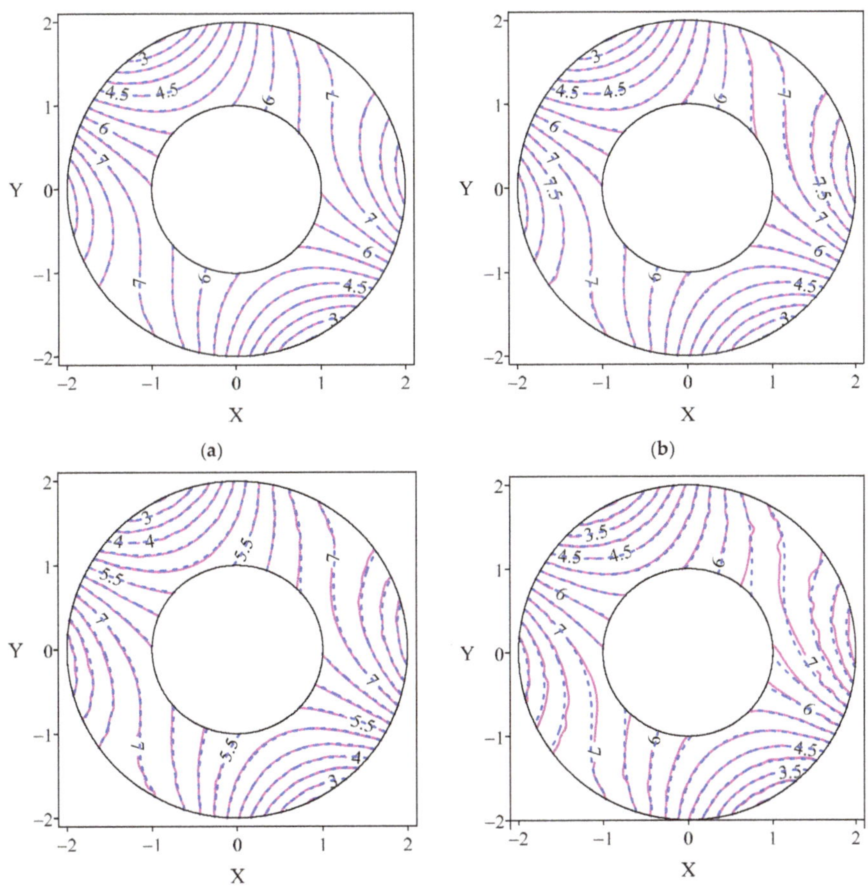

Figure 10. The distributions of numerical (solid lines) and analytical solutions (dashed lines). (**a**) s = 1 (**b**) s = 2 (**c**) s = 3 (**d**) s = 4.

4.4. Case 4

In order to verify the stability of the numerical method, we use the multi-connected domain as the computational domain in this case, as shown in Figure 11. In this case, we take the outer boundary Γ_2 as the unknown boundary and the inner boundary Γ_1 as the known boundary. Therefore, two kinds of boundary conditions are added to the inner boundary. The analytical solution for this example is:

$$u_a = x^2 - y^2 + xy + 5. \tag{23}$$

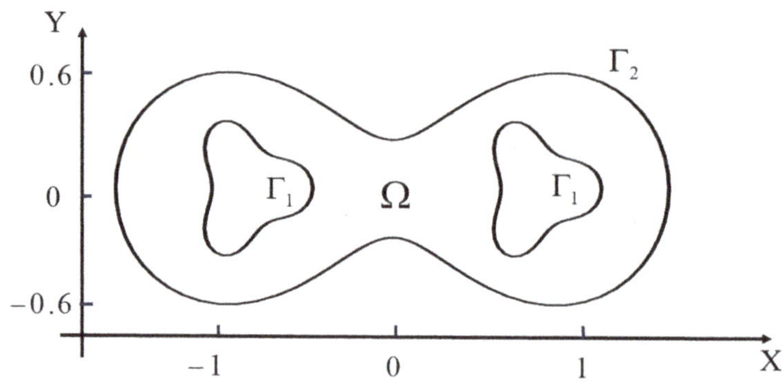

Figure 11. Schematic diagram for case 4.

The boundary of the peanut shape is regarded as an unknown boundary, so the points on the boundary are calculated as internal nodes. Two internal wave elimination blocks are used as known boundaries, and a Dirichlet boundary condition and Neumann boundary condition are added. The parameters used in this example are as follows:

$$N = 3068,\ n_{b1} = 120,\ n_{b2} = 102,\ n_k = 100,\ c = 0.1.$$

In Table 4, we list the maximum relative errors obtained when adding different degrees of noise, and the errors are also stable. A comparison of the analytical and numerical solutions drawn along the unknown boundary is shown in Figure 12. The data from tables and graphs show that the error is relatively stable and small.

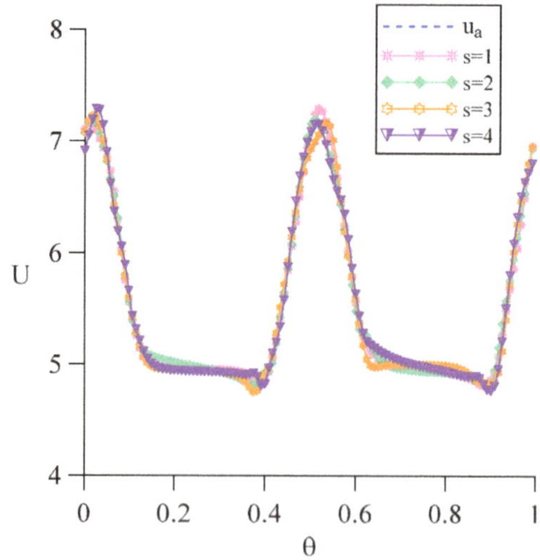

Figure 12. The profiles of numerical solutions along Γ_2 for case 4.

Table 4. The maximum relative error obtained by adding different noise for case 4.

Percentage of Noise	s = 0	s = 1	s = 2	s = 3	s = 4	s = 5	s = 6
Maximum relative error	1.96×10^{-4}	0.0154	0.0196	0.0277	0.0496	0.0590	0.0688

4.5. Case 5

In this example, the geometry of this computational domain is more complex and there are many sharp angles at the boundary; its schematic diagram is shown in Figure 13. The equation for the gear shape is as follows:

$$\partial\Omega = \{\, (x,y)|x = \rho(\theta)\cos(\gamma(\theta)), y = \rho(\theta)\sin(\gamma(\theta))\}, \tag{24}$$

where $\rho(\theta) = 0.2(2 + 0.5\sin(7\theta))$, $\gamma(\theta) = \theta + 0.5\sin(\theta)$, $0 \le \theta \le 2\pi$.

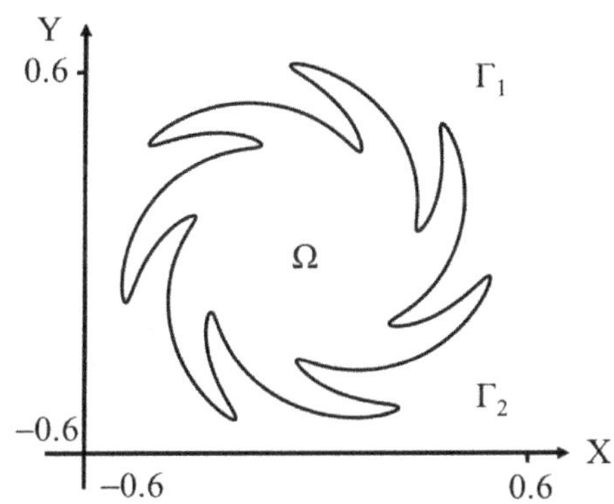

Figure 13. Schematic diagram for case 5.

We set the boundary conditions ($0 < \theta \le \pi$) of the upper half as unknown and the boundary conditions of the lower half ($\pi < \theta \le 2\pi$) as given. The Dirichlet boundary condition and the Neumann boundary condition are given by the following analytical solution:

$$u_a = \cos(x)\sinh(y) + x^2 - y^2 + xy + 1 \tag{25}$$

The following parameters are used: $N = 901$, $n_{b1} = 150$, $n_{b2}= 150$, $n_k = 80$, $c = 0.1$.

From Table 5, it can be observed that even the geometry of the boundary is more complex under the setting of different levels of noise, and we can use the localized boundary knot method to solve this inverse Cauchy problem and still maintain a stable level of accuracy. Additionally, Figure 14 clearly shows the error curves obtained by applying different percentages of noise under different numbers of local points. This means that when the number of local points increases, the maximum relative error from the analytical solution approaches a stable state. In Figure 15, we show that (a) $s = 1$, (b) $s = 2$, (c) $s = 3$ and (d) $s = 4$. These four graphs show that there is indeed a certain degree of deviation in the upper half of the lack of boundary information, but the numerical results in the domain are consistent with the analytical solution.

Table 5. The maximum relative error obtained by adding different noise for case 5.

Percentage of Noise	s = 0	s = 1	s = 2	s = 3	s = 4	s = 5	s = 6
Maximum relative error	7.39×10^{-4}	0.0150	0.0265	0.0376	0.0473	0.0582	0.0675

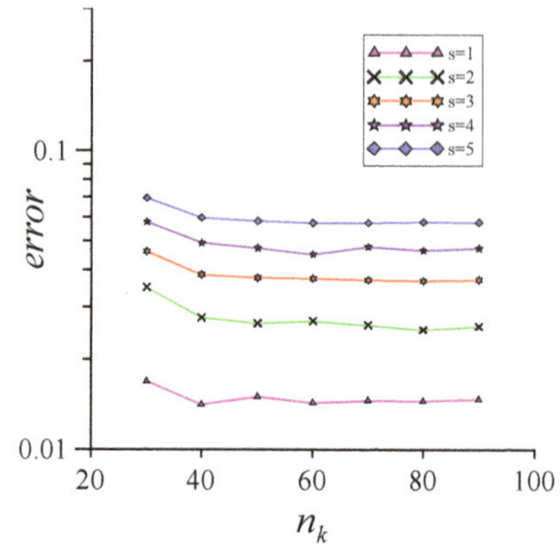

Figure 14. The maximum relative error of the different percentages of noise and local nodes for case 5.

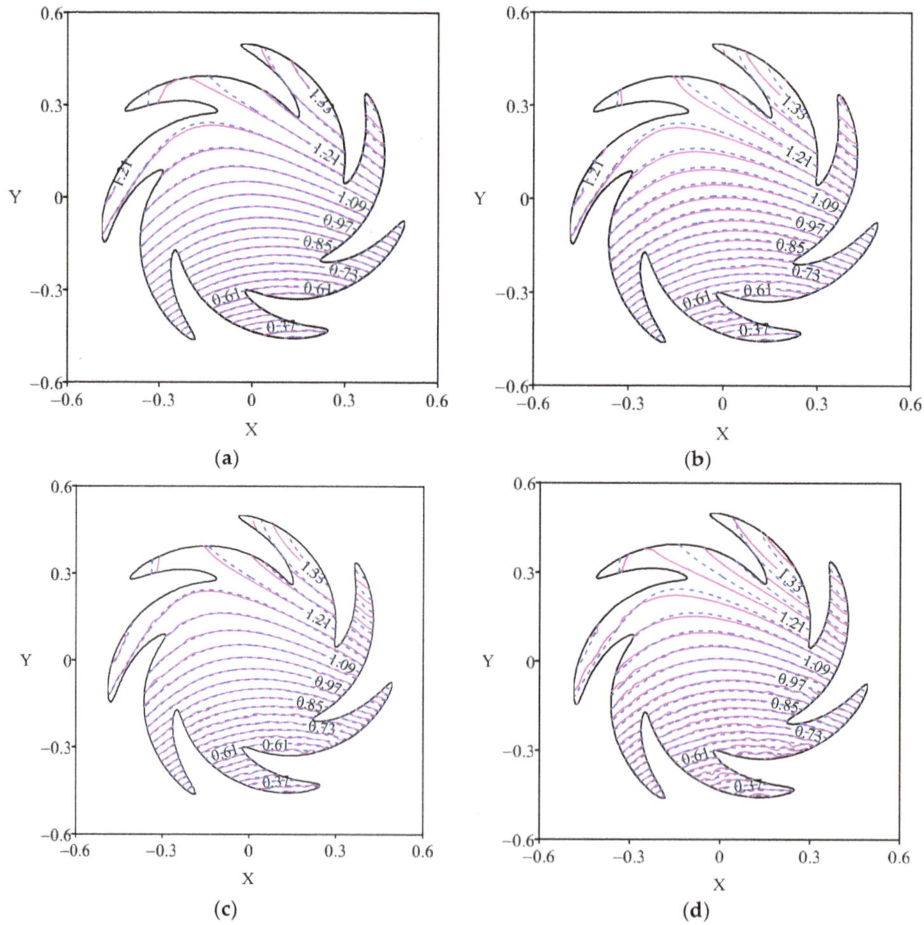

Figure 15. The distributions of numerical (solid lines) and analytical solutions (dashed lines) for Case 6. (**a**) s = 1 (**b**) s = 2 (**c**) s = 3 (**d**) s = 4.

4.6. Case 6

In order to further verify the accuracy of the localized BKM, in the last case, we also use the circle as the calculation domain, where a quarter of the boundary is used as the unknown boundary, namely $\Gamma_2: \left(\frac{3}{2}\pi \leq \theta \leq 2\pi\right)$. We assume that the boundary conditions do not satisfy the analytical solution. This means that the corresponding analytical solution cannot be derived from the governing equations and boundary conditions. The known boundary satisfies the following conditions:

$$u = \left(\sinh\left(\frac{x}{4}\right) + \cosh\left(\frac{x}{4}\right)\right)\cos\left(\frac{y}{4}\right) + 50, \quad x \in \Gamma^D, \tag{26}$$

$$\frac{\partial u(x)}{\partial n} = \frac{1}{10}(x+y), \quad x \in \Gamma^N, \tag{27}$$

In Step 1, the boundary $\Gamma_1: \left(0 \leq \theta < \frac{3}{2}\pi\right)$ is set as the Neumann boundary condition, and the boundary Γ_2 is set as the Dirichlet boundary condition. The numerical solutions $[u]_{\Gamma_1}$ can be solved by LBKM.

In Step 2, Γ_1 is selected as the unknown boundary condition and the numerical solution obtained from the previous solution $[u]_{\Gamma_1}$ and the Neumann boundary condition on the Γ_2 boundary are used. For the first of the step calculation, the total number of nodes is $N = 2949$, the number of boundary nodes is $n_b = 200$, the number of local domain nodes is $n_k = 100$, and the shape parameter is $c = 0.1$, and for the second step of the calculation, the total number of nodes is $N = 4249$, the number of boundary nodes is $n_b = 200$, and the shape parameter is $c = 0.1$. We analyze the maximum relative error of the numerical solutions for Step 1 and Step 2.

To show the stability of the numerical method, we solved this problem by using different numbers of local points, and the maximum relative error is presented in Table 6. The change in maximum relative error corresponding to the change in total points is recorded in Table 7. It can be seen from the test of different total points N and local points n_k that, in the case where the boundary conditions do not use analytical solutions, the maximum relative error can still remain accurate and stable.

Table 6. The maximum relative error obtained with different values of n_k for case 6. ($N = 2949$).

n_k	40	70	100	130	150
Maximum relative error	3.75×10^{-3}	7.22×10^{-4}	1.20×10^{-3}	1.92×10^{-3}	1.72×10^{-3}

Table 7. The maximum relative errors with different values of N for case 6. ($n_k = 100$).

N	3405	4093	5308	6380	8560
Maximum relative error	1.00×10^{-3}	7.89×10^{-4}	9.91×10^{-4}	9.76×10^{-4}	2.14×10^{-3}

The distributions of numerical solutions to the direct and inverse problems are shown in Figure 16. In this figure, it can be seen that numerical solutions to the inverse problem are basically the same as in Step 1, and the maximum relative error is 7.89×10^{-4}.

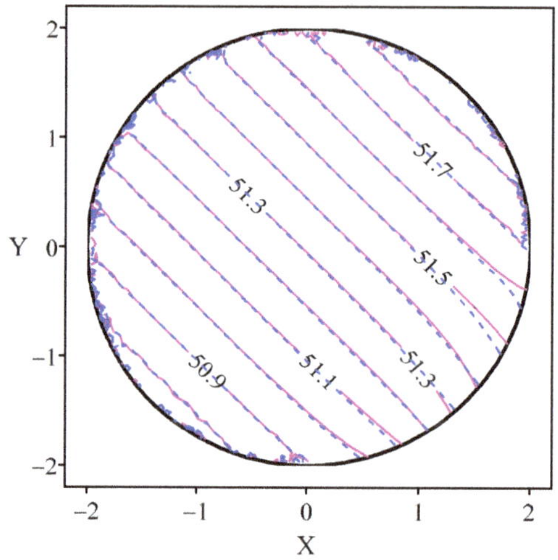

Figure 16. The numerical solution distribution of Step 1 (dashed lines) and Step 2 (solid lines) for case 6. ($N = 4093$, $n_k = 100$).

5. Conclusions

In this paper, the localized BKM was used to solve an inverse Cauchy problem controlled by a two-dimensional Laplace equation. The localized BKM is a method that combines the BKM of the meshless method with the localization concept. This method does not need grid generation and numerical integration, and it eliminates border radius issues with source points. For Cauchy problems, some boundary conditions are not readily available or there are measurement errors, so the numerical simulation is unstable. Therefore, we used the localized BKM to calculate such problems and verify the accuracy of this method.

We presented five examples that illustrate the stability and accuracy of this method for solving inverse problems. With different percentages of noise on the boundaries, the maximum relative error remained stable and within the acceptable range. In particular, in the last case, the direct algorithm was first used to obtain the data with an extra boundary and was then applied to the reverse calculation in the second step. From the results of the error analysis presented in this paper, the localized BKM was shown to be more stable and accurate for solving Cauchy inverse problems.

In the future, the localized BKM will be applied to various mathematical and physical problems as well as more complex problems, for example, moving boundary problems and three-dimensional problems.

Author Contributions: Conceptualization, Y.-C.L.; Data curation, Y.W.; Formal analysis, Y.-C.L. and S.D.; Investigation, J.Z.; Methodology, Y.-C.L.; Software, Y.W. and J.Z.; Supervision, Y.-C.L. and S.D.; Writing—original draft, Y.W. and J.Z.; Writing—review & editing, Y.-C.L. and S.D. All authors have read and agreed to the published version of the manuscript.

Funding: This research received no external funding.

Institutional Review Board Statement: Not applicable.

Informed Consent Statement: Not applicable.

Data Availability Statement: Not applicable.

Conflicts of Interest: The authors declare no conflict of interest.

References

1. Chang, J.R.; Yeih, W.; Shieh, M.H. On the modified Tikhonov's regularization method for the Cauchy problem of the Laplace equation. *J. Mar. Sci. Technol.* **2001**, *9*, 113–121. [CrossRef]
2. Chakib, A.; Nachaoui, A. Convergence analysis for finite element approximation to an inverse Cauchy problem. *Inverse Probl.* **2006**, *22*, 1191–1206. [CrossRef]
3. Vanrumste, B.; Van, H.G.; Van de Walle, R.; D'Havè, M.R.; Lemahieu, I.A.; Boon, P.A. The validation of the finite difference method and reciprocity for solving the inverse problem in EEG dipole source analysis. *Brain Topogr.* **2001**, *14*, 83–92. [CrossRef] [PubMed]
4. Lesnic, D.; Elliott, L.; Ingham, D.B. An iterative boundary element method for solving numerically the Cauchy problem for the Laplace equation. *Eng. Anal. Bound. Elem.* **1997**, *20*, 123–133. [CrossRef]
5. Mera, N.S.; Elliott, L.; Ingham, D.B.; Lesnic, D. An iterative boundary element method for the solution of a Cauchy steady state heat conduction problem. *CMES Comput. Modeling Eng. Sci.* **2000**, *1*, 101–106.
6. Lesnic, D.; Elliott, L.; Ingham, D.B. A alternating boundary element method for solving Cauchy problems for the biharmonic equation. *Inverse Probl. Eng.* **1997**, *5*, 145–168. [CrossRef]
7. Kansa, E.J. Multiquadrics—A scattered data approximation scheme with applications to computational fluid-dynamics—II solutions to parabolic, hyperbolic and elliptic partial differential equations. *Comput. Math. Appl.* **1990**, *19*, 147–161. [CrossRef]
8. Kansa, E.J. Multiquadrics—A scattered data approximation scheme with applications to computational fluid-Dynamics—I surface approximations and partial derivative estimates. *Comput. Math. Appl.* **1990**, *19*, 127–145. [CrossRef]
9. Hardy, R.L. Multiquadric equations of topography and other irregular surfaces. *J. Geophys. Res.* **1971**, *76*, 1905–1915. [CrossRef]
10. Duchon, J. Splines minimizing rotation-invariant semi-norms in Sobolev spaces. In *Constructive Theory of Functions of Several Variables*; Springer: Berlin/Heidelberg, Germany, 1977; pp. 85–100.
11. Franke, R. Scattered data interpolation: Tests of some methods. *Math. Comput.* **1982**, *38*, 181–200.
12. Nam, M.D.; Thanh, T.C. Mesh-free radial basis function network methods with domain decomposition for approximation of functions and numerical solution of Poisson's equations. *Eng. Anal. Bound. Elem.* **2002**, *26*, 133–156.
13. Fan, C.M.; Huang, Y.K.; Li, P.W.; Chiu, C.L. Application of the generalized finite-difference method to inverse biharmonic boundary-value problems. *Numer. Heat Transf. Part B Fundam.* **2014**, *65*, 129–154. [CrossRef]
14. Fan, C.M.; Li, P.W.; Yeih, W. Generalized finite difference method for solving two-dimensional inverse Cauchy problems. *Inverse Probl. Sci. Eng.* **2015**, *23*, 737–759. [CrossRef]
15. Li, P.W.; Fan, C.M.; Grabski, J.K. A meshless generalized finite difference method for solving shallow water equations with the flux limiter technique. *Eng. Anal. Bound. Elem.* **2021**, *131*, 159–173. [CrossRef]
16. Li, P.W. Space–time generalized finite difference nonlinear model for solving unsteady Burgers' equations. *Appl. Math. Lett.* **2021**, *114*, 106896. [CrossRef]
17. Chu, H.F.; Fan, C.M.; Yeih, W.C. Solution of inverse boundary optimization problem by Trefftz method and exponentially convergent scalar homotopy algorithm. *CMC-Comput. Mater. Contin.* **2011**, *24*, 125–142.
18. Liu, C.S.; Atluri, S.N. Numerical solution of the Laplacian Cauchy problem by using a better postconditioning collocation Trefftz method. *Eng. Anal. Bound. Elem.* **2013**, *37*, 74–83. [CrossRef]
19. Kołodziej, J.A.; Grabski, J.K. Many names of the Trefftz method. *Eng. Anal. Bound. Elem.* **2018**, *96*, 169–178. [CrossRef]
20. Liu, C.S. A highly accurate MCTM for direct and inverse problems of biharmonic equation in arbitrary plane domains. *CMES: Comput. Modeling Eng. Sci.* **2008**, *30*, 65–75.
21. Fan, C.M.; Chan, H.F. Modified collocation Trefftz method for the geometry boundary identification problem of heat conduction. *Numer. Heat Transf. Part B Fundam.* **2011**, *59*, 58–75. [CrossRef]
22. Gu, Y.; Chen, W.; Zhang, C.; He, X. A meshless singular boundary method for three-dimensional inverse heat conduction problems in general anisotropic media. *Int. J. Heat Mass Transf.* **2015**, *84*, 91–102. [CrossRef]
23. Fu, Z.; Chen, W.; Zhang, C. Boundary particle method for Cauchy inhomogeneous potential problems. *Inverse Probl. Sci. Eng.* **2012**, *20*, 189–207. [CrossRef]
24. Kupradze, V.D.; Aleksidze, M.A. The method of functional equations for the approximate solution of certain boundary value problems. *USSR Comput. Math. Math. Phys.* **1964**, *4*, 82–126. [CrossRef]
25. Karageorghis, A.; Lesnic, D. Detection of cavities using the method of fundamental solutions. *Inverse Probl. Sci. Eng.* **2009**, *17*, 803–820. [CrossRef]
26. Karageorghis, A.; Lesnic, D.; Marin, L. A survey of applications of the MFS to inverse problems. *Inverse Probl. Sci. Eng.* **2011**, *19*, 309–336. [CrossRef]
27. Young, D.L.; Tsai, C.C.; Chen, C.W.; Fan, C.M. The method of fundamental solutions and condition number analysis for inverse problems of Laplace equation. *Comput. Math. Appl.* **2008**, *55*, 1189–1200. [CrossRef]
28. Fan, C.M.; Li, P.W. Numerical solutions of direct and inverse stokes problems by the method of fundamental solutions and the Laplacian decomposition. *Numer. Heat Transf. Part B Fundam.* **2015**, *68*, 204–223. [CrossRef]
29. Chen, W.; Tanaka, M. A meshless, integration-free, and boundary-only RBF technique. *Comput. Math. Appl.* **2002**, *43*, 379–391. [CrossRef]
30. Chen, W. Symmetric boundary knot method. *Eng. Anal. Bound. Elem.* **2002**, *26*, 489–494. [CrossRef]

31. Jiang, X.; Chen, W.; Chen, C.S. Fast multipole accelerated boundary knot method for inhomogeneous Helmholtz problems. *Eng. Anal. Bound. Elem.* **2013**, *37*, 1239–1243. [CrossRef]
32. Chen, W.; Shen, L.J.; Shen, Z.J.; Yuan, G.W. Boundary knot method for Poisson equations. *Eng. Anal. Bound. Elem.* **2005**, *29*, 756–760. [CrossRef]
33. Jin, B.; Zheng, Y. Boundary knot method for some inverse problems associated with the Helmholtz equation. *Int. J. Numer. Methods Eng.* **2005**, *62*, 1636–1651. [CrossRef]
34. Jin, B.; Zheng, Y. Boundary knot method for the Cauchy problem associated with the inhomogeneous Helmholtz equation. *Eng. Anal. Bound. Elem.* **2005**, *29*, 925–935. [CrossRef]
35. Zheng, H.; Zhang, C.; Wang, Y.; Sladek, J.; Sladek, V. A meshfree local RBF collocation method for anti-plane transverse elastic wave propagation analysis in 2D phononic crystals. *J. Comput. Phys.* **2016**, *305*, 997–1014. [CrossRef]
36. Zheng, H.; Yao, G.; Kuo, L.H.; Li, X. On the selection of a good shape parameter of the localized method of approximated particular solutions. *Adv. Appl. Math. Mech.* **2018**, *10*, 896–911. [CrossRef]
37. Zheng, H.; Yang, Z.; Zhang, C.; Tyrer, M. A local radial basis function collocation method for band structure computation of phononic crystals with scatterers of arbitrary geometry. *Appl. Math. Model.* **2018**, *60*, 447–459. [CrossRef]
38. Zheng, H.; Xiong, J.G.; Yuan, Y.; Wen, P.H. Mixed-mode dynamic stress intensity factors by variation technique with finite block method. *Eng. Anal. Bound. Elem.* **2019**, *106*, 27–33. [CrossRef]
39. Chan, H.F.; Fan, C.M. The local radial basis function collocation method for solving two-dimensional inverse Cauchy problems. *Numer. Heat Transf. Part B Fundam.* **2013**, *63*, 284–303. [CrossRef]
40. Fan, C.M.; Huang, Y.K.; Chen, C.S.; Kuo, S. Localized method of fundamental solutions for solving two-dimensional Laplace and biharmonic equations. *Eng. Anal. Bound. Elem.* **2019**, *101*, 188–197. [CrossRef]
41. Wang, F.; Fan, C.M.; Hua, Q.; Gu, Y. Localized MFS for the inverse Cauchy problems of two-dimensional Laplace and biharmonic equations. *Appl. Math. Comput.* **2020**, *364*, 124658. [CrossRef]
42. Liu, Y.C.; Fan, C.M.; Yeih, W.; Ku, C.Y.; Chu, C.L. Numerical solutions of two-dimensional Laplace and biharmonic equations by the localized Trefftz method. *Comput. Math. Appl.* **2021**, *88*, 120–134. [CrossRef]
43. Wang, F.; Chen, Z.; Li, P.W.; Fan, C.M. Localized singular boundary method for solving Laplace and Helmholtz equations in arbitrary 2D domains. *Eng. Anal. Bound. Elem.* **2021**, *129*, 82–92. [CrossRef]
44. Wang, F.; Gu, Y.; Qu, W.; Zhang, C. Localized boundary knot method and its application to large-scale acoustic problems. *Comput. Methods Appl. Mech. Eng.* **2020**, *361*, 112729. [CrossRef]
45. Xiong, J.; Wen, J.; Liu, Y.C. Localized boundary knot method for solving two-dimensional Laplace and Bi-Harmonic equations. *Mathematics* **2020**, *8*, 1218. [CrossRef]

mathematics

MDPI

Article

"Mixed" Meshless Time-Domain Adaptive Algorithm for Solving Elasto-Dynamics Equations

Maoxiong Liao, Tao Zhang * and Jinggu Cao

School of Mechatronical Engineering, Beijing Institute of Technology, Beijing 100081, China; maoxiong.liao@gmail.com (M.L.); 3120190207@bit.edu.cn (J.C.)
* Correspondence: taozhang@bit.edu.cn

Abstract: A time-domain adaptive algorithm was developed for solving elasto-dynamics problems through a mixed meshless local Petrov-Galerkin finite volume method (MLPG5). In this time-adaptive algorithm, each time-dependent variable is interpolated by a time series function of n-order, which is determined by a criterion in each step. The high-order series of expanded variables bring high accuracy in the time domain, especially for the elasto-dynamic equations, which are second-order PDE in the time domain. In the present mixed MLPG5 dynamic formulation, the strains are interpolated independently, as are displacements in the local weak form, which eliminates the expensive differential of the shape function. In the traditional MLPG5, both shape function and its derivative for each node need to be calculated. By taking the Heaviside function as the test function, the local domain integration of stiffness matrix is avoided. Several numerical examples, including the comparison of our method, the MLPG5–Newmark method and FEM (ANSYS) are given to demonstrate the advantages of the presented method: (1) a large time step can be used in solving a elasto-dynamics problem; (2) computational efficiency and accuracy are improved in both space and time; (3) smaller support sizes can be used in the mixed MLPG5.

Keywords: meshless local Petrov-Galerkin approach (MLPG); finite volume methods; mixed methods; adaptive algorithm; time-domain; moving least squares (MLS)

MSC: 74H15

Citation: Liao, M.; Zhang, T.; Cao, J. "Mixed" Meshless Time-Domain Adaptive Algorithm for Solving Elasto-Dynamics Equations. *Mathematics* **2022**, *10*, 1722. https://doi.org/10.3390/math10101722

Academic Editors: Zhuojia Fu, Yiqian He and Hui Zheng

Received: 16 March 2022
Accepted: 13 May 2022
Published: 18 May 2022

1. Introduction

Structural vibration analysis is an important system dynamics problem in engineering. This dynamics problem is governed by partial differential equations of elasto-dynamics associated with a group of boundary conditions and initial conditions. The elasto-dynamics equation is a second-order PDE in both time and space domains. Exact analyses are usually very difficult, and only few analytical solutions are obtained [1]. Therefore, numerical methods have been developed to solve these complex problems, such as the finite difference method (FDM) [2], the stepwise integration method [3], the Newmark method [4], the Wilson-θ method and the Houbolt method [5] for the time domain; and the FDM [6], the finite element method (FEM) [7], the boundary element method (BEM) [8–11], the differential quadrature method (DQM) [12] and the meshless methods (MMs) [2] for the space domain.

Since the dynamics equation of vibration is a high-order partial differential equation in the time domain, many efforts have been made studying the time-domain methods [13]. Thus, the methods that are commonly used in solving vibration problems can be divided into two categories: mode superposition methods and direct integration methods. In a mode superposition method, the computational cost comes from solving the n-order generalized eigenvalue problem. If the structure vibrates in a short period, this method is less efficient than a direct integration method. In contrast, if the vibration lasts for some time, it is more effective to use the mode superposition method. In the direct integration method, the dynamics equation is directly solved by integration of, e.g., the FDM [2], the Newmark method [4], the Wilson-θ method or the Houbolt method [5]. In these methods, the computational cost in one time step is proportional to the product of the freedom degrees and the square of the average bandwidth of the matrix. All variables are usually constant or linear in every time step, which may lead to inefficient calculation, incomplete accuracy and even divergent results if the time step is selected improperly [14].

To improve the computing accuracy and reduce the error caused by an improper time step size, the time-domain adaptive algorithm was proposed by Haitian. Y. It is an unconditionally stable direct integration method [15]. Differently from the difference method [16], all the time-dependent variables are expanded into series in discrete time steps, and the expansion coefficients can be obtained by solving the recursive equation. Therefore, the variables in each discrete time step can be more accurately described without any assumptions made for nonlinearity. Since the computing accuracy can be controlled by the truncation error, the time step size can be freely selected in a large range. This means large time steps are allowed in the time domain. This method has been successfully used together with FEM in a large time step and has shown advantages in terms of calculation accuracy [17].

Besides the discretization in the time domain, the elasto-dynamics equations also need to be discretized in the space domain. Although the FEM is the most widely used method for structure vibration analysis in engineering, it still encounters many challenges due to the mesh distortion and remeshing when solving large deformation problems, such as high-speed impact, dynamic crack propagation and strain localization [18]. However, these disadvantages of the FEM can be avoided in MMs, as they do not need elements. Over the past two decades, some efforts were devoted to solving the elasto-dynamics equations with MMs [2].

Speaking of MMs, Atluri proposed the meshless local Petrov-Galerkin Method (MLPG) to avoid the background mesh [19]. In this method, the idea of eliminating residuals in the subdomain was firstly proposed. When combined with the moving least squares (MLS) approximation, a true meshless method is realized which does not need interpolation mesh or integral mesh [20]. Since the MLPG method establishes a residual equation on each subdomain separately, the equations from different subdomains are relatively independent, so different weighted residual methods can be easily mixed and used. Additionally, it provides a good platform for the coupling of various methods [21]. Nowadays, the MLPG is a general term for a series of methods (MLPG1–MLPG6) [22]. Nevertheless, MLPG has the problem of low efficiency. An effective way to overcome this shortcoming is to eliminate or simplify the domain integral in the stiffness matrix. In the above six methods, MLPG2, MLPG4 and MLPG5 have no domain integrals. However, MLPG2 relies too much on the configuration of nodes, and MLPG4 has singular integrals. Only MLPG5 includes neither domain integration in the stiffness matrix nor singularity integration, along with only local boundary integrals. Therefore, the MLPG5 is an attractive method that has high computational efficiency [23]. In this paper, MLPG5 is developed for solving elasto-dynamics equations through a "mixed" approach. Independent meshless approximations are used for both strains and displacements. The strain-displacement compatibility is enforced at nodal points by using the collocation method; thus, the independent nodal strains are expressed in terms of nodal displacements. The "mixed" approach eliminates the expensive process of differentiating the shape function, which greatly increases the computational efficiency.

In this paper, attention is devoted to the meshless time-domain adaptive method for structural vibration analyses of two-dimensional solids. Local weak forms are developed using the weighted residual method from the elasto-dynamics equations. In Section 2, the MLS approximation is introduced to establish shape functions for a set of regularly or randomly distributed nodes, and the Heaviside function is used as a test function. In Section 3, all the time related-variables are expanded in every time step, and then the spatiotemporally coupled dynamics equations are converted into a series of recursively solved spatial problems. In Section 4, the validity and accuracy of the proposed method are verified by several numerical examples.

2. Moving Least Square (MLS) Approximation

The moving least square (MLS) interpolation is generally considered to be one of the best schemes with which to interpolate random data with a reasonable accuracy, because of its completeness, robustness and continuity [24]. In this section, a briefing of MLS approximation is given. Consider a local sub-domain Ω_s, which is the neighborhood of a point $\boldsymbol{X} = [x, y]$. The distribution of a function u can be approximated, over a number of scattered local points $\{x_i\}$, $(i = 1, 2, \ldots, n)$, as

$$u(\boldsymbol{X}) \approx u^h(\boldsymbol{X}) = \sum_{j=1}^{m} p_j(\boldsymbol{X}) a_j(\boldsymbol{X}) = \boldsymbol{p}^T(\boldsymbol{X}) \boldsymbol{a}(\boldsymbol{X}) \tag{1}$$

where $\boldsymbol{p}(\boldsymbol{X})$ is a monomial basis function of order m. In two dimensions, it is given by

$$\boldsymbol{p}^T(\boldsymbol{X}) = \left[1, x, y, x^2, xy, y^2, \ldots\right] \tag{2}$$

The vector $\boldsymbol{a}(\boldsymbol{X})$ containing coefficients are functions of the global Cartesian coordinates, depending on the monomial basis. They are determined by minimizing a weighted discrete L_2 norm, defined as:

$$J = \sum_{i=1}^{n} \hat{W}(\boldsymbol{X} - \boldsymbol{X}_i) \left[\boldsymbol{p}^T(\boldsymbol{X}_i) \boldsymbol{a}(\boldsymbol{X}) - u_i\right]^2 \tag{3}$$

where $\hat{W}$ are the weight functions and u_i are the fictitious nodal values.

The stationarity of J in Equation (3) with respect to $\boldsymbol{a}(\boldsymbol{X})$ leads to the following relationship:

$$\boldsymbol{a}(\boldsymbol{X}) = \boldsymbol{A}^{-1}(\boldsymbol{X}) \boldsymbol{B}(\boldsymbol{X}) \boldsymbol{U}_s \tag{4}$$

Substituting $\boldsymbol{a}(\boldsymbol{X})$ into Equation (1), we have

$$u^h(\boldsymbol{X}) = \sum_{i=1}^{n} \phi_i(\boldsymbol{X}) u_i \tag{5}$$

where the MLS shape function $\phi_i(\boldsymbol{X})$ can be defined as:

$$\phi_i(\boldsymbol{X}) = \sum_{j=1}^{m} p_j(\boldsymbol{X}) \left(\boldsymbol{A}^{-1}(\boldsymbol{X}) \boldsymbol{B}(\boldsymbol{X})\right)_{ji} = \boldsymbol{p}^T(\boldsymbol{X}) \left(\boldsymbol{A}^{-1} \boldsymbol{B}\right)_i \tag{6}$$

where $\boldsymbol{A}(\boldsymbol{x})$ and $\boldsymbol{B}(\boldsymbol{x})$ are defined by

$$\boldsymbol{A}(\boldsymbol{X}) = \sum_{i=1}^{n} \hat{W}(\boldsymbol{X} - \boldsymbol{X}_i) p(X_i) \boldsymbol{p}(\boldsymbol{X}) \boldsymbol{p}^T(\boldsymbol{X}_i) = \sum_{i=1}^{n} \hat{W}(\boldsymbol{X} - \boldsymbol{X}_i) \begin{bmatrix} 1 & x_i & y_i \\ x_i & x_i^2 & x_i y_i \\ y_i & x_i y_i & y_i^2 \end{bmatrix} \tag{7}$$

$$\boldsymbol{B}(\boldsymbol{X}) = [W_1(\boldsymbol{X}) \boldsymbol{p}(\boldsymbol{X}_1), W_2(\boldsymbol{X}) \boldsymbol{p}(\boldsymbol{X}_2), \ldots, W_n(\boldsymbol{X}) \boldsymbol{p}(\boldsymbol{X}_n)] \tag{8}$$

The weight function is very important for the MLS interpolation, because the smoothness of the shape function and its derivatives depends on the order of the weight function. In two-dimensional problems, discontinuities in derivatives can be produced if the order of the spline is not sufficient, and unwanted oscillations in nodal shape functions are produced when a high order of spline function is used. It has been found that the best nodal shape function and its first derivative come from 4th order spline function [25]. Thus, in this paper, the following 4-order spline function is used:

$$\hat{W}_i(\mathbf{X}) = \begin{cases} 1 - 6\left(\frac{d_i}{r_w}\right)^2 + 8\left(\frac{d_i}{r_w}\right)^3 - 3\left(\frac{d_i}{r_w}\right)^4 & 0 \le d_i \le r_w \\ 0 & d_i > r_w \end{cases} \tag{9}$$

where $d_i = |\boldsymbol{x}_Q - \boldsymbol{x}_i|$ is the distance from node $\boldsymbol{x}_i$ to the sampling point $\boldsymbol{x}_Q$, and r_w is the support size for the weight function.

3. Recursive Governing Equations

3.1. Recursive Elasto-Dynamics Equations

Consider a linear elastic body in a 2D domain Ω, with a boundary Γ, shown in Figure 1. The solid is assumed to undergo infinitesimal deformations. The governing differential equation for small displacement elasto-dynamics can be written as:

$$\sigma_{ij,j} + b_i - \rho\ddot{u}_i - c\dot{u}_i = 0; \quad \sigma_{ij} = \sigma_{ji} \tag{10}$$

where σ_{ij} is the stress tensor, which corresponds to the displacement field u_i; b_i is the body force; ρ is the mass density; c is the damping coefficient; $\dot{u}_i = \frac{\partial u_i}{\partial t}$ is the velocity; $\ddot{u}_i = \frac{\partial^2 u_i}{\partial t^2}$ is the acceleration.

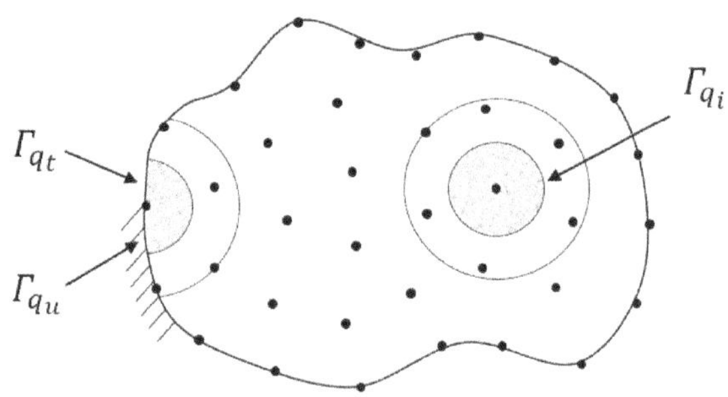

Figure 1. Local domains and boundaries of MLPG.

The boundary conditions are given as follows,

$$u_i = \tilde{u}_i \qquad on\ \Gamma_u \tag{11}$$

$$t_i \equiv n_i\sigma_{ij} = \tilde{p}_i \quad on\ \Gamma_t \tag{12}$$

where $\overline{u}_i$ and $\overline{t}_i$ are the prescribed displacements and tractions, respectively, on the displacement boundary Γ_u and on the traction boundary Γ_t; and n_i is the unit outward normal to the boundaryΓ. The initial conditions are defined by

$$\boldsymbol{u}(\mathbf{X}, t_0) = \boldsymbol{u}_{in}(\mathbf{X}) \quad \mathbf{X} \in \Omega \tag{13}$$

$$\dot{\boldsymbol{u}}(\mathbf{X}, t_0) = \boldsymbol{v}_{in}(\mathbf{X}) \quad \mathbf{X} \in \Omega \tag{14}$$

With $\boldsymbol{u}_{in}$ and $\boldsymbol{v}_{in}$ being the initial displacements and velocities at the initial time t_0, respectively.

To improve the computing accuracy, exploiting a discretized expanding technique is of interest. At each discretized time subdomain, all variables can be described as

$$\sigma = \sum_{m=0} \sigma_m s^m \tag{15}$$

$$\varepsilon = \sum_{m=0} \varepsilon_m s^m \tag{16}$$

$$c = \sum_{m=0} c_m s^m \tag{17}$$

$$b = \sum_{m=0} b_m s^m \tag{18}$$

$$u = \sum_{m=0} u_m s^m \tag{19}$$

$$\widetilde{u} = \sum_{m=0} \widetilde{u}_m s^m \tag{20}$$

$$\widetilde{p} = \sum_{m=0} \widetilde{p}_m s^m \tag{21}$$

$$s = \frac{t - t_{k-1}}{T_k} \tag{22}$$

where t_{k-1} and T_k represent the beginning time and size of time step, respectively; $\widetilde{u}$ and $\widetilde{p}$ represent the prescribed displacement and traction on the boundary, respectively; and σ_m, ε_m, c_m, b_m, u_m, $\widetilde{u}_m$, p_m and $\widetilde{p}_m$ are the expanding coefficients of σ, ε, c, b, u, $\widetilde{u}$, p and $\widetilde{p}$, respectively.

The derivative with respect to t can be written in the form

$$\frac{d}{dt} = \frac{1}{T_k}\frac{d}{ds} \tag{23}$$

Substitute Equations (15), (18) and (19) into Equation (10), and obtain

$$\sum_{m=0} \sigma_{mij,j} s^m + \sum_{m=0} b_{mi} s^m - \rho \sum_{m=0} \frac{(m+2)(m+1)}{T_k^2} u_{m+2i} s^m - c \sum_{m=0} \frac{m+1}{T_k} u_{m+1i} s^m = 0 \tag{24}$$

Equate every power of s^m, $m = 1,2,3\ldots$, and obtain

$$\sigma_{mij,j} + b_{mi} - \rho \frac{(m+2)(m+1)}{T_k^2} u_{m+2i} - c\frac{m+1}{T_k} u_{m+1i} = 0 \tag{25}$$

Equation (25) is the recursive governing equation by the time-domain adaptive method.

In the first time step, u_0 and u_1 are the initial conditions of displacement u and velocity $\dot{u}$, which can be described as:

$$u_0 = u(X,0) \tag{26}$$

$$u_1 = \dot{u}(X,0)T_k \tag{27}$$

Then, u_m can be obtained by solving Equation (37) iteratively. In the $(m+1)$th time step, the displacement and velocity can be obtained by:

$$u_{n+1} = \sum_{m=0}^{n} u_{m_k} \tag{28}$$

$$\dot{u}_{n+1} = \frac{1}{T_k}\sum_{m=0}^{n} m u_{m_k} \tag{29}$$

In each time step, the expanded order m could be obtained adaptively from the following criteria:

$$\frac{||u_m s^m||_2}{||\sum_0^{m-1} u_m s^m||_2} \leq \beta \tag{30}$$

where β is an error bound (for example $\beta = 10^{-6}$)-; $||\ ||_2$ represents the 2-norm of the matrix.

3.2. Numerical Implementation of MLPG5

In the MLPG approaches, one may write a weak form over a local sub-domain Ω_s, which can be: (1) a circle, (2) an ellipse, (3) a rectangle or any other regular or irregular shape. A generalized local weak form of the differential Equation (25) over a local sub-domain Ω_s can be written as:

$$\int_{\Omega_q} W_I(\sigma_{mij,j} + b_{mi} - \rho\frac{(m+2)(m+1)}{T_k^2}u_{m+2i} - c\frac{m+1}{T_k}u_{m+1i})d\Omega = 0 \tag{31}$$

where W_I is the test function. In mixed MLPG5, the Heaviside function is used as the test function in the local weak form. It is defined as:

$$W_I = \begin{cases} 1 & inside\ \Omega_q \\ 0 & outside\ \Omega_q \end{cases} \tag{32}$$

By substituting Equation (32) into Equation (31) and applying the divergence theorem, Equation (31) may be rewritten in a symmetric weak form as:

$$\int_{\Omega_q}\left(\rho\frac{(m+2)(m+1)}{T_k^2}u_{m+2i} + c\frac{m+1}{T_k}u_{m+1i}\right)d\Omega - \int_{\Gamma_{qi}}\sigma_{mij}n_j d\Gamma - \int_{\Gamma_{qu}}\sigma_{mij}n_j d\Gamma = \int_{\Gamma_{qt}}\sigma_{mij}n_j d\Gamma + \int_{\Omega_q} b_{mi}d\Omega \tag{33}$$

where Γ_{qi} is a part of the local boundary, which is inside the solution domain; Γ_{qu} is the intersection between the local boundary and the global displacement boundary; and Γ_{qt} is a part of the boundary over which the natural boundary conditions are specified, as shown in Figure 1.

In this paper, it is assumed that the body force is zero. By substituting the Equation (12) into Equation (33), we have:

$$\int_{\Omega_q}\left(\rho\frac{(m+2)(m+1)}{T_k^2}u_{m+2i} + c\frac{m+1}{T_k}u_{m+1i}\right)d\Omega - \int_{\Gamma_{qi}} t_{m_i}d\Gamma - \int_{\Gamma_{qu}} t_{m_i}d\Gamma = \int_{\Gamma_{qt}} \widetilde{p}_{m_i}d\Gamma \tag{34}$$

with the constitutive relations of an isotropic linear elastic homogeneous solid, the tractions in Equation (34) can be written in terms of the strains:

$$t_{m_i} = \boldsymbol{n}\boldsymbol{\sigma_m} = \boldsymbol{n}\boldsymbol{D}\boldsymbol{\varepsilon_m} \tag{35}$$

$$\boldsymbol{\varepsilon_m} = \boldsymbol{L}\boldsymbol{u_m} \tag{36}$$

where

$$\boldsymbol{n} = \begin{bmatrix} n_x & 0 & n_y \\ 0 & n_y & n_x \end{bmatrix} \tag{37}$$

$$\boldsymbol{D} = \frac{E}{1-\nu^2}\begin{bmatrix} 1 & \nu & 0 \\ \nu & 1 & 0 \\ 0 & 0 & \frac{1-\nu}{2} \end{bmatrix} \quad for\ plane\ stress \tag{38}$$

In the mixed MLPG5 method, the interpolation of nodal displacements $\boldsymbol{u_{m_i}}$ and strains ε_{m_i} can be accomplished by using the shape function mentioned in Section 2, as

$$u_m^h(X) = \sum_{k=1}^{n}\phi_k(X)u_{m_k} = \boldsymbol{\Phi U_m} \tag{39}$$

$$\varepsilon_m^h(X) = \sum_{k=1}^{n}\phi_k(X)\varepsilon_{m_k} = \boldsymbol{\Phi\varepsilon_m} \tag{40}$$

where $\boldsymbol{\Phi}$ is the shape function matrix; and $\boldsymbol{U_m}$ and $\boldsymbol{\varepsilon_m}$ are the vector of virtual nodal displacement and strain, respectively.

With Equations (35)–(40), one may discretize the local symmetric weak-form of Equation (34), as:

$$\frac{(m+2)(m+1)}{T_k^2}\int_{\Omega_q}\rho\mathbf{\Phi}d\Omega\mathbf{U}_{m+2}+\frac{m+1}{T_k}\int_{\Omega_q}c\mathbf{\Phi}d\Omega\mathbf{U}_{m+1}-\int_{\Gamma_{qi}}\mathbf{nD\Phi}d\Gamma(\mathbf{L\Phi U}_m)-\int_{\Gamma_{qu}}\mathbf{nD\Phi}d\Gamma(\mathbf{L\Phi U}_m)=\int_{\Gamma_{qt}}\widetilde{\mathbf{p}}_m d\Gamma \tag{41}$$

Obviously, it can be found that no derivatives of the shape functions are involved in the local integrals. While both shape function and its derivative at each point need to be calculated in the traditional MLPG, which greatly increases the computing cost. The final system equation can be rewritten in a matrix form:

$$\frac{(m+2)(m+1)}{T_k^2}\mathbf{MU}_{m+2}+\frac{m+1}{T_k}\mathbf{CU}_{m+1}-\mathbf{KU}_m=\mathbf{F} \tag{42}$$

where $\mathbf{M}$, $\mathbf{C}$, $\mathbf{K}$ and $\mathbf{F}$ are the matrixes of mass, damping and stiffness, and the vector of force, respectively. They are defined as follows.

$$\mathbf{M}=\rho\int_{\Omega_q}\mathbf{\Phi}d\Omega=\rho\mathbf{S} \tag{43}$$

$$\mathbf{C}=c\int_{\Omega_q}\mathbf{\Phi}d\Omega=c\mathbf{S} \tag{44}$$

$$\mathbf{F}=\int_{\Gamma_{qt}}\widetilde{\mathbf{p}}_m d\Gamma \tag{45}$$

$$\mathbf{K}=\int_{\Gamma_{qi}}\mathbf{nD\Phi}d\Gamma(\mathbf{L\Phi})+\int_{\Gamma_{qu}}\mathbf{nD\Phi}d\Gamma(\mathbf{L\Phi}) \tag{46}$$

Once nonlinear damping is introduced, the system equation can be rewritten in another form:

$$\frac{(m+2)(m+1)}{T_k^2}\mathbf{MU}_{m+2}+\frac{c_0(m+1)}{T_k}\mathbf{SU}_{m+1}+\left(\frac{c_1 m}{T_k}\mathbf{S}-\mathbf{K}\right)\mathbf{U}_m=\mathbf{F} \tag{47}$$

where c_0 and c_1 represent the expanding coefficients of damping coefficient c.

In the present study, the Gauss quadrature is used for the subdomain integration in Equations (43)–(46).

3.3. Natural Frequency Solved by Mixed MLPG5

The natural frequencies and corresponding mode shapes are often referred to as the dynamic characteristics of the structure. While the mass matrix $\mathbf{M}$ and the stiffness matrix $\mathbf{K}$ in the vibration system are obtained from Equation (42), the elasto-dynamics equation of the undamped system can be written as a typical eigenvalue equation as follows:

$$\lambda=eig\left(\mathbf{M}^{-1}\mathbf{K}\right) \tag{48}$$

where λ is the vector of eigenvalues. Finally, the natural frequency can be solved by:

$$f_i=\frac{\sqrt{\lambda_i}}{2\pi} \tag{49}$$

4. Numerical Examples

4.1. Free Vibration Analysis

Example 1: A Variable-Cross-Section Beam

In this example, the presented method is used in free vibration analysis of a cantilever beam with a variable cross-section, as shown in Figure 2. The problem is solved for the plane stress case with the following parameters: the length $L = 10$ m, the height $H1 = 5$ m,

$H2 = 3$ m, the density $\rho = 1$ kg/m^3, the Young's modulus $E = 3 \times 10^7$ Pa and the Poisson ratio $\nu = 0.3$.

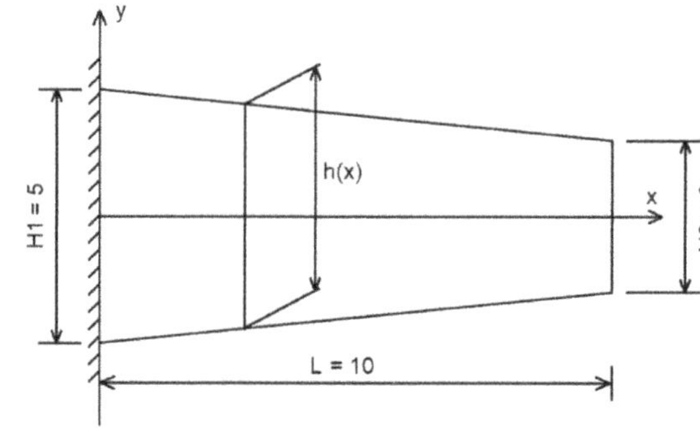

Figure 2. A cantilever beam with a variable cross-section.

Regular and irregular nodal configurations were used, as shown in Figure 3. For comparison, the problem was also analyzed by FEM software ANSYS (Mechanical). Additionally, the number of nodes used in ANSYS was 3978, which is 13 times more that used in the presented method.

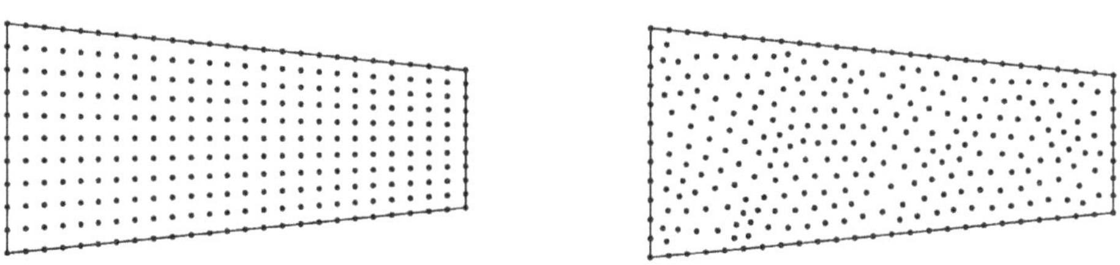

(**a**) (**b**)

Figure 3. Nodal configuration for a variable-cross-section beam. (**a**) regular nodal distribution; (**b**) irregular nodal distribution.

The natural frequencies of the first five modes were calculated by the presented mixed MLPG method and the FEM software, as listed in Table 1. It can be seen that the natural frequencies obtained by the presented method are in good agreement with that of ANSYS, whether a regular or random node distribution is used.

Table 1. Comparison of the natural frequencies of the variable-cross-section beam obtained by the meshless algorithm and ANSYS (FEM).

Mode	Mixed MLPG5 Regular		Mixed MLPG5 Random		ANSYS (FEM) (Hz)
	Frequency (Hz)	Relative Error (%)	Frequency (Hz)	Relative Error (%)	
1	42.65	2.45	42.37	1.78	41.63
2	145.57	0.36	147.43	0.92	146.09
3	153.44	1.27	153.88	1.56	151.51
4	293.04	0.64	293.52	0.48	294.94
5	412.59	0.30	414.02	0.64	411.37

The first four eigenmodes obtained with the present mixed MLPG5 method are plotted in Figure 4. Compared with the FEM results obtained by ANSYS, the results are identical. As fewer nodes are used, the presented method has higher computational efficiency.

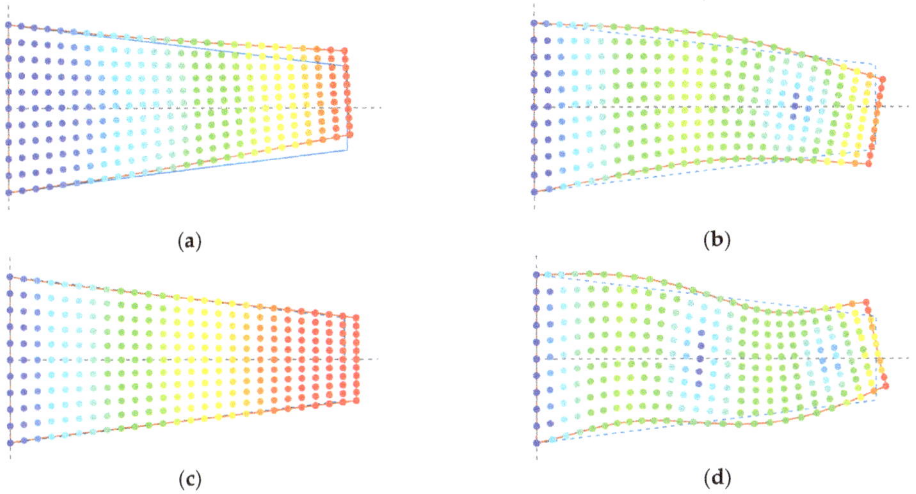

Figure 4. Eigenmodes for the variable-cross-section beam by the mixed MLPG5 method. (a) Mode 1; (b) mode 2; (c) mode 3; (d) mode 4.

4.2. Forced Vibration Analysis

Example 2: A cantilever beam with horizontal traction.

In the second example, the forced vibration analysis of a 2D cantilever beam is considered, as shown in Figure 5. The parameters are taken as, length $L = 20$ m, width $D = 4$ m, Young's modulus $E = 1 \times 10^5$ Pa, Poisson ratio $\nu = 0.3$, density $\rho = 1\ \mathrm{kg/m^3}$ and damping coefficient $c = 1$ Ns/m. The initial conditions are defined as:

$$u_0 = u_{in}(\mathbf{X}, 0) = 0 \tag{50}$$

$$u_1 = \dot{u}_{in}(\mathbf{X}, 0) = 0 \tag{51}$$

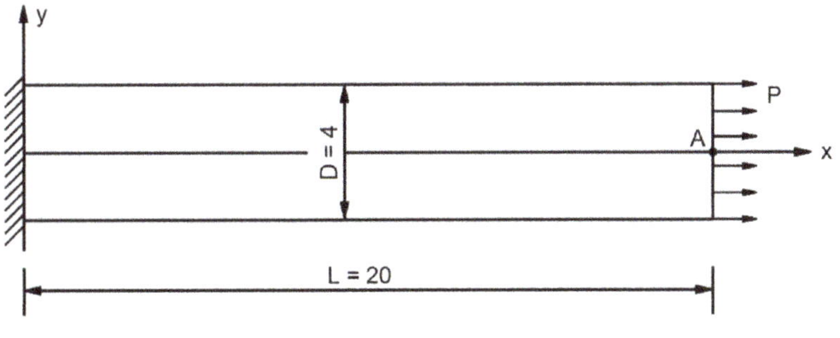

Figure 5. A cantilever beam subjected to horizontal traction.

The transient response of the beam subjected to a suddenly loaded traction P = 300 Pa is considered. A regular uniform nodal configuration is used with nodal distances $d = 1$ m, as shown in Figure 6.

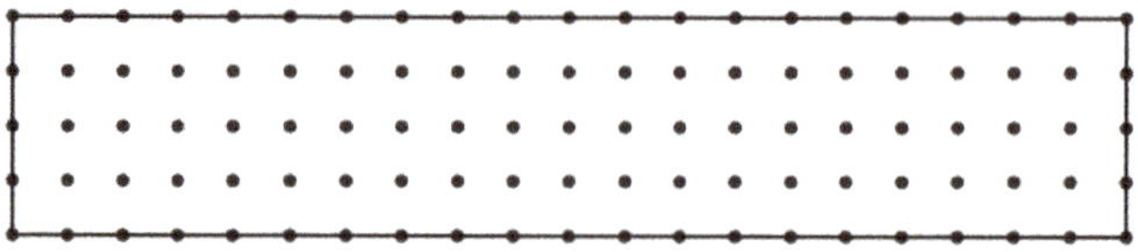

Figure 6. The nodal distribution for a cantilever beam.

The presented method was used to obtain the transient response. The Newmark method and the present time-adaptive method were utilized in this analysis. The results of time steps $\Delta t = 0.001,\ 0.002,\ 0.005,\ 0.01,\ 0.02$ s were obtained. For comparison, solutions for this problem were also obtained using the FEM software ANSYS (Mechanical).

The horizontal displacement u_x at point A of different time steps by the Newmark method is plotted in Figure 7. Additionally, the parameters $\beta = 0.3$ and $\gamma = 0.6$ were used. One can observe that for $\Delta t = 0.001$ s, the results are in good agreement with FEM. However, it should be noted that the computational error would increase with the increase in time step in the Newmark method due to the dissipation and dispersion errors. When the time step is too large (e.g., $\Delta t = 0.02$ s), the accuracy would become unacceptable. Thus, a straightforward way of reducing the dispersion and dissipation error in Newmark method is to use a smaller time step size.

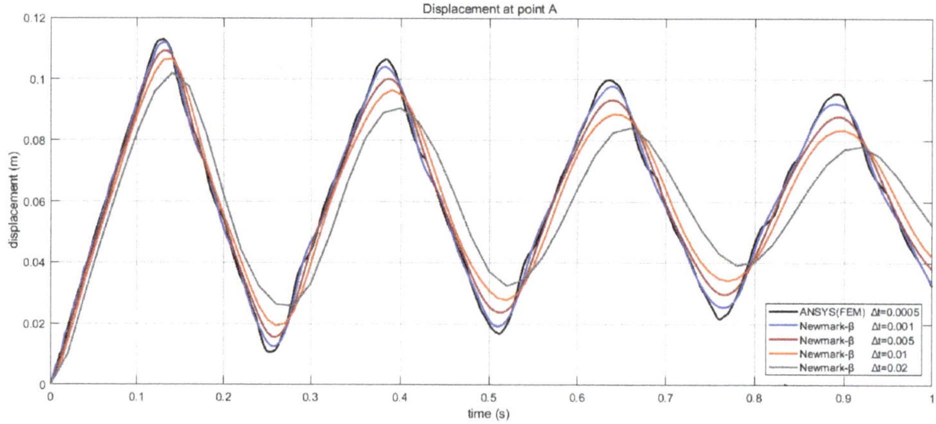

Figure 7. Displacements u_x at point A using Newmark method with different time steps. ($\alpha = 0.3$, $\beta = 0.6$, 105 nodes with nodal distance $d = 1.0$ m).

The horizontal displacement u_x at point A for different time steps via the time-adaptive method is plotted in Figure 8. As the results are quite close to the reference solution when the time steps are 0.001, 0.002 and 0.005 s, it is hard to distinguish them on the figure. Only the results of the time steps $\Delta t = 0.01,\ 0.02,\ 0.04$ s are plotted in Figure 8. It can be found that all the results obtained by time-adaptive methods are in good agreement with FEM, even if the time step is very large and the peak of displacement cannot be accurately obtained. Since high-order expansion in each time step is adopted in a time-domain adaptive method, a high precision result can be obtained by this time-adaptive method.

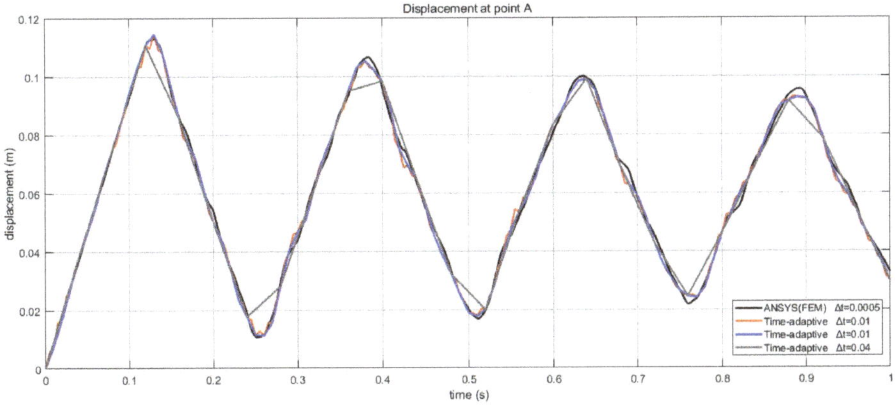

Figure 8. Displacements u_x at point A using a time-adaptive method with different time steps (105 nodes with nodal distance $d = 1.0$ m).

The calculation time and relative error at point A obtained by the two methods at different time steps are shown in Table 2. One can observe that the computing time of the Newmark method is less than that of our method, which shows that efficiency of Newmark method is higher at any sized time step. Although not as fast as the Newmark method, our method has higher accuracy when a large time step is used. Only when $\Delta t = 0.001$, were the efficiency and accuracy of Newmark method higher than those of our method. However, in engineering, it is difficult to predict the "best time step size." As shown in Table 2, the expansion order would increase with the increase in time step while the relative error would remain unchanged. This is very useful for the forced vibration analysis in engineering applications, especially in long-time response analysis, as a large time step is preferred.

Table 2. The computing time, the order of expanding and the mean relative error at point A for two time-discretization methods.

Method	DeltaT (s)	Computing Time (s)	Order of Expanding	Relative Error at Point A (%)
Newmark	0.001	0.283	/	3.30
	0.002	0.164		3.99
	0.005	0.072		7.45
	0.01	0.042		14.40
	0.02	0.026		27.87
	0.04	0.018		52.91
Adaptive	0.001	1.183	7	3.47
	0.002	0.693	9	3.42
	0.005	0.419	15	3.72
	0.01	0.314	24	3.17
	0.02	0.259	42	3.29
	0.04	0.227	79	3.13

The test-domain size S_t and the support size S_s (or the size of the influence domain) are the key components for the mixed MLPG5 method. Both of them affect the computational efficiency and the accuracy. In the present study, the test domain size and the support size were chosen to be proportional to the nodal distance d.

In practice, the test-domain size is chosen to be less than 1.0 d to ensure that the local sub-domains of the internal nodes are entirely within the solution domain, without being intersected by the global boundary. In the present study, five test-domain sizes were used,

0.4, 0.5, 0.6, 0.7 and 0.8 d. Additionally, the support size was fixed as 1.5 d and the nodal distance was fixed as 1 m. The displacements u_x at point A (shown in Figure 5) were used to examine the effects of the different test-domain size, as shown Figure 9. It can be seen that accuracy is excellent when the test-domain size is less than 0.7 d. It is noticeable that the accuracy would become unacceptable when the test-domain size is larger than 0.8 d, as the sub-domains are obviously over-lapping. Our study has found that the test size $S_t = 0.4 - 0.7$ works for most of forced vibration problems. Additionally, $S_t = 0.6$ was used in the following calculations.

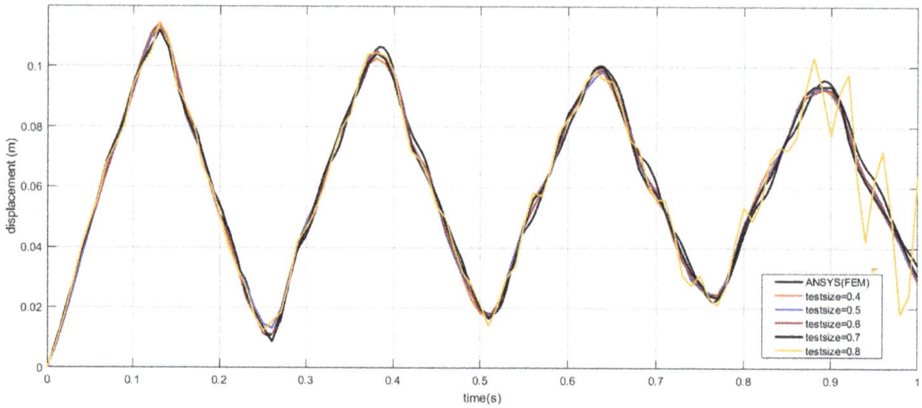

Figure 9. Influence of the test domain size in a cantilever beam under an end load (105 nodes with nodal distance d = 1.0 m, at point A).

For a small support size, the meshless approximation algorithms may be singular, and the shape function cannot be constructed because of too few nodes. In the present study, four support sizes (1.2, 1.5, 1.8 and 2.1 d) were used for the MLPG5 mixed approach. The nodal distance was fixed as 1 m. The displacements u_x at point A (shown in Figure 5) were also used to examine the effects of the support-domain size, as shown in Figure 10.

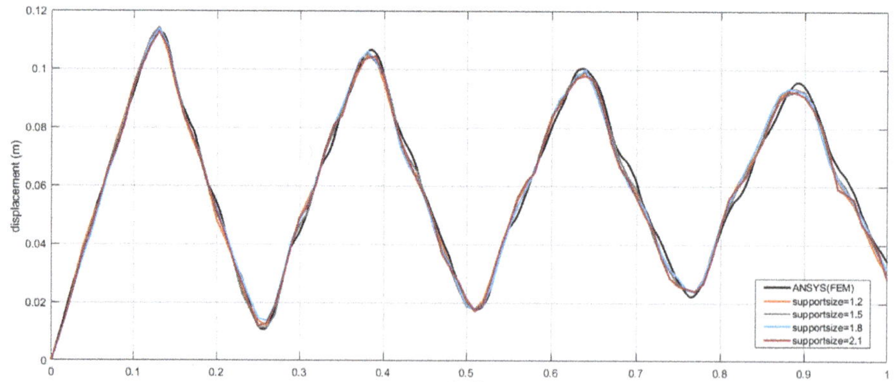

Figure 10. Influence of the support size in a cantilever beam under an end load (105 nodes with nodal distance d = 1.0 m, at point A).

It can be seen that good accuracy is obtained when the support sizes are 1.5 d and 1.8 d. However, the result becomes more unstable when the support size is 2.1 d, as the continuous shape function leads to smoother results but lower accuracy. Our study has found that support sizes of $S_s = 1.2 - 1.8$ work for most of forced vibration problems. Additionally, $S_s = 1.5$ was used in the following calculations.

Example 3: A cantilever beam with vertical traction.

In this example, our method is used to analyze the forced vibration of a cantilever beam subjected to a vertical traction with different damping coefficient, as shown in Figure 11. The problem is solved for the plane stress case with: length $L = 48$ m, width $D = 12$ m, Young's modulus $E = 3 \times 10^7$ Pa, Poisson ratio $\nu = 0.3$ and density $\rho = 1$ kg/m^3. A regular set of 85 scattered nodes with nodal distances d = 3 m is employed here, as shown in Figure 12. The same initial conditions are defined as:

$$u_0 = u_{initial}(\mathbf{X}, 0) = 0 \quad (52)$$

$$u_1 = \dot{u}_{initial}(\mathbf{X}, 0) = 0 \quad (53)$$

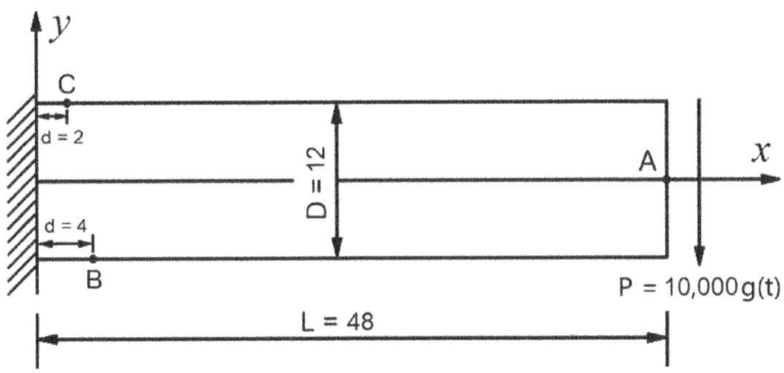

Figure 11. A cantilever beam subjected to a vertical traction.

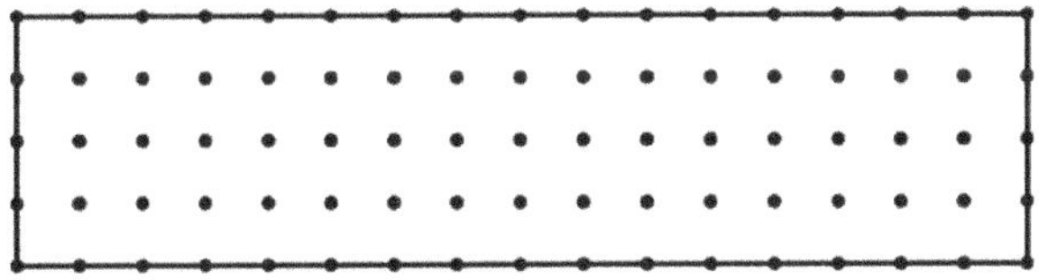

Figure 12. The nodal distribution for a cantilever beam.

Three kinds of traction at the free end of the beam while using $P(x,t) = 10,000$ g(t) N/m are considered in this example: one is a Heaviside step loading, another is a transient loading with a finite decreasing time and the last is a transient loading with a finite increasing time, as shown in Figure 13. Additionally, the g(t) is the time-dependent function. The vertical displacement at point A, and the normal stress at points B and C (shown in Figure 11) were computed. To verify the accuracy of the present algorithm, the problem was also analyzed by FEM software ANSYS (Mechanical), where 2425 nodes (27 times more than our method) were adopted.

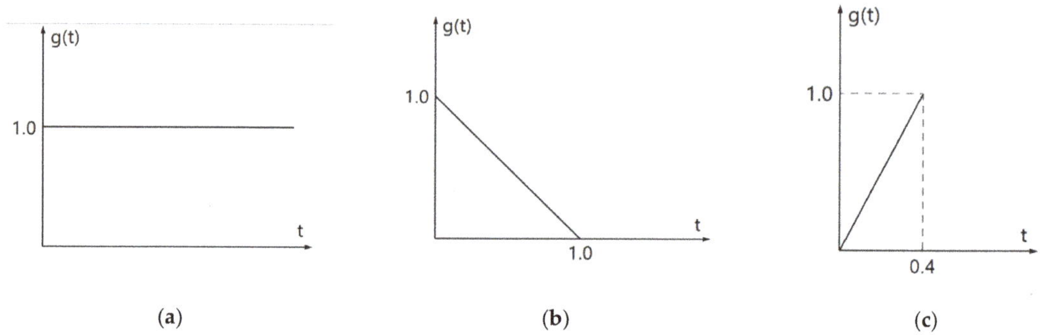

Figure 13. Schematic diagram of dynamic loadings. (**a**) Heaviside step loading with an infinite duration; (**b**) transient loading with a finite decreasing time; (**c**) transient loading with a finite increasing time.

a. Heaviside step loading with an infinite duration

The transient response of the beam subjected to Heaviside step loading with an infinite duration is considered. The loading function is determined by

$$g(t) = 1.0 \tag{54}$$

as shown in Figure 13a. This type of dynamics analysis under impact loading is usually defined as dynamic relaxation [26]. The mixed MLPG5 method was combined with the time-adaptive method and used to obtain the transient response. The displacements u_y of point A with damping coefficients $c = 1,\ 10$ and 20 Ns/m are plotted in Figures 14–16, respectively. It is evident that the response converges to the static deformation ($u_y = 10.682$ m, obtained by ANSYS) once a damping is introduced, and the deformation declines fast with an increase in damping coefficient. All of them are in good agreement with the ANSYS results.

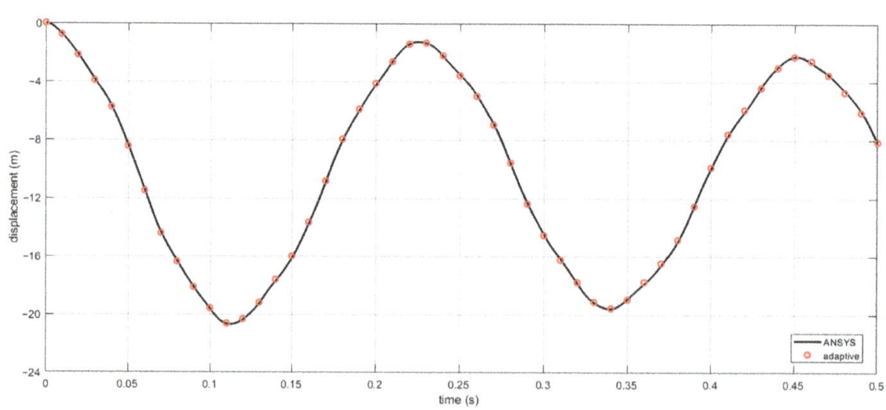

Figure 14. The transient vertical displacement at point A with damping ($c = 1$ Ns/m), $\Delta t = 0.005$ s, under Heaviside step loading with an infinite duration.

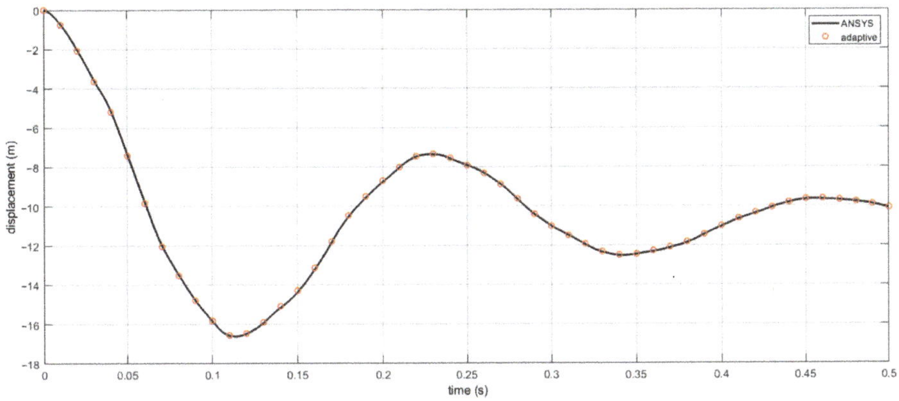

Figure 15. The transient vertical displacement at point A with damping ($c = 10$ Ns/m), $\Delta t = 0.005$ s, under Heaviside step loading with an infinite duration.

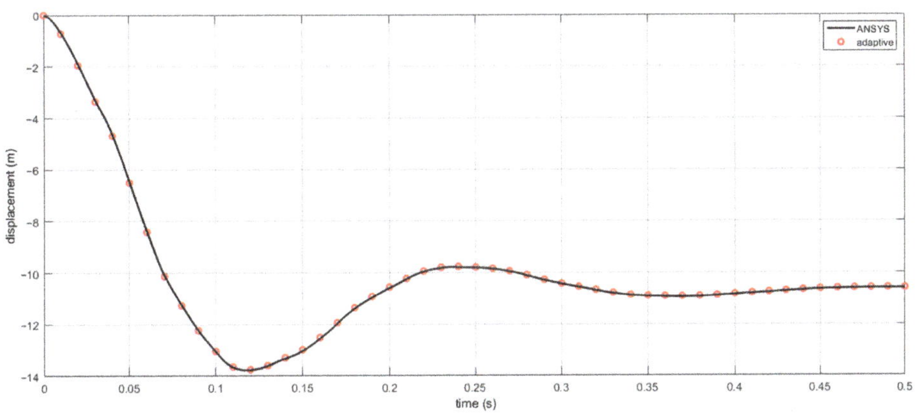

Figure 16. The transient vertical displacement at point A with damping ($c = 20$ Ns/m), $\Delta t = 0.005$ s, under Heaviside step loading with an infinite duration.

In addition, the vertical displacement fields of the deformed cantilever beam at different time steps (t = 0.005, 0.01, and 0.02 s) are shown in Figures 17–19. One can observe that with time, the stress wave propagates from the free end towards the fixed end. Thus, the displacement distribution in elasto-dynamics is quite different from that in static analysis.

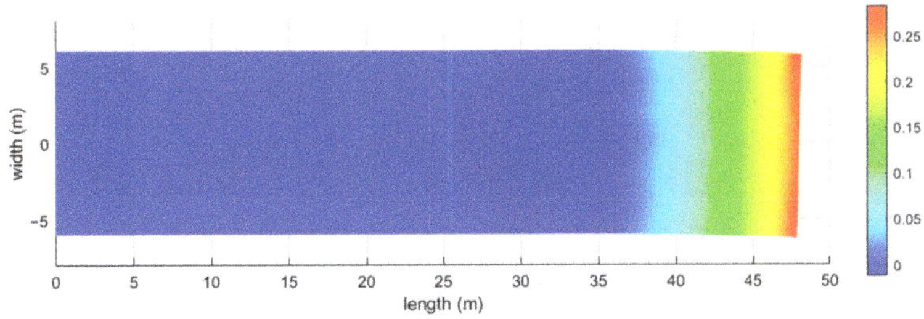

Figure 17. Vertical displacement field of the cantilever beam ($c = 1$ Ns/m, $t = 0.005$ s,), under Heaviside step loading with an infinite duration.

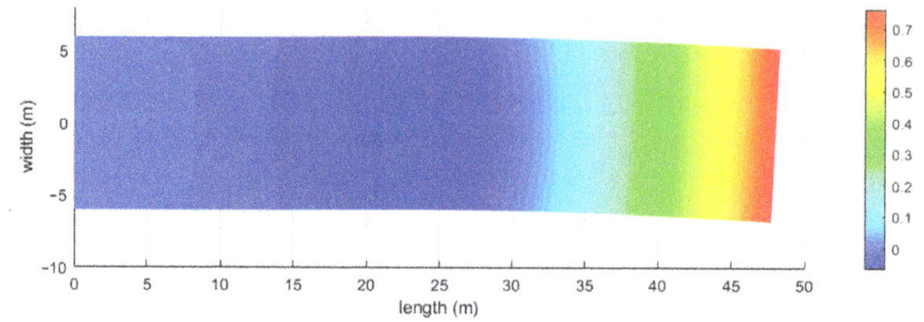

Figure 18. Vertical displacement field of the cantilever beam (c = 1 Ns/m, t = 0.010 s), under Heaviside step loading with an infinite duration.

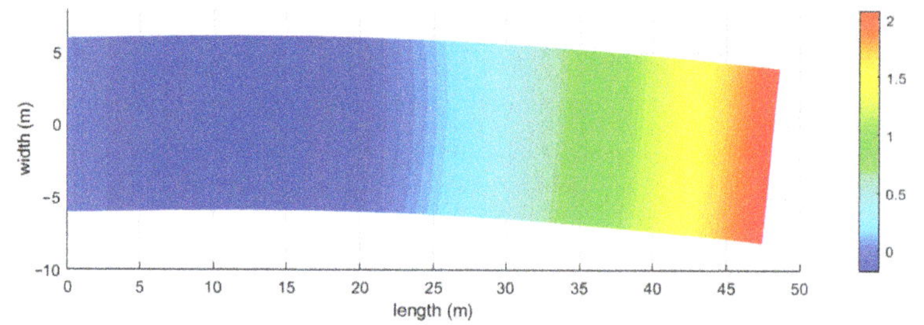

Figure 19. Vertical displacement field of the cantilever beam (c = 1 Ns/m, t = 0.020 s), under Heaviside step loading with an infinite duration.

The normal stress σ_{xx} at point B is shown in Figure 20. The damping coefficient is $c = 1$ Ns/m. It can be seen that the results obtained by Newmark method have larger errors due to the numerical dissipation and dispersion, and the results obtained by our time-adaptive method are in good agreement with those of the reference solution. Thus, our method works very well, and it is more accurate than the Newmark method for the forced vibration analysis.

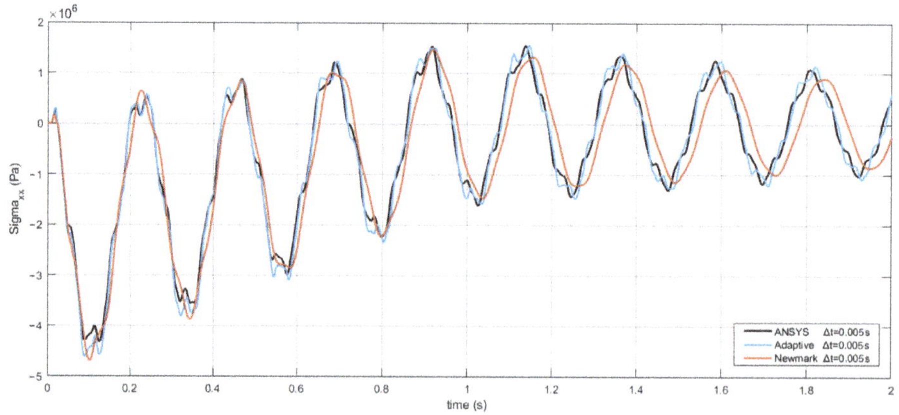

Figure 20. The normal stress σ_{xx} at point B with damping coefficient $c = 1$ Ns/m and $\Delta t = 0.005$ s under Heaviside step loading with an infinite duration.

b. Transient loading with finite decreasing time

The transient response of the beam subjected to a transient loading with a finite decreasing time is considered. The loading function is defined as

$$g(t) = \begin{cases} 1 - t & 0 < t < 1 \\ 0 & t > 1 \end{cases}, \tag{55}$$

as shown in Figure 13b.

The displacements u_y of point A with different damping coefficients are plotted in Figures 21–23. It can be seen that as the damping coefficient increases, the amplitudes decay faster and the duration of vibration is shorter. Very stable results with different damping coefficients were obtained by our method, and they are in good agreement with the results obtained by ANSYS. The computing time with the mixed MLPG5 time-domain adaptive method and ANSYS (FEM) are included in Table 3, for different nodal numbers. Additionally, the time step was fixed to 0.001 s. It also can be seen that our method is more efficient than ANSYS (FEM). From these results, our method shows good approximations to the transient responses of different damps with high efficiency.

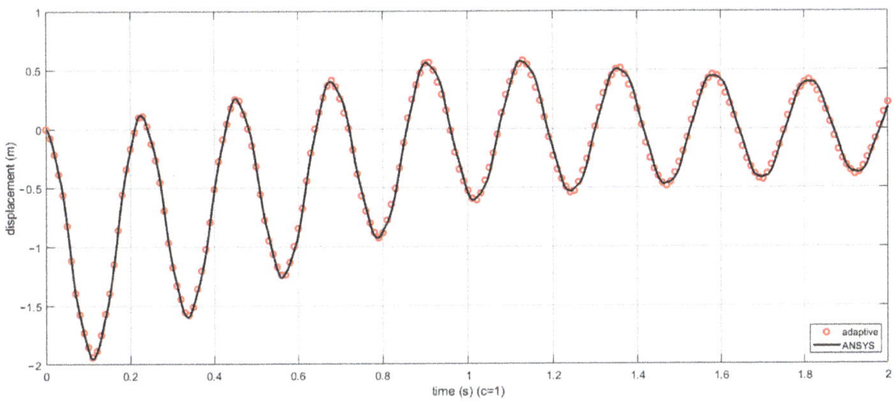

Figure 21. The transient vertical displacement at point A with damping ($c = 1$ Ns/m) and $\Delta t = 0.001$ s under transient loading with finite decreasing time.

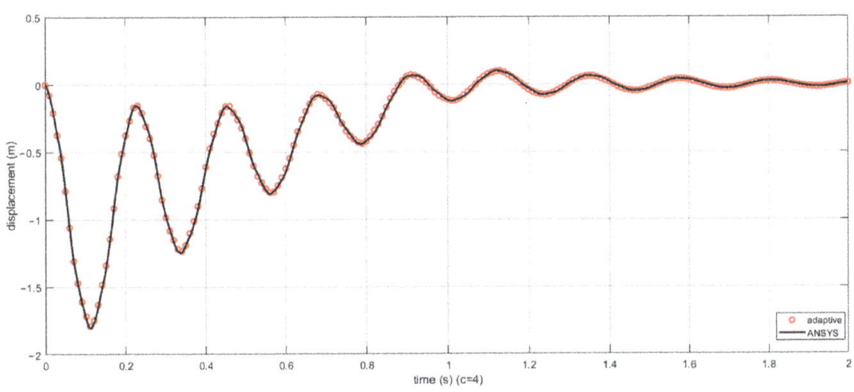

Figure 22. The transient vertical displacement at point A with damping ($c = 4$ Ns/m) and $\Delta t = 0.001$ s under transient loading with finite decreasing time.

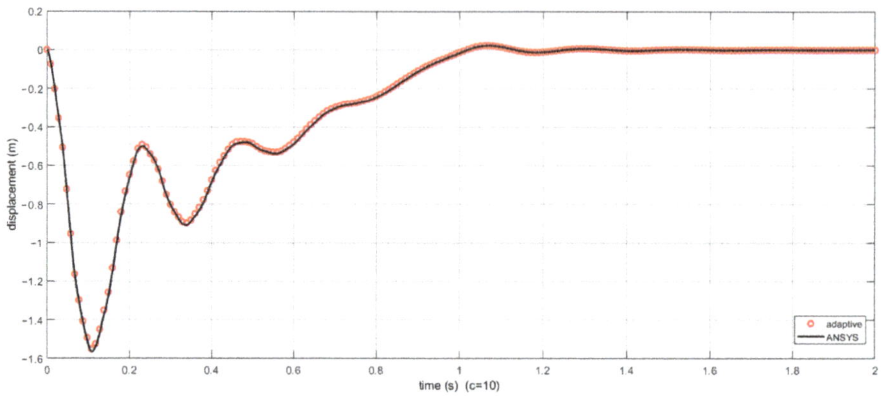

Figure 23. The transient vertical displacement at point A with damping ($c = 10$ Ns/m) and $\Delta t = 0.001$ s under transient loading with finite decreasing time.

Table 3. Computing time of two algorithms.

Numerical Methods	Number of Nodes	Step Size (s)	Computing Time (s)
Mixed MLPG5 time Adaptive Method	85 (17 × 5)	0.001	3.3257
	175 (25 × 7)		10.105
ANSYS(FEM)	85(17 × 5)		10.484
	175 (25 × 7)		21.828

c. Time-dependent damping

In this example, the transient response of the beam subjected to a time dependent loading (shown in Figure 13c) and nonlinear damping is considered. The loading function and the damping coefficient are defined as follows:

$$g(t) = \begin{cases} 2.5t & 0 < t < 0.4 \\ 0 & t > 0.4 \end{cases} \tag{56}$$

$$c = 1 + t \tag{57}$$

The example was solved by our method using different time step sizes. It can be seen in Figure 24 that the normal stress levels σ_{xx} at point C with different time step sizes are quite close to each other. For comparison, the normal stress levels σ_{xx} at point C solved by the Newmark method are plotted in Figure 25. It can be seen that the Newmark method still has large errors due to the numerical dissipation and dispersion. It also cannot accurately capture the stress peaks when a larger time step (Δt = 0.006 s) is adopted.

In addition, the shear stress levels τ_{xy} at different times solved by our method are shown in Figures 26–28. It can be clearly seen in Figures 27 and 28 that the stress concentrated on the center of the beam, as a result of the diffraction and reflection of elastic stress waves. This shows that the stress distribution in the dynamic problem is very different from that in a static problem. The results demonstrate that our method works well for the nonlinear forced vibration analysis.

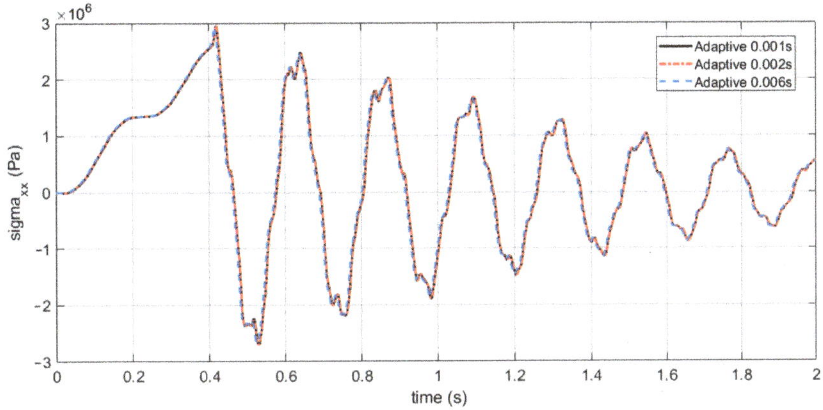

Figure 24. The normal stress σ_{xx} at point C with different time steps (nonlinear damping $c = 1 + t\,\mathrm{Ns/m}$).

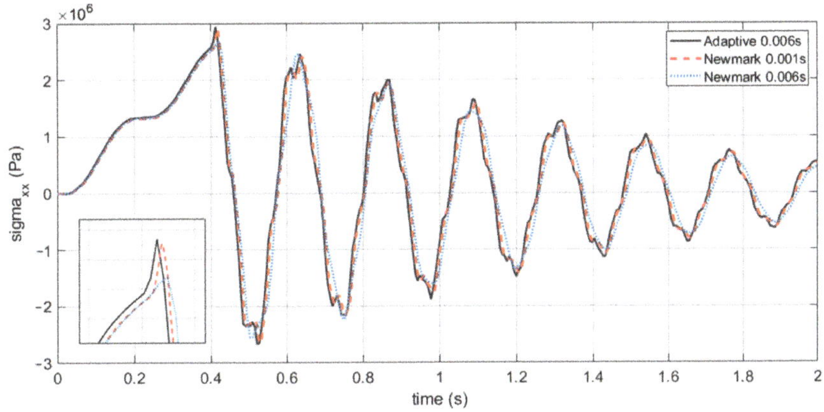

Figure 25. The normal stress σ_{xx} at point C using time-adaptive method and the Newmark method (nonlinear damping $c = 1 + t\,\mathrm{Ns/m}$).

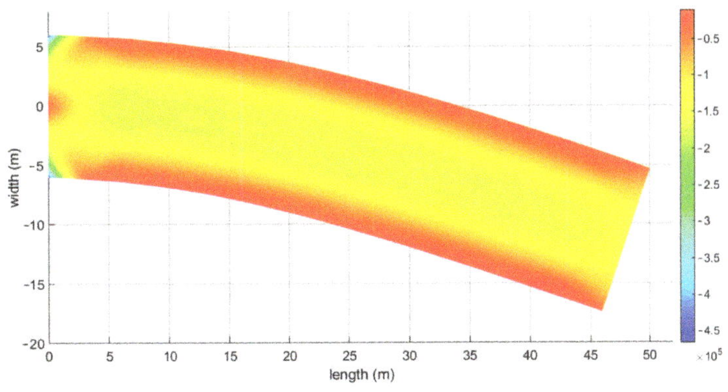

Figure 26. Shear stress τ_{xy} of the cantilever beam (t = 0.4 s), with time-dependent damping.

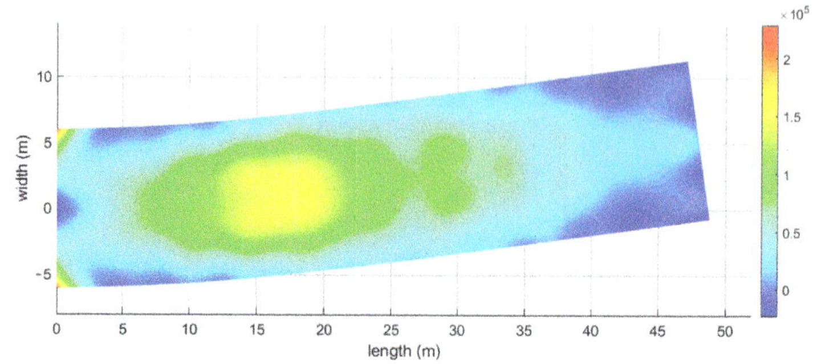

Figure 27. Shear stress τ_{xy} of the cantilever beam (t = 0.48 s), with time-dependent damping.

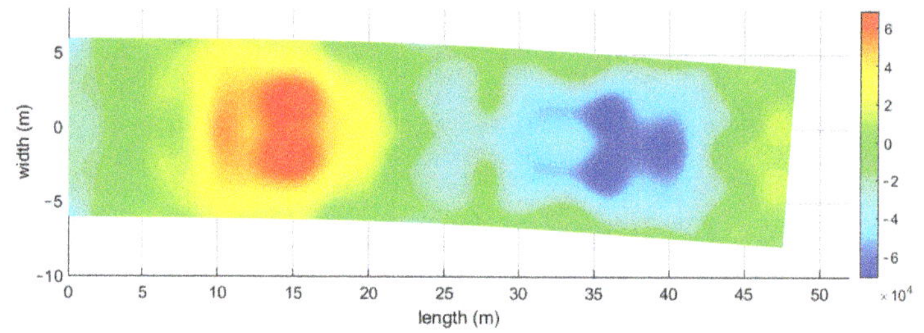

Figure 28. Shear stress τ_{xy} of the cantilever beam (t = 0.58 s), with time-dependent damping.

Example 4: A Perforated Tension Strip

The last example is a perforated strip under axial tension, as shown in Figure 29. This problem has been studied by Kontoni and Beskos, using the dual reciprocity BEM [27]. The strip was subjected to a Heaviside tension step load with initial value P = 20 Pa. The material properties of the strip were taken as: length $L = 1.6$ m, width $D = 1.0$ m, Young's modulus $E = 2 \times 10^3$ Pa, Poisson ratio $\nu = 0.3$, density $\rho = 1$ kg/m^3 and damping coefficient $c = 1$ Ns/m. The initial conditions were defined as:

$$u_0 = u_{in}(\mathbf{X}, 0) = 0 \tag{58}$$

$$u_1 = \dot{u}_{in}(\mathbf{X}, 0) = 0 \tag{59}$$

Symmetry conditions were imposed on the left and right edges, and the inner boundary of the hole had no traction. Regular uniform nodal configurations with nodal distances d = 0.03 m were used in this example, as shown in Figure 30. The time step used in the time-adaptive method was $\Delta t = 0.001$ s. The horizontal displacement of point A (0.00, 0.05) and vertical displacement of point B (0.05, 0.00) are plotted in Figures 31 and 32, respectively. For comparison, solutions for this problem were also obtained using the finite element software ANSYS (Mechanical). It is evident that the results obtained by our method are in very good agreement with those obtained by ANSYS.

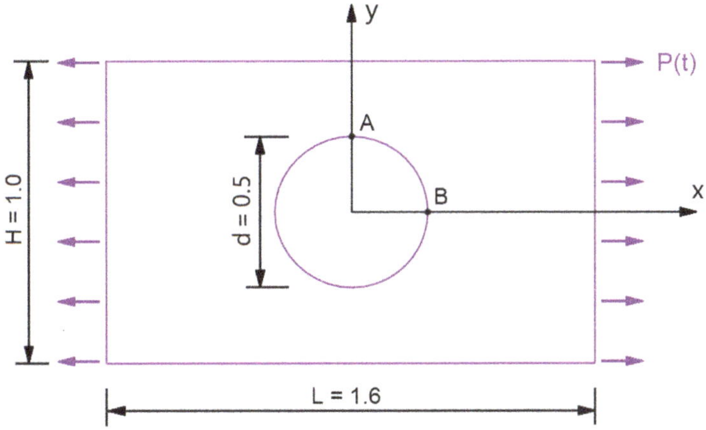

Figure 29. A perforated tension strip subjected to a Heaviside tension step loading.

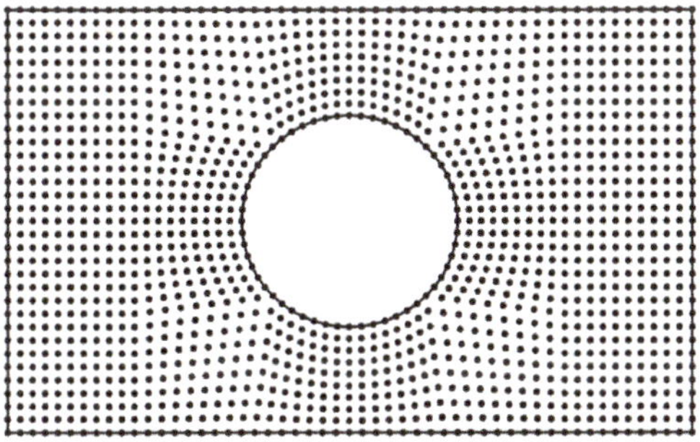

Figure 30. Nodal configurations for a perforated tension strip.

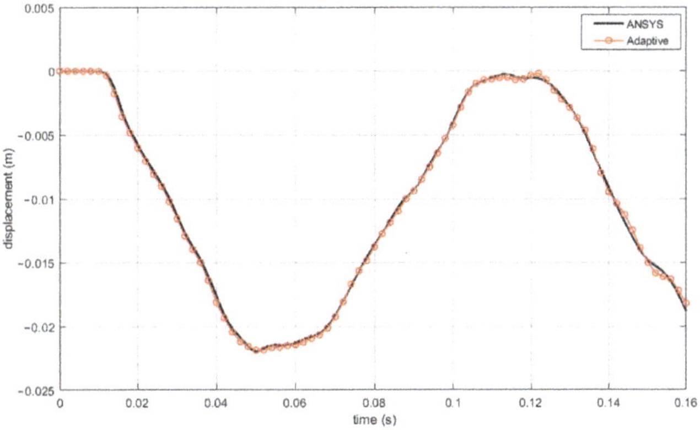

Figure 31. The transient vertical displacement at point A, $\Delta t = 0.001$ s and $c = 1$ Ns/m for the Heaviside tension step loading.

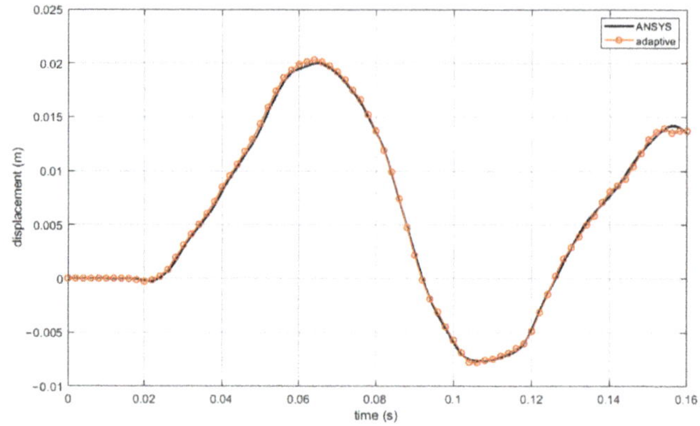

Figure 32. The transient vertical displacement at point B, $\Delta t = 0.001$ s and $c = 1$ Ns/m for the Heaviside tension step loading.

It can be observed that the maximum displacement level for point A and point B occurs at t = 0.065 s, and the maximum displacement of point A in the reverse direction occurs at t = 0.105 s. The displacement fields of this perforated tension strip at t = 0.065 s and t = 0.105 s are shown in Figures 33 and 34. The results prove the efficiency and accuracy of the developed meshless time-adaptive method for forced vibration analysis in multiple connected domains.

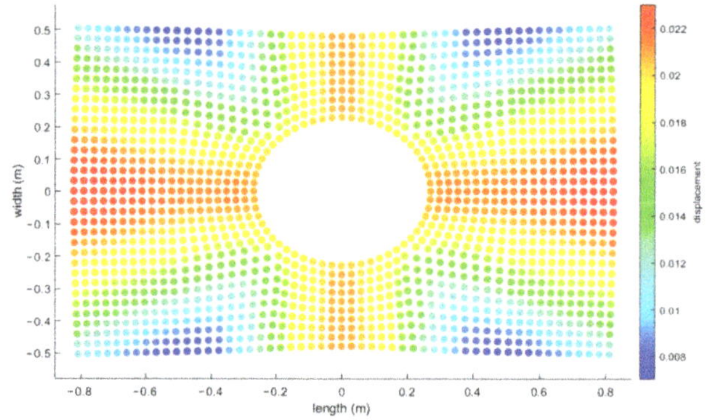

Figure 33. The displacement field of this perforated tension strip at t = 0.065 s.

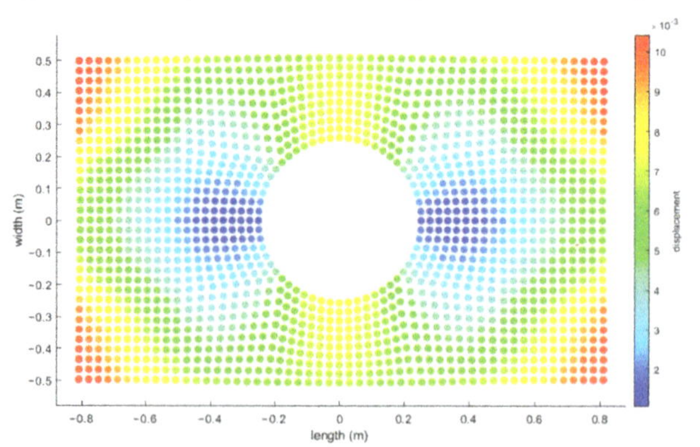

Figure 34. The displacement field of this perforated tension strip at t = 0.105 s.

5. Conclusions

In this paper, a new meshless time-domain adaptive method was presented for vibration analysis through mixed MLPG-FVM (MLPG5). In this method, each variable is interpolated by time series of variable order in the time domain. Thus, more accurate stress and displacement can be obtained, and larger time steps can be used in vibration analysis compared with the Newmark method (when the time step is 0.04, the calculation error of this method is only 1/17 of that of the Newmark method). Furthermore, through the independent interpolation of strain and displacement, the differentiation of the shape function is eliminated and the lower-order polynomial basis can be used in the MLS interpolations. Thus, smaller support sizes ($S_s = 0.4 - 0.7$, and the test sizes S_t were 1.2–1.8) can be used in the MLPG approach. By using the Heaviside function as the weighted function, the domain integral of stiffness matrix is removed and the calculation efficiency is improved. All the numerical results show that the time-domain adaptive method can cooperate well with the meshless method, and the calculation accuracy of the present method is satisfactory with various time step sizes. This high-accuracy time-domain scheme is very attractive for second-order PDE in time as elasto-dynamics equations. Put simply, this method provides a high efficiency and accuracy solution for solving free and forced vibration problems in both simply and multiply-connected domains under large time step sizes without any type of mesh.

Author Contributions: Conceptualization, T.Z. and M.L.; methodology, T.Z. and M.L.; software, M.L. and J.C.; investigation, T.Z. and M.L.; data curation, M.L. and J.C.; writing—original draft preparation, M.L. and J.C.; writing—review and editing, T.Z. and M.L.; visualization, M.L. and J.C.; supervision, T.Z.; project administration, T.Z. All authors have read and agreed to the published version of the manuscript.

Funding: This research received no external funding.

Institutional Review Board Statement: Not applicable.

Informed Consent Statement: Not applicable.

Data Availability Statement: Data sharing not applicable to this article, as no datasets were generated or analyzed during the current study.

Conflicts of Interest: The authors declare no conflict of interest.

References

1. Meirovitch, L. Computational methods in structural dynamics. *J. Vib. Acoust.* **1982**, *49*, 259–260. [CrossRef]
2. Gu, Y.; Liu, G.R. A meshless local Petrov-Galerkin (MLPG) method for free and forced vibration analyses for solids. *Comput. Mech.* **2001**, *27*, 188–198. [CrossRef]
3. Mohebpour, S.R.; Malekzadeh, P.; Ahmadzadeh, A.A. Dynamic analysis of laminated composite plates subjected to a moving oscillator by FEM. *Compos. Struct.* **2011**, *93*, 1574–1583. [CrossRef]
4. Ghafoori, E.; Asghari, M. Dynamic analysis of laminated composite plates traversed by a moving mass based on a first-order theory. *Compos. Struct.* **2010**, *92*, 1865–1876. [CrossRef]
5. Yang, Y.; Lam, C.C.; Kou, K.P. Forced vibration analysis of functionally graded beams by the meshfree boundary-domain integral equation method. *Eng. Anal. Bound. Elem.* **2016**, *72*, 100–110. [CrossRef]
6. Thankane, K.S. Finite Difference Method for Beam Equation with Free Ends Using Mathematica. *S. Afr. J. Pure Appl. Math.* **2009**, *4*, 61–78.
7. Chakravorty, D.; Sinha, P.K.; Bandyopadhyay, J.N. Applications of fem on free and forced vibration of laminated shells. *J. Eng. Mech.* **1998**, *124*, 1–8. [CrossRef]
8. Ahmad, S.; Banerjee, P.K. Free vibration analysis by BEM using particular integrals. *J. Eng. Mech.* **1986**, *112*, 682–695. [CrossRef]
9. Schanz, M. Application of 3d time domain boundary element formulation to wave propagation in poroelastic solids. *Eng. Anal. Bound. Elem.* **2001**, *25*, 363–376. [CrossRef]
10. Israil, A.; Banerjee, P.K. Advanced development of time-domain bem for two-dimensional scalar wave propagation. *Int. J. Numer. Methods Eng.* **2010**, *29*, 1003–1020. [CrossRef]
11. Guoyou, Y.; Mansur, W.J.; Carrer, J.A.M.; Gong, L. Stability of Galerkin and collocation time domain boundary element methods as applied to the scalar wave equation. *Comput. Struct.* **2000**, *74*, 495–506.

12. Malekzadeh, P.; Haghighi, M.R.G.; Gholami, M. Dynamic response of thick laminated annular sector plates subjected to moving load. *Compos. Struct.* **2010**, *92*, 155–163. [CrossRef]
13. Schenk, C.A.; Bergman, L.A.; Asce, M. Response of continuous system with stochastically varying surface roughness to moving load. *J. Eng. Mech.* **2003**, *129*, 759–768. [CrossRef]
14. Ikuno, S.; Fujita, Y.; Hirokawa, Y. Large-Scale Simulation of Electromagnetic Wave Propagation Using Meshless Time-domain Method with Parallel Processing. *IEEE Trans. Magn.* **2013**, *49*, 1613–1616. [CrossRef]
15. Haitian, Y. A new approach of time stepping for solving transfer problems. *Int. J. Numer. Methods Biomed. Eng.* **1999**, *15*, 325–334. [CrossRef]
16. Liu, Q.; Zhang, J.; Yan, L. A numerical method of calculating first and second derivatives of dynamic response based on gauss precise time step integration method. *Eur. J. Mech.* **2010**, *29*, 370–377. [CrossRef]
17. Yang, H.T.; Liu, Y.; Wu, R.F. Solving 2-D nonlinear coupled heat and moisture transfer problems via a self-adaptive precise algorithm in time-domain. *Appl. Math. Mech.* **2005**, *26*, 848–854.
18. Taylor, R.L.; Papadopoulos, P. On a finite element method for dynamic contact/impact problems. *Int. J. Numer. Methods Eng.* **1993**, *36*, 2123–2140. [CrossRef]
19. Atluri, S.N.; Zhu, T. A new meshless local Petrov-Galerkin (MLPG) approach in computational mechanics. *Comput. Mech.* **1998**, *22*, 117–127. [CrossRef]
20. Atluri, S.N.; Zhu, T. The meshless local Petrov-Galerkin (MLPG) approach for solving problems in elasto-statics. *Comput. Mech.* **2000**, *25*, 169–179. [CrossRef]
21. Atluri, S.N.; Han, Z.; Shen, S. Meshless Local Patrov-Galerkin (MLPG) approaches for weakly singular traction & displacement boundary integral equations. *Comput. Model. Eng. Sci.* **2003**, *4*, 507–517.
22. Shen, S.; Atluri, S.N. Multiscale Simulation Based on The Meshless Local Petrov-Galerkin (MLPG) Method. *Comput. Model. Eng. Sci.* **2004**, *5*, 235–255.
23. Shen, S.; Atluri, S.N. The Meshless Local Petrov-Galerkin (MLPG) Method: A Simple & Less-costly Alternative to the Finite Element and Boundary Element Methods. *Comput. Model. Eng. Sci.* **2002**, *3*, 11–51.
24. Atluri, S.N.; Han, Z.D.; Rajendran, A.M. A New Implementation of the Meshless Finite Volume Method, through the MLPG "Mixed" Approach. *Comput. Model. Eng. Sci.* **2004**, *6*, 491–513.
25. Atluri, S.N.; Shen, S. *The Meshless Local Petrov-Galerkin (MLPG) Method*; Tech Science Press: Encino, CA, USA, 2002.
26. Gu, Y.T.; Liu, G.R. A meshfree weak-strong (mws) form method for time dependent problems. *Comput. Mech.* **2005**, *35*, 134–145. [CrossRef]
27. Kontoni, D.P.N.; Beskos, D.E. Transient dynamic elastoplastic analysis by the dual reciprocity BEM. *Eng. Anal. Bound. Elem.* **1993**, *12*, 1–16. [CrossRef]

mathematics

Article

A Multi-View Ensemble Width-Depth Neural Network for Short-Term Wind Power Forecasting

Jing Wan [1,†], Jiehui Huang [2,†], Zhiyuan Liao [2,†], Chunquan Li [2,*] and Peter X. Liu [2,3]

1 The School of Qianhu, Nanchang University, Nanchang 330031, China; 6112119016@email.ncu.edu.cn
2 The School of Information Engineering, Nanchang University, Nanchang 330031, China; 7803018161@email.ncu.edu.cn (J.H.); 6105118084@email.ncu.edu.cn (Z.L.); xpliu@sce.carleton.ca (P.X.L.)
3 The Department of Systems and Computer Engineering, Carleton University, Ottawa, ON K1S 5B7, Canada
* Correspondence: lichunquan@ncu.edu.cn
† These authors contributed equally to this work.

Abstract: Short-term wind power forecasting (SWPF) is essential for managing wind power systems management. However, most existing forecasting methods fail to fully consider how to rationally integrate multi-view learning technologies with attention mechanisms. In this case, some potential features cannot be fully extracted, degenerating the predictive accuracy and robustness in SWPF. To solve this problem, this paper proposes a multi-view ensemble width-depth neural network (MVEW-DNN) for SWPF. Specifically, MVEW-DNN consists of local and global view learning subnetworks, which can effectively achieve more potential global and local view features of the original wind power data. In MVEW-DNN, the local view learning subnetwork is developed by introducing the deep belief network (DBN) model, which can efficiently extract the local view features. On the other hand, by introducing the attention mechanism, a new deep encoder board learning system (deBLS) is developed as the global view learning subnetwork, which provides more comprehensive global information. Therefore, by rationally learning the effective local and global view features, MVEW-DNN can achieve competitive predictive performance in SWPF. MVEW-DNN is compared with the state-of-the-art models in SWPF. The experiment results indicate that MVEW-DNN can provide competitive predictive accuracy and robustness.

Keywords: renewable energy; wind power forecasting; hybrid model; machine learning

MSC: 65-04

Citation: Wan, J.; Huang, J.; Liao, Z.; Li, C.; Liu, P.X. A Multi-View Ensemble Width-Depth Neural Network for Short-Term Wind Power Forecasting. *Mathematics* **2022**, *10*, 1824. https://doi.org/10.3390/math10111824

Academic Editors: Zhuojia Fu, Yiqian He and Hui Zheng

Received: 23 March 2022
Accepted: 17 May 2022
Published: 25 May 2022

1. Introduction

Since wind power has clean and pollution-free features compared with traditional energy sources, it has become an important part of modern power systems [1–3]. In fact, accurate wind power forecasting (WPF) is becoming increasingly important because it can optimize the generation schedules and units, as well as improve the profitability and stability of the power system [4,5]. However, it is still a challenging task to obtain accurate and robust WPF due to the uncertainty, volatility, and intermittency of wind speed [6].

To improve the predictive accuracy and robustness in SWPF, various forecasting methods have been developed. These systems can be divided into physical methods, statistical methods, and machine learning methods [7]. Physical methods mainly rely on numerical weather prediction (NWP) information such as atmospheric pressure, temperature, and relative humidity [8]. For example, Zjavka et al. [9] designed a wind power forecasting system by polynomial decomposition of the general differential equation. Jacondino et al. [10] proposed a weather and research forecasting (WRF) system for forecasting wind power from two different wind farms.

Statistical methods involve the application of autoregressive dynamic adaptive (ARDA) models [11], Bayesian models [12], autoregressive moving average (ARMA) models [13], Gaussian mixture models [14,15], and the quantile regression neural network (QRNN) models [16]. In ultra-short wind power forecasting (UWPF), wind power data are almost linear. Since statistical and physical methods can be easily formulated into linear predictive models, they provide promising predictive results for UWPF [17]. However, different from UWPF, short-term wind power forecasting (SWPF) has higher volatility and more uncertain power load data. Therefore, statistical and physical methods cannot handle such nonlinear characteristics information in SWPF [18].

To obtain better predictive performance in SWPF, various machine learning models have been developed. Because machine learning effectively constructs the nonlinear mapping relationship between the input and output of wind power data, it can effectively learn and mine the nonlinear characteristics from wind power data [19]. The commonly used machine learning models are support vector machines (SVRs) [20], deep belief networks (DBNs) [21], echo state networks (ESNs) [22], extreme learning machines (ELMs) [23], and broad learning systems (BLSs) [24].

For example, as a promising deep learning network, DBN is composed of multiple restricted Boltzmann machines, which provides powerful nonlinear data processing capability. However, DBN can produce high-dimensional features because of multiple BPNN layers. This may limit the prediction performance [25]. BLS is a new single-layer incremental neural network. Its advantages lie in fast computing speed, low computing resource consumption, easy online incremental learning, and easy expansion. However, BLS needs to perform the random nodes selection and pseudo-inverse calculation, so that its predictive accuracy is often inferior to deep-learning networks in the face of large-scale data. Furthermore, a single BLS model may have problems such as over-training, poor generalization ability, or limited prediction accuracy [26].

Wind power can be significantly influenced by many natural factors such as geographical location, weather conditions, and seasonal effects [27]. To overcome the instability and intermittent nature of the time series in SWPF, the combination of the decomposition-based method and the machine learning model has been proven to be an effective solution [28]. Chen et al. [29] used the discrete wavelet transform to decompose PV output power. The decomposed subsequences were then fed into an adaptive neuro-fuzzy inference system (ANFIS) to predict the short-term PV output power. Wang et al. [30] developed the VMD-CISSA-LSSVM model, consisting of the variational modal decomposition (VMD) data preprocessing method, the sparrow search algorithm (SSA), and the least squares support vector machine (LSSVM) model, which has high prediction accuracy and stable prediction results. Devi et al. [31] rationally combined ensemble empirical mode decomposition (EEMD), cuckoo search optimization algorithm, and an improved LSTM to improve forecasting accuracy. Zhang et al. [15] integrated CEEMDAN to Gaussian process regression, which can also obtain promising prediction performance.

Furthermore, to further improve the prediction ability of a single machine learning model, hybrid models are also considered effective solutions. This because the hybrid models can compensate for the disadvantage of each method. For example, Zhao et al. [32] used CNN and attention mechanisms to provide more reliable multitask learning accuracy. In [33], the attention mechanism is combined with the gated recurrent unit (GRU) network, obtaining robust prediction performance. In [34], a novel genetic long short-term memory (GLSTM) framework was developed to provide accurate, reliable, and robust performance in SWPF. The genetic technology is used to automatically optimize LSTM parameters according to different wind power data. Khan et al. [35] combined autoencoder (AE) and bidirectional long short-term memory (BiLSTM) to form a novel hybrid model. Duan et al. [36] proposed a novel hybrid model consisting of VMD, LSTM, and PSO-DBN. Wu et al. [37] used the charged system search (CSS) algorithm to construct a hybrid model, which consists of least-squares-support vector machines (LS-SVM), a modified artificial neural network (ANN), and an adaptive network-based fuzzy inference system (ANFIS) model. Ogliari et al. [38] built a hybrid model by combining the physical and ANN-developed models, which can give some knowledge about the wind turbine characteristics to the ANN model. Hong et al. [39] effectively combined CNN with a radial basis function neural network (RBFNN). Here, RBFNN is built for dealing with uncertain characteristics, and CNN is built for extracting wind power characteristics, so that it also has outstanding prediction performance. Ribeiro et al. [40] proposed an ensemble learning model by introducing bagging and stacking, which integrated the samples through the arithmetic and weighted average values.

Note that some multi-view hybrid models have recently also gained outstanding prediction performance. For example, Lai et al. [41] proposed a multi-view neural network by rationally combining LSTM model with RBFNN model for short- and mid-term load forecast, which has higher generalization ability. Nguyen et al. [42] decomposed time series data into a closely related time series group and a loosely related group, which are fed into a multitask learning model and a multi-view learning part, respectively. Zhong et al. [43] devised a multi-view deep forecast model for solar irradiance forecast, which uses multiple related data sets to feed into the RBFNN model and one hybrid model (MvDF).

Although the existing methods have achieved great success, there are still some problems that need to be further solved as follows:

1. For the SWPF task, the existing machine learning methods rarely consider the compromise between prediction accuracy and computation cost. Although BLS [24] has attracted considerable attention for its fast training speed and incremental learning algorithm, the prediction performance of BLS is also limited. Because BLS has problems such as the randomness of its parameter settings [26] and its sensitivity to the number of enhanced nodes, vulnerability to noise, and lack of uncertainty expression ability. Furthermore, although various deep learning models can achieve promising performance, computation costs are high.
2. Most hybrid machine learning methods rarely consider how to establish a multi-view learning mechanism, which may degenerate the predictive accuracy. Although researchers [15,30,31] have introduced decomposition in single models, the models cannot comprehensively learn original data characteristics, so that the robustness of the models is limited.
3. The attention mechanism is integrated into CNN [32] and GRU [33] for obtaining stable performance and providing feature selection, respectively. However, this technology is rarely considered for adjusting network structures while applying to different regression tasks, which may limit the improvement of model performance on other data sets.
4. Most existing models seldom consider how to effectively and stably connect two distinctly different models. For instance, a fully connected neural network is used to connect two different models in [35], which may cause gradient disappearing or exploding while connecting two much different models.

From the above analysis, our investigation mainly considers how to effectively integrate a decomposition mechanism and a multi-view learning mechanism into machine learning for efficient and stable SWPF. Considering the above motivation, this paper proposes a multi-view ensemble width-depth neural network (MVEW-DNN), which involves a local view learning subnetwork (CEEMDAN-DBN), a global view learning subnetwork (deBLS), and a feature dynamic decisionmaker (FDDM). The local view learning subnetwork covers CEEMDAN and a deep belief network (DBN), which can effectively extract part features of wind power load data. On the other hand, the global view learning subnetwork is an encoder board learning system (deBLS), which can provide more comprehensive features. In addition, the effective feature dynamic decisionmaker (FDDM) is developed to effectively fuse the local view learning subnetwork and the global view learning subnetwork.

The main contributions are as follows:

1. A novel width-depth integration model with a global view and a local view is introduced for short-term wind power forecasting. Different from other multi-view models, our model focuses on improving model performance and reducing the computational cost of the global view learning subnetwork (deBLS) as much as possible.
2. The deBLS model is developed by rationally replacing the feature nodes with the multiple encoder nodes, which can improve the learning ability of BLS. Furthermore, the deBLS introduced an attention mechanism of adjusting the enhancement nodes to achieve higher prediction accuracy.
3. An effective feature fusion model FDDM is proposed for rationally combining the deBLS and CEEMDAN-DBN, which can promise optimal predictive performance.

The rest of this paper is arranged as follows. The framework of the model and related theoretical knowledge are introduced in Section 2. Section 3 analyses the test data and details the concrete case analysis. Section 4 is the conclusion of this paper.

2. The Proposed MVEW-DNN

As shown in Figure 1, the proposed MVEW-DNN is divided into global view and local view learning subnetworks. In the local view learning subnetwork (CEEMDAN-DBN), CEEMDAN decomposes the original wind power data into multiple local view components. Then, the DBN network is used to extract the features of the local view components. In the global view learning subnetwork (deBLS), the original wind power data are regarded as the global view data. The deBLS model is developed to learn the features of the global view data. Finally, the FDDM method is developed to fuse CEEMDAN-DBN and deBLS by dynamically adjusting the fusion parameters. The FDDM method can monitor the performance of deBLS and CEEMDAN-DBN in the training phase, which can obtain the best model fusion performance.

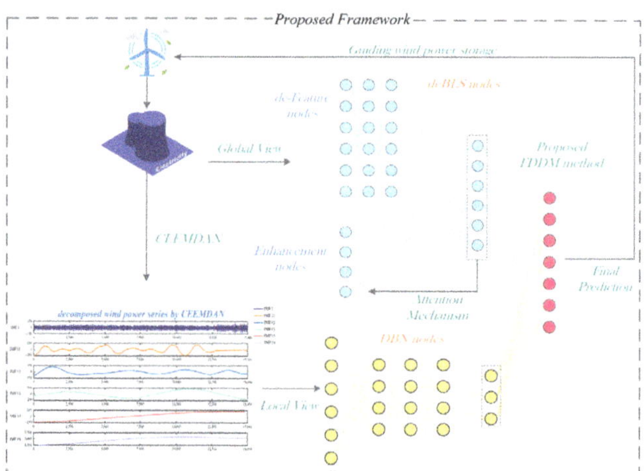

Figure 1. MVEW-DNN consists of the CEEMDAN-DBN, deBLS, and FDDM. deBLS is established for the global view. CEEMDAN-DBN is established for the local view.

2.1. Local View Subnetwork

Wind power data have high uncertainty and volatility, degenerating the predictive accuracy. To address these problems, CEEMDAN is applied to decompose the original wind power data into multiple smooth local view components called eigen-modes [44], and DBN is used to effectively capture more local view characteristics of wind power data.

2.1.1. Empirical Mode Decomposition with Adaptive Noise (CEEMDAN)

In contrast with EMD and EEMD, CEEMDAN overcomes the modal aliasing of EMD and the inefficiency of EEMD on some closely spaced spectral signals. Furthermore, CEEMDAN adds white noise to each decomposition stage so that the noise of the original data and the added white noise are superimposed and cancel each other. Therefore, CEEMDAN gradually eliminates the reconstruction error in the iterative process, which ensures the accuracy of the decomposition and greatly improves the influence of the modal aliasing. The details of CEEMDAN are given as follows:

Assumption 1. *$y_0(t)$ is defined as the original signal. $n^m(t)$ is defined as a Gaussian white noise signal with a standard normal distribution, and $m \in [1, M]$. β is defined as the noise coefficient of $n^m(t)$. $E[*]$ is defined as the EMD decomposition. $\overline{IMF_k}(t)$ is defined as the kth intrinsic mode function obtained by the CEEMDAN.*

Step 1 Add Gaussian white noise to $y_0(t)$ to get a new signal $y_0(t) + (-1)^q \beta_0 n^m(t), q = 1, 2$. Perform EMD on the new signal to get the $IMF_1^m(t)$:

$$E\left(y_0(t) + (-1)^q \beta_0 n^m(t)\right) = IMF_1^m(t) + r^m \tag{1}$$

Step 2 Average $IMF_1^m(t)$ to get $\overline{IMF_1}(t)$, as show in Formula (2). Then, calculate the residual $r_1(t)$ after removing $\overline{IMF_1}(t)$:

$$\overline{IMF_1}(t) = \frac{1}{M} \sum\nolimits_{m=1}^{M} IMF_1^m(t) \tag{2}$$

$$r_1(t) = y_0(t) - \overline{IMF_1}(t) \tag{3}$$

Step 3 Add Gaussian white noise to $r_1(t)$ to get a new signal and perform EMD on the new signal to get the $IMF_2^m(t)$. Then, $\overline{IMF_2}(t)$ and residual $r_2(t)$ can be obtained:

$$\overline{IMF_2}(t) = \frac{1}{M} \sum\nolimits_{m=1}^{M} IMF_2^m(t) \tag{4}$$

$$r_2(t) = r_1(t) - \overline{IMF_1}(t) \tag{5}$$

Step 4 The above steps are repeated until the obtained residual signal is a monotonic function and the decomposition signal cannot be continued. At this time, the number of intrinsic mode function is K. Finally, the original signal $y_0(t)$ is decomposed into

$$y_0(t) = \sum_{k=1}^{K} \overline{IMF_k}(t) + r_K(t) \tag{6}$$

2.1.2. Deep Belief Network (DBN)

DBN is a probability map model that includes multiple restricted Boltzmann machines (RBM). Here, it is used to effectively extract effective local multiple view features from the decomposed smooth signals of CEEMDAN. The training process of DBN can be divided into two phases, namely pretraining and fine-tuning. In the pretraining phase, RBM is trained in an unsupervised manner. In the fine-tuning phase, DBN is treated as a backward propagation neural network for supervised learning that can fine-tune the model parameters.

2.2. Global View

Although decomposition methods such as CEEMDAN can decompose the original wind power load data into multiple smooth local view components, it may lead to the loss of the original wind data during the entire decomposed process. To compensate for the information loss from the above decomposed view components, we develop a deep encoder board learning system (deBLS) to extract global view information from original wind power data.

In the traditional BLS, its feature node generation method is feature mapping, and its number of enhancement nodes is preset. Different from the traditional BLS, deBLS has improvements in how it generates both feature nodes and enhancement nodes. Specifically, the deBLS method of generating feature nodes contains not only feature mapping but also a sparse encoder. Its number of enhanced nodes can also be automatically adjusted via an attention mechanism. The details of deBLS are given as follows:

Definition 1. *X and $\hat{Y}$ are defined as the input and output of deBLS, respectively. J_i is defined as the feature nodes, $i = 1, 2, \cdots, n$. $J^n = [J_1, J_2, \cdots J_n]$ is defined as the combination of all feature nodes; δ_e, and δ_h are defined as bias matrices; and the four matrices are fine-tuned by a sparse encoder.*

Step 1 By feature mapping, the original data X is mapped into n nodes K_i, as shown in Formula (7). Here, $\eta(\cdot)$ is a linear transform. Then, by increasing the depth, a three-layer sparse encoder is used to perform feature extraction on nodes K_i to obtain J^n.

$$K_i = \eta(XW_{e_i} + \delta_{e_i}), i = 1, 2, \cdots, n \quad (7)$$

Step 2 By enhancing and transforming with J^n, the enhancement nodes E_k can be obtained as

$$E_k = tanh(J^n W_{h_k} + \delta_{h_k}), k = 1, 2, \cdots, m \quad (8)$$

Note that the number of enhancement nodes has an impact on the prediction performance. To obtain a suitable number of enhancement nodes, we introduce the attention mechanism to deBLS, which can automatically adjust the number of nodes of deBLS to the most suitable number in the training phase. Here, a detailed pseudo-code for the attention mechanism algorithm is given in Algorithm 1. When the number of enhancement nodes is determined, E^m and B can be obtained.

Algorithm 1: Attention Mechanism Algorithm.

// Our attention mechanism Algorithm is located on lines 11 to 13
Original data X is divided into training set and testing set. The training set consists of train-x and train-y, the testing set consists of test-x and test-y.
Input: *train-x, train-y, test-x*
Output: W
Process:
while 1

1: **if** *the training error threshold is not satisfied* **do**
2: $k = k + 1, m = m + 1;$
3: Random W_{h_k}, δ_k;
4: Calculate $E_m = [\xi(J^n W_k + \delta_{h_k})]$;
5: Set $E^m = [E_1, E_2, \cdots, E_m]$, $B = [J^n | E^m]$;
6: r is the number of rows of matrix B';
7: I is a $r \times r$ unit matrix;
8: Set parameter C as 2^{-30};
9: Calculate W^m by $\frac{B' \times train-y}{(B' \times B + I \times C)}$;
10: Calculate Y by $B \times W^m$;
11: Calculate the cosine similarity between *train-y* and Y as δ;
12: $W^m = W^m + \delta \times \omega$, ω is a parameter $\in [0, 1]$;
13: Update Y by $Y = B \times W^m$;
14: Calculate *the training error* between Y and *train-y*;
15: **else**
16: break;
17: **end**
18: **end**

Step 3 Calculate the weight matrix W. The predictive result $\hat{Y}$ can be expressed as $\hat{Y} = BW$. Furthermore, during the training phase, the actual value Y is known, and therefore, the weight matrix W can be calculated as shown in Formula (9), where B^+ is the pseudo-inverse of B:

$$W = B^+ Y \tag{9}$$

To obtain a suitable W, the ridge regression is used to transform the above problem into $\arg\min_{W}\left(\|\hat{Y} - Y\|_2^2 + \lambda\|W\|_2^2\right)$. Here, λ is the regularization parameter; when $\lambda \to 0$, $W = \left(\lambda I + BB^T\right)^{-1} B^T Y$ where I is the identity matrix. Thus, B^+ can be obtained as

$$B^+ = \lim_{\lambda \to 0}\left((\lambda I + BB^T)^{-1} B^T\right). \tag{10}$$

2.3. FDDM

FDDM was developed to reasonably allocate the fusion weights of deBLS and CEEMDAN-DBN on the training stage and the test stage by dynamically adjusting the fusion parameters. This can achieve the optimal prediction performance of the proposed hybrid MVEW-DNN model (Algorithm 2).

Algorithm 2: FDDM Algorithm.

$\mathcal{M}$: Cross-validation fold
$\mathcal{N}$: The length of the test set (the number of output nodes)
$\mathcal{W}_{\mathcal{B}}$: Fusion weight of deBLS
$V_{\mathcal{B}}(\hat{V_{\mathcal{B}}})$: Prediction validation data (Real validation data) of deBLS
$T_{\mathcal{B}}$: Prediction test data of deBLS
$\mathcal{W}_{\mathcal{D}}$: Fusion weight of DBN
$V_{\mathcal{D}}(\hat{V_{\mathcal{D}}})$: Prediction validation data (Real validation data) of DBN
$T_{\mathcal{D}}$: Prediction test data of DBN
ρ: Correlation test threshold

Error of each node : $\varepsilon(x,y) = \frac{|x_i - y_i|}{\|x-y\|_2},\ i \in [1,\ \mathcal{N}]$ (11)

Correlation value : $\lambda(x,y) = \frac{\left|\sum_{i=1}^{n}(x_i - \overline{x})(y_i - \overline{y})\right|}{\sqrt{\sum_{i=1}^{n}(x_i - \overline{x})^4 \sum_{i=1}^{n}(y_i - \overline{y})^4}}$ (12)

Process:

$\mathcal{W}_{\mathcal{B}} = \mathcal{W}_{\mathcal{D}} = zero[\mathcal{M},\ \mathcal{N}]$;
$\rho = 2$; $\mathcal{M} = 4$;
for $m = 1; m \leq \mathcal{M}$ **do**
  Obtain $V_{\mathcal{B}}^m$ and $\hat{V_{\mathcal{B}}^m}$ from $V_{\mathcal{B}}$ and $\hat{V_{\mathcal{B}}}$, respectively.
  Obtain $V_{\mathcal{D}}^m$ and $\hat{V_{\mathcal{D}}^m}$ from $V_{\mathcal{D}}$ and $\hat{V_{\mathcal{D}}}$, respectively.
  for $n = 1; n \leq \mathcal{N}$ **do**
    Calculate error $\varepsilon_{\mathcal{B}}$ between $V_{\mathcal{B}}^m$ and $\hat{V_{\mathcal{B}}^m}$ by Formula (11).
    Calculate error $\varepsilon_{\mathcal{D}}$ between $V_{\mathcal{D}}^m$ and $\hat{V_{\mathcal{D}}^m}$ by Formula (11).
    if $\varepsilon_{\mathcal{B}}^n > \varepsilon_{\mathcal{D}}^n$ **then**
      $\mathcal{W}_{\mathcal{B}}(m,n) = 1$; // Give deBLS a higher fusion weight.
   else $\mathcal{W}_{\mathcal{D}}(m,n) = 1$;
  end
end
for $m = 1; m \leq \mathcal{M}$ **do**
  Calculate λ between $\mathcal{W}_{\mathcal{B}}(m,:)$ and $\mathcal{W}_{\mathcal{D}}(m,:)$ by Formula (12).
  if $\lambda < \rho$ **then**
    $\mathcal{W}_{\mathcal{B}}(m,:) = \mathcal{W}_{\mathcal{D}}(m,:) = [\ ]$;// Clear $\mathcal{W}_{\mathcal{B}}(m,:)$ and $\mathcal{W}_{\mathcal{D}}(m,:)$.
  end
end

Here, the original data are divided into training data set, validation data set, and the test data set, whose proportion is set as 6:2:2. The cross-validation fold parameter $\mathcal{M}$ is set as 4, which keeps the same weight length of validation data set and test data set. Therefore, the final prediction data can be defined as $P = \mathcal{W}_{\mathcal{B}} * T_{\mathcal{B}} + \mathcal{W}_{\mathcal{D}} * T_{\mathcal{D}}$. Additionally, the parameter ρ is set as 2, which is determined by our experimental tests [45]. In general, MVEW-DNN can effectively provide the prediction of SWPF by rationally combining deBLS and CEEMDAN-DBN.

2.4. Evaluation Criteria

To test the performance of the proposed MVEW-DNN, we use three evaluation indicators: Normalized Root Mean Square Error (NRMSE), Normalized Mean Absolute Error (NMAE), and Theil's inequality coefficient (TIC), as shown in Formulas (13)–(15). NRMSE and NMAE are utilized to measure the deviation between the actual value and the predictive value. TIC is applied to characterize the predictive performance of predictive models. The smaller the NRMSE and NMAE are, the stronger the non-linear approximation capability is. The closer to 0 the TIC is, the stronger the spatial learning ability is:

$$NRMSE = \frac{\sqrt{\frac{1}{N}\sum_{i=1}^{N}(y_i - \hat{y}_i)^2}}{\hat{y}_{max} - \hat{y}_{min}} \tag{13}$$

$$NMAE = \frac{\frac{1}{N}\sum_{i=1}^{N}|\hat{y}_i - y_i|}{\hat{y}_{max} - \hat{y}_{min}} \tag{14}$$

$$TIC = \frac{\sqrt{\frac{1}{N}\sum_{i=1}^{N}(y_i - \hat{y}_i)^2}}{\sqrt{\frac{1}{N}\sum_{i=1}^{N}y_i^2} + \sqrt{\frac{1}{N}\sum_{i=1}^{N}\hat{y}_i^2}} \tag{15}$$

where $\hat{y}_i$ and y_i are the predictive and actual values at the time i, N is the observation size.

3. Results and Discussion

3.1. Data Description and Experiment Settings

3.1.1. Data Description

The real wind power data from the Wind Forecasting track of the Global Energy Forecasting Competition 2021 (GEF-Com2021) are used to test the predictive performance of MVEW-DNN [46]. This data set contains the wind power measurement values and wind speed data from seven wind farms (WF1–WF7). The time resolution of the data is one hour. In [46], the data set was normalized. The data set contains data from 1 a.m. on 1 July 2009 to 12 a.m. on 26 June 2012. The entire data set contains 18,757 samples. In experiments, we consider the forecasts for the next 24 h. To effectively test the predictive models, the data from the last 24 h of the data set is first excluded. Then, the data set is divided into training set (75%) and testing set (25%).

Wind power data form a random, seasonal, nonlinear time series. Figure 2 displays the wind power data characteristics of the seven wind farms (wp1–wp7) in a box diagram. By analyzing the data characteristics of the seven wind farms, we find that there are inevitably abnormal data points in the data set. The abnormal data points are mainly caused by uncontrollable factors such as breakdown and operation planning [47].

Figure 3 shows some data points that correspond to high wind speeds and zero power generation. These abnormal data points are mainly caused by the shutdown of the turbine [48]. Therefore, prediction systems are required to provide high prediction accuracy and robustness when performing SWPF tasks.

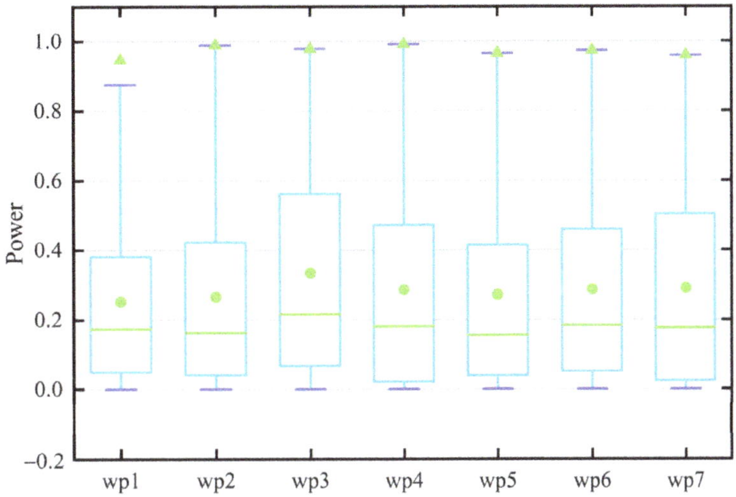

Figure 2. The wind power data characteristics of 7 wind farms. The green triangles and circles represent the outliers and the average values of the data set respectively. The short purple lines on the upper side represent the maximum values, while those on the lower side represent the minimum values. And the short green lines represent the median values.

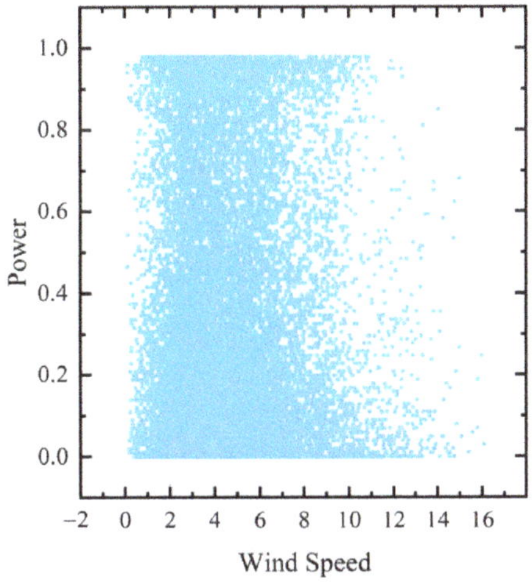

Figure 3. Wind power curve of WF3 under 1-h sampling rate. The blue points refer to the sampling moments. The vertical coordinates of the blue points indicate the wind power measurement values at the sampling moments, and the horizontal coordinates of the points are the corresponding wind speed data.

3.1.2. Experiment Settings

The parameter settings of the proposed MVEW-DNN model are given as follows. MVEW-DNN mainly consists of the local learner (DBN) and the global learner (deBLS). First, when the original data are decomposed by the CEEMDN algorithm, the signal-to-noise ratio of CEEMDAN (N_{std}) is set as 0.01. The number of noise additions is set to 6. The maximum number of iterations is 2000. Then, the sub-models (IMFs) are split into training set (train-x, train-y) and testing set (test-x, test-y) in a ratio of 8 to 2. The training data set is used as input data, and the input layer of the local learner (DBN) has 20 input layer nodes. We adopt three hidden layers of 100 nodes in each layer. Each sigmoid activation function is optimized.

For the global learner, we directly use the original normalized wind power measurement values for the training task. We set the number of mapped features to 73 and the dimension of the mapped features is 6. The mapped features are mapped to the enhancement nodes. Every enhancement node group has 4 enhancement nodes. All experiments are implemented using MATLAB on a laptop equipped with Intel-i7 1.8 GHz CPU.

3.2. Models

To verify the predictive performance of the MVEW-DNN model, we compare it with some state-of-the-art and conventional predictive models in the SWPF task. These models are described as follows:

1. Autoregressive Integrated Moving Average (ARIMA) [49] is a seasonal model expressed as $ARIMA\ (p,d,q)\ (P,D,Q)_m$. Here, m refers to the number of periods in each season, and P, D, and Q refer to autoregressive, differencing, and moving average terms for the seasonal part of the ARIMA model, respectively.
2. Random Vector Functional Link (RVFL) Network [50] is a multilayer perceptron (MLP). Its input and output are directly linked; only the output weights are selected as adaptive parameters. However, the remaining parameters are set to random values that are independently preselected. RVFL can also obtain promising prediction performance on SWPF tasks.
3. MOGWO-ELM [51] can provide promising SWPF by integrating the variational mode decomposition (VMD), the extreme learning machine model, the error factor, and a nonlinear ensemble method.
4. IVMD-SE-MCC-LSTM [52] is composed of the improved variational mode decomposition (IVMD), sample entropy (SE), the maximum correntropy criterion (MCC), and long short-term memory (LSTM) neural network. Here, the parameter K of the IVMD is determined by the MCC; the decomposed subseries is reconstructed by SE to improve the prediction efficiency. Then, the MCC is also utilized to replace the mean square error in the classic LSTM network.
5. Multi-view Neural Network Ensemble [41] is an ensemble of Radial Basis Function Neural Networks (RBFNN). In this ensemble neural network, a long short-term memory network (LSTM) and a multi-resolution wavelet transform are first used to extract the features for training. Then, the extracted feature data is input into multiple RBFNN networks for prediction. The output layer of the Multi-view Neural Network Ensemble is a local generalization error model, which assigns the corresponding weights to the output of multiple RBFNN networks. Finally, these output results of RBFNN are weighted and summed to provide the final predictive results.

3.3. Results

The NRMSE, NMAE, and TIC metrics are used to evaluate the predictive performance of the above six models on wind farm validation data (WF1–WF7). Interestingly, Table 1 shows that the proposed MVEW-DNN model provides lower NRMSR, NMAE, and TIC values than those of ARIMA, RVFL, MOGWO-ELM, IVMD-SE-MCC-LSTM, and Multi-view Neural Network Ensemble on WF1-WF7. For instance, the predictive results given by IVMD-SE-MCC-LSTM for NRMSE, NMAE, and TIC on WF1 are 0.2547, 0.2058, and 0.4131, respectively. On the other hand, the proposed MVEW-DNN gives 0.2103, 0.1603, and 0.3381 from NRMSE, NMAE, and TIC, respectively. Furthermore, we also provide a clear visual prediction display of the above six predictive models on WF3 in Figure 4. An interesting observation is that the proposed MVEW-DNN model has the best predictive performance among all compared models. Table 1 and Figure 4 indicate that our model can provide the best nonlinear approximation capability, robustness, and spatial learning ability among all six models.

Table 1. The NRMSE, NMAE, and TIC assessment results of the 6 models.

Data Set	Metrics	ARIMA	RVFL	MOGWO-ELM	IVMD-SE-MCC-LSTM	Multi-View Neural Network Ensemble	MVEW-DNN
WF1	NRMSE	0.4477	0.3417	0.2534	0.2547	0.2758	0.2103
	NMAE	0.3285	0.2505	0.2042	0.2058	0.1916	0.1603
	TIC	0.5878	0.651	0.4118	0.4131	0.6618	0.3381
WF2	NRMSE	0.4744	0.3494	0.2761	0.2766	0.2944	0.2236
	NMAE	0.3458	0.2575	0.2306	0.2275	0.241	0.173
	TIC	0.571	0.6543	0.4219	0.4253	0.4145	0.3281
WF3	NRMSE	0.5442	0.4566	0.3188	0.3119	0.2839	0.2378
	NMAE	0.4178	0.3373	0.2744	0.268	0.2386	0.1879
	TIC	0.5503	0.7596	0.398	0.3865	0.3714	0.2784
WF4	NRMSE	0.5008	0.4023	0.2992	0.2925	0.2664	0.2264
	NMAE	0.3686	0.2935	0.2505	0.2465	0.1859	0.1784
	TIC	0.5586	0.7166	0.4217	0.4035	0.6372	0.2954
WF5	NRMSE	0.4978	0.425	0.3208	0.3221	0.3863	0.2502
	NMAE	0.36	0.308	0.2591	0.2603	0.2738	0.1988
	TIC	0.5838	0.7119	0.453	0.4535	0.7101	0.3113
WF6	NRMSE	0.4804	0.4057	0.2915	0.2882	0.302	0.2328
	NMAE	0.356	0.2936	0.2414	0.2349	0.208	0.1821
	TIC	0.5504	0.7219	0.4078	0.4092	0.6483	0.2977
WF7	NRMSE	0.5041	0.4058	0.3025	0.2973	0.3872	0.5041
	NMAE	0.368	0.2953	0.2599	0.2541	0.2367	0.368
	TIC	0.5492	0.7502	0.4218	0.4108	0.6439	0.5492

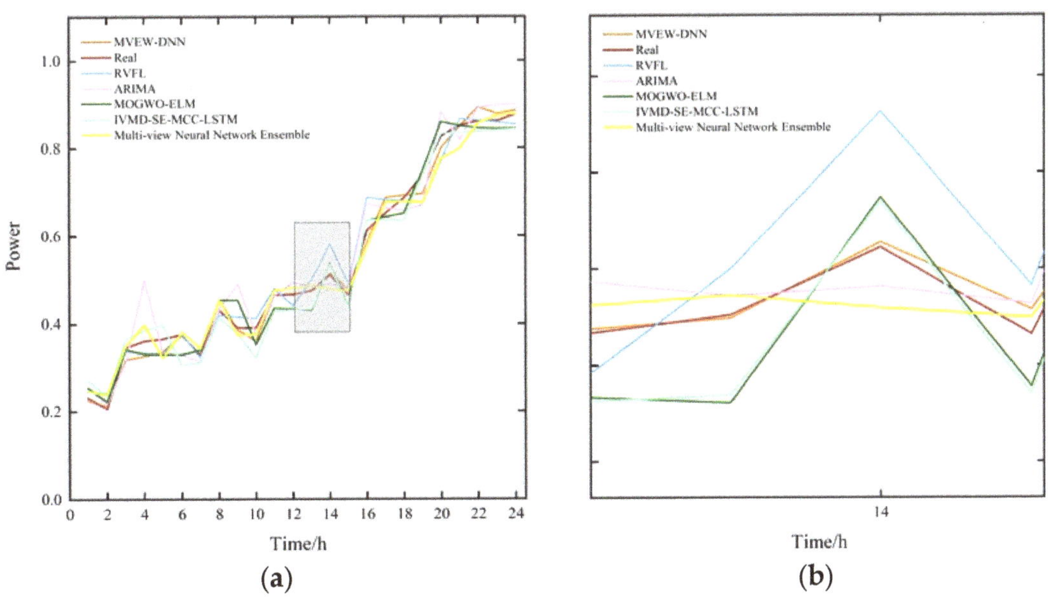

Figure 4. The prediction results are executed by the above models with the data set from WF3. (**a**) Prediction results from 6 models for WF3 wind power data forecasted 24-h in advance. (**b**) Partial enlargement of the 6 model predictions.

Figure 5 shows the NRMSE, NMAE, and TIC results for the six predictive models on WF1-WF7. We can clearly see that the proposed MVEW-DNN model achieves the best predictive performance. This further indicates that our model has the best nonlinear approximation capability, robustness, and spatial learning ability among all six models.

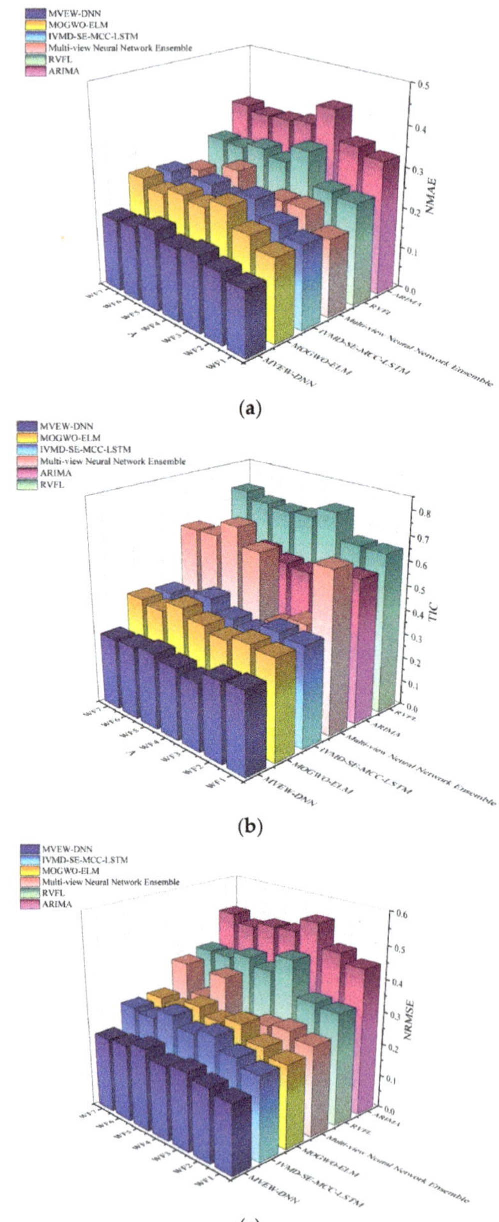

Figure 5. The NRMSE, NMAE, and TIC assessment results: (**a**) comparison of prediction results from 6 models on NMAE; (**b**) comparison of prediction results from 6 models on TIC; (**c**) comparison of prediction results from 6 models on NRMSE.

3.4. Ablation Investigations of MVEW-DNN

Note that the proposed MVEW-DNN model covers the local view learning subnetwork (CEEMDAN-DBN), the global view learning subnetwork (deBLS), and FDDM. To evaluate the effectiveness of the local view learning subnetwork (CEEMDAN-DBN), the global view learning subnetwork (deBLS), and FDDM, ablation investigations are performed.

3.4.1. Effect of the Local View Learning Subnetwork

The local view learning subnetwork covers CEEMDAN and DBN. To evaluate the performance of the local view learning subnetwork (CEEMDAN-DBN), it is compared with DBN. The experimental results are listed in Table 2, where we can observe that CEEMDAN-DBN has better results for NRMSE, NMAE, and TIC on WF1–WF7 than DBN. For instance, CEEMDAN-DBN can provide NRMSE = 0.2555 on WF4, whereas DBN provides NRMSE = 0.3024 on WF4. CEEMDAN-DBN can provide NMAE = 0.2054 on WF4, but DBN provides NMAE = 0.2583 on WF4. These findings indicate that CEEMDAN-DBN has better nonlinear approximation capability than the single DBN. Furthermore, CEEMDAN-DBN can provide TIC = 0.3364 on WF4, whereas the single DBN achieves TIC = 0.4077. This implies that CEEMDAN-DBN has better spatial learning ability than the single DBN. From the above analyses, CEEMDAN-DBN can provide promising predictive performance on WF1–WF7.

Table 2. The assessments results of DBN and CEEMDAN-DBN on three metrics.

Data Set	Metrics	CEEMDAN-DBN	DBN
WF1	NRMSE	**0.2519**	0.2702
	NMAE	**0.1925**	0.2172
	TIC	**0.3388**	0.4146
WF2	NRMSE	**0.2454**	0.2778
	NMAE	**0.1979**	0.2338
	TIC	**0.3595**	0.4141
WF3	NRMSE	**0.2845**	0.3278
	NMAE	**0.2346**	0.2798
	TIC	**0.3275**	0.4021
WF4	NRMSE	**0.2555**	0.3024
	NMAE	**0.2054**	0.2583
	TIC	**0.3364**	0.4077
WF5	NRMSE	**0.2736**	0.3327
	NMAE	**0.2204**	0.2678
	TIC	**0.3592**	0.4561
WF6	NRMSE	**0.2533**	0.3002
	NMAE	**0.2124**	0.2506
	TIC	**0.3155**	0.4049
WF7	NRMSE	**0.2512**	0.3178
	NMAE	**0.2102**	0.2745
	TIC	**0.3296**	0.4195

3.4.2. Effect of the Global Network

The proposed global view learning subnetwork is called deBLS, which is composed of the attention mechanism, the additional enhancement nodes, and BLS. To assess the performance of deBLS, it is compared with BLS, BLS with the additional enhancement nodes (BLS-AEN), and BLS with the attention mechanism (BLS-A). The experimental results are presented in Table 3. It can be seen that deBLS has better results than BLS, BLS-AEN, and BLS-A on the NRMSE, NMAE, and TIC indicators of WF1–WF7. For example, deBLS can provide NRMSE = 0.2956 on WF4, whereas BLS, BLS-AEN, and BLS-A provide NRMSE = 0.3074, NRMSE = 0.3028, and NRMSE = 0.2999 on WF4, respectively. The NMAE for deBLS is 0.245 on WF4, versus 0.2521, 0.2531, and 0.251 for BLS, BLS-AEN, and BLS-A, respectively. These suggest that deBLS has better non-inear approximation capability than either BLS, BLS-AEN, and BLS-A. Furthermore, deBLS provides TIC = 0.4053 on WF4, versus TIC = 0.4174, TIC = 0.4215, and TIC = 0.4206 for BLS, BLS-AEN, and BLS-A, respectively. This implies that deBLS has better spatial learning ability. Based on the above analyses, deBLS has competitive predictive performance on WF1–WF7.

Table 3. The assessment results of BLS, BLS-AEN, BLS-A, and deBLS.

Data Set	Metrics	BLS	BLS-AEN	BLS-A	deBLS
WF1	NRMSE	0.2776	0.2713	0.2628	**0.2548**
	NMAE	0.2223	0.2184	0.213	**0.209**
	TIC	0.4082	0.4128	0.3998	**0.3783**
WF2	NRMSE	0.2817	0.2783	0.2759	**0.2757**
	NMAE	0.2329	0.2313	0.2255	**0.2241**
	TIC	**0.418**	0.4219	0.4257	0.4362
WF3	NRMSE	0.3238	0.3199	0.3127	**0.3126**
	NMAE	0.2731	0.2742	0.2669	**0.2628**
	TIC	0.3863	0.3975	**0.3791**	0.3879
WF4	NRMSE	0.3074	0.3028	0.2999	**0.2956**
	NMAE	0.2521	0.2531	0.251	**0.245**
	TIC	0.4174	0.4215	0.4206	**0.4053**
WF5	NRMSE	0.339	0.3321	0.3205	**0.3179**
	NMAE	0.2727	0.2683	0.2597	**0.2543**
	TIC	0.4451	0.4526	0.4508	**0.4443**
WF6	NRMSE	0.3052	0.2944	0.2925	**0.2892**
	NMAE	0.2462	0.2428	0.2424	**0.2376**
	TIC	0.408	0.4117	0.4071	**0.3917**
WF7	NRMSE	0.3203	0.3054	0.3023	**0.2997**
	NMAE	0.2652	0.2608	0.2576	**0.2521**
	TIC	0.4181	0.4247	**0.4016**	0.4085

3.4.3. Effect of FDDM

Our MVEW-DNN consists of CEEMDAN-DBN, deBLS, and FDDM. To better assess the performance of MVEW-DNN, it is compared with CEEMDAN-DBN and deBLS. The experimental results are displayed in Table 4. We can see that the proposed MVEW-DNN model has better NRMSE, NMAE, and TIC results on WF1–WF7 than either CEEMDAN-DBN or deBLS. For example, the proposed MVEW-DNN model can provide NRMSE = 0.2264 and NMAE = 0.1784 on WF4, versus either NRMSE = 0.2555 and NMAE = 0.2054 for CEEMDAN-DBN or NRMSE = 0.2956 and NMAE = 0.245 for deBLS. This indicates that the proposed MVEW-DNN has better nonlinear approximation capability than CEEMDAN-DBN and deBLS. Furthermore, the proposed MVEW-DNN model can provide TIC = 0.2954 on WF4, versus TIC = 0.3364 and TIC = 0.4053 for CEEMDAN-DBN and deBLS, respectively. This means that the proposed MVEW-DNN model has better spatial learning ability. Moreover, the above analyses also imply that FDDM can effectively integrate CEEMDAN-DBN and deBLS to improve the predictive performance of MVEW-DNN.

To highlight the prediction performance difference, we visualize the data from Tables 2–4 with the radar charts in Figure 6. Interestingly, we can see that CEEMDAN-DBN outperforms DBN in predicting wind power generation on WF1–WF7. It strongly clarifies the effectiveness of CEEMDAN. Moreover, both BLS-AEN and BLS-A have better prediction performance than that of BLS, validating the effectiveness of the attention mechanism and the additional enhancement nodes. The proposed deBLS outperforms BLS-A and BLS-AEN, further suggesting that the combination of the attention mechanism and the additional enhancement nodes can improve the prediction performance of deBLS. MVEW-DNN outperforms CEEMDAN-DBN and deBLS, indicating that FDDM can provide effective combination between CEEMDAN-DBN and deBLS.

Table 4. The results of CEEMDAN-DBN, deBLS, and the proposed MVEW-DNN model.

Data Set	Metrics	CEEMDAN-DBN	deBLS	MVEW-DNN
WF1	NRMSE	0.2519	0.2548	**0.2103**
	NMAE	0.1925	0.209	**0.1603**
	TIC	0.3388	0.3783	**0.3381**
WF2	NRMSE	0.2454	0.2757	**0.2236**
	NMAE	0.1979	0.2241	**0.173**
	TIC	0.3595	0.4362	**0.3281**
WF3	NRMSE	0.2845	0.3126	**0.2378**
	NMAE	0.2346	0.2628	**0.1879**
	TIC	0.3275	0.3879	**0.2784**
WF4	NRMSE	0.2555	0.2956	**0.2264**
	NMAE	0.2054	0.245	**0.1784**
	TIC	0.3364	0.4053	**0.2954**
WF5	NRMSE	0.2736	0.3179	**0.2502**
	NMAE	0.2204	0.2543	**0.1988**
	TIC	0.3592	0.4443	**0.3113**
WF6	NRMSE	0.2533	0.2892	**0.2328**
	NMAE	0.2124	0.2376	**0.1821**
	TIC	0.3155	0.3917	**0.2977**
WF7	NRMSE	0.2512	0.2997	**0.2271**
	NMAE	0.2102	0.2521	**0.1782**
	TIC	0.3296	0.4085	**0.2926**

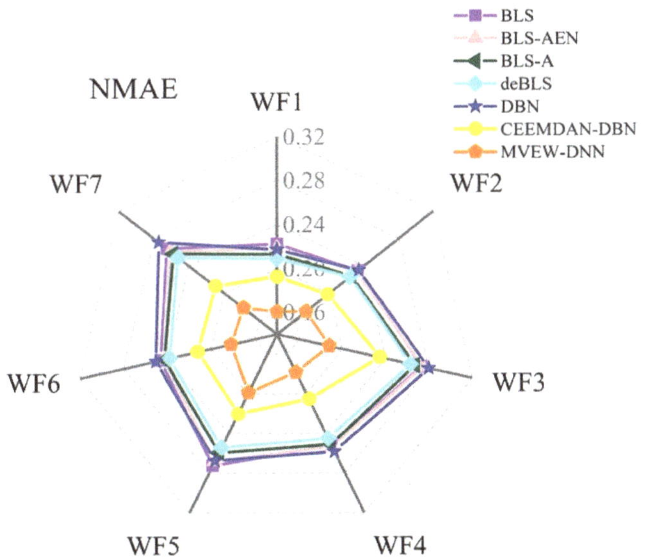

(a)

Figure 6. *Cont.*

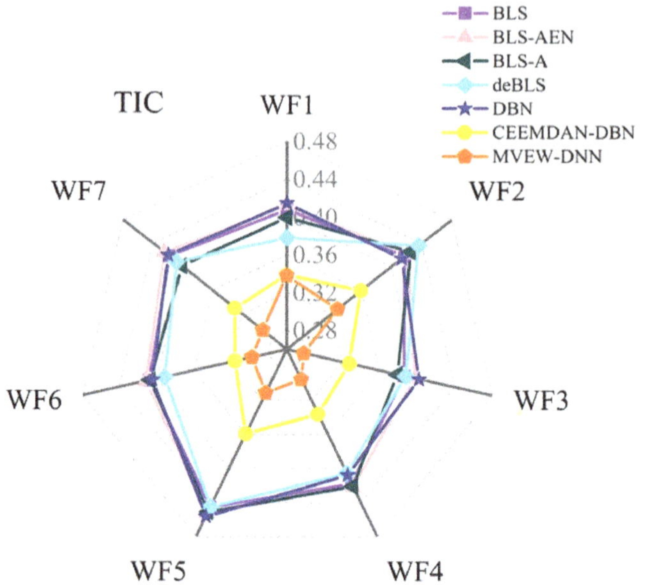

(**b**)

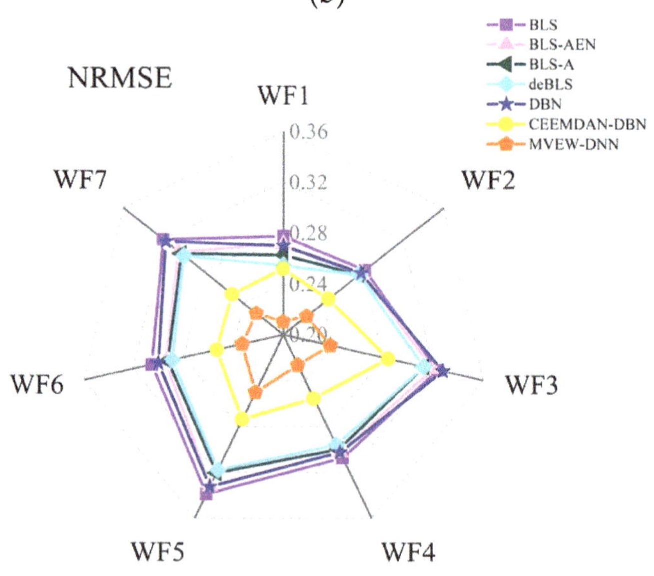

(**c**)

Figure 6. Ablation experiments on NMAE, TIC, and NRMSE evaluation indicators for 7 wind power data sets: (**a**) results of ablation experiments on NMAE evaluation indicators for 7 wind power data sets; (**b**) results of ablation experiments on TIC evaluation indicator for 7 wind power data sets; (**c**) results of ablation experiments on NRMSE evaluation indicator for 7 wind power data sets.

3.5. Parameter Selection Experiments

Our proposed model involves only one key parameter, ω, which is used for the attention mechanism. It serves to adjust the output layer weights W^m (see Algorithm 1). The different values of ω inevitably lead to discrepancies in the global learner predictions.

We apply different values of ω to optimize the global learner on different sub-data sets. Some representative results are listed in Table 5. It can be seen that the different values of ω provide similar results for NRMSE, NMAE, and TIC on WF3. This indicates that MVEW-DNN is insensitive to ω. This further implies that MVEW-DNN has promising robustness in predictive performance.

Table 5. Effect of adjusting parameter ω with the data from WF3.

ω	NRMSE	NMAE	TIC
0.5	0.3275	0.2794	0.3881
0.6	0.3268	0.2692	0.3857
0.7	0.3263	0.2792	0.3835
0.8	0.3257	0.2891	0.3814

3.6. Discussion

Based on the above experiments, our proposed MVEW-DNN has outstanding predictive performance in the SWPF field, mainly for the following reasons:

First, MVEW-DNN provides global and local view learning subnetworks, which can effectively learn more potential feature information to enhance the prediction accuracy.

Second, in MVEW-DNN, deBLS can provide higher predictive accuracy by rationally integrating the attention mechanism and the additional enhancement nodes.

Third, FDDM can provide effective feature fusion between the global and local view learning subnetworks to perfectly complement each other.

Fourth, the local view learning subnetwork provides the combination of CEEMDAN and DBN to achieve more potential local view feature data in SWPF, effectively reducing the impact of data volatility and avoiding the model confounding problem on model prediction results.

4. Conclusions

In this paper, the developed MVEW-DNN model is a new width-depth integrated predictor that consists of a global view learning subnetwork and a local view learning subnetwork. The global view learning subnetwork effectively integrates the attention mechanism and the additional enhancement nodes, which gives it the advantages of low computational cost and high prediction accuracy. The local view learning subnetwork rationally combines CEEMDAN and DBN, which can achieve better potential local view features, enhancing the predictive accuracy and robustness. FDDM can provide an effective feature fusion between the global and local view learning subnetworks, further enhancing the predictive accuracy and robustness. Therefore, the proposed MVEW-DNN provides better predictive performance, e.g., nonlinear approximation capability and spatial learning ability, than that of the state-of-the-art and conventional predictive models on the SWPF task. MVEW-DNN can effectively and significantly improve the wind power schedule and production program, which relieves the pressure on the power system for peak and frequency regulation, to greatly improve the wind energy utilization. Table 6 shows that the high time-computation costs of our model are mainly due to the local view learning subnetwork (CEEMDAN-DBN). Therefore, in the future, we will consider how to effectively reduce the computational costs of the proposed MVEW-DNN.

Table 6. The time computation costs of deBLS, CEEMDAN-DBN, FDDM, and the proposed MVEW-DNN.

Wind Farm	deBLS (s)	CEEMDAN-DBN (s)	FDDM (s)	MVEW-DNN (s)
WF1	0.654	142.582	0.984	144.22
WF2	0.833	135.888	0.994	137.715
WF3	0.438	149.442	0.643	150.523
WF4	0.394	160.626	0.717	161.737
WF5	0.423	188.86	0.815	190.098
WF6	0.417	163.324	0.893	164.634
WF7	0.433	172.055	0.927	173.415

Author Contributions: Conceptualization, J.H., J.W. and Z.L.; methodology, J.H., J.W. and Z.L.; software, J.W., J.H. and Z.L.; validation, J.W.; formal analysis, J.H., J.W. and Z.L.; investigation, J.W.; resources, J.W.; data curation, J.W.; writing—original draft preparation, J.H., J.W. and Z.L.; writing—review and editing, C.L., J.H. and Z.L.; visualization, J.W.; supervision, C.L. and P.X.L.; project administration, C.L. and J.H.; funding acquisition, C.L. All authors have read and agreed to the published version of the manuscript.

Funding: This work was supported in part by the National Natural Science Foundation of China under grants 61863028, 62173176, 81660299, and 61503177, and in part by the Science and Technology Department of Jiangxi Province of China under grants 20204ABC03A39, 20161ACB21007, 20171BBE50071, and 20171BAB202033.

Institutional Review Board Statement: The study did not involve humans or animals.

Informed Consent Statement: The study did not involve humans.

Data Availability Statement: Publicly available data sets were analyzed in this study. These data can be found here: [https://www.kaggle.com/c/GEF2012-wind-forecasting/data] (accessed on 14 October 2021).

Conflicts of Interest: The authors declare no conflict of interest.

Abbreviations

SWPF	Short-term wind power forecasting
CEEMDAN	Complete ensemble empirical mode decomposition with adaptive noise
BLS-AEN	BLS network with Addition Enhancement Nodes
BLS-A	The BLS network with Attention Mechanism
deBLS	Deep encoder board learning system
MVEW-DNN	Multi-view ensemble-based width-depth neural network
Variables	
$X(t)$	The original wind power data
$\overline{IMF_k}(t)$	The kth decomposition in CEEMDAN
W_{e_i}	The randomly generated weight matrix
δ_{e_i}	The randomly generated bias matrix
J_n	The feature nodes
J^n	The feature nodes group
E_m	The enhancement nodes
E^m	The enhancement nodes group
B	The combination matrix of J^n and E_m
P	The output of our proposed model
$\mathcal{W}_{\mathcal{B}}$	The fusion weight of deBLS
$\mathcal{W}_{\mathcal{D}}$	The fusion weight of DBN
Indices	
k	The IMF index
n	The index of the feature nodes
m	The index of the enhancement nodes
N_{std}	The signal-to-noise ratio
ω	The adjusting weights in attention mechanism algorithm
C	The regularization parameter for sparse regularization
S	The shrinkage parameter in deBLS
ρ	The correlation test threshold

References

1. Hong, T.; Pinson, P.; Wang, Y.; Weron, R.; Yang, D.; Zareipour, H. Energy forecasting: A review and outlook. *IEEE Open Access J. Power Energy* **2020**, *7*, 376–388. [CrossRef]
2. Singh, U.; Rizwan, M. A Systematic Review on Selected Applications and Approaches of Wind Energy Forecasting and Integration. *J. Inst. Eng. Ser. B* **2021**, *102*, 1061–1078. [CrossRef]
3. Kerem, A.; Saygin, A.; Rahmani, R. A green energy research: Forecasting of wind power for a cleaner environment using robust hybrid metaheuristic model. *Environ. Sci. Pollut. Res.* **2021**. [CrossRef]

4. Liu, H.; Li, Y.; Duan, Z.; Chen, C. A review on multi-objective optimization framework in wind energy forecasting techniques and applications. *Energy Convers. Manag.* **2020**, *224*, 113324. [CrossRef]
5. Maciejowska, K.; Nitka, W.; Weron, T. Enhancing load, wind and solar generation for day-ahead forecasting of electricity prices. *Energy Econ.* **2021**, *99*, 105273. [CrossRef]
6. Rodriguez, H.; Flores, J.J.; Morales, L.A.; Lara, C.; Guerra, A.; Manjarrez, G. Forecasting from incomplete and chaotic wind speed data. *Soft Comput.* **2019**, *23*, 10119–10127. [CrossRef]
7. Yang, B.; Zhong, L.; Wang, J.; Shu, H.; Zhang, X.; Yu, T.; Sun, L. State-of-the-art one-stop handbook on wind forecasting technologies: An overview of classifications, methodologies, and analysis. *J. Clean. Prod.* **2021**, *283*, 124628. [CrossRef]
8. Foley, A.M.; Leahy, P.G.; Marvuglia, A.; McKeogh, E.J. Current methods and advances in forecasting of wind power generation. *Renew. Energy* **2012**, *37*, 1–8. [CrossRef]
9. Zjavka, L.; Mišák, S. Direct wind power forecasting using a polynomial decomposition of the general differential equation. *IEEE Trans. Sustain. Energy* **2018**, *9*, 1529–1539. [CrossRef]
10. Jacondino, W.D.; da Silva Nascimento, A.L.; Calvetti, L.; Fisch, G.; Beneti, C.A.; da Paz, S.R. Hourly day-ahead wind power forecasting at two wind farms in northeast brazil using WRF model. *Energy* **2021**, *230*, 120841. [CrossRef]
11. Zhang, F.; Li, P.C.; Gao, L.; Liu, Y.Q.; Ren, X.Y. Application of autoregressive dynamic adaptive (ARDA) model in real-time wind power forecasting. *Renew. Energy* **2021**, *169*, 129–143. [CrossRef]
12. Xie, W.; Zhang, P.; Chen, R.; Zhou, Z. A nonparametric Bayesian framework for short-term wind power probabilistic forecast. *IEEE Trans. Power Syst.* **2018**, *34*, 371–379. [CrossRef]
13. Zhang, J.; Wang, C. Application of ARMA model in ultra-short term prediction of wind power. In Proceedings of the 2013 International Conference on Computer Sciences and Applications IEEE, Washington, DC, USA, 14–15 December 2013; pp. 361–364.
14. Jia, M.; Shen, C.; Wang, Z. A distributed incremental update scheme for probability distribution of wind power forecast error. *Int. J. Electr. Power Energy Syst.* **2020**, *121*, 106151. [CrossRef]
15. Zhang, C.; Peng, T.; Nazir, M.S. A novel hybrid approach based on variational heteroscedastic Gaussian process regression for multi-step ahead wind speed forecasting. *Int. J. Electr. Power Energy Syst.* **2022**, *136*, 107717. [CrossRef]
16. He, Y.; Zhang, W. Probability density forecasting of wind power based on multi-core parallel quantile regression neural network. *Knowl.-Based Syst.* **2020**, *209*, 106431. [CrossRef]
17. Pearre, N.S.; Swan, L.G. Statistical approach for improved wind speed forecasting for wind power production. *Sustain. Energy Technol. Assess.* **2018**, *27*, 180–191.
18. Hu, T.; Wu, W.; Guo, Q.; Sun, H.; Shi, L.; Shen, X. Very short-term spatial and temporal wind power forecasting: A deep learning approach. *CSEE J. Power Energy Syst.* **2019**, *6*, 434–443.
19. Zendehboudi, A.; Baseer, M.A.; Saidur, R. Application of support vector machine models for forecasting solar and wind energy resources: A review. *J. Clean. Prod.* **2018**, *199*, 272–285. [CrossRef]
20. Li, R.; Ke, Y.Q.; Zhang, X.Q. Wind power forecasting based on time series and SVM. *Electr. Power* **2012**, *45*, 64–68.
21. Sun, W.; Wang, Y. Short-term wind speed forecasting based on fast ensemble empirical mode decomposition, phase space reconstruction, sample entropy and improved back-propagation neural network. *Energy Convers. Manag.* **2018**, *157*, 1–12. [CrossRef]
22. Hu, H.; Wang, L.; Lv, S.X. Forecasting energy consumption and wind power generation using deep echo state network. *Renew. Energy* **2020**, *154*, 598–613. [CrossRef]
23. Shetty, R.P.; Sathyabhama, A.; Pai, P.S. An efficient online sequential extreme learning machine model based on feature selection and parameter optimization using cuckoo search algorithm for multi-step wind speed forecasting. *Soft Comput.* **2021**, *25*, 1277–1295. [CrossRef]
24. Chen, C.P.; Liu, Z. Broad learning system: An effective and efficient incremental learning system without the need for deep architecture. *IEEE Trans. Neural Netw. Learn. Syst.* **2017**, *29*, 10–24. [CrossRef] [PubMed]
25. Hu, Q.; Zhang, R.; Zhou, Y. Transfer learning for short-term wind speed prediction with deep neural networks. *Renew Energy* **2016**, *85*, 83–95. [CrossRef]
26. Xu, L.; Chen, C.P.; Han, R. Sparse Bayesian broad learning system for probabilistic estimation of prediction. *IEEE Access* **2020**, *8*, 56267–56280. [CrossRef]
27. Yan, J.; Liu, Y.; Han, S.; Wang, Y.; Feng, S. Reviews on uncertainty analysis of wind power forecasting. *Renew. Sustain. Energy Rev.* **2015**, *52*, 1322–1330. [CrossRef]
28. Jiajun, H.; Chuanjin, Y.; Yongle, L.; Huoyue, X. Ultra-short term wind prediction with wavelet transform, deep belief network and ensemble learning. *Energy Convers. Manag.* **2020**, *205*, 112418. [CrossRef]
29. Chen, C.R.; Ouedraogo, F.B.; Chang, Y.M.; Larasati, D.A.; Tan, S.W. Hour-Ahead Photovoltaic Output Forecasting Using Wavelet-ANFIS. *Mathematics* **2021**, *9*, 2438. [CrossRef]
30. Wang, G.; Wang, X.; Wang, Z.; Ma, C.; Song, Z. A VMD–CISSA–LSSVM Based Electricity Load Forecasting Model. *Mathematics* **2022**, *10*, 28.
31. Devi, A.S.; Maragatham, G.; Boopathi, K.; Rangaraj, A.G. Hourly day-ahead wind power forecasting with the EEMD-CSO-LSTM-EFG deep learning technique. *Soft Comput.* **2020**, *24*, 12391–12411. [CrossRef]

32. Zhao, X.; Bai, M.; Yang, X.; Liu, J.; Yu, D.; Chang, J. Short-term probabilistic predictions of wind multi-parameter based on one-dimensional convolutional neural network with attention mechanism and multivariate copula distribution estimation. *Energy* **2021**, *234*, 121306. [CrossRef]
33. Niu, Z.; Yu, Z.; Tang, W.; Wu, Q.; Reformat, M. Wind power forecasting using attention-based gated recurrent unit network. *Energy* **2020**, *196*, 117081. [CrossRef]
34. Shahid, F.; Zameer, A.; Muneeb, M. A novel genetic LSTM model for wind power forecast. *Energy* **2021**, *223*, 120069. [CrossRef]
35. Khan, N.; Ullah, F.U.M.; Haq, I.U.; Khan, S.U.; Lee, M.Y.; Baik, S.W. AB-Net: A Novel Deep Learning Assisted Framework for Renewable Energy Generation Forecasting. *Mathematics* **2021**, *9*, 2456. [CrossRef]
36. Duan, J.; Wang, P.; Ma, W.; Fang, S.; Hou, Z. A novel hybrid model based on nonlinear weighted combination for short-term wind power forecasting. *Int. J. Electr. Power Energy Syst.* **2022**, *134*, 107452. [CrossRef]
37. Wu, Y.K.; Su, P.E.; Hong, J.S. Stratification-based wind power forecasting in a high-penetration wind power system using a hybrid model. *IEEE Trans. Ind. Appl.* **2016**, *52*, 2016–2030. [CrossRef]
38. Ogliari, E.; Guilizzoni, M.; Giglio, A.; Pretto, S. Wind power 24-h ahead forecast by an artificial neural network and an hybrid model: Comparison of the predictive performance. *Renew. Energy* **2021**, *178*, 1466–1474. [CrossRef]
39. Hong, Y.Y.; Rioflorido, C.L.P.P. A hybrid deep learning-based neural network for 24-h ahead wind power forecasting. *Appl. Energy* **2019**, *250*, 530–539. [CrossRef]
40. Ribeiro, M.H.D.M.; da Silva, R.G.; Moreno, S.R.; Mariani, V.C.; dos Santos Coelho, L. Efficient bootstrap stacking ensemble learning model applied to wind power generation forecasting. *Int. J. Electr. Power Energy Syst.* **2022**, *136*, 107712. [CrossRef]
41. Lai, C.S.; Yang, Y.; Pan, K.; Zhang, J.; Yuan, H.; Ng, W.W.; Gao, Y.; Zhao, Z.; Wang, T.; Shahidehpour, M.; et al. Multi-view neural network ensemble for short and mid-term load forecasting. *IEEE Trans. Power Syst.* **2020**, *36*, 2992–3003. [CrossRef]
42. Nguyen, L.H.; Pan, Z.; Openiyi, O.; Abu-gellban, H.; Moghadasi, M.; Jin, F. Self-boosted time-series forecasting with multi-task and multi-view learning. *arXiv* **2019**, arXiv:1909.08181.
43. Zhong, C.; Lai, C.S.; Ng, W.W.; Tao, Y.; Wang, T.; Lai, L.L. Multi-view deep forecasting for hourly solar irradiance with error correction. *Sol. Energy* **2021**, *228*, 308–316. [CrossRef]
44. Torres, M.E.; Colominas, M.A.; Schlotthauer, G.; Flandrin, P. A Complete Ensemble Empirical Mode Decomposition with Adaptive Noise. In Proceedings of the 2011 IEEE International Conference on Acoustics, Speech and Signal Processing (ICASSP), Prague, Czech Republic, 22–27 May 2011; pp. 4144–4147.
45. Flores, J.H.F.; Engel, P.M.; Pinto, R.C. Autocorrelation and Partial Autocorrelation Functions to Improve Neural Networks Models on Univariate Time Series Forecasting. In Proceedings of the The 2012 International Joint Conference on Neural Networks (IJCNN) IEEE, San Diego, CA, USA, 10–15 June 2012; pp. 1–8.
46. Global Energy Forecasting Competition 2012—Wind Forecasting. Available online: https://www.kaggle.com/c/GEF2012-wind-forecasting/data (accessed on 14 October 2021).
47. Kisvari, A.; Lin, Z.; Liu, X. Wind power forecasting—A data-driven method along with gated recurrent neural network. *Renew. Energy* **2021**, *163*, 1895–1909. [CrossRef]
48. Zhu, Y.; Zhu, C.; Song, C.; Li, Y.; Chen, X.; Yong, B. Improvement of reliability and wind power generation based on wind turbine real-time condition assessment. *Int. J. Electr. Power Energy Syst.* **2019**, *113*, 344–354. [CrossRef]
49. Putz, D.; Gumhalter, M.; Auer, H. A novel approach to multi-horizon wind power forecasting based on deep neural architecture. *Renew. Energy* **2021**, *178*, 494–505. [CrossRef]
50. Ren, Y.; Suganthan, P.N.; Srikanth, N.; Amaratunga, G. Random vector functional link network for short-term electricity load demand forecasting. *Inf. Sci.* **2016**, *367*, 1078–1093. [CrossRef]
51. Hao, Y.; Tian, C. A novel two-stage forecasting model based on error factor and ensemble method for multi-step wind power forecasting. *Appl. Energy* **2019**, *238*, 368–383. [CrossRef]
52. Duan, J.; Wang, P.; Ma, W. Short-term wind power forecasting using the hybrid model of improved variational mode decomposition and Correntropy Long Short-term memory neural network. *Energy* **2021**, *214*, 118980. [CrossRef]

mathematics

MDPI

Article

Study on Failure Characteristics and Control Technology of Roadway Surrounding Rock under Repeated Mining in Close-Distance Coal Seam

Yuqi Shang [1], Dezhong Kong [1,2,*], Shijiang Pu [3], Yu Xiong [1], Qiang Li [1] and Zhanbo Cheng [4,*]

[1] College of Mining, Guizhou University, Guiyang 550025, China; gs.yqshang20@gzu.edu.cn (Y.S.); gs.xiongy19@gzu.edu.cn (Y.X.); gs.liq19@gzu.edu.cn (Q.L.)
[2] State Key Laboratory of Public Big Data, Guizhou University, Guiyang 550025, China
[3] Faculty of Land and Resources Engineering, Kunming University of Science and Technology, Kunming 650093, China; pu_shijiang@163.com
[4] School of Engineering, University of Warwick, Coventry CV4 7AL, UK
* Correspondence: dzkong@gzu.edu.cn (D.K.); z.cheng.4@warwick.ac.uk (Z.C.)

Abstract: In this study, taking the Sheng'an coal mine as an engineering background, the failure characteristics of the surrounding rock of a roadway under repeated mining in a close-distance coal seam is comprehensively illustrated through field measurements (e.g., drilling imaging), theory analysis and numerical simulation (finite difference method (FDM)). The results show that although the return airway 10905 remains intact, the apparent failure of the roadway's roof and the coal pillar can be observed. In addition, the expression of floor failure depth caused by upper coal seam mining is obtained through elastic-plastic theory. Meanwhile, the deformation of the surrounding rock of the roadway increases with the increase of repeated mining times, especially for the horizontal displacement of the roadway on the coal pillar side. Moreover, the cracks' evolution of surrounding rock in the roadway can be observed as asymmetric characteristics. Finally, the stability control technology of "asymmetric anchor net cable + I-steel" is proposed to prevent potential mining disasters, and the feasibility of this support scheme is verified by numerical simulation and field practices. It can meet the requirement of safe mining and provide guidelines to effectively solve the failure of a roadway in close-distance coal seam mining.

Keywords: failure characteristics; surrounding rock of roadway; repeated mining; close-distance coal seam; stability control technology

MSC: 86-08; 86-10; 65E05

Citation: Shang, Y.; Kong, D.; Pu, S.; Xiong, Y.; Li, Q.; Cheng, Z. Study on Failure Characteristics and Control Technology of Roadway Surrounding Rock under Repeated Mining in Close-Distance Coal Seam. *Mathematics* **2022**, *10*, 2166. https://doi.org/10.3390/math10132166

Academic Editors: Zhuojia Fu, Yiqian He and Hui Zheng

Received: 19 May 2022
Accepted: 20 June 2022
Published: 21 June 2022

1. Introduction

In the process of coal formation, it will experience many crustal movements, and the coal measure strata are hosted in sedimentary rocks. Therefore, multiple coal seams will appear in the same coal measure strata with a small distance between the adjacent multi-coal seams. Different from the mining of a single coal seam, the mining activities of a close coal seam group can be influenced by each other's coal seams with the characteristics of mutual disturbance, stress concentration and severe damage to the mining roadway [1–4]. The roadway in the lower coal seam is significantly affected by the caving gangue generated after upper coal seam mining and the dynamic pressure due to the mining activities of the adjacent working face. Therefore, the roof management of the working face under repeated mining should be paid more attention in order to prevent the occurrence of mining disasters. In the process of coal formation, it will experience many crustal movements, and the coal measure strata are hosted in sedimentary rocks. Therefore, multiple coal seams will appear in the same coal measure strata with a small distance between the adjacent multi-coal seams. Different from the mining of a single coal seam, the mining activities of a close coal seam group can be influenced by each other's coal seams with the characteristics of mutual disturbance, stress concentration and severe damage to the mining roadway [5–10]. The roadway in the lower coal seam is significantly affected by the caving gangue generated after upper coal seam mining and the dynamic pressure due to the mining activities of the adjacent working face.

Currently, the support theory and control technology of the surrounding rock of a roadway under repeated mining in a close-distance coal seam is comprehensively illustrated. Refs.studied the dynamic stress evolution law of floor in the process of repeated mining and discussed the distribution characteristics of surrounding rock stress and the displacement of floor roadway. Meanwhile, the grouting bolt to strengthen shallow broken surrounding rock and hollow grouting anchor cable to strengthen deep cracks combined with double anchor mesh shotcrete support were proposed to fully mobilize the self-supporting ability of the surrounding rock. In addition, Xiong et al. [11] illustrated the stress distribution of the floor under the repeated mining and the staggered arrangement of the roadway in the lower coal seam. Zhang et al. [12] illustrated that the lower coal mining roadway was prone to instability under the action of the low support strength of the roadway, the over-speed mining and the vertical arrangement of the upper coal seam roadway. Liu et al. [13] proposed the segmented support design technology to control different types of roofs, which can significantly improve the stress state of the surrounding rock. Using numerical simulation, Han et al. [14] conducted the roadway stability under a reinforcement support scheme. The results showed that the instability mechanism of the roadway met the requirements of an extremely close coal seam, and the section shrinkage rate remained at 5.29%. Cheng et al. [15] proposed three schemes of lengthening an anchor bolt combined support to solve the problem of significant roof subsidence in the roadway of the lower coal seam. Geng et al. [16] analyzed the plastic failure characteristics, stress distribution and displacement variation of the roadway under the influence of the superimposed stress after the upper coal seam mining. Then the comprehensive roof control technology of 'broken roof hole + pressure relief hole + high pre-stressed anchor cable + single hydraulic prop' was proposed.

Throughout the literature review, the current research mainly focused on the stress distribution law of a floor under a coal pillar in the close-distance coal seam group mining and the layout offset of a roadway in the lower coal seam. However, there are few studies proposing the stability control technology to support the surrounding rock of a roadway in the lower coal seam while considering the action of the caving gangue generated in the upper coal seam and the dynamic pressure due to the mining activities of the adjacent working face. There may be no residual coal pillar after the upper coal seam mining when the close-distance coal seam group adopts the downward mining method. In addition, the stress and displacement of the surrounding rock of the roadway under the repeated mining in the close-distance coal seam group should be explored in detail. Therefore, taking the Sheng'an coal mine in Guizhou Province (China) as an engineering background, this study aims to illustrate the failure characteristics and instability law of the surrounding rock of the roadway in the lower coal seam and the damage depth of the floor caused by the upper coal seam mining [17,18]. Most importantly, the corresponding support techniques are proposed and applied in engineering practices, which provide the guideline to control the stability of the surrounding rock of the roadway in similar mining conditions.

2. Engineering Background

2.1. Geological Conditions

The Sheng'an coal mine has two main coal seams, named ##6 and ##9, respectively. The coal seam #9 is buried with a depth of 191 m and an average thickness of 1.81 m. Moreover, its roof is silty mudstone, argillaceous siltstone and mudstone, and its floor is mudstone, silty mudstone and argillaceous siltstone. On the other hand, the coal seam #6 with an average thickness of 1.26 m is away from coal seam #9 by 4.14–7.01 m, which is a typical close-distance coal seam group.

The working face 10905 is arranged in coal seam #9 without leaving the coal pillar, located in the south of working face 10903, as shown in Figures 1 and 2. Moreover, the return airway of working face 10905 and the transportation roadway of working face 10903 are separated by coal pillars of 13 m. Therefore, significant roof subsidence and horizontal displacement of the return airway in working face 10905 during the excavation process can be observed due to the influence of upper coal seam #6 mining and the adjacent working face 10903 mining. Notably, various disasters (e.g., roof leakage and roof caving) can be observed, which greatly affect the safe and efficient production of the mine in working face 10905.

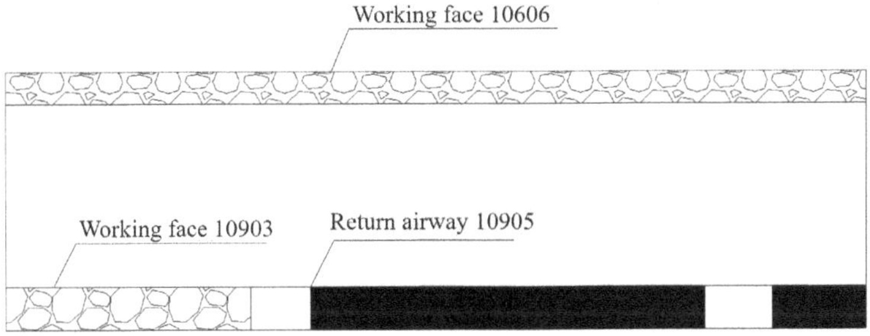

Figure 1. Arrangement of multi-working faces.

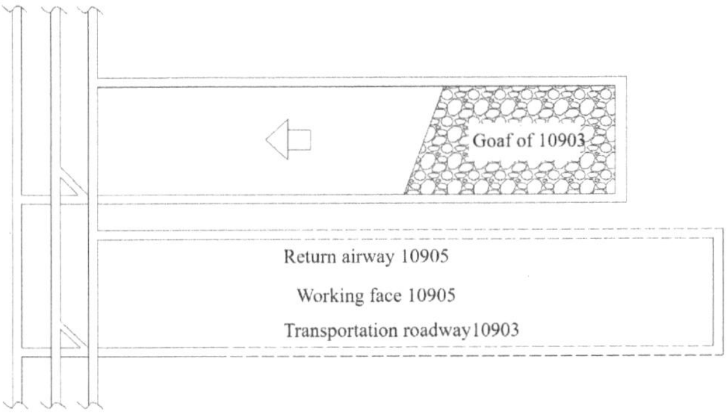

Figure 2. Arrangement of working face 10905.

2.2. *Roof Failure Characteristics of Return Airway in Working Face 10905*

The working face 10905 mined coal seam #9 is arranged below the 10606 working face of coal seam #6. Originally, the bolt + I-steel combined symmetric support scheme was adopted as shown in Figure 3. The row spacing between the bolts is 0.8 × 0.8 m, and the spacing between the sheds and frames is 0.8 m. However, the sidewall of the return airway is not fully supported, and the I-steel is only used to maintain the stability of the roadway. Due to the neglect of the asymmetry of the stress and deformation of the roadway sidewall, severe sidewall heave and roof subsidence deformation can still be observed in the process of roadway excavation, as shown in Figure 4.

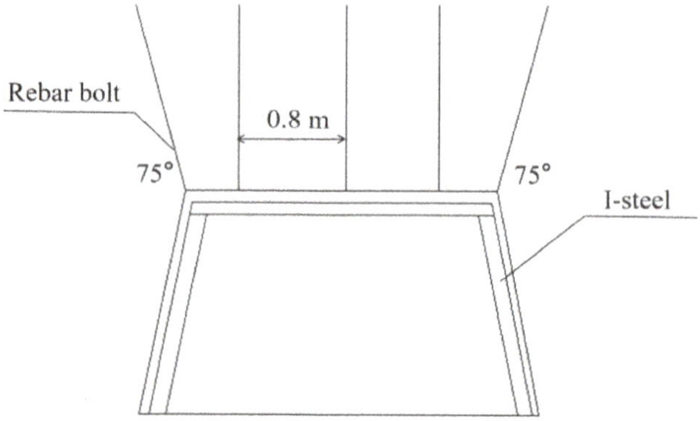

Figure 3. Previous support scheme of return airway of working face 10905.

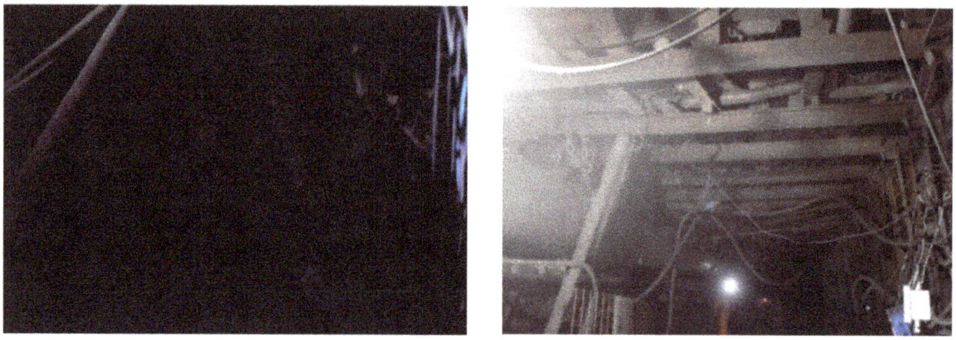

Figure 4. Deformation of surrounding rock during roadway excavation.

Based on the results of drilling images, Figure 5 illustrates that there are few cracks in the upper part of the roadway roof from 2.5 to 3.0 m, while the surrounding rock of the borehole is relatively complete. In addition, an obvious transverse fracture in the upper roof 3.5 m can be observed, which is similar to the annular interval fracture zone. Moreover, the loose fracture of the surrounding rock in the borehole is observed at the upper roof of 4 m, and zoning fracture exists in shallow and deep parts of the roadway roof. On the other hand, the integrity of the surrounding rock in the borehole is good when the borehole depth on the coal pillar side of the roadway reaches 1.5–2 m as shown in Figure 6. When the drilling depth reaches 2.5 m, the coal body begins in a broken state. Meanwhile, the number of cracks is small, and there are few longitudinal cracks when the depth of the borehole on the side of the roadway increases to 1.5 m, as shown in Figure 7. With the increase of drilling depth, the shape of longitudinal fractures decreases, and the integrity of the surrounding rock is good at the drilling depth of 2.5–3 m. The comprehensive analysis shows that the roadway roof of working face 10905 is not fully broken, while the overall bearing capacity is weak. However, the roof and coal pillar side of the roadway are obviously broken in different areas. It is possible that a large deformation in the future working face mining may appear.

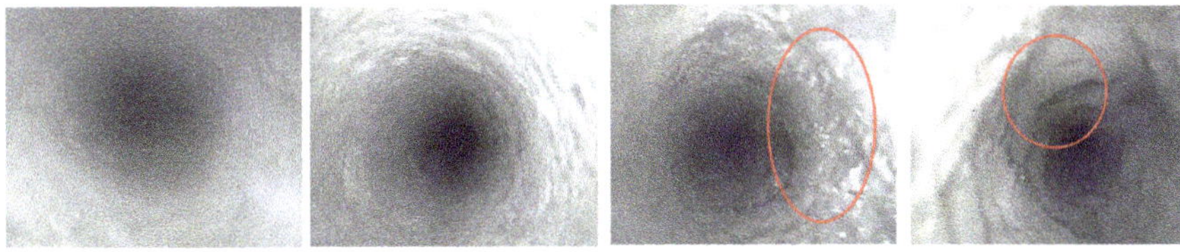

(a) (b) (c) (d)

Figure 5. Drilling images of a borehole at different distances from roadway roof. (**a**) 2.5 m. (**b**) 3.0 m. (**c**) 3.5 m. (**d**) 4.0 m.

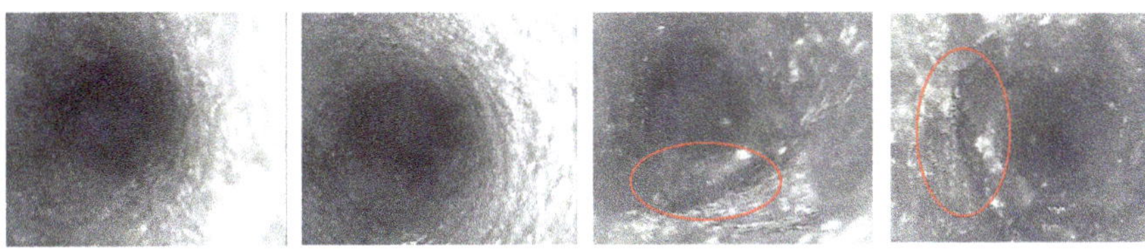

(a) (b) (c) (d)

Figure 6. Drilling images of a borehole at different distances from coal pillar side of roadway. (**a**) 1.5 m. (**b**) 2.0 m. (**c**) 2.5 m. (**d**) 3.0 m.

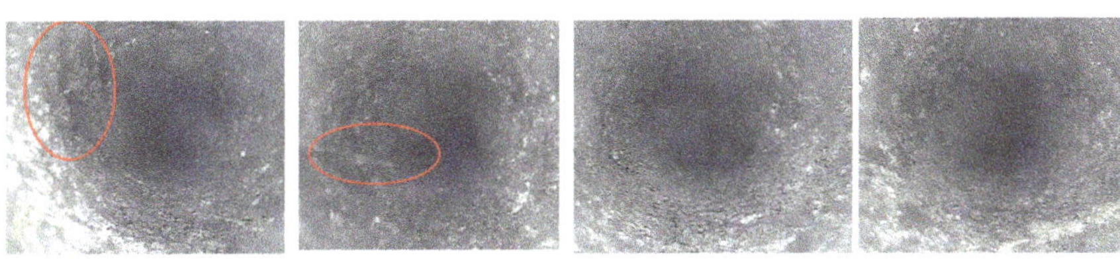

(a) (b) (c) (d)

Figure 7. Drilling images of a borehole at different distances from working face side. (**a**) 1.5 m. (**b**) 2.0 m. (**c**) 2.5 m. (**d**) 3.0 m.

2.3. Instability Factors of Roadway

After coal seam #6 was mined, the floor strata were damaged to influence the mining of lower coal seam #9. Moreover, the coal seam #6 above the working face 10905 was mined without leaving the coal pillar. In addition, the rock strata activity of adjacent working face 10903 has not reached a stable state. The surrounding rock of the roadway in working face 10905 is again experiencing severe deformation and failure, especially in the coal pillar side of the roadway. Most importantly, the support method of the return airway in working face 10905 is unreasonable. Therefore, the roof subsidence of the roadway in working face 10905 is significant, and two sides of the roadway are seriously moved during the excavation process.

3. Calculation of Floor Damage Depth after Coal Seam #6 Mining

A rectangular goaf is generally formed in the rear after the working face is mined, and the ratio of the height of the mined coal seam to the width of the working face is minimal [19–22]. Therefore, the mechanical model of the longwall working face can be simplified, as shown in Figure 8.

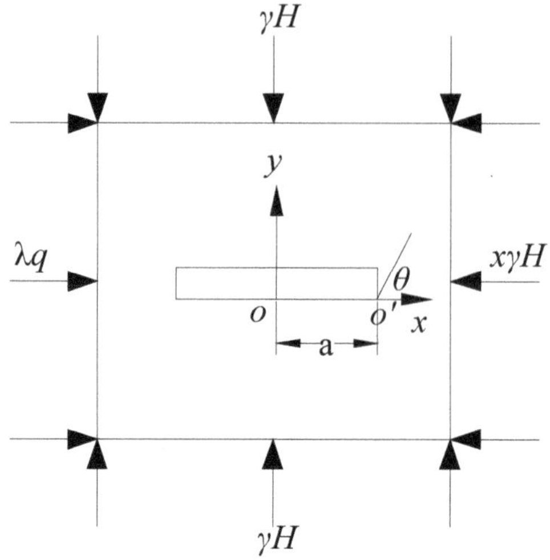

Figure 8. Mechanical model based on elastic-plastic theory.

According to the elastic-plastic theory and using the coordinate system as shown in Figure 9, the vertical stress and shear stress of the surrounding rock can be expressed as follows.

$$\begin{cases} \sigma_x = \gamma H\sqrt{\frac{L}{2r}}\cos\frac{\theta}{2}(1-\sin\frac{\theta}{2}\sin\frac{3\theta}{2}) - (1-x)\gamma H \\ \sigma_y = \gamma H\sqrt{\frac{L}{2r}}\cos\frac{\theta}{2}(1+\sin\frac{\theta}{2}\sin\frac{3\theta}{2}) \\ \tau_{xy} = \gamma H\sqrt{\frac{L}{2r}}\cos\frac{\theta}{2}\sin\frac{\theta}{2}\cos\frac{3\theta}{2} \end{cases} \quad (1)$$

where L and H are the length and buried depth of the working face, γ is the bulk density of rock mass, x is lateral stress ratio, r is the limit failure distance ahead of the working face, θ is the angle between the edge line and the horizontal direction at the maximum yield depth h.

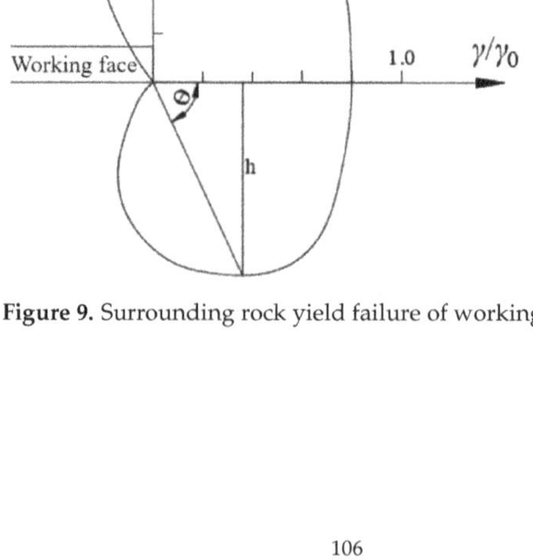

Figure 9. Surrounding rock yield failure of working face.

According to the actual mining situation of the Sheng'an coal mine, the lateral pressure coefficient is 1, and then the principal stress expression of the stope edge can be deduced as follows.

$$\begin{cases} \sigma_1 = \frac{\gamma H}{2}\sqrt{\frac{L}{r}}\cos\frac{\theta}{2}(1+\sin\frac{\theta}{2}) \\ \sigma_2 = \frac{\gamma H}{2}\sqrt{\frac{L}{r}}\cos\frac{\theta}{2}(1-\sin\frac{\theta}{2}) \\ \sigma_3 = \mu\gamma H\sqrt{\frac{L}{r}}\cos\frac{\theta}{2} \end{cases} \quad (2)$$

where μ is the Poisson' s ratio of surrounding rock.

Assuming that the failure of surrounding rock obeys the Mohr-Coufomb criterion, the following expression can be obtained.

$$\sigma_1 - \xi\sigma_3 = R_c \quad (3)$$

$$\xi = \frac{1+\sin\phi}{1-\sin\phi} \quad (4)$$

where R_c is the uniaxial compressive strength of surrounding rock, and φ is the internal friction angle of the surrounding rock.

Therefore, the yield failure depth (h) of floor rock caused by stress concentration in coal seam mining can be obtained as follows.

$$h = \frac{\gamma^2 H^2 L}{4{R_c}^2}\cos^2\frac{\theta}{2}(1+\sin\frac{\theta}{2})^2\sin\theta \quad (5)$$

The maximum failure depth of floor strata under the plane stress state is expressed as follows.

$$h_{\max} = \frac{1.57\gamma^2 H^2 L}{4{R_c}^2} \quad (6)$$

It can be observed that the damage depth of floor rock increases linearly with the square of inclined length and the buried depth of the working face, and decreases linearly with the square of the compressive strength of floor rock.

On the other hand, the failure zone near the stope edge (r') can be expressed as follows.

$$r' = \frac{\gamma^2 H^2 L}{4{R_c}^2}\cos^2\frac{\theta}{2}(1+\sin\frac{\theta}{2}-2\varepsilon\mu)^2 \quad (7)$$

where ε is the strain of the rock element in the plane strain state.

Therefore, the horizontal failure range of stope edge r'_0 at $\theta = 0°$ is shown as follows.

$$r'_0 = \frac{\gamma^2 H^2 L(1-2\varepsilon\mu)^2}{4{R_c}^2} \quad (8)$$

The failure depth of floor strata in lower coal seam (h') can be calculated according to the geometric relationship under the plane strain state as follows.

$$h' = r'\sin\theta = \frac{\gamma^2 H^2 L}{4R^2}\cos^2\frac{\theta}{2}(1+\sin\frac{\theta}{2}-2\xi\mu)^2\sin\theta \quad (9)$$

According to the comparison of the failure depth of floor strata under the plane stress and strain states, it can be seen that the failure range obtained under the plane stress state is larger than that under the plane strain state. Therefore, when the elastic-plastic theory is used to calculate the failure depth of floor strata, the calculation results in plane stress state are used to measure the failure depth of floor strata in coal mining. The influence of the joint fissures of the floor strata on the failure depth is then comprehensively considered, and Equation (6) is transformed as follows.

$$h_{\max} = 1.57\gamma^2 H^2 L / \left(4R_c^2 \bullet \delta^2\right) \tag{10}$$

where δ is the influence coefficient of joint fissure in floor strata.

The average mining height and buried depth of coal seam #6 in Sheng'an Coal Mine is 1.35 m and 185 m, respectively. The length of the working face 10606 is 150 m. According to the experimental test results, the internal friction angle of cohesion of coal body #6 are 25.2° and 1.18 MPa, respectively. In addition, the friction coefficient of the contact surface between coal seam 5# and the floor is 0.32, and the influence coefficient of the joint fracture is 0.39. Moreover, the uniaxial compressive strength of floor strata is 14.9 MPa, and the bulk density of floor strata is 2300 kN/m^3. The maximum stress concentration coefficient is 3.5. Inserting these geological parameters into Equation (10), the failure depth of floor strata caused by the upper coal seam #6 is 4.63 m, as follows.

$$h_{\max} = 1.57\gamma^2 H^2 L / \left(4R^2 \bullet \delta^2\right) = \frac{1.57 \times 23^2 \times 185^2 \times 150}{0.6084 \times 31,900^2} \approx 4.63 \text{ m}$$

4. Numerical Simulation of Roadway Instability under Repeated Mining

4.1. Numerical Model Establishment and Parameter Determination

In order to explore the influence of repeated mining on the instability law of the roadway, FLAC3D is used to illustrate the stress distribution law and the development of the plastic zone in the stope when the upper and lower coal seams are mined [23–25]. The numerical calculation model adopts the Mohr-Coulomb constitutive model because it is a nonlinear model and is widely used in the calculation of the actual bearing capacity and failure load of rock mass in underground space engineering. FLAC 3D can simulate the mechanical properties and plastic flow analysis of three-dimensional structures of soil, rock and other materials by adjusting the polyhedral units. Based on the finite difference method, the computational region is divided into several tetrahedral elements, each of which follows the Moor-Coulomb constitutive model under given boundary conditions.

According to the occurrence conditions of the coal seam in the Sheng'an coal mine, the numerical simulation model is established with the length, width and height of 250 m, 120 m and 108 m, respectively, as shown in Figure 10. The bottom boundary of the model is fixed, and the displacement in the X, Y and Z directions of the bottom boundary is set as zero. In addition, the top of the model is a free boundary. The upper rock layer is applied to the equivalent load, and the self-balancing treatment is carried out before the excavation of the model.

The average buried depth of coal seam #6 is about 185 m, and the uniform load is applied according to the buried depth. The average density of rock strata is 2500 kg/m^3, and the lateral stress coefficient is 1. In addition, according to the experimental tests of rock specimens collected from the Sheng'an coal mine and then conducted in the laboratory of Guizhou University, various physical and mechanical parameters (e.g., volumetric weight, compressive strength, tensile strength, Poisson's ratio, cohesion and internal friction angle) of coal seam and rock mass are obtained and used in the numerical model as listed in Table 1.

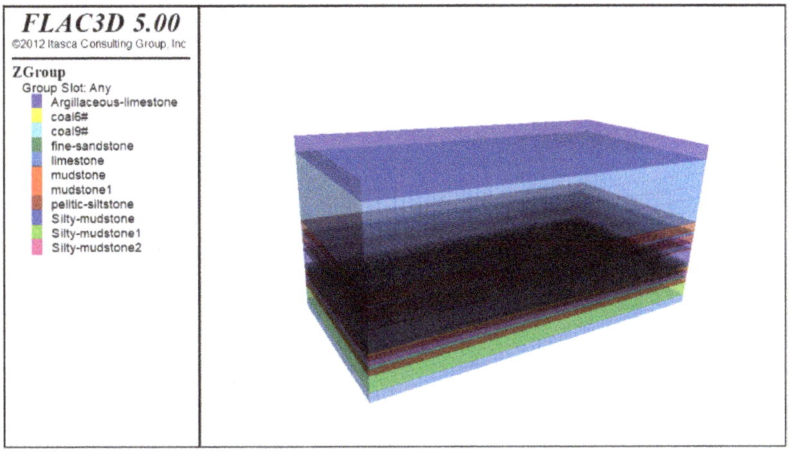

Figure 10. Numerical simulation model.

Table 1. Physical and mechanical properties of coal and rock mass.

Rock Name	Volumetric Weight g/cm^3	Compressive Strength/MPa	Tensile Strength/MPa	Poisson's Ratio	Cohesion/MPa	Internal Friction Angle/°
Coal #6	1.29	13.25	0.33	0.32	1.18	25.16
Mudstone-1	2.13	38.90	0.88	0.31	1.78	23.40
Argillaceous Sandstone	2.32	79.65	1.57	0.28	3.80	34.00
Silty Mudstone	2.44	62.18	1.23	0.21	3.30	30.05
Coal #9	1.30	11.89	0.26	0.36	1.42	24.50
Mudstone-2	2.00	38.20	0.82	0.29	1.80	24.00

4.2. Stress and Displacement Characteristics of Surrounding Rock in Lower Coal Seam

4.2.1. Stress Evolution Law

Figure 11 illustrates the stress distribution of surrounding rock in lower coal seam mining #9 with the working face advancing of 20 m, 40 m, 60 m and 80 m. Specifically, the stress concentration coefficient at the coal wall of the working face on the open-off cut is significantly reduced with the working face advancing of 20 m under the pressure relief effect of coal seam #6 mining. With the working face advancing increasing to 40 m, the small stress value of the roof and floor of coal seam #9 has been extended to an extensive range, and a small range of the stress concentration area appears in front of the coal wall of the working face. Subsequently, part of the pressure relief is reduced to connect into slices, and the force is redistributed again when the advance of the working face is 60 m. With the continuous increase of working face advancing, the pressure relief range of the connected slices increases periodically, while the increased effect of the pressure relief range is not apparent in the upper and lower ranges. It indicates that the rock entirely collapses, the rear of the working face is compacted, and the pressure relief range reaches stability.

4.2.2. Evolution Law of Plastic Zone

Figure 12 illustrates the distribution of plastic zone during the lower coal seam mining. It can be seen that there is a large range of plastic area at the cutting hole, while the plastic range at the coal wall is less under the working face advancing 20 m. Subsequently, the plastic range in the front of the working face and floor strata increase with the advance of working face increasing to 40 m, and the roof of the goaf is still in the elastic area. Moreover, the plastic zones of overlying and floor strata increase significantly at the working face advancing 60 and 80 m.

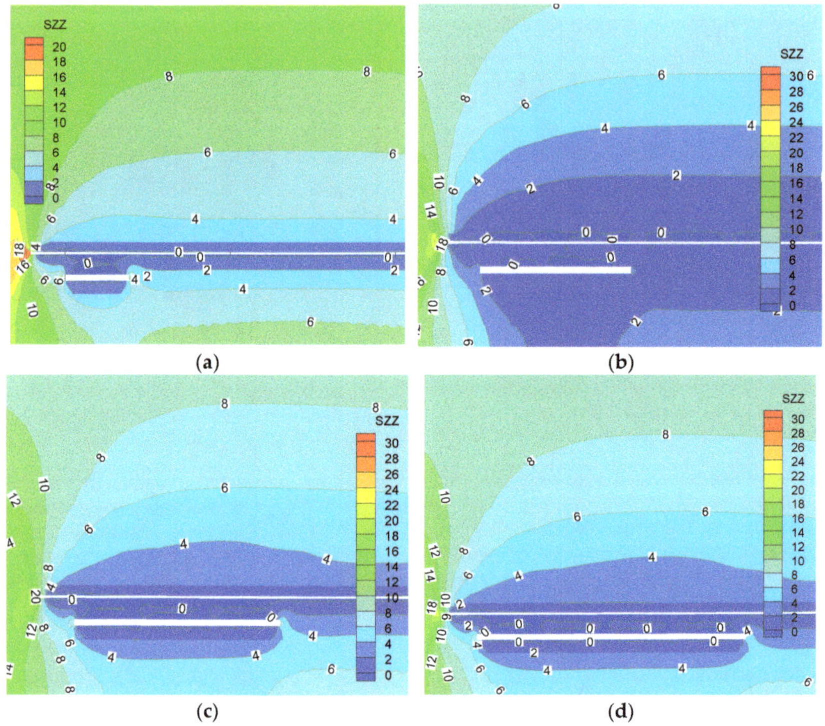

Figure 11. Vertical stress distribution of surrounding rock in lower coal seam #9. (**a**) Advancing 20 m. (**b**) Advancing 40 m. (**c**) Advancing 60 m. (**d**) Advancing 80 m.

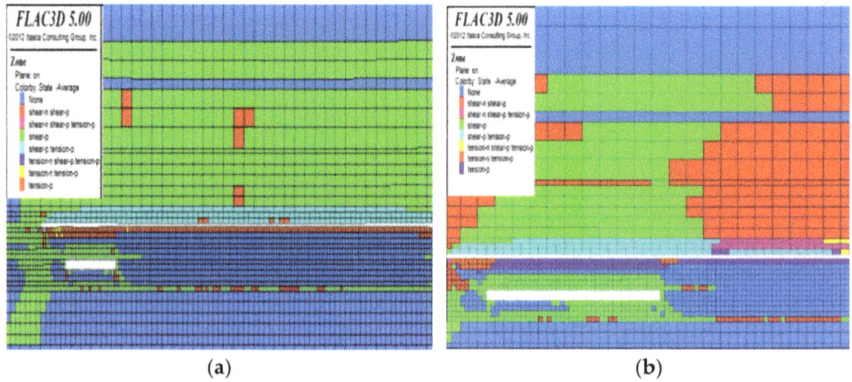

Figure 12. *Cont.*

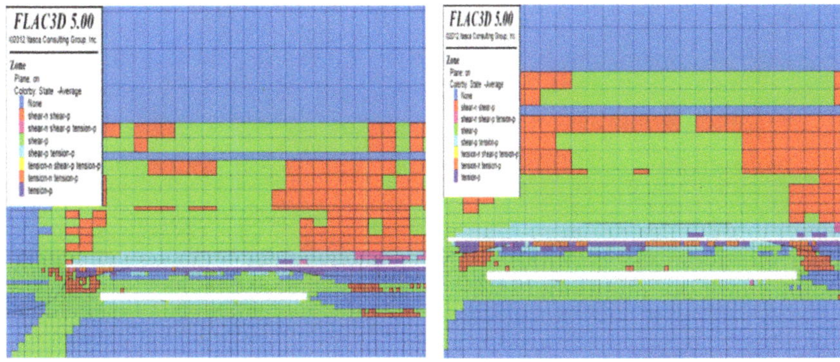

(c) (d)

Figure 12. Plastic zone of coal seam #9 with different advancing distances. (**a**) Advancing 20 m. (**b**) Advancing 40 m. (**c**) Advancing 60 m. (**d**) Advancing 80 m.

4.3. Stress and Deformation Evolution Law of Surrounding Rock under Repeated Mining

Figure 13 illustrates the model excavation scheme to fully mine the upper coal seam and excavate the adjacent roadway of 30 m. Moreover, the gob-side entry retaining technology without the coal pillar is used in the mining of upper coal seam #6.

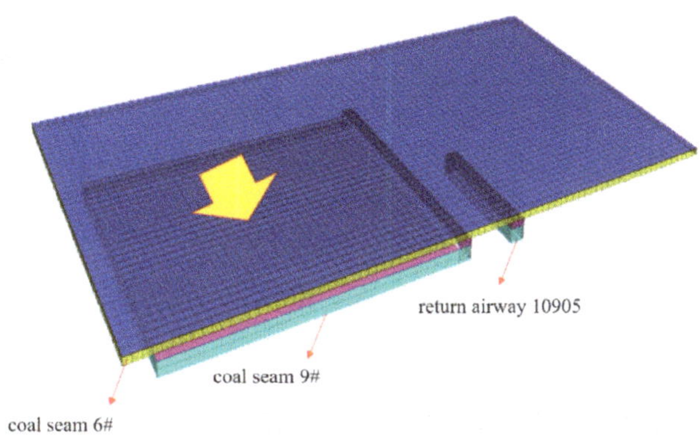

Figure 13. Model excavation scheme.

Figure 14 shows the vertical stress distribution at the position of the reserved roadway and the roof of the coal pillar in the upper coal seam mining. The pressure relief effect at the position of reserved roadway and coal pillar is good with the low stress value due to the small space between the two coal seams. Moreover, the stress value at the position of reserved roadway strike 30 m and 90 m is slightly higher with the average value of about 0.3 MPa due to the influence of the coal pillar boundary in the goaf, and the direction of vertical stress is downward. On the other hand, the direction of vertical stress at the position of the reserved roadway strike 40 m, 50 m, 70 m and 80 m is upward because the lower strata of the goaf is changed from original extrusion pressure into tensile stress and the cracks also begin to be expended after the upper coal seam mining. Meanwhile, the location of a roadway strike at 60 m may be the first weighing site, and the overlying strata is collapsed and compacted resulting in the downward direction of vertical stress.

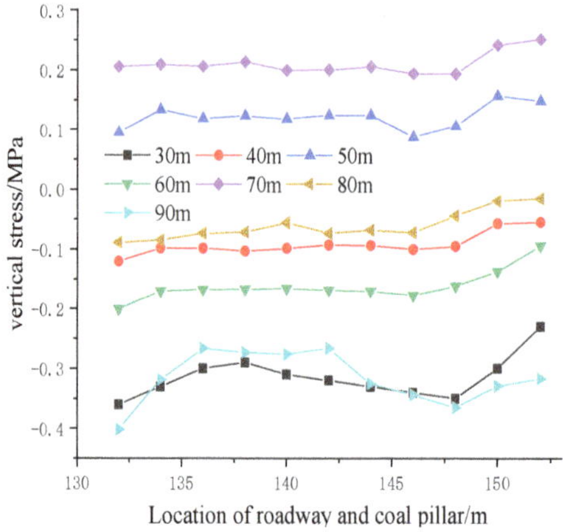

Figure 14. Influence of excavation disturbance on upper coal seam.

Figure 15 illustrates that there exists a certain of lateral pressure concentration because of the adjacent roadway excavation to cause the vertical stress of the reserved roadway and the roof of the coal pillar increasing firstly and then decreasing from near to far. Figure 16 illustrates that the vertical stress distribution at the position of 40 m and 50 m along the roadway has limited change, while the vertical stress distribution is greatly changeable at the position of 30 m and 60 m along the roadway behind the working face. Meanwhile, the stress in the roof of the roadway is large. In summary, the excavation of the upper coal seam has a significant effect on the stress value and distribution of the reserved roadway and coal pillar because of the low rock strength and the small interlay space of two coal seams, while the stress value and range is limited changed under the influence of the excavation of adjacent roadway and local roadway.

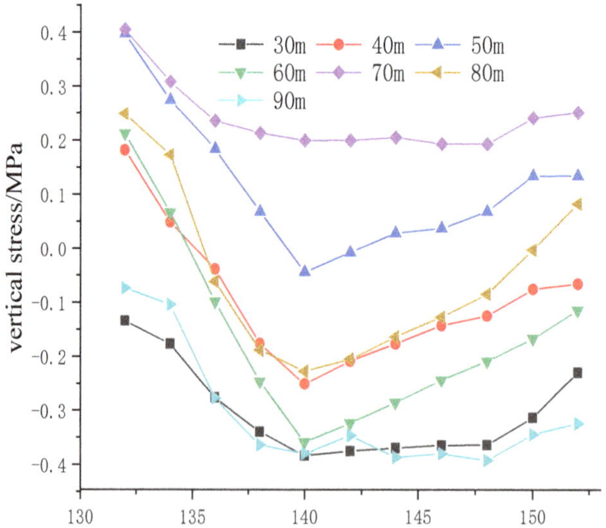

Figure 15. Influence of adjacent roadway excavation disturbance.

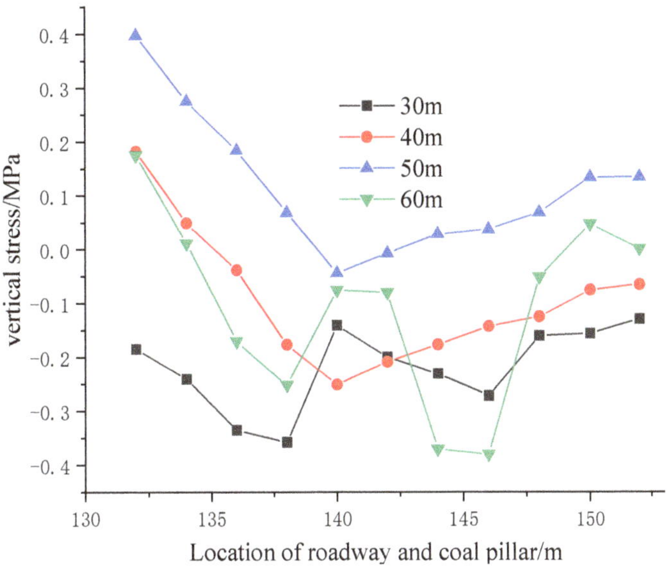

Figure 16. Influence of excavation disturbance on this roadway.

Figure 17 illustrates the variation of horizontal displacement of the roadway along with the strike position. Under the repeated mining, the deformation of surrounding rock in the roadway increases with the increase of mining times, especially for the coal pillar side. The deformation variables of the two sides are prone to have asymmetric situations during the mining process, and the stability maintenance of the coal pillar side needs to be emphasized.

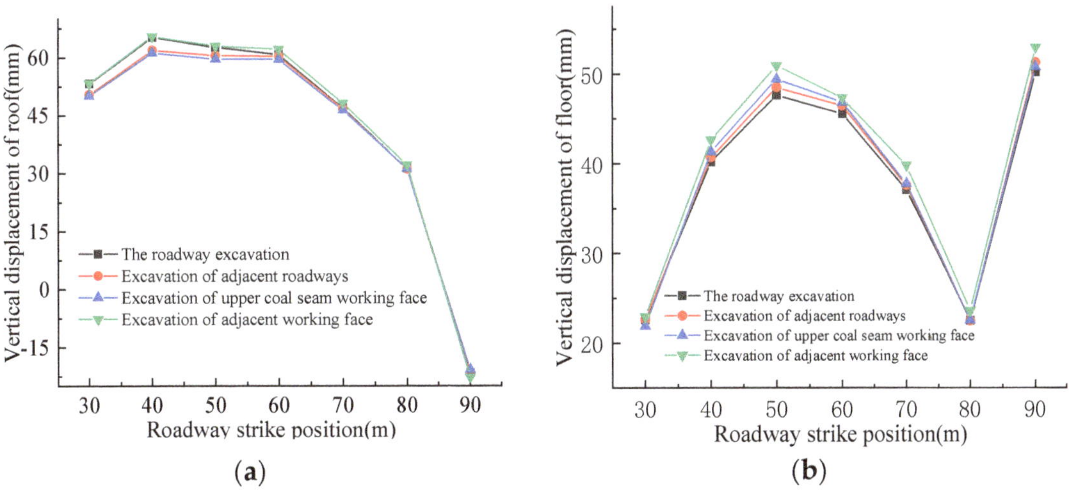

Figure 17. *Cont.*

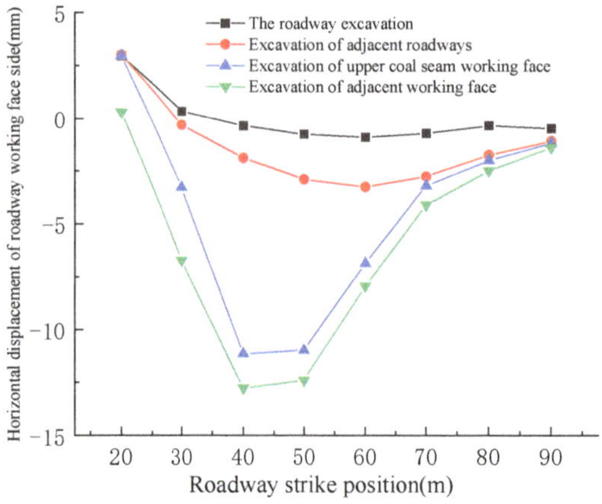

(c)

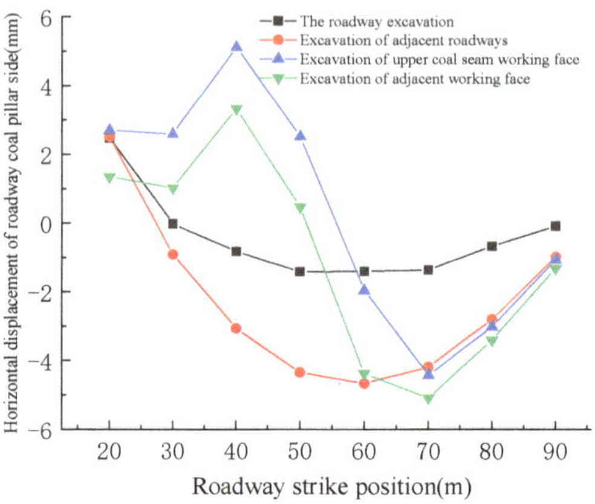

(d)

Figure 17. Displacement of roadway. (**a**) Displacement of roadway roof. (**b**) Displacement of roadway floor. (**c**) Displacement of roadway in working face side. (**d**) Displacement of roadway in coal pillar side.

5. Support Measurements Numerical Simulation Analysis

5.1. Influence of Fracture Angle on Unconfined Compressive Strength

Considering the repeated disturbance of the adjacent working face of the roadway, the asymmetric anchor cable + I-steel support scheme is proposed to effectively prevent the deformation and fracture of the roadway roof as shown in Figure 18. Specifically, five left-handed helical steel bolts (Φ20 × 2200 mm), four left spiral steel anchors (Φ20 × 2400 mm), and three reinforced fiber glass bolts (Φ20 × 2200 mm) are installed in the roof strata of the roadway, the first side of the coal pillar and the first side of the working face with the row spacing of 800 × 800 mm and connected with W-shaped steel strip, respectively. Meanwhile, a high strength drum anchor plate (150 × 150 × 10 mm) is also used. In addition, the anchor cables of Φ22 × 4300 mm are arranged in the roof strata of the roadway with the spacing of 1400 × 2400 mm, and three anchor cables are installed in each row. Similarly, the anchor cables are arranged in the side of the coal pillar and working face with the row spacing of 1600 × 2400 mm, and 2 anchor cables are installed in each row [26–28].

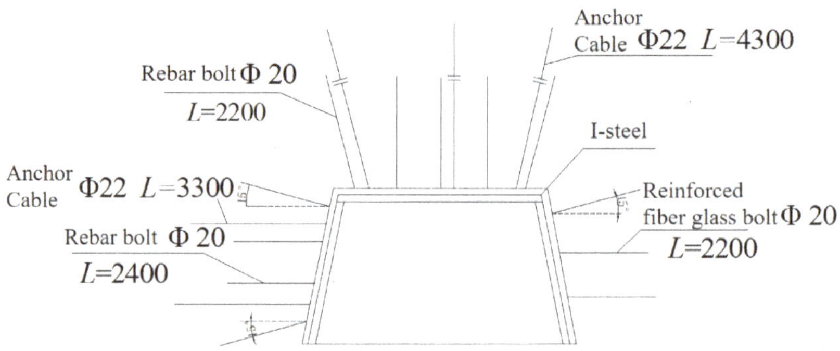

Figure 18. Roadway section support scheme.

5.2. Comparative Analysis of Supporting Effect in Numerical Simulation

Numerical simulation is performed to analyze the feasibility of the surrounding rock control scheme through comparison of the deformation, plastic zone and stress field distribution of surrounding rock in the roadway of the lower coal seam by using the original support scheme and the proposed optimized support scheme (asymmetric anchor cable + I-steel).

As shown in Figure 19a, the surrounding rock of the roadway is mainly shear failure and the plastic zone decreases when the bolt is used in time after the excavation of the roadway, while there is still a large area of the plastic zones in the roof and the two sides by using the original support scheme. In addition, the surrounding rock is unstable again if the support stillness of the roadway is insufficient in the later period of coal seam mining. However, the timely support of the bolt and anchor cable plays a controlling role in the surrounding rock of the roadway, and the plastic zones of surrounding rock are less by using the proposed optimized support scheme as shown in Figure 19c. Meanwhile, the bearing capacity of surrounding rock can also gradually increase from 0–2 MPa to 2–4 MPa. Overall, the asymmetric anchor cable + I-steel can basically realize the temporary support demand to meet the deformation requirement of surrounding rock in the later mining.

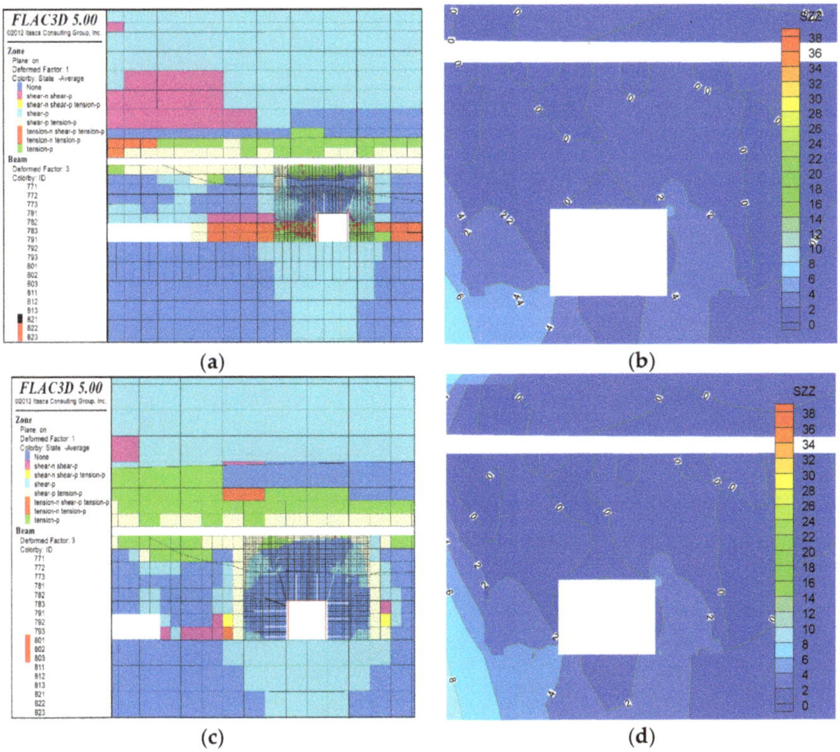

Figure 19. Plastic zone and stress diagram of surrounding rock in two support schemes. (**a**) Plastic zone of original support scheme. (**b**) Vertical stress of original support scheme. (**c**) Plastic zone of proposed support scheme. (**d**) Vertical stress of proposed support scheme.

5.3. Engineering Practices

As shown in Figure 20, 20 monitoring points are arranged to measure the deformation of surrounding rock in the roadway with the distance of each point being 10 m, and Figure 21 illustrates the typical displacement curve of the surrounding rock of roadway in working face 10905. The results show that the maximum displacement of the roadway roof, coal pillar side and working face side is 326 mm, 225 mm and 201 mm, respectively. Moreover, the deformation on both sides of the roadway is asymmetric distribution and its deformation rate is the largest in the range of +20 m to −40 m from the working face. In addition, the displacement of the roadway increases with the advancement of the working face 10903, and the displacement of the roadway far from the working face is small. The overall displacement of the roadway is within the controllable range, and the roadway support effect is shown in Figure 22.

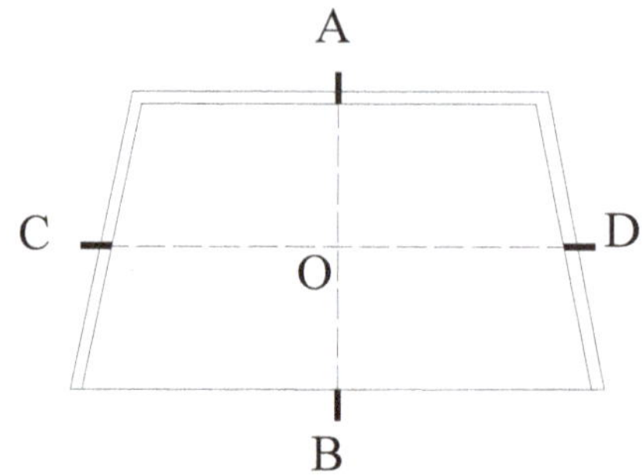

Figure 20. Layout of monitoring points.

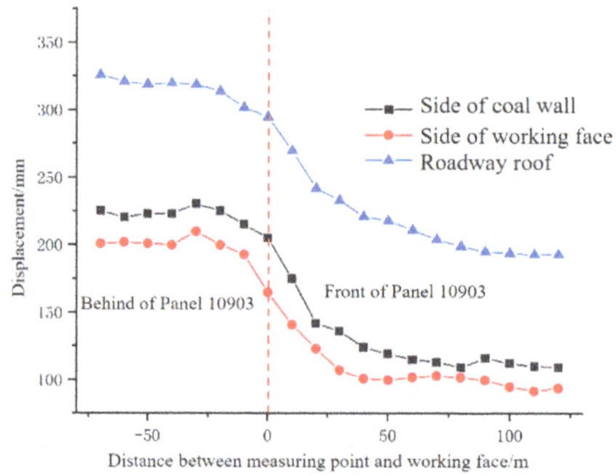

Figure 21. Displacement curve of the surrounding rock of the roadway.

(a) **(b)**

Figure 22. Support effect of return airway in working face 10905. (**a**) Return airway after support. (**b**) test section.

6. Conclusions

In this study, comprehensive research methods (e.g., field test, theory analysis and numerical simulation) are adopted to illustrate the failure characteristics of surrounding rock of a roadway in a lower coal seam under repeated mining in close-distance coal seam considering the caving gangue in the upper coal seam and the mining activities of the adjacent working face. Meanwhile, the corresponding support scheme is also proposed. The main conclusions can be drawn as follows.

(1) Through field investigation and data observation, the surrounding rock of the roadway presents the asymmetric evolution characteristics of cracks. The expression of floor failure depth caused by upper coal seam mining is obtained through the elastic-plastic theory. Combined with the geological conditions of coal seam #6, the floor failure depth caused by coal seam #6 is 4.63 m.

(2) According to the results of numerical simulation, the stress concentration in working face 10905 and roadway without a residual coal pillar is in a low stress environment. After repeated mining, the deformation of the overall surrounding rock of the roadway increases with the increase of mining times. In particular, the horizontal displacement of the roadway coal pillar side changes greatly, and the actual damage degree is the largest. The deformation variables of the two sides are prone to asymmetric situations during mining, and the stability maintenance of the coal pillar side needs to be emphasized.

(3) The asymmetric anchor cable + I-steel support scheme is proposed to effectively prevent the deformation and fracture of the roadway roof in this study. And the bolt-cable timely support plays a controlling role on the surrounding rock of the roadway. In addition, the plastic zone of the surrounding rock of the roadway is the least, and the bearing capacity of surrounding rock in the roadway increases from 0–2 MPa to 2–4 MPa.

(4) Through the field observation of the surrounding rock deformation of the roadway in the test section, the maximum displacement of the roadway roof, coal pillar side and working face side is 326 mm, 225 mm and 201 mm, respectively. Moreover, the deformation on both sides of the roadway is asymmetric in distribution, and its deformation rate is the largest in the range of +20 m to −40 m from the working face. The overall displacement of the roadway is within the controllable range as a result of using the optimized support scheme.

The finite difference method in numerical simulation has a certain limitation to simulate the practice situations of background engineering. In addition, further research should also consider the influence of temperature and humidity on the strength of rock mass, especially for the coal seam under a large buried depth.

Author Contributions: Y.S.: Formal analysis, Numerical simulation, Experimental test, Writing—Original draft; D.K.: Data curation, Methodology, Writing—Original draft, Numerical Simulation, Experimental test, Funding acquisition; S.P.: Formal analysis, Investigation; Y.X.: Numerical simulation, Experimental test; Q.L.: Data curation, Numerical simulation, Experimental test; Z.C.: Formal analysis, Methodology, Validation, Writing—Review and editing. All authors have read and agreed to the published version of the manuscript.

Funding: This research was funded by the National Natural Science Foundation of China (No. 52164002, 52164005, 52064005 and 51904082); And this Supported by Guizhou Provincial Science and Technology Projects (Qianke Science Support [2021] General 399). The authors would also like to thank the editors and anonymous reviewers for their valuable time and suggestions.

Institutional Review Board Statement: Not applicable.

Informed Consent Statement: Not applicable.

Data Availability Statement: All data used during the study appear in the submitted article.

Conflicts of Interest: The authors declare no conflict to interest.

References

1. Kong, D.; Cheng, Z.; Zheng, S. Study on the failure mechanism and stability control measures in a large-cutting-height coal mining face with a deep-buried seam. *Bull. Eng. Geol. Environ.* **2019**, *78*, 6143–6157. [CrossRef]
2. Xiong, Y.; Kong, D.; Cheng, Z.; Wu, G.; Zhang, Q. The Comprehensive Identification of Roof Risk in a Fully Mechanized Working Face Using the Cloud Model. *Mathematics* **2021**, *9*, 2072. [CrossRef]
3. Liu, F.; Guo, Z.; Lv, H.; Cheng, Z. Test and analysis of blast wave in mortar test block. *Int. J. Rock Mech. Min. Sci.* **2018**, *108*, 80–85. [CrossRef]
4. Klemetti, T.M.; Van Dyke, M.A.; Evanek, N.; Compton, C.C.; Tulu, I.B. Insights into the Relationships Among the Roof, Rib, Floor, and Pillars of Underground Coal Mines. *Min. Met. Explor.* **2021**, *38*, 531–538. [CrossRef]
5. Maleki, H. Coal pillar mechanics of violent failure in U.S. Mines. *Int. J. Min. Sci. Technol.* **2017**, *27*, 387–392. [CrossRef]
6. Xue, Y.; Liu, J.; Ranjith, P.G.; Zhang, Z.; Gao, F.; Wang, S. Experimental investigation on the nonlinear characteristics of energy evolution and failure characteristics of coal under different gas pressures. *Bull. Eng. Geol. Environ.* **2022**, *81*, 38. [CrossRef]
7. Xie, J.; Xu, J.; Wang, F.; Guo, J.; Liu, D. Deformation effect of lateral roof roadway in close coal seams after repeated mining. *Int. J. Min. Sci. Technol.* **2014**, *24*, 597–601. [CrossRef]
8. Kong, D.; Xiong, Y.; Cheng, Z.; Wang, N.; Wu, G.; Liu, Y. Stability analysis of coal face based on coal face-support-roof system in steeply inclined coal seam. *Geomech. Eng.* **2021**, *25*, 233–243. [CrossRef]
9. Lv, H.; Cheng, Z.; Dong, Y.; Zhang, J.; Ma, Y. Numerical simulation on the crack initiation and propagation of coal with combined defects. *Struct. Eng. Mech.* **2021**, *79*, 237–245. [CrossRef]
10. Xue, Y.; Liu, J.; Liang, X.; Wang, S. Ecological risk assessment of soil and water loss by thermal enhanced methane recovery: Numerical study using two-phase flow simulation. *J. Clean. Prod.* **2022**, *334*, 130183. [CrossRef]
11. Xiong, Y.; Kong, D.; Cheng, Z.; Wen, Z.; Ma, Z.; Wu, G.; Liu, Y. Instability Control of Roadway Surrounding Rock in Close-Distance Coal Seam Groups under Repeated Mining. *Energies* **2021**, *14*, 5193. [CrossRef]
12. Zhang, Y.; Cheng, Z.; Lv, H. Study on failure and subsidence law of frozen soil layer in coal mine influenced by physical conditions. *Geomech. Eng.* **2019**, *18*, 97–109. [CrossRef]
13. Liu, X.; Cheng, Z. Changes in subsidence-field surface movement in shallow-seam coal mining. *J. S. Afr. Inst. Min. Metal.* **2019**, *119*, 201–206. [CrossRef]
14. Singh, S.K.; Agrawal, H.; Singh, A.P. Rib stability: A way forward for safe coal extraction in India. *Int. J. Min. Sci. Technol.* **2017**, *27*, 1087–1091. [CrossRef]
15. Lv, H.; Cheng, Z.; Liu, F. Study on the mechanism of a new fully mechanical mining method for extremely thick coal seam. *Int. J. Rock Mech. Min. Sci.* **2021**, *142*, 104788. [CrossRef]
16. Cheng, Z.; Geng, X. Soil consistency and interparticle characteristics of various biopolymer types stabilization of clay. *Geomech. Eng.* **2021**, *27*, 103–113. [CrossRef]
17. Liu, X.; Ning, J.; Tan, Y.; Xu, Q.; Fan, D. Coordinated supporting method of gob-side entry retainingin coal mines and a case study with hard roof. *Geomech. Eng.* **2018**, *15*, 1173–1182. [CrossRef]
18. Yu, J.; Liu, G.; Cai, Y.; Zhou, J.; Liu, S.; Tu, B. Time-Dependent Deformation Mechanism for Swelling Soft-Rock Tunnels in Coal Mines and Its Mathematical Deduction. *Int. J. Geomech.* **2020**, *20*, 04019186. [CrossRef]
19. Lv, H.; Tang, Y.; Zhang, L.; Cheng, Z.; Zhang, Y. Analysis for mechanical characteristics and failure models of coal specimens with non-penetrating single crack. *Geomech. Eng.* **2019**, *17*, 355–365. [CrossRef]
20. Cheng, Z.; Li, L.; Zhang, Y. Laboratory investigation of the mechanical properties of coal–rock combined body. *Bull. Eng. Geol. Environ.* **2020**, *79*, 1947–1958. [CrossRef]
21. Cheng, Z.; Pan, W.; Li, X.; Sun, W. Numerical simulation on strata behaviours of TCCWF influenced by coal-rock combined body. *Geomech. Eng.* **2019**, *19*, 269–282. [CrossRef]
22. Cheng, Z.; Yang, S.; Li, L.; Zhang, L. Support working resistance determined on top-coal caving face based on coal-rock combined body. *Geomech. Eng.* **2019**, *19*, 255–268. [CrossRef]
23. Wang, D.; Barakos, G.; Cheng, Z.; Mischo, H.; Zhao, J. Numerical simulation of pressure profile of mining backfill fly-ash slurry in an L-shaped pipe using a validated Herschel-Bulkley model. *J. Sustain. Cem. Based* **2021**, 1–15. [CrossRef]
24. Wang, Y.; Wu, G.; Liu, Y.; Cheng, Z. Study on Overlying Strata Movement and Surface Subsidence of Coal Workfaces with Karst Aquifer Water. *Mathematics* **2022**, *10*, 169. [CrossRef]
25. Yang, S.; Chen, M.; Jing, H.; Chen, K.; Meng, B. A case study on large deformation failure mechanism of deep soft rock roadway in Xin'An coal mine, China. *Eng. Geol.* **2017**, *217*, 89–101. [CrossRef]
26. Lv, H.; Wang, D.; Cheng, Z.; Zhang, Y.; Zhou, T. Study on mechanical characteristics and failure modes of coal-mudstone combined body with prefabricated crack. *Mathematics* **2022**, *10*, 177. [CrossRef]
27. Wang, D.; Cheng, Z.; Shi, Q.; Zhao, J.; Mischo, H. Simulation Study of the Velocity Profile and Deflection Rate of Non-Newtonian Fluids in the Bend Part of the Pipe. *Geofluids* **2022**, *2022*, 7885556. [CrossRef]
28. Xu, C.; Xia, C. A new large strain approach for predicting tunnel deformation in strain-softening rock mass based on the generalized Zhang-Zhu strength criterion. *Int. J. Rock Mech. Min.* **2021**, *143*, 104786. [CrossRef]

mathematics

Article

A Stacking Learning Model Based on Multiple Similar Days for Short-Term Load Forecasting

Qi Jiang [1,†], Yuxin Cheng [1,†], Haozhe Le [1], Chunquan Li [1,*] and Peter X. Liu [1,2]

1 School of Information Engineering, Nanchang University, Nanchang 330031, China; 6104119104@email.ncu.edu.cn (Q.J.); 6108118061@email.ncu.edu.cn (Y.C.); 6108118076@email.ncu.edu.cn (H.L.); xpliu@sce.carleton.ca (P.X.L.)
2 Department of Systems and Computer Engineering, Carleton University, Ottawa, ON K1S 5B7, Canada
* Correspondence: lichunquan@ncu.edu.cn
† These authors contributed equally to this work.

Abstract: It is challenging to obtain accurate and efficient predictions in short-term load forecasting (STLF) systems due to the complexity and nonlinearity of the electric load signals. To address these problems, we propose a hybrid predictive model that includes a sliding-window algorithm, a stacking ensemble neural network, and a similar-days predictive method. First, we leverage a sliding-window algorithm to process the time-series electric load data with high nonlinearity and non-stationarity. Second, we propose an ensemble learning scheme of stacking neural networks to improve forecasting performance. Specifically, the stacking neural networks contain two types of networks: the base-layer and the meta-layer networks. During the pre-training process, the base-layer network integrates a radial basis function (RBF), random vector functional link (RVFL), and backpropagation neural network (BPNN) to provide a robust predictive model. The meta-layer network utilizes a deep belief network (DBN) and the improved broad learning system (BLS) to enhance predictive accuracy. Finally, the similar-days prediction method is developed to extract the relationship of electric load data in different time dimensions, further enhancing the robustness and accuracy of the model. To demonstrate the effectiveness of our model, it is evaluated using real data from five regions of the United States in three consecutive years. We compare our method with several state-of-the-art and conventional neural-network-based models. Our proposed algorithm improves the prediction accuracy by 16.08%, 16.83%, and 22.64% compared to DWT-EMD-RVFL, SWT-LSTM, and EMD-BLS, respectively. Empirical results demonstrate that our model achieves better accuracy and robustness compared with the baselines.

Keywords: short-term load forecasting (STLF); stacking ensemble learning; similar-days forecasting; sliding window; broad learning system–backpropagation (BLS–BP)

MSC: 68T07

Citation: Jiang, Q.; Cheng, Y.; Le, H.; Li, C.; Liu, P.X. A Stacking Learning Model Based on Multiple Similar Days for Short-Term Load Forecasting. *Mathematics* **2022**, *10*, 2446. https://doi.org/10.3390/math10142446

Academic Editors: Zhuojia Fu, Yiqian He and Hui Zheng

Received: 30 May 2022
Accepted: 5 July 2022
Published: 13 July 2022

1. Introduction

Power load forecasting is essential to power system planning [1]. Since it is challenging to store electric energy, an accurate load forecasting algorithm is critical for efficient power consumption and the security of the power grid [2]. The load forecasting task can be classified as long-term, medium-term, or short-term based on the time span of the load forecasting. For medium-term and long-term load forecasting, they are mainly used to develop long-term power generation plans. Due to the short interval of STLF, it can be used to adjust the operation mode of the power grid and promote the stable operation of the power system.

In past decades, various forecasting methods have been proposed to tackle STFL. They can be classified into two categories: One includes statistical models such as autoregressive moving average (ARMA) [3,4] and linear regression (LR) [5]. The other includes machine learning methods including support-vector regression (SVR) [6], backpropagation neural networks (BPNNs), deep neural networks (DBNs) [7], broad learning systems (BLSs) [8], random vector functional link (RVFL) [9], and long short-term memory (LSTM) [10]. Due to the nonlinear and non-stationary characteristics of short-term power load data, statistical methods cannot effectively process such characteristic information. Therefore, machine learning has gradually become the mainstream STLF method, which can effectively extract features from nonlinear time series and provide an effective connection between input and output.

Recently, machine learning has achieved remarkable results in load forecasting [11]. Artificial neural networks (ANNs) are one of the most popular methods [12], which can simulate human brain behavior by training and learning ways to obtain the relationship between input and output. Deep learning methods such as LSTM and DBN have powerful nonlinear data processing capabilities, and are also very popular methods [7,10]. However, a deep neural network requires a lot of computational costs, as it depends on a large amount of training data. To save computational costs, a new single-layer incremental neural network BLS is gradually obtained.

More recently, various hybrid models have been developed to effectively improve the predictive accuracy of STFL. This is because the hybrid models can integrate the advantages of each model to solve the limitations of each mode by weighted combination. Chen et al. [13] presented a new combination model to enhance power load forecasting. In [14,15], multiple artificial neural network models are integrated to improve predictive performance. In [16], artificial neural networks are integrated to improve the accuracy of STLF with a new evolutionary method. In [17], support-vector machines with ant colony optimization are combined to improve the performance of power load forecasting.

To tackle the complexity and nonlinearity of electric signals, various hybrid predictive frameworks have been developed by combining decomposition methods with neural networks. Nengling et al. [18] proposed dividing the load data into different resolutions by wavelet transform and applying different combination forecasting methods based on statistical models to each scale. Ghayekhloo et al. [19] and Ghofrani et al. [20] both used wavelet transform to convert the load data into multiple frequency components. Subsequently, they trained multiple artificial neural networks on the data by linking the weighted outputs of the trained networks in the STLF task. Qiu et al. [7] introduced integrated deep learning based on empirical mode decomposition for load-demand time-series forecasting. Laouafi et al. [21] combined traditional methods and intelligent methods for STLF.

The above hybrid predictive models achieve promising prediction results, as in [22,23]; however, they still cannot solve the following problems:

1. The existing popular empirical mode decomposition [24] often has the problem of modal aliasing. Furthermore, the difficulty of wavelet decomposition [25] lies in how to effectively select the wavelet basis and decomposition scale. In addition, the decomposition methods may introduce some redundant decomposition information to the predictive models, degenerating the predictive computational cost.
2. Each machine learning method—such as LSTM, DBN, and BLS—has its own specific limitations, which may influence its predictive performance in STLF.
3. The selection of the dataset is also a challenging problem. Generally, continuous time series are used, and are divided into training and test sets. This approach can lead to ineffective extraction of correlations between continuous time series and, therefore, may result in lower accuracy of model predictions.

To address the above problems, we propose an improved hybrid predictive model, which includes a sliding-window algorithm, a stacking ensemble neural network model, and a similar-days predictive method. Specifically, a sliding-window algorithm [26] is first introduced to directly process the nonlinearity and non-stationarity of the time-series electric load data. This method effectively mines spatiotemporal features of the time series. Furthermore, a stacking ensemble neural network model is proposed to improve the forecasting performance. The stacking neural networks contain two types of networks: the base-layer network and the meta-layer network. During the pre-training process, the base-layer networks integrate radial basis function (RBF), random vector functional link (RVFL), and backpropagation neural network (BPNN) to provide a robust predictive model; the meta-layer networks utilize a deep belief network (DBN) and the improved broad learning system (BLS) to improve predictive accuracy; the predictive results of RBF, RVFL, BPNN, DBN, and BLS are rationally weighted to obtain the final prediction result. Finally, the similar-days prediction method is developed to extract the relationship of electric load data in different time dimensions, further enhancing the robustness and accuracy of the model. This paper selects the load data of five regions in the United States for three consecutive years to conduct a large number of experiments, proving that the framework has high prediction accuracy and strong robustness.

The main contributions of this paper are as follows:

1. The sliding-window algorithm is an effective method for extracting the spatiotemporal characteristics of load data, which are used to reduce computational costs and improve prediction accuracy.
2. The stacking neural network is proposed to greatly improve the prediction accuracy.
3. The similar-days predictive method is developed to extract the relationship of electric load data in different time dimensions, further enhancing the robustness and accuracy of the model.

The rest of this paper is organized as follows: Section 2 introduces the framework of the proposed model and the theoretical knowledge of interest; Section 3 shows the data analysis; Section 4 introduces the details of the case analysis; Section 5 concludes the paper.

2. Methodology

2.1. Model Framework

We show the overall framework of our proposed method in Figure 1. It contains four parts: (A) data preprocessing, (B) base learners, (C) data processing, and (D) meta-learners. And the detailed pseudo-code of the stacking algorithm is given in Algorithm 1. The proposed model can be described as follows:

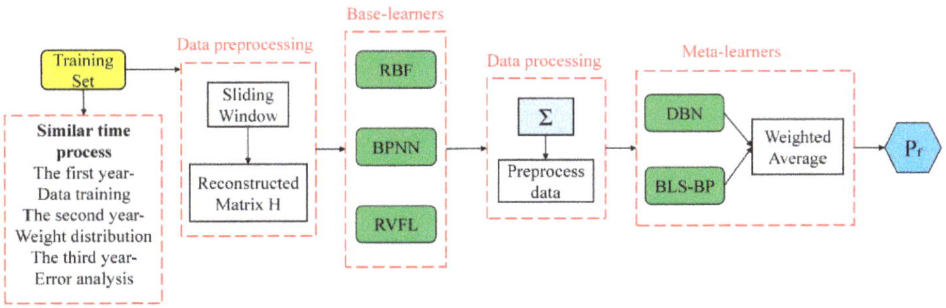

Figure 1. Framework of the proposed model.

Part A: The collected power load data are divided into three parts: (1) the training set, which is used as training data; (2) the validation set, which is used for weight adjustment between meta-learners; and (3) the test set, which is used for evaluation and error analysis. The time series in each of the three parts are input into the sliding-window algorithm to obtain the reconstructed multidimensional matrix H as the data input matrix for the base learner (refer to Section 2.2 for more details).

Part B: The base-layer learning system consists of RBF, BPNN, and RVFL networks for preliminary training (refer to Section 2.3 for more details).

Part C: During data processing, the prediction data of the base-layer learner are recombined as the input of the meta-layer learner (refer to Section 2.3 for more details).

Part D: The meta-layer learning system involves two neural networks: DBN and BLS–BP. BLS–BP is an improved network that is first used in load forecasting (refer to Section 2.3 for more details).

Algorithm 1: Stacking: Based on sliding window

Input: training data

$$D = \{a_i, b_i\}_{i=1}^{m} (x_i \in R^n, y_i \in Y)$$

Step 1: analysis with sliding window
Reconstruct D to H
end for
Step 2: learn base-layer learners
for n: 1 to N **do**
Learn a base learner S_n based on H
end for
Step 3: construct new datasets from H
for i: 1 to m **do**
Construct a new dataset that contains

$$H_s = \left\{x_i^1, y_i\right\},$$

where $x_i^1 = \{s_1(x_i), s_2(x_i), \ldots, s_N(x_i)\}$
end for
Step 4: learn meta-layer learners
for t: 1 to T **do**
Learn a meta-learner S_t based on H_s
end for
Return $S(x) = s^1\{s_1(x), s_2(x), \ldots, s_N(x)\}$
Output: ensemble learner S

2.2. Sliding-Window Algorithm

The principle of the sliding-window algorithm is to reconstruct the original power load data into a multidimensional matrix H by sliding the window. When training and validating the model, the reconstruction matrix H includes both the input and output data (also known as training data and label data, respectively). In the evaluation step, only training data are in the reconstruction matrix H. Figures 2 and 3 illustrate the reconstruction process. In each window slot, three components are included, namely, input data X, output data Y, and delay time T. The window is slid to remove the data at the beginning of the previous window, and then the same amount of new data is added at the end of the window to ensure that the window size is constant. The sliding window will go through the entire dataset until all of the data are covered.

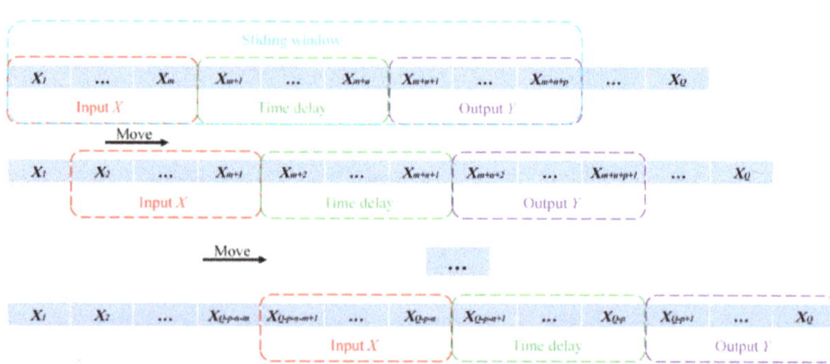

Figure 2. Flowchart of the sliding window.

Input X	Output Y
$X_1, X_2, \ldots, X_{m-1}, X_m$	$X_{m+n+1}, X_{m+n+2}, \ldots, X_{m+n+p-1}, X_{m+n+p}$
$X_2, X_3, \ldots, X_m, X_{m+1}$	$X_{m+n+2}, X_{m+n+3}, \ldots, X_{m+n+p}, X_{m+n+p+1}$
…	…
$X_{Q-p-n-m+1}, X_{Q-p-n-m+2}, \ldots, X_{Q-p-n-1}, X_{Q-p-n}$	$X_{Q-p+1}, X_{Q-p+2}, \ldots, X_{Q-1}, X_Q$

Figure 3. The reconstructed matrix.

2.3. *Stacking Algorithm*

2.3.1. Algorithm Structure

Figures 4 and 5 show the framework structure of the stacking algorithm; the specific process is as follows:

1. First, we leverage the sliding-window method to perform data preprocessing on the original data and obtain a new training set, validation set, and test set. The training set is divided into n parts: {Train(i) | $i = 1, 2, \ldots, n$}, where n is the number of folds in cross-validation (see Section 3.3 for details).
2. Model training: We choose RBF, BPNN, and RVFL as the base-layer learners. After each model is pre-trained, we train the base learners with {Train(i) | $i = 1, 2, \ldots, n$}, in turn. We make the base learners well-trained with the i-folder cross-validation method, as shown in Figure 5. We generate an intermediate dataset A by vertically merging the n predictions of the base learners. Specifically, we name the datasets generated by RBF, BPNN, and RVFL as A(1), A(2), and A(3), respectively, and merge these three datasets horizontally to obtain A(x). We use DBN and BLS–BP as our meta-learners and train the meta-learners on A(x). We repeat the above process for the validation set and the test set using the well-trained base learners to generate two intermediate datasets B(x) and C(x), where $x \in \{1,2,3\}$.
3. Weight adjustment between meta-learners: We obtain a new dataset B(x) from the predictions of the base learners on the validation set, and utilize B(x) to adjust the weights between the meta-learners. The weights between the two meta-learners are updated according to the error between the predictions and the labels.
4. Model Evaluation: We forward the test set to the well-trained base learners to obtain C(x), and forward C(x) to the well-trained meta-learners to make predictions. Finally, the optimal weights are used to obtain a weighted average of the predicted values of the two meta-learners to obtain the final prediction results. The model is evaluated by the error between the final prediction result and the actual value.

2.3.2. Base-Layer Network

The base-layer network consists of a radial basis function (RBF), random vector functional link (RVFL), and backpropagation neural network (BPNN), to provide a robust predictive model for STLF.

The RBF [27] is composed of three layers: The first layer is the input layer, which takes the signal source as input. The second layer is the hidden layer, whose transformation function is the radial basis function. The non-negative transformation function is linear, symmetric, and attenuated. The third layer is the output layer, which responds to the input mode. The output layer leverages a linear optimization strategy to fine-tune the linear weight between the hidden layer and the output layer.

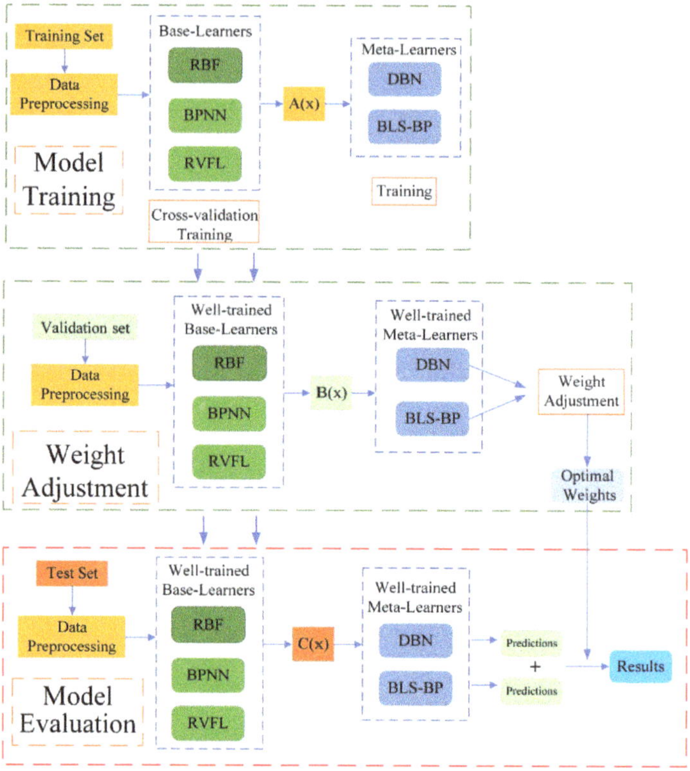

Figure 4. Algorithm structure.

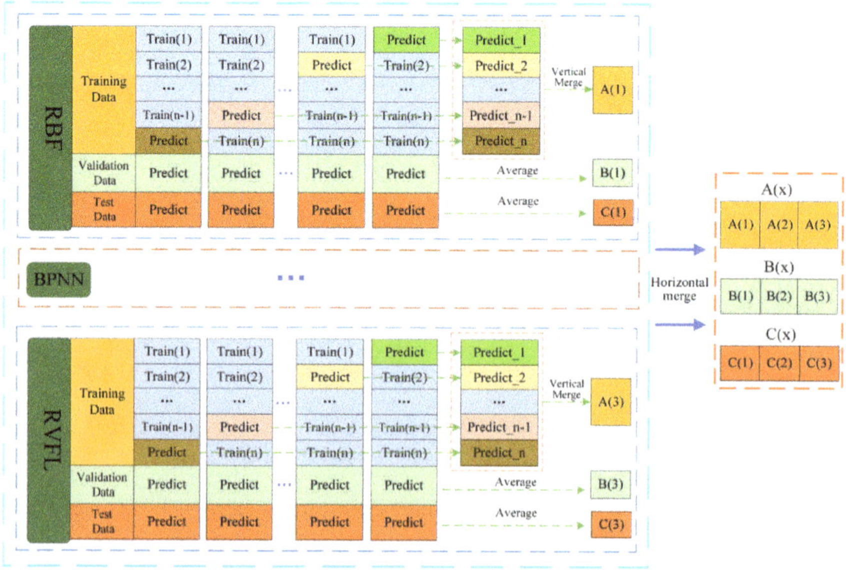

Figure 5. Cross-validation in the training process of the base learners.

RVFL [9] is a neural network based on the learning paradigm. RVFL is more efficient than the conventional iterative learning neural network. This feedforward structure can be regarded as a linear combination of a fixed number of nonlinear expansions of the original inputs. RVFL contains three layers: the input layer, enhanced node layer, and output layer. The principle of RVFL is to use the augmented nonlinear kernel raw data learned at the implicit layer to improve the generalization ability. The neural network has a direct connection from the input layer to the output layer, which is helpful to map the relationship between input and output. It is very suitable for the characteristics of our selected basic learner.

The BPNN [28] is the most basic supervised learning neural network. Its output is rendered by the forward propagation, and the errors are carried out in one-way propagation. The BPNN contains three layers: the input layer, the hidden layer, and the output layer. Specifically, the input of the hidden layer is the output of the input layer. Then, the hidden layer applies an activation function to the hidden features, and the output of the hidden layer is forwarded to the output layer to generate the output results.

The partial derivative gradient descent method is used to obtain the minimum value of the cost function so that the error between the expected value and the output is reduced as much as possible.

2.3.3. Meta-Layer Network

The meta-layer network applies a deep belief network (DBN) and the improved broad learning system (BLS) to improve predictive accuracy.

The DBN [7] is a deep neural network model composed of a stacked RBM and a layer of BP network, and it is also a current mainstream neural network. The structure is shown in Figure 6. The training process of the DBN includes two steps:

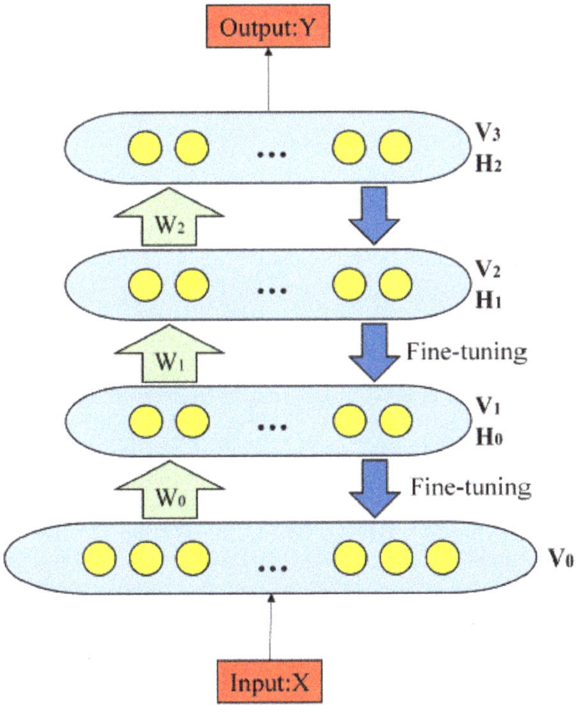

Figure 6. Frame structure of the DBN.

Step 1: Pre-training. The pre-training process involves training each layer of the RBM network in an unsupervised manner. The aim is to keep sufficient feature information when the features are mapped to different feature spaces. The overall training process includes three steps: (1) train the first RBM until convergence; (2) freeze the weight and bias of the well-trained RBM and take the state of its hidden layer as the input of the second RBM; and (3) stack the two RBM models after the second RBM is converged. We repeat the above three steps until the whole network is converged.

Step 2: Fine-tuning. In the fine-tuning step, we set up a supervised network in the last layer of a DBN model. The model takes the output of the RBM as input, and trains the entity relationship in a supervised manner. In addition, the backpropagation process propagates the error information to each RBM model, and fine-tunes the parameters in the DBN network.

As shown in Figure 7, the BLS [8] consists of four parts: input, feature node, enhancement node, and output. In fact, the network performance of the BLS after two training steps is insufficient. We establish the links between the output and input of the network, and fine-tune it by backpropagation. Based on this idea, this paper designs an improved BLS variant, namely, BLS–BP.

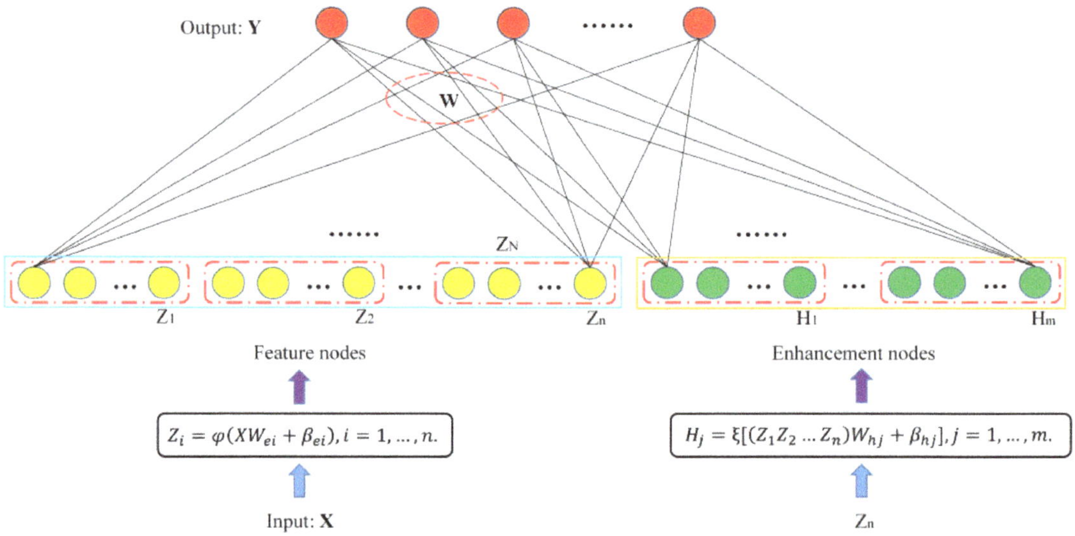

Figure 7. Frame structure of the BLS.

After the load data are trained by the BLS, the error in the output layer is propagated to the input layer for fine-tuning by backpropagation. Then, we calculate the gradient based on the error, and leverage the gradient to update the weights and biases. The training step is stopped if certain conditions are met. We can set the maximum number of iterations or calculate the prediction accuracy of the training set on the network, and stop training after reaching a certain threshold. The training process of the BLS can be viewed as the weight initialization of a BP network, which can help the network get rid of the local optima and shorten the training time. Here, a detailed pseudo-code for the BLS-BP is given in Algorithm 2.

Algorithm 2: Broad Learning: Increment of the backpropagation neural network

Input: training samples X;
Output: the weight matrix between feature nodes, W;
Parameter setting: Z_n (the feature mapping group); H_m (the enhancement nodes group); W (the output weight of the BLS); E (the condition for stopping iteration);

1: **for** $i = 0;\ i \leq n$ **do**
2: **Random** $W_{e_i},\ \beta_{e_i};$
3: Calculate $Z_i = [\varphi(UW_{e_i} + \beta_{e_i})];$
4: **end**
5: Set $Z_n = [Z_1, \ldots, Z_n];$
6: **for** $j = 1;\ j \leq m$ **do**
7: **Random** $W_{h_j}, \beta_{h_j};$
8: Calculate $H_i = \left[\xi_j\left(PW_{h_j} + \beta_{h_j}\right)\right];$
9: **end**
10: Set $H_m = [H_1,\ H_2, \ldots,\ H_m];$
11: Set $Y = [Z_1, Z_2, \ldots, Z_n\ |H_1,\ H_2, \ldots,\ H_m];\ W = [\mathrm{P}|H_m]W;$
12: Calculate $E_p = f' \cdot (Y_p) \cdot (d_p - Y_p);$
13: **while** $E_p > E$ do
14: Return W
15: Calculate $W_{(n)} = W + \cdot E_p \cdot Y_p\ ;$
16: Update $Y_{(n)} = [Z_1, Z_2, \ldots, Z_n\ |H_1,\ H_2, \ldots,\ H_m]\ ; W_n = [\mathrm{P}|H_m]W_{(n)};$
17: $W = W_{(n)};$
18: $n = n + 1;$
19: **end**
20: Repeat steps 12–19
21: **Export** W

3. Numerical Analysis

3.1. Datasets

To demonstrate the effectiveness and robustness of our model, we conducted experiments on five datasets collected in the United States between 2017 and 2019. All datasets were from five regions in the US, and were called CAPITL, CENTRL, DUNWOD, GENESE, and HUDVL. The dataset sampling interval was 30 min, meaning that one day covers 48 load data samples. Figure 8 shows the load data in March to demo the training mode of similar-days [29] prediction in this paper. We selected the similar-days period data of different years to divide the training set, validation set, and test set. Before starting the experiment, we normalized the sample data to the range [0, 1] to eliminate the dominant effect of those data with large values.

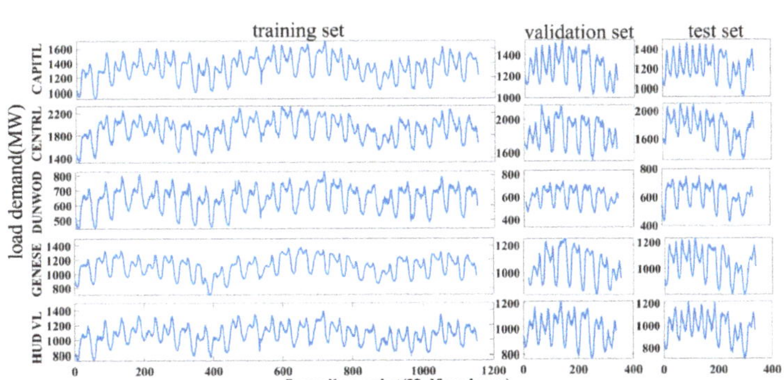

Figure 8. Dataset for March.

The normalization formula was as follows:

$$\hat{y}_m = \frac{y_{max} - y_m}{y_{max} - y_{min}} \quad (1)$$

where $\hat{y}_m$ is the normalized value, y_m represents the actual load data, y_{max} is the maximum value of the load data, and y_{min} is the minimum value of the load data.

3.2. Evaluation Criterion

To effectively evaluate the predictive performance of our proposed model in STLF, we used the following two evaluation criteria: the root-mean-square error (RMSE) [30] and the mean absolute percentage error (MAPE) [31]. They are defined as follows:

$$\text{RMSE} = \sqrt{\frac{1}{M}\sum_{m=1}^{M}\left(\hat{y}_m - y_m\right)^2} \quad (2)$$

$$\text{MAPE} = \frac{100\%}{M}\sum_{m=1}^{M}\left|\frac{\hat{y}_m - y_m}{y_m}\right| \quad (3)$$

where $\hat{y}_m$ represents the prediction data, y_m represents the actual load data, and M is the size of the dataset. For both of the evaluation criteria, a smaller value indicates better performance of the models.

3.3. Parameter Settings

We performed hyperparameter exploration before we started our formal experiment. In our data pre-processing, the window size of the sliding-window algorithm was critical to the final performance. To ensure the optimal window size, we applied the controlled variable method, and adopted RMSE and MAPE as the evaluation metrics. According to the test results in Figure 9, we can see that our model has the smallest RMSE and MAPE when the sliding window takes the value of 96, indicating that the model has the best prediction performance. Since there are 48 samples of load data in a day, and the size of the window needs to be an integer number of days, we need to consider the practical significance of the window size representing a specific time interval. Therefore, we determined the optimal window size for the sliding window to be 96.

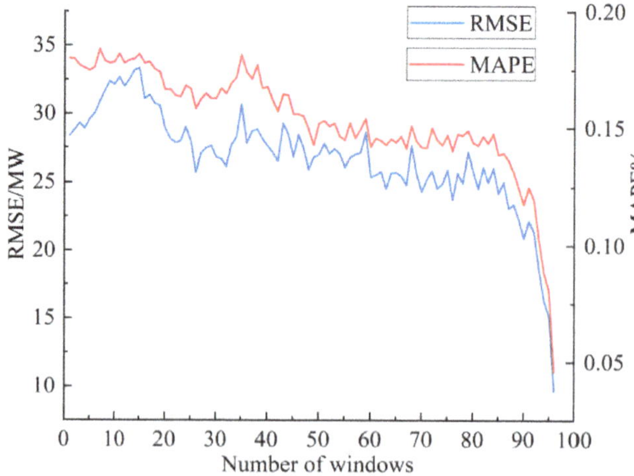

Figure 9. The corresponding error of window size.

In the cross-validation (CV) module [32], an error experiment was carried out to filter out the number of CV folds with the smallest error. We utilized MAPE as the evaluation metric, and plotted the figure of error lines with regard to the power load in the spring for CAPITL. As shown in Figure 10, when the CV is too small, the empirical error is large and the model is not robust. When the CV is too large, the experimental error is not reduced, although the computational effort increases greatly. We set CV to 12 as a compromise of the computational effort and the model prediction performance. Table 1 shows the optimal parameter settings of the machine learning methods used for comparison after many experiments.

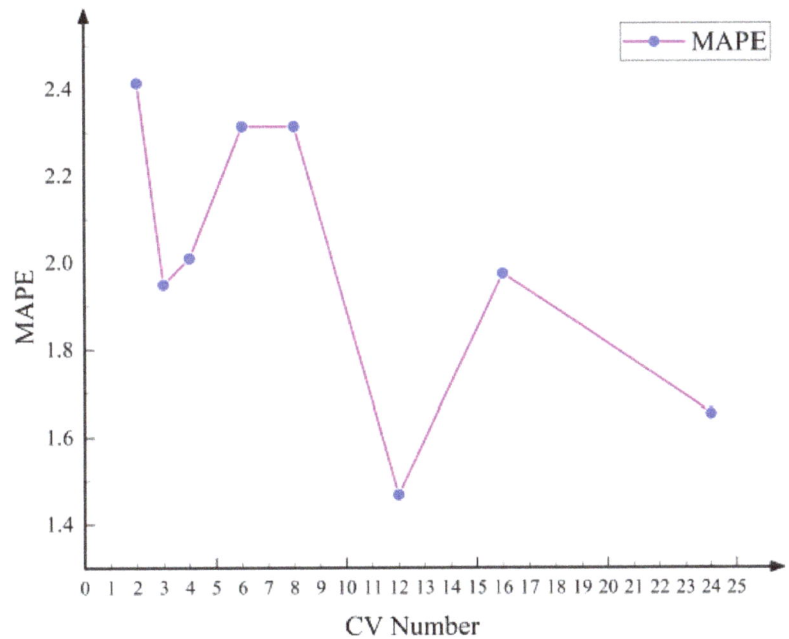

Figure 10. Corresponding error of CV folding number.

Table 1. Comparison of method parameter settings.

Model	Optimal Parameters
BPNN	$n_h = 200,\ m_i = 10,\ a_f = Sigmoid$
DBN	$n_h = 10,\ eta = 0.001,\ a_f = Sigmoid,\ r_b = 1,\ v_m = 0.01,\ m_i = 20$
RBFNN	$f_{RBF} = Gaussian,\ s_{RBF} = 50$
RVFL	$n_e = 10000, a_f = Sigmoid,\ DL = \text{true},\ r_m = Gaussian$
EMD-BLS	$n_f = 24,\ n_e = 15$
SWT-LSTM	$n_h = 200,\ eta = 0.01$
DWT-EMD-RVFL	$n_e = 10000, a_f = Sigmoid,\ DL = \text{true},\ r_m = Gaussian$
EMD-EDBN	$n_h = [100,\ 100],\ eta = 0.001, a_f = Sigmoid, r_b = 2,$ $v_m = 0.01, m_i = 500$

n_h—the number of hidden nodes; n_h—the maximum number of iterations; a_f—activation function; *eta*—learning rate; r_b—the random batch size of each time; v_m—momentum value; f_{RBF}—radial basis functions; s_{RBF}—the spread of radial basis functions; n_e—the number of enhancement nodes; DL—whether to have the direct link between the input layer and output layer; r_m—randomization methods; n_f—the number of feature nodes.

4. Case Study

To demonstrate the effectiveness and robustness of our model, we extensively compared the performance of the proposed model with several baselines. Among the baselines, five approaches are single components of our stacking model: RBFNN, BPNN, RVFL, DBN, BLS–BP, and four models are state-of-the-art in STLF: DWT-EMD-RVFL [9], SWT-LSTM [33], EMD-BLS [8], and EMD-EDBN [7]. We conducted four sets of experiments to show the superiority of our model against the baselines. Our experiments were implemented in MATLAB R2021b (which is produced by US based MathWorks, Inc., Natick, MA, USA) on a laptop equipped with Intel(R) Core (TM) i7-9750H CPU @ 2.60 GHz 2.59 GHz.

1. **Ablation study**: In this experiment, we compared our stacking model with the five components of our model, and verified that the proposed model can outperform all the baselines (see Section 4.1).
2. **Compare to other ensemble models:** In this experiment, we demonstrated the effectiveness of the stacked meta-learners in our model against the baseline models with a single meta-learner. We adopted the same base-layer learners in our model and the baseline models (see Section 4.2).
3. **Compare to state-of-the-art models:** We compared our model with other state-of-the-art models, and demonstrated that our model outperforms other baseline models (see Section 4.3).
4. **Comparison of computation times between models:** We compared the computation times required for each case based on the spring load data in HUDVL (see Section 4.4).
5. **Heavy load test**: In this experiment, we repeated the above three experiments on the data collected on a special holiday. The high demand for electricity on the holiday leads to a heavy power load, and increases the uncertainty of the power load (see Section 4.5).

4.1. Ablation Experiment between Single Models and Hybrid Models

In this experiment, we took five single machine learning methods as baselines, and the results are shown in Table 2. We emphasize the prediction results of our model using the grey background. We can observe that our model outperforms the baselines in each sub-dataset. Specifically, our model can achieve an outstanding performance even when the power load time series is nonlinear and non-stationary (see CAPITL and CENTRL for example). Although DBN can already make good predictions, the improved BLS proposed in this article even has a prediction error less than that of the DBN in many cases. The results demonstrate that the regression-based BLS has an effective predictive ability. In addition, our model significantly outperforms other baseline models. In Figure 11, we can also observe that the proposed method has the lowest MAPE, demonstrating the effectiveness and robustness of our model. The proposed method achieves the best performance in all datasets and forecasting steps. The forecast curves of the various methods on Christmas Day are shown in Section 4.5.

Table 2. The error of comparison with separate neural network models.

Area	Season	Spring		Summer		Autumn		Winter	
	Model	RMSE	MAPE	RMSE	MAPE	RMSE	MAPE	RMSE	MAPE
CAPITL	**OURS**	**21.97**	**1.47**	**27.73**	**1.24**	**24.72**	**1.54**	**25.70**	**1.47**
	RBFNN	60.05	3.93	55.50	2.55	70.27	4.80	38.59	2.34
	BPNN	39.75	2.52	35.70	1.71	37.66	2.59	35.04	2.09
	RVFL	31.13	2.00	38.74	1.77	33.95	2.17	31.29	1.82
	DBN	31.74	2.09	39.39	1.82	33.99	2.17	29.68	1.73
	BLS–BP	37.71	2.38	35.57	1.61	41.29	2.55	26.77	1.48
CENTRL	**OURS**	**41.60**	**1.95**	**41.04**	**1.61**	**36.20**	**1.75**	**38.02**	**1.74**
	RBFNN	79.29	3.69	51.33	1.93	61.56	3.06	66.51	3.03
	BPNN	63.32	2.99	60.29	2.42	46.15	2.28	58.08	2.52
	RVFL	60.14	2.96	44.13	1.74	38.99	1.80	41.17	1.83
	DBN	46.39	2.23	56.13	2.26	37.88	1.78	40.00	1.74
	BLS–BP	50.04	2.37	46.96	1.97	46.45	2.10	42.54	1.88

Table 2. *Cont.*

Area	Season	Spring		Summer		Autumn		Winter	
	Model	RMSE	MAPE	RMSE	MAPE	RMSE	MAPE	RMSE	MAPE
DUNWOD	**OURS**	**14.20**	**1.86**	**22.82**	**1.82**	**17.87**	**2.28**	**16.42**	**2.09**
	RBFNN	28.05	3.68	34.47	2.92	28.59	3.82	25.46	3.28
	BPNN	25.80	3.40	24.32	2.13	32.09	4.52	18.22	2.43
	RVFL	21.17	2.89	27.93	2.08	19.21	2.38	18.09	2.32
	DBN	16.86	2.17	32.22	2.76	18.61	2.48	17.12	2.16
	BLS–BP	18.29	2.37	24.20	1.89	18.59	2.38	16.29	2.10
GENESE	**OURS**	**18.48**	**1.44**	**18.88**	**1.16**	**15.55**	**1.16**	**16.59**	**1.18**
	RBFNN	29.90	2.38	22.10	1.34	23.71	1.84	24.29	1.78
	BPNN	28.51	2.38	38.84	2.61	16.30	1.19	20.93	1.57
	RVFL	32.36	2.67	28.89	1.69	21.28	1.62	23.06	1.66
	DBN	23.23	1.91	35.34	2.04	21.95	1.71	24.21	1.88
	BLS–BP	29.20	2.23	26.79	1.60	21.69	1.68	24.15	1.69
HUDVL	**OURS**	**24.05**	**1.99**	**28.19**	**2.11**	**47.49**	**4.08**	**28.08**	**2.07**
	RBFNN	48.70	4.12	36.44	1.92	64.84	5.31	41.37	3.10
	BPNN	36.69	3.08	47.62	2.78	50.98	4.17	31.40	2.25
	RVFL	37.67	3.11	39.81	2.10	59.71	5.19	31.51	2.40
	DBN	24.69	1.99	44.47	2.43	56.60	4.83	31.25	2.41
	BLS–BP	32.54	2.73	34.97	1.91	51.98	4.27	32.47	2.46

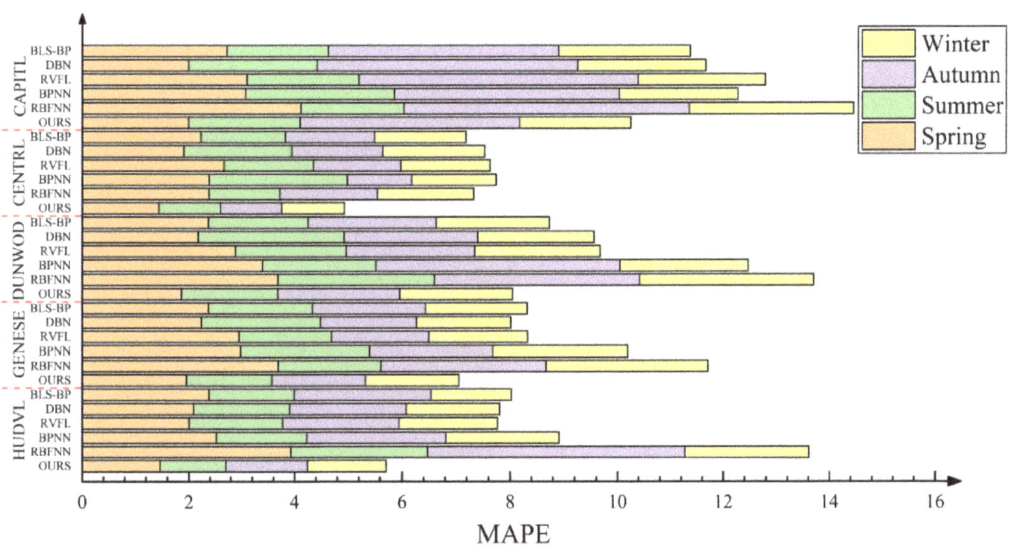

Figure 11. Stacked evaluation indicators of each model.

4.2. Comparison with Other Ensemble Models

Based on the base learners, we utilized DBN and BLS networks as our meta-learners. We further applied the backpropagation algorithm in the BLS network. We renamed the DBN and improved BLS as S-DBN and S-BLS, respectively. The error results are shown in Table 3. From the table, we can observe that the accuracy and stability of the stacked model outperform those of a single model. However, the performance is still insufficient compared to the algorithm proposed in this article, which shows the feasibility of our proposed algorithm. The forecast curves of various methods on Christmas Day are shown in Section 4.5.

Table 3. The error of comparison with other ensemble models.

Area	Season	Spring		Summer		Autumn		Winter	
	Model	RMSE	MAPE	RMSE	MAPE	RMSE	MAPE	RMSE	MAPE
CAPITL	**OURS**	**21.97**	**1.47**	**27.73**	**1.24**	**24.72**	**1.54**	**25.70**	**1.47**
	S-DBN	34.52	2.39	52.53	2.40	34.35	2.26	27.23	1.57
	S-BLS	30.33	1.93	35.28	1.57	31.60	2.01	26.96	1.61
CENTRL	**OURS**	**41.60**	**1.95**	**41.04**	**1.61**	**36.20**	**1.75**	**38.02**	**1.74**
	S-DBN	55.57	2.71	49.04	1.95	36.67	1.79	40.88	1.80
	S-BLS	51.69	2.40	54.28	2.09	58.70	2.77	40.51	1.78
DUNWOD	**OURS**	**14.20**	**1.86**	**22.82**	**1.82**	**17.87**	**2.28**	**16.42**	**2.09**
	S-DBN	15.43	2.06	27.70	2.26	18.00	2.36	16.68	2.14
	S-BLS	15.37	2.05	24.58	1.92	18.98	2.47	20.02	2.52
GENESE	**OURS**	**18.48**	**1.44**	**18.88**	**1.16**	**15.55**	**1.16**	**16.59**	**1.18**
	S-DBN	19.79	1.58	28.20	1.50	17.96	1.34	16.65	1.22
	S-BLS	23.86	1.91	20.77	1.20	17.16	1.26	18.48	1.40
HUDVL	**OURS**	**24.05**	**1.99**	**28.19**	**2.11**	**47.49**	**4.08**	**28.08**	**2.07**
	S-DBN	29.77	2.51	37.57	2.01	60.14	5.39	29.12	2.18
	S-BLS	24.59	2.02	30.12	1.63	48.67	4.08	29.47	2.24

4.3. Comparison with Other Hybrid Models

To date, a variety of hybrid models have been proposed for short-term load forecasting. We took four models as the baselines for our model: DWT-EMD-RVFL [9], SWT-LSTM [33], EMD-BLS [8], and EMD-EDBN [7]. The empirical results show a similar trend with previous experimental results: the proposed model outperforms the hybrid models for each dataset in all forecasting horizons. The respective error experiments are shown in Table 4. We can observe that the EMD-EDBN model has the worst results for all datasets in all forecasting horizons. Figure 12 shows that our method has the smallest errors on each sub-dataset, demonstrating the effectiveness and robustness of our model. The forecast curves of various methods on Christmas Day are shown in Section 4.5.

Table 4. The error of comparison with other hybrid models.

Area	Season	Spring		Summer		Autumn		Winter	
	Model	RMSE	MAPE	RMSE	MAPE	RMSE	MAPE	RMSE	MAPE
CAPITL	**OURS**	**21.97**	**1.47**	**27.73**	**1.24**	**24.72**	**1.54**	**25.70**	**1.47**
	DWT-EMD-RVFL	29.38	1.95	43.22	1.93	27.12	1.75	29.54	1.66
	SWT-LSTM	29.56	1.90	42.37	1.97	25.71	1.60	43.56	2.70
	EMD-BLS	23.28	1.51	30.83	1.43	39.42	3.05	30.93	1.61
	EMD-EDBN	36.00	2.26	74.20	3.64	47.37	3.20	30.93	1.61
CENTRL	**OURS**	**41.60**	**1.95**	**41.04**	**1.61**	**36.20**	**1.75**	**38.02**	**1.74**
	DWT-EMD-RVFL	43.72	2.08	48.46	1.93	39.66	1.86	39.75	1.77
	SWT-LSTM	35.52	1.65	44.14	1.85	37.58	1.79	38.83	1.73
	EMD-BLS	52.07	2.55	47.50	1.92	39.86	1.83	45.50	2.00
	EMD-EDBN	42.34	1.98	88.28	3.64	50.78	2.51	79.92	3.76
DUNWOD	**OURS**	**14.20**	**1.86**	**22.82**	**1.82**	**17.87**	**2.28**	**16.42**	**2.09**
	DWT-EMD-RVFL	16.14	2.20	28.01	2.28	17.94	2.38	17.49	2.16
	SWT-LSTM	15.64	2.06	26.41	1.98	18.70	2.17	18.96	2.45
	EMD-BLS	19.76	2.69	34.56	3.45	30.28	4.71	23.21	3.25
	EMD-EDBN	29.76	4.00	95.57	7.39	45.02	5.93	30.02	4.37

Table 4. *Cont.*

Area	Season	Spring		Summer		Autumn		Winter	
	Model	RMSE	MAPE	RMSE	MAPE	RMSE	MAPE	RMSE	MAPE
GENESE	**OURS**	**18.48**	**1.44**	**18.88**	**1.16**	**15.55**	**1.16**	**16.59**	**1.18**
	DWT-EMD-RVFL	22.53	1.77	28.59	1.65	19.49	1.42	20.94	1.43
	SWT-LSTM	23.75	1.93	27.46	1.70	23.73	1.87	23.01	1.75
	EMD-BLS	26.34	2.08	26.23	1.42	42.30	3.04	30.54	2.22
	EMD-EDBN	46.70	3.89	153.69	9.01	39.91	3.02	77.17	6.00
HUDVL	**OURS**	**24.05**	**1.99**	**28.19**	**2.11**	**47.49**	**4.08**	**28.08**	**2.07**
	DWT-EMD-RVFL	28.93	2.35	40.06	2.09	48.32	4.14	32.67	2.44
	SWT-LSTM	34.30	2.73	30.61	1.70	59.02	5.21	28.20	2.04
	EMD-BLS	34.64	2.93	40.73	2.41	47.95	4.29	33.41	2.46
	EMD-EDBN	64.31	5.85	82.02	4.61	97.17	8.74	50.54	3.60

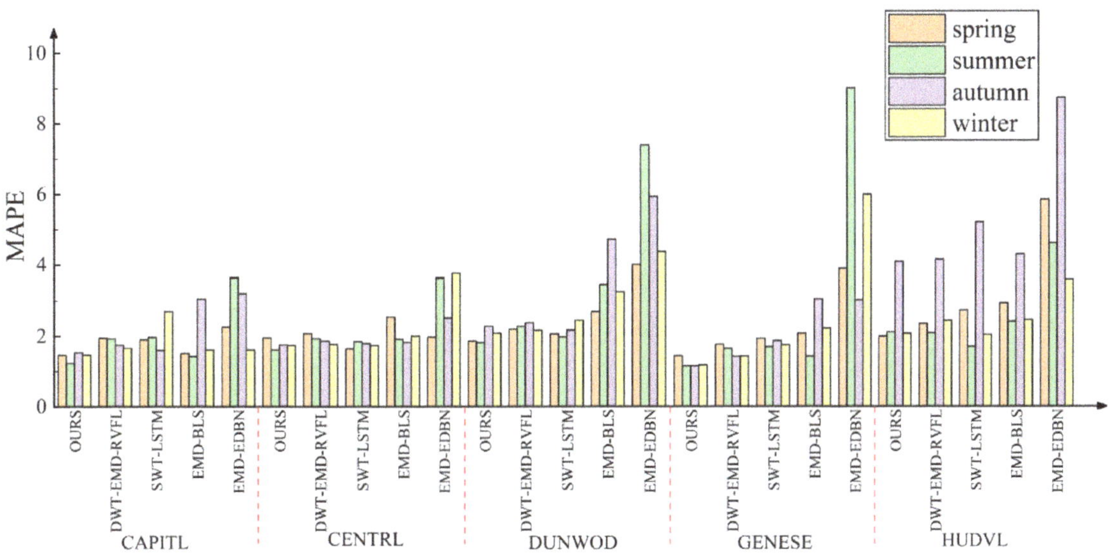

Figure 12. MAPEs of the hybrid models.

4.4. Comparison of Computation Times between Models

Considering that the computational effort should be considered for the prediction performance evaluation of the models, the computation times required for each case are discussed in this section. We selected the computation times of each model in the case of predicting the spring load data in HUDVL, and the computation times for each model are shown in Table 5. As shown in Table 5, the proposed model has a computation time of 83.928 s. Although the proposed model has a longer computation time than most of the individual comparative models, it significantly outperforms the other comparative models in terms of prediction performance, and the time cost of implementation is within acceptable limits. In addition, the experimental results show that the proposed model has a shorter computation time and better prediction performance than a single complex SWT-LSTM model.

Table 5. The computation times required for each case.

Area	Season	Spring
	Model	**Time/Second**
HUDVL	**OURS**	**83.928**
	RBFNN	13.214
	BPNN	15.893
	RVFL	12.039
	DBN	12.901
	BLS–BP	11.574
	S-DBN	81.259
	S-BLS	66.374
	DWT-EMD-RVFL	13.333
	SWT-LSTM	107.791
	EMD-BLS	12.618
	EMD-EDBN	28.211

4.5. Model Performance Analysis on a Heavy Load Test

This section selects a special day in the United States—Christmas—to analyze the performance of the model. Figure 13a–c show the prediction curves of three groups of comparative experiments on Christmas Day. The figures show that although other models can effectively predict the load in some regions where the original electric load increases and decreases steeply, there are still large errors in the prediction results in the regions where the original electric load curve fluctuates widely at the peaks and valleys. In contrast, the load prediction curve of the hybrid network proposed in this paper can fit the original power load curve well. It can predict well even in some areas with large fluctuations of the original power load curve, as well as peaks and troughs. This shows that the method proposed in this paper has strong robustness.

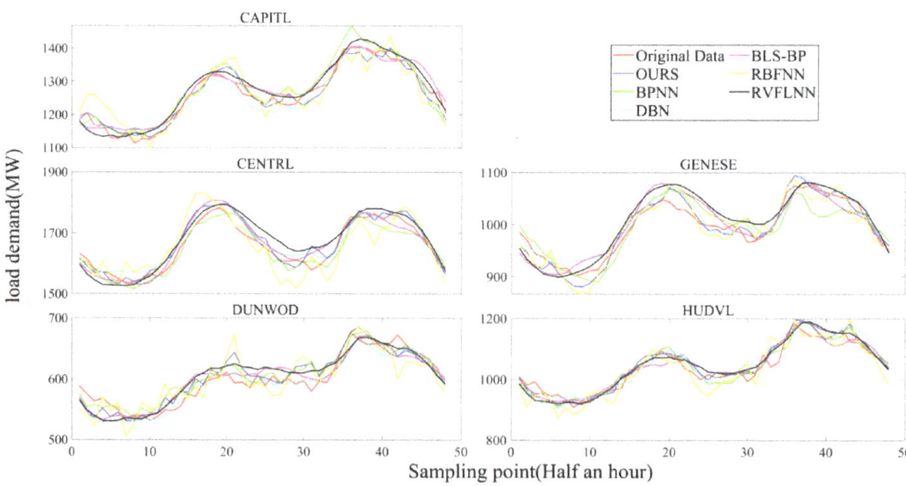

(**a**)

Figure 13. *Cont.*

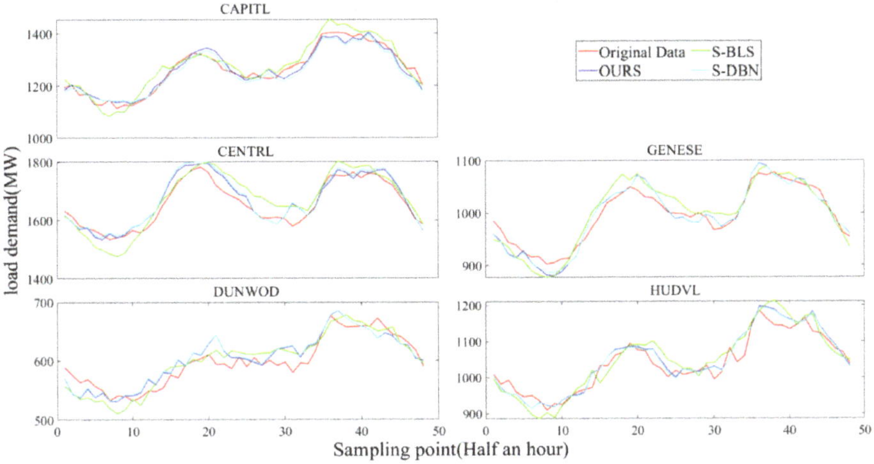

(b)

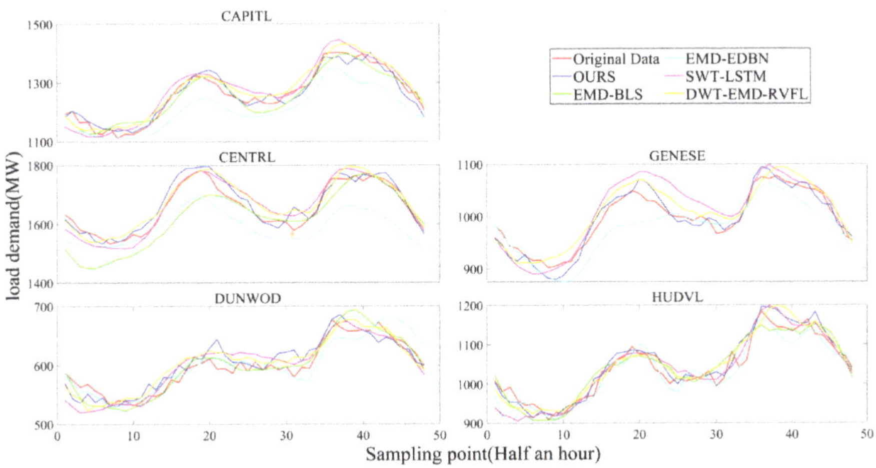

(c)

Figure 13. (**a**) The prediction curve of the comparison with separate neural network models; (**b**) the prediction curve of the comparison with other ensemble models; (**c**) the prediction curve of the comparison with other hybrid models.

4.6. Discussion

The empirical results demonstrate that our model can achieve promising performance, and that our model is more robust than the baseline models for the STLF task. The high-level intuition is that the sliding-window algorithm can smooth the nonlinearity and non-stationarity of the power load data series. In addition, the proposed stacking method can effectively combine multiple neural networks to improve the prediction performance of this method. The forecasting accuracy is further improved by the improved BLS. In addition, the similar-days prediction method is developed for extracting the relationship of electric load data in different time dimensions, proving the robustness of the model.

5. Conclusions

This paper proposes a novel ensemble learning framework for short-term load forecasting. The proposed forecasting framework employs the sliding-window technique to deal with the time-series electric load data. After that, the data are processed in a similar-time prediction method after the training of ensemble learning. Finally, the proposed model is compared with individual neural network models, other ensemble models, and hybrid models. Error analysis is obtained based on MAPE and RMSE evaluation criteria.

In conclusion, the proposed model has advantages in robustness and effectiveness. (i) Robustness: The regression-based broad learning system can achieve outstanding performance when tackling the noise and outliers. The proposed model stacks sub-models to obtain a stacking ensemble model. Our empirical results show that our proposed stacking method can outperform its sub-component, demonstrating the robustness of our model. (ii) Effectiveness: The proposed model can outperform the four existing hybrid baseline models and the sub-component model. The experimental results show that our model can achieve significantly better results than the baseline models because it has a rational framework and design.

However, there are still some limitations to the proposed work. For example, our proposed stacking model has a higher computational cost compared to other individual prediction models. In the future, we plan to explore better model selection for the base- and meta-learners in the stacking approach to tackle this issue, and we intend to use optimization methods to tune the hyperparameters of the prediction models to obtain better prediction accuracy. In addition, we are also interested in investigating electricity load forecasting for individual household customers with higher volatility to validate the robustness and accuracy of our proposed model.

Author Contributions: Conceptualization, Q.J., Y.C. and C.L.; methodology, Y.C.; software, Y.C. and H.L.; validation, Q.J., Y.C. and H.L.; formal analysis, H.L.; investigation, Y.C.; resources, C.L. and P.X.L.; data curation, Y.C.; writing—original draft preparation, Q.J. and Y.C.; writing—review and editing, Q.J. and C.L.; visualization, Q.J. and Y.C.; supervision, C.L. and P.X.L.; project administration, C.L. and P.X.L.; funding acquisition, C.L. All authors have read and agreed to the published version of the manuscript.

Funding: This work was supported in part by the National Natural Science Foundation of China under grants 61863028, 62173176, 81660299, and 61503177, and in part by the Science and Technology Department of Jiangxi Province of China under grants 20204ABC03A39, 20161ACB21007, 20171BBE50071, and 20171BAB202033.

Institutional Review Board Statement: This study did not involve humans or animals.

Informed Consent Statement: This study did not involve humans.

Data Availability Statement: Not applicable.

Conflicts of Interest: The authors declare no conflict of interest.

Abbreviations

ANN	Artificial neural network
ARMA	Autoregressive moving average
BLS	Broad learning system
BLS–BP	Broad learning system–backpropagation
BPNN	Backpropagation neural network
CV	Cross-validation
DBN	Deep belief network
DWT	Discrete wavelet transform
EMD	Empirical mode decomposition
EDBN	Ensemble DBN
LR	Linear regression
LSTM	Long short-term memory
MAPE	Mean absolute percentage error
RBF	Radial basis function
RBM	Restricted Boltzmann machine

RVFL	Random vector functional link
RMSE	Root-mean-square error
S-BLS	Selected BLS
S-DBN	Selected DBN
STLF	Short-term load forecasting
SVR	Support-vector regression
SWT	Stationary wavelet transform

References

1. Simoglou, C.K.; Biskas, P.N. Assessment of the impact of the National Energy and Climate Plan on the Greek power system resource adequacy and operation. *Electr. Power Syst. Res.* **2021**, *194*, 107113. [CrossRef]
2. Li, X.; Jiang, T.; Liu, G.; Bai, L.; Cui, H.; Li, F. Bootstrap-based confidence interval estimation for thermal security region of bulk power grid. *Int. J. Electr. Power Energy Syst.* **2020**, *115*, 105498. [CrossRef]
3. Moon, J.; Hossain, M.B.; Chon, K.H. AR and ARMA model order selection for time-series modeling with ImageNet classification. *Signal Process.* **2021**, *183*, 108026. [CrossRef]
4. Dosiek, L. The Effects of Forced Oscillation Frequency Estimation Error on the LS-ARMA+S Mode Meter. *IEEE Trans. Power Syst.* **2020**, *35*, 1650–1652. [CrossRef]
5. Prion, S.K.; Haerling, K.A. Making Sense of Methods and Measurements: Simple Linear Regression. *Clin. Simul. Nurs.* **2020**, *48*, 94–95. [CrossRef]
6. Alamdar, F.; Mohammadi, F.S.; Amiri, A. Twin Bounded Weighted Relaxed Support Vector Machines. *IEEE Access* **2019**, *7*, 22260–22275. [CrossRef]
7. Qiu, X.; Ren, Y.; Suganthan, P.N.; Amaratunga, G.A.J. Empirical Mode Decomposition based ensemble deep learning for load demand time series forecasting. *Appl. Soft Comput.* **2017**, *54*, 246–255. [CrossRef]
8. Zhu, L.; Lian, C. Wind Speed Forecasting Based on a Hybrid EMD-BLS Method. In Proceedings of the Chinese Automation Congress (CAC), Hangzhou, China, 22–24 November 2019; IEEE: Piscataway, NJ, USA, 2019; pp. 2191–2195.
9. Qiu, X.; Suganthan, P.N.; Amaratunga, A.J.G. Ensemble Incremental Random Vector Functional Link Network for Short-term Crude Oil Price Forecasting. In Proceedings of the IEEE Symposium Series on Computational Intelligence (SSCI), Bangalore, India, 18–21 November 2018; IEEE: Piscataway, NJ, USA, 2018; pp. 1758–1763.
10. Shahid, F.; Zameer, A.; Muneeb, M. A novel genetic LSTM model for wind power forecast. *Energy* **2021**, *223*, 120069. [CrossRef]
11. Potočnik, P.; Škerl, P.; Govekar, E. Machine-learning-based multi-step heat demand forecasting in a district heating system. *Energy Build.* **2021**, *233*, 110673. [CrossRef]
12. Xu, C.; Gordan, B.; Koopialipoor, M.; Armaghani, D.J.; Tahir, M.M.; Zhang, X. Improving Performance of Retaining Walls under Dynamic Conditions Developing an Optimized ANN Based on Ant Colony Optimization Technique. *IEEE Access* **2019**, *7*, 94692–94700. [CrossRef]
13. Chen, G.J.; Li, K.K.; Chung, T.S.; Sun, H.B.; Tang, G.Q. Application of an innovative combined forecasting method in power system load forecasting. *Electr. Power Syst. Res.* **2001**, *59*, 131–137. [CrossRef]
14. Chen, Y.; Luh, P.B.; Guan, C.; Zhao, Y.; Michel, L.D.; Coolbeth, M.A.; Friedland, P.B.; Rourke, S.J. Short-Term Load Forecasting: Similar Day-Based Wavelet Neural Networks. *IEEE Trans. Power Syst.* **2010**, *25*, 322–330. [CrossRef]
15. Matrenin, P.V.; Manusov, V.Z.; Khalyasmaa, A.I.; Antonenkov, D.V.; Eroshenko, S.A.; Butusov, D.N. Improving Accuracy and Generalization Performance of Small-Size Recurrent Neural Networks Applied to Short-Term Load Forecasting. *Mathematics* **2020**, *8*, 2169. [CrossRef]
16. Singh, P.; Dwivedi, P. Integration of new evolutionary approach with artificial neural network for solving short term load forecast problem. *Appl. Energy* **2018**, *217*, 537–549. [CrossRef]
17. Niu, D.; Wang, Y.; Wu, D.D. Power load forecasting using support vector machine and ant colony optimization. *Expert Syst. Appl.* **2010**, *37*, 2531–2539. [CrossRef]
18. Nengling, T.; Stenzel, J.; Hongxiao, W. Techniques of applying wavelet transform into combined model for short-term load forecasting. *Electr. Power Syst. Res.* **2006**, *76*, 525–533. [CrossRef]
19. Ghayekhloo, M.; Menhaj, M.B.; Ghofrani, M. A hybrid short-term load forecasting with a new data preprocessing framework. *Electr. Power Syst. Res.* **2015**, *119*, 138–148. [CrossRef]
20. Ghofrani, M.; Ghayekhloo, M.; Arabali, A.; Ghayekhloo, A. A hybrid short-term load forecasting with a new input selection framework. *Energy* **2015**, *81*, 777–786. [CrossRef]
21. Laouafi, A.; Mordjaoui, M.; Haddad, S.; Boukelia, T.E.; Ganouche, A. Online electricity demand forecasting based on an effective forecast combination methodology. *Electr. Power Syst. Res.* **2017**, *148*, 35–47. [CrossRef]
22. Wang, G.; Wang, X.; Wang, Z.; Ma, C.; Song, Z. A VMD–CISSA–LSSVM Based Electricity Load Forecasting Model. *Mathematics* **2022**, *10*, 28. [CrossRef]
23. Che, J.; Wang, J. Short-term load forecasting using a kernel-based support vector regression combination model. *Appl. Energy* **2014**, *132*, 602–609. [CrossRef]
24. Zhang, T.; Zhang, Y.; Sun, H.; Shan, H. Parkinson disease detection using energy direction features based on EMD from voice signal. *Biocybern. Biomed. Eng.* **2021**, *41*, 127–141. [CrossRef]

25. Hu, M.; Wang, G.; Ma, K.; Cao, Z.; Yang, S. Bearing performance degradation assessment based on optimized EWT and CNN. *Measurement* **2021**, *172*, 108868. [CrossRef]
26. Cheng, Y.; Le, H.; Li, C. A Decomposition-Based Improved Broad Learning System Model for Short-Term Load Forecasting. *J. Electr. Eng. Technol.* **2022**. [CrossRef]
27. Liang, L.; Guo, W.; Zhang, Y.; Zhang, W.; Li, L.; Xing, X. Radial Basis Function Neural Network for prediction of medium-frequency sound absorption coefficient of composite structure open-cell aluminum foam. *Appl. Acoust.* **2020**, *170*, 107505. [CrossRef]
28. Hu, Y.; Li, J.; Hong, M.; Ren, J.; Lin, R.; Liu, Y.; Liu, M.; Man, Y. Short term electric load forecasting model and its verification for process industrial enterprises based on hybrid GA-PSO-BPNN algorithm—A case study of papermaking process. *Energy* **2019**, *170*, 1215–1227. [CrossRef]
29. Sun, G.; Jiang, C.; Cheng, P.; Liu, Y.; Wang, X.; Fu, Y.; He, Y. Short-term wind power forecasts by a synthetical similar time series data mining method. *Renew. Energy* **2018**, *115*, 575–584. [CrossRef]
30. Mentaschi, L.; Besio, G.; Cassola, F.; Mazzino, A. Problems in RMSE-based wave model validations. *Ocean. Model.* **2013**, *72*, 53–58. [CrossRef]
31. Jahan, S.; Riley, I.; Walter, C.; Gamble, R.F.; Pasco, M.; McKinley, P.K.; Cheng, B.H.C. MAPE-K/MAPE-SAC: An interaction framework for adaptive systems with security assurance cases. *Future Gener. Comput. Syst.* **2020**, *109*, 197–209. [CrossRef]
32. Hirano, K.; Wright, J.H. Analyzing cross-validation for forecasting with structural instability. *J. Econ.* **2021**, *226*, 139–154. [CrossRef]
33. Yan, K.; Li, W.; Ji, Z.; Qi, M.; Du, Y. A Hybrid LSTM Neural Network for Energy Consumption Forecasting of Individual Households. *IEEE Access* **2019**, *7*, 157633–157642. [CrossRef]

mathematics

Article

Fluid–Structure Interaction Modeling of Structural Loads and Fatigue Life Analysis of Tidal Stream Turbine

Yuquan Zhang [1,2], Zhiqiang Liu [1], Chengyi Li [2,*], Xuemei Wang [3], Yuan Zheng [1], Zhi Zhang [2], Emmanuel Fernandez-Rodriguez [4] and Rabea Jamil Mahfoud [2]

1 College of Energy and Electrical Engineering, Hohai University, Nanjing 210098, China
2 College of Water Conservancy and Hydropower Engineering, Hohai University, Nanjing 210098, China
3 Chongqing Jiangjin Shipbuilding Industry Co., Ltd., Chongqing 402263, China
4 Technological Institute of Merida, Technological Avenue, Merida 97118, Mexico
* Correspondence: lichengyi@hhu.edu.cn

Abstract: Developing reliable tidal-energy turbines of a large size and capacity links to preservation of the structural safety and stability of the blades. In this study, a bidirectional fluid–structure coupling method was applied to analyze the hydrodynamic performance and structural characteristics of the blade of a tidal-stream turbine. Analyses were conducted on the transient and stable structural stresses, fatigue, and deformations under the influence of water depth and turbine rotational speed. The performance predictions with and without fluid–structure coupling are similar to measurements. The water-depth change has little effect on the stress and deformation change of the blade, while the turbine-speed change has the most significant effect on it. When the turbine just starts, the blade will be subject to a sudden change load. This is due to the increase in turbine speed, resulting in the sudden load. Similar to the trend of blade stress, the blade safety factor is lower near the root of the blade, and the turbine-speed change has a more significant impact on the blade structure's safety. However, the number of stress cycles in the blade at different rotational speeds is within the safety range.

Keywords: tidal stream turbine; CFD; fatigue life; fluid–structure interaction; blade safety factor

MSC: 76E07

Citation: Zhang, Y.; Liu, Z.; Li, C.; Wang, X.; Zheng, Y.; Zhang, Z.; Fernandez-Rodriguez, E.; Mahfoud, R.J. Fluid–Structure Interaction Modeling of Structural Loads and Fatigue Life Analysis of Tidal Stream Turbine. *Mathematics* **2022**, *10*, 3674. https://doi.org/10.3390/math10193674

Academic Editors: Zhuojia Fu, Yiqian He and Hui Zheng

Received: 30 August 2022
Accepted: 29 September 2022
Published: 7 October 2022

1. Introduction

Environmentalists emphasize the imminent animal- and human-habitat disruption from the rising climate temperatures due to the large-scale implementation and burning of fossil fuels. Attempts to reverse the ecological damage are without economical side effects and comprise the carbon residues' elimination and the minimization and eventual substitution of fossil-based systems into renewable power systems. However, the strategy carries obstacles, such as overcoming renewable discontinuous power output, equalizing cost disparities, and improving reception among users. More recently, supporters have stressed the importance of combining renewable resources, named hybrid systems, to achieve economy of scale and solve the cost-inefficient energy accumulators. Tidal-stream energy fits into this concept. It is a high-density, unrenowned, and foreseeable source, and it could supplement wind offshore systems, once viable. The popular mode for current kinetic energy conversion is through rotary machines (three-bladed turbines) stationed in the sea bottom and coupled to electrical generators. Due to its parallelism to offshore wind, the blade profile can be selected to achieve power efficiencies of 48% but may be more in bounded conditions; this is presumed from the multi-member concept and relatively large sweep to incident channel area.

Relevant inquiries, nevertheless, are whether the underwater devices can survive the corrosity and unexpected sea environments, as well as where they can live up to investors' expectations to deliver large low-cost energy over a reasonable time. Since direct field testing is difficult, scientific strategies involve the artificial flow replication, to comprehend the alone and multi-turbine operation, and possible interference in the aquatic life. However, as sites diverge in bathymetry and geographical position, caution in regard to the measured properties must be applied; the current may prompt turbine blockage effects due to shallow depth and mix with omni-directional waves, and the turbulence intensity (TI) can be small (0.1) or critical (0.4), whilst the shear may or not exemplify power laws.

Contrary to uniform flows, the turbine's fluctuating performance is intricate, and thus, the association is unclear between the dynamic blade effects and the main properties of the turbulence and with waves. Tidal-energy turbines are generally arranged in complex marine environments with high flow velocities [1,2]. So, the research methods for tidal-energy turbines are mainly model tests and numerical simulations [3–7]. Allmark et al. [8] conducted model tests of a tidal-energy turbine with a model scale of 1:20 in a recirculating water tank. They found that by using the upstream region of the turbine to achieve acceleration, the turbine could achieve higher power, and the control scheme used had a significant effect on power and load fluctuations. Myers et al. [9] conducted model experiments in a circulating water tank with a turbine diameter of 0.4 m and a ratio of 1:30 and found that, as the inlet flow rate increases, it increases the turbulence around the runner and the change in water-surface height. Zhang et al. [10] evaluated the wake characteristics of a turbine under wave action and showed that the presence of waves has an effect on the intensity of vorticity and turbulence in the near wake field. Gaurier et al. [5] studied load fluctuations in a tank for a turbine model with a scale of 1:20 and showed that fluctuations in turbine load respond directly to fluctuations in low-frequency velocities and are influenced by turbulence shedding from the turbine. This provides substantial suggestions for conducting further fatigue analyses for turbine conditions with high Reynolds-number flow.

Numerical simulations have gradually become a convenient and credible research method through the continuous validation of model experiments conducted by researchers [11]. Tian et al. [12] used available experimental data to verify the reliability of the adopted calculation method, and based on this, the effects of the yaw angle and turbulence-intensity drops on the performance of a horizontal axis tidal energy turbine with a diameter of 3 m were calculated. The results showed that the effects of different turbulence intensities on power coefficient (C_p) and thrust coefficient (C_t) are small, but the effects on wake are large. Ahmadi et al. [13] and others studied the evolution of the wake characteristics of horizontal-axis tidal-energy turbines experimentally, followed by numerical simulations of the flow field, using a combination of Large Eddy Simulation (LES) and Augmented Lagrangian Method (ALM) to partition the turbine wake into different regions, suggesting that to study the characteristics of the turbine wake, it is necessary to understand the variation of flow characteristics in the transition zone.

With the development of tidal-energy turbines to large capacity and large size, their structural safety and stability have received more and more attention [14–17]. On the one hand, the horizontal-axis tidal turbine will produce hydroelastic deformation under the action of water flow, and the deformation produced by the blades will also act on the water flow to produce a certain impact on the flow field; on the other hand, compared with the wind turbine, the tidal turbine will be subject to greater thrust due to the density of seawater [18]. Therefore, the study of fluid–structure coupling for tidal-energy turbines has also attracted the attention of experts and scholars. At present, many scholars have started to conduct fluid–structure coupling analysis on tidal turbines, mainly focusing on their structural reliability, and then achieved the purpose of optimizing the blades.

Some researchers have analyzed the structural performance of tidal turbine blades under different conditions by using the unidirectional fluid–structure coupling method [19]. Hafeez et al. [20] investigated the effect of the velocity shear on the performance and structure of the tidal turbine, comparing the blade deformation in uniform flow and shear flow, and found that the blade deformation of the turbine under velocity shear flow changed significantly. Liu et al. [21] analyzed the structural performance of blades made of stainless steel and structural steel at different rotational speeds, and the results showed that the output power of the turbine was lower at low rotational speeds, but the energy gain efficiency was higher, and the blades of both materials met the structural safety requirements. Ullah et al. [22], on the other hand, performed a fatigue-life analysis and modal analysis of the hydraulic turbine. Some scholars have also used a bidirectional fluid–structure coupling approach in order to obtain the transient structural response of the blades [23–25]. Nicholls-Lee et al. [26] developed an adaptive composite blade design tool and performed a bidirectional fluid–structure coupling analysis on a series of composite bending–torsion coupled blades, and the results showed that practical design of a properly designed blade can achieve a 12% reduction in thrust coefficient and an effective 5% increase in power coefficient. Badshah et al. [27] showed that the difference between CFD calculation results and fluid–structure coupling calculation results is less than 10%, and the two calculation conditions differ in the results of the blade-surface pressure difference. Tatum et al. [28] recognized that wave action would cause the hydraulic turbine's asymmetric loading, so the turbine characteristics were calculated for uncoupled CFD and bidirectional fluid–structure coupling conditions, and the comparison revealed no significant difference between the two calculations; this is a matter of blade-material selection. Khalid et al. [24] simulated the transient structural response of a vertical axis tidal-energy turbine runner, using the fluid–structure coupling method; the blade deformation at each time step was considered in the calculation, and a new calculation method was proposed: transferring the file in ANSYS-APDL to obtain the solution results.

Clearly, an implication of turbine (performance curve and number of blades) and flow operation (turbulence profile) and design (vertical vs horizontal), along with the model differences, raises important questions about the generalizability of the above numerical findings. Therefore, in this study, the hydrodynamic performance and structural characteristics of the turbine were numerically simulated and analyzed based on the bidirectional fluid–structure coupling calculation, and the accuracy of the calculation results was verified by model tests. The prototype is a standard three-bladed horizontal-axis concept, operating in a flow with a turbulence intensity of 7%, and depth variation resembling the logarithmic power law. The fatigue life of the blade was also predicted by considering the influence of the turbine speed and water-depth-variation factors. Our work provides a reference for the design and material application of the blade of the tidal-energy turbine. In our view, these results represent an excellent initial step toward the wider use of the Coupled Fluid Structure model due to high computational accuracy and resource efficiency, as well as further testing in more complex situations, such as incoming waves and currents, and floating turbine systems.

2. Basic Theory

The fluid–structure coupling models the complex interaction between the turbine and water by first treating separately and then coupling the behavior of the incompressible fluid (water) and deformable structure. The strategy has been used to contemplate complex physical phenomena, such as smoking, and can benefit by the use of advanced backed-up separate solvers, applicable to the matter and operating state. Parameters in the method's stability, resource and time requirement, and preciseness comprise the mode and mechanisms of fluid–structure data (interface) communication. If the governing equations of the fluid and structure both satisfy, per time-step calculation, the coupling is said to be strong. The integrated equation is as follows:

$$\begin{bmatrix} A_{FF} & A_{FS} \\ A_{SF} & A_{SS} \end{bmatrix} \begin{bmatrix} \Delta X_F^K \\ \Delta X_S^K \end{bmatrix} = \begin{bmatrix} B_F \\ B_S \end{bmatrix} \tag{1}$$

where A_{FF} is the fluid domain coefficient matrix, ΔX_F^K is the physical solvable quantity, B_F is the external force, and K is the number of time iteration steps; the subscripts F and S

refer to the fluid and solid domain, respectively whilst A_{SF} and A_{FS} are both fluid–structure coupling matrices.

Theoretically, the strong coupling lacks time lag, and the solution's stability, visualization, and accuracy are high. However, the iterative process in the interface becomes time and resource exhaustive, especially for three-dimensional natural-phenomena problems. An alternative to maximize resource efficiency is to satisfy the interface's governing equations, only once per time step, called weak coupling; however, it carries well-known defects: instabilities in strong added-mass circumstances and in solutions, confining the time-step calculation. Additionally, the data transfer between the fluid and the solid modules can be unidirectional, reducing complexity, or reciprocal by assuming the solid deformations alter the surrounding flow, as in the blade against the incident current. The structural dynamics equations of the two-way coupling is as follows:

$$[M]\{x''\} + [C]\{x'\} + [K]\{x\} = \{F(t)\} \tag{2}$$

where the matrix, $[M]$, is the mass; $[C]$ is the damping; and $[K]$ is the stiffness. Moreover, the vector of displacement is $\{x\}$, that of force is $\{F(t)\}$, that of velocity is $\{x'\}$, and that of acceleration is $\{x''\}$.

The following conditions are satisfied for data exchange at the relevant fluid–structure coupled intersection:

$$\begin{cases} u_{s,f} = u_{f,s} \\ v_{s,f} = v_{f,s} \end{cases} \tag{3}$$

where u is the normal-phase displacement component, and v is the normal-phase velocity component.

3. Computational Model

3.1. Numerical Calculation Model

A bidirectional weak coupling fluid–structure model, the ANSYS Workbench platform Fluent, Transient Structural and System Coupling, simulates the turbine transient responses due to incident turbulent current. The CFD-based model is divided into two domains: the blade domain of radius 0.15 m (D/2), and a rectangular prism comprising the outflow field. The width of the prism is set to 4D, consistent with the channel's width, whilst the water depth is set to h = [1.6D, 2D, 2.4D] in order to capture the channel blockage effects on the wake and turbine development. The blade hub is at half-water depth, 8D from the upstream inlet and 30D from the downstream outlet. The blade material is set to Aluminum 6061, with properties summarized in Table 1. To acquire a consistent mesh around the complex blade geometry by virtue of the radial angle variation, the tetrahedral grids are used for the blade domain, with blade sections locally encrypted to increase the result accuracy. The boundary-layer grid is set for the blade boundary, and the height of the first-layer grid is 0.02 mm. The hexahedral grid, known for yielding higher accuracy, distortion resistance, and the number of divided grids, is used for the outflow field. In order to further reduce the influence of the outflow field calculation, the blade domain is encrypted, and the final grid structure is divided as shown in Figure 1. The eddy-viscosity model, SST k-ω, accounts for turbulent shear stresses. The solution of the Navier–Stokes (NS) equations incorporates an implicit scheme. The convective components are discretized with second-order upwind schemes, owing to good convergence and stability features. The pressure–velocity linkage in the NS equation is resolved iteratively via the SIMPLE algorithm. The velocity depth variation is close to the logarithmic power law, as shown in Figure 2. The fitting formula is as follows:

$$V = 0.023\ln\left(\frac{z}{0.0015} + 57.7\right) + 0.25 \tag{4}$$

Table 1. Material properties of 6061 aluminum.

Material	Density (kg·m^{-3})	Young's Modulus (Pa)	Poisson's Ratio
Aluminum 6061	2750	7e + 10	0.33

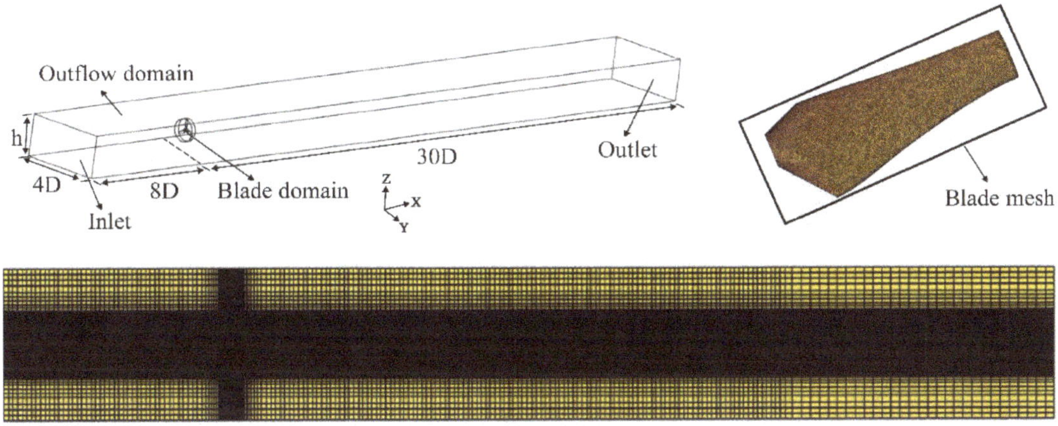

Figure 1. CFD model and the division of the mesh.

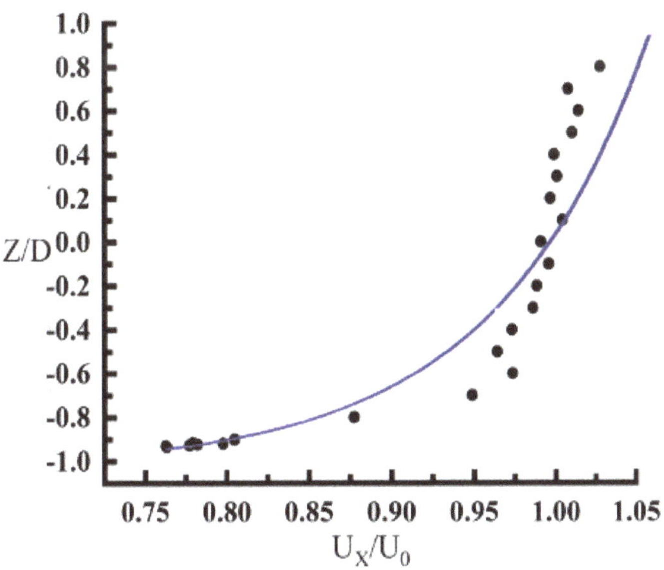

Figure 2. Vertical velocity distribution.

The mean velocity across the swept area is 0.4m/s, with a turbulence intensity of 7%. Consequently, the boundary condition at the inlet is the velocity inlet, and the velocity varies according to Equation (4), whereas at the pressure outlet, the relative atmospheric pressure is set to 0. The free liquid surface is set to symmetry, and the moving mesh is used for the non-constant solution of the fluid domain. Figure 1 shows the mesh structure and main characteristics of the domains.

The solid domain part uses a tetrahedral mesh. The radial and axial displacement constraints are applied to the blade structural body. Gravity is present, and the blade surface is the fluid–structure coupling intersection. The constraints and mesh domain of the solid part are shown in Figure 3.

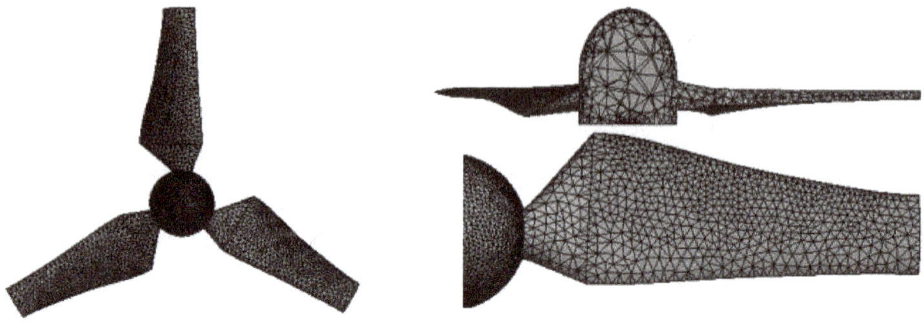

(a)

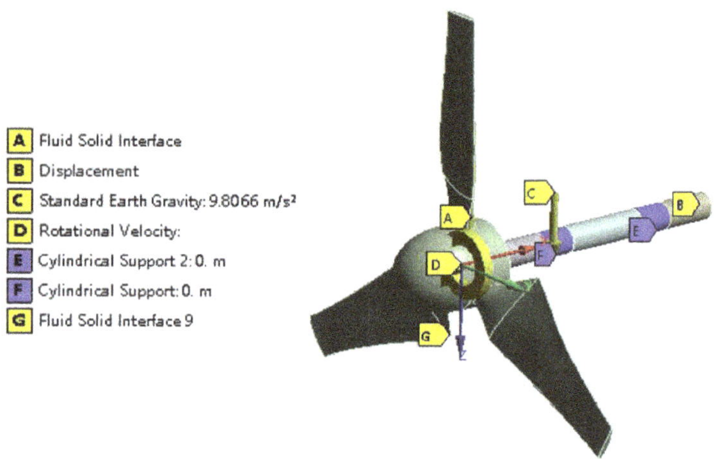

(b)

Figure 3. Mesh division and constraint setting of solid domain model: (**a**) mesh of solid domain and (**b**) constraints on solid domain.

3.2. Grid-Independence Verification

A grid-independence test investigates the method's computational resource with result accuracy. For the fluid domain, the grid number ranges from 3.5 to 7 million, whereas in the solid, the unidirectional fluid–structure coupling uses a grid size of 2 to 6 mm. The water depth is set to 0.6 m, with a blade angular speed of 100 r/min. As shown in Figure 4 and Table 2, the C_p and C_t values quickly decrease from 4.5 to 6 million grids, and then asymptote with numbers over 6 million. The maximum deformation and stress increases with grid reduction and converges with sizes less than 4 mm. Consequently, using a grid size of 3 mm for the solid and 6 million grids for the fluid saves computational resource without sacrificing accuracy level (<0.1%). The bidirectional fluid–solid coupling simulation was conducted by a computer with 32-cores AMD CPU. The final computation time for each case is 132 h.

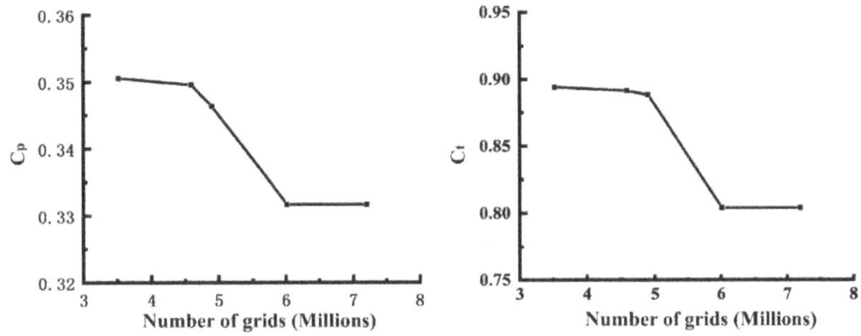

(a) (b)

Figure 4. Grid-independence verification of fluid domain: (**a**) C_p and (**b**) C_t.

Table 2. Grid-independent verification of solid domains.

Segmentation Scheme	Grid Size (mm)	Number of Grids	Maximum Deformation (m)	Maximum Stress (MPa)
1	6	4187	0.012049	979.2
2	5	6409	0.012191	984.68
3	4	9616	0.012376	1122.3
4	3	15,337	0.012614	1307.5
5	2	43,382	0.012691	1337

3.3. Model Test Validation

The power output of the modeled 3-bladed turbine was examined in the hydrodynamic laboratory of Shandong Transportation Institute, using a flume of 50 m in length, 1.2 m in width, and 1.2 m in depth. The pumped water recirculates from the upstream inlet to the downstream via a returning underneath chamber, and the water depth (h) is 0.6 m. The piled turbine is suspended in a metal cage, confining the speed and torque controller and electric cables. This is then fixed by using a crossbeam on the flume, allowing for the adjustment of the hub height (0.3 m). Figure 5 presents the experimental setup.

Figure 5. Layout of circulation pool and turbine.

Figure 6 shows the comparison of results calculated by the FSI method and regular CFD method with the experimental results of the current study. As seen, the predicted power coefficients by BEMT, FSI, and CFD follow an inverted u-curve with a tip–speed ratio (TSR) of TSR = $\omega R/U$, culminating at TSR = 3.9, with C_p = 0.332–0.345. In general, the FSI simulations deviate more from the measurements than the CFD's do due to the non-optimal initial twist blade angle and deformation consideration; however, the error is less than 4.01% for the contemplated study's range (TSR = 3.64–4.32).

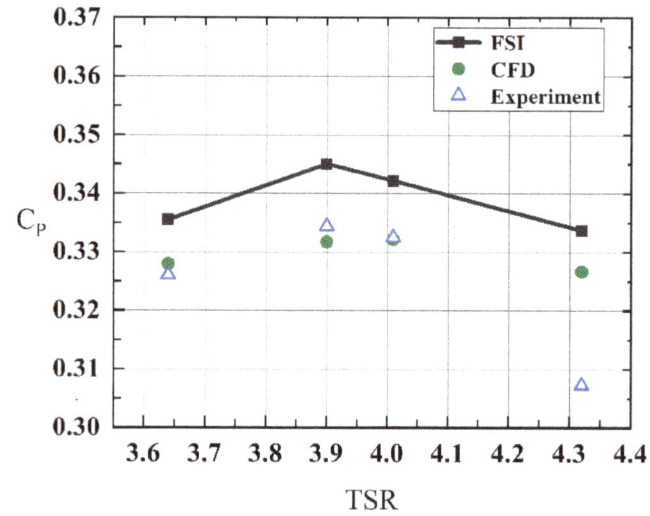

Figure 6. Graph of C_p with TSR.

4. Results Analysis

4.1. Hydrodynamic Performance of Blades

As Figure 7 demonstrates, the pressure simulations follow S-shaped curves, with upper asymptote (near the root) stretching further and lower (at the tip) shifting downwardly with radial distance. This behavior is attributed to two issues: a larger power section performance, apart from the blade root, augmenting the low–high pressure ranges; and the closer cavitation occurrence at the wingtip due to high tangential velocity (ω*r). The only observable simulation difference is at the rear of the blade; it is slightly more negative with than without the fluid–structure coupling condition, due to a small deformation of the blade.

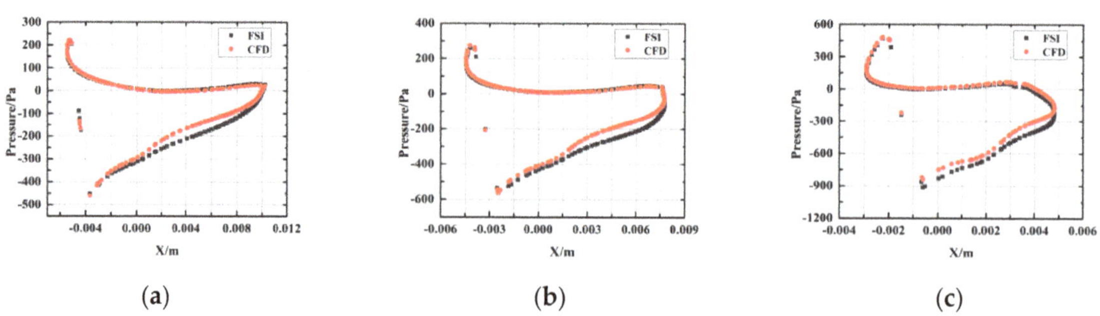

Figure 7. *Cont.*

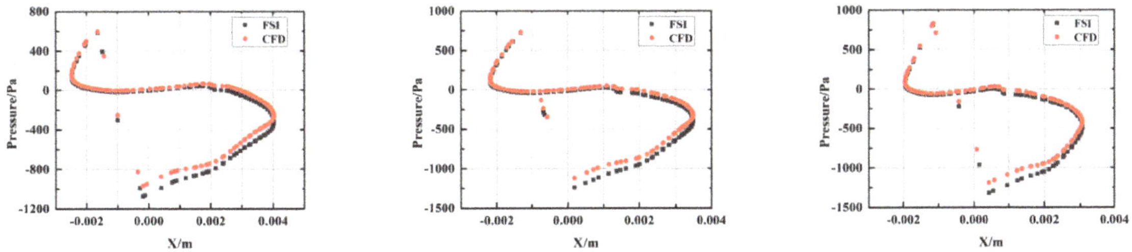

(d) **(e)** **(f)**

Figure 7. Pressure distribution of different blade sections: (**a**) span = 20%, (**b**) span = 40%, (**c**) span = 50%, (**d**) span = 60%, (**e**) span = 70%, and (**f**) span = 80%.

4.2. Blade Structural Stress Analysis

The structural characteristics of the blade were analyzed for a water depth of 0.6 m, an installation height of 0.3 m, and a turbine speed of 100 r/min under fluid–structure coupling conditions. The operation of the tidal-energy turbine for 3 s is calculated, and Figure 8 shows the dynamic stress distribution of the turbine blades at different times. It can be seen that the stress features similar lanceolate contours per blade, extending from the mid-root to almost all the blade, and reducing in intensity radially, reminiscent of an enlarged flame-like shape. Over time, the inner-core strength slightly augments and extends radially. This is because the blade is fixedly connected to the hub, and the blade can be regarded as a cantilever beam, and the bending moment and shear force near the blade root are maximum under the action of fluid loads, such as water thrust. The trend of the stress distribution on the three blades of the blade under each moment is that the maximum stress is at the root of the blade and decreases with an elliptical gradient toward the tip of the blade. When the blade starts to operate, the maximum stress on its surface rises rapidly, with the maximum value reaching 0.596 MPa, and the large stress-distribution area expands rapidly. As the turbine operation gradually stabilizes, the blade's stress distribution is basically similar, and the maximum stress fluctuates in a small range, which is the result of the alternating cyclic load on the blade.

Figure 9 shows the deformation distribution of the blade at different moments. It can be clearly seen that the deformation of the blade's surface at each moment is gradually increasing from the root to the tip of the blade. Combined with Figure 8, it can be found that the maximum blade deformation increases equally rapidly when the turbine is first started and fluctuates in a small range subsequently, due to the stable operation of the blade.

Figure 10 shows the variation of the maximum blade stress with time for 3 s operation under the water depth of 0.48 m, 0.6 m, and 0.72 m operating conditions. From the curves in the figure, it can be seen that the stress initially features an abrupt inverse u-curve before stabilizing, though in a fluctuating manner. The water depth reduces moderately the transient peak but slightly the stable stress. The maximum stress changes in all three water depth conditions show similar small amplitude periodic fluctuations. The turbine is operated under the maximum blocking ratio at the water depth of 0.48 m, and the maximum stress of the blade exists under the three water-depth conditions. Moreover, it can be observed that, under the three water-depth conditions, the maximum stress of the blade tends to decrease with the increase of water depth, but the maximum stress value is very close, so the change of water depth-conditions has little effect on the maximum stress of the blade under stable operation.

Figure 11 shows the variation of the average values of stress and deformation with the water depth during the stable operation of the turbine. It can be seen more directly that, as the water depth decreases, the average stress and average deformation of the blade show an overall decreasing trend, and the average deformation of the blade does not change much after the water depth is lower than 0.6 m.

The influence of the tip–speed ratio (TSR) on the energy conversion of the turbine runner is relatively obvious. As the TSR increases, the runner thrust coefficient increases, and the thrust force acting on the blades also increases. Therefore, it is necessary to investigate the influence of TSR on the blade structure performance under the fluid–structure coupling condition and provide a theoretical basis for the blade strength design of tidal energy turbine. In this calculation, the incoming flow velocity of 0.4 m/s is kept constant, and the TSR is changed by changing the blade's rotational speed. The rotational speeds are 92.69 r/min, 100 r/min, 102.11 r/min, and 110.01 r/min, respectively.

Figure 12 shows the graph of stress variation of the runner at different rotational speeds. When the turbine just started, the blade was also subjected to sudden load changes, and the maximum stress showed periodic fluctuations after 1 s. The higher the rotational speed, the greater the load acting on the blade. Take the rotation speed 100 r/min and 110.01 r/min for example; when the rotation speed increases by about 10%, the sudden stress on the blade at the initial start-up increases by about 30%. Therefore, in the designed operating speed range, the abrupt load changes generated at the start of the turbine cannot be ignored.

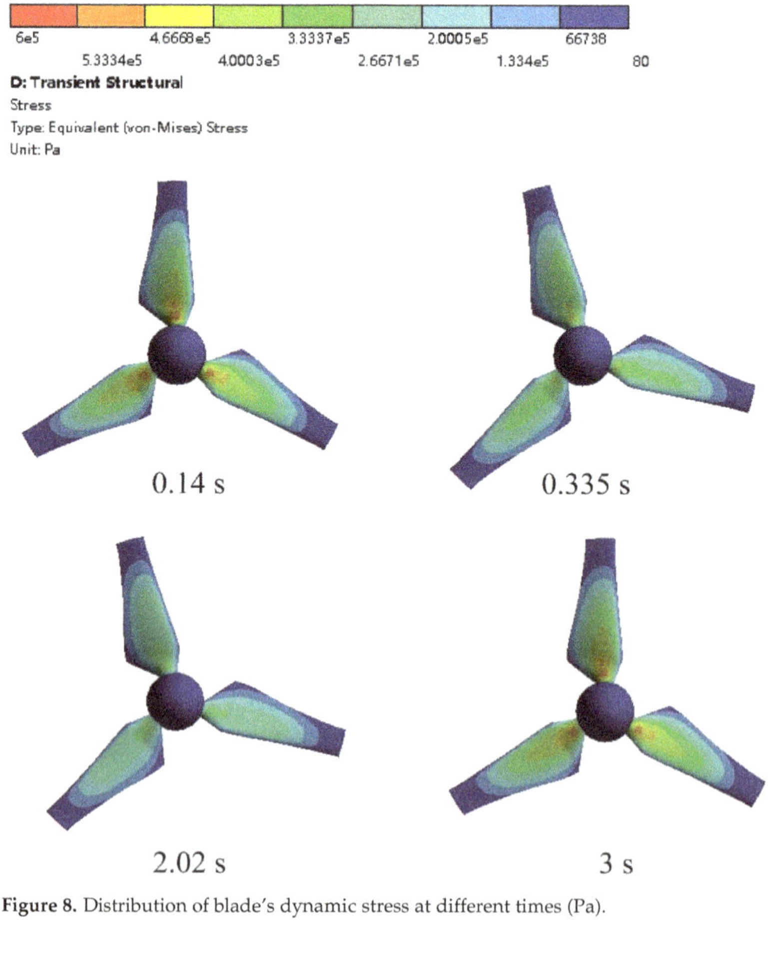

Figure 8. Distribution of blade's dynamic stress at different times (Pa).

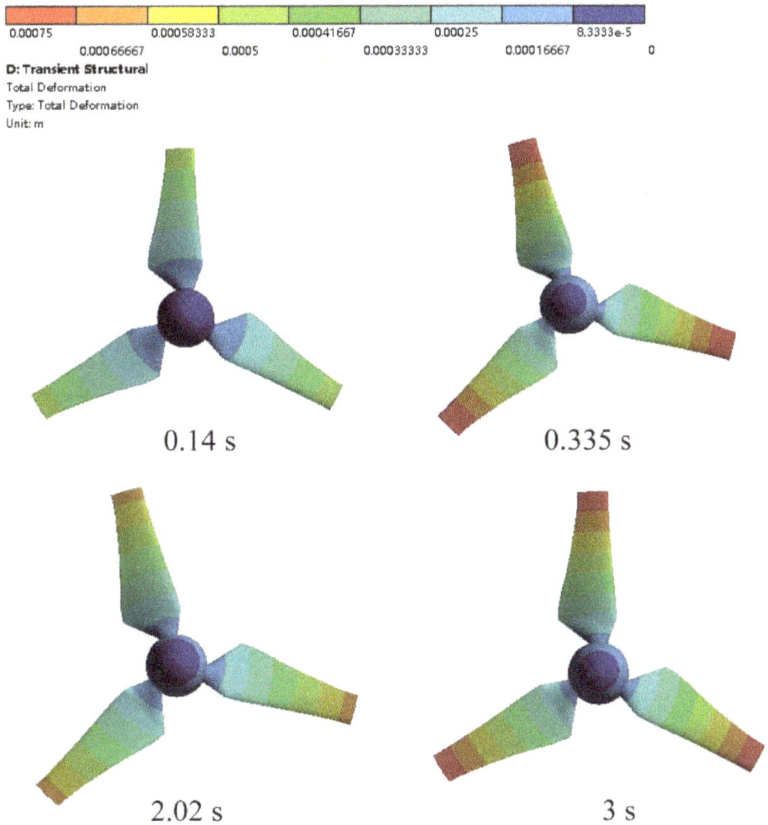

Figure 9. Distribution of blade deformation at different times (m).

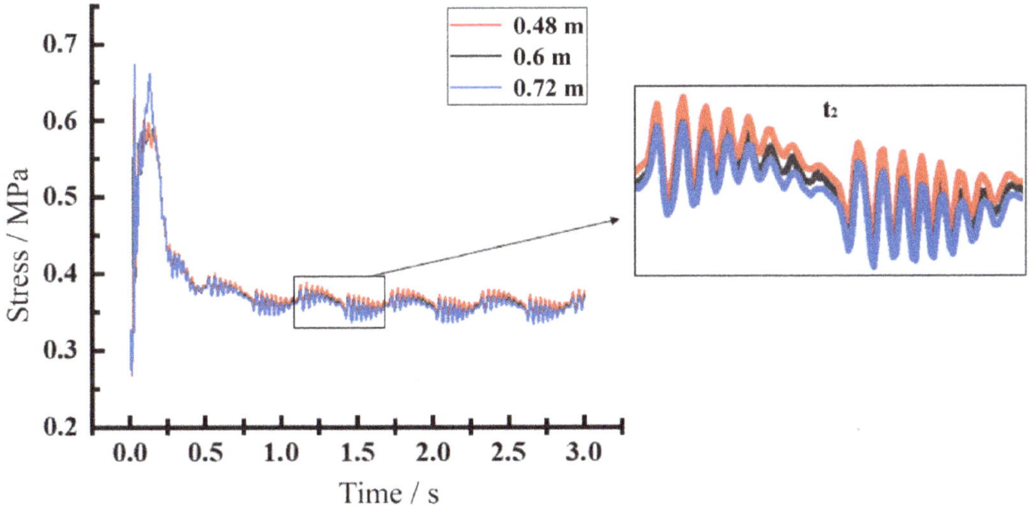

Figure 10. Variation of maximum stress of blade at different water depths.

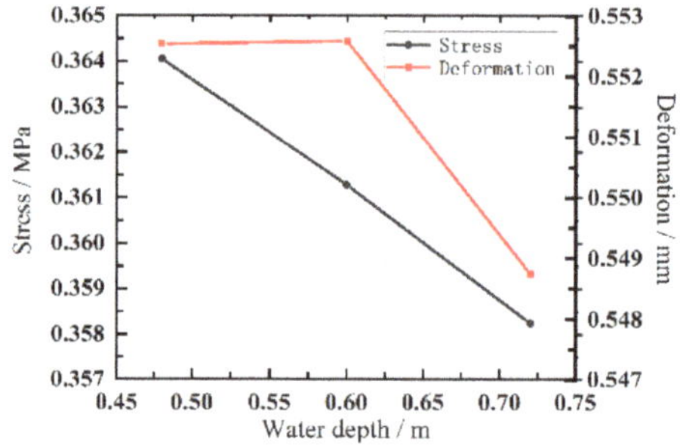

Figure 11. Stable cycle stress and deformation of the blade at different water depths.

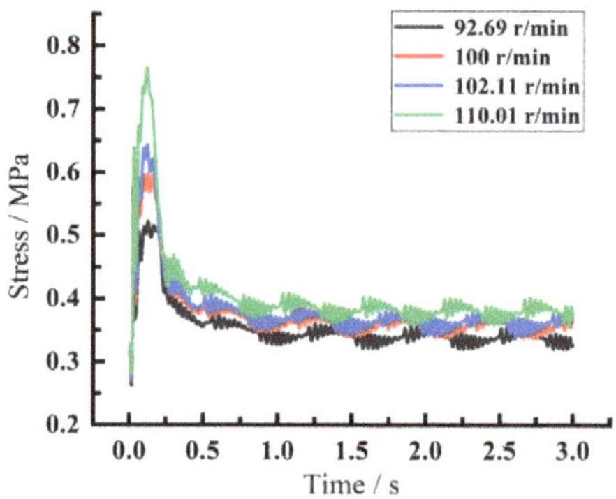

Figure 12. Variation of maximum blade stress at different rotation speeds.

When the turbine operation was stabilized, the average stress and average deformation at four rotational speeds were calculated, as shown in Table 3. It can be found that the average stress and average deformation generally increase with the increase of rotational speed. The average stress becomes larger with the increase of the rotational speed, which is consistent with the trend of the thrust load on the blade. The stress and deformation of the blade are mainly caused by the fluid load [19], and the horizontal-axis tidal-energy turbine is mainly subjected to the axial-thrust force. Moreover, as the speed increases, the axial-thrust force on the turbine increases. The average deformation of the blade decreases at the maximum speed, and this may be due to the second-order oscillation of the blades.

Table 3. Average stress and average deformation.

Rotational Speed (r/min)	Average Stress (MPa)	Average Deformation (mm)
92.69	0.339	0.543
100	0.361	0.550
102.11	0.364	0.551
110.007	0.38	0.544

4.3. Blade-Fatigue-Life Analysis

Figure 13 shows the distribution of the safety coefficient of the blade under different water-depth conditions. The safety factor is uniform, except in near the inner root section of the individual blades; it features irregular elliptical cores of the half safety factor extending along the blade's axis. The depth both slightly affects the distribution and increases the magnitude of the safety factor.

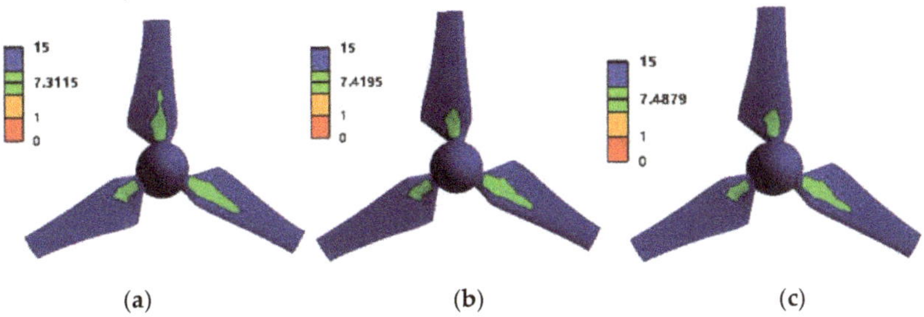

Figure 13. Blade safety factor at different water depths: (**a**) water depth of 0.48 m, (**b**) water depth of 0.6 m, and (**c**) water depth of 0.72 m.

Overall, the low safety coefficient of the blade is located at the root of the blade, which corresponds to the stress distribution of the blade in the previous section, where a large stress concentration occurs at the root of the blade leading to a decrease in the safety coefficient at the root. Meanwhile, with the increase of the water depth, the minimum safety coefficient increases slightly, but the influence range of the blade's minimum safety coefficient is basically the same under different water-depth conditions, and the influence range increases only under the minimum water depth.

Figure 14 depicts the safety-factor distribution of the blade under different TSR conditions. Individually (blade), the half-safety-factor area in the root stretches along the blade axis, though irregularly, with rotational speed. Figure 14d shows the distribution of the safety coefficients on the front and back of the blade at the maximum speed, and it is found that the range of the low safety coefficients on the back of the blade is much larger and has reached the middle of the blade. If the turbine is in a more complex marine environment, the middle of the blade may break, so special attention should be paid when performing the blade's strength calibration.

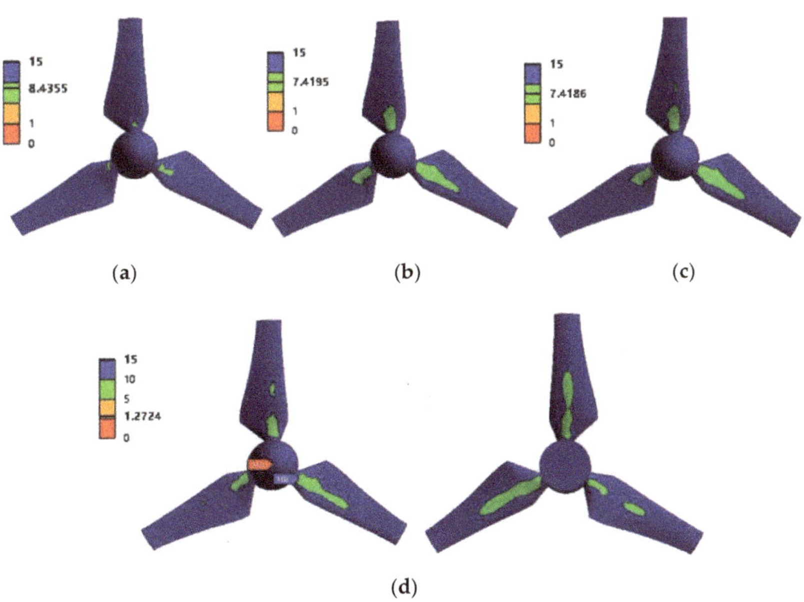

Figure 14. Blade safety factor at different rotational speeds: (**a**) 92.69 r/min, (**b**) 100 r/min, (**c**) 102.11 r/min, and (**d**) 110.01 r/min.

Considering the influence of different rotational speeds on the safety coefficient of the blade, the calculation of the number of stress cycles was carried out for different rotational speeds of the blade. The number of stress cycles of turbine blades under different rotational speeds all reach 108, indicating that the blades are in the safe range under these rotational speeds.

5. Conclusions

This paper calculated and analyzed the hydrodynamic performance and structural characteristics of the tidal stream turbine under bidirectional fluid–structure coupling conditions, and the main conclusions are as follows:

(1) The difference between the calculated hydraulic turbine power coefficients with and without fluid–structure coupling conditions is not significant, and the deformation of the blade under the bidirectional fluid–structure coupling calculation will have a certain impact on the pressure difference on the blade's surface.
(2) As a cantilever beam structure, the blade has its maximum stress concentrated in the root of the leaf, and its maximum deformation is located near the tip of the leaf. The change of water depth has little influence on the stress and deformation of the blade, but the change of rotation speed has the most significant influence on it. The blade will be subjected to abrupt load when it is first started, and the increase of rotation speed will increase the abrupt load.
(3) The fatigue-life prediction of the blade of the tidal-energy turbine was carried out. Similar to the blade stress variation, the lower safety factor of the blade is located near the root of the blade, and the blade's rotation-speed variation has a more significant effect than water depth. The number of stress cycles of the blade at different rotational speeds is within the safety range.
(4) During the design process of the blade, not only the hydraulic performance but also the strength of the blade situation should be taken into consideration.
(5) These results represent an excellent initial step toward the wider use of the coupled fluid structure model due to high computational accuracy and resource efficiency; and toward further testing in more complex situations, such as incoming waves and currents, and floating turbine systems.

Author Contributions: Conceptualization, Y.Z. (Yuquan Zhang) and Z.L.; data curation, Z.L. and C.L.; funding acquisition, Y.Z. (Yuquan Zhang); investigation, Y.Z. (Yuquan Zhang) and X.W.; methodology, Y.Z. (Yuquan Zhang); resources, C.L.; supervision, Y.Z. (Yuan Zheng); validation, Z.L., X.W. and Z.Z.; writing—original draft, Y.Z. (Yuquan Zhang) and C.L.; writing—review and editing, X.W., Z.Z., E.F.-R., and R.J.M. All authors have read and agreed to the published version of the manuscript.

Funding: The research was supported by the following funding programs: National Natural Science Foundation of China (No. 52171257) and Natural Science Foundation of Jiangsu Province (No. BK20220144).

Data Availability Statement: Not applicable.

Conflicts of Interest: The authors declare that they have no known competing financial interests or personal relationships that could have appeared to influence the work reported in this paper.

References

1. Zang, W.; Zheng, Y.; Zhang, Y.; Zhang, J.; Fernandez-Rodriguez, E. Experiments on the mean and integral characteristics of tidal turbine wake in the linear waves propagating with the current. *Ocean Eng.* **2019**, *173*, 1–11. [CrossRef]
2. Gaurier, B.; Ikhennicheu, M.; Germain, G.; Druault, P. Experimental study of bathymetry generated turbulence on tidal turbine behaviour. *Renew. Energy* **2020**, *156*, 1158–1170. [CrossRef]
3. Gaurier, B.; Carlier, C.; Germain, G.; Pinon, G.; Rivoalen, E. Three tidal turbines in interaction: An experimental study of turbulence intensity effects on wakes and turbine performance. *Renew. Energy* **2020**, *148*, 1150–1164. [CrossRef]
4. Derakhshan, S.; Ashoori, M.; Salemi, A. Experimental and numerical study of a vertical axis tidal turbine performance. *Ocean Eng.* **2017**, *137*, 59–67. [CrossRef]

5. Gaurier, B.; Druault, P.; Ikhennicheu, M.; Germain, G. Experimental analysis of the shear flow effect on tidal turbine blade root force from three-dimensional mean flow reconstruction. *Philos. Trans. R. Soc. A* **2020**, *378*, 20200001. [CrossRef]
6. Zhang, Y.; Zhang, J.; Lin, X.; Wang, R.; Zhang, C.; Zhao, J. Experimental investigation into downstream field of a horizontal axis tidal stream turbine supported by a mono pile. *Appl. Ocean Res.* **2020**, *101*, 102257. [CrossRef]
7. Zhang, Y.; Zhang, Z.; Zheng, J.; Zhang, J.; Zheng, Y.; Zang, W.; Lin, X.; Fernandez-Rodriguez, E. Experimental investigation into effects of boundary proximity and blockage on horizontal-axis tidal turbine wake. *Ocean Eng.* **2021**, *225*, 108829. [CrossRef]
8. Allmark, M.; Ellis, R.; Ebdon, T.; Lloyd, C.; Ordonez-Sanchez, S.; Martinez, R.; Mason-Jones, A.; Johnstone, C.; O'Doherty, T. A detailed study of tidal turbine power production and dynamic loading under grid generated turbulence and turbine wake operation. *Renew. Energy* **2020**, *169*, 1422–1439. [CrossRef]
9. Myers, L.; Bahaj, A.S. Wake studies of a 1/30th scale horizontal axis marine current turbine. *Ocean. Eng.* **2005**, *34*, 758–762. [CrossRef]
10. Zhang, Y.; Zang, W.; Zheng, J.; Cappietti, L.; Zhang, J.; Zheng, Y.; Fernandez-Rodriguez, E. The influence of waves propagating with the current on the wake of a tidal stream turbine. *Appl. Energy* **2021**, *290*, 116729. [CrossRef]
11. Peng, B.; Zhang, Y.; Zheng, Y.; Wang, R.; Fernandez-Rodriguez, E.; Tang, Q.; Zhang, Z.; Zang, W. The effects of surge motion on the dynamics and wake characteristics of a floating tidal stream turbine under free surface condition. *Energy Convers. Manag.* **2022**, *266*, 115816. [CrossRef]
12. Tian, W.; VanZwieten, J.H.; Pyakurel, P.; Li, Y. Influences of yaw angle and turbulence intensity on the performance of a 20 kW in-stream hydrokinetic turbine. *Energy* **2016**, *111*, 104–116. [CrossRef]
13. Ahmadim, H.B.; Yang, Z. The evolution of turbulence characteristics in the wake of a horizontal axis tidal stream turbine. *Renew. Energy* **2020**, *151*, 1008–1015. [CrossRef]
14. Yazicioglu, H.; Tunc, K.M.; Ozbek, M.; Kara, T. Simulation of electricity generation by marine current turbines at Istanbul Bosphorus Strait. *Energy* **2016**, *95*, 41–50. [CrossRef]
15. Gonabadi, H.; Oila, A.; Yadav, A.; Bull, S. Fatigue life prediction of composite tidal turbine blades. *Ocean Eng.* **2022**, *260*, 111903. [CrossRef]
16. Finnegan, W.; Fagan, E.; Flanagan, T.; Doyle, A.; Goggins, J. Operational fatigue loading on tidal turbine blades using computational fluid dynamics. *Renew. Energy* **2020**, *152*, 430–440. [CrossRef]
17. Mullings, H.; Stallard, T. Assessment of Dependency of Unsteady Onset Flow and Resultant Tidal Turbine Fatigue Loads on Measurement Position at a Tidal Site. *Energies* **2021**, *14*, 5470. [CrossRef]
18. Bahaj, A.S.; Myers, L.E. Fundamentals applicable to the utilisation of marine current turbines for energy production. *Renew. Energy* **2003**, *28*, 2205–2211. [CrossRef]
19. Badshah, M.; Badshah, S.; Jan, S. Comparison of computational fluid dynamics and fluid structure interaction models for the performance prediction of tidal current turbines. *J. Ocean Eng. Sci.* **2020**, *5*, 164–172. [CrossRef]
20. Hafeez, N.; Badshah, S.; Badshah, M.; Khalil, S.J. Effect of velocity shear on the performance and structural response of a small-scale horizontal axis tidal turbine. *Mar. Syst. Ocean Technol.* **2019**, *14*, 51–58. [CrossRef]
21. Liu, X.F.; Wang, J.B.; Tian, M.L.; Tang, Z.B. Efficiency and Performance Analysis of Tidal Current Energy Turbine Basing on the Unidirectional Fluid-Structure Interaction. *Appl. Mech. Mater.* **2014**, *672*, 386–391. [CrossRef]
22. Ullah, H.; Hussain, M.; Abbas, N.; Ahmad, H.; Amer, M.; Noman, M. Numerical investigation of modal and fatigue performance of a horizontal axis tidal current turbine using fluid–structure interaction. *J. Ocean Eng. Sci.* **2019**, *4*, 328–337. [CrossRef]
23. Li, C.; Zheng, Y.; Zhang, Y.; Kan, K.; Xue, X.; Fernandez-Rodriguez, E. Stability Optimization and Analysis of a Bidirectional Shaft Extension Pump. *J. Fluids Eng.* **2020**, *142*. [CrossRef]
24. Khalid, S.-S.; Zhang, L.; Zhang, X.-W.; Sun, K. Three-dimensional numerical simulation of a vertical axis tidal turbine using the two-way fluid structure interaction approach. *J. Zhejiang Univ. Sci. Appl. Phys. Eng.* **2013**, *14*, 574–582. [CrossRef]
25. Badshah, M.; Badshah, S.; VanZwieten, J.; Jan, S.; Amir, M.; Malik, S.A. Coupled Fluid-Structure Interaction Modelling of Loads Variation and Fatigue Life of a Full-Scale Tidal Turbine under the Effect of Velocity Profile. *Energies* **2019**, *12*, 2217. [CrossRef]
26. Nicholls-Lee, R.F.; Turnock, S.R.; Boyd, S.W. Application of bend-twist coupled blades for horizontal axis tidal turbines. *Renew. Energy* **2013**, *50*, 541–550. [CrossRef]
27. Badshah, M.; Badshah, S.; Kadir, K. Fluid Structure Interaction Modelling of Tidal Turbine Performance and Structural Loads in a Velocity Shear Environment. *Energies* **2018**, *11*, 1837. [CrossRef]
28. Tatum, S.C.; Frost, C.H.; Allmark, M.; O'doherty, D.M.; Mason-Jones, A.; Prickett, P.W.; Grosvenor, R.I.; Byrne, C.B.; O'Doherty, T. Wave–current interaction effects on tidal stream turbine performance and loading characteristics. *Int. J. Mar. Energy* **2016**, *14*, 161–179. [CrossRef]

mathematics

Article

A Fast Singular Boundary Method for the Acoustic Design Sensitivity Analysis of Arbitrary Two- and Three-Dimensional Structures

Liyuan Lan [1], Suifu Cheng [1], Xiatao Sun [2], Weiwei Li [3], Chao Yang [4,*] and Fajie Wang [1,*]

1 National Engineering Research Center for Intelligent Electrical Vehicle Power System, College of Mechanical and Electrical Engineering, Qingdao University, Qingdao 266071, China
2 School of Engineering and Applied Science, University of Pennsylvania, Philadelphia, PA 19104, USA
3 School of Transportation and Vehicle Engineering, Shandong University of Technology, Zibo 255049, China
4 College of Materials Science and Engineering, Qingdao University, Qingdao 266071, China
* Correspondence: yangchao@qdu.edu.cn (C.Y.); wfj88@qdu.edu.cn (F.W.)

Abstract: This paper proposes a fast meshless scheme for acoustic sensitivity analysis by using the Burton–Miller-type singular boundary method (BM-SBM) and recursive skeletonization factorization (RSF). The Burton–Miller formulation was adopted to circumvent the fictitious frequency that occurs in external acoustic analysis, and then the direct differentiation method was used to obtain the sensitivity of sound pressure to design variables. More importantly, RSF was employed to solve the resultant linear system obtained by the BM-SBM. RSF is a fast direct factorization technique based on multilevel matrix compression, which allows fast factorization and application of the inverse in solving dense matrices. Firstly, the BM-SBM is a boundary-type collocation method that is a straightforward and accurate scheme owing to the use of the fundamental solution. Secondly, the introduction of the fast solver can effectively reduce the requirement of computer memory and increase the calculation scale compared to the conventional BM-SBM. Three numerical examples including two- and three-dimensional geometries indicate the precision and efficiency of the proposed fast numerical technique for acoustic design sensitivity analysis associated with large-scale and complicated structures.

Keywords: recursive skeletonization factorization; Burton–Miller-type singular boundary method; fast solver; fundamental solution; acoustic design sensitivity

MSC: 65N35; 76Q05

Citation: Lan, L.; Cheng, S.; Sun, X.; Li, W.; Yang, C.; Wang, F. A Fast Singular Boundary Method for the Acoustic Design Sensitivity Analysis of Arbitrary Two- and Three-Dimensional Structures. *Mathematics* **2022**, *10*, 3817. https://doi.org/10.3390/math10203817

Academic Editor: Yury Shestopalov

Received: 16 September 2022
Accepted: 12 October 2022
Published: 16 October 2022

1. Introduction

In recent years, various methods [1–4] have been proposed to address acoustic problems, such as transient acoustic wave propagation in unbounded domains [5], acoustic transmission across multilayered construction [6], wave diffusion in unbounded domains [7], and acoustic sensitivity analysis [8]. For these problems, numerical simulation plays an irreplaceable role. Common methods for the analysis of acoustic problems include the finite element method (FEM) [9,10], the boundary element method (BEM) [11,12], and some alternative meshless/mesh-free methods. Meshless methods can reduce or even eliminate the tasks of grid generation and numerical integration. Therefore, many scholars and engineers have developed numerous meshless approaches, such as the element-free Galerkin method [13,14], the exponential basis function method [15,16], the localized semi-analytical meshless collocation method [17–19], the method of fundamental solutions (MFS) [20,21], and the singular boundary method (SBM) [22].

Among the above methods, the SBM is a semi-analytical and boundary-type meshless approach using fundamental solutions, which is mathematically simple, numerically accurate, and easy to program. Unlike the MFS, the SBM avoids the singularity of fundamental solutions by introducing the origin intensity factor (OIF), and circumvents the fictitious boundary issue in the traditional MFS. To overcome the influence of the fictitious eigenfrequency issue, the BM-SBM was proposed to deal with sound scattering and radiation [23,24]. Up to now, this scheme has been successfully applied to acoustic simulations [25–27], heat conduction analysis [28,29], electromagnetic problems [30], and other domains.

Similar to the traditional boundary-type methods [31–33], the resultant matrix of the BM-SBM is a dense matrix. Assuming that the number of boundary nodes is N, the storage process needs to occupy the memory of $O(N^2)$, and the operations of $O(N^3)$ are required in the direct calculation. Therefore, insufficient memory and time-consuming computation are often encountered when solving large-scale problems. In order to reduce the calculation time and increase the calculation scale, some scholars have introduced various fast algorithms. The fast multipole (FM) and adaptive cross approximation (ACA) have been used to establish a series of new fast algorithms, such as the fast multipole BEM (FM-BEM) [34–36], the fast multipole MFS (FMM-MFS) [37], the ACA-BEM [38], and the ACA-MFS [39]. Moreover, the ACA-BEM has also been successfully applied to the solution of acoustic sensitivity. The SBM, which draws inspiration from the boundary element technique, has also been combined with fast algorithms to address large-scale problems. Qu et al. [40,41] proposed the fast multipole accelerated SBM (FMM-SBM) to solve large-scale Helmholtz problems, increasing the computational scale of boundary nodes to more than one million. Wei et al. [42] developed an adaptive cross approximation SBM (ACA-SBM) to simulate 2D steady-state heat transfer problems. Li et al. [43–45] developed a precorrected-FFT SBM (PFFT-SBM) to address large-scale 3D Laplace problems, Helmholtz problems, and high-frequency acoustic radiation and scattering problems. Li et al. [46,47] proposed a fast SBM for solving the 2D steady-state heat conduction problem and large-scale 3D potential problem.

This paper aims to present a fast formulation of the BM-SBM for analyzing the acoustic sensitivity of 2D and 3D complex structures. In our earlier works [48,49], we built a BM-SBM framework for acoustic design sensitivity analysis. Benchmark numerical examples confirmed the accuracy and effectiveness of the method. However, the approach still faces the challenge of addressing a large-scale structure. Recursive skeletonization factorization (RSF) [50,51] is a fast and direct scheme based on multilevel matrix compression, and has been successfully applied to various problems. In this paper, RSF is adopted to solve the resultant system of the BM-SBM, and then a new fast method called the RSF-BM-SBM is proposed. Compared with the original BM-SBM, the calculation time is greatly reduced, and the computational scale is significantly increased.

The rest of this paper is organized as follows. In Section 2, we briefly introduce the acoustic sensitivity formula of the BM-SBM and the empirical formula of the OIFs. In Section 3, recursive skeletonization factorization is shown to solve the linear system formed in the sensitivity analysis using the BM-SBM. In Section 4, three examples, including classical models and a complex car model, are demonstrated to verify the accuracy and efficiency of the proposed RSF-BM-SBM for acoustic sensitivity analysis. In Section 5, some conclusions are drawn.

2. Burton–Miller-Type Singular Boundary Method for Acoustic Sensitivity

2.1. Acoustic Sensitivity Analysis

We consider an external sound field problem in two- and three-dimensional spaces, which can be described by the following Helmholtz equation [48,49]:

$$\nabla^2 u(\mathbf{x}) + k^2 u(\mathbf{x}) = 0\,, \mathbf{x} \in \Omega \tag{1}$$

with the following Dirichlet and Neumann boundary conditions:

$$u(\mathbf{x}) = \overline{u}(\mathbf{x}), \mathbf{x} \in \Gamma_u, \tag{2}$$

$$\frac{\partial u(\boldsymbol{x})}{\partial \boldsymbol{n}_x} = \mathrm{i}\rho\omega\overline{v}(\boldsymbol{x}), \boldsymbol{x} \in \Gamma_q, \tag{3}$$

where ∇^2 represents the Laplace operator; $k = \omega/c$ is the wave number; ω is the angular frequency; c is the speed of sound in the propagating medium; and $\overline{u}(\boldsymbol{x})$ and $\overline{v}(\boldsymbol{x})$ are the sound pressure and the normal vibration velocity on Γ_u and Γ_q, respectively.

Considering sound propagation in an infinite field, the sound pressure should satisfy the Sommerfeld radiation condition at infinity:

$$\lim_{r\to\infty} r^{\frac{1}{2}(d-1)}\left(\frac{\partial u(\boldsymbol{x})}{\partial r} - \mathrm{i}ku(\boldsymbol{x})\right) = 0 \tag{4}$$

where d is the spatial dimension (d = 2, 3) and r is the distance between point x and the sound field's center. The fundamental solution employed in the BM-SBM automatically satisfies the aforementioned requirements; therefore, no additional handling is necessary in the numerical computation.

For acoustic sensitivity analysis, the most important thing is to obtain the gradient of the objective function with respect to the design variables. In many applications, the objective function is sound pressure, and the design variables are size, wave number, or frequency.

2.2. Burton–Miller-Type Singular Boundary Method

Assuming the total number of boundary nodes is N, the BM-SBM formulas can be given by [49]:

$$u(\boldsymbol{x}_i) = \sum_{\substack{j=1 \\ i\neq j}}^{N} \alpha_j\left(G(\boldsymbol{x}_i,\boldsymbol{s}_j) + \lambda E(\boldsymbol{x}_i,\boldsymbol{s}_j)\right) + \alpha_i u_{BM},\ \boldsymbol{x}_i \in \Gamma_u,\ \boldsymbol{s}_j \in \Gamma \tag{5}$$

$$\frac{\partial u(\boldsymbol{x}_i)}{\partial \boldsymbol{n}_x} = \sum_{\substack{j=1 \\ i\neq j}}^{N} \alpha_j\left(F(\boldsymbol{x}_i,\boldsymbol{s}_j) + \lambda H(\boldsymbol{x}_i,\boldsymbol{s}_j)\right) + \alpha_i q_{BM},\ \boldsymbol{x}_i \in \Gamma_q,\ \boldsymbol{s}_j \in \Gamma \tag{6}$$

$$E(\boldsymbol{x}_i,\boldsymbol{s}_j) = \frac{\partial G(\boldsymbol{x}_i,\boldsymbol{s}_j)}{\partial \boldsymbol{n}_s},\ F(\boldsymbol{x}_i,\boldsymbol{s}_j) = \frac{\partial G(\boldsymbol{x}_i,\boldsymbol{s}_j)}{\partial \boldsymbol{n}_x},\ H(\boldsymbol{x}_i,\boldsymbol{s}_j) = \frac{\partial^2 G(\boldsymbol{x}_i,\boldsymbol{s}_j)}{\partial \boldsymbol{n}_s \partial \boldsymbol{n}_x} \tag{7}$$

where $\lambda = \frac{\mathrm{i}}{k+1}$ is a complex number [24]; α_j is the unknown coefficient; and $\boldsymbol{x}_i$ and $\boldsymbol{s}_j$ denote ith boundary node and jth source point, respectively. u_{BM} and q_{BM} are the OIFs, which can be computed by the following formulas [52,53]:

$$u_{BM} = u_{ii} - \lambda \sum_{\substack{j=1 \\ j\neq i}}^{N} \zeta_{ji}\frac{\partial G_0(\boldsymbol{x}_i,\boldsymbol{s}_j)}{\partial \boldsymbol{n}_s} \tag{8}$$

$$q_{BM} = q_{ii} + \lambda\left(\frac{k^2}{2}u_{ii} - \sum_{\substack{j=1 \\ j\neq i}}^{N} \zeta_{ji}\frac{\partial^2 G_0(\boldsymbol{x}_i,\boldsymbol{s}_j)}{\partial \boldsymbol{n}_s \partial \boldsymbol{n}_x}\right) \tag{9}$$

where u_{ii} and q_{ii} are given in Refs. [24,48], and $G_0(\boldsymbol{x}_i,\boldsymbol{s}_j)$ is the fundamental solution of the Laplace equation. $G_0(\boldsymbol{x}_i,\boldsymbol{s}_j) = -\frac{\ln|\boldsymbol{x}_i-\boldsymbol{s}_j|}{2\pi}$ for 2D problems; $G_0(\boldsymbol{x}_i,\boldsymbol{s}_j) = \frac{1}{4\pi|\boldsymbol{x}_i-\boldsymbol{s}_j|}$ for 3D problems.

Substituting the boundary conditions into Equations (5) and (6), the following system of equations can be obtained:

$$\mathbf{M}\boldsymbol{\alpha} = \mathbf{b} \tag{10}$$

where $\mathbf{M}_{N\times N}$ is the coefficient matrix, $\boldsymbol{\alpha}_{N\times 1}$ is the undetermined coefficient vector, and $\mathbf{b}_{N\times 1}$ is the known vector. The matrix $\mathbf{M}$ is generated from Burton–Miller-type formulation (a combination of single- and double-layer potentials), and its condition number is related to the number of nodes. Since the method is implemented by MATLAB programming, the condition number of the matrix can be viewed by the routine *cond*(M). By solving Equation (10), $\boldsymbol{\alpha}$ can be obtained. After that, the following formulas can be employed to determine the sound pressure and normal derivative at point x:

$$u(x) = \sum_{j=1}^{N} \alpha_j \left(G(x, s_j) + \lambda E(x, s_j)\right) \tag{11}$$

$$q(x) = \sum_{j=1}^{N} \alpha_j \left(F(x, s_j) + \lambda H(x, s_j)\right) \tag{12}$$

Based on the formulas mentioned above, the direct differentiation approach can be used to compute the sensitivities:

$$\dot{u}(x) = \sum_{j=1}^{N} \begin{bmatrix} \dot{\alpha}_j \left(G(x, s_j) + \lambda E(x, s_j)\right) \\ +\alpha_j \left(\dot{G}(x, s_j) + \dot{\lambda} E(x, s_j) + \lambda \dot{E}(x, s_j)\right) \end{bmatrix} \tag{13}$$

$$\dot{q}(x) = \sum_{j=1}^{N} \begin{bmatrix} \dot{\alpha}_j \left(F(x, s_j) + \lambda H(x, s_j)\right) \\ +\alpha_j \left(\dot{F}(x, s_j) + \dot{\lambda} H(x, s_j) + \lambda \dot{H}(x, s_j)\right) \end{bmatrix} \tag{14}$$

where the superscript ($\dot{}$) denotes the differentiation of a function. For the differentiation calculation in the right hand sides of the above equations, one can refer to Ref. [48].

3. Recursive Skeletonization Factorization

Recursive skeleton factorization is a fast direct solver which allows fast factorization and application of the inverse in the process of solving asymmetric dense matrices.

3.1. Interpolative Decomposition

The present paper adopts interpolative decomposition (ID) to compress the low-rank blocks [46,54]. If the submatrix $\mathbf{M}_{pq} \in \mathbb{R}^{m\times n}$ of $\mathbf{M}$ is a matrix of rank $h \leq \min(m, n)$, then there exist $\mathbf{R}_q \in \mathbb{R}^{h\times(n-t)}$ such that $\mathbf{M}_{pq'} \approx \mathbf{M}_{pq''}\mathbf{R}_q$. It should be pointed out that m and n denote the dimension of the matrix $\mathbf{M}$, which are set as $m = n = N$. Here, p and q represent ordered sets of indices, q' and q'' denote the skeleton and redundant indices, and they satisfy the following relationships: $q = q' \cup q''$ and $|q''| = h$. If $\mathbf{R}_q$ satisfy $\mathbf{M}_{pq'} = \mathbf{M}_{pq''}\mathbf{R}_q$, then

$$\begin{bmatrix}\mathbf{M}_{pq'} \ \mathbf{M}_{pq''}\end{bmatrix} \begin{bmatrix} \mathbf{I} & \\ -\mathbf{R}_q & \mathbf{I} \end{bmatrix} = \begin{bmatrix} 0 \ \mathbf{M}_{pq''} \end{bmatrix} \tag{15}$$

It should be pointed out that ID is commonly applied to cases with an error matrix $\mathbf{E}$, i.e., $\mathbf{M}_{pq'} = \mathbf{M}_{pq''}\mathbf{R}_q + \mathbf{E}$, in which $||\mathbf{E}|| \sim \sigma_{h+1}(\mathbf{M})$, and $\sigma_{h+1}(\mathbf{M})$ stands for the (h + 1)th-largest singular value of $\mathbf{M}$. In this regard, ID can be employed to select h adaptively, so that $||\mathbf{E}|| \leq \varepsilon ||\mathbf{M}||$ for a given tolerance $\varepsilon > 0$. In this paper, ID is achieved by a random sampling scheme [54], which only requires $O\left(mn\log(h) + h^2 n\right)$ operations.

3.2. Skeletonization

In this subsection, ID is adopted to compress a matrix with low-rank off-diagonal blocks. We consider a block matrix $\mathbf{M}$ with index sets p and q:

$$\mathbf{M} = \begin{bmatrix} \mathbf{M}_{pp} & \mathbf{M}_{pq} \\ \mathbf{M}_{qp} & \mathbf{M}_{qq} \end{bmatrix} \tag{16}$$

where $\mathbf{M}_{pq}$ and $\mathbf{M}_{qp}$ are low-rank submatrices. After applying ID to $\mathbf{M}$ with $p = p' \cup p''$, we obtain

$$\mathbf{M} = \begin{bmatrix} \mathbf{M}_{p'p'} & \mathbf{M}_{p'p''} & \mathbf{M}_{p'q} \\ \mathbf{M}_{p''p'} & M_{p''p''} & \mathbf{M}_{p''q} \\ \mathbf{M}_{qp'} & \mathbf{M}_{qp''} & \mathbf{M}_{qq} \end{bmatrix} \tag{17}$$

Let

$$\mathbf{Q}_p = \begin{bmatrix} \mathbf{I} & & \\ -\mathbf{R}_p & \mathbf{I} & \\ & & \mathbf{I} \end{bmatrix} \tag{18}$$

and then

$$\mathbf{Q}_p^{\mathrm{T}}\mathbf{M}\mathbf{Q}_p \approx \begin{bmatrix} \mathbf{N}_{p'p'} & \mathbf{N}_{p'p''} & \\ \mathbf{N}_{p''p'} & \mathbf{M}_{p''p''} & \mathbf{M}_{p''q} \\ & \mathbf{M}_{qp''} & \mathbf{M}_{qq} \end{bmatrix} \tag{19}$$

where

$$\mathbf{N}_{p'p'} = \mathbf{M}_{p'p'} - \mathbf{R}_p^{\mathrm{T}}\mathbf{M}_{p'',p'} - \mathbf{M}_{p'p''}\mathbf{R}_p + \mathbf{R}_p^{\mathrm{T}}\mathbf{M}_{p''p''}\mathbf{R}_p \tag{20}$$

$$\mathbf{N}_{p'p''} = \mathbf{M}_{p'p''} - \mathbf{R}_p^{\mathrm{T}}\mathbf{M}_{p''p''}, \quad \mathbf{N}_{p''p'} = \mathbf{M}_{p''p'} - \mathbf{M}_{p''p''}\mathbf{R}_p \tag{21}$$

Supposing $\mathbf{N}_{p'p'}$ is a nonsingular matrix, and $\mathbf{N}_{p'p''}$ can be decomposed into $\mathbf{L}_{p'}\mathbf{D}_{p'}\mathbf{U}_{p'}$ ($\mathbf{D}_{p'}$ is a diagonal matrix; $\mathbf{L}_{p'}$ and $\mathbf{U}_{p'}$ are unit triangular matrices), we obtain

$$\mathbf{s}_{p'}^{\mathrm{T}}\mathbf{Q}_p^{\mathrm{T}}\mathbf{M}\mathbf{Q}_p\mathbf{T}_{p'} \approx \begin{bmatrix} \mathbf{D}_{p'} & & \\ & \mathbf{N}_{p'',p''} & \mathbf{M}_{p'',q} \\ & \mathbf{M}_{q,p''} & \mathbf{M}_{q,q} \end{bmatrix} \equiv \Psi_p(\mathbf{M}) \tag{22}$$

where $\Psi_p(\cdot)$ is called the skeletonization operator, and

$$\mathbf{s}_{p'}^{\mathrm{T}} = \begin{bmatrix} \mathbf{I} & & \\ -\mathbf{N}_{p''p'}\mathbf{U}_{p'}^{-1}\mathbf{D}_{p'}^{-1} & \mathbf{I} & \\ & & \mathbf{I} \end{bmatrix} \begin{bmatrix} \mathbf{L}_{p'}^{-1} & & \\ & \mathbf{I} & \\ & & \mathbf{I} \end{bmatrix} \tag{23}$$

$$\mathbf{T}_{p'} = \begin{bmatrix} \mathbf{U}_{p'}^{-1} & & \\ & \mathbf{I} & \\ & & \mathbf{I} \end{bmatrix} \begin{bmatrix} \mathbf{I} & -\mathbf{D}_{p'}^{-1}\mathbf{L}_{p'}^{-1}\mathbf{N}_{p'p''} & \\ & \mathbf{I} & \\ & & \mathbf{I} \end{bmatrix} \tag{24}$$

$$\mathbf{N}_{p''p''} = \mathbf{M}_{p''p''} - \mathbf{N}_{p''p'}\mathbf{N}_{p'p'}^{-1}\mathbf{N}_{p'p''} \tag{25}$$

Considering a collection of disjoint index sets C, in which $\mathbf{M}_{c,c^C}$ and $\mathbf{M}_{c^C,c}$ are low-rank for any $c \in C$, $\Psi_C(\mathbf{M})$ can be decomposed into

$$\Psi_C(\mathbf{M}) \approx \mathbf{U}^{\mathrm{T}}\mathbf{M}\mathbf{V} \tag{26}$$

where c^C denotes the complement of the index set c, $\mathbf{U} = \prod_{c \in C} \mathbf{Q}_c\mathbf{S}_{c'}$, and $\mathbf{V} = \prod_{c \in C} \mathbf{Q}_c\mathbf{T}_{c'}$.

3.3. Recursive Skeletonization Factorization (RSF)

Let C_j denote the collection of the skeleton index set at level j. We define the matrix at each level j by using $\mathbf{M}_j$. It should be noted that $\mathbf{M}_0 = \mathbf{M}$. Based on the skeletonization mentioned above, we have

$$\mathbf{M}_{j+1} = \Psi_{C_j}(\mathbf{M}_j) \approx \mathbf{U}_j^{\mathrm{T}}\mathbf{M}_j\mathbf{V}_j, \quad \mathbf{U}_j = \prod_{c\in C_j}\mathbf{Q}_c\mathbf{S}_{c'}, \quad \mathbf{V}_j = \prod_{c\in C_j}\mathbf{Q}_c\mathbf{T}_{c'} \tag{27}$$

By using RSF, each $\mathbf{U}_j$ and $\mathbf{V}_j$ are products of unit triangular matrices, and can be simply inverted and transposed. Then, according to the same principle, the factorization can be written as

$$\mathbf{M}_j \approx \mathbf{U}_{j-1}^{\mathrm{T}} \cdots \mathbf{U}_0^{\mathrm{T}}\mathbf{M}\mathbf{V}_0 \cdots \mathbf{V}_{j-1} \tag{28}$$

Note that the inversion and transposition of matrices $\mathbf{U}_j$ and $\mathbf{V}_j$ can be easily obtained, since they are products of unit triangular matrices. Therefore, $\mathbf{M}$ and $\mathbf{M}^{-1}$ can be calculated by

$$\mathbf{M} \approx \left[\mathbf{U}_0^{-1}\right]^{\mathrm{T}} \cdots \left[\mathbf{U}_{j-1}^{-1}\right]^{\mathrm{T}}\mathbf{M}_j\mathbf{V}_{j-1}^{-1} \cdots \mathbf{V}_0^{-1} \tag{29}$$

$$\mathbf{M}^{-1} \approx \mathbf{V}_0 \cdots \mathbf{V}_{j-1}\mathbf{M}_j\mathbf{U}_{j-1}^{\mathrm{T}} \cdots \mathbf{U}_0^{\mathrm{T}} \tag{30}$$

After obtaining $\mathbf{M}^{-1}$ from Equation (30), the unknown coefficient vector $\boldsymbol{\alpha}$ in Equation (10) can be acquired by the following formula:

$$\boldsymbol{\alpha} = \mathbf{M}^{-1}\mathbf{b} \tag{31}$$

4. Numerical Examples

Here, two benchmark examples are firstly investigated to demonstrate the accuracy of the RSF-BM-SBM, and then the feasibility and effectiveness of the method to solve large-scale problems are verified by calculating the sensitivity of a vehicle model. Assuming that the design variable t is divided into m equidistant nodes, the following relative-root-mean-square error (RRMSE) [24] is adopted to evaluate numerical error:

$$\mathrm{RRMSE} = \frac{\sqrt{\sum_{j=1}^{m}\left(\dot{u}_e(t_j) - \dot{u}_n(t_j)\right)^2}}{\sqrt{\sum_{j=1}^{m}\dot{u}_e(t_j)^2}} \tag{32}$$

where $\dot{u}_e$ and $\dot{u}_n$ denote the exact and numerical solutions of the acoustic sensitivity, respectively. In the following numerical calculation, we have fixed the air density and the sound speed to $\rho = 1.2\ \mathrm{kg/m^3}$ and $c = 341\ \mathrm{m/s}$.

In acoustic sensitivity analysis, the gradient of the objective function with respect to the design variables needs to be obtained. Taking the sound pressure p as the objective function, it can be expressed as $\frac{\partial p(x)}{\partial t}$, where t represents the design variable.

4.1. Example 1

In the first example, we consider an infinite pulsating cylinder [49] with radius $a = 0.1$ m, which can be reduced to a 2D problem as shown in Figure 1.

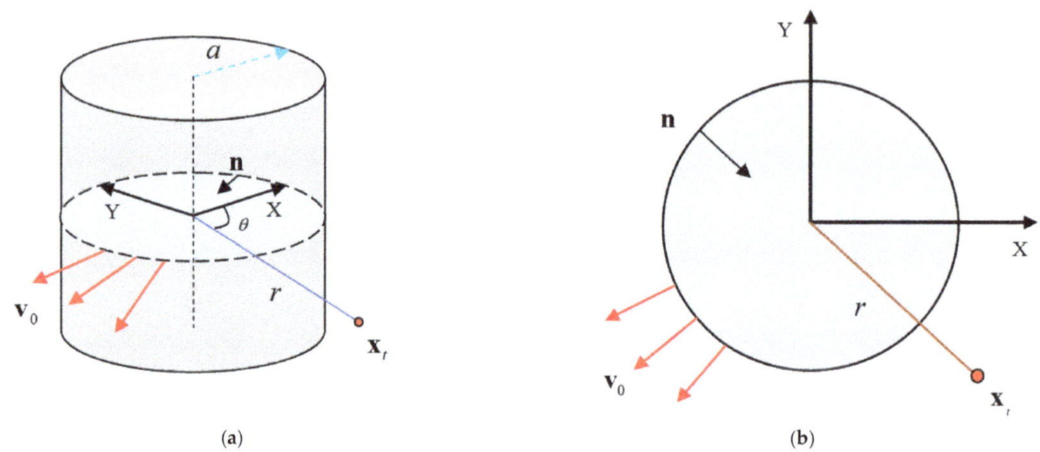

Figure 1. Infinite pulsating cylinder: (**a**) a pulsating cylinder; (**b**) simplified model.

Taking the wave number as the design variable, the analytical solution of the acoustic sensitivity at the test point x_t can be given by

$$\frac{\partial p_e(r)}{\partial k} = \frac{-\mathrm{i}\rho c v_0}{\left(H_1^1(ka)\right)^2}\left[rH_1^1(kr)H_1^1(ka) + \frac{a}{2}H_0^1(kr)\left(H_0^1(ka) - H_2^1(ka)\right)\right] \quad (33)$$

where $v_0 = 1$ m/s(Neumann boundary condition); H_0^1 and H_1^1 are first-kind zero-order and one-order Hankel functions, respectively; and r is the distance between the test point and the center of cylinder.

Firstly, we investigate the influence of compression accuracy on calculation results. Figure 2 displays error curves of sound pressure sensitivity at the test point $\mathbf{x}_t = (3, 3)$ under various values of ID ($\varepsilon = 10^{-4}$, $\varepsilon = 10^{-7}$, and $\varepsilon = 10^{-10}$). In this calculation, the range of the design variable is fixed at 5~6, and the traditional BM-SBM solutions are used for an intuitive comparison. We can see from Figure 2 that the numerical error of the RSF-BM-SBM increases with a decreasing value of ID. When $\varepsilon = 10^{-10}$, the calculation accuracy is basically consistent with the traditional BM-SBM. Therefore, the higher compression accuracy should be chosen to obtain accurate and reliable results.

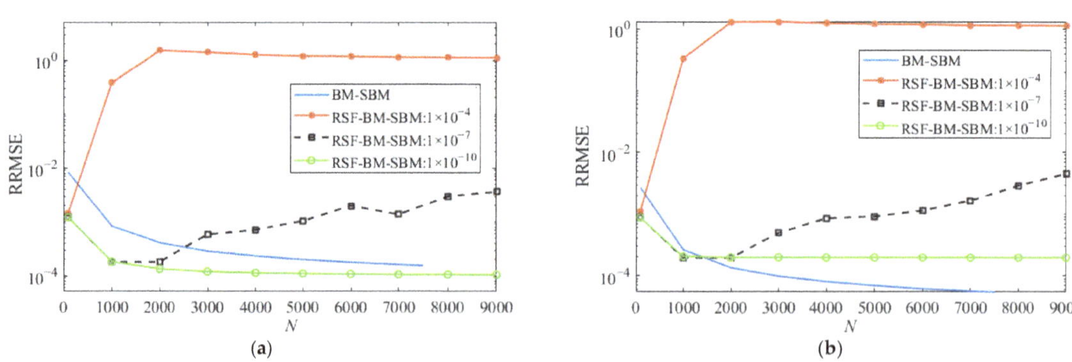

Figure 2. The RRMSEs of the RSF-BM-SBM and conventional BM-SBM: (**a**) real part; (**b**) imaginary part.

In addition, Figure 3 compares the computation times of the RSF-BM-SBM and the BM-SBM under different numbers of nodes. When the number of nodes is small, both the BM-SBM and the RSF-BM-SBM consume less time. However, with an increasing number of nodes, the RSF-BM-SBM requires significantly less time than the BM-SBM.

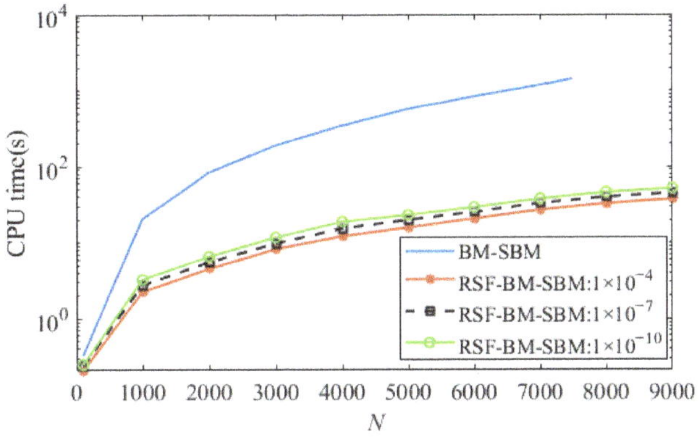

Figure 3. Comparison of CPU computation times under different numbers of nodes.

4.2. Example 2

In this example, we consider a 3D sound radiation problem on a pulsating sphere [48] with radius $a = 0.1$ m, as shown in Figure 4. This acoustic sensitivity analysis takes the wave number k as the design variable. The analytical solution of the acoustic sensitivity is

$$\frac{\partial p_e(r)}{\partial k} = \frac{\mathrm{i}\rho c v_0 a^2 e^{\mathrm{i}k(r-a)}}{r(1-\mathrm{i}ka)^2}\left[(1-\mathrm{i}ka)^2 + \mathrm{i}kr(1-\mathrm{i}ka) + \mathrm{i}ka\right] \tag{34}$$

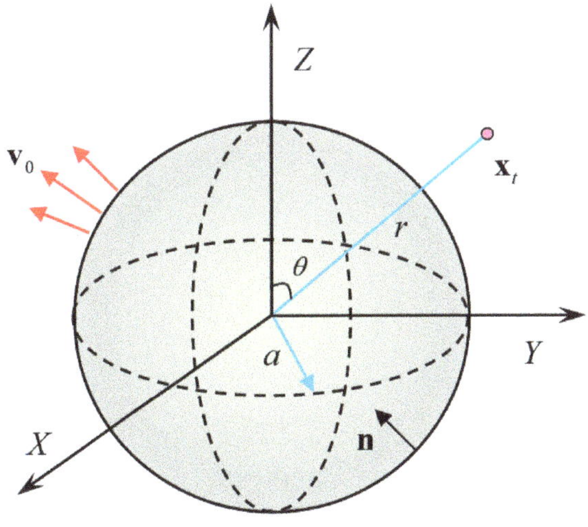

Figure 4. Acoustic radiation from a pulsating sphere.

Table 1 lists the condition numbers and the GPU memories of the conventional BM-SBM and the RSF-BM-SBM with various numbers of nodes. When the number of nodes increases, the memory required by the traditional BM-SBM increases rapidly. Therefore, when the number of nodes increases to a certain number, there will be a problem of insufficient memory. The RSF-BM-SBM requires less memory than the BM-SBM. The traditional BM-SBM will fail when the number of boundary nodes exceeds 10,000, due to the limitation of computer memory. In addition, it should be noted that the condition number is better when using fewer nodes. As the number of nodes increases, the condition number also increases.

Table 1. Memory and condition number of the RSF-BM-SBM and the BM-SBM with various numbers of nodes.

Boundary Nodes N	Condition Number	Memory (MB)	
		Conventional BM-SBM	RSF-BM-SBM (ID: 1×10^7)
100	22.94	0.16	0.32
2000	104.37	64.00	107.82
4000	1.50×10^7	256.00	239.01
7500	3.33×10^7	900.00	530.60
9000	2.79×10^8	1296.00	589.31
58,204	—	—	6772.86
112,722	—	—	14,541.76
150,082	—	—	27,069.25

4.3. Example 3

The last example considers a scaled-down vehicle model, as shown in Figure 5. This is an acoustic scattering problem, and but there is no analytical solution for sound pressure and sensitivity. Due to the complexity of the model, a large number of boundary points need to be configured, and the traditional BM-SBM cannot be calculated, so the acoustic sensitivity of the model is established by applying the RSF-BM-SBM involving 104,896 source points. In this model, a unit amplitude plane wave of wavenumber $k = 4$ propagates in the positive x-axis direction.

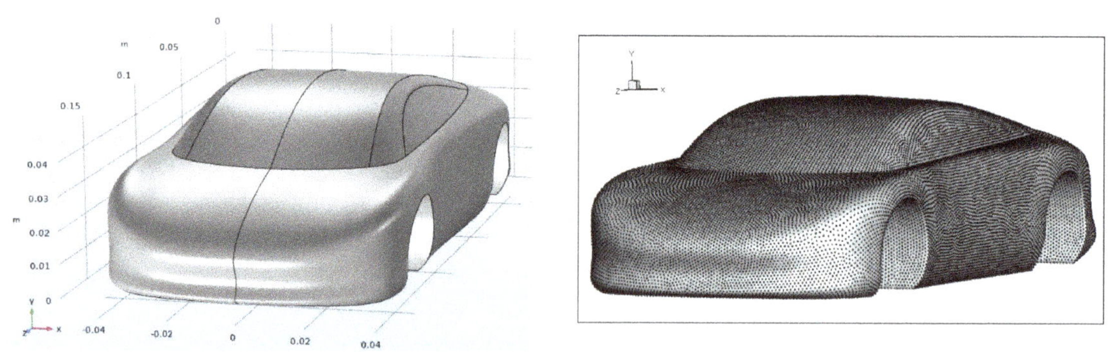

(a) (b)

Figure 5. An irregular rigid vehicle model boundary point configuration ($N = 104,896$): (**a**) vehicle model; (**b**) boundary points.

Firstly, we chose a spherical surface with radius $r = 1$ m in order to test the accuracy of the proposed method in solving the acoustic scattering of this complex structure. The RSF-BM-SBM and COMSOL Multiphysics FEM solver were used to calculate the scattered sound pressure levels on the surface. The FEM needs to set a perfectly matched layer when solving this kind of problem. Numerical results in Figure 6 indicate the capability and reliability of the proposed method for the 3D complex structure.

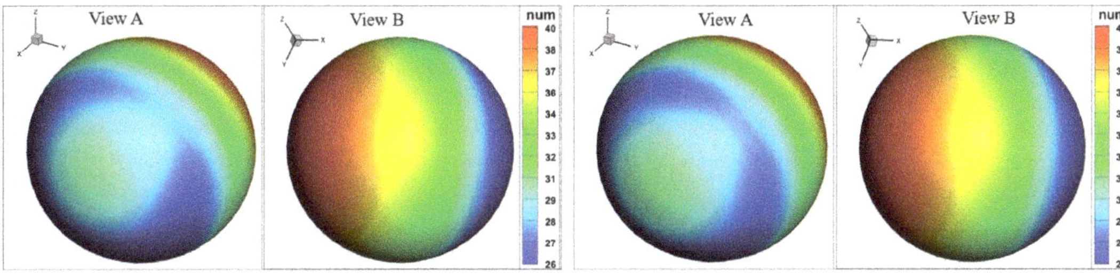

(**a**) (**b**)

Figure 6. Distributions of the scattered sound pressure level on the investigated surface obtained by using the FEM and RSF-BM-SBM: (**a**) FEM; (**b**) RSF-BM-SBM.

We intercepted a limited domain around the car body as shown in Figure 7, and the distributions of sensitivity values with respect to the design variable k were computed by the RSF-BM-SBM. Figure 8 shows the amplitudes of sound pressure sensitivity under different wave numbers. Obvious differences can be observed, which provides a reference for the analysis of acoustic sensitivity of complex structures.

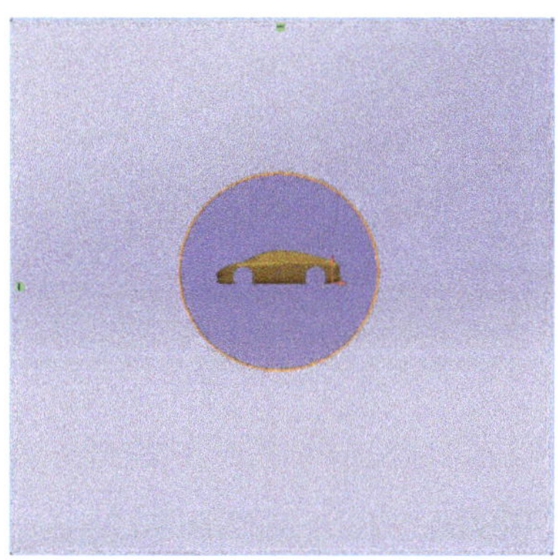

Figure 7. Distributions of boundary source points and test points.

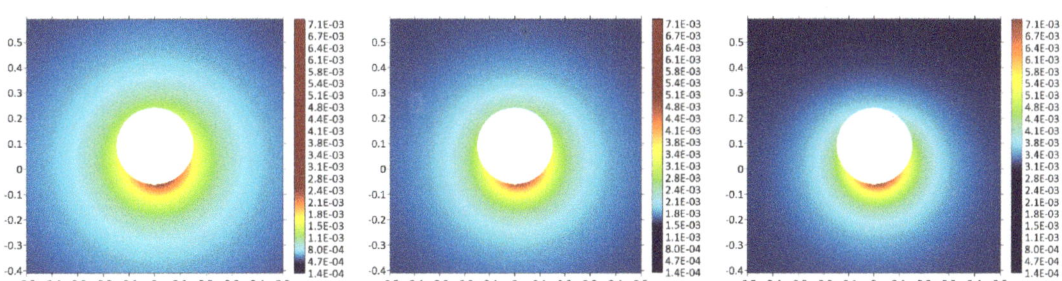

(**a**) (**b**) (**c**)

Figure 8. Acoustic pressure sensitivities ($|\partial p/\partial k|$) on $\{(x, y, z,)|-0.5 \leq y \leq 0.5,\ -0.4 \leq z \leq 0.6, x = 0\}$ cross section under different values of k: (**a**) $k = 3$; (**b**) $k = 6$; (**c**) $k = 9$.

5. Conclusions

In this paper, a fast RSF-BM-SBM has been developed for the acoustic sensitivity analysis of 2D and 3D domains. The present scheme is an accurate and semi-analytical method with the merits of being truly meshless, integration free, mathematically simple, and easy to program. As a boundary-type method based on the fundamental solution, the RSF-BM-SBM is straightforward for addressing exterior acoustic problems encountered in acoustic design sensitivity analysis. In addition, the fictitious frequency issue has been successfully overcome by using the Burton–Miller formulation. Compared with previous approaches [48,49], the proposed fast RSF-BM-SBM greatly reduces the computation time and improves the computation scale by introducing the RSF technique, which makes it possible for the method to analyze the acoustic sensitivity of high-dimensional and large-scale structures.

Through investigating the acoustic scattering problem of an infinite pulsating cylinder, the RSF-SM-SBM shows obvious advantages in solving large-scale problems. Under high compression accuracy (ID: $\varepsilon = 10^{-10}$), the CPU computation time of the RSF-SM-SBM is much shorter than that of the BM-SBM, while the calculation accuracy is basically the same. Numerical results for sound radiation from a pulsating sphere demonstrate that the traditional BM-SBM has a huge demand for memory, which limits its application in large-scale problems. Conversely, the RSF-BM-SBM has significant advantages in reducing computation time and computation cost. For the acoustic sensitivity analysis of a car-like structure, the proposed scheme is also applicable, which indicates the ability and potential of the fast method for 3D complex geometries.

Author Contributions: Conceptualization, L.L. and F.W.; Investigation, X.S. and C.Y.; Methodology, W.L. and F.W.; Resources, S.C.; Supervision, C.Y.; Validation, L.L.; Writing—original draft, S.C.; Writing—review & editing, X.S., W.L., C.Y. and F.W. All authors have read and agreed to the published version of the manuscript.

Funding: The work described in this paper was supported by the National Natural Science Foundation of China (No. 11802151).

Data Availability Statement: Not applicable.

Conflicts of Interest: The authors declare no conflict of interest.

References

1. Gohari, H.; Zarastvand, M.; Talebitooti, R.; Loghmani, A.; Omidpanah, M. Radiated sound control from a smart cylinder sub-jected to piezoelectric uncertainties based on sliding mode technique using self-adjusting boundary layer. *Aerosp. Sci. Technol.* **2020**, *106*, 106141. [CrossRef]
2. Xu, M.; Du, J.; Wang, C.; Li, Y. Hybrid uncertainty propagation in structural-acoustic systems based on the polynomial chaos expansion and dimension-wise analysis. *Comput. Methods Appl. Mech. Eng.* **2017**, *320*, 198–217. [CrossRef]
3. Rahmatnezhad, K.; Zarastvand, M.; Talebitooti, R. Mechanism study and power transmission feature of acoustically stimu-lated and thermally loaded composite shell structures with double curvature. *Compos. Struct.* **2021**, *276*, 114557. [CrossRef]
4. Chen, Q.; Fei, Q.; Wu, S.; Li, Y. Uncertainty propagation of the energy flow in vibro-acoustic system with fuzzy parameters. *Aerosp. Sci. Technol.* **2019**, *94*, 105367. [CrossRef]
5. Shojaei, A.; Mossaiby, F.; Zaccariotto, M.; Galvanetto, U. A local collocation method to construct Dirichlet-type absorbing boundary conditions for transient scalar wave propagation problems. *Comput. Methods Appl. Mech. Eng.* **2019**, *356*, 629–651. [CrossRef]
6. Zarastvand, M.R.; Ghassabi, M.; Talebitooti, R. Prediction of acoustic wave transmission features of the multilayered plate constructions: A review. *J. Sandw. Struct. Mater.* **2022**, *24*, 218–293. [CrossRef]
7. Shojaei, A.; Hermann, A.; Seleson, P.; Cyron, C. Dirichlet absorbing boundary conditions for classical and peridynamic diffu-sion-type models. *Comput. Mech.* **2020**, *66*, 773–793. [CrossRef]
8. Scarpa, F. Parametric Sensitivity Analysis of Coupled Acoustic-Structural Systems. *J. Vib. Acoust.* **2000**, *122*, 109–115. [CrossRef]
9. Dong, J.; Choi, K.K.; Wang, A.; Zhang, W.; Vlahopoulos, N. Parametric design sensitivity analysis of high-frequency structur-al-acoustic problems using energy finite element method. *Int. J. Numer. Methods Eng.* **2005**, *62*, 83–121. [CrossRef]
10. Chai, Y.; Li, W.; Liu, Z. Analysis of transient wave propagation dynamics using the enriched finite element method with interpolation cover functions. *Appl. Math. Comput.* **2022**, *412*, 126564. [CrossRef]
11. Koo, B.-U.; Ih, J.-G.; Lee, B.-C. Acoustic shape sensitivity analysis using the boundary integral equation. *J. Acoust. Soc. Am.* **1998**, *104*, 2851–2860. [CrossRef]
12. Kane, J.H.; Mao, S.; Everstine, G.C. A boundary element formulation for acoustic shape sensitivity analysis. *J. Acoust. Soc. Am.* **1991**, *90*, 561–573. [CrossRef]
13. Belytschko, T.; Lu, Y.; Gu, L. Element-free Galerkin methods. *Int. J. Numer. Methods Eng.* **1994**, *37*, 229–256. [CrossRef]

14. Lu, Y.; Belytschko, T.; Gu, L. A new implementation of the element free Galerkin method. *Comput. Methods Appl. Mech. Eng.* **1994**, *113*, 397–414. [CrossRef]
15. Shojaei, A.; Boroomand, B.; Soleimanifar, E. A meshless method for unbounded acoustic problems. *J. Acoust. Soc. Am.* **2016**, *139*, 2613–2623. [CrossRef] [PubMed]
16. Mossaiby, F.; Shojaei, A.; Boroomand, B.; Zaccariotto, M.; Galvanetto, U. Local Dirichlet-type absorbing boundary conditions for transient elastic wave propagation problems. *Comput. Methods Appl. Mech. Eng.* **2020**, *362*, 112856. [CrossRef]
17. Chen, Z.; Wang, F. Localized Method of Fundamental Solutions for Acoustic Analysis Inside a Car Cavity with Sound-Absorbing Material. *Adv. Appl. Math. Mech.* **2022**. [CrossRef]
18. Chen, Z.; Wang, F.; Cheng, S.; Wu, G. Localized MFS for three-dimensional acoustic inverse problems on complicated do-mains. *Int. J. Mech. Syst. Dyn.* **2022**, *2*, 143–152. [CrossRef]
19. Wang, F.; Gu, Y.; Qu, W.; Zhang, C. Localized boundary knot method and its application to large-scale acoustic problems. *Comput. Methods Appl. Mech. Eng.* **2020**, *361*, 112729. [CrossRef]
20. Fairweather, G.; Karageorghis, A. The method of fundamental solutions for elliptic boundary value problems. *Adv. Comput. Math.* **1998**, *9*, 69–95. [CrossRef]
21. Poullikkas, A.; Karageorghis, A.; Georgiou, G. The method of fundamental solutions for three-dimensional elastostatics problems. *Comput. Struct.* **2002**, *80*, 365–370. [CrossRef]
22. Chen, W. Singular boundary method: A novel, simple, meshfree, boundary collocation numerical method. *Chin. J. Solid Mech.* **2009**, *30*, 592–599.
23. Burton, A.J.; Miller, G.F. The application of integral equation methods to the numerical solution of some exterior boundary-value problems. *Proc. R. Soc. London. Ser. A Math. Phys. Sci.* **1971**, *323*, 201–210. [CrossRef]
24. Fu, Z.-J.; Chen, W.; Gu, Y. Burton–Miller-type singular boundary method for acoustic radiation and scattering. *J. Sound Vib.* **2014**, *333*, 3776–3793. [CrossRef]
25. Li, J.; Chen, W. A modified singular boundary method for three-dimensional high frequency acoustic wave problems. *Appl. Math. Model.* **2018**, *54*, 189–201. [CrossRef]
26. Qu, W.; Zheng, C.; Zhang, Y.; Gu, Y.; Wang, F. A wideband fast multipole accelerated singular boundary method for three-dimensional acoustic problems. *Comput. Struct.* **2018**, *206*, 82–89. [CrossRef]
27. Wei, X.; Luo, W. 2.5D singular boundary method for acoustic wave propagation. *Appl. Math. Lett.* **2021**, *112*, 106760. [CrossRef]
28. Gu, Y.; Chen, W.; He, X. Singular boundary method for steady-state heat conduction in three dimensional general anisotropic media. *Int. J. Heat Mass Transf.* **2012**, *55*, 4837–4848. [CrossRef]
29. Wei, X.; Sun, L.; Yin, S.; Chen, B. A boundary-only treatment by singular boundary method for two-dimensional inhomogeneous problems. *Appl. Math. Model.* **2018**, *62*, 338–351. [CrossRef]
30. Li, W.; Chen, W. Band gap calculations of photonic crystals by singular boundary method. *J. Comput. Appl. Math.* **2017**, *315*, 273–286. [CrossRef]
31. Cheng, A.H.; Hong, Y. An overview of the method of fundamental solutions—Solvability, uniqueness, convergence, and stability. *Eng. Anal. Bound. Elem.* **2020**, *120*, 118–152. [CrossRef]
32. Karageorghis, A.; Johansson, B.; Lesnic, D. The method of fundamental solutions for the identification of a sound-soft obstacle in inverse acoustic scattering. *Appl. Numer. Math.* **2012**, *62*, 1767–1780. [CrossRef]
33. Jin, B.; Zheng, Y. Boundary knot method for some inverse problems associated with the Helmholtz equation. *Int. J. Numer. Methods Eng.* **2005**, *62*, 1636–1651. [CrossRef]
34. Zheng, C.; Matsumoto, T.; Takahashi, T.; Chen, H. A wideband fast multipole boundary element method for three dimensional acoustic shape sensitivity analysis based on direct differentiation method. *Eng. Anal. Bound. Elem.* **2012**, *36*, 361–371. [CrossRef]
35. Chen, L.; Liu, L.; Zhao, W.; Chen, H. 2D Acoustic Design Sensitivity Analysis Based on Adjoint Variable Method Using Different Types of Boundary Elements. *Acoust. Aust.* **2016**, *44*, 343–357. [CrossRef]
36. Xu, Y.; Zhao, W.; Chen, L.; Chen, H. Distribution Optimization for Acoustic Design of Porous Layer by the Boundary Element Method. *Acoust. Aust.* **2020**, *48*, 107–119. [CrossRef]
37. Liu, Y.; Nishimura, N.; Yao, Z. A fast multipole accelerated method of fundamental solutions for potential problems. *Eng. Anal. Bound. Elem.* **2005**, *29*, 1016–1024. [CrossRef]
38. Zheng, C.; Zhao, W.; Gao, H.; Du, L.; Zhang, Y.; Bi, C. Sensitivity analysis of acoustic eigenfrequencies by using a boundary element method. *J. Acoust. Soc. Am.* **2021**, *149*, 2027–2039. [CrossRef]
39. Godinho, L.; Soares, D.; Santos, P. Efficient analysis of sound propagation in sonic crystals using an ACA–MFS approach. *Eng. Anal. Bound. Elem.* **2016**, *69*, 72–85. [CrossRef]
40. Qu, W.; Chen, W.; Gu, Y. Fast multipole accelerated singular boundary method for the 3D Helmholtz equation in low frequency regime. *Comput. Math. Appl.* **2015**, *70*, 679–690. [CrossRef]
41. Qu, W.; Chen, W.; Zheng, C. Diagonal form fast multipole singular boundary method applied to the solution of high-frequency acoustic radiation and scattering. *Int. J. Numer. Methods Eng.* **2017**, *111*, 803–815. [CrossRef]
42. Wei, X.; Chen, B.; Chen, S.; Yin, S. An ACA-SBM for some 2D steady-state heat conduction problems. *Eng. Anal. Bound. Elem.* **2016**, *71*, 101–111. [CrossRef]
43. Li, W.; Chen, W.; Fu, Z. Precorrected-FFT Accelerated Singular Boundary Method for Large-Scale Three-Dimensional Potential Problems. *Commun. Comput. Phys.* **2017**, *22*, 460–472. [CrossRef]

44. Li, W. A fast singular boundary method for 3D Helmholtz equation. *Comput. Math. Appl.* **2019**, *77*, 525–535. [CrossRef]
45. Li, W.; Wang, F. Precorrected-FFT Accelerated Singular Boundary Method for High-Frequency Acoustic Radiation and Scattering. *Mathematics* **2022**, *10*, 238. [CrossRef]
46. Li, W.; Xu, S.; Shao, M. Simulation of two-dimensional steady-state heat conduction problems by a fast singular boundary method. *Eng. Anal. Bound. Elem.* **2019**, *108*, 149–157. [CrossRef]
47. Li, W.; Wu, B. A fast direct singular boundary method for three-dimensional potential problems. *Eng. Anal. Bound. Elem.* **2022**, *139*, 132–136. [CrossRef]
48. Cheng, S.; Wang, F.; Wu, G.; Zhang, C. A semi-analytical and boundary-type meshless method with adjoint variable formulation for acoustic design sensitivity analysis. *Appl. Math. Lett.* **2022**, *131*, 108068. [CrossRef]
49. Cheng, S.; Wang, F.; Li, P.-W.; Qu, W. Singular boundary method for 2D and 3D acoustic design sensitivity analysis. *Comput. Math. Appl.* **2022**, *119*, 371–386. [CrossRef]
50. Ho, K.L.; Greengard, L. A Fast Direct Solver for Structured Linear Systems by Recursive Skeletonization. *SIAM J. Sci. Comput.* **2012**, *34*, A2507–A2532. [CrossRef]
51. Ho, K.L.; Ying, L. Hierarchical Interpolative Factorization for Elliptic Operators: Differential Equations. *Commun. Pure Appl. Math.* **2016**, *69*, 1415–1451. [CrossRef]
52. Xing, W.; Wen, C.; Sun, L.; Chen, B. A simple accurate formula evaluating origin intensity factor in singular boundary method for two-dimensional potential problems with Dirichlet boundary. *Eng. Anal. Bound. Elem.* **2015**, *58*, 151–165.
53. Li, J.; Chen, W.; Fu, Z.; Sun, L. Explicit empirical formula evaluating original intensity factors of singular boundary method for potential and Helmholtz problems. *Eng. Anal. Bound. Elem.* **2016**, *73*, 161–169. [CrossRef]
54. Cheng, H.; Gimbutas, Z.; Martinsson, P.G.; Rokhlin, V. On the Compression of Low Rank Matrices. *SIAM J. Sci. Comput.* **2005**, *26*, 1389–1404. [CrossRef]

mathematics

Article

Transient Dynamic Response Analysis of Two-Dimensional Saturated Soil with Singular Boundary Method

Dongdong Liu [1], Xing Wei [1,*], Chengbin Li [2], Chunguang Han [2], Xiaxi Cheng [1] and Linlin Sun [3,*]

1 Jiangxi Key Laboratory of Disaster Prevention, Mitigation and Emergency Management, School of Civil Engineering & Architecture, East China Jiaotong University, Nanchang 330013, China
2 China Railway Construction Bridge Engineering Bureau Group Co., Ltd., Tianjin 300000, China
3 School of Science, Nantong University, Nantong 226019, China
* Correspondence: weix911@126.com (X.W.); rudong9110@163.com (L.S.); Tel.: +86-791-87046046 (X.W.); +86-513-55003300 (L.S.)

Abstract: In this paper, the singular boundary method (SBM) in conjunction with the exponential window method (EWM) is firstly extended to simulate the transient dynamic response of two-dimensional saturated soil. The frequency-domain (Fourier space) governing equations of Biot theory is solved by the SBM with a linear combination of the fundamental solutions. In order to avoid the perplexing fictitious boundary in the method of fundamental solution (MFS), the SBM places the source point on the physical boundary and eliminates the source singularity of the fundamental solution via the origin intensity factors (OIFs). The EWM is carried out for the inverse Fourier transform, which transforms the frequency-domain solutions into the time-domain solutions. The accuracy and feasibility of the SBM-EWM are verified by three numerical examples. The numerical comparison between the MFS and SBM indicates that the SBM takes a quarter of the time taken by the MFS.

Keywords: singular boundary method; meshless methods; exponential window method; saturated soil; transient dynamic response analysis

MSC: 65N35; 65N80; 74H15

Citation: Liu, D.; Wei, X.; Li, C.; Han, C.; Cheng, X.; Sun, L. Transient Dynamic Response Analysis of Two-Dimensional Saturated Soil with Singular Boundary Method. *Mathematics* **2022**, *10*, 4323. https://doi.org/10.3390/math10224323

Academic Editor: Ravi P. Agarwal

Received: 27 October 2022
Accepted: 15 November 2022
Published: 17 November 2022

1. Introduction

The transient dynamic analysis is of great importance in the geotechnical and mechanical engineering to observe the time-history mechanical response caused by the dynamic loads [1,2]. Although there are some analytical solutions for the regular geometric shapes with isotropic and homogeneous material properties and simple boundary conditions, the numerical tools are usually more flexible and effective for general real-world problems. The transient analysis is usually divided into two parts, viz. spatial discretization and temporal discretization.

For the spatial discretization, the finite element method (FEM) is one of most powerful numerical methods. In light of its theoretical completeness and well-established commercial software, the FEM is robust to different engineering applications [3,4]. Nevertheless, the FEM requires the artificial boundary [5] to analyze the infinite and semi-infinite medium. Besides the FEM, the other domain-type methods [6] encounter the same difficulty. The boundary element method (BEM) has been boosted as an effective alternative in infinite and semi-infinite problems because the fundamental solutions used in the BEM automatically satisfy the Sommerfield radiation condition at infinity. The utilization of the fundamental solutions makes the BEM avoid domain discretization, because the kernel function satisfies governing equations. The superiority of the BEM motivated researchers to develop novel numerical methods based on analytical solutions, such as the fundamental solutions [7–9], the general solutions [10–12] and the particular solutions [13–16]. Among them, most of numerical methods are pertinent to the fundamental solutions, including the method of fundamental solutions (MFS) [8,17], modified method of fundamental solutions [18] and singular boundary method (SBM) [19–21], to just name a few. The SBM was firstly proposed by Chen [19] with introducing the concept of the origin intensity factor (OIF) to desingularize the fundamental solutions. Originally, the OIF was evaluated via a tedious inverse interpolation technique [22]. Later, simple analytical and empirical formulas were developed and extended the application of the SBM to different problems [23–32]. The abovementioned boundary-type methods required expensive operation counts and memory storage in real-world large-scale problems. This promotes the development of fast algorithms accelerated techniques [33–37] and localized methods [38–41]. It is worth noting that the localized variant of the boundary-type method is a domain-type method.

To implement the transient analysis, the boundary methods require special treatment to deal with time-dependent terms, including the direct time integration methods [42–44], transform methods [45–47] and time-domain fundamental solutions [48]. Except the transform method, the other methods require a proper time-step for numerical stability. Nevertheless, the long-time solution may deteriorate as the time increases. The Krylov deferred correction method (KDC) [49] allows larger time step size for the long-time analysis with acceptable temporal accumulation errors. In the transform methods, the frequency-domain governing equation is solved at some discrete sampling frequencies, and then the frequency-domain solutions are transformed back to the time-domain solutions via the inverse transform, namely the Laplace transform or Fourier transform. The inverse transform is carried out by numerical methods, which may consume a lot of time. The Fourier transform is more attractive because its inverse process can be accelerated by the fast Fourier transform (FFT). However, in lightly damped systems or undamped systems, the FFT is inefficient, or even not applicable without the desired attenuation. This problem was circumvented by introducing an artificial damping to the system by the exponential window method (EWM) [50].

There are few works related to the transient dynamic response analysis of saturated soil. In this study, the SBM in conjunction with the EWM is firstly established to solve the transient dynamic problems in two-dimensional saturated soil. The SBM is formulated in the frequency domain (Fourier space). Thanks to the fundamental solutions, the SBM can be directly applied to finite-, semi-infinite and infinite domains. The source singularity of the fundamental solution is bypassed with simple formulas. Subsequently, the frequency-domain SBM solutions are transformed by the EWM. The selection of the parameters in the EWM will be discussed. The stability and accuracy of the SBM will be investigated via three numerical examples.

2. Governing Equations

For the saturated soil, it is better to take the coupling effect of two phases into consideration [51,52]. Thus, the coupling effect is taken into account in the constitute equation [53,54]:

$$\sigma_{ij} = \lambda\delta_{ij}u_{k,k} + 2\mu\varepsilon_{ij} - \alpha\delta_{ij}p,\ i = 1,3, j = 1,3, \tag{1}$$

$$p = -\alpha M u_{i,i} - M w_{i,i}, \tag{2}$$

where σ_{ij} is the effective stress; δ_{ij} the Kronecker delta; $\varepsilon_{ij} = \left(u_{i,j} + u_{j,i}\right)/2$ the strain tensor; w_i the fluid displacement with respect to the solid skeleton; p the pore pressure; u_i the average skeleton displacement; λ and μ the solid skeleton Lamé constants; and α and M the Biot parameters describing the compressibility of the fluid-saturated two-phase material.

Taking Equations (1) and (2) into the equilibrium equations, we obtained the equations of motion for the bulk porous medium and the pore fluid without body forces as [53,54]

$$\mu u_{i,jj} + \left(\lambda + \alpha^2 M + \mu\right) u_{j,ji} + \alpha M w_{j,ji} = \rho\ddot{u}_i + \rho_f \ddot{w}_i, \tag{3}$$

$$\alpha M u_{j,ji} + M w_{j,ji} = \rho_f \ddot{u}_i + m\ddot{w}_i + \frac{\eta}{k} K(t) * \dot{w}_i, \tag{4}$$

where a dot ($\bullet$) denotes the time derivative and a star ($*$) denotes the time convolution; $\rho = (1-\phi)\rho_s + \phi\rho_f$ is the density of the saturated poroelastic medium; ρ_s and ρ_f are the density of the skeleton and fluid; ϕ the porosity; η the viscosity of the pore fluid; k the permeability of the saturated poroelastic medium; $m = \alpha_\infty \rho_f/\phi$; α_∞ is the tortuosity; and $K(t)$ is a time-dependent viscosity correction factor which describes the transition between the viscous flow in the low-frequency range and the inertia-dominated flow in the high-frequency range.

The initial boundary conditions and boundary conditions are given as

$$\boldsymbol{u}^s|_{t=0} = \left.\frac{\partial \boldsymbol{u}^s}{\partial t}\right|_{t=0} = 0,\ \boldsymbol{w}|_{t=0} = 0, \text{ and } p|_{t=0} = 0, \tag{5}$$

$$u_i^s = \hat{u}_i^s, \text{ on } \Gamma_u^s, \tag{6}$$

$$t_i^s = \sigma_{i1}^s n_1 + \sigma_{i3}^s n_3 = \hat{t}_i^s, \text{ on } \Gamma_t^s, \tag{7}$$

$$w_i = \hat{w}_i, \text{ on } \Gamma_w^f, \tag{8}$$

$$p = \hat{p}, \text{ on } \Gamma_p^f, \tag{9}$$

where $\boldsymbol{n} = (n_1, n_3)$ is the normal vector to the boundary, and $\hat{u}_i^s$, $\hat{t}_i^s$, $\hat{w}_i$ and $\hat{p}$ are the prescribed solid displacements, tractions, relative fluid displacements and pore pressure on the boundary, respectively.

We introduce the Fourier transform with respect to time and frequency as

$$\tilde{f}(\omega) = \int_{-\infty}^{+\infty} f(t)e^{-\mathrm{j}\omega t}dt,\ f(t) = \frac{1}{2\pi}\int_{-\infty}^{+\infty} \tilde{f}(\omega)e^{\mathrm{j}\omega t}d\omega, \tag{10}$$

where $\mathrm{j} = \sqrt{-1}$ is the imaginary unit.

After Fourier transform on Equations (3) and (4), the frequency-domain governing equations in terms of solid displacement and fluid pressure [54] are recast as

$$\mu\tilde{u}_{i,jj} + (\lambda+\mu)\tilde{u}_{j,ji} + \rho_g\omega^2\tilde{u}_i - \alpha_g\tilde{p}_{,i} = 0, \tag{11}$$

$$\tilde{p}_{,jj} + \beta_2\omega^2\tilde{p} - \beta_3\tilde{u}_{j,j} = 0, \tag{12}$$

where $\rho_g = \rho - \beta_4\rho_f$, $\alpha_g = \alpha - \beta_4$, $\beta_1 = M/\left[m\omega^2 - \mathrm{j}\omega(\eta/k)\tilde{K}(\omega)\right]$, $\beta_2 = 1/(\beta_1\omega^2)$, $\beta_4 = \rho_f\omega^2\beta_1/M$; $\beta_3 = \rho_f\omega^2 - \alpha\left[m\omega^2 - \mathrm{j}\omega(\eta/k)\tilde{K}(\omega)\right]$, $\tilde{K}(\omega)$ is the Fourier transform of $K(t)$, and "~" denotes the representation in the frequency-domain.

3. Singular Boundary Method in Frequency-Domain

In this section, the SBM formulation is established for the frequency-domain governing equations. The SBM evaluates the frequency-domain solution with a linear combination of fundamental solutions in terms of the source points as [55]

$$\tilde{u}_i^s(\boldsymbol{x}_m) = \sum_{n=1}^{N} \beta_{1n}\tilde{u}_{i1}^s(\boldsymbol{x}_m, \boldsymbol{s}_n) + \sum_{n=1}^{N} \beta_{3n}\tilde{u}_{i3}^s(\boldsymbol{x}_m, \boldsymbol{s}_n) + \sum_{n=1}^{N} \beta_{4n}\tilde{u}_{i4}^s(\boldsymbol{x}_m, \boldsymbol{s}_n),\ i = 1, 3, \tag{13}$$

$$\tilde{p}(\boldsymbol{x}_m) = \sum_{n=1}^{N} \beta_{1n}\tilde{p}_1(\boldsymbol{x}_m, \boldsymbol{s}_n) + \sum_{n=1}^{N} \beta_{3n}\tilde{p}_3(\boldsymbol{x}_m, \boldsymbol{s}_n) + \sum_{n=1}^{N} \beta_{4n}\tilde{p}_4(\boldsymbol{x}_m, \boldsymbol{s}_n), \tag{14}$$

$$\tilde{t}_i^s(\boldsymbol{x}_m) = \sum_{n=1}^{N} \beta_{1n}\tilde{t}_{i1}^s(\boldsymbol{x}_m, \boldsymbol{s}_n) + \sum_{n=1}^{N} \beta_{3n}\tilde{t}_{i3}^s(\boldsymbol{x}_m, \boldsymbol{s}_n) + \sum_{n=1}^{N} \beta_{4n}\tilde{t}_{i4}^s(\boldsymbol{x}_m, \boldsymbol{s}_n),\ i = 1, 3, \tag{15}$$

$$\tilde{q}_{\mathbf{n}}(\boldsymbol{x}_m) = \sum_{n=1}^{N} \beta_{1n}\tilde{q}_1(\boldsymbol{x}_m, \boldsymbol{s}_n) + \sum_{n=1}^{N} \beta_{3n}\tilde{q}_3(\boldsymbol{x}_m, \boldsymbol{s}_n) + \sum_{n=1}^{N} \beta_{4n}\tilde{q}_4(\boldsymbol{x}_m, \boldsymbol{s}_n). \tag{16}$$

where $\boldsymbol{x}_m, \boldsymbol{s}_n$ are the mth field point and nth source point; N is the total number of boundary source points; $\{\beta_{kn}\}_{n=1}^{N}(k = 1,3,4)$ are the coefficients to be determined; and $\widetilde{u}^s_{ik}$, $\widetilde{t}^s_{ik}$, $\widetilde{p}_k$ and $\widetilde{q}_k$ $(i = 1,3,\ k = 1,3,4)$ are the fundamental solutions of solid displacements, traction, pore pressure and flux, which are given as

$$\widetilde{u}^s_{ik} = A\delta_{ik} - Br_{,i}r_{,k},\ \widetilde{u}^s_{i4} = Dr_{,i},\ i,k = 1,3, \tag{17}$$

$$\begin{aligned}\widetilde{t}^s_{ik} &= \lambda\left[A' - B' - \tfrac{B}{r}\right]r_{,k}n_i + \mu\Big[\left(A' - \tfrac{B}{r}\right)(r_{,n}\delta_{ik} + r_{,i}n_k) \\ &\quad - \tfrac{2B}{r}r_{,k}n_i + 2\left(-B' + \tfrac{2B}{r}\right)r_{,i}r_{,k}r_{,n}\Big],\ i,k = 1,3, \\ \widetilde{t}^s_{i4} &= \left[(\lambda + 2\mu)\tfrac{D}{r} + \lambda D'\right]n_i + 2\mu\left(-\tfrac{D}{r} + D'\right)r_{,i}r_{,n},\ i = 1,3,\end{aligned} \tag{18}$$

$$\widetilde{p}_k = Cr_{,k},\ \widetilde{p}_4 = \frac{1}{2\pi}\sum_{d=1,2} r_d h_d K_0(z_d),\ k = 1,3, \tag{19}$$

$$\widetilde{q}_k = \begin{cases} \frac{-\alpha_g}{\beta_3}\left[\frac{C}{r}n_k + \left(C' - \frac{C}{r}\right)r_{,k}r_{,n}\right],\ k = 1,3, \\ \frac{\mathrm{j}\alpha_g r_{,n}}{2\pi\beta_3}\sum_{d=1,2} r_d h_d k_d K_1(z_d),\ k = 4, \end{cases} \tag{20}$$

where

$$A = \frac{1}{2\pi}\left[-\sum_{d=1,2} g_d\frac{K_1(z_d)}{z_d} + g_3\left(K_0(z_3) + \frac{K_1(z_3)}{z_3}\right)\right],\ C = \frac{\mathrm{j}}{2\pi}\left[\sum_{d=1,2}\frac{r_d g_d}{k_d}K_1(z_d)\right]$$

$$B = \frac{1}{2\pi}\left[-\sum_{d=1,2} g_d K_2(z_d) + g_3 K_2(z_3)\right],\ D = \frac{-\mathrm{j}}{2\pi}\sum_{d=1,2} k_d h_d K_1(z_d) z_3 = \mathrm{j}k_3 r$$

$$z_d = \mathrm{j}k_d r,\ r_d = \frac{\omega^2\rho_g - (\lambda + 2\mu)k_d^2}{\alpha_g}(d = 1,2),\ g_1 = \frac{\beta_3 - r_2}{(\lambda + 2\mu)(r_1 - r_2)},$$

$$g_2 = \frac{\beta_3 - r_1}{(\lambda + 2\mu)(r_2 - r_1)},\ g_3 = \frac{1}{\mu},\ h_1 = -\frac{\beta_3}{\alpha_g(r_1 - r_2)},\ h_2 = -\frac{\beta_3}{\alpha_g(r_2 - r_1)}$$

in which $r = \sqrt{(x_1 - y_1)^2 + (x_3 - y_3)^2}$ is the distance between field point $\boldsymbol{x} = (x_1, x_3)$ and source point $\boldsymbol{y} = (y_1, y_3)$. K_n is the modified Bessel function of the second kind of order n, and k_d is

$$k_1 = \sqrt{\frac{\beta_2\omega^2}{2} + \frac{\rho_g\omega^2 - \alpha_g\beta_3 + \sqrt{H}}{2(\lambda + 2\mu)}},\ k_2 = \sqrt{\frac{\beta_2\omega^2}{2} + \frac{\rho_g\omega^2 - \alpha_g\beta_3 - \sqrt{H}}{2(\lambda + 2\mu)}},\ k_3 = \sqrt{\omega^2\rho_g/\mu}$$

where

$$H = \left(\lambda\beta_2\omega^2 - \alpha_g\beta_3 + \rho_g\omega^2\right)^2 + 4(\lambda + \mu)\beta_2\omega^4(\mu\beta_2 - \rho_g) - 4\mu\alpha_g\beta_2\beta_3\omega^2$$

The derivation of the fundamental solutions is detailed in Appendix A.

With the fundamental solutions, Equations (13)–(16) are forced to satisfy the boundary conditions for the determination of the unknown coefficients. Then the boundary conditions with Equations (13)–(16) are formulated as

$$\widetilde{u}^s_i(\boldsymbol{y}_m) = \sum_{k=1,3,4}\sum_{n\neq m}^{N}\beta_{kn}\widetilde{u}^s_{ik}(\boldsymbol{y}_m, \boldsymbol{y}_n) + \sum_{k=1,3,4}\beta_{km}\widetilde{U}^s_{ik}(\boldsymbol{y}_m, \boldsymbol{y}_m),\ i = 1,3, \tag{21}$$

$$\widetilde{t}^s_i(\boldsymbol{y}_m) = \sum_{k=1,3,4}\sum_{n\neq m}^{N}\beta_{kn}\widetilde{t}^s_{ik}(\boldsymbol{y}_m, \boldsymbol{y}_n) + \sum_{k=1,3,4}^{3}\beta_{km}\widetilde{T}^s_{ik}(\boldsymbol{y}_m, \boldsymbol{y}_m),\ i = 1,3, \tag{22}$$

$$\widetilde{p}(y_m) = \sum_{k=1,3,4} \sum_{n \neq m}^{N} \beta_{kn} \widetilde{p}_k(y_m, y_n) + \sum_{k=1,3,4} \beta_{km} \widetilde{P}_k(y_m, y_m), \tag{23}$$

$$\widetilde{q}_{\mathbf{n}}(y_m) = \sum_{k=1,3,4} \sum_{n \neq m}^{N} \beta_{kn} \widetilde{q}_k(y_m, y_n) + \sum_{k=1,3,4} \beta_{km} \widetilde{Q}_k(y_m, y_m). \tag{24}$$

The singular terms, namely, $\widetilde{u}^s_{ik}(y_m, y_m)$, $\widetilde{t}^s_{ik}(y_m, y_m)$, $\widetilde{p}_k(y_m, y_m)$ and $\widetilde{q}_k(y_m, y_m)$, are involved when the boundary data points overlaps the source points. To deal with this issue, some numerical or analytical methods are introduced to desingularize these terms. In the SBM, the diagonal terms are called the origin intensity factors (OIFs), as $\widetilde{U}^s_{ik}(y_m, y_m)$, $\widetilde{T}^s_{ik}(y_m, y_m)$, $\widetilde{P}_k(y_m, y_m)$ and $\widetilde{Q}_k(y_m, y_m)$ in Equations (21)–(24). The OIFs for 2D saturated poroelastic problems [20,21,56], as shown in Equations (21)–(24) are calculated as

$$\widetilde{U}^s_{ik}(y_m, y_m) = \begin{cases} [\hat{g}(y_m, y_m)\chi_1 - \chi_2]\delta_{ik} + \chi_3 \Lambda_{ik}, \ i,k = 1,3, \\ 0, \ k = 4, \ i = 1,3, \end{cases} \tag{25}$$

$$\widetilde{T}^s_{ik}(y_m, y_m) = \begin{cases} \hat{t}_{ik}(y_m, y_m), \ i,k = 1,3, \\ [\hat{g}(y_m, y_m)\chi_4 + \chi_5]n_i, \ k = 4, \ i = 1,3, \end{cases} \tag{26}$$

$$\widetilde{P}_k(y_m, y_m) = \begin{cases} 0, \ k = 1,3, \\ \hat{g}(y_m, y_m)\chi_6 + \chi_7, \ k = 4, \end{cases} \tag{27}$$

$$\widetilde{Q}_k(y_m, y_m) = \begin{cases} [\hat{g}(y_m, y_m)\chi_8 + \chi_9]n_k, \ k = 1,3, \\ \hat{q}(y_m, y_m)\chi_{10}, \ k = 4, \end{cases} \tag{28}$$

where $\chi_1, \ldots, \chi_{10}$ are provided in Appendix B; $\Lambda_{ik} = \lim_{x \to y, x \in \Gamma} r_{,i} r_{,k} = \frac{\tau_i \tau_k}{\tau_1^2 + \tau_3^2}$, $\boldsymbol{\tau} = (\tau_1, \tau_3)$ is the tangent vector of point $\boldsymbol{x}$ on the boundary, $\hat{g}(y_m, y_m)$ and $\hat{q}(y_m, y_m)$ are the OIFs for the fundamental solution of the Laplace operator for Dirichlet and Neumann boundary conditions, and $\hat{t}_{ik}(y_m, y_m)$ is the OIF for the fundamental solution of the traction boundary condition. These terms are computed as

$$\hat{g}(y_m, y_m) = -\frac{1}{2\pi} \ln\left(\frac{l_m}{2\pi}\right), \ \hat{q}(y_m, y_m) = -\frac{1}{2l_m}, \ \hat{t}_{ij}(y_m, y_m) = -\frac{\delta_{ij}}{2l_m} \tag{29}$$

where l_m is a half-length of the arc between source points y_{m+1} and y_{m-1}.

Finally after obtaining the coefficients, the frequency-domain solutions of the variables within the domain can be evaluated via Equations (13)–(16).

4. Exponential Window Method

The frequency-domain solutions can be converted to the transient solutions via the inverse Fourier transform, which is accelerated by the fast Fourier transformation (FFT) [47,57]. It should be noted that the time responses decay slowly in lightly damped systems, and even never decay in undamped systems. In these two cases, the FFT is inefficient. Thus, a powerful numerical technique, the exponential window method (EWM) [58], is introduced. In the EWM, artificial damping is created to produce the desired attenuation, and the artificial damping is removed by scaling back in the final. The detail of the EWM is summarized as follows:

(1) Determine the total calculation time T and the number of sampling frequencies N_ω, then to determine the angular frequency resolution $\Delta\omega = 2\pi/T$ with $\Delta t = T/N_\omega$;

(2) Determine the shifting constant according to the numerical experiments and experience as

$$\vartheta = \frac{\kappa \ln 10}{T}, \tag{30}$$

where κ denote the damping coefficient, and $2 \leq \kappa \leq 3$ is recommended;

(3) Construct a desired damping system with scaling the variables $\xi(x,t)$ (u_i^s, σ_{ik}^s, w_i and p) with the scaling function $e^{-\vartheta t}$ as $\xi_{ew}(x,t) = \xi(x,t)e^{-\vartheta t}$. Bring new variables ξ_{ew} into the governing equations, and a novel frequency-domain boundary value problem Equations (6) and (7) with $\overline{\omega} = \omega - \mathrm{j}\vartheta$ is obtained.

(4) Simultaneously, the boundary condition $P(x,t)$ is scaled into $P_{ew}(x,t) = P(x,t)e^{-\vartheta t}$, and the frequency-domain boundary condition can be obtained via discretized Fourier transform

$$\hat{P}_{ew}(x,\overline{\omega}_k) = \frac{1}{N_\omega}\sum_{n=0}^{N_\omega-1} P_{ew}(x,n\Delta t)e^{-2\pi \mathrm{j}nk/N_\omega} = \frac{1}{N_\omega}\sum_{n=0}^{N_\omega-1} e^{-\vartheta n\Delta t}P(x,n\Delta t)e^{-2\pi \mathrm{j}nk/N_\omega}, \tag{31}$$

where $\overline{\omega}_k = k\Delta\omega - \mathrm{j}\vartheta (k = 0,1,\ldots,N_\omega - 1)$.

(5) Perform the SBM to evaluate the solutions of the frequency-domain problems $R_{ew}^*(\overline{\omega}_k)$ at the frequencies $\overline{\omega}_k = k\Delta\omega - \mathrm{j}\vartheta(k = 0,1,\ldots,N_\omega/2)$. The remaining of results can be obtained through conjugate symmetric property as

$$R_{ew}^*(\overline{\omega}_k) = \mathrm{conj}(R_{ew}^*(\overline{\omega}_{N_\omega-k})),\ k = N_\omega/2+1,\ldots,N_\omega - 1. \tag{32}$$

(6) Perform the IFFT with the inverse DFT with Hanning window function W_k, and obtain the time-domain solutions as

$$R_{ew}(n\Delta t) = \sum_{k=1}^{N_\omega-1} W_k R_{ew}^*(\overline{\omega}_k)e^{2\pi \mathrm{j}nk/N_\omega}, \tag{33}$$

The Hanning window function $W_k = 0.5[1+\cos(2\pi k/N_\omega)]$ is used to alleviate the Gibbs oscillations.

(7) Descale the time-domain solutions and obtain the solutions of the original problems as

$$R(n\Delta t) = e^{\vartheta n\Delta t}R_{ew}(n\Delta t). \tag{34}$$

5. Numerical Examples

In this section, three numerical examples are used to verify the accuracy and effectiveness of the proposed method for the transient dynamic response of two-dimensional saturated soil. The accuracy of the SBM-EWM is evaluated by the absolute error of variable ξ versus time at point x as

$$AE(\xi) = \left|\overline{\xi}\left(\frac{kT}{N_\omega},x\right) - \xi\left(\frac{kT}{N_\omega},x\right)\right|, \tag{35}$$

where $\overline{\xi}$ represents the exact solution, ξ denotes the numerical result obtained by the SBM.

Unless otherwise specified, the parameters of the saturated soil are set as $\lambda = 4.0 \times 10^7$ Pa, $\mu = 2.0 \times 10^7$ Pa, $\rho_s = 2500$ kg/m^3, $\rho_f = 1.0 \times 10^3$ kg/m^3, $a_\infty = 3$, $\alpha = 0.95$, $M = 4.0 \times 10^8$ Pa, $\phi = 0.3$, $\eta = 1.0 \times 10^{-3}$ Pa·s, $k = 1.0 \times 10^{-12}$ m^2. All calculations of this paper are fulfilled on a desktop with an Intel Core (TM) I7-6500U at 2.50 GHz on a 64-bit Windows server with a total of 12GB DDR4 memory. The SBM is implemented via MATLAB software.

5.1. Verification of the Proposed SBM-EWM Method

In the section, a saturated poroelastic column problem (Figure 1) is considered. A uniform normal load on the upper boundary and the rest boundaries is sliding:

$$\begin{cases} \mathrm{t_n^s = -H(t)N/m^2, t_\tau^s = 0N/m^2, p = 0Pa,\ on\ the\ top\ boundary,} \\ \mathrm{u_n^s = 0m, t_\tau^s = 0N/m^2, w_n = 0m,\ on\ the\ other\ boundaries,} \end{cases} \tag{36}$$

where $H(t)$ is the Heaviside step function.

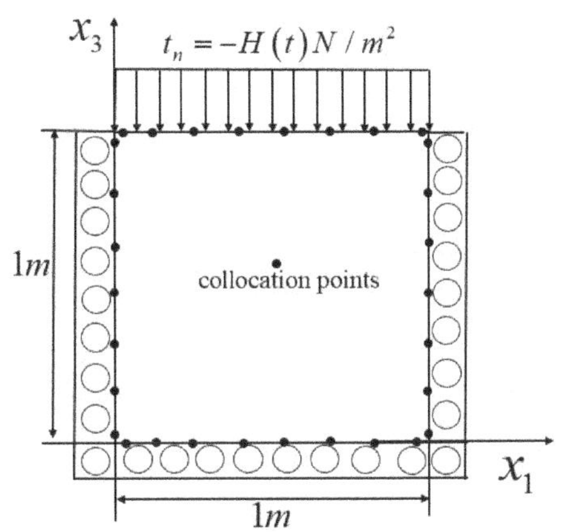

Figure 1. Computational model of saturated column.

Firstly, the transient problem is transformed into the frequency domain. The frequency-domain exact solution for the problem can be constructed as

$$\begin{aligned} \widetilde{u_3^s} &= a_1 \mathrm{j} k_1 e^{\mathrm{j}k_1(x_3-h)} + a_2 \mathrm{j} k_2 e^{\mathrm{j}k_2(x_3-h)} - a_3 \mathrm{j} k_1 e^{-\mathrm{j}k_1 x_3} - a_4 \mathrm{j} k_2 e^{-\mathrm{j}k_2 x_3}, \\ \widetilde{p} &= a_1 r_1 e^{\mathrm{j}k_1(x_3-h)} + a_2 r_2 e^{\mathrm{j}k_2(x_3-h)} + a_3 r_1 e^{-\mathrm{j}k_1 x_3} + a_4 r_2 e^{-\mathrm{j}k_2 x_3}, \end{aligned} \tag{37}$$

in which h = 1 m, and the unknown coefficients a_1, a_2, a_3 and a_4 can be derived from

$$\begin{bmatrix} -k_1^2 & -k_2^2 & -k_1^2 e^{-\mathrm{j}k_1 h} & -k_2^2 e^{-\mathrm{j}k_2 h} \\ r_1 & r_2 & r_1 e^{-\mathrm{j}k_1 h} & r_2 e^{-\mathrm{j}k_2 h} \\ \mathrm{j}k_1 e^{-\mathrm{j}k_1 h} & \mathrm{j}k_2 e^{-\mathrm{j}k_2 h} & -\mathrm{j}k_1 & -\mathrm{j}k_2 \\ \mathrm{j}k_1\left(r_1 - \omega^2 \rho_f\right) e^{-\mathrm{j}k_1 h} & \mathrm{j}k_2\left(r_2 - \omega^2 \rho_f\right) e^{-\mathrm{j}k_2 h} & \mathrm{j}k_1\left(r_1 - \omega^2 \rho_f\right) & \mathrm{j}k_2\left(r_2 - \omega^2 \rho_f\right) \end{bmatrix} \begin{bmatrix} a_1 \\ a_2 \\ a_3 \\ a_4 \end{bmatrix} = \begin{bmatrix} \frac{-1}{\lambda+2\mu} \\ 0 \\ 0 \\ 0 \end{bmatrix}$$

Then the transient exact solution is retrieved via the EWM.

The SBM discretizes the boundary into 400 boundary nodes. The EWM-SBM is employed for the numerical solutions in a duration of T = 18 ms. In the EWM, N_ω and κ are set as 128 and 3.

In Figure 2, some numerical results are picked up to show the accuracy of the present method, including u_3^s at (0.5, 0.8), p at (0.5, 0.5), w_3 at (0.5, 0.7) and σ_{33}^s at (0.5, 0.3). It is shown that the numerical results are in good agreement with the exact solutions. Nevertheless, the results without the Hanning window function drastically oscillate in the end of the duration, which is called Gibbs oscillations. The problem is ameliorated by the Hanning window function. The application of the Hanning window functions does not bring much time. For example, in Figure 2a, the SBM-EWM without and with the Hanning window functions, respectively, take 57.08 s and 56.48 s. As a consequence, it is essential to employ the window function in the EWM-SBM.

It is obvious that the selection of the parameters N_ω, κ has an influence on the accuracy and the stability of the solutions. In the following, the influence is studied.

N_ω is the number of the sample frequencies. More sample frequencies enhance the accuracy of the results but in the meantime bring more operation counts. If the sample frequencies are not enough, the numerical methods may yield inaccurate results. Figure 3 shows the effect of N_ω on the numerical methods via σ_{33}^s at (0.5, 0.8) and p at (0.5, 0.5). In this figure, the number of boundary points is 400 and κ = 2.7. As the number of sampling frequencies increases, the numerical solutions converge to the exact solutions. The solution with N_ω = 64 deviates from the exact solutions most in comparison with N_ω = 128 and 256. However, the case with N_ω = 256 takes 111.7 s in total, which is nearly two times that of the case with $N_\omega = 128$, which consumes 59.3 s. Overall, $N_\omega = 128$ is considered in the following numerical experiments.

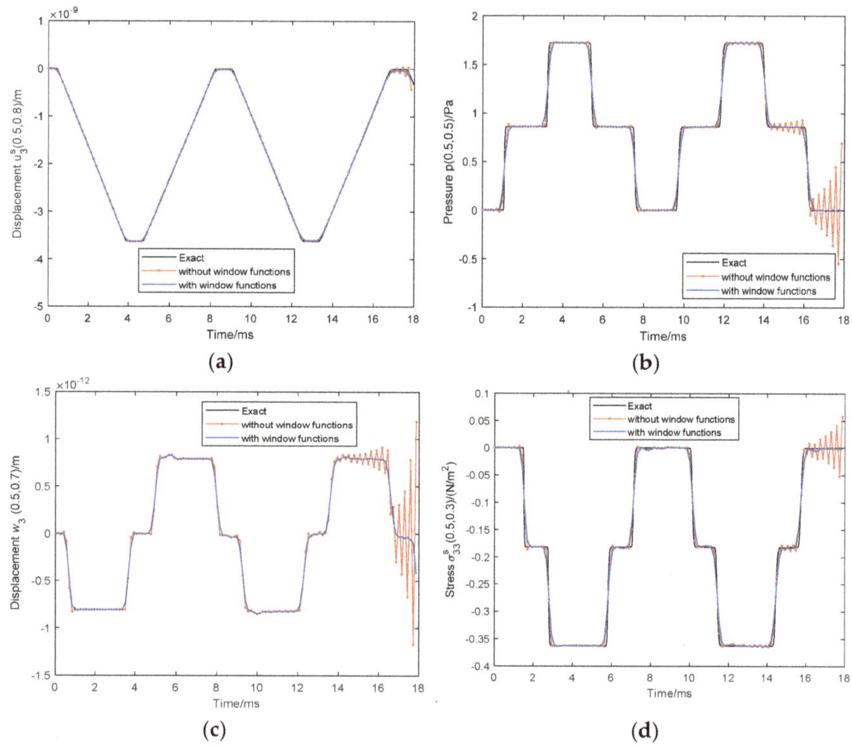

Figure 2. Time history of (**a**) u_3^s at (0.5, 0.8), (**b**) p at (0.5, 0.5), (**c**) w_3 at (0.5, 0.7), (**d**) σ_{33}^s at (0.5, 0.3).

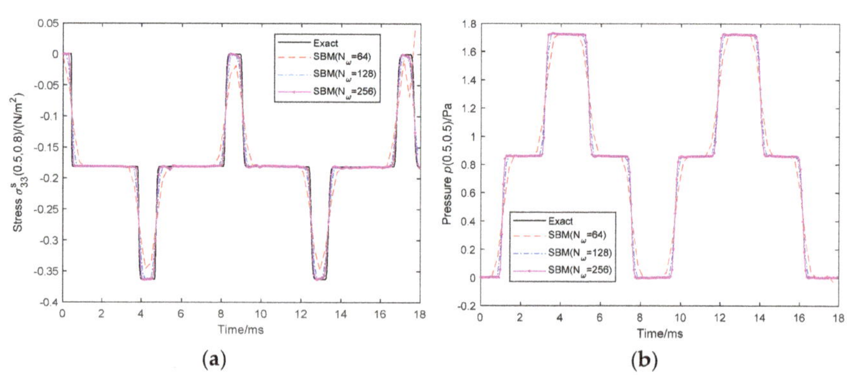

Figure 3. Time history of (**a**) σ_{33}^s at (0.5, 0.8) and (**b**) p at (0.5, 0.5) with respect to the number of sampling frequencies N_ω.

κ is the damping coefficient to determine the artificial damping. A numerical investigation on the κ is given in Figure 4 via the absolute error of u_3^s at (0.5, 0.5) under different damping coefficients. $\kappa = 1.5$, 2, 2.5, 3 and 3.5 are selected. The method with $\kappa = 1.5$ results in the worst solutions. The reason lies in that more sampling frequencies are required in lightly damped systems. In Figure 4, the results with κ = 2, 2.5, 3 and 3.5 are acceptable. Nevertheless, an arbitrary large damping coefficient may lead to loss of numerical precision. As a trade-off, the κ = 2.5 is applied in the subsequent examples.

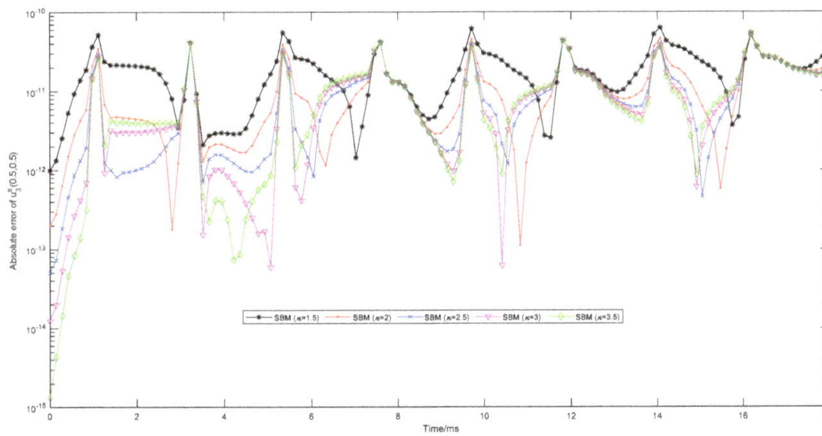

Figure 4. Time history of absolute error of u_3^s at point (0.5, 0.5) under different κ.

In general, the numerical transient results are limited to a short time duration because the results deteriorate if the calculation duration is too long. In this study, the long time behavior of the present method is investigated. In this case, T = 140 ms and N_ω = 1024. Figure 5 plots the history of u_3^s at (0.5, 0.8) and p at (0.5, 0.5). In the entire calculation time, no obvious differences can be observed between the SBM-EWM and exact solutions, which verifies the accuracy and stability of the SBM-EWM in the long-term dynamic simulation.

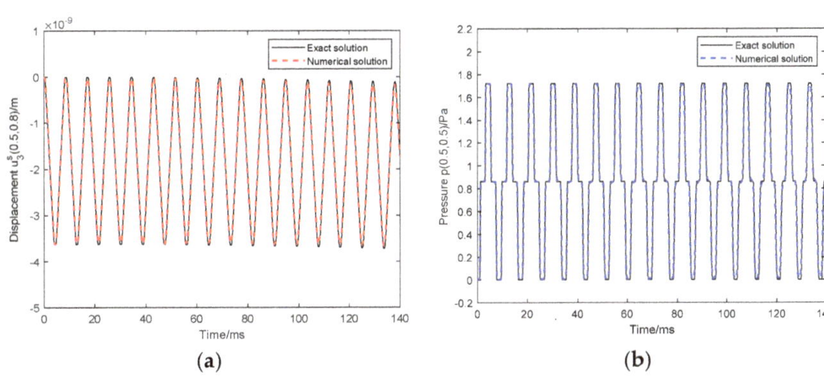

Figure 5. A long time dynamic response of saturated column (**a**) u_3^s at (0.5, 0.8) and (**b**) p at (0.5, 0.5).

5.2. A Half-Space Problem Subjected to a Transient Load

In the section, a saturated poroelastic half-space subjected to transient loads on the ground is shown in Figure 6. Thus, the saturated poroelastic half-space is subjected to the boundary condition expressed as

$$\begin{cases} t_3^s = -H(t)\mathrm{N/m^2}, t_1^s = 0\mathrm{N/m^2}, p = 0\mathrm{Pa},\ x_1 \in [-1,1], x_3 = 0, \\ t_3^s = 0\mathrm{N/m^2}, t_1^s = 0\mathrm{N/m^2}, p = 0\mathrm{Pa\ rest} \end{cases}$$

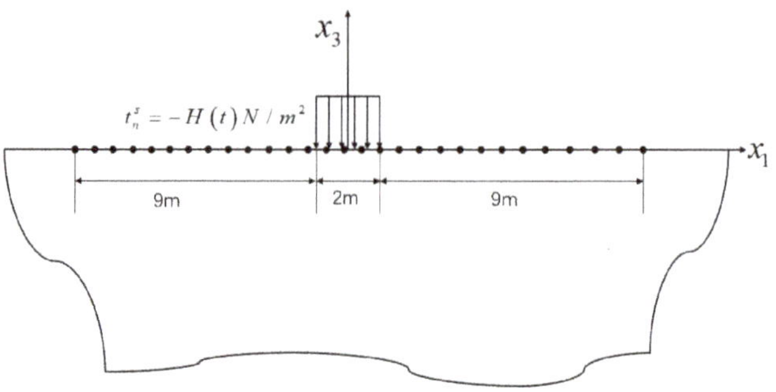

Figure 6. The sketch of the semi-infinite domain.

The boundary is discretized into 500 points. The parameters N_ω, κ are respectively 128 and 2.5 for the SBM. The analytical solution of this problem in frequency-domain is derived by Ba [59]. Then the transient analytical solution is obtained by the EWM with $N_\omega = 256$ and $\kappa = 2.5$. The mesh plots of the analytical solutions and SBM solutions are displayed in Figures 7 and 8. The solutions at different times at different depths are plotted. Good agreement indicates that the SBM is successfully applied to the half-space transient problem.

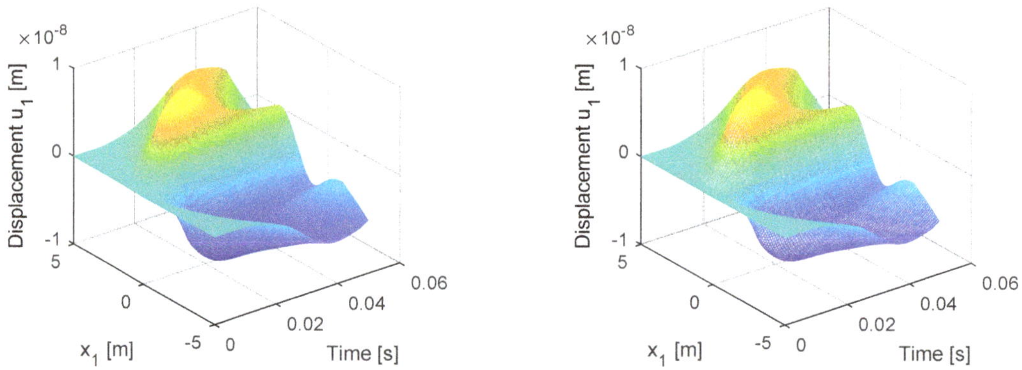

Figure 7. Time history of u_1 at $x_3 = -1$ generated by the analytical solution (**left**) and the SBM-EWM (**right**).

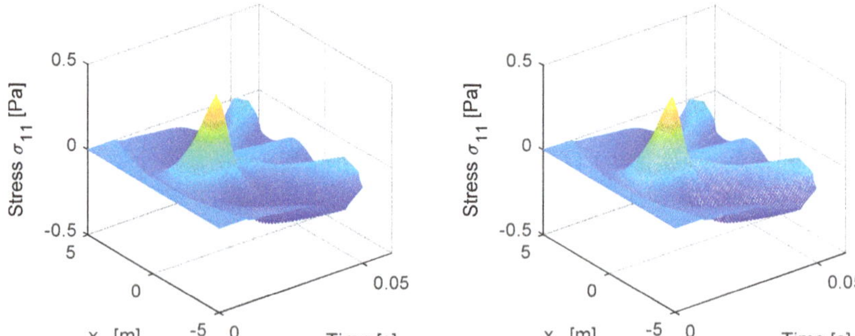

Figure 8. Time history of σ_{11} at $x_3 = -2$ generated by the analytical solution (**left**) and the SBM-EWM (**right**).

Furthermore, the MFS is introduced for comparison with the SBM in Figure 9. All the parameters for the MFS and SBM are the same as the above. The MFS avoids the origin singularity via the artificial boundary outside the computational domain. d is the distance between the artificial boundary and physical boundary. To obtain stable solutions, the MATLAB built-in function pinv is used to solve the linear system of the MFS. As shown in the figure, the MFS and SBM could obtain acceptable solutions. Nevertheless, the results of the MFS are influenced by the location of the artificial boundary. Only the MFS with d = 0.1 converges to the analytical solutions. Otherwise, because of the application of pinv, the MFS takes 357.34 s for the whole process, while the SBM takes 92.96 s. It can be observed that the MFS takes a much longer time than the SBM.

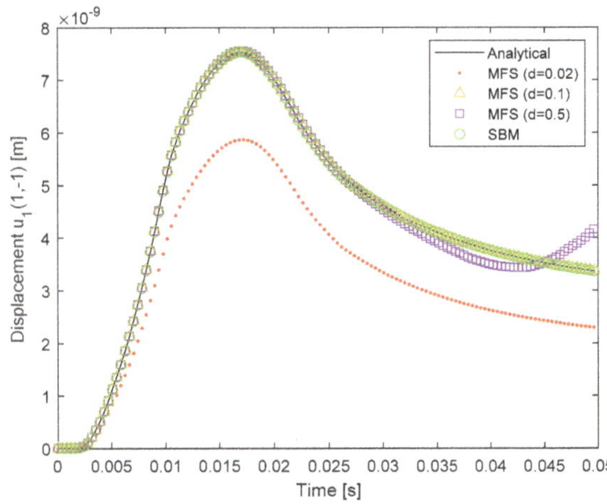

Figure 9. Numerical comparison between the MFS and SBM.

5.3. A Tunnel Embedded in a Saturated Poroelastic Half-Space

In this example, a model of a semi-circular tunnel embedded in a saturated poroelastic half-space in Figure 10 is considered. The radius of the tunnel is R = 3 m and the depth of invert of the tunnel is H = 6 m. A triangularly distributed transient load is imposed at the invert of the tunnel. The ground and the surface of the tunnel are set as permeable. Thus, the boundary conditions are expressed as

$$\begin{cases} t_3^s = ((|x| - 3)P(t))\mathrm{N/m^2},\ t_1^s = 0\mathrm{N/m^2}, p = 0\mathrm{Pa},\ x_1 \in [-3,\ 3],\ x_3 = -6 \\ t_3^s = 0\mathrm{N/m^2}, t_1^s = 0\mathrm{N/m^2}, p = 0\mathrm{Pa},\ \text{otherwise} \end{cases},$$

where

$$P(t) = \begin{cases} 100t\ 0 \le t \le 0.01 \\ 1\ \ 0.01 < t \le 0.03 \\ 4 - 100t\ 0.03 < t \le 0.04 \\ 0\ \text{otherwise} \end{cases}$$

In this case, no analytical solution is available. Thus, the accuracy of the SBM-EWM is presented with different parameters. The total time of tunnel transient response T is 90 ms, and the damping coefficient κ is 2.5. Figure 11 gives σ_{33}^s at (−2, −7) and p at (1, −7) calculated by the SBM-EWM with different numbers of sampling frequencies N_ω (128, 256) and numbers of boundary points N (471, 786). It is observed that the SBM-EWM with different parameters obtains identical results.

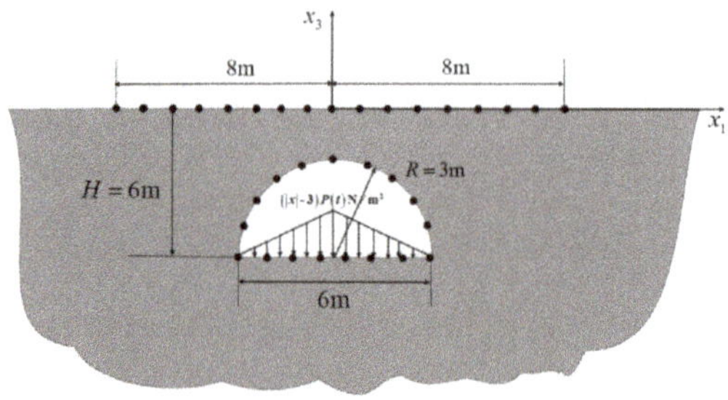

Figure 10. Schematic sketch of the semi-infinite domain tunnel.

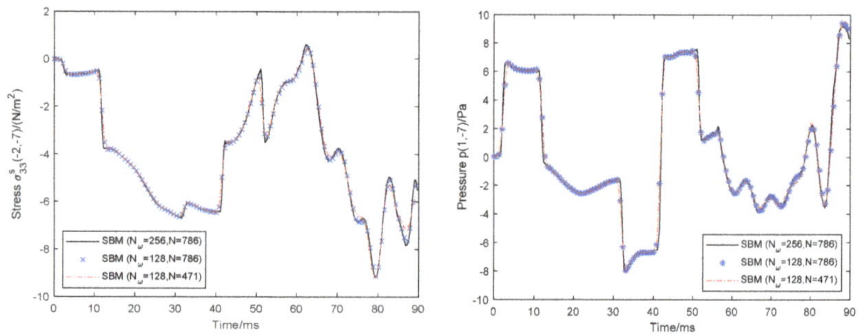

(**a**) (**b**)

Figure 11. Time history of (**a**) σ^s_{33} at $(-2, -7)$ and (**b**) p at $(1, -7)$ under different sampling numbers and boundary points.

To further investigate the numerical results, the time history of the distribution of u^s_3 and p of the domain $(x_1, x_3) \in [-10, 10] \times [-20, 0]$ are plotted in Figures 12 and 13 to observe the wave propagation in the entire time. In all results, the dynamic response is symmetric, which is reasonable according to the symmetry loads. In both figures, it can be seen that the wave is caused by loads at the invert of the tunnel. Then it propagates outward in different directions and around the tunnel to the ground. Theoretically speaking, the whole propagation process complies with the law of wave propagation in solids.

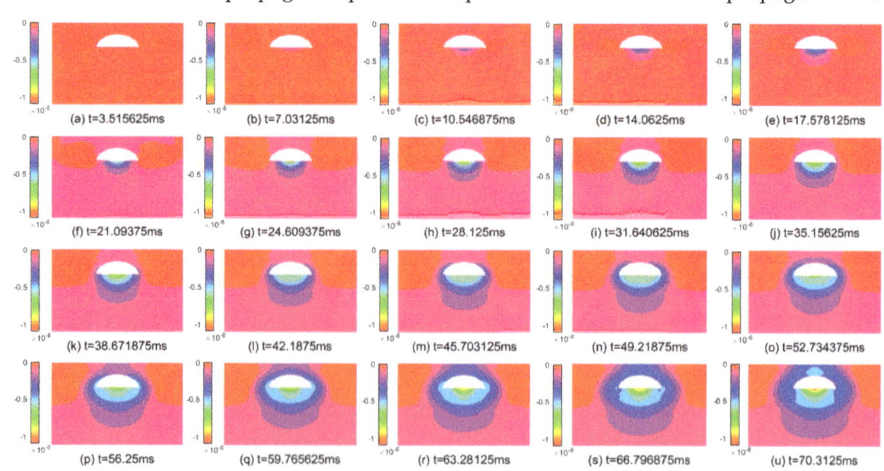

Figure 12. Distribution of u^s_3 with of domain $(x_1, x_3) \in [-10, 10] \times [-20, 0]$ at different times.

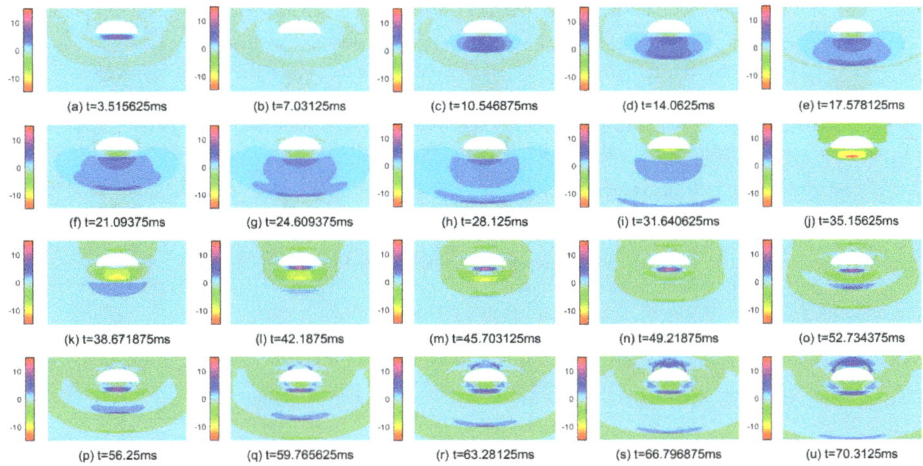

Figure 13. Distribution of p with of domain $(x_1, x_3) \in [-10, 10] \times [-20, 0]$ at different times.

6. Conclusions

In this paper, a novel boundary-only meshless approach is developed to simulate transient dynamic response in the saturated soil. In this method, the SBM is employed to solve the frequency-domain governing equations, while the EWM transforms the frequency-domain solutions into time-domain solutions. In the SBM, the solutions are approximated via the fundamental solutions in terms of boundary points. The boundary-only property makes the SBM very suitable in solving semi-infinite domain problems. The fundamental solutions are derived via the wave decomposition method and eigenanalysis, and their source singularities are removed by the OIFs. The EWM is boasted as an effective inverse Fourier transform method, which incorporates exponential artificial damping into the FFT to enhance its numerical efficiency. The Hanning window function is used to smooth the Gibbs oscillation as the computation period increases. The influence of the parameters in the EWM was investigated in the first numerical experiment. All numerical results validate that the present SBM-EWM is accurate and effective to solve the transient soil dynamic response. Nevertheless, the SBM-EWM is only applicable when the fundamental solutions exist because the fundamental solutions are the kernel function of the SBM.

Author Contributions: Conceptualization, D.L., X.W. and L.S.; Formal analysis, X.W., C.L. and L.S.; Funding acquisition, X.W.; Investigation, C.L. and L.S.; Methodology, D.L., X.W. and L.S.; Software, D.L., X.W. and L.S.; Validation, D.L., X.W., C.L., C.H. and X.C.; Writing—original draft, X.W., C.L. and C.H.; Writing—review and editing, X.C. and L.S. All authors have read and agreed to the published version of the manuscript.

Funding: This work is supported by the National Natural Science Foundation of China (Grant No. 12102135, 51978265, 11602114, 11662003) and Double Thousand Talents Project from Jiangxi Province, The Natural Science Foundation of Jiangxi Province of China (Grant No. 20202BABL201014).

Institutional Review Board Statement: Not applicable.

Informed Consent Statement: Not applicable.

Data Availability Statement: Not applicable.

Acknowledgments: This work is supported by the National Natural Science Foundation of China (Grant No. 12102135, 51978265, 11602114, 11662003) and Double Thousand Talents Project from Jiangxi Province, The Natural Science Foundation of Jiangxi Province of China (Grant No. 20202BABL 201014, 20202ACB211002).

Conflicts of Interest: The authors declare no conflict of interest.

Appendix A. Detailed Derivations of the 2D Fundamental Solutions

The fundamental solution is one of most important parts for the boundary-only methods. However, it is not a trivial work to derive the fundamental solutions for coupled governing equations. This section decouples the governing equations into several simpler scalar governing equations with known fundamental solutions, and then coupled these fundamental solutions with the eigenanalysis.

(1) Solid loads

The singular loads are applied to the solid phase as $\boldsymbol{F}^s = -\delta(\boldsymbol{x}-\boldsymbol{y})\boldsymbol{e}^k (k = 1, 3)$ where $\boldsymbol{e}^1$ and $\boldsymbol{e}^3$ are the unit vectors along x_1 and x_3 direction. The variables in governing Equations (11) and (12) are decomposed into underdetermined potentials A_L, A_T and A_P as

$$\widetilde{\boldsymbol{u}}^s = \nabla\nabla\cdot\left(A_L\boldsymbol{e}^k\right) - \nabla\times\nabla\times\left(A_T\boldsymbol{e}^k\right), \tag{A1}$$

$$\widetilde{p} = \nabla\cdot\left(A_P\boldsymbol{e}^k\right), \tag{A2}$$

The Laplace operator can be decomposed into

$$\Delta\left(\tau\boldsymbol{e}^k\right) = \nabla\nabla\cdot\left(\tau\boldsymbol{e}^k\right) - \nabla\times\nabla\times\left(\tau\boldsymbol{e}^k\right) = -\delta(\boldsymbol{y}-\boldsymbol{x})\boldsymbol{e}^k, \tag{A3}$$

where τ is the fundamental solutions for the Laplace operator.

With Equations (A1) and (A2), we decouple the governing Equations (11) and (12) as

$$(\lambda+2\mu)\nabla^2 A_L + \omega^2\rho_g A_L - \alpha_g A_P = \tau, \tag{A4}$$

$$\mu\nabla^2 A_T + \omega^2\rho_g A_T = \tau, \tag{A5}$$

$$\nabla^2 A_P + \omega^2\beta_2 A_P - \beta_3\nabla^2 A_L = 0. \tag{A6}$$

Potentials A_T can be obtained from Equation (A5) as

$$A_T = -\frac{g_3}{2\pi k_3^2}(\ln r + K_0(jk_3 r)). \tag{A7}$$

The other two potentials A_L and A_P are coupled in Equations (A4) and (A6). To solve A_L and A_P, the eigenanalysis is introduced for the matrix system as

$$M_1\nabla^2\begin{bmatrix} A_L \\ A_P \end{bmatrix} + M_2\begin{bmatrix} A_L \\ A_P \end{bmatrix} = \begin{bmatrix} \tau \\ 0 \end{bmatrix}, \tag{A8}$$

where

$$M_1 = \begin{bmatrix} \lambda+2\mu & 0 \\ -\beta_3 & 1 \end{bmatrix},\ M_2 = \begin{bmatrix} \omega^2\rho_g & -\alpha_g \\ 0 & \beta_2\omega^2 \end{bmatrix}$$

Reformulate Equation (A8) as

$$\nabla^2\begin{bmatrix} A_L \\ A_P \end{bmatrix} + M\begin{bmatrix} A_L \\ A_P \end{bmatrix} = \tau M_1^{-1}\begin{bmatrix} 1 \\ 0 \end{bmatrix} = \tau\boldsymbol{g},\ M = M_1^{-1}M_2 \tag{A9}$$

with matrix $\boldsymbol{g}$ written as

$$g = \frac{1}{\lambda+2\mu}\begin{bmatrix} 1 \\ \beta_3 \end{bmatrix} \tag{A10}$$

Search the solutions through the eigenvector basis as

$$\begin{bmatrix} A_L \\ A_P \end{bmatrix} = \phi_1\begin{bmatrix} 1 \\ r_1' \end{bmatrix} + \phi_2\begin{bmatrix} 1 \\ r_2' \end{bmatrix}, \tag{A11}$$

where $(1, r_i')^T (i = 1, 2)$ denote the eigenvector of $\boldsymbol{M}$ and r_1', r_2' are given by

$$r_i' = \frac{(\lambda + 2\mu)k_i^2 - \omega^2 \rho_g}{-\alpha_g}, \ i = 1, 2, \tag{A12}$$

where $k_i^2 (i = 1, 2)$ are the eigenvalue of $\boldsymbol{M}$ and $k_3^2 = \omega^2 \rho_g / \mu$. Then based on Equations (A11), Equation (A9) can be simplified as

$$\nabla^2 \phi_i + k_i^2 \phi_i = g_i \tau, \tag{A13}$$

where $g_3 = 1/\mu$ and $g_i (i = 1, 2)$ are

$$\boldsymbol{g} = g_1 \begin{bmatrix} 1 \\ r_1' \end{bmatrix} + g_2 \begin{bmatrix} 1 \\ r_2' \end{bmatrix}. \tag{A14}$$

Thus, the solution of Equation (A13) is

$$\phi_i(r) = -\frac{g_i}{2\pi k_i^2} (\ln r + K_0(\mathrm{j} k_i r)), \tag{A15}$$

where K_0 is the modified Bessel function of zero order.

Bringing the potentials into Equations (A1) and (A2), the 2D fundamental solutions are derived as

$$\widetilde{u}_{ik}^s = A\delta_{ik} - B r_{,i} r_{,k}, \ i, k = 1, 3, \tag{A16}$$

$$\widetilde{p}_k = C r_{,k}, \ k = 1, 3. \tag{A17}$$

where

$$A = \frac{1}{2\pi} \left[-\sum_{d=1,2} g_d \frac{K_1(z_d)}{z_d} + g_3 \left(K_0(z_3) + \frac{K_1(z_3)}{z_3} \right) \right]$$

$$C = \frac{\mathrm{j}}{2\pi} \left[\sum_{d=1,2} \frac{r_d g_d}{k_d} K_1(z_d) \right]$$

$$B = \frac{1}{2\pi} \left[-\sum_{d=1,2} g_d K_2(z_d) + g_3 K_2(z_3) \right]$$

$$D = \frac{-\mathrm{j}}{2\pi} \sum_{d=1,2} k_d h_d K_1(z_d), \ z_3 = \mathrm{j} k_3 r, \ z_d = \mathrm{j} k_d r$$

$$r_d = \frac{\omega^2 \rho_g - (\lambda + 2\mu)k_d^2}{\alpha_g} (d = 1, 2), \ g_1 = \frac{\beta_3 - r_2}{(\lambda + 2\mu)(r_1 - r_2)},$$

$$g_2 = \frac{\beta_3 - r_1}{(\lambda + 2\mu)(r_2 - r_1)}, \ g_3 = \frac{1}{\mu}, \ h_1 = -\frac{\beta_3}{\alpha_g (r_1 - r_2)}, \ h_2 = -\frac{\beta_3}{\alpha_g (r_2 - r_1)}$$

in which $r = \sqrt{(x_1 - y_1)^2 + (x_3 - y_3)^2}$ is the distance between field point $\boldsymbol{x} = (x_1, x_3)$ and source point $\boldsymbol{y} = (y_1, y_3)$. K_n is the modified Bessel function of the second kind of order n, and k_d is

$$k_1 = \sqrt{\frac{\beta_2 \omega^2}{2} + \frac{\rho_g \omega^2 - \alpha_g \beta_3 + \sqrt{H}}{2(\lambda + 2\mu)}}, \ k_2 = \sqrt{\frac{\beta_2 \omega^2}{2} + \frac{\rho_g \omega^2 - \alpha_g \beta_3 - \sqrt{H}}{2(\lambda + 2\mu)}}, k_3 = \sqrt{\omega^2 \rho_g / \mu}$$

where

$$H = \left(\lambda \beta_2 \omega^2 - \alpha_g \beta_3 + \rho_g \omega^2 \right)^2 + 4(\lambda + \mu) \beta_2 \omega^4 (\mu \beta_2 - \rho_g) - 4\mu \alpha_g \beta_2 \beta_3 \omega^2$$

With the constitutive relationship, we have the traction fundamental solutions as

$$\begin{aligned}\widetilde{t}^{s}_{ik} = \lambda\left[A' - B' - \tfrac{B}{r}\right]r_{,k}n_i + \mu\Big[\Big(A' - \tfrac{B}{r}\Big)(r_{,n}\delta_{ik} + r_{,i}n_k)\\ - \tfrac{2B}{r}r_{,k}n_i + 2\Big(-B' + \tfrac{2B}{r}\Big)r_{,i}r_{,k}r_{,n}\Big]\ i,k = 1,3,\end{aligned} \tag{A18}$$

where $r_{,i} = \frac{x_i - y_i}{r}$, $r_{,n} = r_{,1}n_1 + r_{,3}n_3$ and $(\bullet)'$ are the derivatives of $\bullet$ with respect to r.

For the fluid, the flux fundamental solutions are

$$\widetilde{q}_k = \frac{-\alpha_g}{\beta_3}\left[\frac{C}{r}n_k + \left(C' - \frac{C}{r}\right)r_{,k}r_{,n}\right],\ k = 1,3. \tag{A19}$$

(2) Fluid load

The singular load $\boldsymbol{F}^p = -\delta(\boldsymbol{x} - \boldsymbol{y})$ is applied to Equation (12). The variables are decomposed by the Helmholtz decomposition as

$$\widetilde{\boldsymbol{u}}^s = \nabla\varphi + \nabla \times \Psi, \tag{A20}$$

Taking Equations (A2) and (A20) into Equations (11) and (12), we have

$$(\lambda + 2\mu)\nabla^2\varphi + \omega^2\rho_g\varphi - \alpha_g p = 0, \tag{A21}$$

$$\mu\nabla^2\Psi + \omega^2\rho_g\Psi = 0, \tag{A22}$$

$$\nabla^2 p + \omega^2\beta_2 p - \beta_3\nabla^2\varphi = -\delta(\boldsymbol{x} - \boldsymbol{y}) \tag{A23}$$

Only Ψ is associated with Equation (A22). For simplicity, let $\Psi = 0$. The other two potentials are derived from

$$\nabla^2\begin{bmatrix}\varphi\\ p\end{bmatrix} + M\begin{bmatrix}\varphi\\ p\end{bmatrix} = \boldsymbol{h}\begin{bmatrix}0\\ -\delta\end{bmatrix}, \tag{A24}$$

where M is the same as in Equation (A9), and $\boldsymbol{h} = (0,1)^T$. Then the eigenanalysis is based on

$$\begin{bmatrix}\varphi\\ p\end{bmatrix} = \phi_1\begin{bmatrix}1\\ r_1'\end{bmatrix} + \phi_2\begin{bmatrix}1\\ r_2'\end{bmatrix}. \tag{A25}$$

Recast Equation (A24) as

$$\nabla^2\phi_i + k_i^2\phi_i = -h_i\delta(\boldsymbol{x} - \boldsymbol{y}), \tag{A26}$$

where $h_i (i = 1,2)$ satisfies

$$\boldsymbol{h} = h_1\begin{bmatrix}1\\ r_1'\end{bmatrix} + h_2\begin{bmatrix}1\\ r_2'\end{bmatrix}. \tag{A27}$$

The solutions of Equation (A26) are

$$\phi_i(r) = \frac{h_i}{2\pi}K_0(jk_i r). \tag{A28}$$

The 2D fundamental solutions can be derived via potentials and decomposition equations as

$$\widetilde{u}^s_{i4} = Dr_{,i},\ i = 1,3, \tag{A29}$$

$$\widetilde{p}_4 = \frac{1}{2\pi}\sum_{d=1,2} r_d h_d K_0(z_d). \tag{A30}$$

Similarly, the fundamental solutions of the traction and flux are

$$\widetilde{t}_{i4} = \left[(\lambda + 2\mu)\frac{D}{r} + \lambda D'\right]n_i + 2\mu\left(-\frac{D}{r} + D'\right)r_{,i}r_{,n},\ i = 1,3, \tag{A31}$$

$$\widetilde{q}_4 = \frac{\mathrm{j}\alpha_g r_{,n}}{2\pi\beta_3}\sum_{d=1,2} r_d h_d k_d K_1(z_d). \tag{A32}$$

Appendix B. The $\chi_1,\ldots,\chi_{10}$ of OIFs for 2D Saturated Poroelastic Problems

$$\chi_1 = \frac{g_1 + g_2 + g_3}{2},\ \chi_3 = -\frac{1}{2\pi}\left(\frac{g_1 + g_2 - g_3}{2}\right),\ \chi_4 = -(\lambda + \mu)\left(\sum_{m=1,2} k_m^2 h_m\right),$$

$$\chi_2 = \frac{1}{2\pi}\left[\frac{g_1 + g_2 + g_3}{2}\overline{\tau} + \frac{g_1}{2}\ln\left(\frac{\mathrm{j}k_1}{2}\right) + \frac{g_2}{2}\ln\left(\frac{\mathrm{j}k_2}{2}\right) + \frac{g_3}{2}\ln\left(\frac{\mathrm{j}k_3}{2}\right) - \frac{g_1 + g_2 - g_3}{4}\right],$$

$$\chi_5 = \frac{1}{2\pi}\left[2(\lambda + \mu)\left(\sum_{m=1,2}\frac{k_m^2 h_m}{2}\left(\overline{\tau} + \ln\left(\frac{\mathrm{j}k_m}{2}\right)\right)\right) - \mu\sum_{m=1,2}\frac{k_m^2 h_m}{2}\right],\ \chi_6 = r_1 h_1 + r_2 h_2,$$

$$\chi_7 = \frac{1}{2\pi}\left[-(r_1 h_1 + r_2 h_2)\overline{\tau} - r_1 h_1 \ln\left(\frac{\mathrm{j}k_1}{2}\right) - r_2 h_2 \ln\left(\frac{\mathrm{j}k_2}{2}\right)\right],\ \chi_8 = -\frac{\alpha_g(r_1 g_1 + r_2 g_2)}{2\beta_3},$$

$$\chi_9 = \frac{\alpha_g}{2\pi\beta_3}\left[\frac{r_1 g_1 + r_2 g_2}{2}\left(\overline{\tau} - \frac{1}{2}\right) + \frac{r_1 g_1}{2}\ln\left(\frac{\mathrm{j}k_1}{2}\right) + \frac{r_2 g_2}{2}\ln\left(\frac{\mathrm{j}k_2}{2}\right)\right],\ \chi_{10} = \sum_{m=1,2} -\frac{\alpha_g r_m h_m}{\beta_3},$$

$\overline{\tau} = 0.57721566490153286$ is the Euler–Mascheroni constant.

References

1. Chen, G.; Yang, J.; Liu, Y.; Kitahara, T.; Beer, M. An energy-frequency parameter for earthquake ground motion intensity measure. *Earthq. Eng. Struct. Dyn.* **2022**, 1–14. [CrossRef]
2. Chen, G.; Li, Q.-Y.; Li, D.-Q.; Wu, Z.-Y.; Liu, Y. Main frequency band of blast vibration signal based on wavelet packet transform. *Appl. Math. Model.* **2019**, *74*, 569–585. [CrossRef]
3. Li, W.; Zhang, Q.; Gui, Q.; Chai, Y. A Coupled FE-Meshfree Triangular Element for Acoustic Radiation Problems. *Int. J. Comput. Methods* **2021**, *18*, 2041002. [CrossRef]
4. Chai, Y.; Li, W.; Liu, Z. Analysis of transient wave propagation dynamics using the enriched finite element method with interpolation cover functions. *Appl. Math. Comput.* **2022**, *412*, 126564. [CrossRef]
5. Pled, F.; Desceliers, C. Review and Recent Developments on the Perfectly Matched Layer (PML) Method for the Numerical Modeling and Simulation of Elastic Wave Propagation in Unbounded Domains. *Arch. Comput. Methods Eng.* **2022**, *29*, 471–518. [CrossRef]
6. Fu, Z.-J.; Xie, Z.-Y.; Ji, S.-Y.; Tsai, C.-C.; Li, A.-L. Meshless generalized finite difference method for water wave interactions with multiple-bottom-seated-cylinder-array structures. *Ocean Eng.* **2020**, *195*, 106736. [CrossRef]
7. Kythe, P.K. *Fundamental Solutions for Differential Operators and Applications*; Birkhauser: Basel, Switzerland, 1996.
8. Chen, C.S.; Karageorghis, A.; Smyrlis, Y.S. *The Method of Fundamental Solutions: A Meshless Method*; Dynamic Publishers: Atlanta, GA, USA, 2008.
9. Wei, X.; Chen, W.; Chen, B. An ACA accelerated MFS for potential problems. *Eng. Anal. Bound. Elem.* **2014**, *41*, 90–97. [CrossRef]
10. Chen, Z.; Sun, L. A boundary meshless method for dynamic coupled thermoelasticity problems. *Appl. Math. Lett.* **2022**, *134*, 108305. [CrossRef]
11. Wang, M.Z.; Xu, B.X.; Gao, C.F. Recent General Solutions in Linear Elasticity and Their Applications. *Appl. Mech. Rev.* **2008**, *61*, 030803–030820. [CrossRef]
12. Sun, L.; Zhang, C.; Yu, Y. A boundary knot method for 3D time harmonic elastic wave problems. *Appl. Math. Lett.* **2020**, *104*, 106210. [CrossRef]
13. Xu, W.-Z.; Fu, Z.-J.; Xi, Q. A novel localized collocation solver based on a radial Trefftz basis for thermal conduction analysis in FGMs with exponential variations. *Comput. Math. Appl.* **2022**, *117*, 24–38. [CrossRef]
14. Xi, Q.; Fu, Z.; Zhang, C.; Yin, D. An efficient localized Trefftz-based collocation scheme for heat conduction analysis in two kinds of heterogeneous materials under temperature loading. *Comput. Struct.* **2021**, *255*, 106619. [CrossRef]
15. Li, Z.C.; Lu, T.T.; Hu, H.Y.; Cheng, A.H.D. *Trefftz and Collocation Methods*; WIT Press: Boston, UK, 2008.
16. Sun, L.; Wei, X.; Chu, L. A 2D frequency-domain wave based method for dynamic analysis of orthotropic solids. *Comput. Struct.* **2020**, *238*, 106300. [CrossRef]

17. Karageorghis, A.; Lesnic, D.; Marin, L. A survey of applications of the MFS to inverse problems. *Inverse Probl. Sci. Eng.* **2011**, *19*, 309–336. [CrossRef]
18. Šarler, B. Solution of potential flow problems by the modified method of fundamental solutions: Formulations with the single layer and the double layer fundamental solutions. *Eng. Anal. Bound. Elem.* **2009**, *33*, 1374–1382. [CrossRef]
19. Chen, W. Singular boundary method: A novel, simple, meshfree, boundary collocation numerical method. *Chin. J. Solid Mech.* **2009**, *30*, 592–599.
20. Wei, X.; Chen, W.; Chen, B.; Sun, L. Singular boundary method for heat conduction problems with certain spatially varying conductivity. *Comput. Math. Appl.* **2015**, *69*, 206–222. [CrossRef]
21. Wei, X.; Chen, W.; Sun, L.; Chen, B. A simple accurate formula evaluating origin intensity factor in singular boundary method for two-dimensional potential problems with Dirichlet boundary. *Eng. Anal. Bound. Elem.* **2015**, *58*, 151–165. [CrossRef]
22. Wei, X.; Chen, W.; Fu, Z.J. Solving inhomogeneous problems by singular boundary method. *J. Mar. Sci. Technol. Taiwan* **2013**, *21*, 8–14. [CrossRef]
23. Wei, X.; Sun, L.; Yin, S.; Chen, B. A boundary-only treatment by singular boundary method for two-dimensional inhomogeneous problems. *Appl. Math. Model.* **2018**, *62*, 338–351. [CrossRef]
24. Wei, X.; Sun, L. Singular boundary method for 3D time-harmonic electromagnetic scattering problems. *Appl. Math. Model.* **2019**, *76*, 617–631. [CrossRef]
25. Wei, X.; Huang, A.; Sun, L. Singular boundary method for 2D and 3D heat source reconstruction. *Appl. Math. Lett.* **2020**, *102*, 106103. [CrossRef]
26. Wei, X.; Luo, W. 2.5D singular boundary method for acoustic wave propagation. *Appl. Math. Lett.* **2021**, *112*, 106760. [CrossRef]
27. Cheng, S.; Wang, F.; Li, P.-W.; Qu, W. Singular boundary method for 2D and 3D acoustic design sensitivity analysis. *Comput. Math. Appl.* **2022**, *119*, 371–386. [CrossRef]
28. Fu, Z.; Xi, Q.; Li, Y.; Huang, H.; Rabczuk, T. Hybrid FEM–SBM solver for structural vibration induced underwater acoustic radiation in shallow marine environment. *Comput. Methods Appl. Mech. Eng.* **2020**, *369*, 113236. [CrossRef]
29. Wei, X.; Rao, C.; Chen, S.; Luo, W. Numerical simulation of anti-plane wave propagation in heterogeneous media. *Appl. Math. Lett.* **2023**, *135*, 108436. [CrossRef]
30. Sun, L.; Wei, X. A frequency domain formulation of the singular boundary method for dynamic analysis of thin elastic plate. *Eng. Anal. Bound. Elem.* **2019**, *98*, 77–87. [CrossRef]
31. Sun, L.; Chen, W.; Cheng, A.H.D. Singular boundary method for 2D dynamic poroelastic problems. *Wave Motion* **2016**, *61*, 40–62. [CrossRef]
32. Sun, L.; Wei, X.; Chen, B. A meshless singular boundary method for elastic wave propagation in 2D partially saturated poroelastic media. *Eng. Anal. Bound. Elem.* **2020**, *113*, 82–98. [CrossRef]
33. Li, W.; Wang, F. Precorrected-FFT Accelerated Singular Boundary Method for High-Frequency Acoustic Radiation and Scattering. *Mathematics* **2022**, *10*, 238. [CrossRef]
34. Li, J.; Gu, Y.; Qin, Q.-H.; Zhang, L. The rapid assessment for three-dimensional potential model of large-scale particle system by a modified multilevel fast multipole algorithm. *Comput. Math. Appl.* **2021**, *89*, 127–138. [CrossRef]
35. Li, J.; Zhang, L.; Qin, Q. A regularized fast multipole method of moments for rapid calculation of three-dimensional time-harmonic electromagnetic scattering from complex targets. *Eng. Anal. Bound. Elem.* **2022**, *142*, 28–38. [CrossRef]
36. Li, J.; Fu, Z.; Gu, Y.; Qin, Q. Recent advances and emerging applications of the singular boundary method for large-scale and high-frequency computational acoustics. *Adv. Appl. Math. Mech.* **2022**, *14*, 315–343. [CrossRef]
37. Qu, W.; Chen, W.; Zheng, C. Diagonal form fast multipole singular boundary method applied to the solution of high-frequency acoustic radiation and scattering. *Int. J. Numer. Methods Eng.* **2017**, *111*, 803–815. [CrossRef]
38. Fu, Z.; Tang, Z.; Xi, Q.; Liu, Q.; Gu, Y.; Wang, F. Localized collocation schemes and their applications. *Acta Mech. Sin.* **2022**, *38*, 422167. [CrossRef]
39. Li, W. Localized method of fundamental solutions for 2D harmonic elastic wave problems. *Appl. Math. Lett.* **2021**, *112*, 106759. [CrossRef]
40. Zhu, T.; Zhang, J.D.; Atluri, S.N. A local boundary integral equation (LBIE) method in Comput. Mech., and a meshless discretization approach. *Comput. Mech.* **1998**, *21*, 223–235. [CrossRef]
41. Sun, L.; Fu, Z.; Chen, Z. A localized collocation solver based on fundamental solutions for 3D time harmonic elastic wave propagation analysis. *Appl. Math. Comput.* **2023**, *439*, 127600. [CrossRef]
42. Zhang, Y.; Dang, S.; Li, W.; Chai, Y. Performance of the radial point interpolation method (RPIM) with implicit time integration scheme for transient wave propagation dynamics. *Comput. Math. Appl.* **2022**, *114*, 95–111. [CrossRef]
43. Qu, W.; He, H. A spatial–temporal GFDM with an additional condition for transient heat conduction analysis of FGMs. *Appl. Math. Lett.* **2020**, *110*, 106579. [CrossRef]
44. Gao, X.-W.; Zheng, B.-J.; Yang, K.; Zhang, C. Radial integration BEM for dynamic coupled thermoelastic analysis under thermal shock loading. *Comput. Struct.* **2015**, *158*, 140–147. [CrossRef]
45. Kuhlman, K. Review of inverse Laplace transform algorithms for Laplace-space numerical approaches. *Numer. Algorithms* **2013**, *63*, 339–355. [CrossRef]
46. Xiao, J.; Ye, W.; Cai, Y.; Zhang, J. Precorrected FFT accelerated BEM for large-scale transient elastodynamic analysis using frequency-domain approach. *Int. J. Numer. Methods Eng.* **2012**, *90*, 116–134. [CrossRef]

47. Phan, A.V.; Gray, L.J.; Salvadori, A. Transient analysis of the dynamic stress intensity factors using SGBEM for frequency-domain elastodynamics. *Comput. Methods Appl. Mech. Eng.* **2010**, *199*, 3039–3050. [CrossRef]
48. Marrero, M.; Domínguez, J. Numerical behavior of time domain BEM for three-dimensional transient elastodynamic problems. *Eng. Anal. Bound. Elem.* **2003**, *27*, 39–48. [CrossRef]
49. Qu, W.; Gao, H.W.; Gu, Y. Integrating Krylov deferred correction and generalized finite difference methods for dynamic simulations of wave propagation phenomena in long-time intervals. *Adv. Appl. Math. Mech.* **2021**, *13*, 1398–1417.
50. Kausel, E.; Roësset, J.M. Frequency Domain Analysis of Undamped Systems. *J. Eng. Mech.* **1992**, *118*, 721–734. [CrossRef]
51. Tong, L.H.; Ding, H.B.; Yan, J.W.; Xu, C.; Lei, Z. Strain gradient nonlocal Biot poromechanics. *Int. J. Eng. Sci.* **2020**, *156*, 103372. [CrossRef]
52. Tong, L.; Yu, Y.; Hu, W.; Shi, Y.; Xu, C. On wave propagation characteristics in fluid saturated porous materials by a nonlocal Biot theory. *J. Sound Vib.* **2016**, *379*, 106–118. [CrossRef]
53. Biot, M.A. Theory of Propagation of Elastic Waves in a Fluid-Saturated Porous Solid. II. Higher Frequency Range. *J. Acoust. Soc. Am.* **1956**, *28*, 179–191. [CrossRef]
54. Lu, J.F.; Jeng, D.S.; Williams, S. A 2.5-D dynamic model for a saturated porous medium: Part I. Green's function. *Int. J. Solids Struct.* **2008**, *45*, 378–391. [CrossRef]
55. Wei, X.; Liu, D.; Luo, W.; Chen, S.; Sun, L. A half-space singular boundary method for predicting ground-borne vibrations. *Appl. Math. Model.* **2022**, *111*, 630–643. [CrossRef]
56. Gu, Y.; Chen, W.; Zhang, C.-Z. Singular boundary method for solving plane strain elastostatic problems. *Int. J. Solids Struct.* **2011**, *48*, 2549–2556. [CrossRef]
57. Ariza, M.P.; Dominguez, J. General BE approach for three-dimensional dynamic fracture analysis. *Eng. Anal. Bound. Elem.* **2002**, *26*, 639–651. [CrossRef]
58. Xiao, J.; Ye, W.; Wen, L. Efficiency improvement of the frequency-domain BEM for rapid transient elastodynamic analysis. *Comput. Mech.* **2013**, *52*, 903–912. [CrossRef]
59. Ba, Z.; Kang, Z.; Lee, V.W. Plane strain dynamic responses of a multi-layered transversely isotropic saturated half-space. *Int. J. Eng. Sci.* **2017**, *119*, 55–77. [CrossRef]

mathematics

Article

Effects of Diffusion-Induced Nonlinear Local Volume Change on the Structural Stability of NMC Cathode Materials of Lithium-Ion Batteries

Noman Iqbal [1], Jinwoong Choi [1], Changkyu Lee [1], Hafiz Muhammad Uzair Ayub [2], Jinho Kim [1], Minseo Kim [1], Younggee Kim [1], Dongjae Moon [1] and Seungjun Lee [1,*]

1 Department of Mechanical, Robotics and Energy Engineering, Dongguk University, Seoul 04620, Republic of Korea
2 Gas Processing Center, College of Engineering, Qatar University, Doha P.O. Box 2713, Qatar
* Correspondence: sjunlee@dgu.ac.kr

Abstract: Electrochemical stress induced by the charging/discharging of electrode materials strongly affects the lifetime of lithium-ion batteries (LIBs) by regulating mechanical failures. Electrochemical stress is caused by a change in the local volume of the active materials associated with the lithium-ion concentration. The local volume change of certain active materials, such as nickel-rich $LiNi_xMn_yCo_zO_2$ (NMC), varies nonlinearly with the lithium content, which has not been considered in the stress calculations in previous studies. In this paper, the influence of nonlinear local volume change on the mechanical response of NMC-active materials is investigated numerically. The goal is achieved by using a concentration-dependent partial molar volume calculated from the previously obtained local volume change experimental results. A two-dimensional axisymmetric model was developed to perform finite element simulations by fully coupling lithium diffusion and stress generation at a single particle level. The numerical results demonstrate that (1) the global volume change of the particle evolves nonlinearly, (2) the stress response correlates with the rate of change of the active particle's volume, and (3) stress–concentration coupling strongly affects the concentration levels inside the particle. We believe this is the first simulation study that highlights the effect of a concentration-dependent partial molar volume on diffusion-induced stresses in NMC materials. The proposed model provides insight into the design of next-generation NMC electrode materials to achieve better structural stability by reducing mechanical cracking issues.

Keywords: lithium-ion battery; concentration-dependent material property; nonlinear volume change; NMC electrode; finite element simulation

MSC: 74F25; 74S05

Citation: Iqbal, N.; Choi, J.; Lee, C.; Ayub, H.M.U.; Kim, J.; Kim, M.; Kim, Y.; Moon, D.; Lee, S. Effects of Diffusion-Induced Nonlinear Local Volume Change on the Structural Stability of NMC Cathode Materials of Lithium-Ion Batteries. *Mathematics* **2022**, *10*, 4697. https://doi.org/10.3390math10244697

Academic Editors: Zhuojia Fu, Yiqian He and Hui Zheng

Received: 16 November 2022
Accepted: 9 December 2022
Published: 11 December 2022

1. Introduction

With the growing demand for energy storage devices, lithium-ion batteries (LIBs) are gaining more interest due to their higher capacity and longer cycle life [1]. LIB applications range from small medical and portable electronic devices to electric vehicles (EVs); however, their capacity decreases over time [2]. One of the main goals of the development of the next-generation batteries is to increase their efficiency by limiting the capacity-fading mechanisms [3]. Layered cathode materials, such as lithium nickel manganese cobalt oxide $LiNi_xMn_yCo_zO_2$ (NMC), are the most promising active materials with lower costs and higher energy density [4,5]. However, the battery capacity quickly decreases due to various mechanical failures caused by diffusion-induced stress (DIS) when lithium is introduced into (lithiation) or extracted from active materials (delithiation) [6,7].

A lot of effort has gone into the development of charging/discharging models to understand the mechanisms underlying DIS generation. One of the pioneering works are the studies of Christensen and Newman [8]. They investigated the lithiation-induced stresses and predicted mechanical failure in a single spherical graphite anode. A thermal analogy was then employed to calculate the DIS using finite element method (FEM) simulations [9]. Later, the DIS model was further updated by including the phase transition effects [10,11], grain boundaries [12–14], charging/discharging rates [15], material properties [16,17], active material morphology [18], surface stresses [19,20], yielding and plastic deformations of the active material [21–24], and solid–electrolyte interface [25–27]. Furthermore, several researchers have developed various stress-regulated charging/discharging strategies to reduce stresses using such DIS models [28–30]. Going a step further, the dynamic growth of failures in LIB model systems under the influence of DIS has also been simulated [31–33]. However, in order to reduce the simulation complexity, the mentioned studies have mainly used constant material properties, whereas most of the active material properties depend on the lithium concentration. Therefore, to accurately predict the charging/discharging behavior of the material, precise property values should be used when performing simulations.

In the last few years, many researchers have devoted themselves to determining the effect of concentration-dependent material properties on the charging and discharging processes of lithium-ion batteries. The researchers included the lithium concentration-dependent elastic properties especially Young's modulus [34–41], yield stress [24,42,43], Poisson's ratio [44], coefficient of chemical expansion or partial molar volume [45,46], toughness [47], and lithium diffusion coefficient [48,49] to DIS simulation models. For example, Deshpande et al. [50] used a simple cylindrical electrode particle to find that Young's modulus variation has a significant effect on the evolution of DIS. Zhang et al. [51] examined the effect of the concentration-dependent elastic modulus on lithium diffusion and DIS generation using composition-gradient LCO cathode particles. They found that lithiation-induced stiffening regulates DIS in composition-gradient electrodes. Hong et al. [44] investigated the effects of concentration-dependent diffusivity, Young's modulus, and Poisson's ratio on stress evolution during lithiation of the Sn particle and concluded that the change in material properties with lithium content significantly alters mechanical failure modes. Cai and Guo [48] examined the effect of changing the diffusion coefficient and elastic modulus hardening with the lithium concentration on DIS in an anisotropic graphite anode particle. They found that diffusivity as a function of concentration increased concentration gradients and thus enhanced DIS because the change in the volume of the active material induced by the lithium concentration change is the main source of DIS. However, the effects of the concentration-dependent chemical expansion coefficient have rarely been investigated in the past. The study of nonlinear volume change and its effects on DIS is essential to determine strategies for avoiding mechanical failures in high-energy-density cathode materials such as NMC.

During charging, both the lattice parameters a and c of the NMC unit cell change strongly, which ultimately leads to a large change in the unit cell volume [52]. This volume change evolves nonlinearly with the lithium content. Distinct changes in the lattice structure are the main sources of stress generation that lead to various modes of mechanical cracks [53]. The disintegration and cracks induced by lithium diffusion in NMC materials disrupt the ionic and electronic conduction pathways [54]. Consequently, structural degradation accelerates the capacity decrease of NMC cathodes. However, the effects of the nonlinear volume change of NMC materials in stress diffusion problems have not yet received much attention.

In this paper, we focus on the effects of diffusion-induced nonlinear volume change on the evolution of lithium concentration distributions and the related stress development. To achieve the goal, we first calculated the partial molar volume (chemical expansion coefficient) based on experimentally obtained volume change values given in reference [52]. Next, we simulated the charging (delithiation) phenomenon in a single NMC particle using the concentration-dependent partial molar volume under galvanostatic charging conditions. We then compared the results of the constant and variable (concentration-dependent) partial molar volumes to evaluate the effects of the nonlinear volume change on the chemomechanical response of the NMC-active material. The main objectives of this paper are as follows:

1. To construct a fully coupled finite element chemomechanical model in order to investigate the effects of a concentration-dependent partial molar volume on the mechanical response of NMC particle.
2. To study and compare the simulation results for the constant and concentration-dependent partial molar volume of the NMC particle during the charging (delithiation) process.
3. To investigate the simultaneous effects of the particle size or the charging rate and the concentration-dependent partial molar volume on the mechanical response of the NMC-active material.

The rest of the paper is organized as follows: we first developed a fully coupled chemomechanical model that considered the local effects of a nonlinear volume change on the distribution of stress and lithium concentration. We then validated the application of the concentration-dependent partial molar volume by comparing the finite element simulation results with the experimentally obtained volume changes. Afterwards, we compared the stress and lithium concentration results for the constant and variable (concentration-dependent) partial molar volumes for the delithiation (charging) process. We then evaluated the effects of the particle size and charge rate. Finally, the article is concluded in the last section.

2. Methodology

For numerical simulations, an isolated active particle with a radius R_s was considered, as shown in Figure 1. The axisymmetric model system and its spatial discretization for a representative case of lithiation are illustrated in Figure 1a,b, respectively. We employed full coupling between lithiation/delithiation kinetics and mechanics of diffusion-induced deformations. The computational modeling of this fully coupled chemomechanical model is presented in the following subsections.

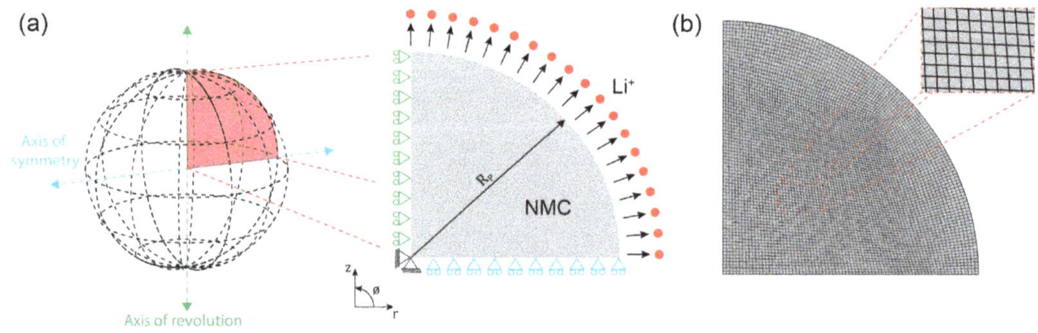

Figure 1. (**a**) Schematic representation and (**b**) spatial discretization of an axisymmetric model system used to perform numerical simulations.

2.1. Fully Coupled Chemomechanical Model

2.1.1. Modeling of Lithium Ion Diffusion in an Active Particle

The diffusion of lithium ions inside the active particle was assumed to follow Fick's law [55]:

$$\frac{\partial c}{\partial t} + \nabla \cdot \mathbf{J} = 0 \tag{1}$$

where c is the lithium ion molar concentration; t is the lithiation/delithiation time, and $\mathbf{J}$ is the lithium ion flux inside the active material. The flux $\mathbf{J}$ is defined as a function of chemomechanical potential as [9]:

$$\mathbf{J} = -M\,c\,\nabla\mu \tag{2}$$

where M is the mobility factor given by $M = D/RT$, and μ is the stress-dependent chemical potential, which can be defined by hydrostatic stress (σ_h) as [9]:

$$\mu = \mu^o + RT\ln X - \Omega\sigma_h \tag{3}$$

where μ^o is the reference state potential; R is the universal gas constant; T is the absolute temperature; X is the molar fraction, and Ω is the partial molar volume. Combining Equations (2) and (3) leads to:

$$\mathbf{J} = -D\left(\nabla c - \frac{c}{RT}\nabla(\Omega\sigma_h)\right) \tag{4}$$

Finally, putting Equation (4) to Equation (1) gives the final form of the partial differential equation for solving lithium concentrations in a coupled stress–concentration manner [56]:

$$\frac{\partial c}{\partial t} - D\nabla^2 c + \frac{D}{RT}\nabla c \cdot \nabla(\Omega\sigma_h) + \frac{Dc}{RT}\nabla^2(\Omega\sigma_h) = 0 \tag{5}$$

The third and fourth terms on the left-hand side of Equation (5) result from the stress–concentration coupling. Thus, without stress–concentration coupling, the partial differential equation above reduces to:

$$\frac{\partial c}{\partial t} - D\nabla^2 c = 0 \tag{6}$$

2.1.2. Modeling of Diffusion-Induced Stress

The DIS in the active particle was solved by the following partial differential equation for mechanical equilibrium [20]:

$$\nabla \cdot \boldsymbol{\sigma} + \mathbf{F}_b = 0 \tag{7}$$

where $\boldsymbol{\sigma}$ is the Cauchy stress tensor, and $\mathbf{F}_b$ is the body fore. In this work, no body force was assumed, so $\mathbf{F}_b = \mathbf{0}$. For elastic deformations during the charging/discharging process, the stress–strain relationship is governed by Hook's law as [33]:

$$\boldsymbol{\sigma} = \mathbf{C} : \boldsymbol{\varepsilon}_e \tag{8}$$

where $\mathbf{C}$ is the fourth-order stiffness matrix, and $\boldsymbol{\varepsilon}_e$ is the elastic strain. The total strain caused by the elastic and diffusion-induced deformations is given as [33]:

$$\boldsymbol{\varepsilon}_t = \boldsymbol{\varepsilon}_e + \boldsymbol{\varepsilon}_d = \frac{1}{2}\left((\nabla u)^{\mathrm{T}} + \nabla u\right) \tag{9}$$

where $\boldsymbol{\varepsilon}_t$ and $\boldsymbol{\varepsilon}_d$ are the total and diffusion-induced strains, and u denotes the displacement field. Thus, the elastic strain is calculated by subtracting the diffusion-induced strain from the total strain as [9,14]:

$$\boldsymbol{\varepsilon}_e = \boldsymbol{\varepsilon}_t - \boldsymbol{\varepsilon}_d \tag{10}$$

For the DIS calculations, the diffusion strain was calculated using the thermal analogy [8,9,57] as:

$$\boldsymbol{\varepsilon}_d = \frac{1}{3}\tilde{c}\Omega\mathbf{I} \tag{11}$$

where $\tilde{c}$ is the concentration difference between the current and the initial state, and $\mathbf{I}$ is the identity matrix. In another method, using directly the volume change ($\Delta V/V_o$) obtained from the experiments, the diffusion-induced strain can be represented by the following diffusion-induced deformation gradient F_d:

$$F_d = \left(1 + \frac{\Delta V}{V_o}\right)^{1/3} \mathbf{I} \tag{12}$$

2.2. Material Properties and Numerical Simulations

To perform the finite element fully coupled chemomechanical simulations, the structural mechanics and transport of the dilute species modules of COMSOL Multiphysics (version 6.0) was employed in this work. The partial differential equation of the mechanical equilibrium was solved in the structural mechanics' module, while the partial differential equations of the mass balance of lithium ions inside the active material were solved using the transport of the dilute species module. The built-in parallel sparse direct solver (PARDISO) transient solver was used to solve the weak forms of partial differential equations in a fully coupled manner. The delithiation phenomenon was modeled by applying a constant negative flux to the exposed surfaces of the active particle. The partial differential equations were solved in time increments until the local minimum state of charge reached the lower limit of the respective NMC-active material. To explore the effects of the concentration-dependent volume change of the active material, a representative case of 2 μm particle size of $LiNi_{1/3}Mn_{1/3}Co_{1/3}O_2$ (NMC-111) at 1C charge/discharge rate was considered, unless otherwise specified. Furthermore, the following initial and boundary conditions were considered to solve the partial differential equations given in Equations (5) and (7).

Initial conditions: At the start of the simulation, it was assumed that the maximum lithium concentrations (c_{max}) were homogeneously distributed throughout the NMC active particles as:

$$c = c_{total} \text{ at } t = 0 \tag{13}$$

where c_{total} is the stoichiometric lithium concentration in the NMC material. To solve the partial differential equation of mechanical equilibrium Equation (7), initially no stress was considered in the particle as:

$$(\nabla \cdot \boldsymbol{\sigma})_{t=0} = \mathbf{0} \tag{14}$$

Boundary conditions: To solve the issue of lithium diffusion inside the particle, a constant lithium flux was applied to the particle surface, such as:

$$\mathbf{J} \cdot \mathbf{n} = -\frac{i_n}{F} = -\frac{C_{rate}\alpha\rho}{F} \times \frac{R_s}{3} \tag{15}$$

where $\mathbf{n}$, i_n, F, and C_{rate} denote the outward normal unit vector on the external surface of the particle, the current density, the Faraday's constant, and the charging rate, respectively. The α, ρ, and R_s are the specific capacity, density, and radius of the active particle, respectively.

To quantify the effects of the nonlinear volume change, during the simulation the total volume change of the active material was calculated as:

$$\frac{\Delta V}{V_o} = \frac{\left(\int dv\right)_{t=t} - V_{t=0}}{V_{t=0}} \tag{16}$$

where ΔV is the change in particle volume between the current (at $t = t$) and initial (at $t = 0$) delithiation state. To explore the mechanical response of active materials, the maximum first principal stress (σ_{max}) was calculated and compared for various cases. Further, to investigate the change in lithium concentration behavior, the difference between the maximum and minimum states of charge (ΔSOC) was evaluated as:

$$\Delta SOC = \frac{c_{max} - c_{min}}{c_{total}} \times 100\% \tag{17}$$

where $c_{\max}$ and $c_{\min}$ are local maximum and minimum lithium concentrations. Finally, to assess the change in charge storage, the normalized capacity (Π) of the active particle was calculated as follows:

$$\Pi = \frac{F\int c dv}{\alpha\rho V_o} \tag{18}$$

where Π will change between 1 and 0 during delithiation.

The convergence of both the maximum stress (σ_{max}) and change in state of charge (ΔSOC) parameters was confirmed by increasing the degrees of freedom by refining the mesh size. According to the mesh independence test, the simulations were carried out with 5673 mesh elements and 46,356 degrees of freedom.

Concentration-Dependent Partial Molar Volume

To calculate the concentration-dependent partial molar volume, the volume change data during the delithiation process of NMC materials were obtained from reference [52]. The concentration-dependent partial molar volume of each NMC structure (i.e., NMC-111, $LiNi_{0.5}Mn_{0.2}Co_{0.3}O_2$ (NMC-523), $LiNi_{0.6}Mn_{0.2}Co_{0.2}O_2$ (NMC-622), and $LiNi_{0.8}Mn_{0.1}Co_{0.1}O_2$ (NMC-811)) was calculated separately. The volumetric strain (λ) due to the volume change caused by the delithiation was calculated as:

$$\lambda = \left(\frac{\Delta V}{V_o} + 1\right)^{1/3} - 1 = \left(\frac{V_{x=x} - V_{x=x_{max}}}{V_{x=x_{max}}} + 1\right)^{1/3} - 1 \tag{19}$$

where ΔV is the volume change that is calculated as the delithiation states increase. The $V_{x=x}$ is current, and $V_{x=x_{max}}$ is the initial (with maximum lithium content) unit cell volume. Based on this strain value, the partial molar volume is given by:

$$\Omega = \frac{3 \times \lambda}{(x - x_{max}) \times c_{total}} \tag{20}$$

Using Equation (20), the concentration-dependent partial molar volume of each NMC was calculated and plotted in Figure 2. For simplicity, we proposed that other material properties, such as Young's modulus and diffusion coefficient of the active material, were independent of the lithium-ion concentrations. Other material properties and simulation parameters used in this work are listed in Table 1.

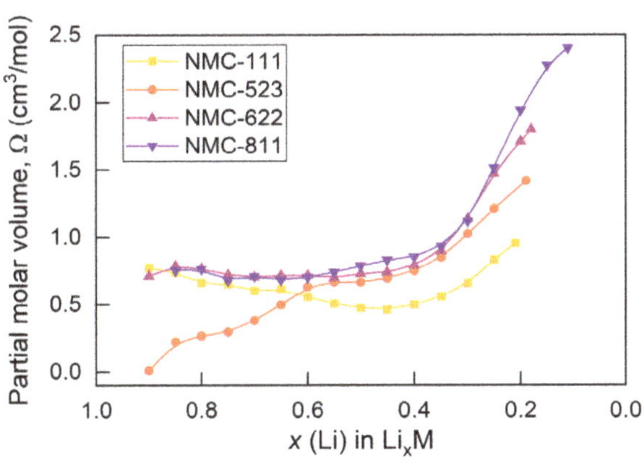

Figure 2. Calculated partial molar volume as the function of normalized lithium concentrations or lithium contents.

Table 1. Summary of simulation parameters and material properties for NMC materials used for numerical simulations.

Parameters	Symbols	Units	Values			
			NMC-111	NMC-523	NMC-622	NMC-811
Young's modulus [1]	E	GPa	202.98	191.79	181.52	194.4
Diffusion coefficient [2]	D	$m^2\ s^{-1}$	3.39×10^{-15}	3.89×10^{-15}	7.5×10^{-15}	4.0×10^{-14}
Specific capacity [3]	α	$mAh\ g^{-1}$	188.75	194.89	203.18	213.42
Stoichiometric lithium concentration [4]	c_{total}	$mol\ m^{-3}$	33,452	34,542	36,009	37,825
Minimum SOC [5]	SOC_{min}	%	21	19	18	11
Maximum SOC [6]	SOC_{max}	%	94	93	93	90
Poisson's ratio [7]	ν	-	0.25			
Density [8]	ρ	$kg\ m^{-3}$	4750			
Faraday's constant	F	$C\ mol^{-1}$	96,487			
Absolute temperature	T	K	300			
Universal gas constant	R	$J\ mol^{-1}\ K^{-1}$	8.314			

[1] Sun and Zhao [58]; [2] Wei et al. [59] and Huang et al. [60]; [3,5,6] de Biasi et al. [52]; [4] Calculated by $c_{total} = \alpha\rho/F$; [7] Cheng et al. [61]; [8] Mistry et al. [62].

3. Results and Discussions

3.1. Validations of Numerical Results

In this section, we validate the calculations of the concentration-dependent partial molar volume of NMC with different nickel contents; NMC-111, NMC-523, NMC-622, and NMC-811. If the distributions of lithium concentration inside the active particle are sufficiently homogenized, then the local volume change will equal the percentage of the total volume change of the active particle. Therefore, in Figure 3, we compare the results by plotting the global volume change obtained by simulating a small particle under a lower charge rate (i.e., $R_s = 2$ μm and $C_{rate} = 1C$) against the normalized charge capacity and the local volume change of the respective NMC material against the lithium content obtained from [52]. The close volume change values obtained from the simulations and the experiments suggest that this concentration-dependent partial molar volume can be used for stress calculations of NMC-active materials.

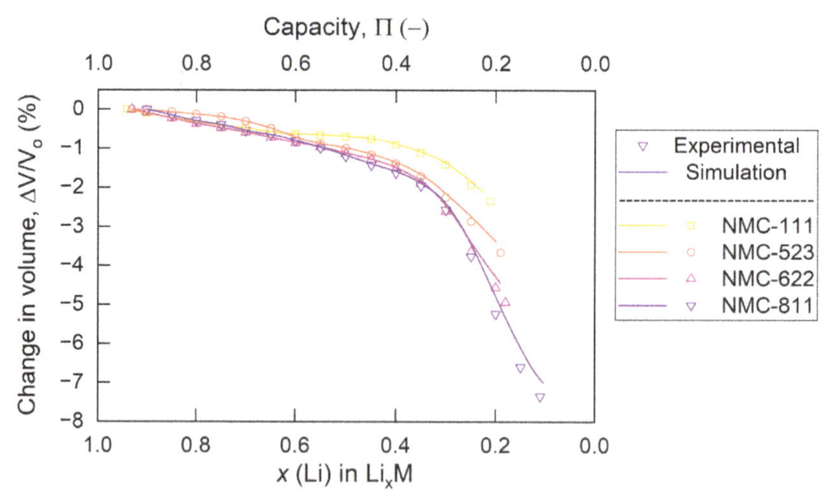

Figure 3. Local and global volume changes obtained by experiments (Adapted with permission from Ref. [52]. Copyright 2017, American Chemical Society.) and finite element simulations, respectively. The local volume change is plotted against the lithium content, and the global volume change is plotted against the normalized capacity of the various NMC materials.

Then, the simulation results obtained by directly using the local volume change as the intercalation strain (Equation (12)) and using the calculated concentration-dependent partial molar volume as the thermal analogy (Equation (11)) are compared in Figure 4. To avoid changes caused by stress–concentration coupling, only uncoupled simulations were performed in this section using Equation (6). All simulation results are similar either by using the intercalation strains or thermal analogy. This, therefore, proves the validity of the thermal analogy method and the use of concentration-dependent partial molar volume instead of the direct use of the local volume change as the volumetric strain in finite element simulations.

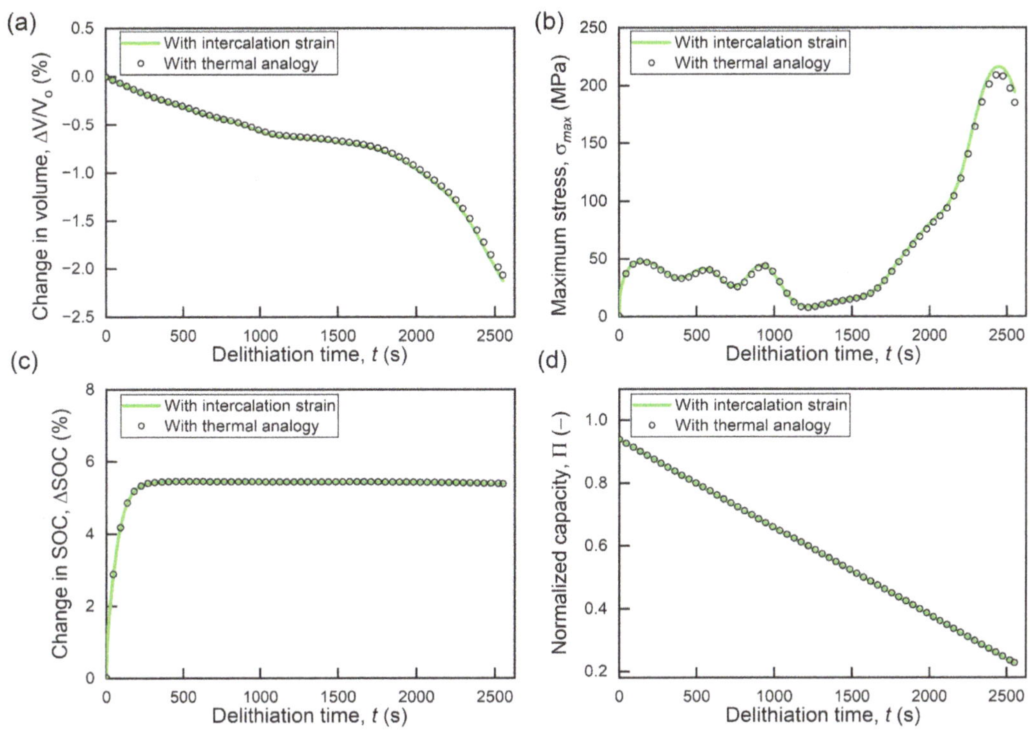

Figure 4. Validation of the use of concentration-dependent partial molar volume by performing simulations by intercalation strain and thermal analogy methods. (**a**) change in the total volume of the active particle ($\Delta V/V_o$), (**b**) the maximum value of the local first principal stress (σ_{max}), (**c**) the difference between maximum and minimum local charge states (ΔSOC), and (**d**) the normalized lithium charge capacity (Π) inside the active particle.

3.2. *Effects of Variable Partial Molar Volume*

Figure 5 compares the simulation results obtained for a representative case of a 2 μm NMC-111 particle at a discharge rate of 1C with and without considering the nonlinear local volume change during the delithiation process. Figure 5a shows that the total volume of the active particle ($\Delta V/V_o$) changes nonlinearly when the variable (concentration-dependent) partial molar volume (Ω_{var}) is considered. On the other hand, using a constant partial volume (Ω_{const}), the change of $\Delta V/V_o$ is linear. This indicates that the local volume change significantly affects the global volume change, suggesting that the local volume change will also increase the stress due to the surrounding constraints provided by the binder, other active particles, current collector, and separator.

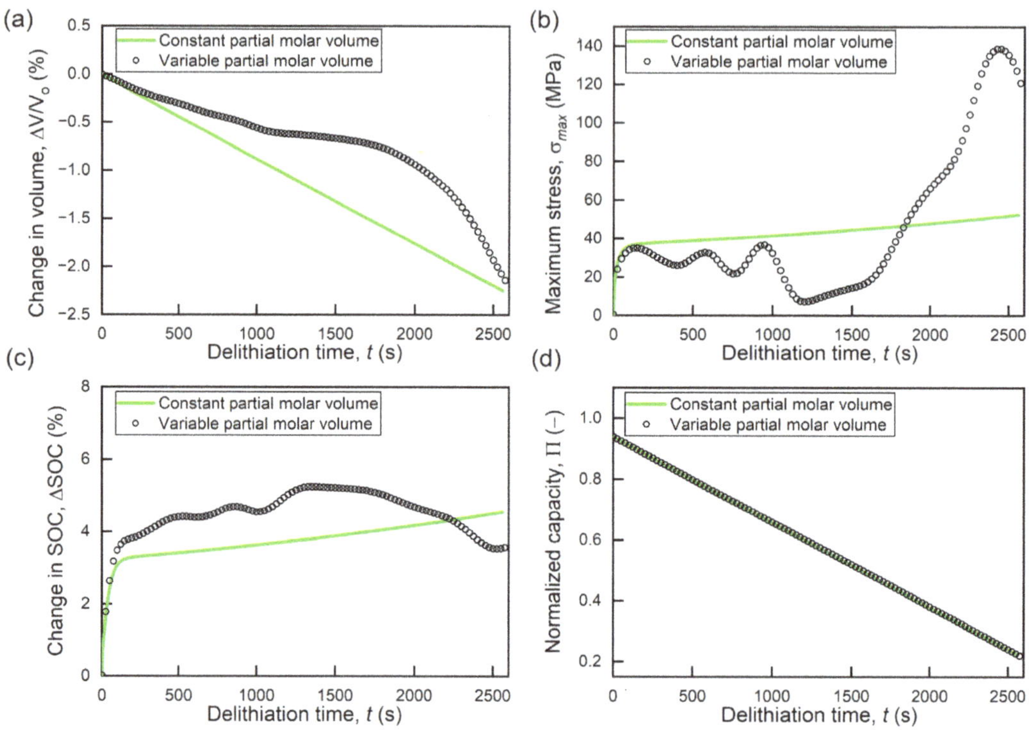

Figure 5. Comparison of the results of the delithiation process simulation with and without considering the concentration-dependent partial molar volume. (**a**) change in the total volume of the active particle ($\Delta V/V_o$), (**b**) the maximum value of the local first principal stress (σ_{max}), (**c**) the difference between the maximum and minimum local states of charge (ΔSOC), and (**d**) the normalized lithium charge capacity (Π) inside the active particle.

The evaluation of the stress generation caused by lithium diffusion is essential for the analysis of mechanical failure. For this purpose, the local maximum of the first principal stress (σ_{max}) was analyzed here. DIS developed because of the local mismatch of lithium concentration levels between the inner and outer regions of the active particle. This mismatch caused the regions to expand/contract based on the magnitude of the partial molar volume. Consequently, using Ω_{var}, the rate of volume change induced by lithium diffusion is different at different concentration levels, and the associated stress increase is different along the radial direction. As a result, σ_{max} evolves differently for Ω_{var}, as illustrated in Figure 5b. The evolution of σ_{max} reveals several smaller peaks before a larger peak toward the end of the delithiation process, while these peaks are not visible when Ω_{const} is used. Instead, σ_{max} increases gradually after achieving a distinct peak in the early stages of the delithiation process. Figure 5b also shows that the peak magnitude of σ_{max} is almost three times higher for the Ω_{var} case compared to the Ω_{const} case indicating a higher probability of mechanical failures. In summary, the evolution and levels of diffusion-induced stress in the active particle are significantly affected by the use of concentration-dependent partial molar volume. The reason for the appearance of such smaller peaks in the evolution of σ_{max} is given in the following paragraphs.

The maximum concentration difference in the active particle measures concentration gradients to some extent. Therefore, the maximum SOC difference (ΔSOC) was evaluated to express the change in the evolution of the concentration gradients. Figure 5c compares the evolution of ΔSOC using Ω_{const} and Ω_{var}. For Ω_{const}, ΔSOC initially increases sharply, and after reaching a distinct peak, the increase becomes more gradual. In the initial stages of a particle's delithiation, only the outermost regions undergo the deintercalation process, so, over time, the SOC difference between the surface and the core increases rapidly, but when the deintercalation front reaches the particle's core, the core starts to delithiate. The change in ΔSOC drops, which is the second stage of a gradual increase in ΔSOC. In contrast, when Ω_{var} is included, the change of ΔSOC becomes irregular. It is affected by either a local volume change or a stress change through stress–concentration coupling.

To explore the effects of the concentration-dependent partial molar volume on the capacity stored inside the active particle, the normalized capacity (Π) was compared for both the Ω_{const} and Ω_{var} cases, as shown in Figure 5c. The same capacity value was observed for both partial volume cases. This indicates that although the nonlinear local volume affects the particle's response to stress, the total stored charge remains the same.

Uncoupled numerical simulations were performed to isolate the effects of stress–concentration coupling and concentration-dependent partial molar volume on the SOC differences. In Figure 6a, the ΔSOC evolution is again plotted for Ω_{const} and Ω_{var}, without considering the coupling between the stress and concentration. The ΔSOC is the same for both partial molar volumes, although changes are still present in the evolution of σ_{max}, as shown in Figure 6b when Ω_{var} is considered. Thus, this proves that (1) changes in ΔSOC are caused by stress–concentration coupling, meaning that inhomogeneous stress levels due to nonlinear volume changes affect the lithium concentration levels, and (2) σ_{max} is not directly affected by the change in ΔSOC.

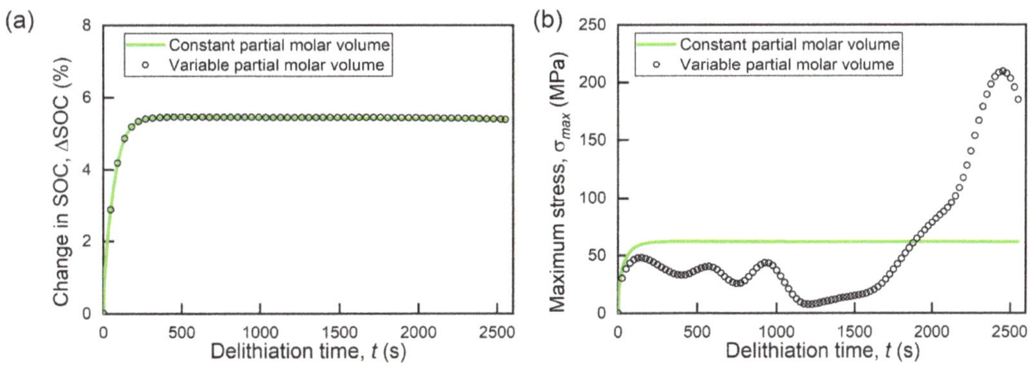

Figure 6. Comparison of results for uncoupled simulations. (**a**) The difference between the maximum and minimum local state of charges (ΔSOC). (**b**) The maximum value of the local first principal stress (σ_{max}).

Further, to figure out the mechanism underlying the stress response caused by the concentration-dependent partial molar volume, we investigated the rate of change of $\Delta V/V_o$ over time. The evolution of the 1st temporal derivative of $\Delta V/V_o$ was plotted with the evolution of σ_{max} in Figure 7. The trend of σ_{max} perfectly matches the trend of the 1st derivative of $\Delta V/V_o$. This proves that the change in maximum stress behavior is directly affected by the rate of change in $\Delta V/V_o$.

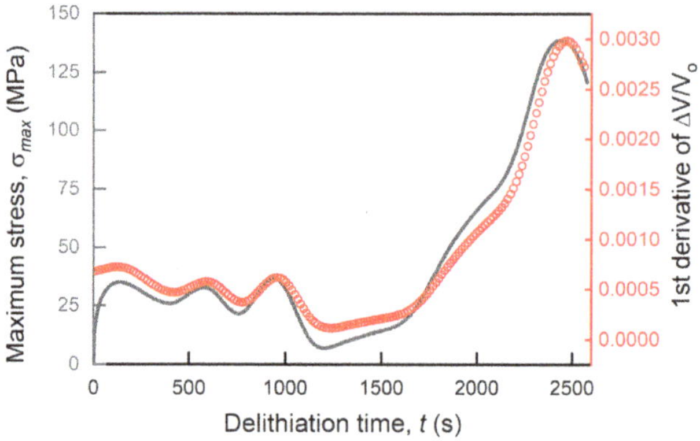

Figure 7. The delithiation time evolution of the maximum stress (σ_{max}) and the 1st derivative of the volume change ($\Delta V/V_o$).

We then investigated the effects of the concentration-dependent partial molar volume on the distribution patterns of the lithium concentration and the associated stress generation. It is clear from the comparison that the distribution patterns of the local lithium concentration and the first principal stress are consistent as the partial molar volume changes from constant to a variable. As shown in Figure 8a,b, the maximum local concentration of lithium occurs at the center of the particle, while the minimum occurs at the surface of the particle. Similarly, the local maximum first principal stress occurs at the surface of the particle, and the minimum stress occurs at the center of the particle, as shown in Figure 8c,d. This indicates that although the use of concentration-dependent partial volume enhances stress levels, it does not change the location of maximum stress.

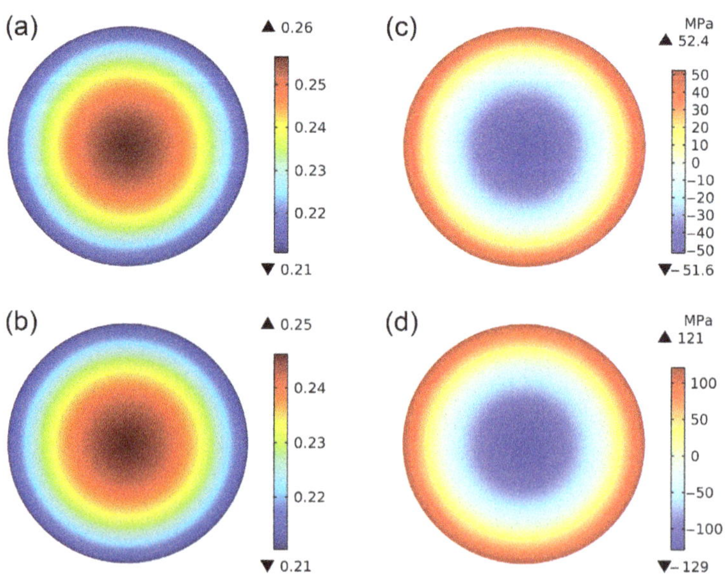

Figure 8. (**a**) Representative contour plots for (**a**,**b**) lithium concentration distributions (c/c_{total}) and (**c**,**d**) first principal stress at the end of the delithiation. The results (**a**,**c**) are based on a constant partial molar volume, and (**b**,**d**) were obtained using a concentration-dependent partial molar volume.

3.3. Effects of Particle Size

Usually, the particle size (R_s) inside the electrode varies. Particle size plays an essential role in the stress increase caused by lithium diffusion. Therefore, in this section, the particle size was changed from $R_s = 1$ μm to $R_s = 30$ μm in order to study the effects of concentration-dependent partial molar volume on the stress increase. Figure 9 compares the simulation results for various particle sizes with and without the use of a diffusion-induced nonlinear local volume change. The red dots to the right of each 3D plot represent the peak value during the delithiation time evolution of the corresponding parameter. The absolute (positive) volume change values are plotted in Figure 9 for better visibility and comparison of trends.

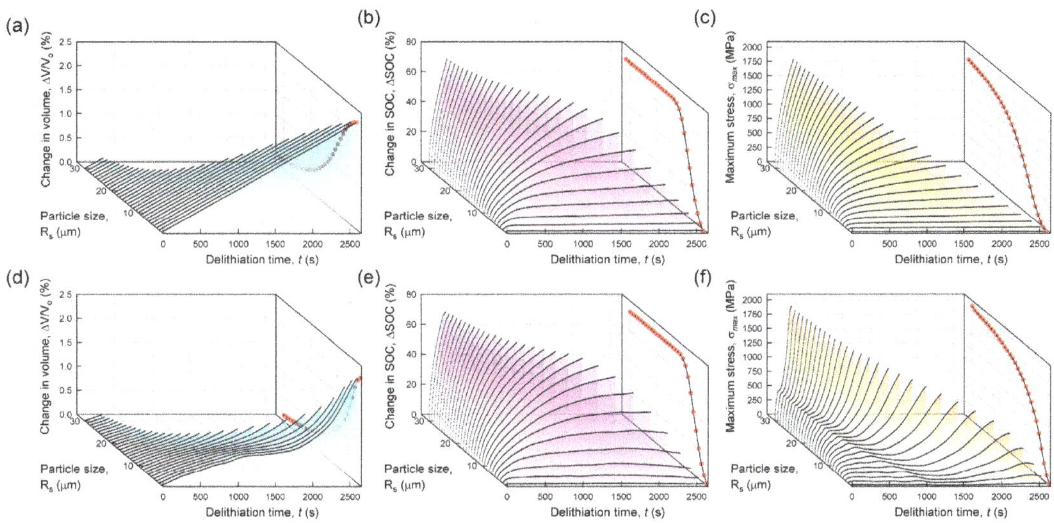

Figure 9. Impact of particle size (R_s) on the transient chemomechanical response during the delithiation process. The results (**a–c**) were obtained using a constant partial molar volume, and the results (**d–f**) were obtained using a variable partial molar volume. The red dots to the right of each graph denote the evolution of the peak values with respect to the particle size increase. (**a**,**d**) Evolution of the volume change ($\Delta V/V_o$) of particle size. (**b**,**e**) Evolution of the maximum difference in this state of charge (ΔSOC). (**c**,**f**) Evolution of the first principle maximum stress (σ_{max}) in the active particle.

In both cases, active particles with different R_s shrink in the same manner. However, for Ω_{const}, the volume change is linear, and for Ω_{var}, the volume change is nonlinear, as illustrated in Figure 9a,d, respectively. Moreover, as R_s increases, the peak values of volume change decrease, which is consistent for both cases of partial molar volume. The peak values of $\Delta V/V_o$ decrease because the stop condition for larger particles is achieved earlier, and the maximum volume achieved decreases. This indicates that the nonlinear volume change will have minimal effects for larger particles.

The ΔSOC curves in Figure 9b,e show that as R_s increases, the magnitude of ΔSOC increases significantly. Larger particles take longer to start delithiating the core, resulting in enhanced concentration gradients within the particle that remain for a longer period of time. As a consequence, ΔSOC increases. However, the trends and magnitude for both Ω_{const} and Ω_{var} remain almost the same, suggesting that the concentration-dependent partial molar volume has a minimal effect on ΔSOC with increasing particle size.

Meanwhile, as the concentration gradients increase, σ_{max} also increases, as shown in Figure 9c,f. Although the evolution in time and magnitude of σ_{max} for both the constants Ω_{const} and Ω_{var} are different, the trend in the rise of the peak value of σ_{max} with increasing R_s is the same. For larger particles, the difference between the peak values of σ_{max} is due to a very small volume change. In summary, the trends in the evolution of $\Delta V/V_o$, ΔSOC, and σ_{max} remain consistent, while R_s increases for both the Ω_{const} and Ω_{var} cases. However, the propensity for mechanical fracture increases with increasing particle size. Meanwhile the effects of concentration-dependent partial molar volume on the stress rise decrease for larger particles.

3.4. *Effects of Charge Rate*

Fast charging is the most desirable aspect of EVs. However, fast charging significantly increases the capacity degradation of lithium-ion batteries. Therefore, to explore the effects of fast charging in combination with the use of a concentration-dependent partial molar volume, the C_{rate} was varied from 0.5 C to 10 C with a difference of 0.5 C. Simulations were performed for $R_s = 2$ μm of the NMC-111-active particle.

Figure 10 shows that the evolution trends of $\Delta V/V_o$, ΔSOC, and σ_{max} are consistent for different C_{rates}, even when Ω_{var} was used. As the stopping condition of the numerical simulations was achieved earlier with an increasing C_{rate}, the peak magnitude of $\Delta V/V_o$ decreases, as presented in Figure 10a,d for Ω_{const} and Ω_{var}, respectively. Although the trends are consistent, the evolution of $\Delta V/V_o$ becomes nonlinear once the concentration-dependent partial molar volume is used.

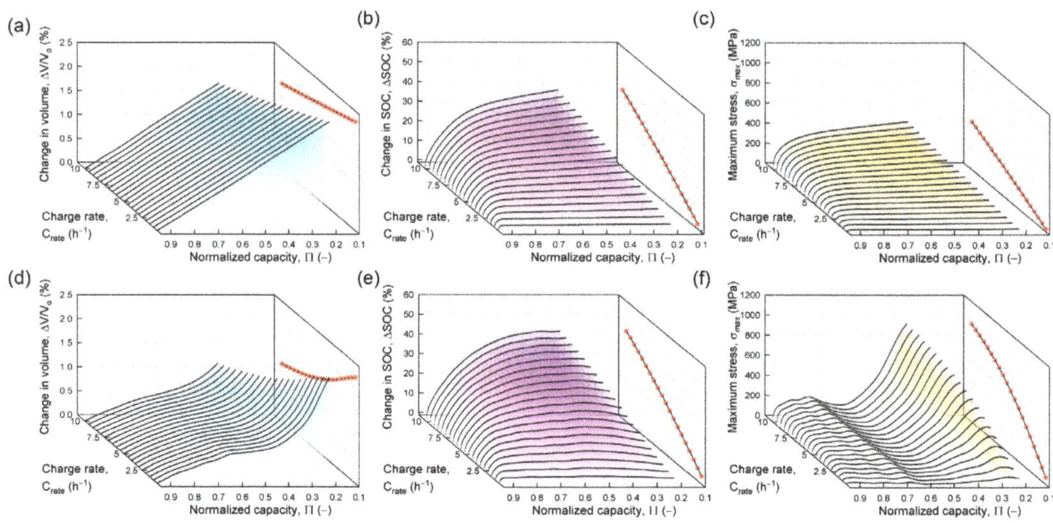

Figure 10. Impact of the charging rate (C_{rate}) on the transient chemomechanical response during the delithiation process. The results (**a–c**) were obtained using a constant partial molar volume, and the results (**d–f**) were obtained using a variable partial molar volume. The red dots to the right of each graph denote the evolution of the respective peak values. (**a**,**d**) Evolution of volume change ($\Delta V/V_o$) of the particle size. (**b**,**e**) Evolution of the maximum difference in this state of charge (ΔSOC). (**c**,**f**) Evolution of the first principle maximum stress (σ_{max}) in the active particle.

Furthermore, increasing the C_{rate} causes an increase in ΔSOC due to enhanced concentration gradients. Figure 10b,e show a slight increase in the ΔSOC values for Ω_{var} compared to Ω_{const}. This is caused by this stress–concentration coupling effect.

Moreover, small SOC differences for a lower C_{rate} indirectly indicate a more uniform distribution of lithium inside the particles and thus exhibit reduced concentration gradients. Since the lithium diffusion-induced strain mismatch is the main cause of stress generation, with smaller SOC differences, stress increase is also reduced for the lower C_{rate}. As the C_{rate} increases, σ_{max} in a given delithiation time increases. The increase in the stress raises the probability of fracture. Although trends in the evolution of σ_{max} remain consistent for

Ω_{const} and Ω_{var}, using Ω_{var}, the stress rise is significantly higher, as shown in Figure 10c,f for Ω_{const} and Ω_{var}, respectively. Thus, the propensity for mechanical failure increases significantly when using a concentration-dependent partial molar volume under fast charging conditions.

4. Conclusions

In this paper, the influence of a concentration-dependently local volume change of active materials on the lithium concentration evolution and diffusion-induced stress generation was studied by performing finite element simulations using a fully coupled chemomechanical model at the particle level. The concentration-dependent partial molar volume was calculated based on the previously obtained local nonlinear volume change of the NMC-active materials. We first validated the calculations of the partial molar volume by comparing the results of the global volume change obtained by finite element simulations with the local volume change values that were previously received in experiments described in the literature. We then compared the chemical and mechanical response of the active material with and without considering the concentration-dependent partial molar volume.

The main findings of this work are given below:

1. The local volume change induced by the concentration-dependent chemical expansion of the active material significantly alters the global volume change of the active particles, which suggests that the stress increase due to the surrounding materials in electrodes will be affected by the concentration-dependent partial molar volume of the active materials.
2. The concentration-dependent partial molar volume significantly changes the stress evolution trends and SOC differences. The peak stress due to diffusion is almost three times greater for a variable partial molar volume. However, the accumulated capacity within the particle remains independent of the change in partial molar volume.
3. The trends of the maximum diffusion-induced stress in the particle correlate with variations in the time rate of $\Delta V/V_0$ change (total volume change of particle). Although changes in the partial molar volume affect the stress response of the active particles, the lithium concentration patterns and stress distributions remain the same.
4. As the particle size increases, the propensity for mechanical failure increases with the use of the concentration-dependent partial molar volume. However, the effect of changing the partial molar volume on the stress rise decreases for larger particles.
5. Faster charging with a concentration-dependent partial molar volume increases diffusion-induced stress levels compared to using a constant partial molar volume.

Author Contributions: Conceptualization, N.I. and S.L.; methodology, N.I.; software, N.I., J.C., C.L., D.M., Y.K., J.K. and M.K.; validation, N.I., H.M.U.A., J.C., C.L., D.M., Y.K., J.K. and M.K.; investigation, N.I., J.C., C.L., D.M., Y.K., J.K. and M.K.; resources, S.L.; writing—original draft preparation, N.I. and J.C.; writing—review and editing, N.I., H.M.U.A. and S.L.; visualization, N.I. and H.M.U.A.; supervision, S.L.; project administration, S.L.; funding acquisition, S.L. All authors have read and agreed to the published version of the manuscript.

Funding: This research was supported by the National Research Foundation of Korea grants, funded by the Ministry of Science and ICT (No. 2018R1A5A7023490 and No. 2022R1A2C1003003).

Data Availability Statement: Not applicable.

Conflicts of Interest: The authors declare no conflict of interest.

References

1. Ding, Y.; Cano, Z.P.; Yu, A.; Lu, J.; Chen, Z. Automotive Li-Ion Batteries: Current Status and Future Perspectives. *Electrochem. Energ. Rev.* **2019**, *2*, 1–28. [CrossRef]
2. Nie, L.; Chen, S.; Liu, W. Challenges and strategies of lithium-rich layered oxides for Li-ion batteries. *Nano Res.* **2022**, 1–12. [CrossRef]
3. Armand, M.; Tarascon, J.-M. Building better batteries. *Nature* **2008**, *451*, 652–657. [CrossRef] [PubMed]

4. Lu, Z.; MacNeil, D.D.; Dahn, J.R. Layered cathode materials Li [Ni x Li (1/3− 2x/3) Mn (2/3− x/3)] O 2 for lithium-ion batteries. *Electrochem. Solid-State Lett.* **2001**, *4*, A191. [CrossRef]
5. Yabuuchi, N.; Ohzuku, T. Novel lithium insertion material of LiCo1/3Ni1/3Mn1/3O2 for advanced lithium-ion batteries. *J. Power Sources* **2003**, *119–121*, 171–174. [CrossRef]
6. Iqbal, N.; Choi, J.; Lee, C.; Khan, A.; Tanveer, M.; Lee, S. A Review on Modeling of Chemo-mechanical Behavior of Particle—Binder Systems in Lithium-Ion Batteries. *Multiscale Sci. Eng.* **2022**, *4*, 79–93. [CrossRef]
7. Ali, Y.; Iqbal, N.; Lee, S. Inhomogeneous stress development at the multiparticle electrode of lithium-ion batteries. *Int. J. Energy Res.* **2021**, *45*, 14788–14803. [CrossRef]
8. Christensen, J.; Newman, J. Stress generation and fracture in lithium insertion materials. *J. Solid State Electrochem.* **2006**, *10*, 293–319. [CrossRef]
9. Zhang, X.; Shyy, W.; Marie Sastry, A. Numerical Simulation of Intercalation-Induced Stress in Li-Ion Battery Electrode Particles. *J. Electrochem. Soc.* **2007**, *154*, A910. [CrossRef]
10. Deshpande, R.; Cheng, Y.-T.; Verbrugge, M.W.; Timmons, A. Diffusion Induced Stresses and Strain Energy in a Phase-Transforming Spherical Electrode Particle. *J. Electrochem. Soc.* **2011**, *158*, A718. [CrossRef]
11. Park, J.; Lu, W.; Sastry, A.M. Numerical Simulation of Stress Evolution in Lithium Manganese Dioxide Particles due to Coupled Phase Transition and Intercalation. *J. Electrochem. Soc.* **2011**, *158*, A201. [CrossRef]
12. Bai, Y.; Zhao, K.; Liu, Y.; Stein, P.; Xu, B.-X. A chemo-mechanical grain boundary model and its application to understand the damage of Li-ion battery materials. *Scr. Mater.* **2020**, *183*, 45–49. [CrossRef]
13. Barai, P.; Higa, K.; Ngo, A.T.; Curtiss, L.A.; Srinivasan, V. Mechanical Stress Induced Current Focusing and Fracture in Grain Boundaries. *J. Electrochem. Soc.* **2019**, *166*, A1752–A1762. [CrossRef]
14. Han, S.; Park, J.; Lu, W.; Sastry, A.M. Numerical study of grain boundary effect on Li+ effective diffusivity and intercalation-induced stresses in Li-ion battery active materials. *J. Power Sources* **2013**, *240*, 155–167. [CrossRef]
15. Zhao, K.; Pharr, M.; Vlassak, J.J.; Suo, Z. Fracture of electrodes in lithium-ion batteries caused by fast charging. *J. Appl. Phys.* **2010**, *108*, 073517. [CrossRef]
16. Lee, S.; Park, J.; Sastry, A.M.; Lu, W. Molecular Dynamics Simulations of SOC-Dependent Elasticity of LixMn2O4 Spinels in Li-Ion Batteries. *J. Electrochem. Soc.* **2013**, *160*, A968–A972. [CrossRef]
17. Schmidt, A.P.; Bitzer, M.; Imre, Á.W.; Guzzella, L. Experiment-driven electrochemical modeling and systematic parameterization for a lithium-ion battery cell. *J. Power Sources* **2010**, *195*, 5071–5080. [CrossRef]
18. Stein, P.; Xu, B. 3D Isogeometric Analysis of intercalation-induced stresses in Li-ion battery electrode particles. *Comput. Methods Appl. Mech. Eng.* **2014**, *268*, 225–244. [CrossRef]
19. Singh, G.; Bhandakkar, T.K. Semianalytical study of the effect of realistic boundary conditions on diffusion induced stresses in cylindrical Lithium ion electrode-binder system. *Int. J. Mech. Sci.* **2019**, *163*, 105141. [CrossRef]
20. Stein, P.; Moradabadi, A.; Diehm, M.; Xu, B.-X.; Albe, K. The influence of anisotropic surface stresses and bulk stresses on defect thermodynamics in LiCoO2 nanoparticles. *Acta Mater.* **2018**, *159*, 225–240. [CrossRef]
21. Pharr, M.; Suo, Z.; Vlassak, J.J. Variation of stress with charging rate due to strain-rate sensitivity of silicon electrodes of Li-ion batteries. *J. Power Sources* **2014**, *270*, 569–575. [CrossRef]
22. Ma, Z.S.; Xie, Z.C.; Wang, Y.; Zhang, P.P.; Pan, Y.; Zhou, Y.C.; Lu, C. Failure modes of hollow core–shell structural active materials during the lithiation–delithiation process. *J. Power Sources* **2015**, *290*, 114–122. [CrossRef]
23. Li, J.; Fang, Q.; Wu, H.; Liu, Y.; Wen, P. Investigation into diffusion induced plastic deformation behavior in hollow lithium ion battery electrode revealed by analytical model and atomistic simulation. *Electrochim. Acta* **2015**, *178*, 597–607. [CrossRef]
24. Wen, J.; Wei, Y.; Cheng, Y.-T. Stress evolution in elastic-plastic electrodes during electrochemical processes: A numerical method and its applications. *J. Mech. Phys. Solids* **2018**, *116*, 403–415. [CrossRef]
25. Colclasure, A.M.; Smith, K.A.; Kee, R.J. Modeling detailed chemistry and transport for solid-electrolyte-interface (SEI) films in Li–ion batteries. *Electrochim. Acta* **2011**, *58*, 33–43. [CrossRef]
26. Deng, J.; Wagner, G.J.; Muller, R.P. Phase Field Modeling of Solid Electrolyte Interface Formation in Lithium Ion Batteries. *J. Electrochem. Soc.* **2013**, *160*, A487–A496. [CrossRef]
27. Liu, L.; Park, J.; Lin, X.; Sastry, A.M.; Lu, W. A thermal-electrochemical model that gives spatial-dependent growth of solid electrolyte interphase in a Li-ion battery. *J. Power Sources* **2014**, *268*, 482–490. [CrossRef]
28. Gao, E.; Lu, B.; Zhao, Y.; Feng, J.; Song, Y.; Zhang, J. Stress-Regulated Protocols for Fast Charging and Long Cycle Life in Lithium-Ion Batteries: Modeling and Experiments. *J. Electrochem. Soc.* **2021**, *168*, 060549. [CrossRef]
29. Iqbal, N.; Haq, I.U.; Lee, S. Chemo-mechanical model predicted critical SOCs for the mechanical stability of electrode materials in lithium-ion batteries. *Int. J. Mech. Sci.* **2022**, *216*, 107034. [CrossRef]
30. Iqbal, N.; Lee, S. Stress-regulated pulse charging protocols via coupled electrochemical-mechanical model for the mechanical stability of electrode materials in lithium-ion batteries. *J. Power Sources* **2022**, *536*, 231376. [CrossRef]
31. Iqbal, N.; Ali, Y.; Haq, I.U.; Lee, S. Progressive interface debonding in composite electrodes of Li-ion batteries via mixed-mode cohesive zone model: Effects of binder characteristics. *Compos. Struct.* **2021**, *259*, 113173. [CrossRef]
32. Klinsmann, M.; Rosato, D.; Kamlah, M.; McMeeking, R.M. Modeling crack growth during Li extraction and insertion within the second half cycle. *J. Power Sources* **2016**, *331*, 32–42. [CrossRef]

33. Xu, R.; Yang, Y.; Yin, F.; Liu, P.; Cloetens, P.; Liu, Y.; Lin, F.; Zhao, K. Heterogeneous damage in Li-ion batteries: Experimental analysis and theoretical modeling. *J. Mech. Phys. Solids* **2019**, *129*, 160–183. [CrossRef]
34. Guo, Z.-S.; Zhang, T.; Zhu, J.; Wang, Y. Effects of hydrostatic pressure and modulus softening on electrode curvature and stress in a bilayer electrode plate. *Comput. Mater. Sci.* **2014**, *94*, 218–224. [CrossRef]
35. He, Y.-L.; Hu, H.J.; Song, Y.-C.; Guo, Z.-S.; Liu, C.; Zhang, J.-Q. Effects of concentration-dependent elastic modulus on the diffusion of lithium ions and diffusion induced stress in layered battery electrodes. *J. Power Sources* **2014**, *248*, 517–523. [CrossRef]
36. Qi, Y.; Hector, L.G.; James, C.; Kim, K.J. Lithium Concentration Dependent Elastic Properties of Battery Electrode Materials from First Principles Calculations. *J. Electrochem. Soc.* **2014**, *161*, F3010. [CrossRef]
37. Sitinamaluwa, H.S.; Wang, M.C.; Will, G.; Senadeera, W.; Zhang, S.; Yan, C. Lithium concentration dependent structure and mechanics of amorphous silicon. *J. Appl. Phys.* **2016**, *119*, 245103. [CrossRef]
38. Xie, H.; Kang, Y.; Song, H.; Zhang, Q. Real-time measurements and experimental analysis of material softening and total stresses of Si-composite electrode. *J. Power Sources* **2019**, *424*, 100–107. [CrossRef]
39. Yang, B.; He, Y.-P.; Irsa, J.; Lundgren, C.A.; Ratchford, J.B.; Zhao, Y.-P. Effects of composition-dependent modulus, finite concentration and boundary constraint on Li-ion diffusion and stresses in a bilayer Cu-coated Si nano-anode. *J. Power Sources* **2012**, *204*, 168–176. [CrossRef]
40. Zhang, T.; Guo, Z. Effects of electrode properties and fabricated pressure on Li ion diffusion and diffusion-induced stresses in cylindrical Li-ion batteries. *Model. Simul. Mater. Sci. Eng.* **2014**, *22*, 025016. [CrossRef]
41. Zhang, Y.; Zhan, S.; Zhang, K.; Zheng, B.; Lyu, L. Buckling behavior of a wire-like electrode with a concentration-dependent elastic modulus based on a deformed configuration. *Eur. J. Mech.-A/Solids* **2021**, *85*, 104111. [CrossRef]
42. Liu, Y.; Guo, K.; Wang, C.; Han, J.; Gao, H. Concentration dependent properties and plastic deformation facilitate instability of the solid-electrolyte interphase in Li-ion batteries. *Int. J. Solids Struct.* **2020**, *198*, 99–109. [CrossRef]
43. Weng, L.; Xu, C.; Chen, B.; Zhou, J.; Cai, R.; Shi, Y. A comparative study on ratcheting deformation between negative Poisson's ratio electrode and thin film electrode in Li-ion battery cyclic operation. *Mech. Mater.* **2020**, *150*, 103567. [CrossRef]
44. Hong, C.S.; Qaiser, N.; Nam, H.G.; Han, S.M. Effect of Li concentration-dependent material properties on diffusion induced stresses of a Sn anode. *Phys. Chem. Chem. Phys.* **2019**, *21*, 9581–9589. [CrossRef]
45. Dora, J.K.; Sengupta, A.; Ghosh, S.; Yedla, N.; Chakraborty, J. Stress evolution with concentration-dependent compositional expansion in a silicon lithium-ion battery anode particle. *J. Solid State Electrochem.* **2019**, *23*, 2331–2342. [CrossRef]
46. Malavé, V.; Berger, J.R.; Martin, P.A. Concentration-Dependent Chemical Expansion in Lithium-Ion Battery Cathode Particles. *J. Appl. Mech.* **2014**, *81*, 091005. [CrossRef]
47. Qian, Y.; Lu, B.; Bao, Y.; Zhao, Y.; Song, Y.; Zhang, J. Prelithiation design for suppressing delamination in lithium-ion battery electrodes. *Appl. Math. Mech.-Engl. Ed.* **2021**, *42*, 1703–1716. [CrossRef]
48. Cai, X.; Guo, Z. Influence of Li Concentration-Dependent Diffusion Coefficient and Modulus Hardening on Diffusion-Induced Stresses in Anisotropic Anode Particles. *J. Electrochem. Soc.* **2021**, *168*, 010517. [CrossRef]
49. Karami, A.; Nayebi, A. Kinematic hardening analysis of Li-ion battery with concentration-dependent material behaviours under cyclic charging and discharging. *J. Power Sources* **2020**, *461*, 228155. [CrossRef]
50. Deshpande, R.; Qi, Y.; Cheng, Y.-T. Effects of Concentration-Dependent Elastic Modulus on Diffusion-Induced Stresses for Battery Applications. *J. Electrochem. Soc.* **2010**, *157*, A967–A971. [CrossRef]
51. Zhang, K.; Li, Y.; Zheng, B. Effects of concentration-dependent elastic modulus on Li-ions diffusion and diffusion-induced stresses in spherical composition-gradient electrodes. *J. Appl. Phys.* **2015**, *118*, 105102. [CrossRef]
52. de Biasi, L.; Kondrakov, A.O.; Geßwein, H.; Brezesinski, T.; Hartmann, P.; Janek, J. Between Scylla and Charybdis: Balancing Among Structural Stability and Energy Density of Layered NCM Cathode Materials for Advanced Lithium-Ion Batteries. *J. Phys. Chem. C* **2017**, *121*, 26163–26171. [CrossRef]
53. Noh, H.-J.; Youn, S.; Yoon, C.S.; Sun, Y.-K. Comparison of the structural and electrochemical properties of layered Li [NixCoyMnz] O2 (x = 1/3, 0.5, 0.6, 0.7, 0.8 and 0.85) cathode material for lithium-ion batteries. *J. Power Sources* **2013**, *233*, 121–130. [CrossRef]
54. Mao, Y.; Wang, X.; Xia, S.; Zhang, K.; Wei, C.; Bak, S.; Shadike, Z.; Liu, X.; Yang, Y.; Xu, R.; et al. High-Voltage Charging-Induced Strain, Heterogeneity, and Micro-Cracks in Secondary Particles of a Nickel-Rich Layered Cathode Material. *Adv. Funct. Mater.* **2019**, *29*, 1900247. [CrossRef]
55. Iqbal, N.; Ali, Y.; Lee, S. Chemo-mechanical response of composite electrode systems with multiple binder connections. *Electrochim. Acta* **2020**, *364*, 137312. [CrossRef]
56. Takahashi, K.; Higa, K.; Mair, S.; Chintapalli, M.; Balsara, N.; Srinivasan, V. Mechanical degradation of graphite/PVDF composite electrodes: A model-experimental study. *J. Electrochem. Soc.* **2016**, *163*, A385–A395. [CrossRef]
57. Ryu, I.; Choi, J.W.; Cui, Y.; Nix, W.D. Size-dependent fracture of Si nanowire battery anodes. *J. Mech. Phys. Solids* **2011**, *59*, 1717–1730. [CrossRef]
58. Sun, H.; Zhao, K. Electronic structure and comparative properties of LiNi x Mn y Co z O2 cathode materials. *J. Phys. Chem. C* **2017**, *121*, 6002–6010. [CrossRef]
59. Wei, Y.; Zheng, J.; Cui, S.; Song, X.; Su, Y.; Deng, W.; Wu, Z.; Wang, X.; Wang, W.; Rao, M.; et al. Kinetics tuning of Li-ion diffusion in layered Li (Ni x Mn y Co z) O2. *J. Am. Chem. Soc.* **2015**, *137*, 8364–8367. [CrossRef]

60. Huang, X.; Zhu, W.; Yao, J.; Bu, L.; Li, X.; Tian, K.; Lu, H.; Quan, C.; Xu, S.; Xu, K.; et al. Suppressing structural degradation of Ni-rich cathode materials towards improved cycling stability enabled by a Li_2 MnO_3 coating. *J. Mater. Chem. A* **2020**, *8*, 17429–17441. [CrossRef]
61. Cheng, E.J.; Hong, K.; Taylor, N.J.; Choe, H.; Wolfenstine, J.; Sakamoto, J. Mechanical and physical properties of LiNi0. 33Mn0. 33Co0. 33O2 (NMC). *J. Eur. Ceram. Soc.* **2017**, *37*, 3213–3217. [CrossRef]
62. Mistry, A.; Juarez-Robles, D.; Stein, M.; Smith, K.; Mukherjee, P.P. Analysis of long-range interaction in lithium-ion battery electrodes. *J. Electrochem. Energy Convers. Storage* **2016**, *13*, 031006. [CrossRef]

mathematics

MDPI

Article

Numerical Investigation on a Diffuser-Augmented Horizontal Axis Tidal Stream Turbine with the Entropy Production Theory

Wei Zang [1], Yuan Zheng [1,2], Yuquan Zhang [1,2,3,*], Xiangfeng Lin [3], Yanwei Li [2] and Emmanuel Fernandez-Rodriguez [4]

[1] College of Water Conservancy and Hydropower Engineering, Hohai University, Nanjing 210098, China
[2] College of Energy and Electrical Engineering, Hohai University, Nanjing 210098, China
[3] College of Harbor Coastal and Offshore Engineering, Hohai University, Nanjing 210098, China
[4] Technological Institute of Merida, Technological Avenue, Merida 97118, Mexico
* Correspondence: zhangyq@hhu.edu.cn

Abstract: An implication of a turbine current is the development of a wake, a reduced speed flow, thus affecting the performance of an adjoined turbine. The aim of this study is to examine the turbine wake properties to offer a basic framework for the exploration of efficient turbine arrangements through the OpenFOAM source package and the entropy production theory. The results indicate that the diffuser inlet produces the largest entropy rate; however, this dissipates quickly after the rotor plane. In terms of vorticity, the Q and λ_2-criterion results are sensitive to the isosurface thresholds. In general, the Ω-Rortex method proves a convenient and accurate solution for vortex visualization and identification. For the overall mean wake structure, the velocity profile follows a tadpole-shape, whilst the velocity deficits above 100% are observed around the nacelle and throat (diffuser) and behind the tower. The concentration of maximum turbulent intensities appears behind the throat of the diffuser and at the top and bottom of the tower. Owing to the swirling effect after rotor, we proposed recommended values of $b_0 = 10^{-5}$ for the hydrodynamic investigation of tidal stream turbines. The present findings extend our knowledge on the flow disruption due to shrouded turbines and are particularly relevant for farm project advisors.

Keywords: diffuser-augmented tidal stream turbine; near wake structure; turbulent intensity; entropy production theory; Rortex criterion

MSC: 76D25

Citation: Zang, W.; Zheng, Y.; Zhang, Y.; Lin, X.; Li, Y.; Fernandez-Rodriguez, E. Numerical Investigation on a Diffuser-Augmented Horizontal Axis Tidal Stream Turbine with the Entropy Production Theory. *Mathematics* **2023**, *11*, 116. https://doi.org/10.3390/math11010116

Academic Editor: Michael Todinov

Received: 30 November 2022
Revised: 17 December 2022
Accepted: 21 December 2022
Published: 27 December 2022

1. Introduction

As petroleum power phases out, researchers focus on renewable and predictable power sources to combine with energy storage systems, with the aim of restoring the ecosystem balance. A promising approach is the deployment of multiple underwater turbines at tidal stream sites with great speeds (1~2 m/s [1]) and smooth profile velocities due to the negative consequences of turbulence, such as excessive response [2] and structural-induced vibration on the turbine components. Although widely considered to be a predictable resource [3], the turbine supports are exclusively for low channel depths, therefore, forbidding large rotor size, although they can produce the same power output of a standard, similar wind turbine using a smaller diameter due to larger flow density. Currently, many authors still focus on the viability of unshrouded 3-bladed horizontal axis turbines as a result of simpleness, competitive capital costs and reliability, although new designs report higher efficiencies using diffuser casings [4,5], despite using a smaller rotor size owing to a higher flow concentration along the blades. This is achieved mainly through the diffuser, owing to the increase of flow pressure in the downstream section, and reduction afterwards the rotor. As a result, the current tends to converge in the inlet section, leading to a greater energy capture per rotor area and velocity across the turbine, compared to the free-stream condition. Despite the power benefits, even at misaligned flows [6] and the possibility of harnessing sites with lower than conventional profitable current speeds; further work is required to not only justify the diffuser costs but also assess the environmental and social risks. In addition, little is known about its performance in unsteady, as well as the effects of channel blockage and water environment, such as marine fouling and cavitation.

It is widely accepted that the positioning of the turbines within the resource is influential in the project assessment, since their functioning emits a wake, a reduction of current speed compared to the upstream section. This effect appears to be linked with the operation of the turbine, configuration of the entire device (e.g., type of support [7]) and inflow characteristics, and may merge with nearby wakes, thus influencing the upstream flow of the turbines afterwards. Although theories of the wake field are abundant, it is alleged that the wake interactions may be understood better through quantifications of the patterns and mechanisms of the single turbine wake in terms of the operating flow characteristics: turbulence intensities, depth-dependent velocity, and length scale profiles [8]. Nonetheless, most experimental and theoretical studies have been focused on single unshrouded rather than shrouded tidal stream turbines operating in low turbulent and with specific wave flows [9,10]. Thereby, it is unclear to what extent the diffuser affects the inflow properties and tower and wingtip vortices, determinants of the device efficiency and wake evolution. One way to investigate the optimum position of arrays is to predict through Computational Fluid Dynamic (CFD) programs the flow induced by the front turbines to the next rows of turbines, in terms of the entropy production [11]. The increase of the turbine downstream flow entropy is known to be inevitable and associated with lower subsequent device efficiency [12], hence the measure can serve as a tool for quantifying the resource potential and determining the parameters of a shrouded turbine system for reducing the overall losses and wake lengths.

Consequently, this paper considers the entropy theory as a main subject, to predict the downstream flow and visualize the vortex structure, along with the developed turbulence intensity. It is divided into three subsequent sections. The second section deals with the methodology, as well as the parameters to measure the entropy production and the vortex identification methods. The third section shows the computational set up and validation against experimental measurements of a scaled rotor. The fourth section discusses findings and results, and the fifth the conclusions.

2. Methodology

2.1. Governing Equation

Assuming that the fluid is incompressible, based on the law of mass and momentum conservation, the continuity and momentum equation of Navier–Stokes equation are evaluated as:

$$\nabla \cdot \boldsymbol{u} = 0 \tag{1}$$

$$\rho \frac{\partial \boldsymbol{u}}{\partial t} + \rho \nabla \cdot (\boldsymbol{u}\boldsymbol{u}) = -\nabla p + \nabla \cdot \boldsymbol{\tau} + \boldsymbol{F}_s \tag{2}$$

where $\boldsymbol{F}_s$ represents the body force which acts on the control volume. For Newtonian fluids, the shear stress tensor $\boldsymbol{\tau}$ has a linear relationship with the velocity vector $\boldsymbol{u}$:

$$\boldsymbol{\tau} = 2\mu S \tag{3}$$

where μ is the dynamic viscosity, $\boldsymbol{S} = 0.5 \cdot \left(\nabla \boldsymbol{u} + \nabla \boldsymbol{u}^{\mathrm{T}}\right)$ is the rate of deformation of the isotropy fluid, and the equation can be further expressed as:

$$\rho \frac{\partial \boldsymbol{u}}{\partial t} + \rho \nabla \cdot (\boldsymbol{u}\boldsymbol{u}) = -\nabla p + \nabla \cdot (\mu \nabla \boldsymbol{u}) + \boldsymbol{F}_s \tag{4}$$

Time averages the instantaneous values of the equation and omits the source term $\boldsymbol{F}_s$, and the equation becomes:

$$\rho \frac{\partial \mathbf{U}}{\partial t} + \rho \nabla \cdot (\mathbf{U}\mathbf{U}) = -\nabla P + \nabla \cdot \overline{\tau} - \nabla \cdot \boldsymbol{\tau}_R \tag{5}$$

According to Reynolds averaging, the instantaneous velocity can be split as $\boldsymbol{u} = \mathbf{U} + \boldsymbol{u}'$; here, $\mathbf{U}$ and $\boldsymbol{u}'$ are mean and fluctuating vectors. $P = \overline{p}$ is time–mean pressure. $\overline{\tau} = \mu(\nabla \mathbf{U} + \nabla \mathbf{U}^{\mathrm{T}})$, and $\boldsymbol{\tau}_R$ represents viscous and Reynolds stress, respectively. In general, Reynolds stress is much greater than the viscous stress in the turbulent core. Hence, it is crucial to model Reynolds stress.

The Boussinesq eddy viscosity assumption determined that Reynolds stress $(\boldsymbol{\tau}_R)$ conforms to the following linear relationship:

$$-\boldsymbol{\tau}_R = \mu_t \left(\nabla \mathbf{U} + \nabla \mathbf{U}^{\mathrm{T}} \right) \tag{6}$$

where $\mu_t = \rho \nu_t$ is dynamic turbulent viscosity, and ν_t is kinematic turbulent viscosity. Let $\nu_{\text{eff}} = \nu + \nu_t$, $P_{\text{eff}} = P + 2/3 \cdot \rho k$ and, substituting $\boldsymbol{\tau}_R$ into Equation (5), RANS (Reynolds averaged Navier–Stokes) equation is expressed as:

$$\frac{\partial \mathbf{U}}{\partial t} + \nabla \cdot (\mathbf{U}\mathbf{U}) = -\frac{1}{\rho} \nabla P_{\text{eff}} + \nabla \cdot (\nu_{\text{eff}} \nabla \mathbf{U}) \tag{7}$$

2.2. Turbulence Model

As proposed by Menter [13,14], the SST $k - \omega$ model is a two-equation eddy-viscosity model whose accuracy has been widely validated. For the SST $k - \omega$ model used in OpenFOAM, the turbulence kinetic energy (k) equation of incompressible fluid is:

$$\frac{\partial k}{\partial t} + \nabla \cdot (\mathbf{U}k) - \nabla \cdot (D_k \nabla k) = P_k - \beta^* k \omega + S_k \tag{8}$$

The equation of specific dissipation rate (ω) can be expressed as:

$$\begin{aligned} \frac{\partial \omega}{\partial t} + \nabla \cdot (\mathbf{U}\omega) - \nabla \cdot (D_\omega \nabla \omega) =& \gamma \cdot \min\left(\frac{G}{\nu_t}, \frac{c_1}{a_1} \beta^* \max\left(a_1 \omega, b_1 F_2 \sqrt{S_2} \right) \right) \\ & - \beta \omega^2 + (1 - F_1) C D_{k\omega} + S_w \end{aligned} \tag{9}$$

The kinematic eddy viscosity (ν_t) can be calculated as:

$$\nu_t = \frac{a_1 k}{\max(\alpha_1 \omega, b_1 F_2 S_2)} \tag{10}$$

where $S_2 = 2 \cdot |\mathbf{S}|^2$, and the auxiliary relations are defined as:

$$\begin{aligned} D_k &= B(F_1, \alpha_{k1}, \alpha_{k2}) \nu_t + \nu \\ D_\omega &= B(F_1, \alpha_{\omega 1}, \alpha_{\omega 2}) \nu_t + \nu \\ \beta &= B(F_1, \beta_1, \beta_2) \\ \gamma &= B(F_1, \gamma_1, \gamma_2) \\ B(a, b, c) &= ab + (1 - a)c \end{aligned} \tag{11}$$

The closure Coefficients in SST $k - \omega$ equations are:

$$
\begin{aligned}
P_k &= \min(G, c_1\beta^* k\omega) \\
CD_{k\omega} &= \frac{2\alpha_{\omega,2}(\nabla k \cdot \nabla\omega)}{\omega} \\
G &= 2\nu_t \cdot (\boldsymbol{S} : \nabla \mathrm{U}) \\
F_1 &= \tanh\left(\min\left(\min\left(\max\left(\frac{\sqrt{k}}{\beta^*\omega y}, \frac{500\nu}{\omega y^2}\right), \frac{4\alpha_{\omega,2}k}{CD_{k\omega}y^2}\right), 10\right)\right)^4 \\
F_2 &= \tanh\left(\min\left(\max\left(\frac{2\sqrt{k}}{\beta^*\omega y}, \frac{500\nu}{\omega y^2}\right), 100\right)\right)^2 \\
F_3 &= 1 - \tanh\left(\min\left(\frac{150\nu}{\omega y^2}, 10\right)\right)
\end{aligned}
\tag{12}
$$

where y is the wall-distance, according to empirical value which was suggested by Menter [15], $\alpha_{k,1} = 0.85$, $\alpha_{k,2} = 1$, $\alpha_{\omega,1} = 0.5$, $\alpha_{\omega,2} = 0.856$, $\gamma_1 = 5/9$, $\gamma_2 = 0.44$, $\beta_1 = 0.075$, $\beta_2 = 0.0828$, $\beta^* = 0.09$, $a_1 = 0.31$, $b_1 = 1$, $c_1 = 10$.

2.3. Entropy Production Analysis

To analyze the energy transfer of free shear flows, the entropy production method can be used to present the irreversibility and energy deficit of the fluid system [16]. According to the Fourier heat conduction equation, for the incompressible fluid, the entropy transport per finite control volume is:

$$
\rho\left[\frac{\partial s}{\partial t} + \boldsymbol{u} \cdot (\nabla s)\right] = \nabla \cdot \left(\frac{\boldsymbol{q}}{T}\right) + \frac{\Phi_I}{T} + \frac{\Phi_{II}}{T^2} \tag{13}
$$

where s is the specific entropy, T is the thermodynamic temperature, and $\boldsymbol{q}$ represents the heat flux. Φ_I and Φ_{II} represent the dissipation functions of the fluid. As the entropy production caused by radiation is negligible, the entropy production rate $\dot{s}$ can be expressed as:

$$
\dot{s} = \frac{\Phi_I}{T} + \frac{\Phi_{II}}{T^2} = \dot{s}_D + \dot{s}_T \tag{14}
$$

As seen in Equation (14), the entropy production rate consists of two terms that represent viscous ($\dot{s}_D$) and thermal ($\dot{s}_T$) contribution, respectively [17]. Since the main content of this article belongs to the field of ocean hydrodynamics, it is convenient to assume that the environment temperature is constant [18–22], and the contribution of the temperature gradient to entropy production is negligible ($\dot{s}_T \approx 0$). To reduce computational resource requirements, the energy equation is not solved in this numerical simulation. The entropy production rate can be further calculated by:

$$
\dot{s}_D = \frac{2\rho\nu \cdot \|\boldsymbol{S}\|^2}{T} \tag{15}
$$

where the notation $\|*\|$ represents a Frobenius norm of strain rate tensor $\boldsymbol{S}$, which can be split as: $\boldsymbol{S} = \overline{\boldsymbol{S}} + \boldsymbol{S}'$. The direct (time-averaged) and indirect (turbulent) entropy production rate ($\dot{s}_{VD}$ and $\dot{s}_{TD}$) are defined by:

$$
\dot{s}_{VD} = \frac{2\rho\nu \cdot \|\overline{\boldsymbol{S}}\|^2}{T} \tag{16}
$$

$$
\dot{s}_{TD} = \frac{2\rho\nu \cdot \|\boldsymbol{S}'\|^2}{T} \tag{17}
$$

With the Reynolds Averaged Navior Stokes method, the strain rate tensor of velocity fluctuation ($\boldsymbol{S}'$) cannot obtained directly from existing equations. However, in high Reynolds number flows, the turbulent production and dissipation rate are considered equal [23], namely: $2\nu \cdot \overline{S'S'} = \overline{u_i'u_j'} \cdot S$. Hence, with Boussinesq eddy viscosity assumption, the following relationship can be derived: $\nu \cdot \|S'\|^2 = \nu_t \cdot \|\overline{S}\|^2$. The entropy production rate ($\dot{s}_D$) per finite control volume can be further expressed as:

$$\dot{s}_D = \dot{s}_{VD} + \dot{s}_{TD} = \frac{2\rho(\nu + \nu_t) \cdot \|\overline{S}\|^2}{T} = \frac{2\rho\nu_{\text{eff}} \cdot \|\overline{S}\|^2}{T} \tag{18}$$

Furthermore, the total entropy production rate $\overline{S}$ can be calculated from the volume integral of $\dot{s}_D$ over the computational domain:

$$\overline{S} = \iiint_V \dot{s}_D \mathrm{d}v \tag{19}$$

2.4. Vortex Identification Methods

In order to analyze the entropy production characteristics in turbine wake, the structure of the vortex must be identified and visualized. It is necessary to outline the most commonly used vortex identification in the field of ocean hydrodynamics.

2.4.1. Vorticity Method

Vorticity is the most convenient method to identify wake vortices. It can be expressed as the curl of velocity vector: $\boldsymbol{\omega} = \nabla \times \boldsymbol{u}$. It is common to quantity the core of the vortex by the magnitude of vorticity ($|\omega|$) in free shear flows. However, the vorticity method cannot effectively extract the fluid swirling in the wall shear layer [24]. Thus, it is a fundamental identification method but not sufficient to identify the vortex in free shear turbulence.

2.4.2. Q and λ_2-Criterion

Q and λ_2-criteria are the most widely used vortex identification methods [25–27]. These methods are eigenvalue-based criteria that can be obtained from a velocity gradient tensor ($\nabla \boldsymbol{u}$). As the measurement of vorticity and strain rate magnitude, the criteria Q is expressed as:

$$Q = \frac{1}{2}\left(\nabla \cdot \boldsymbol{u} + \|\boldsymbol{\Omega}\|^2 - \|\boldsymbol{S}\|^2\right) \tag{20}$$

where $\boldsymbol{\Omega}$ is the rotation rate tensor defined by the skew-symmetric part of the velocity gradient tensor: $\boldsymbol{\Omega} = 0.5 \cdot \left(\nabla \boldsymbol{u} - \nabla \boldsymbol{u}^{\mathrm{T}}\right)$. For incompressible flows, $\nabla \cdot \boldsymbol{u} \equiv 0$, which means that Q is equal to the second invariant of $\nabla \boldsymbol{u}$ [28]. It can be directly calculated with the symmetric ($\boldsymbol{S}$) and skew-symmetric ($\boldsymbol{\Omega}$) terms of the matrix. The Q-criterion indicates the fluid region that has a positive second invariant of the velocity gradient tensor, which means that a larger rotational force component is observed.

Equation (20) indicates that the shear effect of an incompressible fluid is less than the rotational force. As another commonly used vortex identification method [29], λ_2-criterion is defined as the second eigenvalue λ_2 of the tensor $\boldsymbol{\Omega}^2 + \boldsymbol{S}^2$. It essentially represents the vortex core region that is associated with the negative eigenvalues of the matrix [28]; given this, $\lambda_2 < 0$. Nevertheless, for both the Q and λ_2 criteria method, it is difficult to separate the individual vortices in the multiple vortices coexisting environment.

2.4.3. Ω and Ω-Rortex Criterion

According to Liu et al. [30], the vortex identification criterion named Ω has been proposed, which could extract the rotational part from the vorticity of fluid. Ω is defined as a dimensionless scalar that is obtained by the ratio of the skew-symmetric part of the velocity gradient:

$$\Omega = \frac{\|\boldsymbol{\Omega}\|^2}{\|\boldsymbol{\Omega}\|^2 + \|\boldsymbol{S}\|^2 + \varepsilon} \tag{21}$$

where $\varepsilon = b_0 \cdot \max\left(\|\boldsymbol{\Omega}\|^2 - \|S\|^2\right)$ is a positive parameter to avoid dividing by zero and obtain an extremely large Ω. b_0 is a positive constant, which is further discussed in Section 4.

As a systematical definition of the local fluid rotation based on critical point theory [31], the Rortex/Liutex method utilizes the complex conjugate eigenvalues of $\nabla \boldsymbol{u}$ to represent the swirling of the fluid [32–34]. The local vector $\boldsymbol{r}_l$, named the Rortex vector, represents the rotation axis of local velocity gradient tensor and is defined as: $\nabla \boldsymbol{u} \cdot \boldsymbol{r}_l = \lambda_r \cdot \boldsymbol{r}_l$, and λ_r is the real eigenvalue of $\nabla \boldsymbol{u}$. To balance the sign of the Rortex vector, the following conditions must be imposed: $\boldsymbol{\omega} \cdot \boldsymbol{r}_l > 0$, where $\boldsymbol{\omega}$ is the vorticity. The explicit definition of the magnitude of Rortex vector R_l has been given by Wang et al. [35] as:

$$R_l = \boldsymbol{\omega} \cdot \boldsymbol{r}_l - \sqrt{(\boldsymbol{\omega} \cdot \boldsymbol{r}_l)^2 - 4\lambda_{ci}^2} \tag{22}$$

where λ_{ci} is the imaginary part of the complex conjugate eigenvalues of $\nabla \boldsymbol{u}$. Hence, the Rortex vector can be expressed as: $\boldsymbol{R}_l = R_l \cdot \boldsymbol{r}_l$.

Similar to the definition of Ω-criterion, Dong et al. [36] defined a normalized scalar Ω_R, based on the Rortex vector. According to Zhao et al.'s derivation [27], it can be written as the following explicit equation:

$$\Omega_R = \frac{(\boldsymbol{\omega} \cdot \boldsymbol{r}_l)^2}{2 \cdot \left[(\boldsymbol{\omega} \cdot \boldsymbol{r}_l)^2 + 2\left(\lambda_{cr}^2 - \lambda_{ci}^2\right) + \lambda_r^2\right] + \varepsilon} \tag{23}$$

where λ_{ci} and λ_{cr} are the imaginary and real part of the complex conjugate eigenvalues of $\nabla \boldsymbol{u}$. As the definition of Equation (21), ε here is calculated by the eigenvalues as: $\varepsilon = b_0 \cdot \max\left(4\lambda_{ci}^2 - 3\lambda_{cr}^2 - 1.5\lambda_r^2\right)$.

3. Computational Setup and Verification

3.1. Model Turbine and Numerical Method

As illustrated in Figure 1a, the diffuser-augmented horizontal-axis tidal stream turbine (DAHATT) consists of three components: rotor, diffuser, and support structure, represented here by green, dark orange, and blue, respectively. The model of turbine rotor is shown in Figure 1b. The diameter of the horizontal-axis three-bladed rotor is $D = 0.2$ m, and the depth of the flume is $H = 0.8$ m. According to the Froude similarity, the Froude number of the investigation is $\mathrm{Fr} = U_0/\sqrt{gH} = 0.143$. The bulk velocity U_0 is constant at 0.35 m/s with a 1:60 Froude scale, exemplifying a prototype turbine which has a rated power of 0.5 MW and an environmental incoming velocity of 3.1 m/s, consistent with our presented research [37].

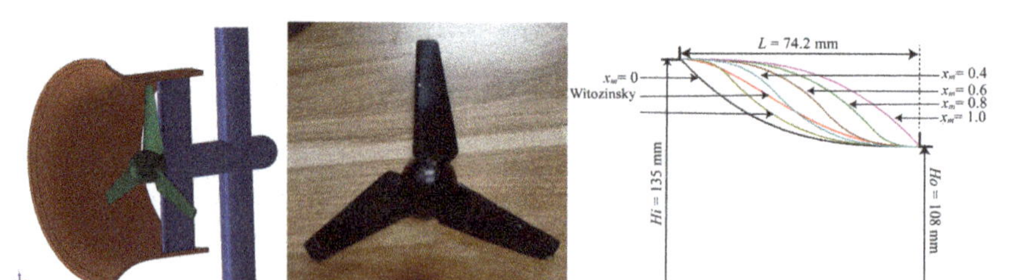

(a) Turbine model (b) Rotor (c) Section of the diffuser shape

Figure 1. Sketch and image of the turbine and diffuser shape.

The rotor follows a unique NREL S822 airfoil, with respect to rotor radius R, the chord (c), and pitch angle (θ) of the cross-section are indicated in Table 1. The model-scaled rotor achieves peak performance similar to the full-size turbine. The diameters of the nacelle and pile are 40 mm.

Table 1. Model turbine specifications.

No. of the Section	r/R	c (mm)	θ (rad)
1	0.2	23.0	0.2380
2	0.3	34.4	0.2078
3	0.4	32.1	0.1775
4	0.5	27.4	0.1473
5	0.6	25.0	0.1170
6	0.7	22.7	0.0868
7	0.8	20.3	0.0565
8	0.9	18.0	0.0263
9	1.0	15.6	−0.0040

As a diffuser-augmented turbine, the tip clearance size (ξ) is constant at 2.5% of the rotor diameter. The center of the diffuser support is located at $0.5D$ from the rotor with a length of 42 mm. Table 2 provides the detailed specifications of the model turbine. As shown in Figure 1c, the diffuser is designed with a cubic B-spline curve, which is expressed in Equation (24):

$$\frac{h - H_o}{H_i - H_o} = \begin{cases} 1 - \frac{1}{x_m^2} \cdot (x/L)^3 & x/L \leq x_m \\ \frac{1}{(1 - x_m)^2} \cdot [1 - (x/L)]^3 & x/L > x_m \end{cases} \tag{24}$$

where L is the length of the tapering section, H_i and H_o are inlet and outlet radii of the diffuser, and h is the local radius with distance x from the diffuser inlet. x_m is the inflection point position of the cubic B-spline curve. These parameters were determined as: $L = 74.2$ mm, $H_i = 135$ mm, $H_o = 108$ mm, and $x_m = 0$. To install the support structure, the diffuser has 75mm straight section, which gives it a total length of $L_D = 139.2$mm.

Table 2. Specifications of the turbine.

Turbine Parameter		Value
Number of the blades	N_b	3
Rotor diameter	D (mm)	200
Hub ratio	α_H	20%
Nacelle diameter	D_N (mm)	40
Length of diffuser	L_D (mm)	149.2
Radius of diffuser inlet	H_i (mm)	135
Radius of diffuser outlet	H_o (mm)	108
Thickness of diffuser	δ_D (mm)	5
Tip clearance size	ξ (mm)	5
Tip speed ratio	TSR	2.5∼4.5
Bulk velocity	U_0 (m/s)	3.5
Reference temperature	T (K)	288

The computations were performed using the Reynolds-Averaged Navier Stokes (RANS) model with the pimpleFoam solver of OpenFOAM. As a finite volume method based solver, pimpleFoam [38] combines the PISO [39,40] and SIMPLE [41,42] algorithms for solving N–S equations for transient incompressible Newtonian fluids. Owing to good convergence, the time and convective components are discretized with Euler and a limited linear scheme. The gradient term is discretized using a cell limited least squares method. To ensure convergence at each time step, there are a maximum of 50 corrections for the SIMPLE algorithm and a constant two iterations for the PISO loop. The time step of the calculation is set to 0.1 deg rotation angle of the rotor, which has a maximum Courant number Co < 40. For this investigation, the rotational region is modeled with a fixed rotating speed relative to the stationary domain and SST $k - \omega$ model is applied to resolve wake turbulence.

3.2. Domain and Boundary Conditions

As illustrated in Figure 2, dimensions of the computational domain are $19D \times 6D \times 4D$, with $4D$ from the upstream inlet and $15D$ from the downstream outlet. The rotor center is set at half depth and mid plane of the computational volume which coincides with the origin of the coordinate. The computational volume can be split into two individual regions, a cylinder region containing the rotor called rotational region, and the other one including the static support and diffuser, which is called the background region. In our case, the field data are transmitted through the AMI interface of each region. To avoid possible numerical oscillation on the interface, the diameter of rotational region is set to $1.05D$.

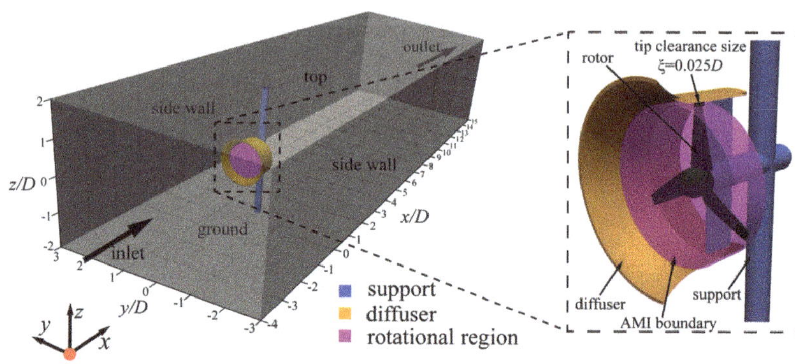

Figure 2. Schematic of computational domain and boundary conditions.

The boundary conditions of the computational domain are presented in Table 3. The free surface patch (top) is set as a slip wall. The moving wall boundary is used for blade and hub surfaces, which is stationary relative to the rotational region. The rotational speed of the rotor ω_r is varied from 8.75 rad/s to 17.5 rad/s corresponding to tip–speed ratio (TSR $= \omega_r R / U_0$) from 2.5 to 5.0.

Table 3. The boundary conditions of each patch.

Patch	Velocity (U)	Pressure (p)	Turbulent Kinetic Energy (k)
inlet	codedFixedValue	inletOutlet	fixedValue
outlet	inletOutlet	zeroGradient	zeroGradient
top	slip	zeroGradient	zeroGradient
staticWalls	fixedValue	zeroGradient	kqRWallFunction
rotationWalls	movingWallVelocity	zeroGradient	kqRWallFunction

The environmental turbulence intensity (**I**) approximates 6%. The depth-variation inflow velocity (U_{inc}) follows the logarithmic law near the ground and gradually transitions to a linear distribution as the bottom distance ($d = z + 2D$) increases. With a velocity-based inlet boundary condition, the velocity varies according to Equation (25), whereas at inlet and outlet, the relative atmospheric pressure is set to zero.

$$U_{\text{inc}} = \begin{cases} u^* \cdot \left[\frac{1}{\kappa}\ln\left(\frac{u^* d}{\nu}\right) + 5.0\right] & d \le 0.45D \\ 1.6506 \cdot d^3 - 1.8122 \cdot d^2 + 0.6684 \cdot d + 0.2696 & 0.45D < d < 1.75D \\ 0.0065 \cdot d + 0.3500 & d \ge 1.75D \end{cases} \tag{25}$$

where $u^* = 0.01411$ m/s denotes the estimation of friction velocity, and $\kappa = 0.41$ is the von Kármán constant. Figure 3 presents the velocity and turbulence intensity profiles along the vertical direction at $x = y = 0$ without the turbine installed. Here, the turbulence intensity refers to as the turbulence level. For RANS simulation, it can be defined as:

$$\mathbf{I} = \frac{\overline{u'}}{|\mathbf{U}|} = \frac{\sqrt{2/3 \cdot k}}{|\mathbf{U}|} \tag{26}$$

where $k = 0.5 \cdot \sum u_i'^2$ is the turbulent kinetic energy, and $|\mathbf{U}| = \sqrt{\sum U_i^2}$ is the magnitude of the local velocity vector.

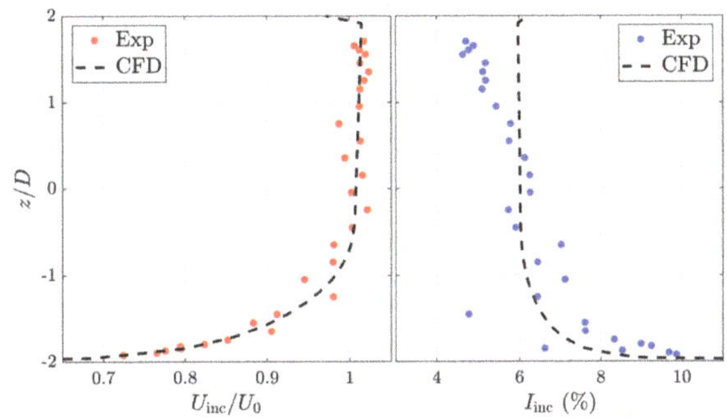

Figure 3. Vertical profile of normalized incoming velocity and turbulence intensities.

3.3. Mesh and Its Independence Assessment

The hexahedral-dominated mesh of the investigation is generated by ANSYS ICEM with a maximum wall $y^+ \approx 16$ of the rotation region. Figure 4 illustrates the overall and magnified computational mesh. The layered-grid near the rotor surface is produced to improve the overall quality of the grid with a maximum height of 0.5 mm and growth rate of 1.07. Mixed mesh of prisms and hexahedra are used near the nose of the rotor hub. With 1.3 million grids in the rotation region and 6.1 million grids of the flume, the total number of grids is approximately 7.4 million.

A grid-independence test was performed to reduce the requirement computing resource requirements. As mentioned in Table 4, the grid number ranges from 2.9 to 11.3 million. The computations were conducted by two AMD EPYC workstations, and the end time of calculation is one rotor rotation cycle. Results indicate that, when the number of grids is 'Medium', fewer computational resources are used with the relative error of mean power coefficient less than 1%.

Table 4. Mesh independence verification of computational domain.

Case	No. of Celles	Clock Time (hour)	Max Wall y^+ of Rotation Region	Mean Power Coefficient $\overline{C_P}$	Relative Error (%)
Coarsest	2,898,716 (2.9 M)	15.9	>70	0.337	11.59
Coarse	3,574,652 (3.6 M)	18.4	≈50	0.331	9.60
Medium	7,446,432 (7.4 M)	83.1	≈16	0.304	0.66
Fine	9,847,484 (9.8 M)	108.6	≈13	0.301	0.33
Finest	11,304,968 (11 M)	130.3	≈11	0.302	–

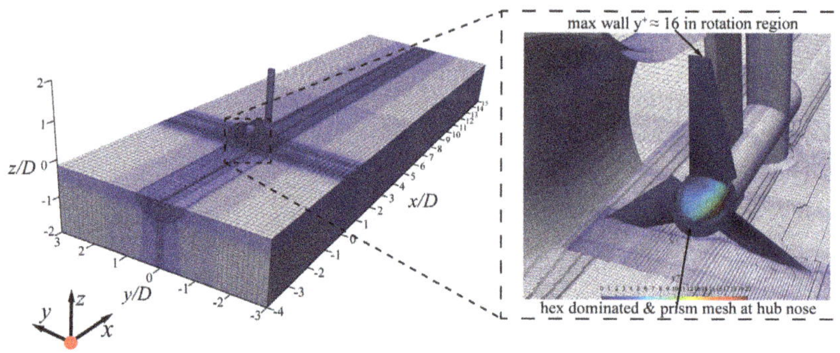

Figure 4. Overall and magnified computational mesh.

4. Results and Discussion

4.1. Performance Validation

The hydrodynamic performance of diffuser-augmented tidal stream turbine can be defined as a normalized power coefficient C_P that varies with the tip–speed ratio (TSR) as:

$$C_p = \frac{M\omega_r}{0.5\rho A U_0^3} \tag{27}$$

where M is the torque of all rotation surfaces, and $A = \pi R^2$, the swept area of the rotor.

To validate the accuracy of the numerical method, the results are compared with experimental results, which are shown in Figure 5. The power coefficients follow an inverted u-shape curve with maximum $C_p = 0.296$ at TSR ≈ 3.72 for the experiment, whilst peak $C_p = 0.301$ at TSR ≈ 3.6 for CFD investigation. At the range of TSR $= 3.4 \sim 3.8$, numerical and experimental curves experience a good agreement, whereas, it deviates more when the tip–speed ratio is out of the range. The relative error is less than 3% for the contemplated study range, while the maximum value occurs at TSR $= 2.76$. Eventually, the result provides confidence in the ability of the numerical simulation to accurately replicate hydrodynamic experimental investigation.

4.2. Near Wake Structure

4.2.1. Mean Velocity Deficit

As defined as $\Delta_1 = 1 - U_1/U_{\text{inc}}$, the velocity deficit represents the change of time-averaged longitudinal velocity (U_1) relative to the incoming velocity (U_{inc}) from Equation (25). Figure 6 is the contour map of transverse (xOy) and the vertical (xOz) plane.

Over the mid-depth plane (see Figure 6a), maximum deficit ($\Delta_1 \approx 1.4$) occurs after the outer edge of the diffuser ($|y/D| = 0.675$), where the reverse flow is found. In order to compensate for the rapid momentum dissipation, an increment of velocity is observed in the region of $|y/D| = 0.8 \sim 1.2$, which presents a sharply velocity acceleration ($\Delta_1 < 0$). However, this accelerated portion does not extend more than $3D$ downstream. The flow separation that occurs within this area is caused by the momentum losses induced by the diffuser inlet. As mentioned in Cresswell et al.'s research [6], owing to the tip gap jet generated by the inside wall of the diffuser, the velocity deficit remains low in a narrow region bypassing the rotor. The second large deficit zone is noticeable between rotor and the support, where an increment of the local velocity appears. This is caused by less energy losses induced by the root of the blades. Over the region of $1 \leq x/D \leq 6$, sub-figure (a) indicates the maximum deficit ($\approx$0.95) at the closest center point ($x/D = 1, y = 0$). Overall, the wake exhibits a tadpole-shape with a width covering three rotor diameter and the inner core behind the support at the transverse plane. Furthermore, 5.5D downstream, the time-averaged deficit is almost constant at 10%, which reveals that it has a significantly momentum dissipation in the near wake region ($x/D \leq 4$).

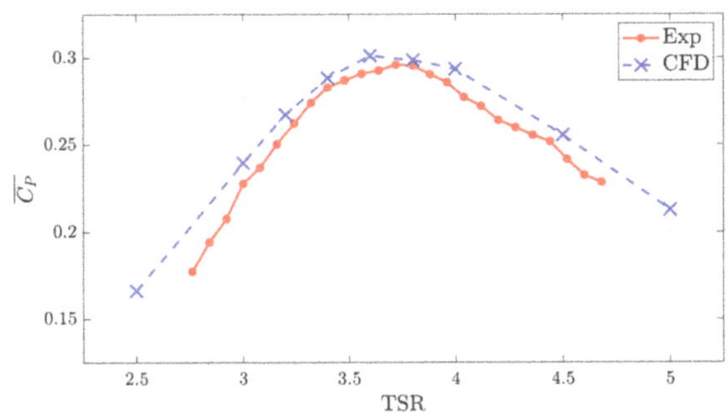

Figure 5. Vertical profile of normalized incoming velocity and turbulence intensities.

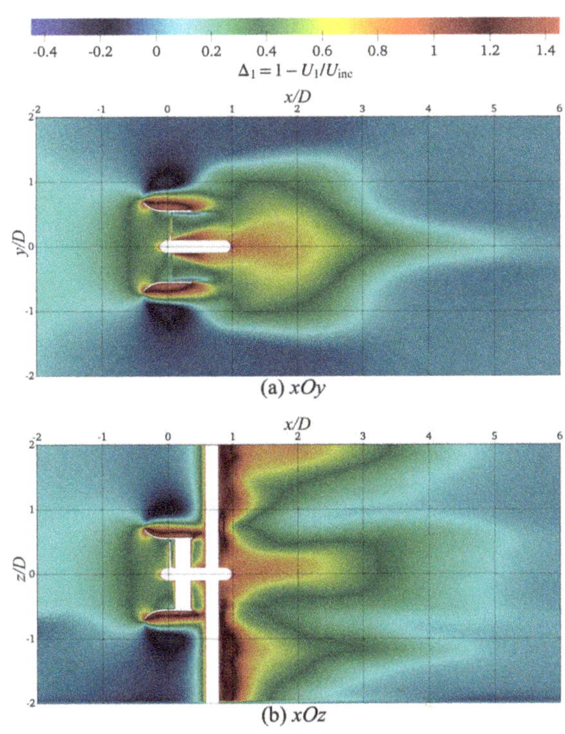

Figure 6. Contours of velocity deficit (Δ_1) on horizontal and vertical plane (TSR = 3.6).

As plotted in Figure 6b, the cloud map of the vertical velocity deficit indicates similar behavior to the transverse distribution outside of the diffuser. Due to the significant effect of the robust support, it is noticeable that the wake region with maximum $\Delta_1 \approx 1.3$ is existing close to the support. The vertical profiles of Δ_1 exhibit a triple peak distribution in the near wake. Among $z/D \geq 1.5$, the peak tilts up towards the water surface. Before the $2D$ section, the velocity deficit is slightly influenced by the bed shear layer. Owing to the combined effect of wake swirling and support shadow, the magnitude of middle plateau is lower than the other, but still remains until $5D$ downstream.

4.2.2. Turbulence Characteristics

Figure 7 illustrates the contour of total turbulence intensities (Equation (26)) of the diffuser-augmented turbine. According to this figure, the high turbulence regions are close to the position behind the diffuser inlet, blade root, and support structures.

Similar to the maximum velocity gradient locations mentioned in Figure 6, the distributions of turbulence intensity, which are illustrated in Figure 7a, are almost symmetrical with respect to the rotor centerline on the horizontal plane. Among the range of $x/D = -0.3 \sim 0.7$, there are three high turbulence plateaus which the turbulence intensity $\mathbf{I} > 90\%$: mid plateau after the rotor hub; top and bottom plateaus outside the diffuser. Inside the diffuser, a low-turbulence core exists due to the bypass flow through rotor tip clearance. In the near wake region, the maximum turbulence intensity occurs at $x/D \approx 1$ near the centerline and its $|\mathbf{U}| \approx 0$; thus, $\mathbf{I} \gg 100\%$. Three high turbulence plateaus are mixed in the range of $1.5 \sim 2D$. Further downstream, the turbulence intensity exponentially reduced and converged to around 6% after a $4.5D$ section.

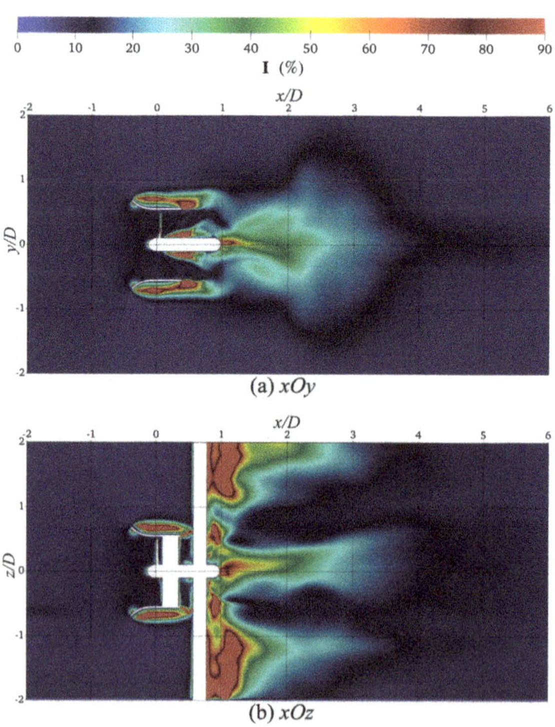

Figure 7. Contours of turbulence intensity (**I**) on horizontal and vertical plane (TSR = 3.6).

On the other hand, the turbulent flow is slightly asymmetrical to the centerline on the vertical plane (Figure 7b). Similar to its distributions on the horizontal plane, turbulence intensities experience two high value zones above and below the diffuser. In the wake region, the turbulence intensity is higher behind the supporting pile due to the blockage effect. The enhancement occurs especially in the zones close to the free surface ($z/D > 1.2$) and sea bed ($z/D < -1$). As a similar phenomenon to the mean wake deficit, the centerline of turbulent flow tilts up towards the water surface, and it expands in a convex upward shape with the focal point at the rotor center. In the presence of the diffuser, the turbulence intensity in the near wake region is increasing, and the higher values are located close to the rotor tips and the free surface.

4.3. Entropy Production

Figure 8 depicts the entropy production rate distribution (Equation (18)) with TSR = 3.6. As a result of flow separation behind the diffuser inlet, it can be observed that higher $\dot{s}_D$ is revealed at $x/D = -0.3{\sim}0.7$ outside the diffuser, across horizontal plane (xOy). Moreover, a high entropy production rate region exists behind the blade tip and hub of the turbine. This is because of the appearance of the blade vortex, which is generated by the pressure difference of blade surfaces. However, because of the vortex breakup caused by the support structure, the entropy production rate experiences a rapid dissipation before the turbulent flow enters the wake region. Due to a certain flow separation at the outlet of the diffuser, a part of the vortex falls off from the trailing edge of the duct and propagates downstream, and the outlet of the diffuser is also a region of a high entropy production rate. Owing to the large range of flow separation, most of the entropy is produced behind diffuser surfaces, which contributes to the main entropy production. Moreover, the intensity of entropy production rate in the near wake region continues to propagate downstream, but it converges to $\dot{s}_D < 0.015$ (W/m^3/K).

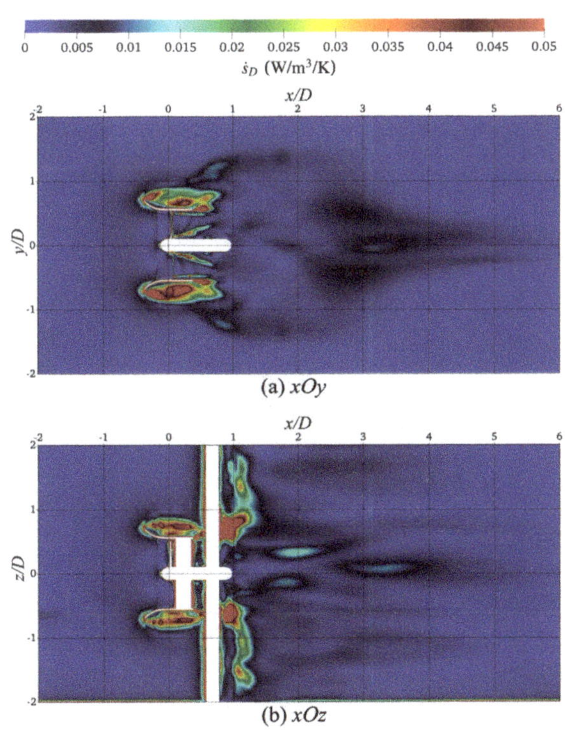

Figure 8. Contours of entropy production rate ($\dot{s}_D$) on horizontal and vertical plane (TSR = 3.6).

As shown in Figure 8b, the entropy production rate presents continuous high $\dot{s}_D$ regions around the diffuser across vertical plane (xOz). These regions are highly consistent with the high turbulence regions that are illustrated in Figure 7b. With the presence of the diffuser, two extremely large zones ($\dot{s}_D > 0.1$) appear behind the support structure at $z/D = 0.4{\sim}0.9$ and $z/D = -0.8{\sim}-0.5$. Due to the diffusion of turbulence viscosity, the distribution of entropy production rate is depicted as deflecting towards the free surface and bottom of the flume at $1D$ downstream. Furthermore, as the wake develops, the entropy production presents a discontinuous characteristic with $\dot{s}_D \approx 0.015$, and slowly tilts up towards the free surface similar to the distribution of turbulence intensities.

Figure 9 shows the distribution of the entropy production rate at different longitudinal sections that $|y/D|$ and $|z/D| \leq 0.7$. Sub-figure (a) is the 30 mm upstream section from the origin; (b) is the rotor plane ($x = 0$); (c)–(e) are the specific sections inside the diffuser; (f) is the mid-section between the outlet of the diffuser and support pile; (g) is the immediately downstream plane ($x/D = 1$) in the near wake region. It can be seen from Figure 9b,c that the energy loss of the turbulent flow is concentrated in the area attached to the rotor surfaces and especially near the tip clearance and presents anticlockwise characteristics, which is the same as the rotation direction. As illustrated in Figure 9d,e, it is obvious that the dissipation of $\dot{s}_D$ is evident in the tip clearance. The radius of the center of blade-roots energy loss is gradually increasing along $x/D = 0.1{\sim}0.6$. Note that, in sub-figure (f), the large magnitude of the entropy production rate is concentrated on the outlet of the diffuser and four corners, which means lower effective viscosity (ν_{eff}) along horizontal and vertical directions. This phenomenon is caused by the rear support pile and nacelle, which hinders the spread of the vortex in a certain direction.

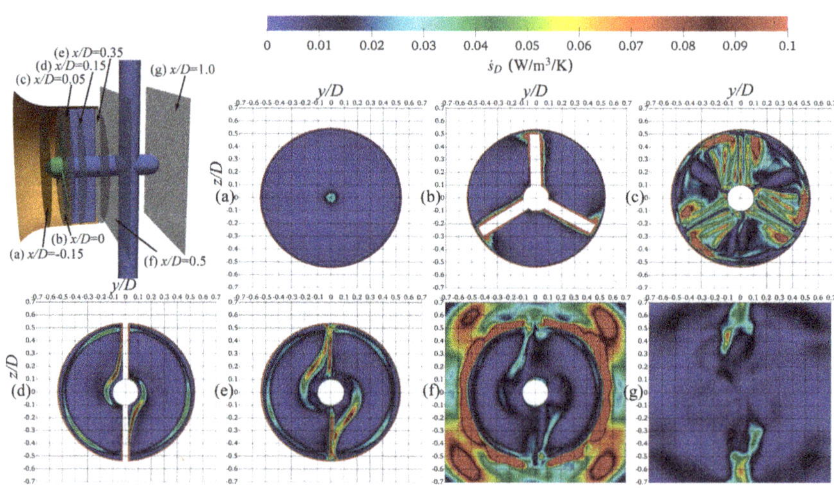

Figure 9. $\dot{s}_D$ distribution of the turbine at different longitudinal positions (TSR = 3.6).

The wake structure of the diffuser-augmented turbine shows a rapidly dissipation tendency, and it can be separated into two high entropy rate regions in the near wake. Meanwhile, it can be clearly seen that the morphology of the high intensity region of $\dot{s}_D$ changes from $-0.15D$ to $1.0D$, which relates to the diffuser and support structures of the turbine.

4.4. Vortex Identification

Figures 10–12 depict the visualizations of the instantaneous flows for the diffuser-augmented horizontal-axis tidal stream turbine. These vortical structures are identified by different criteria with TSR = 3.6 and colored by the intensity of entropy production rate ($\dot{s}_D$). As illustrated in these figures, the dominant wake structures follow clockwise tip vortices, which are generated by the turbine whilst the rotor blades rotate in an anticlockwise direction.

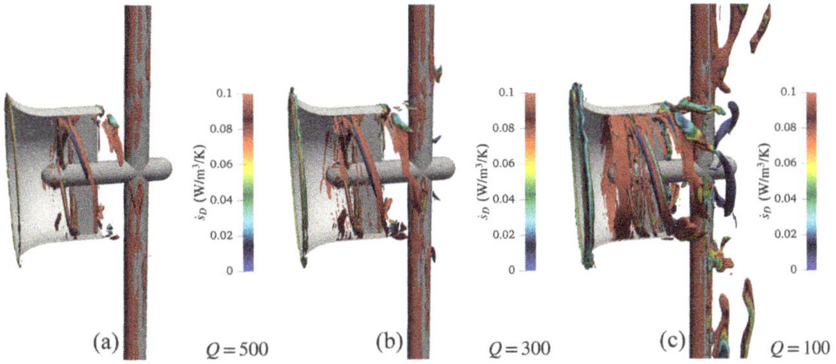

Figure 10. Vortical structure of the turbine. Isosurfaced by different Q, colored by $\dot{s}_D$ (TSR = 3.6).

Figure 10 presents the vortical structure of the turbine, which is resolved by the isosurfaces of different Q-criteria. As can be seen in these sub-figures, the extracted tip vortices are clearly illustrated as the value of Q decreases. However, the vortices identified by Q-criteria contain redundant motions in the wall shear layer of the diffuser. Similar to the study on the ship propeller [27], these deformations are excluded in Figure 12 when resolving the vortices by Ω-Rortex criteria.

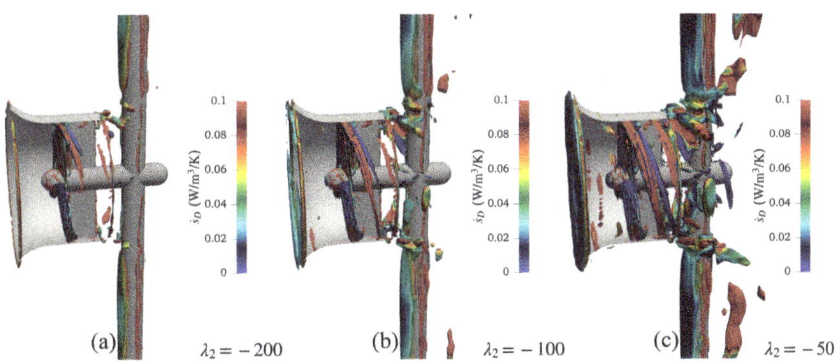

Figure 11. Vortical structure of the turbine, isosurfaced by different λ_2 (TSR = 3.6).

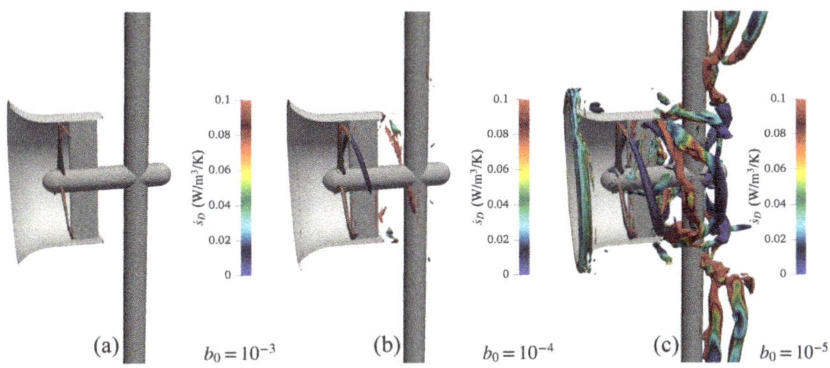

Figure 12. Vortical structure of the turbine, isosurfaced by $\Omega_R = 0.52$ with different b_0 (TSR = 3.6).

Figure 11 shows the contours of vortical structure with different λ_2 values. Compared to the Q isosurfaces, a λ_2-criterion cannot distinguish the vortical tubes with certain distinct boundaries. The vortex has a discontinuous intermittent structure after passing the rotor and behind the outlet of the diffuser. Notice that both Q and λ_2 criteria are sensitive to the isosurface thresholds. In general, it is different to identify the vortex structure inside the diffuser of a horizontal-axis tidal stream turbine with the vortex identification methods that are based on a velocity gradient [43].

Figure 12 depicts the vortical structure of DAHATT with Ω-Rortex criteria. Owing to the clear physical meaning of Ω_R defined by Liu et al. [32], $\Omega_R = 0.52$ is recommended to illustrate the rotation strength of vortices. However, when the strong swirling vortex is broken due to the presence of the supporting structure, ε (in Equation (23)) will not be large enough to identify the vortical structure even if the rotational strength is stronger than the deformation. Hence, it is crucial to study the sensitivity of b_0 for the vortex identification using the Ω-Rortex method. As mentioned in Zhao et al.'s research [27], $b_0 = 10^{-6}$ is reasonable for most marine hydrodynamic investigations. According to our investigation, $b_0 = 10^{-6}$ is too large, so the wrong vortical structure, which contains extra shear motion near the tip clearance, is captured. For our case, the threshold value of $b_0 = 10^{-5}$ is suitable for extracting the vortices inside the diffuser and behind the support structure.

5. Conclusions

The presented investigation focused on the near wake structure, entropy production analysis, and vortex identification of diffuser-augmented horizontal-axis tidal stream turbine (DAHATT). After the detailed discussions, the following conclusions are drawn:

(1) The overall mean wake structure follows a tadpole-shape on the horizontal plane, whilst it has the maximum velocity deficit after the outer edge of the diffuser. In the near wake, the vertical profiles exhibit a triple peak distribution and significant recovery within $6D$ downstream.

(2) On the whole, the region that is behind the tip of the diffuser inlet accounts for the greatest proportion of entropy production rate ($\dot{s}_D$). Inside the diffuser, entropy production rate ($\dot{s}_D$) experiences a rapid dissipation after passing the rotor. Moreover, in the near wake region, the distribution of $\dot{s}_D$ can be depicted as deflecting towards the free surface and the bottom of the flume.

(3) Q and λ_2-criteria are sensitive to their isosurface thresholds. The vortices identified by Q-criteria contain redundant wall shear motions, and λ_2-criteria cannot distinguish the vortical structure with certain distinct boundaries. Thus, the Ω-Rortex method provides reliable vortex identification results for DAHATT.

(4) Owing to the vortex breakup of the strong swirling flows, b_0 should be a small value that distinguishes the rotational part from the overall vortical structure. For the investigation of DAHATT, we suggest that b_0 should be set to 10^{-5}.

Author Contributions: Methodology, X.L.; Validation, W.Z. and Y.L.; Formal analysis, E.F.-R.; Resources, Y.Z. (Yuquan Zhang); Data curation, Y.Z. (Yuquan Zhang); Writing—original draft, W.Z.; Writing—review and editing, E.F.-R.; Supervision, Y.Z. (Yuan Zheng). All authors have read and agreed to the published version of the manuscript.

Funding: The research was supported by the following funding: Graduate Research and Innovation Program of Jiangsu Province (SJKY19_0493), Fundamental Research Funds for the Central Universities (No. 2019B71714), and the National Natural Science Foundation of China (52171257).

Data Availability Statement: Not applicable.

Conflicts of Interest: The authors declare no conflict of interest.

References

1. Vyshnavi, P.; Venkatesan, N.; Samad, A.; Avital, E. Tidal Current Energy for Indian Coastal Lines—A State Art of Review. *J. Phys. Conf. Ser.* **2020**, *1716*, 012008. [CrossRef]
2. Fernandez-Rodriguez, E.; Stallard, T.; Stansby, P. Experimental study of extreme thrust on a tidal stream rotor due to turbulent flow and with opposing waves. *J. Fluids Struct.* **2014**, *51*, 354–361. [CrossRef]
3. Zhou, Z.; Scuiller, F.; Charpentier, J.F.; Benbouzid, M.; Tang, T. An up-to-date review of large marine tidal current turbine technologies. In Proceedings of the 2014 International Power Electronics and Application Conference and Exposition, Shanghai, China, 5–8 November 2014; pp. 480–484.
4. Gaden, D.L.; Bibeau, E.L. A numerical investigation into the effect of diffusers on the performance of hydro kinetic turbines using a validated momentum source turbine model. *Renew. Energy* **2010**, *35*, 1152–1158. [CrossRef]
5. Nunes, M.M.; Mendes, R.C.; Oliveira, T.F.; Junior, A.C.B. An experimental study on the diffuser-enhanced propeller hydrokinetic turbines. *Renew. Energy* **2019**, *133*, 840–848. [CrossRef]
6. Cresswell, N.; Ingram, G.; Dominy, R. The impact of diffuser augmentation on a tidal stream turbine. *Ocean. Eng.* **2015**, *108*, 155–163. [CrossRef]
7. Zhang, Y.; Zhang, J.; Lin, X.; Wang, R.; Zhang, C.; Zhao, J. Experimental investigation into downstream field of a horizontal axis tidal stream turbine supported by a mono pile. *Appl. Ocean. Res.* **2020**, *101*, 102257. [CrossRef]
8. Cacciali, L.; Battisti, L.; Dell'Anna, S. Free Surface Double Actuator Disc Theory and Double Multiple Streamtube Model for In-Stream Darrieus Hydrokinetic Turbines. *Ocean. Eng.* **2022**, *260*, 112017. [CrossRef]
9. Zang, W.; Zheng, Y.; Zhang, Y.; Zhang, J.; Fernandez-Rodriguez, E. Experiments on the mean and integral characteristics of tidal turbine wake in the linear waves propagating with the current. *Ocean. Eng.* **2019**, *173*, 1–11. [CrossRef]
10. Zhang, Y.; Zang, W.; Zheng, J.; Cappietti, L.; Zhang, J.; Zheng, Y.; Fernandez-Rodriguez, E. The influence of waves propagating with the current on the wake of a tidal stream turbine. *Appl. Energy* **2021**, *290*, 116729. [CrossRef]
11. Wang, X.; Yan, Y.; Wang, W.Q.; Hu, Z.P. Evaluating energy loss with the entropy production theory: A case study of a micro horizontal axis river ducted turbine. *Energy Convers. Manag.* **2023**, *276*, 116553. [CrossRef]
12. Wang, Z.; Xie, B.; Xia, X.; Yang, H.; Zuo, Q.; Liu, Z. Energy loss of radial inflow turbine for organic Rankine cycle using mixture based on entropy production method. *Energy* **2022**, *245*, 123312. [CrossRef]
13. Menter, F. Zonal two equation kw turbulence models for aerodynamic flows. In Proceedings of the 23rd Fluid Dynamics, Plasmadynamics, and Lasers Conference, Orlando, FL, USA, 6–9 July 1993; p. 2906.
14. Menter, F.R. Two-equation eddy-viscosity turbulence models for engineering applications. *AIAA J.* **1994**, *32*, 1598–1605. [CrossRef]
15. Menter, F.R.; Kuntz, M.; Langtry, R. Ten years of industrial experience with the SST turbulence model. *Turbul. Heat Mass Transf.* **2003**, *4*, 625–632.
16. Herwig, H.; Kock, F. Local entropy production in turbulent shear flows: A tool for evaluating heat transfer performance. *J. Therm. Sci.* **2006**, *15*, 159–167. [CrossRef]
17. Kock, F.; Herwig, H. Local entropy production in turbulent shear flows: A high-Reynolds number model with wall functions. *Int. J. Heat Mass Transf.* **2004**, *47*, 2205–2215. [CrossRef]
18. Li, D.; Wang, H.; Qin, Y.; Han, L.; Wei, X.; Qin, D. Entropy production analysis of hysteresis characteristic of a pump-turbine model. *Energy Convers. Manag.* **2017**, *149*, 175–191. [CrossRef]
19. Nazeryan, M.; Lakzian, E. Detailed entropy generation analysis of a Wells turbine using the variation of the blade thickness. *Energy* **2018**, *143*, 385–405. [CrossRef]
20. Haghighi, M.H.S.; Mirghavami, S.M.; Ghorani, M.M.; Riasi, A.; Chini, S.F. A numerical study on the performance of a superhydrophobic coated very low head (VLH) axial hydraulic turbine using entropy generation method. *Renew. Energy* **2020**, *147*, 409–422. [CrossRef]
21. Yu, Z.F.; Wang, W.Q.; Yan, Y.; Liu, X.S. Energy loss evaluation in a Francis turbine under overall operating conditions using entropy production method. *Renew. Energy* **2021**, *169*, 982–999. [CrossRef]
22. Cacciali, L.; Battisti, L.; Dell'Anna, S.; Soraperra, G. Case study of a cross-flow hydrokinetic turbine in a narrow prismatic canal. *Ocean. Eng.* **2021**, *234*, 109281. [CrossRef]
23. White, F.M.; Majdalani, J. *Viscous Fluid Flow*; McGraw-Hill: New York, NY, USA, 2006; Volume 3.
24. Jeong, J.; Hussain, F. On the identification of a vortex. *J. Fluid Mech.* **1995**, *285*, 69–94. [CrossRef]
25. Xing, T.; Bhushan, S.; Stern, F. Vortical and turbulent structures for KVLCC2 at drift angle 0, 12, and 30 degrees. *Ocean. Eng.* **2012**, *55*, 23–43. [CrossRef]
26. Wang, L.Z.; Guo, C.Y.; Su, Y.M.; Wu, T.C. A numerical study on the correlation between the evolution of propeller trailing vortex wake and skew of propellers. *Int. J. Nav. Archit. Ocean. Eng.* **2018**, *10*, 212–224. [CrossRef]
27. Zhao, W.w.; Wang, J.h.; Wan, D.c. Vortex identification methods in marine hydrodynamics. *J. Hydrodyn.* **2020**, *32*, 286–295. [CrossRef]
28. Haller, G. An objective definition of a vortex. *J. Fluid Mech.* **2005**, *525*, 1–26. [CrossRef]
29. Fureby, C.; Anderson, B.; Clarke, D.; Erm, L.; Henbest, S.; Giacobello, M.; Jones, D.; Nguyen, M.; Johansson, M.; Jones, M.; et al. Experimental and numerical study of a generic conventional submarine at 10 yaw. *Ocean. Eng.* **2016**, *116*, 1–20. [CrossRef]
30. Liu, C.; Wang, Y.; Yang, Y.; Duan, Z. New omega vortex identification method. *Sci. China Phys. Mech. Astron.* **2016**, *59*, 1–9. [CrossRef]

31. Chong, M.S.; Perry, A.E.; Cantwell, B.J. A general classification of three-dimensional flow fields. *Phys. Fluids A Fluid Dyn.* **1990**, *2*, 765–777. [CrossRef]
32. Liu, C.; Gao, Y.; Tian, S.; Dong, X. Rortex—A new vortex vector definition and vorticity tensor and vector decompositions. *Phys. Fluids* **2018**, *30*, 035103. [CrossRef]
33. Gao, Y.; Liu, C. Rortex and comparison with eigenvalue-based vortex identification criteria. *Phys. Fluids* **2018**, *30*, 085107. [CrossRef]
34. Gao, Y.; Liu, C. Rortex based velocity gradient tensor decomposition. *Phys. Fluids* **2019**, *31*, 011704. [CrossRef]
35. Wang, Y.q.; Gao, Y.s.; Liu, J.m.; Liu, C. Explicit formula for the Liutex vector and physical meaning of vorticity based on the Liutex-Shear decomposition. *J. Hydrodyn.* **2019**, *31*, 464–474. [CrossRef]
36. Dong, X.; Gao, Y.; Liu, C. New normalized Rortex/vortex identification method. *Phys. Fluids* **2019**, *31*, 011701. [CrossRef]
37. Zhang, Z.; Zhang, Y.; Zheng, Y.; Zhang, J.; Fernandez-Rodriguez, E.; Zang, W.; Ji, R. Power fluctuation and wake characteristics of tidal stream turbine subjected to wave and current interaction. *Energy* **2022**, *264*, 126185. [CrossRef]
38. Holzmann, T. *Mathematics, Numerics, Derivations and OpenFOAM®*; Holzmann CFD: Loeben, Germany, 2016; Chapter 11, pp. 99–103.
39. Issa, R.I. Solution of the implicitly discretised fluid flow equations by operator-splitting. *J. Comput. Phys.* **1986**, *62*, 40–65. [CrossRef]
40. Issa, R.I.; Gosman, A.; Watkins, A. The computation of compressible and incompressible recirculating flows by a non-iterative implicit scheme. *J. Comput. Phys.* **1986**, *62*, 66–82. [CrossRef]
41. Patankar, S.V.; Spalding, D.B. A calculation procedure for heat, mass and momentum transfer in three-dimensional parabolic flows. In *Numerical Prediction of Flow, Heat Transfer, Turbulence and Combustion*; Elsevier: Amsterdam, The Netherlands, 1983; pp. 54–73.
42. Ferziger, J.H.; Perić, M.; Street, R.L. *Computational Methods for Fluid Dynamics*; Springer: Berlin/Heidelberg, Germany, 2002; Volume 3.
43. Bai, X.; Zhang, W.; Fang, Q.; Wang, Y.; Zheng, J.; Guo, A. The visualization of turbulent coherent structure in open channel flow. *J. Hydrodyn.* **2019**, *31*, 266–273. [CrossRef]

mathematics

MDPI

Article

A Novel and Robust Wind Speed Prediction Method Based on Spatial Features of Wind Farm Cluster

Mumin Zhang [1], Yuzhi Wang [1], Haochen Zhang [2], Zhiyun Peng [3] and Junjie Tang [4,*]

[1] University of Cincinnati Joint Co-op Institute, Chongqing University, Chongqing 400044, China
[2] Department of Electrical and Computer Engineering, University of California, Los Angeles, CA 90095, USA
[3] School of Computing Science, Simon Fraser University, Burnaby, BC V5A 1S6, Canada
[4] State Key Laboratory of Power Transmission Equipment & System Security and New Technology, Chongqing University, Chongqing 400044, China
* Correspondence: tangjunjie@cqu.edu.cn

Abstract: Wind energy has been widely used in recent decades to achieve green and sustainable development. However, wind speed prediction in wind farm clusters remains one of the less studied areas. Spatial features of cluster data of wind speed are not fully exploited in existing work. In addition, missing data, which dramatically deteriorate the forecasting performance, have not been addressed thoroughly. To tackle these tough issues, a new method, termed input set based on wind farm cluster data–deep extreme learning machine (IWC-DELM), is developed herein. This model builds an input set based on IWC, which takes advantage of the historical data of relevant wind farms to utilize the spatial characteristics of wind speed sequences within such wind farm clusters. Finally, wind speed prediction is obtained after the training of DELM, which results in a better performance in forecasting accuracy and training speed. The structure IWC, complete with the multidimensional average method (MDAM), is also beneficial to make up the missing data, thus enhancing data robustness in comparison to the traditional method of the moving average approach (MAA). Experiments are conducted with some real-world data, and the results of gate recurrent unit (GRU), long- and short-term memory (LSTM) and sliced recurrent neural networks (SRNNs) are also taken for comparison. These comparative tests clearly verify the superiority of IWC-DELM, whose accuracy and efficiency both rank at the top among the four candidates.

Keywords: wind speed forecasting; wind farm cluster; input set based on wind farm cluster data; robustness analysis; deep extreme learning machine; multidimensional average method

MSC: 68T07

Citation: Zhang, M.; Wang, Y.; Zhang, H.; Peng, Z.; Tang, J. A Novel and Robust Wind Speed Prediction Method Based on Spatial Features of Wind Farm Cluster. *Mathematics* **2023**, *11*, 499. https://doi.org/10.3390/math11030499

Academic Editors: Zhuojia Fu, Yiqian He and Hui Zheng

Received: 18 December 2022
Revised: 8 January 2023
Accepted: 12 January 2023
Published: 17 January 2023

1. Introduction

Clean energy is largely needed to achieve peak carbon emission and carbon neutrality [1]. Wind power, as a renewable and widely distributed energy source, has received increasing attention in the past two decades [2]. Large-scale wind energy integration brings challenges for grid security due to the intermittent and random nature of wind speed [2–4]. Therefore, accurate forecasting of wind speed among wind farms in the cluster has gradually taken on a key role in operating strategies, capacity planning and power balance [5].

Existing work on wind speed and wind power forecasting can be classified as single-wind-farm prediction and wind farm cluster prediction according to the scale of research objects. Single-wind-farm forecasting methods mainly include four categories: physical models, traditional statistical models, artificial-intelligence-based models and hybrid models [6]. Deep learning methods have emerged as a powerful tool in wind speed and wind power prediction due to their ability to realize nonlinear fitting [7,8]. Gate recurrent unit (GRU) and sliced recurrent neural networks (SRNNs) are used in wind speed forecasting in [9,10]. References [11,12] adopt deep extreme learning machine (DELM) to predict wind power. However, the prediction of a single farm only focuses on its own data analysis without considering surrounding environmental factors including humidity, temperature, latitude and orography, leading to insufficient prediction accuracy [13,14]. These environmental factors can be reflected by the historical data of adjacent wind farms [15]. Additionally, the data capacity of a wind farm cluster is several times that of a single wind farm, which indicates that single-wind-farm forecasting methods may be not suitable for wind farm cluster forecasting.

Wind farm cluster prediction imposes a significant influence on the generation schedule and reserve capacity of the power system compared with a single wind farm [16,17]. Taking spatial–temporal correlation into consideration, a wind farm cluster fully utilizes information of the surrounding environment. Existing works related to multi-wind-farm prediction mainly focus on wind power prediction (WPP). In [18], three coefficients representing the characteristics of a wind farm in a wind cluster are weighted by the Shapley value method. The characteristics of the wind cluster are extracted by a convolutional neural network (CNN), and then such characteristics are fed into a long- and short-term memory (LSTM) neural network to establish the relationship between key characteristics and power generation. Peng et al. [19] proposed a regional WPP method called multifeature similarity matching (MFSM) on the basis of the single feature similarity matching (SFSM) method. The four key parameters in MFSM are proposed while the impact of each parameter on forecasting error and the method applicability in varying regional scales are analyzed.

There are few studies concerning wind speed forecasting (WSF) of wind farm clusters. However, WSF has a wider range of applications, including meteorological uses and energy uses. Additionally, unlike wind power data, historical wind speed sequences can directly represent the relevance between different wind farms. In [20], a prediction method based on collaborative filtering against a virtual edge expansion graph structure is proposed in order to tackle the problem of underutilization of wind speed sequences. This method ensures that the spatial correlation can be fully learned by extending the scale of the dataset. It connects the wind turbines in different wind farms through virtual edges and takes LSTM as the main body for wind speed prediction. In [15], the CNN and LSTM are combined to build a deep architecture termed predictive spatiotemporal network (PSTN). CNNs at the bottom of the prediction model are used to extract spatial features from the spatial wind speed matrices, and LSTM captures the temporal dependencies amongst the spatial characteristics. This model is trained by a loss function in an end-to-end manner to learn the temporal correlations along with spatial correlations. Reference [21] proposed a predictive deep convolutional neural network (PDCNN), which is an integration of CNNs and a multilayer perceptron (MLP). Spatial characteristics are extracted by CNNs, and MLP is intended to construct a relationship between temporal and spatial features. However, the structure of [15,21] cannot be directly applied to WSF of wind farm clusters, since these two studies focus on wind turbines that are neatly arranged, and the CNN is intended to solve graphic issues [22].

It can be found that most existing works apply hybrid models, which bring about framework complications and calculation costs, thus reducing efficiency. They tend to have a longer training time period.

Additionally, few of them consider the robustness training of the input set [23]. The prediction accuracy cannot maintain a high degree of accuracy when the input data are continuously missing in a time interval, for instance, due to damage to the measuring devices or data transmission failure. Interpolation methods are always used to solve this problem, typically from two perspectives, spatial characteristics and temporal characteristics [24]. From a spatial perspective, the "1/7 power law", "revised power law" and "ANFIS" are typical interpolation methods for dealing with wind speed prediction at different heights. Recently, a new method, the vertically correlated echelon model (VCEM), which utilizes vertical correlation of wind speeds, is proposed with a significant improvement in the prediction accuracy [25]. From a temporal perspective, there are a few interpolation methods based on a time sequence. The most commonly used method is the moving average approach (MAA), which entirely neglects the spatiotemporal features of wind speed data. Therefore, the multidimensional average method (MDAM) is first proposed in this paper to utilize spatial characteristics so as to enhance data robustness.

To address the issues of insufficient utilization of the spatiotemporal features and inefficiency in large-volume data processing, as well as to improve the input data robustness, this paper proposes a new model termed input set based on wind farm cluster data–deep extreme learning machine (IWC-DELM). This model enlarges the input dataset by utilizing the historical data of adjacent wind farms with full consideration of their data correlation. This model constructs DELM as the main body for achieving high prediction efficiency. By means of adopting the multidimensional input set, this model can also enhance the wind speed prediction robustness. It is demonstrated in [26,27] that the RNN has a better performance than the CNN in time series data prediction. Therefore, some variants of CNNs, for instance, GRU, LSTM and SRNN, are selected to prove the validity of IWC-DELM.

The main contributions of this paper can be summarized as follows:

1. A new input configuration of the wind speed prediction model, i.e., an input set based on wind farm cluster data (IWC), is built. The capacity of the input set has been expanded by utilizing historical data of adjacent wind farms, thus fully considering the spatial features of wind speed sequences.
2. A new machine learning architecture, IWC-DELM, is proposed for the WSF within wind farm clusters. This model contributes to more accurate and efficient prediction compared to some promising deep learning methods. Three algorithms, GRU, LSTM and SRNN, are selected to verify the superiority of the proposed method.
3. Robustness analysis on the input set is performed. The forecasting accuracy is required to maintain a high level even if some input data are missing in a time interval. The MDAM, which completes the temporal features of data with the spatial features of the wind farm cluster, is first proposed for this purpose.

The rest of this paper is organized as follows: Section 2 introduces the main methods in data preprocessing, and Section 3 illustrates the model structure of the proposed method. A case study located in the USA is discussed in Section 4. Section 5 provides the conclusion.

2. Data Preprocessing Theory

2.1. Weighted Mean Filtering

Weighted mean filtering (WMF) is employed as a denoise method to replace the traditional methods in order to overcome the boundary effects issue [28]. Its transfer function can be described as:

$$\frac{D_{(d)}(Z)}{D(Z)} = \frac{\sum\limits_{i=0}^{L} \alpha_{\tau-i} \cdot Z^{-i}}{\sum\limits_{i=0}^{L} \alpha_{\tau-i}} \tag{1}$$

The denoised wind speed data and the corresponding raw data are represented by $D_{(d)}(Z)$ and $D(Z)$, respectively. *(Z)* denotes its Z-transform. $\alpha_{\tau-i}$ denotes the weight for each timestamp, and $L-1$ represents the window size. Accordingly, the output of WMF in the time domain can be defined as:

$$D_{(d)}[\tau] = \frac{\sum\limits_{i=0}^{L} \alpha_{\tau-i} \cdot D[\tau]}{\sum\limits_{i=0}^{L} \alpha_{\tau-i}} \tag{2}$$

where $D[\tau]$ is the original wind speed data and $D_{(d)}[\tau]$ is the denoised data at a particular time instant τ.

2.2. Multidimensional Average Method

Traditional interpolation methods, for example, the MAA, make the missing data be determined as the average of the preceding data number with a defined autoregressive order [24]. In this paper, it is modified to apply in the cluster, which is defined as:

$$x_j = \frac{1}{\omega} \sum_{i=j-\omega}^{j-1} x_i \tag{3}$$

where x_j is the first missing data and ω is the autoregressive order. However, this method only uses the temporal characteristics of wind speed data.

To better utilize the spatiotemporal characteristics of wind speed, the MDAM is first proposed in this paper. As shown in Figure 1, the relevant data sequences from other wind farms within the same wind farm cluster are adopted in the MDAM to make up for the missing data. Assuming there are k relevant sequences with the same length, $x_{1,j}$, which stands for the first missing data of wind farm speed series x_1, can be represented as:

$$x_{1,j} = \frac{x_{2,j} + x_{3.j} + \ldots + x_{k,j}}{k-1} \tag{4}$$

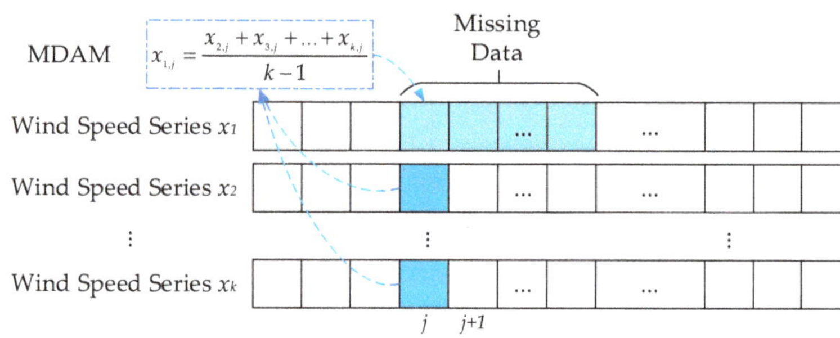

Figure 1. Schematic diagram of MDAM.

3. The Ensembled Model IWC-DELM

3.1. Deep Extreme Learning Machine

Extreme learning machine (ELM) is a popular feed-forward neural network for classification or regression uses, which was first proposed by Huang et al. in [29]. ELM has a good generalization performance along with a comparatively fast speed. Its trainable parameters connecting the input layer and hidden layer are randomly assigned instead of backpropagation [30]. Its output weights are obtained by calculating the generalized inverse operation of the hidden matrix [31]. Assuming there are l training samples, the output of ELM with L hidden neurons can be represented as:

$$y = \sum_{i=1}^{L} \eta_i h_i(x) = H\eta, for\ i = 1, 2, \ldots l \tag{5}$$

$$H = g(wx + b) \tag{6}$$

where y represents the output vector and η_i represents output weight connecting the ith hidden layer and output neuron. H is the hidden layer matrix, and $g(\cdot)$ is the activation function. w and b denote input weight and bias, respectively. We can also have

$$H\eta = T \tag{7}$$

where T is the matrix of targets. η is determined by reaching the smallest training error between the output y and the target T.

$$\eta = \min\|T - H\eta\|_2^2 = H^{\dagger}T \tag{8}$$

where $H^{\dagger}$ is the generalized inverse matrix of H.

Due to the shallow architecture of ELM, it is incapable of capturing the complex characteristics of input data [32]. To tackle this issue, deep extreme learning machine (DELM) was proposed in [33], whose configuration is shown in Figure 2. This model, utilizing a multilayer extreme learning machine (MLELM) and based on an extreme learning machine autoencoder (ELM-AE), takes advantage of both deep learning and ELM. The output of ELM-AE is the same as (6) and (9) is used to ensure the orthogonality of w and b.

$$w^T w = 1, b^T b = 1 \tag{9}$$

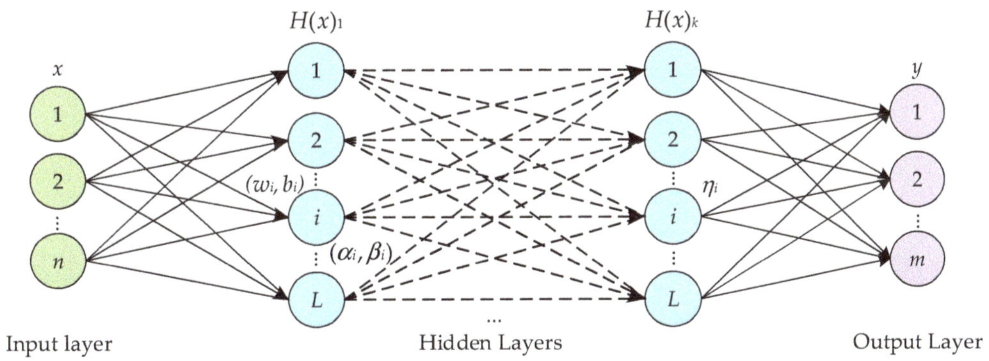

Figure 2. DELM configuration with n inputs and L-length hidden layer.

The relationship between the adjacent hidden layers can be expressed as:

$$H_j = g(\alpha_i H_{j-1} + \beta_i), for\ i = 1, 2, ...L; j = 1, 2, ...k; \tag{10}$$

where α_i and β_i denote the weight and bias of the ith hidden neuron.

Unlike traditional machine learning methods using a gradient-based method, which include many iterations and deep learning models, which contain a memory unit leading to a slow procession, DELM determines the output weight by calculation of a hidden matrix [34]. Therefore, DELM shows great efficiency in processing big-capacity data.

3.2. Input Set Based on Wind Farm Cluster Data

Figure 3 illustrates a newly proposed approach, IWC, for input set construction. It is defined as follows:

$$X = \begin{bmatrix} x_{a,1} & x_{a,2} & \cdots & x_{a,m} \\ x_{b,1} & x_{b,2} & \cdots & x_{b,m} \\ \vdots & \vdots & \ddots & \vdots \\ x_{n,1} & x_{n,2} & \cdots & x_{n,m} \end{bmatrix} \tag{11}$$

where X is the constructed n-dimensional input set, x_a, x_b, ... , and x_n is wind speed series from wind farm a, b, ... , and n.

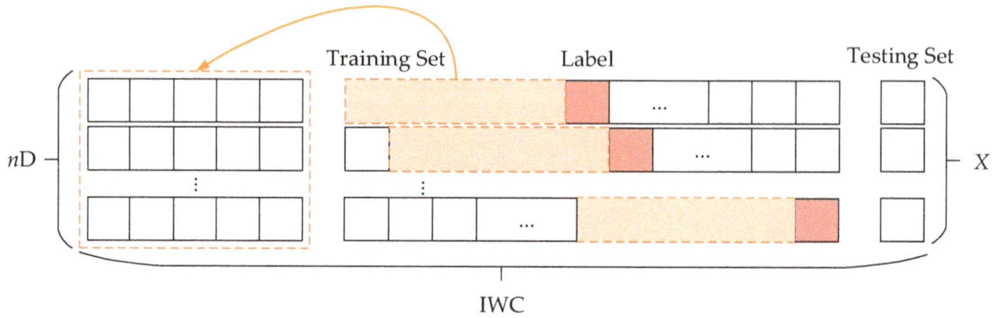

Figure 3. Schematic diagram of IWC configuration.

In Figure 3, an n-dimensional training set is constructed based on wind farm cluster data containing n wind farms. X contains both the training set and the testing set. The overall process is named the IWC approach.

3.3. The Proposed IWC-DELM

Figure 4 illustrates a newly proposed model for IWC-DELM that consists of n-dimensional input sets and three major steps.

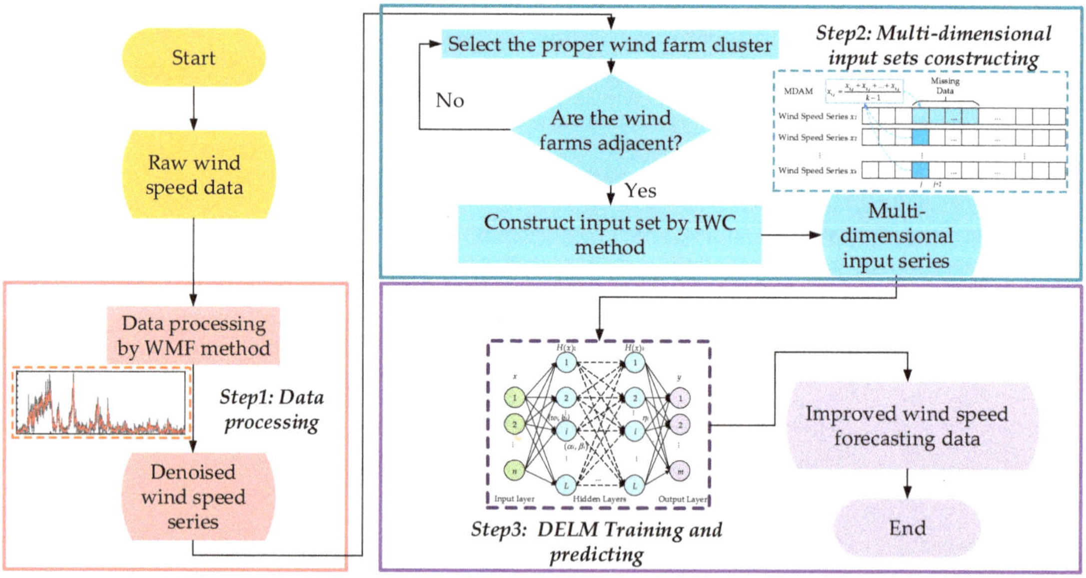

Figure 4. Flowchart of IWC-DELM.

Step 1: During the data cleaning preprocess, the original wind speed data is filtered by WMF to suppress the white noise in the original time series. WMF can maintain the causality of the whole system and reduce the noise at the same time [28].

Step 2: Once the denoised wind speed series is obtained, a proper wind farm cluster should be selected to construct a multidimensional input set of DELM using the IWC method. Moreover, whenever the wind speed of any wind farm in a cluster is unavailable, the model will make up for the continuous missing data via the MDAM.

Step 3: As described in Section 3.2, the multidimensional input set is used to train the prediction model of DELM. Then, it is applied to future prediction to obtain improved wind speed forecasting data.

Parameters of the IWC-DELM model can be found in Table 1.

Table 1. Configuration of the proposed ensemble model IWC-DELM.

Type	Configuration	
WMF	Batch extent Weights	5 [0.80, 0.64, 0.51, 0.41, 0.33]
IWC	$X = \begin{bmatrix} x_{a,1} & x_{a,2} & \cdots & x_{a,m} \\ x_{b,1} & x_{b,2} & \cdots & x_{b,m} \\ \vdots & \vdots & \ddots & \vdots \\ x_{n,1} & x_{n,2} & \cdots & x_{n,m} \end{bmatrix}$	X_a data series of wind farm a X_b data series of wind farm b $\cdots$ X_n data series of wind farm n
DELM	Layers	Hyperparameters
	Hidden layer 1	Input: 5×3 Nodes: 30
	Hidden layer 2	Input: 10×1 Nodes: 15

4. Case Study

4.1. Datasets and Evaluation Indices

The datasets used in this paper are shown in Figure 5 with their longitudes and latitudes. Further information, both data and maps, can be found in the data availability statement. Site 1 to Site 5 are adjoining to one other, and Site 6 and Site 7 are apart from these five wind farms. Figure 6 illustrates the data preprocessing of seven selected wind farms by WMF.

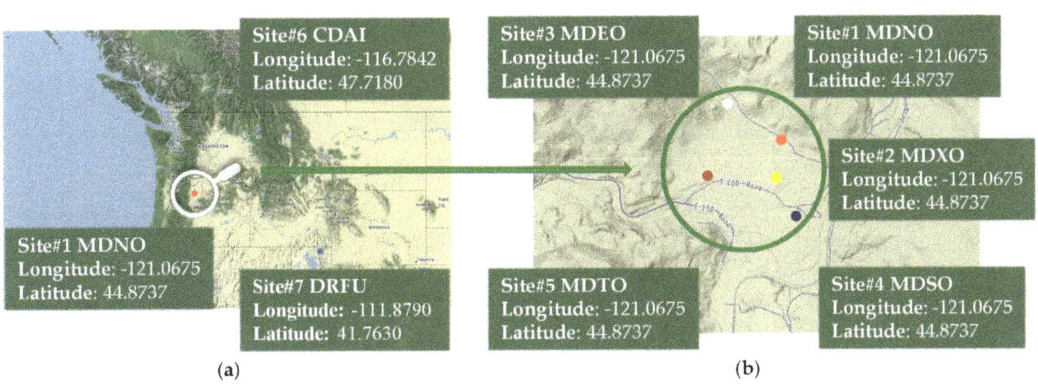

Figure 5. Seven selected wind farms with their longitudes and latitudes: (**a**) nonadjacent wind farms from Site 1 to Site 6 to Site 7; (**b**) adjacent wind farms from Site 1 to Site 5.

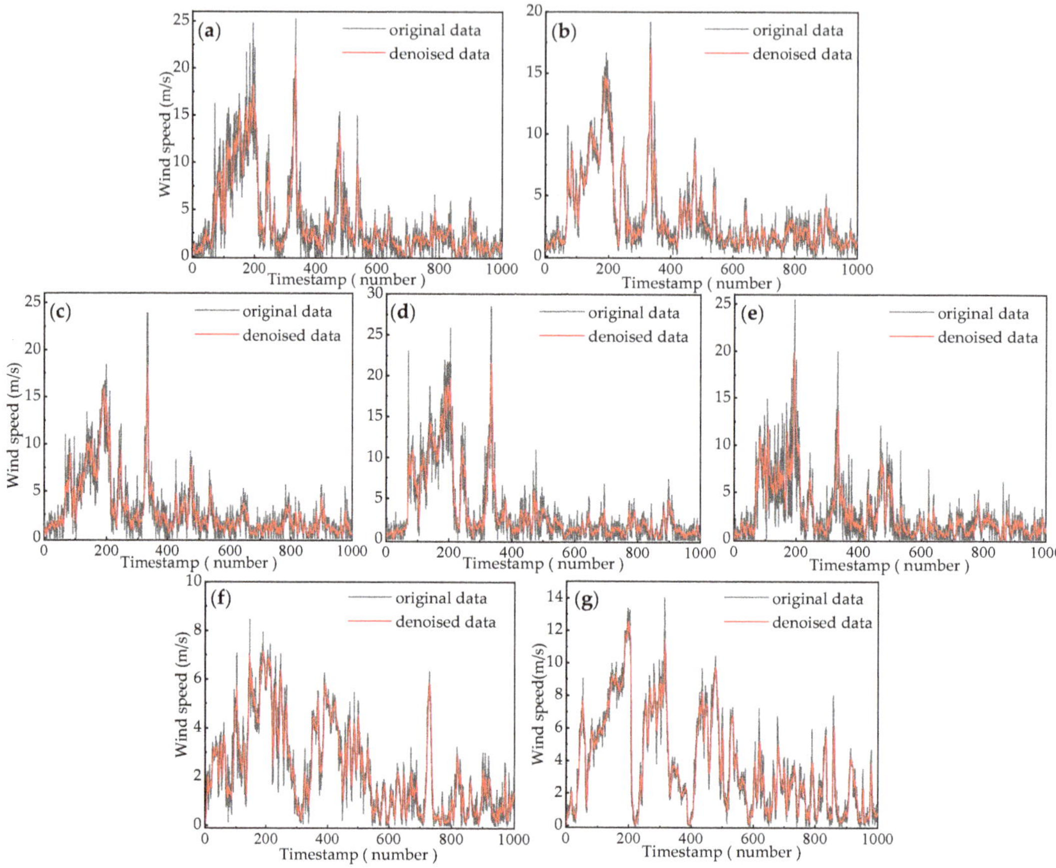

Figure 6. Data preprocessing on the historical wind speed sequences of seven selected wind farms: (**a**) Site#1, (**b**) Site#2, (**c**) Site#3, (**d**) Site#4, (**e**) Site#5, (**f**) Site#6, (**g**) Site#7.

Four indices, the root mean squared error (RMSE), mean absolute error (MAE), mean absolute percentage error (MAPE) and R-squared (R^2), are used for evaluation [28,35]. Their definitions are available below:

$$\text{RMSE} = \sqrt{\frac{1}{\mu}\sum_{i=1}^{\mu}(y_i^p - y_i)^2} \tag{12}$$

$$\text{MAE} = \frac{1}{\mu}\sum_{i=1}^{\mu}\left|y_i^p - y_i\right| \tag{13}$$

$$\text{MAPE} = \frac{1}{\mu}\sum_{i=1}^{\mu}\left|\frac{y_i^p - y_i}{y_i}\right| \tag{14}$$

$$\text{R}^2 = 1 - \frac{\sum_{i=1}^{\mu}\left(y_i^p - y_i\right)^2}{\sum_{i=1}^{\mu}(\overline{y} - y_i)^2} \tag{15}$$

where y^p denotes the wind speed prediction, y is the real data and $\overline{y}$ represents the mean value of real data. μ represents the wind speed sequence length.

To measure the improvement of these four indices, η_I is defined as:

$$\eta_I = -\frac{I' - I}{I} \times 100\% \quad (16)$$

where the I represents any of the four indices and I' is the improved one. If η_I is positive, it indicates lower error and better performance, and vice versa.

4.2. Tests under Various Influential Factors

4.2.1. Accuracy Analysis of Different Methods Operated on Different Input Sets

Historical data of the adjacent wind farms are involved in the input dataset in order to utilize the spatial relevance of wind sequences in wind farm clusters. The number of adopted wind farms changes from one to five, which means the input dataset can be from one-dimensional to five-dimensional (i.e., 1D to 5D). Three models, GRU, LSTM and SRNN, are adopted as candidate algorithms for comparison.

Table 2 and Figure 7 illustrate the performance of three promising algorithms and the selected algorithm DELM. SRNN and DELM obtain a similar performance, which is better than those of GRU and LSTM. DELM shows more competitive capability in terms of all error indices at 3D input, with an RMSE of 0.288, MAE of 0.224, MAPE of 0.140 and R^2 of 0.898. Four indices of GRU and LSTM become larger along with an increase in input dimension, indicating a drop in prediction accuracy. For instance, the RMSE of GRU increases from 0.316 to 0.628. Their lack of capabilities of addressing large-volume data and overfitting issues may result in this phenomenon, which indicates that GRU and LSTM are not suitable for the prediction of wind farm clusters herein. In contrast, the forecasting accuracies of SRNN and DELM are improved when enlarging the input dimension. The RMSE of DELM declines from 0.325 to 0.287. The fitting lines shown in Figure 8 clearly represent their capacities for prediction. Prediction of DELM is always the closest to the real wind speed data. These experimental results indicate that utilizing relevant spatial data plays a significant role in prediction accuracy improvement.

Table 2. Performance of different models with diverse input dimensions from 1 to 5 *.

Model	Indices	1D	2D	3D	4D	5D
GRU	RMSE	**0.316**	0.452	0.564	0.658	0.628
	MAE	0.267	0.353	0.442	0.507	0.489
	MAPE	0.529	0.674	1.412	1.978	1.979
	R^2	**0.898**	0.831	0.766	0.765	0.723
LSTM	RMSE	0.319	0.390	0.452	0.722	0.725
	MAE	**0.257**	0.301	0.344	0.558	0.585
	MAPE	0.438	0.364	0.648	1.911	2.458
	R^2	0.896	0.858	0.874	0.763	0.728
SRNN	RMSE	0.352	0.302	0.289	**0.267**	0.298
	MAE	0.280	0.241	0.235	**0.216**	**0.234**
	MAPE	**0.235**	**0.137**	0.266	0.226	**0.237**
	R^2	0.841	**0.872**	0.891	**0.903**	0.872
DELM (selected algorithm)	RMSE	0.325	**0.301**	**0.288**	0.286	**0.287**
	MAE	0.262	**0.234**	**0.224**	0.228	0.236
	MAPE	0.354	0.168	**0.140**	**0.145**	0.297
	R^2	0.777	0.809	**0.898**	0.886	**0.875**

* The minimum error of 4 indices among candidate algorithms with different input dimensions are in bold.

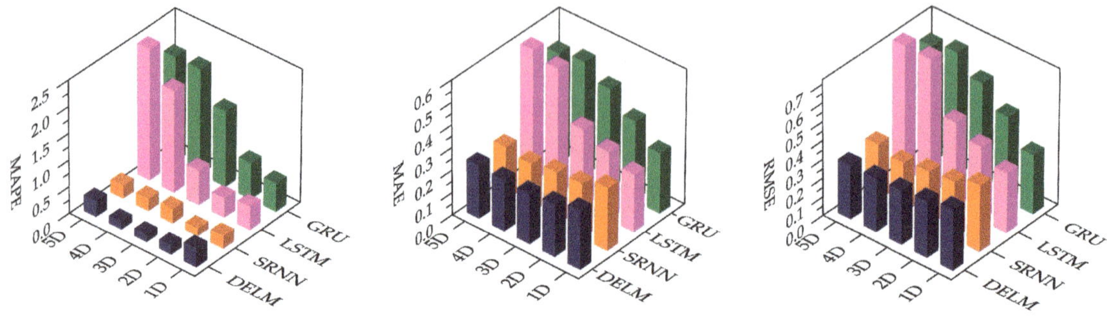

Figure 7. Error indices of different models.

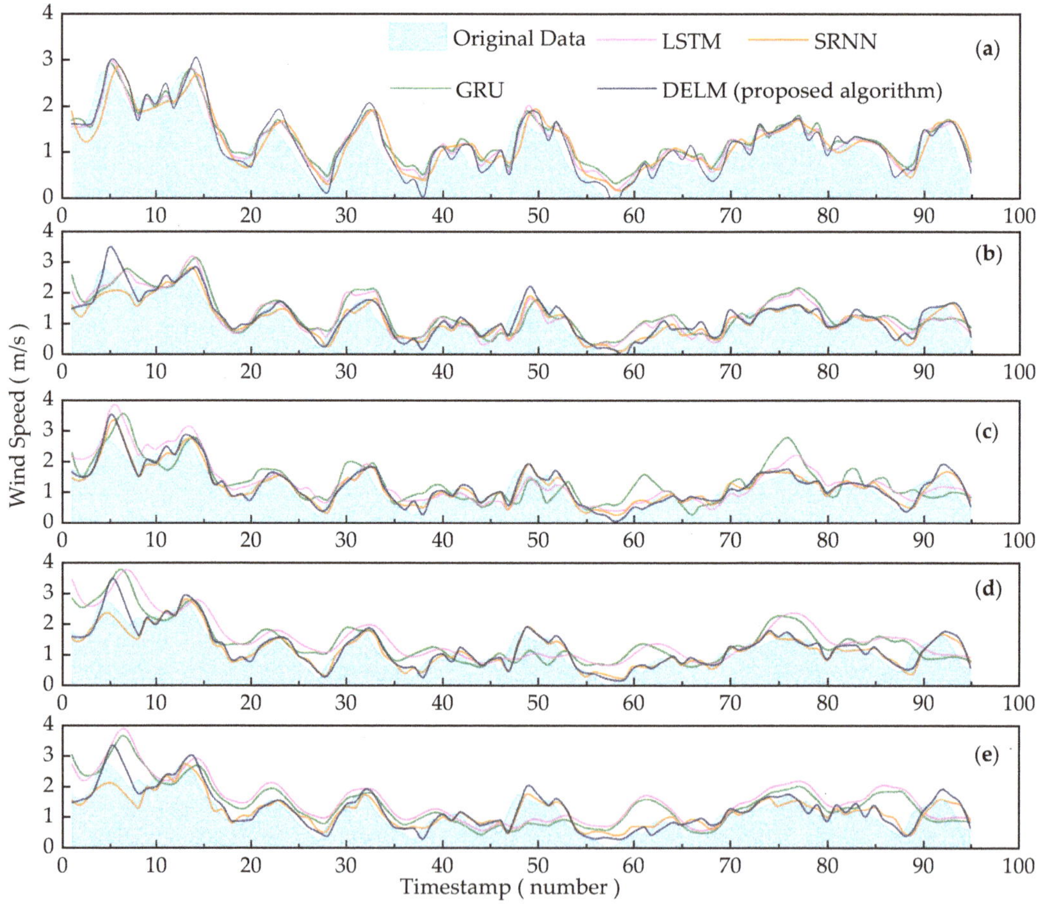

Figure 8. Fitting lines of different models with input dimensions from 1 to 5: (**a**) 1D input set; (**b**) 2D input set; (**c**) 3D input set; (**d**) 4D input set; (**e**) 5D input set.

4.2.2. Efficiency Analysis of Different Methods Operated on Different Input Sets

To measure the efficiency of different prediction methods, their training periods are displayed in Table 3. Three comparative methods and DELM are conducted with 1D to

5D input set conditions. Figure 9 shows the efficiency improvement percentage of three candidates compared to DELM.

Table 3. CPU time for both training and testing sets of different models (s) *.

Model	1D	2D	3D	4D	5D
GRU	105.225	165.201	195.250	227.745	306.538
LSTM	140.558	240.385	342.736	410.983	501.438
SRNN	51.800	55.793	57.255	58.372	56.018
DELM (selected algorithm)	**0.228**	**0.268**	**0.279**	**0.343**	**0.462**

* The minimum training time with different input dimensions is in bold.

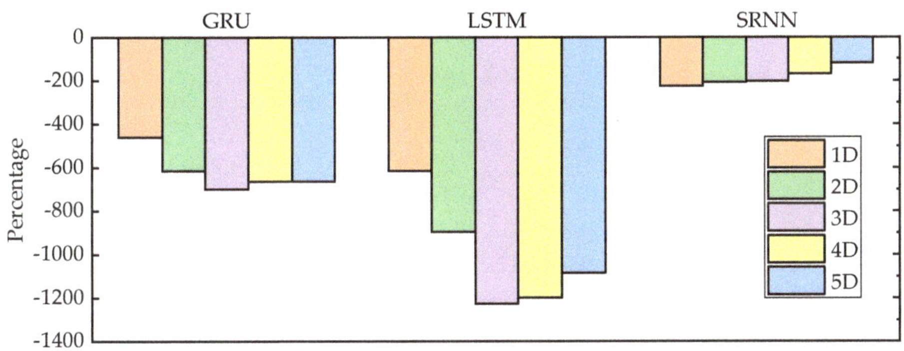

Figure 9. The efficiency improvement percentage of three candidates compared to DELM.

According to Table 3, when the input dimension ranges from one to five, the training times of GRU and LSTM increase sharply from 105.225 s to 306.538 s and from 140.558 s to 501.438 s, respectively. The time cost of SRNN and DELM shows a slight rise. The SRNN period increases by 4.218 s, and the DELM period with five dimensions is only 0.234 s longer than with one dimension. Despite the fact that the training time of DELM increases by 102.63% compared to the 1D input, its absolute CPU time is comparatively shorter than others. These results mainly stem from different model configurations. GRU and LSTM cannot be computed in parallel owing to their recurrent structure [10]. Every current input is connected to its previous step, so the larger the input database is, the longer it will take for computation. However, SRNN, as an improvement of this recurrent structure, slices input data into subsequences so that each subsequence can be operated simultaneously, leading to a markable reduction in training time [36]. The larger the input dataset is, the more significant the speed advantage SRNN achieves. When the input dimension reaches five, SRNN only needs 56.018 s, while GRU and LSTM take 306.538 s and 501.438 s, respectively.

It is mentioned that the parameters of the three comparison models are consistent with those in [1,9,10] as shown in Table 4. Among the mentioned four models, the selected DELM markedly surpasses the other models in training time. As shown in Figure 9 and Table 4, its speed is hundreds or even thousands of times faster than the other three candidate methods as it has the least parameters. The learning period of DELM is extremely fast, which can be completed within one second [36,37].

Table 4. Number of parameters of different methods.

Model	GRU	LSTM	SRNN	DELM (Selected Algorithm)
Number of parameters	845,601	1,849,441	4137	3600

4.2.3. Comparison of Datasets with Different Correlation Degrees

To evaluate the validity of IWC-DELM model, we chose the prediction results of a single wind farm as a blank control group and compared the results of wind farm clusters with high relevance and weak relevance. Adjacent wind farms and nonadjacent wind farms represent strong and weak correlations, respectively, since the distance between wind farms is positively related to correlation.

The performance of three different input datasets is displayed in Table 5. When the input set includes adjacent wind farm data, the RMSE declines by 11.38%, MAE drops by 14.50%, MAPE dramatically falls by 60.56% and R^2 increases by 5.40% compared to the single-wind-farm prediction. Inversely, nonadjacent farm data input leads to the RMSE, MAE and MAPE experiencing a rise of 2.15%, 5.34% and 1.98%, respectively. Figure 10 intuitively shows the fitting lines of the three conditions mentioned above. It can be obviously observed that forecasting of adjacent wind farms is most close to the original data.

Table 5. Performance of different input datasets *.

	Single Wind Farm	Wind Farm Cluster			
		Nonadjacent Farms	Improvement	Adjacent Farms	Improvement
RMSE	0.325	0.332	−2.15%	**0.288**	**11.38%**
MAE	0.262	0.276	−5.34%	**0.224**	**14.50%**
MAPE	0.354	0.361	−1.98%	**0.140**	**60.45%**
R^2	0.777	0.748	−3.73%	**0.819**	**5.40%**

* The minimum error and maximum improvement are in bold.

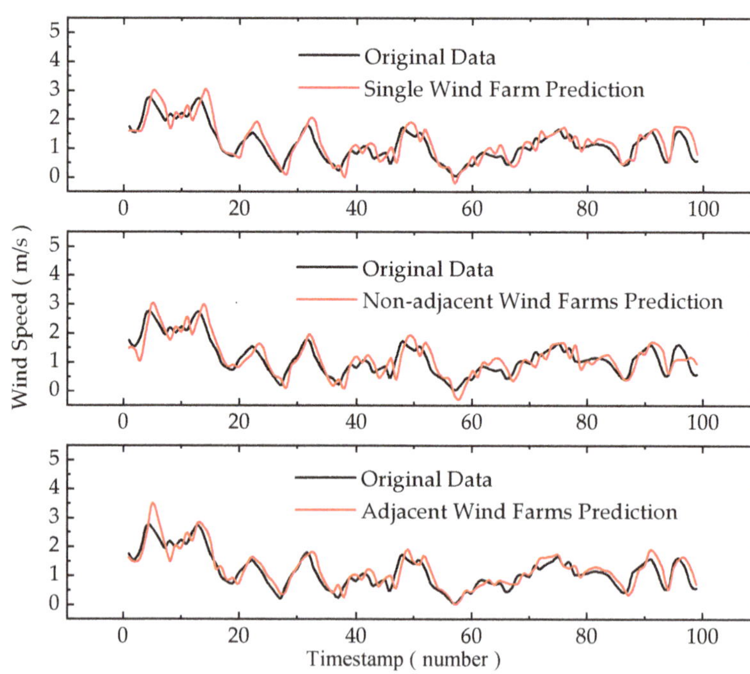

Figure 10. Fitting lines of different data inputs.

Therefore, a conclusion can be drawn that the forecasting accuracy is improved with a highly correlated historical data input, which verifies the effectiveness of the proposed model utilizing spatial corrections of wind speed sequences in wind farm clusters.

4.2.4. Discussion

According to the experiment results shown above, the prediction accuracies of SRNN and DELM are higher than those of GRU and LSTM. In addition, the operation efficiency of DELM is outstanding. Therefore, DELM is selected as the main body of the model, and the 3D input is designed due to the balance between training cost and prediction accuracy. The input dataset is constructed by wind farm data with a strong correlation. This proposed model, termed IWC-DELM and proved validly, can achieve a better wind speed forecasting result.

The main advantages of the proposed model can be summarized as follows:

1. DELM has boasted its operational efficiency as it determines the output weight by simple computations of the hidden matrix. It also employs the multi-hidden-layer structure to capture complex nonlinear characteristics. Hence, using DELM as the main body of the model is critical for forecasting accuracy and training speed improvement.
2. Considering the spatial correlation, the multidimension input can improve the forecasting capacity. The proposed model is an integration of DELM and IWC, which outperforms the other candidate algorithms with a smaller prediction fluctuance, better adaptiveness and greatly enhanced efficiency.

4.3. Input Dataset Robustness Analysis

Robustness analysis is conducted to prevent the prediction capability from a significant drop in extreme cases. Figure 11 shows the selected two periods that experience 5, 10 and 15 missing points, respectively. Those missing points in single-farm prediction are made up by the MAA [25], while those in wind farm cluster prediction are made up by the MDAM. Error indices of prediction results of the single wind farm and wind farm cluster are displayed in Table 6. Their improvement compared to the original forecasting is shown in Table 7.

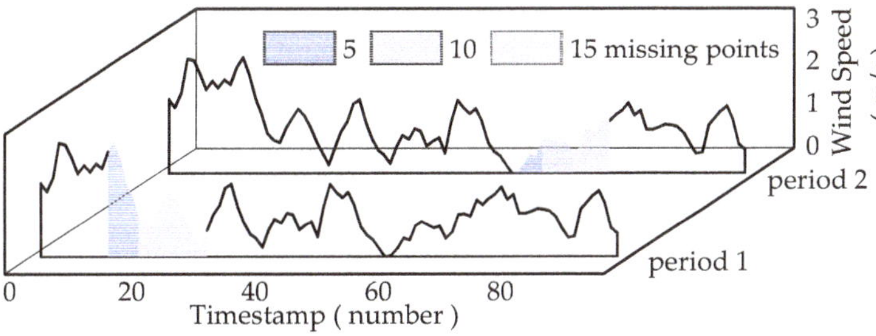

Figure 11. Selected two periods where data are missing.

Table 6. Comparison of single-farm and wind farm cluster performance in different conditions of missing data *.

Missing Period	Indices	Original Prediction	Single Farm			Wind Farm Cluster		
			MAA			MDAM (Proposed Method)		
			5 Missing	10 Missing	15 Missing	5 Missing	10 Missing	15 Missing
Period 1	RMSE	0.288	0.340	0.386	0.448	**0.296**	**0.312**	**0.331**
	MAE	0.224	0.267	0.303	0.342	**0.234**	**0.245**	**0.257**
	MAPE	0.140	0.373	0.439	1.078	**0.153**	**0.168**	**0.308**
	R^2	0.898	0.724	0.548	0.238	**0.858**	**0.734**	**0.702**
Period 2	RMSE	0.288	0.328	0.445	0.454	**0.291**	**0.288**	**0.292**
	MAE	0.224	0.263	0.352	0.365	**0.231**	**0.226**	**0.230**
	MAPE	0.140	0.386	0.281	0.306	**0.145**	**0.144**	**0.145**
	R^2	0.898	0.827	0.582	0.292	**0.796**	**0.726**	**0.705**

* The minimum error in the different missing conditions is in bold.

Table 7. Improvement of single-farm and wind farm cluster prediction in different conditions of missing data *.

Missing Period	Indices	Single Farm			Wind Farm Cluster		
		MAA			MDAM (Proposed Method)		
		5 Missing	10 Missing	15 Missing	5 Missing	10 Missing	15 Missing
Period 1	η_{RMSE}	−18.06%	−34.03%	−55.56%	**−2.78%**	**−8.33%**	**−14.93%**
	η_{MAE}	−19.20%	−35.27%	−52.68%	**−4.46%**	**−9.38%**	**−14.73%**
	η_{MAPE}	−166.43%	−213.57%	−670.00%	**−9.29%**	**−20.00%**	**−120.00%**
	η_{R2}	−19.38%	−38.98%	−73.50%	**−4.45%**	**−18.26%**	**−21.83%**
Period 2	η_{RMSE}	−13.89%	−54.51%	−57.64%	**−1.04%**	**−0.32%**	**−1.39%**
	η_{MAE}	−17.41%	−57.14%	−62.95%	**−3.13%**	**−0.89%**	**−2.68%**
	η_{MAPE}	−175.71%	−100.71%	−118.57%	**−3.57%**	**−2.86%**	**−3.57%**
	η_{R2}	**−7.91%**	−35.19%	−67.48%	−11.36%	**−19.15%**	**−21.49%**

* The maximum improvement ratios in the different missing conditions are in bold.

According to Table 6, as a result of missing data, the negative η_I indicates that the performance of both the single farm and wind farm cluster are worse than the original one without missing data. As the numbers of lost data increase, the four indices decline in both prediction forms and in both periods. Table 7 illustrates that a wind farm cluster can achieve a better prediction than a single wind farm. Especially in the 15-point-missing condition in period 2, the improvement of the RMSE in the wind farm cluster only falls by 1.39% compared to 57.64% in the single wind farm. This can be attributed to different interpolation methods. Our MDAM adopts the historical wind speed sequences of two adjacent wind farms, which characterize the original wind speed data.

Additionally, the accuracy reduction in period 2 is not as serious as in period 1, which is mainly arisen from the sharp variation in wind speed in period 1. For instance, in the 15-point-missing condition, the RMSE in period 2 drops by 1.39%, while that in period 1 declines by 14.93%.

Using a paired t-test to study the differences in experimental data [38], it can be seen from the Table 8 that there are six groups of paired data in total, amongst which five groups of paired data show differences ($p < 0.05$). With the increase in missing data, the p value becomes smaller ($p < 0.01$), and this indicates a more significant difference between the MAA and MDAM.

Table 8. Results of paired t-test analysis of missing data in both MAA and MDAM methods *.

Missing Period	Paired Name	Pair (Mean ± Standard Deviation)		Difference (Pair 1–Pair 2)	t	p
		Pair 1	Pair 2			
Period 1	MAA(5) vs. MDAM(5)	1.17 ± 0.48	1.15 ± 0.48	0.03	0.664	0.517
	MAA(10) vs. MDAM(10)	1.55 ± 0.62	1.28 ± 0.47	0.27	4.144	0.001 ***
	MAA(15) vs. MDAM(15)	1.57 ± 0.00	1.37 ± 0.29	0.21	2.756	0.015 **
Period 2	MAA(5) vs. MDAM(5)	0.71 ± 0.29	1.01 ± 0.32	−0.30	−2.611	0.021 **
	MAA(10) vs. MDAM(10)	0.53 ± 0.37	0.98 ± 0.35	−0.45	−3.822	0.002 ***
	MAA(15) vs. MDAM(15)	0.62 ± null	1.02 ± 0.34	−0.40	−4.578	0.000 ***

* MAA(5), MAA(10) and MAA(15) mean 5, 10 and 15 missing values in MAA method, while the same rule holds for MDAM as well. ** $p < 0.05$; *** $p < 0.01$

From these experimental results, it can be concluded that the proposed MDAM can enhance the data robustness, thus leading to a reduction in accuracy loss in some special cases.

5. Conclusions

Existing studies focus on WSF in wind farm clusters without consideration of spatial correlation. Additionally, there are few effective solutions for dealing with missing data conditions. Therefore, IWC-DELM is proposed in this paper based on a combination of IWC and MDAM. IWC takes advantage of spatial correlations within wind farm clusters by employing the historical data of adjacent wind farms. DELM is selected as the main body of this proposed model for its extremely fast speed in processing. Robustness analysis is conducted using the MDAM to prevent prediction accuracy from a dramatic drop in the missing data conditions. Therefore, IWC-DELM outperforms some promising deep learning algorithms, for instance, GRU, LSTM and SRNN, in both accuracy and efficiency, especially when processing large volumes of wind farm cluster data. It is mentioned above that the parameters of the three comparison models are consistent with those in [1,9,10]. Four indices, RMSE, MAE, MAPE and R^2, in the 3D input condition using DELM are improved by 48.94%, 49.32%, 90.08% and 17.23%, respectively, compared to GRU and are improved by 36.28%, 34.88%, 78.40% and 2.75%, respectively, compared to LSTM. As for different input datasets, IWC-DELM used in adjacent wind farms achieves an improvement in RMSE, MAE, MAPE and R^2 of 11.38%, 14.50%, 60.45% and 5.40%, respectively, compared to nonadjacent wind farms. When dealing with missing data, the proposed method, MDAM, also performs better than the MAA. For instance, the MAE is improved by 9.38~25.89% with 5, 10 and 15 missing data. Such an accurate prediction can be applied in broad fields, such as the making of grid operation strategies, and is available for meteorological usage.

Meanwhile, there is still room for improvement. Firstly, the selected DELM could be not the best option with the advent of other state-of-the-art forecasting methods. Moreover, hybrid state-of-the-art approaches in both wind prediction studies and other AI-assisted contributions can be applied in terms of handling missing data. Some promising statistics and probability methods should be taken into consideration as well. Numerical weather prediction (NWP) can be also adopted to further expand the input dataset since the current dataset only includes historical data on wind speed.

Author Contributions: Methodology, M.Z. and J.T.; software, M.Z. and H.Z.; writing—original draft preparation, Y.W.; writing—review and editing, M.Z., Y.W., H.Z, Z.P. and J.T.; supervision, J.T. All authors have read and agreed to the published version of the manuscript.

Funding: This research was funded by National Natural Science Foundation of China [52177071] and Chongqing Municipal Training Program of Innovation and Entrepreneurship for Undergraduates [S 202110611442]. And the APC was funded by [52177071].

Data Availability Statement: The datasets used in this paper are available at the website: https://www.usbr.gov/pn/agrimet/webaghrread.html, accessed on 16 January 2023. The main prediction method code used in this article can be accessed at the following website for reference. In addition, the codes written by the authors, which are not available below, will be provided by the corresponding author via email once they are required by the readers. GRU: https://github.com/keras-team/keras/blob/v2.11.0/keras/layers/rnn/gru.py, accessed on 16 January 2023. LSTM: https://github.com/keras-team/keras/blob/v2.11.0/keras/layers/rnn/lstm.py#L382-L893, accessed on 16 January 2023. SRNN: https://github.com/zepingyu0512/srnn, accessed on 16 January 2023. DELM: https://github.com/atefeta/Deep-Extreme-Learning-Machine, accessed on 16 January 2023.

Conflicts of Interest: The authors declare no conflict of interest.

References

1. Zhou:, B.; Ma, X.; Luo, Y.; Yang, D. Wind Power Prediction Based on LSTM Networks and Nonparametric Kernel Density Estimation. *IEEE Access* **2019**, *7*, 165279–165292. [CrossRef]
2. Qin, Y.; Li, K.; Liang, Z.; Lee, B.; Zhang, F.; Gu, Y.; Zhang, L.; Wu, F.; Rodriguez, D. Hybrid forecasting model based on long short term memory network and deep learning neural network for wind signal. *Appl. Energy* **2019**, *236*, 262–272. [CrossRef]
3. Liu, X.; Yang, L.; Zhang, Z. Short-Term Multi-Step Ahead Wind Power Predictions Based on A Novel Deep Convolutional Recurrent Network Method. *IEEE Trans. Sustain. Energy* **2021**, *12*, 1820–1833. [CrossRef]
4. Alanis, A.Y.; Sanchez, O.D.; Alvarez, J.G. Time Series Forecasting for Wind Energy Systems Based on High Order Neural Networks. *Mathematics* **2021**, *9*, 1075. [CrossRef]
5. Wang, H.Z.; Wang, G.B.; Li, G.Q.; Peng, J.C.; Liu, Y.T. Deep belief network based deterministic and probabilistic wind speed forecasting approach. *Appl. Energy* **2016**, *182*, 80–93. [CrossRef]
6. Wang, Y.; Zou, R.; Liu, F.; Zhang, L.; Liu, Q. A review of wind speed and wind power forecasting with deep neural networks. *Appl. Energy* **2021**, *304*, 117766. [CrossRef]
7. Zhang, H.; Liu, Y.; Yan, J.; Han, S.; Li, L.; Long, Q. Improved Deep Mixture Density Network for Regional Wind Power Probabilistic Forecasting. *IEEE Trans. Power Syst.* **2020**, *35*, 2549–2560. [CrossRef]
8. Khan, N.; Ullah, F.U.M.; Haq, I.U.; Khan, S.U.; Lee, M.Y.; Baik, S.W. AB-Net: A Novel Deep Learning Assisted Framework for Renewable Energy Generation Forecasting. *Mathematics* **2021**, *9*, 2456. [CrossRef]
9. Peng, Z.; Peng, S.; Fu, L.; Lu, B.; Tang, J.; Wang, K.; Li, W. A novel deep learning ensemble model with data denoising for short-term wind speed forecasting. *Energy Convers. Manag.* **2020**, *207*, 112524. [CrossRef]
10. Yu, Z.; Liu, G. Sliced recurrent neural networks. *arXiv* **2018**, arXiv:1807.02291.
11. Meng, A.; Zhu, Z.; Deng, W.; Ou, Z.; Lin, S.; Wang, C.; Xu, X.; Wang, X.; Yin, H.; Luo, J. A novel wind power prediction approach using multivariate variational mode decomposition and multi-objective crisscross optimization based deep extreme learning machine. *Energy* **2022**, *260*, 124957. [CrossRef]
12. An, G.; Jiang, Z.; Chen, L.; Cao, X.; Li, Z.; Zhao, Y.; Sun, H. Ultra Short-Term Wind Power Forecasting Based on Sparrow Search Algorithm Optimization Deep Extreme Learning Machine. *Sustainability* **2021**, *13*, 10453. [CrossRef]
13. Chen, N.; Qian, Z.; Nabney, I.T.; Meng, X. Wind Power Forecasts Using Gaussian Processes and Numerical Weather Prediction. *IEEE Trans. Power Syst.* **2014**, *29*, 656–665. [CrossRef]
14. Pinhão, M.; Fonseca, M.; Covas, R. Electricity Spot Price Forecast by Modelling Supply and Demand Curve. *Mathematics* **2022**, *10*, 2012. [CrossRef]
15. Zhu, Q.; Chen, J.; Shi, D.; Zhu, L.; Bai, X.; Duan, X.; Liu, Y. Learning Temporal and Spatial Correlations Jointly: A Unified Framework for Wind Speed Prediction. *IEEE Trans. Sustain. Energy* **2020**, *11*, 509–523. [CrossRef]
16. Wang, Q.; Martinez-Anido, C.B.; Wu, H.; Florita, A.R.; Hodge, B.-M. Quantifying the Economic and Grid Reliability Impacts of Improved Wind Power Forecasting. *IEEE Trans. Sustain. Energy* **2016**, *7*, 1525–1537. [CrossRef]
17. Hu, Q.; Zhang, S.; Yu, M.; Xie, Z. Short-Term Wind Speed or Power Forecasting with Heteroscedastic Support Vector Regression. *IEEE Trans. Sustain. Energy* **2016**, *7*, 241–249. [CrossRef]
18. Zhang, J.; Liu, D.; Li, Z.; Han, X.; Liu, H.; Dong, C.; Wang, J.; Liu, C.; Xia, Y. Power prediction of a wind farm cluster based on spatiotemporal correlations. *Appl. Energy* **2021**, *302*, 117568. [CrossRef]
19. Peng, X.; Chen, Y.; Cheng, K.; Wang, H.; Zhao, Y.; Wang, B.; Che, J.; Liu, C.; Wen, J.; Lu, C.; et al. Wind Power Prediction for Wind Farm Clusters Based on the Multifeature Similarity Matching Method. *IEEE Trans. Ind. Appl.* **2020**, *56*, 4679–4688. [CrossRef]
20. Ying, X.; Zhao, K.; Liu, Z.; Gao, J.; He, D.; Li, X.; Xiong, W. Wind Speed Prediction via Collaborative Filtering on Virtual Edge Expanding Graphs. *Mathematics* **2022**, *10*, 1943. [CrossRef]
21. Zhu, Q.; Chen, J.; Zhu, L.; Duan, X.; Liu, Y. Wind Speed Prediction with Spatio–Temporal Correlation: A Deep Learning Approach. *Energies* **2018**, *11*, 705. [CrossRef]
22. Ali, M.; Prasad, R.; Xiang, Y.; Sankaran, A.; Deo, R.C.; Xiao, F.; Zhu, S. Advanced extreme learning machines vs. deep learning models for peak wave energy period forecasting: A case study in Queensland, Australia. *Renew. Energy* **2021**, *177*, 1031–1044. [CrossRef]
23. Wan, J.; Huang, J.; Liao, Z.; Li, C.; Liu, P.X. A Multi-View Ensemble Width-Depth Neural Network for Short-Term Wind Power Forecasting. *Mathematics* **2022**, *10*, 1824. [CrossRef]
24. Lotfi, B.; Mourad, M.; Najiba, M.B.; Mohamed, E. Treatment methodology of erroneous and missing data in wind farm dataset. In Proceedings of the Eighth International Multi-Conference on Systems, Signals & Devices, Sousse, Tunisia, 22–25 March 2011; pp. 1–6.
25. Lin, Q.; Wang, J. Vertically Correlated Echelon Model for the Interpolation of Missing Wind Speed Data. *IEEE Trans. Sustain. Energy* **2014**, *5*, 804–812. [CrossRef]
26. O'Leary, C.; Lynch, C.; Bain, R.; Smith, G.; Grimes, D. A Comparison of Deep Learning vs Traditional Machine Learning for Electricity Price Forecasting. In Proceedings of the 2021 4th International Conference on Information and Computer Technologies (ICICT), Kahului, HI, USA, 11–14 March 2021; pp. 6–12.
27. Peña-Gallardo, R.; Medina-Rios, A. A comparison of deep learning methods for wind speed forecasting. In Proceedings of the 2020 IEEE International Autumn Meeting on Power, Electronics and Computing (ROPEC), Ixtapa, Mexico, 4–6 November 2020; pp. 1–6.

28. Zhang, H.; Peng, Z.; Tang, J.; Dong, M.; Wang, K.; Li, W. A multi-layer extreme learning machine refined by sparrow search algorithm and weighted mean filter for short-term multi-step wind speed forecasting. *Sustain. Energy Technol. Assess.* **2022**, *50*, 101698. [CrossRef]
29. Huang, G.B.; Zhu, Q.Y.; Siew, C.K. Extreme learning machine: A new learning scheme of feedforward neural networks. In Proceedings of the 2004 IEEE International Joint Conference on Neural Networks, Budapest, Hungary, 25–29 July 2004; Volume 1–4, pp. 985–990.
30. Zhao, Y.; Ye, L.; Li, Z.; Song, X.; Lang, Y.; Su, J. A novel bidirectional mechanism based on time series model for wind power forecasting. *Appl. Energy* **2016**, *177*, 793–803. [CrossRef]
31. Fu, W.; Wang, K.; Li, C.; Tan, J. Multi-step short-term wind speed forecasting approach based on multi-scale dominant ingredient chaotic analysis, improved hybrid GWO-SCA optimization and ELM. *Energy Convers. Manag.* **2019**, *187*, 356–377. [CrossRef]
32. Wei, J.; Liu, H.; Yan, G.; Sun, F. Robotic grasping recognition using multi-modal deep extreme learning machine. *Multidimens. Syst. Signal Process.* **2016**, *28*, 817–833. [CrossRef]
33. Ding, S.; Zhang, N.; Xu, X.; Guo, L.; Zhang, J. Deep Extreme Learning Machine and Its Application in EEG Classification. *Math. Probl. Eng.* **2015**, *2015*, 129021. [CrossRef]
34. Wan, C.; Xu, Z.; Pinson, P.; Dong, Z.Y.; Wong, K.P. Probabilistic Forecasting of Wind Power Generation Using Extreme Learning Machine. *IEEE Trans. Power Syst.* **2014**, *29*, 1033–1044. [CrossRef]
35. Farsi, B.; Amayri, M.; Bouguila, N.; Eicker, U. On Short-Term Load Forecasting Using Machine Learning Techniques and a Novel Parallel Deep LSTM-CNN Approach. *IEEE Access* **2021**, *9*, 31191–31212. [CrossRef]
36. Huang, G.-B.; Zhu, Q.-Y.; Siew, C.-K. Extreme learning machine: Theory and applications. *Neurocomputing* **2006**, *70*, 489–501. [CrossRef]
37. Chorowski, J.; Wang, J.; Zurada, J.M. Review and performance comparison of SVM- and ELM-based classifiers. *Neurocomputing* **2014**, *128*, 507–516. [CrossRef]
38. Menke, J.; Martinez, T.R. In Using permutations instead of student's t distribution for p-values in paired-difference algorithm comparisons. In Proceedings of the 2004 IEEE International Joint Conference on Neural Networks (IEEE Cat. No.04CH37541), Budapest, Hungary, 25–29 July 2004; Volume 2, pp. 1331–1335.

mathematics

MDPI

Article

The Meshfree Radial Point Interpolation Method (RPIM) for Wave Propagation Dynamics in Non-Homogeneous Media

Cong Liu [1], Shaosong Min [1], Yandong Pang [2] and Yingbin Chai [3,4,*]

[1] College of Naval Architecture and Ocean Engineering, Naval University of Engineering, Wuhan 430033, China
[2] College of Weapon Engineering, Naval University of Engineering, Wuhan 430033, China
[3] School of Naval Architecture, Ocean and Energy Power Engineering, Wuhan University of Technology, Wuhan 430063, China
[4] State Key Laboratory of Ocean Engineering, Shanghai Jiao Tong University, Shanghai 200240, China
* Correspondence: chaiyb@whut.edu.cn

Abstract: This work presents a novel simulation approach to couple the meshfree radial point interpolation method (RPIM) with the implicit direct time integration method for the transient analysis of wave propagation dynamics in non-homogeneous media. In this approach, the RPIM is adopted for the discretization of the overall space domain, while the discretization of the time domain is completed by employing the efficient Bathe time stepping scheme. The dispersion analysis demonstrates that, in wave analysis, the amount of numerical dispersion error resulting from the discretization in the space domain can be suppressed at a very low level when the employed nodal support domain of the interpolation function is adequately large. Meanwhile, it is also mathematically shown that the amount of numerical error resulting from the time domain discretization is actually a monotonically decreasing function of the non-dimensional time domain discretization interval. Consequently, the present simulation approach is capable of effectively handling the transient analysis of wave propagation dynamics in non-homogeneous media, and the disparate waves with different speeds can be solved concurrently with very high computation accuracy. This numerical feature makes the present simulation approach more suitable for complicated wave analysis than the traditional finite element approach because the waves with disparate speeds always cannot be concurrently solved accurately. Several numerical tests are given to check the performance of the present simulation approach for the analysis of wave propagation dynamics in non-homogeneous media.

Keywords: meshfree techniques; numerical methods; spatial discretization; transient analysis; time integration

MSC: 35A08; 35A09; 35A24; 65L60; 74S05

Citation: Liu, C.; Min, S.; Pang, Y.; Chai, Y. The Meshfree Radial Point Interpolation Method (RPIM) for Wave Propagation Dynamics in Non-Homogeneous Media. *Mathematics* **2023**, *11*, 523. https://doi.org/10.3390/math11030523

Academic Editors: Zhuojia Fu, Yiqian He and Hui Zheng

Received: 9 December 2022
Revised: 15 January 2023
Accepted: 16 January 2023
Published: 18 January 2023

1. Introduction

In many engineering application areas, transient wave propagation dynamics are frequently encountered [1,2]. In essence, solving this type of engineering problem is to effectively handle the time-continuous governing partial differential equations via numerical approaches. In practice, the finite element approach with the direct time integration algorithm is widely utilized to solve complex transient wave propagation dynamics [3]. The finite element method (FEM) is mainly adopted to achieve the discretization of the overall space domain. Then, a series of semi-discrete dynamic equations, which are discrete in the space domain and continuous in the time domain, can be obtained. By using the appropriate time integration algorithms, the required discretization in the time domain can also be realized, and then the considered transient wave propagations can finally be solved.

Although a large number of spatial discretization schemes can be exploited to discretize the involved problem domain spatially (such as the finite difference method [4–7], the spectral element method [8], the smoothed FEM [9–19], the meshless techniques [20–29], and the boundary element or boundary-based numerical algorithms [30–41]), the traditional finite element approach is still dominantly employed in practice due to its relatively firm mathematical background and easy implementation. Nevertheless, the finite element approach also suffers from several inherent shortcomings in wave analysis [1,3,42]. One intractable issue of them is that the concomitant spatial discretization error always arises in the numerical solutions and cannot be completely avoided [42]. Actually, the resultant spatial discretization error is closely related to the number of employed elements per wavelength. More elements in one wavelength can lead to a smaller amount of discretization error. In engineering practice, only the relatively low vibration modes can be accurately represented when a fixed mesh pattern is used. For the relatively high-vibration modes, the obtained spatial discretization error is usually quite large because they are not spatially resolved with sufficiently high accuracy. In solving the transient wave propagation dynamics, these spatial discretization errors in high-order vibration modes will pollute the obtained numerical solutions and can give rise to many spurious oscillations [3].

Compared to the conventional finite element approach, meshless numerical techniques might be a powerful alternative to enhance the performance of traditional FEM in spatial discretization for wave analysis [20]. In the meshless framework, only a set of scattered field nodes are used to represent the involved physical space domain, and the pre-defined meshes or elements are not required [20]. In consequence, the computed numerical solutions from the meshless techniques are usually insensitive to the employed node distribution schemes, while this factor can severely affect the solution quality of the traditional FEM because the distorted meshes can lead to very inaccurate solutions. Additionally, the higher-order numerical approximation can always be achieved by meshless techniques, and then in wave analysis, the possible spatial discretization errors can be largely suppressed. Consequently, the high-order vibration modes also can be well represented, and the spurious oscillations in the solutions can be effectively eliminated. During the past few decades, various meshfree numerical techniques have been developed and used in a large range of engineering and scientific computation fields, such as the smoothed particle hydrodynamics (SPH) [43], the reproducing kernel particle method (RKPM) [44], the element-free Galerkin method (EFGM) [45–47], the method of finite spheres (MFS) [48] and various strong-form collocation methods [49–53]. Due to the relatively high numerical performance of the RPIM in a large number of numerical tests and the possession of the Kronecker delta function property [20], the meshless RPIM is utilized in this work to achieve the required spatial discretization in transient wave analysis.

In addition to spatial discretization, discretization in the time domain is also an indispensable step to handle complex time-continuous dynamic equations. The widely used numerical treatment for this step is to use a direct time integration algorithm. In the direct time integration schemes, the required discretization in the time domain can be achieved without any additional numerical treatments on the obtained system mass and stiffness matrices. Generally, the frequently used direct time integration algorithms in practice can be classified into two types, namely the explicit direct time integration algorithm [54,55] and the implicit direct time integration algorithm [56,57]. In the explicit time integration algorithm, only the information of the field function variables (such as displacements, velocities, and accelerated velocities) at the previous time point is needed to calculate the response at the current time point. The treatment of the simultaneous equations can be easily avoided in an explicit time integration algorithm. However, the explicit time integration algorithm is always conditionally stable. Consequently, there always exists a critical time step increment in the numerical integration process. Due to this issue, stable and reliable numerical solutions can be yielded unless the employed time step for time integration is not larger than the critical time step increment.

In contrast to the explicit time integration algorithm, in the implicit time integration scheme, both the variable information at the previous and current time points are required to compute the responses at the current time point. In general, the treatment of the simultaneous equations cannot be avoided in an implicit method. However, the implicit direct time integration algorithm is always unconditionally stable, and there exists no so-called critical time step increment. As a result, a relatively large time integration step can be used for a stable numerical solution, and then the required number of time steps can be largely reduced. Similar to the discretization in the space domain, the discretization in the time domain can also give rise to considerable numerical errors. In general, the numerical errors induced by temporal discretization are mainly determined by the order of the computational accuracy and the temporal discretization step used.

In this work, the two-step implicit Bathe time integration algorithm is employed to complete the discretization in the time domain due to the fact that excellent numerical features can be obtained in solving complex linear and nonlinear structural dynamics [58]. It should be noted that the numerical spatial discretization error induced by the RPIM can be suppressed at a very low level; hence, it is reasonable to expect that the RPIM with the Bathe time integration algorithm might be a powerful numerical approach to solve the transient wave propagation dynamic problems. Actually, this novel simulation approach has been developed to handle the transient wave propagations in homogeneous media [59]. It has been demonstrated by the numerical tests and dispersion analysis that quite fine numerical solutions can be yielded. More importantly, it is very interesting to find that the so-called monotonic convergence property can be basically reached by this numerical approach in transient wave analysis; namely, the quality of the obtained numerical solutions will be better when the non-dimensional temporal discretization step used gets smaller. Due to this good and valuable numerical feature, this numerical approach is particularly suitable for the analysis of complicated transient wave propagation problems, such as wave propagation in non-homogeneous media and composite structures. The contents of this work are mainly motivated by this idea, and the potential powerful ability of this simulation approach in solving the transient wave propagations in non-homogeneous media is investigated in great detail in this work.

2. Problem Statement

We consider the involved wave propagation domain contains two different regions, Ω_1 and Ω_2, with the interface Γ (See Figure 1). Suppose that the different regions are occupied with different acoustic fluid media. When the considered acoustic fluid media are inviscid and compressible, for the linear theory of acoustics, the acoustic pressure p is governed by the following equations:

$$\begin{cases} \nabla^2 p_1 - \frac{1}{c_1^2}\frac{\partial^2 p_1}{\partial t^2} = 0, \text{ in } \Omega_1 \\ \nabla^2 p_2 - \frac{1}{c_2^2}\frac{\partial^2 p_2}{\partial t^2} = 0, \text{ in } \Omega_2 \end{cases}, \tag{1}$$

in which ∇^2 represents the Laplace operator, p_i (i = 1,2) are the acoustic pressures in different acoustic fluid regions, c_i (i = 1,2) are the corresponding acoustic wave speeds, and t denotes the time variable.

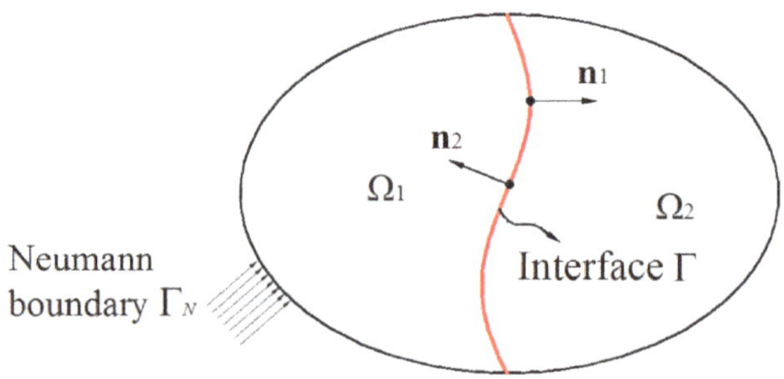

Figure 1. The involved wave propagation domain in which non-homogeneous media are considered.

On the interface of the different wave propagation regions, the following continuity conditions of acoustic pressure and normal acoustic particle velocity should be satisfied:

$$\left\{ \begin{array}{l} p_1 = p_2 \\ \frac{1}{\rho_1}\nabla p_1 \cdot \mathbf{n}_1 + \frac{1}{\rho_2}\nabla p_2 \cdot \mathbf{n}_2 = 0 \end{array} \right., \text{ on } \Gamma, \tag{2}$$

in which ρ_i (i = 1,2) are the mass densities of the considered acoustic fluid media in different regions, and $\mathbf{n}_i$ (i = 1,2) stand for the outward normal unit vector on interface Γ.

According to the principle of virtual work, the governing equations of acoustic wave propagation in non-homogeneous media can be written in the following integral form [1,60–62]:

$$\sum_{i=1}^{2} \int_{\Omega_i} \overline{p}(\nabla^2 p_i - \frac{1}{c_i^2}\frac{\partial^2 p_i}{\partial t^2})d\Omega = 0, \tag{3}$$

in which $\overline{p}$ denotes the assumed "virtual" acoustic pressure distributions.

It should be noted that $\overline{p}$ in Equation (3) is arbitrary, hence the satisfaction of Equation (3) requires that the field variables in the bracket should be zero. Therefore, Equation (3) is actually equivalent to the original governing equation in Equation (1).

In order to decrease the order of derivatives in Equation (3), by using the divergence theorem, the following equation can be obtained:

$$\sum_{i=1}^{2} \left(\int_{\Omega_i} \nabla\overline{p} \cdot \nabla p_i d\Omega + \frac{1}{c_i^2}\int_{\Omega_i} \overline{p}\frac{\partial^2 p_i}{\partial t^2} d\Omega - \int_{\Gamma_N} \overline{p}(\nabla p_i \cdot \mathbf{n}_i) d\Gamma \right) = 0, \tag{4}$$

in which Γ_N denotes the involved Neumann boundary conditions (see Figure 1).

In this work, the Lagrange multipliers are employed to handle the acoustic wave propagation in non-homogeneous media in which the discontinuities in the gradient fields of acoustic pressure are usually involved in the interface of different acoustic fluid media. By using the usual field function approximation in the standard finite element approach and the well-known Lagrange multiplier technique, the following equations in matrix form can be obtained from Equation (4):

$$\left\{ \begin{array}{l} \frac{1}{c_1^2}\int_{\Omega_1} \mathbf{N}_{f_1}^T \mathbf{N}_{f_1} \frac{\partial^2 \mathbf{p}_1}{\partial t^2} d\Omega + \int_{\Omega_1} \left(\nabla \mathbf{N}_{f_1}\right)^T \nabla \mathbf{N}_{f_1} \mathbf{p}_1 d\Omega - \int_{\Gamma_N} \mathbf{N}_{f_1}^T (\nabla p_1 \cdot \mathbf{n}_1) d\Gamma \\ -\int_{\Gamma} \left(\nabla \mathbf{N}_{f_1}\right)^T \mathbf{n}_1 \mathbf{N}_\lambda \frac{1}{\rho_1} \boldsymbol{\lambda} d\Gamma = \mathbf{0} \\ \frac{1}{c_2^2}\int_{\Omega_2} \mathbf{N}_{f_2}^T \mathbf{N}_{f_2} \frac{\partial^2 \mathbf{p}_2}{\partial t^2} d\Omega + \int_{\Omega_2} \left(\nabla \mathbf{N}_{f_2}\right)^T \nabla \mathbf{N}_{f_2} \mathbf{p}_2 d\Omega - \int_{\Gamma_N} \mathbf{N}_{f_2}^T (\nabla p_2 \cdot \mathbf{n}_2) d\Gamma \\ -\int_{\Gamma} \left(\nabla \mathbf{N}_{f_2}\right)^T \mathbf{n}_2 \mathbf{N}_\lambda \frac{1}{\rho_2} \boldsymbol{\lambda} d\Gamma = \mathbf{0} \\ -\int_{\Gamma} \mathbf{N}_\lambda^T \mathbf{n}_1 \left(\nabla \mathbf{N}_{f_1}\right) \frac{1}{\rho_1} \mathbf{p}_1 d\Gamma - \int_{\Gamma} \mathbf{N}_\lambda^T \mathbf{n}_2 \left(\nabla \mathbf{N}_{f_2}\right) \frac{1}{\rho_2} \mathbf{p}_2 d\Gamma = \mathbf{0} \end{array} \right., \tag{5}$$

in which $\mathbf{N}_{f_1}$ and $\mathbf{N}_{f_2}$ represent the constructed nodal interpolation functions for the acoustic pressure in different regions, and $\mathbf{N}_\lambda$ is the nodal interpolation function for the Lagrange multiplier $\boldsymbol{\lambda}$ on the interface Γ.

Of course, Equation (5) can also be expressed in the following simplified form:

$$\begin{bmatrix} \mathbf{M}_1 & \mathbf{0} & \mathbf{0} \\ \mathbf{0} & \mathbf{M}_2 & \mathbf{0} \\ \mathbf{0} & \mathbf{0} & \mathbf{0} \end{bmatrix} \begin{bmatrix} \ddot{\mathbf{p}}_1 \\ \ddot{\mathbf{p}}_2 \\ \ddot{\boldsymbol{\lambda}} \end{bmatrix} + \begin{bmatrix} \mathbf{K}_1 & \mathbf{0} & \mathbf{A} \\ \mathbf{0} & \mathbf{K}_2 & \mathbf{G} \\ \mathbf{A}^T & \mathbf{G}^T & \mathbf{0} \end{bmatrix} \begin{bmatrix} \mathbf{p}_1 \\ \mathbf{p}_2 \\ \boldsymbol{\lambda} \end{bmatrix} = \begin{bmatrix} \mathbf{R}_1 \\ \mathbf{R}_2 \\ \mathbf{0} \end{bmatrix}, \tag{6}$$

in which

$$\begin{array}{l} \mathbf{M}_1 = \frac{1}{c_1^2}\int_{\Omega_1} \mathbf{N}_{f_1}^T \mathbf{N}_{f_1} d\Omega,\ \mathbf{M}_2 = \frac{1}{c_2^2}\int_{\Omega_2} \mathbf{N}_{f_2}^T \mathbf{N}_{f_2} d\Omega \\ \mathbf{K}_1 = \int_{\Omega_1} \left(\nabla \mathbf{N}_{f_1}\right)^T \nabla \mathbf{N}_{f_1} d\Omega,\ \mathbf{K}_2 = \int_{\Omega_2} \left(\nabla \mathbf{N}_{f_2}\right)^T \nabla \mathbf{N}_{f_2} d\Omega \\ \mathbf{A} = -\int_{\Gamma} \left(\nabla \mathbf{N}_{f_1}\right)^T \mathbf{n}_1 \mathbf{N}_{\lambda} \frac{1}{\rho_1} d\Gamma,\ \mathbf{G} = -\int_{\Gamma} \left(\nabla \mathbf{N}_{f_2}\right)^T \mathbf{n}_2 \mathbf{N}_{\lambda} \frac{1}{\rho_2} d\Gamma \\ \mathbf{R}_1 = \int_{\Gamma_N} \mathbf{N}_{f_1}^T (\nabla p_1 \cdot \mathbf{n}_1) d\Gamma,\ \mathbf{R}_2 = \int_{\Gamma_N} \mathbf{N}_{f_2}^T (\nabla p_2 \cdot \mathbf{n}_2) d\Gamma \end{array}, \tag{7}$$

3. A Brief Review of the Meshfree RPIM

In the meshfree RPIM framework, the constructed numerical approximation for the considered field function is obtained by using a series of scattered field points in the problem domain (see Figure 2). In addition, the numerical approximation is also enforced to pass through the function values at the involved field points. In the classical and well-developed RPIM, the radial basis functions (RBFs) are combined with the frequently used polynomial basis functions (PBFs) to create the required numerical approximation.

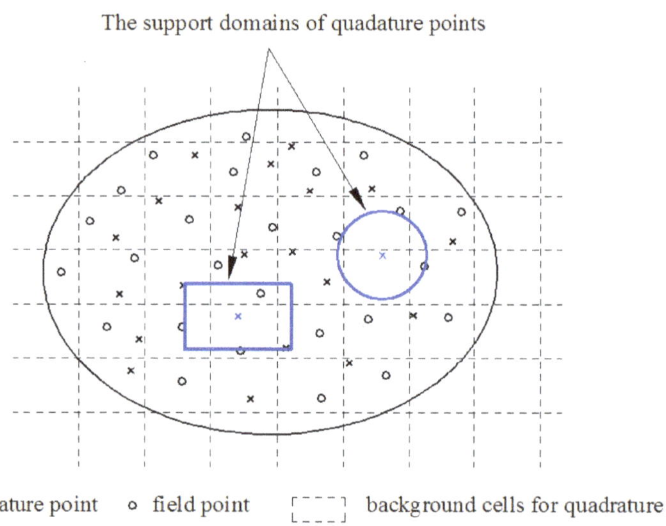

Figure 2. The description of constructed numerical approximation for the considered field function using the typical meshfree RPIM.

For an involved problem domain that is represented by a series of field nodes, suppose that a scalar function $u(\mathbf{x})$ is defined on it, and the corresponding field function approximation using RPIM for $u(\mathbf{x})$ can be expressed by [20]

$$u_h(\mathbf{x}) = \sum_{i=1}^{n} R_i(\mathbf{x}) a_i + \sum_{j=1}^{m} p_j(\mathbf{x}) b_j = \mathbf{R}^T(\mathbf{x})\mathbf{a} + \mathbf{p}^T(\mathbf{x})\mathbf{b}, \tag{8}$$

in which $R_i(\mathbf{x})$ is the employed RBF in creating the numerical approximation for node i, and a_i is the corresponding interpolation coefficient; $p_j(\mathbf{x})$ is the employed PBF, and b_j is the corresponding interpolation coefficient; and n and m are the numbers of the employed RBFs and PBFs, respectively.

In this work, we only use the linear PBF. For the numerical approximation in two-dimensional space, m = 3. On the contrary, the number of the used RBF for numerical approximation is determined by the size of the employed local support domain. In general, the vector of RBF in Equation (8) can be written by

$$\mathbf{R}^T(\mathbf{x}) = \begin{bmatrix} R_1(\mathbf{x}) & R_2(\mathbf{x}) & R_3(\mathbf{x}) & \cdots & R_n(\mathbf{x}) \end{bmatrix}, \tag{9}$$

In practice, the required RBF can be constructed in different ways, and different types of RBF usually have different numerical features [20,63]. In this work, the classical multi-quadric (MQ) basis, which is frequently used in surface fitting, is employed to construct the RBF. The explicit expression of MQ is given by

$$R_i(\mathbf{x}) = \left[r_i^2 + (\alpha_c d_c)^2 \right]^q, \tag{10}$$

in which r_i is the distance from the field node $\mathbf{x}_i$ to the interest point $\mathbf{x}$, d_c is the defined characteristic length of the used field node distribution pattern, and α_c and q are two related parameters to control the shape of the MQ. Here, $q = 1.03$ and $\alpha_c = 1$ are directly used due to the fact that very good numerical performance can be obtained with these parameters by a large number of numerical experiments in computational solid and fluid mechanics [20,64,65].

For the linear PBF in Equation (8), the vector of PBF is

$$\begin{cases} \mathbf{p}^T(\mathbf{x}) = \begin{bmatrix} 1 & x \end{bmatrix}, & \text{for 1D space} \\ \mathbf{p}^T(\mathbf{x}) = \begin{bmatrix} 1 & x & y \end{bmatrix}, & \text{for 2D space}, \\ \mathbf{p}^T(\mathbf{x}) = \begin{bmatrix} 1 & x & y & z \end{bmatrix}, & \text{for 3D space} \end{cases} \tag{11}$$

Suppose that the numerical approximation in Equation (8) is satisfied at n involved field nodes in the local support domain, namely

$$u_i(\mathbf{x}) = \sum_{i=1}^{n} R_i(\mathbf{x}) a_i + \sum_{j=1}^{m} p_j(\mathbf{x}) b_j, \; i = 1, 2, \cdots, n, \tag{12}$$

In order to make the interpolation coefficients a_i and b_j unique, the following constraints are also required:

$$\sum_{i=1}^{n} p_j(\mathbf{x}_i) a_i = 0, \; j = 1, 2, \cdots, m, \tag{13}$$

By combining Equations (12) and (13), we can have

$$\begin{bmatrix} \mathbf{u} \\ \mathbf{0} \end{bmatrix} = \underbrace{\begin{bmatrix} \mathbf{R}_Q & \mathbf{P}_m \\ \mathbf{P}_m^T & \mathbf{0} \end{bmatrix}}_{\mathbf{G}} \underbrace{\begin{bmatrix} \mathbf{a} \\ \mathbf{b} \end{bmatrix}}_{\mathbf{a}_0} = \mathbf{G}\mathbf{a}_0, \tag{14}$$

in which

$$\mathbf{R}_Q = \begin{bmatrix} R_1(r_1) & R_2(r_1) & \cdots & R_n(r_1) \\ R_1(r_2) & R_2(r_2) & \cdots & R_n(r_2) \\ \vdots & \vdots & \ddots & \vdots \\ R_1(r_n) & R_2(r_n) & \cdots & R_n(r_n) \end{bmatrix}_{n \times n}, \tag{15}$$

$$\mathbf{P}_m = \begin{bmatrix} P_1(\mathbf{x}_1) & P_2(\mathbf{x}_1) & \cdots & P_m(\mathbf{x}_1) \\ P_1(\mathbf{x}_2) & P_2(\mathbf{x}_2) & \cdots & P_m(\mathbf{x}_2) \\ \vdots & \vdots & \ddots & \vdots \\ P_1(\mathbf{x}_n) & P_2(\mathbf{x}_n) & \cdots & P_m(\mathbf{x}_n) \end{bmatrix}_{n \times m}, \tag{16}$$

$$\mathbf{a}_0^T = \begin{bmatrix} a_1 & a_2 & \cdots & a_n & b_1 & b_2 & \cdots & b_m \end{bmatrix}, \tag{17}$$

Following the standard formulation of the RPIM, the following matrix equation can be obtained [20,64]:

$$\begin{cases} u_h(\mathbf{x}) = \mathbf{R}^T(\mathbf{x})\mathbf{a} + \mathbf{p}^T(\mathbf{x})\mathbf{b} = \left[\mathbf{R}^T(\mathbf{x})\mathbf{S}_a + \mathbf{p}^T(\mathbf{x})\mathbf{S}_b\right]\mathbf{u}_s = \mathbf{\Phi}(\mathbf{x})\mathbf{u} \\ \mathbf{S}_a = \left(\mathbf{R}_Q^{-1} - \mathbf{R}_Q^{-1}\mathbf{P}_m\mathbf{S}_b\right) \\ \mathbf{S}_b = \left[\mathbf{P}_m^T\mathbf{R}_Q^{-1}\mathbf{P}_m\right]\mathbf{P}_m^T\mathbf{R}_Q^{-1} \end{cases}, \tag{18}$$

in which $\mathbf{\Phi}(\mathbf{x})$ is the constructed nodal interpolation function matrix in the classical RPIM framework.

4. Numerical Error Evaluation in Transient Wave Analysis

In engineering practice, the governing equation for transient wave propagation is continuous both in the space and time domains. To effectively handle this problem by means of the numerical approaches, both the discretization schemes in the space and time domains are needed. Unfortunately, not only the discretization in the space domain but also the discretization in the time domain are able to cause a considerable amount of numerical errors in the computed numerical solutions. In this section, the resultant numerical errors in transient wave analysis will be systemically investigated. Owing to the excellent numerical properties which have been demonstrated in previously published papers [20,64,65], the classical meshfree RPIM and the two-stage time stepping Bathe method are respectively responsible for the required discretization in space and time domain.

For the linear theory of acoustics, the governing equation of transient acoustic wave propagation in an ideal acoustic fluid can be easily obtained by

$$\nabla^2 p - \frac{1}{c^2}\frac{\partial^2 p}{\partial t^2} = 0, \tag{19}$$

As usual, when the considered acoustic pressure variable p is time-harmonic, the following reduced governing equation for wave propagation can be obtained from Equation (19):

$$\nabla^2 P + k^2 P = 0, \tag{20}$$

in which P is the spatial distribution of acoustic pressure, and k stands for the wave number.

It should be noted that Equation (20) is actually the well-known Helmholtz equation in state steady wave analysis, and it is clear that Equation (20) is time-independent. To solve Equation (20) numerically, only the related discretization in the space domain is required. Here, we first investigate the numerical error properties when different spatial discretization techniques are exploited to handle Equation (20). The evenly placed node distribution shown in Figure 3 is employed for numerical error evaluation in this section.

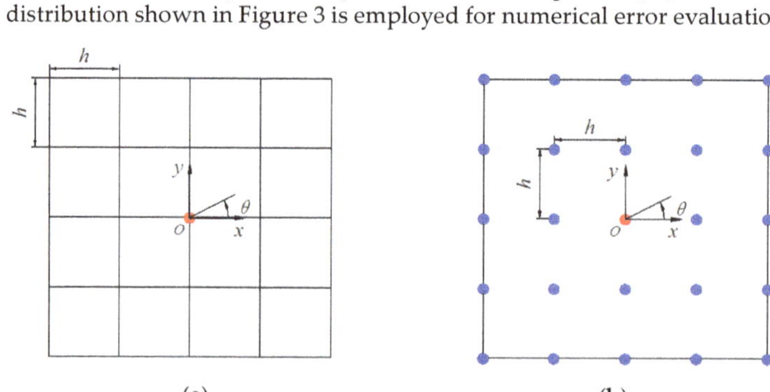

Figure 3. The evenly placed node distributions for numerical error evaluation using different numerical approaches: (**a**) FEM-Q4; (**b**) RPIM.

Using the classical Galerkin weighted residual numerical techniques, the following matrix equation can be obtained from Equation (20) [60,66–69]:

$$\mathbf{KP} - k^2\mathbf{MP} = \mathbf{0}, \tag{21}$$

in which **P** is the nodal unknowns for the acoustic pressure, and **K** and **M** are the resultant matrices corresponding to the system stiffness and mass, respectively [60].

It is clear that Equation (21) has the following fundamental numerical solutions:

$$\mathbf{P} = \mathbf{A}e^{jk_h\mathbf{x}\cdot\mathbf{n}}, \tag{22}$$

In which **x** is a position vector of the point of interest, **A** is the amplitude of the acoustic pressure distribution vector, and k_h denotes the wave number of numerical solutions.

Since no boundary conditions are involved here, the amplitude of acoustic pressure distribution for all nodes should hence be identical.

Taking Equation (22) into Equation (21), the following characteristic equation can be arrived at [60]:

$$\left(D_{\text{stiffness}} - k^2 D_{\text{mass}}\right)\mathbf{A} = \mathbf{0}, \tag{23}$$

in which $D_{\text{stiffness}}$ and D_{mass} are two characteristic parameters that are closely related to the system stiffness and mass, respectively. $D_{\text{stiffness}}$ and D_{mass} can be directly computed using the related formulations in Refs. [60,66].

For the non-trivial solutions of Equation (23), we have

$$k = \sqrt{\frac{D_{\text{stiffness}}}{D_{\text{mass}}}}, \tag{24}$$

From Refs. [60,66], it is known that both $D_{\text{stiffness}}$ and D_{mass} are functions of the numerical wave number k_h. Therefore, the relationship between the exact wave number k and the numerical wave number k_h can be successfully built via Equation (24).

In this work, the following error indicator is employed to perform the numerical error evaluation from the discretization in space domain:

$$\varepsilon = \frac{k}{k_h}. \tag{25}$$

To compare the numerical performance of the different spatial discretization schemes in tackling the Helmholtz equation, the meshfree RPIM with different support domain sizes of the quadrature points and the traditional bilinear quadrilateral elements (FEM-Q4) are mainly considered in this work. For simplicity, in all numerical experiments, the standard four-node quadrilateral mesh patterns for the FEM-Q4 are directly employed as the background numerical integration cells for the RPIM.

Figure 4 compares the numerical spatial discretization error results along different angles of wave travel ($\theta = 0°$, $\theta = 15°$, $\theta = 30°$, and $\theta = 45°$) as the functions of the non-dimensional wave numbers $k_h h$ (h stands for the characteristic length of the nodal space) from the above-mentioned spatial discretization methods. Looking at Figure 4d, it is apparent that the calculated numerical errors from the FEM-Q4 grow quickly when the considered non-dimensional wave numbers get larger. This means that the traditional FEM-Q4 is not able to behave sufficiently well in suppressing the numerical errors from the discretization in the space domain. Figure 4 also displays the computed numerical errors from the RPIM when different support domain sizes ($\alpha_s = h$, $\alpha_s = 2h$, and $\alpha_s = 3h$) of quadrature points are employed; here, α_s stands for the characteristic length of the employed local square support domain.

The numerical results in Figure 4 illustrate that the RPIM is able to produce much smaller numerical errors than the conventional FEM-Q4.This is because the high-order numerical approximation can be reached in formulating the RPIM. In addition, one clear trend can also be observed from Figure 4 that the abilities of the RPIM in suppressing the numerical will become stronger when the used local support domain size gets larger. In particular, the computed numerical errors along all angles are very close to zero when the local support domain size $\alpha_s = 3h$. Due to this observation, in the following numerical tests, we only consider the local support domain size $\alpha_s = 3h$.

As stated in previous texts, in addition to the discretization in the space domain, the discretization in the time domain also can lead to numerical errors in transient wave analysis. From the related research in Ref. [60], it is known that the total numerical errors (both the numerical errors from the spatial and temporal discretizations are contained) can be explicitly expressed by the following equation:

$$\frac{c_h}{c} = \frac{k}{k_h}\frac{T}{T_h}, \tag{26}$$

in which c is the acoustic wave speed, and T represents the period of the considered wave mode; the subscript "h" means that the corresponding field variables are from the numerical solutions.

In the right hand of Equation (26), the first term k/k_h stands for the numerical errors from the discretization in the space domain, and the second term T/T_h is mainly caused by the temporal discretization. In this work, the Bathe method, which is a typical two-stage time-stepping implicit temporal discretization numerical technique [1], is employed for the required temporal discretization. It has been demonstrated mathematically that the temporal discretization errors T/T_h from the Bathe method are actually a monotonically decreasing function of the non-dimensional temporal discretization interval CFL [60] (CFL = $c\Delta t/h$, Δt is the time increment for time integration). When the used CFL trends to zero, the resultant temporal discretization error will also trend to zero, i.e., $T/T_h \to 1$. With this numerical property, the total numerical error in transient wave analysis can also be roughly regarded as a monotonically decreasing function of the non-dimensional temporal discretization interval CFL when the numerical errors from the discretization in the space domain are sufficiently small (in particular, $k/k_h \to 1$ is required).

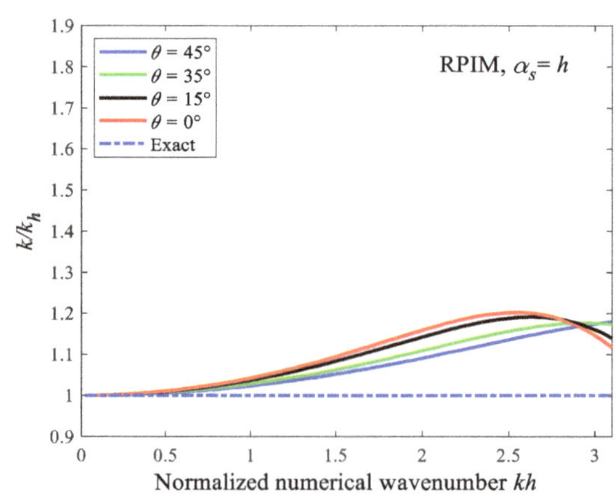

(a)

Figure 4. *Cont.*

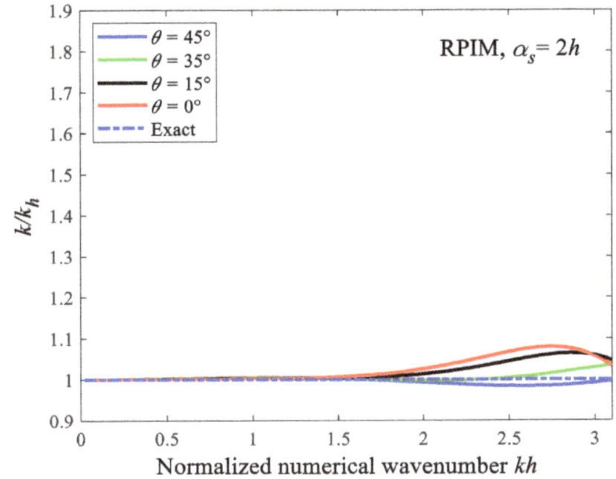

(**b**)

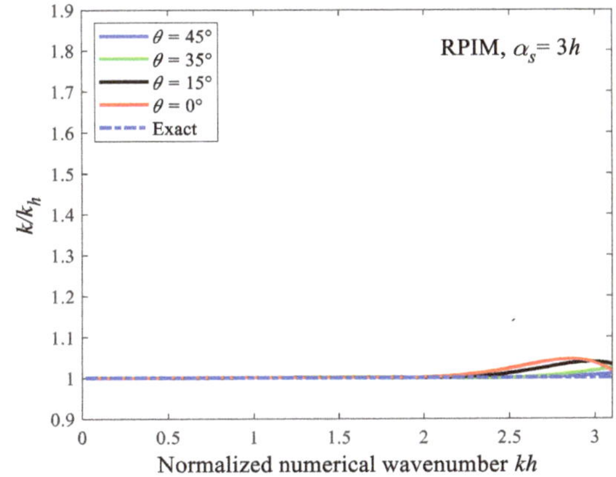

(**c**)

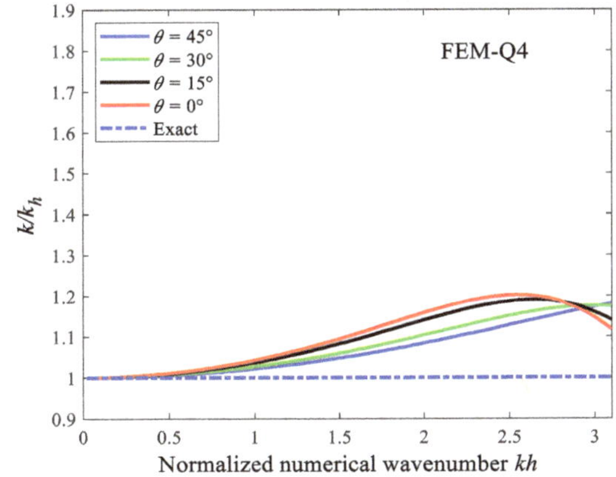

(**d**)

Figure 4. Comparisons of the numerical spatial discretization error results along different angles of wave travel as the functions of the non-dimensional wave numbers from disparate spatial discretization methods: (**a**) RPIM with $\alpha_s = h$; (**b**) RPIM with $\alpha_s = 2h$; (**c**) RPIM with $\alpha_s = 3h$; (**d**) FEM-Q4.

From the previous analysis and discussion, it is clearly displayed that the meshfree RPIM is able to generate close-to-zero spatial discretization errors when the employed local support domain size $\alpha_s = 3h$. Therefore, it is very reasonable to expect that the computed numerical solutions can become more accurate when the employed temporal discretization interval CFL becomes smaller. In other words, the present meshfree RPIM with the Bathe method has the so-called monotonic convergence property in handling the transient wave propagation dynamics [59,60]. However, the traditional numerical approach in transient wave analysis does not have this interesting and important numerical feature. Due to this good numerical feature, the wave propagation property of different wave components at different wave speeds can be simulated very accurately. Therefore, the numerical approach presented in this work is particularly suitable for solving very complex wave propagations. In the next section, the numerical feature of the present approach will be examined carefully by solving three typical numerical experiments in which the transient wave propagations in non-homogeneous media are considered.

5. Numerical Results

5.1. One Two-Dimensional Tube Filled with Different Media

As shown in Figure 5, one two-dimensional tube, which is filled with two different types of acoustic fluid media, is first considered here. This two-dimensional tube has a length of L = 1 m and a width of b = 0.1 m. The left and right halves of this tube are filled with different media with fluid density ρ and acoustic wave speed c. The related material constants are $\rho_1 = \rho_2$, c_1 = 1 m/s, and c_2 = 0.5 m/s. The required spatial discretization of the involved problem domain for this numerical example is first achieved by using the evenly placed node distributions with the nodal interval h = 0.0125 m. The corresponding spatial discretization patterns for different methods are given in Figure 6. Suppose that a sinusoidal acoustic wave, $p = \sin 16\pi t$ Pa with $t \in [0, 0.0625]$s, is traveling along this tube from the left end. In this numerical example, the non-dimensional time integration step size used is measured by CFL = $c_1 \Delta t / h$.

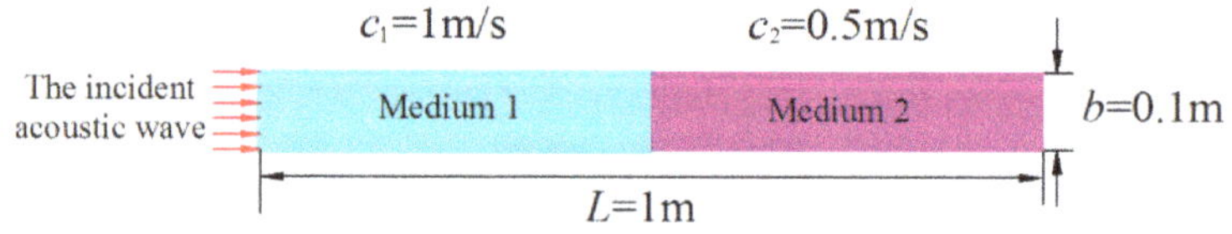

Figure 5. The transient wave propagation in a two-dimensional tube filled with different media.

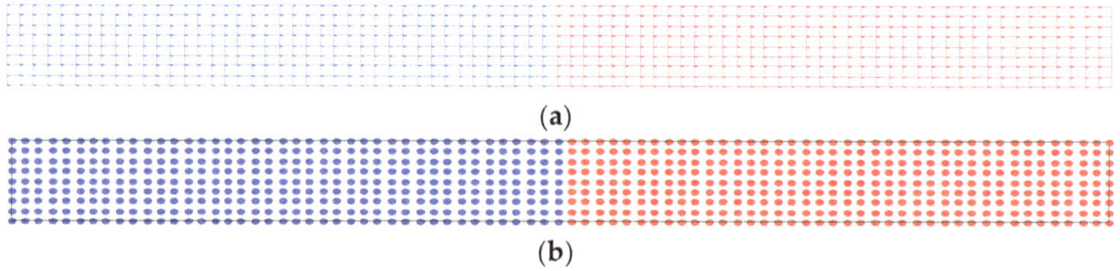

Figure 6. The used spatial discretization of the two-dimensional tube for different methods: (**a**) FEM-Q4; (**b**) RPIM.

Figure 7 compares the computed numerical solutions of the acoustic pressure distributions from the standard FEM-Q4 and the present meshfree RPIM with the identical node distribution schemes (see Figure 6) when the considered time point t = 0.4 s and the employed non-dimensional time integration step size CFL = 0.1. With the aim to compare the numerical performance of different numerical approaches in terms of computation accuracy, the exact solutions are also provided in the figures here. One important finding from Figure 7 is that the FEM-Q4 solutions are not sufficiently accurate because the obvious spurious oscillations can be clearly seen behind the wave front. In contrast to the FEM-Q4 solutions, the present meshfree RPIM is able to generate much more accurate solutions which are quite consistent with the exact solutions. Additionally, when the time point t = 0.8 s, the corresponding numerical solutions of acoustic pressure distributions from different numerical approaches are also computed and displayed in Figure 8. In this situation, both the reflected and transmitted acoustic waves can be induced by the interface of the two different fluid media. Figure 8 indicates that the outcome for this case is quite similar to that when the time point t = 0.4 s because the FEM-Q4 solutions exhibit clear spurious oscillations in both the reflected and transmitted acoustic waves, while the meshfree RPIM solutions are very close to the exact solutions and the resultant spurious oscillations are much smaller compared to those from the FEM-Q4 solutions. A possible explanation for these observations might be that the present meshfree RPIM is able to yield much smaller numerical dispersion errors from spatial discretization than the standard FEM-Q4, which has been reported in Figure 4.

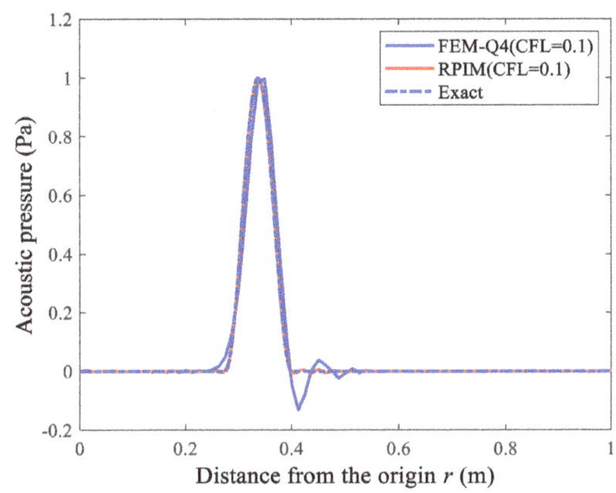

Figure 7. The computed numerical solutions of the acoustic pressure distributions for the two-dimensional tube from different numerical approaches when the time point t = 0.4 s.

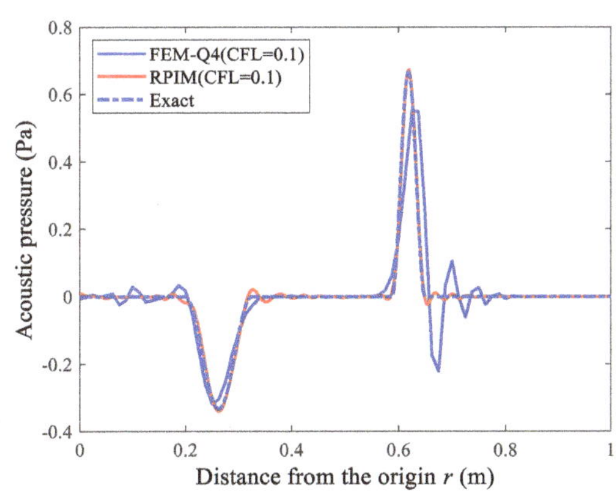

Figure 8. The computed numerical solutions of the acoustic pressure distributions for the two-dimensional tube from different numerical approaches when the time point t = 0.8 s.

Additionally, the acoustic pressure distribution results from different numerical approaches are also computed when the varying non-dimensional time integration steps are employed (CFL = 1, CFL = 0.5, CFL = 0.25, and CFL = 0.1). For the time points t = 0.4 s and t = 0.8 s, the corresponding numerical solutions are displayed in Figures 9 and 10, respectively. The results in these figures show that the quality of the numerical results from the standard FEM-Q4 does not become better when the smaller non-dimensional time integration step is used. In particular, more unwanted spurious oscillations can be observed in the FEM-Q4 solutions when the non-dimensional time integration step CFL = 0.1. In contrast to the observations which can be seen in the FEM-Q4 solutions, it is quite surprising that the present meshfree RPIM is able to generate more accurate and reliable acoustic pressure distribution results when we use smaller non-dimensional time integration steps. Therefore, we can reach one important conclusion that in transient wave analysis, the present meshfree RPIM with the Bathe temporal discretization scheme possesses the ability to achieve better numerical solutions by decreasing the employed non-dimensional time integration steps, namely the so-called monotonic convergence property in transient wave analysis can be broadly reached. Owing to this valuable numerical feature, the present meshfree RPIM is able to stand out clearly from the existing conventional numerical approaches in transient wave analysis. The above findings from Figures 9 and 10 may be explained by the fact that the present meshfree RPIM is able to generate almost no dispersion errors, which is related to the discretization in the space domain, while the corresponding dispersion errors from FEM-Q4 are relatively large. Meanwhile, the additional numerical errors from the Bathe temporal discretization scheme are actually a monotonically decreasing function of the employed non-dimensional time integration step. As a result, the monotonic convergence property in transient wave analysis can be broadly reached by the meshfree RPIM and cannot be reached by the traditional FEM-Q4.

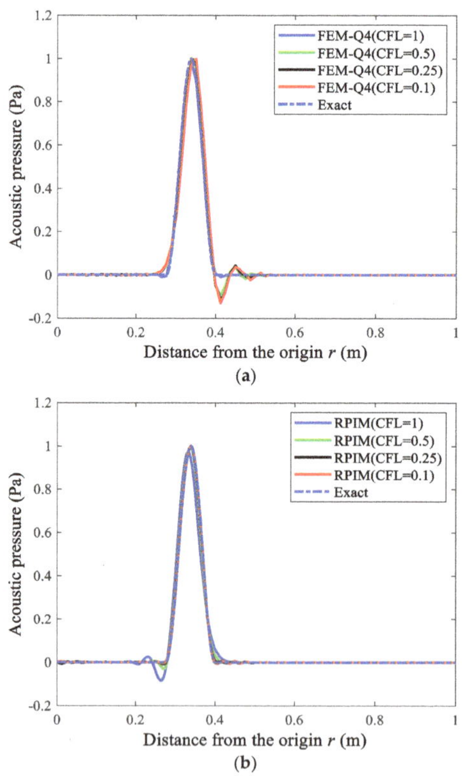

Figure 9. The computed acoustic pressure distribution results from different numerical approaches for the time point t = 0.4 s when the varying non-dimensional time integration steps are employed: (**a**) FEM-Q4; (**b**) RPIM.

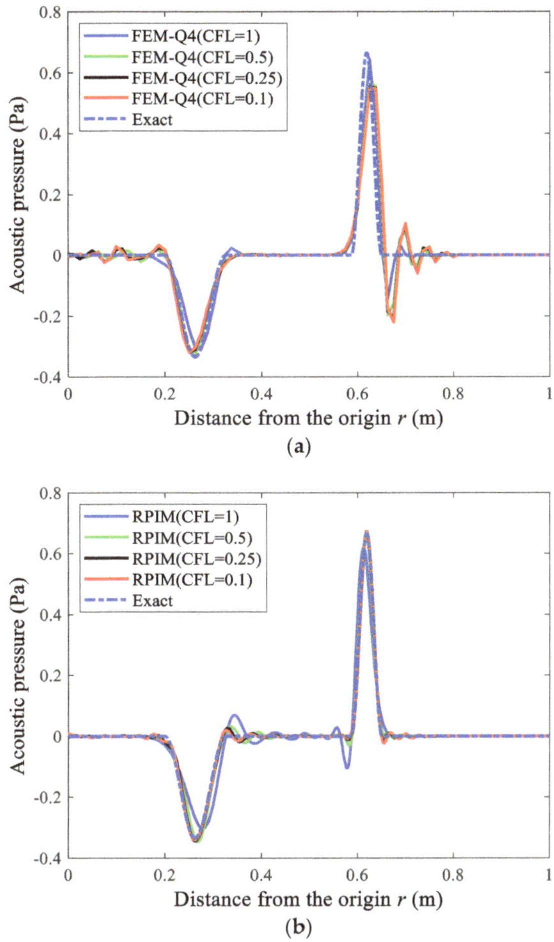

Figure 10. The computed acoustic pressure distribution results from different numerical approaches for the time point t = 0.8 s when the varying non-dimensional time integration steps are employed: (**a**) FEM-Q4; (**b**) RPIM.

Note that the regular node distributions are employed in a previous analysis. This numerical example is further studied by using the irregular node distributions with an average nodal interval of h = 0.0125 m (see Figure 11). Here the employed non-dimensional temporal interval for time integration is CFL = 0.1 m, and the considered time point is t = 0.8 s. The comparisons of the acoustic pressure distribution results for different meshes and different numerical approaches are exhibited in Figure 12. It is quite apparent from these figures that the FEM-Q4 solutions will become worse when the used regular mesh is replaced by the irregular mesh. The main factor for this is that the performance of the traditional FEM-Q4 in numerical analysis is usually sensitive to mesh distortions, and more numerical errors will arise when the distorted mesh patterns are employed. Unlike the traditional FEM-Q4, the present meshfree RPIM shows more powerful abilities in tackling the mesh distortions because the corresponding acoustic pressure distribution results almost cannot be affected when the irregular node distributions are employed for numerical computation. These results may be broadly explained by the fact that the used field function approximation in the meshfree RPIM is usually constructed regardless of the node distributions. This is also one main advantage of the meshfree RPIM compared to the FEM. This numerical feature can further strengthen the abilities of the present meshfree RPIM in transient wave analysis.

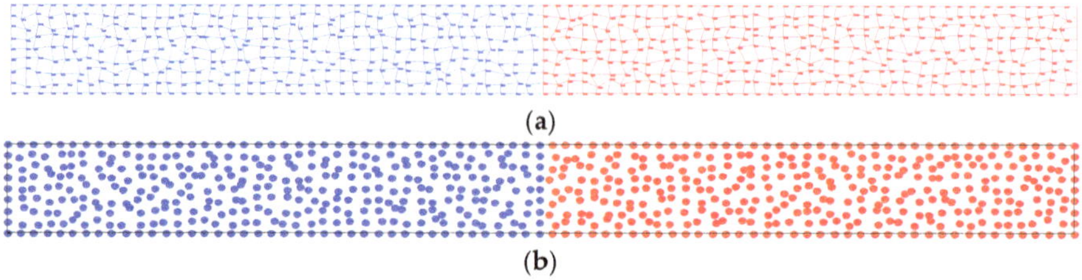

Figure 11. The employed irregular node distributions for the two-dimensional tube: (**a**) FEM-Q4; (**b**) RPIM.

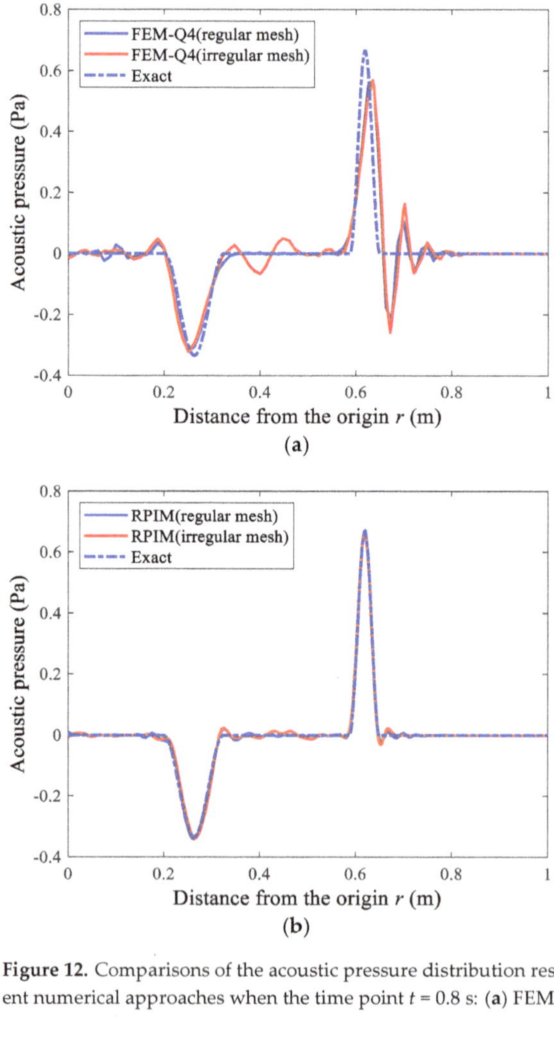

Figure 12. Comparisons of the acoustic pressure distribution results for different meshes and different numerical approaches when the time point $t = 0.8$ s: (**a**) FEM-Q4; (**b**) RPIM.

5.2. The Two-Dimensional Acoustic Wave Scattering Problem by Circular Objects

Another numerical experiment considered here is the two-dimensional acoustic wave scattering problem. Figure 13 displays the geometry configuration of this problem. As shown in Figure 13, several totally identical circular regions are evenly placed in the involved square problem region. The different problem regions are occupied with different acoustic fluid media. The material constants of the involved acoustic fluid media are $\rho_1 = \rho_2$, $c_1 = 2$ m/s, and $c_2 = 1$ m/s. The external excitation, $F = 8\pi \sin(20\pi t)$ with $t \in [0, 0.05]$ s, is imposed at the center of the problem domain. In the numerical computation process, only one quadrant problem domain needs to be modeled due to the fact that this transient acoustic wave scattering problem has the symmetry feature (see Figure 13). The standard four-node quadrilateral mesh with an average mesh size of $h = 0.01$ m is used to perform the required spatial discretization for this numerical experiment. Note that as the exact solution to this problem is not easy to derive, the corresponding numerical solutions from the high-order finite elements using very refined mesh are also provided here as the reference solutions for comparison. In this numerical example, the used non-dimensional time integration step size is measured by CFL = $c_2\Delta t/h$.

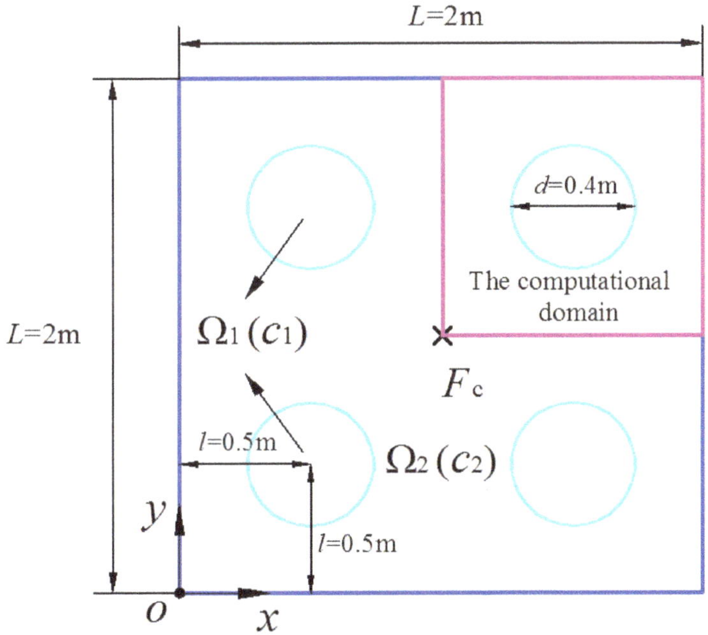

Figure 13. The geometry description of the two-dimensional acoustic wave scattering problem.

For the wave travel angle of $\theta = 45°$ and the non-dimensional time integration size CFL = 0.1, the transient responses of the acoustic pressure distributions at two different time points ($t = 0.4$ s and $t = 0.7$ s) are first computed by using different numerical approaches, and the corresponding results are plotted in Figures 14 and 15. In Figure 15, both reflected and transmitted acoustic waves are induced by the interface of different acoustic fluid media; the positions of the interface are also given in Figure 15 using pink lines. The results provided by these figures show that the FEM-Q4 solutions are obviously worse than the meshfree RPIM ones, which match very well with the reference solutions, while the FEM-Q4 solutions obviously deviate quite substantially from the reference solutions. Additionally, the related numerical computations are further performed by considering the different wave travel angles ($\theta = 0°$, $\theta = 22.5°$, and $\theta = 45°$). Figure 16 gives the obtained acoustic pressure distribution results from different numerical approaches.

Figure 16a reveals that the wave travel angle can severely affect the quality of the FEM-Q4 solutions; notably, the numerical anisotropy issue can be clearly observed. While one interesting point that can be seen from Figure 16b is that the above numerical anisotropy issue can be relieved quite substantially by the present meshfree RPIM because the numerical solutions with very similar accuracy can be yielded when the different wave travel angles are considered.

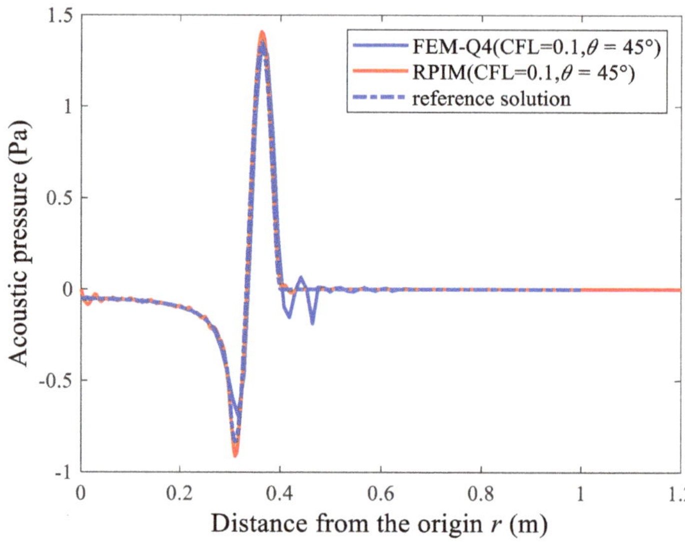

Figure 14. The transient responses of the acoustic pressure distributions from different methods for the two-dimensional scattering problem when the time point $t = 0.4$ s.

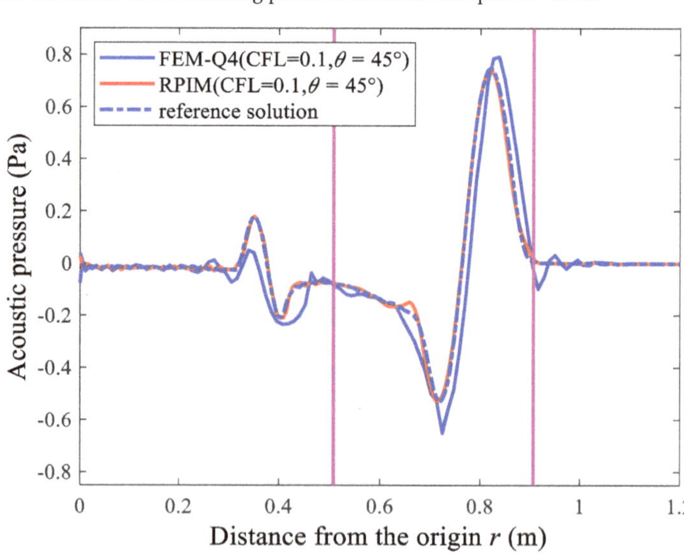

Figure 15. The transient responses of the acoustic pressure distributions from different methods for the two-dimensional scattering problem when the time point $t = 0.7$ s.

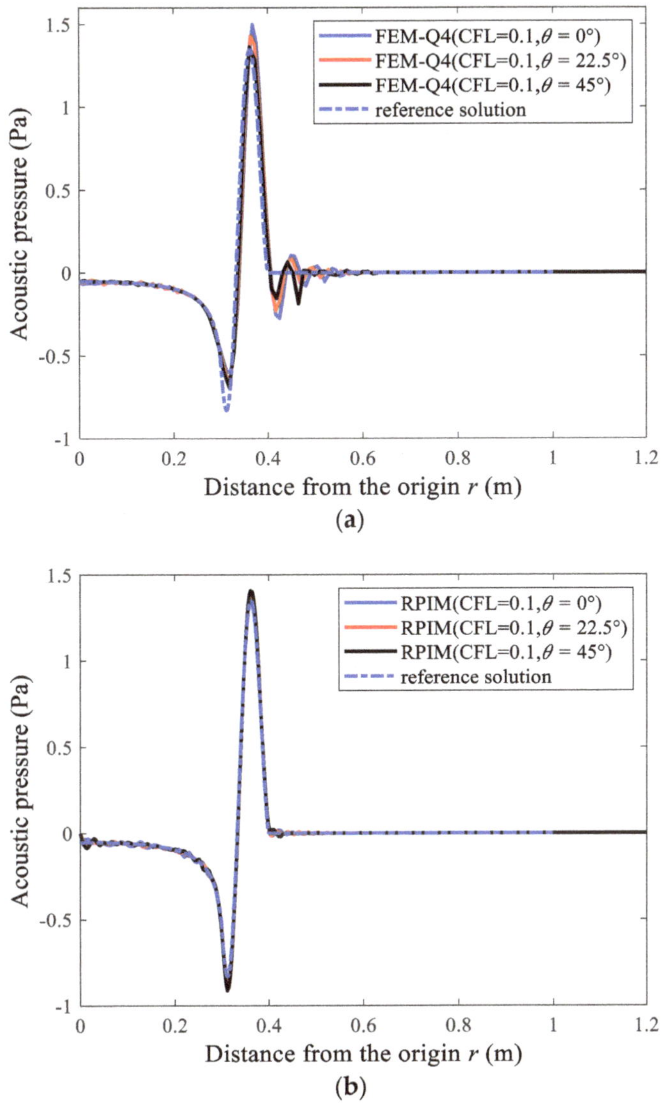

Figure 16. The transient responses of the acoustic pressure distributions from different methods for the two-dimensional scattering problem by considering the different wave travel angles: (**a**) FEM-Q4; (**b**) RPIM.

Next, the varying non-dimensional time integration steps (CFL = 1, CFL = 0.5, CFL = 0.25, and CFL = 0.1) are exploited in the numerical analysis to check whether the monotonic convergence property can be reached in transient wave analysis. For two different time points(t = 0.4 s and t = 0.7 s) and two different angles of wave travel ($\theta = 22.5°$ and $\theta = 45°$), the computed acoustic pressure distributions from different numerical techniques are presented in Figures 17 and 18. The relevant observations from these figures are quite similar to those found in a previous numerical experiment; in particular, the monotonic convergence numerical feature can broadly be reached by the meshfree RPIM and cannot be reached by the conventional FEM-Q4.

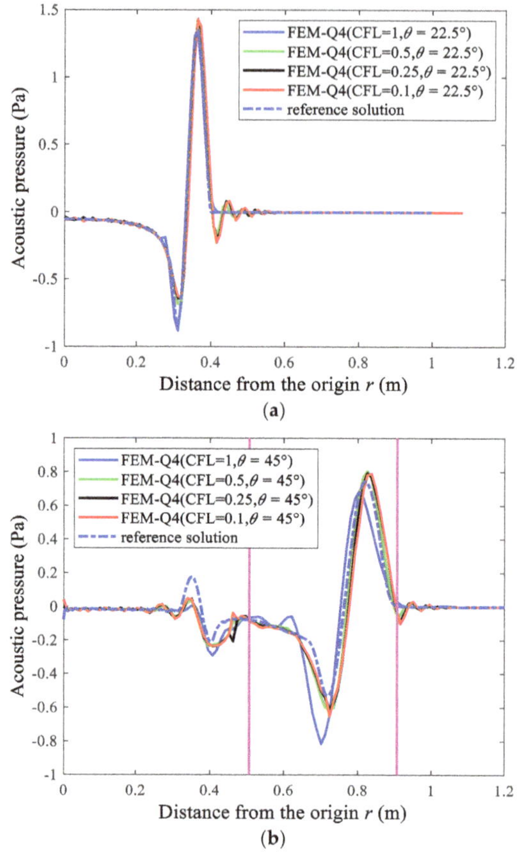

Figure 17. The transient responses of the acoustic pressure distributions at different time points from FEM-Q4 for the two-dimensional scattering problem by using the varying non-dimensional time integration steps: (**a**) $t = 0.4$ s; (**b**) $t = 0.7$ s.

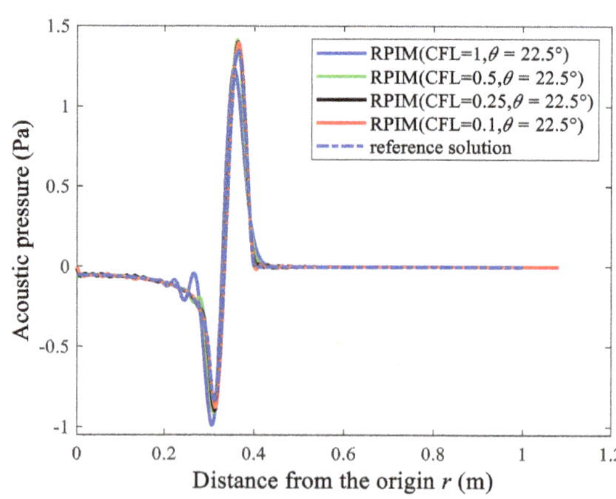

Figure 18. *Cont.*

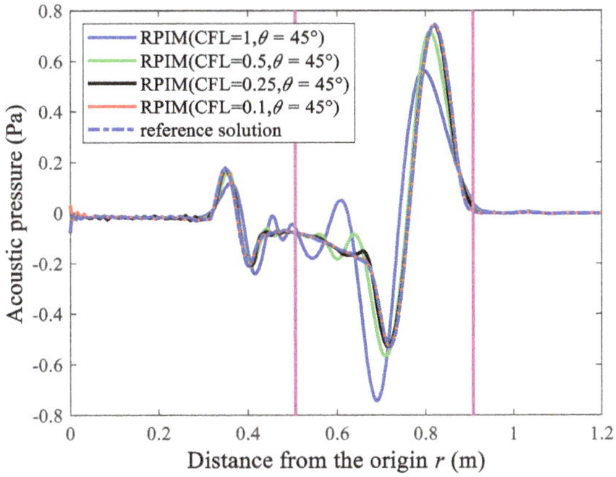

(**b**)

Figure 18. The transient responses of the acoustic pressure distributions at different time points from RPIM for the two-dimensional scattering problem by using the varying non-dimensional time integration steps: (**a**) $t = 0.4$ s; (**b**) $t = 0.7$ s.

All of the above numerical solutions suggest that the proposed RPIM with the Bathe time integration method shows stronger abilities and is more suitable for solving transient wave propagations than the conventional FEM-Q4 with totally identical node distributions.

5.3. The Two-Dimensional Acoustic Wave Scattering Problem by Irregular Objects

In the third numerical example, the acoustic wave scattering by irregular objects in two dimensions is considered in testing the numerical performance of the above-mentioned methods in handling irregular problem domains. The details of this numerical experiment are given in Figure 19. The physical constants of acoustic media in different problems are acoustic wave speed $c_1 = 2$ m/s and $c_2 = 1$ m/s, acoustic media mass density $\rho_1 = \rho_2$. For this numerical example, the conventional four-node quadrilateral mesh is again employed as the background mesh, and the mean node interval is $h = 0.01$ m. In this numerical experiment, the employed non-dimensional time interval for time integration is defined as CFL = $c_2\Delta t/h$(Δt is the used time step), and the point excitation at the corner of the problem domain (see Figure 19) is of the following Ricker wavelet form [60]:

$$F = 0.4\left[1 - 2\pi^2 f_p^2 (t - t_s)^2\right] \exp\left(-\pi^2 f_p^2 (t - t_s)^2\right), \tag{27}$$

in which $t_s = 0.1$ s and $f_p = 10$Hz are the defined characteristic parameters.

For the non-dimensional time step CFL = 0.1 and several observation time points ($t = 0.7$ s, $t = 0.8$ s, $t = 0.9$ s and $t = 1$ s), the computed numerical results of this numerical wave propagation problem in the whole problem domain are displayed in Figures 20 and 21. For comparison purposes, both the standard FEM-Q4 and the present RPIM ($\alpha_h = 3h$) results are furnished here. From the results, it is obvious that considerable numerical errors can be seen in the standard FEM-Q4 solutions. On the contrary, the solutions from the present RPIM are much smoother and show higher computation precision than those from the FEM-Q4. This numerical experiment again demonstrates that the present meshfree RPIM has more excellent numerical performance than the FEM-Q4 in transient wave propagation analysis, even if the irregular problem domains are considered.

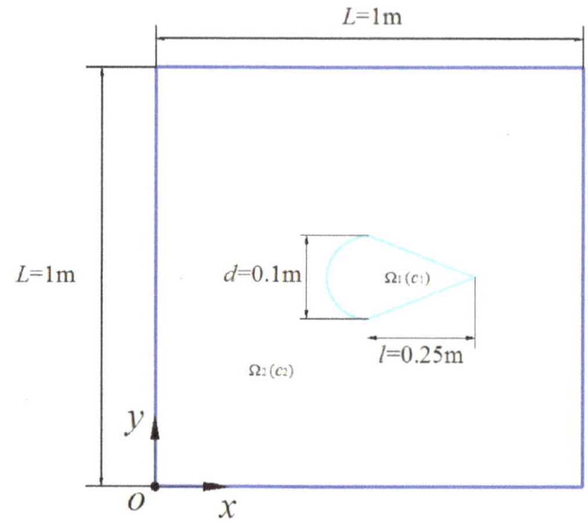

Figure 19. The geometry parameters of the two-dimensional acoustic wave scattering problem by irregular objects.

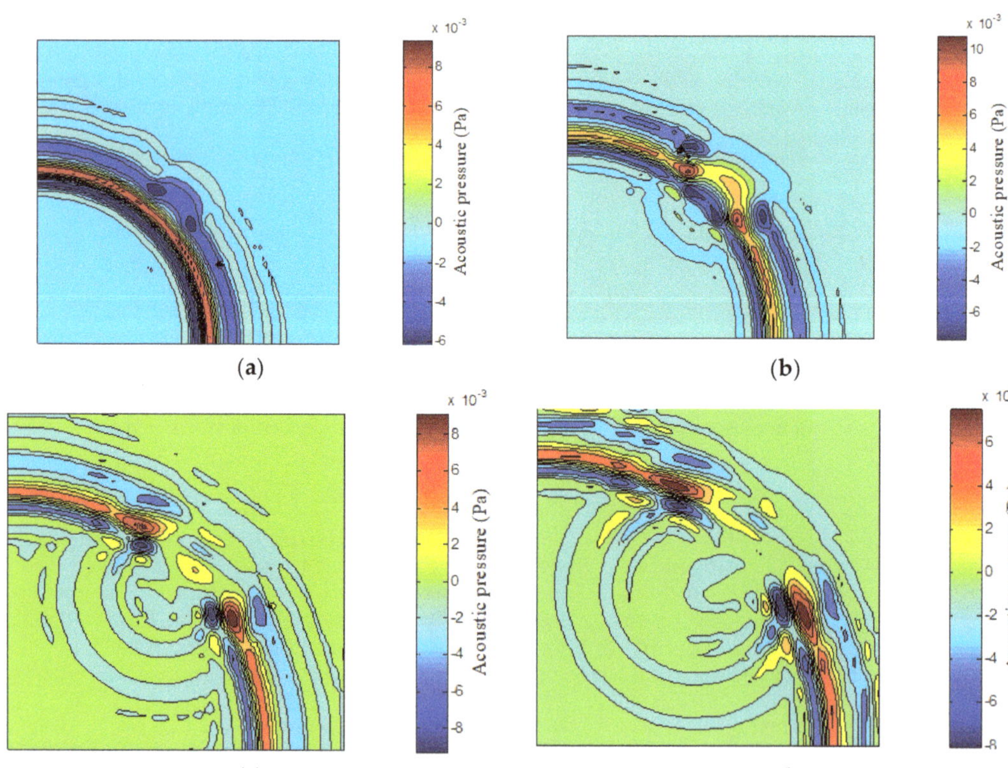

Figure 20. The computed FEM-Q4 results of the acoustic wave scattering by irregular object in the whole problem domain for several observation time points: (**a**) t = 0.7 s; (**b**) t = 0.8 s; (**c**) t = 0.9 s; (**d**) t = 1 s.

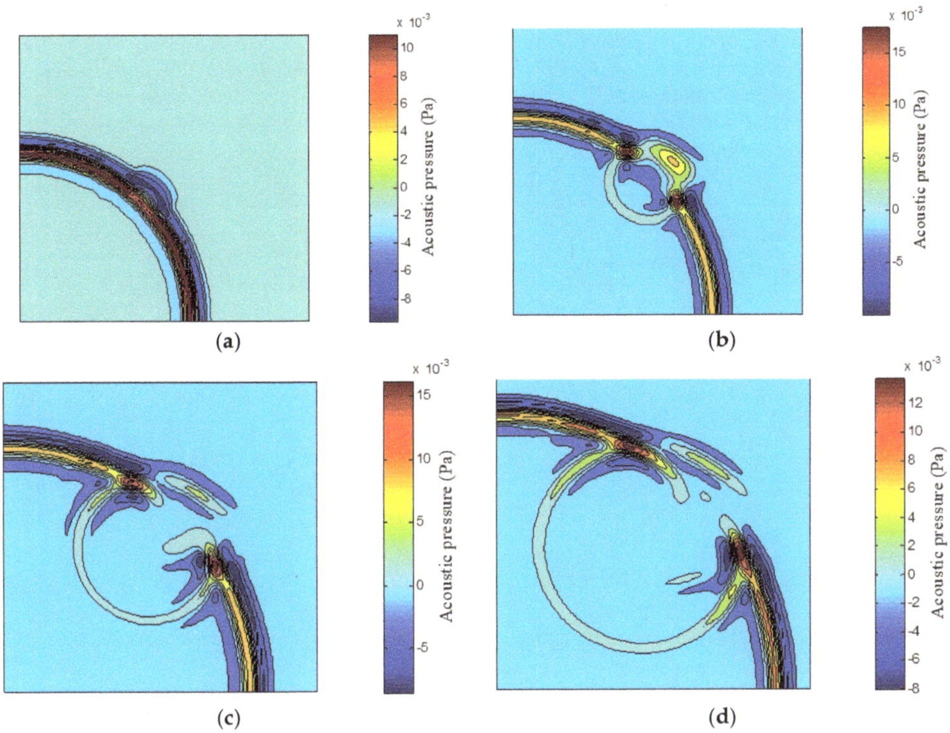

Figure 21. The computed RPIM (α_s = 3 h)results of the acoustic wave scattering by irregular object in the whole problem domain for several observation time points: (**a**) t = 0.7 s; (**b**) t = 0.8 s; (**c**) t = 0.9 s; (**d**) t = 1 s.

5.4. Study on the Computational Cost and Computation Efficiency

In previous numerical analysis, we mainly examine the numerical performance of different spatial discretization techniques (FEM-Q4 and RPIM) in treating the transient wave propagation in non-homogeneous media when the varying non-dimensional time integration step CFL numbers are employed. The important finding is that the present RPIM with adequately large support domains has the valuable monotonic convergence property in transient wave analysis when the Bathe time integration scheme is employed for temporal discretization, while the standard FEM-Q4 does not have this ideal numerical property. Nevertheless, so far, the computational cost and computation efficiency of different spatial discretization methods has not been systemically studied. To examine the abilities of different methods in depth, these issues are studied in this sub-section in great detail. To measure the solution accuracy of the obtained numerical results, the following L^2 relative error norm is employed [70]:

$$e_r = \sqrt{\frac{\int_V (u - u_h)^2 \mathrm{d}V}{\int_V u^2 \mathrm{d}V}}, \tag{28}$$

in which u_h is the numerical solutions, and u represents the corresponding exact solutions or reference solutions.

For the numerical experiments performed in Sections 5.1 and 5.2, the numerical results of computational cost and computational efficiency are detailed and provided in Tables 1 and 2. With the aim to further evaluate the numerical performance of the present meshfree RPIM, the results of another well-developed meshfree technique, which is called the element-free Galerkin method (EFGM), are also given for comparison here. All the involved numerical computation processes are performed in a laptop with a single-core Intel 2.1 GHz CPU and 8Gb RAM. From these two tables, the following valuable remarks can be summarized:

Table 1. The detailed computational cost of different numerical methods in solving the numerical experiment in Section 5.1.

Methods	Number of DOFs	Non-Zero Entities in the System Matrices	CPU Time for Spatial Discretization (s)	Non-Dimensional Time Steps	CPU Time for Temporal Discretization (s)	Total CPU Time (s)	Time Points (s)	Total Numerical Error(%)
FEM-Q4	729	6025	0.78	CFL = 1	3.11	3.89	$t = 0.4$ $t = 0.8$	3.8 14.1
				CFL = 0.5	5.87	6.65	$t = 0.4$ $t = 0.8$	6.04 27.34
				CFL = 0.25	10.09	10.87	$t = 0.4$ $t = 0.8$	8.78 33.89
				CFL = 0.1	14.58	15.36	$t = 0.4$ $t = 0.8$	9.69 36.17
RPIM ($\alpha_s = 3h$)	729	58,029	1.03	CFL = 1	3.56	4.59	$t = 0.4$ $t = 0.8$	5.88 20.14
				CFL = 0.5	6.61	7.64	$t = 0.4$ $t = 0.8$	1.59 7.28
				CFL = 0.25	12.21	13.51	$t = 0.4$ $t = 0.8$	0.89 5.65
				CFL = 0.1	19.09	20.12	$t = 0.4$ $t = 0.8$	0.59 1.58
EFGM ($\alpha_s = 3h$)	729	58,029	1.02	CFL = 1	4.12	5.14	$t = 0.4$ $t = 0.8$	5.13 18.13
				CFL = 0.5	7.23	8.25	$t = 0.4$ $t = 0.8$	1.14 6.17
				CFL = 0.25	13.19	14.21	$t = 0.4$ $t = 0.8$	0.77 4.89
				CFL = 0.1	20.01	21.03	$t = 0.4$ $t = 0.8$	0.37 1.12

(1) For different spatial discretization schemes, the required number of DOFs is totally identical, while the non-zero entities in the obtained system matrices are clearly different. This is because the required number of nodes to assemble the element matrices in the meshfree methods is usually larger than that in the standard FEM.

(2) In performing transient wave propagation analysis, the required total computational time mainly comes from two parts, namely the computing time for spatial discretization and temporal discretization, respectively. Compared to the standard FEM-Q4, more computing time is needed to perform the spatial discretization when the meshfree techniques (RPIM and EFGM) are employed. The reason for this is that in the meshfree approaches, more complex numerical approximation and more expensive numerical integration are always needed.

(3) For all the considered spatial discretization schemes (FEM-Q4, RPIM, and EFGM). The required computing time for temporal discretization is much more than that for spatial discretization. This means that in transient wave propagation analysis, the main required computational cost is from the time integration.

(4) Among the three disparate considered spatial discretization schemes, the standard FEM-Q4 has the highest computational efficiency, while the computation efficiency of the RPIM is the lowest. Though the EFGM is numerically cheaper than the present RPIM, the EFGM always possesses other disadvantages compared to the present RPIM in the numerical process; the related detailed discussion and comparison of RPIM and EFGM can be seen in Ref. [20].

(5) For the RPIM and EFGM, the obtained total relative error can basically become smaller when the smaller non-dimensional time integration step CFL number is employed,

namely the monotonic convergence numerical property can be basically achieved, while the standard FEM-Q4 obviously does not possess this important numerical property.

(6) Although the standard FEM-Q4 is usually numerically cheaper than the meshfree RPIM in solving the transient wave propagation problems, the ideal monotonic convergence property usually can be achieved. This is because the standard FEM-Q4 can always furnish relatively large numerical dispersion errors from the spatial discretization (see Figure 4d). On the contrary, the present RPIM has this ideal numerical property because the meshfree RPIM can generate adequately small spatial discretization errors (see Figure 4c). It is this important numerical property that makes the present RPIM more suitable than the FEM-Q4 in solving the relatively complex transient wave propagation problems (such as wave propagation in non-homogeneous media). This is also the core and main contribution of the present work.

Table 2. The detailed computational cost of different numerical methods in solving the numerical experiment in Section 5.2.

Methods	Number of DOFs	Non-Zero Entities in the System Matrices	CPU Time for Spatial Discretization (s)	Non-Dimensional Time Steps	CPU Time for Temporal Discretization (s)	Total CPU Time (s)	Time Points (s)	Total Numerical Error(%)
FEM-Q4	11,023	97,995	10.89	CFL = 1	54.83	65.72	$t = 0.4$ $t = 0.7$	1.39 10.12
				CFL = 0.5	107.42	118.31	$t = 0.4$ $t = 0.7$	4.09 24.21
				CFL = 0.25	206.83	217.72	$t = 0.4$ $t = 0.7$	7.19 36.84
				CFL = 0.1	419.23	430.12	$t = 0.4$ $t = 0.7$	9.9 46.01
RPIM ($\alpha_s = 3h$)	11,023	1,626,915	17.71	CFL = 1	63.12	80.83	$t = 0.4$ $t = 0.7$	4.12 13.71
				CFL = 0.5	129.53	147.24	$t = 0.4$ $t = 0.7$	3.14 7.63
				CFL = 0.25	264.73	282.44	$t = 0.4$ $t = 0.7$	2.08 3.08
				CFL = 0.1	548.93	466.64	$t = 0.4$ $t = 0.7$	0.51 1.26
EFGM ($\alpha_s = 3h$)	11,023	1,626,915	17.46	CFL = 1	64.18	81.64	$t = 0.4$ $t = 0.7$	3.76 11.23
				CFL = 0.5	132.75	150.21	$t = 0.4$ $t = 0.7$	2.87 6.13
				CFL = 0.25	268.35	285.81	$t = 0.4$ $t = 0.7$	1.64 2.46
				CFL = 0.1	554.27	571.73	$t = 0.4$ $t = 0.7$	0.38 0.76

6. Concluding Remarks

The present work sets out to examine the numerical performance of the meshfree RPIM with the Bathe implicit temporal discretization technique in the transient analysis of wave propagations in non-homogeneous media. The evaluation of the numerical errors is investigated in great detail, and the effects of the required discretizations in the space and time domains on the numerical errors in transient wave analysis are separately analyzed. The results of the dispersion analysis show that the meshfree RPIM has the ability to yield close-to-zero spatial discretization errors as long as the support domain size used for quadrature points is sufficiently large, while this kind of dispersion errors from the standard FEM-Q4 are generally very large. Additionally, it is also shown that the resultant temporal discretization error from the Bathe method is actually a monotonically decreasing function of the non-dimensional time integration steps. Owing to these two factors, the present meshfree RPIM shows distinct advantages over the conventional FEM-Q4 in transient wave analysis.

The strengths of the meshfree RPIM in solving transient wave propagations are confirmed by considering three typical numerical experiments in which the acoustic wave propagations in non-homogeneous media are considered. Since the important monotonic convergence numerical feature with respect to the non-dimensional time integration step can be broadly reached by the present RPIM, the different waves with different travel speeds can be simulated simultaneously with very high computation accuracy. However, the conventional FEM-Q4 generally cannot provide similar numerical solutions. The findings in this research provide further insights into the abilities of different numerical approaches in the analysis of transient wave propagations and also demonstrate that the present meshfree RPIM with the Bathe method can be regarded as a quite competitive alternative to the existing numerical approaches in solving very complex transient wave propagation problems in the practical engineering applications.

Author Contributions: Conceptualization, C.L. and Y.C.; methodology, Y.C.; software, S.M.; validation, C.L. and Y.P.; formal analysis, C.L.; investigation, C.L.; resources, Y.P.; data curation, C.L.; writing—original draft preparation, C.L. and S.M.; writing—review and editing, C.L. and S.M.; visualization, C.L.; supervision, Y.C.; funding acquisition, Y.C. All authors have read and agreed to the published version of the manuscript.

Funding: This research was funded by State Key Laboratory of Ocean Engineering (Shanghai Jiao Tong University) (Grant No. GKZD010081) and the Open Fund of Key Laboratory of High Performance Ship Technology (Wuhan University of Technology), Ministry of Education (Grant No. gxnc21112701).

Institutional Review Board Statement: Not applicable.

Informed Consent Statement: Not applicable.

Data Availability Statement: The data used to support the findings of this study are available from the corresponding author upon request.

Acknowledgments: We thank Zhang for the helpful suggestions to revise the present paper.

Conflicts of Interest: The authors declare no conflict of interest.

References

1. Bathe, K.J. *Finite Element Procedures*, 2nd ed.; Prentice Hall: Watertown, MA, USA, 2014.
2. Li, Y.C.; Dang, S.N.; Li, W.; Chai, Y.B. Free and Forced Vibration Analysis of Two-Dimensional Linear Elastic Solids Using the Finite Element Methods Enriched by Interpolation Cover Functions. *Mathematics* **2022**, *10*, 456. [CrossRef]
3. Noh, G.; Ham, S.; Bathe, K.J. Performance of an implicit time integration scheme in the analysis of wave propagations. *Comput. Struct.* **2013**, *123*, 93–105. [CrossRef]
4. Zheng, Z.Y.; Li, X.L. Theoretical analysis of the generalized finite difference method. *Comput. Math. Appl.* **2022**, *120*, 1–14. [CrossRef]
5. Ju, B.R.; Qu, W.Z. Three-dimensional application of the meshless generalized finite difference method for solving the extended Fisher-Kolmogorov equation. *App. Math. Lett.* **2023**, *136*, 108458. [CrossRef]
6. Qu, W.Z.; He, H. A GFDM with supplementary nodes for thin elastic plate bending analysis under dynamic loading. *Appl. Math. Lett.* **2022**, *124*, 107664. [CrossRef]
7. Fu, Z.J.; Xie, Z.Y.; Ji, S.Y.; Tsai, C.C.; Li, A.L. Meshless generalized finite difference method for water wave interactions with multiple-bottom-seated-cylinder-array structures. *Ocean Eng.* **2020**, *195*, 106736. [CrossRef]
8. Lee, U.; Kim, J.; Leung, A.Y.T. The spectral element method in structural dynamics. *Shock Vib. Dig.* **2000**, *32*, 451–465. [CrossRef]
9. Chai, Y.B.; Gong, Z.X.; Li, W.; Li, T.Y.; Zhang, Q.F. A smoothed finite element method for exterior Helmholtz equation in two dimensions. *Eng. Anal. Bound. Elem.* **2017**, *84*, 237–252. [CrossRef]
10. Chai, Y.B.; Li, W.; Gong, Z.X.; Li, T.Y. Hybrid smoothed finite element method for two-dimensional underwater acoustic scattering problems. *Ocean Eng.* **2016**, *116*, 129–141. [CrossRef]
11. Chai, Y.B.; Li, W.; Gong, Z.X.; Li, T.Y. Hybrid smoothed finite element method for two dimensional acoustic radiation problems. *Appl. Acoust.* **2016**, *103*, 90–101. [CrossRef]
12. Li, W.; You, X.Y.; Chai, Y.B.; Li, T.Y. Edge-Based Smoothed Three-Node Mindlin Plate Element. *J. Eng. Mech.* **2016**, *142*, 04016055. [CrossRef]
13. Li, W.; Gong, Z.X.; Chai, Y.B.; Cheng, C.; Li, T.Y.; Zhang, Q.F.; Wang, M.S. Hybrid gradient smoothing technique with discrete shear gap method for shell structures. *Comput. Math. Appl.* **2017**, *74*, 1826–1855. [CrossRef]
14. Chai, Y.B.; Li, W.; Li, T.Y.; Gong, Z.X.; You, X.Y. Analysis of underwater acoustic scattering problems using stable node-based smoothed finite element method. *Eng. Anal. Bound. Elem.* **2016**, *72*, 27–41. [CrossRef]

15. Chai, Y.B.; Gong, Z.X.; Li, W.; Li, T.Y.; Zhang, Q.F.; Zou, Z.H.; Sun, Y.B. Application of smoothed finite element method to two dimensional exterior problems of acoustic radiation. *Int. J. Comput. Methods* **2018**, *15*, 1850029. [CrossRef]
16. Wang, T.T.; Zhou, G.; Jiang, C.; Shi, F.C.; Tian, X.D.; Gao, G.J. A coupled cell-based smoothed finite element method and discrete phase model for incompressible laminar flow with dilute solid particles. *Eng. Anal. Bound. Elem.* **2022**, *143*, 190–206. [CrossRef]
17. Jiang, C.; Hong, C.; Wang, T.T.; Zhou, G. N-Side cell-based smoothed finite element method for incompressible flow with heat transfer problems. *Eng. Anal. Bound. Elem.* **2023**, *146*, 749–766. [CrossRef]
18. Chai, Y.B.; You, X.Y.; Li, W.; Huang, Y.; Yue, Z.J.; Wang, M.S. Application of the edge-based gradient smoothing technique to acoustic radiation and acoustic scattering from rigid and elastic structures in two dimensions. *Comput. Struct.* **2018**, *203*, 43–58. [CrossRef]
19. Li, W.; Chai, Y.B.; Lei, M.; Li, T.Y. Numerical investigation of the edge-based gradient smoothing technique for exterior Helmholtz equation in two dimensions. *Comput. Struct.* **2017**, *182*, 149–164. [CrossRef]
20. Liu, G.R. *Mesh Free Methods: Moving beyond the Finite Element Method*; CRC Press: Boca Raton, FL, USA, 2009.
21. Chai, Y.B.; You, X.Y.; Li, W. Dispersion Reduction for the Wave Propagation Problems Using a Coupled "FE-Meshfree" Triangular Element. *Int. J. Comput. Methods* **2020**, *17*, 1950071. [CrossRef]
22. You, X.Y.; Li, W.; Chai, Y.B. Dispersion analysis for acoustic problems using the point interpolation method. *Eng. Anal. Bound. Elem.* **2018**, *94*, 79–93. [CrossRef]
23. Lin, J.; Bai, J.; Reutskiy, S.; Lu, J. A novel RBF-based meshless method for solving time-fractional transport equations in 2D and 3D arbitrary domains. *Eng. Comput.* **2022**. [CrossRef]
24. Li, W.; Zhang, Q.; Gui, Q.; Chai, Y.B. A coupled FE-Meshfree triangular element for acoustic radiation problems. *Int. J. Comput. Methods* **2021**, *18*, 2041002. [CrossRef]
25. Wang, C.; Wang, F.J.; Gong, Y.P. Analysis of 2D heat conduction in nonlinear functionally graded materials using a local semi-analytical meshless method. *AIMS Math.* **2021**, *6*, 12599–12618. [CrossRef]
26. Gui, Q.; Zhang, Y.; Chai, Y.B.; You, X.Y.; Li, W. Dispersion error reduction for interior acoustic problems using the radial point interpolation meshless method with plane wave enrichment functions. *Eng. Anal. Bound. Elem.* **2022**, *143*, 428–441. [CrossRef]
27. You, X.Y.; Li, W.; Chai, Y.B. A truly meshfree method for solving acoustic problems using local weak form and radial basis functions. *Appl. Math. Comput.* **2020**, *365*, 124694. [CrossRef]
28. Qu, J.; Dang, S.N.; Li, Y.C.; Chai, Y.B. Analysis of the interior acoustic wave propagation problems using the modified radial point interpolation method (M-RPIM). *Eng. Anal. Bound. Elem.* **2022**, *138*, 339–368. [CrossRef]
29. Liu, G.R.; Gu, Y.T. A meshfree method: Meshfree weak–strong (MWS) form method for 2-D solids. *Comput. Mech.* **2003**, *33*, 2–14. [CrossRef]
30. Cheng, S.; Wang, F.J.; Li, P.W.; Qu, W. Singular boundary method for 2D and 3D acoustic design sensitivity analysis. *Comput. Math. Appl.* **2022**, *119*, 371–386. [CrossRef]
31. Chen, Z.; Sun, L. A boundary meshless method for dynamic coupled thermoelasticity problems. *App. Math. Lett.* **2022**, *134*, 108305. [CrossRef]
32. Cheng, S.F.; Wang, F.J.; Wu, G.Z.; Zhang, C.X. semi-analytical and boundary-type meshless method with adjoint variable formulation for acoustic design sensitivity analysis. *Appl. Math. Lett.* **2022**, *131*, 108068. [CrossRef]
33. Li, J.P.; Zhang, L. High-precision calculation of electromagnetic scattering by the Burton-Miller type regularized method of moments. *Eng. Anal. Bound. Elem.* **2021**, *133*, 177–184. [CrossRef]
34. Li, J.P.; Zhang, L.; Qin, Q.H. A regularized fast multipole method of moments for rapid calculation of three-dimensional time-harmonic electromagnetic scattering from complex targets. *Eng. Anal. Bound. Elem.* **2022**, *142*, 28–38. [CrossRef]
35. Gu, Y.; Fan, C.M.; Fu, Z.J. Localized method of fundamental solutions for three-dimensional elasticity problems: Theory. *Adv. Appl. Math. Mech.* **2021**, *13*, 1520–1534.
36. Li, J.P.; Fu, Z.J.; Gu, Y.; Qin, Q.H. Recent advances and emerging applications of the singular boundary method for large-scale and high-frequency computational acoustics. *Adv. Appl. Math. Mech.* **2022**, *14*, 315–343. [CrossRef]
37. Gu, Y.; Lei, J. Fracture mechanics analysis of two-dimensional cracked thin structures (from micro- to nano-scales) by an efficient boundary element analysis. *Results Math.* **2021**, *11*, 100172. [CrossRef]
38. Fu, Z.J.; Xi, Q.; Gu, Y.; Li, J.P.; Qu, W.Z.; Sun, L.L.; Wei, X.; Wang, F.J.; Lin, J.; Li, W.W.; et al. Singular boundary method: A review and computer implementation aspects. *Eng. Anal. Bound. Elem.* **2023**, *147*, 231–266. [CrossRef]
39. Chen, Z.; Wang, F. Localized Method of Fundamental Solutions for Acoustic Analysis Inside a Car Cavity with Sound-Absorbing Material. *Adv. Appl. Math. Mech.* **2022**, *15*, 182–201. [CrossRef]
40. Wei, X.; Rao, C.; Chen, S.; Luo, W. Numerical simulation of anti-plane wave propagation in heterogeneous media. *App. Math. Lett.* **2023**, *135*, 108436. [CrossRef]
41. Fu, Z.J.; Xi, Q.; Li, Y.; Huang, H.; Rabczuk, T. Hybrid FEM–SBM solver for structural vibration induced underwater acoustic radiation in shallow marine environment. *Comput. Methods Appl. Mech. Eng.* **2020**, *369*, 113236. [CrossRef]
42. Zienkiewicz, O.C. Achievements and some unsolved problems of the finite element method. *Int. J. Numer. Methods Eng.* **2000**, *47*, 9–28. [CrossRef]
43. Monaghan, J.J. Smoothed particle hydrodynamics. *Annu. Rev. Astron. Astrophys.* **1992**, *30*, 543–574. [CrossRef]
44. Liu, W.K.; Jun, S.; Li, S.; Adee, J.; Belytschko, T. Reproducing Kernel particle methods for structural dynamics. *Int. J. Numer. Methods Eng.* **1995**, *38*, 1655–1679. [CrossRef]

45. Belytschko, T.; Lu, Y.Y.; Gu, L. Element-free Galerkin methods. *Int. J. Numer. Methods Eng.* **1994**, *37*, 229–256. [CrossRef]
46. Li, X.; Li, S. A fast element-free Galerkin method for the fractional diffusion-wave equation. *App. Math. Lett.* **2021**, *122*, 107529. [CrossRef]
47. Li, X.; Li, S. A linearized element-free Galerkin method for the complex Ginzburg–Landau equation. *Comput. Math. Appl.* **2021**, *90*, 135–147. [CrossRef]
48. Lai, B.; Bathe, K.J. The method of finite spheres in three-dimensional linear static analysis. *Comput. Struct.* **2016**, *173*, 161–173. [CrossRef]
49. Li, X.; Li, S. A finite point method for the fractional cable equation using meshless smoothed gradients. *Eng. Anal. Bound. Elem.* **2022**, *134*, 453–465. [CrossRef]
50. Fu, Z.J.; Tang, Z.C.; Xi, Q.; Liu, Q.G.; Gu, Y.; Wang, F.J. Localized collocation schemes and their applications. *Acta Mech. Sinica* **2022**, *38*, 422167. [CrossRef]
51. Fu, Z.J.; Yang, L.W.; Xi, Q.; Liu, C.S. A boundary collocation method for anomalous heat conduction analysis in functionally graded materials. *Comput. Math. Appl.* **2021**, *88*, 91–109. [CrossRef]
52. Tang, Z.; Fu, Z.J.; Sun, H.; Liu, X. An efficient localized collocation solver for anomalous diffusion on surfaces. *Fract. Calc. Appl. Anal.* **2021**, *24*, 865–894. [CrossRef]
53. Xi, Q.; Fu, Z.J.; Rabczuk, T.; Yin, D. A localized collocation scheme with fundamental solutions for long-time anomalous heat conduction analysis in functionally graded materials. *Int. J. Heat Mass Tran.* **2021**, *180*, 121778. [CrossRef]
54. Noh, G.; Bathe, K.J. An explicit time integration scheme for the analysis of wave propagations. *Comput. Struct.* **2013**, *129*, 178–193. [CrossRef]
55. Kim, W.; Reddy, J.N. Novel explicit time integration schemes for efficient transient analyses of structural problems. *Int. J. Mech. Sci.* **2000**, *172*, 105429. [CrossRef]
56. Noh, G.; Bathe, K.J. Further insights into an implicit time integration scheme for structural dynamics. *Comput. Struct.* **2018**, *202*, 15–24. [CrossRef]
57. Song, C.M.; Eisenträger, S.; Zhang, X.R. High-order implicit time integration scheme based on Padé expansions. *Comput. Methods Appl. Mech. Eng.* **2022**, *390*, 114436. [CrossRef]
58. Bathe, K.J. Conserving energy and momentum in nonlinear dynamics: A simple implicit time integration scheme. *Comput. Struct.* **2007**, *85*, 437–445. [CrossRef]
59. Zhang, Y.O.; Dang, S.N.; Li, W.; Chai, Y.B. Performance of the radial point interpolation method (RPIM) with implicit time integration scheme for transient wave propagation dynamics. *Comput. Math. Appl.* **2022**, *114*, 95–111. [CrossRef]
60. Chai, Y.B.; Bathe, K.J. Transient wave propagation in inhomogeneous media with enriched overlapping triangular elements. *Comput. Struct.* **2020**, *237*, 106273. [CrossRef]
61. Chai, Y.B.; Li, W.; Liu, Z.Y. Analysis of transient wave propagation dynamics using the enriched finite element method with interpolation cover functions. *Appl. Math. Comput.* **2022**, *412*, 126564. [CrossRef]
62. Sun, T.T.; Wang, P.; Zhang, G.J.; Chai, Y.B. Transient analyses of wave propagations in nonhomogeneous media employing the novel finite element method with the appropriate enrichment function. *Comput. Math. Appl.* **2023**, *129*, 90–112. [CrossRef]
63. Fasshauer, G.E.; Zhang, J.G. On choosing "optimal" shape parameters for RBF approximation. *Numer. Algorithms* **2007**, *45*, 345–368. [CrossRef]
64. Liu, G.R.; Gu, Y.T. Assessment and applications of point interpolation methods for computational mechanics. *Int. J. Numer. Meth. Eng.* **2004**, *59*, 1373–1397. [CrossRef]
65. Liu, G.R.; Gu, Y.T. *An Introduction to Meshfree Methods and Their Programming*; Springer Science & Business Media: Dordrecht, The Netherlands, 2005.
66. Li, Y.C.; Liu, C.; Li, W.; Chai, Y.B. Numerical investigation of the element-free Galerkin method (EFGM) with appropriate temporal discretization techniques for transient wave propagation problems. *Appl. Math. Comput.* **2023**, *442*, 127755. [CrossRef]
67. Wu, F.; Zhou, G.; Gu, Q.Y.; Chai, Y.B. An enriched finite element method with interpolation cover functions for acoustic analysis in high frequencies. *Eng. Anal. Bound. Elem.* **2021**, *129*, 67–81. [CrossRef]
68. Gui, Q.; Zhou, Y.; Li, W.; Chai, Y.B. Analysis of two-dimensional acoustic radiation problems using the finite element with cover functions. *Appl. Acoust.* **2022**, *185*, 108408. [CrossRef]
69. Chai, Y.B.; Gong, Z.X.; Li, W.; Zhang, Y.O. Analysis of transient wave propagation in inhomogeneous media using edge-based gradient smoothing technique and bathe time integration method. *Eng. Anal. Bound. Elem.* **2020**, *120*, 211–222. [CrossRef]
70. Kim, K.T.; Zhang, L.; Bathe, K.J. Transient implicit wave propagation dynamics with overlapping finite Elements. *Comput. Struct.* **2018**, *199*, 18–33. [CrossRef]

mathematics MDPI

Article

Mechanical Stability of the Heterogenous Bilayer Solid Electrolyte Interphase in the Electrodes of Lithium–Ion Batteries

Yasir Ali [1], Noman Iqbal [2], Imran Shah [1] and Seungjun Lee [2,*]

[1] Department of Aerospace Engineering, College of Aeronautical Engineering, National University of Science and Technology, Risalpur 24090, Pakistan
[2] Department of Mechanical, Robotics and Energy Engineering, Dongguk University, Seoul 04620, Republic of Korea
* Correspondence: sjunlee@dgu.ac.kr

Abstract: Mechanical stability of the solid electrolyte interphase (SEI) is crucial to mitigate the capacity fade of lithium–ion batteries because the rupture of the SEI layer results in further consumption of lithium ions in newly generated SEI layers. The SEI is known as a heterogeneous bilayer and consists of an inner inorganic layer connecting the particle and an outer organic layer facing the electrolyte. The growth of the bilayer SEI over cycles alters the stress generation and failure possibility of both the organic and inorganic layers. To investigate the probability of mechanical failure of the bilayer SEI, we developed the electrochemical-mechanical coupled model with the core–double-shell particle/SEI layer model. The growth of the bilayer SEI is considered over cycles. Our results show that during charging, the stress of the particle changes from tensile to compressive as the thickness of bilayer SEI increases. On the other hand, in the SEI layers, large compressive radial and tensile tangential stress are generated. During discharging, the compressive radial stress of the bilayer SEI transforms into tensile radial stress. The tensile tangential and radial stresses are responsible for the fracture and debonding of the bilayer SEI, respectively. As the thickness ratio of the inorganic to organic layers increases, the fracture probability of the inorganic layer increases, while that of the organic layer decreases. However, the debonding probability of both layers is decreased. In addition, the SEI covering large particles is more vulnerable to fracture, while that covering small particles is more susceptible to debonding. Therefore, tailoring the thickness ratio of the inorganic to organic layers and particle size is important to reduce the fracture and debonding of the heterogeneous bilayer SEI.

Keywords: SEI formation; core–double-shell structure; stress; fracture; debonding; electrochemical model

MSC: 74F25; 74S05; 78A57

Citation: Ali, Y.; Iqbal, N.; Shah, I.; Lee, S. Mechanical Stability of the Heterogenous Bilayer Solid Electrolyte Interphase in the Electrodes of Lithium–Ion Batteries. *Mathematics* **2023**, *11*, 543. https://doi.org/10.3390/math11030543

Academic Editor: Zhuojia Fu

Received: 2 January 2023
Revised: 16 January 2023
Accepted: 17 January 2023
Published: 19 January 2023

1. Introduction

Lithium–ion batteries are considered a prominent energy storage device, ranging from consumer electronics to electric vehicles [1,2]. The solid electrolyte interphase formation (SEI) inside the electrode is crucial to battery performance [3]. The developed SEI layer leads to degradation and capacity loss by consuming cyclable lithium ions [4]. Current research is focused on the development of a mechanically stable bilayer SEI, as during cycling, the rupture of the SEI layer additionally consumes the cyclable lithium content [5,6].

The decomposition of the electrolyte during initial charge–discharge cycles forms a passivating layer on the electrode surface termed the SEI layer [7]. The SEI layer allows lithium ion transport and blocks electrons to prevent further electrolyte decomposition. The SEI layer grows over cycles causing capacity fade [8]. Many studies on the bilayer structure of the SEI have been reported. For example, the bilayer SEI develops on the particle surface in the form of a shell, consisting of both inorganic and organic compounds [9,10]. Smith et al. reported a heterogeneous bilayer SEI comprised of inorganic (Li_2CO_3) and organic ($(CH_2OCO_2Li)_2$) species [11]. Peled et al. concluded that the SEI comprises inner inorganic and outer organic layers [9,12]. Lan et al. experimentally proved the double-layer hybrid SEI on a SnO_2 electrode [13]. Ha et al. prepared a 3D-structured inorganic–organic hybrid bilayer SEI with enhanced mechanical stability [14]. Lee et al. observed a bilayer SEI with a 3.7 nm inner inorganic layer and a 15.4 nm outer organic layer [15]. Aspern et al. observed that after 1171 charge–discharge cycles, half of the developed SEI layer was inorganic, while the other half was the organic layer [16]. Li et al. developed an in situ inner inorganic and outer organic bilayer SEI for zinc aqueous batteries [17]. Zhao et al. synthesized an organic–inorganic SEI layer with sufficient mechanical strength [18].

In addition, SEI formation in solid-state batteries has been studied. Fitzhugh et al. developed an ab inito computational method to study the properties of the SEI layer formed at the interface of the solid-state electrolyte [19]. Tu et al. investigated the mechanical fracture and debonding of the SEI layer formed on the surface of lithium metal inside solid-state batteries [20]. In addition, many efforts have been made to enhance lithium conductivity and reduce the interfacial resistance of the solid-state electrolyte [21–24]. Qin et al. added La_2O_3 nanoparticles to a garnet-type solid electrolyte to enhance lithium conductivity [25]. Using thermodynamic analysis, Qin et al. increased the lithium conductivity of a Ta-doped solid-state electrolyte [26].

The developed SEI layer varies in composition and physiochemical properties, which alters its mechanical stability [27–29]. Since the continuous conversion of organic SEI to inorganic SEI occurs over several cycles, the actual mechanical properties of the developed SEI cannot be well predicted [30–32]. In addition, different electrolyte additives also alter the actual thickness and porosity of the developed SEI [33,34]. Zheng et al. reported that the SEI layer has an inhomogeneous multilayered structure with varied mechanical properties [35]. Moeremans et al. studied the mechanical properties of the heterogeneous bilayer SEI in situ [36]. They addressed that the mechanical properties of the developed layers can be controlled via the addition of additives or electrolyte formulations [36]. Using the AFM topographical imaging technique, Zhang et al. confirmed that the SEI is inhomogeneous in morphology and mechanical properties [37]. Shin et al. investigated that the stiffness of SEI layers widely varies between 0.2 and 80 GPa. Moreover, the inorganic LiF exhibited a peak value of 135.3 GPa [38].

Significant efforts are devoted to developing a mechanically stable bilayer SEI. One example is to develop an elastic SEI [7,39,40]. The elastic polymeric films and inherently bonded lithium salts provided considerable mechanical strength [7]. In addition, artificial single- [41–43] and double-layer SEIs are constructed to enhance mechanical stability, suppressing the fracture and debonding of the SEI layer [44,45].

Various attempts have been made to understand the mechanical failure of the heterogeneous bilayer SEI [46–48]. For instance, Chen et al. studied the impact of SEI inhomogeneities on the fracture of the SEI layer in Si electrodes [49]. Guo et al. examined the cracks in the outer SEI layer. The produced cracks stopped at the inorganic/organic interface [50]. He et al. studied the stress in the heterogeneous SEI. They concluded that the peak tensile stress occurred at the active material/inorganic SEI layer interface. They further observed that the strength of SEI layers largely varies with the thickness of the inorganic layer, compared to the organic layer [51]. Yuanpeng et al. studied the wrinkling and ratcheting of the SEI layer during lithiation with varying SEI thicknesses [52].

In most of the theoretical models, the bilayer SEI has been assumed to be a continuum with homogenized properties throughout the thickness. This idealized assumption cannot capture the interfacial debonding at the inorganic/organic interfaces [51]. In addition, a constant thickness of the bilayer SEI has been assumed over cycles. The constant SEI thickness does not consider the effect of the increased mechanical constraint as the SEI layer grows. Furthermore, the impact of the inorganic/organic thickness ratio of the SEI layer on stress generation and electrochemical performance is rarely studied. In this article, we analyze the mechanical stability of a heterogeneous bilayer SEI, while considering the combined effect of a reduction in the state of charge (SOC) because of lithium consumption and an increase in the mechanical constraint as a result of the growing thickness of the bilayer SEI. The particle–SEI layer is modeled in the form of a core–double-shell, where the inner and outer shells represent the inorganic and organic SEI layers, respectively. A one-dimensional (1D) electrochemical model fully coupled with a two-dimensional (2D) core–double-shell model is developed to evaluate stress generation inside the particle while considering the growth of the bilayer SEI. The stresses are calculated for different inorganic-to-organic-layer-thickness ratios. Furthermore, using the elastic strain energies, the fracture and debonding probability of both inorganic and organic SEI layers are analyzed. Finally, the impact of microstructural variation on the mechanical failure probability of the bilayer SEI is studied.

2. Electrochemical Model

Figure 1 shows the coupling between the 1D electrochemical model (Model 1) and the 2D core–double-shell model (Model 2). Model 1 consists of negative and positive electrodes, a separator, an electrolyte, and current collectors. The active particle and the bilayer SEI are modeled as a core–double-shell, where the active particle is modeled as a core, the inorganic SEI layer (SEI_{in}) as an inner shell, and the organic SEI layer (SEI_{or}) as an outer shell. The formation of the bilayer SEI is studied at the negative electrode in Model 1. Using direct projection coupling, the interfacial current density and the SEI current density, which are computed in Model 1, are applied to the particle/inorganic SEI interface (P/SEI_{in}) in Model 2. During lithiation/delithiation, the electrode region facing the separator experience large stresses. Therefore, the flux calculated from this region in Model 1 is input into Model 2.

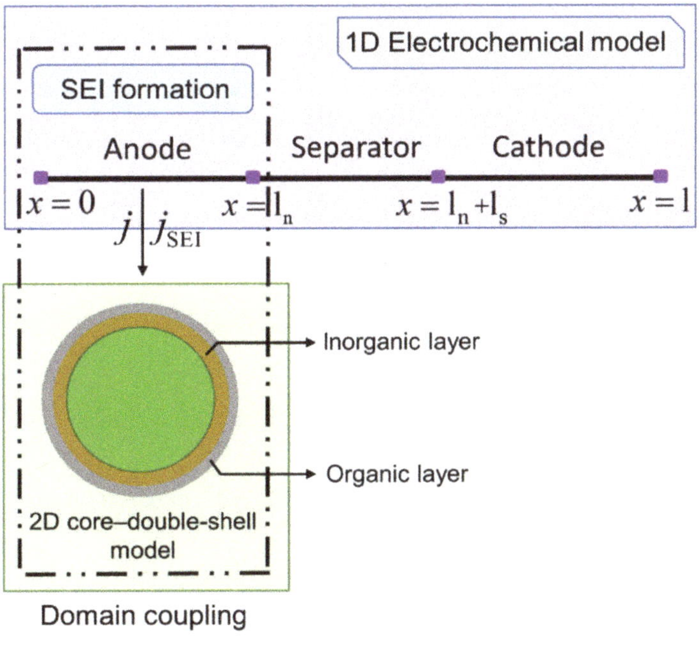

Figure 1. Simulation model showing the coupling between the 1D electrochemical model and the 2D core–double-shell model.

The SEI thickness computed in Model 1 is mapped to the thickness of SEI_{in} and SEI_{or} in Model 2. The thickness of the shells is increased every cycle to consider the growth of the bilayer SEI. Table 1 shows the cell-level parameters.

2.1. Cell-Level Model

The time-dependent lithium concentration inside the electrolyte is described by:

$$\varepsilon_l \frac{\partial c_l}{\partial t} = \nabla \cdot (D_l \nabla c_l) + (\frac{1-t_+}{F}) a_s j \quad (1)$$

where D_l and ε_l are the diffusivity and effective porosity, respectively, t_+ is the ion transport number, and j is the interfacial current density applied at the P/SEI_{in} interface. The boundary conditions for the electrolyte current density are given in Equation (2) and illustrated in Figure 1:

$$\begin{aligned} &-D_l \nabla c_{l\, x=0} = 0, \\ &-D_l \nabla c_{l\, x=1} = 0, \\ &-D_l \nabla c_{l\, x=(l_n)^-} = -D_l \nabla c_{l\, x=(l_n)^+}, \\ &-D_l \nabla c_{l\, x=(l_n+l_s)^-} = -D_l \nabla c_{l\, x=(l_n+l_s)^+}. \end{aligned} \quad (2)$$

Inside the electrolyte, the ionic charge balance follows the governing equation [53]:

$$\nabla \cdot \left(k_l \nabla \varphi_l - \frac{2RT(1-t_+)}{F} k_l \nabla \ln c_l \right) = -a_s j \quad (3)$$

with the following boundary conditions:

$$-k_l \nabla \varphi_l|_{x=0} = -k_l \nabla \varphi_l|_{x=1} = 0 \quad (4)$$

The lithium diffusion in the particles is written by:

$$\frac{\partial C(r,t)}{\partial t} = D_s \nabla^2 C(r,t) \quad (5)$$

where $C(r,t)$ is the lithium concentration and D_s represents the lithium ions diffusivity. The mass flux inside the particle is related to interfacial current density as [54]

$$-D_s \nabla C(r,t) = \frac{j}{F} \quad (6)$$

2.2. Interfacial Kinetics

The lithium current density applied at the P/SEI_{in} interface follows the Butler–Volmer equation:

$$j = kF(c_l(c_m - c_{surf})c_{surf})^{0.5} \left\{ \exp\left(\frac{\alpha_a \eta F}{RT}\right) - \exp\left(\frac{-\alpha_c \eta F}{RT}\right) \right\} \quad (7)$$

where k is the reaction rate constant. c_{surf} and c_l are the lithium concentration on the particle surface and electrolyte, respectively. The overpotential η on the P/SEI_{in} interface is calculated as $\eta = \varphi_s - \varphi_l - E_{eq} - \Delta\varphi_s^{SEI}$, where φ_s is the electrode potential and φ_l represents the electrolyte potentials. E_{eq} is the equilibrium potential and $\Delta\varphi_s^{SEI}$ represents the reduction in potential due to SEI layer resistance. The charge conservation inside the electrode obeys Ohm's law:

$$k_s \nabla^2 \varphi_s = a_s j \quad (8)$$

The boundary conditions for charge balance are written as:

$$-k_s \nabla \varphi_s|_{x=0} = 0, \quad -k_s \nabla \varphi_s|_{x=1} = i_{app} \quad (9)$$

2.3. Effect of SEI Formation

During battery charging and discharging, the ethylene carbonate (EC) is reduced to lithium ethylene di-carbonate $(CH_2OCO_2Li)_2$, consuming the cyclable lithium ions: [55]

$$EC + 2Li^+ + 2e^- \rightarrow [CH_2O\,CO_2Li]_2 \tag{10}$$

The SEI formation follows the equation: [56]

$$j_{SEI} = -j^0_{SEI}\exp\left(\frac{-\alpha_{SEI}\eta_{SEI}F}{RT}\right) \tag{11}$$

where j^0_{SEI} is the SEI exchange current density. $\eta_{SEI} = \varphi_s - \varphi_l - E^{SEI}_{eq} - \Delta\varphi^{SEI}_s$ represents the overpotential of the SEI layer. In Model 1, the side reaction is coupled with the electrode reaction to simulate the formation of bilayer SEI and accompanied SOC variation. To solve this, the interfacial kinetics responsible for lithiation and SEI formation reaction are separately defined on the electrode/electrolyte interface [57]. The volume fraction of lithium consumed in the bilayer SEI is given as:

$$\frac{\partial c_{SEI}}{\partial t} = -a_s\frac{v_{SEI}j_{SEI}}{nF} \tag{12}$$

The temporal evolution of SEI layer volume fraction follows:

$$\frac{\partial \varepsilon_{SEI}}{\partial t} = \frac{\partial \varepsilon_{SEI,In}}{\partial t} + \frac{\partial \varepsilon_{SEI,Or}}{\partial t} = \left(h_{SEI}\frac{M_{SEI,In}}{\rho_{SEI,In}} + (1-h_{SEI})\frac{M_{SEI,Or}}{\rho_{SEI,Or}}\right)\frac{\partial c_{SEI}}{\partial t} \tag{13}$$

where $M_{SEI,In}$ is the molecular mass of the SEI_{in}, and $\rho_{SEI,In}$ is the SEI_{in} density. As the volumetric fraction of the bilayer SEI increases, the electrode porosity is reduced. $\varepsilon_l|_n$ is the electrode porosity at the nth cycle. In any cycle, the electrode porosity is calculated as:

$$\varepsilon_l|_n = \varepsilon_l|_{n-1} - \Delta\varepsilon_{SEI}|_n \tag{14}$$

where $\Delta\varepsilon_{SEI}|_n$ depicts the change in the volume content of the bilayer SEI. The increase in the SEI thickness is: [58]

$$\frac{\partial th_{SEI}}{\partial t} = \frac{\partial th_{SEI,In}}{\partial t} + \frac{\partial th_{SEI,Or}}{\partial t} = -\frac{j_{SEI}}{F}\left(h_{SEI}\frac{M_{SEI,In}}{\rho_{SEI,In}} + (1-h_{SEI})\frac{M_{SEI,Or}}{\rho_{SEI,Or}}\right) \tag{15}$$

Over cycles, the thickness of the SEI layer increases as: $th_{SEI}|_n = th_{SEI}|_{n-1} + \Delta th_{SEI}|_n$.

2.4. Reduction in State of Charge

The battery capacity is defined as:

$$Q = \varepsilon_s c_m F(x_{max} - x_{min}) \tag{16}$$

where ε_s is the volumetric fraction of the active material inside the positive electrode and c_m is the stoichiometric lithium concentration of the material. x_{max} and x_{min} represent the maximum and minimum SOC of the electrode. In this model, no degradation and side reactions are considered at the positive electrode. Part of the available lithium is used during SEI formation, which reduces the discharge capacity, ΔQ_{SEI}. $Q|_n$ is the discharge capacity of the nth cycle. Over charge–discharge cycles, the net cell capacity can be obtained as:

$$Q|_n = Q|_{n-1} - \Delta Q_{SEI}|_n \tag{17}$$

Substituting Equation (16) into Equation (17) and solving for x_{max}:

$$x_{max}|_n = x_{max}|_{n-1} - \frac{1}{\varepsilon_s c_m}\Delta c_{SEI}|_n \tag{18}$$

The decrease in $x_{\max}$ of the positive electrode correspondingly reduces the $x_{\max}$ of the anode.

3. Mechanical Model

During lithium intercalation deintercalation, the stress in Model 2 can be obtained as [59]

$$\varepsilon_{ij} = \frac{1}{E}\left[(1+\nu)\sigma_{ij} - \nu\sigma_{\mathrm{kk}}\delta_{ij}\right] + \frac{C(r,t)\Omega}{3}\delta_{ij} \tag{19}$$

where ε_{ij} and σ_{ij} represents the strain and stress tensors, respectively, $\sigma_{\mathrm{kk}} = \mathrm{tr}(\sigma) = \sigma_1 + \sigma_2 + \sigma_3$. Ω represents the change in volume of the electrode per one addition of lithium. In the current study, the radial σ_r and tangential σ_θ stress are studied inside Model 2. During charging and discharging, the stress–strain relationship is given as [60,61]

$$\frac{\mathrm{d}u(r,t)}{\mathrm{d}r} = \frac{1}{E}(\sigma_r - 2\nu\sigma_\theta) + \frac{\Omega}{3}\{C(r,t) - C(r,0)\} \tag{20}$$

$$\frac{u(r,t)}{r} = \frac{1}{E}\{\sigma_\theta - \nu(\sigma_r + \sigma_\theta)\} + \frac{\Omega}{3}\{C(r,t) - C(r,0)\} \tag{21}$$

In Equations (20) and (21), the last term on the right-hand side represents the diffusion-induced strain. The mechanical equilibrium is expressed:

$$\frac{1}{2}\frac{\mathrm{d}\sigma_r}{\mathrm{d}r} + \frac{\sigma_r}{r} = \frac{\sigma_\theta}{r} \tag{22}$$

The governing equation for radial displacement can be obtained by plugging Equations (20) and (21) into Equation (22).

$$\frac{\mathrm{d}^2u}{\mathrm{d}r^2} + \frac{2}{r}\left(\frac{\mathrm{d}u}{\mathrm{d}r} - \frac{u}{r}\right) = k\frac{\mathrm{d}C(r,t)}{\mathrm{d}r} \tag{23}$$

where $k = \frac{\Omega}{3}\frac{(1+\nu)}{(1-\nu)}$. Integrating Equation (23) yields: [62]

$$u(r,t) = \frac{k}{r^2}\int_\alpha^r Cr^2dr + \mathrm{A}r + \mathrm{B}r^{-2} \tag{24}$$

For the particle, the lower limit of integration is α = 0. For the inorganic and organic SEI layers, α = $\mathrm{R_p}$, and $\mathrm{R_p} + \mathrm{th_{SEI,In}}$, respectively, where $\mathrm{R_p}$ is the particle radius. When there is no SEI layer, the boundary conditions become: [63]

$$u_r^{\mathrm{P}}\Big|_{r=\mathrm{R_p}} = 0,\ \ \sigma_r^{\mathrm{P}}\Big|_{r=\mathrm{R_p}} = 0 \tag{25}$$

The boundary conditions during the SEI layer formation are:

$$\begin{gathered}
u_r^{\mathrm{P}}\Big|_{r=\mathrm{R_p}} = u_r^{\mathrm{SEI,In}}\Big|_{r=\mathrm{R_p}},\ u_r^{\mathrm{SEI,In}}\Big|_{r=\mathrm{R_p}+\mathrm{th_{SEI,In}}} = u_r^{\mathrm{SEI,Or}}\Big|_{r=\mathrm{R_p}+\mathrm{th_{SEI,In}}} \\
\sigma_r^{\mathrm{P}}\Big|_{r=\mathrm{R_p}} = \sigma_r^{\mathrm{SEI,In}}\Big|_{r=\mathrm{R_p}},\ \sigma_r^{\mathrm{SEI,In}}\Big|_{r=\mathrm{R_p}+\mathrm{th_{SEI,In}}} = \sigma_r^{\mathrm{SEI,Or}}\Big|_{r=\mathrm{R_p}+\mathrm{th_{SEI,In}}} \\
\sigma_r^{\mathrm{SEI,Or}}\Big|_{r=\mathrm{R_t}} = 0
\end{gathered} \tag{26}$$

where u_r^{P}, u_r^{SEI}, and σ_r^{P}, σ_r^{SEI} are the radial displacements and corresponding stresses of the particle and the bilayer SEI, respectively. The radial displacement u is plugged into Equations (20) and (21) to obtain the corresponding stresses inside the SEI shell and the core.

3.1. Stress inside the Bilayer SEI

Applying the appropriate boundary conditions shown in Equation (26), the σ_r and σ_θ in the SEI_{In} ($R_p \le r \le R_p + th_{SEI,In}$) are calculated as:

$$\sigma_r^{SEI,In} = 2(1-3b_1)\frac{E_{SEI,In}\frac{\Omega_p}{3}\left(1-\frac{(R_p+th_{SEI,In})^3}{r^3}\right)\times\left(\frac{1}{R_p^3}\int_0^{R_p} Cr^2dr\right)}{3(1-\nu_{SEI})+\left\{E_{eff,In}(1-2\nu_p)-(1-2\nu_{SEI})\right\}6b_1} \tag{27}$$

$$\sigma_\theta^{SEI,In} = \frac{E_{SEI,In}\frac{\Omega_p}{3}\left(\frac{1}{r^3}+\frac{2}{(R_p+th_{SEI,In})^3}\right)\times\left(\frac{1}{R_p^3}\int_0^{R_p} Cr^2dr\right)}{3(1-\nu_{SEI})+\left\{E_{eff,In}(1-2\nu_p)-(1-2\nu_{SEI})\right\}6b_1} \tag{28}$$

Similarly, the stresses inside the organic SEI layer ($R_p + th_{SEI,In} \le r \le R_t$), are:

$$\sigma_r^{SEI,Or} = 2(1-3b_2)\frac{E_{SEI,Or}\frac{\Omega_p}{3}\left(1-\frac{(R_t)^3}{r^3}\right)\times\left(\frac{1}{R_p^3}\int_0^{R_p} Cr^2dr\right)}{3(1-\nu_{SEI})+\left\{E_{eff,Or}(1-2\nu_p)-(1-2\nu_{SEI})\right\}6b_2} \tag{29}$$

$$\sigma_\theta^{SEI,Or} = \frac{E_{SEI,Or}\frac{\Omega_p}{3}\left(\frac{1}{r^3}+\frac{2}{(R_t)^3}\right)\times\left(\frac{1}{R_p^3}\int_0^{R_p} Cr^2dr\right)}{3(1-\nu_{SEI})+\left\{E_{eff,Or}(1-2\nu_p)-(1-2\nu_{SEI})\right\}6b_2} \tag{30}$$

where $b_1 = \frac{th_{SEI,In}}{R_p+th_{SEI,In}}$, $b_2 = \frac{th_{SEI,Or}}{R_t}$, $E_{eff,In} = \frac{E_{SEI,In}}{E_p}$, and $E_{eff,Or} = \frac{E_{SEI,Or}}{E_p}$.

In the presence of the SEI layer constraint, the σ_r and σ_θ inside the particle are calculated as:

$$\sigma_r^p = \frac{2E_p\Omega_p}{3(1-\nu_p)}\left(m\frac{1}{R_p^3}\int_0^{R_p} Cr^2dr - \frac{1}{r^3}\int_0^{r} Cr^2dr\right) \tag{31}$$

$$\sigma_\theta^p = \frac{E_p\Omega_p}{3(1-\nu_p)}\left(2m\frac{1}{R_p^3}\int_0^{R_p} Cr^2dr + \frac{1}{r^3}\int_0^{r} Cr^2dr - C(r,t)\right) \tag{32}$$

where m is:

$$m = \frac{E_{eff}(1-2b)-\nu_{SEI}E_{eff}(1-4b)-b(1+\nu_p)}{2b(1-2\nu_p)+E_{eff}(1-2b)-\nu_{SEI}E_{eff}(1-4b)} \tag{33}$$

where $E_{eff} = E_p/(h_{SEI}E_{eff,In} + (1-h_{SEI})E_{eff,Or})$, and $b = \frac{th_{SEI}}{R_t}$. When no SEI layer is formed, m =1 and Equations (31) and (32) transform into general analytical equations to calculate the σ_r and σ_θ [64].

3.2. Numerical Simulations

The models are numerically solved using COMSOL software. The Transport of diluted species (tds) module is adopted to solve the lithium concentration of the core, whereas the Solid mechanics module is used to compute the stresses in the core and bilayer SEI. After the mesh independence tests are conducted, the final mesh contained 257,830 triangular elements with 1,985,032 degrees of freedom. During the simulation, the charge–discharge process of the battery is controlled by varying the applied current. The battery is constantly charged at 1 C (cc_ch), until the maximum voltage of 4.25 V is achieved. The battery is further charged at the maximum voltage (cv_ch), while decreasing the current until it decreases to 0.05 C. Then, the battery is discharged at 1 C to 2.7 V (cc_dch).

4. Results and Discussion

4.1. Capacity Fading

Figure 2A depicts the discharge profiles for the first 2000 cycles. Over cycles, the capacity decreases to 80.2% of the initial capacity. This decrease in capacity is solely due to the formation of the bilayer SEI, which decreases the available cyclable lithium content. Figure 2B shows the reduction in SOC of the anode from the initial (33 to 27) % in 2000 cycles. The consumed ions are used in the formation of the bilayer SEI on the particle surface. Figure 2C shows the evolution of the heterogeneous bilayer SEI thickness. In 2000 cycles, the SEI_{in} and SEI_{or} increase to 0.308 and 0.462 μm, respectively. Figure 2D shows the thickness of SEI_{in} and SEI_{or} with different h_{SEI}. The total thickness of the SEI layer is $SEI_{total} = SEI_{in} + SEI_{or} = h_{SEI}SEI_{total} + (1 - h_{SEI})SEI_{total}$. The h_{SEI} is the ratio of SEI_{in} to SEI_{total}.

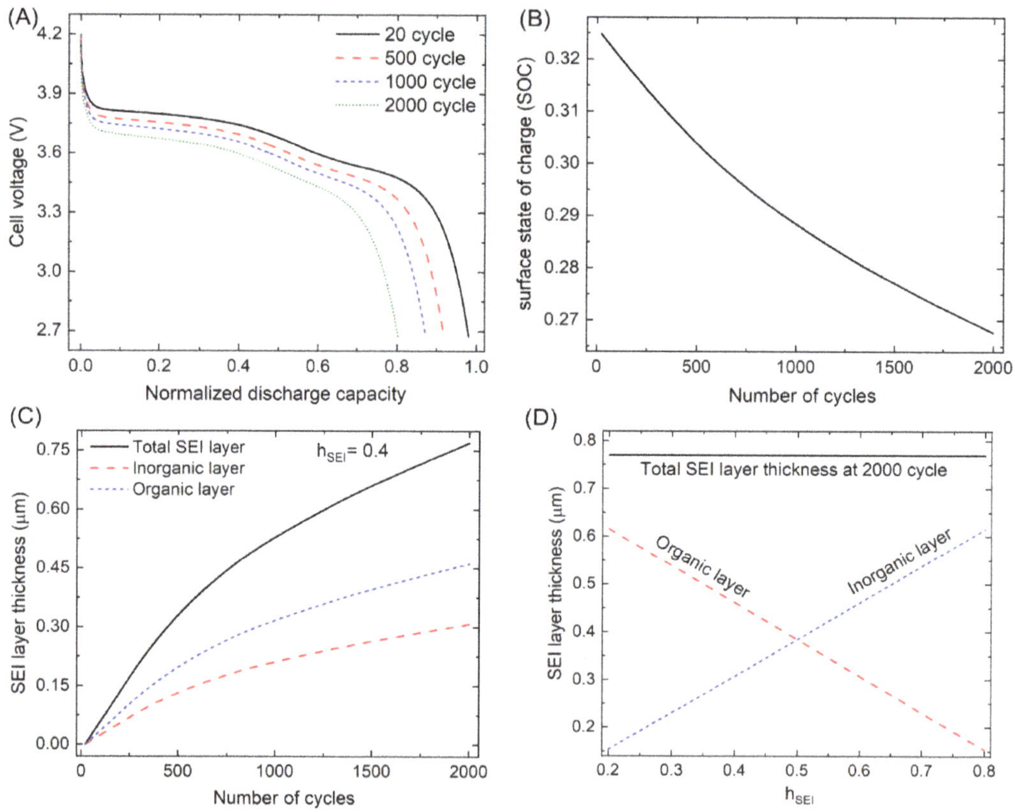

Figure 2. (**A**) Discharge curves over cycles. (**B**) Decrease in SOC of the negative electrode due to SEI formation. (**C**) Evolution of SEI layer thickness. (**D**) Thickness of the inorganic and organic SEI layer according to h_{SEI}.

4.2. Stress Analysis

The developed bilayer SEI increases the mechanical constraint to the swelling and shrinkage of the particle during lithiation and delithiation. Over cycles, the bilayer SEI continuously grows on the particle surface, forming a core–double-shell structure. Figure 3a shows the radial stress contours inside Model 2 at 2000 cycles during lithiation. The zoomed view shows that the largest compressive radial stress occurs at the P/SEI_{in} interface and decreases toward the center of the particle center and the surface of SEI_{or}. Figure 3b depicts the tangential stress contour inside Model 2 at 2000 cycles during lithiation. The extended view shows the stress discontinuity at the interfaces. The maximum tangential stress occurred at the P/SEI_{in} interface. Figure 3c shows the detailed contour maps of the tangential stress in the separate domain of the particle, inorganic, and organic SEI layers. The largest compressive stress inside the particle occurs at the surface as shown in Figure 3c(i). Figure 3c(ii) depicts that the highest tensile tangential stress in SEI_{in} occurs at the P/SEI_{in} interface and decreases along the thickness. Figure 3c(iii) illustrates that the tensile stress in SEI_{or} is smaller than that in SEI_{in}. Inside the organic layer, the largest stress happens at the SEI_{in}/SEI_{or} interface and decreases along the thickness. The compressive stress of the particle and bilayer SEI is caused by the simultaneous effect of diffusion-induced stress and mechanical confinement from the bilayer SEI.

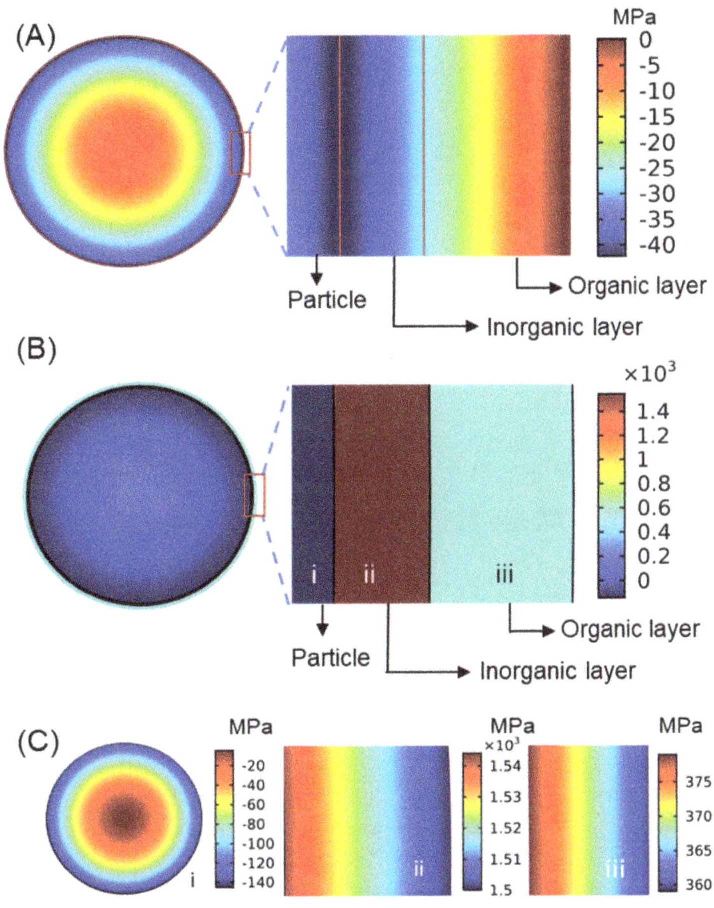

Figure 3. Stress contours in the particle and SEI layer at the end of 2000 cycles. (**A**) Radial stress with magnified view in the inorganic and organic SEI layers. (**B**) Tangential stress with magnified view in the inorganic and organic SEI layers. (**C**) Detailed tangential stress distribution (i) inside the particle, (ii) inorganic SEI layer, and (iii) organic SEI layer. The results are plotted for $h_{SEI} = 0.4$.

Figure 4A shows the radial stress distribution inside Model 2 for $h_{SEI} = 0.4$ at the end of lithiation. At the initial cycles, tensile radial stress occurred inside the particle. As the bilayer SEI becomes thicker during charge–discharge cycles, the corresponding mechanical constraint against the particle expansion increases, causing a reduction in the tensile behavior. After 800 cycles, the SEI layer confinement is sufficient to transform the tensile radial stress to compressive. The compressive stress of the particle increases outward from the particle center, reaches the maximum at the P/SEI$_{in}$ interface, and then decreases to zero along the SEI thickness.

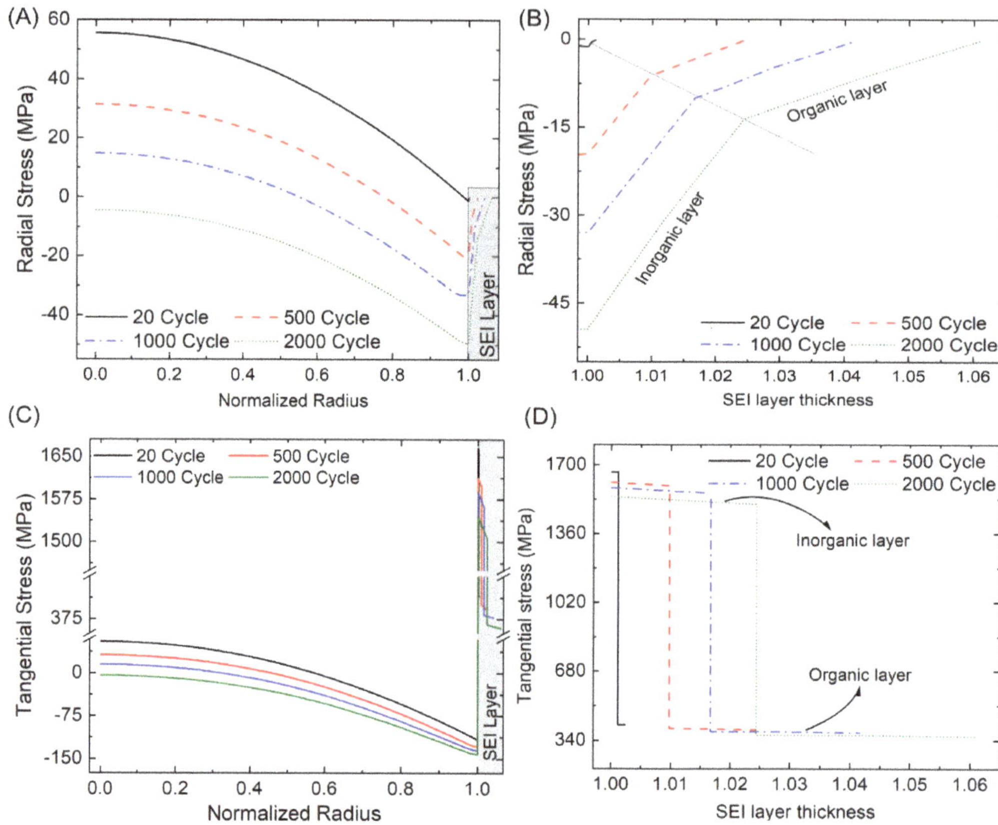

Figure 4. Evolution of radial and tangential stress inside the particle and SEI layer during lithiation. (**A**) Radial stress inside the particle and SEI layer, with (**B**) magnified view inside the inorganic and organic SEI layer. (**C**) Tangential stress inside the particle and SEI layer, with (**D**) magnified view inside the inorganic and organic SEI layer.

Figure 4B depicts the magnified view of the compressive radial stress of the bilayer SEI, showing that the compressive stress is decreased in a linear manner. The gradient of the stress reduction is decreased at the interface of SEI$_{in}$ and SEI$_{or}$.

Figure 4C illustrates the tangential stress inside Model 2. Compared to the particle, significantly large tensile tangential stress occurred in the bilayer SEI. The maximum tensile tangential stress occurs in SEI$_{in}$ and decreases along the SEI thickness. Inside the bilayer SEI, the tangential stress shows discontinuities twice at the P/SEI$_{in}$ and SEI$_{in}$/SEI$_{or}$ interfaces. However, the tangential stress in the SEI$_{or}$ is smaller than that in SEI$_{in}$.

4.3. Effect of h_{SEI}

In this section, we discuss how the variation in h_{SEI} affects the stress distribution in Model 2. Figure 5A depicts the radial stress distribution inside Model 2 with different h_{SEI}. The results are plotted for 2000 cycles. As h_{SEI} increases, the tensile radial stress tends to become compressive stress because thick SEI$_{in}$ provides a larger mechanical constraint to the particle expansion than thin SEI_{in}. Figure 5B shows the magnified view of the stress inside the bilayer SEI. Figure 5C illustrates the tangential stress inside Model 2 with different h_{SEI}. Similar to the radial stress, an increase in h_{SEI} transforms the tangential stress in the core from tensile to compressive. However, the tensile tangential stress of the SEI_{in} is reduced, as shown in Figure 5D. These stresses cause the fracture and debonding of the bilayer SEI.

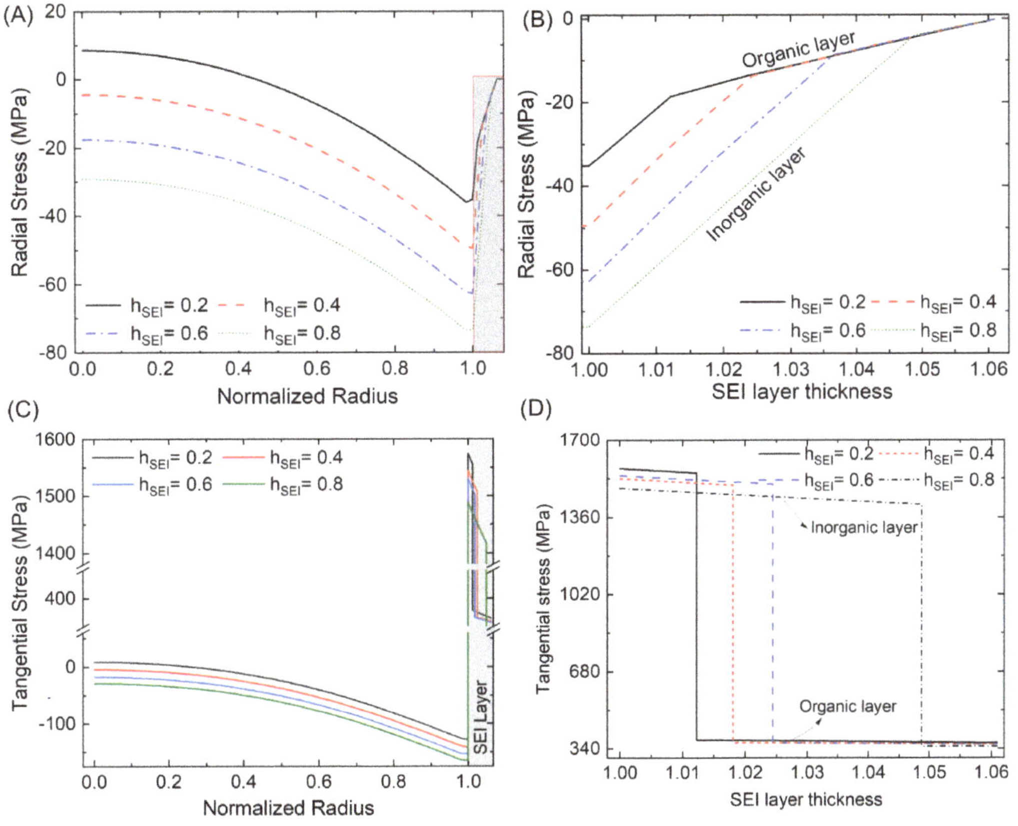

Figure 5. Effect of h_{SEI} on radial and tangential stress inside the particle and SEI layer during lithiation. The results are plotted for 2000 cycles. (**A**) Radial stress inside the particle and SEI layer, with (**B**) magnified view inside the inorganic and organic SEI layer. (**C**) Tangential stress inside the particle and SEI layer, with (**D**) magnified view of inside the inorganic and organic layers.

4.4. Fracture and Debonding Analysis

The tensile tangential stress that occurred in the bilayer SEI may cause a fracture of the bilayer SEI. In the core–double-shell structure, the elastic strain energy responsible for the cracking of the bilayer SEI can be calculated as [65]

$$G_{f,x} = \frac{2\left(\sigma_\theta^{SEI,x}\right)^2 th_{SEI,x}}{E_{SEI,x}} \tag{34}$$

where x = 'in' or 'or' represents the inorganic or organic portion of the bilayer SEI. The maximum tensile tangential stresses at the P/SEI_{in} and SEI_{in}/SEI_{or} interfaces are chosen for the calculation of elastic strain energy. Figure 6A,B show the evolution of tensile tangential stress inside SEI_{in} and SEI_{or}, respectively, over 2000 cycles. In the initial cycles, the stresses are higher and decrease as the cycling continues. In addition, as h_{SEI} decreases, the tangential stress increases. Figure 6C,D show the corresponding elastic strain energies responsible for SEI rupture. For small h_{SEI}, the fracture possibility of the inorganic layer is low in all cycles, although the stress is large, as shown in Figure 6A. This is because the increase in thickness has a stronger effect than the stress in Equation (34). On the other hand, the cracking possibility of the organic layer is high for small h_{SEI} after 800 cycles, as shown in Figure 6D. As h_{SEI} increases, the fracture probability of the SEI_{in} increases, while that of the SEI_{or} decreases. Therefore, for small h_{SEI}, a fracture in SEI is more likely to occur at the organic layer, while for large h_{SEI}, it occurs at the inorganic layer. The simulation results suggest that having a similar thickness of the inorganic and organic layers is preferred to avoid a fracture of the SEI layers.

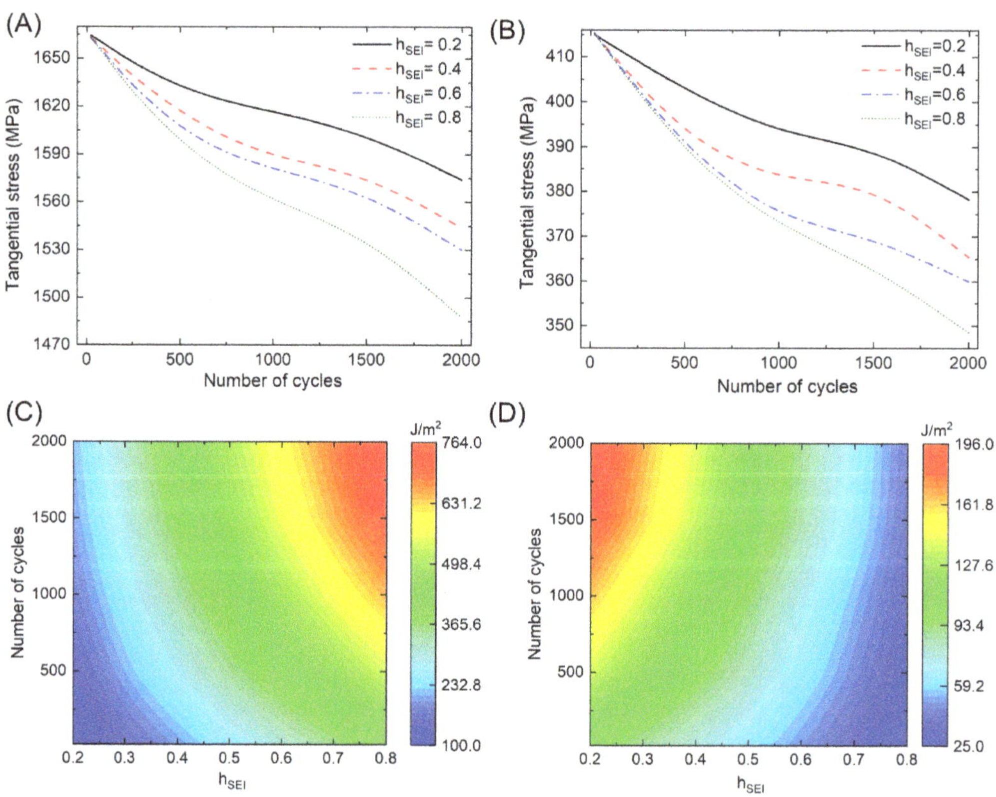

Figure 6. Evolution of tangential stress at the (**A**) P/SEI_{in} interface and (**B**) SEI_{in}/SEI_{or} interface, with different h_{SEI}. Contour plot of fracture energy release rate G_f as a function of h_{SEI} and cycle numbers for the (**C**) inorganic and (**D**) organic SEI layer.

In addition to the fracture, debonding of the bilayer SEI can occur when tensile radial stress develops at the interface. The tensile radial stress develops during delithiation as the shrinkage of the particle is prevented by the surrounding bilayer SEI. The debonding energy release rate for the inorganic SEI layer is given as: [61]

$$G_{d,in} = \frac{\pi\left(\sigma_r^{SEI,in}\right)^2 th_{SEI,in}}{2E_p E_{SEI,in}}(E_p + E_{SEI,in}) \tag{35}$$

Similarly, for the organic layer, Equation (35) becomes:

$$G_{d,or} = \frac{\pi \left(\sigma_r^{SEI,or}\right)^2 th_{SEI,or}}{2E_{SEI,in}E_{SEI,or}} (E_{SEI,in} + E_{SEI,or}) \tag{36}$$

Figure 7A shows the radial stress distribution along the particle and bilayer SEI at the 500th cycle with h_{SEI} = 0.4. Figure 7B shows the zoomed view near the bilayer SEI. During the charging process (cc_ch), the radial stresses at the P/SEI_{in} and SEI_{in}/SEI_{or} interfaces are compressive, as the swelling of the particle is confined by the bilayer SEI. After the constant current charging (cc_ch) is changed to the constant voltage charging (cv_ch), the compressive radial stress at the interfaces further increases. However, in subsequent discharging (cc_dch), the radial stress at the interfaces transforms from a compressive to a tensile state, because the particle shrinks upon delithiation. This tensile radial stress inside the bilayer SEI increases over cycles as shown in Figure 7C. Figure 7D depicts the debonding energy release rate for whole cycles. Over cycles, the debonding probability of both SEI_{in} and SEI_{or} increases.

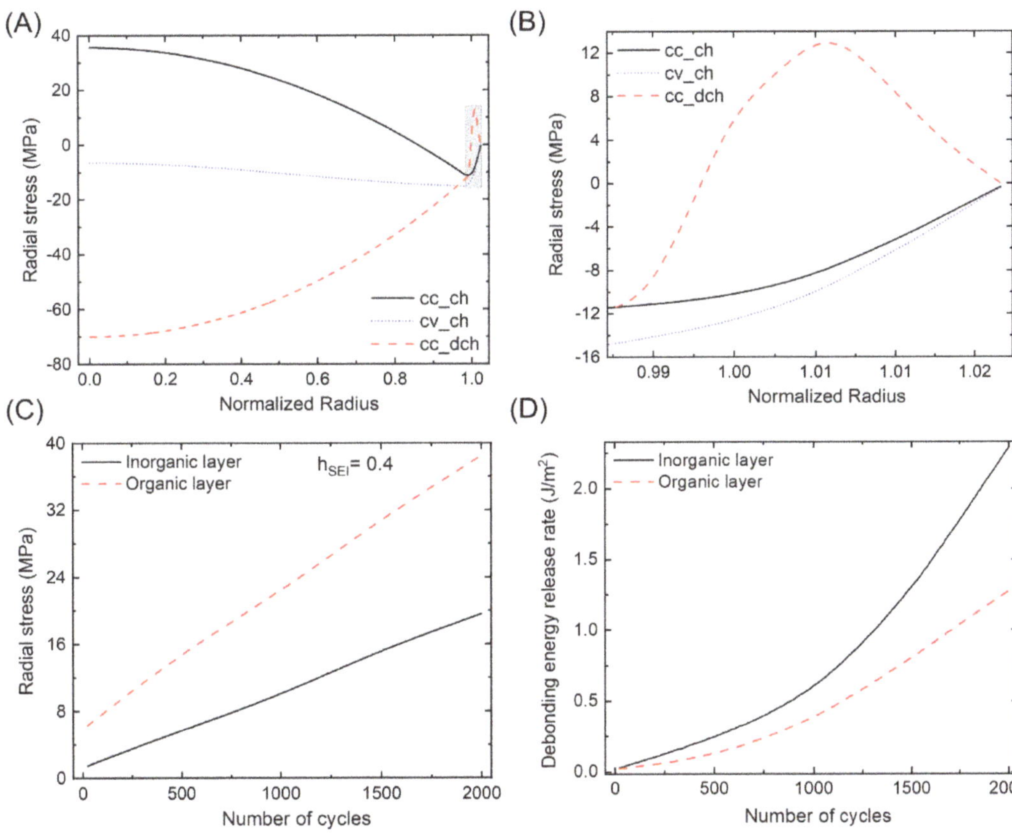

Figure 7. (**A**) Radial stress profile along the radius of particle at the end of constant current charge (cc_ch), constant voltage charge (cv_ch), and discharge (cc_dch). (**B**) Magnified view of the particle/SEI interface and SEI layers. The magnified area is shown in (**A**). (**C**) Evolution of radial stress in the inorganic and organic SEI layer interface (h_{SEI} = 0.4). (**D**) Evolution of debonding energy release rate in the SEI layers (h_{SEI} = 0.4).

Figure 8A,B show the contour plot of radial stress for the whole range of cycles and h_{SEI} at the P/SEI_{in} and SEI_{in}/SEI_{or} interfaces, respectively. The maximum stress occurred at later cycles and small h_{SEI}. As the h_{SEI} increases, the stress decreases. Moreover, the radial stress at the P/SEI_{in} interface is compressive in low cycles and at large h_{SEI}. As the cycling proceeds, the radial stress transforms from the compressive to the tensile state. The stress of the SEI_{in}/SEI_{or} interface is greater than that of the P/SEI_{in} interface.

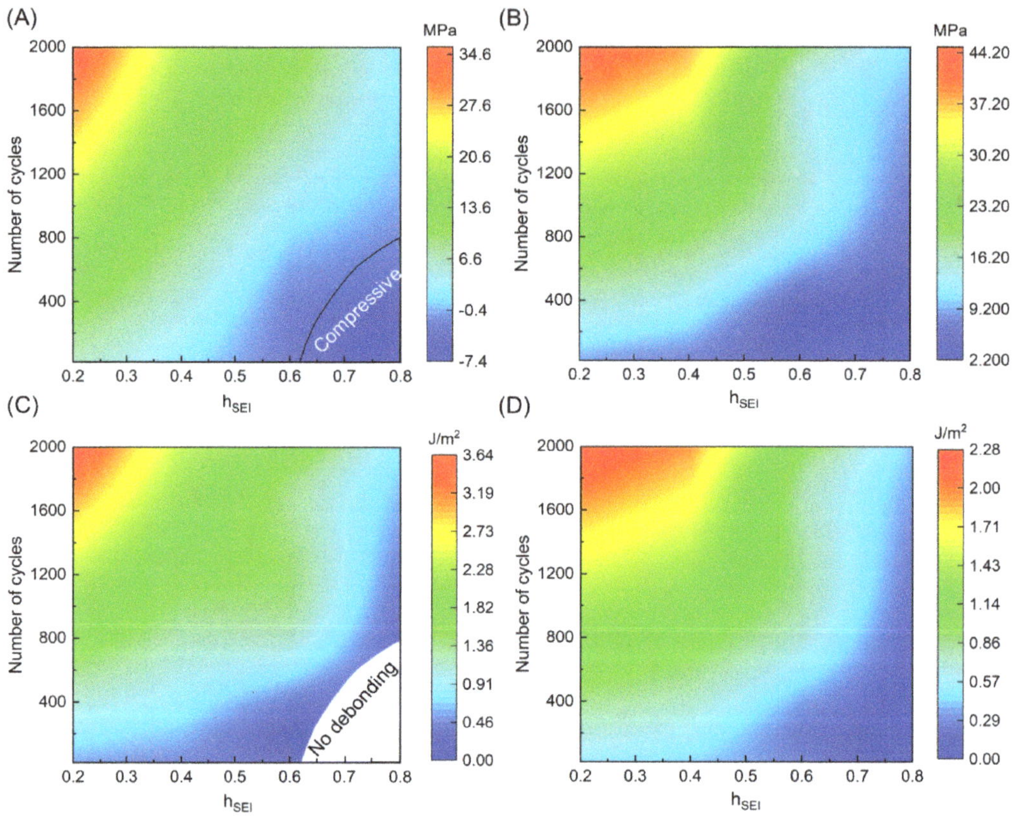

Figure 8. Contour plots of radial stress and debonding energy release rate G_d as a function of cycle number and h_{SEI}. Radial stress inside the (**A**) inorganic and (**B**) organic SEI layers. Debonding energy release rate G_d inside the (**C**) inorganic and (**D**) organic SEI layers. In (**C**), the white area indicates no debonding onset, due to the compressive stresses.

Figure 8C,D show the debonding strain energy of the P/SEI_{in} and SEI_{in}/SEI_{or} interface, respectively. The contour map indicates that debonding is more likely to occur as the cycle increases and as h_{SEI} decreases. The white area in Figure 8C depicts the no-debonding region, where the stress is compressive. In our simulation, debonding of the P/SEI_{in} interface does not occur up to 800 cycles for h_{SEI} = 0.8.

4.5. Effect of Particle Size on Fracture and Debonding

A series of simulations are carried out to study the effect of particle size on the fracture and debonding of the bilayer SEI. The particle size is varied from 5 to 25 um. Figure 9 shows the fracture and debonding energy release rate of the inorganic and organic SEI layers. As the particle size increases, the fracture is more dominant, while debonding is more likely to occur with the decrease in particle size. Since the fracture energy release rate of the SEI_{in} is higher than that of the SEI_{or}, fracture highly occurs at the inner SEI layer (inorganic layer) of large particles. On the other hand, the debonding energy release rate of the SEI_{or} is greater than that of the SEI_{in}, and debonding highly occurs at the SEI_{in}/SEI_{or} interface of small particles. Our simulation results suggest that tuning the particle size to approximately 13 μm is a better choice to minimize both SEI fracture and debonding.

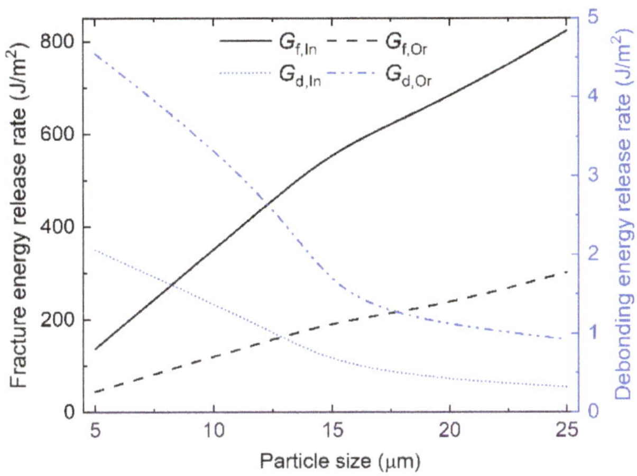

Figure 9. Fracture and debonding energy release rate of the inorganic and organic SEI layers as a function of particle size.

5. Conclusions

In this paper, we developed a 1D electrochemical model fully coupled with a core–double-shell particle/SEI model to investigate the mechanical stability of the heterogeneous bilayer SEI over multiple cycles. The SEI layer is considered a double-layer shell consisting of the inorganic layer as the inner shell and the organic layer as the outer shell. Our simulation results show that the increase in the mechanical constraint due to the growth of the bilayer SEI transforms the tensile stress inside the particle into compressive stress. Tensile tangential stress occurs at the particle/SEI interfaces, which leads to the initiation of a fracture inside the inorganic SEI layer, and the total fracture of both inorganic and organic SEI layers. As the thickness ratio of the inorganic layer increases, the compressive radial stress at the interface increases, while tangential stress decreases. At the end of discharge, the compressive radial stress at the interface converts to tensile stress, which leads to debonding of the interfaces.

As the thickness ratio of the inorganic layer increases, the fracture probability of the inorganic layer increases, while that of the organic layer decreases. On the other hand, the debonding probability of both inorganic and organic layers increases as the thickness ratio of the inorganic layer decreased. In addition, for the effect of particle size, the simulation results suggest that, in a multiparticle electrode, fracture of the SEI layers is more likely to occur for large particles, while the debonding of SEI layers is more likely to occur for small particles. Therefore, tailoring the thickness ratio of the inorganic layer and particle size is important to reduce the fracture and debonding of the heterogeneous bilayer SEI.

Table 1. Parameters for the Cell level.

Parameter	Unit	Negative	Ref.	Positive	Ref.	Separator
Thickness of Electrode	μm	90		52		70
Radius of Particle	μm	(5–25)				8
Volume fraction of active material		0.471	[57]	0.297	[57]	
Electrolyte phase volume fraction		0.357	[66]	0.44		1
Conductivity of active material	S/m	100		3.8		
Active material diffusion coefficient	m^2/s	3.9×10^{-14}	[67]	1×10^{-13}		
Initial electrolyte concentration	mol/m^3	1000		1000		1000
Electrolyte diffusivity	m^2/s	7.5×10^{-11}	[66]	7.5×10^{-11}		7.5×10^{-11}
Charge transfer coefficient		0.5		0.5		
Reaction rate constant	$m^{2.5}/(mol^{0.5}s)$	2×10^{-11}	[66]	2×10^{-11}		
Faraday constant	C/mol	96,485				
Youngs modulus of active material	GPa	12	[68]	10	[68]	
Elastic modulus of inorganic SEI layer	GPa	40				
Elastic modulus of organic SEI layer	GPa	10				
Poisson's ratio		0.3	[68]	0.3		
Partial molar volume	m^3/mol	3.64×10^{-6}	[69]			

Author Contributions: Conceptualization, Y.A.; Methodology, Y.A. and S.L.; Software, Y.A., N.I. and I.S.; Formal analysis, Y.A.; Investigation, Y.A.; Data curation, Y.A.; Writing—original draft, Y.A.; Writing—review & editing, S.L.; Visualization, Y.A.; Supervision, S.L.; Project administration, S.L.; Funding acquisition, S.L. All authors have read and agreed to the published version of the manuscript.

Funding: This research was supported by the National Research Foundation of Korea grants, funded by the Ministry of Science and ICT (No. 2018R1A5A7023490 and No. 2022R1A2C1003003).

Data Availability Statement: Not applicable.

Conflicts of Interest: The authors declare no conflict of interest.

References

1. Wang, A.; Kadam, S.; Li, H.; Shi, S.; Qi, Y. Review on Modeling of the Anode Solid Electrolyte Interphase (SEI) for Lithium-Ion Batteries. *npj Comput. Mater.* **2018**, *4*, 15. [CrossRef]
2. Astaneh, M.; Andric, J.; Löfdahl, L.; Stopp, P. Multiphysics Simulation Optimization Framework for Lithium-Ion Battery Pack Design for Electric Vehicle Applications. *Energy* **2021**, *239*, 122092. [CrossRef]
3. Gauthier, N.; Courrèges, C.; Demeaux, J.; Tessier, C.; Martinez, H. Probing the In-Depth Distribution of Organic/Inorganic Molecular Species within the SEI of LTO/NMC and LTO/LMO Batteries: A Complementary ToF-SIMS and XPS Study. *Appl. Surf. Sci.* **2020**, *501*, 144266. [CrossRef]
4. Ekström, H.; Lindbergh, G. A Model for Predicting Capacity Fade Due to SEI Formation in a Commercial Graphite/$LiFePO_4$ Cell. *J. Electrochem. Soc.* **2015**, *162*, A1003–A1007. [CrossRef]
5. Tsai, W.-Y.; Thundat, T.; Nanda, J. Toward a Mechanically Stable Solid Electrolyte Interphase. *Matter* **2021**, *4*, 2119–2122. [CrossRef]
6. Deng, Q.; Hu, R.; Xu, C.; Chen, B.; Zhou, J. Modeling Fracture of Solid Electrolyte Interphase in Lithium-Ion Batteries during Cycling. *J. Solid State Electrochem.* **2019**, *23*, 2999–3008. [CrossRef]
7. Shi, Q.; Heng, S.; Qu, Q.; Gao, T.; Liu, W.; Hang, L.; Zheng, H. Constructing an Elastic Solid Electrolyte Interphase on Graphite: A Novel Strategy Suppressing Lithium Inventory Loss in Lithium-Ion Batteries. *J. Mater. Chem. A* **2017**, *5*, 10885–10894. [CrossRef]
8. Kindermann, F.M.; Keil, J.; Frank, A.; Jossen, A. A SEI Modeling Approach Distinguishing between Capacity and Power Fade. *J. Electrochem. Soc.* **2017**, *164*, E287–E294. [CrossRef]
9. Peled, E.; Golodnitsky, D.; Ardel, G. Advanced Model for Solid Electrolyte Interphase Electrodes in Liquid and Polymer Electrolytes. *J. Electrochem. Soc.* **1997**, *144*, L208. [CrossRef]
10. Fu, X.; Yu, D.; Zhou, J.; Li, S.; Gao, X.; Han, Y.; Qi, P.; Feng, X.; Wang, B. Inorganic and Organic Hybrid Solid Electrolytes for Lithium-Ion Batteries. *CrystEngComm* **2016**, *18*, 4236–4258. [CrossRef]

11. Spotte-Smith, E.W.C.; Kam, R.L.; Barter, D.; Xie, X.; Hou, T.; Dwaraknath, S.; Blau, S.M.; Persson, K.A. Toward a Mechanistic Model of Solid–Electrolyte Interphase Formation and Evolution in Lithium-Ion Batteries. *ACS Energy Lett.* **2022**, *7*, 1446–1453. [CrossRef]
12. Peled, E.; Menkin, S. Review—SEI: Past, Present and Future. *J. Electrochem. Soc.* **2017**, *164*, A1703–A1719. [CrossRef]
13. Lan, X.; Cui, J.; Xiong, X.; He, J.; Yu, H.; Hu, R. Multiscale Observations of Inhomogeneous Bilayer SEI Film on a Conversion-Alloying SnO2 Anode. *Small Methods* **2021**, *5*, 2101111. [CrossRef] [PubMed]
14. Ha, S.; Yoon, H.J.; Jung, J.I.; Kim, H.; Won, S.; Kwak, J.H.; Lim, H.-D.; Jin, H.-J.; Wie, J.J.; Yun, Y.S. 3D-Structured Organic-Inorganic Hybrid Solid-Electrolyte-Interface Layers for Lithium Metal Anode. *Energy Storage Mater.* **2021**, *37*, 567–575. [CrossRef]
15. Lee, C.H.; Dura, J.A.; LeBar, A.; DeCaluwe, S.C. Direct, Operando Observation of the Bilayer Solid Electrolyte Interphase Structure: Electrolyte Reduction on a Non-Intercalating Electrode. *J. Power Sources* **2019**, *412*, 725–735. [CrossRef]
16. von Aspern, N.; Leissing, M.; Wölke, C.; Diddens, D.; Kobayashi, T.; Börner, M.; Stubbmann-Kazakova, O.; Kozel, V.; Röschenthaler, G.-V.; Smiatek, J.; et al. Non-Flammable Fluorinated Phosphorus(III)-Based Electrolytes for Advanced Lithium-Ion Battery Performance. *ChemElectroChem* **2020**, *7*, 1499–1508. [CrossRef]
17. Li, D.; Cao, L.; Deng, T.; Liu, S.; Wang, C. Design of a Solid Electrolyte Interphase for Aqueous Zn Batteries. *Angew. Chem. Int. Ed.* **2021**, *60*, 13035–13041. [CrossRef]
18. Zhao, Y.; Li, G.; Gao, Y.; Wang, D.; Huang, Q.; Wang, D. Stable Li Metal Anode by a Hybrid Lithium Polysulfidophosphate/Polymer Cross-Linking Film. *ACS Energy Lett.* **2019**, *4*, 1271–1278. [CrossRef]
19. Fitzhugh, W.; Chen, X.; Wang, Y.; Ye, L.; Li, X. Solid–Electrolyte-Interphase Design in Constrained Ensemble for Solid-State Batteries. *Energy Environ. Sci.* **2021**, *14*, 4574–4583. [CrossRef]
20. Tu, Q.; Barroso-Luque, L.; Shi, T.; Ceder, G. Electrodeposition and Mechanical Stability at Lithium-Solid Electrolyte Interface during Plating in Solid-State Batteries. *Cell Rep. Phys. Sci.* **2020**, *1*, 100106. [CrossRef]
21. Qin, Z.; Meng, X.; Xie, Y.; Qian, D.; Deng, H.; Mao, D.; Wan, L.; Huang, Y. Fast Li-Ion Transport Pathways via 3D Continuous Networks in Homogeneous Garnet-Type Electrolyte for Solid-State Lithium Batteries. *Energy Storage Mater.* **2021**, *43*, 190–201. [CrossRef]
22. Qin, Z.; Xie, Y.; Meng, X.; Qian, D.; Mao, D.; Ma, X.; Shan, C.; Chen, J.; Wan, L.; Huang, Y. Recycling Garnet-Type Electrolyte toward Superior Cycling Performance for Solid-State Lithium Batteries. *Energy Storage Mater.* **2022**, *49*, 360–369. [CrossRef]
23. Qin, Z.; Xie, Y.; Meng, X.; Qian, D.; Mao, D.; Zheng, Z.; Wan, L.; Huang, Y. Grain Boundary Engineering in Ta-Doped Garnet-Type Electrolyte for Lithium Dendrite Suppression. *ACS Appl. Mater. Interfaces* **2022**, *14*, 40959–40966. [CrossRef]
24. Qin, Z.; Xie, Y.; Meng, X.; Qian, D.; Shan, C.; Mao, D.; He, G.; Zheng, Z.; Wan, L.; Huang, Y. Interface Engineering for Garnet-Type Electrolyte Enables Low Interfacial Resistance in Solid-State Lithium Batteries. *Chem. Eng. J.* **2022**, *447*, 137538. [CrossRef]
25. Qin, Z.; Xie, Y.; Meng, X.; Qian, D.; Li, J.; Li, C.; Cao, J.; Wan, L.; Huang, Y. Oriented Attachment Strategy Toward Enhancing Ionic Conductivity in Garnet-Type Electrolytes for Solid-State Lithium Batteries. *ACS Appl. Mater. Interfaces* **2021**, *13*, 34385–34396. [CrossRef]
26. Qin, Z.; Xie, Y.; Meng, X.; Shan, C.; He, G.; Qian, D.; Mao, D.; Wan, L.; Huang, Y. High Cycling Stability Enabled by Li Vacancy Regulation in Ta-Doped Garnet-Type Solid-State Electrolyte. *J. Eur. Ceram. Soc.* **2022**, *43*, 2023–2032. [CrossRef]
27. Keefe, A.S.; Weber, R.; Hill, I.G.; Dahn, J.R. Studies of the SEI Layers in $Li(Ni_{0.5}Mn_{0.3}Co_{0.2})O_2$/Artificial Graphite Cells after Formation and after Cycling. *J. Electrochem. Soc.* **2020**, *167*, 120507. [CrossRef]
28. Shen, Z.; Zhang, W.; Li, S.; Mao, S.; Wang, X.; Chen, F.; Lu, Y. Tuning the Interfacial Electronic Conductivity by Artificial Electron Tunneling Barriers for Practical Lithium Metal Batteries. *Nano Lett.* **2020**, *20*, 6606–6613. [CrossRef]
29. Ye, S.; Wang, L.; Liu, F.; Shi, P.; Wang, H.; Wu, X.; Yu, Y. G-C_3N_4 Derivative Artificial Organic/Inorganic Composite Solid Electrolyte Interphase Layer for Stable Lithium Metal Anode. *Adv. Energy Mater.* **2020**, *10*, 2002647. [CrossRef]
30. Guo, L.; Huang, F.; Cai, M.; Zhang, J.; Ma, G.; Xu, S. Organic–Inorganic Hybrid SEI Induced by a New Lithium Salt for High-Performance Metallic Lithium Anodes. *ACS Appl. Mater. Interfaces* **2021**, *13*, 32886–32893. [CrossRef]
31. Ng, B.; Faegh, E.; Lateef, S.; Karakalos, S.G.; Mustain, W.E. Structure and Chemistry of the Solid Electrolyte Interphase (SEI) on a High Capacity Conversion-Based Anode: NiO. *J. Mater. Chem. A* **2021**, *9*, 523–537. [CrossRef]
32. Ali, Y.; Lee, S. An Integrated Experimental and Modeling Study of the Effect of Solid Electrolyte Interphase Formation and Cu Dissolution on $CuCo_2O_4$-Based Li-Ion Batteries. *Int. J. Energy Res.* **2022**, *46*, 3017–3033. [CrossRef]
33. Wang, M.; Huai, L.; Hu, G.; Yang, S.; Ren, F.; Wang, S.; Zhang, Z.; Chen, Z.; Peng, Z.; Shen, C.; et al. Effect of LiFSI Concentrations To Form Thickness- and Modulus-Controlled SEI Layers on Lithium Metal Anodes. *J. Phys. Chem. C* **2018**, *122*, 9825–9834. [CrossRef]
34. Guan, P.; Liu, L.; Lin, X. Simulation and Experiment on Solid Electrolyte Interphase (SEI) Morphology Evolution and Lithium-Ion Diffusion. *J. Electrochem. Soc.* **2015**, *162*, A1798. [CrossRef]
35. Zheng, J.; Zheng, H.; Wang, R.; Ben, L.; Lu, W.; Chen, L.; Chen, L.; Li, H. 3D Visualization of Inhomogeneous Multi-Layered Structure and Young's Modulus of the Solid Electrolyte Interphase (SEI) on Silicon Anodes for Lithium Ion Batteries. *Phys. Chem. Chem. Phys.* **2014**, *16*, 13229–13238. [CrossRef] [PubMed]
36. Moeremans, B.; Cheng, H.-W.; Merola, C.; Hu, Q.; Oezaslan, M.; Safari, M.; Van Bael, M.K.; Hardy, A.; Valtiner, M.; Renner, F.U. In Situ Mechanical Analysis of the Nanoscopic Solid Electrolyte Interphase on Anodes of Li-Ion Batteries. *Adv. Sci.* **2019**, *6*, 1900190. [CrossRef]

37. Zhang, J.; Wang, R.; Yang, X.; Lu, W.; Wu, X.; Wang, X.; Li, H.; Chen, L. Direct Observation of Inhomogeneous Solid Electrolyte Interphase on MnO Anode with Atomic Force Microscopy and Spectroscopy. Available online: https://pubs.acs.org/doi/abs/10.1021/nl300570d (accessed on 10 September 2022).
38. Shin, H.; Park, J.; Han, S.; Sastry, A.M.; Lu, W. Component-/Structure-Dependent Elasticity of Solid Electrolyte Interphase Layer in Li-Ion Batteries: Experimental and Computational Studies. *J. Power Sources* **2015**, *277*, 169–179. [CrossRef]
39. Liu, Y.; Lin, D.; Li, Y.; Chen, G.; Pei, A.; Nix, O.; Li, Y.; Cui, Y. Solubility-Mediated Sustained Release Enabling Nitrate Additive in Carbonate Electrolytes for Stable Lithium Metal Anode. *Nat. Commun.* **2018**, *9*, 3656. [CrossRef]
40. Yu, J.; Zhao, L.; Huang, Y.; Hu, Y.; Chen, L.; He, Y.-B. Progress and Perspective of Constructing Solid Electrolyte Interphase on Stable Lithium Metal Anode. *Front. Mater.* **2020**, *7*, 71. [CrossRef]
41. Xu, R.; Zhang, X.-Q.; Cheng, X.-B.; Peng, H.-J.; Zhao, C.-Z.; Yan, C.; Huang, J.-Q. Artificial Soft–Rigid Protective Layer for Dendrite-Free Lithium Metal Anode. *Adv. Funct. Mater.* **2018**, *28*, 1705838. [CrossRef]
42. Li, Z.; Ding, X.; Feng, W.; Han, B.-H. Aligned Artificial Solid Electrolyte Interphase Layers as Versatile Interfacial Stabilizers on Lithium Metal Anodes. *J. Mater. Chem. A* **2022**, *10*, 10474–10483. [CrossRef]
43. Gao, S.; Sun, F.; Liu, N.; Yang, H.; Cao, P.-F. Ionic Conductive Polymers as Artificial Solid Electrolyte Interphase Films in Li Metal Batteries—A Review. *Mater. Today* **2020**, *40*, 140–159. [CrossRef]
44. Liu, Y.; Wu, J.; Yang, Y. A Double-Layer Artificial SEI Film Fabricated by Controlled Electrochemical Reduction of LiODFB-FEC Based Electrolyte for Dendrite-Free Lithium Meal Anode. *J. Electrochem. Soc.* **2020**, *167*, 160535. [CrossRef]
45. Zhao, Y.; Amirmaleki, M.; Sun, Q.; Zhao, C.; Codirenzi, A.; Goncharova, L.V.; Wang, C.; Adair, K.; Li, X.; Yang, X.; et al. Natural SEI-Inspired Dual-Protective Layers via Atomic/Molecular Layer Deposition for Long-Life Metallic Lithium Anode. *Matter* **2019**, *1*, 1215–1231. [CrossRef]
46. Efaw, C.M.; Lu, B.; Lin, Y.; Pawar, G.M.; Chinnam, P.R.; Hurley, M.F.; Dufek, E.J.; Meng, Y.S.; Li, B. A Closed-Host Bi-Layer Dense/Porous Solid Electrolyte Interphase for Enhanced Lithium-Metal Anode Stability. *Mater. Today* **2021**, *49*, 48–58. [CrossRef]
47. Kolzenberg, L.v.; Latz, A.; Horstmann, B. Chemo-Mechanical Model of SEI Growth on Silicon Electrode Particles. *Batter. Supercaps* **2022**, *5*, e202100216. [CrossRef]
48. McBrayer, J.D.; Apblett, C.A.; Harrison, K.L.; Fenton, K.R.; Minteer, S.D. Mechanical Studies of the Solid Electrolyte Interphase on Anodes in Lithium and Lithium Ion Batteries. *Nanotechnology* **2021**, *32*, 502005. [CrossRef]
49. Chen, C.; Zhou, T.; Danilov, D.L.; Gao, L.; Benning, S.; Schön, N.; Tardif, S.; Simons, H.; Hausen, F.; Schülli, T.U.; et al. Impact of Dual-Layer Solid-Electrolyte Interphase Inhomogeneities on Early-Stage Defect Formation in Si Electrodes. *Nat. Commun.* **2020**, *11*, 3283. [CrossRef]
50. Guo, K.; Kumar, R.; Xiao, X.; Sheldon, B.W.; Gao, H. Failure Progression in the Solid Electrolyte Interphase (SEI) on Silicon Electrodes. *Nano Energy* **2020**, *68*, 104257. [CrossRef]
51. He, Y.; Hu, H.; Zhang, K.; Li, S.; Chen, J. Mechanical Insights into the Stability of Heterogeneous Solid Electrolyte Interphase on an Electrode Particle. *J. Mater. Sci.* **2017**, *52*, 2836–2848. [CrossRef]
52. Liu, Y.; Guo, K.; Wang, C.; Gao, H. Wrinkling and Ratcheting of a Thin Film on Cyclically Deforming Plastic Substrate: Mechanical Instability of the Solid-Electrolyte Interphase in Li–Ion Batteries. *J. Mech. Phys. Solids* **2019**, *123*, 103–118. [CrossRef]
53. Jin, N.; Danilov, D.L.; Van den Hof, P.M.J.; Donkers, M.C.F. Parameter Estimation of an Electrochemistry-Based Lithium-Ion Battery Model Using a Two-Step Procedure and a Parameter Sensitivity Analysis. *Int. J. Energy Res.* **2018**, *42*, 2417–2430. [CrossRef]
54. Ramadass, P.; Haran, B.; Gomadam, P.M.; White, R.; Popov, B.N. Development of First Principles Capacity Fade Model for Li-Ion Cells. *J. Electrochem. Soc.* **2004**, *151*, A196–A203. [CrossRef]
55. Yan, J.; Xia, B.J.; Su, Y.C.; Zhou, X.Z.; Zhang, J.; Zhang, X.G. Phenomenologically Modeling the Formation and Evolution of the Solid Electrolyte Interface on the Graphite Electrode for Lithium-Ion Batteries. *Electrochim. Acta* **2008**, *53*, 7069–7078. [CrossRef]
56. Lawder, M.T.; Northrop, P.W.C.; Subramanian, V.R. Model-Based SEI Layer Growth and Capacity Fade Analysis for EV and PHEV Batteries and Drive Cycles. *J. Electrochem. Soc.* **2014**, *161*, A2099–A2108. [CrossRef]
57. Lin, X.; Park, J.; Liu, L.; Lee, Y.; Lu, W.; Sastry, A.M. A Comprehensive Capacity Fade Model and Analysis for Li-Ion Batteries. *J. Electrochem. Soc.* **2013**, *160*, A1701–A1710. [CrossRef]
58. Kotak, N.; Barai, P.; Verma, A.; Mistry, A.; Mukherjee, P.P. Electrochemistry-Mechanics Coupling in Intercalation Electrodes. *J. Electrochem. Soc.* **2018**, *165*, A1064–A1083. [CrossRef]
59. Iqbal, N.; Lee, S. Mechanical Failure Analysis of Graphite Anode Particles with PVDF Binders in Li-Ion Batteries. *J. Electrochem. Soc.* **2018**, *165*, A1961–A1970. [CrossRef]
60. Laresgoiti, I.; Käbitz, S.; Ecker, M.; Sauer, D.U. Modeling Mechanical Degradation in Lithium Ion Batteries during Cycling: Solid Electrolyte Interphase Fracture. *J. Power Sources* **2015**, *300*, 112–122. [CrossRef]
61. Zhao, K.; Pharr, M.; Hartle, L.; Vlassak, J.J.; Suo, Z. Fracture and Debonding in Lithium-Ion Batteries with Electrodes of Hollow Core-Shell Nanostructures. *J. Power Sources* **2012**, *218*, 6–14. [CrossRef]
62. Ali, Y.; Iqbal, N.; Lee, S. Role of SEI Layer Growth in Fracture Probability in Lithium-Ion Battery Electrodes. *Int. J. Energy Res.* **2021**, *45*, 5293–5308. [CrossRef]
63. Deshpande, R.D.; Bernardi, D.M. Modeling Solid-Electrolyte Interphase (SEI) Fracture: Coupled Mechanical/Chemical Degradation of the Lithium Ion Battery. *J. Electrochem. Soc.* **2017**, *164*, A461–A474. [CrossRef]

64. Cheng, Y.T.; Verbrugge, M.W. Evolution of Stress within a Spherical Insertion Electrode Particle under Potentiostatic and Galvanostatic Operation. *J. Power Sources* **2009**, *190*, 453–460. [CrossRef]
65. Wu, B.; Lu, W. Mechanical Modeling of Particles with Active Core–Shell Structures for Lithium-Ion Battery Electrodes. *J. Phys. Chem. C* **2017**, *121*, 19022–19030. [CrossRef]
66. Wu, W.; Xiao, X.; Wang, M.; Huang, X. A Microstructural Resolved Model for the Stress Analysis of Lithium-Ion Batteries. *J. Electrochem. Soc.* **2014**, *161*, A803–A813. [CrossRef]
67. Iqbal, N.; Ali, Y.; Lee, S. Debonding Mechanisms at the Particle-Binder Interface in the Li-Ion Battery Electrode. *J. Electrochem. Soc.* **2020**, *167*, 060515. [CrossRef]
68. Xiao, X.; Wu, W.; Huang, X. A Multi-Scale Approach for the Stress Analysis of Polymeric Separators in a Lithium-Ion Battery. *J. Power Sources* **2010**, *195*, 7649–7660. [CrossRef]
69. Lee, S.; Yang, J.; Lu, W. Debonding at the Interface between Active Particles and PVDF Binder in Li-Ion Batteries. *Extrem. Mech. Lett.* **2016**, *6*, 37–44. [CrossRef]

mathematics

MDPI

Article

DNN-MLVEM: A Data-Driven Macromodel for RC Shear Walls Based on Deep Neural Networks

German Solorzano [1,*] and Vagelis Plevris [2]

1 Department of Civil Engineering and Energy Technology, OsloMet–Oslo Metropolitan University, 0166 Oslo, Norway
2 Department of Civil and Architectural Engineering, Qatar University, Doha P.O. Box 2713, Qatar; vplevris@qu.edu.qa
* Correspondence: germanso@oslomet.no

Abstract: This study proposes the DNN-MVLEM, a novel macromodel for the non-linear analysis of RC shear walls based on deep neural networks (DNN); while most RC shear wall macromodeling techniques follow a deterministic approach to find the right configuration and properties of the system, in this study, an alternative data-driven strategy is proposed instead. The proposed DNN-MVLEM is composed of four vertical beam-column elements and one horizontal shear spring. The beam-column elements implement the fiber section formulation with standard non-linear uniaxial material models for concrete and steel, while the horizontal shear spring uses a multi-linear force–displacement relationship. Additionally, three calibration factors are introduced to improve the performance of the macromodel. The data-driven component of the proposed strategy consists of a large DNN that is trained to predict the force–displacement curve of the shear spring and the three calibration factors. The training data is created using a parametric microscopic FEM model based on the multi-layer shell element formulation and a genetic algorithm (GA) that optimizes the response of the macromodel to match the behavior of the microscopic FEM model. The DNN-MVLEM is tested in two types of examples, first as a stand-alone model and then as part of a two-bay multi-story frame structure. The results show that the DNN-MVLEM is capable of reproducing the results obtained with the microscopic FEM model up to 100 times faster and with an estimated error lower than 5%.

Keywords: shear wall; macromodel; deep neural network; genetic algorithm; OpenSees

MSC: 68T07; 74S05; 74-10

Citation: Solorzano, G.; Plevris, V. DNN-MLVEM: A Data-Driven Macromodel for RC Shear Walls Based on Deep Neural Networks. *Mathematics* **2023**, *11*, 2347. https://doi.org/10.3390/math11102347

Academic Editors: Zhuojia Fu, Yiqian He and Hui Zheng

Received: 8 April 2023
Revised: 13 May 2023
Accepted: 15 May 2023
Published: 18 May 2023

1. Introduction

The modeling of reinforced concrete (RC) shear walls is an essential area of research in earthquake engineering [1]. Engineers have sought to create numerical models of RC shear walls that can be reliably used for the analysis and design of structures under earthquake hazards [2,3]. Over the years, the research and development of modeling strategies have resulted in two main distinguished categories: macroscopic and microscopic models [4].

Microscopic modeling (micromodels) strategies attempt to create a model with an elevated level of detail and refinement to reproduce the complex interaction between the concrete and the reinforcement steel at a microscopic level [5,6]. The most popular micromodeling technique is the implementation of finite element method (FEM) models utilizing solid, shell, and beam/truss elements combined with state-of-the-art material models for concrete and reinforcement steel [7–9]. One such example is the 3D FEM model developed by Fei-Yu et al. [10], where each reinforcement bar is modeled independently, including the corresponding contact interaction between steel and concrete. Micromodels stand out for their good performance in reproducing the realistic behavior of RC shear walls [11]. Their effectiveness has been extensively demonstrated in various studies [12–15]. However, their main disadvantage is their high computational cost, significantly reducing their practical applicability for the analysis of large-scale real-world structures. For example, the model in Figure 1 contains more than 100,000 degrees of freedom and takes 22 h to run 100 steps of a static non-linear pushover analysis on four cores with a computer equipped with an Intel Core i7-6700HQ CPU @2.60 GHz.

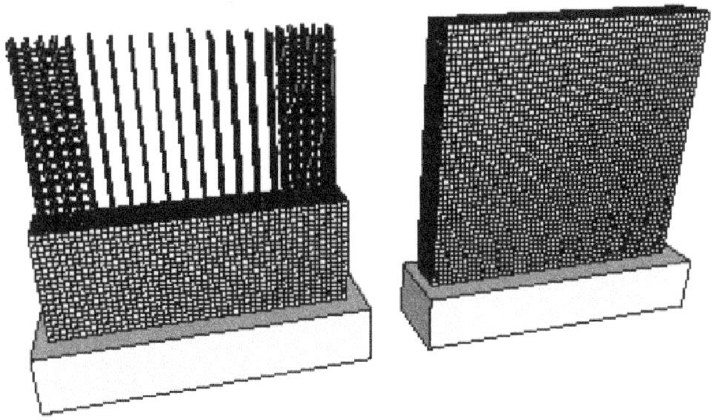

Figure 1. RC shear wall microscopic 3D FEM model using solid elements.

Macroscopic modeling (macromodels) techniques, on the other hand, attempt to reproduce the overall behavior of RC shear walls at the macro scale with a much simpler model [16]; thus, their computational cost is significantly lower. These models typically combine springs and axial bars connected through rigid elements to mimic the wall geometry. They implement non-linear material laws for both the concrete and the reinforcement steel. However, the shear and flexural response in these systems is usually uncoupled, meaning that the element can experience shear and flexure deformations independently, which is normally not physically possible. Hence, their efficacy to model certain effects is limited [17]. Nonetheless, the research and development of macromodeling techniques is a popular and active area of research as the analysis and design paradigm is shifting towards performance-based techniques [18], where the assessment of the non-linear behavior of the structure plays a central role. Therefore, creating reliable macromodels that contribute to reducing the computational cost of the non-linear analysis of structures is of particularly high interest.

Macroscopic modeling techniques have been around for a few decades; among the first proposed macromodels is the three-vertical-line-element model by Kabeyasawa et al. [19]. It consists of two axial springs, one rotational spring for flexure, and one horizontal spring for shear deformation; see Figure 2a. Vulcano et al. [20,21] improved the model by removing the rotational spring and using several vertical axial fibers in parallel instead, creating the multiple-vertical-lines-element-model (MVLEM); see Figure 2b. Since then, the MVLEM has become widely popular and has been thoroughly tested and verified in numerous studies [22–26]. The MVLEM has also been included in various popular FEM packages, such as in the OpenSees framework [27]. Additionally, it has served as the base and motivation for developing similar models with enhanced properties, such as the SFI-MVLEM [28,29] depicted in Figure 2c, the V-MVLEM [30], and others [31,32].

Despite the efforts to find the perfect macromodel, some of their disadvantages are too difficult to overcome due to the underlying assumptions and simplifications implicit in their formulations. For instance, they may be unable to fully capture the RC shear wall's complex behavior to its full extent. A comparative study by Kolozvari et al. [17] found that some macromodels were not reliable in predicting the local strains at the base (where the higher strains are localized). In such cases, the tensile strains were overestimated as much as a factor of 2.0, while the compressive strains were underestimated up to 2.0–3.0 times. Overall, RC shear walls' behavior is a complex phenomenon challenging to model using simplified methods based on deterministic strategies. Deterministic methods usually cannot capture complex phenomena to their full extent, becoming subject to many limitations that restrict their applicability. In contrast, data-driven strategies that do not follow the deterministic road have proven to be a better alternative for complex problems [33], provided that sufficient and high-quality data are used in their formulation.

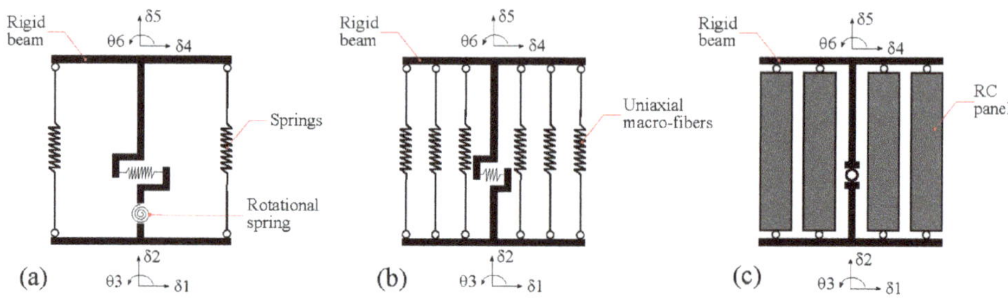

Figure 2. Popular macromodels for RC shear wall analysis. (**a**) Model proposed by Kabeyasawa et al. [19]. (**b**) The MVLEM, proposed by Vulcano et al. [20]. (**c**) The SFI-MVLEM proposed by Kolozvari et al. [28].

In this study, a novel data-driven macromodel for modeling RC shear walls is developed based on deep learning techniques. The macromodel, referred to as DNN-MVLEM, is composed of four vertical beam-column elements that implement the fiber section formulation and a non-linear horizontal shear spring. All the elements are connected together with rigid elements to mimic the RC shear wall geometry. The material models for the vertical elements are based on well-established non-linear models commonly used for concrete and reinforcement steel. For the shear spring, a multi-linear material model is implemented. The final piece of the macromodel is three factors that are introduced to calibrate it and improve its accuracy. The data-driven component of the macromodel consists of a deep neural network (DNN) trained in a two-phase procedure. In the first phase, the DNN is trained to predict the force–displacement curve to define the multi-linear curve for the shear spring material model. To that end, a parametric microscopic FEM model generates the corresponding data. In the second phase, several macromodels are built and calibrated to match the results of the microscopic FEM model using a genetic algorithm (GA). The results are used to re-train the DNN to add the calibration factors to its predictions. Hence, the final DNN is able to predict all the required information to construct the macromodel.

The DNN-MVLEM is a novel approach inspired by the effectiveness of data-driven strategies to substitute intricate hard-computing models for solving complex problems with reliable approximations that require significantly less computational effort. Notably, in structural engineering [34], these strategies are quickly gaining momentum and acceptance for both research and industrial applications [35]. Several recent examples can be found, such as the following: using artificial neural networks (ANN) to predict the lateral capacity of RC shear walls [36]; predicting the non-linear response of 3D buildings under seismic actions with ANNs [37]; using ANNs as non-linear constitutive materials [38]; autonomous design of structures using optimization algorithms [39–42]; speeding up the solution procedure of FEM equations [43,44]; surrogate modeling of large FEM structures [45–47]; using the ensemble wavelet-neural networks [48] and physical informed neural networks (PINN) [49] to estimate the properties of complex materials such as concrete composites; and many other exciting applications [50,51].

The remainder of the paper is organized as follows. Section 2 presents the basic structure and components of the DNN-MVLEM. Section 4 explains the data-driven component of the model, which includes a description of the microscopic FEM model used for the data generation. Section 5 presents various numerical examples of the DNN-MVLEM compared to the microscopic FEM model. Finally, the results are discussed in Section 6, and the conclusions are presented in Section 7.

2. The DNN-MVLEM

2.1. Base Elements

The DNN-MLVEM has been implemented using the FEM framework provided by the OpenSeesPy library [52,53]. It is composed of four vertical columns—two columns K_{eb1} and K_{eb2} for the boundary elements, and another two K_{web1} and K_{web2} for the web part of the wall. Each of the columns is positioned at the center of the tributary area of the portion of the wall that is intended to represent. Additionally, to simulate the shear resistance, there is a horizontal axial spring S_h in the middle of the model positioned at a distance of 0.4 h from the bottom. The whole system is held together by rigid beam elements. The resulting configuration of the macromodel is depicted in Figure 3.

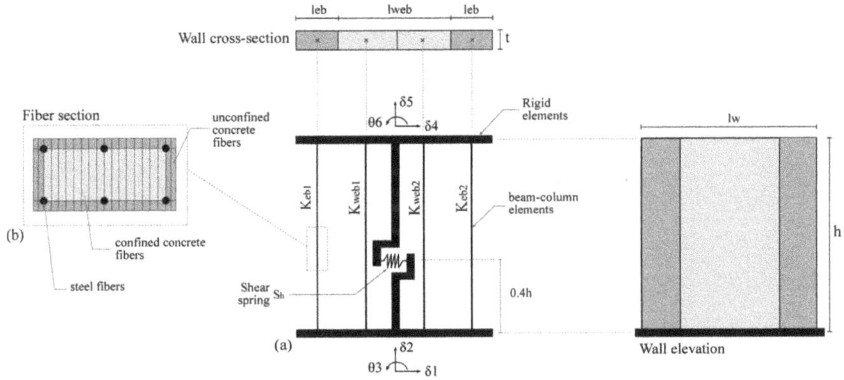

Figure 3. The DNN-MVLEM macromodel. (**a**) Main components and geometry. (**b**) Fiber-based discretization of the cross section used for all the vertical elements.

The columns are modeled using beam-column elements with the fiber section formulation [54]. Their corresponding commands in OpenSees are the "forceBeamColumn" element and the "fiber" section. For the four vertical elements, the cross-section is discretized into 20 rectangular fibers in the direction of the wall length for the concrete area. The total quantity for the reinforcement steel is distributed into six fibers, with four positioned in the corners and two in the middle of the larger edges. Figure 3b depicts the resulting fiber section. The shear spring S_h consists of a uni-axial element that provides only stiffness in the horizontal direction, modeled using the "zeroLenght" element in OpenSees. The rigid beams at the top and bottom of the macromodel and the additional elements holding the shear spring are modeled using the "elasticBeamColumn" element command with a large cross-section assigned to simulate the rigid behavior.

2.2. Material Models for Vertical Elements

The material model for the concrete fibers in the columns is the Kent–Scott–Park model, which does not include tensile strength in its formulation. It is denoted as "Concrete01" in OpenSees, and its definition requires four parameters: the concrete compressive strength f'_c; the strain at the maximum compressive strength ϵ_{co}, taken as -0.002; the crushing strength f_{cu}, taken as $0.2f'_c$; and the strain at the crushing strength ϵ_{cu}, taken as -0.01. A second concrete material model is defined for the confined regions. The material parameters for the unconfined concrete model are the same as those previously mentioned but with the values of $f_{cu} = 0$ and $\epsilon_{cu} = -0.005$.

For the reinforcement steel fibers in the columns, the Giuffre–Menegotto–Pinto model that includes the characteristic post-yielding and the Bauschinger effects have been used. It is identified as "Steel02" in OpeenSees, and its definition requires three parameters: the yield stress f_y; the initial elastic tangent, taken as $E_0 = 210$ GPa; and the strain-hardening ratio, taken as $b = 0.01$ (b is the ratio between the elastic tangent E_0 and the post-yield tangent E_p).

The values for the material parameters for the concrete and the reinforcement steel sections are taken from well-established studies found in the literature, such as [55–60]. A representative stress–strain curve for both material models is presented in Figure 4. Note that the curves are not scaled; their only intention is to provide a visual definition of the required parameters.

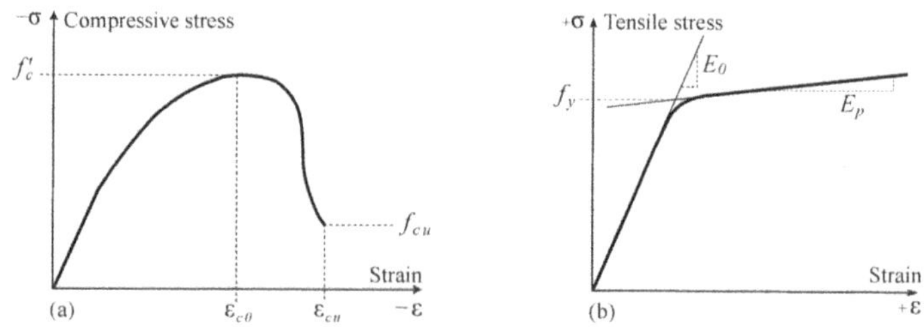

Figure 4. Illustrative uni-axial curves for the material models. (**a**) Concrete. (**b**) Reinforcement steel.

2.3. Material Model for Shear Spring

For the shear spring S_h, a multi-linear material is used with the "MultiLinear" uniaxial material command in OpenSees. The force–displacement coordinates of the multi-linear curve are obtained in the following way. Suppose that a more sophisticated FEM model is used to model the RC shear wall and perform a static non-linear lateral pushover analysis. Then, the computed pushover curve (horizontal force–displacement relation measured at the top of the model through the analysis) is discretized into six segments so that six force–displacement coordinates are obtained. These six force–displacement coordinates define the multi-linear material model for the shear spring. A representative force–displacement curve of the multi-linear model is given in Figure 5. Such a curve serves as the basic shape of the multi-linear model that is later calibrated with a process described in Section 4.

Using the pushover curve obtained with FEM analysis as the curve for the multi-linear material may seem counter-intuitive as it implies the solution of a computationally expensive analysis first. However, this is not the case. The six points defining the multi-linear model are obtained by calling a DNN previously trained with thousands of static non-linear pushover FEM analyses of RC shear walls. The complete description of the methodology to develop the DNN is given in Section 4.

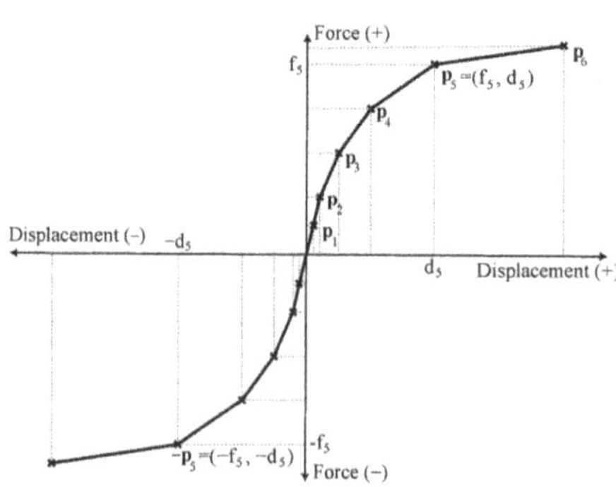

Figure 5. Illustrative force–displacement curve of the multi-linear model used in the shear spring obtained using an DNN.

2.4. Calibration Factors

The DNN-MVLEM is constructed on top of various assumptions and simplifications, which, depending on multiple parameters such as the geometry and reinforcement quantity, may deviate its performance from the actual behavior of the RC shear wall. Thus, a simple data-driven calibration method has been developed. The strategy consists of using three factors to adjust its behavior, namely k_c, k_s, and k_m. The factor k_c multiplies the thickness t of the cross-sections, while k_s multiplies the strength of reinforcement steel f_y. The third factor k_m multiplies the six force coordinates used to define the multi-linear model, shifting the curve up or down.

The calibration is performed by solving an optimization problem using a genetic algorithm. The decision to include these three factors to calibrate the macromodel's behavior comes after several attempts to improve its accuracy without sacrificing its simplicity or computational efficiency. For instance, instead of adding more elements or implementing more complex material models, the optimization algorithm calibrates its performance by simply adjusting the response with three factors.

In principle, the macromodel is calibrated to match the results of a more sophisticated microscopic FEM model. The strategy may seem paradoxical because it implies computing the solution with an expensive microscopic FEM model to calibrate a simpler macromodel. However, this is where the benefits of the data-driven paradigm are genuinely harnessed. Instead of conducting the calibration process each time the macromodel is used, an extensive database of macromodels is calibrated beforehand. Then, that database is used to train a DNN to predict the calibration factors. Thus, the computationally expensive operation is transferred to an external process where the database is generated, and the DNN model is trained. After those processes are finalized, the DNN becomes ready to be used at any given time, predicting the calibration factors in a few milliseconds. The process is described in more detail in Section 4.

3. Parametric FEM Model for Data Generation

The required data for the DNN-MVLEM methodology are generated using a microscopic FEM model based on the multi-layer shell element (MLSE) formulation, particularly the implementation developed by Lu et al. [61,62]. The MLSE has proven to be an effective and practical modeling approach capable of reproducing the in-plane and out-of-plane bending and the characteristic in-plane shear and coupled bending–shear behavior of RC shear walls [63,64]. In the MLSE approach, the shell thickness is discretized into several fully-bonded layers, including the vertical and transverse reinforcement steel as smeared orthotropic layers.

The model consists of a rectangular RC shear wall with special boundary elements (BE) on both sides with a beam element added at the top to distribute the loads to all the nodes on the top edge. The model is parameterized into 11 different variables that describe the geometry and properties of the wall. These parameters are described in Table 1.

The model is subjected to a two-stage analysis procedure. In the first stage, a vertical load is applied to simulate the gravity actions. In the second stage, a static non-linear lateral pushover analysis with a target displacement of 20 mm applied at the top-left node at a rate of 0.05 per step is conducted. The final form of the model and an illustration of the multi-layer shell element discretization is shown in Figure 6.

The chosen bounding values in Table 1 are derived from design guidelines provided by the American Concrete Institute (ACI318-19) [65] and from engineering criteria. The bounding values are selected to produce realistic wall geometries and configurations. For instance, the ACI318-19 specifies that the minimum thickness allowed for a structural wall is $t = 12.5$ cm, and the smallest length-to-thickness ratio is $l_w/t = 6$. As a result, the lower bound for the wall length is set to $t \cdot 6$. Additionally, Section 18.10.6.4 of the ACI318-19 recommends a transverse reinforcement quantity of $\rho_{t_{be}}$ for the boundary element range of 0.0075 to 0.020, depending on the material properties. The longitudinal reinforcement $\rho_{l_{be}}$ is similar to concrete columns, so a value between 0.01 and 0.05 is reasonably selected. Note that reinforcement is expressed as a ratio of the corresponding concrete cross-sectional area. The compressive strength f'_c and yield strength f_y range from traditional values commonly used in the construction of modern buildings. The wall length l_w and height h are based on typical wall dimensions found in medium-rise buildings. The axial load value q_a is expressed as a ratio of the maximum axial strength for concrete sections according to

Equation 22.4.2.2 of ACI318-19. The range of 0.010 to 0.1 is chosen based on the assumption that a value of 0.1 represents the loading of a wall in the bottom story of a medium-height building [66].

Table 1. Parameters that define the properties and dimensions of an RC shear wall.

n	Symbol	Lower Bound	Upper Bound	Description
1	f'_c	25	60	Concrete compressive strength [MPa]
2	f_y	380	600	Reinforcing steel yield stress [MPa]
3	h	300	350	Wall height [cm]
4	t	12.5	40	Wall thickness [cm]
5	l_w	$t \cdot 6$	300	Wall total length [cm]
6	l_{be}	$0.15 \cdot l_w$	$0.30 \cdot l_w$	BE length [cm]
7	$\rho_{l_{be}}$	0.01	0.05	BE longitudinal reinforcement ratio
8	$\rho_{t_{be}}$	0.0075	0.02	BE transversal reinforcement ratio
9	$\rho_{l_{web}}$	0.0025	$0.75 \cdot \rho_{l_{be}}$	Web longitudinal reinforcement ratio
10	$\rho_{t_{web}}$	0.0025	$0.75 \cdot \rho_{t_{be}}$	Web transversal reinforcement ratio
11	q_a	0.005	0.1	Axial load ratio, $P = q_a \cdot 0.85 \cdot f'_c \cdot t \cdot l_w$

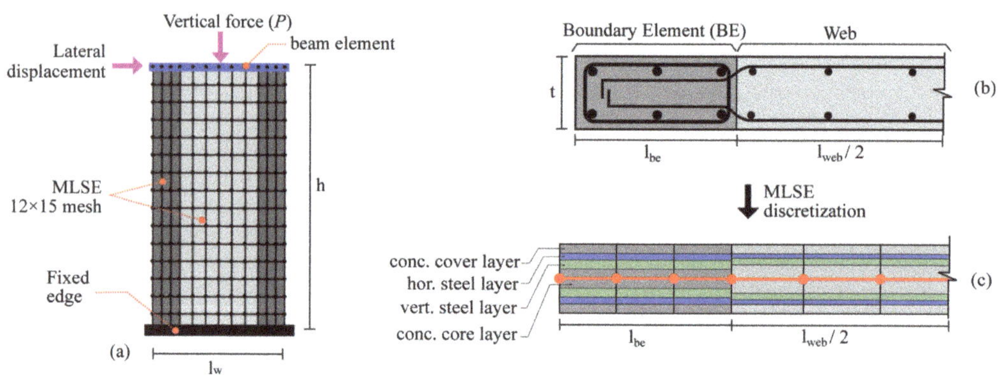

Figure 6. MLSE-based microscopic FEM model. (**a**) Elevation and mesh. (**b**) Realistic cross-section. (**c**) MLSE discretization of the cross-section.

3.1. Validation

The selected MLSE approach is validated with two numerical examples by comparing the results to some of the popular experimental tests available in the literature. For the first case, the specimen labeled as SW22 taken from the study conducted by Lefas et al. [66] is selected. The input values are: $f'_c = 50.6$ MPa, $f_y = 470$ MPa, $h = 130$ cm, $t = 7$ cm, $l_w = 65$ cm, $l_{be} = 0.215$ (14 cm), $\rho_{l_{be}} = 0.033$, $\rho_{t_{be}} = 0.008$, $\rho_{l_{web}} = 0.025$, $\rho_{t_{web}} = 0.008$, $q_a = 0.1$. The second case corresponds to the specimen SW1-1 taken from the database [67]. The input values are: $f'_c = 20.7$ MPa, $f_y = 392$ MPa, $h = 200$ cm, $t = 12.5$ cm, $l_w = 100$ cm, $l_{be} = 0.20$ (20 cm), $\rho_{l_{be}} = 0.0188$, $\rho_{t_{be}} = 0.0028$, $\rho_{l_{web}} = 0.0037$, $\rho_{t_{web}} = 0.0018$, and $q_a = 0.11$. The results for both examples are shown in Figure 7a,b.

The presented numerical examples demonstrate that the implemented RC shear wall FEM model based on the MLSE formulation reproduces the experimental results reasonably, even when two different databases are used. Although only two specimens were analyzed in this study, the same MLSE implementation has been tested extensively in other studies [61,62,68].

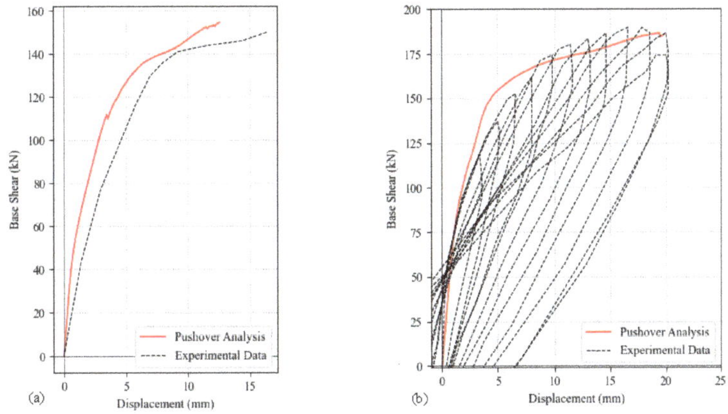

Figure 7. Comparison of the MLSE-based microscopic FEM model to experimental test results. (**a**) Specimen SW22 [66]. (**b**) Specimen SW1-1 [67].

4. Data-Driven Component

The key ingredient of the DNN-MVLEM is adding the data-driven component, which consists of a large deep neural network trained with thousands of non-linear analyses of RC shear walls. The DNN is trained to predict the force–displacement curve for the multi-linear model used in the shear spring and the three factors required to calibrate its performance, as illustrated in Figure 8.

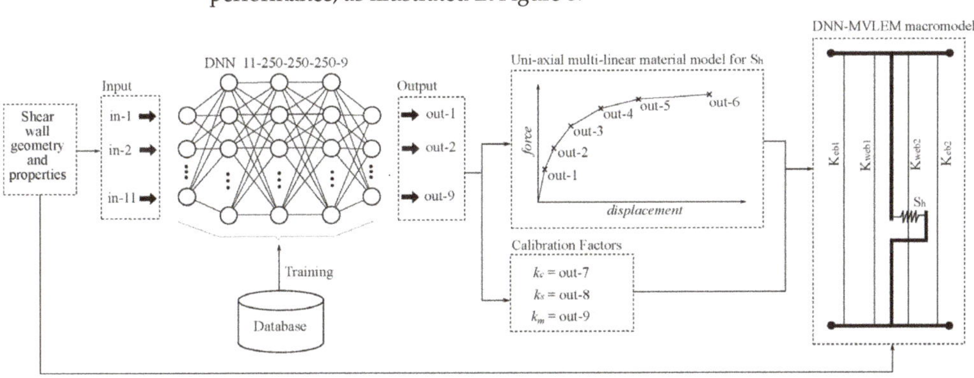

Figure 8. A diagram showing the methodology that is followed to create the DNN-MVLEM.

The data-driven component is summarized in eight steps. In the first phase (Steps 1 to 4), a database is generated that contains thousands of RC shear walls and their corresponding analysis results obtained with the FEM model described in Section 3. The database is used to train a temporary DNN to predict the multi-linear model for the shear spring. In the second phase (Steps 5 to 8), for every RC shear wall in the database, the corresponding macromodel is generated and calibrated to match the FEM results using a genetic algorithm. The calibration factors for each data point are added to the initial database so that a second larger DNN is trained to predict the two parts: the multi-linear curve for the shear spring and the calibration factors, thus obtaining a single DNN that predicts the complete information required to define the DNN-MVLEM. The eight steps are described in more detail in the following paragraphs.

Step 1. A vector **w** that contains the 11 input values is generated using a uniform random distribution based on the bounding values specified in Table 1. The vector has the following form.

$$\mathbf{w} = \{f'_c, f_y, h, t, l_w, l_{be}, \rho_{l_{be}}, \rho_{t_{be}}, \rho_{l_{web}}, \rho_{t_{web}}, q_a\}$$

Step 2. The vector **w** is used to generate the microscopic FEM model described in Section 3. The model is subjected to a static non-linear lateral pushover analysis. The obtained pushover curve is discretized into six segments by reading the force at the displacement values of 0.5, 1.0, 2.5, 5.0, 10.0, and 20.0 mm. Step 2 can be conveniently summarized into a single function as:

$$p(\mathbf{w}) = \{p_1, \ldots, p_6\} \quad (1)$$

where p_i are the force coordinates of the discretized pushover curve obtained with the microscopic FEM model.

Step 3. Steps 1 and 2 are repeated several times until a large database of analysis results is generated. The database is denoted as 11 × 6 because it contains 11 input and 6 output values per data point.

Step 4. A temporary DNN, referred to as DNNb, is created and trained with the 11 × 6 database; thus, obtaining a DNN that predicts the 6 values corresponding to the 6 force coordinates of the discretized pushover curve.

Step 5. From the 11 × 6 database, a data point is selected, and the 11 input values are used to build the corresponding macromodel according to the process described in Section 2. The DNNb is used to obtain the force–displacement curve of the shear spring S_h, and the calibration coefficients are set to an initial value of $k_c = k_s = k_m = 1$. Similarly to Step 2, the following function is defined:

$$q(\mathbf{w}, k_c, k_s, k_m) = \{q_1, \ldots, q_6\} \quad (2)$$

where q_i are the force coordinates of the discretized pushover curve obtained with the macromodel after performing the same static pushover analysis, and applying the same six-value discretization as in Step 2.

Step 6. The calibration procedure is formulated as an optimization problem:

$$\min \quad e = |p(\mathbf{w}) - q(\mathbf{w}, k_c, k_s, k_m)|$$

$$\begin{aligned} 0.1 \leq & k_c \leq 2 & k_c \in \mathbb{R} \\ 0.1 \leq & k_s \leq 2 & k_s \in \mathbb{R} \\ 0.1 \leq & k_m \leq 5 & k_m \in \mathbb{R} \end{aligned} \quad (3)$$

The calibration coefficients are computed by solving the optimization problem with a genetic algorithm. To that end, the genetic algorithm in the multi-objective optimization Python library known as "pymoo" [69] is used. The GA is run for a total of 50 generations using the default parameters provided by the library, which include a population size of 100 and the genetic operators of SBX crossover, polynomial mutation, and tournament selection. The optimization problem is unconstrained, but the solution vector is limited to the space dictated by the bounding values of the variables k_c, k_s, k_m.

Step 7. Steps 5 and 6 are repeated until the calibration coefficients of all the RC shear walls in the database are computed, obtaining a larger 11 × 9 database with nine output values (the six values obtained in Step 2 and the three values obtained in Step 6).

Step 8. With the 11 × 9 database, a second larger DNN model is created and trained to predict the complete information (the six output values used for the multi-linear model and the three calibration factors). The DNN details, such as the architecture and its performance, are given in Section 4.1.

4.1. DNN Architecture and Performance

The DNN has been created using the TensorFlow library [70]. The chosen architecture is a back-propagation neural network with 11 input neurons at the input layer, 3 hidden layers with 250 neurons each, and an output layer with 9 neurons. Its size can be expressed in the following way: $11 - 250 - 250 - 250 - 9$. The total number of trainable parameters is equal to $(11+1) \times 250 + (250+1) \times 200 + (250+1) \times 250 + (250+1) \times 9 = 130{,}759$.

The database is composed of 3000 data points that are generated using the procedure described in Section 4. The inputs and the outputs are normalized to add flexibility and stability to the DNN. A validation subset of 10% of the training data is used to monitor the training process and avoid over-fitting. Other relevant characteristics are the usage of the Adams optimizer, ReLu activation functions, a batch size of 5, and a random uniform initialization of the weights.

After the training, the DNN is tested using a freshly generated data set containing 200 new data points. The testing set is processed by the DNN and the predictions are compared with the ground truth using two metrics, the correlation coefficient (R) and the coefficient of determination (R^2) [71]. The results are shown in Figure 9 for the first 8 outputs. The average values of R and R^2 are 0.9909 and 0.9806, respectively. Such results indicate good correlation values with R and R^2 close to 1, implying that the error is low and that the DNN predicts the results with high accuracy.

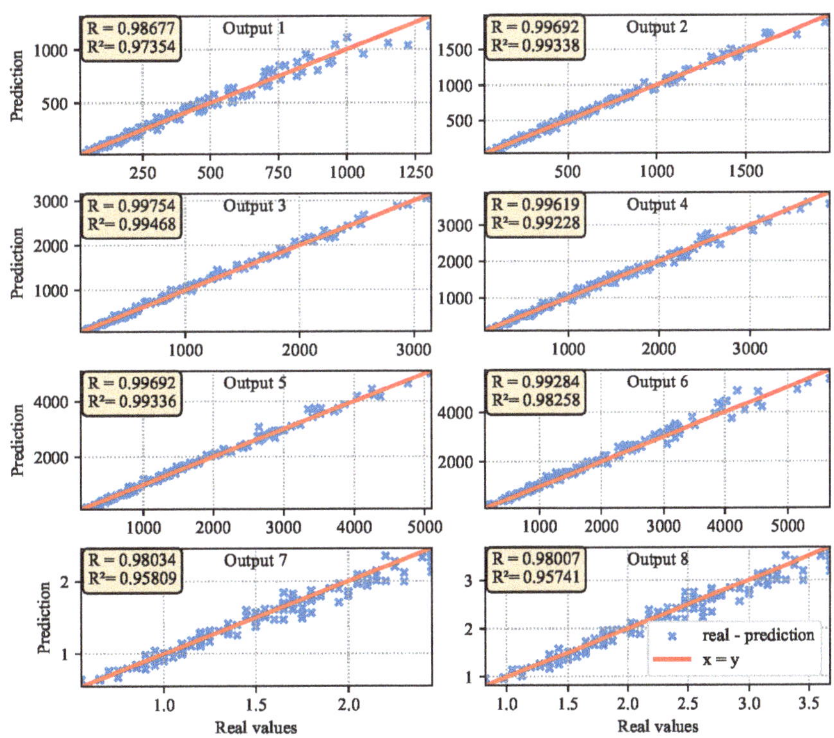

Figure 9. Results of the correlation coeficients R and R^2 of the first 8 output variables for the testing set.

The temporary DNNb model defined in Step number 4 of the process described in Section 4 uses the same parameters described in this section, with the only difference that its size is 11-200-200-200-6.

5. Numerical Examples

This section presents a series of numerical examples to demonstrate the effectiveness of the macromodel. For simplicity, the parameters used to build the microscopic and macroscopic models of the tested walls are presented in Table 2.

Table 2. Properties of all the RC shear walls used in the numerical examples.

Parameters			Wall Identifier					
n	var.	Unit	A	B	C	D	E	F
1	f'_c	MPa	45.1	33.7	55	35	40	30
2	f_y	MPa	530	462	580	420	558	400
3	h	cm	320	335	342	320	340	330
4	t	cm	21	27	36	25	30	20
5	l_w	cm	187	242	165	200	275	160
6	l_{be}	cm	41	48	40	50	68	40
7	$\rho_{l_{be}}$	-	0.031	0.039	0.045	0.035	0.025	0.03
8	$\rho_{t_{be}}$	-	0.0092	0.0102	0.0087	0.0075	0.006	0.0085
9	$\rho_{l_{web}}$	-	0.011	0.009	0.013	0.0125	0.01	0.0095
10	$\rho_{t_{web}}$	-	0.0078	0.0067	0.0091	0.005	0.0075	0.0060
11	q_a	-	0.025	0.018	0.02	0.05	0.075	0.075
1	v_1	kN	206	377	350	263	676	106
2	v_2	kN	361	651	601	459	1184	190
3	v_3	kN	605	1131	1071	790	2009	324
4	v_4	kN	810	1447	1381	1047	2476	435
5	v_5	kN	1086	2035	2101	1393	3357	601
6	v_6	kN	1189	2177	2278	1501	3539	673
7	k_c	-	1.65	1.47	1.57	1.63	1.27	1.51
8	k_s	-	0.43	0.49	0.38	0.41	0.54	0.44
9	k_m	-	4.65	4.63	3.44	3.32	4.81	4.15

5.1. Stand-Alone RC Shear Wall

The first testing round consists of three numerical examples (A, B, C) where the wall is modeled as a stand-alone structure subjected to a static non-linear pushover analysis. The dimensions and properties for the three examples are generated randomly and correspond to the walls labeled as A, B, and C according to Table 2. The analysis is performed using both the microscopic FEM model described in Section 3, and the developed DNN-MVLEM. The boundary conditions are set so that the wall is fixed at the bottom, and a vertical load equal to $P = q_a \cdot 0.85 \cdot f'_c \cdot t \cdot l_w$ is added at the top-middle node. The prescribed displacement for the pushover analysis is set to 20 mm, which is applied at a rate of 0.1 mm per step (200 total steps). The results for each example are presented and compared in Figure 10 and Table 3.

Table 3. Scenario A, B, and C error and computational cost comparisons.

Scenario	Error			Computational Efficiency			
	MAE [kN]	Peak Force [kN]	Total %	FEM 8 × 10 [s]	FEM 12 × 15 [s]	DNN-MVLEM [s]	Speed Factor (8 × 10)/(12 × 15)
A	37	1320	2.8	27	81	0.247	109/327
B	109	2622	4.16	36	97	0.245	146/395
C	107	2292	4.66	30	86	0.252	119/341
Averages	-	-	3.87	31	88	0.248	125/355

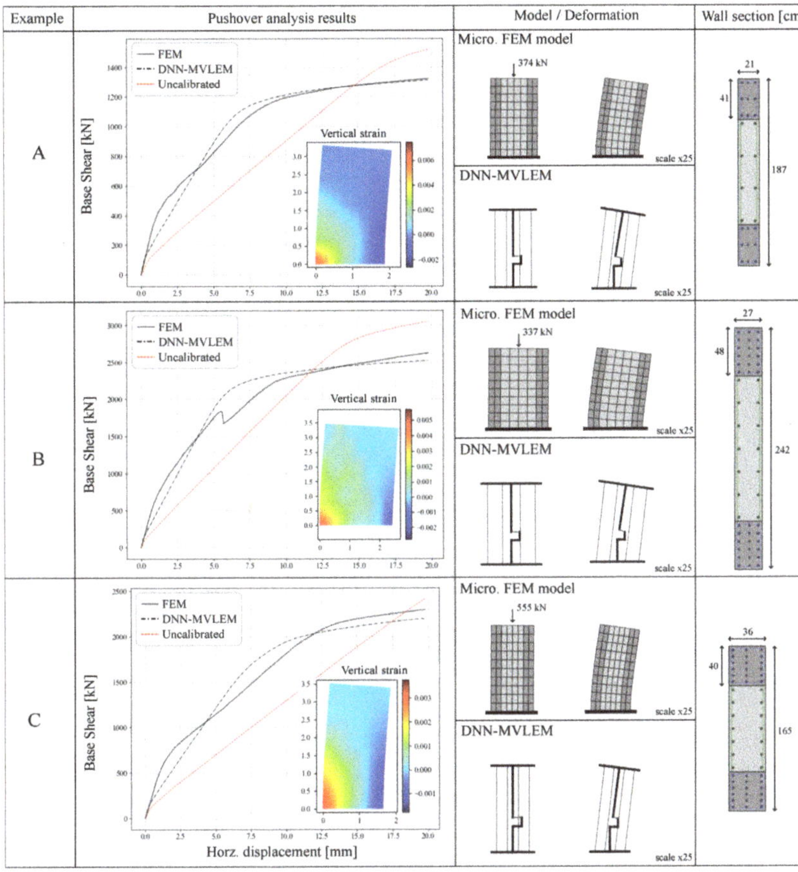

Figure 10. Comparison of results between the microscopic FEM model and the developed DNN-MVLEM for the three stand-alone analysis examples labeled **A**, **B**, and **C**.

5.2. Multi-Story Frame

For the second round of tests, three additional numerical examples (D, E, F) are prepared in which the macromodel has been incorporated into a larger structure that consists of a two-bay multi-story frame. Each structure is modeled using both approaches—the microscopic FEM model and the DNN-MVLME macromodel. The additional columns and beams that form the framed structure are modeled using the same fiber section approach and the non-linear material models described in Section 2.3. For scenarios D and E, the column dimensions are set to 40 × 40 cm with $r_c = 3$ cm of concrete cover and a quantity of reinforcement steel equal to $q_c = 3\%$ of the concrete cross-section gross area. The beam dimensions are 30 × 50 cm with $r_c = 3$ cm and $q_c = 1\%$. For the third scenario F, the structure is intentionally made softer to test the methodology under extreme deformations. For such a scenario, the column dimensions are 25 × 25 cm with $r_c = 2.5$ cm and $q_c = 2\%$; the beam dimensions are 20 × 30 cm with $r_c = 2.5$ cm and $q_c = 1\%$. A static-nonlinear pushover analysis is performed for each scenario and each model. For the D and E scenarios, the prescribed displacement for the pushover analysis is 60 mm applied at a rate of 0.5 per step (120 total steps). For the third scenario, a larger target displacement of 600 mm applied at a rate of 1 mm per step is used (total 600 steps). The boundary conditions for all scenarios are set so that the bottom of the frame is fully fixed. Additionally, the vertical point load is added at the top-middle node of the top story with a magnitude equal to $P = q_a \cdot 0.85 \cdot f'_c \cdot t \cdot l_w$ according to the values specified at Table 2. The results for each example are presented and compared in Figure 11 and Table 4.

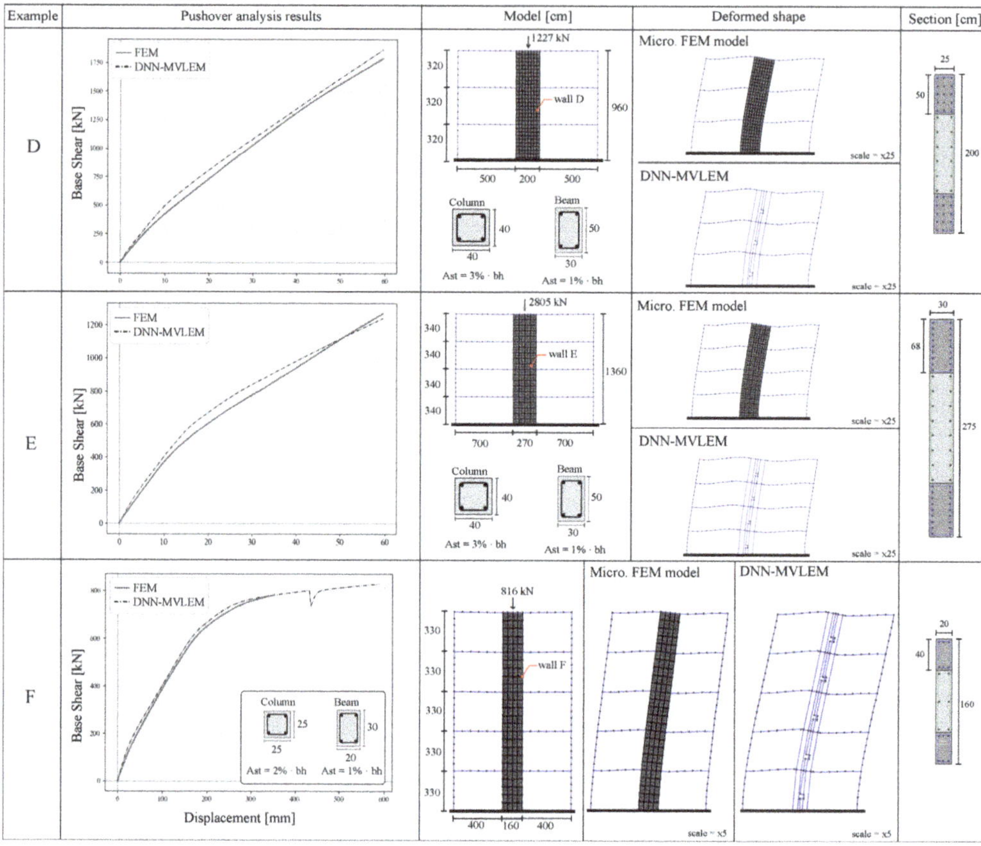

Figure 11. Comparison of results between the microscopic FEM model and the developed DNN-MVLEM for the three multi-story frame analysis examples labeled as **D**, **E**, and **F**.

Table 4. Scenario D, E, and F error and computational cost comparisons.

Scenario	Error			Computational Efficiency		
	MAE [kN]	Peak Force [kN]	Total %	FEM [s]	DNN-MVLEM [s]	Speed Factor
D	50	1757	2.85	82	0.979	83
E	62	1243	4.99	214	2.01	106
F	24	889	2.70	1578	10.75	146

6. Discussion of the Results

6.1. Accuracy

From the numerical examples, it can be appreciated that the computed pushover curve using the microscopic FEM model follows a highly non-linear path with a different shape in each case, thus illustrating the complex non-linear behavior of RC shear walls under intense lateral loading. However, despite the curves' complex shape, the DNN-MVLEM can approximate the results with reasonable accuracy every time. The mean average error

(MAE) between the pushover curve obtained with the microscopic FEM model and the one obtained with the DNN-MVLEM is computed as follows:

$$MAE = \sum_{i=1}^{nStep} \frac{|forceFEM_i - forceDNN_i|}{nStep} \tag{4}$$

$$e_{total} = \frac{MAE}{PeakForce} \tag{5}$$

where $nStep$ is the total number of steps in the pushover analysis; the term $forceFEM_i$ is equal to the base shear obtained with the microscopic FEM model at Step i; the term $forceDNN_i$ is equal to the base shear obtained with the DNN-MVLEM at the Step i; $PeakForce$ is the maximum base shear measured in the entire pushover analysis. Hence, the value e_{total} is a normalization of the mean average error and provides a reasonable estimation of the overall error. With that in mind, the obtained results show that $e_{total} <$ 5% in all scenarios, which indicates a reasonably good approximation from an engineering point of view; see Tables 3 and 4.

The accuracy referred to in this section is the approximation of the DNN-MVLEM to the reference microscopic FEM model. As it is well-known in FEM analysis, the reference FEM model is itself an approximation of the actual behavior of the structure. In Section 3.1, the accuracy of the reference FEM model is discussed.

6.2. Calibrated vs. Uncalibrated Response

In the first three scenarios, A, B, and C, the uncalibrated response of the DNN-MVLEM is also presented (i.e., the response when $k_c = K_s = K_m = 1$); see Figure 10. It can be appreciated that the calibration process is an essential step, as the uncalibrated version deviates from the actual response. Such a deviation in the uncalibrated response may be explained by the inability of the macromodel to simulate the coupled shear and flexural behavior properly, among other disparities, such as using different material models for the concrete. Nonetheless, the proposed calibration procedure using an optimization algorithm has proven to be a simple and effective solution that does not increase the complexity of the model, transferring the added computational cost to an external process to generate the database and train the DNN model.

6.3. Computational Efficiency

This study's computational operations have been performed with a conventional PC with the following characteristics: CPU Intel Core i7-6700HQ @2.60 GHz with 16 GB RAM. These operations include creating the database, solving the calibration optimization problem using GA, training and testing the DNN, and solving the numerical examples.

The gains obtained by using the DNN-MVLEM are evident regarding the computational efficiency. For the first three scenarios, the computational cost is compared using two different mesh sizes for the microscopic FEM model, a mesh of 8×10 and another of 12×15 elements. Each pushover analysis using 200 steps takes, on average, 31 and 88 s for each case, respectively. In contrast, the DNN-MVLEM takes an average of 0.248 s. Thus, the analysis is accelerated by 125 and 355 for each case. The results are equally impressive for scenarios D, E, and F, where the speed acceleration factors obtained are 83, 106, and 146 for each case, respectively. The results are presented in Table 3 and 4 in the columns are labeled as "Computational Efficiency".

On the other hand, generating the database may be a computationally expensive operation. However, the proposed microscopic FEM model based on the MLSE formulation is significantly faster than other microscopic models and poses a viable option for creating large data quantities. Each data point in the database takes approximately 1 min to be generated (30 s for the FEM analysis and 30 for the genetic algorithm). Therefore, generating the 3000 data points to train the DNN model would take about 50 h using a single PC and a single core. Nonetheless, the procedure can be significantly accelerated using parallel processing with multiple cores and computers. For example, for this study, using two computers with the same characteristics described above and running the process on multiple cores, the 3000 data points are generated in 14 h. The training of the DNN with 130,759 features takes an additional 30 s. Once the DNN is trained and ready to be used, it can be serialized into a file with a digital size of less than 5 megabytes. Loading the DNN from a file takes merely 678 milliseconds, and predicting the output for a set of input values takes less than 1 millisecond.

6.4. Advantages Summary

The advantages of the DNN-MVLEM can be summarized as follows.

- **Computational Efficiency**. The DNN-MVLEM can substantially speed up the nonlinear analysis of large structures. In the presented numerical example labeled scenario D, a five-story frame is analyzed using both approaches. The analysis for the structure where the walls are modeled with the DNN-MVLEM is 116 times faster, taking 10.75 s to finalize compared to the 1253 s (or about 20 min) for the analysis with the walls modeled with the microscopic FEM model.
- **Simplicity**. The full DNN-MVLEM can be created based only on the basic properties of the RC shear wall and the pre-trained DNN model. There are no difficult-to-obtain parameters required for its definition. Furthermore, the implemented material models and element formulations are typically included in most commercial FEM packages.
- **Adaptability**. The methodology developed to create the DNN-MVLEM could be easily enhanced or adapted to tackle new challenges. For instance, increasing the lower and upper bound of the input values or adding additional variables to the problem. These improvements are relatively easy to implement by adding more data points to the training data and re-training the model. Similarly, the same strategy could be adapted to other types of RC shear walls, such as L-shaped or T-shaped geometries.
- **Improved convergence rate**. The DNN-MVLEM has been shown to have fewer convergence problems than those encountered with the microscopic FEM model. This can be appreciated in example F, where the FEM model failed to converge to the target displacement of 600 mm, but the DNN-MVLEM reached the target without issue. One potential explanation is that the elements conforming to the macromodel are based on simpler element and material formulations, making them less sensitive to convergence problems.

6.5. Scope and Applicability of DNN-MVLEM

In order to fully assess the advantages and limitations discussed in this section, it is essential to mention the objectives and motivations that led to the creation of the proposed strategy. Although the results are highly promising, DNN-MVLEM is not designed to replace traditional FEM models of RC shear walls that are grounded in well-established theoretical frameworks and have been extensively tested and verified over time. Instead, DNN-MVLEM is conceived as a more straightforward and significantly more computationally efficient alternative for certain types of analyses and problems. For example, uncertainty analysis, failure analysis, and risk assessment of structures. In these types of studies, the structure must be modeled multiple times under various conditions to determine quantities such as failure probabilities. Hence, a simpler and significantly faster model approximating the results is preferred as long as the approximation quality is good enough. For DNN-MVLEM, the obtained error for the tested examples is between 2% and 5%, which is within a reasonable range for such engineering applications.

Similarly, during the preliminary stages of a building's design process, numerous iterations are typically needed to identify the optimal shape or layout of walls and braces to achieve the best possible performance of the building under lateral loads. Trading some accuracy for a simpler and much faster model is usually preferred at this stage. The faster model may be used for the pre-design, and once the ideal configuration has been established, the structure can be re-analyzed using a more sophisticated (and precise) model to ensure higher confidence in the final design.

6.6. Current Limitations and Future Enhancements

There are some limitations that one needs to be aware of when using DNN-MVLEM in its current form. For instance, the calibration factors slightly adjust the model's stiffness to match the FEM results in terms of displacements. This has turned out to be a simple and straightforward solution. However, other properties of the structure, such as modal frequencies, have not been taken into account. In future versions of DNN-MVLEM, such additional quantities may be considered by including them into the optimization problem that is solved to obtain the calibration coefficients.

Another inconvenience may be encountered when defining the axial load required as input in the DNN. However, one simple solution is to perform a linear static analysis for the gravitational load case with the uncalibrated form of the macromodel (i.e., $k_c = k_s = k_m = 1$), thus obtaining an estimate of the axial load, which can then be used to define the calibrated macromodel prior to the non-linear procedure.

There are also two common concerns for applying data-driven strategies in practical applications. One is the availability of the data to train the model. Nonetheless, for DNN-MVLEM that is not the case, as the data are generated using a parametric microscopic FEM model and the quantity of data is only limited by the time or computational resources, which have been discussed in Section 6.3. The second concern is the expertise that the user requires to fully comprehend and apply these methodologies. However, in this regard, big tech companies are constantly developing multiple tools that facilitate the application of machine learning techniques. Hence, nowadays, it is becoming easier to build reliable data-driven solutions.

7. Conclusions

In this study, a macromodel denoted as DNN-MVLEM has been developed for the analysis of RC shear walls. The model is created based on a novel data-driven methodology using deep neural networks. The DNN-MVLEM is composed of two main parts. The structural part, which is comprised of four vertical elements and one horizontal shear spring, and the data-driven part, which is a DNN trained to predict the properties of the shear spring and three coefficients required to calibrate the macromodel's behavior. The data utilized to train the DNN have been generated in a two-step procedure using a microscopic FEM model based on the multi-layer shell formulation, and a genetic algorithm that determines the calibration coefficients. The DNN-MVLEM was tested in two sets of examples: as a stand-alone wall in cantilever mode and as part of a multi-story frame structure subjected to a static non-linear lateral pushover analysis. The results obtained with the DNN-MVLEM were compared to those from the microscopic FEM model, showing an estimated error of less than 5% between the two pushover curves. Moreover, the DNN-MVLEM demonstrated significantly improved computational efficiency, being up to 140 times faster than the microscopic FEM model, depending on the total number of elements in the FEM model.

This study has shown that alternative methods based on data-driven solutions are exceptionally effective in reducing the computational time of the non-linear analysis of structures with a minimum compromise in accuracy with respect to more sophisticated FEM models. In essence, the computational effort is transferred to the database creation and the DNN model's training process. However, these heavy-duty operations can be conveniently automated using parametric modeling techniques and high-performance computing systems. Hence, significantly speeding the workflow process and enabling the practical application of such data-driven techniques. In particular, the DNN-MVLEM is suitable for applications where a large number of analysis are needed, and the engineer (or designer) is willing to sacrifice a bit of accuracy for significantly greater computational efficiency. Some examples of such applications are uncertainty analysis, failure analysis, risk assessment of structures, and optimization of buildings in preliminary design stages.

We are entering an era where artificial intelligence and data-driven solutions are becoming much more efficient and mature, thus quickly taking over traditional deterministic approaches, while the full implications of such fast phased progress is still uncertain for structural engineering, its effect is already taking place notoriously. This study serves as an example of how AI-driven techniques could revolutionize the analysis and simulation of structures in the future.

Author Contributions: Conceptualization, G.S. and V.P.; methodology, G.S. and V.P.; software, G.S. and V.P.; formal analysis, G.S. and V.P.; investigation, V.P. and G.S.; resources, V.P. and G.S.; data curation, G.S.; writing—original draft preparation, G.S. and V.P.; writing—review and editing, G.S. and V.P.; visualization, G.S. and V.P.; supervision, V.P.; project administration, V.P.; funding acquisition, G.S. All authors have read and agreed to the published version of the manuscript.

Funding: The APC was funded by Oslo Metropolitan University.

Data Availability Statement: The data presented in this study are available on request from the corresponding author.

Conflicts of Interest: The authors declare that the research was conducted in the absence of any commercial or financial relationships that could be construed as a potential conflict of interest.

References

1. Tuna, Z. Seismic Performance, Modeling, and Failure Assessment of Reinforced Concrete Shear Wall Buildings. Ph.D. Thesis, UCLA, Los Angeles, CA, USA, 2012.
2. Fintel, M. Performance of Buildings With Shear Walls in Earthquakes of the Last Thirty Years. *PCI J.* **1995**, *40*, 62–80. [CrossRef]
3. Mo, Y.; Zhong, J.; Hsu, T. Seismic simulation of RC wall-type structures. *Eng. Struct.* **2008**, *30*, 3167–3175. [CrossRef]
4. Jalali, A.; Dashti, F. Nonlinear behavior of reinforced concrete shear walls using macroscopic and microscopic models. *Eng. Struct.* **2010**, *32*, 2959–2968. [CrossRef]
5. Mulas, M.; Coronelli, D.; Martinelli, L. Multi-scale modelling approach for the pushover analysis of existing RC shear walls—Part I: Model formulation. *Earthq. Eng. Struct. Dyn.* **2007**, *36*, 1169–1187. [CrossRef]
6. Mulas, M.; Coronelli, D.; Martinelli, L. Multi-scale modelling approach for the pushover analysis of existing RC shear walls—Part II: Experimental verification. *Earthq. Eng. Struct. Dyn.* **2007**, *36*, 1189–1207. [CrossRef]
7. Ayoub, A.; Filippou, F. Nonlinear finite-element analysis of RC shear panels and walls. *J. Struct. Eng.* **1998**, *124*, 298–308. [CrossRef]
8. Wang, J.J.; Liu, C.; Nie, X.; Fan, J.S.; Zhu, Y.J. Nonlinear model updating algorithm for biaxial reinforced concrete constitutive models of shear walls. *J. Build. Eng.* **2021**, *44*, 103215. [CrossRef]
9. Luu, C.; Mo, Y.; Hsu, T. Development of CSMM-based shell element for reinforced concrete structures. *Eng. Struct.* **2017**, *132*, 778–790. [CrossRef]
10. Liao, F.Y.; Han, L.H.; Tao, Z. Performance of reinforced concrete shear walls with steel reinforced concrete boundary columns. *Eng. Struct.* **2012**, *44*, 186–209. [CrossRef]
11. Dong, Y.R.; Xu, Z.D.; Zeng, K.; Cheng, Y.; Xu, C. Seismic behavior and cross-scale refinement model of damage evolution for RC shear walls. *Eng. Struct.* **2018**, *167*, 13–25. [CrossRef]
12. Dashti, F.; Dhakal, R.P.; Pampanin, S. Numerical Modeling of Rectangular Reinforced Concrete Structural Walls. *J. Struct. Eng.* **2017**, *143*, 04017031. [CrossRef]
13. Epackachi, S.; Whittaker, A.S. A validated numerical model for predicting the in-plane seismic response of lightly reinforced, low-aspect ratio reinforced concrete shear walls. *Eng. Struct.* **2018**, *168*, 589–611. [CrossRef]
14. El-Kashif, K.F.O.; Adly, A.K.; Abdalla, H.A. Finite element modeling of RC shear walls strengthened with CFRP subjected to cyclic loading. *Alex. Eng. J.* **2019**, *58*, 189–205. [CrossRef]
15. Kolozvari, K.; Gullu, M.F.; Orakcal, K. Finite Element Modeling of Reinforced Concrete Walls Under Uni- and Multi-Directional Loading Using Opensees. *J. Earthq. Eng.* **2021**, *26*, 6524–6547. [CrossRef]
16. Wu, Y.T.; Lan, T.Q.; Xiao, Y.; Yang, Y.B. Macro-Modeling of Reinforced Concrete Structural Walls: State-of-the-Art. *J. Earthq. Eng.* **2017**, *21*, 652–678.
17. Kolozvari, K.; Arteta, C.; Fischinger, M.; Gavridou, S.; Hube, M.; Isakovic, T.; Lowes, L.; Orakcal, K.; Vásquez, G.J.; Wallace, J. Comparative Study of State-of-the-Art Macroscopic Models for Planar Reinforced Concrete Walls. *ACI Struct. J.* **2018**, *115*, 1637–1657. [CrossRef]
18. Goel, S.; Liao, W.; Bayat, M.; Chao, S. Performance-based plastic design (PBPD) method for earthquake-resistant structures: An overview. *Struct. Des. Tall Spec. Build.* **2010**, *19*, 115–137. [CrossRef]
19. Kabeyasawa, T.; Shioara, H.; Otani, S. U.S.-Japan Cooperative Research on R/C Full-Scale Building Test, Part 5: Discussion of Dynamic Response System. In Proceedings of the Eighth World Conference on Earthquake Engineering, San Francisco, CA, USA, 21–28 July 1984; Volume 6, pp. 627–634.
20. Vulcano, A.; Bertero, V.; Colotti, V. Analytical Modeling of R/C Structural Walls. In Proceedings of the 9th World Conference on Earthquake Engineering, Tokyo/Kyoto, Japan, 2–9 August 1988; Volume 6.

21. Vulcano, A. Macroscopic modeling for nonlinear analysis of RC structural walls. In *Nonlinear Seismic Analysis and Design of Reinforced Concrete Buildings*; CRC Press: Boca Raton, FL, USA, 1992; p. 10.
22. Orakcal, K.; Wallace, J.; Conte, J. Nonlinear modeling and analysis of slender reinforced concrete walls. *ACI Struct. J.* **2004**, *101*, 688–698.
23. Lu, X.; Chen, Y. Modeling of Coupled Shear Walls and Its Experimental Verification. *J. Struct. Eng.* **2005**, *131*, 75–84. [CrossRef]
24. Orakcal, K.; Wallace, J. Flexural modeling of reinforced concrete walls—Experimental verification. *ACI Struct. J.* **2006**, *103*, 196–206.
25. Rezapour, M.; Ghassemieh, M. Macroscopic modelling of coupled concrete shear wall. *Eng. Struct.* **2018**, *169*, 37–54. [CrossRef]
26. Isakovic, T.; Fischinger, M. Assessment of a force–displacement based multiple-vertical-line element to simulate the non-linear axial–shear–flexure interaction behaviour of reinforced concrete walls. *Bull. Earthq. Eng.* **2019**, *17*, 6369–6389. [CrossRef]
27. Kolozvari, K.; Orakcal, K.; Wallace, J.W. New opensees models for simulating nonlinear flexural and coupled shear-flexural behavior of RC walls and columns. *Comput. Struct.* **2018**, *196*, 246–262. [CrossRef]
28. Kolozvari, K.; Orakcal, K.; Wallace, J.W. Modeling of Cyclic Shear-Flexure Interaction in Reinforced Concrete Structural Walls. I: Theory. *J. Struct. Eng.* **2015**, *141*, 04014135.
29. Kolozvari, K.; Tran, T.A.; Orakcal, K.; Wallace, J.W. Modeling of Cyclic Shear-Flexure Interaction in Reinforced Concrete Structural Walls. II: Experimental Validation. *J. Struct. Eng.* **2015**, *141*, 04014136.
30. Zhang, H.; Fang, Y.; Duan, Y.; Du, G. The V-MVLE model for cyclic failure behavior simulation of planar RC members. *Thin-Walled Struct.* **2022**, *181*, 110159. [CrossRef]
31. Esmaeiltabar, P.; Vaseghi, J.; Khosravi, H. Nonlinear macro modeling of slender reinforced concrete shear walls. *Struct. Concr.* **2019**, *20*, 899–910. [CrossRef]
32. Fu, W. Macroscopic numerical model of reinforced concrete shear walls based on material properties. *J. Intell. Manuf.* **2021**, *32*, 1401–1410. [CrossRef]
33. Solorzano, G.; Plevris, V. Computational intelligence methods in simulation and modeling of structures: A state-of-the-art review using bibliometric maps. *Front. Built Environ.* **2022**, *8*. [CrossRef]
34. Plevris, V.; Lagaros, N.D. Artificial Intelligence (AI) Applied in Civil Engineering. *Appl. Sci.* **2022**, *12*, 7595. [CrossRef]
35. Plevris, V.; Tsiatas, G.C. Computational Structural Engineering: Past Achievements and Future Challenges. *Front. Built Environ.* **2018**, *4*, 21.
36. Solorzano, G.; Plevris, V. ANN-based surrogate model for predicting the lateral load capacity of RC shear walls. In Proceedings of the ECCOMAS Congress 2022—8th European Congress on Computational Methods in Applied Sciences and Engineering, Oslo, Norway, 5–9 June 2022. [CrossRef]
37. Lagaros, N.; Papadrakakis, M. Neural network based prediction schemes of the non-linear seismic response of 3D buildings. *Adv. Eng. Softw.* **2012**, *44*, 92–115. [CrossRef]
38. Plevris, V.; Asteris, P.G. Modeling of Masonry Failure Surface under Biaxial Compressive Stress Using Neural Networks. *Constr. Build. Mater.* **2014**, *55*, 447–461. [CrossRef]
39. Moayyeri, N.; Gharehbaghi, S.; Plevris, V. Cost-Based Optimum Design of Reinforced Concrete Retaining Walls Considering Different Methods of Bearing Capacity Computation. *Mathematics* **2019**, *7*, 1232.
40. Liu, J.; Xia, Y. A hybrid intelligent genetic algorithm for truss optimization based on deep neutral network. *Swarm Evol. Comput.* **2022**, *73*, 101120. [CrossRef]
41. Solorzano, G.; Plevris, V. Optimum Design of RC Footings with Genetic Algorithms According to ACI 318–319. *Buildings* **2020**, *10*, 110.
42. Kallioras, N.; Kazakis, G.; Lagaros, N. Accelerated topology optimization by means of deep learning. *Struct. Multidiscip. Optim.* **2020**, *62*, 1185–1212. [CrossRef]
43. Jung, J.; Yoon, K.; Lee, P.S. Deep learned finite elements. *Comput. Methods Appl. Mech. Eng.* **2020**, *372*, 113401. [CrossRef]
44. Samaniego, E.; Anitescu, C.; Goswami, S.; Nguyen-Thanh, V.M.; Guo, H.; Hamdia, K.; Zhuang, X.; Rabczuk, T. An energy approach to the solution of partial differential equations in computational mechanics via machine learning: Concepts, implementation and applications. *Comput. Methods Appl. Mech. Eng.* **2020**, *362*, 112790. [CrossRef]
45. Kudela, J.; Matousek, R. Recent advances and applications of surrogate models for finite element method computations: A review. *Soft Comput.* **2022**, *26*, 13709–13733. [CrossRef]
46. Mai, H.T.; Kang, J.; Lee, J. A machine learning-based surrogate model for optimization of truss structures with geometrically nonlinear behavior. *Finite Elem. Anal. Des.* **2021**, *196*, 103572. [CrossRef]
47. Abueidda, D.W.; Koric, S.; Sobh, N.A. Topology optimization of 2D structures with nonlinearities using deep learning. *Comput. Struct.* **2020**, *237*, 106283. [CrossRef]
48. Linghu, J.; Dong, H.; Cui, J. Ensemble wavelet-learning approach for predicting the effective mechanical properties of concrete composite materials. *Comput. Mech.* **2022**, *70*, 335–365. [CrossRef]
49. Lee, S.; Popovics, J. Applications of physics-informed neural networks for property characterization of complex materials. *Rilem Tech. Lett.* **2022**, *7*, 178–188. [CrossRef]
50. Solorzano, G.; Plevris, V. Design of Reinforced Concrete Isolated Footings under Axial Loading with Artificial Neural Networks. In Proceedings of the 14th ECCOMAS Thematic Conference on Evolutionary and Deterministic Methods for Design, Optimization and Control (EUROGEN 2021), Athens, Greece, 28–30 June 2021; pp. 118–131. [CrossRef]

51. Ben Seghier, M.E.A.; Corriea, J.A.F.O.; Jafari-Asl, J.; Malekjafarian, A.; Plevris, V.; Trung, N.T. On the modeling of the annual corrosion rate in main cables of suspension bridges using combined soft computing model and a novel nature-inspired algorithm. *Neural Comput. Appl.* **2021**, *33*, 15969–15985. [CrossRef]
52. McKenna, F.; Scott, M.H.; Fenves, G.L. Nonlinear Finite-Element Analysis Software Architecture Using Object Composition. *JOurnal Comput. Civ. Eng.* **2010**, *24*, 95–107.
53. Zhu, M.; McKenna, F.; Scott, M.H. OpenSeesPy: Python library for the OpenSees finite element framework. *SoftwareX* **2018**, *7*, 6–11. [CrossRef]
54. Taucer, F.; Spacone, E.; Filippou, F. A Fiber Beam-Column Element for Seismic Response Analysis of Reinforced Concrete Structures. Ph.D. Thesis, University of California, Berkeley, CA, USA, 1991.
55. Shah, S.P.; Swartz, S.E.; Ouyang, C. *Fracture Mechanics of Concrete: Applications of Fracture Mechanics to Concrete, Rock and Other Quasi-Brittle Materials*; John Wiley & Sons: Hoboken, NJ, USA, 1995.
56. Kent, D.C.; Park, R. Flexural Members with Confined Concrete. *J. Struct. Div.* **1971**, *97*, 1969–1990.
57. Mander, J.B.; Priestley, M.J.N.; Park, R. Theoretical Stress-Strain Model for Confined Concrete. *J. Struct. Eng.* **1988**, *114*, 1804–1826. [CrossRef]
58. Bangash, M.Y.H. *Concrete and Concrete Structures: Numerical Modelling and Applications*; Elsevier Applied Science: London, UK, 1989.
59. Menegotto, M. *Method of Analysis of Cyclically Loaded RC Plane Frames including Changes in Geometry and Non-Elastic Behavior of Elements under Normal Force and Bending*; ETH Zürich: Zürich, Schweiz, 1973; pp. 15–22.
60. Filippou, F.C.; Popov, E.P.; Bertero, V.V. *Effects of Bond Deterioration on Hysteretic Behavior of Reinforced Concrete Joints*; Technical Report; Earthquake Engineering Research Center, University of California: Berkeley, CA, USA, 1983.
61. Xie, L.; Lu, X.; Lu, X.; Huang, Y.; Ye, L. *Multi-Layer Shell Element for Shear Walls in OpenSees*; American Society of Civil Engineers: Reston, VA, USA, 2014; pp. 1190–1197, ISBN 9780784413616. [CrossRef]
62. Lu, X.; Xie, L.; Guan, H.; Huang, Y.; Lu, X. A shear wall element for nonlinear seismic analysis of super-tall buildings using OpenSees. *Finite Elem. Anal. Des.* **2015**, *98*, 14–25. [CrossRef]
63. Guan, H.; Loo, Y.C. Flexural and Shear Failure Analysis of Reinforced Concrete Slabs and Flat Plates. *Adv. Struct. Eng.* **1997**, *1*, 71–85.
64. Hallinan, P.; Guan, H. Layered Finite Element Analysis of One-Way and Two-Way Concrete Walls with Openings. *Adv. Struct. Eng.* **2007**, *10*, 55–72. [CrossRef]
65. ACI Committee 318. *Building Code Requirements for Structural Concrete (ACI 318-19)*; ACI: Farmington Hills, MI, USA, 2019.
66. Lefas, I.; Kotsovos, M. Behavior of reinforced concrete structural walls. Strength, deformation characteristics, and failure mechanism. *ACI Struct. J.* **1990**, *87*, 23–31.
67. Lu, X.; Zhou, Y.; Yang, J.; Qian, J.; Song, C.; Wang, Y. *SLDRCE Database on Static Tests of Structural Members and Joint Assemblies —Shear Walls R11*; Technical Report; Institute of Structural Engineering and Disaster Reduction, Tongji University: Shanghai, China, 2008.
68. Petrone, F.; McKenna, F.; Do, T.; McCallen, D. A versatile numerical model for the nonlinear analysis of squat-to-tall reinforced-concrete shear walls. *Eng. Struct.* **2021**, *242*, 112406. [CrossRef]
69. Blank, J.; Deb, K. pymoo: Multi-Objective Optimization in Python. *IEEE Access* **2020**, *8*, 89497–89509. [CrossRef]
70. Abadi, M.; Agarwal, A.; Barham, P.; Brevdo, E.; Chen, Z.; Citro, C.; Corrado, G.S.; Davis, A.; Dean, J.; Devin, M.; et al. TensorFlow: Large-Scale Machine Learning on Heterogeneous Systems. 2015. Available online: https://www.tensorflow.org (accessed on 18 January 2022).
71. Plevris, V.; Solorzano, G.; Bakas, N.; Seghier, M.E.A. Investigation of performance metrics in regression analysis and machine learning-based prediction models. In Proceedings of the ECCOMAS Congress 2022—8th European Congress on Computational Methods in Applied Sciences and Engineering, Oslo, Norway, 5–9 June 2022. [CrossRef]

mathematics

MDPI

Article

Studies on Finite Element Analysis in Hydroforming of Nimonic 90 Sheet

Fakrudeen Ali Ahamed J and Pandivelan Chinnaiyan *

School of Mechanical Engineering, Vellore Institute of Technology, Vellore 632014, India; fakrudeen.2018@vitstudent.ac.in
* Correspondence: cpandivelan@vit.ac.in

Abstract: The primary goal of this study was to investigate the formability of Nimonic 90 sheet which performs well at high temperatures and pressures, making it ideal for applications in the aerospace, processing, and manufacturing industries. In this present study, finite element analysis (FEA) and optimization of process parameters for formability of Nimonic 90 in sheet hydroforming were investigated. The material's mechanical properties were obtained by uniaxial tensile tests as per the standard ASTM E8/E8M. The sheet hydroforming process was first simulated to obtain maximum pressure (53.46 MPa) using the FEA and was then validated using an experiment. The maximum pressure obtained was 50.5 MPa in experimentation. Since fully experimental or simulation designs are impractical, the Box–Behnken design (BBD) was used to investigate various process parameters. Formability was measured by the forming limit diagram (FLD) and maximum deformation achieved without failure. Analysis of variance (ANOVA) results also revealed that pressure and thickness were the most effective parameters for achieving maximum deformation without failure. Response surface methodology (RSM) optimizer was used to predict optimized process parameter to achieve maximized response (deformation) without failure. Experimental validation was carried out for the optimized parameters. The percentage of error between experimental and simulation results for maximum deformation was less than 5%. The findings revealed that all the aspects in the presented regression model and FEM simulation were effective on response values.

Keywords: simulation; sheet hydroforming; optimization; Nimonic 90; mechanical properties; formability; design of experiments; finite element analysis; Box–Behnken design

MSC: 65-04; 65-05; 65K10

Citation: Ahamed J, F.A.; Chinnaiyan, P. Studies on Finite Element Analysis in Hydroforming of Nimonic 90 Sheet. *Mathematics* **2023**, *11*, 2437. https://doi.org/10.3390/math11112437

Academic Editors: Zhuojia Fu, Yiqian He and Hui Zheng

Received: 27 April 2023
Revised: 20 May 2023
Accepted: 23 May 2023
Published: 24 May 2023

1. Introduction

In most the industries, including the automotive and aerospace sectors, hydroforming was used to manufacture components which are challenging in metal forming [1]. It produces structurally strong components with complex geometry quickly, efficiently, and cost-effectively [1–3]. The benefits of hydroformed parts include improved strength to weight ratios, weight savings from section designs that are more effective, fewer parts, and reduced costs associated with tooling development, better dimensional stability and reproducibility of produced components, and subassemblies [4]. Since there are no welding joints, the parts produced in hydroforming can absorb more crash energy. This means that vehicles are more crashworthy, which translates into improved safety for vehicle occupants in the event of a crash [2]. All complex geometries of automotive components, such as rear axle subframe, a front axle, twin elbow exhaust manifold, fuel tank and roofs for luxury class cars, can be obtained through hydroforming [2,5]. Hydroforming processes are eco-friendly, as they reduce the amount of scrap, emit less noise pollution, and protect the environment, as forming is carried out only by the liquid medium [2]. Tube hydroforming and sheet hydroforming are the two primary divisions of the hydroforming process [4].

Sheet hydroforming is a near net shape manufacturing process, which means the parts it produces are very close to the final specified geometry and require very little rework [1]. This process will result in a reduction in the number of production steps and components in an assembly. This would reduce dimensional variations and make assembly easier [3]. The sheet hydroforming process, as shown in Figure 1, uses high pressure fluid for deformation of a blank (sheet) into a desired shape with die.

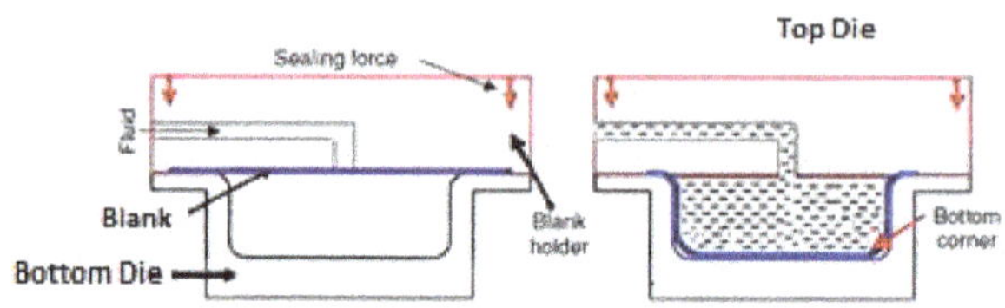

Figure 1. The Schematic of the Sheet Hydroforming Process.

The most common material instabilities in sheet metals are wrinkling and tearing. Parameters of the sheet hydroforming process must be adequately modified to produce the desired results without wrinkling and tearing. The forming process parameters of sheet hydroforming includes pressure, blank holder force, sheet thickness, etc. Although most hydroforming operations are kept under 1000 bar, pressure intensification systems on high pressure hydroforming equipment can reach pressures ranging from 1000 to 4000 bar. Exceeding 4000 bar is possible, but it reduces the equipment's service life while drastically increasing its complexity [6,7]. Blank holding force (BHF) will depend on the magnitude of the fluid pressure and the area of the blank in contact with the blank holder. It should be noted that in sheet hydroforming, the area of the blank in contact with the blank holder continuously decreases, and so, proper BHF is required to avoid wrinkling and rupture [8]. Sheet thickness influences formability and forming limits [9].

Improved formability in hydroforming is primarily caused by more evenly distributed strain, which results in less thinning at the corners [10]. In all forming operations using sheet metal as an input material, it is critical to understand the conditions that cause necking (instability of material) or fracture. Such limits can be represented as a forming limit diagram (FLD) shown in Figure 2, which plots the curve of major and minor strain coordinates [11]. The strain in the direction of the maximum strain is defined as the major strain. The strain perpendicular to the major strain is known as the minor strain. The major strain is always positive and is plotted vertically, while the minor strain is plotted horizontally [12]. The combinations of major and minor strains lying below the forming limit curve (FLC) define a safe operating region and failure is represented by the region above the FLC. FLD offers a useful summary. Formability helps to quickly identify key areas that need additional investigation, especially for early feasibility studies.

As the experimental procedure for the metal forming process is costly and time-consuming, the finite element method (FEM) has the advantage of lowering production costs by predicting part defects such as spring-back, rupture, wrinkling, buckling, and shape errors, as well as optimizing process parameters [13].

Design of experiments (DOE) approaches were used to maximize response variables in the presence of multiple factors. DOE is the process of using geometric concepts to statistical sampling in order to produce desired outputs. The DOE's primary goal is to obtain the desired response with the fewest possible trials because conducting fewer experiments results in a reduction in the cost and time needed to carry out the experiments [14].

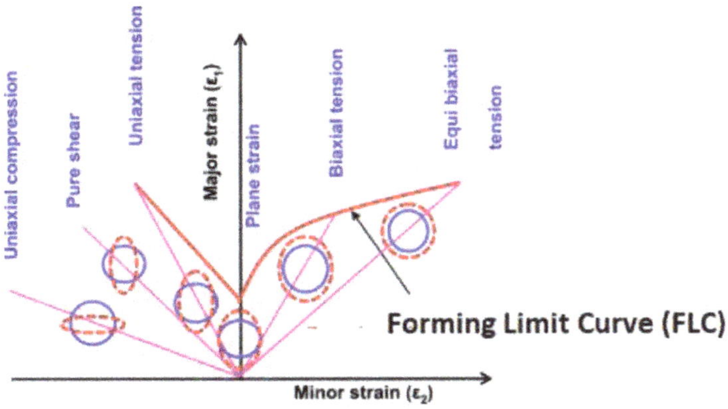

Figure 2. The Schematic of Forming Limit Diagram.

Nickel alloys are long-lasting materials known for their ability to operate at extremely high temperatures for extended periods of time. Nickel-based superalloys with outstanding high-temperature tensile strength, improved oxidation resistance, weldability, fatigue resistance, corrosion resistance, and long-term structural stability were used in high-temperature parts of aeroengines and industrial gas turbines [15]. Single crystal superalloys based on nickel have outstanding high-temperature mechanical properties and are commonly employed as turbine blade materials in current aviation gas turbine engines [16]. Although strong, nickel alloys are also relatively ductile, allowing them to be formed using a variety of different processes, although at higher pressures than other metals [17]. Nimonic 90, an nickel alloy, is an ideal material to use in aircraft parts, exhaust nozzles, and gas turbine components where the pressure and heat are extreme [18]. Nimonic 90 has high strength at high temperature levels, and it is highly resistant to scaling, oxidation, heat, and corrosion [19].

Existing studies lack in hydroforming Nimonic 90 sheet. The aim of this study is to propose an FEA model for formability analysis in the hydroforming of Nimonic 90 sheets. The following objectives will help to achieve this goal:

- Derivation of FEA model for sheet hydroforming;
- Validation of FEA result with experimentation;
- Evaluation of forming limit diagram;
- Determination of optimum process parameters for hydroforming of Nimonic 90 sheet;
- Discussion of the FEA model's accuracy.

In this present study, first, mechanical properties of Nimonic 90 sheet were obtained by uniaxial tensile test as per the standard ASTM E8/E8M. Secondly, finite element method (FEM) simulation of the process was run to obtain the maximum pressure and blank holder force and was compared to experimental results. Thirdly, Box–Behnken design (BBD) of response surface methodology (RSM) was used to design the experiments by using lower and higher levels of variable parameters. Fourthly, FEM simulations were carried out as per the design of experiments (DOE). Fifthly, the impact of process factors (Pressure, Blank Holder Force, and Sheet Thickness) during the hydroforming of Nimonic 90 sheets was analyzed using RSM. Sixth, RSM optimizer was used to predict the optimized process parameter to achieve maximized response (deformation) without failure (crack or wrinkling). Lastly, a validation experiment was conducted, and the findings were discussed.

2. Material and Methodology

In this section, details of material properties, computer-aided design (CAD) modeling, FEM simulation, experimentation DOE, and optimization are discussed.

2.1. Material and Its Properties

In this study, the material used was Nimonic 90. The material was tested in the AUM Meta Lab, Mumbai, India, to obtain the chemical composition that is illustrated in Table 1.

Table 1. Composition of Nimonic 90.

Ni	Cr	Co	Ti	Al	Fe	Mn	Si	Cu	C	P	S
Bal	18.65	16.7	2.37	1.38	0.98	0.67	0.34	0.085	0.082	0.008	0.007

Uniaxial tensile tests were carried out as per the standard ASTM E8/E8M as shown in Figure 3. The specimens were cut using electrical discharge machining, as shown in Figure 4.

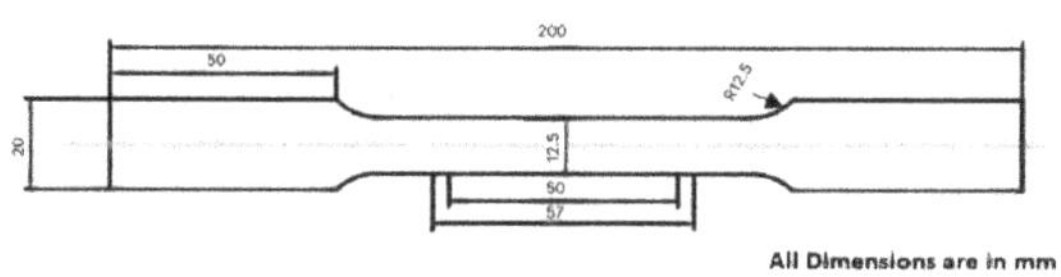

Figure 3. Schematic of tensile test specimen.

Figure 4. Tensile Test Specimen.

The mechanical properties of the Nimonic 90 sheet as determined from the tensile test are given in Table 2. True stress (σ_t) and True strain (ε_t) [20] were calculated using Equation (1).

$$\sigma_t = \sigma_e\,(1 + \varepsilon_e), \text{ and } \varepsilon_t = \ln(1 + \varepsilon_e), \tag{1}$$

where σ_e is Engineering stress and ε_e is Engineering strain.

Table 2. Mechanical Properties of Nimonic 90.

Material Properties	Value
Yield stress (0.2%)	587 MPa
Young's Modulus	105.95 GPa
Poisson's Ratio	0.28
Ultimate Tensile Stress	1271 MPa
Strain Hardening Exponent at *n* value	0.30398
Strength Coefficient at *n* value	1555.36974

The multilinear points of the stress–strain curve can be obtained using Ramberg–Osgood equation [21]. Where ε is strain, E is Young's modulus, σ is stress, σ_y is yield strength, and n is strain-hardening coefficient

$$\varepsilon = \frac{\sigma}{E} + 0.002\left(\frac{\sigma}{\sigma y}\right)^{(1/n)} \tag{2}$$

This Ramberg–Osgood equation shown in Equation (2) was used to approximate the non-linear relationship between strain and stress.

2.2. *CAD Modeling and Finite Element Simulation*

2.2.1. CAD Modeling

In this study, Autodesk Fusion 360 software was used to model components as shell elements for FEA simulations, as shown in Figure 5 Shell elements were used in FEA to achieve better results, because they allowed modelling of narrow features with fewer mesh components [22], and computational time was reduced. As per the approximation model shown in Figure 6, thin shell approximation was applied in this model as the ratio between thickness and length (h/L Chart) was within 0.3 [23].

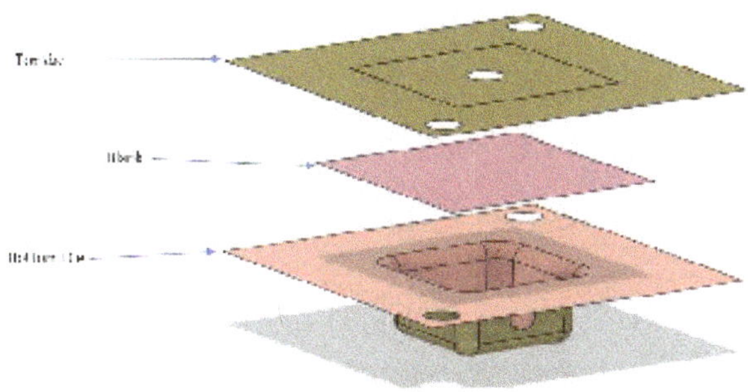

Figure 5. CAD model.

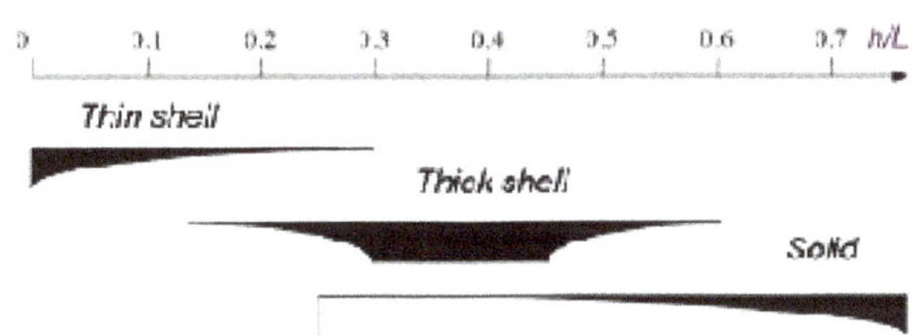

Figure 6. h/L Chart.

Thickness of all surface components were assigned in FEA simulation. Dimensions of all components used in CAD modeling are shown in Table 3. The die corner radius should be greater than four times the material thickness [24].

Table 3. Dimensions of Die and Sheet.

Component	Dimension (mm)
Top Die	100 × 100
Bottom Die	100 × 100
Sheet	65 × 65
Sheet Thickness	0.8, 1 and 1.2
Die Cavity	38 × 38 × 20

2.2.2. Development of Finite Element Model

To input the properties of Nimonic 90, two regions, elastic and plastic regions, were considered. The elastic properties were assigned as listed in Table 2 and true stress and true strain of the plastic region of the material were given as per Figure 7.

Meshing was carried out using Ansys Mechanical. The elements used for meshing were quadrilateral elements as they produced far smoother surfaces than triangular elements, as triangular elements frequently produced visible anomalies on the surface [25]. All the free elements were set to quad type and the element size was 2 mm. Some of the critical areas such as the blank surface, fillets, and corner surfaces were defined with smaller element sizes of 1 mm using the face sizing option. Figure 8a–c shows the FEA mesh model. Once the mesh was generated, it was exported in STL format to LS Dyna. In this work, mesh refinement for convergence study was performed. Simulations were run for various mesh refinement stages.

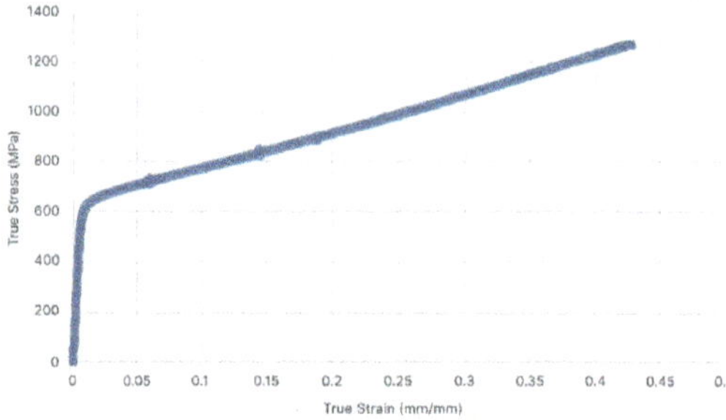

Figure 7. True Stress—True Strain Curve of Nimonic 90.

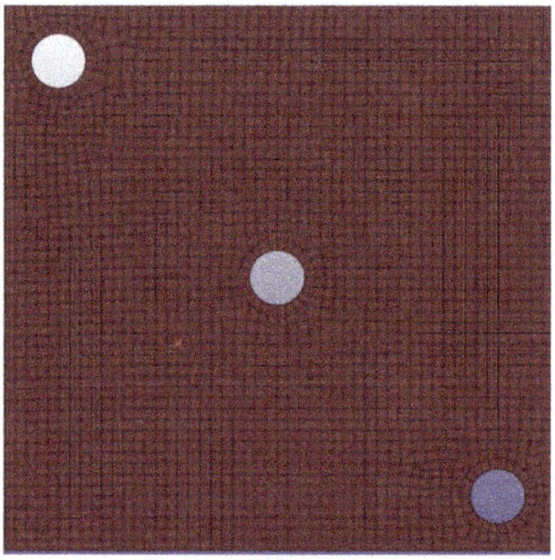

(a)

(b)

Figure 8. *Cont.*

(c)

Figure 8. (**a**) FEA mesh model of top die. (**b**) FEA mesh model of bottom die. (**c**) FEA mesh model of sheet.

2.3. Development of Experiment Model

To validate the outcomes of numerical simulations and identify the optimum process parameters, experimental work was carried out using a 100-ton hydraulic press, as shown in Figure 9, and 1000 bar pressure pump.

Figure 9. Hydraulic Press.

The dies shown in Figures 10 and 11 were made of P20 tool steel material which has a high degree of resistance to the deformation [26].The top plate and the bottom plate were attached to the respective dies with M8 bolts, which allowed the die to be clamped with the hydraulic press. The dimension of die and sheet used are given in Table 3. The specimen, Nimonic 90, was cut as per the dimension shown in Figure 12 using a laser cutting machine.

Figure 10. Top Die with Plate.

Figure 11. Bottom Die with Plate.

Figure 12. Specimen-Nimonic 90.

The validation experiment was conducted for maximum pressure and for the optimum process parameters that were obtained using an RSM optimizer.

Since the finite element simulation was validated using the experimental model and it was in the permissible limit, the same was proceeded with in the design of experiments approach.

2.4. Design of Experiments

The Box–Behnken design (BBD) of RSM was used in this study to analyze the regression model and determine the effects of variable parameters on the outputs. In the present study, three processing parameters including pressure (Pr), blank holder force (BHF), and thickness (T) of sheet were considered and their effects on the deformation without failure were investigated using RSM. The experiments were designed in accordance with the BBD by using lower and higher levels of variable parameters, procuring 15 experiments to run using Minitab software. Table 4 illustrates the conditions under which the simulations were performed.

Table 4. BBD- Design of Experiments.

Std Order	Run Order	Pt Type	Blocks	Pressure (MPa)	BHF (kN)	Thickness (mm)
14	1	0	1	40	180	1
4	2	2	1	50	220	1
12	3	2	1	40	220	1.2
1	4	2	1	30	140	1
3	5	2	1	30	220	1
15	6	0	1	40	180	1
6	7	2	1	50	180	0.8
8	8	2	1	50	180	1.2
9	9	2	1	40	140	0.8
10	10	2	1	40	220	0.8
11	11	2	1	40	140	1.2
13	12	0	1	40	180	1
7	13	2	1	30	180	1.2
2	14	2	1	50	140	1
5	15	2	1	30	180	0.8

The primary goal of RSM was to achieve an optimal response through a series of designed experiments. In most cases, the RSM regression model was a quadratic full equation [13] as Equation (3), where y is the response variable. Additionally, α_0, α_1, α_2, and α_3 are constant, linear, quadratic, and interaction coefficients, respectively. Additionally, x_i and x_j are the independent variables and E is the statistical error. The effectiveness of the regression model was then assessed using R^2 as Equation (3), which can be obtained from ANOVA.

$$y = \alpha 0 + \sum_{i=0}^{n} \alpha 1 \text{ xi} + \sum_{i=0}^{n} \alpha 0 \text{ xi}^2 + \sum_{i=0}^{n}\sum_{i=0}^{n} \alpha 3 \text{ xixj} + E \quad (3)$$

$$R^2 = 1 - \frac{S_r}{S_t} \quad (4)$$

3. Results and Discussion

Figure 13 shows the analysis result of maximum pressure for failure. The simulation result for maximum pressure was validated using experimentation. Figure 14 represents the validation result of maximum pressure for failure during hydroforming.

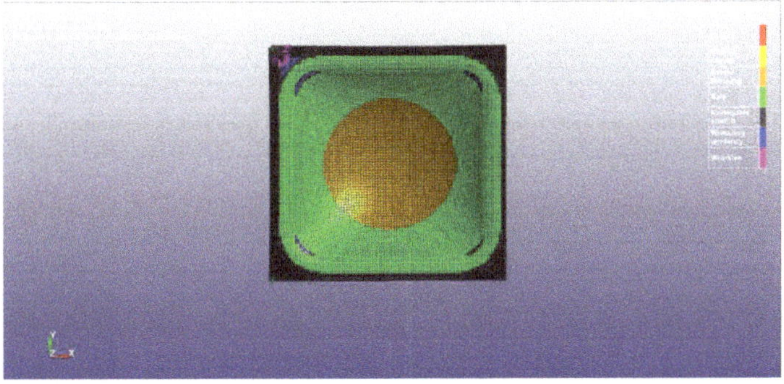

Figure 13. FEA analysis for maximum pressure.

Figure 14. Experimentation result for maximum pressure.

Table 5 represents the maximum pressure obtained during hydroforming in FEA simulation and experimentation. Then, the finite element simulation process was carried out under different conditions according to the design of experiments (Table 4), and the response variable, i.e., deformation (De), was obtained, as shown in Table 6. Forming limit diagram obtained using LSdyna, as shown in Figure 15, depicts the major and minor strain of Nimonic 90 in hydroforming. Strain combinations over the FLC will result in fracture, whereas those below the wrinkling limit line will result in wrinkles. For a fixed minor strain, a larger gap between the FLC and wrinkling limit lines signifies more potential for forming [27]. In Figure 15, the gap between the FLC and wrinkling limit line was more, the Nimonic 90 sheet was more suitable for forming.

Table 5. Maximum Pressure obtained by FEA Simulation and Experiment.

	Maximum Pressure (MPa)	Percentage Error (%)
FEA Simulation	53.46	5.53
Experimentation	50.5	

Table 6. Deformation results obtained from FEA Simulation.

	Inputs			Output
Run Order	Pr (MPa)	BHF (kN)	T (mm)	De (mm)
1	40	180	1	7.88
2	50	220	1	9.62
3	40	220	1.2	6.65
4	30	140	1	6.19
5	30	220	1	6.16
6	40	180	1	7.88
7	50	180	0.8	11.9
8	50	180	1.2	8.11
9	40	140	0.8	9.7
10	40	220	0.8	9.66
11	40	140	1.2	6.68
12	40	180	1	7.88
13	30	180	1.2	5.27
14	50	140	1	9.65
15	30	180	0.8	7.52

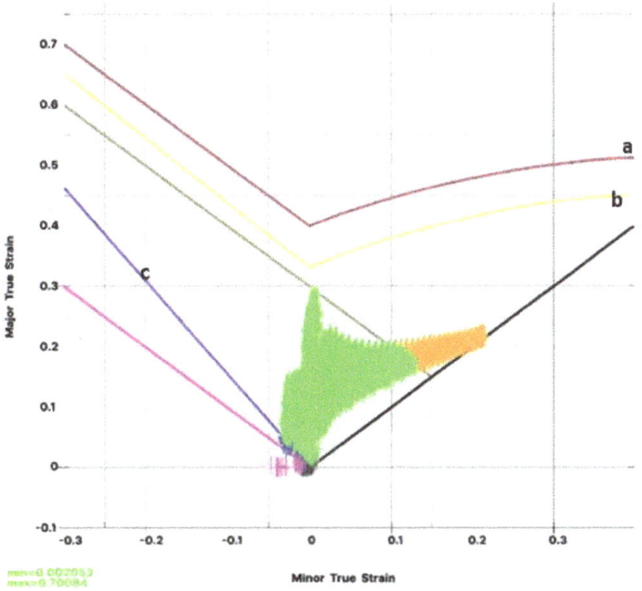

Figure 15. Forming Limit Diagram for Nimonic 90 Safe Severe thinning. (**a**) Forming limit curve (FLC), (**b**) Risk of Failure. (**c**) Wrinkling limit line.

The ANOVA analysis yielded regression models for estimating the value of deformation (De) for Nimonic 90 as Equation (5).

$$\begin{aligned} De = 8.52 + 0.3483 \times Pr - 0.00044 \times BHF - 14.59 \times T + 0.000262 \times Pr \times Pr - 0.000001 \times BHF \times BHF \\ + 7.344 \times T \times T - 0.000000 \times Pr \times BHF - 0.1925 \times Pr \times T + 0.00031 \times BHF \times T \end{aligned} \quad (5)$$

During this study, a confirmatory experiment was carried out to validate the optimized RSM solutions. Figure 16 shows the deformed Nimonic 90 sheet. Table 7 compares the predicted and experimental results of the response (deformation) in the formability of Nimonic 90. The table shows that the error percentage between predicted and experimental results was less than 5%.

Figure 16. Deformed Nimonic 90 sheet for optimized parameter.

Table 7. Confirmatory test results.

Process Parameter			Predicted Deformation (mm)	Experimental Deformation (mm)	Percentage Error (%)
Pressure (MPa)	BHF (kN)	T (mm)			
42.32	144.04	0.8	10.199	9.72	4.92

ANOVA (analysis of variance) generally helps to understand the influence of independent input parameters on dependent output parameter(s). ANOVA helps the users to prove cause and effect relationships in various forms such as R^2 value, pareto chart, *p*-values, etc. Here, the Pareto chart shown in Figure 17 depicts the standardized effects of input parameters on output parameter (i.e., deformation). The R^2 value for the present regression model of deformation regarding formability of Nimonic 90 was greater than 95%, indicating the authenticity of model [17]. Furthermore, according to Table 8, the *p* value for most of the input terms were less than 0.05, implying that these terms had a significant influence on the value of deformation in the sheet [28].

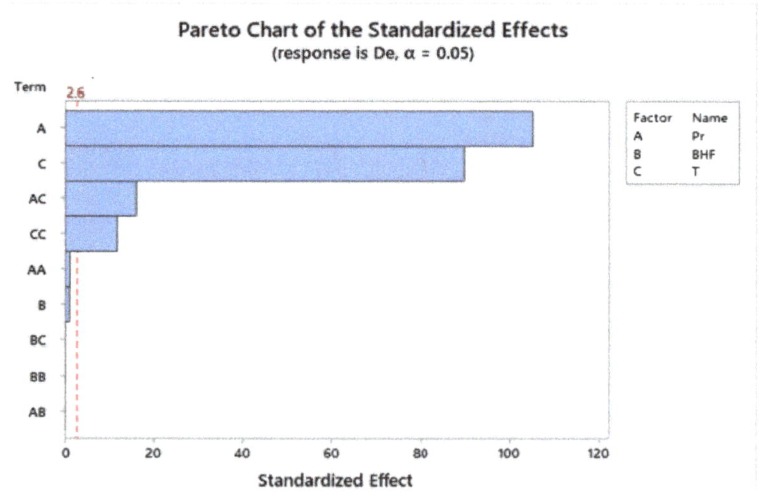

Figure 17. Pareto chart.

Table 8. ANOVA results for each coefficient for deformation.

Coefficient of Regression Model	*p*-Value
Model	0.000
Linear	0.000
Pr	0.000
BHF	0.378
T	0.000
Square	0.000
Pr × Pr	0.337
BHF × BHF	0.962
T × T	0.000
2-Way Interaction	0.000
Pr × BHF	1.000
Pr × T	0.000
BHF × T	0.920

Figure 18 shows the optimized process parameter achieved in RSM optimizer. In experimental validation, the error percentage between experimental and simulation was less than 10%. This indicates that the proposed simulation model is capable of making accurate predictions [28,29]. Figure 19 shows the mesh convergence study.

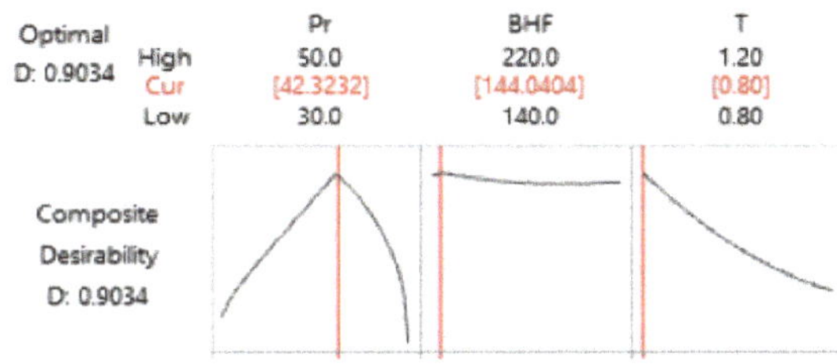

Figure 18. Optimized parameters.

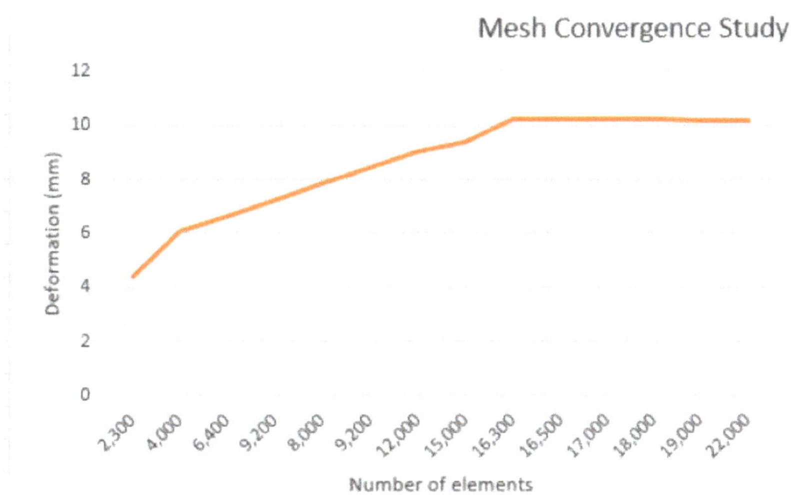

Figure 19. Mesh Convergence Study.

4. Conclusions

In this study, a finite element simulation of formability of Nimonic 90 in sheet hydroforming for investigating required pressure, blank holder force, and thickness reductions was conducted. The main conclusions from this study can be concisely summarized as follows.

- The Nimonic 90 sheet tested showed good formability. The formability was higher in the plane strain and biaxial tension condition compared to the tension–compression condition;
- The fluid pressure in sheet hydroforming caused the sheet to stretch in the flange area, forcing strains above the wrinkling limit curve in the forming limit diagram (FLD);
- Since the FLD indicated no failure zone, these process parameter values were acceptable;
- As p value in the two-way interaction between pressure and thickness was less than 0.05, it was vital in achieving maximum deformation;
- Based on finite element analysis and verified experiments, BHF of 144.04 kN, pressure of 42.32 MPa, and sheet thickness of 0.8 mm were the key parameters to prevent wrinkling under the forming state for achieving the maximum deformation;

- The statistical results revealed that the models proposed in analysis had a high accuracy to estimate the optimum pressure, blank holder force, and thickness for achieving maximum deformation in formability of Nimonic 90 sheets in sheet hydroforming;
- The results demonstrated that the most effective parameters on deformation were pressure and thickness;
- The proposed FEA model is capable of accurate predictions, as the error percentage between the experiment and simulation was less than 5%

Future research will include unconventional optimization techniques to predict the optimum process parameters for better formability and applying the same methodology for different super alloys and different shapes that are more complex. An optimization code will be utilized to create the multiple response optimization for hydroforming complex automotive parts.

Author Contributions: F.A.A.J. designed and performed the FEA and optimization; P.C. was responsible for the tensile test, experimentation study, and behavior study. All authors have read and agreed to the published version of the manuscript.

Funding: This research received no external funding and the APC was funded by the authors.

Data Availability Statement: The data presented in this study are available on request from the corresponding author.

Conflicts of Interest: The authors declare no conflict of interest.

References

1. Bell, C.; Corney, J.; Zuelli, N.; Savings, D. A state of the art review of hydroforming technology: Its applications, research areas, history, and future in manufacturing. *Int. J. Mater. Form.* **2020**, *13*, 789–828. [CrossRef]
2. Pavithra, E.; Kumar, V.S.S. Hydroforming developments: Insights of other researchers. In *Proceedings of the Applied Mechanics and Materials*; Trans Tech Publications Ltd.: Zurich, Switzerland, 2012; Volume 110–116, pp. 1748–1752.
3. Bakhshi-Jooybari, M.; Gorji, A.; Elyasi, M. Developments in Sheet Hydroforming for Complex Industrial Parts. In *Metal Forming-Process, Tools, Design*; InTech: Houston TX, USA, 2012.
4. Oh, S.I.; Jeon, B.H.; Kim, H.Y.; Yang, J.B. Applications of hydroforming processes to automobile parts. *J. Mater. Process. Technol.* **2006**, *174*, 42–55. [CrossRef]
5. Hu, H.; Wang, J.-F.; Fan, K.-T.; Chen, T.; Wang, S.-Y. Development of sheet hydroforming for making an automobile fuel tank. *Proc. Inst. Mech. Eng. Part B J. Eng. Manuf.* **2015**, *229*, 654–663. [CrossRef]
6. Bell, C.; Dixon, C.; Blood, B.; Corney, J.; Savings, D.; Jump, E.; Zuelli, N. Enabling sheet hydroforming to produce smaller radii on aerospace nickel alloys. *Int. J. Mater. Form.* **2019**, *12*, 761–776. [CrossRef]
7. Gürün, H.; Karaağaç, İ. The Experimental Investigation of Effects of Multiple Parameters on the Formability of the DC01 Sheet Metal. *Strojniški Vestn.-J. Mech. Eng.* **2015**, *61*, 651–662. [CrossRef]
8. Abedrabbo, N.; Zampaloni, M.A.; Pourboghrat, F. Wrinkling control in aluminum sheet hydroforming. *Int. J. Mech. Sci.* **2005**, *47*, 333–358. [CrossRef]
9. Anand, D.; Ravi Kumar, D. Effect of Sheet Thickness and Grain Size on Forming Limit Diagrams of Thin Brass Sheets. In *Innovations in Infrastructure*; Springer: Berlin/Heidelberg, Germany, 2019; pp. 435–444. [CrossRef]
10. Feyissa, F.T.; Kumar, D.R. Enhancement of drawability of cryorolled AA5083 alloy sheets by hydroforming. *J. Mater. Res. Technol.* **2019**, *8*, 411–423. [CrossRef]
11. Rubešová, K.; Rund, M.; Rzepa, S.; Jirková, H.; Jeníček, Š.; Urbánek, M.; Kučerová, L.; Konopík, P. Determining Forming Limit Diagrams Using Sub-Sized Specimen Geometry and Comparing FLD Evaluation Methods. *Metals* **2021**, *11*, 484. [CrossRef]
12. Uijl, N.J.D.; Carless, L.J. Advanced metal-forming technologies for automotive applications. In *Advanced Materials in Automotive Engineering*; Elsevier: Amsterdam, The Netherlands, 2012; pp. 28–56. [CrossRef]
13. Kahhal, P.; Ahmadi Brooghani, S.Y.; Deilami Azodi , H. Multi-objective optimization of sheet metal forming die using FEA coupled with RSM. *J. Mech. Sci. Technol.* **2013**, *27*, 3835–3842. [CrossRef]
14. Hasan Nejad, S.J.; Hasanzadeh, R.; Doniavi, A.; Modanloo, V. Finite element simulation analysis of laminated sheets in deep drawing process using response surface method. *Int. J. Adv. Manuf. Technol.* **2017**, *93*, 3245–3259. [CrossRef]
15. Ma, K.; Wang, J. Microstructural Characteristics and Mechanical Properties of an Additively Manufactured Nickel-Based Superalloy. *Crystals* **2022**, *12*, 1358. [CrossRef]
16. Feng, Z.; Wen, Z.; Lu, G.; Zhao, Y. Influence of Cooling Scenarios on the Evolution of Microstructures in Nickel-Based Single Crystal Superalloys. *Crystals* **2022**, *12*, 74. [CrossRef]
17. Horke, K.; Meyer, A.; Singer, R.F. Metal injection molding (MIM) of nickel-base superalloys. In *Handbook of Metal Injection Molding*; Elsevier: Amsterdam, The Netherlands, 2019; pp. 575–608. [CrossRef]

18. Madderla Sandhya, D.; Ramasamy, I.K.; Anil, K.S.; Chandramouli, G.; Vinod, K. Optimization of process parameters in machining of nimonic super-alloy on EDM using genetic algorithm. *Maejo Int. J. Energy Environ. Commun.* **2020**, *2*, 35–44. [CrossRef]
19. Henry Wiggin & Company Ltd. NIMONIC 90: Heat and Corrosion Resistant Nickel-Base Alloy. *Alloy Dig.* **1961**, *10*, Ni-6. [CrossRef]
20. Arasaratnam, P.; Sivakumaran, K.S.; Tait, M.J. True Stress-True Strain Models for Structural Steel Elements. *ISRN Civ. Eng.* **2011**, *2011*, 1–11. [CrossRef]
21. Lanzagorta, J.L.; Martín-Meizoso, A. 3-Point Bending of Bars and Rods Made of Materials Obeying a Ramberg-Osgood Criterion. *World J. Mech.* **2011**, *1*, 71–77. [CrossRef]
22. Nakasumi, S.; Suzuki, K.; Ohtsubo, H.; Fujii, D. Mixed analysis of shell and solid elements using overlaying mesh method. *J. Soc. Nav. Archit. Japan* **2001**, *2001*, 219–224. [CrossRef]
23. Akin, J.E. *Finite Element Analysis Concepts: Via SolidWorks*; Rice University: Houston, TX, USA, 2010; p. 348. [CrossRef]
24. SCHULER GmbH. Sheet metal forming and blanking. In *Metal Forming Handbook*; Springer: Berlin/Heidelberg, Germany, 1998; pp. 123–404. [CrossRef]
25. Docampo-Sanchez, J.; Haimes, R. Towards fully regular quad mesh generation. In Proceedings of the AIAA Scitech 2019 Forum, San Diego, CA, USA, 7–11 January 2019; American Institute of Aeronautics and Astronautics: Reston, Virginia, 2019. [CrossRef]
26. Priyadarshini, M.; Behera, A.; Biswas, C.K.; Rajak, D.K. Experimental Analysis and Mechanical Characterization of AISI P20 Tool Steel through Heat-Treatment Process. *J. Bio-Tribo-Corrosion* **2022**, *8*, 3. [CrossRef]
27. Narayanasamy, R.; Narayanan, C.S. Forming, fracture and wrinkling limit diagram for if steel sheets of different thickness. *Mater. Des.* **2008**, *29*, 1467–1475. [CrossRef]
28. Foster, F.D.; Smith, T.; Whaley, R.E. Assessing Goodness-Of-Fit of Asset Pricing Models: The Distribution of the Maximal R 2. *J. Financ.* **1997**, *52*, 591. [CrossRef]
29. Jankovic, A.; Chaudhary, G.; Goia, F. Designing the design of experiments (DOE)—An investigation on the influence of different factorial designs on the characterization of complex systems. *Energy Build.* **2021**, *250*, 111298. [CrossRef]

mathematics

MDPI

Article

Magnetohydrodynamics Williamson Nanofluid Flow over an Exponentially Stretching Surface with a Chemical Reaction and Thermal Radiation

Hillary Muzara [1] and Stanford Shateyi [2,*]

[1] Department of Mathematics and Computational Sciences, University of Zimbabwe, Mt. Pleasant, Harare P.O. Box MP167, Zimbabwe; hmuzara@science.uz.ac.zw

[2] Department of Mathematical and Computational Sciences, University of Venda, P. Bag X5050, Thohoyandou 0950, South Africa

* Correspondence: stanford.shateyi@univen.ac.za

Abstract: Presented in this current study is the numerical analysis of magnetohydrodynamics Williamson nanofluid flow over an exponentially stretching surface. The most important aspect of the investigation is that the effects of the magnetic field, chemical reaction and thermal radiation in the fluid flow are taken into account. The partial differential equations governing the present Williamson nanofluid flow problem were observed to be highly nonlinear and coupled. Suitable similarity transformations were used to transmute the coupled system of nonlinear partial differential equations governing the fluid flow into a linear system. The linear system was solved numerically using the spectral quasi-linearization method. The MATLAB bvp4c numerical technique and a comparison with existing results for the skin friction coefficient were used to confirm the appropriateness of the method in solving the current problem. The influence of some pertinent physical parameters on the fluid's velocity, temperature and concentration profiles were displayed graphically. The effects of all the physical parameters on the skin friction coefficient, Nusselt number and Sherwood number were portrayed in a tabular form. It was noted that enhancing the thermal radiation parameter reduces the fluid's temperature, Nusselt number and the skin friction coefficient, while the Sherwood number is improved.

Keywords: magnetohydrodynamics; Williamson nanofluid; quasi-linearization; chemical reaction; thermal radiation

MSC: 65N12; 76M22; 76M25; 80M25

Citation: Muzara, H.; Shateyi, S. Magnetohydrodynamics Williamson Nanofluid Flow over an Exponentially Stretching Surface with a Chemical Reaction and Thermal Radiation. *Mathematics* **2023**, *11*, 2740. https://doi.org/10.3390/math11122740

Academic Editors: Zhuojia Fu, Yiqian He and Hui Zheng

Received: 29 April 2023
Revised: 5 June 2023
Accepted: 13 June 2023
Published: 16 June 2023

1. Introduction

Non-Newtonian fluids occur most often in industrial and engineering applications. The rheological properties of the non-Newtonian fluids cannot be explained using the famous Navier–Stokes equations. As a consequence, a number of models have been used to describe the characteristics of non-Newtonian fluids. These models include the Ellis model [1], Carreaus model [2], power law model [3], Cross model [4] and Casson model [5], to mention but a few. One special type of non-Newtonian model is the Williamson model [6], which was proposed to describe the flow of pseudoplastic materials. The boundary layer flow of the pseudoplastic materials has found applications in bio-engineering, chemical and nuclear industry, material processing and geophysics.

In fluid dynamics, Sakiadis [7] was the first researcher to study the boundary layer flow over a continuous stretching surface. An inaguaral study of fluid flow of Blasius type past a stretching surface was initiated by Crane [8]. The study of fluid flow over a stretching sheet has been a subject of interest in recent years due to its significant importance in areas such as metallurgical processes, polymer extrusion, plastic films, metal spinning, etc. There are quite a number of studies that have been performed on fluid flow past a stretching sheet, i.e., [9–13], among others.

In thermal engineering, the enhancement of the thermal characteristics of heat transfer fluids is a priority. The thermal conductivity and heat transfer qualities of the base fluid can be improved by dispersing nanosized (1–100 nm) solid particles into the fluid. These nanoparticles are usually metals, carbon nanotubes, oxides or carbines. The enhancement of heat transfer in fluids as a result of dispersing ultra-fine particles was first reported by Masuda et al. [14]. The term 'nanofluid', a fluid that contains dispersed nanoparticles, was introduced by Choi and Eastman [15]. A significant number of studies have been carried out on nanofluids, which inlcude the works by Elboughdiri et al. [16], Ashraf et al. [17], Nabwey et al. [18], Selimefendigil et al. [19] and Lou et al. [20].

Alfven [21] was the first to study the magnetic properties and the characteristics of fluids that are electrical conductors. Typical examples of such magnetofluids include electrolytes, plasmas, salt water and liquid metals. There has been growing interest in studying the MHD Williamson nanofluid. Abbas et al. [22] investigated the effects of heat generation and viscous dissipation on an MHD Williamson nanofluid that flows past a linear stretching sheet in a porous medium. The characteristics of MHD flow and heat transfer of a Williamson nanofluid flowing past a stretching sheet were examined by Reddy et al. [23]. Shawky et al. [24] used the Runge–Kutta method to analyze the heat and mass transfer of magnetohydrodynamic Williamson nanofluid flowing over a stretching sheet. The influence of Joule heating, heat generation/absorption, thermal radiation and chemical reaction on the MHD Williamson nanofluid flow over a stretching sheet through a porous medium was investigated by Bouslimi et al. [25]. Other notable works on the MHD Williamson nanofluid are [26–33], among others.

This current study mainly focuses on the Williamson nanofluid flow past an exponentially stretching surface with a chemical reaction and thermal radiation. This study has many applications in engineering and industrial processes. The Williamson fluid model with a chemical reaction has applications in water and air pollution, atmospheric flows and in chemical engineering problems such as food processes. Thermal radiation has applications in processes such as drying and distribution of temperature and moisture over agricultural fields [34]. Nadeen and Hussain [35] used the homotopy analysis method to explore heat transfer effects on Williamson nanofluid flow over a porous exponentially stretching sheet. The Runge–Kutta–Fehlberg method was used to study the MHD flow of a Williamson nanofluid flow over an exponentially stretching surface by Kumar et al. [34]. Two cases of heat transfer, PEST and PEHF, were investigated on an MHD Williamson nanofluid flow over an exponentially stretching surface by Ahmed and Akbar [36]. Temperature-dependent viscosity and thermal conductivity in a Williamson nanofluid flow over an exponentially stretching sheet were studied by Amjad et al. [37]. Li et al. [38] used MATLAB's bvp4c package to analyze heat and mass transfer in MHD Williamson nanofluid flow over an exponentially porous stretching surface.

Based on the aforementioned studies, it can be noted that there are many studies that have been performed on the Williamson nanofluid flow past an exponentially stretching surface. The novelty of this current study is the addition of thermophoresis and Brownian motion effects in the momentum equation. Additionally, the effects of the magnetic field, thermal radiation, chemical reaction, heat source and injection/suction parameters are simultaneously investigated in this model. The highly non-linear partial differential equations that govern the Williamson nanofluid flow are reduced into non-linear ordinary differential equations using suitable similarity transformations and then solved using the spectral quasi-linearization method (SQLM), developed by Motsa et al. [39]. The effects of some chosen pertinent parameters on the fluid velocity, temperature, concentration, skin friction coefficient, heat transfer rate and mass transfer rate were displayed using graphs and tables. The numerical results obtained in this current research work were validated by comparing the present results with those from MATLAB's bvp4c routine and those results from already-published work. A very good agreement was established.

2. Fluid Model

The Williamson fluid model is used to describe the rheological behaviour of pseudoplastic materials over a wide range of shear stresses and shear rates. The continuity and momentum equations of an incompressible Williamson model are given, respectively, by [40]:

$$div\mathbf{V} = 0, \tag{1}$$

$$\rho_f \frac{d\mathbf{V}}{dt} = div\mathbf{S} + \rho_f \mathbf{b}, \tag{2}$$

where $\frac{d}{dt}$ is the time derivative and $\mathbf{b}$ is the specific body force vector. The Cauchy stress tensor $S = -pI + \tau^*$, [41], where p is the pressure term and I the identity vector. The extra stress tensor is given by:

$$\tau^* = \left(\mu_\infty + \frac{\mu_0 - \mu_\infty}{1 - \Gamma\dot{\gamma}}\right) A_1,$$

where the respective viscosities at zero and infinity shear rate are μ_0 and μ_∞, respectively. The terms A_1 and Γ are the first Revlin–Ericksen tensor and time constant, respectively. Additionally:

$$\dot{\gamma} = \sqrt{\frac{\pi}{2}}, \; \pi = \text{trace}(A_1^2).$$

Choosing $\mu_\infty = 0$ and $\Gamma\dot{\gamma} < 1$ and applying the Binomial expansion, we have the extra stress tensor $\tau^* = \mu_0[1 + \Gamma\dot{\gamma}]A_1$.

3. Mathematical Analysis

Investigated in this current study is a two-dimensional flow of a steady incompressible Williamson nanofluid over a sheet that stretches exponentially. In this flow problem, the coordinate system is chosen in such a way that the x axis is along the stretching sheet and the y axis is measured normal to the sheet. At $y = 0$, the sheet is assumed to be stretching with a velocity $U_w = U_0 e^{\frac{x}{l}}$. The variable magnetic field $B(x) = B_0 e^{\frac{x}{2l}}$ (B_0 is a constant magnetic field) is applied perpendicular to the direction of flow. At the sheet, the fluid has temperature $T_w = T_\infty + T_0 e^{\frac{x}{2l}}$ and nanoparticle fraction $C_w = C_\infty + C_0 e^{\frac{x}{2l}}$. The ambient values of temperature and nanoparticle fraction, far way from the sheet, are denoted by T_∞ and C_∞, respectively. Figure 1 displays the schematic flow diagram and the coordinate system of the problem. Assuming that there is no pressure gradient and applying boundary layer approximations, the continuity, momentum and energy equations governing the flow are given by [25,40]:

$$\frac{\partial u}{\partial x} + \frac{\partial v}{\partial y} = 0, \tag{3}$$

$$u\frac{\partial u}{\partial x} + v\frac{\partial u}{\partial y} = \nu\frac{\partial}{\partial y}\left\{\frac{\partial u}{\partial y} + \frac{\Gamma}{\sqrt{2}}\left(\frac{\partial u}{\partial y}\right)^2\right\} + g\beta_T(T - T_\infty) + g\beta_C(C - C_\infty) - \frac{\sigma B^2}{\rho_f}u, \tag{4}$$

$$u\frac{\partial T}{\partial x} + v\frac{\partial T}{\partial y} = \alpha\frac{\partial^2 T}{\partial y^2} + \frac{Q}{(\rho c_p)_f}(T - T_\infty) + \tau\left\{D_B\frac{\partial T}{\partial y}\frac{\partial C}{\partial y} + \frac{D_T}{T_\infty}\left(\frac{\partial T}{\partial y}\right)^2\right\} - \frac{1}{(\rho c_p)_f}\frac{\partial q_r}{\partial y}, \tag{5}$$

$$u\frac{\partial C}{\partial x} + v\frac{\partial C}{\partial y} = D_B\frac{\partial^2 C}{\partial y^2} + \frac{D_T}{T_\infty}\frac{\partial^2 T}{\partial y^2} - K(C - C_\infty), \tag{6}$$

where u and v are the fluid velocity components in the x and y directions, respectively, ν is the kinematic viscosity of the fluid, g is the acceleration due to gravity, β_T is the thermal expansion coefficient, β_C is the concentration expansion coefficient, σ is the electrical conductivity, α is thermal diffusivity, $Q(x)(= Q_0 e^{\frac{x}{l}})$ is the variable heat source, ρ_f is the fluid density, D_B is the Brownian diffusion coefficient, D_T is the thermophoresis coefficient, $K(x)(= K_0 e^{\frac{x}{l}})$ is the chemical reaction parameter and $\tau = \frac{(\rho c_p)_p}{(\rho c_p)_f}$ is the ratio of the effective heat capacity of the nanoparticle material and heat capacity of the fluid.

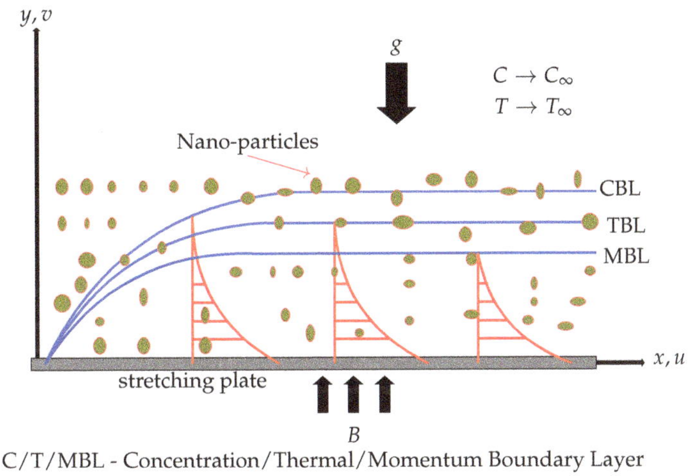

Figure 1. Schematic flow diagram and coordinate system.

The energy Equation (5) can be simplified by using the Rosseland approximation [42], which states that the radiative heat flux:

$$q_r = \frac{4\sigma^*}{3k^*}\frac{\partial T^4}{\partial y},$$

where σ^* is the Stefan–Boltzmann constant and k^* is the mean absorption coefficient. Assuming that the temperature differences within the flow are so small, the linear Taylor series expansion of T^4 about T_∞ gives $T^4 \approx 4TT_\infty^3 - 3T_\infty^3$ such that:

$$\frac{\partial q_r}{\partial y} = -\frac{16\sigma^* T_\infty^3}{3k^*}\frac{\partial^2 T}{\partial y^2}. \tag{7}$$

Using Equation (7) in Equation (5) gives:

$$u\frac{\partial T}{\partial x} + v\frac{\partial T}{\partial y} = \left(\alpha + \frac{16\sigma^* T_\infty^3}{3(\rho c_p)_f k^*}\right)\frac{\partial^2 T}{\partial y^2} + \frac{Q}{(\rho c_p)_f}(T - T_\infty) + \tau\left\{D_B\frac{\partial T}{\partial y}\frac{\partial C}{\partial y} + \frac{D_T}{T_\infty}\left(\frac{\partial T}{\partial y}\right)^2\right\}, \tag{8}$$

The suitable boundary conditions for the system of Equations (3)–(6) are:

$$\begin{aligned} &u = U_w = U_0 e^{\frac{x}{l}},\ v = -\gamma(x),\ \text{where } \gamma(x) = -V_0 e^{\frac{x}{2l}}, \\ &T = T_w = T_\infty + T_0 e^{\frac{x}{2l}},\ C = C_w = C_\infty + C_0 e^{\frac{x}{2l}},\ \text{at } y = 0, \\ &u \to 0,\ T \to T_\infty,\ C \to C_\infty,\ \text{as } y \to \infty. \end{aligned} \tag{9}$$

The similarity transformations which are used to solve the governing equations are defined as follows [43]:

$$u = U_0 e^{\frac{x}{l}} f'(\eta),\ v = -\sqrt{\frac{\nu U_0}{2l}} e^{\frac{x}{2l}} [f(\eta) + \eta f'(\eta)],\ \eta = \sqrt{\frac{U_0}{2\nu l}} y e^{\frac{x}{2l}},$$
$$T = T_\infty + T_0 e^{\frac{x}{2l}} \theta(\eta),\ C = C_\infty + C_0 e^{\frac{x}{2l}} \phi(\eta) \tag{10}$$

Using similarity transformations Equation (10), the continuity Equation (3) is identically satisfied and Equations (4)–(6) take the following form:

$$f''' + ff'' - 2f'^2 + \lambda f'' f''' - M^2 f' + 2G_T\theta + 2G_C\phi = 0, \tag{11}$$
$$\left(1 + \frac{4}{3}R_d\right)\theta'' + Pr(f\theta' - f'\theta + N_b\phi'\theta' + N_t\theta'^2 + \delta\theta) = 0, \tag{12}$$
$$\phi'' + Sc(f\phi' - f'\phi - K_r\phi) + \frac{N_t}{N_b}\theta'' = 0, \tag{13}$$

subject to boundary conditions:

$$f(0) = -S,\ f'(0) = 1,\ \theta(0) = 1,\ \phi(0) = 1,$$
$$f'(\infty) \to 0,\ \theta(\infty) \to 0,\ \phi(\infty) \to 0. \tag{14}$$

where $\lambda\left(= \Gamma\sqrt{\frac{U_0^3 e^{\frac{3x}{l}}}{\nu l}}\right)$ is the Williamson fluid parameter, $M^2 (= \frac{2l\sigma B_0^2}{\rho U_0})$ is the magnetic field parameter, $G_T (= \frac{glB_T T_0}{U_0^2})$ is the thermal Grashof number, $G_C (= \frac{glB_C C_0}{U_0^2})$ is the mass Grashof number, $Pr (= \frac{\nu}{\alpha})$ is the Prandlt number, $R_d (= \frac{4\sigma^* T_\infty^3}{k^*\kappa})$ is the radiation parameter, $N_b (= \frac{\tau D_B}{\nu}(C_w - C_\infty))$ is the Brownian motion parameter, $N_t (= \frac{\tau D_T}{\nu T_\infty}(T_w - T_\infty))$ is the thermophoresis parameter, $\delta (= \frac{2lQ_0}{\rho c_p U_0})$ is the heat generation parameter, $Sc (= \frac{\nu}{D_B})$ is the Schmidt number, $S (= V_0\sqrt{\frac{2l}{\nu U_0}})$ is the suction $(S < 0)$ or the injection $(S > 0)$ parameter and $K_r (= \frac{2lK_0}{U_0})$ is the chemical reaction parameter.

The skin friction coefficient (c_f), the local Nusselt number (Nu_x) and the local Sherwood number (Sh_x) are the physical quantities of engineering significance discussed in this study. Following the work by Ahmed and Akbar [36]:

$$c_f = \frac{1}{\rho U_w^2}\left(\mu\left(\frac{\partial u}{\partial y} + \frac{\Gamma}{\sqrt{2}}\left(\frac{\partial u}{\partial y}\right)^2\right)\right)_{y=0},$$
$$Nu_x = -\frac{\sqrt{2}l}{(T_w - T_\infty)e^{\frac{x}{2l}}}\left(\frac{\partial T}{\partial y}\right)_{y=0},$$
$$Sh_x = -\frac{\sqrt{2}l}{(C_w - C_\infty)e^{\frac{x}{2l}}}\left(\frac{\partial C}{\partial y}\right)_{y=0}.$$

Using similarity transformations in Equation (10), the following dimensionless forms are obtained:

$$\sqrt{2Re_x}c_f = \left(f''(0) + \frac{\lambda}{2}(f''(0))^2\right),$$
$$\frac{Nu_x}{\sqrt{Re_x}} = -\theta'(0),\ \frac{Sh_x}{\sqrt{Re_x}} = -\phi'(0),$$

where $Re_x = \frac{U_w l}{\nu}$ is the Reynolds number.

4. Method of Solution

In this study, the spectral quasi-linearization method is used to seek the numerical solution of the coupled system of Equations (11)–(13) subject to boundary conditions Equation (18). A Newton–Raphson-based quasi-linearization method [44], which uses first-order Taylor series expansion, is used to linearize the non-linear terms. Denote the respective solutions of Equations (11)–(13) at iteration level s by f_s, θ_s and ϕ_s, respectively. Assuming that the difference between solutions at iteration level s and $s+1$ are sufficiently close, quasi-linearization gives the following iterative sequence of linear differential equations:

$$a_{0,s}f'''_{s+1} + a_{1,s}f''_{s+1} + a_{2,s}f'_{s+1} + a_{3,s}f_{s+1} + a_{4,s}\theta_{s+1} + a_{5,s}\phi_{s+1} = R_{1,s}, \tag{15}$$
$$b_{0,s}\theta''_{s+1} + b_{1,s}\theta''_{s+1} + b_{2,s}\theta_{s+1} + b_{3,s}f'_{s+1} + b_{4,s}f_{s+1} + b_{5,s}\phi'_{s+1} = R_{2,s}, \tag{16}$$
$$c_{0,s}\phi''_{s+1} + c_{1,s}\phi'_{s+1} + c_{2,s}\phi_{s+1} + c_{3,s}f'_{s+1} + c_{4,s}f_{s+1} + c_{5,s}\theta''_{s+1} = R_{3,s}, \tag{17}$$

where the variable coefficients known at iteration level s are defined as:

$$a_{0,s} = 1 + \lambda f''_s,\ a_{1,s} = f_s + \lambda f'''_s,\ a_{2,s} = -4f'_s - M,\ a_{3,s} = f''_s,\ a_{4,s} = 2G_T,\ a_{5,s} = 2G_C,$$
$$b_{0,s} = 1 + \frac{4}{3}R_d,\ b_{1,s} = Pr(f_s + N_b\phi'_s + 2N_t\theta'_s),\ b_{2,s} = -Pr(f'_s - \delta),\ b_{3,s} = -Pr\theta_s,$$
$$b_{4,s} = Pr\theta'_s,\ b_{5,s} = PrN_b\theta'_s,\ c_{0,s} = 1,\ c_{1,s} = Scf_s,\ c_{2,s} = -Sc(f'_s + K_r),$$
$$c_{3,s} = -Sc\phi_s,\ c_{4,s} = Sc\phi'_s,\ c_{5,s} = \frac{N_t}{N_b}.$$

The boundary conditions given in Equation (18) are transformed to:

$$\begin{aligned} &f'_{s+1}(0) = 1,\ f_{s+1}(0) = -S,\ \theta_{s+1}(0) = 1,\ \phi_{s+1}(0) = 1, \\ &f'_{s+1}(\infty) \to 0,\ \theta_{s+1}(\infty) \to 0,\ \theta_{s+1}(\infty) \to 0. \end{aligned} \tag{18}$$

The terms on the right hand side are:

$$R_{1,s} = f_sf''_s - 2f'^2_s + \lambda f''_s f'''_s,\ R_{2,s} = Pr(f_s\theta'_s - f'_s\theta + N_b\theta'_s\phi'_s + N_t\theta'^2_s),$$
$$R_{3,s} = Sc(f_s\phi'_s - f'_s\phi_s)$$

The unknown functions f_{s+1}, θ_{s+1} and ϕ_{s+1} are approximated using Chebyshev interpolating polynomials, such that the their derivatives evaluated at Gauss–Lobatto collocation points $\eta_i = \cos\frac{\pi i}{N}(i = 0, 1, 2, \cdots, N)$ are given by:

$$\begin{aligned} \frac{d^n f_{s+1}}{d\eta}(\eta_i) &= \sum_{k=0}^{N} D^n_{ik} f_{s+1}(\eta_k) = \mathbf{D}^n\mathbf{F}_{s+1}, \\ \frac{d^n \theta_{s+1}}{d\eta}(\eta_i) &= \sum_{k=0}^{N} D^n_{ik} \theta_{s+1}(\eta_k) = \mathbf{D}^n\mathbf{\Theta}_{s+1}, \\ \frac{d^n \phi_{s+1}}{d\eta}(\eta_i) &= \sum_{k=0}^{N} D^n_{ik} \phi_{s+1}(\eta_k) = \mathbf{D}^n\mathbf{\Phi}_{s+1}, \end{aligned} \tag{19}$$

where
$\mathbf{D} = \frac{2}{L_\infty}D$, $\mathbf{F}_{s+1} = [f_{s+1}(\eta_0), f_{s+1}(\eta_1), \cdots, f_{s+1}(\eta_{N-1}), f_{s+1}(\eta_N)]^T$,
$\mathbf{\Theta}_{s+1} = [\theta_{s+1}(\eta_0), \theta_{s+1}(\eta_1), \cdots, \theta_{s+1}(\eta_{N-1}), \theta_{s+1}(\eta_N)]^T$,
$\mathbf{\Phi}_{s+1} = [\phi_{s+1}(\eta_0), \phi_{s+1}(\eta_1), \cdots, \phi_{s+1}(\eta_{N-1}), \phi_{s+1}(\eta_N)]^T$.
Using derivatives in Equation (19) in the system of Equations (15)–(17) yields a system in vector matrix form:

$$\begin{bmatrix} \mathbf{A11} & \mathbf{A12} & \mathbf{A13} \\ \mathbf{A21} & \mathbf{A22} & \mathbf{A23} \\ \mathbf{A31} & \mathbf{A32} & \mathbf{A33} \end{bmatrix} \begin{bmatrix} \mathbf{F}_{s+1} \\ \mathbf{\Theta}_{s+1} \\ \mathbf{\Phi}_{s+1} \end{bmatrix} = \begin{bmatrix} \mathbf{R}_{1,s} \\ \mathbf{R}_{2,s} \\ \mathbf{R}_{3,s} \end{bmatrix},$$

where

$$\begin{aligned}
&\mathbf{A11} = \mathbf{a}_{0,s}\mathbf{D}^3 + \mathbf{a}_{1,s}\mathbf{D}^2 + \mathbf{a}_{2,s}\mathbf{D} + \mathbf{a}_{3,s},\ \mathbf{A12} = a_{4,s}\mathbf{I},\ \mathbf{A13} = a_{5,s}\mathbf{I},\\
&\mathbf{A21} = \mathbf{b}_{3,s}\mathbf{D} + \mathbf{b}_{4,s},\ \mathbf{A22} = b_{0,s}\mathbf{D}^2 + \mathbf{b}_{1,s}\mathbf{D} + \mathbf{b}_{2,s},\ \mathbf{A23} = \mathbf{b}_{5,s}\mathbf{D},\\
&\mathbf{A31} = \mathbf{c}_{3,s}\mathbf{D} + \mathbf{c}_{4,s},\ \mathbf{A32} = c_{5,s}\mathbf{D}^2,\ \mathbf{A33} = c_{0,s}\mathbf{D}^2 + \mathbf{c}_{1,s}\mathbf{D} + \mathbf{c}_{2,s}.
\end{aligned}$$

where $\mathbf{I}$ is an $(N+1)\times(N+1)$ identity matrix. The spectral boundary conditions are:

$$\begin{aligned}
&f_{s+1}(\eta_N) = S,\ \sum_{k=0}^{N} D_{N,k}f_{s+1}(\eta_N) = 1,\ \theta_{s+1}(\eta_N) = 1,\ \phi_{s+1}(\eta_N) = 1,\\
&\sum_{k=0}^{N} D_{0,k}f_{s+1}(\eta_0) = 0,\ \theta_{s+1}(\eta_0) = 0,\ \phi_{s+1}(\eta_0) = 0.
\end{aligned}$$

The numerical iteration of the SQLM, coded in MATLAB R2022b on an Intel(R) Core(TM) i5, is started by using the initial guesses that satisfy the boundary conditions Equation (18), given by:

$$f_0(\eta) = 1 - e^{-\eta} + S,\ \theta_0(\eta) = e^{-\eta},\ \phi_0(\eta) = e^{-\eta}.$$

5. Results and Discussion

5.1. Validation of Results

To confirm the accuracy of the SQLM used in this study, the values of the skin friction $-(f''(0) + \frac{\lambda}{2}(f''(0))^2)$ are compared against the MATLAB bvp4c solver results and the homotopy analysis method results obtained by Nadeem and Hussain [40] and Amjad et al. [45]. Considering the values $G_T = G_C = 0$, Equation (11) reduces to the problem by Amjad et al. [45], which is given by:

$$f''' + ff'' - 2f'^2 + \lambda f''f''' - M^2 f' = 0, \tag{20}$$

subject to boundary conditions:

$$f(0) = -S,\ f'(0) = 1,\ f'(\infty) \to 0. \tag{21}$$

Using $N = 40$ collocation points, $\eta_\infty = 5.0$, the MATLAB SQLM algorithm for solving Equation (20) involves iteratively solving the following recursive sequence:

$$\left[\begin{array}{ccccc}
D_{0,0} & D_{0,1} & \cdots & D_{0,N-1}, & D_{0,N}\\
\hline
 & & \mathbf{A} & & \\
\hline
D_{N,0} & D_{N,1} & \cdots & D_{N,N-1} & D_{N,N}\\
0 & 0 & \cdots & & 1
\end{array}\right]
\left[\begin{array}{c}
f_{s+1}(\eta_0)\\
\hline
\mathbf{F}_{s+1}\\
\hline
f_{s+1}(\eta_{N-1})\\
f_{s+1}(\eta_N)
\end{array}\right]
=
\left[\begin{array}{c}
0\\
\hline
\mathbf{R}_s\\
\hline
1\\
-S
\end{array}\right], \tag{22}$$

where $\mathbf{A} = \mathbf{a}_{0,s}\mathbf{D}^3 + \mathbf{a}_{1,s}\mathbf{D}^2 + \mathbf{a}_{2,s}\mathbf{D} + \mathbf{a}_{3,s}$, $\mathbf{F}_{s+1} = [f_{s+1}(\eta_1), f_{s+1}(\eta_2), \cdots, f_{s+1}(\eta_{N-3}), f_{s+1}(\eta_{N-2})]^T$ and $\mathbf{R}_s = -2\mathbf{F}'_s \circ \mathbf{F}'_s + \mathbf{F}_s \circ \mathbf{F}''_s) + \lambda\mathbf{F}''_s \circ \mathbf{F}'''_s$. Performing 20 iterations, the results obtained for $-(f''(0) + \frac{\lambda}{2}(f''(0))^2)$ are displayed in Table 1.

Table 1 displays the computed values of the skin friction coefficient compared against the results by Amjad et al. [45] for different values of λ, S and M. A good match of the results is observed. The accuracy of the SQLM was validated by a direct comparison with the reported results.

Considering $G_T = G_C = 0 = M = 0$, Equation (11) reduces to the problem by Nadeem and Hussain [40], which can be solved using MATLAB's bvp4c solver by first using the following substitutions:

$$y(1) = f,\ y(2) = f',\ y(3) = f'' \tag{23}$$

$$f''' = y(3)' = \frac{2(y(2))^2 - y(1)y(3)}{(1 + \lambda y(3))} \tag{24}$$

and the boundary conditions are given as $y_a(1) + S,\ y_a(2) - 1,\ y_b(2)$. The three first-order equations are coded in the MATLAB's bvp4c solver with the function name "odeBVP", and with "odeBc" handling the boundary conditions. Choosing the interval of integration to $[0, 40]$, the solutions from the function "bvp4c" are given by:

```
sol = bvp4c(@odeBVP, @odeBc, solinit ,options).
```

A comparison of the SQLM skin friction coefficient values against those from MATLAB's bvp4c routine and the results by Nadeem and Hussain [40] is shown in Table 2. A perfect agreement was observed.

Table 1. Table of present values of $\sqrt{2Re}C_f$ compared against published results for varying values of λ, S and M.

			$-(f''(0) + \frac{\lambda}{2}(f''(0))^2)$	
λ	S	M	Amjad et al. [45]	SQLM
0.1	0.2	2.0	1.754213	1.754213105760364
0.2	0.2	2.0	1.678675	1.678675073146794
0.3	0.2	2.0	1.579827	1.578533717157394
0.1	0.1	2.0	1.799249	1.799249869955796
0.1	0.2	2.0	1.754213	1.754213105760364
0.1	0.3	2.0	1.710489	1.710489423953702
0.1	0.2	0.1	1.201556	1.201559983439274
0.1	0.2	0.2	1.237223	1.237224345281889
0.1	0.2	0.3	1.271816	1.271816653083256

Table 2. Table of present values of $\sqrt{2Re}C_f$ compared against MATLAB's bvp4c results for selected values of λ and $S = 0.1$.

		$-(f''(0) + \frac{\lambda}{2}(f''(0))^2)$	
λ	Nadeem and Hussain [40]	MATLAB's bvp4c	SQLM
0.0	1.32930	1.329302736062721	1.329308462412963
0.1	1.29801	1.298017071294807	1.298022829158239
0.2	1.26310	1.263103796098337	1.263109548733657
0.3	1.22276	1.222776617114427	1.222781418705920

5.2. Results

The SQLM algorithm was implemented using MATLAB R2022b software. For all the numerical results, unless otherwise stated, the default parameters considered are: $N = 60$, $M = 0.1$, $G_T = 0.1$, $\lambda = 0.3$, $G_C = 0.1$, $N_t = 0.1$, $N_b = 0.1$, $Pr = 0.5$, $\delta = 0.2$, $S = 0.0$, $Kr = 0.1$, $Sc = 1.0$. The convergence and accuracy of the spectral quasi-linearization method were verified using the solution error norms and residual errors, respectively. The solution error norms, defined as the difference between values of successive iterations are denoted by [46]:

$$Err[F(\eta)] = ||F_{s+1}(\eta) - F_s(\eta)||_\infty,\ Err[\Theta(\eta)] = ||\Theta_{s+1}(\eta) - \Theta_s(\eta)||_\infty,\ Err[\Phi(\eta)] = ||\Phi_{s+1}(\eta) - \Phi_s(\eta)||_\infty.$$

The residual error gives a measure of the extent to which the SQLM solution approximates the true solution. The residual L^∞ norms are given by Alharbey et al. [47] as:

$$Res(f) = ||f''' + ff'' - 2f'^2 + \lambda f'' f''' - M^2 f' + 2G_T\theta + 2G_C\phi||_\infty,$$
$$Res(\theta) = ||(1 + (4/3)R_d\theta'' + Pr(f\theta' - f'\theta + N_b\phi'\theta' + N_t\theta'^2 + \delta\theta)||_\infty,$$
$$Res(\phi) = ||\phi'' + Sc(f\phi' - f'\phi - K_r\phi) + (N_t/N_b)\theta''||_\infty,$$

Figure 2a reveals that the SQLM converges after only five iterations with a solution based error of order $\approx 10^{-10}$. Additionally, after three iterations, the SQLM achieves an accuracy of order $\approx 10^{-9}$, as shown in Figure 2b.

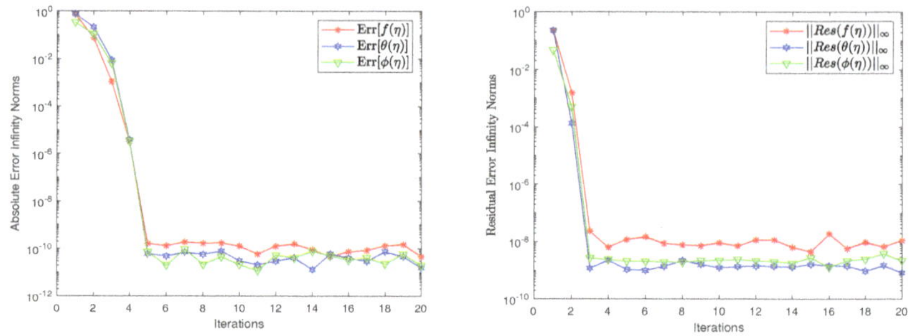

(a) (b)

Figure 2. Error graphs of $f(\eta)$, $\theta(\eta)$ and $\phi(\eta)$.

Figures 3–5 display the effects of the magnetic parameter (M), suction/injection parameter (S) and the Williamson parameter (λ), respectively, on the fluid velocity profiles. Figure 3 shows that the fluid velocity is depressed as the magnetic parameter is increased. Physically, the fluid velocity drops due to the resistive Lorentz force, which is induced by the magnetic parameter. It is depicted in Figure 4 that the Williamson nanofluid velocity profiles are depressed when the suction parameter is increased. Additionally, it is revealed in Figure 5 that there is an inverse relationship between the fluid velocity distribution and the non-Newtonian Williamson parameter. An increase in the values of λ causes a decrease in the fluid movement and reduces the boundary layer thickness.

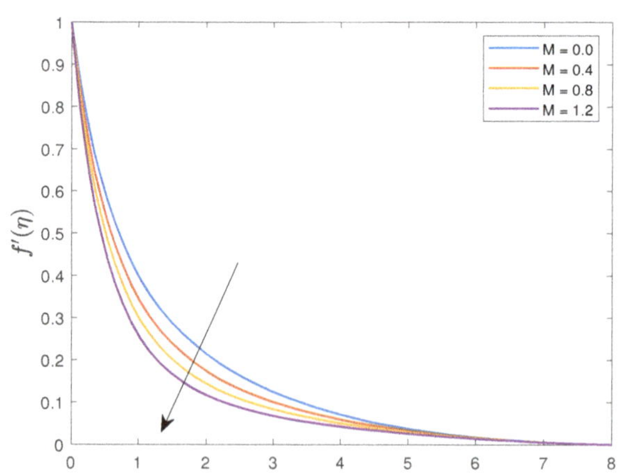

Figure 3. Influence of M on the nanofluid velocity.

The influences of the Prandtl number (Pr), Brownian motion parameter (N_b), thermal Grashof parameter (G_T) and thermal radiation parameter (R_d) on the Williamson nanofluid dimensionless temperature (θ) are depicted in Figures 6–9, respectively. It is displayed in Figure 6 that the fluid temperature and thermal boundary layer are reduced as the Prandtl number increases. The Prandtl number can be viewed as the ratio of momentum to thermal boundary layers. Physically, a high Prandtl number means a small thermal boundary layer. It is revealed in Figure 7 that an increase in the values of the Brownian motion parameter increases the fluid temperature profile. An increase in the Brownian motion parameter results in an increased kinetic energy of the Williamson nanoparticles, and hence, a temperature increase. Figure 8 depicts that the fluid temperature is depressed as the thermal Grashof number is enhanced. Essentially, the Grashof number signifies the ratio of buoyancy to viscous forces. Increasing G_T results in an addition of more thermal energy in the fluid molecules, which in turn increases the fluid local heat transfer rate. The thermal boundary layer is reduced, and hence, the temperature profiles decrease. It is shown in Figure 9 that temperature is an increasing function of the thermal radiation parameter. The effect of increasing the thermal radiation parameter is thickening the thermal boundary layer, and hence, the temperature profiles are increased.

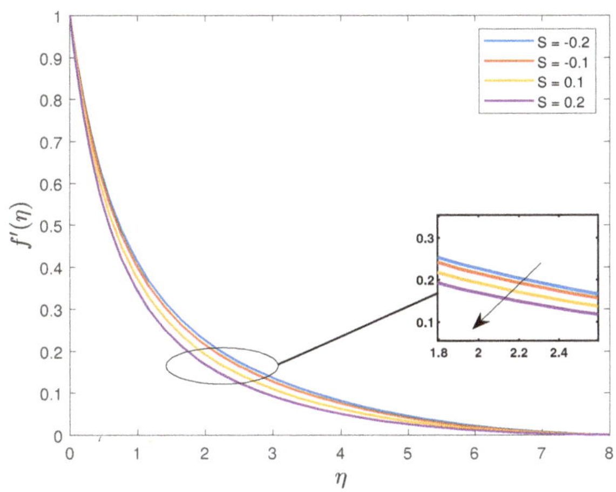

Figure 4. Influence of S on the nanofluid velocity.

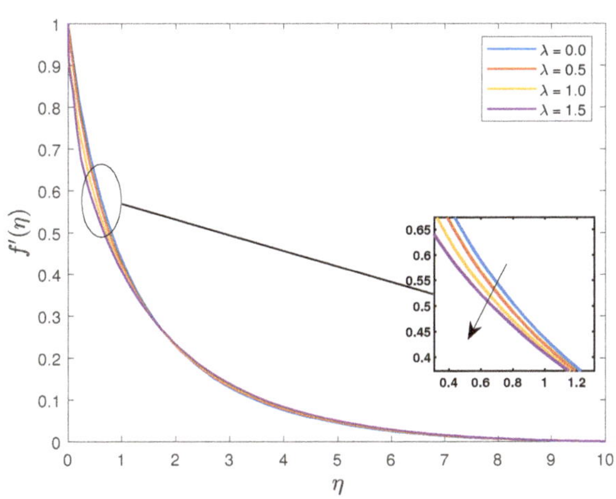

Figure 5. Influence of λ on fluid velocity.

Figure 10 portrays the influence of the Schmidt number (Sc) on the Williamson nanoparticle concentration. Sc can be defined as the ratio of momentum diffusivity and mass diffusivity. High values of Sc corresponds to a weaker solute diffusivity and the concentration distribution and solute boundary layer decrease as a consequence. The fluid dimensionless concentration profiles are depressed when the chemical reaction parameter is increased as seen in Figure 11. Physically, when the chemical reaction parameter is increased, quite a number of solute molecules will undergo chemical reaction, and hence, the reduction in the concentration. The influence of the mass Grashof number (G_C) on the concentration is displayed in Figure 12. G_C relates species buoyancy force to the viscous hydrodynamic force. Increasing G_C causes an enhancement of the concentration gradient, which in turn boosts the buoyancy effect. A resulting induced flow will cause a decrease in concentration, and hence, a decrease in the concentration profile, as depicted in Figure 12.

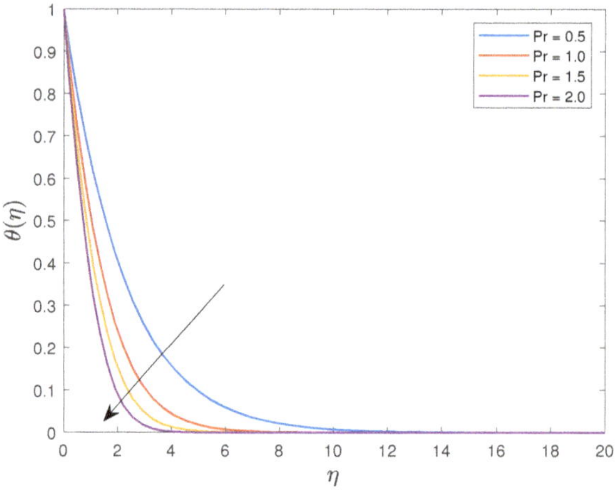

Figure 6. Influence of Pr on fluid temperature.

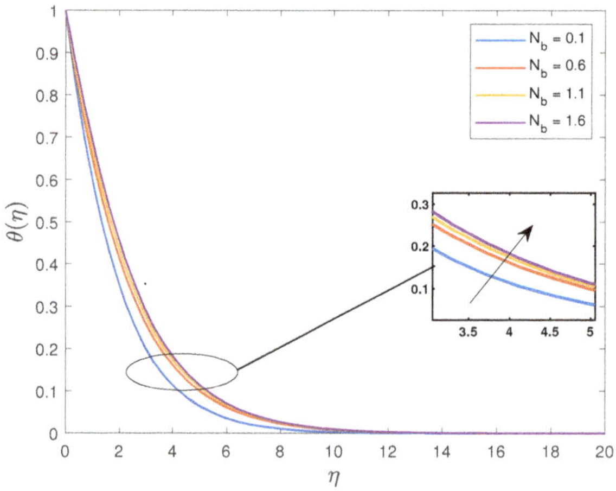

Figure 7. Influence of N_b on fluid temperature.

Table 3 displays the effects of all the pertinent thermo-physical parameters involved in the current problem on the skin friction, Nusselt number and Sherwood number. The skin friction coefficient upsurges as the values of injection parameter, Prandtl number, magnetic parameter, Brownian motion parameter and Schmidt number are increased. The fluid flow is improved by the functioning magnetic field regarding the Williamson nanofluid, and thus, increases the surface friction. The increase of $\sqrt{2Re}C_f$ with an increasing Prandtl number is attributed to increased fluid momentum. The opposite trend is observed when the Williamson fluid parameter, mass Grashof number, thermal Grashof number, thermal radiation parameter, thermophoresis parameter, heat generation parameter and chemical reaction parameter are increased.

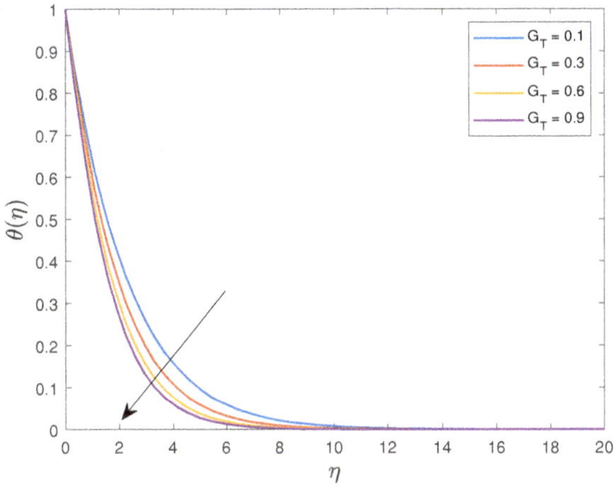

Figure 8. Influence of G_T on fluid temperature.

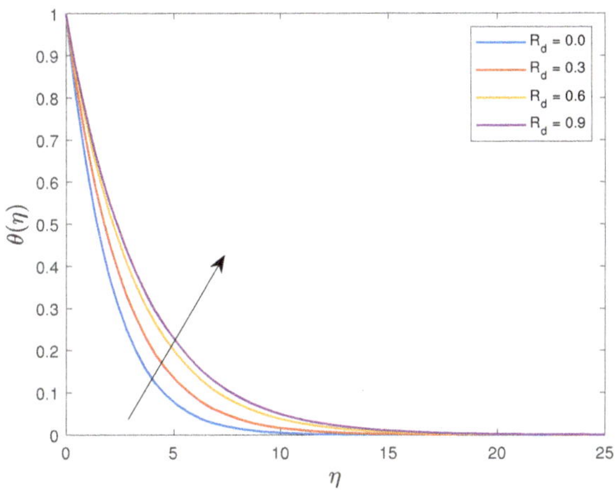

Figure 9. Influence of R_d on fluid temperature.

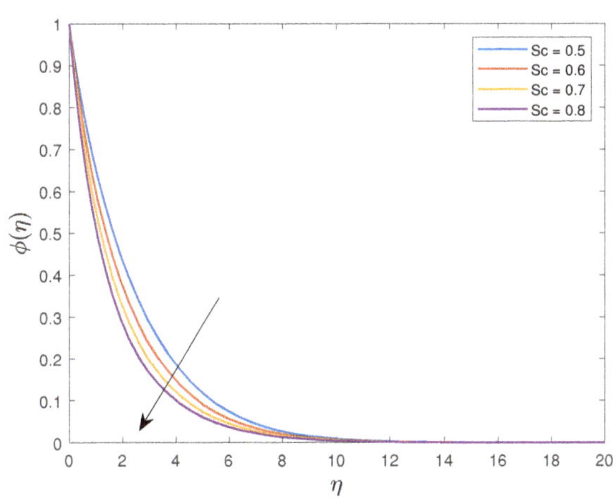

Figure 10. Influence of Sc on fluid concentration.

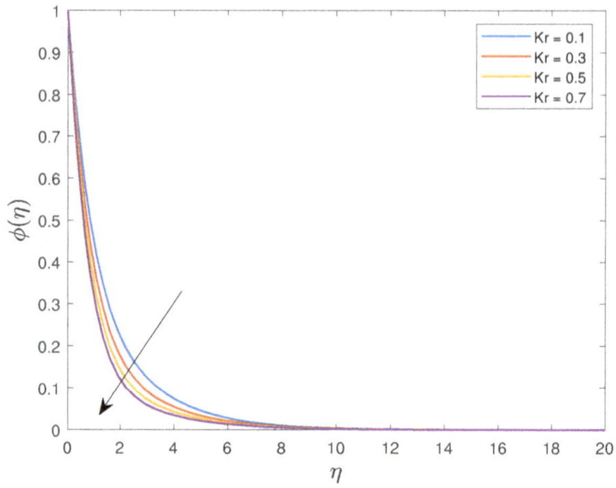

Figure 11. Influence of Kr on fluid concentration.

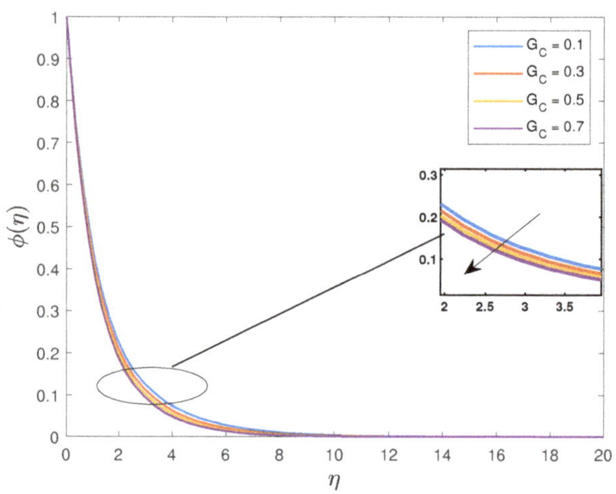

Figure 12. Influence of Gc on fluid concentration.

It is also noted that the mass Grashof number and the thermal Grashof number are the only parameters whose increment enhances the Nusselt number. Increasing the values of the Williamson fluid parameter, injection parameter, magnetic parameter, Prandtl number, thermal radiation, Brownian motion parameter, thermophoresis parameter, heat generation parameter, Schmidt number and chemical reaction parameter suppresses the heat transfer rate. It is noted that Nusselt number is a decreasing function of N_b and N_t. Physically, the effects of both Brownian motion and themorphoresis effects move the Williamson nanoparticles away from the stretching sheet sheet, intensifying the the diffusion of the nanoparticles into the boundary layer, and hence, causing a decrease in the Nusselt number.

The Sherwood number is improved as the values of mass Grashof number, thermal Grashof number, thermal radiation parameter, Brownian motion parameter, heat generation parameter, Schmidt number and chemical reaction parameter are increased and depreciates as the Williamson fluid parameter, injection parameter, magnetic parameter, Prandtl number and thermophoresis parameter are increased. The Schmidt number is the relative effectiveness of the momentum and mass transport by diffusion in the hydrodynamic and species boundary layers. An increase in Sc will result in an increase in the Sherwood number. An increased chemical reaction parameter means there will be more interaction of species concentration with the momentum boundary, and hence, an increase in the Sherwood number.

Table 3. The numerical values of the skin friction coefficient, Nusselt number and Sherwood number for all the thermo-physical parameters.

λ	S	M	Pr	G_C	G_T	R_d	N_b	N_t	δ	Sc	Kr	$\sqrt{2Re}C_f$	$-\frac{Nu_x}{\sqrt{Re_x}}$	$-\frac{Sh_x}{\sqrt{Re_x}}$
0.1	0.2	2.0	0.5	0.1	0.1	0.1	0.5	0.5	0.1	1.0	0.1	1.776767	0.308282	0.700530
0.3												1.706494	0.295463	0.687057
0.9												1.608996	0.169515	0.539204
0.1	0.1											1.730004	0.323907	0.736618
	0.2											1.776768	0.308282	0.700530
	0.3											1.824988	0.294009	0.665454
	0.2	0.1										1.174219	0.434167	0.794308
		0.2										1.213171	0.426083	0.787275
		0.3										1.251027	0.418169	0.780543
		2.0	0.1									1.771939	0.147223	0.810761
			0.2									1.773217	0.191519	0.780377
			0.3									1.774461	0.233031	0.751949
			0.5	0.3								1.635586	0.347227	0.724385
				0.6								1.430563	0.391337	0.757335
				0.9								1.232356	0.424697	0.786362
				0.1	0.3							1.474263	0.368464	0.735159
					0.6							1.246002	0.419482	0.777179
					0.9							1.027907	0.454621	0.811112
					0.1	0.3						1.470957	0.273691	0.724148
						0.5						1.468421	0.248889	0.741101
						0.7						1.466412	0.230255	0.753849
						0.1	0.1					1.390481	0.316343	0.032976
							0.3					1.461652	0.312301	0.593189
							0.5					1.474263	0.308282	0.700530
							0.5	0.1				1.491310	0.358320	0.807764
								0.3				1.482646	0.324544	0.753061
								0.5				1.474263	0.308282	0.700530
								0.1	0.0			1.477366	0.382548	0.658192
									0.1			1.474263	0.308282	0.700530
									0.2			1.470240	0.198753	0.756672
									0.1	0.6		1.446575	0.322304	0.458305
										0.8		1.461864	0.314201	0.587691
										1.0		1.474263	0.308282	0.700530
										1.0	0.2	1.479727	0.303787	0.778334
											0.4	1.488552	0.297958	0.906974
											0.6	1.495533	0.294169	1.015232

6. Conclusions

In this manuscript, the spectral quasi-linearization method was applied to numerically analyze the magnetoxhydrodynamics Williamson nanofluid flow over an exponentially stretching surface with chemical reaction and thermal radiation nanofluid flow. A comparison of the skin friction coefficient results obtained from MATLAB's bvp4c solver and published work confirmed that the method is reliable for solving the current problem. The key findings from the study are as follows:

1. The dimensionless velocity $(f'(\eta))$ diminishes as the values of the magnetic parameter are increased from 0 to 1.2;
2. The dimensionless temperature $(\theta(\eta))$ is an increasing function of $0.1 \leq N_b \leq 1.6$ and $0.0 \leq R_d \leq 0.9$;
3. The dimensionless concentration $(\phi(\eta))$ decreases for $0.5 \leq Sc \leq 0.8$ and $0.1 \leq Kr \leq 0.7$;
4. The skin friction coefficient increases as $M(0.1 \leq M \leq 0.3)$ and $N_b(0.1 \leq N_b \leq 0.5)$ increase and depressed for increased values of $N_t(0.1 \leq N_t \leq 0.5)$;
5. The Nusselt number diminishes as $M(0.1 \leq M \leq 0.3)$, $N_b(0.1 \leq N_b \leq 0.5)$ and $N_t(0.1 \leq N_t \leq 0.5)$ are increased;
6. The Sherwood number decreases as $M(0.1 \leq M \leq 0.3)$ and $N_t(0.1 \leq N_t \leq 0.37)$ increase and decreases as $N_b(0.3 \leq N_b \leq 0.7)$ increases.

Author Contributions: Conceptualization, H.M. and S.S.; Methodology, H.M.; Validation, S.S.; Formal analysis, H.M.; Investigation, S.S.; Writing—original draft, H.M. and S.S.; Writing—review & editing, H.M. and S.S.; Supervision, S.S.; Funding acquisition, S.S. All authors have read and agreed to the published version of the manuscript.

Funding: This research received no external funding.

Data Availability Statement: Data is contained within the article.

Conflicts of Interest: The authors declare no conflict of interest.

Nomenclature

x, y	Cartesian coordinates [m]
u, v	Velocity components in the x and y directions, respectively [m s^{-1}]
U_0	Reference velocity [m s^{-1}]
β_T	Thermal expansion coefficient
β_C	Concentration expansion coefficient
B_0	Magnetic field strength [NmA^{-1}]
C_f	Skin friction coefficient
Pr	Prandtl number
M	Magnetic parameter [Te]
T	Fluid temperature [T]
C_w	Concentration of nanoparticles at the surface [mol m^{-3}]
C	Concentration of nanoparticles [mol m^{-3}]
U_w	Velocity at the wall [m s^{-1}]
Q	Heat source
K_r	Chemical reaction parameter [Ms^{-1}]
T_0	Reference temperature [K]
C_0	Reference concentration [mol m^{-3}]
R_d	Thermal radiation parameter
q_r	Radiative heat flux [J]
S	Suction/injection parameter
$\theta(\eta)$	Dimensionless temperature
$\phi(\eta)$	Dimensionless concentration
N_t	Thermophoretic parameter
Nu_x	Local Nusselt number
Sh_x	Local Sherwood number
T_w	Surface temperature [K]
T_∞	Ambient temperature [K]
f	Dimensionless stream function
g	Acceleration due to gravity [m s^{-2}]
Sc	Schmidt number
D_B	Brownian diffusion coefficient [m^2 s^{-1}]

D_T	Thermophoresis diffusion coefficient [$m^2\ s^{-1}$]
μ_∞	Infinite viscosity [Nsm^{-2}]
$(\rho c_p)_f$	Heat capacity of the nanofluid [$Jm^{-3}K^{-1}$]
Re_x	Reynolds number
$f'(\eta)$	Velocity profile
η	Dimensionless similarity variable
σ	Electrical conductivity [Sm^{-1}]
Γ	Positive time constant
α	Thermal diffusivity [$m^{-2}\ s^{-1}$]
$(\rho c_p)_p$	Heat capacity of the nanoparticles [$Jm^{-3}\ K^{-1}$]
ν	Kinematic viscosity [$m^2\ s^{-1}$]
ρ_f	Fluid density [$kg\ m^{-3}$]
λ	Williamson fluid parameter
Gr_T	Thermal Grashof number
Gr_C	Concentration Grashof number

References

1. Matsuhisa, S.; Bird, R.B. Analytical and numerical solutions for laminar flow of the non-Newtonian ellis fluid. *AIChE J.* **1965**, *11*, 588–595. [CrossRef]
2. Carreau, P.J. Rheological Equations from Molecular Network Theories. *Trans. Soc. Rheol.* **1972**, *16*, 99–127. 10.1122/1.549276. [CrossRef]
3. Ostwald, W. Ueber die rechnerische Darstellung des Strukturgebietes der Viskosität. *Kolloid Z.* **1929**, *47*, 176–187. [CrossRef]
4. Cross, M.M. Rheology of non-Newtonian fluids: A new flow equation for pseudoplastic systems. *J. Colloid Sci.* **1965**, *20*, 417–437. [CrossRef]
5. Casson, N. A Flow Equation for Pigment-Oil Suspensions of the Printing Ink Type. In *Rheology of Disperse Systems*; Mill, C.C., Ed.; Pergamon Press: Oxford, UK, 1959; pp. 84–104.
6. Williamson, R.V. The Flow of Pseudoplastic Materials. *Ind. Eng. Chem.* **1929**, *21*, 1108–1111. [CrossRef]
7. Sakiadis, B.C. Boundary-layer behavior on continuous solid surfaces: I. Boundary-layer equations for two-dimensional and axisymmetric flow. *AIChE J.* **1961**, *7*, 26–28. [CrossRef]
8. Crane, L.J. Flow past a stretching plate. *Z. Angew. Math. Phys. ZAMP* **1970**, *21*, 645–647. [CrossRef]
9. Khan, S.; Selim, M.M.; Khan, A.; Ullah, A.; Abdeljawad, T.; Ikramullah; Ayaz, M.; Mashwani, W.K. On the Analysis of the Non-Newtonian Fluid Flow Past a Stretching/Shrinking Permeable Surface with Heat and Mass Transfer. *Coatings* **2021**, *11*, 566. [CrossRef]
10. Zeb, H.; Bhatti, S.; Khan, U.; Wahab, H.A.; Mohamed, A.; Khan, I. Impact of Homogeneous-Heterogeneous Reactions on Flow of Non-Newtonian Ferrofluid over a Stretching Sheet. *J. Nanomater.* **2022**, *2022*, 2501263. [CrossRef]
11. Mahabaleshwar, U.S.; Maranna, T.; Sofos, F. Analytical investigation of an incompressible viscous laminar Casson fluid flow past a stretching/shrinking sheet. *Sci. Rep.* **2022**, *12*, 18404. [CrossRef]
12. Abbas, N.; Nadeem, S.; Shatanawi, W. Effects of radiation and heat generation for non-Newtonian fluid flow over slendering stretching sheet: Numerically. *J. Appl. Math. Mech.* **2022**, *103*, e202100299. [CrossRef]
13. Akbar, N.S.; Al-Zubaidi, A.; Saleem, S.; Alsallami, S.A.M. Variable fluid properties analysis for thermally laminated 3-dimensional magnetohydrodynamic non-Newtonian nanofluid over a stretching sheet. *Sci. Rep.* **2023**, *13*, 3231. [CrossRef]
14. Masuda, H.; Ebata, A.; Teramae, K.; Hishinuma, N. Alteration of Thermal Conductivity and Viscosity of Liquid by Dispersing Ultra-Fine Particles. Dispersion of Al2O3, SiO2 and TiO2 Ultra-Fine Particles. *Netsu Bussei* **1993**, *7*, 227–233. [CrossRef]
15. Choi, S.U.S.; Eastman, J.A. Enhancing thermal conductivity of fluids with nanoparticle. In Proceedings of the 1995 International Mechanical Engineering Congress and Exhibition, San Francisco, CA, USA, 12–17 November 1995.
16. Elboughdiri, N.; Ghernaout, D.; Muhammad, T.; Alshehri, A.; Sadat, R.; Ali, M.R.; Wakif, A. Towards a novel EMHD dissipative stagnation point flow model for radiating copper-based ethylene glycol nanofluids: An unsteady two-dimensional homogeneous second-grade flow case study. *Case Stud. Therm. Eng.* **2023**, *45*, 102914. [CrossRef]
17. Ashraf, M.Z.; Rehman, S.U.; Farid, S.; Hussein, A.K.; Ali, B.; Shah, N.A.; Weera, W. Insight into Significance of Bioconvection on MHD Tangent Hyperbolic Nanofluid Flow of Irregular Thickness across a Slender Elastic Surface. *Mathematics* **2022**, *10*, 2592. [CrossRef]
18. Nabwey, H.A.; Rahbar, F.; Armaghani, T.; Rashad, A.M.; Chamkha, A.J. A Comprehensive Review of Non-Newtonian Nanofluid Heat Transfer. *Symmetry* **2023**, *15*, 362. [CrossRef]
19. Selimefendigil, F.; Şenol, G.; Öztop, H.F.; Abu-Hamdeh, N.H. A Review on Non-Newtonian Nanofluid Applications for Convection in Cavities under Magnetic Field. *Symmetry* **2022**, *15*, 41. [CrossRef]
20. Lou, Q.; Ali, B.; Rehman, S.U.; Habib, D.; Abdal, S.; Shah, N.A.; Chung, J.D. Micropolar Dusty Fluid: Coriolis Force Effects on Dynamics of MHD Rotating Fluid When Lorentz Force Is Significant. *Mathematics* **2022**, *10*, 2630. [CrossRef]

21. Alfven, H. Existence of Electromagnetic-Hydrodynamic Waves. *Nature* **1942**, *150*, 405–406. [CrossRef]
22. Abbas, A.; Jeelani, M.B.; Alnahdi, A.S.; Ilyas, A. MHD Williamson Nanofluid Fluid Flow and Heat Transfer Past a Non-Linear Stretching Sheet Implanted in a Porous Medium: Effects of Heat Generation and Viscous Dissipation. *Processes* **2022**, *10*, 1221. [CrossRef]
23. Reddy C, S.; Naikoti, K.; Rashidi, M.M. MHD flow and heat transfer characteristics of Williamson nanofluid over a stretching sheet with variable thickness and variable thermal conductivity. *Trans. A. Razmadze Math. Inst.* **2017**, *171*, 195–211. [CrossRef]
24. Shawky, H.M.; Eldabe, N.T.M.; Kamel, K.A.; Abd-Aziz, E.A. MHD flow with heat and mass transfer of Williamson nanofluid over stretching sheet through porous medium. *Microsyst. Technol.* **2019**, *25*, 1155–1169. [CrossRef]
25. Bouslimi, J.; Omri, M.; Mohamed, R.A.; Mahmoud, K.H.; Abo-Dahab, S.M.; Soliman, M.S. MHD Williamson nanofluid flow over a stretching sheet through a porous medium under effects of joule heating, nonlinear thermal radiation, heat generation/absorption, and chemical reaction. *Adv. Math. Phys.* **2021**, *2021*, 9950993. [CrossRef]
26. Hayat, T.; Bashir, G.; Waqas, M.; Alsaedi, A. MHD 2D flow of Williamson nanofluid over a nonlinear variable thicked surface with melting heat transfer. *J. Mol. Liq.* **2016**, *223*, 836–844. [CrossRef]
27. Ibrahim, W.; Negera, M. The Investigation of MHD Williamson Nanofluid over Stretching Cylinder with the Effect of Activation Energy. *Adv. Math. Phys.* **2020**, *2020*, 9523630. [CrossRef]
28. Eswara Rao, M.; Siva Sankari, M.; Nagalakshmi, C.; Rajkumar, S. On the Role of Bioconvection and Activation Energy for MHD-Stretched Flow of Williamson and Casson Nanofluid Transportation across a Porous Medium Past a Permeable Sheet. *J. Nanomater.* **2023**, *2023*, 3995808. [CrossRef]
29. Asjad, M.I.; Zahid, M.; Ali, B.; Jarad, F. Unsteady MHD Williamson Fluid Flow with the Effect of Bioconvection over Permeable Stretching Sheet. *Math. Probl. Eng.* **2022**, *2022*, 7980267. [CrossRef]
30. Wang, F.; Asjad, M.I.; Rehman, S.U.; Ali, B.; Hussain, S.; Gia, T.N.; Muhammad, T. MHD Williamson Nanofluid Flow over a Slender Elastic Sheet of Irregular Thickness in the Presence of Bioconvection. *Nanomaterials* **2021**, *11*, 2297. [CrossRef]
31. Ahmed, K.; Akbar, T.; Muhammad, T.; Alghamdi, M. Heat transfer characteristics of MHD flow of Williamson nanofluid over an exponential permeable stretching curved surface with variable thermal conductivity. *Case Stud. Therm. Eng.* **2021**, *28*, 101544. [CrossRef]
32. Patil, V.S.; Humane, P.P.; Patil, A.B. MHD Williamson nanofluid flow past a permeable stretching sheet with thermal radiation and chemical reaction. *Int. J. Model. Simul.* **2023**, *43*, 185–199. [CrossRef]
33. Khan, M.; Malik, M.Y.; Salahuddin, T.; Hussian, A. Heat and mass transfer of Williamson nanofluid flow yield by an inclined Lorentz force over a nonlinear stretching sheet. *Results Phys.* **2018**, *8*, 862–868. [CrossRef]
34. Kumar, P.B.S.; Gireesha, B.J.; Gorla, R.S.R.; Mahanthesh, B. Magnetohydrodynamic Flow of Williamson Nanofluid Due to an Exponentially Stretching Surface in the Presence of Thermal Radiation and Chemical Reaction. *J. Nanofluids* **2017**, *6*, 264–272. [CrossRef]
35. Nadeem, S.; Hussain, S.T.; Lee, C. Flow of a Williamson fluid over a stretching sheet. *Braz. J. Chem. Eng.* **2013**, *30*, 619–625. [CrossRef]
36. Ahmed, K.; Akbar, T. Numerical investigation of magnetohydrodynamics Williamson nanofluid flow over an exponentially stretching surface. *Adv. Mech. Eng.* **2021**, *13*, 168781402110198. [CrossRef]
37. Amjad, M.; Ahmed, I.; Ahmed, K.; Alqarni, M.S.; Akbar, T.; Muhammad, T. Numerical Solution of Magnetized Williamson Nanofluid Flow over an Exponentially Stretching Permeable Surface with Temperature Dependent Viscosity and Thermal Conductivity. *Nanomaterials* **2022**, *12*, 3661. [CrossRef]
38. Li, Y.-X.; Alshbool, M.H.; Lv, Y.-P.; Khan, I.; Riaz Khan, M.; Issakhov, A. Heat and mass transfer in MHD Williamson nanofluid flow over an exponentially porous stretching surface. *Case Stud. Therm. Eng.* **2021**, *26*, 100975. [CrossRef]
39. Motsa, S.S.; Dlamini, P.G.; Khumalo, M. Spectral Relaxation Method and Spectral Quasilinearization Method for Solving Unsteady Boundary Layer Flow Problems. *Adv. Math. Phys.* **2014**, *2014*, 341964. [CrossRef]
40. Nadeem, S.; Hussain, S.T. Heat transfer analysis of Williamson fluid over exponentially stretching surface. *Appl. Math. Mech.* **2014**, *35*, 489–502. [CrossRef]
41. Dapra, I.; Scarpi, G. Perturbation solution for pulsatile flow of a non-Newtonian Williamson fluid in a rock fracture. *Int. J. Rock Mech. Min. Sci.* **2007**, *44*, 271–278. [CrossRef]
42. Rosseland, S. *Theoretical Astrophysics*; Oxford University Press: Oxford, UK, 1936.
43. Seini, Y.I.; Makinde, O.D. MHD Boundary Layer Flow due to Exponential Stretching Surface with Radiation and Chemical Reaction. *Math. Probl. Eng.* **2013**, *2013*, 163614. [CrossRef]
44. Bellman, R.; Kalaba, R. *Quasilinearization and Nonlinear Boundary-Value Problems*; American Elsevier Publishing Company: New York, NY, USA, 1965.
45. Amjad, M.; Ahmed, K.; Akbar, T.; Muhammad, T.; Ahmed, I.; Alshomrani, A.S. Numerical investigation of double diffusion heat flux model in Williamson nanofluid over an exponentially stretching surface with variable thermal conductivity. *Case Stud. Therm. Eng.* **2022**, *36*, 102231. [CrossRef]

46. Motsa, S. On the New Bivariate Local Linearisation Method for Solving Coupled Partial Differential Equations in Some Applications of Unsteady Fluid Flows with Heat and Mass Transfer. In *Mass Transfer—Advancement in Process Modelling*; InTech: Vienna, Austria, 2015. [CrossRef]
47. Alharbey, R.A.; Mondal, H.; Behl, R. Spectral Quasi-Linearization Method for Non-Darcy Porous Medium with Convective Boundary Condition. *Entropy* **2019**, *21*, 838. [CrossRef]

mathematics

Article

Multi-Step-Ahead Wind Speed Forecast Method Based on Outlier Correction, Optimized Decomposition, and DLinear Model

Jialin Liu [1], Chen Gong [2], Suhua Chen [2] and Nanrun Zhou [2,*]

[1] School of Qianhu, Nanchang University, Nanchang 330031, China; 6003120150@email.ncu.edu.cn
[2] School of Information Engineering, Nanchang University, Nanchang 330031, China; 406100220032@email.ncu.edu.cn (C.G.); chensuhua@ncu.edu.cn (S.C.)
* Correspondence: nrzhou@ncu.edu.cn (N.Z.)

Abstract: Precise and dependable wind speed forecasting (WSF) enables operators of wind turbines to make informed decisions and maximize the use of available wind energy. This study proposes a hybrid WSF model based on outlier correction, heuristic algorithms, signal decomposition methods, and DLinear. Specifically, the hybrid model (HI-IVMD-DLinear) comprises the Hampel identifier (HI), the improved variational mode decomposition (IVMD) optimized by grey wolf optimization (GWO), and DLinear. Firstly, outliers in the wind speed sequence are detected and replaced with the HI to mitigate their impact on prediction accuracy. Next, the HI-processed sequence is decomposed into multiple sub-sequences with the IVMD to mitigate the non-stationarity and fluctuations. Finally, each sub-sequence is predicted by the novel DLinear algorithm individually. The predictions are reconstructed to obtain the final wind speed forecast. The HI-IVMD-DLinear is utilized to predict the real historical wind speed sequences from three regions so as to assess its performance. The experimental results reveal the following findings: (a) HI could enhance prediction accuracy and mitigate the adverse effects of outliers; (b) IVMD demonstrates superior decomposition performance; (c) DLinear has great prediction performance and is suited to WSF; and (d) overall, the HI-IVMD-DLinear exhibits superior precision and stability in one-to-four-step-ahead forecasting, highlighting its vast potential for application.

Keywords: wind speed forecasting; Hampel identifier; improved variational mode decomposition; grey wolf optimization; DLinear

MSC: 65-04

Citation: Liu, J.; Gong, C.; Chen, S.; Zhou, N. Multi-Step-Ahead Wind Speed Forecast Method Based on Outlier Correction, Optimized Decomposition, and DLinear Model. *Mathematics* **2023**, *11*, 2746. https://doi.org/10.3390/math11122746

Academic Editors: Zhuojia Fu, Yiqian He and Hui Zheng

Received: 22 May 2023
Revised: 7 June 2023
Accepted: 8 June 2023
Published: 17 June 2023

1. Introduction

The finite and non-renewable nature of fossil fuels has rendered the development and utilization of renewable energy an indispensable choice [1]. A report published in 2021 stated that the cumulative installed capacity of wind farms globally skyrocketed to 744 GW [2]. However, the inherent volatility and instability of wind energy led to frequent fluctuations in wind power, thereby causing continuous oscillations in grid voltage and frequency, which severely impairs power quality. Precise and dependable WSF are important for all aspects of wind power systems, including electricity market operation, energy storage system management, network planning, etc.

Recently, numerous forecasting methods have been developed to achieve WSF based on different time scales. These methods primarily include physical methods, statistical methods, machine learning methods, and neural network models. Physical methods rely on physical factors such as altitude and atmospheric pressure to construct models to predict the changes in wind speed. However, most physical factors are difficult to obtain in the vast majority of situations. Additionally, the construction and the calculation of physical models are complex, which makes it difficult to obtain accurate WSF in a short period [3–5]. Luckily, statistical methods such as the autoregressive (AR) [6] and autoregressive integrated moving average (ARIMA) methods [7,8] operate at a fast pace. These models were constructed mainly based on historical wind speed operational data. However, statistical methods can only deal with linear data, but not with nonlinear wind speed series. In addition, machine learning methods such as XGBoost [9], support vector regression (SVR) [10,11], and least squares support vector machine (LSSVM) [12] can identify more complex nonlinear relationships in sequences with good generalization abilities. Usually, the predictive performance of machine learning models on large datasets is limited. Compared with conventional machine learning models, neural networks are favorite due to their unique fully connected structure, which promises better prediction accuracy on large datasets. However, neural networks have not fully considered the temporal properties of wind speed sequences. There exists a loss of temporal information in wind speed sequences since neural networks treat time series as unordered and assign equal weight to all time points [13–15].

To address this issue, the recurrent neural network (RNN) was proposed. The self-connection among hidden layers in the RNN enables the retention of prior states, which are then incorporated into the current step. This mechanism facilitates the consideration of temporal information during the processing of sequential data [16]. It has two main variations: long short-term memory (LSTM) [17–19] and gated recurrent unit (GRU) [20–22]. LSTM resolves the problem of gradient vanishing and exploding encountered in RNN by introducing gate mechanisms and a special memory cell structure. Satyam et al. designed a wind speed prediction method with LSTM [17]. GRU is an improvement of LSTM based on a simpler memory cell structure with only two gates (reset gate and update gate) than LSTM. GRU outperforms LSTM in terms of computational efficiency and storage space [20–22]. Syu et al. introduced a WSF model based on GRU to provide more precise WSF than RNN and LSTM [23]. Although LSTM and GRU have shown good performance, they usually only model short-term dependencies, while the transformer can handle longer sequences of dependencies since it does not have a recurrent structure and can simultaneously view the entire sequence at all time steps. Furthermore, the self-attention mechanism of the transformer can capture local and global dependencies in a sequence, which can better handle key information in the sequence [24–26]. Wu et al. devised a multi-step WSF model based on the transformer, treating the problem as a sequence-to-sequence mapping. The transformer-based model has better prediction performance than the GRU [26]. However, Zeng et al. indicated that the comparatively elevated long-term forecasting accuracy of the transformer does not substantially correlate with its capability to extract temporal dependencies, and proposed a structurally simple DLinear model with better performance than the complex transformer model in most cases [27]. The effectiveness of WSF based on the transformer model should be reevaluated. Currently, the transformer model is widely employed in the field of WSF, yet its effectiveness in this domain is questionable. Its intricate structure does not improve the forecasting accuracy. To validate this proposition about the transformer, this study utilizes the DLinear as the foundational model for prediction, considering the transformer model as a comparable model. Furthermore, another reason to adopte the DLinear mode is its remarkably simple structure, which has exceptional forecasting accuracy.

Numerous studies have shown that, because of the non-stationarity and strong volatility of wind speed sequences, models with decomposition methods perform better in predicting wind speed than those without decomposition [25,28–30]. Decomposition-based models usually decompose the wind speed sequence into multiple sub-sequences, then forecast each sub-sequence, and then the ultimate prediction can be obtained by aggregating the results. Currently, the popular decomposition methods include wavelet transform (WT) [31,32], empirical mode decomposition (EMD) [33,34], and ensemble empirical mode decomposition (EEMD) [35,36]. Zhang et al. decomposed the initial wind speed sequence into finite sub-sequences by the complete ensemble empirical mode decomposition with adaptive noise (CEEMDAN) algorithm [37]. Subsequently, prediction models were applied to each sub-sequence to make individual forecasts. On the other hand, Pan et al. introduced the VMD method to decompose wind speed signals and exploit their latent information for more accurate forecasting results [38]. Li et al. decomposed ship-radiated noise signals, extracting feature information of different frequencies and amplitudes with successive variational mode decomposition (SVMD) [39]. Furthermore, VMD displays superior performance in decomposing non-stationary signals when compared to EMD and its improved methods [40]. Nevertheless, VMD lacks adaptability because critical parameters, e.g., the number of decomposition modes and regularization, require manual adjustment. The choice of these two parameters can impact the decomposition results and performance significantly. Moreover, the grey wolf optimization (GWO) algorithm exhibits superior optimization capabilities compared to renowned algorithms including particle swarm optimization, gravitational search algorithm, and evolution strategy [41]. Consequently, in this paper, the hyperparameters of VMD will be optimized by the GWO algorithm, thereby addressing the challenge of selecting the appropriate hyperparameters of VMD.

Additionally, there are few researches focusing on detecting and correcting outliers in the original wind speed sequence. It is reported that the predictive accuracy could be enhanced by rectifying outliers within the original sequence [42]. To detect and rectify outliers in the original wind speed sequence, the HI algorithm [43] is introduced to enhance the final accuracy of wind speed prediction.

In recent years, various metrics such as entropy [44] and correlation dimension [45] have been extensively employed in signal analysis across various research domains. Li et al. introduced an innovative technique known as simplified coded dispersion entropy (SCDE) to identify nonlinear dynamic transitions in signals [44]. A novel approach called FuzzDEα was developed to detect dynamic changes in time series data for signal analysis and fault diagnosis in bearings [46]. To assess the level of optimization of the hyperparameters of VMD by GWO, the envelope entropy (EE) [47] as the fitness function for GWO was employed. The magnitude of the EE serves as a criterion to evaluate the quality of the hyperparameters obtained by GWO. The magnitude of SampEn reflects the complexity level of a time series. If the series exhibits higher complexity, the corresponding SampEn value will be larger; conversely, a lower complexity will result in a smaller SampEn value [48]. Therefore, in this study, the SampEn will be utilized to assess the effectiveness of the HI.

Synthetically speaking, to achieve high accuracy and stability in WSF, a hybrid model is proposed based on outlier correction, heuristic algorithms, signal decomposition methods, and DLinear. The model begins by employing the HI to detect and rectify outliers in the original wind speed sequence. Subsequently, the GWO algorithm is utilized to optimize the hyperparameters of the VMD. Then, employing the VMD algorithm based on the optimal hyperparameters, the sequence processed by HI is decomposed into several sub-sequences. Lastly, each sub-sequence is forecasted by the DLinear algorithm individually. The final wind speed forecast is obtained by reconstructing the predictions. The primary contributions of this study are as follows:

(1) To detect and rectify outliers in the wind speed sequence, an outlier detection technique based on the Hampel identifier (HI) is utilized to enhance the accuracy of WSF.
(2) To optimize the hyperparameters of VMD, the variational mode decomposition is improved by the grey wolf optimization (GWO). The decomposition of the complex non-stationary windspeed sequence with the improved VMD (IVMD) algorithm can reduce the non-stationarity and the complexity of the sequence, thus improving the prediction stability and accuracy.
(3) DLinear is introduced as a fundamental prediction model including only one decomposition scheme and two linear networks. Its performance is significantly superior to both LSTM and the currently popular transformer models.

(4) The proposed method combining HI and IVMD with DLinear is utilized for the multi-step WSF of three real windspeed sequences. The performance of the HI-IVMD-DLinear is validated with comparative experiments from various aspects.

The rest of the paper is organized as follows: In Section 2, HI, GWO, VMD, DLinear, and the proposed method are described in detail. Section 3 elucidates the experimental configuration and elaborates, based on multiple evaluation criteria, on the performance of the proposed model. Section 4 provides a detailed discussion on the computational efficiency and the complexity of the HI-IVMD-DLinear. Finally, a concise conclusion is stated in Section 5.

2. Materials and Methods

2.1. Hampel Identifier

Hampel identifier (HI) is a robust algorithm to detect and replace outliers in datasets [43]. This method identifies any value that falls outside of a certain distance window from the median as an outlier and replaces it with the median value within that window. For dataset $D = [y_1, y_2, \ldots, y_n]$, let the window size be $w = 2k + 1$. Typically, window sizes of 5 or 7 are commonly used. The evaluation parameter α is set as 0.6745. By utilizing the median absolute deviation (MAD) and α, the standard deviation σ_i can be determined [49].

The HI method is composed of the following steps:

(1) Computing median, MAD, and standard deviation: For each data point, the median and the MAD of the neighboring points within the window size are calculated, and then the standard deviation based on the median and MAD can be computed as [42]:

$$m_i = \text{median}(y_{i-n}, y_{i-n+1}, \ldots, y_i, \ldots, y_{i+n-1}, y_{i+n}) \tag{1}$$

$$\text{MAD}_i = \text{median}(|y_{i-n} - m_i|, |y_{i-n+1} - m_i|, \ldots, |y_i - m_i|, \ldots, |y_{i+n-1} - m_i|, |y_{i+n} - m_i|) \tag{2}$$

$$\sigma_i = \text{MAD}_i / \alpha \tag{3}$$

(2) Detecting outlier points: A sample point is considered as an outlier if its value satisfies [50]:

$$|y_i - m_i| > 3\sigma_i \tag{4}$$

(3) Substituting outlier points: For the identified outlier points, the median of the window is used for substitution.

(4) Performing steps (1)–(3) for each sample point.

The HI method has more advantages over other similar methods in terms of robustness to outliers. Additionally, the HI method is highly efficient in computation, making it suitable for large-scale datasets. Processing the dataset with HI can effectively correct its outliers and enhance the accuracy in WSF.

2.2. Variational Mode Decomposition

The VMD is an adaptive decomposition algorithm [51]. Compared to traditional modal decomposition methods, the VMD could avoid aliasing and is more robust to noise.

The VMD method is capable of decomposing complex raw sequences into several relatively simple intrinsic mode functions (IMFs). The VMD is composed of the following steps:

(1) Construct the variational problem: It is essential for the variational problem to minimize the sum of central frequencies of the IMFs [51]:

$$\min_{\{u_k\},\{\omega_k\}} \left\{ \sum_{k=1}^{K} \| \partial_t \left[\left(\delta(t) + \frac{j}{\pi t} \right) * u_k(t) \right] e^{-j\omega_k t} \|_2{}^2 \right\} \tag{5}$$

$$\text{s.t.} \sum_{k=1}^{K} u_k(t) = f(t) \tag{6}$$

where u_k and ω_k are the $k-$th IMF and its corresponding center frequency, respectively; $\delta(t)$ is Dirac function; $f(t)$ is the original input signal; and K is the number of IMFs.

(2) Transform variational problems: To make it easier to solve the variational problem above, a Lagrange function is introduced [51]:

$$\begin{aligned} L(\{u_k\},\{\omega_k\},\lambda) = \alpha \sum_k \partial_t \left[\left(\delta(t) + \tfrac{j}{\pi t} \right) * u_k(t) \right] e^{-j\omega_k t}{}_2^2 \\ + f(t) - \sum_k u_k(t)_2^2 + \lambda(t), f(t) - \sum_k u_k(t) \end{aligned} \tag{7}$$

where α represents the penalty factor, and λ represents the Lagrange multiplier.

(3) Solve the variational problem: To achieve the best solution to the variational problem, the decomposition signal u_k and their corresponding center frequencies ω_k were updated by the alternate direction method of multipliers (ADMM). The cyclic updating rules and termination conditions for u_k and ω_k are as follows [51]:

$$\sum_k \frac{u_k^{n+1} - u_{k2}^{n2}}{u_{k2}^{n2}} < \varepsilon, n < N \tag{8}$$

$$u_k^{n+1}(\omega) = \frac{f(\omega) - \sum_{i \neq k}^{k} u_i^n(\omega) + \frac{\lambda^n(\omega)}{2}}{1 + 2a\left(\omega - \omega_k^n\right)^2} \tag{9}$$

$$\omega_k^{n+1} = \frac{\int_0^\infty \omega \left| u_k^n(\omega) \right|^2 d\omega}{\int_0^\infty \left| u_k^n(\omega) \right|^2 d\omega} \tag{10}$$

where $f(\omega)$, $u_i^n(\omega)$, and $\lambda^n(\omega)$ denote the Fourier transform of $f(t)$, $u_i^n(t)$, and $\lambda^n(t)$, respectively; and n and N are the number and the maximal number of iterations, respectively.

2.3. Grey Wolf Optimization

As a novel heuristic intelligent algorithm, Grey wolf optimization (GWO) [41] seeks the best solution based on the hunting characteristics of wolf packs and the social hierarchy system of grey wolves. There are four social ranks within a wolf pack: the alpha wolf (α), the wolves that obey the alpha (β), the wolves that obey the top two wolves (δ), and the wolves that obey higher-ranked wolves (ω). Their hunting process is:

(1) Wolves surround their prey:

$$D = \left| C \cdot Y_p(i) - Y(i) \right| \tag{11}$$

$$Y(i+1) = Y_p(i) - AD \tag{12}$$

where i denotes the current iteration, and D represents the distance between $Y_p(i)$ (prey) and $Y(i)$ (grey wolves). A and C (the coefficient vector) can be represented as:

$$A = 2br_1 - b \tag{13}$$

$$C = 2br_2 \tag{14}$$

where b is linearly diminished from 2 to 0 throughout the iterations; and r_1 and r_2 represent vector compositions comprising random elements, with the values of these elements ranging from 0 to 1. The grey wolves change their positions according to Equation (12).

(2) Capturing prey: As the location of prey cannot be determined, the optimal strategy cannot be identified either. Therefore, assuming that the α wolf is closest to the prey, followed by β and δ wolves, their distances from the prey are calculated with Equation (11). By iteratively updating the positions of these three types of wolves with Equation (12), the other wolves will also gradually approach the prey. Ultimately, the position of the α wolf is considered to be the location of the prey, leading to the optimal solution.

$$D_\alpha = |C_1 Y_\alpha - Y| \tag{15}$$

$$D_\beta = |C_2 Y_\beta - Y| \tag{16}$$

$$D_\delta = |C_3 Y_\delta - Y| \tag{17}$$

$$Y_1 = Y_\alpha - A_1 D_\alpha \tag{18}$$

$$Y_2 = Y_\beta - A_2 D_\beta \tag{19}$$

$$Y_3 = Y_\delta - A_2 D_\delta \tag{20}$$

$$Y(i+1) = \frac{Y_1 + Y_2 + Y_3}{3} \tag{21}$$

where $Y_j(j = \alpha, \beta, \delta)$ represents the position of the corresponding individual.

2.4. VMD Optimized by GWO

In practical applications, the hyperparameters K and α of VMD are directly related to the quality of the decomposition results and are often difficult to determine, although the VMD technique exhibits exceptional decomposition capabilities for wind speed sequences. An appropriate value of K can fully decompose the modal sequence, circumventing the emergence of mode-blending issues. α determines the accuracy of signal reconstruction. Therefore, appropriate K and α are crucial for the wind speed sequence decomposition process.

Therefore an improved VMD (IVMD) based on the GWO is proposed. The IVMD method determines K and α with the GWO. The range of K is set as [3, 12] and that of α is set as [0, 2000]. When the decomposed signal has less noise, the EE is smaller, and vice versa. Therefore, the minimal EE E_p is utilized as the fitness function for the GWO.

$$E_p = -\sum_{i=1}^{N} p_i \lg p_i \tag{22}$$

$$p_i = \frac{c(i)}{\sum_{i=1}^{N} c(i)} \tag{23}$$

$$c(i) = \sqrt{x^2(i) + x'^2(t)} \tag{24}$$

where N is the length of the signal, $x(i)$ represents the value of the i−th sample point of the decomposed sequence (IMF), and $x'(i)$ represents the demodulated result of Hibert of $x(i)$. The minimal envelope entropy is:

$$\min\{E_p\} = \min\{E_{p1}, E_{p2}, \ldots, E_{pK}\} \tag{25}$$

where E_{pj} represents the value of the EE of the j−th IMF.

The flowchart of IVMD is shown in Figure 1, and the steps of IVMD are as follows:

(1) Initialize the search space, encompass the ranges of K and α. Additionally, initiate the parameters of the grey wolf optimization algorithm, such as population size, maximum number of iterations, and so forth.

(2) Generate the initial population of grey wolves randomly within the provided search space. For each grey wolf denoted by $i = 1, 2, \ldots, N$ (where N represents the total number of grey wolves), the position Y_i is initialized as (K_i, α_i).

(3) Calculate the envelope entropy of each grey wolf with Equation (22). The positions of the three grey wolves with the lowest envelope entropy values are updated by Y_α, Y_β, and Y_δ, respectively. Y_α with the best fitness value is recognized as the optimal solution.

(4) Compute the distance between the remaining grey wolf individuals (ω) and the top three grey wolf individual locations Y_α, Y_β and Y_δ according to Equations (15)–(17).

(5) According to Equations (18)–(21), update the position of individual grey wolves.

(6) If the iteration of GWO reaches maximum, the algorithm ends and outputs an optimal solution Y_α; otherwise, return to (3) and continue the optimization search.

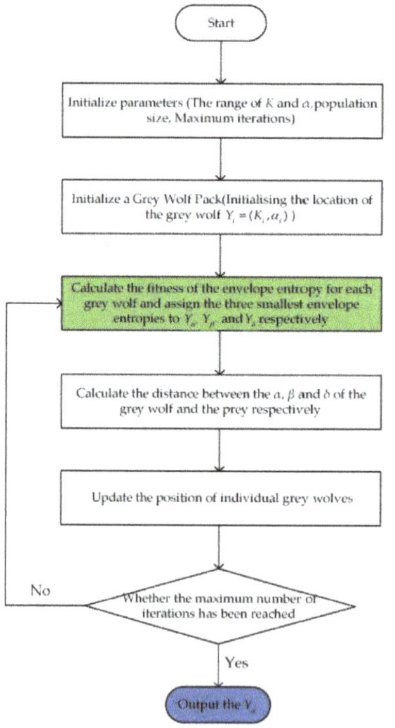

Figure 1. Flowchart of IVMD.

2.5. DLinear

DLinear is a novel high-precision time-series forecasting model proposed by Zeng et al. in 2022 [27]. Despite its simple structure, consisting solely of a decomposition scheme and two linear networks, its predictive accuracy exceeds that of the more complex transformer model.

During the prediction process, the DLinear first decomposes the original sequence X into a trend component X_t and a residual one $X_r(X_r = X - X_t)$. Subsequently, two single-layer linear networks are utilized to forecast each of these decomposed components, respectively.

The foundational architecture of DLinear is depicted in Figure 2a. The output results of the two single-layer linear networks are combined to yield the final predicted outcome $\hat{X}$ [27].

$$H_r = W_r X_r \tag{26}$$

$$H_t = W_t X_t \tag{27}$$

$$\hat{X} = H_t + H_r \tag{28}$$

where H_r and H_t are the output values of the single-layer linear networks for the residual and trend components, respectively. Similarly, W_r and W_t represent the single-layer linear networks for the residual and the trend components, as depicted in Figure 2b.

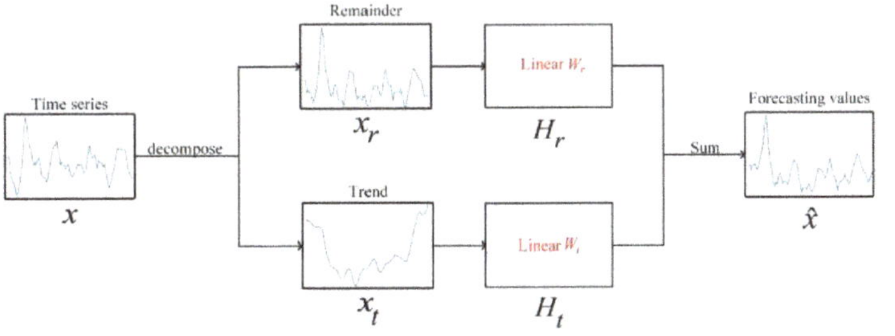

(a)

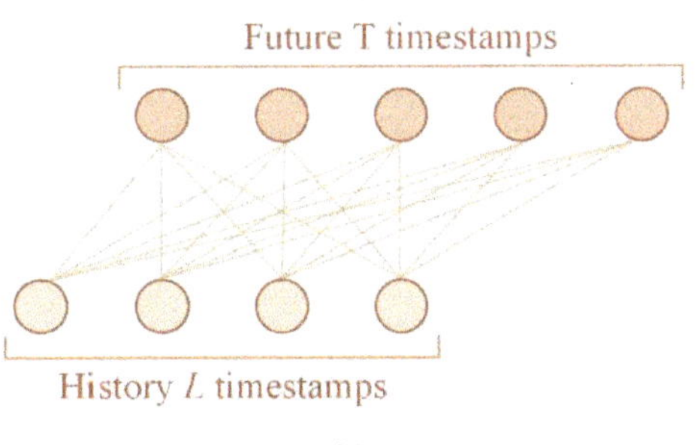

(b)

Figure 2. Illustration of DLinear. (**a**): architecture of DLinear; (**b**): architecture of single-layer linear networks.

2.6. Framework of the Proposed Model

The HI-IVMD-DLinear model is designed to achieve accurate multi-step WSF. The basic framework of this hybrid WSF model is illustrated in Figure 3, which mainly consists of three steps as follows:

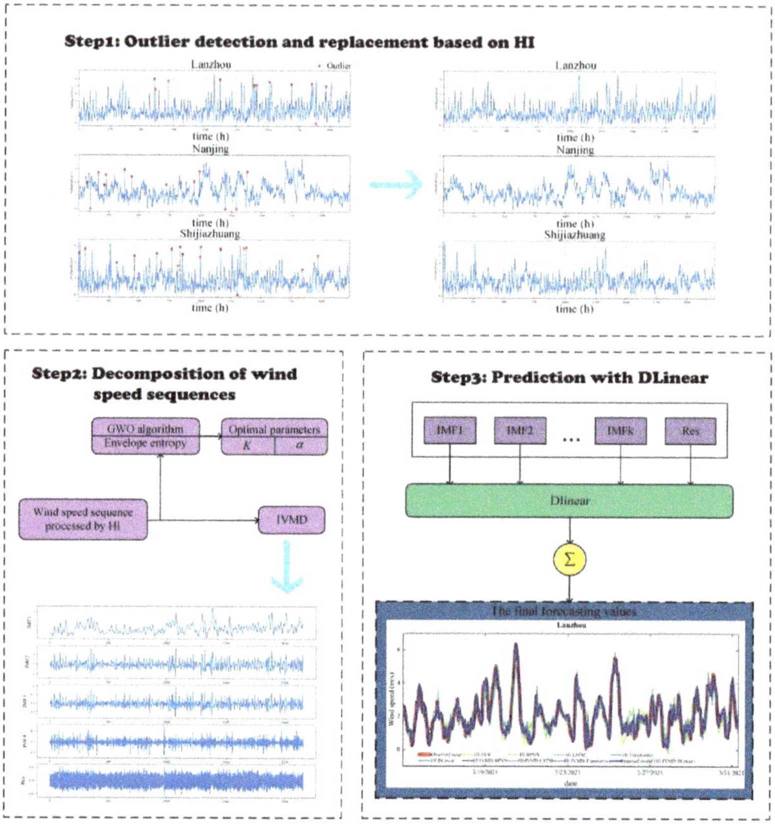

Figure 3. The basic framework of HI-IVMD-DLinear model.

Step 1: Outlier detection and replacement based on HI. Due to equipment malfunctions, human factors, and other reasons, it is inevitable that the collected wind speed data will contain outliers during the data collection process. The HI method is used to detect and replace outliers in the dataset, which is beneficial to improve the accuracy of WSF.

Step 2: Decomposition of wind speed sequences. The sequence processed by the HI is considered as input for the VMD. The GWO is then employed to optimize the hyperparameters K and α of the VMD with the minimal envelope entropy as the fitness function. Based on the optimized values of K and α, the VMD decomposes the sequence into K IMFs.

Step 3: Prediction with DLinear. The DLinear model is constructed to predict each of the K IMFs obtained from the decomposition. Subsequently, the predicted results are summed to derive the ultimate wind speed prediction.

3. Results

3.1. Design of the Experiment

3.1.1. Data Source

The historical wind speed datasets collected from three regions in China serve as the experimental dataset. These three regions are, respectively, located in Shijiazhuang, Hebei Province; Lanzhou, Gansu Province; and Nanjing, Jiangsu Province. Their latitudes and longitudes are significantly different. Lanzhou and Shijiazhuang are situated in the northwestern and northern inland regions, respectively, both possessing abundant wind energy resources. On the other hand, Nanjing is located in the southeastern coastal area and consistently ranks among the top in terms of offshore wind power installed capacity nationwide. The wind speed sequences from all three regions were measured at a height of ten meters above ground level at hourly intervals. The basic information of the three wind speed datasets is presented in Table 1.

Table 1. Basic information of three datasets.

Dataset	Time Interval	Sample Size	Minimum	Mean	Maximum	Standard Deviation
Lanzhou	1 January 2021–31 March 2021	2160	0.000	1.830	6.765	1.317
Nanjing	1 August 2021–1 November 2021	2232	0.000	2.849	7.657	1.705
Shijiazhuang	1 July 2021–1 October 2021	2232	0.000	1.844	6.408	1.585

3.1.2. Evaluation Metrics

To evaluate the accuracy of the prediction methods, the mean absolute error (MAE), root mean square error (RMSE), and mean absolute percentage error (MAPE) are employed

$$\mathrm{MAE} = \frac{1}{N}\sum_{t=1}^{N}\left|\hat{Y}_t - Y_t\right| \tag{29}$$

$$\mathrm{RMSE} = \sqrt{\frac{1}{N}\sum_{t=1}^{N}\left(\hat{Y}_t - Y_t\right)^2} \tag{30}$$

$$\mathrm{MAPE} = \frac{\sum_{t=1}^{N}\left|\frac{\hat{Y}_t - Y_t}{Y_t}\right|}{N} \times 100\% \tag{31}$$

where $\hat{Y}_t$ represents the predicted value of the wind speed, Y_t represents the observed value, and N refers to the number of test-set samples. Generally speaking, as the values of these metrics decrease, the prediction accuracy of the model increases.

Furthermore, improvement percentage is utilized to quantitatively evaluate the proposed model. P_{RMSE}, P_{MAE}, and P_{MAPE} are the improvement percentages for RMSE, MAE, and MAPE, respectively.

$$P_{\mathrm{RMSE}} = \frac{\mathrm{RMSE}_i - \mathrm{RMSE}_j}{\mathrm{RMSE}_i} \times 100\% \tag{32}$$

$$P_{\mathrm{MAE}} = \frac{\mathrm{MAE}_i - \mathrm{MAE}_j}{\mathrm{MAE}_i} \times 100\% \tag{33}$$

$$P_{\mathrm{MAPE}} = \frac{\mathrm{MAPE}_i - \mathrm{MAPE}_j}{\mathrm{MAPE}_i} \times 100\% \tag{34}$$

where RMSE_i, MAE_i, and MAPE_i represent the errors of the comparative methods, while RMSE_j, MAE_j, and MAPE_j represent the errors of the HI-IVMD-DLinear method. The larger the P_{RMSE}, P_{MAE}, and P_{MAPE} are, the more superior the precision of the proposed model is.

In addition, the variance of absolute error (VAE) is introduced to assess the stability of the model.

$$\mathrm{VAE} = \mathrm{Var}\left(\left|Y_t - \hat{Y}_t\right|\right) \tag{35}$$

Simultaneously, the improvement percentage of VAE is also introduced to compare the proposed model with the comparative model.

$$P_{\mathrm{VAE}} = \frac{\mathrm{VAE}_i - \mathrm{VAE}_j}{\mathrm{VAE}_i} \times 100\% \tag{36}$$

where VAE_i and VAE_j represent the VAE of the comparative model and the proposed one, respectively.

3.1.3. Model Development

To assess the performance of HI-IVMD-DLinear, a machine learning model, SVR, two prevalent neural network models, namely, back propagation neural network (BPNN) and LSTM, as well as a popular deep learning algorithm, the transformer, are incorporated as comparative models.

The input for predicting the output values includes the true values from the previous 24 h; i.e., the time window size is 24 h. Table 2 provides the parameter settings for all relevant models, along with the methods used to confirm these parameters. The dataset is divided into training, validation, and testing sets at a ratio of 7:1:2. Additionally, all models employ mean squared error (MSE) as the loss function. To optimize the weights and enhance the prediction performance, the Adam algorithm is employed as an optimizer [52].

Table 2. Parameters of all related methods.

Methods	Parameters	Values
IVMD	Population size	50
	Maximum iterations	30
	K	[3, 11]
	α	[0, 1000]
SVR	C	[0, 10]
	Epsilon	[0, 1]
	Gamma	[0, 2]
BPNN	Dropout	[0.05, 0.2]
	Batchsize	64
	Epochs	100
	Initial lr	0.1
	Hidden_units	[10, 100]
LSTM	Dropout	[0.05, 0.2]
	Batchsize	64
	Epochs	100
	Initial lr	0.1
	Hidden_units	[10, 100]
Transformer	Dropout	[0.05, 0.2]
	Batchsize	64
	Epochs	100
	Initial lr	0.1
	Model dimension	[64, 256]
	Feedforward dimension	[128, 256]
	Heads number	[1, 5]
	Enc_layers	[1, 5]
	Dec_layers	[1, 5]
DLinear	Batchsize	64
	Epochs	100
	Initial lr	0.1

3.2. *Analysis of Hampel Identifier*

The performance of utilizing HI for the data cleaning of the wind speed sequence is explored in this section. As illustrated in Figure 4, all three wind speed datasets exhibit some outliers. Failure to clean these outliers would adversely impact the accuracy of the final WSF. Therefore, the HI method can be utilized to handle the outliers in the wind speed sequences. The effectiveness of the HI can generally be evaluated by calculating the sample entropy of the sequences. The magnitude of the SampEn value reflects the complexity of the sequence [48]. If the complexity of the sequence is greater, the SampEn value will be larger, and vice versa. The SampEn values of the original wind speed sequences and the HI-processed wind speed sequences are presented in Table 3. It is evident that the SampEn values of all three wind speed sequences are reduced after applying the HI method. It indicates that the HI method can reduce the complexity of the original sequences.

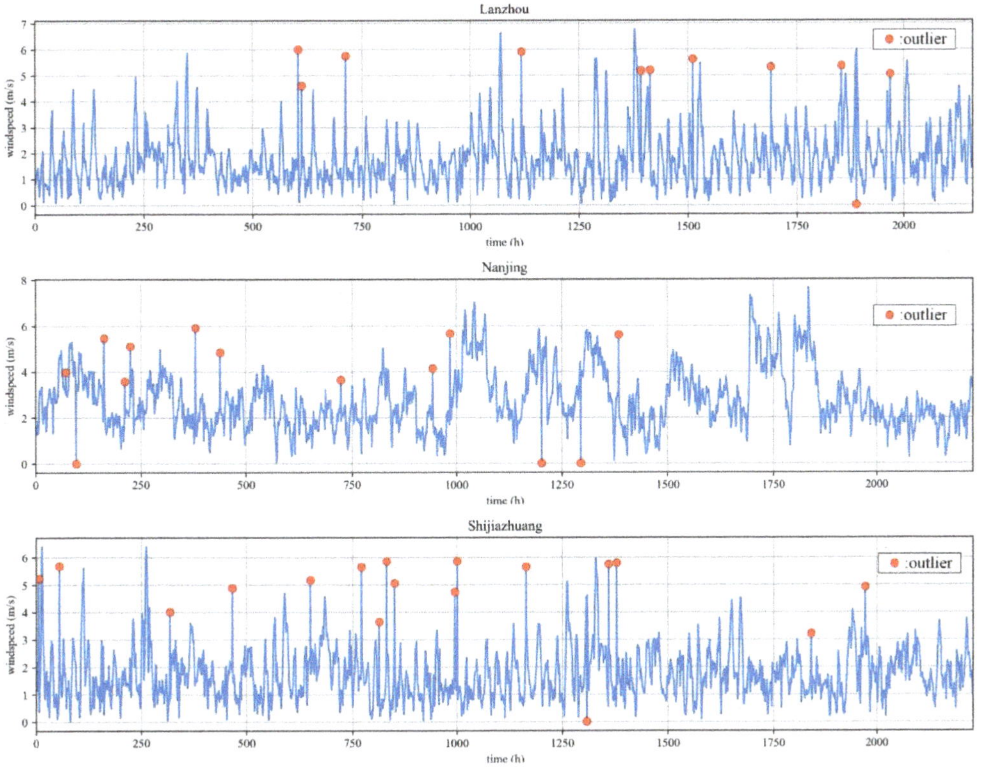

Figure 4. Original wind speed sequences of Lanzhou, Nanjing, and Shijiazhuang.

Table 3. The SampEn value of original and HI-processed datasets.

SampEn	Lanzhou	Nanjing	Shijiazhuang
Original sequence	1.0562	1.0230	1.0658
Sequence after HI	1.0497	0.9534	0.9570

The predictive performances of models with and without HI are also compared. Table 4 gives the forecasting accuracy of models with HI processing and without HI processing under the three datasets. It can be observed that the improvement percentages of MAPE are 1.2316%, 2.1240%, and 2.1531% compared with the HI-IVMD-DLinear with IVMD-DLinear, respectively. Other HI-based models also reduce the RMSE, MAE, and MAPE values. Therfore the HI can enhance the accuracy of WSF, since HI is able to identify and rectify outliers in the original wind speed sequence, which can efficiently mitigate the interference caused by such outliers.

Table 4. Improvement percentages with HI.

Dataset	Model	P_{MAE} (%)	P_{RMSE} (%)	P_{MAPE} (%)
Lanzhou	HI-SVR vs. SVR	2.1206	4.1472	2.5125
	HI-LSTM vs. LSTM	1.2452	3.5612	2.0106
	HI-Transformer vs. Transformer	0.8921	3.5125	2.2215
	HI-DLinear vs. DLinear	0.9915	1.1305	1.7683
	HI-IVMD-DLinear vs. IVMD-DLinear	0.7624	1.0614	1.2316
Nanjing	HI-SVR vs. SVR	1.5125	3.8903	1.7246
	HI-LSTM vs. LSTM	2.2092	5.2137	3.0165
	HI-Transformer vs. Transformer	1.2875	5.1751	3.1062
	HI-DLinear vs. DLinear	2.1785	2.1867	2.1554
	HI-IVMD-DLinear vs. IVMD-DLinear	1.0126	1.8751	2.1240
Shijiazhuang	HI-SVR vs. SVR	3.5613	3.1451	6.1246
	HI-LSTM vs. LSTM	2.5146	0.8915	4.1256
	HI-Transformer vs. Transformer	1.8745	1.3271	4.6012
	HI-DLinear vs. DLinear	2.0761	1.0512	3.1251
	HI-IVMD-DLinear vs. IVMD-DLinear	1.5612	0.7951	2.1531

3.3. Decomposition Results

According to the augmented Dickey–Fuller (ADF) test results presented in Table 5, the ADF statistics of the three datasets, after undergoing HI processing, are all below the critical values at the 1%, 5%, and 10% confidence levels. Additionally, their p-values are greater than 0.1. It is evident that the three wind speed sequences are non-stationary. Hence, it is imperative to decompose the wind speed sequences appropriately to reduce their complexity. The parameters of VMD are optimized by the GWO. The obtained hyperparameters K and α for VMD on the three datasets are 4 and 1.2771, 4 and 0.4501, 5 and 0.2580, respectively.

Table 5. ADF test results.

Datasets	t-Statistic	p-Value	1% Level	5% Level	10% Level
Lanzhou	−1.714	0.3704	−3.2334	−2.6828	−2.3674
Nanjing	−1.227	0.5513	−2.8910	−2.2150	−1.9674
Shijiazhuang	−1.827	0.3207	−3.3517	−2.7124	−2.4512

Taking Lanzhou as an example, the decomposition results of the wind speed sequence, after undergoing HI processing, are illustrated in Figure 5a. IVMD decomposes the sequence of Lanzhou into four IMFs. Among them, IMF1 has the lowest frequency and displays the long-term trend of the wind speed sequence. IMF2 and IMF3 belong to the mid-frequency range signals, reflecting the fluctuations within smaller periods. IMF4 represents the high-frequency range signal. Evidently, the sequence exhibits a more regular pattern after the IVMD decomposition.

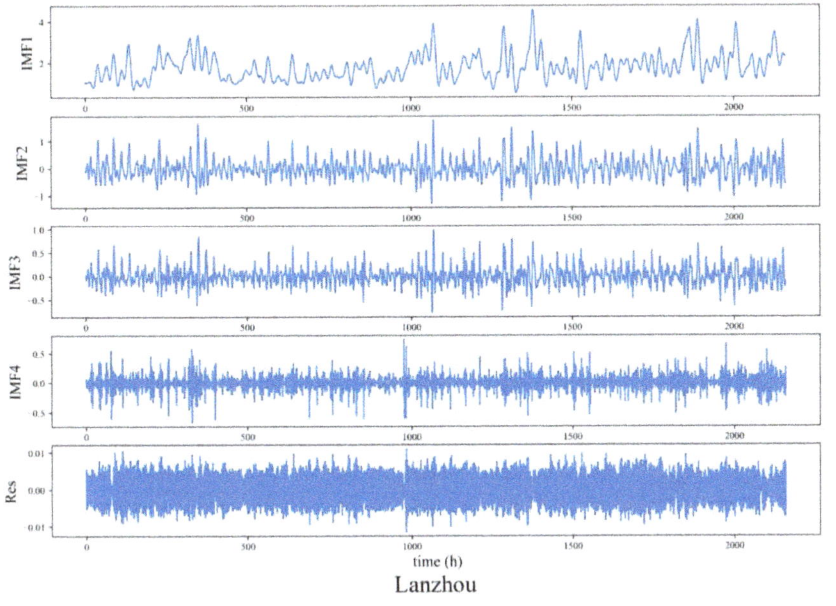

(**a**)

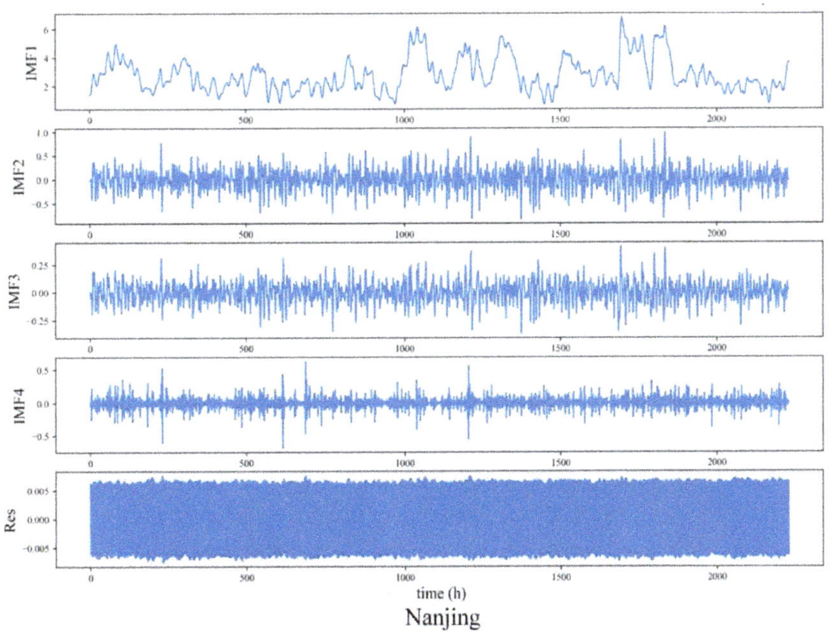

(**b**)

Figure 5. *Cont.*

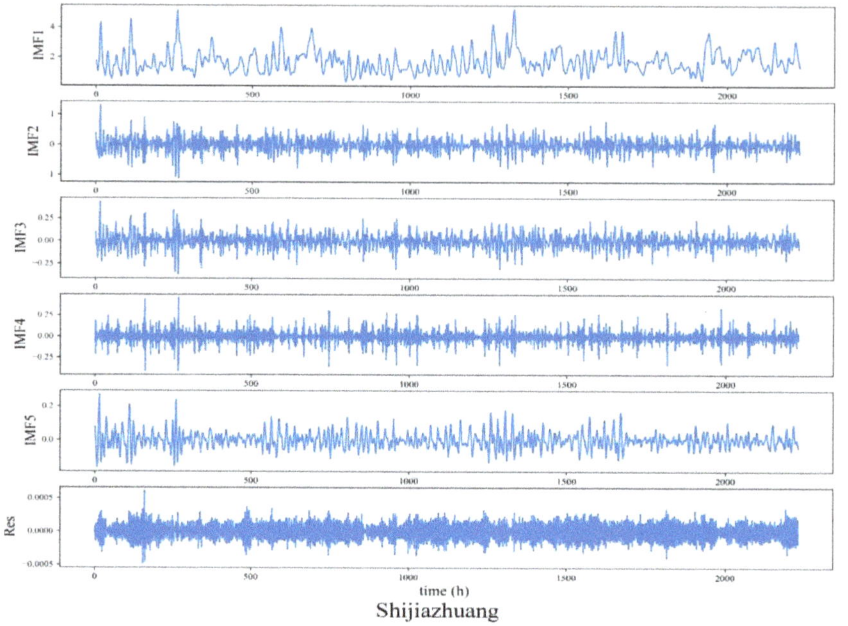

(c)

Figure 5. Decomposition results of the three wind speed sequences: (**a**) Lanzhou, (**b**) Nanjing, and (**c**) Shijiazhuang. Res is the noise after decomposition.

3.4. Forecasting Results

The HI-processed dataset is utilized for IVMD decomposition, with the subsequent prediction of each modal component with DLinear. Summing the predicted outcomes of these components yields the final WSF. Specifically, during training, only the training set should undergo decomposition, ensuring the data in the test set remain unknown. This safeguards against the inflated accuracy resulting from test set leakage. Subsequently, the IMFs derived from the training set decomposition are employed to train the model, while hyperparameter selection is performed on the validation set. Finally, test is conducted on the designated subsequence of the complete dataset. To assess the performance of the HI-IVMD-DLinear, HI-SVR, HI-BPNN, HI-LSTM, HI-Transformer, HI-DLinear, HI-IVMD-BPNN, HI-IVMD-LSTM, and HI-IVMD-Transformer are considered.

During the process of WSF, it is important to forecast wind speeds for multiple hours in advance. For instance, multi-step WSF assists wind power generation companies in accurately anticipating changes in wind speed over a specific period. This enables them to devise more efficient power generation plans and scheduling strategies to enhance the capacity and the efficiency of wind power generation. Therefore, the introduction of multi-step WSF is crucial. Given the wind speed sequence $\{Y_1, Y_2, Y_3, \ldots, Y_T\}$, the forecasting value for the $k-$th step can be calculated as

$$\hat{Y}_{t+k} = f\left(Y_t, Y_{t-1}, \ldots, Y_{t-(w-1)}\right), t = 1, 2, \ldots, T \tag{37}$$

where $\hat{Y}_{t+k}$ represents the predicted value at time $t+k$, Y_t represents the observed value at time t, and w refers to the lag order. The value of w is set as 24, in other words, the model takes the past 24 h wind speed sequence as its input. The horizon k ranges from 1 to 4.

3.4.1. Forecasting Accuracy

The forecasting results of three metrics for HI-IVMD-DLinear and other comparative models are presented in Tables 6–8. In all three datasets, the HI-IVMD-DLinear model outperforms the others in terms of MAE, RMSE, and MAPE. The HI-IVMD-DLinear exhibits the best predictive accuracy among the comparative models and is better suitable for the WSF task.

Table 6. Results of three evaluation metrics of multi-step-ahead prediction in Lanzhou.

Estimation Horizon	Metric	HI-SVR	HI-BPNN	HI-LSTM	HI-Transformer	HI-DLinear	HI-IVMD-BPNN	HI-IVMD-LSTM	HI-IVMD-Transformer	HI-IVMD-DLinear
1-step	MAE	0.3179	0.2773	0.2689	0.2366	0.2064	0.1688	0.1213	0.0767	**0.0501**
	RMSE	0.4116	0.3750	0.3592	0.3261	0.2582	0.2038	0.1452	0.1069	**0.0641**
	MAPE	0.1535	0.1494	0.1362	0.1213	0.1023	0.0745	0.0700	0.0421	**0.0237**
2-step	MAE	0.4391	0.4380	0.3345	0.3301	0.2826	0.2273	0.2025	0.1512	**0.1207**
	RMSE	0.6031	0.5832	0.4533	0.4426	0.3779	0.3152	0.2898	0.2124	**0.1578**
	MAPE	0.2240	0.2251	0.1785	0.1844	0.1596	0.1223	0.1065	0.0814	**0.0601**
3-step	MAE	0.4512	0.4405	0.385	0.3816	0.3434	0.2877	0.2587	0.2223	**0.1398**
	RMSE	0.6001	0.5813	0.5164	0.5173	0.4567	0.4045	0.3649	0.2882	**0.1909**
	MAPE	0.2356	0.2304	0.212	0.2098	0.1799	0.1765	0.1528	0.1103	**0.0687**
4-step	MAE	0.5240	0.5114	0.4412	0.4133	0.3713	0.3437	0.3381	0.2512	**0.1666**
	RMSE	0.6861	0.6732	0.5942	0.5559	0.4898	0.4125	0.3538	0.3051	**0.2136**
	MAPE	0.2523	0.2581	0.2345	0.2295	0.2034	0.2010	0.1782	0.1312	**0.0839**

Table 7. Results of three evaluation metrics of multi-step-ahead prediction in Nanjing.

Estimation Horizon	Metric	HI-SVR	HI-BPNN	HI-LSTM	HI-Transformer	HI-DLinear	HI-IVMD-BPNN	HI-IVMD-LSTM	HI-IVMD-Transformer	HI-IVMD-DLinear
1-step	MAE	0.4463	0.4080	0.3691	0.3572	0.3295	0.1325	0.1152	0.0911	**0.0705**
	RMSE	0.5533	0.5324	0.471	0.4694	0.4332	0.1668	0.1472	0.1253	**0.0881**
	MAPE	0.3839	0.3082	0.292	0.2705	0.2418	0.0917	0.0792	0.0632	**0.0479**
2-step	MAE	0.5244	0.5035	0.4785	0.4696	0.3797	0.2258	0.208	0.1717	**0.1113**
	RMSE	0.6814	0.6615	0.6172	0.6118	0.4699	0.2989	0.2752	0.229	**0.1477**
	MAPE	0.4356	0.4045	0.3905	0.3766	0.2557	0.1562	0.1511	0.1118	**0.0773**
3-step	MAE	0.5724	0.5620	0.5368	0.5304	0.4531	0.2592	0.211	0.1871	**0.1381**
	RMSE	0.7621	0.7394	0.6977	0.7005	0.6014	0.3488	0.3001	0.2624	**0.1834**
	MAPE	0.4761	0.4300	0.4477	0.4459	0.3346	0.1825	0.1629	0.1412	**0.0956**
4-step	MAE	0.6348	0.6034	0.5716	0.5615	0.4495	0.3071	0.2509	0.2215	**0.1648**
	RMSE	0.8500	0.8108	0.7718	0.7457	0.6271	0.4024	0.3583	0.2918	**0.2289**
	MAPE	0.5298	0.5009	0.4826	0.4682	0.3532	0.2206	0.2012	0.1811	**0.1266**

Table 8. Results of three evaluation metrics of multi-step-ahead prediction in Shijiazhuang.

Estimation Horizon	Metric	HI-SVR	HI-BPNN	HI-LSTM	HI-Transformer	HI-DLinear	HI-IVMD-BPNN	HI-IVMD-LSTM	HI-IVMD-Transformer	HI-IVMD-DLinear
1-step	MAE	0.3073	0.3041	0.2697	0.2540	0.2060	0.1441	0.1277	0.0939	**0.0669**
	RMSE	0.3937	0.3908	0.3564	0.3383	0.2847	0.2013	0.1765	0.1283	**0.0861**
	MAPE	0.2506	0.2281	0.1935	0.1936	0.1510	0.1225	0.1022	0.0661	**0.0480**
2-step	MAE	0.4121	0.4139	0.4026	0.3745	0.2976	0.2255	0.1768	0.1202	**0.0814**
	RMSE	0.5261	0.5286	0.5188	0.5040	0.3945	0.3132	0.2371	0.1612	**0.1054**
	MAPE	0.2799	0.2823	0.3379	0.2642	0.2215	0.1946	0.1268	0.0912	**0.0569**
3-step	MAE	0.4625	0.4574	0.4396	0.3995	0.3246	0.2752	0.2248	0.1512	**0.1000**
	RMSE	0.6031	0.5997	0.5657	0.5401	0.4224	0.3674	0.2903	0.2342	**0.1338**
	MAPE	0.3412	0.3275	0.3392	0.3114	0.2551	0.2157	0.1735	0.1023	**0.0690**
4-step	MAE	0.4951	0.4941	0.4871	0.4519	0.3814	0.3502	0.2861	0.2215	**0.1439**
	RMSE	0.6431	0.6335	0.6195	0.5761	0.4745	0.4264	0.3683	0.3012	**0.2141**
	MAPE	0.3620	0.3639	0.3530	0.3614	0.3095	0.2849	0.2543	0.2202	**0.1023**

Taking Lanzhou as an example, compared with other models, the HI-IVMD-DLinear model achieves lower MAE, RMSE, and MAPE values. The MAE, RMSE, and MAPE values for the HI-IVMD-DLinear's one-step-ahead prediction are 0.0705, 0.0881, and 0.0479, respectively, which are smaller than those of other models. Specifically, the MAPE values for HI-SVR, HI-BPNN, HI-LSTM, HI-Transformer, HI-DLinear, HI-IVMD-BPNN, HI-IVMD-LSTM, HI-IVMD-Transformer, and HI-IVMD-DLinear are 0.3839, 0.3082, 0.2920, 0.2705, 0.2418, 0.0917, 0.0792, 0.0632, and 0.0479, respectively. Among them, the HI-IVMD-DLinear achieves the smallest MAPE value. Moreover, for one-step-ahead to four-steps-ahead predictions, the HI-IVMD-DLinear obtains the optimal MAPE values of 0.0773, 0.0956, and

0.1266, respectively. Additionally, the HI-IVMD-DLinear also obtains the best MAE and RMSE values.

Furthermore, according to Tables 6–8, it is evident that the hybrid methods based on IVMD outperform the individual models in terms of accuracy. Taking the one-step-ahead forecasting in Lanzhou as an example, the MAPE value of the HI-DLinear is 0.2418, while that of the HI-IVMD-DLinear is 0.0479. Therefore the IVMD method helps diminish the complexity of the wind speed series enables the forecasting model to capture valuable patterns within the wind speed series, and effectively improves the forecasting performance.

The comparison between the predicted and the observed wind speed values in the three datasets is illustrated in Figure 6. It can be observed that the prediction curve of the HI-IVMD-DLinear hybrid model closely resembles that of the observed wind speed values. This highlights better predictive accuracy of the HI-IVMD-DLinear model in the field of WSF than other comparative models.

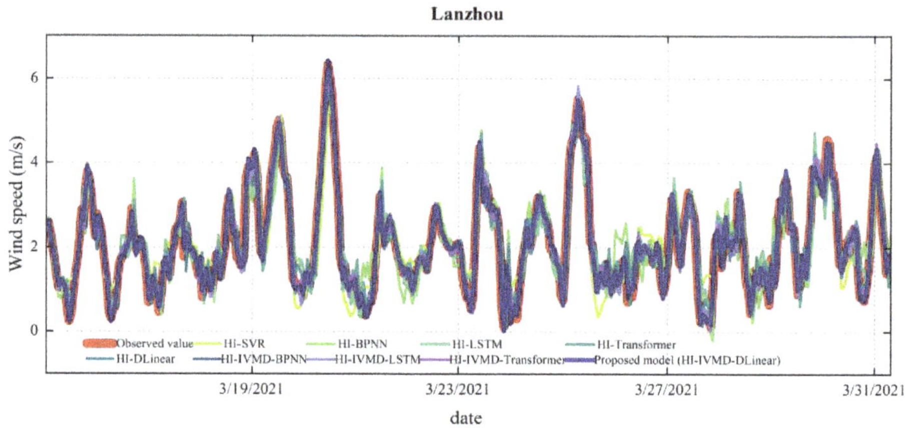

(a)

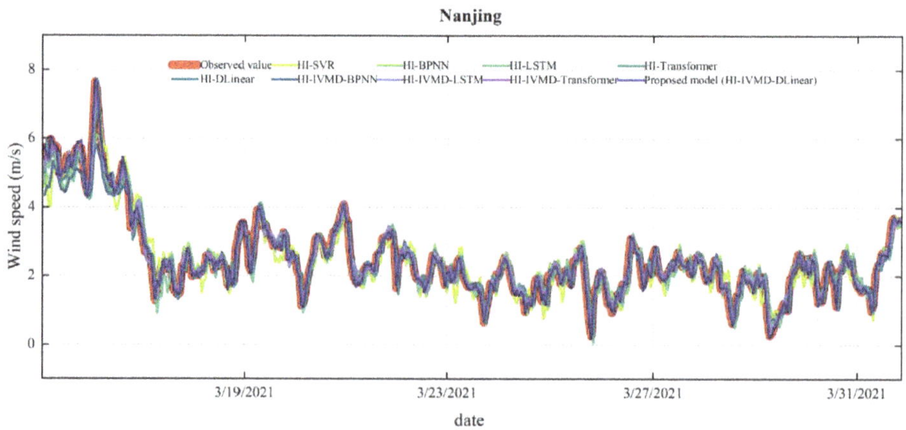

(b)

Figure 6. *Cont.*

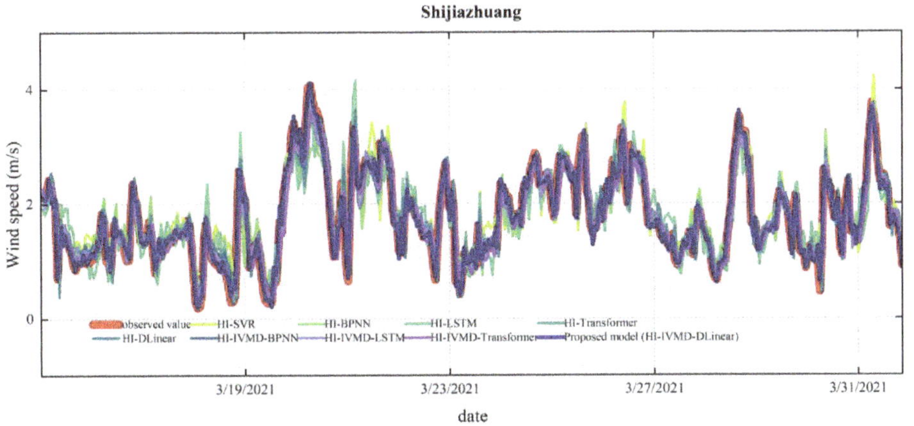

(c)

Figure 6. Results of one-step-ahead prediction: (**a**) Lanzhou; (**b**) Nanjing; (**c**) Shijiazhuang.

Meanwhile, compared with the individual HI-SVR, HI-BPNN, HI-LSTM, HI-Transformer, and HI-DLinear models, the prediction curves of HI-IVMD-SVR, HI-IVMD-BPNN, HI-IVMD-LSTM, HI-IVMD-Transformer, and HI-IVMD-DLinear across the three datasets exhibit a higher degree of similarity to the observed wind speed curves. Thus the IVMD decomposition is helpful in WSF.

3.4.2. Improvement Percentage in Accuracy

The improvement percentages of accuracy metrics for the HI-IVMD-DLinear model are presented in Tables 9–11. It can be seen that the proposed model consistently achieves the lowest prediction errors across all four forecasting horizons on the three wind speed datasets. Thus the accuracy of the proposed model is acceptable.

Table 9. Improvement percentages on three metrics of HI-IVMD-DLinear compared with comparable models in Lanzhou.

Estimation Horizon	Metric	HI-SVR	HI-BPNN	HI-LSTM	HI-Transformer	HI-DLinear	HI-IVMD-BPNN	HI-IVMD-LSTM	HI-IVMD-Transformer
1-step	P_{MAE} (%)	84.2033	82.7196	80.9005	80.2659	78.6032	46.7841	38.8104	22.6125
	P_{RMSE} (%)	84.0766	83.4535	81.2947	81.2296	79.6612	47.1681	40.1372	29.6887
	P_{MAPE} (%)	87.5236	84.4584	83.5969	82.2938	80.1936	47.7605	39.5475	24.2089
2-step	P_{MAE} (%)	78.7740	77.8952	76.7398	76.3006	70.6891	50.7040	46.4791	35.1776
	P_{RMSE} (%)	78.3228	77.6722	76.0693	75.8583	68.5685	50.5914	46.3353	35.5022
	P_{MAPE} (%)	82.2549	80.8899	80.2049	79.4739	69.7645	50.5266	48.8467	30.8587
3-step	P_{MAE} (%)	75.8735	75.4275	74.2732	73.9633	69.5241	46.7304	34.5396	26.1892
	P_{RMSE} (%)	75.9363	75.1968	73.7148	73.8202	69.5041	47.4129	38.8968	30.1067
	P_{MAPE} (%)	79.9212	77.7699	78.6447	78.5622	71.4304	47.6040	41.3313	32.2946
4-step	P_{MAE} (%)	74.0380	72.6866	71.1707	70.6518	63.3334	46.3339	34.3082	25.5982
	P_{RMSE} (%)	73.0713	71.7671	70.3405	69.3023	63.4987	43.1154	36.1221	21.5559
	P_{MAPE} (%)	76.1047	74.7235	73.7673	72.9588	64.1566	42.6058	37.0858	30.0939

Table 10. Improvement percentages on three metrics of HI-IVMD-DLinear compared with comparable models in Nanjing.

Estimation Horizon	Metric	HI-SVR	HI-BPNN	HI-LSTM	HI-Transformer	HI-DLinear	HI-IVMD-BPNN	HI-IVMD-LSTM	HI-IVMD-Transformer
1-step	P_{MAE} (%)	84.2409	81.9333	81.3657	78.8260	75.7224	70.3199	58.6831	34.6806
	P_{RMSE} (%)	84.4272	82.9060	82.1564	80.3460	75.1727	68.5442	55.8529	40.0374
	P_{MAPE} (%)	84.5591	84.1313	82.5998	80.4556	76.8356	68.1678	66.1645	43.7055
2-step	P_{MAE} (%)	72.5134	72.4446	63.9205	63.4358	57.2882	46.8873	40.3826	20.1904
	P_{RMSE} (%)	73.8362	72.9428	65.1858	64.3458	58.2394	49.9432	45.5538	25.6908
	P_{MAPE} (%)	73.1711	73.2950	66.3302	67.4084	62.3519	50.8716	43.5630	26.1879
3-step	P_{MAE} (%)	69.0184	68.2667	63.6840	63.3623	59.2891	51.4043	45.9572	37.1233
	P_{RMSE} (%)	68.1908	67.1616	63.0349	63.0957	58.1990	52.8060	47.6892	33.7700
	P_{MAPE} (%)	70.8416	70.1822	67.5903	67.2581	61.8191	61.0778	55.0276	37.7379
4-step	P_{MAE} (%)	68.2063	67.4222	62.2392	59.6876	55.1269	51.5240	50.7219	33.6865
	P_{RMSE} (%)	68.8684	68.2711	64.0548	61.5750	56.3870	48.2202	39.6268	29.9954
	P_{MAPE} (%)	66.7518	67.4935	64.2221	63.4508	58.7554	58.2622	52.9276	36.0750

Table 11. Improvement percentages on three metrics of HI-IVMD-DLinear compared with comparable models in Shijiazhuang.

Estimation Horizon	Metric	HI-SVR	HI-BPNN	HI-LSTM	HI-Transformer	HI-DLinear	HI-IVMD-BPNN	HI-IVMD-LSTM	HI-IVMD-Transformer
1-step	P_{MAE} (%)	78.2167	77.99	75.18	73.65	67.50	53.54	47.59	28.72
	P_{RMSE} (%)	78.1334	77.97	75.84	74.55	69.76	57.24	51.21	32.90
	P_{MAPE} (%)	80.8590	78.98	75.22	75.23	68.24	60.86	53.09	27.44
2-step	P_{MAE} (%)	80.2491	80.33	79.78	78.26	72.65	63.90	53.96	32.25
	P_{RMSE} (%)	79.9665	80.06	79.68	79.09	73.28	66.35	55.54	34.62
	P_{MAPE} (%)	79.6722	79.84	83.16	78.46	74.31	70.77	55.11	37.63
3-step	P_{MAE} (%)	78.3790	78.14	77.25	74.97	69.19	63.66	55.51	33.88
	P_{RMSE} (%)	77.8146	77.69	76.35	75.23	68.32	63.59	53.91	42.88
	P_{MAPE} (%)	79.7793	78.93	79.66	77.84	72.96	68.01	60.22	32.56
4-step	P_{MAE} (%)	70.9363	70.87	70.46	68.16	62.27	58.91	49.71	35.02
	P_{RMSE} (%)	66.7056	66.20	65.44	62.84	54.88	49.79	41.87	28.93
	P_{MAPE} (%)	71.7365	71.89	71.02	71.70	66.94	64.09	59.77	53.53

As shown in Table 10, for the Nanjing dataset, the improvement percentages of MAPE for one-step-ahead prediction by the HI-IVMD-DLinear relative to HI-SVR, HI-BPNN, HI-LSTM, HI-Transformer, and HI-DLinear are 87.5236%, 84.4584%, 83.5969%, 82.2938%, and 80.1936% respectively. This indicates the necessity of decomposing the original sequence with IVMD in the WSF process.

Furthermore, like HI-IVMD-BPNN, HI-IVMD-LSTM, and HI-IVMD-Transformer, HI-IVMD-DLinear also demonstrates significantly higher prediction accuracy. As shown in Table 10, compared with HI-IVMD-BPNN, HI-IVMD-LSTM, and HI-IVMD-Transformer, the HI-IVMD-DLinear exhibits improvement percentages 58.2622%, 52.9276%, and 36.0750% in MAPE for the one-step-ahead and two-steps-ahead predictions, respectively.

Therefore the HI-IVMD-DLinear outperforms the other models in the field of WSF in terms of accuracy.

3.4.3. Analysis of Forecasting Errors

Figure 7 is the frequency distribution of the predictive errors with the proposed model and eight other comparative models, regarding one-step-ahead predictions. The graph indicates that the error of the model based on the IVMD is small. Additionally, it can be observed that the HI-IVMD-DLinear presents the smallest errors among the majority of the data points in the test set.

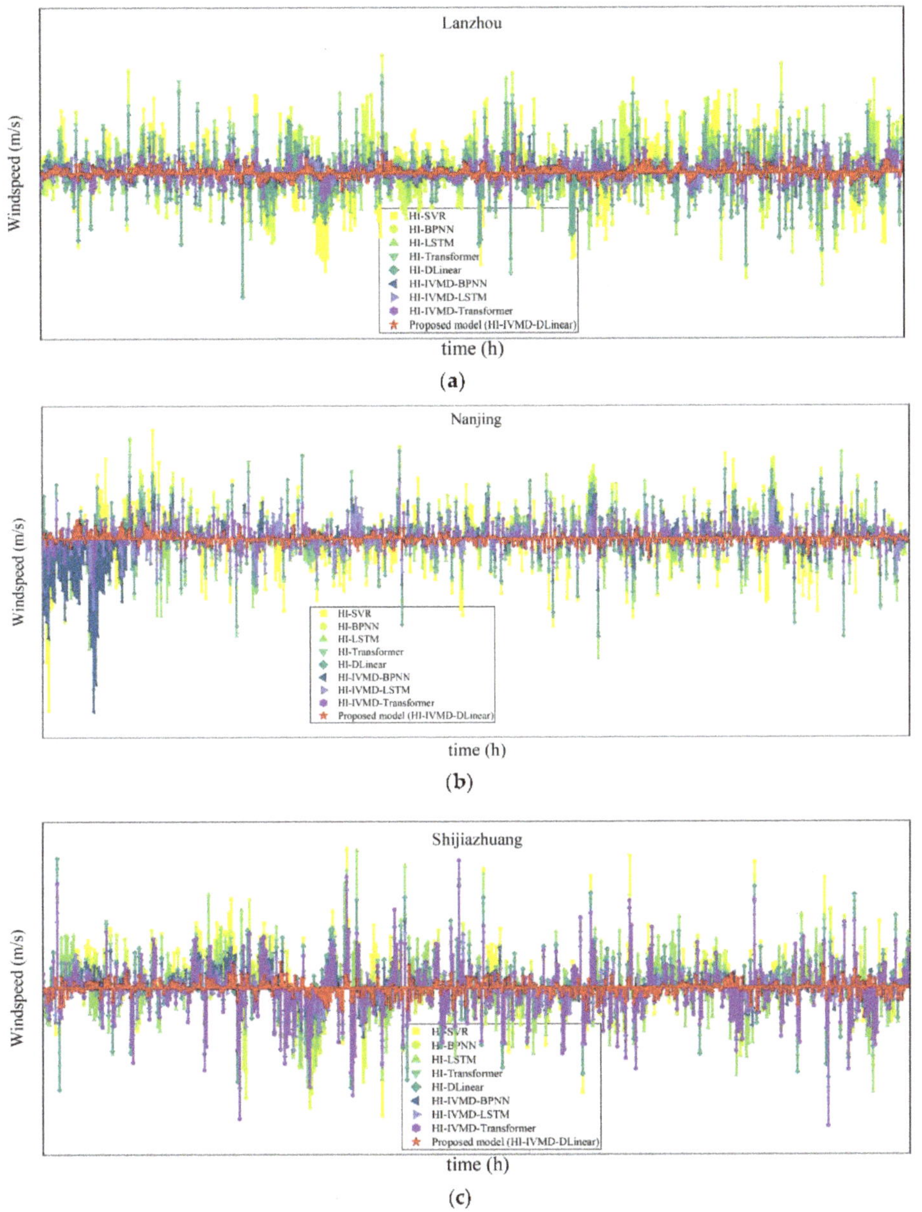

Figure 7. One-step-ahead prediction errors on the three datasets: (**a**) Lanzhou; (**b**) Nanjing; (**c**) Shijiazhuang.

Figure 8 illustrates the distribution of errors for each model. It is noticeable that the HI-IVMD-DLinear exhibits a higher concentration of prediction errors around zero for each dataset than the other models, with a smaller range of error variation. This implies that the HI-IVMD-DLinear possesses exceptional predictive accuracy and robustness.

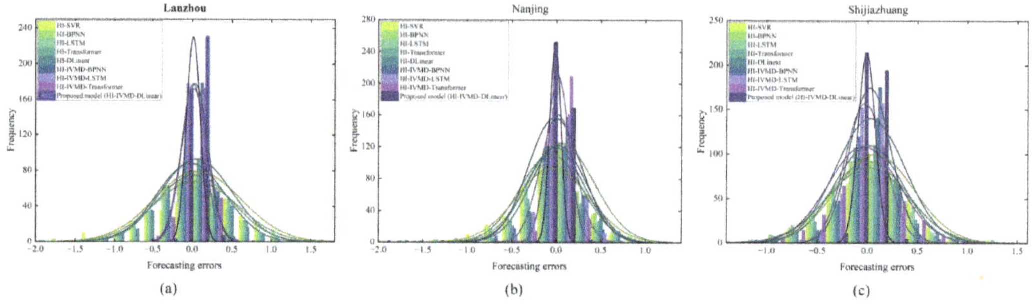

Figure 8. The error distribution for one-step-ahead predictions across the three datasets: (**a**) Lanzhou; (**b**) Nanjing; (**c**) Shijiazhuang.

3.4.4. Stability Analysis

Table 12 is the variance of absolute errors (VAE) with the proposed model and all comparative models across three datasets for multi-step ahead predictions. It reveals that the proposed model has good stability since it obtains the lowest VAE for one-to-four-steps-ahead predictions across all three datasets. For instance, in the Lanzhou dataset, the HI-IVMD-DLinear achieves VAE values of 0.0028, 0.0084, 0.0178, and 0.0264 for one-to-four-steps-ahead predictions, respectively. These values are consistently lower than those of the other comparative models.

Table 12. Predictive stability results (VAE) in three datasets.

Estimation Horizon	HI-SVR	HI-BPNN	HI-LSTM	HI-Transformer	HI-DLinear	HI-IVMD-BPNN	HI-IVMD-LSTM	HI-IVMD-Transformer	HI-IVMD-DLinear
					Lanzhou				
1-step	0.1200	0.1100	0.0893	0.1102	0.0513	0.0197	0.0129	0.0211	**0.0028**
2-step	0.1920	0.1890	0.1541	0.1899	0.1127	0.0383	0.0313	0.0316	**0.0084**
3-step	0.2112	0.2216	0.1873	0.2012	0.1577	0.0512	0.0544	0.0412	**0.0178**
4-step	0.2635	0.2539	0.2367	0.2524	0.2025	0.0551	0.0676	0.0518	**0.0264**
					Nanjing				
1-step	0.0667	0.0571	0.0536	0.0610	0.0506	0.0327	0.0114	0.0110	**0.0052**
2-step	0.1098	0.0835	0.0997	0.0811	0.0710	0.0477	0.0327	0.0411	**0.0173**
3-step	0.1371	0.1380	0.1178	0.1225	0.1048	0.0902	0.0669	0.0624	**0.0353**
4-step	0.1620	0.1610	0.1503	0.1503	0.1303	0.1333	0.1047	0.1009	**0.0603**
					Shijiazhuang				
1-step	0.0651	0.0610	0.0652	0.0782	0.0514	0.0137	0.0100	0.0416	**0.0044**
2-step	0.1021	0.1019	0.0922	0.0956	0.0781	0.0412	0.0266	0.0210	**0.0096**
3-step	0.1241	0.1221	0.1170	0.1018	0.0921	0.0810	0.0591	0.0411	**0.0336**
4-step	0.1407	0.1395	0.1301	0.1312	0.1139	0.1065	0.0872	0.0721	**0.0655**

The improvement percentages of VAE for the HI-IVMD-DLinear together with other comparative models are depicted in Figure 9. Compared to HI-SVR, HI-BPNN, HI-LSTM, HI-Transformer, and HI-DLinear, the HI-IVMD-DLinear exhibits a reduction in VAE of over 50% under the three datasets,. The IVMD decomposition also enhances the stability of predictions. Furthermore, compared to HI-IVMD-BPNN, HI-IVMD-LSTM, and HI-IVMD-Transformer, the HI-IVMD-DLinear achieves a reduction in VAE ranging from 9.0707% to 85.8084%. Hence, the DLinear-based model is more stable than BPNN, LSTM, and transformer.

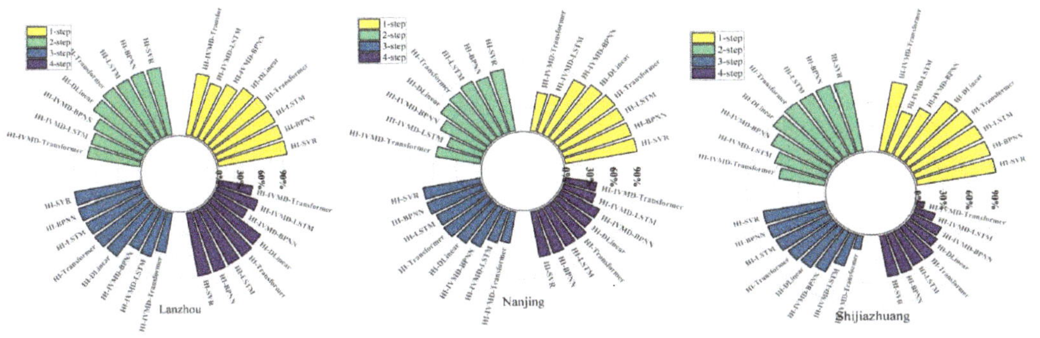

Figure 9. Improvement percentages of VAE for HI-IVMD-DLinear compared to other comparative models.

3.5. Comparative Analysis of Decomposition Strategies

To validate the decomposition performance of IVMD, IVMD is compared with the decomposition strategies including EMD [53], CEEMDAN [37], and the recently published CEEMDAN-VMD [54] and CEEMDAN-LMD [55]. Additionally, the strategy without decomposition methods is also compared. The CEEMDAN-VMD method begins by decomposing the wind speed sequence into several IMFs with CEEMDAN, followed by another decomposition of the highest-frequency IMF with VMD. Similarly, the CEEMDAN-LMD method involves decomposing the wind speed sequence into multiple IMFs with CEEMDAN, and subsequently decomposing the IMF1 generated from the CEEMDAN decomposition with LMD. The comparative results are presented in Table 13.

Based on the data presented in Table 13, the following conclusions can be inferred:

- Compared with the other decomposition strategies, the predictive models based on IVMD demonstrate the minimal RMSE values, specifically, 0.1712, 0.1668, 0.1472, 0.1253, and 0.0881. This further validates the superior performance of IVMD over the other decomposition strategies. CEEMDAN-VMD and CEEMDAN-LMD fail to address the inherent mode-mixing issue in the CEEMDAN algorithm, although they employ secondary decomposition, which reduces the complexity of sequences once again to some extent. This is why both have lower performance than IVMD.
- Compared to traditional machine learning methods like SVR, deep learning methods including BPNN, LSTM, transformer, and DLinear present significant improvement in predictive accuracy when combined with decomposition methods. For instance, the RMSE of IVMD-SVR and the SVR are 0.3015 and 0.5533, respectively. The RMSE is reduced by only 45.50% when incorporating IVMD. However, IVMD-DLinear and DLinear achieve an RMSE of 0.4332 and 0.0881, respectively. It is demonstrated that a remarkable RMSE reduction of 79.66% is achieved when combined with IVMD.
- For the same decomposition strategy, DLinear consistently obtains the lowest RMSE, implying DLinear generally has optimal accuracy.
- Among different combinations of decomposition strategies and original prediction models, IVMD-DLinear achieves the lowest RMSE of 0.0881. Therefore IVMD-DLinear has best predictive performance than the aforementioned combinations.

Table 13. The RMSE in Lanzhou obtained by basic forecasting models combined with different decomposition strategies.

Strategy	SVR	BPNN	LSTM	Transformer	DLinear
Non-decomposition	0.5533	0.5324	0.4710	0.4694	0.4332
EMD	0.4119	0.3992	0.3611	0.3574	0.3192
CEEMDAN	0.3633	0.2731	0.2632	0.2427	0.174
CEEMDAN-VMD	0.3211	0.2031	0.1754	0.1641	0.1259
CEEMDAN-LMD	0.3275	0.1832	0.1618	0.1517	0.1187
IVMD	**0.3015**	**0.1668**	**0.1472**	**0.1253**	**0.0881**

4. Discussion

WSF is a complex task influenced by various factors, such as temperature, humidity, and air pressure. These factors contribute to the non-stationary and nonlinear characteristics of wind speed sequences. It is challenging to forecast wind speeds with a single prediction model accurately. Precise WSF holds significant importance in the energy industry, as higher accuracy forecasts can help reduce operational costs of power systems.

4.1. Discussion of Computational Efficiency

In terms of computational efficiency, the proposed method outperforms the other prediction models. Specifically, the VMD allows for higher computational efficiency with distributed storage and parallel computing techniques, since each IMF's prediction is independent of the others. Furthermore, the DLinear model has high efficiency, with each branch containing only a single linear layer. Significantly lower memory and fewer parameters are involved than the transformer, and faster calculation speeds.

4.2. Discussion of Computational Complexity

Compared with the other non-decomposition methods, the IVMD-DLinear increases the computational complexity within an acceptable range. The predictions for each IMF are obtained by applying the DLinear model to each IMF and the hyperparameter in VMD is optimized by the GWO algorithm, which significantly increases the computational complexity. However, it is reasonable since the substantial improvement in prediction accuracy augments the economic efficacy of wind power systems significantly.

5. Conclusions

Accurate and robust WSF is of great importance for the advancement of the wind power industry. Nevertheless, the intricate and non-stationary nature of wind speed sequences poses a significant challenge to achieve precise predictions. Therefore, a WSF model (HI-IVMD-DLinear) based on outlier correction, heuristic algorithms, and sequence decomposition is proposed to achieve high precision and robust wind speed forecasting. Firstly, the outliers in the wind speed sequence are detected and corrected with the outlier correction method HI to reduce the adverse effects of outliers on prediction accuracy. Secondly, the hyperparameters K and α of the VMD are optimized by the GWO. Thirdly, with the optimized K and α, the wind speed sequence processed by HI is decomposed into several IMFs by the VMD, and the non-stationarity and the complexity of the sequence are reduced. Finally, each IMF is individually predicted by the novel DLinear algorithm, and the predicted outputs are summed to obtain the final wind speed prediction.

The experimental results conducted on wind speed datasets from three cities in China validate the predictive performance of the HI-IVMD-DLinear. Based on the experiments, the following conclusions can be drawn:

- HI assists in mitigating the detrimental effects of outliers on prediction accuracy, and enhances the overall precision of the predictions. HI can detect and correct outliers in wind speed series and reduce their interference in prediction.

- The IVMD algorithm demonstrates significant advantages compared to the EEMD, CEEMDAN, CEEMDAN-VMD, and CEEMDAN-LMD algorithms. The CEEMDAN algorithm shows spurious modes during decomposition, which can affect the accuracy of predictions to some extent. CEEMDAN-VMD and CEEMDAN-LMD fail to address the mode-mixing issue in CEEMDAN, although they employ secondary decomposition to reduce sequence complexity to some extent.
- The DLinear model has better optimal performance than the SVR, BPNN, LSTM, and transformer models. Simultaneously, DLinear is stable with higher prediction accuracy than that of the widely used and highly accurate transformer or LSTM models in the field of WSF, and it is not necessary to adjust its hyperparameters. Therefore, DLinear is more suitable for WSF than transformer and LSTM.
- In the one-to-four-steps-ahead forecasting on the three datasets, the HI-IVMD-DLinear model demonstrates excellent prediction accuracy compared with the other eight comparative models. This hybrid model utilizes HI for outlier correction, IVMD for sequence decomposition, and DLinear for prediction. The performance of the hybrid model has been validated at each stage.

Nevertheless, our study does possess certain limitations. Primarily, it relies heavily on simulations due to the current cost constraints that prevent us from conducting field measurements.

Author Contributions: Conceptualization, J.L.; methodology, J.L.; investigation, J.L., C.G., S.C. and N.Z.; data curation, J.L. and S.C.; writing—original draft preparation, J.L. and C.G.; validation, C.G. and N.Z.; writing—reviewing and editing, S.C. and N.Z.; supervision, N.Z.; funding acquisition, N.Z.; project administration, N.Z.; resources, N.Z. All authors have read and agreed to the published version of the manuscript.

Funding: This research was supported in part by the National Natural Science Foundation of China, grant number 62162041; in part by the Science & Technology Planning Project of Shanghai, grant number 23010501800; and in part by the Top Double 1000 Talent Programme of Jiangxi Province, grant number JXSQ2019201055.

Institutional Review Board Statement: The study did not involve humans or animals.

Informed Consent Statement: The study did not involve humans.

Data Availability Statement: Publicly available datasets and code were analyzed in this study. These data and code can be found here: https://github.com/2076959577/PaperCode (accessed on 7 June 2023).

Conflicts of Interest: The authors declare no conflict of interest.

References

1. Dong, F.; Li, W. Research on the Coupling Coordination Degree of "Upstream-Midstream-Downstream" of China's Wind Power Industry Chain. *J. Clean. Prod.* **2021**, *283*, 124633. [CrossRef]
2. World Wind Energy Association. *Worldwide Wind Capacity Reaches 744 Gigawatts—An Unprecedented 93 Gigawatts Added in 2020*; World Wind Energy Association: Bonn, Germany, 2021.
3. Wang, L.; Li, J. Estimation of Extreme Wind Speed in SCS and NWP by a Non-Stationary Model. *Theor. Appl. Mech. Lett.* **2016**, *6*, 131–138. [CrossRef]
4. Zhao, J.; Guo, Z.-H.; Su, Z.-Y.; Zhao, Z.-Y.; Xiao, X.; Liu, F. An Improved Multi-Step Forecasting Model Based on WRF Ensembles and Creative Fuzzy Systems for Wind Speed. *Appl. Energy* **2016**, *162*, 808–826. [CrossRef]
5. Yang, J.; Astitha, M.; Delle Monache, L.; Alessandrini, S. An Analog Technique to Improve Storm Wind Speed Prediction Using a Dual NWP Model Approach. *Mon. Weather. Rev.* **2018**, *146*, 4057–4077. Available online: https://journals.ametsoc.org/view/journals/mwre/146/12/mwr-d-17-0198.1.xml (accessed on 30 April 2023). [CrossRef]
6. Karakuş, O.; Kuruoğlu, E.E.; Altınkaya, M.A. One-day Ahead Wind Speed/Power Prediction Based on Polynomial Autoregressive Model. *IET Renew. Power Gener.* **2017**, *11*, 1430–1439. Available online: https://ietresearch.onlinelibrary.wiley.com/doi/10.1049/iet-rpg.2016.0972 (accessed on 30 April 2023). [CrossRef]
7. Aasim; Singh, S.N.; Mohapatra, A. Repeated Wavelet Transform Based ARIMA Model for Very Short-Term Wind Speed Forecasting. *Renew. Energy* **2019**, *136*, 758–768. [CrossRef]

8. Yatiyana, E.; Rajakaruna, S.; Ghosh, A. Wind Speed and Direction Forecasting for Wind Power Generation Using ARIMA Model. In Proceedings of the 2017 Australasian Universities Power Engineering Conference (AUPEC), Melbourne, Australia, 19–22 November 2017; pp. 1–6.
9. Phan, Q.T.; Wu, Y.K.; Phan, Q.D. A Hybrid Wind Power Forecasting Model with XGBoost, Data Preprocessing Considering Different NWPs. *Appl. Sci.* **2021**, *11*, 1100. [CrossRef]
10. Santamaría-Bonfil, G.; Reyes-Ballesteros, A.; Gershenson, C. Wind Speed Forecasting for Wind Farms: A Method Based on Support Vector Regression. *Renew. Energy* **2016**, *85*, 790–809. [CrossRef]
11. Chen, J.; Zeng, G.-Q.; Zhou, W.; Du, W.; Lu, K.-D. Wind Speed Forecasting Using Nonlinear-Learning Ensemble of Deep Learning Time Series Prediction and Extremal Optimization. *Energy Convers. Manag.* **2018**, *165*, 681–695. [CrossRef]
12. Wang, G.; Wang, X.; Wang, Z.; Ma, C.; Song, Z. A VMD–CISSA–LSSVM Based Electricity Load Forecasting Model. *Mathematics* **2021**, *10*, 28. [CrossRef]
13. Ren, C.; An, N.; Wang, J.; Li, L.; Hu, B.; Shang, D. Optimal Parameters Selection for BP Neural Network Based on Particle Swarm Optimization: A Case Study of Wind Speed Forecasting. *Knowl.-Based Syst.* **2014**, *56*, 226–239. [CrossRef]
14. Yang, Z.; Wang, J. A Hybrid Forecasting Approach Applied in Wind Speed Forecasting Based on a Data Processing Strategy and an Optimized Artificial Intelligence Algorithm. *Energy* **2018**, *160*, 87–100. [CrossRef]
15. Wang, Z.; Wang, B.; Liu, C.; Wang, W. Improved BP Neural Network Algorithm to Wind Power Forecast. *J. Eng.* **2017**, *2017*, 940–943. [CrossRef]
16. Duan, J.; Zuo, H.; Bai, Y.; Duan, J.; Chang, M.; Chen, B. Short-Term Wind Speed Forecasting Using Recurrent Neural Networks with Error Correction. *Energy* **2021**, *217*, 119397. [CrossRef]
17. Gangwar, S.; Bali, V.; Kumar, A. Comparative Analysis of Wind Speed Forecasting Using LSTM and SVM. *EAI Endorsed Trans. Scalable Inf. Syst.* **2020**, *7*, e1. [CrossRef]
18. Ying, X.; Zhao, K.; Liu, Z.; Gao, J.; He, D.; Li, X.; Xiong, W. Wind Speed Prediction via Collaborative Filtering on Virtual Edge Expanding Graphs. *Mathematics* **2022**, *10*, 1943. [CrossRef]
19. Mousavi, S.M.; Ghasemi, M.; Dehghan Manshadi, M.; Mosavi, A. Deep Learning for Wave Energy Converter Modeling Using Long Short-Term Memory. *Mathematics* **2021**, *9*, 871. [CrossRef]
20. Liu, H.; Mi, X.; Li, Y.; Duan, Z.; Xu, Y. Smart Wind Speed Deep Learning Based Multi-Step Forecasting Model Using Singular Spectrum Analysis, Convolutional Gated Recurrent Unit Network and Support Vector Regression. *Renew. Energy* **2019**, *143*, 842–854. [CrossRef]
21. Xiang, L.; Li, J.; Hu, A.; Zhang, Y. Deterministic and Probabilistic Multi-Step Forecasting for Short-Term Wind Speed Based on Secondary Decomposition and a Deep Learning Method. *Energy Convers. Manag.* **2020**, *220*, 113098. [CrossRef]
22. Zhang, G.; Liu, D. Causal Convolutional Gated Recurrent Unit Network with Multiple Decomposition Methods for Short-Term Wind Speed Forecasting. *Energy Convers. Manag.* **2020**, *226*, 113500. [CrossRef]
23. Syu, Y.-D.; Wang, J.-C.; Chou, C.-Y.; Lin, M.-J.; Liang, W.-C.; Wu, L.-C.; Jiang, J.-A. Ultra-Short-Term Wind Speed Forecasting for Wind Power Based on Gated Recurrent Unit. In Proceedings of the 2020 8th International Electrical Engineering Congress (iEECON), Chiang Mai, Thailand, 4–6 March 2020; pp. 1–4.
24. Wu, N.; Green, B.; Ben, X.; O'Banion, S. Deep Transformer Models for Time Series Forecasting: The Influenza Prevalence Case. *arXiv* **2020**, arXiv:2001.08317.
25. Bommidi, B.S.; Teeparthi, K.; Kosana, V. Hybrid Wind Speed Forecasting Using ICEEMDAN and Transformer Model with Novel Loss Function. *Energy* **2023**, *265*, 126383. [CrossRef]
26. Wu, H.; Meng, K.; Fan, D.; Zhang, Z.; Liu, Q. Multistep Short-Term Wind Speed Forecasting Using Transformer. *Energy* **2022**, *261*, 125231. [CrossRef]
27. Zeng, A.; Chen, M.; Zhang, L.; Xu, Q. Are Transformers Effective for Time Series Forecasting? *arXiv* **2022**, arXiv:2205.13504.
28. Büyükşahin, Ü.Ç.; Ertekin, Ş. Improving Forecasting Accuracy of Time Series Data Using a New ARIMA-ANN Hybrid Method and Empirical Mode Decomposition. *Neurocomputing* **2019**, *361*, 151–163. [CrossRef]
29. Zhang, J.; Wei, Y.; Tan, Z. An Adaptive Hybrid Model for Short Term Wind Speed Forecasting. *Energy* **2020**, *190*, 115615. [CrossRef]
30. Shang, Z.; He, Z.; Chen, Y.; Chen, Y.; Xu, M. Short-Term Wind Speed Forecasting System Based on Multivariate Time Series and Multi-Objective Optimization. *Energy* **2022**, *238*, 122024. [CrossRef]
31. Liu, D.; Niu, D.; Wang, H.; Fan, L. Short-Term Wind Speed Forecasting Using Wavelet Transform and Support Vector Machines Optimized by Genetic Algorithm. *Renew. Energy* **2014**, *62*, 592–597. [CrossRef]
32. Liu, H.; Mi, X.; Li, Y. Wind Speed Forecasting Method Based on Deep Learning Strategy Using Empirical Wavelet Transform, Long Short Term Memory Neural Network and Elman Neural Network. *Energy Convers. Manag.* **2018**, *156*, 498–514. [CrossRef]
33. Wang, J.; Zhang, W.; Li, Y.; Wang, J.; Dang, Z. Forecasting Wind Speed Using Empirical Mode Decomposition and Elman Neural Network. *Appl. Soft Comput.* **2014**, *23*, 452–459. [CrossRef]
34. Liu, H.; Chen, C.; Tian, H.; Li, Y. A Hybrid Model for Wind Speed Prediction Using Empirical Mode Decomposition and Artificial Neural Networks. *Renew. Energy* **2012**, *48*, 545–556. [CrossRef]
35. A Complete Ensemble Empirical Mode Decomposition with Adaptive Noise. Available online: https://ieeexplore.ieee.org/document/5947265/ (accessed on 7 April 2023).
36. Wang, S.; Zhang, N.; Wu, L.; Wang, Y. Wind Speed Forecasting Based on the Hybrid Ensemble Empirical Mode Decomposition and GA-BP Neural Network Method. *Renew. Energy* **2016**, *94*, 629–636. [CrossRef]

37. Zhang, W.; Qu, Z.; Zhang, K.; Mao, W.; Ma, Y.; Fan, X. A Combined Model Based on CEEMDAN and Modified Flower Pollination Algorithm for Wind Speed Forecasting. *Energy Convers. Manag.* **2017**, *136*, 439–451. [CrossRef]
38. Zhang, Y.; Pan, G.; Chen, B.; Han, J.; Zhao, Y.; Zhang, C. Short-Term Wind Speed Prediction Model Based on GA-ANN Improved by VMD. *Renew. Energy* **2020**, *156*, 1373–1388. [CrossRef]
39. Li, Y.; Tang, B.; Jiao, S. SO-Slope Entropy Coupled with SVMD: A Novel Adaptive Feature Extraction Method for Ship-Radiated Noise. *Ocean Eng.* **2023**, *280*, 114677. [CrossRef]
40. Liu, H.; Mi, X.; Li, Y. Smart Multi-Step Deep Learning Model for Wind Speed Forecasting Based on Variational Mode Decomposition, Singular Spectrum Analysis, LSTM Network and ELM. *Energy Convers. Manag.* **2018**, *159*, 54–64. [CrossRef]
41. Mirjalili, S.; Mirjalili, S.M.; Lewis, A. Grey Wolf Optimizer. *Adv. Eng. Softw.* **2014**, *69*, 46–61. [CrossRef]
42. Liu, H.; Xu, Y.; Chen, C. Improved Pollution Forecasting Hybrid Algorithms Based on the Ensemble Method. *Appl. Math. Model.* **2019**, *73*, 473–486. [CrossRef]
43. Liu, H.; Shah, S.; Jiang, W. On-Line Outlier Detection and Data Cleaning. *Comput. Chem. Eng.* **2004**, *28*, 1635–1647. [CrossRef]
44. Li, Y.; Geng, B.; Tang, B. Simplified Coded Dispersion Entropy: A Nonlinear Metric for Signal Analysis. *Nonlinear Dyn.* **2023**, *111*, 9327–9344. [CrossRef]
45. Grassberger, P.; Procaccia, I. Characterization of Strange Attractors. *Phys. Rev. Lett.* **1983**, *50*, 346–349. [CrossRef]
46. Li, Y.; Tang, B.; Geng, B.; Jiao, S. Fractional Order Fuzzy Dispersion Entropy and Its Application in Bearing Fault Diagnosis. *Fractal Fract.* **2022**, *6*, 544. [CrossRef]
47. Zhu, K.; Song, X.; Xue, D. Fault Diagnosis of Rolling Bearings Based on IMF Envelope Sample Entropy and Support Vector Machine. *J. Inf. Comput. Sci.* **2013**, *10*, 5189–5198. [CrossRef]
48. Chen, W.; Zhuang, J.; Yu, W.; Wang, Z. Measuring Complexity Using FuzzyEn, ApEn, and SampEn. *Med. Eng. Phys.* **2009**, *31*, 61–68. [CrossRef]
49. Pearson, R.K. Outliers in Process Modeling and Identification. *IEEE Trans. Control Syst. Technol.* **2002**, *10*, 55–63. [CrossRef] [PubMed]
50. Wang, J.; Du, P.; Hao, Y.; Ma, X.; Niu, T.; Yang, W. An Innovative Hybrid Model Based on Outlier Detection and Correction Algorithm and Heuristic Intelligent Optimization Algorithm for Daily Air Quality Index Forecasting. *J. Environ. Manag.* **2020**, *255*, 109855. [CrossRef]
51. Dragomiretskiy, K.; Zosso, D. Variational Mode Decomposition. *IEEE Trans. Signal Process.* **2014**, *62*, 531–544. [CrossRef]
52. Kingma, D.P.; Ba, J. Adam: A Method for Stochastic Optimization. *arXiv* **2017**, arXiv:1412.6980.
53. Huang, N.E.; Shen, Z.; Long, S.R.; Wu, M.C.; Shih, H.H.; Zheng, Q.; Yen, N.-C.; Tung, C.C.; Liu, H.H. The Empirical Mode Decomposition and the Hilbert Spectrum for Nonlinear and Non-Stationary Time Series Analysis. *Proc. R. Soc. London Ser. A Math. Phys. Eng. Sci.* **1998**, *454*, 903–995. [CrossRef]
54. Peng, T. Multi-Step Ahead Wind Speed Forecasting Using a Hybrid Model Based on Two-Stage Decomposition Technique and AdaBoost-Extreme Learning Machine. *Energy Convers. Manag.* **2017**, *153*, 589–602. [CrossRef]
55. Emeksiz, C.; Tan, M. Multi-Step Wind Speed Forecasting and Hurst Analysis Using Novel Hybrid Secondary Decomposition Approach. *Energy* **2022**, *238*, 121764. [CrossRef]

mathematics

MDPI

Article

Calculation of the Electrostatic Field of a Circular Cylinder with a Slot by the Wiener–Hopf Method

Seitkerim Bimurzaev [1,†], Seil Sautbekov [2,*,†] and Zerde Sautbekova [1,†]

[1] Department of Science and Commercialization, G. Daukeev Almaty University of Power Engineering and Telecommunication, Almaty 050013, Kazakhstan; s.bimurzaev@aues.kz (S.B.); z.sautbekova@aues.kz (Z.S.)
[2] Department of Physics and Technology, Al-Farabi Kazakh National University, Almaty 050040, Kazakhstan
* Correspondence: seilsautbekov@gmail.com; Tel.: +7-701-924-1167
† These authors contributed equally to this work.

Abstract: The paper presents an exact solution to the internal boundary value problem of the field distribution in an electrostatic lens formed by two identical semi-infinite coaxially located round cylinders separated by a slit of finite width and located inside an infinite outer cylinder. The problem is reduced to a system of singular Wiener–Hopf integral equations, which is further solved by the Wiener–Hopf method using factorized Bessel functions. Solutions to the problem for each region inside the infinite outer cylinder are presented as exponentially converging series in terms of eigenfunctions and eigenvalues. Using the obtained formulas, a numerical calculation of the axial distribution of the potential of a two-electrode lens was made for various values of the radii of the outer and inner cylinders.

Keywords: time-of-flight mass spectrometer; electron microscope; electrostatic lens; electrostatic mirror; relativistic effect; system of singular integral equations; factorized functions; eigenfunctions; eigenvalues

MSC: 45F15; 45E10; 47A68; 30E20

Citation: Bimurzaev, S.; Sautbekov, S.; Sautbekova, Z. Calculation of the Electrostatic Field of a Circular Cylinder with a Slot by the Wiener–Hopf Method. *Mathematics* **2023**, *11*, 2933. https://doi.org/10.3390/math11132933

Academic Editors: Zhuojia Fu, Yiqian He and Hui Zheng

Received: 29 April 2023
Revised: 21 June 2023
Accepted: 25 June 2023
Published: 30 June 2023

1. Introduction

Electrostatic mirrors have become indispensable structural elements of modern scientific and technological instrumentation, which determine the quality of focusing of such instruments as time-of-flight mass spectrometers and electron microscopes. In this regard, electrostatic mirrors of rotational symmetry are of particular interest, since they perform stigmatic focusing of electron beams, i.e., create the correct electron optical image of the object. However, the most studied and highly demanded in practical implementation are the designs of mirrors constructed as sets of coaxial circular cylinders. The advantage of cylindrical electrodes is the possibility of shielding the beam from scattered electric fields. For this reason, it is expedient to solve the internal boundary value problem for such structures rather than the external one. In works [1,2], devoted to the study of the focusing properties of electrostatic mirrors with cylindrical electrodes, the calculation of the field was performed under the assumption that the width of the gap between the electrodes is infinitely small. However, practical application of such mirrors in high-voltage electron microscopy [3,4] imposes high requirements on the width of the gap between the electrodes in terms of ensuring electrostatic strength at high field intensity. However, with an increase in the width of the inter-electrode gap, the effect of scattered electric fields on the quality of electron beam focusing increases. The aim of the work is to use the Wiener–Hopf (WH) method to solve the problem of field distribution in an electrostatic lens formed by two identical semi-infinite coaxially located circular cylinders, separated by gaps (slits) of finite width and located inside an infinite outer cylinder. Such an electrode design makes it possible to simultaneously provide electrostatic strength at high field intensities and the screening of the electron beam from external electric fields at large gap widths between the internal electrodes. It should be noted that it was N.N. Lebedev [5] who first used the WH method to solve the boundary value problem of the electrostatic field of an electron lens consisting of a semi-infinite circular cylinder coaxially located inside an infinite cylinder, which is a key for solving a number of other problems. However, a well-known powerful WH method has not been used since then even to calculate the field of the simplest system of electrodes with two semi-infinite cylinders, not to mention the case when the finite width between the electrodes is taken into account. The studied boundary value problem, as a rule, is reduced to solving pairwise integral equations with kernels of Bessel functions, which were studied by L.A. Weinstein [6], Titchmarsh [7], Noble [8], Erdelyi and Sneddon [9], and others.

A comprehensive review of the historical development of pairwise integral equations is given by Eswaran [10] and Sneddon [11], where they are reduced to a system of algebraic equations or to a Fredholm-type equation. The methodology for solving paired integral equations is considered in detail in the works of N.N. Lebedev [5], V.A. Fock, P.L. Kapitsa, and L.A. Weinstein [12].

In these works, pairwise integral equations describing the problem of a conducting hollow cylinder of finite length were reduced to the Fredholm integral equation of the second kind [13] or solved by the variational method when the length of the cylinder is large enough compared to its diameter [14,15]. However, the proposed methods are very cumbersome and require a large amount of computational time.

It is known that the WH method [6,8,10,16–19], like the Riemann method, is a rigorous method for solving pairwise singular integral equations (SIEs) for semi-infinite structures whose solutions automatically satisfy the additional Meixner condition or the so-called condition on a sharp edge, which determines the uniqueness of the solution to the problem as well as the behavior of the field at small distances from the sharp edge. Note that, as a rule, this condition is not mentioned in approximate methods. It should be recalled that the classical WH method was previously used mainly for solving dynamic problems, for example, in the theory of electromagnetic wave diffraction.

2. Statement of the Problem

Let us consider a lens consisting of two thin semi-infinite cylinders of radius a with a common axis z and given potentials V_1 and V_2, coaxially located towards each other inside a shielding infinite cylinder of radius b, which is at zero potential (Figure 1).

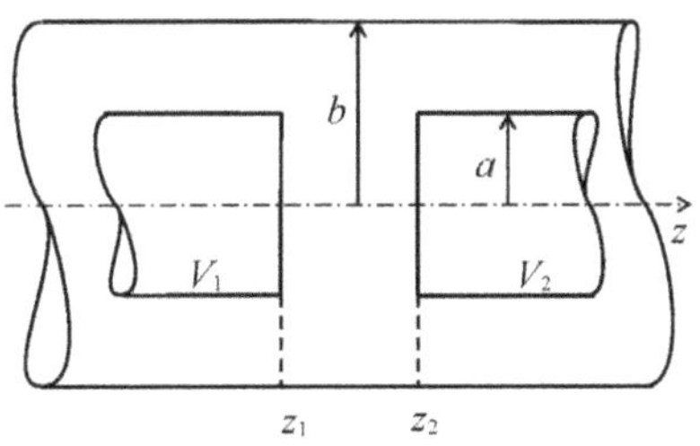

Figure 1. Electrostatic lens with a slit $(z_2 - z_1)$ of finite width.

The desired potential $\varphi(r, z)$ satisfies the Laplace equation

$$\triangle\varphi(r,z) = 0$$

and boundary conditions

$$\varphi(b,z) = 0, \quad \varphi(a,z<a) = V_1, \quad \varphi(a,z>a) = V_2, \tag{1}$$

$$\varphi(a-0,z) - \varphi(a+0,z) = 0, \tag{2}$$

$$\left(\frac{\partial}{\partial r}\varphi(r-0,z) - \frac{\partial}{\partial r}\varphi(r+0,z)\right)\Big|_{r=a} = 0 \quad \text{at} \quad z_1 < z < z_2, \tag{3}$$

$$\varphi(a \pm 0) = \lim_{0<\epsilon\to 0} \varphi(a \pm \epsilon).$$

Let us introduce the notations

$$\begin{gathered} L(r,w) = \frac{\pi}{2\ln\frac{a}{b}\mathrm{J}_0(vb)}\begin{cases}\mathrm{J}_0(vr)(a,b), & \text{at } 0 \le r \le a;\\ \mathrm{J}_0(va)(r,b), & \text{at } a \le r \le b,\end{cases}\\ (r,b) = \mathrm{N}_0(vr)\mathrm{J}_0(vb) - \mathrm{N}_0(vb)\mathrm{J}_0(vr),\\ v = \sqrt{k^2 - w^2}, \quad \mathrm{Im}v > 0, \end{gathered} \tag{4}$$

where $\mathrm{J}_0(vr)$, $\mathrm{N}_0(vr)$ are zero-order Bessel and Neumann functions, and (r,b) is a combination of Bessel functions, and search for a solution in the form

$$\varphi(r,z) = \frac{1}{2\pi i}\int_{-\infty}^{\infty} e^{iwz} L(r,w)\frac{F(w)}{L(a,w)}dw \tag{5}$$

with respect to the desired function $F(w)$.

For electrostatic problems, k should be assumed to have a vanishingly small positive imaginary part, and we transfer to the limit $|k| \to 0$ only in finite expressions.

The cuts of the function $L(r,w)$ in (4) are located in the plane of the complex variable w on the curves $\mathrm{Im}\, v = 0$.

Due to the properties of the Bessel functions and boundary conditions (1) and (3), we obtain a system of singular integral equations (SIE)

$$\frac{1}{2\pi i}\int_{-\infty}^{\infty} e^{iwz}F(w)dw = V_1, \quad z \le z_1, \tag{6}$$

$$\frac{1}{2\pi i}\int_{-\infty}^{\infty} e^{iwz}F(w)dw = V_2, \quad z \ge z_2, \tag{7}$$

$$\int_{-\infty}^{\infty} e^{iwz}L^{-1}(a,w)F(w)dw = 0, \quad z_1 < z < z_2. \tag{8}$$

The last, Equation (8), can be obtained from the boundary condition (3) due to the property of the Bessel functions

$$\frac{\partial}{\partial r}\left(\frac{\mathrm{J}_0(vr)(a,b)}{\mathrm{J}_0(vb)} - \frac{\mathrm{J}_0(va)(r,b)}{\mathrm{J}_0(vb)}\right)\Big|_{r=a} \equiv -\frac{2}{\pi a}.$$

3. Solution of a System of Integral Equations

The solution of SIE (6)–(8) is constructed by the Wiener–Hopf method in the form [20]

$$\begin{aligned} F(w) = {} & L_-(a,w)\Big(A^1_+(w) + B^1_+(w)\Big)e^{-iwz_1} + \\ & + L_+(a,w)\Big(A^2_-(w) + B^2_-(w)\Big)e^{-iwz_2}. \end{aligned} \tag{9}$$

Here, the subscripts '+' and '−' denote holomorphic functions in the upper half-plane (UHP) $\mathrm{Im}\, w \geq 0$, and lower half-plane (LHP) $\mathrm{Im} w \leq 0$, respectively, which do not have zeros and poles there, and the functions L_+ and L_- are factorized functions, $L = L_- \cdot L_+$ [6,8].

It should be noted that for the SIE solution to be unique, the desired function $F(w)$ must satisfy the Meixner condition [21,22] on the edge or the so-called sharp edge condition ($E_z, E_r \sim \rho^{-1/2}$, $E_\phi \sim \sqrt{\rho}$), which is equivalent to the behavior of the function $F(|w|) \sim |w|^{-3/2}$ at infinity $|w| \to \infty$.

For convenience, we introduce the notations for the eigenvalues for each region inside the infinite tube of radius b: (a), (b), (c). The regions (a) and (b) correspond to the regions inside and outside the semi-infinite circular cylinder of radius a, respectively. The region $0 < r < b$ and $z_1 < z < z_2$ is denoted as (c). Further, the superscripts of the eigenvalues will denote the corresponding region. Note that L_+ has zeros at the points $-w_n^a$, $-w_n^c$ and poles in $-w_n^b$ $(n = 1, 2, \dots)$ in the LHP of the complex variable w. The function L_- has the same zeros and poles only in the UHP, due to the property of factorized functions:

$$L_+(a, -w) = L_-(a, w). \tag{10}$$

The roots of the functions $\mathrm{J}_0(va)$, $\mathrm{J}_0(vb)$, and (a, b) with respect to the variable v in (4) are $v_n^a = \gamma_n / a$; $v_n^b = \gamma_n / b$ and $v_n^c = \delta_n / (b - a)$ $(n = 1, 2, \dots)$, where γ_n and δ_n denote the roots of the equations with respect to arguments γ and δ [23]:

$$\mathrm{J}_0(\gamma) = 0,$$
$$\mathrm{N}_0\left(\tfrac{a\delta}{b-a}\right)\mathrm{J}_0\left(\tfrac{b\delta}{b-a}\right) - \mathrm{N}_0\left(\tfrac{b\delta}{b-a}\right)\mathrm{J}_0\left(\tfrac{a\delta}{b-a}\right) = 0.$$

Equation (6), due to the function A_+^1, will satisfy the solution if the function $F(w)$ is holomorphic everywhere in LHP ($\mathrm{Im} w \leq 0$) except for a single simple pole at the point $w = -k$ and uniformly tends to zero as $|w| \to \infty$. Therefore, the remaining poles contained in the LHP at the points $w = -w_n^b$ $(n = 1, 2, \dots)$ of the function L_+ must be compensated using the function $B_+^1(w)$.

To find a solution to Equation (7), we require the same conditions for the functions $A_-^2(w)$ and $B_-^2(w)$ in the UHP ($\mathrm{Im} w \geq 0$).

Using the theory of residues to calculate the integrals (6) and (7), as well as compensating all singular points inside the integration contour (IC), except for the poles $\pm k$, we obtain the desired functions in (9):

$$\begin{cases} A_+^1(w) = -\dfrac{V_1}{w + k}, \\ \\ A_-^2(w) = \dfrac{V_2}{w - k} \quad (0 < \mathrm{Im}(k),\ |k| \to 0), \end{cases} \tag{11}$$

$$\begin{cases} B_+^1(w) = -\displaystyle\sum_{n=1}^{\infty} \frac{e^{iw_n^b(z_2 - z_1)}}{(w + w_n^b)} \frac{L_+^*(a, -w_n^b)}{L_-(a, -w_n^b)} \left(A_-^2(-w_n^b) + B_-^2(-w_n^b)\right), \\ \\ B_-^2(w) = -\displaystyle\sum_{n=1}^{\infty} \frac{e^{iw_n^b(z_2 - z_1)}}{(w - w_n^b)} \frac{L_-^*(a, w_n^b)}{L_+(a, w_n^b)} \left(A_+^1(w_n^b) + B_+^1(w_n^b)\right), \end{cases} \tag{12}$$

where

$$L_+^*(a, -w_n^b) = \lim_{w \to -w_n^b} (w + w_n^b) L_+(a, w) =$$
$$- \lim_{w \to w_n^b} (w - w_n^b) L_-(a, w) = -L_-^*(a, w_n^b).$$

The validity of the obtained solution of SIE (6)–(8) can be checked directly by substituting it into the Equations (6)–(8) and closing the IC in the LHP or UHP w, according to the Jordan lemma, then calculating the residues at all poles of the integrand inside this IC.

It should be noted that the resulting solution (9) automatically satisfies (8), since the integrand turns out to be holomorphic inside the corresponding IC.

Solution of a System of Functional Equations

The exact solution of the system of functional Equation (12) can be represented in the form of rapidly convergent infinite series

$$\begin{aligned} B_+^1(w) = & -V_2\Bigg(\sum_{n_1}^{\infty}\frac{g_{n_1}}{(w+w_{n_1}^b)l^{(1)}}+\sum_{n_1,n_2,n_3}^{\infty}\frac{g_{n_1}g_{n_2}g_{n_3}}{(w+w_{n_3}^b)l^{(3)}}+\dots \\ & +\sum_{n_1,\dots,n_{2i-1}}^{\infty}\frac{\prod_{k=1}^{2i-1}g_k}{(w+w_{2i-1}^b)l^{(2i-1)}}\Bigg)-V_1\Bigg(\sum_{n_1,n_2}^{\infty}\frac{g_{n_1}g_{n_2}}{(w+w_{n_2}^b)l^{(2)}}+ \\ & \sum_{n_1,n_2,n_3,n_4}^{\infty}\frac{g_{n_1}g_{n_2}g_{n_3}g_{n_4}}{(w+w_{n_4}^b)l^{(4)}}+\dots\sum_{n_1,\dots,n_{2i}}^{\infty}\frac{\prod_{k=1}^{2i}g_k}{(w+w_{2i}^b)l^{(2i)}}\Bigg), \end{aligned} \tag{13}$$

$$\begin{aligned} B_-^2(w) = & V_1\Bigg(\sum_{n_1}^{\infty}\frac{g_{n_1}}{(w-w_{n_1}^b)l^{(1)}}+\sum_{n_1,n_2,n_3}^{\infty}\frac{g_{n_1}g_{n_2}g_{n_3}}{(w-w_{n_3}^b)l^{(3)}}+\dots \\ & +\sum_{n_1,\dots,n_{2i-1}}^{\infty}\frac{\prod_{k=1}^{2i-1}g_k}{(w+w_{2i-1}^b)l^{(2i-1)}}\Bigg)+V_2\Bigg(\sum_{n_1,n_2}^{\infty}\frac{g_{n_1}g_{n_2}}{(w-w_{n_2}^b)l^{(2)}}+ \\ & +\sum_{n_1,n_2,n_3,n_4}^{\infty}\frac{g_{n_1}g_{n_2}g_{n_3}g_{n_4}}{(w-w_{n_4}^b)l^{(4)}}+\dots\sum_{n_1,\dots,n_{2i}}^{\infty}\frac{\prod_{k=1}^{2i}g_k}{(w-w_{2i}^b)l^{(2i)}}\Bigg), \end{aligned} \tag{14}$$

where the following notations are used:

$$\begin{aligned} g_n &= \frac{L_-^*(a,w_n^b)}{L_+(a,w_n^b)}e^{iw_n^b(z_2-z_1)}, \\ l^{(k)} &= \underbrace{w_{n_1}^b(w_{n_1}^b+w_{n_2}^b)\cdots(w_{n_{k-1}}^b+w_{n_k}^b)}_{k}, \\ n_k &= 1,2,\dots,\ k=1,2,\dots. \end{aligned} \tag{15}$$

Factorized function $L_-^*(a,w_n^b)$ is calculated by Formula (22). Indeed, system (12) can be easily divided into separate recursive equations

$$\begin{aligned} B_+^1(w) = & -V_2\sum_{n_1=1}^{\infty}\frac{g_{n_1}}{(w+w_{n_1}^b)w_{n_1}^b}-V_1\sum_{n_1,n_2=1}^{\infty}\frac{g_{n_1}g_{n_2}}{(w+w_{n_1}^b)(w_{n_1}^b+w_{n_2}^b)w_{n_2}^b}+ \\ & +\sum_{n_1,n_2=1}^{\infty}\frac{g_{n_1}g_{n_2}}{(w+w_{n_1}^b)(w_{n_1}^b+w_{n_2}^b)}B_+^1(w_{n_2}^b), \\ B_-^2(w) = & V_1\sum_{n_1=1}^{\infty}\frac{g_{n_1}}{(w-w_{n_1}^b)w_{n_1}^b}+V_2\sum_{n_1,n_2=1}^{\infty}\frac{g_{n_1}g_{n_2}}{(w-w_{n_1}^b)(w_{n_1}^b+w_{n_2}^b)w_{n_2}^b}+ \\ & +\sum_{n_1,n_2=1}^{\infty}\frac{g_{n_1}g_{n_2}}{(w-w_{n_1}^b)(w_{n_1}^b+w_{n_2}^b)}B_-^2(-w_{n_2}^b), \end{aligned} \tag{16}$$

from which we directly obtain solutions in (16), cyclically using the equation itself in its right side.

4. Potential Distribution in the Lens

Substituting the resulting solution $F(w)$ (9) into (5) and calculating the integral along the real axis w using the residue theory, we determine the potential φ.

Let us consider each case for different cylinder regions separately.

1. $z \le z_1, 0 \le r \le a$.

In the region (a) to the left from z_1, the IC should be closed in the LHP w. After making calculations and passing to the limit $k \to 0$, we obtain the potential distribution inside the semi-infinite cylinder

$$\varphi(r,z) = V_1 - \sum_{n=1}^{N} \frac{\mathrm{J}_0(v_n^a r)}{\mathrm{J}_0^*(-w_n^a a)} \{L_-(a,w)(A_+^1(w) + B_+^1(w))e^{iw(z-z_1)}\}_{w=-w_n^a} =$$
$$V_1 - \sum_{n=1}^{N} e^{\frac{\gamma_n}{a}(z-z_1)} \frac{\mathrm{J}_0(\gamma_n \frac{r}{a})}{\gamma_n \mathrm{J}_1(\gamma_n)} L_+(a, i\tfrac{\gamma_n}{a})\Big(V_1 + i\frac{\gamma_n}{a} B_+^1(-i\tfrac{\gamma_n}{a})\Big). \quad (17)$$

Here we took into account that

$$\mathrm{J}_0^*(-w_n^a a) = \lim_{w \to -w_n^a} (w + w_n^a)^{-1} \mathrm{J}_0(va) = -ia\,\mathrm{J}_1(v_n^a a) = -ia\,\mathrm{J}_1(\gamma_n) \quad (18)$$

and the property of factorized functions $L_\pm$ in (10).

2. $z \le z_1, a \le r \le b$.

In this case for the region (c) to the left from z_1, integration along the real axis w in this case must also be closed, according to the Jordan lemma, in the LHP, then the integral can be easily transformed into a series of residues

$$\varphi(r,z) = V_1 \frac{\ln \frac{b}{r}}{\ln \frac{b}{a}} - \sum_{n=1}^{N} \left\{ \frac{(r,b)}{(a,b)^*} L_-(a,w)(A_+^1(w) + B_+^1(w))e^{iw(z-z_1)} \right\}_{-w_n^c} =$$
$$V_1 \frac{\ln \frac{b}{r}}{\ln \frac{b}{a}} - \frac{\pi}{2} \sum_{n=1}^{N} \frac{\mathrm{J}_0(\frac{\delta_n a}{b-a})\mathrm{J}_0(\frac{\delta_n b}{b-a})}{\mathrm{J}_0^2(\frac{\delta_n b}{b-a}) - \mathrm{J}_0^2(\frac{\delta_n a}{b-a})} (\mathrm{N}_0(\tfrac{\delta_n r}{b-a})\mathrm{J}_0(\tfrac{\delta_n b}{b-a}) - \mathrm{N}_0(\tfrac{\delta_n}{b-a} b)\mathrm{J}_0(\tfrac{\delta_n r}{b-a})) \quad (19)$$
$$L_+(a, i\tfrac{\delta_n}{b-a})\Big(V_1 + \frac{i\delta_n}{b-a} B_+^1(-i\tfrac{\delta_n}{b-a})\Big) e^{\frac{\delta_n}{b-a}(z-z_1)}.$$

Note that there is a transformation

$$(a,b)^*_{-w_n^c} = \lim_{w \to -w_n^c} (w + w_n^c)^{-1}(a,b) = -i\frac{2}{\pi v_n^c}\Big(\frac{(a',b)}{(a',a)} - \frac{(a,b')}{(b,b')}\Big)_{v_n^c} =$$
$$-i\frac{2(b-a)}{\pi \delta_n}\left(\frac{\mathrm{J}_0(\frac{\delta_n b}{b-a})}{\mathrm{J}_0(\frac{\delta_n a}{b-a})} - \frac{\mathrm{J}_0(\frac{\delta_n a}{b-a})}{\mathrm{J}_0(\frac{\delta_n b}{b-a})}\right), \quad (20)$$

where in the derivation the Wronskian $(z',z) = \mathrm{N}_0(z)\mathrm{J}_1(z) - \mathrm{N}_1(z)\mathrm{J}_0(z) = 2/(\pi z)$ is used [23]. Here the primes in the combination of Bessel functions (a,b) denote their derivatives.

3. $z_1 \le z \le z_2, 0 \le r \le b$.

For area (a) between semi-infinite round cylinders, according to the Jordan lemma, closing the IC in (5) for terms with an exponential factor $e^{iw(z-z_1)}$ in the UHP, and with a factor $e^{iw(z-z_2)}$ in the LHP w, taking into account all the contributions of the poles inside the IC, we similarly find the potential distribution in the slit region

$$\varphi(r,z) = \sum_{n=1}^{N} \frac{\mathrm{J}_0(\gamma_n \frac{r}{b})}{\mathrm{J}_0(\gamma_n \frac{a}{b})} L_-^*(a, w_n^b)\Big((-V_1/w_n^b + B_+^1(w_n^b))e^{iw_n^b(z-z_1)} +$$
$$(V_2/w_n^b + B_-^2(-w_n^b))e^{-iw^b(z-z_2)}\Big),$$

or it can be written as

$$\varphi(r,z) = \frac{1}{\ln\frac{b}{a}} \sum_{n=1}^{N} \frac{J_0(\gamma_n \frac{r}{b}) J_0(\gamma_n \frac{a}{b})}{\gamma_n^2 J_1^2(\gamma_n)} L_+^{-1}(a, i\tfrac{\gamma_n}{b}) \Big(e^{-\frac{\gamma_n}{b}(z-z_1)} (V_1 - \tfrac{i\gamma_n}{b} B_+^1(i\tfrac{\gamma_n}{b})) + e^{\frac{\gamma_n}{b}(z-z_2)} (V_2 - \tfrac{i\gamma_n}{b} B_-^2(-i\tfrac{\gamma_n}{b})) \Big), \quad (21)$$

using the properties of the Bessel functions

$$\frac{(a,b)_{v_n^b}}{J_0(\gamma_n \frac{a}{b})} = \frac{(b',b)_{v_n^b}}{J_1(\gamma_n)} = -\frac{2}{\pi \gamma_n J_1(\gamma_n)},$$

in the expression for

$$L_-^*(a, w_n^b) = \lim_{w \to w_n^b} (w - w_n^b) L_-(a,w) = \frac{i}{b \ln\frac{a}{b}} \frac{J_0^2(\gamma_n \frac{a}{b})}{\gamma_n J_1^2(\gamma_n) L_+(a, w_n^b)}. \quad (22)$$

4. $z_2 \le z, 0 \le r \le a$.

Similarly, in the region (a) to the right from the semi-infinite tube, closing the IC in the UHP of the complex variable w, we obtain

$$\varphi(r,z) = V_2 - \sum_{n=1}^{N} e^{-\frac{\gamma_n}{a}(z-z_2)} \frac{J_0(\gamma_n \frac{r}{a})}{\gamma_n J_1(\gamma_n)} L_+(a, i\tfrac{\gamma_n}{a}) \Big(V_2 + i\frac{\gamma_n}{a} B_-^2(i\tfrac{\gamma_n}{a}) \Big). \quad (23)$$

5. $z_2 \le z, a \le r \le b$.

In region (c) to the right outside the semi-infinite circular cylinder, deforming the IC upwards, we also obtain

$$\varphi(r,z) = V_2 \frac{\ln\frac{b}{r}}{\ln\frac{b}{a}} - \frac{\pi}{2} \sum_{n=1}^{N} \frac{J_0(\frac{\delta_n a}{b-a}) J_0(\frac{\delta_n b}{b-a})}{J_0^2(\frac{\delta_n b}{b-a}) - J_0^2(\frac{\delta_n a}{b-a})} L_+(a, i\tfrac{\delta_n}{b-a}) (r,b)|_{v_n^c} \Big(V_2 + \frac{i\delta_n}{b-a} B_-^2(i\tfrac{\delta_n}{b-a}) \Big) e^{-\frac{\delta_n}{b-a}(z-z_2)}. \quad (24)$$

5. Numerical Calculation of the Potential in a Lens

The numerical implementation of the factorized Bessel functions can be performed optimally using Formula (A5) with a given accuracy, which is expressed through the functions P and Q [5] (Appendix A). It should be noted that the potential distribution is ultimately expressed by a real function in the form of exponentially convergent series in (17)–(24). In particular, let us consider the distribution of the potential along the lens axis calculated by Formulas (17), (21) and (23).

Figures 2 and 3 show the results of calculating the potential in a two-electrode electrostatic lens depending on the radii of its inner and outer electrodes. The linear dimensions are given in units of the radius of the inner cylinders: $a = 1, b \to b/a, z \to z/a$. The width of the slit $z_2 - z_1 = 2$ ($z_1 = -1, z_2 = 1$).

As can be seen from Figure 2, as the radius of the semi-infinite cylinder increases, the steepness of the curve decreases.

It should be noted, as calculations show (see Figure 3), that the radius of an infinite cylinder b has an insignificant effect on the potential distribution along the z axis.

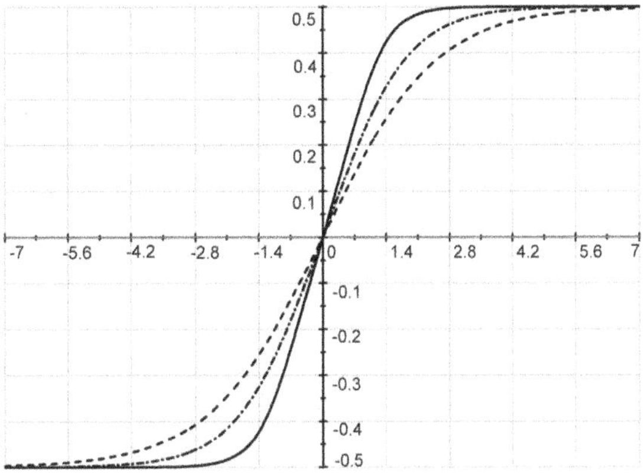

Figure 2. Potential distribution along the lens axis. $b = 6$: $a = 1$ is a solid line, $a = 2$ is a dash–dotted line, $a = 3$ is a dashed line.

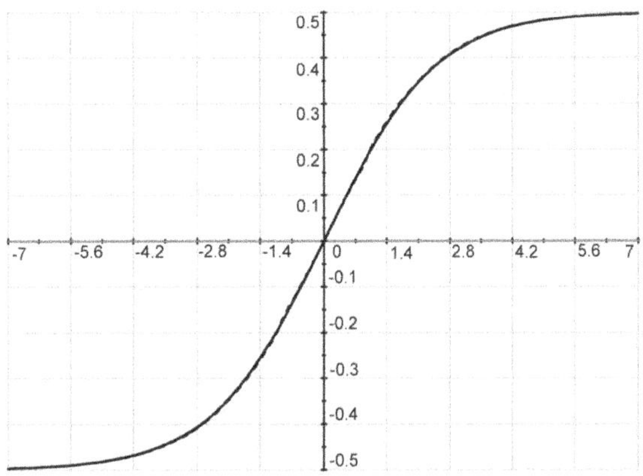

Figure 3. Influence of the outer cylinder radius on the potential distribution. $a = 1$: $b = 2$ is a solid line, $b = 4$ is a dashed line.

6. Discussion

Thus, the exact solution (9) of the boundary value problem for the potential φ in (5) is found, where the auxiliary functions B^1_+ and B^2_- are represented as rapidly convergent infinite series, as well as the factorized Bessel functions (see Appendix A).

As expected, when passing to the limit $z_1 \to -\infty$, when the end of the first semi-infinite cylinder is shifted by a considerable distance to the left, the expressions for the potential (21)–(24) coincide with the final results of N.N. Lebedev [5].

For each area (a), (b), and (c) inside an infinite round tube, the graphs of the distribution of potentials are calculated through their eigenfunctions and plotted for demonstration, for example, on the z axis (see Figures 2 and 3). As can be seen in the above figures, the curves turned out to be quite smooth, especially at the junctions of these regions, which shows that the calculation of factorized functions is sufficiently accurate.

Note that the problem for a nonzero wavenumber k transforms into the corresponding problem of wave diffraction in electrodynamics [20].

It should be expected that it will not be difficult to apply the WH method to similar problems with three or more electrodes, since only the rank of the system of algebraic equations will increase.

So, the internal boundary value problem of the distribution of the electrostatic field in a lens formed by two identical semi-infinite circular cylinders coaxially located inside an infinite outer cylinder is reduced to solving a system of singular integral equations WH and further solved by the WH method using factorized Bessel functions, which is reduced to a system of linear algebraic equations, splitting into separate recursive equations. Solutions to the problem for each region inside the infinite outer cylinder are presented as exponentially converging series in terms of eigenfunctions and eigenvalues.

The final results of this problem can be useful for testing approximate methods as the WH method is one of the mathematically rigorous methods.

7. Conclusions

The WH method was used to solve the internal boundary value problem of the elliptic type on the distribution of the electrostatic potential inside the structure formed by a round cylinder with a slot of finite width coaxially located inside an infinite round cylinder. The potentials of the cylinders are assumed to be constant and are set arbitrarily. The studied problem is first, with the help of boundary conditions, reduced to a system of singular integral Wiener–Hopf equations, the exact solution of which is constructed by the WH method in the class of meromorphic functions with respect to two desired auxiliary functions interconnected by a system of linear algebraic functions. This system breaks down into recursive equations, as a result of which the solution of the problem is obtained in the form of an infinite exponentially convergent series. It should be noted that the rigorous solution automatically satisfies the so-called edge condition or the Meixner condition, which, in fact, is responsible for the uniqueness of the solution to the boundary value problem, since the electric field must tend to infinity according to a given power law as it approaches the edge. Thus, the solution of the boundary value problem φ for each region is represented by eigenfunctions in the form of Bessel functions and eigenvalues, which are their roots at the corresponding radius of the cylinder inside the infinite outer cylinder. On the basis of analytical formulas, a quantitative analysis of the axial distribution of the potential of a two-electrode lens was carried out for various values of the radii of the outer and inner cylinders. The WH method can be applied without significant changes to similar boundary value problems with three or more internal electrodes. Undoubtedly, similar external boundary value problems are also of theoretical interest for the WH method. In modern electron microscopes, high resolution is provided by the use of aberration correctors, which eliminate the main reason that limits the resolution of an electron microscope—spherical and axial chromatic aberration of the electron lens that acts as its objective [1,24]. However, the use of a two-electrode mirror enables us to eliminate only one of these aberrations, either spherical or chromatic [1]. The development of aberration correctors with the simultaneous elimination of both spherical and axial chromatic aberrations using electron mirrors with three or more internal electrodes opens up great opportunities for increasing the resolving power of a new generation of transmission electron microscopes. At the same time, such an electrode design simultaneously provides electrostatic strength at high field strengths and screening of the electron beam from scattered electric fields at large gap widths between the internal electrodes.

Author Contributions: Conceptualization, S.B. and S.S.; methodology, S.S.; software, Z.S.; visualization, Z.S.; data curation, Z.S.; formal analysis, Z.S. and S.B.; investigation, S.S. and S.B.; writing—original draft preparation, S.S. and S.B.; writing—review and editing, S.S., S.B. and Z.S.; funding acquisition, S.B. All authors have read and agreed to the published version of the manuscript.

Funding: This research was funded by the Science Committee of the Ministry of Education and Science of the Republic of Kazakhstan (Grant No. AP14869293).

Data Availability Statement: Not applicable.

Acknowledgments: The authors are grateful to L.E. Strautman for her help in translating the text into English.

Conflicts of Interest: The authors declare no conflict of interests. The funders had no role in the design of the study; in the collection, analyses, or interpretation of data; in the writing of the manuscript; or in the decision to publish the results.

Abbreviations

The following abbreviations are used in this manuscript:

WH	Wiener–Hopf
SIE	Singular integral equation
UHP	Upper half-plane
LHP	Lower half-plane
IC	Integration contour

Appendix A. Factorization of Bessel Functions

Using a standard decomposition of integer functions into factorized functions, we can represent the Bessel functions and their combinations as

$$L(a,w) = L(a,w)_+ \cdot L(a,w)_-,$$

where [6,8]

$$L(a,w)_+ = \frac{\prod_{n=1}^{\infty}\left(1+\frac{w}{w_n^a}\right)e^{-\frac{w}{w_n^a}}\prod_{n=1}^{\infty}\left(1+\frac{w}{w_n^c}\right)e^{-\frac{w}{w_n^c}}}{\prod_{n=1}^{\infty}\left(1+\frac{w}{w_n^b}\right)e^{-\frac{w}{w_n^b}}}e^{-iw\left(T/\pi+(b-a)S\right)},$$
$$T = a\ln a + (b-a)\ln(b-a) - b\ln b,\ S = \sum_{n=1}^{\infty}\left(\tfrac{1}{\delta}_n - \tfrac{1}{\gamma}_n\right). \tag{A1}$$

As the function L_+ in its poles and zeros, which are imaginary, takes real values, it is convenient to express it through the gamma function

$$L(a,\alpha)_+ = \frac{e^{\alpha\frac{T}{\pi}}\,\Gamma(\frac{3}{4}+\alpha\frac{b}{\pi})}{\Gamma(\frac{3}{4}+\alpha\frac{a}{\pi})\Gamma(1+\alpha\frac{b-a}{\pi})}$$
$$\prod_{n=1}^{\infty}\left(\frac{1+\alpha\frac{a}{\gamma_n}}{1+\alpha\frac{a}{\gamma_n'}}\right)\left(\frac{1+\alpha\frac{b-a}{\delta_n}}{1+\alpha\frac{b-a}{\pi n}}\right)\left(\frac{1+\alpha\frac{b}{\gamma_n}}{1+\alpha\frac{b}{\gamma_n'}}\right)^{-1}. \tag{A2}$$

Here, as can be seen, the fast convergence in infinite products occurs due to the asymptotics of the roots of the Bessel functions $\gamma_n' = \pi(n-\frac{1}{4})$ and $\delta_n' = \pi n\ (n = 1,2,\ldots)$. For convenience, denoting the infinite products in (A2) as

$$P(x) = \prod_{n=1}^{\infty}\frac{1+\frac{x}{\gamma_n}}{1+\frac{x}{\gamma_n'}} = \exp\sum_{n=1}^{\infty}\left(\ln(1+\tfrac{x}{\gamma_n}) - \ln(1+\tfrac{x}{\gamma_n'})\right), \tag{A3}$$

$$Q(x) = \prod_{n=1}^{\infty}\frac{1+\frac{x}{\delta_n}}{1+\frac{x}{\pi n}} = \exp\sum_{n=1}^{\infty}\left(\ln(1+\tfrac{x}{\delta_n}) - \ln(1+\tfrac{x}{\pi n})\right), \tag{A4}$$

we finally obtain the optimal formula for the numerical calculation with sufficient accuracy:

$$L(a,\alpha)_+ = \frac{e^{\alpha\frac{T}{\pi}}\,\Gamma(\frac{3}{4}+\alpha\frac{b}{\pi})}{\Gamma(\frac{3}{4}+\alpha\frac{a}{\pi})\Gamma(1+\alpha\frac{b-a}{\pi})}\,\frac{P(a\alpha)Q((b-a)\alpha)}{P(b\alpha)}$$
$$(L(a,+w)_\pm = L(a,-w)_\mp). \tag{A5}$$

References

1. Bimurzaev, S.; Aldiyarov, N.; Yakushev, E. The objective lens of the electron microscope with correction of spherical and axial chromatic aberrations. *Microscopy* **2017**, *66*, 356–365. [CrossRef] [PubMed]
2. Bimurzaev, S.B.; Aldiyarov, N.; Sautbekova, Z. High dispersive electrostatic mirrors of rotational symmetry with the third order time-of-flight focusing by energy. *Tech. Phys.* **2020**, *65*, 1150–1155. [CrossRef]
3. Bimurzaev, S.; Yakushev, Y. An Electron Mirror as an Objective Lens of the Transmission Electron Microscope. *Microsc. Microanal.* **2021**, *27*, 1600–1601. [CrossRef]
4. Bimurzaev, S.; Yakushev, E. Relativistic theory of aberrations of electrostatic electron-optical systems. *Nucl. Instrum. Methods Phys. Res. Sect. A Accel. Spectrom. Detect. Assoc. Equip.* **2022**, *1022*, 165956. [CrossRef]
5. Lebedev, N.; Skal'skaya, I. Electrostatic field of an electron lens consisting of two coaxial cylinders. *Zh. Tekh. Fiz.* **1960**, *30*, 472–479.
6. Weinstein, L. *The Theory of Diffraction and the Factorization Method*; Golem Press: Boulder, CO, USA, 1969.
7. Titchmarsh, E. *Introduction to the Theory of Fourier Integrals*; Oxford University Press: Oxford, UK, 1937.
8. Noble, B.; Weiss, G. Methods based on the Wiener-Hopf technique for the solution of partial differential equations. *Phys. Today* **1959**, *12*, 50. [CrossRef]
9. Erdélyi, A.; Sneddon, I. Fractional Integration and Dual Integral Equations. *Can. J. Math.* **1962**, *14*, 685–693. [CrossRef]
10. Eswaran, K.; Jones, D.S. On the solutions of a class of dual integral equations occurring in diffraction problems. *Proc. R. Soc. Lond. Ser. A Math. Phys. Sci.* **1990**, *429*, 399–427. [CrossRef]
11. Sneddon, I. *Mixed Boundary Value Problems in Potential Theory*; North-Holland Publishing Company: Amsterdam, The Netherlands, 1966.
12. Kapitsa, P.L.; Fock, V.A.; Vainshtein, L.A. Static boundary problems for a hollow cylinder of finite length. *Zh. Tekh. Fiz.* **1959**, *29*, 1177–1187.
13. Lebedev, N.; Skal'skaya, I. Application of Dual Integral Equations to the Electrostatic Problem of a Hollow Conducting Cylinder of Finite Length. *Sov. Phys. Tech. Phys.* **1973**, *18*, 28.
14. Vainshtein, L. Static boundary problems for a hollow cylinder of finite length. II. Numerical results. *Zh. Tekh. Fiz.* **1962**, *32*, 1157–1164.
15. Vainshtein, L. Static boundary problems for a hollow cylinder of finite length. III. Approximate formulas. *Zh. Tekh. Fiz.* **1962**, *32*, 1165–1173.
16. Wiener, N.; Hopf, E. Über eine Klasse singulärer Integralgleichungen. *Sem.—Ber. Preuss. Akad. Wiss* **1931**, *B*, 696–706.
17. Sautbekova, M.; Sautbekov, S. Solution of the Neumann Problem of Diffraction by a Strip Using the Wiener–Hopf Method: Short-Wave Asymptotic Solutions. *IEEE Trans. Antennas Propag.* **2017**, *65*, 4797–4802. [CrossRef]
18. Sautbekov, S. Diffraction of plane wave by strip with arbitrary orientation of wave vector. *Prog. Electromagn. Res. M* **2011**, *21*, 117–131. [CrossRef]
19. Sautbekov, S. Factorization method for finite fine structure. *Prog. Electromagn. Res. B* **2010**, *25*, 1–21. [CrossRef]
20. Sautbekov, S.; Alkina, G.; Sautbekova, M. Wiener-Hopf method for problems of diffraction of asymmetric waves by a circular cylinder. In Proceedings of the Progress in Electromagnetics Research Symposium, Taipei, Taiwan, 25–28 March 2013; pp. 446–449.
21. Meixner, J. The behavior of electromagnetic fields at edges. *IEEE Trans. Antennas Propag.* **1972**, *20*, 442–446. [CrossRef]
22. Lewin, L. *Theory of Waveguides: Techniques for the Solution of Waveguide Problems*; Newnes-Butterworths: London, UK, 1975.
23. Abramowitz, M.; Stegun, I.A. *Handbook of Mathematical Functions with Formulas, Graphs, and Mathematical Tables*, ninth dover printing, tenth gpo printing ed.; Dover: New York, NY, USA, 1964.
24. Hartel, P.; Preikszas, D.; Spehr, R.; Müller, H.; Rose, H. Mirror corrector for low-voltage electron microscopes. In *Advances in Imaging and Electron Physics*; Elsevier: Amsterdam, The Netherlands, 2003; Volume 120, pp. 41–133.

mathematics

Article

Modeling the Five-Element Windkessel Model with Simultaneous Utilization of Blood Viscoelastic Properties for FFR Achievement: A Proof-of-Concept Study

Maria Fernandes [1,2], Luisa C. Sousa [1,2], Carlos A. Conceição António [1,2,*] and Sónia I. S. Pinto [1,2,*]

1 Faculty of Engineering, University of Porto, Rua Dr. Roberto Frias, s/n, 4200-465 Porto, Portugal; mcfernandes@fe.up.pt (M.F.); lcsousa@fe.up.pt (L.C.S.)
2 Institute of Science and Innovation in Mechanical and Industrial Engineering (LAETA-INEGI), Campus FEUP, Rua Dr. Roberto Frias, 400, 4200-465 Porto, Portugal
* Correspondence: cantonio@fe.up.pt (C.A.C.A.); spinto@fe.up.pt (S.I.S.P.)

Abstract: Coronary artery diseases (CADs) are a leading cause of death worldwide. Accurate numerical simulations of coronary blood flow, especially in high-risk atherosclerotic patients, have been a major challenge for clinical applications. This study pioneers a novel approach combining the physiologically accurate five-element Windkessel and sPTT models to enhance the accuracy of the hemodynamics and the fractional flow reserve (FFR) parameter. User-defined functions (UDFs) of the outlet pressure boundary condition (Windkessel model) and the viscoelastic characteristics of blood (sPTT model) were developed and dynamically loaded with ANSYS® 2023 software. In a proof-of-concept study, a patient's left coronary artery with 40% stenosis was provided by the hospital for further analysis. The numerical FFR value obtained in the present work skews only 0.37% from the invasive measurement in the hospital. This highlights the important roles of both blood viscoelasticity and the five-element Windkessel model in hemodynamic simulations. This proof-of-concept of the FFR numerical calculation tool provides a promising comprehensive assessment of atherosclerosis in a fast, accurate, more affordable, and fully non-invasive manner. After validation with more patient cases in the future, this tool could be employed in hospitals and offer a more accurate and individualized approach for the diagnosis and treatment of CAD.

Keywords: computational programming; user-defined functions; hemodynamic simulations; coronary arteries; Windkessel model; viscoelastic property of blood

MSC: 90-08; 90-10; 90-11

Citation: Fernandes, M.; Sousa, L.C.; António, C.A.C.; Pinto, S.I.S. Modeling the Five-Element Windkessel Model with Simultaneous Utilization of Blood Viscoelastic Properties for FFR Achievement: A Proof-of-Concept Study. *Mathematics* **2023**, *11*, 4877. https://doi.org/10.3390/math11244877

Academic Editors: Zhuojia Fu, Yiqian He and Hui Zheng

Received: 23 October 2023
Revised: 14 November 2023
Accepted: 30 November 2023
Published: 5 December 2023

1. Introduction

Coronary artery disease (CAD) occurs when there is partial or total obstruction of the coronary arteries through the development of plaque in the lumen (stenosis), reducing the capacity of this organ (ischemia). This disease represents approximately one in three deaths in developed countries since it is potentiated by population aging and poor lifestyle choices [1]. Stenoses are assessed by medical doctors through the analysis of images obtained with computed tomography (CT) scans [2]. There is an objective parameter used to measure the impact that the stenosis has on the blood flow—the fractional flow reserve (FFR)—which is a measure of pressure drop that occurs in the lumen of the artery. This parameter is non-dimensional, with values between zero (the artery is completely blocked) and one (there are no obstructions to blood flow).

The current invasive method for calculating FFR involves introducing a wire into the stenosed artery while under hyperemic circumstances (maximum vasodilation induced by administration of adenosine), measuring two pressure values, namely the aortic pressure and then the pressure distal to the stenosis at exactly 20 mm downstream [3]. The FFR is defined as the ratio between distal and aortic pressures, p_d and p_a, respectively.

A stenosis is considered significant if the FFR is less than 0.75, and revascularization procedures are conducted to assure reasonable blood flow. Moreover, the narrowing is seen as having a mild impact if this parameter is greater than 0.8. For this case, the patient is provided with medication and a set of preventive measures is recommended, such as lifestyle changes. However, for intermediate values, the clinician is the one that determines which treatment would produce the best outcome, which may not always be the one chosen [4].

As alternatives to the invasive method, a growing body of research has focused on using computational fluid dynamics (CFD) in conjunction with CT images to create artificial models of the diseased arteries and solve numerical simulations of fluid dynamics for coronary blood flow and determine FFR values non-invasively [5–9]. Thus, the non-invasive process would be a viable and cost-free alternative, with no risk for the patient, aimed at improving the accuracy of the diagnostic process.

Windkessel models are lumped-parameter models used to represent the entire circulatory system and are based on the simplified representation of the different cardiovascular elements such as the heart and venous and arterial vessel structures [10]. Applying these models as boundary conditions allows for the creation of a pressure distribution profile along the entire vessel, eliminating the need to model the full circulatory system.

Jonášová et al. (2021) utilized several accurate Windkessel models with 3, 5, and 7 elements, to numerically assess coronary circulation, but they used the Newtonian and shear-thinning blood models, and did not evaluate the fractional flow reserve [11]. Kim et al. (2014) compared the invasive and the computed FFR measures of patient-specific left coronary arteries and found remarkably similar results. However, the study does not disclose the used boundary conditions, namely, which lumped-parameter model was used to model pressure, as well as the rheological model used to model the viscosity of blood. In addition, the numerical FFR results presented in the paper were calculated in the patient's resting conditions [12]. Nakazato et al. (2013) performed a numerical study with 252 patients using blood as a Newtonian model and a lumped-parameter model. Though the model was able to overall match the invasive FFR, the simulation settings are not disclosed [13]. The accuracy of the simulation results is heavily linked to the used boundary conditions, so their study is essential for creating this non-invasive diagnostic tool. Csippa et al. (2021) measured the FFR parameter and the coronary flow reserve (CFR) in vivo and numerically. They also achieved good correlations utilizing patient-specific boundary conditions that were measured through invasive methods [14]. The study considered blood as a Newtonian fluid. Even though both parameters are commonly employed in the study of the physiological impact the stenoses have on blood circulation, the CFR is a function of numerous variables. In fact, CFR depends on properties such as the heartbeat rate. The contribution of collateral flow to myocardial perfusion is not taken into account by this parameter [15], unlike the FFR.

Blood is a series of different heterogeneous cells, such as erythrocytes, leukocytes, and thrombocytes, suspended in plasma, a liquid. The blood suspensions grant blood its non-Newtonian characteristics, that lead to very complex behavior [16]. In the literature, blood is frequently modeled as a shear-thinning fluid that does not factor in the viscoelasticity [11,17–19]. In the study conducted by Pinto et al. (2020), three different viscoelastic constitutive models were used to model blood and the results using a Newtonian and a Carreau model for numerical simulations in right coronary arteries (RCAs) were compared. The differences were significant [20]. In addition, from the studies of Campo-Deano et al. (2013), Bodnár et al. (2011), and Good et al. (2016), it was concluded that the viscoelasticity is the most accurate property of blood and hence, the viscoelastic effects should not be neglected [21–23]. Other works have showcased the importance of viscoelastic blood models for an accurate modeling of blood [24,25]. The simplified Phan-Thien/Tanner (sPTT) model led to the most precise results, and thus it was chosen in this study [20,21].

The primary goal of this work is to create a numerical model that can faithfully mimic the hemodynamics of real left coronary artery (LCA) circulation of a patient and, as a result, correctly forecast the onset of ischemia. This is a significant step towards creating a secure, non-invasive method of measuring the FFR, which, to the authors' knowledge, is still not attainable in the clinical settings. This work is innovative, by simultaneously using a five-element Windkessel model as the boundary condition for the pressure in the outlets of a patient-specific LCA model, and of the viscoelastic sPTT rheological model for blood. The proposed boundary condition representing the pressure conditions influenced by the entire circulatory system was implemented through a user-defined function in ANSYS® 2023 software, which can be dynamically loaded. This implementation was completed in alliance with the use of a pulsatile Womersley velocity profile at the inlet of the arteries and the representation of the complex blood rheology through a simplified Phan-Thien/Tanner (sPTT) viscoelastic model, which was still not reported in the literature.

The present study is a proof-of-concept where a patient-specific LCA model with 40% stenosis was created through image segmentation methods of Computed Tomography (CT) scans provided by the Vila Nova de Gaia/Espinho Hospital Centre (CHVNG/E). After implementation and running the hemodynamic simulations, the computed FFR was compared with the invasive FFR obtained in the hospital. Moreover, results considering the viscoelastic property of blood or blood as a Newtonian fluid were achieved in order to verify the importance of using the viscoelasticity of blood in hemodynamic simulations.

2. Materials and Methods

The entire process used to determine the computed FFR is detailed in this section, including the data of the studied patient, the creation of the patient-specific coronary artery, the replication of the artery in the hyperemia condition, the definition of all boundary conditions, and the rheological model. The mesh convergence test, and the numerical settings used in the CFD numerical simulations, conducted in ANSYS Fluent® 2023 software are also included.

2.1. Data of the Patient Case

A patient from CHVNG/E with a degree of stenosis was evaluated in this study. The patient is a 63-year-old man with a 40% stenosis located in the proximal region of the left anterior descending artery (LAD). Moreover, other patient information was provided, including the systolic blood pressure (SBP), the diastolic blood pressure (DBP), the FFR measured invasively, and the resting heartbeat rate (HBR_{rest}) (Table 1). The patient gave informed consent for inclusion before participating in the study. The study was conducted in accordance with the Declaration of Helsinki, and the protocol was approved by the Ethics Committee of CHVNG/E 53945 2021-01-27.

Table 1. Data of the patient measured invasively: systolic blood pressure (SBP), diastolic blood pressure (DBP), fractional flow reserve (FFR), and resting heartbeat rate (HBR_{rest}).

SBP [Pa]	DBP [Pa]	FFR	HBR_{rest} [bpm]
16,705.3	11,279.1	0.93	59

2.2. Geometric Model

CT images provided by CHVNG/E were used and, through MIMICS® (v20.0) software, a 3D model that represents the LCA of the patient was created, as well as the LAD and the left circumflex artery (LCX). After loading the images in the program and selecting the aorta, the inlet, and the outlets of the coronary tree, the software automatically generated a 3D model of the selected domain (Figure 1a).

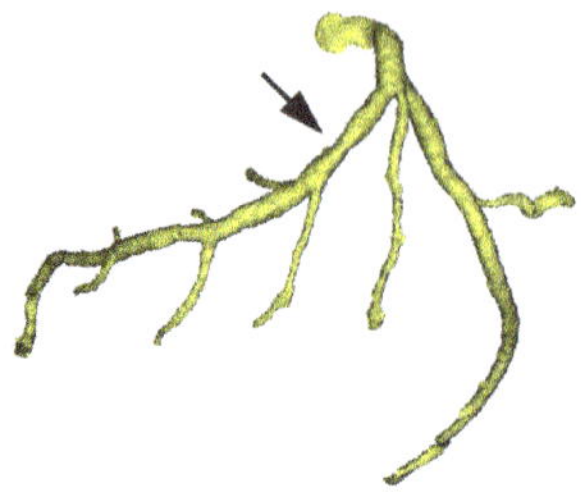

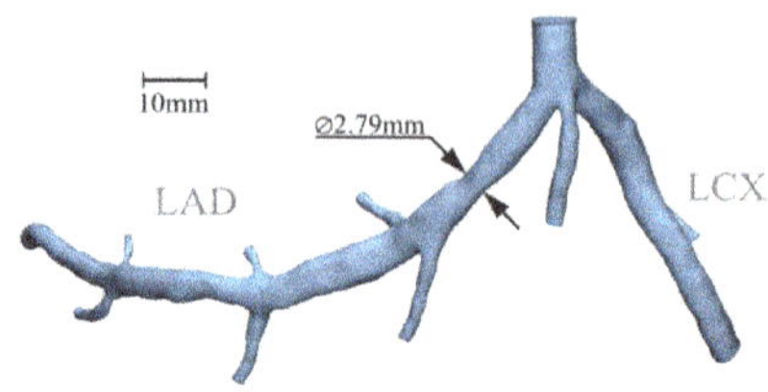

Figure 1. (**a**) LCA lumen model of the patient obtained in Mimics® (v20.0) software; (**b**) LCA lumen model of the patient obtained in 3-matic® (v20.0) software. The stenosis is highlighted with a black arrow, and it has an average diameter of 2.79 mm.

The model was further improved in 3-matic® software, where the geometry was smoothed, and the inlet and outlets were trimmed to form a flat surface onto which the boundary conditions must be applied in the numerical simulation process (Figure 1b). The created model represents the normal resting conditions of the patient, and the visualization of the three-dimensional geometry allows for an easier assessment of the severity of the stenoses.

2.3. Hyperemia Condition for Simulations

For an accurate determination of the non-invasive FFR, maximal hyperemia conditions, under which invasive FFR is determined, should be modeled. In clinical practice, both in invasive FFR or in ischemia testing, a hyperemic status is induced through the intravenous infusion of a pharmacologic vasodilator agent, in the present case adenosine (dose of 140 µg/kg/min). This pharmacologic stress agent causes several hemodynamic modifications that resemble the normal physiological response to stress or exercise [26], including a decrease in the mean systemic arterial pressure (6 mmHg) and vessel resistance (4.17 times), and an increase in heart rate (24 bpm) and absolute myocardial blood flow (4.4 times), relative to the resting conditions.

The vessel resistance depends on the blood viscosity, on the artery length and on the radius/cross-sectional area of the artery [27]. Therefore, the ratio between the cross-section area of the artery in hyperemia conditions and in resting conditions is always 2.04, since blood viscosity and artery length are the same for whatever the condition is (hyperemia or resting). Thus, the radius in each point of the 3D geometry of the artery needs to be increased 1.42 times relative to the resting conditions, and the resistance in hyperemia conditions is 0.24 times lower relative to resting conditions.

Consider that the resistance of a Hagen–Poiseuille flow is given by:

$$Res = \frac{8\mu L}{\pi R^4} \tag{1}$$

where *Res* is the resistance, μ is the dynamic viscosity, L is the length, and R is the radius of the vessel. With the resistance of the hyperemic vessel being 0.24 times lower than the resting vessel, it is possible to deduce that, approximating the artery's cross-sections to circles, the cross-sectional area, A, of the vessel changes:

$$\frac{Res_{hyper}}{Res_{rest}} = 0.24 \therefore \frac{R_{hyper}}{R_{rest}} = \frac{1}{\sqrt[4]{0.24}} \therefore \frac{A_{hyper}}{A_{rest}} = 2.04 \tag{2}$$

Thus, to accurately depict the geometry during maximum hyperemia, the entire LCA model must be scaled by 2.04 in its cross-sectional area. To achieve this goal, the resting 3D model was imported to Mimics®, and over forty values of diameter from differently located LCA cross-sections were measured using the tools of this software. Their values, augmented by the factor deduced in Equation (2), were used as the diameter values to rebuild the vasodilated model, approximating the cross-sections of the artery to perfect circles. Then, these sections were connected to form the hyperemic model (Figure 2). To assure a better representation of the stenosis, more diameter measurements were taken in that region, both downstream and upstream of the stenosis. The authors assumed that the coronary artery has rigid walls because the consideration of elastic walls in past works led to excessive computational times without considerable improvement in the obtained numerical results [28].

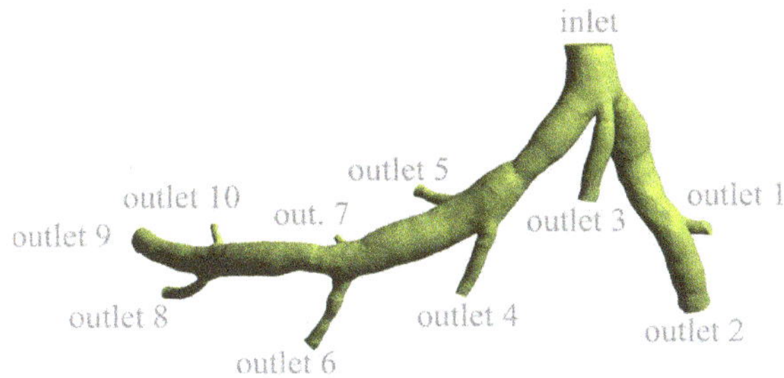

Figure 2. LCA lumen model of the patient under maximum hyperemic conditions. The inlet and outlets are marked accordingly.

2.4. Boundary Condition Definitions

The heart drives the circulatory system, and because of its distinctive motion, it allows blood to flow in a pulsatile manner. Additionally, because the circulatory system is a closed loop, vessels in other parts of the body inevitably influence blood pressure in the coronary arteries. The velocity and pressure boundary conditions defined in the control volume should mimic real hemodynamic flows, and these properties are modeled through a Womersley model and a lumped-parameter model (Windkessel model), respectively, which are presented in this section.

2.4.1. Velocity Boundary Condition

Coronary blood flow is pulsatile and periodic over a cardiac cycle, which has a duration, T, and an angular frequency, ω, defined as:

$$T = \frac{2\pi}{\omega} \tag{3}$$

$$\omega = \frac{2\pi\, HBR}{60} \tag{4}$$

The Womersley mathematical model of pulsatile flow is commonly used in the literature to represent blood flow [14,16,17,29], and a non-dimensional number, Wo, was developed to measure the ratio between transient inertial forces and viscous forces for the inlet of the artery:

$$Wo = R_{inlet}\sqrt{\frac{\rho\omega}{\mu}} \tag{5}$$

where ρ is the density of blood. The previous parameters are displayed in Table 2.

Table 2. Parameters used to calculate the Womersley number in hyperemia conditions.

R_{inlet} [m]	ρ [kg m^{-3}]	ω [rad s^{-1}]	T [s]	HBR [bpm]	Wo
3.406	1060	8.692	0.72	83	5.566

Because blood flow is oscillatory, the velocity profile in the direction of the flow, u, is described through a tailored Poiseuille profile:

$$u(r,t) = \frac{\hat{A}i}{\omega}\left(1 - \frac{J_0\left(i^{\frac{3}{2}}\, Wo\, \frac{r}{R}\right)}{J_0\left(i^{\frac{3}{2}}\, Wo\right)}\right)e^{i\omega t} \tag{6}$$

where J_0 is a null-order Bessel function of the first kind, i is the imaginary number, $\hat{A}$ is the amplitude, r is the radial coordinate, and t is the time instant (Figure 3). This velocity profile, applied in the inlet of the artery, was developed based on [30–32], where a velocity waveform was approximated using a Fourier series in MATLAB® [33–35]. Using the patient-specific values of R, ω, and, consequently, Wo, this profile approximates the real pulsatile blood flow of the patient. The concept of normalized time, t^*, calculated as the ratio between the time instance and the cardiac cycle period, was introduced to better establish the boundary conditions of the patient.

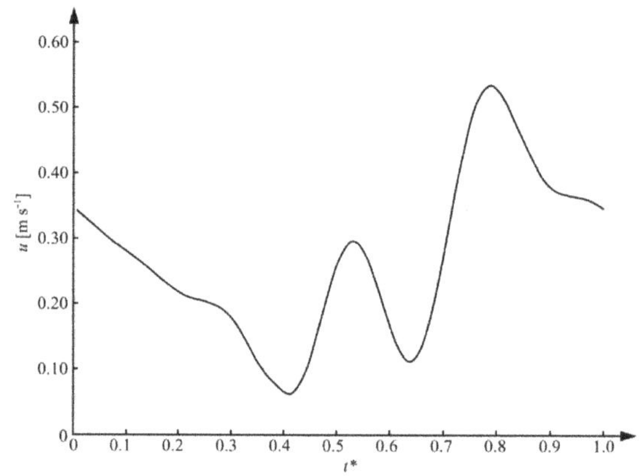

Figure 3. Velocity waveform at the inlet vs. nondimensional instant time (1 cardiac cycle) for the patient-specific case.

2.4.2. Pressure Boundary Condition

The resistances and capacitances of electrical circuits can also be explained in blood vessels [10]. In fact, both fluid inertia and wall elasticity can provoke resistance to the flow, and from Equation (1), it became clear that smaller vessels result in higher resistances. The capacitance (or compliance) of a blood vessel, C, is related to the level of inflating and deflating throughout the cardiac cycle, and the amount of change in the pressure gradient needed to produce a unit change of volume:

$$C = \frac{\Delta V}{\Delta p} \tag{7}$$

A Windkessel model is the direct application of the previous principles, and it is applied exclusively to the hemodynamic description of the arterial circulation [10]. In this work, a five-element Windkessel model was used (Figure 4) as the boundary condition of the outlets. Here, Res_a, Res_v, $Res_{a,micro}$, and $Res_{v,micro}$ represent the resistance of the arterial, venous, and both arterial and venous capillary levels. C_a and C_{im} are the arterial and intramyocardial compliances, and p_a, p_v, and p_{im} correspond to the arterial, venous, and variable intramyocardial pressures, respectively [11]. Moreover, the external pressure, p_{ext}, and the heart's right atrium pressure, p_{ra}, were considered null.

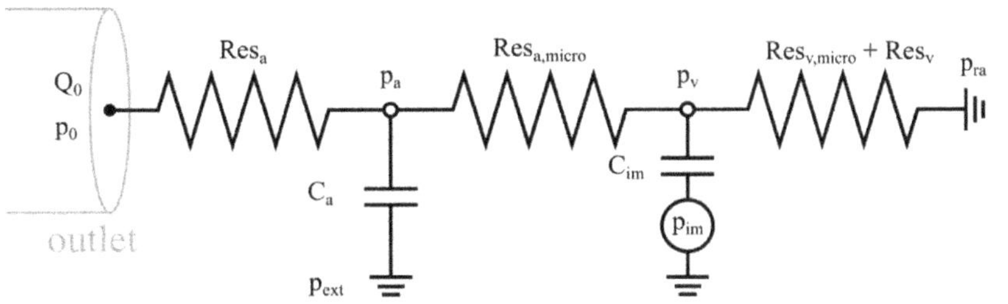

Figure 4. The five-element Windkessel model used as the outlet boundary conditions. Adapted from [11].

The governing equations of flow that are derived from this model are:

$$p_0 = p_a + Res_a Q_0, \tag{8}$$

$$\frac{dp_a}{dt} = \frac{Q_0}{C_a} - \frac{p_a - p_v}{C_a Res_{a,\ micro}}, \tag{9}$$

$$\frac{dp_v}{dt} = \frac{dp_{im}}{dt} + \frac{1}{C_{im}}\left(\frac{p_a - p_v}{Res_{a,\ micro}} + \frac{p_v}{Res_{v,\ micro} + Res_v}\right). \tag{10}$$

The involved parameters are calculated based on the data of the patient. Other considerations must be made. During the systole, the intramyocardial pressure can be equated to the left ventricular pressure, which is the pressure at the inlet of the coronary artery. The transition between systole and diastole was neglected and the pressure during the diastole was considered null. The total resistance to flow, Res_{total}, which involves both the arterial and venous circulation, was determined by:

$$Res_{total} = \frac{\frac{1}{3}SBP + \frac{2}{3}DBP}{\overline{Q_i}}, \tag{11}$$

where the numerator is the *MAP* and the average flow rate in the inlet is $\overline{Q}_i$. The resistance to blood flow in each outlet, Res_i, and the micro-circulatory arterial resistance, Res_m, are given by:

$$Res_i = Res_{total}\frac{A_i}{\sum_{i=1}^{N} A_i}, \tag{12}$$

$$Res_m = Res_{a,\ micro} + Res_a. \tag{13}$$

The resistance in the venous circulation, the sum of Res_v and $Res_{v,\ micro}$, was obtained considering that the average pressure in the veins is equal to 2666.45 Pa [36]:

$$Res_{v_i} + Res_{v,\ micro_i} = 2666.45\,\frac{A_i}{\sum_{i=1}^{N} A_i}\,. \tag{14}$$

The arterial resistance can be calculated through:

$$Res_{a_i} = \frac{\rho\sqrt{\frac{2}{3\rho}\left(k_1 \cdot e^{k_2 R_i} + k_3\right)}}{A_i}, \tag{15}$$

where blood is considered incompressible (and therefore, ρ is constant, equal to 1060 kg m^{-3}), R_i is the radius of the outlet, and the constants k_1, k_2, and k_3 are equal to 2000 kg^2 s^{-1} m^{-1}, -2253 m^{-1}, and 86.5 kg^2 s^{-1} m^{-1}, respectively [36].

Moreover, the arterial microcirculation resistance can be obtained through:

$$Res_{a,\ micro_i} = Res_{total} - (R_{vi} + R_{v,\ microi}) - R_{a_i}, \tag{16}$$

and this was used to calculate the resistances of each outlet of the patient. The values of the total arterial and intra-myocardial capacitances, $C_{a,tot}$ and $C_{im,tot}$, are 1.998×10^{-10} m^3 Pa^{-1} and 3.904×10^{-9} m^3 Pa^{-1}, respectively [36]. The authors assume that the myocardium mass of this patient is 204.9 g based on the works of the analysis of male cadaveric hearts completed by [37], since there are no works in the literature that measure the myocardial mass of ischemic live patients. Moreover, the ventricular mass index could not be calculated since there is not enough clinical information of the patient provided by the hospital.

Thus, in order to model the 5-element Windkessel, scripts in C language were written as user-defined functions (UDFs) to be compiled in ANSYS Fluent®. To implement this model, the equations need to be discretized using a second-order implicit method, which is described following the ANSYS Fluent Theory Guide [38]. The variable ϕ is an arbitrary variable and I is the calculation time step:

$$\frac{d\phi}{dt} = \frac{3\phi^{i+1} - 4\phi^{i} + \phi^{i-1}}{2\Delta t}. \tag{17}$$

Numerically, the constitutive equations were discretized, where Q is the mass flow rate and aux is an auxiliary variable:

$$\frac{dq}{dt} = \frac{3Q_0^{i+1} - 4Q_0^{i} + Q_0^{i-1}}{2\Delta t} \tag{18}$$

$$\frac{dp_{im}}{dt} = \frac{3p_{im}^{i+1} - 4p_{im}^{i} + p_{im}^{i-1}}{2\Delta t} \tag{19}$$

$$aux = \frac{3C_m}{2\Delta t} + \frac{1}{Res_m} + \frac{1}{Res_{v,\ micro} + Res_v} \tag{20}$$

$$p_0^{i+1} = \frac{\left(1 + \frac{Res_a}{Res_m}\right)Q_0^{i+1} + C_a\left(Res_a dq - \frac{-4p_0^i + p_0^{i-1}}{2\Delta t}\right)}{\frac{3C_a}{2\Delta t} + \frac{1}{Res_m} - \frac{1}{aux\ Res_m^2}} \tag{21}$$

$$p_v^{i+1} = \frac{1}{aux}\left(\frac{p_0^{i+1}}{Res_m} + C_m\left(dp_{im} - \frac{-4p_v^i + p_v^{i-1}}{2\Delta t}\right) - \frac{Res_a}{Res_m}Q_0^{i+1} + \frac{p_{ra}}{Res_{v,\ micro} + Res_v}\right) \tag{22}$$

2.5. Blood Rheological Model

Blood is a viscoelastic fluid due to its composition. Thus, to achieve realistic simulation results, the numerical modeling should take into account the elastic component of blood [21–23]. The general linear momentum conservation equation is given by:

$$\rho g - \nabla p + \nabla \cdot \boldsymbol{\tau} = \rho \frac{Du}{Dt} \tag{23}$$

where g is the gravitational acceleration, p is the pressure, and $\boldsymbol{\tau}$ is the stress tensor. The sPTT model for blood is modeled through the stress tensor, which is divided into an elastic and a solvent part:

$$\tau_{i,j} = \tau_{i,j_s} + \tau_{i,j_e} \tag{24}$$

This contributes differently to the overall viscosity values. In the solvent part (Equation (25)), the solvent viscosity, μ_s, is usually deemed constant (and equal to 0.0012 Pa.s) and $D_{i,j}$ is the shear strain rate tensor components. The elastic component (Equation (26)) is the sum of the different k modal shear stress tensor components:

$$\tau_{i,j_s} = 2\mu_s D_{i,j} \tag{25}$$

$$\tau_{i,j_e} = \sum_{k=1}^{N} \tau_{i,j_k} \tag{26}$$

The values for $\tau_{i,j}$ in Equation (26) are calculated through:

$$\left(1 + \frac{\lambda_k \varepsilon_k}{\mu_{e_k}} tr\left(\tau_{i,j_k}\right)\right)\tau_{i,j_k} + \lambda_k \overset{\nabla}{\tau}_{i,j_k} = 2\mu_{e_k} D_{i,j_k} \tag{27}$$

where λ_k is the relaxation time, ε_k is the extensibility coefficient and μ_e is the elastic dynamic viscosity. The upper convected derivative of the elastic stress tensor for each mode, $\overset{\nabla}{\boldsymbol{\tau}}_k$, is equal to:

$$\overset{\nabla}{\boldsymbol{\tau}}_k = \frac{D\boldsymbol{\tau}_k}{Dt} - (\nabla \cdot \mathbf{u})^T \boldsymbol{\tau}_k - \boldsymbol{\tau}_k (\nabla \cdot \mathbf{u}) \tag{28}$$

The experimental study of Campo-Deaño et al. (2013) concluded that four modes (N = 4) were sufficient to fit experimental data of rheological measurements of blood. Therefore, they obtained the different coefficients involved (Table 3) [20,21].

Table 3. Properties of the multi-modal sPTT model. Adapted from [21].

Mode, k	1	2	3	4	Solvent
$\mu_{e,k}$ [Pa s]	0.05	0.001	0.001	0.0016	0.0012
λ_k [s]	7	0.4	0.4	0.006	0
ε_k	0.2	0.5	0.5	0.5	0

2.6. Numerical Settings

The FFR is calculated as the ratio between the distal pressure and the aortic pressure. The positions occupied by the pressure sensor in the measurement of the invasive FFR—the standardized method [3]—and the positions where the computed FFR is calculated must be the same. Thus, two planes were generated in ANSYS Fluent® whose flow properties were recorded (Figure 5). The aortic plane was defined parallel to the inlet at a small distance of 0.01 mm. The distal plane was positioned 20 mm downstream the center of the stenosis and perpendicular to the direction of the flow.

Figure 5. Location of the aortic and distal planes.

The SIMPLE algorithm was used to solve the governing equations. A second order implicit approach was employed in the temporal formulation for the resolution of the pressure and flow fields as well as for the boundary condition—the five-element Windkessel model—in the outlets. A second order upwind discretization method was applied to the scalars produced by the usage of the viscoelastic non-Newtonian model (sPTT) for blood.

The time step duration was set at 0.005 s, with 20 iterations per time step, in order to maintain a Courant number below one throughout the entire pulsatile cycle [17,20,26]. The convergence criteria of the different scalars used to describe the different sPTT modes and the continuity and momentum equations had a value of 1×10^{-6}. This value was chosen to ensure numerical stability and computational efficiency to have accurate simulations results as shown in [20]. In addition, except for the pressure in the aortic and distal planes and the outlets, which were saved every time step, the instantaneous results of the hemodynamic simulations were saved every 0.02 s. The pressure values were averaged through a trapezoidal rule to be able to achieve representative distal and aortic pressure values used in the calculation of the numerical FFR.

2.7. Meshing

In CFD simulations, the quality of the results is highly dependent on the quality of the chosen mesh. A courser mesh can lead to inaccurate results and, also, meshes that are unnecessarily fine bring on large computational times unnecessarily. Thus, an accurate mesh for the lowest computational time possible must be achieved. The meshes of the models were created in ANSYS Meshing® 2023 software and tetrahedron elements were chosen, with the options of patch independent mesh and no refinement, to create a uniform mesh across the artery.

The maximum element size (MES) is the parameter that must be optimally selected. Three mesh sizes were chosen, such as 6.70×10^{-4} m, 5.30×10^{-4} m, and 4.22×10^{-4} m (Table 4), in order to double the number of elements with each mesh. Furthermore, the parameter Skewness is usually used to evaluate the quality of the mesh. Its value should not be above 0.95 for the calculation procedure to be stable and convergent [39].

Table 4. Mesh size and skewness parameters for the patient case.

Mesh Number	MES [m]	Number of Elements	Maximum Skewness	Average Skewness
Mesh 1	6.70×10^{-4}	126,568	0.754	0.154
Mesh 2	5.30×10^{-4}	255,996	0.867	0.136
Mesh 3	4.22×10^{-4}	507,641	0.684	0.125

Every mesh complied with the necessary skewness requirements, so a second criterion based on mesh convergence was employed to choose the mesh. The degree of convergence of the results was conducted with the Richards Interpolation method: considering p^* as the average pressure in the distal plane (Equation (29)) and p_i and p_{finest} as the current and the finest mesh (MES = 4.22×10^{-4} m), respectively:

$$p^* = p_i + \frac{p_i - p_{finest}}{r^2 - 1}, \tag{29}$$

where r is the ratio of the maximum element size of the finest mesh and the current mesh. The relative error value, e_r, can be calculated by:

$$e_{r_i} = \frac{p^* - p_i}{p_i}. \tag{30}$$

The tetrahedron meshes 1, 2, and 3 took a computational time of 0.92 h, 1.64 h, and 3.02 h, respectively. Table 5 shows the relative error of mesh 1 and mesh 2 relative to the finest mesh, mesh 3. All blood flow simulations were performed using mesh 2, which returned the smallest error (1.345%) for the patient even though it took 56% longer in computational time than mesh 1.

In conclusion, mesh 2 has the best balance between the lowest computational time and the highest result accuracy.

Table 5. Relative error values of p^* for the different mesh sizes.

	Mesh 1 (MES = 6.7×10^{-4} m)	Mesh 2 (MES = 5.3×10^{-4} m)
e_r [%]	4.010	1.345

3. Results and Discussion

The FFR value of the patient that was acquired invasively was compared with the one obtained using hemodynamic simulations of coronary flow. The computed FFR was determined considering blood as viscoelastic or blood as a Newtonian fluid. This comparison is important for highlighting the effects of the rheological model in the hemodynamic results.

In addition to the computed FFR, the average pressure in the outlets as well as the velocity and pressure fields throughout the artery model were examined. These results were used to evaluate the impact that the presence of stenosis has on the hemodynamic flow, considering the viscoelastic property of blood and Newtonian model of blood in the numerical simulations.

In summary, we examined the influence of blood rheology in the hemodynamic flow and consequently in the computed FFR. The results were treated through a post-process program, the ANSYS CFD-Post® 2023 software. Five cardiac cycles were computed, and data from the last one were collected, since the errors associated with the initialization of the computational process had diminished.

3.1. Velocity Fields

According to Figure 3, the minimum velocity occurs when the dimensionless time, t^*, is equal to 0.425 and the maximum one is equal to 0.79, during the diastole and the systolic peak, respectively. The velocity fields in those times instances were retrieved, and they are displayed for the sPTT model (Figure 6a,b) and the Newtonian blood model (Figure 6c,d).

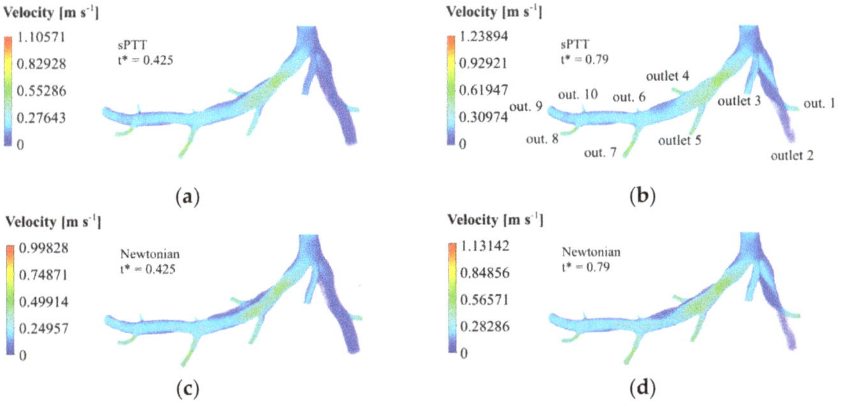

Figure 6. Velocity fields for the patient case: sPTT model at (**a**) minimum velocity (t* = 0.425); (**b**) maximum velocity (t* = 0.79); Newtonian model at (**c**) minimum velocity (t* = 0.425); (**d**) maximum velocity (t* = 0.79).

Due to the rise in dynamic pressure, thinner cross-sections have higher velocity magnitudes, such as in the case of the stenosis region and the outlet arteries. This happens for both rheological models. Moreover, in the LAD, it is clear to see that downstream the narrowed vessel, provoked by the stenosis, the velocity gradually decreases to values like the ones registered in the inlet before the bifurcation. Near the walls, friction losses are the cause of the witnessed velocity decreases. In the region near the wall surface before and after outlet 4, there is a stagnant blood flow since the velocity values are near zero. This region is bigger in the Newtonian case and in both time instances.

The sPTT simulations returned higher maximum velocities than the Newtonian model simulations. In fact, the maximum velocity achieved in $t^* = 0.425$ was 9.72% larger and, for the instant $t^* = 0.79$, the maximum velocity was 8.68% higher. It could be concluded that the Newtonian blood model underestimates the maximum velocity that occurs in the stenosis, not accounting for its real impact on blood flow.

3.2. *Pressure Fields and Profiles*

For the calculation of the FFR, the pressures in the aorta and 20 mm downstream the stenosis are required. The spatial-averaged pressure waveforms at the distal and aortic planes (displayed on Figure 5) are shown in Figure 7 as a function of non-dimensional time, for both sPTT and Newtonian models of blood.

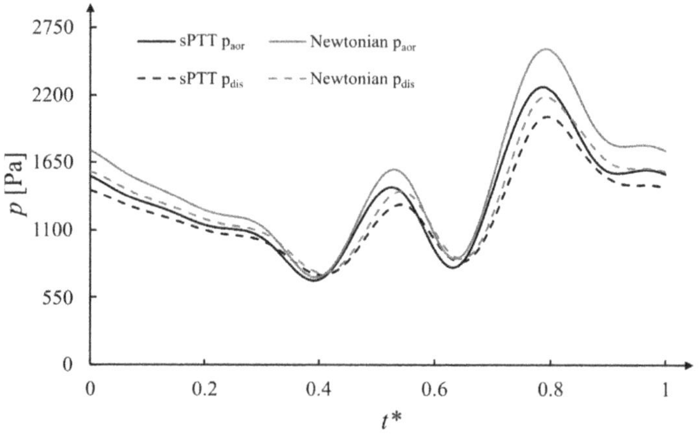

Figure 7. Pressure waveform for the patient case in the aortic and the distal planes for the Newtonian and the sPTT models.

The pressure peak and valley occur approximately in the same instances as the velocity ones. The distal pressure profile reaches lower pressure values, confirming the pressure drop that occurs because of the existence of the stenosis. This happens considering both models for blood. Additionally, the propagation of the pressure pulse from the entrance through the branches of the coronary tree is what causes the observed lag between the minimum and maximum pressure peaks from the aortic to the distal planes. The Newtonian model returned slightly higher pressure values for the aortic and distal plane than the sPTT model since the latter accounts for viscoelastic impacts of blood flow, which lead to lower pressure values.

The pressure fields for the patient are displayed for the minimum and the maximum velocity time instances for the sPTT model (Figure 8a,b) and the Newtonian blood model (Figure 8c,d).

For both rheological models, the maximum pressure reached in $t^* = 0.425$ (Figure 8a,c) is lower than the maximum pressure reached in $t^* = 0.790$ (Figure 8b,d). Since the LCX branch, which is upstream of the stenosis, manages to retain greater pressure values lengthwise, a comparison of the pressure values with the LAD branch denotes the obvious influence the stenosis has on blood flow. The stenosis leads to a pressure drop in the artery that is slowly overturned downstream of the vessel, but the pressure never recovers to the inlet pressure values. This conclusion is supported by Bernoulli's principle, since the increase in cross-sectional area after the stenosis leads to a pressure increase.

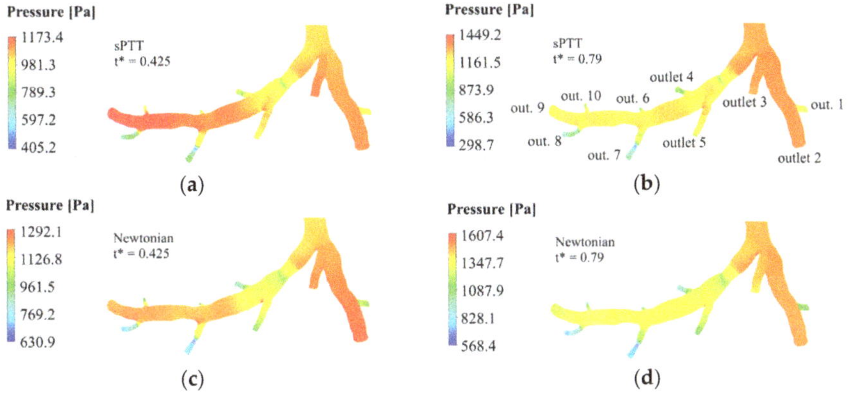

Figure 8. Pressure fields for the patient case: sPTT model at (**a**) minimum velocity (t* = 0.425); (**b**) maximum velocity (t* = 0.79); Newtonian model at (**c**) minimum velocity (t* = 0.425); (**d**) maximum velocity (t* = 0.79).

Looking at the pressure contours, it is evident that the pressure decreases in the stenosis area and starts increasing with the downstream distance to the stenosis. However, the pressure considering the viscoelastic model (Figure 8a,b) recuperates over a shorter distance than the Newtonian model (Figure 8c,d). The sPTT simulations returned maximum and minimum pressure values that were lower than the ones using the Newtonian blood model. Quantitatively, in the sPTT case, the maximum pressure reached in t^* = 0.425 was 10.12% lower, and the minimum pressure obtained was 55.7% smaller. Similarly, for t^* = 0.79, the maximum pressure was 10.92% lower and the minimum pressure obtained was 90.29% smaller.

If the artery had only been numerically studied with the Newtonian model, it could be assumed that the pressure downstream the stenosis would never recuperate and affect the entire circulatory system. Such a conclusion would be misleading and, therefore, a more accurate blood model needs to be computed. Thus, the rheological model to be used in hemodynamic simulations of coronary arteries should take into consideration the viscoelastic property of blood, which is more accurate [20–24].

In the smaller arteries, such as the outlets, the pressure tends to be lower (Figure 8) due to a greater preponderance of viscous strains, the reverse of what occurred with the velocity (Figure 6). To better assess the stenosis impact downstream, the temporal distribution of the spatial-average pressure in each outlet was calculated. These results are displayed considering the sPTT (Figure 9a) and the Newtonian blood models (Figure 9b).

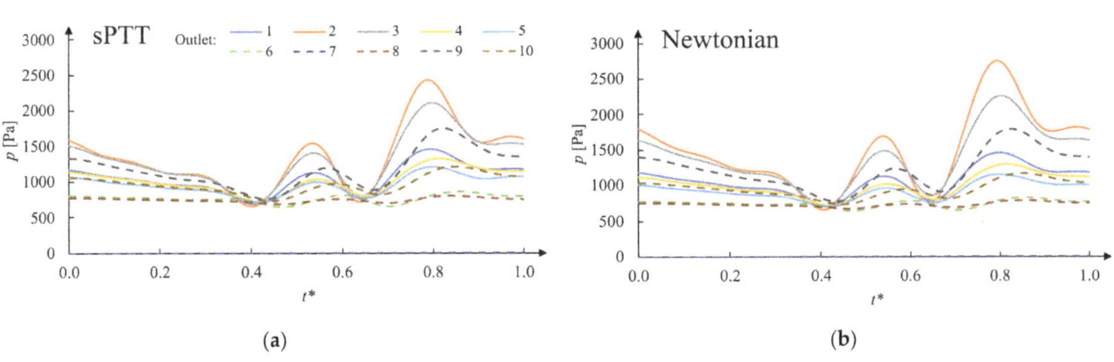

Figure 9. Outlet pressure waveforms of the patient case: (**a**) sPTT model; (**b**) Newtonian model.

The results of the pressure curves for the sPTT and the Newtonian blood models have similar magnitude and shape. The pressure peaks occur in the same time instances. Before the stenosis, outlet 1 to 3 returned higher pressure values. Then, after the stenosis, its closest exits are outlets 4 and 5, where the recorded pressure is significantly lower in comparison with the first three outlets. The pressure continues to decrease in outlets 6 and 7. The magnitude of pressure is much lower, but it recovers downstream, as is evident by the increase in the pressure values in outlets 8 to 10. Outlet 9 is the furthest from the stenosis, and the pressure values, although larger than the ones of outlets upstream, are still below the initial pressure values. This suggests that the presence of stenosis alters the flow in the arteries and, consequently, of the capacity of the cardiac muscle.

For a better comparison of the results obtained using the two different rheological models, the pressure peaks obtained in each outlet were recovered for both the Newtonian and the sPTT blood models. The pressure values are presented in Table 6, where the relative error between them is displayed.

Table 6. Maximum outlet pressure for the sPTT and the Newtonian blood models and the relative error values.

Outlet	Maximum Outlet Pressure (sPTT) [Pa]	Maximum Outlet Pressure (Newtonian) [Pa]	Relative Error [%]
Outlet 1	1449.8	1473.5	1.6
Outlet 2	2695.8	2835.0	5.2
Outlet 3	2119.7	2292.0	8.1
Outlet 4	1323.8	1235.4	6.7
Outlet 5	1210.0	1237.4	2.3
Outlet 6	837.4	710.9	15.1
Outlet 7	881.7	1321.3	49.9
Outlet 8	804.0	797.5	0.8
Outlet 9	1746.5	1840.6	5.4
Outlet 10	1233.2	1204.5	2.3

The calculated relative error values are diverse, ranging from 0.8% to 49.9% in outlets 8 and 7, respectively. The average relative error is 9.7%. This measure indicates that, since the relative error values are high, the sPTT model must be used in the numerical simulations.

3.3. Non-Invasive FFR

The previous data were used to calculate the temporal and spatial-averaged pressure values for the distal and the aortic planes of the artery to obtain the non-invasive FFR. For both locations, the spatial-average pressure values in different time steps were averaged through a trapezoidal rule. With the ratio of the two values, the FFR value for the patient case was calculated, as well as the relative error to the invasive measurement (Table 7).

Table 7. Comparison between invasive and non-invasive FFR for the patient case considering the Newtonian and the sPTT blood models.

Blood Model	Invasive FFR	Non-Invasive FFR	e_r [%]
Newtonian	0.930	0.904	2.74
sPTT		0.934	0.37

The non-invasive method captured the hemodynamics of the LCA, given the fact that the computed FFR of the patient is practically equivalent to the invasive FFR, recording a relative error of 0.37%. This error value is much smaller than the one registered in the numerical simulations considering the Newtonian blood model (2.74%). This is due to the fact that the sPTT model considers the viscoelasticity of blood, and it is a more accurate representation of its fluid properties [20–24]. In addition, the use of the Womersley velocity model and the five-element Windkessel flow are essential for reproducing the realistic waveforms of this patient.

Moreover, it is crucial to compare our results with those reported in the recent literature in order to validate the reliability of the implemented method. In a study conducted by Xue et al. (2023), the outlet blood flow conditions were determined based on CT perfusion and outlet diameter, while maintaining a constant pressure at the artery inlet. They assumed blood to be a Newtonian fluid. Like the present work, these authors performed the reconstruction of a coronary artery through 2D images and used clinical information to determine patient-specific boundary conditions. The outlet boundary conditions used were coronary outlet resistance based on the myocardial perfusion territory, extracted from medical imaging of the heart during a cardiac cycle. The mesh used by the authors exceeds 1×10^6 elements, and the software OpenFOAM was used in the numerical simulations. The results showed a relative error of 4.35% and 2.25% between invasive and computed FFR for two patient cases [40]. On the other hand, Gao et al. (2020) utilized a machine learning algorithm to predict the FFR based on CT imaging. The authors created a tree-structured recurrent neural network. The hemodynamic results were obtained through simulations using the finite element method of 1D models of coronary artery trees. The work used outlet pressure and inlet velocity values based on lumped-parameter models. The neural network was trained with 13,000 synthetic coronary trees authors, and eight patient cases were used in the validation stage. The authors achieved an average relative error of 2.85% between invasive and computed FFR for eight patients. Given the low relative error obtained in their work in comparison with state-of-the-art methods, it could be stated that the implemented methods are valid and reliable [41].

4. Conclusions

In this work, a patient-specific geometry of a left coronary artery was generated to perform hemodynamic simulations using computational fluid dynamics, with the objective of calculating the value of the FFR. This parameter is considered the gold standard in the assessment of the severity of a lesion due to the existence of stenosis and the possible need for revascularization. In order to assess the accuracy of the developed numerical model, the non-invasive computed FFR value was compared with the invasively measured one, obtained by the Vila Nova de Gaia/Espinho Hospital Centre.

The geometry of the LCA was modeled through CT scans provided by the CHVNG/E. Using Mimics® (v20.0) and 3-matic® (v20.0) software, the geometry under resting conditions was reconstructed. Then, its cross-sectional area was scaled by a factor of 2.04 to replicate the FFR measurement procedure in hyperemic conditions. In order to simulate coronary blood flow, a patient-specific Womersley velocity profile was used as the inlet velocity boundary condition. A simplified Phan-Thien/Tanner rheological model was implemented to model the viscoelastic properties of blood. Moreover, a five-element Windkessel model was modeled as the pressure boundary condition for the outlets of the patient-specific artery geometry. User-defined functions were implemented in ANSYS Fluent® to consider the previous conditions.

The numerical tool allows for the creation of pressure and velocity domains in the artery along a cardiac cycle, which, due to the accuracy of the chosen boundary conditions and rheological model, would be very approximate to the real-life waveforms of the patients. In addition, this tool allows for the calculation of the non-invasive FFR, a parameter used in clinical settings to assess coronary artery disease and the level of constriction of the coronary arteries. Hence, this work has clinical importance for potentially returning accurate values custom to each patient case, aiding medical doctors in the diagnosis and treatment of their patients with atherosclerosis.

The implemented model produced an FFR value of 0.934 for the patient, which corresponds to a relative error of 0.37% in comparison with the invasive measurement. This error value is lower than the one obtained in the numerical simulations that took into consideration the Newtonian model (2.74%). The results confirm the need to consider the viscoelasticity of blood in realistic blood flow simulations, in alliance with accurate boundary conditions for pressure (Windkessel model) and velocity (Womersley profile).

This work deals with a relevant problem in medical practice since obtaining a computational measure of FFR would aid in clinical practice by replacing invasive FFR procedures. The non-invasive procedure could be a cost-free alternative, with no risk for the patient, which improves the diagnosis and treatment of the disease. After validation with many patient-specific cases, in the future, the final goal of this project is to create software to be used by the medical doctors on-site to obtain an accurate computed FFR avoiding invasive procedures.

Study Limitations

Even though this study returned promising results, some limitations are worth mentioning. Since the 3D geometric model of the patient artery is scaled manually, there can be a loss in patient geometry information, which could be particularly more relevant for higher stenosis severities. Moreover, the authors assumed that the hyperemia condition impacts the vessel in the same constant proportion of 2.04. The ability of the artery to dilate may be different in the stenotic region because of the material properties of the plaque.

Regarding the five-element Windkessel model, it allows for downstream vasculature compliance but ignores coronary artery compliance. The used Windkessel model assumes a Newtonian behavior downstream of the artery, but still considers a viscoelastic model in the artery itself. Since the FFR pressure values are measured around the stenosis in the artery model, where the viscoelastic model was implemented and the corresponding results were very accurate when compared to the invasive measure, this consideration was not relevant.

Moreover, in the coronary artery numerical simulations of the present study, the fluid–structure interaction (FSI) method was not applied since our past works have shown that the implementation of FSI in numerical simulations increased the computational time without improving the accuracy of the hemodynamic results [28]. However, according to the research of Amabili et al. (2020), the human aorta, larger than the coronary artery, possesses a certain degree of flexibility, giving it a pulsatile diameter expansion (10% for a young human aorta) [42].

The myocardial mass used to calculate the compliance parameters corresponds to an average of cadaveric heart weight of healthy adults, and not of live ischemic hearts, because of a lack of data from the hospital and the literature. The knowledge of the myocardial mass index could better assist the authors in using a more accurate myocardial mass value for other patient cases. Moreover, the authors did not consider the possibility of the thickening of arterioles that can occur on ischemic hearts, which would consequently increase their resistance to blood flow.

Evidently, the current study constitutes proof-of-concept, since only one patient has been studied. Thus, in the near future and before clinical use, the numerical software must be further validated with many patient cases, with different stenosis severities in separate locations of the coronary artery.

Author Contributions: Conceptualization, M.F. and S.I.S.P.; methodology, M.F., L.C.S., C.A.C.A. and S.I.S.P.; software, M.F., L.C.S., C.A.C.A. and S.I.S.P.; validation, M.F. and S.I.S.P.; formal analysis, M.F. and S.I.S.P.; investigation, M.F., L.C.S., C.A.C.A. and S.I.S.P.; resources, C.A.C.A.; data curation, M.F.; writing—original draft preparation, M.F.; writing—review and editing, L.C.S. and S.I.S.P.; visualization, M.F. and S.I.S.P.; supervision, C.A.C.A. and S.I.S.P.; project administration, S.I.S.P.; funding acquisition, L.C.S., C.A.C.A. and S.I.S.P. All authors have read and agreed to the published version of the manuscript.

Funding: This research was funded by Foundation for Science and Technology, (Portugal), grant number "PTDC/EMD-EMD/0980/2020".

Institutional Review Board Statement: The study was conducted in accordance with the Declaration of Helsinki and approved by the Ethics Committee of CHVNG/E (protocol code 53945 and date of approval 27 January 2021).

Informed Consent Statement: Informed consent was obtained from all subjects involved in the study.

Data Availability Statement: The data presented in this study are available on request from the corresponding author.

Acknowledgments: The authors gratefully acknowledge the financial support of FCT, the Foundation for Science and Technology, (Portugal) regarding the R&D Project "CADS-FACT—PTDC/EMD-EMD/0980/2020", the Engineering Faculty of University of Porto (FEUP), the Institute of Science and Innovation in Mechanical and Industrial Engineering (INEGI), the Cardiovascular R&D Unit of the Medicine Faculty of University of Porto (FMUP), and the Cardiology Department of Gaia/Espinho Hospital Center (CHVNG/E).

Conflicts of Interest: The authors declare no conflict of interest.

References

1. Khan, M.A.; Hashim, M.J.; Mustafa, H.; Baniyas, M.Y.; Al Suwaidi, S.K.B.M.; AlKatheeri, R.; Alblooshi, F.M.K.; Almatrooshi, M.E.A.H.; Alzaabi, M.E.H.; Al Darmaki, R.S.; et al. Global Epidemiology of Ischemic Heart Disease: Results from the Global Burden of Disease Study. *Cureus* **2020**, *12*, 9349. [CrossRef] [PubMed]
2. Cohen, J.C. Genetic Approaches to Coronary Heart Disease. *J. Am. Coll. Cardiol.* **2006**, *48*, 5–9. [CrossRef]
3. Toth, G.G.; Johnson, N.P.; Jeremias, A.; Pellicano, M.; Vranckx, P.; Fearon, W.F.; Barbato, E.; Kern, M.J.; Pijls, N.H.J.; De Bruyne, B. Standardization of Fractional Flow Reserve Measurements. *J. Am. Coll. Cardiol.* **2016**, *68*, 742–753. [CrossRef] [PubMed]
4. Chahour, K.; Aboulaich, R.; Habbal, A.; Abdelkhirane, C.; Zemzemi, N. Numerical Simulation of the Fractional Flow Reserve (FFR). *Math. Model. Nat. Phenom.* **2018**, *13*, 2018069. [CrossRef]
5. Dash, A.; Jain, K.; Ghosh, N.; Patra, A. Non-Invasive Detection of Coronary Artery Disease from Photoplethysmograph Using Lumped Parameter Modelling. *Biomed. Signal Process. Control* **2022**, *77*, 103781. [CrossRef]
6. Meimoun, P.; Clerc, J.; Ardourel, D.; Djou, U.; Martis, S.; Botoro, T.; Elmkies, F.; Zemir, H.; Luycx-Bore, A.; Boulanger, J. Assessment of Left Anterior Descending Artery Stenosis of Intermediate Severity by Fractional Flow Reserve, Instantaneous Wave-Free Ratio, and Non-Invasive Coronary Flow Reserve. *Int. J. Cardiovasc. Imaging* **2017**, *33*, 999–1007. [CrossRef]
7. Zhang, J.M.; Luo, T.; Huo, Y.; Wan, M.; Chua, T.; Tan, R.S.; Kassab, G.S.; Tan, S.Y.; Zhong, L. Area Stenosis Associated with Non-Invasive Fractional Flow Reserve Obtained from Coronary CT Images. In Proceedings of the 2013 35th Annual International Conference of the IEEE Engineering in Medicine and Biology Society (EMBC), Osaka, Japan, 3–7 July 2013; pp. 3865–3868. [CrossRef]
8. Tsompou, P.I.; Siogkas, P.K.; Sakellarios, A.I.; Lemos, P.A.; Michalis, L.K.; Fotiadis, D.I. Non-Invasive Assessment of Coronary Stenoses and Comparison to Invasive Techniques: A Proof-of-Concept Study. In Proceedings of the 2017 IEEE 30th International Symposium on Computer-Based Medical Systems (CBMS), Thessaloniki, Greece, 22–24 June 2017; pp. 328–331. [CrossRef]
9. Liu, J.; Wang, X.; Li, B.; Huang, S.; Sun, H.; Zhang, L.; Sun, Y.; Liu, Z.; Liu, J.; Wang, L.; et al. Non-Invasive Quantification of Fraction Flow Reserve Based on Steady-State Geometric Multiscale Models. *Front. Physiol.* **2022**, *13*, 881826. [CrossRef]
10. Westerhof, N.; Lankhaar, J.W.; Westerhof, B.E. The Arterial Windkessel. *Med. Biol. Eng. Comput.* **2009**, *47*, 131–141. [CrossRef]
11. Jonášová, A.; Vimmr, J. On the Relevance of Boundary Conditions and Viscosity Models in Blood Flow Simulations in Patient-Specific Aorto- Coronary Bypass Models. *Int. j. Numer. Method. Biomed. Eng.* **2021**, *37*, e3439. [CrossRef]
12. Kim, K.-H.H.; Doh, J.-H.H.; Koo, B.-K.K.; Min, J.K.; Erglis, A.; Yang, H.M.; Park, K.W.; Lee, H.Y.; Kang, H.J.; Kim, Y.J.; et al. A Novel Noninvasive Technology for Treatment Planning Using Virtual Coronary Stenting and Computed Tomography-Derived Computed Fractional Flow Reserve. *JACC Cardiovasc. Interv.* **2014**, *7*, 72–78. [CrossRef]
13. Nakazato, R.; Park, H.B.; Berman, D.S.; Gransar, H.; Koo, B.K.; Erglis, A.; Lin, F.Y.; Dunning, A.M.; Budoff, M.J.; Malpeso, J.; et al. Noninvasive Fractional Flow Reserve Derived from Computed Tomography Angiography for Coronary Lesions of Intermediate Stenosis Severity Results from the DeFACTO Study. *Circ. Cardiovasc. Imaging* **2013**, *6*, 881–889. [CrossRef] [PubMed]
14. Csippa, B.; Üveges, Á.; Gyürki, D.; Jenei, C.; Tar, B.; Bugarin-Horváth, B.; Szabó, G.T.; Komócsi, A.; Paál, G.; Kőszegi, Z. Simplified Coronary Flow Reserve Calculations Based on Three-Dimensional Coronary Reconstruction and Intracoronary Pressure Data. *Cardiol. J.* **2021**, *XX*, 1–10. [CrossRef] [PubMed]
15. Pijls, N.H.J.; Van Gelder, B.; Van der Voort, P.; Peels, K.; Bracke, F.A.L.E.; Bonnier, H.J.R.M.; El Gamal, M.I.H. Fractional Flow Reserve. *Circulation* **1995**, *92*, 3183–3193. [CrossRef] [PubMed]

16. Bessonov, N.; Sequeira, A.; Simakov, S.; Vassilevskii, Y.; Volpert, V. Methods of Blood Flow Modelling. *Math. Model. Nat. Phenom.* **2016**, *11*, 1–25. [CrossRef]
17. Pinho, N.; Sousa, L.C.; Castro, C.F.; António, C.C.; Carvalho, M.; Ferreira, W.; Ladeiras-Lopes, R.; Ferreira, N.D.; Braga, P.; Bettencourt, N.; et al. The Impact of the Right Coronary Artery Geometric Parameters on Hemodynamic Performance. *Cardiovasc. Eng. Technol.* **2019**, *10*, 257–270. [CrossRef] [PubMed]
18. Sandeep, S.; Shine, S.R. Effect of Stenosis and Dilatation on the Hemodynamic Parameters Associated with Left Coronary Artery. *Comput. Methods Programs Biomed.* **2021**, *204*, 106052. [CrossRef] [PubMed]
19. Chahour, K.; Aboulaich, R.; Habbal, A.; Zemzemi, N.; Abdelkhirane, C. Virtual FFR Quantified with a Generalized Flow Model Using Windkessel Boundary Conditions. *Comput. Math. Methods Med.* **2020**, *2020*, 3942152. [CrossRef]
20. Pinto, S.I.S.; Romano, E.; António, C.C.; Sousa, L.C.; Castro, C.F. The Impact of Non-Linear Viscoelastic Property of Blood in Right Coronary Arteries Hemodynamics—A Numerical Implementation. *Int. J. Non. Linear. Mech.* **2020**, *123*, 103477. [CrossRef]
21. Campo-Deaño, L.; Dullens, R.P.A.; Aarts, D.G.A.L.; Pinho, F.T.; Oliveira, M.S.N. Viscoelasticity of Blood and Viscoelastic Blood Analogues for Use in Polydymethylsiloxane in Vitro Models of the Circulatory System. *Biomicrofluidics* **2013**, *7*, 4804649. [CrossRef]
22. Bodnár, T.; Sequeira, A.; Prosi, M. On the Shear-Thinning and Viscoelastic Effects of Blood Flow under Various Flow Rates. *Appl. Math. Comput.* **2011**, *217*, 5055–5067. [CrossRef]
23. Good, B.C.; Deutsch, S.; Manning, K.B. Hemodynamics in a Pediatric Ascending Aorta Using a Viscoelastic Pediatric Blood Model. *Ann. Biomed. Eng.* **2016**, *44*, 1019–1035. [CrossRef] [PubMed]
24. Romano, E.; Sousa, L.C.; António, C.C.; Castro, C.F.; Pinto, S.I.S. Non-Linear or Quasi-Linear Viscoelastic Property of Blood for Hemodynamic Simulations. *Adv. Struct. Mater.* **2020**, *132*, 127–139. [CrossRef]
25. Romano, E.; Sousa, L.C.; António, C.C.; Castro, C.F.; Pinto, S.I.S. WSS Descriptors in a Patient RCA Taking into Account the Non-Linear Viscoelasticity of Blood. *Adv. Struct. Mater.* **2020**, *132*, 141–152. [CrossRef]
26. Wilson, R.F.; Wyche, K.; Christensen, B.V.; Zimmer, S.; Laxson, D.D. Effects of Adenosine on Human Coronary Arterial Circulation. *Circulation* **1990**, *82*, 1595–1606. [CrossRef] [PubMed]
27. Sharma, P.; Itu, L.; Zheng, X.; Kamen, A.; Bernhardt, D.; Suciu, C.; Comaniciu, D. A Framework for Personalization of Coronary Flow Computations during Rest and Hyperemia. In Proceedings of the 2012 Annual International Conference of the IEEE Engineering in Medicine and Biology Society, San Diego, CA, USA, 28 August–1 September 2012; pp. 6665–6668. [CrossRef]
28. Miranda, E.; Sousa, L.C.; Castro, C.F.; António, C.C.; Pinto, S.I.S. On the Impact of Using the Non-Linear Viscoelastic Property of Blood and FSI Simultaneously for Arterial Hemodynamic Simulations. In Proceedings of the Proceedings IRF2020: 7th International Conference Integrity-Reliability-Failure, Funchal, Portugal, 6–10 September 2020; pp. 1017–1022.
29. Pijls, N.H.J.; de Bruyne, B.; Peels, K.; van der Voort, P.H.; Bonnier, H.J.R.M.; Bartunek, J.; Koolen, J.J. Measurement of Fractional Flow Reserve to Assess the Functional Severity of Coronary-Artery Stenoses. *N. Engl. J. Med.* **1996**, *334*, 1703–1708. [CrossRef] [PubMed]
30. Dong, J.; Sun, Z.; Inthavong, K.; Tu, J. Fluid–Structure Interaction Analysis of the Left Coronary Artery with Variable Angulation. *Comput. Methods Biomech. Biomed. Engin.* **2015**, *18*, 1500–1508. [CrossRef]
31. Chaichana, T.; Sun, Z.; Jewkes, J. Computation of Hemodynamics in the Left Coronary Artery with Variable Angulations. *J. Biomech.* **2011**, *44*, 1869–1878. [CrossRef]
32. Chaichana, T.; Sun, Z.; Jewkes, J. Computational Fluid Dynamics Analysis of the Effect of Plaques in the Left Coronary Artery. *Comput. Math. Methods Med.* **2012**, *2012*, 504367. [CrossRef]
33. Pinho, N.; Castro, C.F.; António, C.C.; Bettencourt, N.; Sousa, L.C.; Pinto, S.I.S. Correlation between Geometric Parameters of the Left Coronary Artery and Hemodynamic Descriptors of Atherosclerosis: FSI and Statistical Study. *Med. Biol. Eng. Comput.* **2019**, *57*, 715–729. [CrossRef]
34. Sousa, L.C.; Castro, C.F.; António, C.C.; Santos, A.M.F.; dos Santos, R.M.; Castro, P.M.A.C.; Azevedo, E.; Tavares, J.M.R.S. Toward Hemodynamic Diagnosis of Carotid Artery Stenosis Based on Ultrasound Image Data and Computational Modeling. *Med. Biol. Eng. Comput.* **2014**, *52*, 971–983. [CrossRef]
35. Womersley, J.R. Method for the Calculation of Velocity, Rate of Flow and Viscous Drag in Arteries When the Pressure Gradient Is Known. *J. Physiol.* **1955**, *127*, 553–563. [CrossRef] [PubMed]
36. Boileau, E.; Pant, S.; Roobottom, C.; Sazonov, I.; Deng, J.; Xie, X.; Nithiarasu, P. Estimating the Accuracy of a Reduced-order Model for the Calculation of Fractional Flow Reserve (FFR). *Int. J. Numer. Method. Biomed. Eng.* **2018**, *34*, 2908. [CrossRef] [PubMed]
37. Dadgar, S.K.; Tyagi, S.P. Importance of Heart Weight, Weights of Cardiac Ventricles and Left Ventricle Plus Septum/Right Ventricle Ratio in Assessing Cardiac Hypertrophy. *Jpn. Heart J.* **1979**, *20*, 63–73. [CrossRef] [PubMed]
38. ANSYS® Tutorial Guide. Temporal Discretization. Available online: https://www.afs.enea.it/project/neptunius/docs/fluent/html/th/node367.htm (accessed on 4 April 2021).
39. Kohnk, P. Ansys Theory Reference for the Mechanical APDL and Mechanical Applications. *Ansys* **2009**, *3304*, 724–746.
40. Xue, X.; Liu, X.; Gao, Z.; Wang, R.; Xu, L.; Ghista, D.; Zhang, H. Personalized Coronary Blood Flow Model Based on CT Perfusion to Non-Invasively Calculate Fractional Flow Reserve. *Comput. Methods Appl. Mech. Eng.* **2023**, *404*, 115789. [CrossRef]

41. Gao, Z.; Wang, X.; Sun, S.; Wu, D.; Bai, J.; Yin, Y.; Liu, X.; Zhang, H.; de Albuquerque, V.H.C. Learning Physical Properties in Complex Visual Scenes: An Intelligent Machine for Perceiving Blood Flow Dynamics from Static CT Angiography Imaging. *Neural Netw.* **2020**, *123*, 82–93. [CrossRef]
42. Amabili, M.; Balasubramanian, P.; Bozzo, I.; Breslavsky, I.D.; Ferrari, G.; Franchini, G.; Giovanniello, F.; Pogue, C. Nonlinear Dynamics of Human Aortas for Material Characterization. *Phys. Rev. X* **2020**, *10*, 011015. [CrossRef]

mathematics

Article

Calculation of Stationary Magnetic Fields Based on the Improved Quadrature Formulas for a Simple Layer Potential

Igor Reznichenko [1], Primož Podržaj [1,*] and Aljoša Peperko [1,2]

[1] Faculty of Mechanical Engineering, University of Ljubljana, 1000 Ljubljana, Slovenia; ir4016@student.uni-lj.si (I.R.); aljosa.peperko@fs.uni-lj.si (A.P.)
[2] Institute of Mathematics, Physics and Mechanics, 1000 Ljubljana, Slovenia
* Correspondence: primoz.podrzaj@fs.uni-lj.si

Abstract: This research deals with precision calculations of stationary magnetic fields of volumetric bodies. The electrostatics analogy allows for the use of a scalar magnetic potential, which reformulates the original task as a boundary value problem for the Laplace equation. We approach this with the boundary element method, specifically in distance ranges close to the magnetized surface, where existing standard numerical methods are known to struggle. This work presents an approach based on the improved quadrature formulas for the simple layer potential and its normal derivative. Numerical tests confirm significant improvements in calculating the field at any distance from the surface of the magnet.

Keywords: boundary element method; magnetic fields; numerical integration; Laplace equation; Fredholm integral equation

MSC: 35J05; 35J25; 35Q60; 45E05; 65D30; 65D32; 65M38

Citation: Reznichenko, I.; Podržaj, P.; Peperko, A. Calculation of Stationary Magnetic Fields Based on the Improved Quadrature Formulas for a Simple Layer Potential. *Mathematics* **2024**, *12*, 21. https://doi.org/10.3390/math12010021

Academic Editors: Zhuojia Fu, Yiqian He and Hui Zheng

Received: 9 November 2023
Revised: 12 December 2023
Accepted: 19 December 2023
Published: 21 December 2023

1. Introduction

In order to accurately simulate and control a magnetic system, one needs a reliable way of obtaining the values of the fields involved. This research deals with calculations of stationary magnetic fields at close proximity to a magnetized object. Standard numerical methods in the 3D case are known to struggle when the point of interest shifts towards the surface of the object. In order to achieve an adequate representation of the field under such conditions, one may need to heavily reduce the size of mesh elements, which greatly increases computational costs. The boundary element method approach is a valid choice, since it is known to yield a significant benefit because of the unit reduction in the dimensions of the original system of equations. Here, we aim to develop a calculation approach that provides uniform convergence and uniform approximation of stationary magnetic fields, that is, at any distance from the surface.

Magnetic fields are used in various physical applications [1]. Coil design is crucial in magnetic resonance imaging [2]. In transcranial magnetic stimulation, coils are used for individualized field targeting. A magnetically induced electric field is adopted to modulate brain tissue activity as a means of non-invasive scanning technology. Computational optimization of coil placement improves the performance of such medical imaging systems [3]. Linearized models are widely used to determine controller parameters of magnetic systems. However, the settings of a model usually fluctuate in relation to the operating point. A robust closed-loop control strategy for systems with active magnetic bearings requires calculations of the mentioned parameters over the entirety of the operating range [4]. Precision calculations of magnetic fields are required to successfully implement complicated magnetic phenomena, like magnetic levitation [5,6]. A more detailed expression of the magnetic force is an important optimization approach to controlling open-loop unstable magnetic systems [5]. Overall, magnets are parts of various mechanical systems and are still studied with new methods [7,8].

All these devices go through a design stage where it is in the best interest of the developer to find out more about the future performance of magnetic components. This is the reason why various calculation techniques are used in magnetism, like the finite element method, variational computing, the boundary element method and so on. For simple surfaces and volumetric bodies, quite often, there exist explicit expressions for the magnetic fields of such objects. A symmetry axis, for example, reduces the dimensions of the problem and thus makes it much easier to acquire an exact formula. An infinite dimension of a body like the infinitely long cylinder often used in theoretical endeavors allows for a limit passage. Real magnetic objects, on the other hand, often possess complicated geometries. For this reason, numerical methods are the only means of calculation in such situations. But even in numerical calculations, one can see that standard quadrature formulas have their limitations and may diverge under certain conditions [9]. Therefore, the development of numerical methods that provide uniform approximation is important.

The Boundary Element Method

When modeling a physical process, the main efforts are usually aimed at solving differential equations that characterize a physical system in a specific area, whose boundaries may have a complex shape. The presence of complex boundaries in practice does not allow for the construction of an explicit solution to the problem, so numerical methods have become the only means of obtaining sufficient results. Standard numerical methods often consider differential equations directly in the form in which they are obtained, without special mathematical transformations [10]. In the finite difference method (FDR), differential operators are approximated by simpler algebraic (difference) operators acting in a sequence of nodes located in the region of interest. The finite element method (FEM) approximates the desired solution in the area under consideration by a sum of elements that are not infinitely small. However, there is a range of tasks in which these approaches face certain difficulties. Since accuracy directly depends on the density of the grid that determines the nodal points, a need to discretize an entire region of interest may lead to a large number of finite elements [11]. The resulting systems of a high order may be too large even for modern computers. This is especially noticeable in external three-dimensional problems, for example, in acoustic wave scattering [12].

The boundary element method (BEM) is viewed by many as a bit rarer alternative to the dominating approaches, like FEM and FDR. It is a collection of numerical methods for solving various boundary value problems for differential and integral equations [13]. A layer potential transforms the original problem into a boundary integral equation, which means that we only have to discretize the boundaries of the area of interest. Since a numerical solution to a boundary integral equation is usually found as a solution to a system of algebraic equations, the dimensions of the problem are reduced by one. When using the BEM for external boundary value problems, one does not need to stretch the calculation mesh for large distances, as it satisfies the conditions at infinity by default. This decrease in many applied problems has a decisive influence on the choice of this solution method [1,14,15]. Some researchers aim to combine, where possible, the benefits of both finite and boundary element methods [16,17].

The BEM is also know as the potential or the boundary integral equation method. It uses the principle of superposition. Simple and double layer potentials are used to prove the existence of solutions to boundary value problems for the Laplace and Helmholtz equations in simply connected domains [18,19]. It is a process of transition from the original problem to the integral Fredholm equation of the second kind [20]. The numerical algorithm for solving boundary value problems with layer potentials consists of two stages. First, we need to find the values of the potential density on the surface. These values are the numerical solutions to the boundary integral equation. Next, they are substituted into a quadrature formula for the designated layer potential; thus, we find the solution to the boundary value problem at any point in space.

Standard quadrature formulas for the simple layer potential for the Laplace equation do not provide uniform approximation and convergence. When reaching the surface where the potential density is defined, the values of the simple layer potential tend to infinity, wherein the simple layer potential is a continuous function everywhere, including the surface itself. Thus, the property of boundedness and continuity of the potential on the surface [9] is not satisfied. The insufficient accuracy in calculating potentials near the surface using standard quadrature formulas is called the boundary layer effect [21]. The problem of calculating surface potentials near singularity points is widely known [22,23]. The article [24] discusses the need to move from standard numerical integration formulas to more advanced ones when calculating surface potentials near the surface on which the potential density is specified.

In [25], a quadrature formula for the simple layer potential which preserves the property of continuity was obtained. Unlike standard formulas of numerical integration, the developed method provides uniform convergence and uniform approximation when moving the point of interest through a given surface. This provides additional accuracy at close proximity without the need for mesh refinement. In [26], this approach was applied to obtain a quadrature formula for the direct value of the normal derivative of the simple layer potential. It can be applied to solving boundary integral equations that occur when dealing with various problems in mathematical physics. This research applies these results to the physical task of determining stationary magnetic fields in a three-dimensional case. We are going to see if these formulas should be used to numerically determine the magnetic potential at any point in 3D space.

2. Materials and Methods

2.1. Electrostatics Analogy: A Scalar Magnetic Potential

A permanent magnet can be viewed as a collection of the so-called imaginary magnetic charges. The idea behind it is the analogy between the electrostatic and magnetostatic fields [1]. If the area of interest does not possess conduction currents, $\sum \mathbf{j} = 0$, then $\operatorname{div} \mathbf{B} = 0$, and

$$\mathbf{B} = \mu_0(\mathbf{H} + \mathbf{M}), \tag{1}$$

where $\mathbf{B}$ is the magnetic flux density vector, μ_0 is the vacuum permeability, $\mathbf{H}$ is the magnetic field strength vector and $\mathbf{M}$ is the magnetization vector. Then, the density of imaginary magnetic charges ρ_m can be formally introduced as

$$\operatorname{div} \mathbf{B} = \mu_0(\operatorname{div} \mathbf{H} - \rho_m) = 0. \tag{2}$$

Since $\operatorname{rot} \mathbf{H} = \mathbf{j}$ and $\mathbf{j} = 0$,

$$\begin{cases} \operatorname{div} \mathbf{H} = -\operatorname{div} \mathbf{M} = \rho_m, \\ \operatorname{rot} \mathbf{H} = 0. \end{cases} \tag{3}$$

Now, let us compare (3) with the electrostatic equations

$$\begin{cases} \operatorname{div} \mathbf{E} = \dfrac{\rho}{\epsilon_0}, \\ \operatorname{rot} \mathbf{E} = 0, \end{cases} \tag{4}$$

where ρ is the density of electrical charges and ϵ_0 is the dielectric permeability of vacuum. There is an analogy between Equations (3) and (4). The original magnetostatic problem can be addressed as an equivalent problem of electrostatics. The solution to (4) with constitutions $\mathbf{E} \to \mathbf{H}$ and $\rho/\epsilon_0 \to \rho_m$ is the solution to the original problem in (3).

If magnetization vector $\mathbf{M}$ is constant, then $\rho_m = 0$. However, one also needs to consider the surface imaginary magnetic charge density (σ_m). It can be defined as

$$\sigma_m = (\mathbf{n}, \mathbf{M_2} - \mathbf{M_1}), \tag{5}$$

where $\mathbf{M_1}$ and $\mathbf{M_2}$ are the magnetization vectors of media 1 and 2, with $\mathbf{n}$ being the normal vector from the first to the second area (see Figure 1).

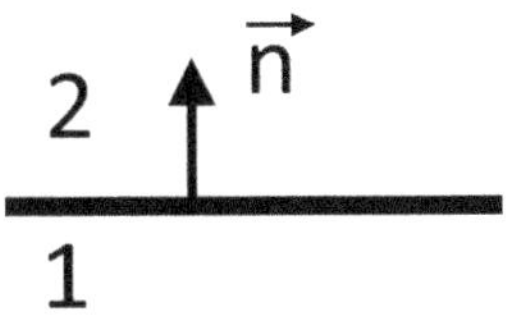

Figure 1. The normal vector ($\mathbf{n}$) between the two magnetized media ($\mathbf{M_1}$ and $\mathbf{M_2}$).

So, if surface magnetization is presented in this method, we also have to formally constitute $\sigma/\epsilon_0 \to \sigma_m$, where σ is the density of the surface electric charges. Also, if in the electrostatic solution we also estimate polarization vector $\mathbf{P}$, then $\mathbf{P}/\epsilon_0 \to \mathbf{M}$ is also required. The same formal procedure can be constructed for a magnetic field induced by stationary currents.

After solving the analogous electrostatic problem, the formal substitution is in place:

$$\begin{cases} \mathbf{E} \to \mathbf{H}, \\ \rho/\epsilon_0 \to \rho_m, \\ \sigma/\epsilon_0 \to \sigma_m, \\ \mathbf{P}/\epsilon_0 \to \mathbf{M} \end{cases} \tag{6}$$

which gives the solution to the original magnetostatic problem.

Let us assume the absence of free currents and that the electric fields ($\mathbf{E}$) (if any) present in the area of interest are constant. A scalar magnetic potential (u) is analogous to an electric potential. It is used to determine the field of a permanent magnet when its magnetization is known. Potential u uniquely provides the magnetic field at a given point in space. In a magnetic levitation train, for example, the field is determined in the vicinity of the accelerating channel [27]. A scalar magnetic potential (u) is introduced, so the magnetic field is found as

$$\mathbf{B} = -\operatorname{grad} u. \tag{7}$$

This is appropriate when the free currents and the gradient of electric field $\mathbf{E}$ are absent or can be neglected.

2.2. Exterior Neumann Boundary Value Problem for the Laplace Equation in a Three-Dimensional Domain

Let us introduce in space the Cartesian coordinate system $x = (x_1, x_2, x_3) \in \mathbb{R}^3$. We consider a simple, smooth, closed surface Γ of class C^2 enclosing a simply connected inner region D. Let the electric fields (if any) in region D be constant. The normal component of the magnetic flux vector ($\mathbf{B}_n$) is set as a boundary condition and is assumed to be a continuous function on Γ. Let us study an exterior Neumann boundary value problem for the Laplace equation.

$$\begin{cases} \Delta u = 0, & u \in C^1(\overline{\mathbb{R}^3 \setminus D}) \cap C^2(\mathbb{R}^3 \setminus \overline{D}), \\ \left.\dfrac{\partial u(x)}{\partial \mathbf{n}}\right|_{\Gamma} = f(x), & x \in \Gamma,\ f(x) \in C^1(\Gamma), \\ u = O\left(\dfrac{1}{|x|}\right), & |x| \to +\infty, \end{cases} \tag{8}$$

where $\partial/\partial\mathbf{n}$ is the normal derivative [20] on surface Γ from the outside at a point x. We assume that $u(x)$ has a normal derivative on Γ. The solution is found in the form of a simple layer potential $\mathcal{V}_0[\mu](x)$.

$$\mathcal{V}_0[\mu](x) = \frac{1}{4\pi} \int_{y \in \Gamma} \mu(y) \frac{1}{|x-y|} dS_y, \tag{9}$$

where $\mu = \mu(y) \in C^0(\Gamma)$ is the potential density. The simple layer potential $\mathcal{V}_0[\mu](x)$ is a harmonic function in the region $\mathbb{R}^3 \setminus \overline{D}$.

The normal derivative from the outside of surface Γ is given by the expression [20,26]

$$\frac{1}{2}\mu(x) + \left.\frac{\partial \mathcal{V}_0[\mu](x)}{\partial \mathbf{n}_x}\right|_\Gamma, \; x \in \Gamma, \tag{10}$$

where

$$\frac{\partial \mathcal{V}_0[\mu](x)}{\partial \mathbf{n}_x} = \frac{1}{4\pi}\int_\Gamma \mu(y)\frac{\partial}{\partial \mathbf{n}_x}\frac{1}{|x-y|}dS_y \tag{11}$$

is the direct value of the normal derivative of the simple layer potential for the Laplace equation at a point $x \in \Gamma$, while $\mathbf{n}_x$ is a unit normal directed inwardly. By equating this expression to the function defined on Γ, we obtain the following equation for the values of the potential density ($\mu(x)$):

$$\frac{1}{2}\mu(x) + \left.\frac{\partial \mathcal{V}_0[\mu](x)}{\partial \mathbf{n}_x}\right|_\Gamma = f(x), \; x \in \Gamma. \tag{12}$$

Equation (12) is a linear Fredholm integral equation of the second kind, which, under given assumptions, is known to be uniquely solvable [20,28].

2.3. Surface Parametrization

Consider the following parametrization of surface Γ:

$$\begin{gathered} y = (y_1, y_2, y_3) \in \Gamma, \quad y_1 = y_1(u,v), \; y_2 = y_2(u,v), \; y_3 = y_3(u,v); \\ u \in [0,A], \quad v \in [0,B]; \\ y_j(u,v) \in C^2([0,A] \times [0,B]), \quad j = 1,2,3. \end{gathered} \tag{13}$$

Let us introduce N points u_n with step h on the segment $[0,A]$ and M points v_m with step H on the segment $[0,B]$ and consider a partition of the rectangle $[0,A] \times [0,B]$ (see Figure 2):

$$\begin{gathered} A = Nh, \quad B = MH, \quad u_n = (n+1/2)h, \quad n = 0,...,N-1; \\ v_m = (m+1/2)H, \quad m = 0,...,M-1. \end{gathered} \tag{14}$$

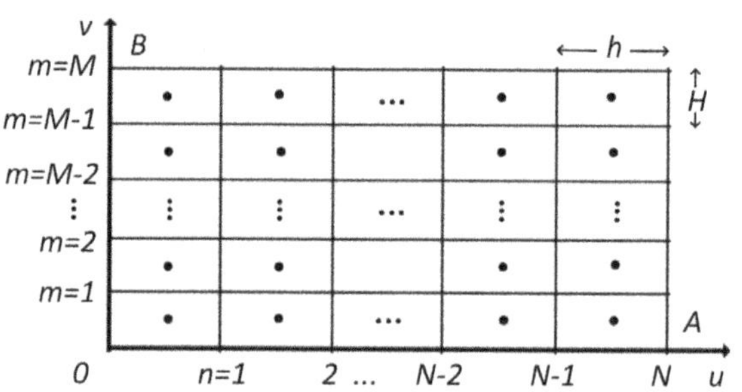

Figure 2. The rectangle $[0,A] \times [0,B]$ is divided into $N \times M$ small rectangles, whose centers are denoted as (u_n, v_m) and are used as reference points in Equation (12).

Let us introduce the continuous numbering of all of the small rectangles sized $h \times H$:

$$p = mN + n, \tag{15}$$

then, $0 \le p \le NM - 1$. If the number p is defined, then n, m are uniquely found as follows:

$$m = [p/N], \quad n = p - [p/N]N, \tag{16}$$

where $[\cdot]$ denotes the integer part of a non-negative real number. Under $y^p = y(u_n, v_m)$, $p = 0, 1, ...NM-1$, we shall consider a central point of a small rectangle (u_n, v_m), where n and m are determined by (16).

It is known that at a point $y = (y_1, y_2, y_3) \in \Gamma$, the components of a non-unit normal vector $\eta(y) = (\eta_1(y), \eta_2(y), \eta_3(y))$ can be expressed as matrix determinants by the expressions

$$\eta_1 = \begin{vmatrix} (y_2)_u & (y_3)_u \\ (y_2)_v & (y_3)_v \end{vmatrix}, \quad \eta_2 = \begin{vmatrix} (y_3)_u & (y_1)_u \\ (y_3)_v & (y_1)_v \end{vmatrix}, \quad \eta_3 = \begin{vmatrix} (y_1)_u & (y_2)_u \\ (y_1)_v & (y_2)_v \end{vmatrix}. \tag{17}$$

Let $|\eta(y)| = \sqrt{(\eta_1(y))^2 + (\eta_2(y))^2 + (\eta_3(y))^2}$. For a surface integral of the first kind, it is known that

$$\int_\Gamma F(y) ds_y = \int_0^A du \int_0^B F(y(u,v)) |\eta(y(u,v))| dv. \tag{18}$$

Note that if $|\eta(y(u,v))| = 0$ at some point, then the function $|\eta(y(u,v))|$ may be non-differentiable at this point. Therefore, we additionally require that

$$|\eta(y(u,v))| \in C^2([0,A] \times [0,B]). \tag{19}$$

In addition, we require that

$$|\eta(y(u,v))| > 0, \quad \forall\, (u,v) \in ((0,A) \times (0,B)). \tag{20}$$

With such parametrization of surface Γ, the simple layer potential with density $\mu(y) \in C^0(\Gamma)$ is expressed as

$$\mathcal{V}_0[\mu](x) = \frac{1}{4\pi} \int_\Gamma \frac{\mu(y)}{|x-y|} dS_y = \frac{1}{4\pi} \int_0^A du \int_0^B \frac{\mu(y(u,v))}{|x - y(u,v)|} |\eta(y(u,v))| dv =$$

$$= \frac{1}{4\pi} \sum_{n=0}^{N-1} \sum_{m=0}^{M-1} \int_{u_n - h/2}^{u_n + h/2} \int_{v_m - H/2}^{v_m + H/2} \frac{\mu(y(u,v))}{|x - y(u,v)|} |\eta(y(u,v))| du dv, \tag{21}$$

where

$$|x - y(u,v)| = \sqrt{(x_1 - y_1(u,v))^2 + (x_2 - y_2(u,v))^2 + (x_3 - y_3(u,v))^2}.$$

On the other hand, the direct value of the normal derivative of the simple layer potential is expressed as

$$\frac{\partial \mathcal{V}_0[\mu](x)}{\partial \mathbf{n}_x} = \frac{1}{4\pi} \int_\Gamma \mu(y) \frac{\partial}{\partial \mathbf{n}_x} \frac{1}{|x-y|} ds_y = -\frac{1}{4\pi |\eta(x)|} \times$$

$$\times \int_0^A du \int_0^B \mu(y(u,v)) |\eta(y(u,v))| \sum_{j=1}^{3} \frac{\eta_j(x)(x_j - y_j(u,v))}{|x - y(u,v)|^3} dv =$$

$$= -\frac{1}{4\pi |\eta(x)|} \sum_{n=0}^{N-1} \sum_{m=0}^{M-1} \int_{u_n - h/2}^{u_n + h/2} du \int_{v_m - H/2}^{v_m + H/2} \mu(y(u,v)) |\eta(y(u,v))| \times$$

$$\times \sum_{j=1}^{3} \frac{\eta_j(x)(x_j - y_j(u,v))}{|x - y(u,v)|^3} dv. \tag{22}$$

The double integrals in (21) and (22) are referred to as the canonical integrals. The numerical calculation of these expressions is the subject of rigorous research. In most applications, standard quadrature formulas of numerical integration are used for this task. But, as stated above, this approach struggles in ranges close to surface Γ. In this work, we are going to apply certain results in numerical methods [25,26] to the solution to the boundary value problem for the Laplace equation, which originates from the problem of finding the scalar magnetic potential. However, we shall use the standard formulas of numerical integration as a means of comparison.

2.4. Application of the Standard Quadrature Formulas for the Simple Layer Potential and Its Normal Derivative

The standard quadrature formula for the direct value of the simple layer potential on surface Γ is often used in applied calculations (Chapter 2, [9]) It is obtained by replacing the canonical integrals at points $x \neq y(u_{\hat{n}}, v_{\hat{m}})$ with their approximate values at the centers of the corresponding rectangles while zeroing the canonical integral over a piece of surface Γ centered at the point $x = y(u_{\hat{n}}, v_{\hat{m}})$

$$\left.\frac{\partial \mathcal{V}_0[\mu](x)}{\partial \mathbf{n}_x}\right|_{x=y(u_{\hat{n}},v_{\hat{m}})\in\Gamma} \approx \frac{1}{4\pi|\eta_{\hat{n}\hat{m}}|} \sum_{\substack{n=0,\, m=0 \\ (n,m)\neq(\hat{n},\hat{m})}}^{n=N-1,\, m=M-1} \mu_{nm}|\eta_{nm}|\mathcal{B}_{nm}(x), \tag{23}$$

where

$$\mathcal{B}_{nm}(x) = hH\sum_{j=1}^{3} \frac{\eta_j(x)(y_j(u_n, v_m) - x_j)}{|x - y(u_n, v_m)|^3}. \tag{24}$$

Using continuous numbering (15), Formula (23) takes the form

$$\left.\frac{\partial \mathcal{V}_0[\mu](x)}{\partial \mathbf{n}_x}\right|_{x=y(u_{\hat{n}},v_{\hat{m}})\in\Gamma} \approx \frac{1}{4\pi|\eta_{\hat{p}}|} \sum_{\substack{p=0 \\ p\neq\hat{p}}}^{NM-1} \mu_p|\eta_p|\mathcal{B}_p(x), \tag{25}$$

where $\mu_p = \mu(y^p) = \mu_{nm}$ are the potential density values at the centers of small rectangles y^p and $\mathcal{B}_p(x) = \mathcal{B}_{nm}(x)$.

Thus, for a given parametrization of surface Γ, integral Equation (12) is reduced to a system of linear algebraic equations with respect to $N \cdot M$ values of the unknown potential density function $\mu(y^p) = \mu_p$ at points $y^p = y(u_n, v_m)$.

$$\frac{1}{2}\mu_{\hat{p}} + \frac{1}{4\pi|\eta_{\hat{p}}|} \sum_{\substack{p=0 \\ p\neq\hat{p}}}^{NM-1} \mu_p|\eta_p|\mathcal{B}_p^{\hat{p}} = f_{\hat{p}}, \quad \hat{p} = 0, 1, 2, \ldots, NM-1, \tag{26}$$

where $f_{\hat{p}} = f(y^{\hat{p}})$ are the values of the boundary condition function on surface Γ and $\mathcal{B}_p(x) = \mathcal{B}_p(y(u_{\hat{n}}, v_{\hat{m}})) = \mathcal{B}_p(y^{\hat{p}}) = \mathcal{B}_p^{\hat{p}}$. Let us multiply system (26) by 4π and write it in the general form

$$\sum_{p=0}^{NM-1} \left(2\pi\Delta_p^{\hat{p}} + \frac{|\eta_p|}{|\eta_{\hat{p}}|}\mathcal{B}_p^{\hat{p}}\left(1 - \Delta_p^{\hat{p}}\right)\right)\mu_p = 4\pi f_{\hat{p}}, \tag{27}$$

where $\hat{p} = 0, 1, 2, \ldots, NM-1$ and

$$\Delta_p^{\hat{p}} = \begin{cases} 1, & \text{if } p = \hat{p}, \\ 0, & \text{if } p \neq \hat{p}. \end{cases}$$

We multiply each $\hat{p}$-th equation of the system by $|\eta_{\hat{p}}|$

$$\sum_{p=0}^{NM-1} \left(2\pi|\eta_{\hat{p}}|\Delta_p^{\hat{p}} + |\eta_p|\mathcal{B}_p^{\hat{p}}\left(1 - \Delta_p^{\hat{p}}\right)\right)\mu_p = 4\pi|\eta_{\hat{p}}|f_{\hat{p}}, \tag{28}$$

where $\hat{p} = 0, 1, 2, \ldots, NM-1$. Equation (28) can be written in matrix form as seen in (A1) in Appendix A. From this system of equations, we obtain the values of the potential density $\mu_{\hat{p}} = \mu(y^{\hat{p}})$ at the centers of small rectangles $y^{\hat{p}}$, which will then be used to calculate the simple layer potential everywhere outside Γ, thus solving the original boundary value problem.

To calculate the potential itself, as a means of comparison, we are going use the standard quadrature formula:

$$\mathcal{V}_0[\mu](x) \approx \frac{1}{4\pi} \sum_{n=0,\, m=0}^{n=N-1,\, m=M-1} \mu_{nm}\mathcal{D}_{nm}(x) = \frac{1}{4\pi} \sum_{p=0}^{NM-1} \mu_p \mathcal{D}_p(x), \tag{29}$$

where

$$\mathcal{D}_{nm} = \frac{hH|\eta(y(u_n, v_m))|}{|x - y(u_n, v_m)|}$$

and $\mathcal{D}_p(x) = \mathcal{D}_{nm}(x)$. It is obtained by replacing the canonical integrals at points $y(u_n, v_m) \in \Gamma$ to its approximate values at the centers of the corresponding rectangles. This formula, as we are going to see in the Results and Discussion section, tends to infinity when point x tends to the surface. In this case, the same is often true about more complex numerical integration formulas [9,24]. Thus, one of the ways to reduce the calculation error is the reduction in steps h, H which leads to a large number of boundary elements. This eliminates the main benefit of the boundary element method in close proximity to a surface [9].

2.5. Application of the Improved Quadrature Formulas for the Simple Layer Potential and Its Normal Derivative

In [26], a quadrature formula for the direct value of the normal derivative of the simple layer potential on surface Γ was explicitly obtained.

$$\left.\frac{\partial \mathcal{V}_k[\mu](x)}{\partial \mathbf{n}_x}\right|_{x=y(u_{\hat{n}}, v_{\hat{m}})\in\Gamma} \approx \frac{1}{4\pi}\mu_{\hat{n}\hat{m}}\mathcal{J}_{\hat{n}\hat{m}} + \frac{1}{4\pi|\eta(x)|} \times \tag{30}$$

$$\times \sum_{\substack{n=0,\, m=0 \\ (n,m)\neq(\hat{n},\hat{m})}}^{n=N-1,\, m=M-1} \mu_{nm}|\eta(y(u_n, v_m))|T_{nm}(x),$$

where the integrals $\mathcal{J}_{\hat{n}\hat{m}}$ and $T_{nm}(x)$ are calculated explicitly in [26]. Using continuous numbering (15), Formula (30) becomes

$$\left.\frac{\partial \mathcal{V}_0[\mu](x)}{\partial \mathbf{n}_x}\right|_{x=y(u_{\hat{n}}, v_{\hat{m}})\in\Gamma} \approx \frac{1}{4\pi}\mu_{\hat{n}\hat{m}}\mathcal{J}_{\hat{n}\hat{m}} + \frac{1}{4\pi|\eta_{\hat{n}\hat{m}}|} \sum_{\substack{n=0,\, m=0 \\ (n,m)\neq(\hat{n},\hat{m})}}^{n=N-1,\, m=M-1} \mu_{nm}|\eta_{nm}|T_{nm}(x) =$$

$$= \frac{1}{4\pi}\mu_{\hat{p}}\mathcal{J}^{\hat{p}} + \frac{1}{4\pi|\eta_{\hat{p}}|} \sum_{\substack{p=0 \\ p\neq\hat{p}}}^{NM-1} \mu_p|\eta_p|T_p(x), \tag{31}$$

where $\mu_p = \mu(y^p) = \mu_{nm}$ are the values of the potential density at the centers of small rectangles y^p, $T_p(x) = T_{nm}(x)$ and $|\eta_p| = |\eta(y^p)| = |\eta_{nm}|$ are the absolute values of the normal vector at y^p. The integral $\mathcal{J}^{\hat{p}} = \mathcal{J}_{\hat{n}\hat{m}}$, the density value $\mu_{\hat{p}} = \mu(y^{\hat{p}}) = \mu_{\hat{n}\hat{m}}$ and the absolute value of the normal vector $|\eta_{\hat{p}}| = |\eta(y^{\hat{p}})| = \eta_{\hat{n}\hat{m}}$ correspond to the case when point x lies in the region of integration. In this case, the integration is carried out over a small rectangle centered at the point $(u_{\hat{n}}, v_{\hat{m}})$, to which the dot $y^{\hat{p}} = y(u_{\hat{n}}, v_{\hat{m}}) = x$ on surface Γ corresponds.

Therefore, with the given parametrization of surface Γ, integral Equation (12) is reduced to the system of linear algebraic equations for $N \cdot M$ values of the unknown potential density function $\mu(y^p) = \mu_p$ at the points $y^p = y(u_n, v_m)$.

$$\frac{1}{2}\mu_{\hat{p}} + \frac{1}{4\pi}\mu_{\hat{p}}\mathcal{J}^{\hat{p}} + \frac{1}{4\pi|\eta_{\hat{p}}|} \sum_{\substack{p=0 \\ p\neq\hat{p}}}^{NM-1} \mu_p|\eta_p|T_p^{\hat{p}} = f_{\hat{p}}, \quad \hat{p} = 0, 1, 2, \ldots, NM-1, \tag{32}$$

where $f_{\hat{p}} = f(y^{\hat{p}})$ are the values of the boundary condition function given on surface Γ, while $T_p(x) = T_p(y(u_{\hat{n}}, v_{\hat{m}})) = T_p(y^{\hat{p}}) = T_p^{\hat{p}}$. Here, we multiply system (32) by 4π and write it in a general form:

$$\sum_{p=0}^{NM-1}\left(\left(\mathcal{J}^{\hat{p}}+2\pi\right)\Delta_p^{\hat{p}}+\frac{|\eta_p|}{|\eta_{\hat{p}}|}T_p^{\hat{p}}\left(1-\Delta_p^{\hat{p}}\right)\right)\mu_p=4\pi f_{\hat{p}}, \tag{33}$$

where $\hat{p}=0,1,2,...,NM-1$ and

$$\Delta_p^{\hat{p}}=\begin{cases}1, & \text{if } p=\hat{p},\\ 0, & \text{if } p\neq\hat{p}.\end{cases}$$

Next, each $\hat{p}$-th equation of system (33) is multiplied by $|\eta_{\hat{p}}|$.

$$\sum_{p=0}^{NM-1}\left(|\eta_{\hat{p}}|\left(\mathcal{J}^{\hat{p}}+2\pi\right)\Delta_p^{\hat{p}}+|\eta_p|T_p^{\hat{p}}\left(1-\Delta_p^{\hat{p}}\right)\right)\mu_p=4\pi|\eta_{\hat{p}}|f_{\hat{p}}, \tag{34}$$

where $\hat{p}=0,1,2,...,NM-1$. Equation (34) can be written in matrix form as seen in (A2) in Appendix A. By reversing the matrix on the left side of the equality in (A2) and multiplying the inverse matrix on the left by the column with the values of the boundary condition function, we obtain the density value capacity $\mu_{\hat{p}}=\mu(y^{\hat{p}})$ at the centers of small rectangles $y^{\hat{p}}$, which will then be used to calculate the simple layer potential everywhere outside Γ, thereby solving the original boundary value problem.

To calculate the simple layer potential, we use the quadrature formula obtained in [25]

$$\mathcal{V}_0[\mu](x)\approx\frac{1}{4\pi}\sum_{n=0}^{N-1}\sum_{m=0}^{M-1}\mu_{nm}\theta_{nm}(x), \tag{35}$$

where the integral $\theta_{nm}(x)$ is explicitly derived in [25]. This formula preserves the property of continuity of the simple layer potential and approximates this function uniformly.

3. Results and Discussion

In [25], a quadrature formula for the simple layer potential which provides uniform approximation was obtained. A quadrature formula for the normal derivative of the simple layer potential with improved accuracy over standard numerical integration was suggested in [26]. We adopt these results to solve a particular magnetostatics problem, which is an external Neumann boundary value problem for the values of a scalar magnetic potential.

3.1. Numerical Tests

Testing was carried out for the case where surface Γ is a sphere of unit radius which is given parametrically by

$$y_1(u,v)=\cos u\sin v,\quad y_2(u,v)=\sin u\sin v,\quad y_3(u,v)=\cos v, \tag{36}$$

where $(u,v)\in[0,2\pi]\times[0,\pi]$.

Test 1. Under a boundary condition of the form $f(x)=3/5\cdot P_2(\cos\vartheta),\ x\in\Gamma$, the solution to the external Neumann boundary value problem for the Laplace equation is known and is given by the expression

$$u(x)=\frac{P_2(\cos\vartheta)}{5|x|^2}\ \text{when}\ |x|>1. \tag{37}$$

In this case, the density of the simple layer potential is equal to

$$\mu(x)=P_2(\cos\vartheta),\ x\in\Gamma, \tag{38}$$

where ϑ is the zenith angle in spherical coordinates centered at the origin and

$$P_2(\cos\vartheta)=\frac{3\cos^2\vartheta-1}{2}$$

is a Legendre polynomial.

Test 2. Under a boundary condition of the form $f(x) = 4/7 \cdot P_3(\cos\vartheta),\ x \in \Gamma$, the solution to the external Neumann boundary value problem for the Laplace equation is known and is given by the expression

$$u(x) = \frac{P_3(\cos\vartheta)}{7|x|^3} \text{ when } |x| > 1. \tag{39}$$

In this case, the density of the simple layer potential is equal to

$$\mu(x) = P_3(\cos\vartheta),\ x \in \Gamma, \tag{40}$$

where ϑ is the zenith angle in spherical coordinates centered at the origin and

$$P_3(\cos\vartheta) = \frac{5\cos^3\vartheta - 3\cos\vartheta}{2}$$

is a Legendre polynomial.

Test 3. Under a boundary condition of the form $f(x) = 5/9 \cdot P_4(\cos\vartheta),\ x \in \Gamma$, the solution to the external Neumann boundary value problem for the Laplace equation is known and is given by the expression

$$u(x) = \frac{P_4(\cos\vartheta)}{9|x|^4} \text{ when } |x| > 1. \tag{41}$$

In this case, the density of the simple layer potential is equal to

$$\mu(x) = P_4(\cos\vartheta),\ x \in \Gamma, \tag{42}$$

where ϑ is the zenith angle in spherical coordinates centered at the origin and

$$P_4(\cos\vartheta) = \frac{35\cos^4\vartheta - 30\cos^2\vartheta + 3}{8}$$

is a Legendre polynomial.

Test 4. Under a boundary condition of the form $f(x) = 3/5 \cdot \cos 2\varphi \sin^2\vartheta,\ x \in \Gamma$, the solution to the external Neumann boundary value problem for the Laplace equation is known and is given by the expression

$$u(x) = \frac{\cos 2\varphi \sin^2\vartheta}{5|x|^2} \text{ when } |x| > 1. \tag{43}$$

In this case, the density of the simple layer potential is equal to

$$\mu(x) = \cos 2\varphi \sin^2\vartheta,\ x \in \Gamma, \tag{44}$$

where ϑ and φ are the zenith and azimuth angles in spherical coordinates centered at the origin.

Test 5. Under a boundary condition of the form $f(x) = 4/7 \cdot \cos 3\varphi \sin^3\vartheta,\ x \in \Gamma$, the solution to the external Neumann boundary value problem for the Laplace equation is known and is given by the expression

$$u(x) = \frac{\cos 3\varphi \sin^3\vartheta}{7|x|^3} \text{ when } |x| > 1. \tag{45}$$

In this case, the density of the simple layer potential is equal to

$$\mu(x) = \cos 3\varphi \sin^3\vartheta,\ x \in \Gamma, \tag{46}$$

where ϑ and φ are the zenith and azimuth angles in spherical coordinates centered at the origin.

Test 6. Under a boundary condition of the form $f(x) = 5/9 \cdot \cos 4\varphi \sin^4\vartheta,\ x \in \Gamma$, the solution to the external Neumann boundary value problem for the Laplace equation is known and is given by the expression

$$u(x) = \frac{\cos 4\varphi \sin^4 \vartheta}{9|x|^4} \text{ when } |x| > 1. \tag{47}$$

In this case, the density of the simple layer potential is equal to

$$\mu(x) = \cos 4\varphi \sin^4 \vartheta,\ x \in \Gamma, \tag{48}$$

where ϑ and φ are the zenith and azimuth angles in spherical coordinates centered at the origin.

3.2. Calculations of the Potential Density

The solution to the external Neumann boundary value problem by the described method consists of two stages. In the first stage, using one of the two given quadrature formulas for the direct value of the normal derivative of the simple layer potential, we obtain the values of the potential density μ_p, $p = 0, 1, ..., NM - 1$, at the centers of small rectangles, solving the corresponding system of linear algebraic equations. This can be either quadrature Formula (31), constructed in [26], or the standard quadrature formula for the normal derivative of the simple layer potential in (25). The point coordinates that were used to estimate the maximum absolute error are (see Figure 3)

$$x_j^{ql} = y_j(u_q, v_l), \quad j = 1, 2, 3,$$

$$u_q = \frac{2\pi}{2N} q, \quad q = 0, \ldots, 2N; \quad v_l = \frac{\pi}{2M} l, \quad l = 1, \ldots, 2M - 1, \tag{49}$$

where $y_j(u, v)$ is determined by the expressions in (36). That is, these points are located on the unit sphere at the centers of the small rectangles (see Figure 2), the midpoints of the boundaries between them and the intersections of these boundaries. Note that these points are distributed over the entire unit sphere.

The calculations were carried out for various values of M and N. The step values are determined as $h = 2\pi/N$, $H = \pi/M$. If $N/2 = M = 10$, then $h = H \approx 0.31$; if $N/2 = M = 20$, then $h = H \approx 0.16$; if $N/2 = M = 40$, then $h = H \approx 0.079$.

First, let us consider the calculation error of potential density. The first number in the cells of Table 1 is the maximum absolute value of error of potential density μ_p, acquired with the standard quadrature Formula (25) for the normal derivative of the simple layer potential. The second number after the semicolon is the maximum absolute value of error of potential density μ_p, acquired with the improved quadrature Formula (31) for the normal derivative [26].

Table 1. The maximum absolute error of potential density in tests 1–3.

Test Number	$N/2 = M = 10$	$N/2 = M = 20$	$N/2 = M = 40$
Test 1	0.039; 0.015	0.021; 0.0096	0.019; 0.0057
Test 2	0.038; 0.014	0.02; 0.0091	0.018; 0.0055
Test 3	0.031; 0.014	0.019; 0.0088	0.018; 0.0054
Test 4	0.081; 0.0035	0.042; 0.0011	0.021; 0.0003
Test 5	0.087; 0.0038	0.044; 0.0014	0.022; 0.00039
Test 6	0.088; 0.0037	0.043; 0.0015	0.022; 0.00047

Let us also consider the average absolute error over all reference points (15) in Equation (12). The first number in the cells of Table 2 is the mean absolute error of potential density μ_p, acquired with the standard quadrature Formula (25). The second number (after the semicolon) is the mean absolute error of potential density μ_p, acquired with the improved quadrature Formula (31).

Table 2. The mean absolute error of potential density in tests 1–3.

Test Number	$N/2 = M = 10$	$N/2 = M = 20$	$N/2 = M = 40$
Test 1	0.023; 0.0043	0.013; 0.0014	0.0066; 0.00047
Test 2	0.02; 0.0041	0.012; 0.0013	0.0059; 0.00045
Test 3	0.018; 0.0045	0.01; 0.0014	0.0053; 0.00046
Test 4	0.024; 0.0012	0.012; 0.00035	0.0059; 9.5×10^{-5}
Test 5	0.023; 0.0011	0.011; 0.00036	0.0054; 9.9×10^{-5}
Test 6	0.021; 0.001	0.0099; 0.00036	0.0051; 0.00011

3.3. Calculations of the Potential—The Solution to the Neumann Problem

In the second stage, the obtained values of potential density μ_p are used to calculate the simple layer potential at any point in the region $\mathbb{R}^3 \setminus \overline{D}$ using one of the two formulas. It can be either (35) from [25] or the standard quadrature formula for the simple layer potential (29).

In the numerical tests, the values of potential density μ_p, obtained using the improved Formula (31), are only used in Formula (35). Similarly, the values of the potential density μ_p obtained using the standard Formula (25) we will use only in Formula (29).

The calculations of the simple layer potential solutions of the original external Neumann boundary value problem were carried out at some points on the auxiliary spheres with centers at the origin and radii $R = 1 + \Delta R$. Thus, the auxiliary spheres are outside of the sphere of unit radius, on which the boundary condition or the potential density is given, at a distance ΔR from it. Then, the values of absolute errors at these points were calculated. For each auxiliary sphere the maximum values of these errors are determined.

The point coordinates that were used to estimate the maximum absolute error are (see Figure 3)

$$x_j^{ql} = Ry_j(u_q, v_l), \quad j = 1,2,3,$$
$$u_q = \frac{2\pi}{2N}q, \quad q = 0,\ldots,2N; \quad v_l = \frac{\pi}{2M}l, \quad l = 1,\ldots,2M-1, \tag{50}$$

where $y_j(u,v)$ is determined by the expressions in (36) and R is the auxiliary sphere radius.

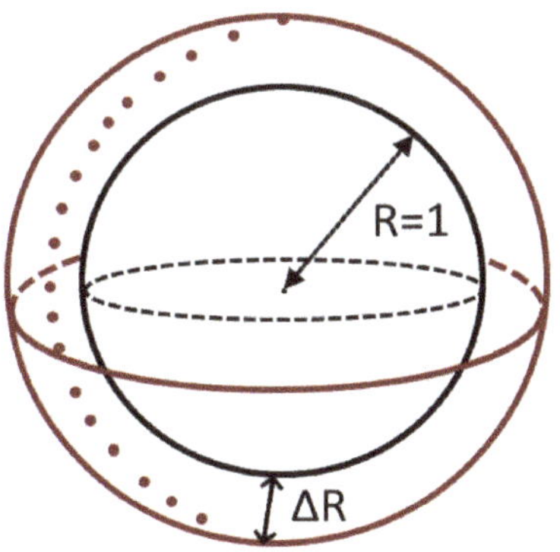

Figure 3. Points x on the test spheres of radii equal to $1 + \Delta R$ are chosen according to (50). The maximum values of absolute error of the simple layer potential among all of these points are used in Tables 3–8. If $\Delta R = 0$, then it is the first stage of the numerical solution, which is the determination of the potential density values (μ_p).

That is, these points are located at a distance ΔR outside of the unit sphere above the centers of the small rectangles (see Figure 2), the midpoints of the boundaries between them and the intersections of these boundaries. Note that these points are distributed over the entire sphere.

Table 3. Maximum absolute values of error of quadrature formulas in test 1.

ΔR	$N/2 = M = 10$	$N/2 = M = 20$	$N/2 = M = 40$
0.1	0.018; 0.013	0.0047; 0.0056	0.0021; 0.0018
0.06	0.039; 0.015	0.0077; 0.0077	0.0024; 0.0029
0.03	0.098; 0.016	0.02; 0.0094	0.004; 0.0045
0.01	0.35; 0.016	0.083; 0.01	0.017; 0.0056
0.001	3.86; 0.016	0.98; 0.01	0.24; 0.0058
0.0001	38.9; 0.016	9.97; 0.01	2.48; 0.0058

Table 4. Maximum absolute values of error of quadrature formulas in test 2.

ΔR	$N/2 = M = 10$	$N/2 = M = 20$	$N/2 = M = 40$
0.1	0.017; 0.011	0.0040; 0.0050	0.0010; 0.0016
0.06	0.030; 0.013	0.0069; 0.0070	0.0017; 0.0027
0.03	0.082; 0.014	0.015; 0.0087	0.0034; 0.0042
0.01	0.30; 0.014	0.066; 0.0094	0.013; 0.0054
0.001	3.36; 0.014	0.80; 0.0094	0.19; 0.0056
0.0001	33.9; 0.014	8.18; 0.0094	2.01; 0.0056

Table 5. Maximum absolute values of error of quadrature formulas in test 3.

ΔR	$N/2 = M = 10$	$N/2 = M = 20$	$N/2 = M = 40$
0.1	0.017; 0.011	0.0036; 0.0047	0.00076; 0.0015
0.06	0.028; 0.013	0.0065; 0.0067	0.0014; 0.0026
0.03	0.059; 0.014	0.014; 0.0083	0.0031; 0.0041
0.01	0.22; 0.014	0.058; 0.0090	0.012; 0.0053
0.001	2.4; 0.014	0.70; 0.0090	0.18; 0.0055
0.0001	24.2; 0.014	7.19; 0.0090	1.84; 0.0055

Table 6. Maximum absolute values of error of quadrature formulas in test 4.

ΔR	$N/2 = M = 10$	$N/2 = M = 20$	$N/2 = M = 40$
0.1	0.020; 0.015	0.0098; 0.015	0.012; 0.015
0.06	0.065; 0.010	0.0067; 0.010	0.0069; 0.010
0.03	0.19; 0.0068	0.033; 0.0057	0.0035; 0.0055
0.01	0.70; 0.010	0.16; 0.0026	0.032; 0.0021
0.001	7.74; 0.015	1.96; 0.0035	0.48; 0.00044
0.0001	78.2; 0.016	20; 0.0041	4.96; 0.00097

Table 7. Maximum absolute values of error of quadrature formulas in test 5.

ΔR	$N/2 = M = 10$	$N/2 = M = 20$	$N/2 = M = 40$
0.1	0.022; 0.012	0.0065; 0.01	0.0077; 0.0099
0.06	0.067; 0.0095	0.0055; 0.0073	0.0046; 0.0069
0.03	0.19; 0.0072	0.033; 0.0045	0.0028; 0.0039
0.01	0.72; 0.013	0.16; 0.0024	0.031; 0.0016
0.001	7.97; 0.018	1.98; 0.0041	0.48; 0.00049
0.0001	80.5; 0.019	20.1; 0.0047	4.97; 0.0011

Table 8. Maximum absolute values of error of quadrature formulas in test 6.

ΔR	$N/2 = M = 10$	$N/2 = M = 20$	$N/2 = M = 40$
0.1	0.020; 0.019	0.012; 0.015	0.013; 0.015
0.06	0.062; 0.016	0.010; 0.011	0.0086; 0.010
0.03	0.19; 0.013	0.028; 0.0069	0.0055; 0.0061
0.01	0.72; 0.017	0.15; 0.0034	0.030; 0.0024
0.001	7.98; 0.022	1.88; 0.0049	0.47; 0.00067
0.0001	80.6; 0.022	19.2; 0.0055	4.92; 0.0013

The calculations were carried out for various values of M and N. The step values were determined as $h = 2\pi/N$, $H = \pi/M$. If $N/2 = M = 10$, then $h = H \approx 0.31$; if $N/2 = M = 20$, then $h = H \approx 0.16$; if $N/2 = M = 40$, then $h = H \approx 0.079$.

Now, let us consider the calculation error of the solution to the external Neumann boundary problem. The first numbers in the cells of Tables 3–8 are the maximum absolute values of error of the solution, acquired with the standard quadrature formula for the simple layer potential (29). The second numbers after the semicolon are the maximum absolute values of error of the solution, acquired with the improved quadrature Formula (35) for the simple layer potential [25].

Table 1 shows that the maximum absolute values of error of potential density μ_p, acquired with the improved quadrature Formula (31) from [26], are a few times lower than those of the standard quadrature Formula (25). The same can be observed about the mean absolute values of error of potential density in Table 2, while in tests 4-6, the values acquired with the improved quadrature Formula (31) are lower by an order of magnitude. In both tables, Formula (31) shows the first order of convergence in H for tests 1-3 and the third order of convergence in H for tests 4–6.

Let us perform an estimate of the maximum absolute value of error of the numerical solution to the original problem in tests 1–6 from Tables 3–8. From them, it follows that the standard Formula (29) for the simple layer potential does not provide uniform approximation and uniform convergence of the solution in the form of the simple layer potential, since at a fixed step H, the error tends to infinity when approaching surface Γ. That is why this formula is not the priority choice for solving boundary value problems for the Laplace equation near a surface Γ.

Quadrature Formula (35) provides uniform approximation of the solution to the original problem. This remains true even for increasingly oscillating test functions, like in test 3 or 6. Therefore, Formula (35) retains the property of continuity of the simple layer potential while heading towards surface Γ. This is why both Formulas (31) and (35) should be used for numerically solving various boundary value problems for the Laplace equation, like the scalar magnetic potential.

4. Conclusions

1. In this work, a new method for determining three-dimensional stationary magnetic fields is proposed. Based on the conception of a magnetic potential, this task can be formulated as a boundary value problem for the Laplace equation with a Neumann condition on a magnetized surface. This work presents a full solution using the boundary element method (BEM). With the use of a simple layer potential, a three-dimensional magnetostatic problem is reduced to a two-dimensional boundary Fredholm integral equation that is uniquely solvable.
2. While, in an external boundary value problem, the BEM automatically satisfies the conditions at infinity, it is known to struggle in close proximity to the boundary. The non-integrable singularity is addressed by applying the improved quadrature formulas for the simple layer potential (35) and its normal derivative (31) [25,26]. For the values of the potential density, a system of linear algebraic equations was constructed, the matrix form of which can be seen in Appendix A. For the same task, standard quadrature Formulas of numerical integration were used as a reference.

3. With the mean and maximum absolute values of error of the potential density being significantly lower (up to an order of magnitude) than that, when acquired with the standard approach, Formula (31) shows improved accuracy. The improved Formula (35) for the simple layer potential provides uniform approximation of the solution, unlike the standard Formula (29), which tends to infinity. The developed approach provides improved accuracy and approximates to the solution uniformly at any distance from the surface, as was confirmed with numerical tests. This remains true even for increasingly oscillating test functions. Therefore, the developed approach can be used to solve the magnetostatic problem at any distance from a volumetric body.

Author Contributions: Conceptualization, I.R., P.P. and A.P.; methodology, I.R., P.P. and A.P.; software, I.R.; validation, I.R., P.P and A.P.; formal analysis, I.R.; investigation, I.R.; resources, I.R., P.P. and A.P.; data curation, I.R., P.P. and A.P.; writing—original draft preparation, I.R.; writing—review and editing, I.R., P.P. and A.P.; visualization, I.R., P.P. and A.P.; supervision, P.P. and A.P. All authors have read and agreed to the published version of the manuscript.

Funding: P. Podržaj was supported by Slovenian Research Agency, grant number P2-0270. A. Peperko was partially supported by ARIS-Slovenian Agency for Research and Innovation (grants P1-0222 and J2-2512).

Data Availability Statement: The data used in this research are available from the corresponding author upon reasonable request.

Conflicts of Interest: The authors declare no conflict of interest.

Appendix A

Here, we write system (28) in matrix form:

$$\begin{pmatrix} 2\pi|\eta_0| & |\eta_1|\mathcal{B}_1^0 & \cdots & |\eta_{\hat{p}-1}|\mathcal{B}_{\hat{p}-1}^0 & |\eta_{\hat{p}}|\mathcal{B}_{\hat{p}}^0 & |\eta_{\hat{p}+1}|\mathcal{B}_{\hat{p}+1}^0 & \cdots & |\eta_{NM-1}|\mathcal{B}_{NM-1}^0 \\ |\eta_0|\mathcal{B}_0^1 & 2\pi|\eta_1| & \cdots & |\eta_{\hat{p}-1}|\mathcal{B}_{\hat{p}-1}^1 & |\eta_{\hat{p}}|\mathcal{B}_{\hat{p}}^1 & |\eta_{\hat{p}+1}|\mathcal{B}_{\hat{p}+1}^1 & \cdots & |\eta_{NM-1}|\mathcal{B}_{NM-1}^1 \\ \vdots & \vdots & \ddots & \vdots & \vdots & \vdots & \vdots & \vdots \\ \vdots & \vdots & \vdots & \ddots & \vdots & \vdots & \vdots & \vdots \\ |\eta_0|\mathcal{B}_0^{\hat{p}} & |\eta_1|\mathcal{B}_1^{\hat{p}} & \cdots & |\eta_{\hat{p}-1}|\mathcal{B}_{\hat{p}-1}^{\hat{p}} & 2\pi|\eta_{\hat{p}}| & |\eta_{\hat{p}+1}|\mathcal{B}_{\hat{p}+1}^{\hat{p}} & \cdots & |\eta_{NM-1}|\mathcal{B}_{NM-1}^{\hat{p}} \\ |\eta_0|\mathcal{B}_0^{\hat{p}+1} & |\eta_1|\mathcal{B}_1^{\hat{p}+1} & \cdots & |\eta_{\hat{p}-1}|\mathcal{B}_{\hat{p}-1}^{\hat{p}+1} & |\eta_{\hat{p}}|\mathcal{B}_{\hat{p}}^{\hat{p}+1} & 2\pi|\eta_{\hat{p}+1}| & \cdots & |\eta_{NM-1}|\mathcal{B}_{NM-1}^{\hat{p}+1} \\ \vdots & \vdots & \vdots & \vdots & \vdots & \vdots & \ddots & \vdots \\ |\eta_0|\mathcal{B}_0^{NM-1} & |\eta_1|\mathcal{B}_1^{NM-1} & \cdots & |\eta_{\hat{p}-1}|\mathcal{B}_{\hat{p}-1}^{NM-1} & |\eta_{\hat{p}}|\mathcal{B}_{\hat{p}}^{NM-1} & |\eta_{\hat{p}+1}|\mathcal{B}_{\hat{p}+1}^{NM-1} & \cdots & 2\pi|\eta_{NM-1}| \end{pmatrix} \times$$

$$\times \begin{pmatrix} \mu_0 \\ \mu_1 \\ \vdots \\ \mu_{NM-1} \end{pmatrix} = 4\pi \begin{pmatrix} |\eta_0|f_0 \\ |\eta_1|f_1 \\ \vdots \\ |\eta_{NM-1}|f_{NM-1} \end{pmatrix}. \tag{A1}$$

Also, let us write system (34) in matrix form:

$$\begin{pmatrix} |\eta_0|(\mathcal{J}^0+2\pi) & |\eta_1|T_1^0 & \cdots & |\eta_{\beta-1}|T_{\beta-1}^0 & |\eta_\beta|T_\beta^0 & |\eta_{\beta+1}|T_{\beta+1}^0 & \cdots & |\eta_{NM-1}|T_{NM-1}^0 \\ |\eta_0|T_0^1 & |\eta_1|(\mathcal{J}^1+2\pi) & \cdots & |\eta_{\beta-1}|T_{\beta-1}^1 & |\eta_\beta|T_\beta^1 & |\eta_{\beta+1}|T_{\beta+1}^1 & \cdots & |\eta_{NM-1}|T_{NM-1}^1 \\ \vdots & \vdots & \ddots & \vdots & \vdots & \vdots & \vdots & \vdots \\ \vdots & \vdots & \vdots & \ddots & \vdots & \vdots & \vdots & \vdots \\ |\eta_0|T_0^\beta & |\eta_1|T_1^\beta & \cdots & |\eta_{\beta-1}|T_{\beta-1}^\beta & |\eta_\beta|(\mathcal{J}^\beta+2\pi) & |\eta_{\beta+1}|T_{\beta+1}^\beta & \cdots & |\eta_{NM-1}|T_{NM-1}^\beta \\ |\eta_0|T_0^{\beta+1} & |\eta_1|T_1^{\beta+1} & \cdots & |\eta_{\beta-1}|T_{\beta-1}^{\beta+1} & |\eta_\beta|T_\beta^{\beta+1} & |\eta_{\beta+1}|(\mathcal{J}^{\beta+1}+2\pi) & \cdots & |\eta_{NM-1}|T_{NM-1}^{\beta+1} \\ \vdots & \vdots & \vdots & \vdots & \vdots & \vdots & \ddots & \vdots \\ |\eta_0|T_0^{NM-1} & |\eta_1|T_1^{NM-1} & \cdots & |\eta_{\beta-1}|T_{\beta-1}^{NM-1} & |\eta_\beta|T_\beta^{NM-1} & |\eta_{\beta+1}|T_{\beta+1}^{NM-1} & \cdots & |\eta_{NM-1}|(\mathcal{J}^{NM-1}+2\pi) \end{pmatrix} \times$$

$$\times \begin{pmatrix} \mu_0 \\ \mu_1 \\ \vdots \\ \mu_{NM-1} \end{pmatrix} = 4\pi \begin{pmatrix} |\eta_0|f_0 \\ |\eta_1|f_1 \\ \vdots \\ |\eta_{NM-1}|f_{NM-1} \end{pmatrix}. \tag{A2}$$

References

1. Reznichenko, I.; Podržaj, P.; Peperko, A. Control theory and numerical analysis of magnetic field involving mechanical systems. In Proceedings of the 17th International Symposium on Operational Research in Slovenia, SOR'23, Slovenian Society Informatika (SSI), Section for Operational Research (SOR), Bled, Slovenia, 20–22 September 2023.
2. Cobos Sanchez, C.; Power, H.; Garcia, S.G.; Rubio Bretones, A. Quasi-static multi-domain inverse boundary element method for MRI coil design with minimum induced E-field. *Eng. Anal. Bound. Elem.* **2011**, *35*, 264–272. [CrossRef]
3. Gomez, L.J.; Dannhauer, M.; Peterchev, A.V. Fast computational optimization of TMS coil placement for individualized electric field targeting. *NeuroImage* **2021**, *228*, 117696. [CrossRef] [PubMed]
4. Polajžer, B.; Štumberger, G.; Ritonja, J.; Dolinar, D. Variations of Active Magnetic Bearings Linearized Model Parameters Analyzed by Finite Element Computation. *IEEE Trans. Magn.* **2008**, *44*, 1534–1537. [CrossRef]
5. Reznichenko, I.; Podržaj, P. Design Methodology for a Magnetic Levitation System Based on a New Multi-Objective Optimization Algorithm. *Sensors* **2023**, *23*, 979. [CrossRef] [PubMed]
6. Chen, Q.; Li, J. Field Dynamic Balancing for Magnetically Suspended Turbomolecular Pump. *Sensors* **2023**, *23*, 6168. [CrossRef] [PubMed]
7. Pashkovskiy, A.; Tkachev, A.; Bahvalov, U. New Standard Elements for Calculating Magnetic Fields of Electromechanical and Magnetic Systems with Permanent Magnets. In Proceedings of the 2018 International Conference on Industrial Engineering, Applications and Manufacturing (ICIEAM), Moscow, Russia, 15–18 May 2018; pp. 1–5. [CrossRef]
8. Yu, Y.; Yue, H.; Wen, F.; Zhao, H.; Zhou, A. Electromagnetic Force on an Aluminum Honeycomb Sandwich Panel Moving in a Magnetic Field. *Sensors* **2023**, *23*, 8577. [CrossRef] [PubMed]
9. Brebbia, C.A.; Telles, J.C.F.; Wrobel, L.C. *Boundary Element Techniques Theory and Applications in Engineering*; Springer: Berlin/Heidelberg, Germany, 1984.
10. Samarskii, A.A.; Nikolaev, E.S. *Numerical Methods for Grid Equations*; Birkhauser: Basel, Switzerland, 1989.
11. Samarskii, A.A.; Matus, P.P.; Vabishchevich, P.N. *Difference Schemes with Operator Factors*; Springer: Berlin/Heidelberg, Germany, 2010.
12. Colton, D.; Kress, R. *Integral Equation Methods in Scattering Theory*; John Wiley & Sons: New York, NY, USA, 1983.
13. Banerjee, P.; Butterfield, R. *Boundary Element Methods in Engineering Science*; McGraw-Hill Inc.: London, UK, 1981.
14. Kalitkin, N.N.; Alshina, E.A. *Numerical Methods: Numerical Analysis*; Academia: Moscow, Russia, 2013.
15. Kalitkin, N.N.; Koryakin, P.V. *Numerical Methods: Mathematical Physics*; Academia: Moscow, Russia, 2013.
16. Lobry, J. A FEM-Green Approach for Magnetic Field Problems with Open Boundaries. *Mathematics* **2021**, *9*, 1662. [CrossRef]
17. Radcliffe, A. Quasi-Stable, Non-Magnetic, Toroidal Fluid Droplets in a Ferrofluid with Annular Magnetic Field. *Magnetism* **2022**, *2*, 380–391. [CrossRef]
18. Sun, Y.; Wei, X.; Zhuang, Z.; Luan, T. A Numerical Method for Filtering the Noise in the Heat Conduction Problem. *Mathematics* **2019**, *7*, 502. [CrossRef]
19. Sun, Y.; Hao, S. A Numerical Study for the Dirichlet Problem of the Helmholtz Equation. *Mathematics* **2021**, *9*, 1953. [CrossRef]
20. Vladimirov, V.S. *Equations of Mathematical Physics*; Mir Publishers: Moscow, Russia, 1981.
21. Khatri, S.; Kim, A.; Cortez, R.; Carvalho, C. Close evaluation of layer potentials in three dimensions. *J. Comput. Phys.* **2020**, *423*, 109798. [CrossRef]
22. Klockner, A.; Barnett, A.; Greengard, L.; O'Neil, M. Quadrature by expansion: A new method for the evaluation of layer potentials. *J. Comput. Phys.* **2013**, *252*, 332–349. [CrossRef]

23. Epstein, C.L.; Greengard, L.; Klockner, A. On the convergence of local expansions of layer potentials. *Siam J. Numer. Anal.* **2013**, *51*, 2660–2679. [CrossRef]
24. Af Klinteberg, L.; Sorgentone, C.; Tornberg, A.K. Quadrature error estimates for layer potentials evaluated near curved surfaces in three dimensions. *Comput. Math. Appl.* **2022**, *111*, 1–19. [CrossRef]
25. Krutitskii, P.A.; Fedotova, A.D.; Kolybasova, V.V. Quadrature formula for the simple layer potential. *Differ. Equations* **2019**, *55*, 1226–1241. [CrossRef]
26. Krutitskii, P.A.; Reznichenko, I.O.; Kolybasova, V.V. Quadrature formula for the direct value of the normal derivative of the single layer potential. *Differ. Equations* **2020**, *56*, 1237–1255. [CrossRef]
27. Han, H.S.; Kim, D.S. *Magnetic Levitation: Maglev Technology and Applications*; Springer: Berlin/Heidelberg, Germany, 2016.
28. Krutitskii, P.A. A mixed problem for the Laplace equation in three-dimensional multiply connected domains. *Differ. Equ.* **1999**, *35*, 1193–1200.

Σ mathematics

Article

Evolutionary Approach for DISCO Profit Maximization by Optimal Planning of Distributed Generators and Energy Storage Systems in Active Distribution Networks

Rabea Jamil Mahfoud [1,2], Nizar Faisal Alkayem [1,3], Emmanuel Fernandez-Rodriguez [4], Yuan Zheng [1,2], Yonghui Sun [2], Shida Zhang [5] and Yuquan Zhang [1,2,*]

1 College of Water Conservancy and Hydropower Engineering, Hohai University, Nanjing 210098, China
2 College of Energy and Electrical Engineering, Hohai University, Nanjing 210098, China
3 College of Civil and Transportation Engineering, Hohai University, Nanjing 210098, China
4 Technological Institute of Merida, Technological Avenue, Merida 97118, Mexico
5 Key Laboratory of Smart Grid of Ministry of Education, Tianjin University, Nankai District, Tianjin 300072, China
* Correspondence: zhangyq@hhu.edu.cn

Abstract: Distribution companies (DISCOs) aim to maximize their annual profits by performing the optimal planning of distributed generators (DGs) or energy storage systems (ESSs) in the deregulated electricity markets. Some previous studies have focused on the simultaneous planning of DGs and ESSs for DISCO profit maximization but have rarely considered the reactive powers of DGs and ESSs. In addition, the optimization methods used for solving this problem are either traditional or outdated, which may not yield superior results. To address these issues, this paper simultaneously performs the optimal planning of DGs and ESSs in distribution networks for DISCO profit maximization. The utilized model not only takes into account the revenues of trading active and reactive powers but also addresses the active and reactive powers of DGs and ESSs. To solve the optimization problem, a new hybrid evolutionary algorithm (EA) called the oppositional social engineering differential evolution with Lévy flights (OSEDE/LFs) is proposed. The OSEDE/LFs is applied to optimize the planning model using the 30-Bus and IEEE 69-Bus networks as test systems. The results of the two case studies are compared with several other EAs. The results confirm the significance of the planning model in achieving higher profits and demonstrate the effectiveness of the proposed approach when compared with other EAs.

Keywords: active distribution networks; DISCO profit; distributed generators; energy storage systems; evolutionary computation

MSC: 68T20

Citation: Mahfoud, R.J.; Alkayem, N.F.; Fernandez-Rodriguez, E.; Zheng, Y.; Sun, Y.; Zhang, S.; Zhang, Y. Evolutionary Approach for DISCO Profit Maximization by Optimal Planning of Distributed Generators and Energy Storage Systems in Active Distribution Networks. *Mathematics* **2024**, *12*, 300. https://doi.org/10.3390/math12020300

Academic Editor: Pedro A. Castillo Valdivieso

Received: 6 December 2023
Revised: 13 January 2024
Accepted: 15 January 2024
Published: 17 January 2024

1. Introduction

In recent years, research on active distribution networks (ADNs) has rapidly improved, with a focus on numerous applications that integrate the latest technologies into such systems [1]. Distributed generators (DGs) are among the best technologies to integrate into ADNs due to their high availability, cost-effectiveness, efficiency, and overall advantages [2]. Several benefits can be achieved by installing DGs in ADNs, such as reliability improvement, loss reduction, voltage improvement, etc. [3]. Recent research studies suggest that even more advantages can be gained from the integrated DGs if energy storage systems (ESSs) are planned alongside them [4]. ESSs are becoming more involved in energy and power system planning due to their ability to provide techno-economic advantages, such as improving power quality, peak shaving, and energy management [5]. However, improper planning of energy sources in any power or energy system can result in the loss of desired benefits and create additional performance problems, which can negatively impact the overall functioning of the system [6]. Therefore, research on the effective coordination between DG and ESS units is of vital importance in the power and energy sector [7,8].

1.1. Literature Review

Various objectives, such as overall performance improvement [9], loss reduction [10], voltage profile improvement [11], and cost minimization [12–14], have been adopted to achieve optimal planning of DGs or ESSs in ADNs. However, the role of ADNs has evolved significantly compared to that of conventional (passive) networks. ADNs locally contribute to the power generation process through the integration of DG and ESS units. As a result, rather than minimizing total planning and operating costs, distribution companies (DISCOs) tend to increase their profit from selling energy to end users [15]. In deregulated electricity markets, electricity companies at different levels aim to maximize their revenues. Meanwhile, the system operators focus on maintaining the safe and secure operation of the corresponding networks [16]. In this regard, DISCOs can effectively utilize DG and ESS units to maximize their profit. The planning of DGs and ESSs for DISCO profit maximization was performed in [17], where the model was solved using the particle swarm optimization (PSO) method. The bi-level model proposed in [18] included techno-environmental criteria in the developed objective function to maximize the DISCO profit as well as the electric vehicle (EV) parking lot owner's profit. A dynamic reliability planning model of DGs in ADNs for DISCO profit maximization under load uncertainty was used in the study presented in [19]. However, most of the previous studies on maximizing DISCO profit in deregulated electricity markets have focused on planning either DG or ESS. Moreover, these studies only included the revenue from active power trading in their models, considering the active power of the integrated generation units.

As mentioned before, it is necessary to optimize the utilization of DGs and ESSs in ADNs to obtain the maximum benefits from their installation. This has been achieved in previous works using different optimization methods. Conventional methods, such as the analytical method proposed in [11], have been used. Linear programming (LP) [20], mixed-integer LP (MILP) [21], and mixed-integer nonlinear programming (MINLP) [13,15] have been applied to build the proposed models. The main advantage of LP and NLP methods is their solvability with a variety of commercial solvers such as MOSEK [13] and IPOPT [15]. Nonetheless, the functions and codes of these solvers are masked and cannot be edited or modified. This reduces flexibility, especially for complex systems. Various concepts from game theory [16] and Karush-Kuhn-Tucker (KKT) conditions [18] have been adopted to solve the developed models. However, conventional methods suffer from increased complexity and inaccurate results in most applications, especially for complex systems. On the other hand, evolutionary algorithms (EAs) have been used to achieve the optimal planning of DGs and ESSs in ADNs. EA techniques provide more flexibility than conventional methods even when system nonlinearity increases. PSO has been applied with various objective functions such as cost minimization [12] and DISCO profit maximization [17]. The authors of [14] proposed an equilibrium optimization (EO) method to determine the optimal locations and sizes of PVs and ESSs by total cost minimization. In [22], the locations and sizes of wind turbines and batteries were optimized by GA based on a techno-economic model. Moreover, some hybrid methods have been developed. In [9], the original artificial bee colony (ABC) algorithm was combined with two other methods: fitness scaling and chaotic methods to avoid being trapped in local optima. The harmony search algorithm (HSA) was integrated with the firefly algorithm (FA) in [19]. This provided a more efficient method in terms of accuracy, convergence, and computation time. Other EA methods have been used in previous papers, such as the artificial ecosystem optimization (AEO) [23], the hybrid arithmetic optimization algorithm-sine-cosine approach (AOA-SCA) [24], and the hybrid gradient-based optimizer with moth–flame algorithm [25]. As observed from the literature, most of the methods do not guarantee obtaining global optima. Hence, it is still necessary to develop effective methods that are particularly compatible with the corresponding problem. This can be achieved by advanced hybrid methods. In this context, various state-of-the-art EAs have been recently proposed but not yet used to solve the optimal planning of DGs and ESSs in ADNs. An example of these EAs is the social engineering optimizer (SEO) algorithm proposed by Fathollahi-Fard et al. [26] in 2018. The original SEO and several modified versions have been applied to various optimization problems in many research areas. However, SEO still has significant potential for unique improvements and applications to other engineering problems.

1.2. Research Motivations and Contributions

The following research motivations and contributions can be highlighted based on the literature reviewed in this paper:

- Existing research on maximizing DISCO profit in deregulated electricity markets separately performs the planning of DGs or ESSs, while planning both technologies simultaneously has been rarely addressed. Therefore, this paper simultaneously investigates the optimal planning of DGs and ESSs in ADNs to maximize the DISCO profit;
- Unlike most previous studies, the model presented in this paper includes both active and reactive power of DGs and ESSs. This can greatly increase the reactive power support and enhance their role as effective ancillary services;
- In deregulated electricity markets, not only active power but also reactive power is traded between the upstream grid and customers. Therefore, the revenues from trading both active and reactive power are included in the model, which has not been properly studied in previous relevant papers;
- The optimization techniques used so far for the DISCO profit maximization are either traditional, software-based, or outdated EAs, which may not provide superior solutions. Therefore, developing hybrid methods to be specifically compatible with the studied model is necessary and worth investigation;
- Moreover, although SEO has been applied to solve various optimization problems, it has not yet been applied to solve the optimal planning of DGs and ESSs in ADNs for DISCO profit maximization;
- However, despite the remarkable results obtained by the SEO in solving the above problems, it may require further improvements to specifically solve the optimal planning of DGs and ESSs in ADNs;
- Hence, this paper proposes a new hybrid approach that combines the optimization mechanisms of SEO, differential evolution (DE), Lévy flights (LFs), and quasi-oppositional-based learning (QOBL). With this developed combination, the global best of SEO is improved by distinctively applying the search mechanisms of DE and LFs. In addition, the QOBL technique is applied to improve the initial population of the proposed algorithm;
- The new algorithm called the oppositional social engineering differential evolution with Lévy flights (OSEDE/LFs) is benchmarked and compared to several state-of-the-art EAs;
- Furthermore, the developed OSEDE/LFs is applied to solve the optimal planning problem of DGs and ESSs in ADNs for DISCO profit maximization. The standard 30-Bus and IEEE 69-Bus distribution networks are used as test systems. The results are obtained for two case studies and compared to various algorithms, including the original SEO.

The rest of this paper is structured as follows: Section 2 demonstrates the integration of DGs and ESSs in distribution networks, while Section 3 presents the mathematical model of the DISCO profit maximization problem. The proposed OSEDE/LFs algorithm is introduced in detail in Section 4, and its application to the standard 30-Bus and IEEE 69-Bus networks is provided in Section 5 with several discussions and comparisons. Finally, Section 6 summarizes the conclusions.

2. Integrating DGs and ESSs into Distribution Networks

DG units are integrated into the distribution network to generate electrical power locally near the end user. Although a DG is mainly considered to be an active power source, it can also produce reactive power [13]. As shown in Figure 1a, for a typical DG system, active power (P kW) is generated and supplied to the grid. At the same time, reactive power (Q kVAr) can be produced or absorbed (bidirectional) [17]. Hence, a DG unit could be used as a reactive power compensator by setting the active power output to "zero" and generating only reactive power. A DG can be modeled as a P-Q bus or P-V bus. However, the P-Q model is more appropriate for distribution network applications, where the DG is considered to be a specified load with fixed values of P and Q [22].

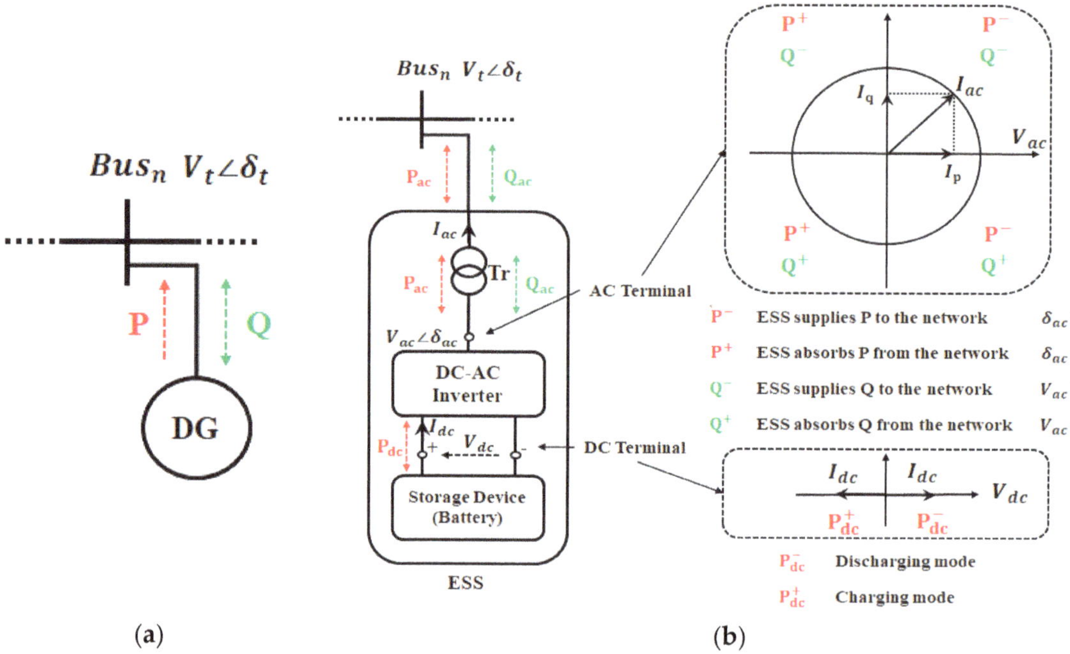

Figure 1. Typical units connected to the distribution network: (**a**) DG; (**b**) ESS.

Electrical energy can also be generated locally in distribution networks through the integration of ESSs. Nonetheless, the main difference between DG and ESS in this respect is that both P and Q of the ESS can flow bidirectionally, as depicted in Figure 1b.

As a controllable load or generator, an ESS can absorb P from the network and store it for later use. This power can then be injected back into the network on demand [9]. As shown in Figure 1b, a generic battery ESS unit needs to include a storage device, an inverter, and a transformer [12]. A DC voltage V_{dc} is generated by the storage device, which is then converted into a controllable AC voltage V_{ac} by means of the DC–AC inverter. To deliver this AC voltage to the distribution network, it must be raised by a suitable transformer. At the DC terminal, the storage device only absorbs (in charge mode) or injects (in discharge mode) active DC power. The inverter then connects the storage device to the transformer, where the power is converted to AC power at the AC terminal (the inverter output) [12]. By controlling the voltage magnitude and angle ($V_{ac}\angle\delta_{ac}$), P and Q delivered to the network by the transformer can be controlled independently. This provides four possible supply/absorption cases for both P and Q [5,22,27].

3. Mathematical Model of the DISCO Profit Maximization Problem

As discussed above, the optimal planning of DGs and ESSs (batteries) in ADNs is performed in this paper to maximize the DISCO profit subject to several constraints and take into account the active and reactive power of DGs and ESSs. Therefore, the decision variables of this problem are the locations and sizes of DG and ESS units (including their active and reactive power).

3.1. Objective Function

The objective function of the problem, represented by the net profit of the DISCO ($PROFIT_{DIS}$ (USD/year)), is to be maximized. The year is divided into 4 seasons of 91 days each, and each day is divided into 24 h. The objective function, including the active and reactive power of the system, is given as follows [6,17]:

$$\begin{gathered}\text{Max } (PROFIT_{DIS}), \\ PROFIT_{DIS} = [PR_P + PR_Q] - [Cost_{DG} + Cost_{ESS}],\end{gathered} \tag{1}$$

where PR_P and PR_Q denote the DISCO revenues from selling active and reactive power to the customers (loads) (USD/year) as given in Equations (2) and (3), respectively:

$$PR_P = \sum_{s=1}^{4} 91 \times \sum_{t=1}^{T} \left(\alpha_{DIS} \times P_{t,s}^{sold} \times \alpha_{t,s}^{P} - P_{t,s}^{purch.} \times \alpha_{t,s}^{P} \right), \tag{2}$$

$$PR_Q = \sum_{s=1}^{4} 91 \times \sum_{t=1}^{T} \left(\alpha_{DIS} \times Q_{t,s}^{sold} \times \alpha_{t,s}^{Q} - Q_{t,s}^{purch.} \times \alpha_{t,s}^{Q} \right), \tag{3}$$

where $P_{t,s}^{sold}$ (kW) and $Q_{t,s}^{sold}$ (kVAr) represent the active and reactive power sold to the customers at time t in season s, and $P_{t,s}^{purch.}$ (kW) and $Q_{t,s}^{purch.}$ (kVAr) are the active and reactive power purchased by DISCO from the upstream grid at time t in season s, respectively. The prices of active and reactive power at time t in season s are denoted by $\alpha_{t,s}^{P}$ (USD/kWh) and $\alpha_{t,s}^{Q}$ (USD/kVArh), while α_{DIS} is a percentage that defines the DISCO profit from this process.

The third term of Equation (1) represents the total cost of DGs in the ADN, which is calculated by:

$$Cost_{DG} = Cost_{DG}^{inv.} + Cost_{DG}^{O\&M}, \tag{4}$$

where $Cost_{DG}^{inv.}$ and $Cost_{DG}^{O\&M}$ (USD/year) denote the investment and operation and maintenance costs of DGs. The investment cost of a DG is mainly related to its apparent power. The maintenance cost is related to the performance, service fees, and the price of other equipment, and its value is usually fixed. The operation cost depends on the type of DG and its output power. However, for conventional DG units, the operation and maintenance cost is slightly increased on a seasonal basis, which is considered in this paper [6]. The investment and operation and maintenance costs of DGs are given in Equations (5) and (6), respectively:

$$Cost_{DG}^{inv.} = \left[\sum_{n=1}^{N_{DG}} \left(S_n^{DG} \times C_{inv.}^{DG} \right) \right] \times EAC, \tag{5}$$

$$Cost_{DG}^{O\&M} = \sum_{n=1}^{N_{DG}} \sum_{s=1}^{4} 91 \times \sum_{t=1}^{T} \left(P_{n,t}^{DG} \times CP_{O\&M,s}^{DG} + Q_{n,t}^{DG} \times CQ_{O\&M,s}^{DG} \right), \tag{6}$$

where S_n^{DG} represents the apparent power (kVA) of the nth DG, N_{DG} is the number of DG units, while $P_{n,t}^{DG}$ (kWh) and $Q_{n,t}^{DG}$ (kVArh) are the active and reactive power of the nth DG at time t. The parameters $C_{inv.}^{DG}$ (USD/kVA), $CP_{O\&M,s}^{DG}$ (USD/kWh), and $CQ_{O\&M,s}^{DG}$ (USD/kVArh) denote the investment unit cost of DG and seasonal operation and maintenance unit costs of active and reactive power, respectively. To convert the investment cost of DGs to the annual value, the equivalent annual cost (EAC) factor is used in Equation (5), which is calculated as follows:

$$EAC = \frac{d \times (1+d)^Y}{(1+d)^Y - 1}, \tag{7}$$

where d represents the discount rate, and Y (years) is the selected lifetime [5,6,17].

Moreover, the total cost of ESSs in the ADN represented by the fourth term of Equation (1) is given by:

$$Cost_{ESS} = Cost_{ESS}^{inv.} + Cost_{ESS}^{O\&M}, \tag{8}$$

where $Cost_{ESS}^{inv.}$ and $Cost_{ESS}^{O\&M}$ (USD/year) are the investment and operation and maintenance costs of ESSs as given in Equations (9) and (10), respectively:

$$Cost_{ESS}^{inv.} = \left[\sum_{n=1}^{N_{ESS}} \left(S_n^{ESS} \times CS_{inv.}^{ESS} + E_n^{ESS} \times CE_{inv.}^{ESS}\right)\right] \times EAC, \tag{9}$$

$$Cost_{ESS}^{O\&M} = \sum_{n=1}^{N_{ESS}} \sum_{s=1}^{4} 91 \times \sum_{t=1}^{T} \left(S_{n,t}^{ESS} \times C_{O\&M,s}^{ESS}\right). \tag{10}$$

The investment cost of ESSs should be calculated for batteries and inverters, as shown in Equation (9). Hence, for the total number of ESS units N_{ESS}, S_n^{ESS} denotes the apparent power (kVA) of the nth ESS's inverter and E_n^{ESS} is the nth ESS's capacity (kWh). To calculate the operation and maintenance cost in Equation (10), the apparent power $S_{n,t}^{ESS}$ (kVAh) of the nth ESS's inverter at time t is used. The parameters $CS_{inv.}^{ESS}$ (USD/kVA) and $CE_{inv.}^{ESS}$ (USD/kWh) are the investment unit costs of the inverter and ESS capacity, respectively, while $C_{O\&M,s}^{ESS}$ (USD/kVAh) is the seasonal operation and maintenance unit cost [6].

3.2. Constraints

DISCO profit is maximized subject to several constraints on network power flow and DG and ESS operation. Network power balance is maintained for active and reactive power as defined in Equations (11) and (12), respectively [5,6,17]:

$$\sum_{b=1}^{N_B} P_{b,t}^{IN} = \sum_{b=1}^{N_B} P_{b,t}^{OUT}, \tag{11}$$

$$\sum_{b=1}^{N_B} Q_{b,t}^{IN} = \sum_{b=1}^{N_B} Q_{b,t}^{OUT}, \tag{12}$$

where $P_{b,t}^{IN}$ and $Q_{b,t}^{IN}$ represent the active and reactive power entering bus b at time t; $P_{b,t}^{OUT}$ and $Q_{b,t}^{OUT}$ denote the active and reactive power leaving bus b at time t, and N_B is the set of network buses.

Network voltages are also constrained as follows [18,28]:

$$V_{min} \leq V_{b,t} \leq V_{max}; b = 1, \ldots, N_B, \tag{13}$$

where V_b denotes the voltage on bus b at time t, and V_{min} and V_{max} are the maximum and minimum voltage limits.

The apparent power of the nth DG at time t should not exceed the maximum limit S_{max}^{DG} as described in Equation (14):

$$S_{n,t}^{DG} \leq S_{max}^{DG}; n = 1, \ldots, N_{DG}, \tag{14}$$

where the relationship between $S_{n,t}^{DG}$, $P_{n,t}^{DG}$, and $Q_{n,t}^{DG}$ is defined as follows [13,17,22]:

$$S_{n,t}^{DG} = \sqrt{\left(P_{n,t}^{DG}\right)^2 + \left(Q_{n,t}^{DG}\right)^2}. \tag{15}$$

The operation of ESS units (batteries) is also constrained, where the apparent power of the nth ESS's inverter at time t must be maintained within the permissible limit as described below:

$$S_{n,t}^{ESS} \leq S_{max}^{ESS}; n = 1, \ldots, N_{ESS}, \tag{16}$$

where $S_{n,t}^{ESS}$ is calculated based on the inverter's active power $P_{n,t}^{ESS}$ and reactive power $Q_{n,t}^{ESS}$ at time t as follows [22,27]:

$$S_{n,t}^{ESS} = \sqrt{\left(P_{n,t}^{ESS}\right)^2 + \left(Q_{n,t}^{ESS}\right)^2}. \tag{17}$$

The nth ESS's capacity is also restricted, where its value at time t should not exceed the maximum limit E_{max}^{ESS} as given below:

$$E_{n,t}^{ESS} \leq E_{max}^{ESS}; n = 1, \ldots, N_{ESS}, \tag{18}$$

where $E_{n,t}^{ESS}$ is calculated as follows [5,12,28]:

$$E_{n,t}^{ESS} = E_{n,t-1}^{ESS} + P_{n,t-1}^{ESS} \times \eta_{ch} - \frac{P_{n,t-1}^{ESS}}{\eta_{dis}}, \tag{19}$$

where η_{ch} and η_{dis} (%) represent the charge and discharge efficiencies of the inverter.

The initial energy stored in ESS at time $t = 0$ should be predefined, which is described as follows:

$$E_{n,t}^{ESS} = E_{n,0}^{ESS}; \; for \; t = 0. \tag{20}$$

In this paper, $E_{n,0}^{ESS}$ is taken as 10% of the maximum capacity, i.e., the depth of discharge is 0.9.

Moreover, the energy balance of the ESS should be preserved at the end of the day ($t = T = 24$). Hence, the following equation is required:

$$E_{n,t}^{ESS} = E_{n,0}^{ESS}; \; for \; t = T. \tag{21}$$

4. The Proposed Algorithm for DISCO Profit Maximization

In this section, the proposed OSEDE/LFs algorithm is presented in detail. First, the mechanisms and steps of the algorithm are explained. Then, the performance analysis is performed by solving benchmark functions and comparing the results with those obtained by other original algorithms. Finally, the proposed approach is applied to solve the DISCO profit maximization problem.

4.1. Mechanisms of the Proposed Algorithm

The proposed algorithm is a unique hybridization of three mechanisms, namely SEO, DE, and LFs. In addition, QOBL is applied to improve the initial population. On this basis, the developed algorithm is called "oppositional social engineering differential evolution with Lévy flights" (OSEDE/LFs).

4.1.1. Oppositional and Quasi-Oppositional-Based Learning

Several EAs suffer from performance-related drawbacks, such as being trapped around local optima or slow convergence. This especially occurs for complex and high-dimensional optimization problems. Recently, the concept of oppositional-based learning (OBL) has been presented to further enhance the performance of EAs in terms of convergence, local optima avoidance, and computational time [29]. The main advantages of OBL are the simplicity and effectiveness when processing EA-based populations, either in the initialization step or within the main loop [30]. The OBL is structured by comparing the current population with its opposite, as the latter could be closer to the global optimum. Furthermore, the quasi-opposite number has been shown to be even closer to the global optimum than the opposite number [31]. Thus, the quasi-opposite population is calculated by a random probabilistic value and compared to the current population, then the best candidate between them is selected, as shown in Figure 2.

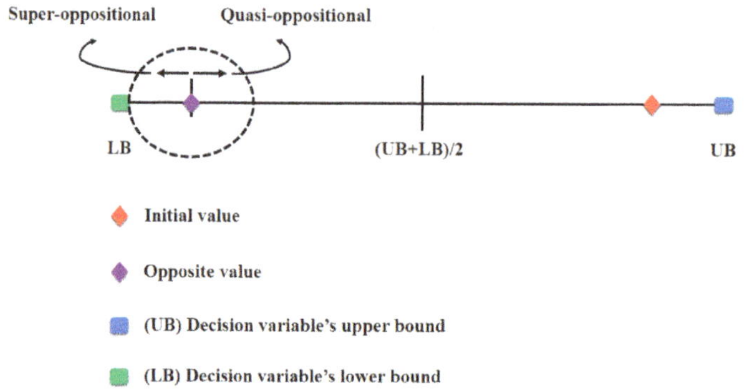

Figure 2. The QOBL concept.

The mathematical definition of quasi-oppositional-based learning (QOBL) is presented as follows [30,31]:

$$X_{ij}(It+1) = \begin{cases} C_j + rand() \times (C_j - X_{ij}(It)), if(X_{ij}(It) < C_j), \\ C_j - rand() \times (X_{ij}(It) - C_j), if(X_{ij}(It) \geq C_j), \end{cases} \tag{22}$$

where $X_{ij}(It+1)$ denotes the quasi-opposition number in dimension j of solution i at iteration $It+1$, *rand*() represents a random number, and C_j is the midpoint of the distance between the upper bound (UB) and the lower bound (LB) in dimension j, which is calculated as follows:

$$C_j = \frac{(UB + LB)}{2}. \tag{23}$$

4.1.2. Social Engineering Optimizer (SEO)

The original SEO was developed as a single-solution metaheuristic algorithm by Fathollahi-Fard et al. [26], inspired by the social interrelationship between individuals, i.e., how a person and his counterpart might interact given their conditions and environment. Based on this principle, each potential solution in SEO is a vector containing an individual and its counterpart. The characteristics of each member in this vector symbolize its social abilities to represent the variables of each solution. To initialize the SEO, two random individuals (representing two initial solutions) are generated and compared. After that, the better solution between them is defined as (attacker), while the other is defined as (defender). Then, the search process is led by the attacker trying to evaluate the defender by its merits through a process called training-retraining. During this random pattern process, the attacker replaces some of its variables with the best merits found in the defender, and then the fitness function is tested once again. The training-retraining mechanism continues the search until the best attacker-defender pair is found, which will guide the searching process by defining a set of trait-exchange experiments that are calculated as follows:

$$N_{tr} = round\{\propto, N_{var}\}, \tag{24}$$

where N_{tr} denotes the number of tested traits (merits), $\propto$ is the selected trait's percent, and N_{var} represents the total number of a person's traits, i.e., decision variables.

The algorithm then proceeds to the process of spotting an attack by performing four unique techniques, as illustrated in Figure 3. During this process, a key parameter β is used as input to improve the exploration of the search space. These four techniques are briefly described as follows [26]:

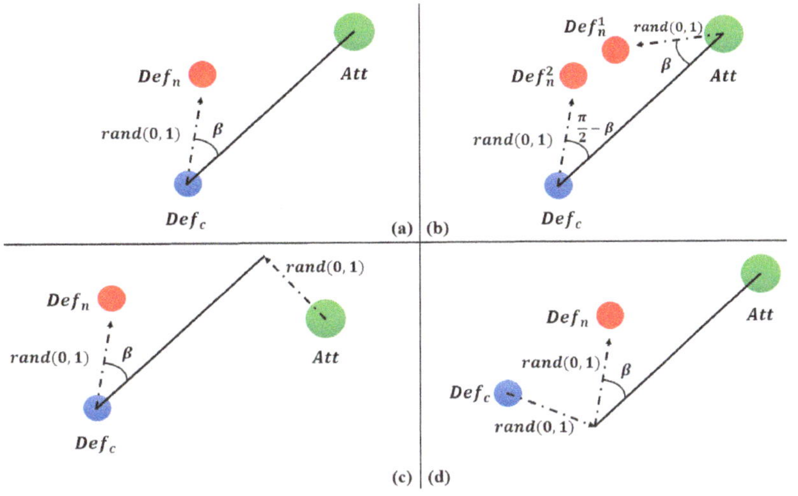

Figure 3. The techniques of SEO: (**a**) Obtaining. (**b**) Phishing. (**c**) Diversion theft. (**d**) Pretext.

1. The first technique is known as "obtaining", in which the attacker directly mistreats the defender to effectively obtain its desired traits. Based on that, the defender's new position is updated using the following equation:

$$Def_n = Def_c \times (1 - \sin\beta) \times rand_1(0,1) + \frac{(Def_c + Att)}{2} \times \sin\beta \times rand_2(0,1), \quad (25)$$

where Def_n and Def_c denote the new and current positions of the defender, Att represents the attacker's current position, and $rand_{1,2}(0,1)$ are randomly generated numbers;

2. The second technique, known as "phishing", involves the attacker faking an attack against the defender. The defender then reacts by moving to a safe place. As a result, two new positions of the defender are generated based on the movement of both the attacker and defender, as described in the following equations:

$$Def_n^1 = Att \times (1 - \sin\beta) \times rand_1(0,1) + \frac{(Def_c + Att)}{2} \times (1 - \sin\beta) \times rand_2(0,1), \quad (26)$$

$$Def_n^2 = Def_c \times \left(1 - \sin\left(\frac{\pi}{2} - \beta\right)\right) \times rand_1(0,1) + \frac{(Def_c + Att)}{2} \times \sin\left(\frac{\pi}{2} - \beta\right) \times rand_2(0,1), \quad (27)$$

3. The next technique is called "diversion theft", in which the attacker deceives the defender by leading the defender to a desired position (set by the attacker). This is achieved using the average distance between the defender and a scaled amount of the attacker. The defender's new position is then updated by:

$$Def_n = Def_c \times (1 - \sin\beta) \times rand_1(0,1) + \frac{(Def_c + Att \times \sin\left(\frac{\pi}{2} - \beta\right) \times rand_2(0,1))}{2} \times \sin\beta \times rand_3(0,1), \quad (28)$$

4. The final technique is defined as "pretext", in which the attacker uses some of the defender's favorite traits as bait to completely guide and defeat the defender. By the end of this process, the defender's new position is re-updated using a scaled amount

of the defender's current position and the average distance between the weighted attacker and defender as follows:

$$Def_n = \left(Def_c \times \sin\left(\tfrac{\pi}{2} - \beta\right) \times rand_1(0,1)\right) \times \left(1 - \sin\beta \times rand_2(0,1)\right) + \frac{\left(\left(Def_c \times \sin\left(\frac{\pi}{2} - \beta\right) \times rand_3(0,1)\right) + Att\right)}{2} \times \sin\beta \times rand_4(0,1), \tag{29}$$

Finally, after the completion of the four techniques, the eventual position of the defender is evaluated by comparing it with its old position, where the best position is selected. Moreover, if the selected defender's position is better than the attacker's, it will be defined as the new attacker, while another position of the defender will be randomly generated. The whole procedure will be iteratively repeated until the termination condition is met.

4.1.3. Differential Evolution (DE)

The well-known DE is an effective technique for solving optimization problems in various applications. Mutation, crossover, and greedy selection are the three main mechanisms that define the structure of DE [32]. Based on the mutation process, new mutant solutions S_M are generated in each iteration as follows:

$$S_M = S_B + AP \cdot ((S_{A1} - S_{A2}) + (S_{A3} - S_{A4})), \tag{30}$$

where S_B represents the best solution in every iteration while S_{A1}, S_{A2}, S_{A3}, and S_{A4} denote arbitrary solutions. The amplifying parameter AP is calculated as follows:

$$AP = \overline{AP} - (It - 1) \cdot (\overline{AP} - \underline{AP}) / (It_{max} - 1), \tag{31}$$

where $\underline{AP} = 0$, $\overline{AP} = 2$ are the limits of AP; It and It_{max} denote the current and maximum number of iterations, respectively.

The obtained mutated solution is then improved by applying the crossover process, evolving a trail solution S_T in the next iteration by:

$$S_T^{It+1} = \begin{cases} S_M^{It+1} \; if \; R \leq R_{CO} \\ S^{It} \; if \; R \geq R_{CO} \end{cases}, \tag{32}$$

where R represents a parameter within the range [0, 1] and R_{CO} represents the crossover rate.

After that, S_M^{It+1} and S_T^{It+1} are compared by greedy selection to keep the best solution in the population [32].

4.1.4. Lévy Flights (LFs)

The LFs is a powerful search mechanism defined as the mathematical representation of the random walks of the creatures as given in Equation (33), where the new solution is obtained by [33]:

$$S^{It+1} = S^{It} + STEP, \tag{33}$$

where $STEP$ represents the step size given by:

$$STEP = C \cdot \left(S_{A1}^{It} - S_{A2}^{It}\right) \bigoplus Levy(\beta) \approx 0.01 \frac{x_1}{|x_2|^{\frac{1}{\beta}}} \left(S_{A1}^{It} - S_{A2}^{It}\right), \tag{34}$$

where C denotes a constant, S_{A1}^{It} and S_{A2}^{It} are arbitrary solutions, $\bigoplus$ stands for the entry-wise multiplication, $Levy(\beta)$ is the Lévy probability distribution function of β, and x_1 and x_2 are calculated by the normal distribution function as follows:

$$\begin{array}{l} x_1 = N\left(0, \sigma_{x_1}^2\right) \\ x_2 = N\left(0, \sigma_{x_2}^2\right)' \end{array} \tag{35}$$

where $\sigma_{x_1} = \left[\frac{\Gamma(1+\kappa)\sin\left(\frac{\pi\kappa}{2}\right)}{\Gamma\left[\frac{(1+\kappa)}{2}\right]\kappa 2^{\frac{(\kappa-1)}{2}}} \right]^{\frac{1}{\eta}}$, κ is an index within the range [1,2], Γ represents the gamma function, $\eta = 1.5$, and $\sigma_{x_2} = 1$.

4.1.5. The Proposed OSEDE/LFs Algorithm

To build the proposed algorithm, the above optimization mechanisms are uniquely combined. The flowchart of the OSEDE/LFs algorithm showing its detailed steps is demonstrated in Figure 4. A stepwise variation process is applied to the stochastic parameters of the algorithm to determine their optimal values, which guarantees that the best performance is achieved by the combined mechanisms. As depicted in Figure 4, the algorithm starts by initializing a random population and defining the required operating parameters. At this stage, the initial values of the attacker and the defender are also defined. The randomly generated initial population is then improved by applying the QOBL mechanism. It is worth mentioning that the QOBL technique is used only at the initialization stage to enhance the initial population without its application within the main loop of the algorithm. After that, the main loop begins by applying SEO, where the training-retraining mechanism is performed. Then, a social attack is spotted and responded to through an iterative process until all attacks are over. Subsequently, a new defender is selected, and the global best is updated according to the value of the new attacker. This updated global best is then improved using the DE mechanisms (mutation, crossover, and greedy selection). Furthermore, greedy LFs are performed, where the LF perturbation is improved by reapplying crossover and greedy selection. This ensures achieving the best performance. Then, the global best is updated and set as the new attacker. The main loop is executed iteratively until the termination criteria are met. Finally, global optima are obtained.

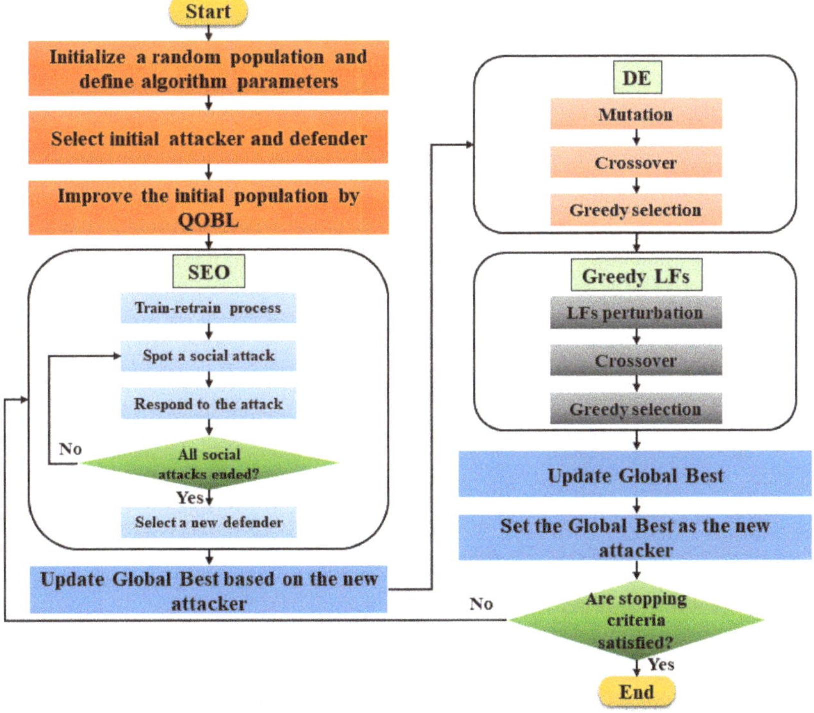

Figure 4. Flowchart of the proposed OSEDE/LFs algorithm.

4.2. Benchmarking of the OSEDE/LFs Algorithm

In this subsection, the performance of the proposed OSEDE/LFs is verified by solving a set of benchmark functions (BFs). These BFs include unimodal, multimodal, fixed-dimensional, and free-dimensional objective functions. A total of 23 BFs with multiple local minima and different shapes (valley, bowl, and plate shapes) are used. Their detailed mathematical formulations can be found in [34,35]. Hence, by solving these BFs, the performance of OSEDE/LFs is compared to that of 9 well-known state-of-the-art algorithms from the literature: the ant lion optimizer (ALO) [36], dragonfly algorithm (DA) [37], grasshopper optimization algorithm (GOA) [38], grey wolf optimizer (GWO) [39], moth–flame optimizer (MFO) [40], multi-verse optimizer (MVO) [34], sine cosine algorithm (SCA) [35], salp swarm algorithm (SSA) [41], and whale optimization algorithm (WOA) [42]. This comparison is carried out using the original parameters of each algorithm, as recommended by their developers and using the same 23 BFs. For a fair comparison, the population size and maximum iterations are set to 100 and 500, respectively, for all algorithms. The results of 20 individual runs of each algorithm are recorded as given in Table 1 for fixed-dimensional BFs (F_1 to F_{13}) and free-dimensional BFs (F_{14} to F_{23}). As shown in this table, the average (Avg) and standard deviation (STD) values are used for a comprehensive analysis of the obtained results. Then, by ranking the performance of each algorithm for all the BFs, it is observed that the best rank among all the compared algorithms is recorded by the proposed OSEDE/LFs (the best total rank of 49 and the best average rank of 2.13). Moreover, Figure 5 depicts the convergence curves of the compared algorithms for some of the BFs, which further validates the performance of the proposed OSEDE/LFs against several powerful original algorithms found in the literature. In addition, the Wilcoxon signed rank test is applied to all the algorithms corresponding to the solved BFs, as shown in Table 2. By conducting this nonparametric test, the p-values for the compared algorithms are obtained. These values demonstrate that the proposed OSEDE/LFs is statistically significant compared to the other algorithms since most of the resulting p-values are below the 5% significance level. Therefore, the proposed OSEDE/LFs can be recommended as a powerful method for solving real-world problems and engineering applications.

Table 1. The benchmarking of the proposed OSEDE/LFs.

Function		ALO	DA	GOA	GWO	MFO	MVO	SCA	SSA	WOA	OSEDE/LFs
F_1	Avg	1.03×10^{-8}	3.949819	1.42×10^{-8}	1.67×10^{-27}	1.241253	0.014665	1.58×10^{-12}	2.69×10^{-7}	1.64×10^{-74}	1.94×10^{-229}
	STD	8.12×10^{-9}	9.015141	9.60×10^{-9}	3.28×10^{-27}	0.837278	0.005057	3.00×10^{-12}	4.86×10^{-7}	5.58×10^{-74}	0
	Rank	5	10	6	3	9	8	4	7	2	1
F_2	Avg	0.468302	1.599196	1.405281	7.46×10^{-17}	23.15880	0.037429	5.18×10^{-10}	0.000147	6.99×10^{-51}	6.33×10^{-116}
	STD	1.135663	1.284330	2.105733	5.56×10^{-17}	20.41869	0.010797	8.11×10^{-10}	0.000341	2.26×10^{-50}	2.32×10^{-115}
	Rank	7	9	8	3	10	6	4	5	2	1
F_3	Avg	0.057536	413.5663	1.15×10^{-5}	2.48×10^{-5}	17309.75	0.107485	0.002350	3.86×10^{-6}	42423.25	2.93×10^{-228}
	STD	0.114693	1254.954	3.48×10^{-5}	7.41×10^{-5}	9753.122	0.082220	0.005775	1.63×10^{-5}	15003.66	0
	Rank	6	8	3	4	9	7	5	2	10	1
F_4	Avg	0.002035	3.347957	0.000246	7.15×10^{-7}	40.44441	0.095011	0.001631	2.34×10^{-5}	52.05566	9.89×10^{-116}
	STD	0.002150	2.075659	0.000441	8.15×10^{-7}	10.34281	0.031363	0.005651	1.03×10^{-5}	29.41085	2.27×10^{-115}
	Rank	6	8	4	2	9	7	5	3	10	1
F_5	Avg	84.75871	1453.581	245.0097	26.88655	23671.32	260.3831	7.531969	268.6981	27.85087	28.689685
	STD	154.9974	1966.364	598.7379	0.731425	39396.17	471.3051	0.561004	641.2532	0.413844	0.0212941
	Rank	5	9	6	2	10	7	1	8	3	4
F_6	Avg	6.90×10^{-9}	20.02457	2.76×10^{-8}	0.713936	1.120453	0.013753	0.374948	0.547076	0.494683	9.06×10^{-10}
	STD	2.36×10^{-9}	31.59926	5.67×10^{-8}	0.354781	0.896267	0.006095	0.133507	0.141783	0.321910	3.99×10^{-10}
	Rank	2	10	3	8	9	4	5	7	6	1
F_7	Avg	0.027927	0.026891	0.026351	0.001713	2.231993	0.003225	0.003166	0.016537	0.003342	2.17×10^{-5}
	STD	0.014574	0.015940	0.038760	0.001462	6.655355	0.001524	0.003221	0.011196	0.002799	1.87×10^{-5}
	Rank	9	8	7	2	10	4	3	6	5	1
F_8	Avg	−2294.46	−2611.78	−1502.40	−6216.58	−8779.65	−2981.60	−5987.54	−2862.42	−9428.42	−2207.91
	STD	422.8099	312.7750	175.4154	619.3926	919.0249	374.4465	860.8516	318.0720	1492.768	252.9189
	Rank	2	3	4	8	9	6	7	5	10	1
F_9	Avg	26.76432	27.10466	9.728792	3.484453	127.0368	18.16475	1.325983	20.34688	1.14×10^{-14}	0
	STD	13.63410	13.54998	8.528671	4.477779	46.11280	7.303766	4.098378	8.942808	3.50×10^{-14}	0
	Rank	8	9	5	4	10	6	3	7	2	1
F_{10}	Avg	0.356285	2.999678	1.789284	1.03×10^{-13}	12.71217	0.109276	2.67×10^{-6}	0.937622	4.26×10^{-15}	8.88×10^{-16}
	STD	0.658060	1.104676	3.609173	2.05×10^{-14}	8.279653	0.248928	9.34×10^{-6}	1.026054	3.15×10^{-15}	0
	Rank	6	9	8	3	10	5	4	7	2	1

Table 1. *Cont.*

Function		ALO	DA	GOA	GWO	MFO	MVO	SCA	SSA	WOA	OSEDE/LFs
F_{11}	Avg	0.194509	0.665993	0.139938	0.005206	14.26329	0.341601	0.100953	0.235602	0	0
	STD	0.104195	0.365076	0.059471	0.008578	32.85796	0.106914	0.151824	0.140456	0	0
	Rank	6	9	5	3	10	8	4	7	1	1
F_{12}	Avg	1.846053	2.098039	0.033959	0.042583	3.188568	0.052179	0.109533	0.354158	0.031228	0.095399
	STD	2.207358	1.551511	0.142477	0.016548	3.829839	0.170313	0.038326	0.538863	0.042258	0.031320
	Rank	8	9	2	3	10	4	6	7	1	5
F_{13}	Avg	0.004241	0.840557	2.869110	0.547333	4.282131	0.005557	0.342977	0.002747	0.431719	0.001131
	STD	0.008568	1.215182	0.329120	0.208381	3.569888	0.007426	0.085893	0.004881	0.247168	0.003385
	Rank	3	8	9	7	10	4	5	2	6	1
F_{14}	Avg	11.87036	11.51923	289.5171	9.702993	203.7239	9.958775	6.62373	6.336665	7.455311	0.998004
	STD	6.678188	7.662714	227.8556	5.229677	217.4068	6.613166	4.770185	4.018664	4.929486	9.30×10^{-12}
	Rank	8	7	10	5	9	6	3	2	4	1
F_{15}	Avg	0.011380	0.039980	2.064983	0.001570	0.327337	0.018534	0.001430	0.005387	0.001545	0.001493
	STD	0.017426	0.050395	7.749271	0.004541	1.386298	0.027542	0.000476	0.007532	0.002281	0.004136
	Rank	6	8	10	4	9	7	1	5	3	2
F_{16}	Avg	−0.95001	−0.70088	178.4440	−1.01906	77.97936	−1.03159	−1.03038	−1.03163	−1.00860	−1.03163
	STD	0.251210	0.408504	368.3589	0.015822	215.1951	3.51×10^{-5}	0.001595	2.36×10^{-13}	0.033520	4.73×10^{-9}
	Rank	7	8	10	5	9	3	4	1	6	2
F_{17}	Avg	0.397887	0.518911	13.61041	0.397961	7.499672	0.397959	1.817831	10.88912	0.724203	0.397887
	STD	1.83×10^{-10}	0.344932	17.48689	0.000156	13.10111	0.000120	2.164800	10.22242	1.046828	2.96×10^{-8}
	Rank	1	5	10	4	8	3	7	9	6	2
F_{18}	Avg	11.1	85.69132	757.7885	11.11088	6094.757	38.10078	7.088386	3	33.92338	3.000001
	STD	19.78277	182.3800	986.2936	19.78185	21684.51	36.22453	18.11531	2.87×10^{-12}	51.15743	1.14×10^{-6}
	Rank	4	8	9	5	10	7	3	1	6	2
F_{19}	Avg	−3.84879	−3.61741	−2.61897	−3.57359	−3.47050	−3.86112	−3.66962	−3.86071	−3.70897	−3.86239
	STD	0.01954	0.347895	0.968000	0.879876	0.669847	0.002963	0.727990	0.004423	0.190813	0.000588
	Rank	4	7	10	8	9	2	6	1	5	3
F_{20}	Avg	−3.26794	−2.93263	−2.45848	−3.26838	−3.15473	−3.25628	−2.44660	−3.21957	−2.93217	−3.24402
	STD	0.077511	0.686012	0.672128	0.123730	0.179302	0.067931	0.719194	0.070374	0.403542	0.062463
	Rank	2	7	9	1	6	3	10	5	8	4

Table 1. *Cont.*

Function		ALO	DA	GOA	GWO	MFO	MVO	SCA	SSA	WOA	OSEDE/LFs
F_{21}	Avg	−4.47386	−3.77144	−1.65018	−5.64516	−3.95988	−5.73927	−0.79106	−5.51181	−3.86936	−5.05515
	STD	1.771646	1.899046	1.761302	3.554868	3.106963	2.797988	0.968610	3.268046	2.583665	8.35×10^{-5}
	Rank	5	8	9	2	6	1	10	3	7	4
F_{22}	Avg	−5.45753	−4.56419	−1.03874	−8.58711	−3.88754	−5.97999	−1.38504	−5.71782	−4.41368	−5.61545
	STD	3.449533	3.064162	0.714230	2.95061	1.981279	3.746717	1.161892	3.25645	2.421325	1.62468
	Rank	5	6	10	1	8	2	9	3	7	4
F_{23}	Avg	−6.75264	−4.66103	−0.91397	−8.45723	−4.15571	−6.53090	−2.16716	−6.25604	−3.87789	−5.12839
	STD	3.598021	2.814268	0.324818	3.336493	3.298330	4.116066	1.672882	3.715353	2.273931	0.000214
	Rank	2	6	10	1	7	3	9	4	8	5
Total rank		117	179	167	88	206	113	118	107	120	49
Average rank		5.09	7.78	7.26	3.83	8.96	4.91	5.13	4.65	5.22	2.13

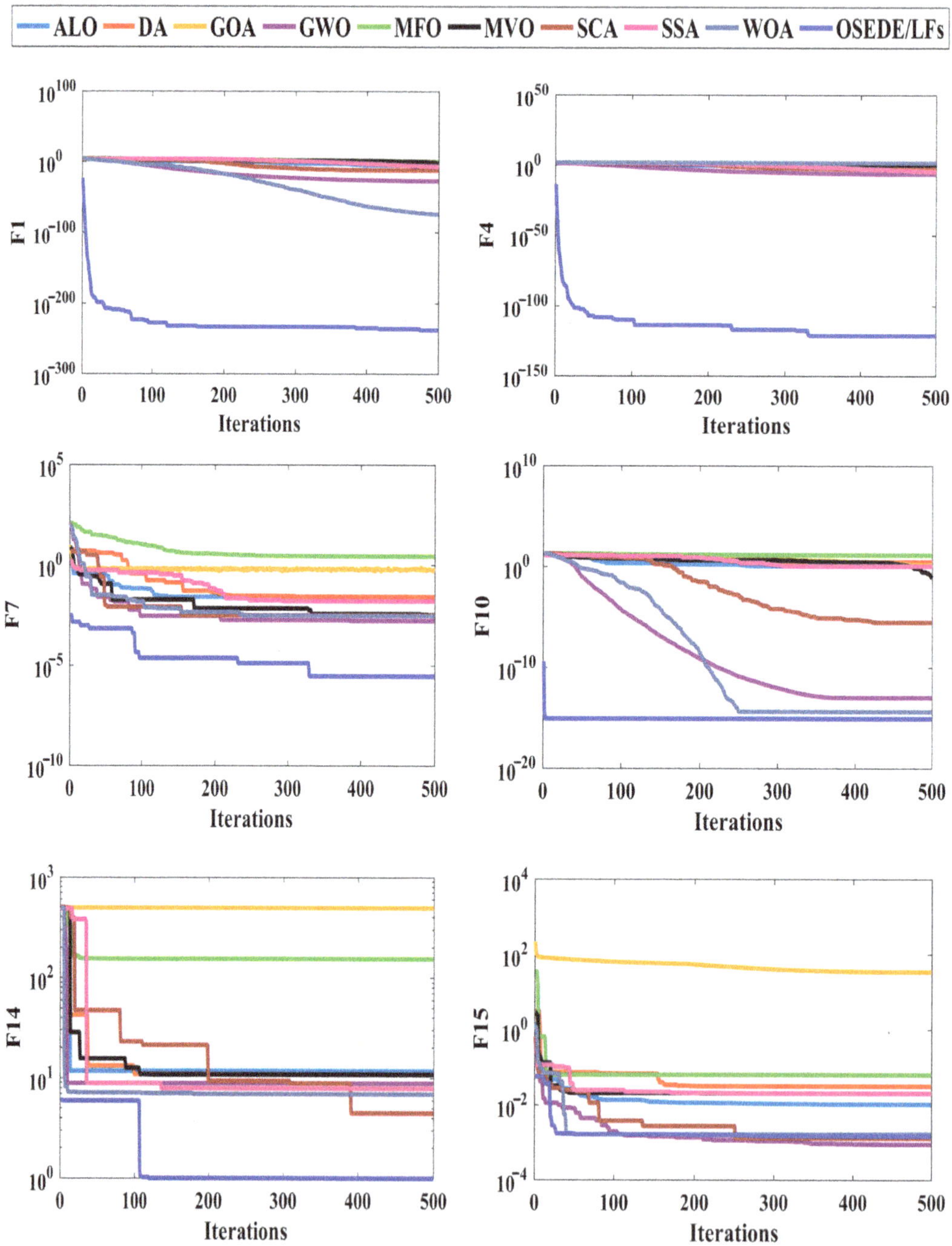

Figure 5. *Cont.*

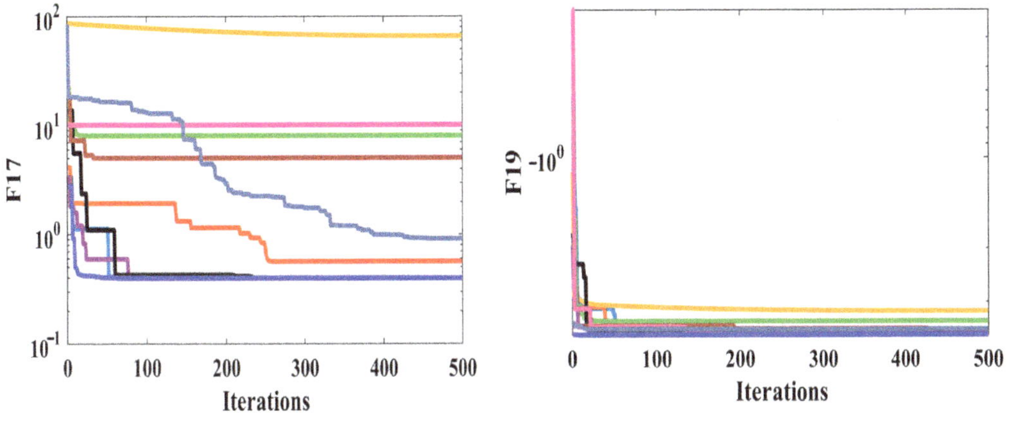

Figure 5. The convergence characteristics of the proposed OSEDE/LFs against other algorithms for some BFs.

Table 2. The Wilcoxon signed rank test results.

Function	p-Value								
	ALO	DA	GOA	GWO	MFO	MVO	SCA	SSA	WOA
F_1	8.86×10^{-5}	8.86×10^{-5}	8.86×10^{-5}	8.86×10^{-5}	8.86×10^{-5}	8.86×10^{-5}	8.86×10^{-5}	8.86×10^{-5}	8.86×10^{-5}
F_2	8.86×10^{-5}	1.03×10^{-4}	8.86×10^{-5}	8.86×10^{-5}	8.86×10^{-5}	8.86×10^{-5}	8.86×10^{-5}	8.86×10^{-5}	8.86×10^{-5}
F_3	8.86×10^{-5}	8.86×10^{-5}	8.86×10^{-5}	8.86×10^{-5}	8.86×10^{-5}	8.86×10^{-5}	8.86×10^{-5}	8.86×10^{-5}	8.86×10^{-5}
F_4	8.86×10^{-5}	8.86×10^{-5}	8.86×10^{-5}	8.86×10^{-5}	8.86×10^{-5}	8.86×10^{-5}	8.86×10^{-5}	8.86×10^{-5}	8.86×10^{-5}
F_5	0.601200	8.86×10^{-5}	0.550300	8.86×10^{-5}	8.86×10^{-5}	0.145400	8.86×10^{-5}	0.601200	1.03×10^{-4}
F_6	8.86×10^{-5}	3.90×10^{-4}	8.86×10^{-5}	0.052200	0.001700	8.86×10^{-5}	0.002200	8.86×10^{-5}	0.350700
F_7	8.86×10^{-5}	8.86×10^{-5}	8.86×10^{-5}	8.86×10^{-5}	8.86×10^{-5}	8.86×10^{-5}	8.86×10^{-5}	8.86×10^{-5}	8.86×10^{-5}
F_8	8.86×10^{-5}	8.86×10^{-5}	8.86×10^{-5}	0.295900	8.86×10^{-5}	8.86×10^{-5}	8.86×10^{-5}	8.86×10^{-5}	8.86×10^{-5}
F_9	8.86×10^{-5}	8.86×10^{-5}	8.86×10^{-5}	8.75×10^{-5}	8.86×10^{-5}	8.86×10^{-5}	1.32×10^{-4}	8.77×10^{-5}	0.500000
F_{10}	8.86×10^{-5}	8.86×10^{-5}	8.86×10^{-5}	7.69×10^{-5}	8.86×10^{-5}	8.86×10^{-5}	8.86×10^{-5}	8.82×10^{-5}	0.000488
F_{11}	8.86×10^{-5}	8.86×10^{-5}	8.86×10^{-5}	0.031250	8.86×10^{-5}	8.86×10^{-5}	8.86×10^{-5}	8.86×10^{-5}	1.00000
F_{12}	0.009996	8.86×10^{-5}	0.001507	0.000120	0.000103	0.013741	0.390530	0.295880	0.000254
F_{13}	8.86×10^{-5}	0.000254	8.86×10^{-5}	8.86×10^{-5}	0.191330	8.86×10^{-5}	8.86×10^{-5}	8.86×10^{-5}	8.86×10^{-5}
F_{14}	0.000130	8.86×10^{-5}	8.86×10^{-5}	0.000130	8.86×10^{-5}	8.86×10^{-5}	8.73×10^{-5}	0.000282	8.43×10^{-5}
F_{15}	0.000892	0.000681	8.86×10^{-5}	0.217960	8.86×10^{-5}	8.86×10^{-5}	0.002204	0.001507	0.033340
F_{16}	0.226560	8.86×10^{-5}	8.86×10^{-5}	8.86×10^{-5}	8.86×10^{-5}	8.86×10^{-5}	8.86×10^{-5}	0.000488	0.000103
F_{17}	8.83×10^{-5}	8.86×10^{-5}	8.86×10^{-5}	8.86×10^{-5}	0.000103	8.86×10^{-5}	8.86×10^{-5}	8.86×10^{-5}	0.000103
F_{18}	0.247140	0.000103	8.86×10^{-5}	8.86×10^{-5}	8.86×10^{-5}	8.86×10^{-5}	8.86×10^{-5}	8.86×10^{-5}	8.86×10^{-5}
F_{19}	0.004550	0.000120	8.86×10^{-5}	0.001713	0.000120	0.040044	8.86×10^{-5}	0.278960	8.86×10^{-5}
F_{20}	0.108430	0.005111	8.86×10^{-5}	0.125860	0.191330	0.501590	8.86×10^{-5}	0.262720	0.000120
F_{21}	8.86×10^{-5}	8.86×10^{-5}	8.86×10^{-5}	0.525650	0.116890	0.601210	8.86×10^{-5}	0.708910	0.015240
F_{22}	0.550290	0.156000	8.86×10^{-5}	0.005111	0.006425	0.708910	8.86×10^{-5}	0.851920	0.012374
F_{23}	0.092963	0.370260	8.86×10^{-5}	0.001507	0.232230	0.061953	0.000140	0.217960	0.003592

4.3. Applying OSEDE/LFs Algorithm to Maximize DISCO Profit

In this subsection, the proposed OSEDE/LFs is applied to solve the mathematical model established in Section 2 for DISCO profit maximization. This application is demonstrated in detail below Algorithm 1.

Algorithm 1: OSEDE/LFs for DISCO profit maximization

I—Input the distribution network's data, define the algorithm's parameters, and decision variables (number and type).
II—Run the power flow and calculate the base-case value of the objective function (before adding DGs or ESSs).
III—The algorithm's initialization:
1. Generate a random population of initial solutions (IP_1) containing locations and sizes of DGs and ESSs. Active and reactive powers of DGs and ESSs are considered, and charging and discharging schedules of ESSs are defined.
2. Initialize random values for the attacker and defender.
3. Run the power flow and evaluate IP_1 by the objective function (OF) using Equation (1) subject to all constraints using Equations (11)–(21).
4. Regenerate an initial population by QOBL technique (IP_2) using Equation (22) and run the power flow to evaluate it by the OF subject to all constraints.
5. Compare IP_1 and IP_2, save the best population, and assign it as the input population to the main loop.
IV—Main loop:
6. **While** stopping criteria are not satisfied:
7. Perform SEO on the current population:
- Train-retrain process.
- Set the 1st social attack.
- **While** number of attacks < max. number of attacks:
    ➢ Spot a social attack by the "obtaining," Equation (25), "phishing," Equations (26) and (27), "diversion theft," Equation (28), and "pretext," Equation (29).
    ➢ Respond to the social attack.
    ➢ Number of attacks is increased by 1.

End while
- Evaluate the population by the OF subject to all constraints.
- Select a new defender.

8. Update the Global Best based on the new attacker.
9. Apply DE to the current population:
- Mutation using Equation (30) and evaluation of the population using the OF subject to all constraints.
- Crossover using Equation (32) and evaluate the population using the OF subject to all constraints.
- Greedy selection to compare the populations and save the best.

10. Execute LF perturbation on the best population using Equation (33) and evaluate it using the OF subject to all constraints.
11. Crossover using Equation (32) and evaluate the population using the OF subject to all constraints.
12. Greedy selection to compare the populations and save the best.
13. Update the Global Best and set its value as the new attacker.
14. **End while.**

V—Save the global best solutions and display the final results.

---

5. Results and Discussion

The optimal planning of DGs and ESSs in ADNs for DISCO profit maximization is performed using the proposed OSEDE/LFs. The standard 30-Bus and IEEE 69-Bus distribution networks shown in Figure 6 are used as test systems, and the full line and load data can be obtained from [24,30]. The base power and voltage are 10 MVA and 11 kV for the 30-Bus system and 100 MVA and 12.66 kV for the 69-Bus system. Moreover, all parameters required to perform the simulations are given in Tables 3 and 4, which are taken from the relevant literature references [6,17,18,24]. The seasonal prices of active and reactive power $\alpha_{t,s}^{P}$ (USD/kWh) and $\alpha_{t,s}^{Q}$ (USD/kVArh) are taken in which the prices in autumn and winter are the same, and the prices in spring and summer are the same. Accordingly, the operation and maintenance unit costs of active and reactive power of DGs $CP_{O\&M,s}^{DG}$ (USD/kWh) and $CQ_{O\&M,s}^{DG}$ (USD/kVArh) are the same in autumn and winter. Then, these prices are increased by 20% in spring and summer. Since the operation and maintenance cost of ESS is mainly dependent on its apparent power, the operation and maintenance unit cost $C_{O\&M,s}^{ESS}$ (USD/kVAh) is fixed for all seasons [6]. The maximum apparent power of DGs (S_{max}^{DG}) and ESSs (S_{max}^{ESS}) given in Equations (14) and (16), respectively, should not exceed the sum of total load and network loss without DGs or ESSs [6,17,24].

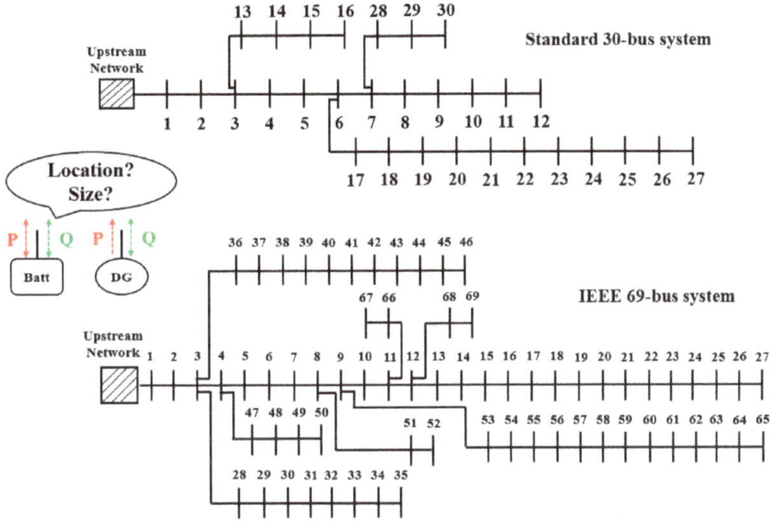

Figure 6. The standard 30-Bus and IEEE 69-Bus distribution networks used as test systems.

Table 3. Load levels and hourly energy prices during the day (24 h) [6,17].

Hours	1–5	6–8	9–10	11–14	15–16	17–20	21–22	23–24
Load (%)	50	60	70	80	90	100	90	70
Energy prices in autumn and winter								
$\alpha_{t,s}^{P}$ (USD/kWh)	0.14	0.14	0.22	0.22	0.30	0.30	0.30	0.22
$\alpha_{t,s}^{Q}$ (USD/kVArh)	0.028	0.028	0.044	0.044	0.060	0.060	0.060	0.044
Energy prices in spring and summer								
$\alpha_{t,s}^{P}$ (USD/kWh)	0.18	0.20	0.24	0.24	0.26	0.33	0.33	0.24
$\alpha_{t,s}^{Q}$ (USD/kVArh)	0.036	0.04	0.048	0.048	0.05	0.066	0.066	0.048

Table 4. Simulation parameters [6,17,18,24].

Parameter	Value	Parameter	Value
α_{DIS} (%)	15	$CE_{inv.}^{ESS}$ (USD/kWh)	81
d (%)	20	η_{ch}, η_{dis} (%)	95
Y (years)	5	$C_{O\&M,s}^{ESS}$ (USD/kVAh)	0.02
V_{min} (p.u.)	0.9	$CP_{O\&M,s}^{DG}$ (USD/kWh), autumn and winter	0.189
V_{max} (p.u.)	1.05	$CQ_{O\&M,s}^{DG}$ (USD/kVArh), autumn and winter	0.021
$C_{inv.}^{DG}$ (USD/kVA)	1150	$CP_{O\&M,s}^{DG}$ (USD/kWh), spring and summer	0.2268
$CS_{inv.}^{ESS}$ (USD/kVA)	805	$CQ_{O\&M,s}^{DG}$ (USD/kVArh), spring and summer	0.0252

For each system, the simulation is carried out considering two cases: the planning of DGs only (Case 1) and the planning of DGs and ESSs simultaneously (Case 2). To validate the performance of the proposed OSEDE/LFs, the model is also solved by the original state-of-the-art algorithms: DE, SEO, GWO, MVO, WOA, and PSO for all cases to compare the results. The comparisons are performed based on the original parameters of each algorithm. The parameters of OSEDE/LFs are defined by a stepwise variation to achieve the best performance. For a fair comparison, the population size and the maximum number of iterations are fixed to 50 and 200 for all algorithms, 10 independent runs are executed for each case, and the best solutions are recorded and analyzed using the minimum (Min), maximum (Max), Avg, and STD. Coding and simulations are carried out using Matlab-R2016a on a PC with an Intel Core (TM) i7 processor, 3.2 GHz speed, and 8 GB RAM.

5.1. The 30-Bus Network

5.1.1. Case 1: The Optimal Planning of DGs

In this case, only DG units are considered. Hence, Equations (8)–(10) and (16)–(21) are excluded, where the decision variables are the locations and sizes of DGs (for active and reactive power). The results are obtained for all algorithms and listed in Table 5. As can be seen in this table, the DISCO profit increased from 109,960.54 USD/year, which is the base case before adding DGs to the network, to 167,003.63 USD/year by PSO. This value is further increased to 167,276.76 USD/year by DE, 167,308.25 USD/year by WOA, 167,354.22 USD/year by SEO, 167,518.23 USD/year by GWO, and 167,639.37 USD/year by MVO. However, when using the proposed ODEDE/LFs, the DISCO profit reaches 168,383.40 USD/year, which is obviously the maximum value compared to the other algorithms.

Table 5. The optimal planning of DGs for the 30-Bus network (Case 1).

Algorithm	Optimal Locations	Optimal Sizes		$PROFIT_{DIS}$ (USD/Year)			
		P (kW)	Q (kVAr)	Max	Min	Avg	STD
Base case	-	-	-	109,960.54			
DE	11	102.64	68.71	167,276.76	167,209.48	167,270.00	21.28
	22	170.92	111.74				
	27	77.48	51.46				
SEO	11	78.27	52.80	167,354.22	167,278.66	167,346.70	23.89
	21	137.95	94.86				
	25	136.29	93.01				
GWO	10	112.75	75.18	167,518.23	167,480.62	167,510.70	15.86
	22	154.58	102.27				
	26	89.25	60.44				
MVO	10	112.45	75.86	167,639.37	167,592.21	167,634.70	14.91
	22	155.04	103.79				
	26	88.51	60.17				
WOA	11	99.07	66.57	167,308.25	167,214.94	167,298.90	29.51
	21	124.11	81.46				
	25	130.36	86.92				
PSO	11	102.76	65.84	167,003.63	166,923.33	166,995.60	25.39
	22	164.25	107.38				
	26	87.06	55.33				
OSEDE/LFs	10	110.58	79.48	168,383.40	168,359.84	168,381.00	7.43
	22	154.02	111.91				
	26	86.33	61.60				

In addition, the STD of the results obtained by ODEDE/LFs (7.43) is smaller than those of the other algorithms. These results verify the robustness of the proposed ODEDE/LFs, further illustrated in Figure 7, which shows the convergence characteristics of all compared algorithms for Case 1. The ODEDE/LFs require a smaller number of iterations to reach the optimal solution.

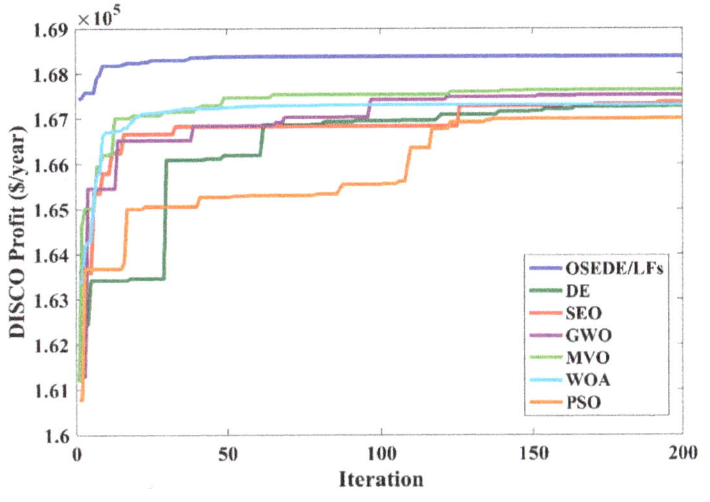

Figure 7. Convergence characteristics of the OSEDE/LFs compared to other algorithms for the 30-Bus network (Case 1).

5.1.2. Case 2: The Optimal Planning of DGs and ESSs Simultaneously

In this case, DG and ESS units are considered. Hence, the decision variables are the locations and sizes of DGs and ESSs (for active and reactive power). The locations and sizes of DGs and ESSs obtained by all the algorithms are listed in Table 6. Comparing the results of Case 1 (Table 5) to those of Case 2 (Table 6), it can be observed that the locations of DG units obtained by each algorithm are not the same compared to Case 1. This is because the algorithms consider the simultaneous planning of DGs and ESSs in Case 2 rather than only DGs in Case 1. This demonstrates the importance of this strategy as it affects the final results. It is also worth mentioning that all the algorithms are programmed to freely select the locations of ESSs to obtain the maximum profit, even if these locations would be the same as the locations of DGs. However, as can also be seen in Table 6, the optimal locations of ESSs are different from the locations of DGs for all algorithms. This demonstrates that when the DGs and ESSs are planned simultaneously, it is not necessary to allocate DG and ESS units at the same location.

Table 6. The optimal planning of DGs and ESSs for the 30-Bus network (Case 2).

Algorithm	DG Units			ESS Units		
	Optimal Locations	Optimal Sizes		Optimal Locations	Optimal Sizes	
		P (kW)	Q (kVAr)		P (kW)	Q (kVAr)
DE	12	39.83	24.99	6	56	112
	23	161.02	100.21	9	43	79
	28	27.32	17.22	27	42	87

Table 6. *Cont.*

Algorithm	DG Units			ESS Units		
	Optimal Locations	Optimal Sizes		Optimal Locations	Optimal Sizes	
		P (kW)	Q (kVAr)		P (kW)	Q (kVAr)
SEO	12	20.03	12.47	6	101	200
	21	102.79	63.98	10	29	55
	24	99.75	61.82	27	34	67
GWO	11	70.75	45.70	3	41	85
	21	97.16	61.74	8	53	101
	26	84.41	53.20	23	61	114
MVO	10	57.74	38.35	5	48	96
	12	35.63	23.57	18	54	103
	23	157.50	104.61	27	39	74
WOA	11	75.67	51.05	3	51	103
	20	78.64	52.23	8	45	86
	23	113.16	75.75	27	50	96
PSO	21	114.09	71.30	6	59	116
	24	93.72	60.05	10	47	88
	30	21.04	13.26	27	39	76
OSEDE/LFs	11	65.52	40.78	9	40	74
	22	124.63	77.24	18	59	113
	25	54.60	33.98	27	35	68

In addition, as can also be seen in Table 6, the reactive power of ESS units is higher than their active power (these active and reactive powers represent the size of the ESS inverter). This explains the high impact of reactive power control on the network. When there is no exchange of active power (P is zero), the ESS unit can still exchange reactive power with the network. In other words, when the inverter is neither charging nor discharging active power, it can still draw or inject reactive power. During these periods, the ESS operates as a capacitor bank, which greatly improves the performance of the network. However, this exchange of reactive power is limited as the apparent power of the inverter must satisfy the technical constraints given in Equations (16) and (17).

Based on the results of the optimal planning of DGs and ESSs shown in Table 6, the DISCO profit is further maximized compared to Case 1, as detailed in Table 7. When PSO is applied, the DISCO profit is increased to 176,734.33 USD/year. The profit reaches 176,975.90 USD/year, 177,097.47 USD/year, 177,100.48 USD/year, 177,282.74 USD/year, and 177,359.65 USD/year by DE, WOA, SEO, GWO, and MVO, respectively. However, the profit reaches its maximum value when the OSEDE/LFs is applied (178,314.58 USD/year). These results emphasize the usefulness of considering the revenues from active and reactive power trading when calculating the DISCO profit, where higher profits could be achieved. Moreover, the simultaneous planning of DGs and ESSs, considering their active and reactive power in the model, proves to be efficient as the profit is further maximized.

In addition, the effectiveness of the proposed algorithm is validated as the highest profits are obtained when the OSEDE/LFs are applied. As also illustrated in Table 7, the proposed algorithm achieves the optimal solutions with higher robustness as the STD is the lowest among all compared algorithms (9.23). The robustness of ODEDE/LFs is maintained even when the number of decision variables is increased. Accordingly, the proposed algorithm can be applied to larger models with higher complexity. These findings are further illustrated in Figure 8, which depicts the convergence characteristics of all the algorithms compared to Case 2. The ODEDE/LFs require fewer iterations to reach the optimal solution.

Table 7. DISCO profit for the 30-Bus network, Case 2 (based on the results given in Table 6).

Algorithm	$PROFIT_{DIS}$ **(USD/Year)**			
	Max	**Min**	**Avg**	**STD**
Base case	109,960.54			
DE	176,975.90	176,907.66	176,969.10	21.58
SEO	177,100.48	177,023.97	177,092.80	24.20
GWO	177,282.74	177,223.70	177,276.80	18.67
MVO	177,359.65	177,322.13	177,352.15	15.82
WOA	177,097.47	177,010.40	177,088.77	27.53
PSO	176,734.33	176,655.29	176,726.40	24.99
OSEDE/LFs	178,314.58	178,295.48	178,308.80	9.23

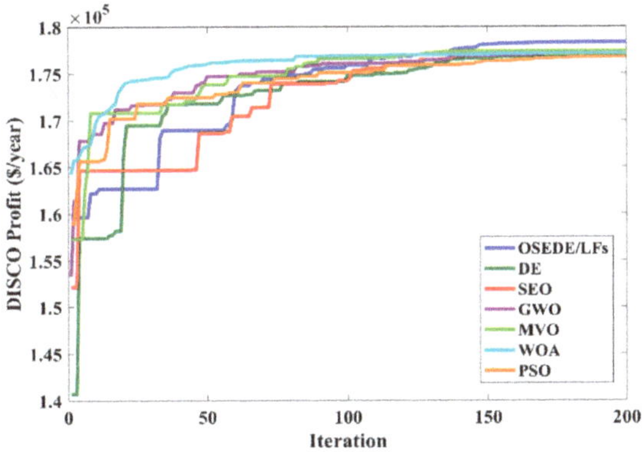

Figure 8. Convergence characteristics of the OSEDE/LFs compared to other algorithms for the 30-Bus network (Case 2).

To demonstrate the operation of ESS during the optimization process using the OSEDE/LFs, the charging and discharging powers, as well as the stored energy of the ESS unit on Bus 18, are shown in Figure 9. It can be seen that the ESS is charged, discharged, and disconnected in accordance with the load levels given in Table 3. During the light-load hours, the ESS operates in charge mode, where the maximum charge power does not exceed the maximum active power of the ESS. To avoid unnecessary power losses, the ESS is disconnected from the network during the medium-load hours, while it operates in discharge mode during full-load hours. This figure also shows that the applied strategy is sufficient to maintain the energy balance of the ESS, where at the end of the day ($t = T = 24$), the residual energy is equal to the initial stored energy ($t = 0$).

5.1.3. Technical Impacts of DGs and ESSs

To analyze the technical impacts of DGs and ESSs on the 30-Bus network, the active power loss is calculated when the OSEDE/LFs are applied for Cases 1 and 2 and compared to that of the base case, as illustrated in Figure 10a.

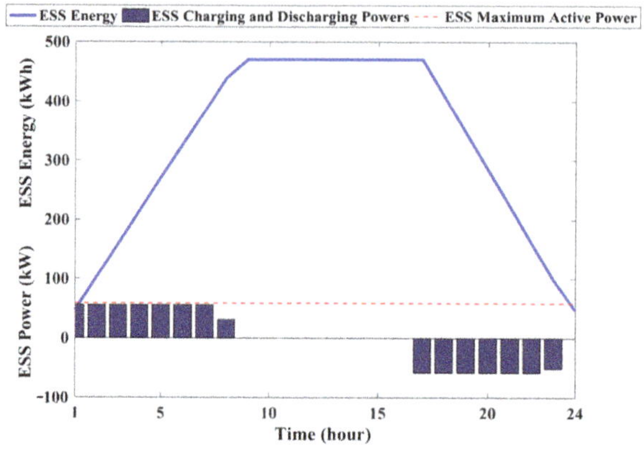

Figure 9. The power and stored energy of the ESS unit on Bus 18 of the 30-Bus network using the OSEDE/LFs.

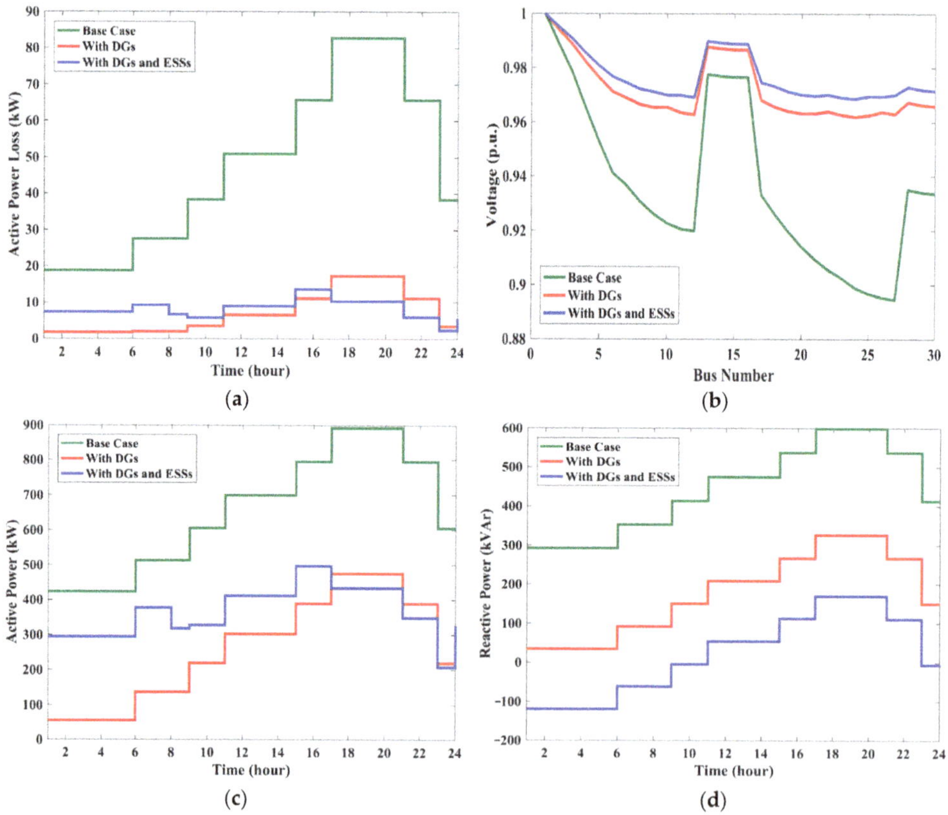

Figure 10. The technical impacts of DGs and ESSs on the 30-Bus network using the OSEDE/LFs: (**a**) Active power loss; (**b**) Voltage profile at Hour 17; (**c**) Active power; and (**d**) Reactive power exchanged with the upstream network.

It is obvious that maximizing the DISCO profit also reduces the active power losses in both studied cases, especially during the full-load hours, where the impact is remarkably significant. Nonetheless, when DG and ESS units are considered, the active power losses are still slightly higher during the ESS charging hours. This is reasonable since the ESS units are considered to be loads during this period. However, when the ESS units operate in discharge mode, the losses of Case 2 are further reduced compared to those of Case 1 during the same period. As a result, more benefits can be achieved if the DGs and ESSs are integrated into the network simultaneously, considering their active and reactive power.

To better visualize the impact of the planning strategy on the network voltage, Figure 10b depicts the voltage profile of all buses at Hour 17 (network fully loaded and ESS units in discharge mode). It is validated that the voltages of all buses are greatly improved compared to the base-case voltages. These improvements are clearly seen on the bus with the lowest base-case voltage (the voltage on Bus 27 is improved from 0.8944 p.u. to 0.9631 in Case 1 and to 0.9701 p.u. in Case 2). Hence, the safe and secure operation of the network is maintained in both cases since all voltages are within permissible limits. Nevertheless, the voltages in Case 2 are better improved throughout the network than in Case 1. More precisely, the worse the base-case voltages are, the better Case 2 improves over Case 1.

Finally, it is necessary to demonstrate the active and reactive power that the DISCO exchanges with the upstream network during the day. This will further justify the above results. It will also validate the effectiveness of the planning strategy. Figure 10c shows the active power exchanged with the upstream network using the OSEDE/LFs for Cases 1 and 2. When only DGs are added to the network (Case 1), the received power from the upstream network is well reduced compared to the base case. However, when DGs and ESSs are added (Case 2), the power received is also lower than the base case but higher than that of Case 1 during ESS charging and disconnecting hours. This is because more power is needed to charge the ESS units. Starting from Hour 17, the power received in Case 2 becomes lower than that of Case 1 since the power stored in ESS units is discharged and used. Thus, the DISCO can make more profit when DGs and ESSs are added because the power used to charge the ESS units (during light-load hours) is cheaper than when ESS units are discharged (the load levels are between 100% and 70%).

The reactive power exchanged with the upstream network is also analyzed, as illustrated in Figure 10d. After adding DG units to the network, the DISCO still must receive reactive power but with a lower amount compared to that before adding DGs. Nevertheless, in Case 2, the reactive power is sold to the upstream network during hours 1 to 9 instead of receiving reactive power compared to Case 1 during the same period. Moreover, the DISCO sells more reactive power in the last two hours of the day. Furthermore, during the rest of the day, the reactive power received from the upstream network is clearly lower in Case 2 than in Case 1. This was previously explained since the ESS is still exchanging reactive power with the network when there is no active power being exchanged. Therefore, by adding DGs and ESSs to the network considering their active and reactive power, the DISCO can obtain more income by exchanging higher amounts of reactive power and reducing the amount of power received from the upstream network.

5.2. The 69-Bus Network

5.2.1. Case 1: The Optimal Planning of DGs

Similar to the 30-Bus network, 3 DGs are added. The results for all of the compared algorithms are listed in Table 8, which demonstrates that the DISCO profit increases from 729,008.14 USD/year (base case) to 871,266.96 USD/year, 871,500.15 USD/year, 871,831.28 USD/year, 872,448.63 USD/year, 873,201.55 USD/year, 873,765.87 USD/year, and 875,457.79 USD/year by PSO, SEO, WOA, DE, GWO, MVO, and OSEDE/LFs, respectively. The maximum profit is obtained by the proposed algorithm. Moreover, the STD of the results obtained by ODEDE/LFs (9.80) is smaller than those of the other algorithms. Comparing the results of Case 1 for the 30-Bus and 69-Bus networks, it can be noticed that the STD values of all algorithms are higher for the 69-Bus network. This is because the search space is increased, and thus, the complexity of the problem is increased. However, the proposed OSEDE/LFs maintains its robustness, as the optimal solution is obtained with the smallest STD value compared to the other algorithms. These results are further illustrated in Figure 11, showing the convergence characteristics of all compared algorithms for Case 1. The ODEDE/LFs require fewer iterations to reach the optimal solution.

Table 8. The optimal planning of DGs for the 69-Bus network (Case 1).

Algorithm	Optimal Locations	Optimal Sizes		$PROFIT_{DIS}$ (USD/Year)			
		P (kW)	Q (kVAr)	Max	Min	Avg	STD
Base case	-	-	-	729,008.14			
DE	22	86.58	54.79	872,448.63	872,360.19	872,439.80	27.97
	61	1003.17	655.84				
	65	20.00	12.76				
SEO	20	168.26	111.76	871,500.15	871,445.35	871,483.70	26.47
	61	146.47	94.99				
	62	853.11	575.52				
GWO	24	72.46	48.88	873,201.55	873,145.33	873,195.90	17.78
	61	976.67	646.15				
	65	43.91	28.82				
MVO	21	90.52	60.60	873,765.87	873,715.50	873,760.80	15.93
	61	786.28	518.14				
	64	231.27	151.20				
WOA	17	68.23	44.78	871,831.28	871,751.03	871,817.00	30.44
	21	21.56	13.93				
	61	1020.37	661.76				
PSO	61	147.01	99.18	871,266.96	871,110.72	871,267.00	49.41
	62	244.06	161.47				
	63	640.21	440.21				
OSEDE/LFs	24	88.03	60.53	875,457.79	875,438.81	875,450.20	9.80
	61	765.34	530.23				
	64	240.87	169.38				

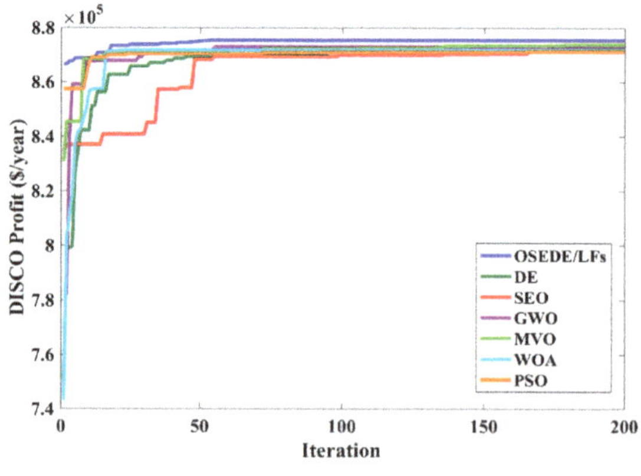

Figure 11. Convergence characteristics of the OSEDE/LFs compared to other algorithms for the 69-Bus network (Case 1).

5.2.2. Case 2: The Optimal Planning of DGs and ESSs Simultaneously

In this case, the decision variables are the locations and sizes of 3 DGs and 3 ESSs (for active and reactive power). The locations and sizes of DGs and ESSs obtained by all the algorithms are listed in Table 9. The results of Case 1 (Table 8) and Case 2 (Table 9) show the difference between planning only DGs and planning DGs and ESSs simultaneously in terms of optimal locations. However, unlike the 30-Bus network, the 69-Bus network requires some DG and ESS units to be placed at the same locations to achieve the maximum profit, as shown in Table 9. These results emphasize that the simultaneous planning of DG and ESS units is also related to the nature and topology of the network under study.

Table 9. The optimal planning of DGs and ESSs for the 69-Bus network (Case 2).

Algorithm	DG Units			ESS Units		
	Optimal Locations	Optimal Sizes		Optimal Locations	Optimal Sizes	
		P (kW)	Q (kVAr)		P (kW)	Q (kVAr)
DE	17	81.14	54.52	19	136	295
	61	398.98	270.19	40	42	141
	64	347.69	230.93	61	181	433
SEO	10	30.78	20.53	8	174	390
	22	180.25	122.07	49	278	747
	61	620.86	410.75	61	289	528
GWO	18	58.618	36.48	61	199	366
	25	41.51	26.27	64	118	221
	61	670.89	429.85	67	212	446
MVO	17	20.27	12.93	42	17	38
	26	20.00	12.61	61	316	584
	61	690.55	449.66	69	159	322
WOA	22	42.90	28.27	62	243	491
	23	62.03	41.84	63	13	24
	62	689.98	460.08	66	114	302
PSO	27	181.65	122.07	56	204	393
	60	155.16	100.23	60	115	262
	62	436.43	289.87	62	176	274
OSEDE/LFs	61	478.16	320.08	12	111	232
	64	178.24	122.09	21	88	178
	65	55.11	36.61	61	281	526

Based on the results of Case 2 shown in Table 10, the DISCO profit is further maximized to reach 889,726.09 USD/year (by PSO), 891,756.92 USD/year (SEO), 897,791.51 USD/year (WOA), 898,119.76 USD/year (DE), 900,334.02 USD/year (GWO), 900,813.13 USD/year (MVO), and 904,013.05 USD/year (ODEDE/LFs), respectively.

Subsequently, it is proved that the utilized optimization model is effective for DISCO profit maximization. It is also observed that as the complexity of the problem increases (increasing the search space between the 30-Bus and 69-Bus networks), the compared algorithms may perform differently. For example, the results of the SEO algorithm are better than those of PSO, DE, and WOA for the 30-Bus system but worse than those of DE and WOA for the 69-Bus system. Moreover, for both test systems, the SEO performs worse than GWO, MVO, and the proposed OSEDE/LFs, especially for the 69-Bus system. These results confirm that the original SEO needs improvements to handle complex optimization problems like the model used in this paper, especially for large-scale systems. This has been achieved by the proposed OSEDE/LFs algorithm.

Table 10. DISCO profit for the 69-Bus network, Case 2 (based on the results given in Table 9).

Algorithm	$PROFIT_{DIS}$ (USD/Year)			
	Max	**Min**	**Avg**	**STD**
Base case	729,008.14			
DE	898,119.76	898,054.43	898,100.20	31.56
SEO	891,756.92	891,629.72	891,744.20	40.23
GWO	900,334.02	900,253.20	900,325.90	25.56
MVO	900,813.13	900,767.78	900,799.50	21.91
WOA	897,791.51	897,721.00	897,770.40	34.06
PSO	889,726.09	889,551.00	889,708.60	55.37
OSEDE/LFs	904,013.05	903,979.67	904,006.40	14.07

It is clear that the highest profits with the lowest STD values are obtained for all cases when the OSEDE/LFs are applied. Using the proposed algorithm, the performance of SEO and DE is remarkably improved to overcome even the powerful state-of-the-art GWO, MVO, and WOA algorithms. To further validate these results, the convergence characteristics of all the algorithms compared to Case 2 are depicted in Figure 12, showing that the ODEDE/LFs reach the optimal solution with fewer iterations.

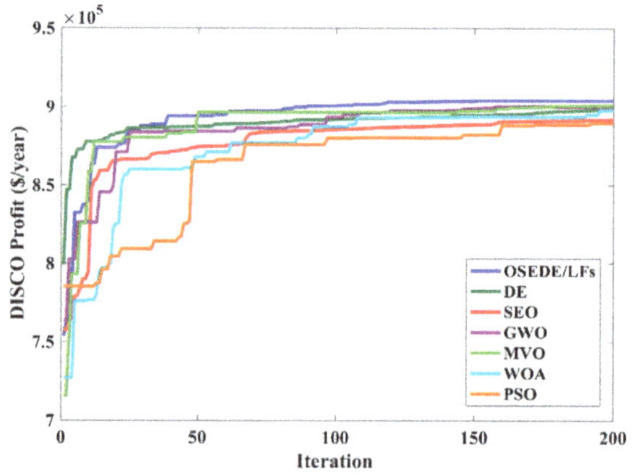

Figure 12. Convergence characteristics of the OSEDE/LFs compared to other algorithms for the 69-Bus network (Case 2).

Furthermore, the charging and discharging powers and the stored energy of the ESS unit on Bus 21 are shown in Figure 13, demonstrating that the energy balance of the ESS is maintained.

5.2.3. Technical Impacts of DGs and ESSs

The technical impacts of DGs and ESSs on the 69-Bus network when the OSEDE/LFs are applied for Cases 1 and 2 are shown in Figure 14, analyzing the (a) active power losses, (b) voltage profile at Hour 17, (c) active power and (d) reactive power exchanged with the upstream network.

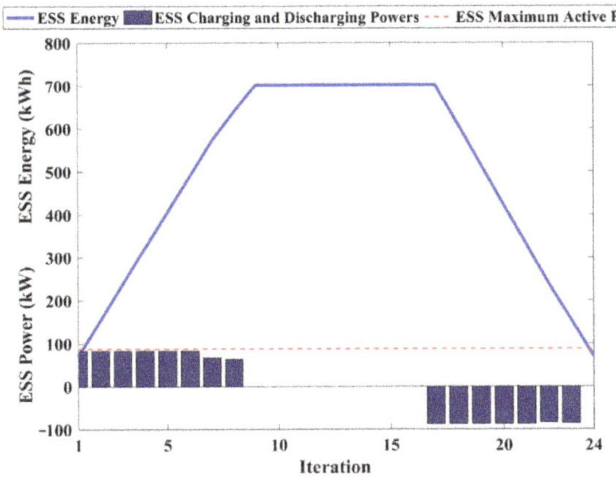

Figure 13. The power and stored energy of the ESS unit on Bus 21 of the 69-Bus network using the OSEDE/LFs.

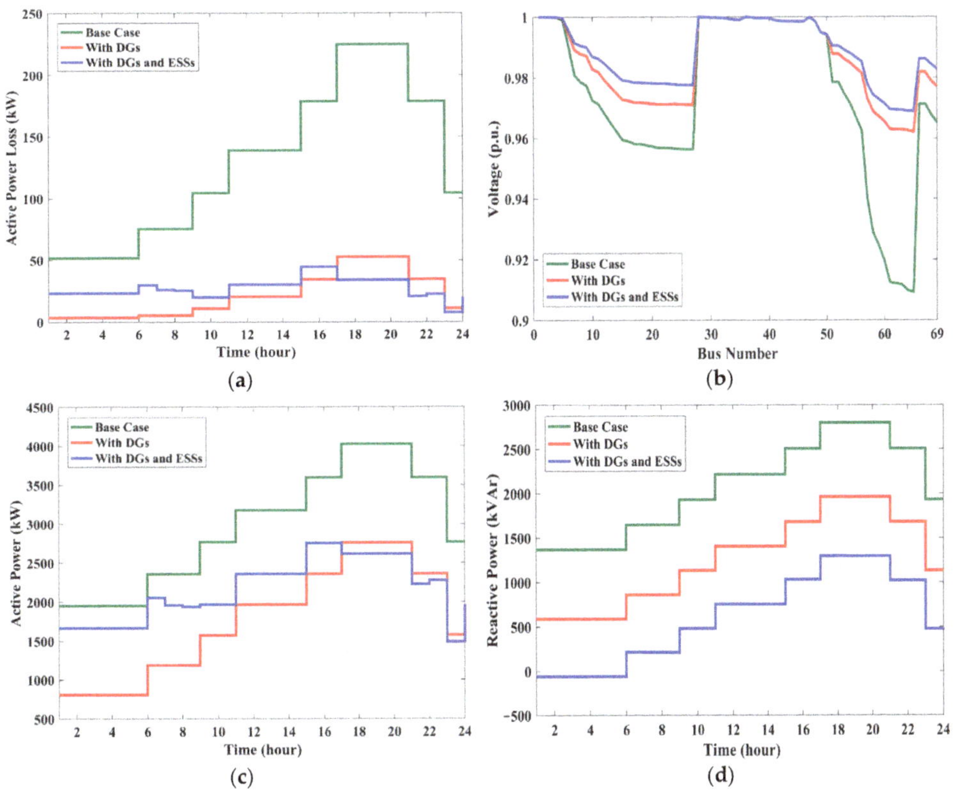

Figure 14. The technical impacts of DGs and ESSs on the 69-Bus network using the OSEDE/LFs: (**a**) Active power loss; (**b**) Voltage profile at Hour 17; (**c**) Active power; and (**d**) Reactive power exchanged with the upstream network.

Similar observations can be made when compared to the results of the 30-Bus network. As shown in Figure 14a, the power losses are well reduced in both cases, especially during the full-load hours. In Case 2, the active power losses are higher during ESS charging hours, and during the discharging hours, the losses are further reduced, which leads to higher profits. Figure 14b illustrates that the voltages of all buses are significantly improved, especially in Case 2. The lowest base-case voltage (on Bus 65) is improved from 0.9092 p.u. to 0.9621 in Case 1 and to 0.9690 p.u. in Case 2. Figure 14c shows the active power exchange with the upstream network using the OSEDE/LFs for Cases 1 and 2. In Case 1, the power received from the upstream network is well reduced compared to the base case. In Case 2, the received power is also reduced compared to the base case, but it is higher than that of Case 1 during the charging and disconnecting hours of the ESSs. From Hour 17, the received power in Case 2 becomes lower than in Case 1. This leads to higher profits due to the difference in energy prices. The reactive power exchange with the upstream network is illustrated in Figure 14d. In Case 1, the DISCO receives less reactive power than in the base case. In Case 2, the reactive power is sold to the upstream network during hours 1 to 6. During the rest of the day, the reactive power received from the upstream network in Case 2 is clearly lower than in Case 1. This is because the ESS is still exchanging reactive power with the network when there is no active power being exchanged. Thus, the DISCO can generate more income through the exchange of higher amounts of reactive power and the reduction of the power received from the upstream network.

6. Conclusions

This paper has addressed the simultaneous planning of DGs and ESSs in deregulated electricity markets for DISCO profit maximization. The revenues from trading active and reactive power have been considered in the optimization model to further improve the accuracy of the results. Meanwhile, the active and reactive power of DGs and ESSs have also been included in the optimization process, which maximizes their utilization in the reactive power support. Thus, the decision variables have been set to be the locations and sizes (active and reactive power) of DGs and ESSs simultaneously. To solve the designated model, a new hybrid EA called the OSEDE/LFs has been proposed based on the recently developed SEO algorithm. The OSEDE/LFs exploits the advantages of the search mechanisms of DE and LFs to improve the performance of SEO by their distinctive combination within the main loop. Furthermore, the initial population of the algorithm is generated using the QOBL technique. The proposed OSEDE/LFs has been benchmarked and compared with the other nine state-of-the-art EAs using a set of well-known BFs. The results obtained for most of the tested BFs have confirmed the outstanding performance of the OSEDE/LFs over the other algorithms in terms of obtaining the global optima, fast convergence, and robustness with the best total and average ranks achieved. Moreover, the Wilcoxon signed rank test has proved the statistical significance of the OSEDE/LFs. Based on this, the proposed algorithm has been applied to solve the planning model of DISCO profit maximization using the standard 30-Bus and IEEE 69-Bus distribution networks. Two case studies have been considered for each network, namely the optimal planning of DGs and the optimal planning of DGs and ESSs simultaneously. For both networks, the maximum DISCO profits with faster convergence and higher robustness have been obtained by the OSEDE/LFs compared to other original algorithms. In addition, by comparing the results of Case 2 with Case 1 for each network, it has been verified that the proposed algorithm maintains its robustness even when the number of decision variables and the search space are increased, especially for the 69-Bus network. The results have also shown that some algorithms, such as the original SEO, may have worse performance as the complexity of the optimization model increases. This has justified the need to improve its performance for complex optimization problems. Thus, the OSEDE/LFs can be recommended as a robust method for solving more complex and larger-scale problems in different engineering applications, which may be promising for future research. Moreover, the comparisons made between Cases 1 and 2 have highlighted the importance of considering the revenues from active and reactive power trading to achieve higher DISCO profits. This has been done by including the active and reactive power of DGs and ESSs in the optimization model, which has remarkably increased the reactive power support. These results have been validated by observing the reduced power losses, improved voltage profile, and power exchanged with the upstream network.

Finally, several potential directions are worthy of investigation in future research, such as including renewable DGs in the planning model, developing an objective function that considers the environmental revenues, and comparing different types of storage systems. For example, the utilization of pumped hydro storage or gravity energy storage in ADNs for DISCO profit optimization could be an interesting trend for further research.

Author Contributions: Conceptualization, R.J.M. and N.F.A.; methodology, R.J.M. and N.F.A.; software, R.J.M. and N.F.A.; validation, R.J.M., N.F.A., E.F.-R., Y.Z. (Yuan Zheng), Y.S., S.Z. and Y.Z. (Yuquan Zhang); formal analysis, R.J.M., N.F.A., E.F.-R. and Y.Z. (Yuquan Zhang); investigation, R.J.M., N.F.A. and Y.Z. (Yuquan Zhang); resources, R.J.M. and Y.Z. (Yuquan Zhang); data curation, R.J.M. and S.Z.; writing—original draft preparation, R.J.M.; writing—review and editing, R.J.M., N.F.A., E.F.-R., Y.Z. (Yuan Zheng), Y.S., S.Z. and Y.Z. (Yuquan Zhang); visualization, R.J.M., N.F.A., E.F.-R. and Y.Z. (Yuquan Zhang); supervision, Y.Z. (Yuan Zheng), Y.S. and Y.Z. (Yuquan Zhang); project administration, Y.Z. (Yuan Zheng), Y.S. and Y.Z. (Yuquan Zhang); funding acquisition, R.J.M., Y.Z. (Yuan Zheng), Y.S. and Y.Z. (Yuquan Zhang). All authors have read and agreed to the published version of the manuscript.

Funding: This research was funded by the Fundamental Research Funds for the Central Universities (No. B220201034), the National Natural Science Foundation of China (No. 52271275), the National Natural Science Foundation of China for Young International Scientists (No. 52250410359), and the 2022 National Young Foreign Talents Program of China (No. QN2022143002L).

Data Availability Statement: Data sharing does not apply to this article as no datasets were generated or analyzed during the current study.

Conflicts of Interest: The authors declare no conflict of interest.

References

1. Zhang, D.; Shafiullah, G.M.; Das, C.K.; Wong, K.W. A systematic review of optimal planning and deployment of distributed generation and energy storage systems in power networks. *J. Energy Storage* **2022**, *56*, 105937. [CrossRef]
2. Prakash, P.; Meena, D.C.; Malik, H.; Alotaibi, M.A.; Khan, I.A. A Novel Hybrid Approach for Optimal Placement of Non-Dispatchable Distributed Generations in Radial Distribution System. *Mathematics* **2021**, *9*, 3171. [CrossRef]
3. Elseify, M.A.; Kamel, S.; Abdel-Mawgoud, H.; Elattar, E.E. A Novel Approach Based on Honey Badger Algorithm for Optimal Allocation of Multiple DG and Capacitor in Radial Distribution Networks Considering Power Loss Sensitivity. *Mathematics* **2022**, *10*, 2081. [CrossRef]
4. Ma, M.; Huang, H.; Song, X.; Peña-Mora, F.; Zhang, Z.; Chen, J. Optimal sizing and operations of shared energy storage systems in distribution networks: A bi-level programming approach. *Appl. Energy* **2022**, *307*, 118170. [CrossRef]
5. Mehrjerdi, H. Simultaneous load leveling and voltage profile improvement in distribution networks by optimal battery storage planning. *Energy* **2019**, *181*, 916–926. [CrossRef]
6. Li, Y.; Feng, B.; Wang, B.; Sun, S. Joint planning of distributed generations and energy storage in active distribution networks: A Bi-Level programming approach. *Energy* **2022**, *245*, 123226. [CrossRef]
7. Xiang, Y.; Lu, Y.; Liu, J. Deep reinforcement learning based topology-aware voltage regulation of distribution networks with distributed energy storage. *Appl. Energy* **2023**, *332*, 120510. [CrossRef]
8. Zhang, Y.; Zang, W.; Zheng, J.; Cappietti, L.; Zhang, J.; Zheng, Y.; Fernandez-Rodriguez, E. The influence of waves propagating with the current on the wake of a tidal stream turbine. *Appl. Energy* **2021**, *290*, 116729. [CrossRef]
9. Das, C.K.; Bass, O.; Mahmoud, T.S.; Kothapalli, G.; Masoum, M.A.S.; Mousavi, N. An optimal allocation and sizing strategy of distributed energy storage systems to improve performance of distribution networks. *J. Energy Storage* **2019**, *26*, 100847. [CrossRef]
10. Adegoke, S.A.; Sun, Y.; Wang, Z. Minimization of Active Power Loss Using Enhanced Particle Swarm Optimization. *Mathematics* **2023**, *11*, 3660. [CrossRef]
11. Anuradha, K.B.J.; Jayatunga, U.; Perera, H.Y.R. Loss-Voltage Sensitivity Analysis Based Battery Energy Storage Systems Allocation and Distributed Generation Capacity Upgrade. *J. Energy Storage* **2021**, *36*, 102357. [CrossRef]
12. Saboori, H.; Hemmati, R.; Abbasi, V. Multistage distribution network expansion planning considering the emerging energy storage systems. *Energy Convers. Manag.* **2015**, *105*, 938–945. [CrossRef]
13. Bai, L.; Jiang, T.; Li, F.; Chen, H.; Li, X. Distributed energy storage planning in soft open point based active distribution networks incorporating network reconfiguration and DG reactive power capability. *Appl. Energy* **2018**, *210*, 1082–1091. [CrossRef]

14. El-Ela, A.A.A.; El-Seheimy, R.A.; Shaheen, A.M.; Wahbi, W.A.; Mouwafi, M.T. PV and battery energy storage integration in distribution networks using equilibrium algorithm. *J. Energy Storage* **2021**, *42*, 103041. [CrossRef]
15. Wang, Y.; Qiu, J.; Tao, Y. Robust energy systems scheduling considering uncertainties and demand side emission impacts. *Energy* **2022**, *239*, 122317. [CrossRef]
16. Zarenia, O.; Shabani, M.J.; Salehpour, M.J.; Zhang, J.; Wang, L. A new two-stage game-based approach for energy storage pricing in radial distribution system considering uncertainty. *J. Energy Storage* **2021**, *38*, 102510. [CrossRef]
17. Saboori, H.; Hemmati, R. Maximizing DISCO profit in active distribution networks by optimal planning of energy storage systems and distributed generators. *Renew. Sustain. Energy Rev.* **2017**, *71*, 365–372. [CrossRef]
18. Sadati, S.M.B.; Moshtagh, J.; Shafie-khah, M.; Rastgou, A.; Catalão, J.P.S. Bi-level model for operational scheduling of a distribution company that supplies electric vehicle parking lots. *Electr. Power Syst. Res.* **2019**, *174*, 105875. [CrossRef]
19. Jeddi, B.; Vahidinasab, V.; Ramezanpour, P.; Aghaei, J.; Shafie-khah, M.; Catalão, J.P.S. Robust optimization framework for dynamic distributed energy resources planning in distribution networks. *Int. J. Electr. Power Energy Syst.* **2019**, *110*, 419–433. [CrossRef]
20. Weckesser, T.; Dominković, D.F.; Blomgren, E.M.V.; Schledorn, A.; Madsen, H. Renewable Energy Communities: Optimal sizing and distribution grid impact of photovoltaics and battery storage. *Appl. Energy* **2021**, *301*, 117408. [CrossRef]
21. Rajabzadeh, M.; Kalantar, M. Improving the resilience of distribution network in coming across seismic damage using mobile battery energy storage system. *J. Energy Storage* **2022**, *52*, 104891. [CrossRef]
22. Khaki, B. Joint sizing and placement of battery energy storage systems and wind turbines considering reactive power support of the system. *J. Energy Storage* **2021**, *35*, 102264. [CrossRef]
23. Thanh Nguyen, T.; Trung Nguyen, T.; Le, B. Artificial ecosystem optimization for optimizing of position and operational power of battery energy storage system on the distribution network considering distributed generations. *Expert Syst. Appl.* **2022**, *208*, 118127. [CrossRef]
24. Abdel-Mawgoud, H.; Fathy, A.; Kamel, S. An effective hybrid approach based on arithmetic optimization algorithm and sine cosine algorithm for integrating battery energy storage system into distribution networks. *J. Energy Storage* **2022**, *49*, 104154. [CrossRef]
25. Mohamed, A.A.; Kamel, S.; Hassan, M.H.; Mosaad, M.I.; Aljohani, M. Optimal Power Flow Analysis Based on Hybrid Gradient-Based Optimizer with Moth–Flame Optimization Algorithm Considering Optimal Placement and Sizing of FACTS/Wind Power. *Mathematics* **2022**, *10*, 361. [CrossRef]
26. Fathollahi-Fard, A.M.; Hajiaghaei-Keshteli, M.; Tavakkoli-Moghaddam, R. The Social Engineering Optimizer (SEO). *Eng. Appl. Artif. Intell.* **2018**, *72*, 267–293. [CrossRef]
27. Pires, V.F.; Pombo, A.V.; Lourenço, J.M. Multi-objective optimization with post-pareto optimality analysis for the integration of storage systems with reactive-power compensation in distribution networks. *J. Energy Storage* **2019**, *24*, 100769. [CrossRef]
28. Saini, P.; Gidwani, L. An investigation for battery energy storage system installation with renewable energy resources in distribution system by considering residential, commercial and industrial load models. *J. Energy Storage* **2022**, *45*, 103493. [CrossRef]
29. Tizhoosh, H.R. Opposition-Based Learning: A New Scheme for Machine Intelligence. In Proceedings of the International Conference on Computational Intelligence for Modelling, Control and Automation and International Conference on Intelligent Agents, Web Technologies and Internet Commerce (CIMCA-IAWTIC'06), Vienna, Austria, 28–30 November 2005; pp. 1–7.
30. Mahfoud, R.J.; Alkayem, N.F.; Sun, Y.; Haes Alhelou, H.; Siano, P.; Parente, M. Improved Hybridization of Evolutionary Algorithms with a Sensitivity-Based Decision-Making Technique for the Optimal Planning of Shunt Capacitors in Radial Distribution Systems. *Appl. Sci.* **2020**, *10*, 1384. [CrossRef]
31. Alkayem, N.F.; Shen, L.; Al-hababi, T.; Qian, X.; Cao, M. Inverse Analysis of Structural Damage Based on the Modal Kinetic and Strain Energies with the Novel Oppositional Unified Particle Swarm Gradient-Based Optimizer. *Appl. Sci.* **2022**, *12*, 11689. [CrossRef]
32. Storn, R.; Price, K. Differential Evolution—A Simple and Efficient Heuristic for Global Optimization over Continuous Spaces. *J. Glob. Optim.* **1997**, *11*, 341–359. [CrossRef]
33. Yang, X.S.; Deb, S. Cuckoo search via Lévy flights. In Proceedings of the 2009 World Congress on Nature & Biologically Inspired Computing (NaBIC), Coimbatore, India, 9–11 December 2009; pp. 210–214.
34. Mirjalili, S.; Mirjalili, S.M.; Hatamlou, A. Multi-Verse Optimizer: A nature-inspired algorithm for global optimization. *Neural Comput. Appl.* **2016**, *27*, 495–513. [CrossRef]
35. Mirjalili, S. SCA: A Sine Cosine Algorithm for solving optimization problems. *Knowl.-Based Syst.* **2016**, *96*, 120–133. [CrossRef]
36. Mirjalili, S. The Ant Lion Optimizer. *Adv. Eng. Softw.* **2015**, *83*, 80–98. [CrossRef]
37. Mirjalili, S. Dragonfly algorithm: A new meta-heuristic optimization technique for solving single-objective, discrete, and multi-objective problems. *Neural Comput. Appl.* **2016**, *27*, 1053–1073. [CrossRef]
38. Saremi, S.; Mirjalili, S.; Lewis, A. Grasshopper Optimisation Algorithm: Theory and application. *Adv. Eng. Softw.* **2017**, *105*, 30–47. [CrossRef]
39. Mirjalili, S.; Mirjalili, S.M.; Lewis, A. Grey Wolf Optimizer. *Adv. Eng. Softw.* **2014**, *69*, 46–61. [CrossRef]
40. Mirjalili, S. Moth-flame optimization algorithm: A novel nature-inspired heuristic paradigm. *Knowl.-Based Syst.* **2015**, *89*, 228–249. [CrossRef]

41. Mirjalili, S.; Gandomi, A.H.; Mirjalili, S.Z.; Saremi, S.; Faris, H.; Mirjalili, S.M. Salp Swarm Algorithm: A bio-inspired optimizer for engineering design problems. *Adv. Eng. Softw.* **2017**, *114*, 163–191. [CrossRef]
42. Mirjalili, S.; Lewis, A. The Whale Optimization Algorithm. *Adv. Eng. Softw.* **2016**, *95*, 51–67. [CrossRef]

mathematics

Article

Numerical Investigation of Wind Flow and Speedup Effect at a Towering Peak Extending out of a Steep Mountainside: Implications for Landscape Platforms

Mohammed Nabil, Fengqi Guo *, Lizhong Jiang, Zhiwu Yu and Qiuliang Long

School of Civil Engineering, Central South University, Changsha 410075, China; monabil@csu.edu.cn (M.N.)
* Correspondence: fengqiguo@csu.edu.cn

Abstract: Wind flow over complex terrain is strongly influenced by the topographical features of the region, resulting in unpredictable local wind characteristics. This paper employs numerical simulation to study the wind flow at a towering peak extending out of a steep mountainside and the wind-induced effect on onsite landscape platforms. First, the wind flow from seven different directions is explored via 3D numerical simulations, and the wind load distribution on the platforms is highlighted. Second, a 2D numerical simulation is conducted to evaluate the wind speedup effect at the side peak, examining the influence of the side peak height and the mountainside steepness on the wind speedup factor. The numerical simulations presented in this research were validated by replicating a published numerical and experimental study. The results illustrate the amplifying and blocking effects of the surrounding topography, yielding unpredictable and nonuniform wind pressure distribution on the platforms. The presence of the side peak leads to a significant increase in the speedup factor, and the side peak height and the mountainside steepness have a moderate influence on the value of the speedup factor. Additionally, the speedup factor obtained from this study varies significantly, especially near the surface, from the recommendations of several wind load standards. Consequently, the impact of the local terrain and the wind speedup effect must be thoroughly assessed to ensure the structural integrity of structures installed at a similar topography.

Keywords: numerical simulation; speedup factor; computational fluid dynamic; complex structure; simulation accuracy

MSC: 74F10; 76F40

Citation: Nabil, M.; Guo, F.; Jiang, L.; Yu, Z.; Long, Q. Numerical Investigation of Wind Flow and Speedup Effect at a Towering Peak Extending out of a Steep Mountainside: Implications for Landscape Platforms. *Mathematics* **2024**, *12*, 467. https://doi.org/10.3390/math12030467

Academic Editor: Sergey Ershkov

Received: 8 January 2024
Revised: 26 January 2024
Accepted: 29 January 2024
Published: 1 February 2024

1. Introduction

The atmospheric boundary layer (ABL) over mountainous regions is significantly affected by the local topography, resulting in its complex behavior. This complexity poses challenges for scientists and engineers who require comprehensive evaluations of the wind field within the relevant terrains. Moreover, this need becomes even more pronounced with the escalating expansion of human projects—such as transportation infrastructures and wind farms—into intricate regions. Over the past few decades, scholars have relied on field measurements to extract local wind data. However, this approach poses certain economic and technical challenges, especially when studying the wind field at a larger scale. Researchers have employed alternative methods, primarily wind tunnel tests and numerical simulations, to overcome these limitations.

Recent significant technological advancements, combined with the constant improvement in computational fluid dynamics (CFD) software, have promoted the utilization of numerical simulations to investigate wind field characteristics over mountainous valleys. Hu et al. [1] numerically studied the wind flow over hilly terrain and proposed a novel turbulence generating method. The numerical simulation successfully predicted the wind field characteristics over realistic hilly terrain and three-dimensional hills with different slopes. Song et al. [2] conducted numerical simulation for the wind field in complex terrain. The results were validated by the wind tunnel test, and it was established that the k-models produced superior predictions to those of other RANS models. Blocken et al. [3] utilized CFD simulation and field measurements to evaluate the wind characteristics in intricate terrains. The results obtained by applying the steady realizable k-ε model show great consistency with the experimental data. Moreira et al. [4] assessed the ability of various RANS turbulence models to simulate airflow over the complex terrain of Askervein Hill accurately. Han et al. [5] proposed a multiscale coupling approach suitable for determining the inlet mean wind speed for numerical simulations of the wind field in mountain gorges. In addition to conducting CFD simulations of wind fields in natural topography, researchers have extensively studied wind flow over typical circular hills [6–9].

The intricate nature of real terrains often subjects the wind flow to a speeding-up effect, a phenomenon that has been extensively discussed by many scholars [10–13]. Flay et al. [14] conducted a comprehensive investigation of the speedup effect in the Belmont Hill region to enhance wind speed predictions. This study involved a comparison of various national wind standards with speedup predictions based on field observations. Chen et al. [15] utilized wind tunnel tests and numerical simulations to assess the speedup effect at the peaks of coastal island mountains, and the influence of the large-scale topography on the speedup effect was highlighted. Pirooz et al. [16] performed numerical simulations for 2D and 3D bell-shaped hills to evaluate the accuracy of speedup multipliers suggested by various wind load standards. The results, validated by a wind tunnel test, revealed certain variations from the recommended values.

Despite abundant research focusing on the wind flow around and through structures on flat surfaces [17–19], understanding the wind-induced effects on structures in complex terrains remains inadequate. Meng et al. [20] conducted a CFD simulation for a tall building with a rectangular section in relatively complex topography. The study revealed significant negative pressure on the building's side surfaces caused by flow separation induced by the front terrain. Han et al. [21] employed numerical simulation to evaluate the impact of surrounding hilly terrain on the wind-induced pressure of a traditional temple within a complex terrain. Lee-Sak et al. [22] conducted wind tunnel tests to assess the influence of terrain complexity on the wind load of low-rise buildings. The experiment also highlighted the effect of terrain roughness on wind flow characteristics such as turbulence intensity.

In the last few decades, the Chinese economy and local individuals' incomes have grown exponentially. This growth led to a significant expansion in the local tourism industry. Many local governments and businesses have capitalized on the local natural features, including hills, waterfalls, and forests, to leverage this growth and attract the largest possible number of visitors. This study presents a comprehensive 3D and 2D simulation investigation of the wind field at a towering peak protruding from a steep mountainside, as depicted in Figure 1. This peak serves as the site for a front butterfly-lookalike landscape platform, which will be connected—via a glass bridge over a narrow col—to a second platform on the mountainside. This platform will hover over the astonishing landscapes of Dajue Mountain, becoming a new tourist attraction and contributing to the region's economic growth.

As ecotourism gains popularity, the emergence of structures in similar locations is expected to increase. Given the limited existing research on the wind loads experienced by complex structures at unique sites, such as towering peaks, a thorough investigation of the local wind field and its impact on structures is highly needed. This research aims to enhance the understanding of the wind flow around architecturally sophisticated structure and analyze the influence of surrounding topography on its behavior. The study provides essential information for designing engineers to ensure the stability of the structure under various wind speeds and directions. Additionally, the research evaluates the speedup effect at the side peak, emphasizing the impact of the side peak height and the mountainside steepness on the speedup factor. The CFD simulation results are compared to the recommendations of several national wind load standards. This investigation holds practical merit and offers valuable guidance for relevant future research. The remainder of this paper is as follows: Section 2 presents numerical simulations of the wind flow over complex terrain, focusing on the impact of the surrounding topography on the platforms wind-induced pressure. Section 3 examines the speedup effect at the side peak and the influence of different side peak heights and mountainside slopes. Section 2 lists the findings of this research.

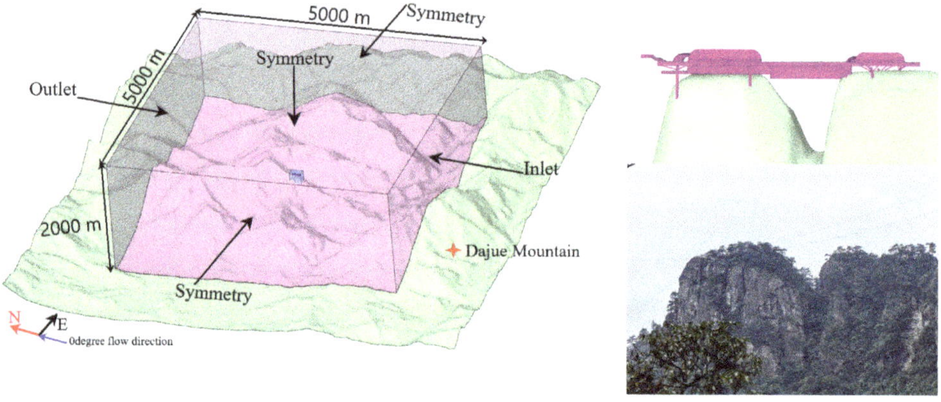

Figure 1. The local topography and 3D model of the computational domain and platforms.

2. 3D Numerical Simulation

2.1. Computational Domain and Flow Directions

The targeted simulation domain is within Dajue Mountain Jiangxi Province, China. The side peak stands at approximately 90 m on the steep mountainside. This towering peak is isolated from the main body of the mountain by a narrow col with a width of 10 m. The steel butterfly-lookalike landscape platforms have maximum dimensions of 60 m in length and 75 m in width. The overall height of the platform is 29 m, and the glass bridge spans a length of 40.5 m, as illustrated in Figure 1.

The model of the local topography of Dajue Mountain was generated using digital elevation model (DEM) data provided by NASA, with a resolution of 12.5 m per pixel. The contour lines of the region were extracted by Global Mapper, and the terrain surface was modeled using Rhinoceros. The platform models were created in Ansys SpaceClaim (2021 R1) based on the provided architectural drawings.

According to available wind field observations, the wind flow mainly blows at high speeds from the south and the west. Furthermore, the mountain body blocks the wind flow from the north, leading to a significant decrease in the wind speed to less than 2 m/s at the platforms site, as shown in Figure 2. Consequently, this study did not investigate the wind flow from the direct north. The other seven wind directions, every 45 degrees, are studied with the initial case (0 degrees) signifying the flow from the south. Additionally, the numerical simulations are conducted on scaled models at a ratio of 1/100.

2.2. Mesh Arrangement

Mesh settings highly influence the wind field numerical simulation results, and poor mesh quality could prevent the convergence of the solution. To address this, scholars have introduced various meshing guidelines, including the aerodynamic roughness suggested by Blocken et al. [23]. In this context, the aerodynamic roughness of the terrain surface is represented by an equivalent sand grain size k_S, and the height of the first mesh layer cannot be less than 6 m, according to Equation (1).

$$k_s = \frac{9.793 z_0}{C_s} \tag{1}$$

$$k_s = 29.6z_0 \tag{2}$$

where $z_0 = 0.05$ is the roughness height, and $C_s = 0.16$ is the roughness constant according to the Chinese wind resistance code [24].

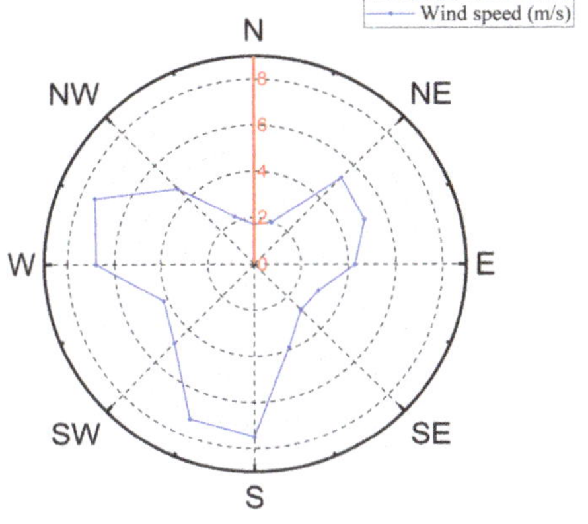

Figure 2. Mean wind speed and direction.

Currently, researchers are utilizing several software and tools, such as Gambit and Ansys ICEM tool, to generate mesh for wind field numerical simulation. However, due to the geometric complexity of the landscape platforms and the natural terrain, Ansys (Fluent meshing) (2021 R1) was used to generate the mesh, and the poly-hexacore mesh type was chosen, as shown in Figure 3. Selecting an appropriate mesh arrangement is a repetitive process that takes into account the simulation equality and calculation time requirements. In this study, a grid independence test was conducted to select the ideal mesh scheme, and three approaches with total mesh cell numbers of 11.0, 16.7, and 23.2 million were examined. The test showed that the maximum wind speed difference of the three schemes at the front platform was only 2.64%, as illustrated in Figure 4. Consequently, the second scheme with 16.7 million mesh cells was applied for the subsequent simulations. In this grid arrangement, the inner domain surrounding the platforms has a maximum cell length of 1 m, and the entire simulation domain has mesh cells with minimum and maximum lengths of 0.1 m and 50 m, respectively. This wide mesh size range ensures that the minor details of complex geometry are captured while keeping the calculation time manageable.

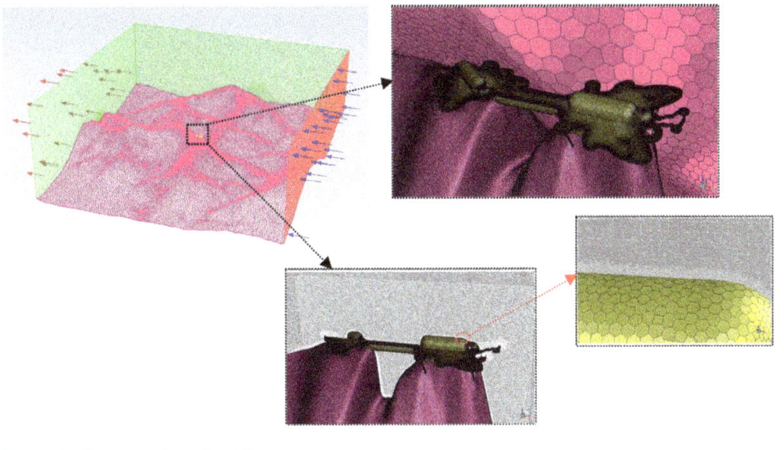

Figure 3. Computational grid.

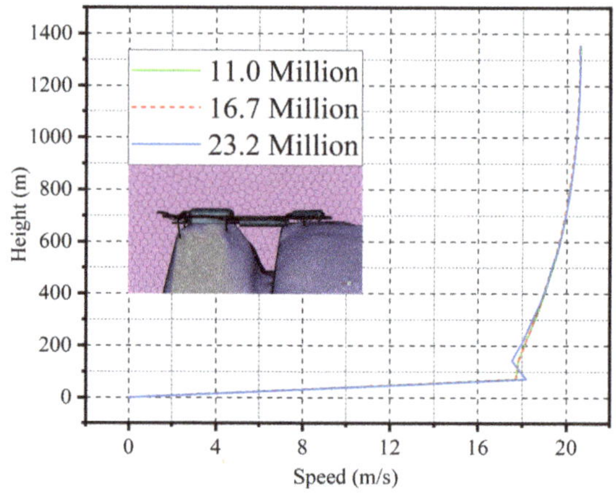

Figure 4. Mesh independency test.

2.3. Atmosphere Boundary Layer and Boundary Conditions

The atmospheric boundary layer (ABL) numerical simulation has been of great interest to researchers, and the currently common approaches involve wall-shear-driven and pressure-driven models. However, since the wind flow within the ABL is generated primarily through differences in regional atmospheric pressure, many scholars have utilized pressure-driven models to simulate the airflow over natural topographies. Additionally, the accuracy of this approach in predicting wind field characteristics in complex terrains has been validated via comparisons with wind tunnel tests and field measurements [16]. This study utilized the pressure-driven mathematical model developed by Deaves and Harris [25] as follows:

$$U(z) = \frac{u^*}{\kappa}\left(\ln\left(\frac{z}{z_0}\right) + 5.75\left(\frac{z}{h}\right) - 1.875\left(\frac{z}{h}\right)^2 - 1.333\left(\frac{z}{h}\right)^3 + 0.25\left(\frac{z}{h}\right)^4\right) \quad (3)$$

where u^* is the fraction velocity, $\kappa = 0.4$ is the Von Karman constant, h is the gradient height, and f is the Coriolis parameter.

$$h = \frac{u^*}{6f} \quad (4)$$

The turbulence model applied in this research is the (k-ε; Realizable) model, and the inlet profile is defined according to Richards and Norris [26] as follows:

$$U(z) = \frac{u^*}{\kappa}\left(\ln\left(\frac{z}{z_0}\right) + C_{U1}\left(\frac{z}{H}\right) + C_{U2}\left(\frac{z}{H}\right)^2 + C_{U3}\left(\frac{z}{H}\right)^3 + C_{U4}\left(\frac{z}{H}\right)^4\right) \quad (5)$$

$$k(z) = u^{*2}\left(C_{k1} + C_{k2}\left(1 - \frac{z}{H}\right)^2 + C_{k3}\left(1 - \frac{z}{H}\right)^4 + C_{k4}\left(1 - \frac{z}{H}\right)^6\right) \quad (6)$$

$$\varepsilon(z) = \frac{C_\mu k(z)^2}{\kappa u^* z}\left(1 + (1 + C_{U1})\left(\frac{z}{H}\right) + (1 + C_{U1} + 2C_{U2})\left(\frac{z}{H}\right)^2 + (1 + C_{U1} + 2C_{U2} + 3C_{U3})\left(\frac{z}{H}\right)^3\right) \quad (7)$$

$$\tau = \rho u^{*2} \quad (8)$$

where $U(z)$ is the wind speed, $k(z)$ is the turbulence kinetic energy, $\varepsilon(z)$ is the turbulence dissipation rate, τ is the wall shear stress, and $\rho = 1.225$ kg m^{-3} is the air density. The values of the constants mentioned in Equations (5)–(7) were previously calculated by Richards and Norris [26].

The symmetry boundary condition is assigned to the top and side surfaces, and the pressure outlet boundary condition with zero-gauge pressure is applied at the outlet of the domain. The terrain's surface and platforms are selected as no-slip walls, and the surface roughness of the terrain due to the vegetation cover is represented by the corresponding wall function parameters k_S and C_S, as in Equation (1). This method simulates the impact of the forest on the airflow development throughout the domain by altering the surface initial roughness length z_0 with the equivalent sand grain size roughness height k_S. Additionally, this approach is widely applied by researchers, and has produced high-quality wind numerical simulations [3]. Furthermore, the scalable wall function is applied to the terrain surface to ensure the accuracy of the near-ground wind simulation. The airflow simulated in this study maintains the initial settings of Ansys Fluent, with a density of 1.225 kg m^{-3}. The simulation convergence criteria were set to 1×10^{-6}, and the solution reached stability within 5000 steps.

2.4. Results

The results obtained from the 3D numerical simulation conducted using Ansys Fluent (2021 R1) are presented in this section, and the impact of the local terrain on the wind-induced effects on the platforms is highlighted.

2.4.1. Platforms Wind-Induced Effects

The platforms' wind-induced pressure resulting from the wind flow from seven different directions is depicted in Figure 5 and Figure 7. The figures show that the sides of the platform facing the wind flow direction experience significant pressure and lifting forces. This effect is particularly evident in Cases 5 and 6, where the wind-induced positive pressure reaches a maximum value of approximately 750 Pa. This is attributed to the relatively open topography of the western and northwestern regions of the terrain. As in Case 6, the wind flow experienced a speeding-up effect by the relatively shorter mountain in the west. In Case 7, the northwestern mountains redirected the wind flow toward the side peak, resulting in higher wind pressure. However, due to the shading effect of the mountains in the northeast direction (Case 4), the platforms, especially the one on the mountainside, were subjected to a significant negative wind pressure. This pressure results from the large vortex formed behind the mountains, attempting to lift the platforms off their bases.

Due to the complex shape of the landscape platforms and the unique installation location, a towering peak, the wind flow undergoes critical separation, resulting in local vortices, as depicted in Figure 6. The figure illustrates the wind flow streamlines from the west (Case 6) and northwest directions (Case 6). As can be seen, the wind flow from the west separates around the edges and domes of the platforms, creating small vortices. These vortices led to the nonuniform distribution of wind pressure on the platforms and the appearance of negative pressure. Furthermore, as the wind flow reattached, a positive wind pressure occurred on the other side of the platforms. This force distribution, coupled with the lifting forces resulting from the upwards redirected wind flow, imposes a significant torsional wind load on the platforms. This torsional effect threatens the structural stability of such lightweight metal structures, and under extreme weather conditions, this may cause uplift or detachment of the platforms' wings. Additionally, the glass bridge connecting the two platforms appears to be more susceptible to damage, and wind-induced vibrations may occur.

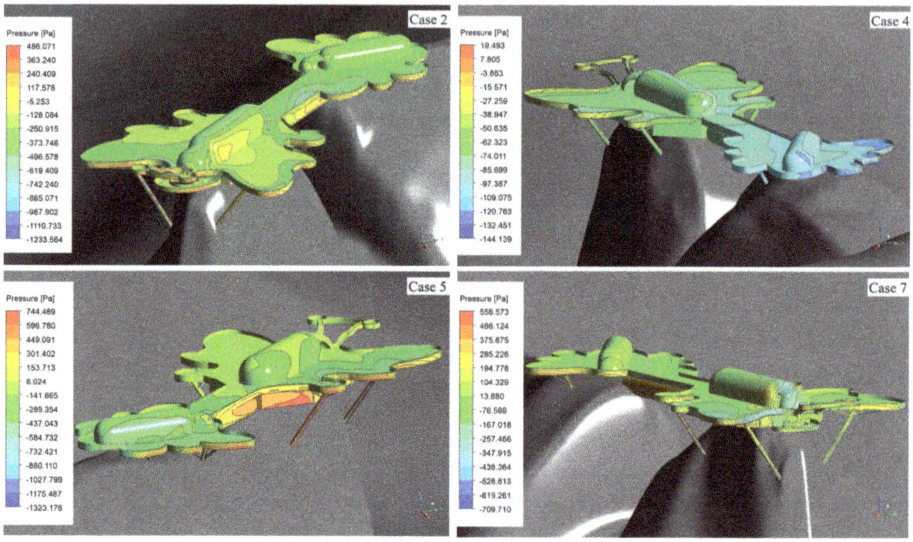

Figure 5. Platforms' mean surface pressure for Cases 2, 4, 5, and 7.

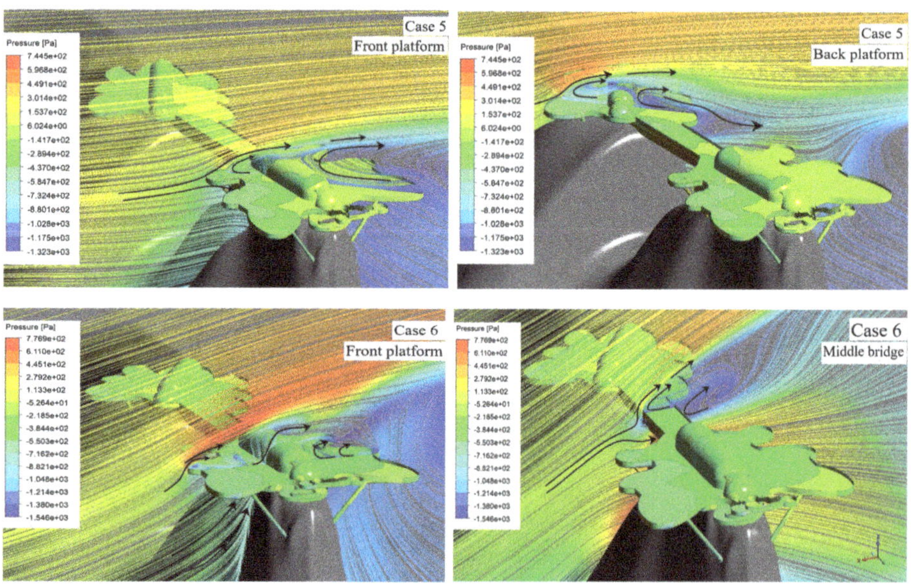

Figure 6. Streamlines of mean velocity for Cases 5 and 6.

2.4.2. Effect of Local Topography

The complex terrain surrounding the landscape platforms significantly influences the approaching airflow and plays a crucial role in determining the wind-induced effects on the structure. To closely examine the local topography effect, additional numerical simulations of the wind flow from the front and two sides of platforms on a plain surface were conducted. Furthermore, the same domain boundary conditions and mesh settings used for the real terrain are applied in these CFD simulations. The numerical simulation results of the wind flow over the real terrain and the plain surface are shown in Figure 7.

The figure demonstrates the substantial amplifying effect imposed by the local topography on the platforms' wind-induced pressure. The wind pressure shows a significant increase, reaching over five times that of the plain surface, particularly in Case 1 and Case 6, where the relatively open area of the terrain provides an unobstructed path for the speedup effect to occur. The following section extensively investigates the speedup effect at the site of the front platform under Case 1, and the findings predicted a speedup factor near the surface of around three. This threefold increase in the wind speed at the side peak is close to the observed pressure increase of around 3.5 times on the front face of the platform. This conclusion highlights the accuracy of the wind speedup effect predictions provided by the second half of this study.

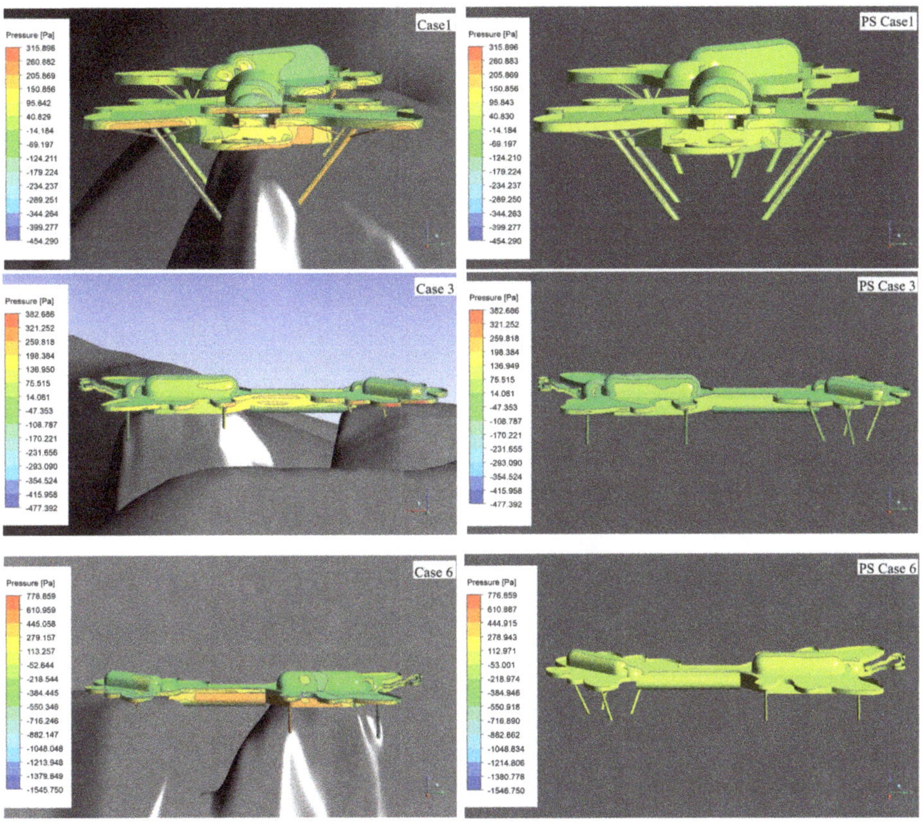

Figure 7. Platforms' mean surface pressure for Cases 1, 3, and 6.

Furthermore, the comparison reveals significant variations in the distribution of negative wind pressure, resulting in lifting and torsional forces. Therefore, a thorough evaluation of the wind behavior and the effect of the surrounding topography is highly recommended when undertaking construction projects or installing wind turbines at similar sites. Failing to do so may result in structural failure, especially under intense weather conditions and powerful storms.

3. Wind Speedup Effect

3.1. Wind Load Standards and Speedup Effect

The wind speedup factor refers to the ratio of the wind speed at a certain height above the hill or escarpment to the wind speed at the same height on flat ground. The wind speedup factor has proven essential in determining the wind load on structures in complex terrains. According to the previous investigation, the speedup phenomenon resulting from the local topography could significantly amplify the wind load on local structures, potentially causing unpredictable structural damage.

Many national wind load standards have addressed the wind speedup effect by introducing a topographic multiplier and developing straightforward mathematical approaches to calculating this multiplier. These calculations consider various factors, such as the height of the hill/escarpment and the horizontal distance from the hill's peak to the targeted hillside location. More explicit details regarding the calculation process can be found in the listed references. This study compares the speedup factor at the side peak obtained from 2D numerical simulations under different side peak heights (90 and 135 m) and mountainside slopes (0.2, 0.31, and 0.5), with the topography multipliers suggested by four wind load standards, namely AS/NZS 1170.2 (2021) [27], NBC-2020 [28], BS-EN (2005–2010) [29,30], and ASCE-7 (2022) [31].

3.2. Computational Domain and Grid

The mountain profile used for this simulation represents a vertical section at the side peak of the 3D model of the actual topography of Dajue Mountain, as shown in Figure 6. Furthermore, the mountain extends upwind to the valley's lowest point at 2185 m from the mountain peak. The overall height of the mountain is 685 m, and the side peak extends 90 m from the mountainside. Additionally, the front mountain, located over 2800 m from the side peak, was omitted and treated as a flat surface. This prevents the possible blocking effect of the distant mountain, which could disturb the wind flow and divert the results. As the backside of the mountain is not considered in this simulation, nor does it affect the speedup factor at the side peak, it was replaced by the Witozinsky transition curve [32] and positioned 720 m from the mountain peak. The dimensions of the computational domain are shown in Figure 8, and the scale ratio of the simulation model is 25:100.

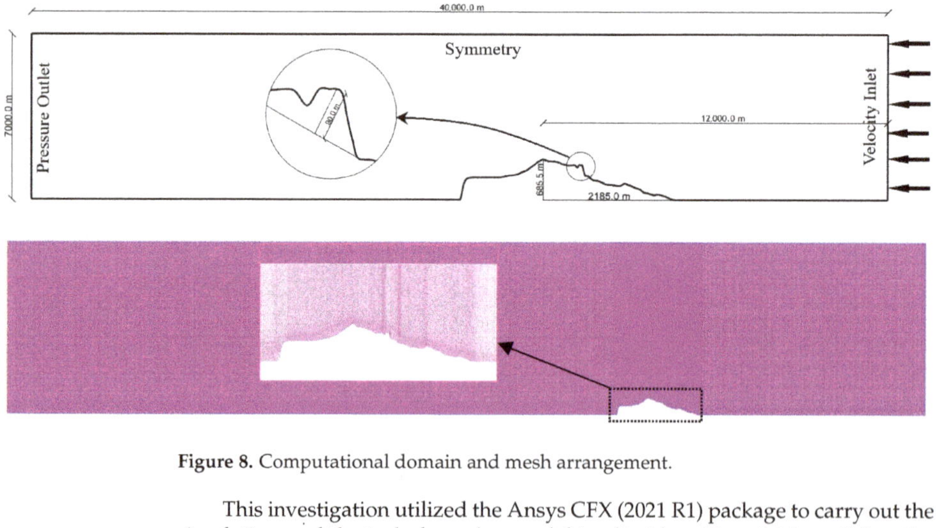

Figure 8. Computational domain and mesh arrangement.

This investigation utilized the Ansys CFX (2021 R1) package to carry out the numerical simulation, and the turbulence k-ε model (realizable with scalable wall functions) and the inlet profile defined by Equations (5)–(7) were applied. Furthermore, a zero-gauge pressure outlet boundary condition was assigned to the domain outlet, and the symmetry boundary condition was applied to the top boundary. As for the ground, the equivalent roughness height $k_S = 1.5$ and roughness constant $C_S = 0.16$ were applied with scalable wall function treatment to reflect the realistic aerodynamic resistance of the terrain vegetation cover, as shown in Equation (2).

Due to the relative simplicity of the 2D mountain profile, the Ansys ICEM (2021 R1) meshing tool was utilized to generate the structure mesh, as shown in Figure 8. Furthermore, the mesh arrangement had a first layer height of 3 m and a maximum cell length of 10 m.

3.3. Numerical Simulation Validation

The boundary conditions and turbulence model applied in this study were also utilized in the wind tunnel and numerical simulation study by Pirooz et al. [16]. This study examined the speedup effect at a bell-shaped hill under varying slopes. The reliability of the current CFD simulations was validated by replicating the published study (Pirooz et al. [16]), and the obtained results were compared with the original ones, as shown in Figure 9. The results show that the wind speedup factor from the conducted simulation (blue line) is almost identical to the published result, with a maximum difference of 5.4% occurring below 1.5 m in height. This highlights the accuracy of the numerical simulations presented in the following discussion.

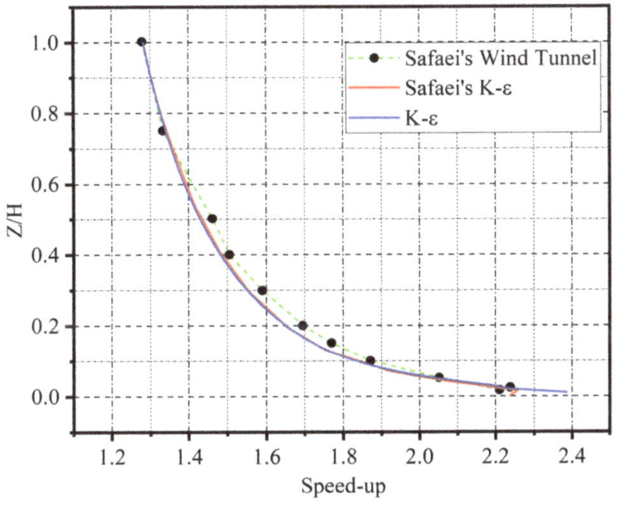

Figure 9. Validation of the numerical simulation accuracy.

A noticeable reduction in the inlet wind velocity and turbulence profile of numerical simulations that employ the k-ε model was reported by Hargreaves et al. [33]. This phenomenon could occur even prior to the presence of an obstacle. To ensure that this did not affect the findings reached in this study, a numerical simulation for the same domain was conducted before introducing the mountain profile, and the homogenous development of the wind field throughout the CFD domain was evaluated. The results demonstrate an evident consistency of the wind velocity, turbulence kinetic energy (TKE), and turbulence dissipation rate throughout the domain, as shown in Figure 10. Furthermore, an insignificant variation in the TKE profile emerged as the flow developed, and the maximum value of divergence was around 3.27% which decreased as the height increased.

3.4. 2D Numerical Simulation Results

3.4.1. Wind Profile at the Side Peak

The wind speed profile at the side peak extending from the mountainside is plotted in Figure 11. The figure shows the influence of the present side peak, with different heights, on the wind speed. The plot illustrates that the incoming wind flow from the inlet experiences a speeding-up effect due to the mountain, without the side peak, reaching 9.5% at a height of 100 m (black line). However, the presence of the extending side peak amplified this effect to 28.5% and 37.3% for the 90 and 135 m high side peaks at 10 m above the top, respectively. This significant increase in wind speed critically enhances the wind influence and loads on structures at such a site. Additionally, the speedup factor extracted from the 3D simulation, which includes the entire realistic topography of Dajue Mountain, is compared with the results from the 2D simulation. The calculation shows a maximum difference of around 10% between the two, which falls to 7% under a height of 200 m. Considering the variations that may occur due to the surrounding topography and the minor differences in results between Ansys Fluent and Ansys CFX, maximum variations of 10% and 7% verify the accuracy of the 3D numerical simulations conducted in Section 2.

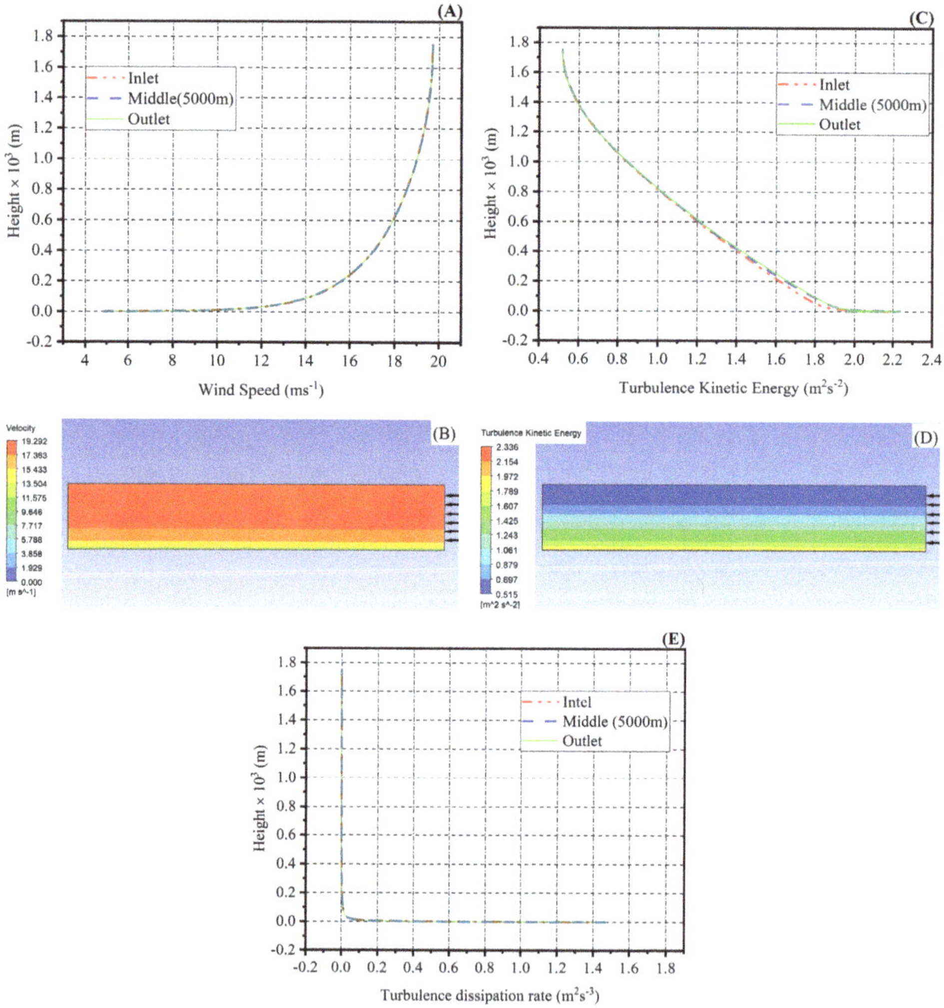

Figure 10. Horizontal homogeneity of the ABL: (**A**) wind speed; (**B**) wind speed development through empty domain; (**C**) TKE; (**D**) TKE development through empty domain; (**E**) turbulence dissipation rate.

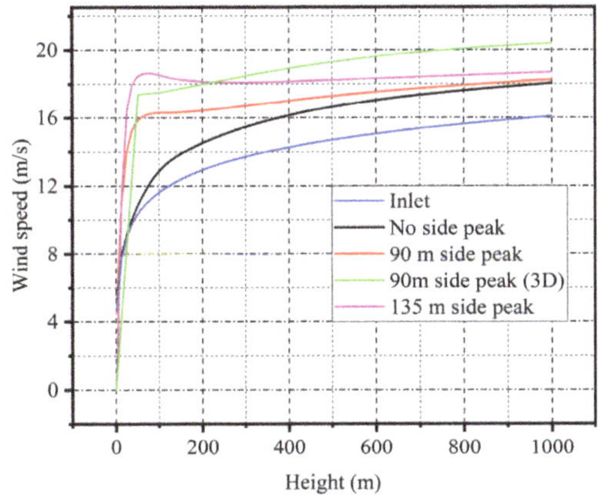

Figure 11. Wind speed profile for different height side peaks.

3.4.2. Speedup Effect at the Mountain Peak

The ability of different wind load standards to predict the speedup effect at the mountain peak is evaluated via comparison with the numerical simulation findings, as shown in Figure 12. The result reveals significant variations between the numerically obtained speedup factors and the recommendations, especially under 50 m high. However, the speedup factor predictions of the ASCE (2022) and AS/NZ (2021) standards over 50 m closely agree with the simulation result.

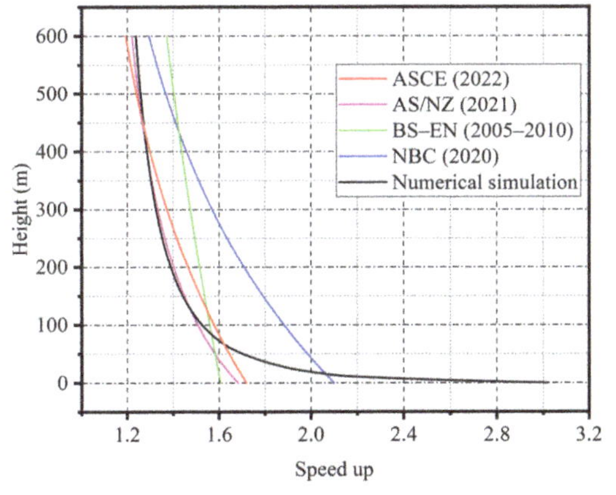

Figure 12. Speedup profile at the mountain peak.

3.4.3. Effect of Different Mountainside Slopes

The mountainside slope directly affects the wind speedup phenomenon, especially near the mountain surface. Figure 13 compares the speedup factor at the position of the side peak after being replaced with a straight line of the same mountain slope under three different slopes; 0.2, 0.31 (original slope), and 0.5. The result shows that under around 25 m, the speedup effect decreases and then surges again; this occurred due to the presence of the short crest before the measurement position, which causes a shading effect.

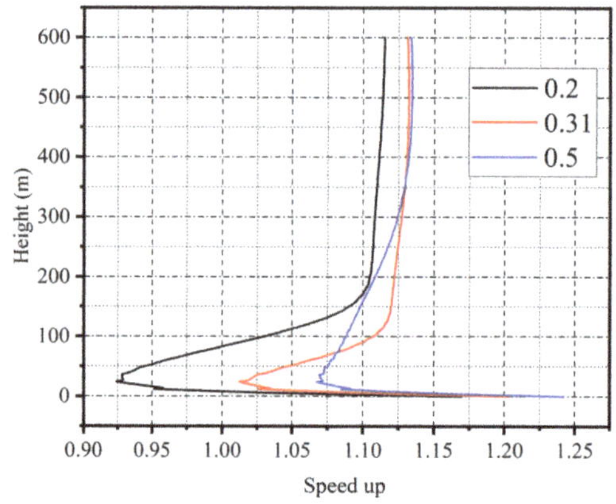

Figure 13. Speedup profile for different mountainside steepness.

Additionally, the difference in the speedup effect of various slopes did not surpass 14% and diminished as the height increased.

3.4.4. Effect of Different Side Peak Heights

Another factor that significantly affects the occurrence of a speedup effect is the presence and height of the side peak. The effects of various side peak heights under different mountainside slopes are plotted in Figure 14. The plots illustrate the significant impact of the side peak on the speedup factor, which led to an increase of approximately 60% near the surface. Additionally, as the height of the side peak increased by 45 m, the speedup factor increased by about 10%. Furthermore, the impact of the side peak on the speedup factor diminishes as the mountainside slope increases. This is attributed to the overall speeding effect caused by the mountain, which, under a certain height, increases with the mountainside slope. This overall speeding effect reduces the significance of the local speedup effect by the side peak.

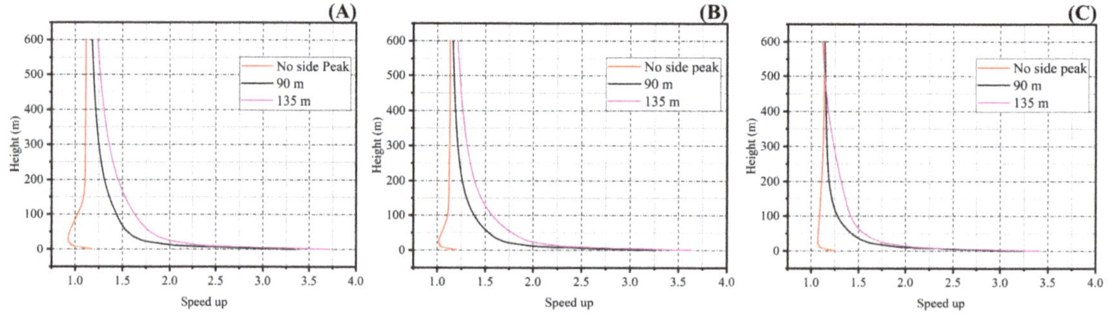

Figure 14. Speedup profile of different side peak heights with various mountainside slopes: (**A**) 0.2; (**B**) 0.31; (**C**) 0.5.

3.4.5. Comparison with Different National Wind Load Standards

The wind speedup factors obtained from the numerical simulation and the recommendations of various wind load specifications are compared in Figure 15. The figure illustrates the speedup effect of the 90 and 135 m high side peaks with different mountainside slopes.

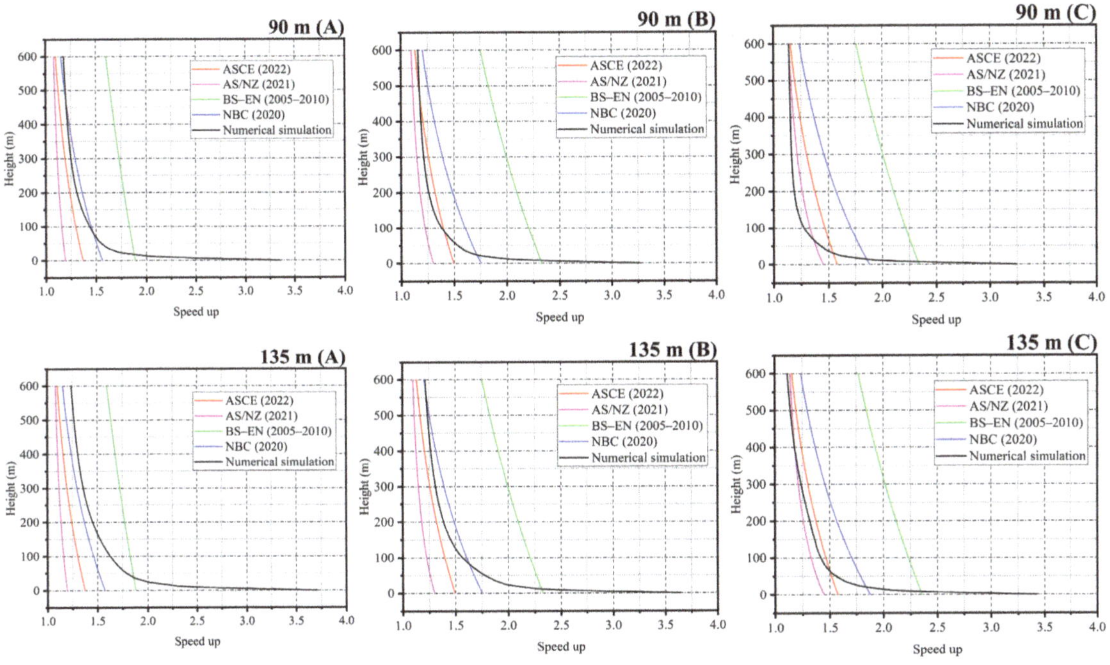

Figure 15. Comparison between the speedup effect of CFD and various national wind load codes under different mountainside slopes: (**A**) 0.2; (**B**) 0.31; (**C**) 0.5.

It is evident that the speedup factor suggested by the standards differs significantly from the simulation results, especially near the peak. Furthermore, apart from BS-EN (2005–2010), these variations diminish with increasing height. Therefore, a thorough evaluation of the wind speedup effect is highly recommended when installing structures at a similar topography. Otherwise, this may result in an unpredictable increase in wind loads, leading to structural damage or, in extreme cases, posing a threat to the safety of occupants or visitors.

4. Conclusions

Numerical simulations have been conducted to investigate the wind flow at a side peak extending out of a mountainside in intricate terrain, where landscape platforms will be installed. The k-e turbulence model was utilized to simulate the wind flow from seven different directions and to evaluate the resulting platforms' wind-induced pressure. This study examined the speedup effect at the towering peak, and the influence of different peak heights and mountainside slopes was explored. The major conclusions of this study are drawn as follows:

- The landscape platforms at the side peak experienced complex patterns of wind pressure due to the influence of surrounding topography, including amplifying and blocking, on the wind and the flow separation around the platforms. This nonuniform wind pressure generates critical torsional and lifting forces that could threaten the structural stability of the platforms.
- The complex terrain substantially amplified the platforms' wind-induced pressure, which in some cases, reached 3.5 times that of when the structure was on flat ground. Therefore, it is crucial to thoroughly evaluate and address this amplifying effect during the design process of structures at such topography, especially lightweight steel structures with complex geometries.

- The investigation of the speedup effect at the towering peak showed that the presence of the peak significantly magnified the speedup effect by approximately 60%, and the variation in the peak height and mountainside steepness has a moderate impact (around 10%) on the resulting speedup factor.
- A comparison of the numerically obtained speedup factor at the side peak and the recommendations of several wind load standards revealed significant variations, especially near the surface. Consequently, further attention should be given to the speedup effect of the actual topography to ensure the accurate assessment of the additional wind load essential for the onsite structure wind resistance design.

Author Contributions: Conceptualization, M.N. and G.F; methodology, M.N.; software, M.N.; validation, L.J. and Z.Y.; formal analysis, M.N.; resources, F.G.; writing—original draft preparation, M.N.; writing—review and editing, M.N. and F.G.; visualization, M.N. and Q.L.; supervision, F.G.; project administration, Q.L. and L.J.; funding acquisition, F.G. and Z.Y. All authors have read and agreed to the published version of the manuscript.

Funding: This research was funded by Zhuzhou CRRCTK under project No: 738011925, focused on the development of the Monorail Elevated Steel Structure Rapid Transit System.

Data Availability Statement: Data will be made available on request.

Conflicts of Interest: The authors affirm that they do not possess any known conflicting financial interests or personal relationships that could have potentially influence the findings presented in this study.

References

1. Hu, W.; Yang, Q.; Chen, H.P.; Yuan, Z.; Li, C.; Shao, S.; Zhang, J. Wind field characteristics over hilly and complex terrain in turbulent boundary layers. *Energy* **2021**, *224*, 120070. [CrossRef]
2. Song, J.; Li, J.W.; Flay, R.G.J.; Pirooz, A.A.S.; Fu, J.Y. Validation and application of pressure-driven RANS approach for wind parameter predictions in mountainous terrain. *J. Wind Eng. Ind. Aerodyn.* **2023**, *240*, 105483. [CrossRef]
3. Blocken, B.; Hout, A.; Dekker, J.; Weiler, O. CFD simulation of wind flow over natural complex terrain: Case study with validation by field measurements for Ria de Ferrol, Galicia, Spain. *J. Wind Eng. Ind. Aerodyn.* **2015**, *147*, 43–57. [CrossRef]
4. Moreira, G.A.; Dos Santos, A.A.; Do Nascimento, C.A.; Valle, R.M. Numerical study of the neutral atmospheric boundary layer over complex terrain. *Boundary-Layer Meteorol.* **2012**, *143*, 393–407. [CrossRef]
5. Han, Y.; Lian, S.; Xu, G.; Cai, C.S.; Hu, P.; Zhang, J. Multiscale simulation of wind field on a long-span bridge site in mountainous area. *J. Wind Eng. Ind. Aerodyn.* **2018**, *177*, 260–274. [CrossRef]
6. Chen, X.; Liu, Z.; Wang, X.; Chen, Z.; Xiao, H.; Zhou, J. Experimental and Numerical Investigation of Wind Characteristics over Mountainous Valley Bridge Site Considering Improved Boundary Transition Sections. *Appl. Sci.* **2020**, *10*, 751. [CrossRef]
7. Liu, Z.; Ishihara, T.; Tanaka, T.; He, X. LES study of turbulent flow fields over a smooth 3-D hill and a smooth 2-D ridge. *J. Wind Eng. Ind. Aerodyn.* **2016**, *153*, 1–12. [CrossRef]
8. Abdi, D.; Bitsuamlak, G.T. Wind flow simulations on idealized and real complex terrain using various turbulence models. *Adv. Eng. Softw.* **2014**, *75*, 30–41. [CrossRef]
9. Yan, S.; Shi, S.; Chen, X.; Wang, X.; Mao, L.; Liu, X. Numerical simulations of flow interactions between steep hill terrain and large scale wind turbine. *Energy* **2018**, *153*, 740–747. [CrossRef]
10. Cunden, T.S.M.; Doorga, J.; Lollchund, M.R.; Rughooputh, S.D.D.V. Multi-level constraints wind farms siting for a complex terrain in a tropical region using MCDM approach coupled with GIS. *Energy* **2020**, *211*, 118533. [CrossRef]
11. Miller, C.; Gibbons, M.; Beatty, K.; Boissonnade, A. Topographic Speed-Up Effects and Observed Roof Damage on Bermuda following Hurricane Fabian (2003). *WAF* **2013**, *28*, 159–174. [CrossRef]
12. Conan, B.; Chaudhari, A.; Aubrun, S.; Beeck, J.V.; Hamalainen, J.; Hellsten, A. Experimental and Numerical Modelling of Flow over Complex Terrain: The Bolund Hill. *Boundary-Layer Meteorol.* **2016**, *158*, 183–208. [CrossRef]
13. Parkinson, D.D.; Pirooz, A.A.S.; Flay, R.G.J. Investigation of Speed-up in Atmospheric Boundary Layer Flow Over Two-dimensional Complex Terrain. In Proceedings of the 21st Australasian Fluid Mechanics Conference, Adelaide, Australia, 10–13 December 2018.
14. Flay, R.G.J.; King, A.B.; Revell, M.; Carpenter, P.; Turner, R.; Cenek, P.; Pirooz, A.A.S. Wind speed measurements and predictions over Belmont Hill, Wellington, New Zealand. *J. Wind Eng. Ind. Aerodyn.* **2019**, *195*, 104018. [CrossRef]
15. Chen, F.; Wang, W.; Gu, Z.; Zhu, Y.; Li, Y.; Shu, Z. Investigation of hilly terrain wind characteristics considering the interference effect. *J. Wind Eng. Ind. Aerodyn.* **2023**, *241*, 105543. [CrossRef]
16. Pirooz, A.A.S.; Flay, R.G.J. Comparison of Speed-Up Over Hills Derived from Wind-Tunnel Experiments, Wind-Loading Standards, and Numerical Modelling. *Boundary-Layer Meteorol.* **2018**, *168*, 213–246. [CrossRef]

17. Zhao, Y.; Li, R.; Feng, L.; Wu, Y.; Niu, J.; Gao, N. Boundary layer wind tunnel tests of outdoor airflow field around urban buildings: A review of methods and status. *Renew. Sust. Energ. Rev.* **2022**, *167*, 112717. [CrossRef]
18. Ricci, A.; Burlando, M.; Freda, A.; Repetto, M.P. Wind tunnel measurements of the urban boundary layer development over a historical district in Italy. *Build. Environ.* **2017**, *111*, 192–206. [CrossRef]
19. Shi, L.; Tao, L.; Zhang, Y.; Li, Y.; Jiang, X.; Yang, Z.; Qi, X.; Qiu, J. CFD simulations of wind-driven rain on typical football stadium configurations in China's hot-summer and cold-winter zone. *Build. Environ.* **2022**, *225*, 109598. [CrossRef]
20. Meng, M.; Tamura, T.; Katsumura, A.; Fugo, Y. LES application to wind pressure prediction for tall building on complex terrain. *J. Wind Eng. Ind. Aerodyn.* **2023**, *242*, 105582. [CrossRef]
21. Han, Y.; Chun, Q.; Xu, X.; Teng, Q.; Dong, Y.; Lin, Y. Wind effects on Chinese traditional timber buildings in complex terrain: The case of Baoguo Temple. *J. Build. Eng.* **2022**, *59*, 105088. [CrossRef]
22. An, L.; Jung, S. Experimental investigation on influence of terrain complexity for wind pressure of low-rise building. *J. Build. Eng.* **2024**, *83*, 108350. [CrossRef]
23. Blocken, B.; Stathopoulos, T.; Carmeliet, J. CFD simulation of the atmospheric boundary layer: Wall function problems. *Atmos. Environ.* **2007**, *41*, 238–252. [CrossRef]
24. *JTG/T 3360-01*; Wind-Resistant Design Specification for Highway Bridges. Ministry of Communications of PRC: Beijing, China, 2018.
25. Deaves, D.M.; Harris, R.I. *A Mathematical Model of the Structure of Strong Winds*; Construction Industry Research and Information Association: London, UK, 1978; Report 76.
26. Richards, P.J.; Norris, S.E. Appropriate boundary conditions for a pressure driven boundary layer. *J. Wind Eng. Ind. Aerodyn.* **2015**, *142*, 43–52. [CrossRef]
27. *AS/NZS1170.2*; Australia/New Zealand Standard, Structural Design Actions, Part 2: Wind Actions, 3d ed. Standards Australia Limited/the Crown in Right of New Zealand: Sydney, New Zealand, 2021; pp. 30–40.
28. *NR24-28-2018*; National Building Code of Canada, volume 1, 15th ed. National Research Council of Canada (NRC): Ottawa, ON, Canada, 2020; 4-32/33.
29. *EN 1991-1-4 (2005) (English)*; Eurocode 1: Actions on Structures–General Actions–Part 1-4: Wind Actions. European Committee for Standardization (CEN): Brussels, Belgium, 2004; pp. 97–102.
30. *BS NA EN 1991-1-4 (2010) (English)*; UK National Annex to Eurocode 1. Actions on Structures. General Actions. Wind Actions. British Standards Institution (BSI): London, UK, 2008; p. 21.
31. *ASCE/SEI 7-22*; Minimum Design Loads and Associated Criteria for Buildings and Other Structures. American Society of Civil Engineers: Reston, Virginia, 2022; pp. 275–277.
32. Wang, Z.; Zou, Y.; Yue, P.; He, X.; Liu, L.; Luo, X. Effect of Topography Truncation on Experimental Simulation of Flow over Complex Terrain. *Appl. Sci.* **2022**, *12*, 2477. [CrossRef]
33. Hargreaves, D.M.; Wright, N.G. On the use of the k–ε model in commercial CFD software to model the neutral atmospheric boundary layer. *J. Wind Eng. Ind. Aerodyn.* **2007**, *95*, 355–369. [CrossRef]

MDPI
St. Alban-Anlage 66
4052 Basel
Switzerland
www.mdpi.com

Mathematics Editorial Office
E-mail: mathematics@mdpi.com
www.mdpi.com/journal/mathematics

www.ingramcontent.com/pod-product-compliance
Lightning Source LLC
Chambersburg PA
CBHW041935260926
51850CB00018B/194